THE LITERATURE OF THE NONPROFIT SECTOR
A Bibliography with Abstracts
VOLUME I

Margaret Chandler Derrickson

The Foundation Center
1989

CONTRIBUTING STAFF

Director of Information Systems   Martha David
Database Assistant   Ila Slimowitz
Production Manager   Rick Schoff
Editorial Associate   Kevin Michael Kurdylo

Copyright © 1989 The Foundation Center
Library of Congress Catalog Card Number 89-084358
ISBN 0-87954-287-X
Printed and bound in the United States of America

CONTENTS

Foreword by Stanley N. Katz..v
Preface vii

Part One. PHILANTHROPY AND THE FOUNDATION WORLD
    1. Philanthropy and Philanthropists 3
    2. Foundations 39
    3. Corporate Philanthropy 85
    4. International Philanthropy 111

Part Two. THE NONPROFIT SECTOR
    5. Nonprofit Organizations 129
    6. Nonprofit Organization Administration 159
    7. Fundraising..189
    8. Proposal Development 237
    9. Tax and Legal Implications for Nonprofits 243
    10. Voluntarism 265
    11. Government Funding and the Nonprofit Sector 275

Part Three. RELATED AND REFERENCE WORKS
    12. General Works Related to Philanthropy 285

Part Four. INDEXES
    Subject Index 301
    Author Index 317
    Title Index 339

Part Five. FOUNDATION CENTER SERVICES
    Foundation Center Library Network 393
    Foundation Center Publications and Services 397

FOREWORD

by Stanley N. Katz
President, American Council of Learned Societies
Chairman, Research Committee, Independent Sector

The Foundation Center's commitment to provide bibliographic control of the literature of the nonprofit sector began with the creation of the Bibliographic Information Service. The Center has now converted its own bibliographic holdings into machine-readable form, and is prepared to continue its work to include all future acquisitions. The volume in hand and the projected annual supplements will constitute the single most indispensable resource for research into the printed record of the nonprofit field. Until now, our most valuable aid has been another Center publication (in association with the American Association of Colleges), Daphne Niobe Layton's invaluable annotated bibliography, *Philanthropy and Voluntarism* (1987), which remains the best selected guide to the field. *The Literature of the Nonprofit Sector* marks an entirely new phase in the development of philanthropy as a scholarly field.

Scholars have never been able to agree on the definition of "professionalism," but most have acknowledged that the capacity for sustained introspection and self-analysis are integral to professional development. Until very recently, such activity was both rare and difficult of accomplishment in the field of philanthropy. Records of philanthropic institutions were (and still are) poorly and inconsistently kept, there was little published scholarship, and the existing materials were hard to locate. The Foundation Center has for many years been one of the shining exceptions to this dismal situation, but only since 1982 has it found the resources to turn its attention to the problem of bibliographic control.

Scholars will recognize that information is useful only when it can be found. Philanthropic information, when it exists, has been notably hard to find. This is mainly because "philanthropy" was not until recently a scholarly, archival or library category, and thus the researcher had no ready path to find the larger groupings of philanthropic materials in existing bibliographies and indexes.

For a variety of reasons, that remains a problem, but it diminishes in importance with the publication of this ongoing project. We now know what the significant collections of the Foundation Center hold, and we will shortly be able to determine the character of holdings elsewhere. The categories employed are well-conceived, the arrangement is user-friendly, and the abstracts are invaluable. Both academic researchers and professionals in the field with research needs will find their work improved by this project.

Research on philanthropy has broadened and deepened over the past fifteen years to a remarkable extent. Both Independent Sector and the Council on Foundations have established research committees, a significant number of university-based philanthropy research centers are in operation, and a growing number of academics in the humanities and social sciences recognize the importance of philanthropic problems. The institutionalization of research as part of the ordinary conduct of philanthropy itself has been disappointingly slow, but here too there are fugitive signs of creeping introspection. One lives in hope.

There can be no doubt that the Bibliographic Information Service and *The Literature of the Nonprofit Sector* mark a significant step forward in the professionalization of knowledge about philanthropy. For that, those of us who toil in the vineyards will remain grateful to Tom Buckman, President of the Foundation Center, and Margaret Derrickson.

PREFACE

BACKGROUND OF THE BIBLIOGRAPHIC INFORMATION SERVICE

The Literature of the Nonprofit Sector is the culmination of nearly a decade of Foundation Center planning to systematically organize, compile and disseminate information about the literature of philanthropy. Foundation Center President Thomas R. Buckman stated in a 1984 *Foundation News* article that the Foundation Center's "goals are pretty much the same as when we started. We simply want to do better what we've been trying to do: reach the people who need the information we provide." This cumulative bibliography is but one of the new or expanded services which the Center has initiated to provide better public access to information on the philanthropic world in fulfillment of its mission.

Historically, the Foundation Center has provided users with access to information on foundations through our libraries in New York, Washington, D.C., Cleveland, and San Francisco as well as through the network of Cooperating Collections and through Foundation Center publications. The Center staff realized that its collection, opened in 1956, held a wealth of otherwise inaccessible literature pertaining to such subjects as philanthropy, foundations, nonprofit organizations, nonprofit administration, fundraising, and voluntarism. In the early 1980s discussions began on the development of a Philanthropy Literature Project which would allow collection access to researchers. By the mid-1980s, the project's concept had expanded to include abstracting as well as indexing the literature.

In May 1987, the literature indexing and abstracting project entered a new phase when the Center began on-line processing of all newly acquired bibliographic materials. By 1988 a retrospective conversion of all the historical Foundation Center holdings—books, articles, pamphlets, project reports, and other literature—was completed. The online processing and the retrospective conversion occurred simultaneously with expanded acquisition, thus allowing access to both the retrospective literature and to timely new research and information.

THE BIBLIOGRAPHIC INFORMATION SERVICE

In mid-1988 the Bibliographic Information Service became a new unit within the Publications Department. The Service indexes and selectively abstracts Foundation Center Library acquisitions and other philanthropic literature. This cumulative volume of the complete Foundation Center collection is the first Bibliographic Information Service publication. Subsequent annual updates published by the Foundation Center will include both new materials collected by the Foundation Center and literature from other sources.

BIBLIOGRAPHIC CONTENTS

The Literature of the Nonprofit Sector includes both historical and current literature. However, it is not a definitive bibliography of philanthropic literature nor does inclusion in this bibliography represent a recommendation of the literature by the Foundation Center. This volume contains 4,992 bibliographic entries; of these entries, 1,519 contain abstracts. The bulk of the abstracted literature has been published since 1985, with the major part published since 1987.

The bibliography contains literature of interest to foundations and nonprofit organizations and their staffs, to fundraisers and to philanthropic researchers, scholars and students of the independent sector.

The Literature of the Nonprofit Sector includes literature on philanthropy, the foundation world, the nonprofit sector, and the works related to philanthropy including project reports, studies and statistical analyses.

This volume does not include bibliographic entries for general reference items which are readily available to the public in libraries and it contains only selected entries dealing with funding to individuals for scholarships and fellowships. Funding information and a bibliography on individual funding can be found in *Foundation Grants to Individuals*, 6th ed. NY: Foundation Center, 1988.

ARRANGEMENT

This bibliography has been compiled and arranged to provide the user with as many access points to the literature as possible. Because this edition is an accumulation of entries analyzed and processed by many people over more than three decades, the indexing for some items is not as extensive as some users may desire or need. To enhance subject access and assist users who may wish to browse only in certain subject areas, the bibliography has been arranged in five parts and further subdivided into twelve broad subject areas. Each chapter represents a subject area. For indexing purposes, every entry in the publication has been assigned a sequential book number; all numeric references pertaining to an entry are to that book number, not to a page number.

The following is an explanation of the contents within each part and chapter:

Part One. Philanthropy and the Foundation World

This section includes literature on the theory, philosophy and workings of both domestic and international philanthropy as well as biographies, autobiographies and memoirs of individual philanthropists. This section also contains the histories of individual foundations and several fictional accounts about philanthropy and philanthropists. Literature on all aspects of foundations and corporate giving programs (foundation, direct giving, and non-cash contributions) is also contained in this section. Part One includes the following chapters:

1. Philanthropy and Philanthropists
2. Foundations
3. Corporate Philanthropy
4. International Philanthropy

Part Two. The Nonprofit Sector

This section includes the literature pertaining to the nonprofit sector, its organizations and its administration or management including such topics as fundraising and proposal development (research and writing). This section includes publications which discuss the impact of governmental policies and funding upon the nonprofit sector as well as the tax and legal implications of local, state, and federal legislation and regulations. Literature on all aspects of voluntarism is also included in this section. Part Two includes the following chapters:

5. Nonprofit Organizations
6. Nonprofit Organization Administration
7. Fundraising
8. Proposal Development
9. Tax and Legal Implications for Nonprofits
10. Voluntarism
11. Government Funding and the Nonprofit Sector

Part Three. Related and Reference Works

This section predominately includes selected materials which have been issued by foundations or nonprofit organizations, or resulted from studies or projects funded by foundations or nonprofit organizations. Part Three includes the following chapter:

12. General Works Related to Philanthropy

The part and chapter arrangement of this book allows for easy access to broad subject areas. However, users will want to use the indexes which are provided for far greater specificity.

Part Four. Indexes

This section contains a subject, an author, and a title index. All bibliographic entries are designated with a unique book number. These book numbers follow the subject or index term, the author, or the title; the numbers after each index citation are not page numbers. The book numbers in bold type in all indexes designate abstracted entries.

The **Subject Index** is alphabetically arranged by subject or index term. Because of indexing differences over the years the user is advised to review general terms such as *Foundations* in addition to such specific terms as *Foundations, individual histories* when searching for pre-1986 literature.

The **Author Index** is alphabetically arranged by the author, editor, compiler, or corporate name.

The **Title Index** is alphabetically arranged by the title of the entry; book titles appear in italic print and journal titles are designated by quotation marks.

Part Five. Foundation Center Services and Publications

Informational material including a list of the Foundation Center Libraries and their network of Cooperating Collections, the Foundation Center Associates Program as well as a list of publications available from the Center has been added to this bibliography for the user's convenience.

ACKNOWLEDGMENTS

The Literature of the Nonprofit Sector would not be complete without acknowledging the work of two people who greatly enhanced this first annual edition. They are Daphne Niobe Layton, author of *Philanthropy and Voluntarism: An Annotated Bibliography,* NY: Foundation Center, 1987, who prepared a number of the abstracts in this current publication and Catherine Barinas who worked diligently on the retrospective conversion project.

Margaret Chandler Derrickson
Bibliographic Information Service

PART ONE

PHILANTHROPY AND THE FOUNDATION WORLD

1

PHILANTHROPY AND PHILANTHROPISTS

1. Abbott, Edith, ed. *Some American Pioneers in Social Welfare: Select Documents with Editorial Notes.* New York: Russell and Russell, 1963.

   This volume presents a documentary history of social welfare in America, through selected writings of and about such important social reformers of the eighteenth and nineteenth centuries as Benjamin Rush, Stephen Girard, Dorothea Dix, Benjamin Franklin, Samuel Gridley Howe, and Charles Loring Brace. The use of primary materials lends an important historical perspective to Abbott's editorial commentary; it is not only interesting, but enlightening to read of pioneering social reforms in the language and context of their day. The latter is especially true when issues being discussed have contemporary relevance, as in the congressional/presidential debate about public vs. private eleemosynary responsibilities in regard to Dorothea Dix's plea for federal aid for the insane and homeless. Abbott prepared the volume expressly for classroom use.

2. Abels, Jules. *The Rockefeller Billions: The Story of the World's Most Stupendous Fortune.* New York: Macmillan, [1965].

3. Ackerman, Carl William. *George Eastman.* Boston: Houghton Mifflin, 1930.

4. Adams, Herbert. *Notes on the Literature of Charities.* New York: Johnson Reprint Corp., 1973.

5. Addams, Jane. *Democracy and Social Ethics.* Cambridge, Mass.: Belknap Press, 1964.

   Complemented by an excellent, brief biography of Jane Addams written by Anne Firor Scott, this collection of seven essays lays the groundwork of Addams' developing thought for the next forty years. Dissatisfied with the eighteenth-century conception of democracy as the franchise, Addams called for a broader definition that took into account social interdependence and respect for every individual's worth—an ethic of social responsibility. Addams based her thought not on abstract or moral reflection, but on experience, much of it gained at Hull House. In fact, she rejected any doctrine that is not successfully practicable. She saw the poor and working classes as the first to recognize and manifest her ethic of social responsibility by forming associations, and concluded that social equality was essential to progress. See especially *Charitable Effort.*

6. Addams, Jane, Bernard Bosanquet, Franklin Giddings, et al. *Philanthropy and Social Progress: Seven Essays.* Montclair, N.J.: Patterson Smith, 1970.

   These essays were delivered before the School of Applied Ethics in Plymouth, Massachusetts in 1892. Jane Addams wrote two essays about Hull House, one based on her personal experience founding it and the other about Hull House's role in Chicago and that of social settlements generally. Robert A. Woods' essay, *The University Settlement Idea,* propounds the idea of greater cooperation between universities and the cities in which they are located through college men and women who live in poor sections of town. The students provide education opportunities to the poor as well as study them and their lifestyles. Two long essays by the Rev. James O.S. Huntington, both well worth reading, warn against the tendency to view philanthropic acts as ends in themselves, not as steps in a ladder toward social progress. He also argues against the double standards of societal expectation of the rich and poor, among other things. *The Ethics of Social Progress* are analyzed by Franklin Giddings, and Bernard Bosanquet writes about the administration of charity.

7. Addams, Jane. *Twenty Years at Hull House, with Autobiographical Notes.* New York: Macmillan, 1910.

   Jane Addams founded Hull House, a social settlement in the middle of an industrial, immigrant section of Chicago, in 1889. This volume describes Hull House's first twenty years from the perspective of its dedicated, involved founder. It is arranged topically rather than chronologically and is flavored throughout with the taste of Addams' own beliefs and aspirations as she struggled to make a success out of an untested idea. The book covers everything from the settlement's activities to the intellectual and social trends and movements that informed its inhabitants. The autobiographical chapters that discuss her original conception of Hull House and how it came about make very interesting reading, especially for those who may sometimes doubt that ideas have consequences.

8–23 PHILANTHROPY AND PHILANTHROPISTS

8. Adventist World Headquarters. *Accent on Philanthropy*. Washington: Adventist World Headquarters, 1981.

9. Alderson, Barnard. *Andrew Carnegie: The Man and His Work*. New York: Doubleday, 1902.

10. Allen, Michael Patrick. *The Founding Fortunes: A New Anatomy of the Super-Rich Families in America*. New York: Truman Talley Books, 1987.

    Based exclusively on information available, although not always readily accessible, from various public records, Allen elucidates the facts concerning the accumulation and perpetuation of great wealth within a few hundred capitalist American families. Of particular interest is a chapter entitled *Practical Philanthropy*, which briefly recounts the activities of several private foundations, and a directory listing 160 families worth at least $200 million in 1986.

11. Allen, William Harvey. *Modern Philanthropy: A Study of Efficient Appealing and Giving*. New York: Dodd, Mead, & Co., 1912.

12. Alper, Sirota and Pfau. *Giving and Volunteering in New York City*. New York: Daring Goals for a Caring New York, 1988.

    Results and implications of interviews with a representative sample of 2,759 adult New York City residents (which breaks down to approximately 550 respondents from each of the five boroughs) concerning their attitudes and behavior in regards to charitable giving and volunteering. In comparisons with a 1988 national survey sponsored by Independent Sector and studies conducted in various other U.S. cities, New Yorkers are more active contributers than the U.S. population as a whole: seventy-one percent of all U.S. citizens made charitable donations last year, while eighty percent of New Yorkers gave money. A large majority (eighty-six percent of those surveyed) believe everyone should volunteer their time to help those less fortunate than themselves, although only thirty-two percent report having volunteered last year. The report suggests that charitable volunteering could be easily increased, for a significant number of respondents said they did not volunteer simply because no one asked them or because they did not know how to go about volunteering. Overall, twenty-eight percent of the New York City population both contributed and volunteered in the last year, fifty-two percent contributed only, four percent volunteered only, and seventeen percent neither contributed nor volunteered. Among the U.S. population as a whole, forty percent contributed and volunteered, thirty-two percent contributed only, five percent volunteered only, and twenty-three percent neither contributed nor volunteered.

13. *An Analysis of Southern California Charitable Giving: 1986 Member Survey*. Los Angeles: Southern California Association for Philanthropy, 1986.

    Survey of the annual giving by members of the Southern California Association for Philanthropy (SCAP) reveals, in summary, that 34.1 percent of 1985's more than 233 million dollars in charitable giving went to education; 20.6 percent went to social services; 14.7 percent went to arts and humanities; 12.7 percent went to health and hospitals, 7.4 percent went to civic affairs and community organizations; 1.3 percent went to religious activities; and 9.2 percent went to miscellaneous and unspecified grants. Includes breakdowns for giving by private foundations, corporations, corporate foundations, corporate contribution programs, and all others. Provides current list of SCAP's more than ninety members.

14. Andrews, Frank Emerson. *Attitudes toward Giving*. New York: Russell Sage Foundation, 1953.

    This book presents data and quotations from ninety-one interviews conducted by the National Opinion Research Center, designed to answer these questions: "What are the present motives of givers? Does giving spring from sympathy for a suffering fellowman, or from a desire to feel superior? How do givers feel about solicitation at their place of employment, street-corner tag days, home visits, collections from their children at school? How far does the social group determine the giving pattern? What sorts of people give, and how much, and why?" While no scientific conclusions could be drawn from such a small sample, the results are presented in a more or less descriptive fashion and organized by topics such as attitudes toward social welfare, fundraising techniques, religious giving, and attitudes toward individual agencies.

15. Andrews, Frank Emerson. *Bibliography*. Unpublished, [1973].

16. Andrews, Frank Emerson. *Philanthropic Giving*. New York: Russell Sage Foundation, 1950.

    This book represents one of the first attempts to take a comprehensive look at the phenomenon of philanthropic giving in the United States and to provide guidance for philanthropists of all kinds in what Andrews refers to as "a new era of giving"—one in which the federal government has largely alleviated private philanthropy from the burden of providing "mere relief." Andrews gives a brief historical account of the evolution of philanthropy and an overview of its current state, domestic and international, before devoting several chapters to methods of giving, legal and tax issues, and various problems and pitfalls. While the statistics are obviously dated, the discussion remains informative, drawing on more than eight thousand references and heavy correspondence.

17. Andrews, Frank Emerson. *Philanthropy in the United States: History and Structure*. New York: Foundation Center, 1978.

    Pamphlet presents brief history of private foundations and philanthropy, emphasizing the structure and dimensions of the philanthropic world in the 1970s.

18. Anthony, Alfred Williams, ed. *Changing Conditions in Public Giving*. Wise Public Giving Series, no. 32. New York: Federal Council of the Churches of Christ in America, 1929.

19. Anthony, Alfred Williams, ed. *Philanthropy for the Future*. Wise Public Giving Series, no. 36. New York: Federal Council of the Churches of Christ in America, 1931.

20. Anthony, Alfred Williams, ed. *Trusts and Trusteeships*. Wise Public Giving Series, no. 39. New York: Federal Council of the Churches of Christ in America, 1932.

21. *Appreciations of Frederick Paul Keppel by Some of His Friends*. New York: Columbia University Press, 1951.

22. Astor, Brooke. *Footprints*. New York: Doubleday, 1980.

23. Astor, Brooke. *Twenty-Five Years of Giving in New York City: The Vincent Astor Foundation*. New York: Vincent Astor Foundation, 1985.

24. Auten, Gerald, and Gabriel Rudney. *The Variability of the Charitable Giving of the Wealthy.* Program on Non-Profit Organizations, no. 126. New Haven, Conn.: Institution for Social and Policy Studies, [1988].

Study uses panel data to analyze the variability of individual high income giving over a five year span (1971-1975) as well as variability of giving among individuals in single years. Two basic samples are used in this study: a permanent income sample culled from federal income tax returns for individuals with a permanent (average) expanded income of at least $100,000, and an annual income sample that included returns with expanded income of at least $100,000 in one or more years during the five year period. These samples limit the study to approximately the top one percent of taxpayers, with 116,178 taxpayers in the permanent income sample (fewer than 1,000 reported expanded income of $1 million or more), and over 700,000 in the annual income sample. The major finding is the high degree of variability in high income giving; in the $1 million or more income group giving in the top quartile is more than sixty times higher than giving in the bottom quartile. In addition, the largest annual giving by an individual is more than ten times his smallest giving over a five year period for forty-five percent of the individuals in the highest income class; such wide fluctuations over time suggest that the pattern of giving by such individuals can be influenced by effective fundraising and development efforts. Another significant finding notes that a small proportion of high income givers account for a large proportion of total high income giving, while a large proportion of high income individuals give less than one percent of income.

25. Bailward, William Amias. *The Slippery Slope, and Other Papers on Social Subjects.* London: John Murray, 1920.

26. Bakal, Carl. "American Way of Giving: Inside the World of Charity. Part 2." *Town & Country* (December 1981): 201-12.

27. Bakal, Carl. *Charity U.S.A.: An Investigation into the Hidden World of the Multi-Billion Dollar Charity Industry.* New York: Times Books, 1979.

In this probing, critical investigative work, Bakal sets out to answer the questions: "Who gives to charity—and why? Is enough money given and is it given where it is most needed? Are the funds collected sensibly and efficiently? How well are they spent to carry out the ostensible purposes for which they are collected? How can one distinguish the worthy charities from the unworthy? And, most fundamentally, are charities really desirable or necessary in today's society? Or should their functions be the responsibility of government?" Bakal looked into the operations of hundreds of charitable organizations, including those of churches, social welfare organizations, libraries, hospitals, and symphony orchestras. Much of the book is based on firsthand experience and observations gained during extensive travels. Bakal's controversial foray into the world of American charity is a comprehensive, interesting, and enlightening, but not always pleasant, examination of an institution "others have thought too pious to probe or question, at least in the depth this book attempts to." Notes and sources.

28. Baltzell, E. Digby. *Philadelphia Gentlemen: The Making of a National Upper Class.* Rev. ed. Philadelphia: University of Pennsylvania Press, 1979.

Baltzell's book is a study of Philadelphia's hereditary upper class, a group based on business wealth and power which has established itself since the city's founding in 1682. He is interested here in presenting an historical analysis of the structure and functions of upper-class institutions. He assumes the desirability of established institutions which create an upper-class consciousness and a more or less primary group solidarity, while at the same time referring to the abuses of privilege and the inevitable human frailties which prevent the proper functioning of such institutions. In many ways, he states, this is an analysis of the adequacy of American institutions in fostering, among the rich and the powerful, a sense of *noblesse oblige*—an old sociological concept which seems to have found no place in the literature of contemporary American social science.

29. Barrett, Nina. "You Have to Be Rude." *Foundation News* 28 (September-October 1987): 34-9.

Profiles Eleanor Petersen, thirteen-year president of the Donors Forum of Chicago and founder of Women in Foundations/Corporate Philanthropy, focusing on her use of "strategic rudeness" to promote awareness for the status of blacks and women.

30. Barrett, William P. "Citizens Rich." *Forbes* (14 December 1987): 141-43, 146-48.

Profiles the profitable success of the Hearst Corporation, thanks in large part to the acquisitions program and upgrade of quality being managed by current president and chief executive Frank A. Bennack Jr., and also to William Randolph Hearst's ingenious will, which is structured to avoid the breakup of the company by his heirs by putting 100 percent of the voting stock in the hands of a family trust.

31. Barron, Clarence W. *More They Told Barron: Conversations and Revelations of an American Pepys in Wall Street.* Edited by Arthur Pound and Samuel Taylor Moore. New York: Harper & Bros., 1931.

32. Barron, Clarence W. *They Told Barron: Conversations and Revelations of an American Pepys in Wall Street.* Edited by Arthur Pound and Samuel Taylor Moore. New York: Harper & Bros., 1930.

33. Barzun, Jacques. *The House of Intellect.* New York: Harper & Row, 1959.

34. Becker, Stephen. *Marshall Field III.* New York: Simon & Schuster, 1964.

35. Behar, Richard. "The 400 Richest People in America." *Forbes 400* (1 October 1984): 69+.

36. Behar, Richard. "A Tempting Target." *Forbes* (18 April 1988): 41-2.

Portrays the changing fortunes of Reader's Digest Association, whose increasing profits make it a potential target for would-be acquisitors.

37. Bellah, Robert N., ed. *Habits of the Heart: Individualism and Commitment in American Life.* Berkeley, Calif.: University of California Press, 1985.

Its title borrowed from Alexis de Tocqueville's *Democracy in America*, this book explores the beliefs and practices that shape our character and give form to our social order. Through the stories of individual lives, the authors—three sociologists, a philosopher, and a theologian—examine American attitudes towards private life—finding oneself, love and marriage, reaching out, individualism—and public life—getting involved, citizenship, religion, and the national society. The fundamental question they pose is "how to preserve or create a morally coherent life." Their basic concern is that individualism "may be destroying those social integuments that de Tocqueville saw as moderating its more destructive potentialities," perhaps "threatening the survival of freedom itself." The authors concentrate on the relationship between public and private life, including forms of participation such as traditional voluntary associations.

38. Bender, Marylin. "Director Who Remembered to Bring Her Credentials." *New York Times* (10 June 1973): 7.

39. Bernhard, Virginia. "Cotton Mather and the Doing of Good: A Puritan Gospel of Wealth." *The New England Quarterly* 49 (1976): 225-41.

Bernhard uses Cotton Mather's *Bonifacius: Essays to Do Good*, published in 1710, as an indicator of the ideological underpinnings of a "distinctively American society whose ideals about social mobility and class lines were already quite different from those of its English parent." Sermons devoted to charity, inspired by Mather, were also inspired by the growing numbers of poor, problems of the economy, and fragmentation of a society where individualism ran rampant. Societies for the doing of good began to be formed in Puritan society, designed to be "engines of piety" (Mather), in further efforts to strengthen social cohesiveness. To gauge the differences in American and English assumptions about class and social mobility, Bernhard compares *Essays to Do Good* with two similar English tracts, published in 1682 and 1715, respectively: Richard Baxter's *How to Do Good to Many* and Robert Nelson's *An Address to Persons of Quality and Estate*. She concludes that by providing a justification for pursuing material wealth (doing good), Mather inadvertently encouraged the economic individualism he was trying to combat.

40. Birmingham, Stephen. *Our Crowd: The Great Jewish Families of New York.* New York: Harper & Row, 1967.

41. Blitz, Mark. *Philanthropy and the Spirit of Voluntarism.* Foundation Officers Forum Occasional Papers, no. 4. New York: Institute for Educational Affairs, 1982.

42. Bob, Murray L. "The Bureaucratization of Begging: A Donor with Shell(out) Shock Looks Back to a Time When the Giving Was Easy." *Grantsmanship Center News* 11 (November-December 1983): 48-51.

43. Bolton, Sarah Knowles. *Famous Givers and Their Gifts.* New York: Thomas Y. Crowell Co., 1986.

Bolton uses brief chapters to describe the lasting contributions of each of more than thirty famous philanthropists of the nineteenth century, including John Lowell, Jr. (The Lowell Institute of Boston), Sophia Smith (Smith College), James Smithson (the Smithsonian Institution), Asa Packer (Lehigh University), John D. Rockefeller (the University of Chicago), and others. While the accounts are not scholarly or objective, they do furnish interesting personal detail about what motivated each person to give in precisely the way he or she did, and for what purposes.

44. Boorstin, Daniel J. *The Decline of Radicalism: Reflections on America Today.* New York: Random House, 1969.

In the chapter entitled *From Charity to Philanthropy*, Boorstin looks at the American idea of community and its manifestation in the uniquely large and important role that the philanthropic and voluntary sector plays in the United States. This notion of community, argues Boorstin, makes it impossible to frame a debate about American social politics in terms of "individualism" vs. "socialism," or collectivism, as it is in Europe. He explores the roots of community in a nation of immigrants, suggesting that the "decisive contrasting fact" between America and Europe is that in the former communities existed before governments. He goes on to note that American philanthropy is the best illustration of this community sentiment and uses the example of Julius Rosenwald's philanthropic activities to make his point. Boorstin concludes with a look at how the emergence of very large foundations in the early decades of the twentieth century, and subsequent rapid increase in their numbers, reflects on the underpinnings of community spirit. For an analytical discussion of philanthropy in a general historical context, this essay is a must.

45. Boorstin, Daniel J. *Hidden History.* Reprint. New York: Harper & Row, 1987.

46. Boris, Elizabeth Trocolli. "Increasing What We Know." *Foundation News* 26 (May-June 1985): 60.

47. Bornet, Vaughn Davis. *Welfare in America.* Norman, Okla.: University of Oklahoma Press, 1960.

Bornet sees the evolution of social welfare in twentieth-century America as the product of a convergence of three seemingly exclusive forces: the individualist creed of personal responsibility for one's own well-being and that of one's family, the growth in popularity and effectiveness of voluntary organizations that address social ills, and the increasingly perceived need for government provision of basic human services on a grand scale and in a systematic fashion. He examines the manifestations of each of these forces during this century and how they worked with—or without—each other to form "the American pattern in social welfare." Bornet concludes by presenting some of his own concerns about the future directions of welfare in this country.

48. Bothwell, Robert O., and Timothy Saasta. "New Nonprofits Are Being Undermined." *Grantsmanship Center News* 13 (May-June 1985): 58+.

49. Boulding, Kenneth E. *A Preface to Grants Economics: The Economy of Love and Fear.* Praeger Special Studies. New York: Praeger, 1981.

Dissatisfied with the inadequacy of exchange economics to account for grants (one-way transfers), Boulding has developed a theory of grants economy. Grants economics contends that grants, usually regarded as an exotic fringe element of the economic system proper, must be integrated into both the theory and the empirical study of the economy. According to Boulding, grants are a measure of an integrative relationship—that is, a relationship dealing with "status, identity, community, legitimacy, loyalty, benevolence, and so on, and...the appropriate opposites." He sees grants as products of two different motivations: either the integrative system—gifts arising out of love, or the threat system—gifts arising out of fear. These motivations are clearly mixed in many instances, so the grants economy cannot be neatly divided into an integrative sector and a threat sector.

50. Boulding, Kenneth E., and Thomas Frederick Wilson, eds. *Redistribution through the Financial System: The Grants Economics of Money and Credit.* New York: Praeger, 1978.

51. Bowen, Louise Hadduck. *Growing Up with a City.* New York: Macmillan, 1926.

This autobiographical account of Bowen's involvement in several of Chicago's social organizations, including Hull House, the Woman's City Club, and the United Charities, yields an interesting personal perspective on both the failures and successes of various social experiments and efforts to provide relief for the poor. It is interesting, as well, to read Bowen's accounts and opinions of contemporaries such as Jane Addams, founder of Hull House, at which Bowen served on the Woman's Club for seventeen years. Bowen also recounts her experiences in churches and hospitals, with the juvenile court system and the suffragist movement, her war work, and the emergence of women in public affairs. The book serves as a testament to the critical role of affluent women like Bowen in meeting the needs of the urban poor in the late nineteenth century and beyond.

52. Brace, Charles Loring. *The Dangerous Classes of New York and Twenty Year's Work among Them.* Montclair, N.J.: Patterson Smith, 1967.

The introduction states, "My great object in the present work is to prove to society the practical truth...that the cheapest and most efficacious way of dealing with the 'Dangerous Classes' of large cities, is not to punish them, but to prevent their growth, to so throw the influences of education and discipline and religion about the abandoned and destitute youth of our large towns; to so change their material circumstances, and draw them under the influence of the moral and fortunate classes, that they shall grow up as useful producers and members of society, able and inclined to aid it in its progress." This he proceeds to do in thirty-seven chapters covering 450 pages. The volume draws largely on Brace's twenty years of work in this field, trying to assure New York's poor, abandoned, and neglected children an opportunity to rise in the world and become self-sufficient.

53. Brakeley, George A., Jr. "The Psychology of Money." *Philanthropy Monthly* 15 (December 1982): 26-9.

54. Brakeley, John Price Jones. *American Philanthropy for Higher Education.* 1966-1987. New York: John Price Jones Co., 19—.

A continuing study of gifts and bequests to seventy-one colleges and universities, now in its sixty-sixth year.

55. Brawley, Benjamin. *Doctor Dillard of the Jeanes Fund.* New York: Fleming H. Revell Co., 1930.

56. Bremner, Robert Hamlett. *American Philanthropy.* 2nd ed. The Chicago History of American Civilization. Chicago: University of Chicago Press, 1988.

Bremner's pioneering and classic volume is required reading for students of American philanthropy. Bremner traces the evolution and character of philanthropy in the United States from the Pilgrims (and notes that the first American philanthropists were the native Indians) to the 1950s. He examines the peculiarly American circumstances that gave rise to different expressions of philanthropy, like voluntary poverty relief, social work and social services, foundations, and government programs. He also explores tensions between the philanthropic impulse and the ideals of individualism, equal opportunity, and democracy that have pervaded American history. The book includes a timeline of important dates and an excellent *Suggested Reading* section for those who wish to delve more deeply into particular aspects of the American philanthropic tradition. This second edition of *American Philanthropy* includes a new introduction, revised *Suggested Reading* and *Important Dates* sections, and new chapters covering developments since 1960, a period in which total giving by individuals, foundations, and corporations has more than doubled in real terms and in which major revisions of tax laws have changed patterns of giving.

57. Bremner, Robert Hamlett. *From the Depths: The Discovery of Poverty in the United States.* New York: New York University Press, 1956.

Bremner states in the preface, "This book is a study of America's awakening to poverty as a social problem...My objectives are to trace the growth of factual information about social conditions, to characterize and account for changing attitudes toward poverty, to describe the ways in which writers and artists have handled the subject of poverty in their work, and to present the experiences and influences that led to the enactment of legislation affecting housing, child labor, women in industry, and industrial accidents. Broadly stated, the purpose of the book is to show how philanthropic movements have added to our awareness and understanding of the poverty problem." The book deals most substantively with the period from 1830-1920, an era in which, Bremner says, American public consciousness of the poverty problem and what to do about it underwent significant alterations. It is centrally concerned with the roles of "do-gooders," or philanthropists, in recognizing and alleviating poverty. Extensive bibliography.

58. Bremner, Robert Hamlett. "The Impact of the Civil War on Philanthropy and Social Welfare." *Civil War History* 12 (1966): 293-303.

Bremner focuses on the response of civilians to the demands of war and on efforts to maintain and advance civilian welfare during wartime. The North was somewhat surprised to find that war had engendered unforeseen economic prosperity, which resulted in better general welfare and less need for charitable work, although some poor—women, the aged, and the handicapped—found themselves worse off. Charitable contributions increased at the same time. Conversely, shortages of food, clothing, and medicine were experienced in the Confederacy, followed by ruinous inflation and devastation. In the face of this, southern states adopted public relief programs without precedent in the South. Bremner says this great expansion of southern state welfare was one of the major, unexpected consequences of the war. Patriotic philanthropy—private aid for the war—flourished on both sides, and there was considerable rivalry between charitable organizations, illustrated by Bremner in a discussion of the Sanitary Commission and the Christian Commission.

59. Bremner, Robert Hamlett. *The Public Good: Philanthropy and Welfare in the Civil War Era.* New York: Alfred A. Knopf, 1980.

In this in-depth study of public and private American philanthropic activity during the late nineteenth century, Bremner touches not only on the works of individual philanthropists, but also on the formation of, activity by, and competition between voluntary associations as well as social movements or groundswells seeking government adoption of selected charitable responsibilities. Philanthropic support for schooling for freedmen during and after the Civil War, higher education in general, cultural events, and other popular needs, as well as charitable needs occasioned by the war, are also discussed. Bremner examines the underlying desire of Civil War-era philanthropists to discipline the charitable impulse "so that good will and benevolent intentions would be enlightened and directed by intelligence." He acknowledges that a tendency toward social control may contribute to this desire, but does not thereby lessen its good intentions and effects. Bibliographical note.

60. Brenner, Marie. "Fast and Luce." *Vanity Fair* 51 (March 1988): 158+.

Profiles the life of Clare Boothe Luce, author of *The Women* and *Stuffed Shirts*, managing editor of *Vanity Fair*, wife of *Time* magazine founder Henry Luce, and the first woman to be made American ambassador to a major country.

61. Breunig, Robert. "Personal Values: The Reason for Philanthropic Exchange." *Fund Raising Management* 15 (December 1984): 54-5.

Describes motives of philanthropists, giving several examples.

62. Bridge, James H. *The Carnegie Millions and the Men Who Made Them: Being the Inside History of the Carnegie Steel Co.* London: Limpus, Baker, & Co., 1903.

63. Broaddus, Will. "Learning to Save Lebanon." *Foundation News* 29 (May-June 1988): 32-6.

Outlines the history and objectives of the Hariri Foundation, dedicated by Lebanese businessman Rafiq Hariri to educating young Lebanese in the U.S. so they might return as strong leaders to the war-torn nation.

64. Broaddus, Will. "Stirrings in the Shadows." *Foundation News* 28 (September-October 1987): 25-33.

Broaddus examines the sense of self and its relationship to society among those coming of age in this decade. He looks back to the attitudes of the Sixties to find continuity and differences in the younger generation of today; evidence of caring and a sensitivity for human values still exists, he contends, but "the peace movement of the Eighties is a story of hundreds of small parts, and not one cataclysmic outpouring" as it appeared twenty years ago. Campus Compact, a national coalition of college and university presidents dedicated to increasing public service among students, reports increased student participation in voluntary activities over the last five years; Broaddus points out that the initiative of Campus Compact, Public Interest Research Groups (which have shown a recent rise in membership) and other similar organizations are necessary to help foster the values of a caring society within the younger generation and provide them with the means to express their idealism. Includes profiles of Yale University's Dwight Hall, the 101-year-old organization that coordinates and encourages student volunteering, and recent legislative proposals modeled on the idea of national service.

65. Brookings Institution. *The Economics of Public Finance.* Washington: Brookings Institution, 1974.

66. Brooks, Elizabeth. *Philanthropy and International Affairs: A Typology and Study of Grantmaking by San Francisco Bay Area Foundations.* San Francisco: Bay Area and the World, 1984.

Seeks to provide a means of identifying a grant or an issue as being international in scope by developing a more accurate and efficient vocabulary and by diminishing the distinction between domestic and international issues. Establishes connections between locally-focused priorities and international dimensions which could be eligible for funding by recognizing the complex interdependence of today's world and the international dimension which exists in almost every aspect of human experience or human need. Also provides an overview of international grantmaking in the San Francisco Bay Area to identify the kinds of international activities or problems which are being addressed, and which are not.

67. Brown, Susan Love. *The Incredible Bread Machine.* San Diego, Calif.: World Research, 1974.

68. Bubnic, Anne M. *The Charitable Behavior of San Francisco Bay Area Physicians.* Working Papers, no. 5. San Francisco: Institute for Nonprofit Organization Management, 1988.

Provides a review of the literature on the history of philanthropy among physicians, reports on the findings of a questionnaire administered by mail to 1,451 San Francisco Bay Area physicians (with 531 respondents), and formulates a set of recommendations for increasing the charitable dollar contributions from doctors. Among the findings: one hundred percent of the physician respondents made charitable contributions in 1985, and they gave an average of 2.5 percent of their annual income; physicians are heavily solicited and they respond to many charities; and as income levels and total contributions to charity increase, physicians have a tendency to increase the number, rather than the size, of their individual gifts. Recommendations are made that development professionals and volunteers consider the personal and professional characteristics of physicians when identifying them as donor prospects rather than targeting doctors for gifts solely on the basis of their occupation.

69. Buckley, William F., Jr. *The Future of Philanthropy: Part 2.* Columbia, S.C.: Southern Educational Communications Association, 1982.

70. "A Busch Family Heritage." *Town & Country* 138 (December 1984): 202+.

Describes and shows photographs of Busch brewery family home in Cooperstown, New York.

71. Butler, Nicholas Murray. *Across the Busy Years: Recollections and Reflections.* New York: Charles Scribner's Sons, 1939.

72. Butler, Nicholas Murray. "The Fruits of a Fortune." *New York Herald Tribune* (24 November 1935): 5, 23, 25.

73. Butler, Stuart M. *Philanthropy in America: The Need for Action. Fiscal Issues 2.* Washington: Heritage Foundation, 1980.

74. Cagney, Penelope. "Thank You, Japan." *NonProfit Times* 2 (October 1988): 21-2.

Addresses American criticism of Japanese corporate philanthropy and urges cooperation to help the new programs become successful. The Japanese lack a cultural, legal and philosophical framework for philanthropy, and "much of what is funded privately here is taken care of by the government there;" therefore their efforts to adopt American methods of philanthropy constitute a new way of thinking for them. While Japanese foundations are naturally interested in projects that promote their culture or that build bridges between East and West, the "record of grants given by Japanese corporations to-date show a conscientious effort to look beyond mere self-promotion to the geniune needs of the community." Indeed, the Hitachi Foundation, which is highlighted in the article, is headed by Delwin Roy, an American, to prevent perceptions of a self-serving institution.

75. Cameron, Frank. *Cottrell, Samaritan of Science.* New York: Doubleday, 1952.

76. Candler, Charles Howard. *Asa Griggs Candler.* Atlanta, Ga.: Emory University, 1950.

77. Carlson, Martin E. *Why People Give.* New York: National Council of the Churches of Christ in the U.S.A., 1968.

78. Carmichael, Leonard, and John Cuthbert Long. *James Smithson and the Smithsonian Story.* New York: Putnam, [1965].

79. Carnegie, Andrew. *Autobiography of Andrew Carnegie.* Boston: Houghton Mifflin, 1920.

80. Carnegie, Andrew. *The Gospel of Wealth and Other Timely Essays.* New York: Century Co., 1900.

81. Carnegie, Andrew. *The Gospel of Wealth and Other Timely Essays.* Edited by Edward C. Kirkland. Cambridge, Mass.: Belknap Press, 1962.

The editor's introduction to this collection of autobiographical essays sets them into the context of Carnegie's life and the late nineteenth-century values and perceptions that influenced him. *The Gospel of Wealth* argues that industrial capitalism (referred to by Carnegie as "intense individualism") is the best possible social and economic system and represents an evolution from a misguided communism. The extreme accumulation of wealth by a few is thought to be in the best interests of society, but only if it is judiciously administered for public purposes—Carnegie's secular concept of stewardship—and this during the life of the wealthy individual. His rationale is that "the millionaire will be but a trustee for the poor, intrusted for a season with a great part of the increased wealth of the community, but administering it for the community far better than it could or would have done itself." The second part of the essay is devoted to the best methods for administering wealth for philanthropic purposes. Other essays of interest include *The Advantages of Poverty* and *Popular Illusions About Trusts.*

82. Carnegie, Andrew. *Triumphant Democracy.* New York: Johnson Reprint Corp., 1971.

83. Carnegie Corporation of New York. *Andrew Carnegie Centenary, 1835-1935.* New York: Carnegie Corporation of New York, 1935.

84. Carnegie Dunfermline Trust. *Andrew Carnegie Sesquicentenary Gathering.* 1985. Dunfermline, Fife, Scotland: Carnegie Dunfermline Trust, 1987.

Speeches include *The Enduring Value of Philanthropy in a Changing World,* by Alan Pifer; *Charitable Foundations and the Advance of Science,* by Sir Andrew Huxley; *Voluntary Effort in a High-Tech Society,* by Lord Thomson of Monifieth; and *The Carnegie Legacy: A Truly Independent International Relations "Establishment",* by Kingman Brewster. Discussion topics on *Interdependence, Education and Peace, Progress and the Arts, Science and Technology,* and *The Carnegie Hero Funds.*

85. Carnegie Endowment for International Peace. *A Manual of the Public Benefactions of Andrew Carnegie.* Washington: Carnegie Endowment for International Peace, 1919.

86. Carr, William H. *The Du Ponts of Delaware.* New York: Dodd, Mead, & Co., [1964].

87. Carson, Emmett D. "Despite Long History, Black Philanthropy Gets Little Credit As 'Self-Help' Tool." *Focus* 15 (June 1987): 3-4, 7.

An essay challenging the myth that blacks do not have a history of philanthropic involvement. Carson, a research associate at the Joint Center for Political Studies (JCPS), expands the definition of philanthropy to include the giving of time and goods as well as money. He cites groups such as the black churches, mutual aid societies and fraternal organizations. These groups were instrumental in the development and support of black education, banks, insurance companies and civil rights. Current information on black philanthropy was obtained from a 1986 Gallup Poll done for the JCPS. The survey results show that the historical tradition of black charitable giving and voluntarism remains strong.

88. Carson, Emmett D. *Pulling Yourself Up by Your Bootstrap: The Evolution of Black Philanthropic Activity.* Unpublished, [1987].

89. Carson, Emmett D. "Survey Dispels Myth That Blacks Receive But Do Not Give to Charity." *Focus* (March 1987): 5-6.

Analysis of organized charitable giving and voluntarism within the black community based on information gathered in a national survey which the Joint Center for Political Studies (JCPS) commissioned the Gallup Organization to conduct. The black community contributes more than two-thirds of its charitable dollars to the church. When analyzing giving by income group, blacks and whites contribute similar amounts to charity. In addition, the survey results indicate that blacks and whites at all income levels are equally involved in volunteer activity. The findings challenge widely held views that blacks are less active in volunteer activity than whites.

90. Carter, Paul C. *Arnaud Cartwright Marts.* New York: Algonquin Press, 1970.

91–104 PHILANTHROPY AND PHILANTHROPISTS

91. Center for the Study of Philanthropy. *Women and Philanthropy: Past, Present and Future.* Center for the Study of Philanthropy Working Papers. New York: Center for the Study of Philanthropy, [1988].

Essays first presented at a 1987 conference at the Center for the Study of Philanthropy address two issues: the traditional roles played by feminine giving and voluntarism, and the impact of the women's movement on these activities. The first section focuses on the American scene, providing an historical overview and a chronological framework for studying women's voluntary associations. Other essays in this section examine the impact of class, ethnic, religious and racial differences in defining the direction of feminine giving; the shifting fortunes of Anglo and Hispanic women's voluntary associations in Tampa; the enduring importance of feminine voluntarism within the black community; and how upper class women have used their activities to forge entrepreneurial careers beyond the realm of paid employment, while at the same time serving the class interests of their families and peers. The second section focuses on the social and political context of feminine philanthropy, including a discussion of why women's voluntary associations developed differently in the United States and England; a comparison of feminine participation in the infant health movement in France and the U.S.; and a look at how traditional feminine charities widened, rather than bridged, the enormous chasm separating middle class women from their impoverished sisters in Brazil.

92. Chambers, Clarke A. *Seedtime of Reform: American Social Service and Social Action, 1918-1933.* Reprint. Westport, Conn.: Greenwood Press, 1980.

Chambers focuses on the roles of voluntary reform associations "of concerned but disinterested" citizens and social welfare leaders and social service agencies during the Jazz Age of the 1920s. The overall question guiding his study is "what happened to the reform impulse between the New Nationalism and the New Freedom, on the one hand, and the New Deal on the other...the years of normalcy." Chambers pays attention to the crusade for children, women's rights, social work, the social settlements, the unemployment crisis, and the drive toward federal action on social problems that heralded the New Deal. He takes a detailed look at the works and guiding spirits of social reformers and voluntary associations during a formative and little understood decade in American history. He concludes that the successes of the New Deal owed much to the reform and welfare leaders who pioneered new programs and maintained a tradition of human liberalism during the 1920s. Bibliographical essay.

93. Chaney, Lindsay, and Michael Cieply. *The Hearsts. Family and Empire: The Later Years.* New York: Simon & Schuster, 1981.

94. "Charles Stewart Mott, 1875-1973." *Flint Journal (Flint, MI)* (24 February 1973): 1-16.

95. Chemical Bank. *Giving and Getting: A Chemical Bank Study of Charitable Contributions 1983 through 1988.* New York: Chemical Bank, 1983.

96. Chemical Bank. *Giving and Getting: A Chemical Bank Study of Charitable Contributions through 1984.* New York: Chemical Bank, [1981].

97. Churcher, Sharon. "Making It by Doing Good: Nouvelle Society Ladies Win Peer Approval Working for 'the Arts and Diseases'." *New York Times Magazine* (3 July 1988): 16-7, 33-4.

98. Clark, James A. *A Biography of Robert Alonzo Welch.* Houston, Tex.: Clark Book Co., 1963.

99. Clarke, Gerald. "A Portrait of the Donor: For a Connoisseur, Living Well Can Also Be a Work of Art." *Time* (8 May 1978): 78-9.

100. Collier, Peter, and David Horowitz. *The Fords: An American Epic.* New York: Summit Books, 1987.

101. Collier, Peter, and David Horowitz. *The Rockefellers: An American Dynasty.* New York: Holt, Rinehart & Winston, [1976].

This enormous biography of the Rockefeller family is divided into four major parts: *The Father*, about John Davison Rockefeller's (1839-1937) rise to fortune in the late nineteenth century and his establishment of the philanthropies that have caused his name to endure long after his death; *The Son*, about John D. Rockefeller, Jr. (1874-1960), who carried on the work of making and maintaining the Rockefeller fortune; *The Brothers*, describing the lives and exploits of John Jr.'s sons, John D. 3rd, Nelson, Laurance, Winthrop, and David; and *The Cousins*, about the brother's children, almost all of whom are still alive today, trying to fit a legacy of money and responsibility into modern lifestyles and diverse occupations. Full of personal accounts, letters, and fascinating biographical detail, this well-documented and exhaustively researched volume is a window into the world of a family whose beneficence has touched millions and whose wealth has angered as many. Extensive notes.

102. Commission on Private Philanthropy and Public Needs. *Giving in America: Toward a Stronger Voluntary Sector. Report of the Commission on Private Philanthropy and Public Needs.* Washington: Commission on Private Philanthropy and Public Needs, [1975].

Formed in 1973 to study the role of private philanthropy in the U.S., the Filer Commission's final report summarizes the findings of its two-year study and presents recommendations for broadening the base of philanthropy and improving the philanthropic process.

103. Cornuelle, Richard. *Healing America.* New York: G.P. Putnam, 1983.

104. Council for Financial Aid to Education. *Survey of the Public's Recollection of 1981 Charitable Donations.* Princeton, N.J.: Gallup Organization, 1982.

Gallup survey which looks at 1981 charitable donations contributed by people who itemize their deductions and people who take the standard deduction when filing Federal income tax returns. The results are compared with the results of a previous survey based on 1978 charitable donations. Includes trend analyses by subject areas of giving and of total charitable donations.

105. Council of Michigan Foundations. *Five Blue-Ribbon Ways to Give Away Your Money.* Grand Haven, Mich.: Council of Michigan Foundations, [1986].

Describes various giving options for individuals and companies, and describes the various kinds of gifts donated.

106. Council on Foundations. *Community Changes/Corporate Responses.* Occasional Paper, no. 3. Washington: Council on Foundations, 1987.

Highlights the discussion at the 1986 Autumn Conference for Corporate Grantmakers, including the nature of community change in the 1980s; the pitfalls and potentials in responding to community change; how corporations strike bargains with communities and how corporate grantmakers can find, retain, and recycle wealth in disinvested communities; and the shift to results-oriented grantmaking by corporations.

107. Council on Foundations. *Philanthropy in the 70's: An Anglo-American Discussion.* Washington: Council on Foundations, 1972.

108. Council on Foundations. *The Philanthropy of Organized Religion.* Washington: Council on Foundations, 1985.

Unique, important study of the philanthropy of organized religion. Based on the 485 responses to a survey of 2,700 national and regional religious organizations concerning their philanthropic activities, report describes the nature of religious giving, looks at the extent of religious philanthropy, identifies grantmaking religious organizations, and discusses trends in religious giving. Comments on current cooperation in religious giving and the future prospects for greater collaborative activities, both with each other and with secular funders. Appendixes provide the survey instrument, additional examples of funding, a selected bibliography, and a list of religious organizations making grants, loans, or alternative investments.

109. Council on Foundations. *Press Clippings.* 1982. Washington: Council on Foundations, 1982.

110. Council on Foundations. *Report and Recommendations to the Commission on Private Philanthropy and Public Needs on Private Philanthropic Foundations.* Unpublished, 1974.

111. Curti, Merle Eugene. "American Philanthropy and the National Character." *American Quarterly* 10 (Winter 1958): 420-37.

In this important article, Curti examines the ways in which philanthropy is integral to the national expression of American character, if there is such a thing. Subjects range from how the term *philanthropy* has been perceived throughout American history, to the amount of attention it has received in traditional scholarship, to notable philanthropic movements and events, to comparisons with Europe, and to the role philanthropy has played in making possible much broader improvements and innovations in American life (e.g., opening the doors of universities to women). More than forty footnotes provide many bibliographic references on almost every major subtopic covered in the article.

112. Curti, Merle Eugene, Judith Green, and Roderick Nash. "Anatomy of Giving: Millionaires in the Late 19th Century." *American Quarterly* 15 (1963): 416-35.

The authors investigated the allocation of gifts and bequests by millionaires between 1851 and 1913 in two related studies. They also attempted to assemble data on motivations. They were hampered severely by the lack of records on the activities of the individuals they chose as a sample, culled from a list of 4,047 reputed millionaires assembled in 1892 by the *New York Tribune*. Nevertheless, they were able to make some observations: 1) virtually all giving was local, 2) virtually no giving went to social or natural science research, 3) education in a broad sense was health and welfare's largest competitor, 4) bequests generally reflected lifelong philanthropic patterns, 5) residence did not affect propensity to give, and 6) "self-made" millionaires were much more philanthropic than those who inherited their wealth. Welfare and liberal arts education dominated the attention of philanthropists during the period studied.

113. Curti, Merle Eugene. "The History of American Philanthropy As a Field of Research." *American Historical Review* 62 (January 1957): 352-63.

In what is essentially an amplification of the Report of the Princeton Conference on the History of Philanthropy (1956), Curti suggests areas of research that could be profitably explored in the field of the history of philanthropy. While this essay is thirty years old now, the fact is that many of the gaps in the literature cited by Curti remain. He calls our attention to the following: 1) the need for studies of the role of charity and philanthropy in other cultures and at other times, 2) the contribution of religion to philanthropy, 3) economics and public policy as factors affecting philanthropy, 4) the effects on philanthropy of changing standards of living, 5) corporate philanthropy, 6) the legal history of philanthropy, 7) the effects of urbanization, 8) regional differences, 9) the growth in and methods of fundraising, 10) the relation of social status and mobility to philanthropy, and much more. There are occasional references to seminal texts in the field.

114. Curti, Merle Eugene, and Roderick Nash. *Philanthropy in the Shaping of American Higher Education.* New Brunswick, N.J.: Rutgers University Press, [1965].

Curti and Nash describe three centuries of voluntary philanthropic support of higher education, beginning with John Harvard's bequest to a struggling college in the Massachusetts Bay Colony in 1638. They always ask what effect the dependence on private sources has had. The scope of their study includes the colonial colleges, the hundreds of new colleges established between the Revolution and the Civil War, the growth of "practical" higher education in the nineteenth century, and the development of institutions for women and blacks. The authors delve into the role of the big foundations early in this century, the growing involvement of alumni, and the emergence of corporate donations to higher education. In a final chapter they appraise the advantages and disadvantages of higher education's dependence on philanthropic support. The authors stress that philanthropy did not merely enable developments in higher educations—in many instances it shaped them for years to come. Note on the sources.

115. Curtis, Charlotte. "A Restless Philanthropist." *New York Times* (3 April 1984): C-13.

116–132 PHILANTHROPY AND PHILANTHROPISTS

116. Curtis, Jody. "In Their Own Style." *Foundation News* 29 (March-April 1988): 43-3.

Profiles the Scrivner Award, which honors grantmakers whose creativity and accomplishments stand apart from the rest. The Council on Foundations' selection committee looks for a creative grantmaker who is active rather than passive; who can construct an original approach when problem-solving, one that will serve as a model for others to replicate or adapt; who builds networks and forges coalitions among disparate elements; and who works with others without seeking self-aggrandizement. Discusses the award's namesake, Robert Winston Scrivner, who for fourteen years directed the Rockefeller Family Fund (his personal passion was the prevention of nuclear war); and provides details on the three grantmakers to have received the Scrivner award so far.

117. Dane, John Hunter. *An Analysis of Trends of the Financial Support by Philanthropic Foundations to General Programs in U.S. Higher Education, 1955-1970.* Pittsburgh: University of Pittsburgh, 1974.

118. Davis, Allen F. *American Heroine: The Life and Legend of Jane Addams.* New York: Oxford University Press, 1973.

Davis, frustrated by the excessively laudatory tone of most writing about Jane Addams, endeavors to present a critical biographical study. He attempts to place an understanding of Addams and her works into the context of the American past and the history of women in the United States. He considers the way people viewed her and the legends she engendered as clues to the character of American society between 1889 and 1935. He is interested in how her symbolic image intertwined with her actions and beliefs. His detailed study of the influences and circumstances that led Addams to found Hull House in 1889 suggests that she shared much in common with other women of her generation who did not achieve the same notoriety. The rest of the book concerns itself with her public image and the ways in which she became a symbol of her age and a representative American woman—and what that means about the society in which she lived and worked.

119. Davis, Allen F. *Spearheads for Reform: The Social Settlements and the Progressive Movement, 1890-1914.* Reprint. New Brunswick, N.J.: Rutgers University Press, 1985.

Davis examines the involvement of settlement house workers in local and regional politics, which led to their involvement in national progressivism at the turn of the century. He demonstrates that from its founding in the 1880s, the settlement house movement was concerned not only with bettering the lives of people in urban slums, but also with transforming the entire environment to benefit future generations. This activity often culminated in legislation or increased governmental responsibility. The movement itself contributed to Progressivism's middle-class character and broadened its concern with welfare. Davis concentrates on Boston, Chicago, and New York and divides his analysis topically according to areas of reform concern. He focuses on the particular women and men who were active in the settlement house movement, as opposed to the institutions and organizations that they created. Note on the sources and extensive chapter notes.

120. Davis, John H. *The Guggenheims: An American Epic.* New York: William Morrow, 1978.

121. Davis, William. *The Rich: A Study of the Species.* New York: Franklin Watts, 1983.

122. De Grazia, Alfred, and Ted Gurr. *American Welfare.* New York: New York University Press, 1961.

123. Desruisseaux, Paul. "Celebrating the Legacy of Andrew Carnegie's Philanthropy." *Chronicle of Higher Education* 31 (11 September 1985): 29+.

124. Desruisseaux, Paul. "$5-Billion Sale Makes Institute Richest Charity." *Chronicle of Higher Education* 30 (12 June 1985): 1+.

125. Desruisseaux, Paul. "Philanthropy Courses and Tax Incentive Backed by Fund-Raisers' Trust." *Chronicle of Higher Education* 31 (4 December 1985): 32.

126. Desruisseaux, Paul. "Philanthropy 'Has to Be Talked about on Campus,' Foundation Head Says." *Chronicle of Higher Education* (24 October 1984): 18.

127. Desruisseaux, Paul. "There's More Asking and More Giving: Individual Donations Top $61-Billion." *Chronicle of Higher Education* 30 (29 May 1985): 1+.

128. Desruisseaux, Paul. "What Would Andrew Carnegie Think about How His Money Is Used Today?" *Chronicle of Higher Education* 30 (7 August 1985): 10-2.

129. Desruisseaux, Paul. "With $2.2-Billion in Its Till, Getty Aims to Make World a Better Place for Art." *Chronicle of Higher Education* 30 (5 June 1985): 1+.

130. Devine, Edward T. *The Principles of Relief.* New York: Macmillan, 1904.

131. Dickinson, Frank G. *The Changing Position of Philanthropy in the American Economy.* Occasional Paper, no. 110. New York: National Bureau of Economic Research, 1970.

Dickinson offers an economic analysis of how philanthropy changed in America between 1929 and 1959, a period of substantial evolution due to the unprecedented growth of the public sector. He is concerned with all charitable giving, not only private giving, emphasizing the flow of funds from those who give to those who receive—the fundamental relationship inherent in philanthropy. Private philanthropy, domestic and foreign, and public philanthropy are all treated, as are the relationships between them. As Dickinson says, "It would have been possible...to exclude one or more of the quadrants, and, instead, call the expenditures classified therein substitutes for philanthropy, or income transfers, or benefits guaranteed by government... [but] it will probably become abundantly clear that the use of such terms would have narrowly confined the treatment of a dynamic subject in a very dynamic period of social, economic and political change, thereby blurring historical patterns."

132. Dickinson, Frank G., ed. *Philanthropy and Public Policy.* New York: National Bureau of Economic Research, 1962.

This volume contains the proceedings of a 1961 conference cosponsored by the National Bureau of Economic Research and the Murill Center for Economics, organized to examine economic aspects of philanthropy, especially relating to public policy. The book includes the following essays: *An Economist's View of Philanthropy* (Solomon Fabricant), *The Growth of Private and Public Philanthropy* (Frank Dickinson), *One Economist's View of Philanthropy* (William Vickrey), *Notes on a Theory of Philanthropy* (Kenneth Boulding), *Hospitals and Philanthropy* (Eli Ginzberg), *Philanthropy and the Business Corporation: Existing Guidelines-Future Policy* (Covington Hardee), *Highlights of the Conference* (Frank Dickinson), and *The Poor Law Revisited* (Williard Thorp). The papers address key policy questions such as the role of government and private philanthropy in meeting human needs; tax law and incentives for giving; respective roles of federal, state, and local governments; media of private giving; and the necessity of redefining philanthropy in the modern world.

133. Dodge, Phyllis B. *Tales of the Phelps-Dodge Family: A Chronicle of Five Generations.* Princeton, N.J.: Princeton University Press, 1987.

Chronicles the lives and events of several generations of Phelps-Dodges, a family which prospered from the booming industry of nineteenth-century America and used its wealth to express strong charitable, religious, educational, and humanitarian impulses. Of great interest to economic and social historians, this biography also wryly details individual eccentricities with an appropriate sense of irony, from David Low Dodge, one of the first prominent pacifists in this country and founder of the New York Peace Society in 1815, who was a tyrant in his own household, to Grace Hoadley Dodge, an early social worker and first president of the National Board of the YWCA, described as "devout, earnest, and completely humorless." Of particular interest is a chapter devoted to Cleveland Hoadley Dodge, benefactor of the American University of Beirut, of Robert College in Istanbul, and of Princeton University, as well founder of the Cleveland Hoadley Dodge Foundation in 1917, who established a close friendship with Woodrow Wilson. As the editor of a Brooklyn newspaper wrote in 1926, "Heredity counts for more than some cynics are willing to believe....Possibly no American family has for so long a time and in so many phases participated in philanthropic activities on a large scale."

134. Doherty, Elizabeth M., ed. *A Window on the World of Philanthropy: A Compilation of Insights, 1973-1983.* Arlington, Va.: Council of Better Business Bureaus, 1984.

A compilation of articles from the Philanthropic Advisory Service's monthly newsletter covering business giving, government funding, tax exemption, and standards and laws governing charitable solicitation.

135. Dorian, Max. *The Du Ponts: From Gunpowder to Nylon.* Translated by Edward B. Garside. Boston: Little, Brown, 1962.

136. Douglas, James. *Why Charity? The Case for the Third Sector.* Beverly Hills, Calif.: Sage Publications, 1983.

Douglas presents a preliminary rationale and justification for the third sector from the point of view of the twin failures of market and government to provide certain needed services or products. He pulls together strands of political theory, including the Arrow Impossibility Theorem and Mancur Olson's theory of collective action. He explores the limitations of traditional concepts of market failure and the self-interest model of conventional economics in providing a sufficient definition and rationale for the sector. He then turns to the theoretical limits on what can be achieved (toward maximizing welfare) by government, given the constraints of democratic norms. His belief is that the case of government is more analogous to charity than the market. He elaborates a concept of categorical constraint—the necessity of universal application of authority—to characterize government and suggests a role for the third sector in serving the values and preferences of individuals or groups (minorities) not served by either government or the market. Brief bibliography.

137. "Douglas Fairbanks Jr. to Be Honored at Int'l Ball." *Coral Gables News* (6 April 1984).

138. Duke, Marc. *The Du Ponts: Portrait of a Dynasty.* New York: Saturday Review Press, 1976.

139. Duncan, Robert F. *John Price Jones: A Memoir by Robert F. Duncan.* New York: John Price Jones Co., 1969.

140. Dykeman, Wilma, and James Stokley. *Seeds of Southern Change: The Life of Will Alexander.* Chicago: University of Chicago Press, 1962.

141. Eisenberg, Pablo. "In Search of More Responsible Philanthropy." *Foundation News* 28 (January-February 1987): 51-3.

Remarks by Pablo Eisenberg, president of the Center for Community Change in Washington, D.C., delivered at a Minnesota Council on Foundations meeting for grantmakers and grantees in which he calls for a self-examination and genuine change in philanthropy. A crisis of serious proportions is being experienced in the nonprofit sector caused by both external and internal problems. Externally, he cites the problems of massive federal cutbacks in domestic spending, federal retrenchment, and the call from President Reagan for the private sector, especially philanthropy, to fill the economic void. Internally, the problems include unchanging priorities, lack of accountability and communications, reluctance to provide general support, double-standards for donees, failure to exercise tough judgements, and the "arrogance of power—a view that the donee is a second-class citizen." A partnership is needed, one in which "both sides of the philanthropic equation decide to get together, not as beggar and giver, but as partners."

142. Elkins, Ken. "Businessman Donates $100,000 to Vo-Tech School." *Enquirer (Columbus, GA)* (18 October 1983).

143. Elliot, Charles. *Mr. Anonymous: Robert W. Woodruff of Coca Cola.* Atlanta, Ga.: Cherokee Publishing Co., 1982.

144. England, Robert. "Giving a Wealth of Goodwill." *Insight* 3 (21 December 1987): 8-13.

Examines the current state of philanthropy in America: charitable donations by individuals are at their highest level in at least seventeen years; one study finds that those who regularly attend religious services tend to be more generous; some Americans feel that president Reagan's Private Sector Initiative has made charity much more effective and personal than the government's attempts to meet the needs of the poor; and celebrities, who have always lent their names to charities, have responded to the new needs with some of the most innovative and creative efforts in the history of charitable giving.

145. Epstein, Joseph. *Ambition: The Secret Passion.* New York: Dutton & Co., 1980.

146. "The Esquire Register." *Esquire* 108 (December 1987).

147. Evangelauf, Jean. "Scientist Donates $40-Million to U. of Illinois for Research on Intelligence." *Chronicle of Higher Education* 31 (9 October 1985): 29.

148. Failing, Patricia. "How the J. Paul Getty Trust Will Spend $90 Million a Year." *Art News* 83 (April 1984): 64-72.

149. Farrell, John C. *Beloved Lady: A History of Jane Addams' Ideas on Reform and Peace.* Baltimore, Md.: Johns Hopkins University Press, 1967.

An intellectual biography of Jane Addams, founder of Chicago's Hull House, this volume deals with her contribution to the social and political ferment of her time, the Progressive era. The author is particularly concerned with Addams' break from the views of most urban Progressives in opposing American participation in World War I, a position which resulted in a flood of public attacks against her and great personal doubt. But in other ways he holds her up as an example of noteworthy Progressive beliefs and actions, seeking to refute "fashionable" efforts to "dismiss Progressivism and prewar reform as nostalgic, complacent, moralistic, and rhetorical rather than concrete and realistic." Farrell asserts that the ideals of culture and democracy guided Addams' social and political activities, including her pacifism, and sustained her in the intellectual crisis she endured during World War I. Very extensive bibliography.

150. Feron, James. "Seven Hundred Forty-Three Acres Given by Rockefellers for a State Park." *New York Times* (22 December 1983): A-1, B-7.

151. Fidler, Kathleen. *The Man Who Gave Away Millions: The Story of Andrew Carnegie.* New York: Roy Publishers, 1956.

152. Fisher, James L. "The Growth of Heartlessness: The Need for Studies in Philanthropy." *Fund Raising Review* (July-August 1986): 4-6.

The author, outgoing president of Council for Advancement and Support of Education (CASE), believes a primary cause for lower giving of personal income is the nation's lack of academic courses in philanthropy.

153. Flexner, Abraham. *Henry S. Pritchett: A Biography.* New York: Columbia University Press, 1943.

154. Flexner, Abraham. *I Remember: The Autobiography of Abraham Flexner.* New York: Simon & Schuster, 1940.

Autobiography dealing primarily with the author's professional accomplishments. Flexner was author of the famous *Flexner Report* on medical education commissioned by the Carnegie Foundation for the Advancement of Teaching, secretary of the General Education Board, and principal advisor to John D. Rockefeller on medical education between 1913 and 1928. He had a long and important career in the service of foundations. He is referred to, cited, and invoked in so many other books and articles, that his autobiography offers an opportunity to test other accounts against his own.

155. Flexner, Simon, and James Thomas. *William Henry Welch and the Heroic Age of American Medicine.* New York: Viking, 1941.

156. Flynn, John T. *God's Gold: The Story of Rockefeller and His Times.* New York: Harcourt, Brace, 1932.

157. Folks, Homer. *The Care of Destitute, Neglected, and Delinquent Children.* Reprint. Poverty, U.S.A.: the Historical Record. Philadelphia: Ayer Press, 1971.

Folks wrote this book in 1900, but it documents the methods of public and private support of children who have been removed from their earlier environment and from parental control for the entire preceding century. Nine papers are presented topically: the situation in 1801; public care of destitute children, 1801-1875; private charities for destitute children, 1801-1875; removal of children from almshouses; public systems, other than almshouse care, 1875-1900; neglected children; private charities for destitute and neglected children, 1875-1900; delinquent children; and present tendencies. It is a comprehensive account of the available services and methods to care for unfortunate children in the nineteenth century, with topics often divided up by city or region. Folks notes in his last chapter what he considers a favorable trend toward increased emphasis on public support. Bibliography.

158. "The Forbes Four Hundred." *Forbes* 136 (28 October 1985): 108+.

159. Ford, David S. *Data on Philanthropy in New Jersey: Alternatives for Data Collection and Analysis. Preliminary Report.* Madison, N.J.: Resource Consultant Services, 1983.

160. Fosdick, Raymond Blaine. *Chronicle of a Generation: An Autobiography.* New York: Harper & Bros., [1958].

161. Fosdick, Raymond Blaine. *John D. Rockefeller Jr.: A Portrait.* New York: Harper & Bros., 1956.

162. Frantzreb, Arthur C. "Philanthropy Is Both Giving and Receiving." *Fund Raising Management* 14 (January 1984): 76+.

163. Freedman, Estelle B. *Their Sister's Keepers: Women's Prison Reform in America, 1830-1930.* Ann Arbor, Mich.: University of Michigan Press, 1981.

This book explores the origins of women's concerns for female prisoners in the United States, beginning with the response of white, middle-class women to the problem in the first half of the nineteenth century. A history of the first state prisons run by and for women from 1870 to 1910 follows, and a third section examines the work of women criminologists and penologists during the Progressive era. The study takes as its larger context much of the scholarship on women in the nineteenth century, the history of American feminism, and the history of prison reform in general. Freedman concentrates on these broad historical questions: "Why did reformers think and act as they did? What internal and external forces influenced the history of their institutions? How, and why, did their movement change from the nineteenth to the early twentieth centuries? And why has the legacy of "their sisters' keepers" remained so powerful?" 150-item bibliography.

164. Friedman, B.H. *Gertrude Vanderbilt Whitney.* New York: Doubleday, 1978.

165. Frisch, Ephraim. *An Historical Survey of Jewish Philanthropy.* New York: Macmillan, 1924.

166. Fromm, Erich. *To Have or to Be?* New York: Harper & Row, 1976.

This volume, building on Fromm's earlier work, presents a "radical-humanistic psychoanalytical" account of selfishness and altruism—the mode of having and the mode of being. Fromm rejects the notions that pleasure (the satisfaction of desires) is the aim of life (radical hedonism) and that egotism, selfishness, and greed, generated by the system, lead to harmony and peace (unlimited egotism), both thought to be principles guiding our economic behavior. He argues that a need for profound human change has emerged not only as an ethical, religious, and psychological imperative resulting from our pathogenic social character, but also as a condition for the sheer survival of the human race. The final chapters of the book deal with the relevance of the modes of having and being "in the formation of a New Man and a New Society and address themselves to the possibilities of alternatives to debilitating individual ill-being, and to catastrophic socioeconomic development of the whole world." Brief bibliography.

167. Fuller, John G. *The Great Soul Trial: The Gripping Story of the Prospector Who Left a Fortune to a Study of the Soul.* New York: Macmillan, 1969.

168. Gallup Omnibus. *Survey of the Public's Recollection of 1978 Charitable Donations.* Princeton, N.J.: Gallup Organization, 1979.

169. Gamarekian, Barbara. "A Prince Whose Mission Is UNICEF." *New York Times* (23 March 1983): A-20.

170. Garrow, David J. *Philanthropy and the Civil Rights Movement.* Working Papers. New York: Center for the Study of Philanthropy, [1987].

Examines the increasingly clear and unified view that has been emerging within the scholarly community about the relationship between the civil rights movement and its non-black, non-southern contributing supporters; two basic conclusions are being articulated in the growing body of literature: first, a social change movement preferably ought to draw upon member beneficiaries for its financial needs, rather than be in a position of relying upon the unpredictable interest or support of non-member outsiders, and thus relinquishing control to outside forces; and second, while philanthropy may thus be potentially bad for a movement, radicalism in a movement is good, for as the behavior of the foundation community in the late 1960s seems to suggest, only the threat of dangerous, irresponsible, uncontrolled extremism will be enough to urge outside philanthropists into substantial and active support for more mainstream movement proponents of meaningful social change.

171. Gates, Frederick Taylor. *Chapters in My Life.* New York: Free Press, 1977.

This autobiography of John D. Rockefeller's chief philanthropic advisor, Frederick Taylor Gates (1853-1929), is divided into two parts. The first, *The Early Years*, encompasses his life from birth in Broome County, New York, childhood, early religious influences, college, and on through to the higher education of his sons and marriages of his daughters. It deals primarily with his personal evolution and the fabric of his family life. The second part, *My Years With Mr. Rockefeller and His Philanthropies*, begins in 1891, when John D. Rockefeller summoned Gates to New York to assist him in screening charitable inquiries. It was an activity that had become too demanding and time-consuming for Rockefeller to do alone. It was Gates who gradually developed and introduced into all Rockefeller's charities the principles of scientific giving. His role in the Rockefeller philanthropies increased exponentially thereafter, until well beyond his formal resignation in 1912.

172. Gates, Frederick Taylor. "The Memoirs of Frederick T. Gates." *American Heritage* 6 (April 1955): 65-86.

173. Geldof, Bob, and Paul Vallely. *Is That It?* New York: Weinfeld & Nicolson, 1987.

Autobiography of Bob Geldof who organized Band Aid and Live Aid for the benefit of famine-stricken Ethiopia. The book traces Geldof's life from his youth in Dublin, Ireland through the years of his rise from rock singer to rock star with the Boomtown Rats and the creation of the Band Aid and the Live Aid benefit concerts which brought him global recognition for his African relief work. [See: FUNDRAISING. Williams, Roger M. *What Hath Geldof Wrought?*].

174. Gettleman, Marvin E. "Charity and Social Classes in the United States, 1874-1900." *The American Journal of Economics and Sociology* 22 (1963): 417-26.

Gettleman attempts to show that simultaneous recognition and evasion of the problem of social classes were the dominant characteristics of the formative years of the American profession and institution of social work. He examines the conceptions of human nature, philanthropic duty, and sources of poverty that underlay the philosophy of the Charity Organization Societies, which emerged in England and the United States in the late nineteenth century. He interestingly asserts that leaders and proponents of organized charity held to many of the notions of social Darwinism, which seemed so antithetical to charity. To reconcile this opposition, they conceived of "the spiritual nature" of humans, the rise of which (in both givers and receivers of charity) is the ultimate good, even over the material progress to which the Darwinian argument applied. They also invoked a distinction between "worthy" and "unworthy" poor, with the claim that poverty had individual causes.

175. Gillin, John Lewis. *Poverty and Dependency.* New York: Appleton-Century Co., 1937.

176. *Giving USA.* 1956-1988. New York: American Association of Fund-Raising Counsel, 19—.

Statistical analysis of charitable giving contributions, distribution, donors, recipients, sources of philanthropy, and areas of philanthropic opportunity in 1986. Sources analyzed include individuals, bequests, foundations, corporations, and volunteers. Areas of philanthropic opportunity reviewed are religion; education; health; human service; arts, culture, and humanities; and public/society benefit. The publication contains numerous charts, lists, and statistical tables. Of particular note are the special listings—*Large Gifts To...*—which are included for individuals, bequests, foundations, corporations, education, and health. (The lists are arranged in descending order of donation amount.) Among the statistical tables are total giving; sources of philanthropy; private foundation ranking by grants and assets; grants by subject; state distribution of grants; corporate contributions; summaries of religious statistics; health expenditures; United Way statistics; federal appropriations; public broadcasting income; and state arts agencies legislative appropriations. Contains a list of AAFRC officers, staff and members, and a list of organizations related to philanthropy.

177. Gladden, Washington. "Tainted Money." *Outlook* 52 (30 November 1985): 886-7.

Gladden argues passionately against the acceptance of "tainted money"—that which has been accumulated dishonestly, through cruelty, trickery, robbery, and the like—by churches, educational institutions, and other charities, claiming that its corrupting influence will far outweigh any good it can do. At the center of his argument is the fear that because institutions cannot really criticize their donors, but instead even eulogize them, their bad, immoral acts will be forgotten by the public, and they will be remembered only for their philanthropic good works. It is interesting to try to extrapolate from Gladden's argument whether the same principle would render Robin Hood's donations to the poor from the pockets of the rich similarly suspect. While he names no names, Gladden is clearly referring to the robber barons of his era, including John D. Rockefeller.

178. Goldin, Milton. "Where Is the Private Money President Reagan Promised?" *New York Times* (11 November 1984): WC-28.

179. Goldin, Milton. *Why They Give: American Jews and Their Philanthropies.* New York: Macmillan, 1976.

180. Goldstein, Richard. "Culture's Hidden Persuaders." *Cue* (28 March 1980): 23-5.

181. Gonzalez, A. Miren, and Philip Tetlock. *A Literature Review of Altruism and Helping Behavior.* Program on Non-Profit Organizations, no. 16. New Haven, Conn.: Institution for Social and Policy Studies, [1980].

182. Goodale, Frances A., ed. *The Literature of Philanthropy.* New York: Harper & Bros., 1893.

This small volume is part of a large collection that represents the periodical literature of women in New York State from the mid-nineteenth century on. Frances Goodale, in her introduction, asserts that periodical literature "mirrors faithfully the passing shadow of the age," and that "some of it shall outlive the stately and treasured book." The volume contains essays on criminal reform, the tenement neighborhood idea, nurses, the Red Cross, Indians, anti-slavery, "the negro and civilization," and the education of the blind. All of the contributing women are practitioners as well as advocates of philanthropy.

183. Goodman, Paul. "Ethics and Enterprise: The Values of the Boston Elite, 1800-1860." *American Quarterly* 18 (1966): 437-51.

Goodman's study of the values and aspirations of Boston's merchant elite in the first half of the nineteenth century reveals that a strong ethic of stewardship dominated their activities, flavored by a belief in progress, personal achievement, and the virtues of honor and wisdom. Boston's educational, charitable, and philanthropic societies increased in number by a factor of five between 1830 and 1850, and large gifts such as Amos Lawrence's gift to Harvard for a scientific school were not uncommon. The merchants were also active patrons of culture in Boston, sharing a deep conviction in the ability of the arts and letters to uplift and enrich one spiritually. While the excitement of business and the gratification of amassing personal wealth were their principal concerns, Goodman trys to show that the city's elite were governed by ethics in many important ways.

184. Goodspeed, Thomas Wakefield. *The University of Chicago Biographical Sketches.* Chicago: University of Chicago Press, 1922.

185. "Great Family Fortunes." *Forbes 400* (1 October 1984): 166+.

Provides brief descriptions of very wealthy families in the U.S.

186. Greene, Bert, and Phillip Stephen Schultz. *Pity the Poor Rich.* Chicago: Contemporary Books, 1978.

187. Greenleaf, William. *From These Beginnings: The Early Philanthropies of Henry and Edsel Ford, 1911-1936.* Detroit: Wayne State University Press, 1964.

This is a systematic study of the philanthropies of Henry Ford, his wife Clara, and his son Edsel, before the establishment of the Ford Foundation. The philanthropies supported by the Fords had a limited scope but wide diversity. They brought support to medicine and medical research, education, historic preservation, community welfare, social work, the arts, and scientific exploration under the general rubric of "advancing human welfare." Greenleaf contends that while Ford was "fumbling, inept, and puerile" in the realm of social judgement, his engineer's horror of waste and inefficiently-utilized human energy prompted him, an "avowed opponent of philanthropy, to help his fellow man help himself." Ford believed strongly that charity is useless unless it is applied to the roots of principle. Skeptical of institutionalized philanthropy, he did not create the Ford Foundation itself until economic pressures and tax incentives practically forced the decision on him in 1936.

188. Gronbjerg, Kirsten A. "Private Welfare in the Welfare State: Recent U.S. Patterns." *Social Service Review* 56 (1982): 1-26.

According to the introduction, "this paper examines recent trends in American philanthropy and relates these to changes in the composition of and size of both the private and public welfare sectors in the United States. The findings reveal that private welfare has been overwhelmed—but not replaced—by the growth in public welfare. Although private welfare maintains some of its traditional functions, it has become more closely linked to and in some cases dependent on public welfare. Consequently, there have been significant changes in the institutional character and organizational format and operations of private welfare. These transformations of the American welfare system are interpreted within the mass-society perspective." Gronbjerg concludes that increased pressures on private agencies for accountability and competition for scarce resources have resulted in more bureaucratic and professional forms of service than in the past.

189. Gronbjerg, Kirsten A. "Private Welfare: Its Future in the Welfare State." *American Behaviorial Scientist* 26 (1983): 773-93.

Gronbjerg examines the evolving role of private sources of welfare in the context of a general movement toward an authentic welfare state—a system in which such services are provided entirely by government. She discusses the desirability—or lack thereof—of such an outcome from a number of vantage points, and suggests that private welfare is in a better position than public welfare to perform two functions: provide some intervening structure by which distinctive individual or group claims may regain prominence, and play an integrative role in a society in which regional, ethnic, or racial identities are highly salient, by providing a structure and purpose for such group organizations. Gronbjerg touches on organizational links between public and private welfare, the system of entitlements and obligations, and the future of private welfare in the United States. She concludes that, in the short term at least, private welfare is more necessary than ever in the face of federal retrenchment.

190. Gunther, John. *Taken at the Flood: The Story of Albert D. Lasker.* New York: Harper, 1960.

191. Gurin, Maurice G. "Courses in Philanthropy: A First in U.S. Colleges." *Fund Raising Management* 18 (August 1987): 60-3.

This 1987-88 academic year the Program for Studying Philanthropy's pilot courses begin at seven institutions of higher learning. The program is designed and conducted by the Association of American Colleges (AAC) and funded by the American Association of Fund-Raising Counsel Trust for Philanthropy (AAFRC) and major foundations. The initial seven institutions will be joined by seven others during this three year project. The courses are interdisciplinary in nature and are diverse in their curricula. For example, among the seven courses, one course will highlight and analyze the diversity of American expressions of philanthropy by focusing on philanthropy as a force in American culture, in the provisions and definition of social service, and as a force in scientific research; another will explore service and charitable giving in America. Fundraising techniques or management of nonprofit organizations, however, will not be a part of the curricula. The final phase of the Program for Studying Philanthropy will be a report on the program, including an evaluation of the pilot courses.

192. Hacker, Louis Morton. *The World of Andrew Carnegie, 1865-1901.* Philadelphia: Lippincott, 1968.

193. Halberstam, David. "The Very Expensive Education of McGeorge Bundy: A Study in the Uses of Power and How It Is Manipulated in the Upper Reaches Where the Nation's Elite Operates." *Harper's Magazine* (July 1969): 21-41.

194. Hammer, Armand, and Neil Lyndon. *Hammer.* New York: Putnam, 1987.

Autobiography of Dr. Armand Hammer, the chairman and CEO of Occidental Petroleum. Statesman, envoy, industrialist, entrepreneur, physician, collector, and philanthropist—this is the story of a man distinguished in public life and business, a true citizen of the world. Hammer has known all the great leaders of the world (he was a man who could call Lenin by his first name). From the 1960's through to the present, Hammer has traveled to Moscow, promoting peace, cultural exchanges, and missions of mercy such as the plight of Soviet Jews and organizing medical assistance for the Chernobyl survivors.

195. Handlin, Oscar, and Mary F. Handlin. *The Wealth of the American People: A History of American Affluence.* New York: McGraw-Hill, 1975.

196. Hands, A.R. *Charities and Social Aid in Greece and Rome.* Ithaca, N.Y.: Cornell University Press, 1968.

In this important history, Hands provides a backdrop for a discussion of ancient philanthropic activity by devoting his initial chapters to the "social ethos" of the age—the philosophy of life or the theory of the city-state. The subsequent chapters—*The Poor, Pity for the Destitute, The Provision of Basic Commodities, Education and Culture,* and *Health and Hygiene*—deal with the applications of this theory, or ethos, as they examine life in Greece and Rome. Hands attempts to define the spirit of classical beneficence and illustrate its main features by consulting a wide range of sources "unlikely to be contaminated by non-classical ideas." The history goes no later than A.D. 250. For a general discussion of motives for giving in classical society, see especially *Giving for a Return*, also reprinted in Brian O'Connell's book, *America's Voluntary Spirit* (1983).

197. Hardin, Garrett. *The Limits of Altruism: An Ecologist's View of Survival.* Bloomington, Ind.: Indiana University Press, 1977.

In this provocative book, Hardin argues that altruism has necessary limitations in large groups, such as social policy institutions, which should seek instead to follow his *Cardinal Rule of Policy*: Never ask a person to act against his own self-interest. When reaching for the best of all possible (not conceivable) worlds, Hardin argues that "in the intimacy of small groups altruism may be substantial and important; in large groups enlightened egoism is the most powerful motive. It is in fact the best motive we can rely on." Hardin, an ecologist, draws on many examples from biological systems to illustrate his arguments. He rejects the ideal of a universal brotherhood, or Family of Man, as not only paradoxical (if there are only brothers, there are no others), but also survival-threatening. He suggests that altruism requires limited antagonism toward others in order to survive.

198. Hardin, John R. *The Marcus L. Ward Home at Maplewood, N.J.* N.p.: Marcus L. Ward Estate, 1928.

199. Harrar, J. George. *Raymond Blaine Fosdick.* Reprint. Newark, Del.: American Philosophical Association, 1972.

200. Harris, Leon. "Charity in Texas. Part 1: Charity, Inc." *Ultra* 3 (January 1984): 54+.

201. Harvey, George. *Henry Clay Frick: The Man.* New York: Charles Scribner's Sons, 1928.

202. "Hauck Gives City Money for Pavilion." *Cincinnati Enquirer* (13 May 1983).

203. Haymarket Peoples Fund. *Inherited Wealth: Your Money and Your Life.* New York: Funding Exchange, 1980.

204. Heale, M.J. "Patterns of Benevolence: Associated Philanthropy in the Cities of New York, 1830-1860." *New York History* 57 (1976): 53-79.

This article examines the challenges posed to New York philanthropy by the growth of cities, foreign immigration, and increasing population. It also examines the response to these challenges: the emergence of associated philanthropy, which could discriminate between the deserving and undeserving poor and give aid with the greatest moral effect. By the 1830s even smaller towns were turning to associated philanthropy. Able-bodied male paupers became legitimate subjects for philanthopic concern in these years, in addition to the traditionally cared-for widows, orphans, and handicapped. Heale goes into some detail about particular charities in certain communities, including New York City, Buffalo, Rochester, Albany, and Brooklyn. The role of evangelical Protestantism in spurring reform is noted, and Heale demonstrates how associated philanthropy became a vehicle for accculturation as well as almsgiving.

205. Heale, M.J. "Patterns of Benevolence: Charity and Morality in Rural and Urban New York, 1783-1830." *Societas—A Review of Social History* 3 (1973): 337-59.

Heale analyzes the development of charity directed not only at providing for the needs of the poor and unfortunate, but also at reforming their characters, in New York in the early Republic. Heale sees this development partly as an attempt on the part of "pious and respectable" Americans to maintain order in a changing society. He highlights the differences and similarities between rural and urban benevolence. He notes that while benevolence in rural environments remained largely informal and personal, in cities the growth of philanthropic associations was necessary to adapt to urban conditions. In rural communities charity could apply more or less equally to people, but the associated philanthropies of urban centers tended to assist widows, orphans, and others about whom it could not be said that idleness and vice had been the cause of their downfall. According to Heale, the charitable association emerged as a means of reconciling the traditional concept of charity as a Christian duty with the new perception of the poor as a potentially dangerous class.

206. Healey, Edna. *Lady Unknown: The Life of Angela Burdett-Coutts.* London: Sidgwick & Jackson, 1978.

207. Held, Walter J. *The Technique for Proper Giving.* New York: McGraw-Hill, 1959.

208. Helderman, Leonard C. *George Washington: Patron of Learning.* New York: Century Co., [1932].

209. Hendrick, Burton J. *The Life of Andrew Carnegie.* 2 Vols. New York: Doubleday, 1932.

210. Hendrick, Burton J., and Daniel Henderson. *Louise Whitfield Carnegie.* New York: Hastings House, 1950.

211. Henry, William A., III. "An Open and Shut Case." *Foundation News* 28 (March-April 1987): 46-7.

A critical examination of foundations' tendency towards secrecy and its impact on media coverage. One major reason that charities and foundations do not receive better media coverage is because "they prefer to work largely in secret," states the author. In return, the media are suspicious of writing selected stories about good works when they cannot obtain the most basic information on the procedures behind the grants, the relationship of donor and donee, and the motives of the donors. The author also believes that the journalists are indolent. The journalistic silence surrounding foundations is based on both ignorance and laziness. They do no investigative reporting on philanthropic abuses or on philanthropic good. While many in philanthropy desire media coverage, "the 'independent sector' has played hard to get, and seemingly has reconciled itself to missing out on the coverage that it would like to have, in order to avoid the accountability that it would not."

212. Henry, Yvette, ed. *People in Philanthropy: A Guide to Funding Connections.* 8th ed. Washington: Taft Group, 1988.

Brief biographical profiles for more than 8,000 foundation trustees, corporate executives, and professional members at more than 1,000 of America's largest philanthropies. Indexed by place of birth; alma mater; office address; and corporate, nonprofit, and philanthropic affiliations. Useful resource in cultivating the individuals who make philanthropic decisions.

213. Herrick, Cheesman A. *Stephen Girard: Founder.* Philadelphia: Girard College, 1923.

214. Hersh, Burton. *The Mellon Family: A Fortune in History.* New York: William Morrow, 1978.

215. Hersh, Burton. "Paul Mellon." *Town & Country* 132 (May 1978): 111-3,160,162,166-7.

216. Hewins, Ralph. *Mr. Five Percent: The Story of Calouste Gulbenkian.* New York: Rinehart & Co., 1958.

217. Hewitt, Edward Ringwood. *Those Were the Days: Tales of a Long Life.* New York: Duell, Sloan, & Pearce, 1943.

218. Heyns, Roger W. *The National Climate for Philanthropy and the Private Sector.* Washington: Independent Sector, 1982.

219. Hill, Frank Pierce. *James Bertram: An Appreciation by Frank Pierce Hill.* New York: Carnegie Corporation of New York, 1936.

220. Hodge, Paul. "Loudoun Man at Ninety-Two Leads Rugged Life: Spry Retired Doctor Made Fortune in Land." *Washington Post* (21 March 1984).

221. Hodgkinson, Virginia A. *Dimensions of the Independent Sector: A Statistical Profile.* Washington: Independent Sector, 1984.

This statistical compilation provides a wealth of data on the characteristics, growth, and financial status of all types of funders and nonprofit organizations. Section 3 details the changing sources of revenues for nonprofit organizations.

222. Hodgkinson, Virginia A. *Dimensions of the Independent Sector: A Statistical Profile.* 2nd ed. Washington: Independent Sector, 1986.

Second in a biennial series of statistical profiles on the U.S. independent sector, which focuses on major trends affecting voluntary organizations, foundations, social responsibility programs of corporations and people who contribute time and money. Includes an overview of the independent sector and its place in the U.S. economy; summary of the total sources and examination of trends in the uses of support for the independent sector; detailed description and analysis of private support sources; profiles for subsectors of the independent sector (e.g., health services, education, religion, social services, etc.) with information on trends in employment, wages, salaries, sources and uses of funds, and operating expenditures. Appendix includes a description of the framework study's methodology and a glossary of terms.

223. Hoffman, William. *David: Report on a Rockefeller.* Secaucus, N.J.: Lyle Stuart, 1971.

224. Hollis, Ernest Victor. *Philanthropic Foundations and Higher Education.* New York: Columbia University Press, 1938.

225. Holman, Louis A. *Scenes from the Life of Benjamin Franklin.* Boston: Small, Maynard & Co., 1916.

226. Holton, Felicia Antonelli. "In a Secular Society, How Can We Teach People about Philanthropy? A Conversation with Robert L. Payton." *University of Chicago Magazine* (Fall 1985): 2-7.

President of Exxon Education Foundation, Robert L. Payton questions and analyzes the lack of formal training in and research of the philanthropic tradition, or what he calls "the wellspring of most of the social change in our society, [which] is directly related to our survival as a free and open democratic society."

227. Horowitz, Daniel. *The Morality of Spending: Attitudes toward the Consumer Society in America, 1875-1940.* New Studies in American Intellectual and Cultural History. Baltimore, Md.: Johns Hopkins University Press, 1985.

An intellectual history of American attitutes towards consumption, seeking to understand how American social thinkers have treated changes in the standard of living. Horowitz insists on the benefit of exploring the interplay between the related stories of how Americans spent their money (focusing primarily on the years from 1875 to 1940) and how social, economic, and intellectual writers thought they should. His approach is to use investigations of household expenditures principally as cultural artifacts that enable us to understand the writers' attitudes to the dilemmas and opportunities of the phenomena they witnessed. Especially interesting for the philanthropic sector are the arguments made against indulging overmuch in mass, commercial consumption and the persistently expressed hope that Americans would aspire to something higher, i.e., a commitment to public life and nonmaterial satisfactions as a way for individuals and groups to construct meaning in their lives.

228. "How Will Philanthropy Fare in the New Congress?" *Philanthropy Monthly* 15 (October 1982): 5-14.

229. Hyman, Sidney, ed. *Gaylord Freeman of First Chicago. 2 Vols.* Chicago: First National Bank of Chicago, 1975.

230. Independent Sector. *Analysis of the Economic Recovery Program's Direct Significance for Philanthropic and Voluntary Organizations and the People They Serve.* Washington: Independent Sector, 1982.

231. Independent Sector. *Daring Goals for a Caring Society: A Blueprint for Substantial Growth in Giving and Volunteering in America.* Washington: Independent Sector, 1986.

Summary of the Final Report of the Task Force on Measurable Growth in Giving and Volunteering, calling for a doubling of charitable giving and a fifty percent increase in volunteer activity by 1991. In order to achieve the overall goal for giving and volunteering, two broad goals have been established: (1) create a climate for giving and volunteering that conditions society as a whole and individuals in particular to the importance of private philanthropy and voluntary service, and (2) develop a far greater ability of voluntary organizations to raise money and involve volunteers.

232. Independent Sector. *Discussion Draft of Report and Recommended Program Plan for Measurable Growth in Giving and Volunteering.* Washington: Independent Sector, 1985.

233. Independent Sector. "'Fairness' and the Charitable Deduction for Nonitemizers." *Government Relations Info and Action* 7 (15 April 1985): D.

234. Independent Sector. *Looking Forward to the Year 2000: Public Policy and Philanthropy.* Spring Research Forum Working Papers. Washington: Independent Sector, 1988.

The 1988 Spring Research Forum's working papers reflect the growing scholarly interest in the independent sector. Topics include public policy and philanthropy; shifting boundaries among the sectors; accountability issues; public policy and nonprofit organizations; values and ethics; demographic trends and new information about the sector; philanthropy, public policy, and the poor; financing nonprofit organizations; regional and community issues; public policy among the major subsectors; the nonprofit sector abroad; issues in corporate giving; and foundation issues and public policy. Each author was asked to consider three questions on their topics: What are the current trends in each of the specific theme areas? What will result if current policies and/or practices are maintained? And what other policies or practices should be considered?

235. Independent Sector. *Measurable Growth in Giving and Volunteering.* Washington: Independent Sector, 1985.

Working from the abiding belief that giving and volunteering are essential to the core fiber of American society, Independent Sector's Task Force presents its conclusions and recommendations for maintaining current levels and influencing significant growth in charitable behavior. Among the findings that justify optimism about future growth: approximately thirteen percent of adult Americans (or twenty million people) already give five percent or more of their income to charity; approximately fourteen percent of adult Americans (or twenty-three million people) already volunteer an average of five hours or more per week. The largest single reason people volunteer (or provide financial support) is that someone asks them. Goals for the recommended program plan to achieve measurable growth in giving and volunteering include: providing a clear indication of what is expected of all of us in the way of personal service to create a free and caring society; maintaining and improving public policies that encourage giving and voluntary action; and helping to develop the far greater ability of voluntary organizations to raise money and involve volunteers.

236. Independent Sector, and United Way Institute. *Philanthropy, Voluntary Action and the Public Good.* Spring Research Forum Working Papers. Washington: Independent Sector, 1986.

237. Independent Sector. *Religion and Philanthropy.* [Cassette tape]. Washington: Independent Sector, 1985.

238. Independent Sector. *Religion and Philanthropy Project: Progress Report, May 15, 1987.* Unpublished, [1987].

After a 1985 survey and Gallup poll revealed that seventy-two percent of all individual giving goes to religious institutions and nearly half of all volunteering was done for the same, Independent Sector (IS) initiated the IS Religion and Philanthropy Project. Its goals are: to increase funding for research on the subject; to increase public awareness of the importance of the religious sector to the charitable behavior of Americans, and of the variety of services provided and supported by religious institutions that improve the quality of life in their communities, in the nation, and in other nations; and to encourage the incorporation of such knowledge into college curricula. This progress report includes drafts for questionnaires, updates on activities related to the project, and a mailing list of persons interested in the Religion and Philanthropy Project to encourage and facilitate the exchange of information and resources.

239. Ireland, Thomas R., and David B. Johnson. *The Economics of Charity.* Blacksburg, Va.: Center for the Study of Public Choice, 1970.

240. Jaffee, Larry. "How Paul Newman's Hobby Grew Up into a Major Grantor." *Fund Raising Management* 16 (September 1985): 38+.

Describes Newman's charity...donating all the profits from his own brand of salad dressing and spaghetti sauce.

241. James, Marquis. *Alfred I. Du Pont: The Family Rebel.* New York: Bobbs-Merrill Co., 1941.

242. "Japanese Philanthropy in the United States. Part 1." *Enterprise* 7 (April 1988): 5.

Profiles the United States Japan Foundation, created in 1980 to improve understanding and cooperation between the two countries. Its programs include pre-college teacher-training, an exchange program between New York City Managers and the Tokyo Metropolitan Government, a conference on a joint U.S.-Japan study of the Soviet Union, and broad public information projects, aided by increased funding for National Public Radio reporters covering Japan and the Far East.

243. "Japanese Philanthropy in the United States. Part 2." *Enterprise* 7 (July 1988): 5, 8, 11.

244. Jarchow, Merrill E. *Amherst H. Wilder and His Enduring Legacy to St. Paul.* St. Paul, Minn.: Amherst H. Wilder Foundation, 1981.

245. Jarrette, Alfred Q. *Julius Rosenwald, Benefactor of Mankind.* Greenville, S.C.: Southeastern University Press, 1975.

246. Jenkins, Edward C. *Philanthropy in America.* New York: Association Press, 1950.

247. Jenkins, Frederick Warren. *Bulletin of the Russell Sage Foundation Library.* New York: Russell Sage Foundation, 1920.

248. Jenkins, John Wilbur. *James B. Duke, Master Builder: The Story of Tobacco, Development of Southern and Canadian Water Power and the Creation of a University.* New York: George H. Doran Co., 1927.

249. Jenkins, Simon. "Paying for the Arts." *Economist* (17 November 1984).

250. Johnson, Alvin. *Andrew Carnegie: Educator.* New York: Carnegie Corporation of New York, 1936.

251. Johnson, Joseph E., and Bernard Bush. *Andrew Carnegie, Apostle of Peace.* Reprint. Washington: Carnegie Endowment for International Peace, 1960.

252. Johnson, Robert Matthews. "Altruism's Own Rewards." *Foundation News* 29 (May-June 1988): 44-7.

Essay examining the "subtle and obscure" benefits of altruism, especially in the context of giving to grassroots community organizations, ranging from self-realization to recognition to reciprocity.

253. Johnson, Robert Matthews. *The First Charity: How Philanthropy Can Contribute to Democracy in America.* Washington: Seven Locks Press, 1988.

Johnson advances the argument that democracy needs to be given top priority in planning for grants and contributions in American communities. In the face of increasing alienation (from the big systems of government, employment, schools and other institutions over which we feel we have so little control; from each other because the sense and resources of community have withered; and from our own potentialities because too often we feel we have no qualifications, no control, and no support) community organizing offers a way to overcome our isolation and strengthen our ability to determine what society should mean for the people. Johnson builds his case, sets up specifications for programs, shows the types of community organizations that effectively meet those specifications, and provides practical guides for giving in ways that are responsible, creative, and satisfying. Appendixes include sources of assistance to community organizations, grantmaking associations and resources, and a bibliography of particularly distinguished, readable books, each with its own clear bearing on philanthropy.

254. Jones, John Price. *The American Giver: A Review of American Generosity.* New York: Inter-River Press, 1954.

255. Jones, John Price, ed. *Philanthropy Today: An Interim Report.* New York: Inter-River Press, 1949.

256. Jones, John Price, ed. *The Yearbook of Philanthropy, 1940-1948. 9 Vols.* New York: Inter-River Press, 1940.

257. Jordan, David Starr. *The Story of a Good Woman: Jane Lathrop Stanford.* Stanford, Calif.: American Unitarian Association, 1912.

258. Joseph, James A. "Five Challenges Outlined at Battle Creek Gathering." *Michigan Scene* 9 (Spring 1983): 1+.

259. Joseph, James A. "The Interrelationships of Organized Philanthropy." *Codel News* (November-December 1986).

260. Joseph, James A. "The Meaning of 1983 for the Mission of 1984." *Foundation News* 25 (May-June 1984): 68-9.

261. Joseph, James A. *What Lies Ahead for Philanthropy.* Occasional Paper, no. 2. Washington: Council on Foundations, 1986.

James A. Joseph, president and chief executive officer of the Council on Foundations, examines the current status of the grantmaking sector and predicts trends for its future. Provides an overview of the nonprofit sector, public policy and the Congress, the creation, growth and other trends in organized philanthropy, trends in individual giving, influence of the advisors to the wealthy, governance and managing issues, and a summary of key trends and planning assumptions. Among the trends cited by Joseph: renewed efforts by policymakers to push more money out of grantmaking organizations; increasing opportunity for grantmakers to be involved in public policy deliberations; a changing mix of organized philanthropy, with a greater role being played by religious organizations, especially in providing charity to the poor; and an increased demand for accountability and information.

262. Josephson, Matthew. *The Robber Barons: The Great American Capitalists, 1861-1901.* New York: Harcourt, Brace, 1934.

263. Kahn, Arnold D. *Family Security through Estate Planning.* New York: McGraw-Hill, 1979.

264. Kahn, E.J., Jr. *Jock: The Life and Times of John Hay Whitney.* New York: Doubleday, 1981.

265. Kahn, E.J., Jr. "Profiles: Blue Chip off the Old Block (Stewart Rawlings Mott)." *New Yorker* (27 November 1971): 56-87.

266. Kahn, E.J., Jr. "Profiles: Resources and Responsibilities." *New Yorker* (9 (& 16) January 1965): (37-83; 40-73).

267. Kalas, John W. *The Grant System.* Albany, N.Y.: State University of New York Press, 1987.

The past thirty years have witnessed massive growth in the giving and receiving of grants, resulting in the formation of a major social and economic system with its own rules and network of institutional relationships. Up to now most literature on the grant system has been devoted to developing skills in grant administration, or has dealt with specific grant programs or with particular operational aspects of the system. This scholarly book analyzes the grant system in its entirety, arranging various particular insights into a comprehensive, multidisciplinary picture that highlights interactions among the parts of a rapidly evolving and dynamic system. Covers the history, scope, social and economic impact, importance, and future of what has become, according to Kalas, a permanent and self-perpetuating structure of society.

268. Kammen, Michael. *The Philanthropic Impulse and the Democratization of Tradition in America.* Washington: Independent Sector, 1986.

269. Katz, Harvey. *Give! Who Gets Your Charity Dollar?* Garden City, N.Y.: Anchor Press, 1974.

270. Kellogg Foundation, W.K. *I'll Invest My Money in People.* Battle Creek, Mich.: W.K. Kellogg Foundation, 1980.

271. Kennedy, Gail, ed. *Democracy and the Gospel of Wealth.* Problems in American Civilization. Lexington, Mass.: D.C. Heath, 1949.

272. Keppel, David. *FPK: An Intimate Biography of Frederick Paul Keppel.* Privately Printed, [1950].

273. Keppel, Frederick Paul. *Philanthropy and Learning: With Other Papers.* New York: Columbia University Press, 1936.

274. Kettering, Charles F. *Prophet of Progress: Selections from the Speeches of Charles F. Kettering.* Edited by T.A. Boyd. New York: Dutton & Co., 1961.

275. Kilman, Ed, and Theon Wright. *Hugh Roy Cullen: A Story of American Opportunity.* Englewood Cliffs, N.J.: Prentice-Hall, 1954.

276. King, Cornelia S., comp. *American Philanthropy, 1731-1860.* New York: Garland Publishing, 1984.

277. King, Willford Isbell. *Trends in Philanthropy: A Study in a Typical American City.* New York: National Bureau of Economic Research, 1928.

278. Kirkland, Richard I., Jr. "Should You Leave All to the Children?" *Fortune* 114 (29 September 1986): 18-26.

Richard Kirkland focuses on what he calls a "peculiarly American obsession"—the determination of if, how much, and when to leave one's accumulated wealth to one's heirs. Other nations have developed rigid legal processes and social patterns for the disposition of inherited wealth, and now estate planning is quickly becoming a major concern of even middle class Americans. The author profiles the attitudes of the super rich towards inherited wealth. The spectrum of personal beliefs range from the "old" money folks who wouldn't think of not leaving all their wealth to the family to the "new" money multi-millionaires who use a wide variety of creative methods to dispose of their wealth. A major portion of the article cites examples of these creative methods. Statements from the rich about their personal philosophies towards inheritance are enlightening. What appears to trouble the entrepreneurs and executives is the fear that large inheritances "will encourage their offspring to do nothing useful with their lives." Included in the article are some pointers for the super rich and the general estate planner. Don't play hide and seek with the will and plan for the distribution of wealth; shelve the silver spoon—lack of work experience alienates heirs from humanity and contributes to insecurity about their ability to survive without their inheritance; don't be afraid to experiment; give later rather than sooner; take the short view—make bequests a generation at a time; don't live and die in Louisiana (they adhere to the Napoleonic Code which requires forced heirship); and put child rearing before estate planning.

279. Kirstein, George G. *Better Giving: The New Needs of American Philanthropy.* Boston: Houghton Mifflin, 1975.

280. Kirstein, George G. *The Rich: Are They Different?* Boston: Houghton Mifflin, 1968.

281. Knauft, E.B. "The World of Philanthropy in the Eighties." *Foundation News* (July-August 1980): 25-30.

282. Kneerim, Jill, ed. *Homelessness: Critical Issues for Policy and Practice.* Boston: Boston Foundation, 1987.

Based on talks given at a major national conference held in Boston and Cambridge, Massachusetts during March of 1986, text examines the extraordinary complexity of the problem of homelessness, both in its causes and in the attempts to aid its victims. Experts in diverse aspects of the problem discuss homelessness from its root causes to possible solutions, including analyses of the dynamics of a housing market that is "squeezing more and more frightened families and individuals out of their homes;" the challenge of delivering any kind of functional health care to people who live on the streets; and the backgrounds and needs of families, "the fastest-growing group among the homeless today." With the recognition that homelessness is now a nationwide crisis, this text serves as an excellent introduction, a guide to how to begin thinking about homelessness.

283. Knowles, Louis L. *Stewardship and Philanthropy: The Unique Ministry of the Endowed Parish.* Indianapolis, Ind.: Consortium of Endowed Episcopal Parishes, 1986.

By comparing and contrasting stewardship with the concept of philanthropy, Dr. Knowles explores the unique contributions that endowed congregations (as Christian stewards) and foundations (as philanthropists) can make to each other. Stresses the need for increased dialogue between the worlds of stewardship and philanthropy, which should focus on issues of community welfare, the future of the family, the nature of shared civic values, and the future of nonprofit, private institutions, both philanthropic and religious.

284. Knudsen, Raymond B. *New Models for Creative Giving.* 2nd ed. Wilton, Conn.: Morehouse-Barlow Co., 1985.

285. Koch, Robert. *Louis C. Tiffany: Rebel in Glass.* New York: Crown Publishers, 1964.

286. Koch, Theodore Wesley. *A Book of Carnegie Libraries.* New York: H.W. Wilson Co., 1917.

287. Kohr, Russell Vernon. *Early History and Influence of Harvard College's Hollis Professorship of Divinity (the First Endowed Professorial Chair in America).* Unpublished, 1981.

Thesis explores the creation and effects of the Hollis Professorship of Divinity, the first endowed professorial chair in America, established 1721 at Harvard College. Sketches the personality of Thomas Hollis of London, his religious inclinations, and his contacts with Harvard College. His establishment of the chair had three effects, Kohr asserts: it raised prominent minister-professors to a position capable of influencing most of the clergy of eighteenth century Massachusetts; it began the vertical, or departmental, system of curricular organization; and it stimulated other colleges to also secure similar endowed professorships. 200-item bibliography.

288. Koskoff, David E. *The Mellons: The Chronicle of America's Richest Family.* New York: Thomas Y. Crowell Co., 1978.

289. Kramer, Ralph M. "The Future of the Voluntary Agency in a Mixed Economy." *Journal of Applied Behavioral Science* 21 (1985): 377-91.

Kramer points out that now, as opposed to in the past, the growing reliance of voluntary nonprofit organizations on governmental funds ties their future to the fate of the welfare state. A mixed, three-sector, social service economy has blurred organizational differences and made a more rational division of responsibility unlikely. This article suggests that the traditional roles of voluntary agencies can still be reformulated to suggest a more realistic view of their distinctive areas of competence and vulnerability. Kramer concludes that voluntary agencies, to avoid being deflected from their true goals in the future, must learn to cope effectively with the dilemmas of entrepreneurialism (the growing reliance on internally generated income from increased fees and charges and from commercial ventures) and vendorism (a tendency to become public service agents through government grants and contracts).

290. Kutz, Myer. *Rockefeller Power: America's Chosen Family.* New York: Simon & Schuster, 1974.

291. Lamont, Thomas W. *Henry P. Davison: The Record of a Useful Life.* New York: Harper & Bros., 1933.

292. Lampman, Robert J. *The Share of the Top Wealth Holders in National Wealth, 1922-1956.* National Bureau of Economic Research. General Series, no. 74. Princeton, N.J.: Princeton University Press, 1962.

293. Lasch, Christopher, ed. *The Social Thought of Jane Addams.* New York: Irvington, 1982.

By collecting some of Jane Addams' writing in one volume, Lasch is pointing out "the less familiar, but...more important side of Jane Addams' life. [The book] shows her as theorist and intellectual—a thinker of originality and daring." The legacy of her thought has been obscured, says Lasch, by the natural tendency to praise her goodness and saintliness, to the intellectual impoverishment of us all. This anthology of her written views includes correspondence, lectures, articles, and monographs. It spans a number of the areas that engaged Addams during her busy lifetime—the idea of social settlements and Hull House, the city, immigrants, youth, political and social reform, women's rights, racial relations, education, democracy, and peace. The volume also contains a brief biography, a select bibliography, and a chronology of her life.

294. Layton, Daphne Niobe. *Philanthropy and Voluntarism: An Annotated Bibliography.* New York: Foundation Center, 1987.

Bibliography of 1,614 monographs and articles which analyze American and international philanthropy and voluntarism. (244 of the included items are annotated.) The materials are arranged in three parts covering the concept of philanthropy, the manifestations of philanthropy, and functional areas. Part 4 is devoted to periodicals, references, and organizational resources. The readings include materials which give an overview of the field, the historical origins of philanthropy, philanthropy's relationship with the state, the types of philanthropic activity, and philanthropy in other countries, among other topics. Not included are guides or aids to fundraising, grantseeking, proposal writing, and volunteer management. The volume is for scholars and students as well as the general public, and is particularly useful as a text for undergraduate study or research in philanthropy.

295. Layton, Daphne Niobe. "Studying Philanthropy: Bibliographies and Beginnings." *Fund Raising Review* (July-August 1987): 1-8.

296. "Leaders Examine Philanthropy: Stress Need for Greater Education about Its Role in Society." *Fund Raising Review* (June 1983): 1+.

297. Lenzner, Robert. *The Great Getty.* New York: Crown Publishers, 1985.

298. Lester, Robert M. *Forty Years of Carnegie Giving.* New York: Charles Scribner's Sons, 1941.

299. Levitt, Theodore. *The Third Sector: New Tactics for a Responsive Society.* New York: Amacom, 1973.

This is a book about the links between the public and private sectors, as well as "the awful contradictions and gaps in the way they conduct their affairs." Levitt asserts that for the first time since the Civil War, American society is being forced to grapple with an issue that is capable of disrupting "its undeviating attention to its own vaulting economic growth." He describes a condition that underlies all particular social problems: the way in which social power is distributed and how decisions are made by those in possession of it. Levitt calls the new agenda of social activists the desire for a more responsive society. He then examines reasons for the evolution of this new form of social activism and the ostensible failures of government and business that nurtured it. The proponents of the new activism are organizations that have sprung up to confront problems ignored for years by the public and private sectors and much of society. The groups, like the Black Panthers, Common Cause, Nader's Raiders, and SDS, comprise the third sector.

300. Littlejohn, Edward, and Charles Wohlstetter. *The Future of Private Philanthropy.* Foundation Officers Forum Occasional Papers, no. 5. New York: Institute for Educational Affairs, 1982.

301. Lockhart-Moss, Eunice J. *In Search of Partnerships: Black Colleges and Universities/Private Philanthropy.* Wingspread Conference Report. Racine, Wis.: Johnson Foundation, 1984.

Report of Wingspread Conference of presidents and chancellors of historically black colleges and universities and foundation executives.

302. Lomask, Milton. *Seed Money: The Guggenheim Story.* New York: Farrar, Straus & Co., 1964.

303. Lomax, John A. *Will Hogg: Texan.* Austin, Tex.: University of Texas, 1956.

304. Lord, Benjamin, ed. *America's Hidden Philanthropic Wealth: Tomorrow's Potential Foundation Giants.* 2nd ed. Washington: Taft Group, 1988.

Directory focuses on the principal donor(s) of a foundation (e.g., Laurence and Preston Tisch of the Tisch Foundation). The individuals who are profiled have personal assets of at least $10 million. Each report describes the past and present background of the donor such as personal history, sources and estimates of wealth, nature of their business and whether it has a foundation or direct giving program, additional foundations in which the donor is an officer, other foundations established by family members and contribution amounts. The section *Giving Analysis* provides a prioritized, statistical breakdown of giving for a recent year in the categories of arts and humanities, civic and public affairs, education, health, international, religion, science, and social science. Parallels between the donor's background and the foundation's giving pattern are analyzed and discussed. Biographical information on the directors and officers of the foundations is also included. Profiles accessed through index of foundations by state and type of recipient; major grants by category and state of recipients; individuals by name and alma mater. Over 300 donors and their foundations are featured.

305. Lord, Benjamin, ed. *America's Wealthiest People: Their Philanthropic and Nonprofit Affiliations.* Washington: Taft Group, 1984.

306. Lord, Benjamin, ed. *Fund Raiser's Guide to Private Fortunes.* 2nd ed. Washington: Taft Group, 1988.

Directory of information on 1,200 of America's wealthiest individuals and families. Those included were chosen using two criteria: a) having identifiable assets of at least $10 million and b) having shown substantial participation in either the nonprofit or philanthropic sectors. In addition, 150 "super rich" people are included although there was no public information available on their charitable or philanthropic commitments; they are included because of their potential as donors. Individual profiles were compiled for each of the 1,200 from information obtained from the Library of Congress; regional libraries; newspapers and magazines; biographies of wealthy people and families; stockholdings disclosed through the Securities and Exchange Commission; and foundation data disclosed through the Internal Revenue Service. Profiles contain information, when available, on publicly-disclosed wealth, personal history, charitable activities, and philanthropic affiliations. Also included are the place of birth, the place of residence, schools attended, and the place of business. In the case of family wealth or business, information is included on the parents, siblings, spouses, children and other important relatives. The directory is indexed to individuals by state of residence, state of office, alma mater, industry affiliations, nonprofit affiliation (arranged in subject areas), philanthropy, and state of philanthropy.

307. Loth, David. *The Story of Woodrow Wilson.* New York: Woodrow Wilson Foundation, 1957.

308. Louis, Arthur M. "America's Centimillionaires." *Fortune* (May 1968): 152-6, 192, 195-6.

309-322 PHILANTHROPY AND PHILANTHROPISTS

309. Lowell, Josephine Shaw. *Public Relief and Private Charity.* 1884. Edited by David J. Rothman. Reprint. Poverty, U.S.A.: the Historical Record. New York: Arno Press, 1971.

Written in 1884 by one of the century's most active social reformers, this little book lays out the "scientific" principles of charity, or how to deal with "the poor and degraded." Lowell presents a theory of public outdoor relief (relief given to the poor at their own homes—not in a workhouse or almshouse) before discussing its practice in England, Europe, and the United States. She then proposes principles of public relief and calls for three departments to be established in every city for children, public dependents, and crime. The second part of the book is devoted to private charity, with a discussion of types of institutions, principles and rules, methods in rural and urban areas, and practical suggestions. Lowell draws on many contemporary and historical examples to justify or illustrate her conclusions, which are presented in the manner of essentially unchallengable facts—commonly perceived to be obvious and true.

310. Lubove, Roy. *The Professional Altruist: The Emergence of Social Work As a Career, 1880-1930.* New York: Atheneum, 1969.

Lubove analyzes the development of social work as a profession. He looks at how it replaced adhoc volunteer philanthropic efforts, which were seen as increasingly inadequate in the face of intensified problems of social control and economic deprivation by the late nineteenth century. He devotes particular attention to such influences as functional specialization, the formation of a professional subculture, and the impact of formal organization and bureaucracy. He shows how professionalism radically altered the nature of private philanthropy after the turn of the century. The emergence of therapeutically oriented casework, rooted in a psychiatric rather than environmental explanation of human behavior, was one of the chief legacies of the new social work. While individuals may have profited from this, Lubove argues, functions of liaison between groups and the stimulation of social legislation and institutional change have suffered since the demise of volunteer-driven reform movements. Bibliographical note.

311. Lubove, Roy. *The Progressives and the Slums: Tenement House Reforms in New York City, 1890-1917.* Reprint. Westport, Conn.: Greenwood Press, 1974.

Lubove's analysis of tenement reform in New York during the Progressive era focuses on housing reform as a key to social progress. The book highlights the roles of particular individuals with differing motives and backgrounds in bringing about changes. His analysis reveals that, pursuant to the dominant cultural ethos of the times, it was the rules of the marketplace, and not charitable instincts, that drove the middle and upper classes to undertake housing reform. Their works were as much, if not more, a reflection of desire for social control as social good. Lubove discusses the emergence of full-time salaried philanthropic professionals—the "social engineers" of the Progressive era—after 1900. He sees reform in this era less as a product of mass protest movements than of a small group of people who saw possibilities for social engineering through organized effort, private and public.

312. Lundberg, Ferdinand. *America's Sixty Families.* New York: Vanguard Press, 1937.

313. Lundberg, Ferdinand. *The Rockefeller Syndrome.* Secaucus, N.J.: Lyle Stuart, 1975.

314. Lutz, Alma. *Emma Willard: Daughter of Democracy.* Boston: Houghton Mifflin, 1929.

315. Lynch, Frederick. *Personal Recollections of Andrew Carnegie.* New York: Fleming H. Revell Co., 1920.

316. Lyon, Peter. "The Adventurous Angels." *Horizon* 1 (May 1959): 4-19.

317. Lyon, Peter. "The Artful Banker." *Horizon* 3 (November 1960): 4-11.

318. MacIntyre, Alasdair. *After Virtue: A Study in Moral Theory.* 2nd ed. Notre Dame, Ind.: University of Notre Dame Press, 1984.

MacIntyre is a Scottish philosopher who describes the fragmentation of Western civilization's collective sense of morality over the past several centuries. The book seeks to understand why so many contemporary moral arguments seem unresolvable and how morality has fallen from a social enterprise to a matter of personal taste. By contrasting modern versions of morality with earlier ones, MacIntyre develops a general understanding of morality as a continuous dialogue about the traditions of practices and customs within a community. A challenging and engaging work, this book provides a good philosophical background for discussions of the motives, ethics, and obligations of philanthropy.

319. Mack, Edward C. *Peter Cooper: Citizen of New York.* New York: Duell, Sloan, & Pearce, 1949.

Peter Cooper (1791-1883), founder of Cooper Union and beloved New York philanthropist, was seen in the days before Carnegie's *Gospel of Wealth* as a possible justification for America's ruthless individualism. He had risen from the depths, acquired his wealth honestly, and treated it as a trust. Mack's biography chronicles Cooper's life in detail. He tells how Cooper began planning for Cooper Union, a tuition-free institution of higher learning, two decades before it became a reality, and how he made his one real aim the amassing of enough money to establish it. He writes, "Peter Cooper had done the exact opposite of most rich men, who give money for an institution to be erected after they are dead. He conceived the idea when young, helped bring it to detailed realization, and then had the good fortune to live a quarter of a century to watch over it...seldom absent from it a day."

320. Magat, Richard. "Wilmer Shields Rich: The First Lady of Organized Foundations." *Foundation News* 23 (November-December 1982): 46+.

321. "Management: The Corporate Cezanne." *Time* 85 (4 June 1965): 74-80.

322. Mann, Arthur. *Yankee Reformers in the Urban Age: Social Reform in Boston, 1880-1900.* Reprint. Chicago: University of Chicago Press, 1974.

This history of urban social reform from 1880-1900 focuses on Boston. Mann seeks "to demonstrate that the New England capital did not fall from grace after the age of Emerson; to prove that modern liberalism owes its beginnings to the city as well as the farm; and to trace the origins of reform thinking to the character of a community, especially to the kinds of people in the community." The efforts of Protestant, Catholic, and Jewish religious leaders, as well as academics, intellectuals, trade unionists, and feminists, to bring reality closer to the ideal of equality are all examined. The development of liberalism as a dominant intellectual tradition in the United States is also a theme, since Mann considers a liberal or a progressive synonymous with a social reformer—someone who refuses to accept the status quo, believes that by changing institutions he or she can change the behavior of people, and fights for the disadvantaged. Brief bibliography.

323. Margolis, Richard J. "The Perfect Fit: When Albert Kunstadter Sold His Famous Corset and Brassiere Firm and Started a Foundation, He Couldn't Have Known What a Model It Would Become." *Foundation News* 26 (March-April 1985): 38-41.

Profiles the Albert Kunstadter Foundation, which is known as a risk-taker.

324. Marts, Arnaud Cartwright. *The Generosity of Americans, Its Source, Its Achievements.* Englewood Cliffs, N.J.: Prentice-Hall, [1966].

325. Marts, Arnaud Cartwright. *George Lundy of Iowa.* Privately Printed, 1967.

326. Marts, Arnaud Cartwright. *Man's Concern for His Fellow Man. A Swift Review of Civilized Man's Philanthropic Nature and Efforts.* New York: Marts & Lundy, 1961.

327. Marts, Arnaud Cartwright. *The Outlook for Gifts to Colleges and Philanthropy.* Tampa, Fla.: Arnaud C. Marts, 1948.

328. Marts, Arnaud Cartwright. *Philanthropy's Role in Civilization: Its Contribution to Human Freedom.* New York: Harper & Bros., 1953.

Written by a fundraiser of thirty years, this volume attempts to describe the major attributes of the then 500,000 voluntary agencies in the United States and the techniques used to induce Americans to support them with monetary contributions and time. With emphasis on religion, Marts calls private colleges, hospitals, and social progress the chief fruits of philanthropy, explores religious and secular motivations for giving, describes the process of fundraising and assesses the effect of taxes on giving, and outlines present and future trends in American philanthropy. Marts makes no secret of his approval of philanthropy, calling the "self-directed private citizens" who furnish their time and money voluntarily "the real artifices of our Republic," whose agencies "have been constantly pumping into the body politic transfusions of the vital lifeblood of morality—true liberalism and enlightened humanitarianism—without which the body would inevitably deteriorate."

329. Mauss, Marcel. *The Gift: Forms and Functions of Exchange in Archaic Societies.* New York: W.W. Norton & Co., 1967.

Originally written in 1925, this work by a noted French sociologist examines the exhanges of archaic societies in as total a context as possible and sees them as economic, juridical, moral, aesthetic, religious, mythological, and sociomorphological phenomena. Mauss seeks to understand the function of gift exchange in the social order. The essay is divided into four parts: *Gifts and Obligation to Return Gifts* (using Samoa and Moari as examples); *Distribution of the System: Generosity, Honour and Money* (Andaman Islands, Melanesia, N.W. America); *Survivals in Early Literature* (Ancient Rome, Hindu Classical Period and Germanic societies); and *Conclusions*—moral, political and economic, and social and ethical. Mauss isolates in this study gifts that are, in theory, voluntarily given, disinterested, and spontaneous, but which are in fact obligatory and interested. The key inquiries of the study are these questions: In primitive or archaic societies what is the principle whereby the gift received has to be repaid? What force is there in the thing given which compels the recipient to make a return?

330. Maxwell, Joan, and Suzanne Medgyesi-Mitschang. *Giving: A Comparison of the Philanthropic Resources of Seven Metropolitan Areas.* Washington: Greater Washington Research Center, 1985.

Unique research report looks at the philanthropic resources of seven metropolitan areas: Atlanta, Boston, Cleveland, Dallas/Ft. Worth, Minneapolis/St. Paul, San Francisco/Oakland, and Washington, DC. The study analyzes the philanthropic resources of these communities from the perspectives of individual wealth, individual giving, foundation assets and grants, corporate giving, and the geographic focus of local nonprofit organizations. Shows that Washington, DC ranked at or near the bottom in per capita measures of philanthropic resources. Includes numerous informative tables comparing the seven metropolitan areas.

331. Maxwell, Joan, and Suzanne Medgyesi-Mitschang. *Giving: A Comparison of the Philanthropic Resources of Seven Metropolitan Areas. Supplementary Tables.* Washington: Greater Washington Research Center, 1985.

332. McAuley, John J., and Robin Balding. "Giving and Getting. The Non-Profit Outlook, 1983-88." *Fund Raising Management* 14 (February 1984): 24-31.

333. McCarthy, Kathleen D. *Noblesse Oblige: Charity and Cultural Philanthropy in Chicago, 1849-1929.* Chicago: University of Chicago Press, 1982.

Citing civic stewardship as a "uniquely urban interpretation" of noblesse oblige, McCarthy traces the manifestations of this guiding ideal in the Chicago of 1849-1929. She focuses on family welfare, medical charities, and cultural institutions and examines the pervasive traits of Chicago's civic stewards in each of four generations: the volunteers of the 1850s, Gilded Age plutocrats, progressive iconoclasts, and Jazz Age donors and dilettantes. Through it all she explores the trend from active to monetary beneficence, or from service ethic to leisure ethic, seeking to explain the development of large-scale community apathy by the early 1920s in Chicago and elsewhere in the United States. She describes, as well, changing patterns of social service, from institutional to family solutions, from centralized institutions to neighborhoods, and from limited to expansive roles for women. 300-item bibliography; extensive chapter notes.

334. Merrill, Charles E. *The Checkbook: The Politics and Ethics of Foundation Philanthropy.* Boston: Oelgeschlager, Gunn & Hain, 1986.

Charles E. Merrill served for twenty years as chairman of the Charles E. Merrill Trust which was established by Charles E. Merrill Sr., the founder of Merrill Lynch Co. The book combines an historical account of the workings of the Trust with an analysis of establishment philanthropy and the future difficulties it faces in the 80's. In the major portion of the book

Merrill analyzes the trends and changes in the giving areas on which the Trust concentrated, such as education, religion, blacks, societal issues, medicine, culture, international development, environment, and conservation. He describes how the money was spent and why. In addition, Merrill examines the broader issue of philanthropy, its accomplishments and its relationship to society. In this context he openly discusses classism, elitism, racism, inequality, and society's changing values and priorities.

335. Meyer, Jack A., ed. *Meeting Human Needs toward a New Public Philosophy.* Washington: American Enterprise Institute, 1982.

336. *Mid-Continent Conference on Philanthropy.* Unpublished, 1964.

337. Mill, John Stuart. *Dissertations and Discussions.* London: George Routledge & Sons, [1910].

338. Miller, Howard S. *Dollars for Research: Science and Its Patrons in Nineteenth-Century America.* Seattle, Wash.: University of Washington Press, 1970.

Unlike today, nineteenth-century science had few established sources of financial support. Miller's study focuses on the resulting logistical problems, the people who solved them, and the institutions they created. Unlike other avenues of research and scholarship, the growing complexity of science as the nineteenth century progressed was not understood by most philanthropists and left them uninterested. Their interest had to be cultivated, nurtured, and directed into some special arena of investigation. Scientists thus had to develop an aggressive and entrepreneurial attitude; they had to capitalize on events, contacts, and circumstances to secure funding for their work. Miller shows how the early gifts to science created a self-perpetuating structure, which eventually resulted in the great research endowments and foundations of the early twentieth century. He also shows how private support, which was more flexible and adventurous than public appropriations, helped usher in the social organization of modern science in the United States. Essay on the sources.

339. Miller, J. Irwin. "Time to Listen." *Foundation News* 25 (May-June 1984): 16-23.

340. Miller, Russell. *The House of Getty.* New York: Henry Holt & Co., 1985.

341. "Million-Dollar Gifts, Grants, Pledges and Requests of 1986." *Philanthropic Digest* 33 (January 1987): 1-10.

342. Minnesota Council of Nonprofits. *Minnesota Philanthropy and Disadvantaged People. Supplementary Tables.* Minneapolis, Minn.: Minnesota Council of Nonprofits, [1986].

Supplementary tables complementing the 1986 Philanthropy Project report *Minnesota Philanthropy and Disadvantaged People.* Tables show the forty largest Minnesota foundations, the distribution of 1985 monies to individual constituencies, the type of organizations funded, and multi-year grants.

343. Minnesota Council on Foundations. *Giving in Minnesota, 1977-1978.* Minneapolis, Minn.: Minnesota Council on Foundations, 1979.

344. Minnesota Council on Foundations. *Philanthropy Is... .* [Video recording]. Minneapolis, Minn.: Minnesota Council on Foundations, 1986.

345. Moscow, Alvin. *The Rockefeller Inheritance.* New York: Doubleday, 1977.

346. Murray, Charles A. *In Pursuit of Happiness and Good Government.* New York: Simon & Schuster, 1988.

A polemic which contends that global post-industrial societal ills can be cured not with government programs but with "leaving people alone" and with voluntarism. Bibliography.

347. National Charities Information Bureau. *Charitable Giving: What Contributors Want to Know.* New York: National Charities Information Bureau, 1988.

Results of a national survey on attitudes toward charitable organizations and charitable giving, conducted for the National Charities Information Bureau by the Roper Organization. Three factors were found to be most important to contributors (more than eighty percent rated them as extremely or very important in deciding whether or not to contribute): whether the charitable organization has a clearly stated purpose or mission; how well the charity's programs serve the basic purpose or mission; and whether the organization is spending an adequate amount of its income on charitable programs. Eight in ten contributors say that the charitable organizations they contribute to are doing an excellent or good job in keeping them informed about the first two factors, but only fifty-four percent feel the third factor is attended to well enough to satisfy them. Contributors also expressed concern that fundraising techniques not involve undue pressure (seventy-one percent), and that charitable organizations describe their programs accurately in their advertising and promotion (seventy percent).

348. National Committee for Responsive Philanthropy. *Evaluating Private Philanthropy: A Practical Guide.* Washington: National Committee for Responsive Philanthropy, 1979.

349. National Council on Philanthropy. *National Conference on Solicitations.* Cleveland: National Council on Philanthropy, 1965.

350. National Puerto Rican Coalition. *Major U.S. Foundations' and Corporations' Responsiveness to Puerto Rican Needs and Concerns.* NPRC Report, no. 87-1. Alexandria, Calif.: National Puerto Rican Coalition, 1987.

An important step in the implementation of the National Puerto Rican Coalition's strategy to double private sector support over the next five years, this report surveys the pattern of giving to Puerto Rican institutions and causes by 125 of the largest private foundations, 125 of the largest corporate-sponsored foundations, and the ten largest community foundations in nine states with the largest Puerto Rican populations (New York, Illinois, Ohio, California, Pennsylvania, New Jersey, Connecticut, Massachusetts, and Florida). Among the major findings: overall, slightly more than one-quarter of the 260 foundations surveyed were found to support Puerto Rican organizations; of the nine states surveyed, more than four-fifths of the funding documented for Puerto Rican causes came from New York, Illinois and Pennsylvania foundations, although foundations in Massachusetts, New Jersey, and Connecticut were found to be the most likely to give to Puerto Rican causes; and the ten community foundations in the sample were found to be more likely than private or corporate foundations to give to Puerto Rican institutions.

351. Nelson, Ralph L. *The Amount of Total Personal Giving in the United States, 1948-1982 with Projections to 1985.* Alexandria, Va.: United Way of America, 1986.

352. Nevins, Allan. *Abram S. Hewitt, with Some Account of Peter Cooper.* New York: Harper & Bros., 1935.

353. Nevins, Allan. *Study in Power: John D. Rockefeller, Industrialist and Philanthropist.* 2 Vols. New York: Charles Scribner's Sons, 1953.

This is a revision and vast expansion of Nevins' earlier biography, *John D. Rockefeller* (1940), occasioned by the discovery of "an immense additional body of correspondence, long thought lost." This discovery made it possible "to illustrate with more point and graphic detail the methods by which the oil business was organized and the personalities of the chief figures in that undertaking," as well as to shed "new light on the benefactions of Rockefeller and on his relations with those who aided him." Nevins calls this biography "an effort to tell the truth about perhaps the most impressive single figure in the transformation of the American economy, 1865-1900." Discussion of Rockefeller's philanthropic works is incorporated into the chronologically arranged biography of his professional and personal life, beginning with his donation of ten percent of his earnings to charity in 1855, the first year he worked, and continuing to the creation of the great foundations of the early twentieth century.

354. Newberry, J.O. "By Any Other Name: Altruism, Self-Help, Charity, Philanthropy, Voluntarism, Nonprofit." *Philanthropy Monthly* 16 (February 1983): 20-1.

355. Newman, Peter C. *King of the Castle.* New York: Atheneum, 1979.

356. "Newman Donates $25G to Connecticut Library." *New York Daily News (Mamaroneck)* (25 November 1983): A-14.

357. Nielsen, Waldemar A. *The Endangered Sector.* New York: Columbia University Press, 1979.

Nielsen undertakes a broad overview of the American nonprofit sector, giving detailed attention to the subsectors of higher education, basic science, health, culture, and social action. He is concerned with the extraordinary dependence of private, nonprofit institutions on government support and warns that their autonomy and diversity, as well as solvency, are threatened by this situation. Nielsen attempts to define the major elements of American pluralism, analyzes the problems of nonprofit institutions, and presents a program of public policy initiatives which would, if adapted, reverse what he sees as a "poisonous mixture of benign indifference and impulsive intrusion" on the part of government. He calls for structural and procedural reforms of government activity to take the third sector into account and for political leadership in defining national policy toward it.

358. Nielsen, Waldemar A. "Needy Arts: Where Have All the Patrons Gone?" *New York Times* (26 October 1980): D-l, D26-7.

359. Norton, Michael. *Leaving Money to Charity.* London: Directory of Social Change, 1983.

Guide for the intending philanthropist, covering topics such as: the importance of making a Will; deciding who to leave your money to; reasons for leaving money to charity; organizing charitable bequests; and how to choose a charity. Also provides detailed information on the rights of family and dependents to inherit, taxation on gifts made during one's lifetime and on death, and sample forms for the wording of a bequest to charity.

360. *Notre Dame Institute on Charitable Giving, Foundations, and Trusts.* Notre Dame, Ind.: Notre Dame Institute on Charitable Giving, 1976.

361. Oates, Marylouise. "Philanthropist Joan Pavlevsky's Heart Is in Giving and Research." *Los Angeles Times* (22 August 1983).

362. O'Connell, Brian. *Philanthropy in Action.* New York: Foundation Center, 1987.

This book presents descriptions of numerous randomly selected philanthropic gifts made by individuals, corporations, and foundations. The gifts are organized into nine "roles": to discover new frontiers of knowledge, to support and encourage excellence, to enable all people to exercize their abilities, to relieve human misery, to help government and other basic institutions to fulfill their roles, to make communities a better place to live, to nourish the spirit, to create understanding and tolerance among people, and to remember the dead. A special section describes unique opportunities of corporate philanthropy, of community foundations, for cooperative benevolence, and for leadership. The book includes a recommended reading list of primary sources for students. 600-item bibliography.

363. O'Connor, Harvey. *Mellon's Millions: The Biography of a Fortune. The Life and Times of Andrew W. Mellon.* New York: Blue Ribbon Books, 1933.

364. "Of Partnerships, Profits and Philanthropy." *Community Relations Letter* 2 (May-June 1988): 1-2.

Addresses the poor record of professional firms involved in charity and public service. Law and accounting firms rarely make philanthropic donations on a scale with corporations, but instead give time in the form of pro bono work. Lawyers and acccountants provide needed services to nonprofit organizations, as well as to artistic and educational institutions, and the issue of homelessness has received attention in several states where lawyers are providing free or reduced-fee legal services to groups building affordable housing for the homeless. Still, the national percentage of professionals participating in organized pro bono programs is small, and several methods are being introduced to increase the numbers, including editorials in the ABA Journal and the Journal of the American Medical Association urging attorneys and physicians to contribute at least fifty hours a year, the introduction of required hours of pro bono work in order for law students to graduate (in an effort to make pro bono service an early-acquired habit), and proposals of mandatory pro bono, which generate intense opposition. It is hoped that increased competition will force professional firms to reexamine their current marketing efforts and become more active in charitable contributions and community relations.

365. O'Grady, John, ed. *Catholic Charities in the United States: History and Problems.* Poverty, U.S.A.: the Historical Record. New York: Arno Press, 1971.

366. Olasky, Marvin N. *The Council on Foundations.* Studies in Philanthropy, no. 1. Washington: Capital Research Center, 1985.

Historical study and review of the programs of the Council on Foundations. Presents arguments against the Council's current policies and procedures.

367. O'Toole, Patricia. "Tisch, Tisch: The Billionaire Brothers Built Loews with One Strategy: Wait and Seize." *Manhattan, Inc.* 2 (March 1985): 54-62.

Biographical sketch of Bob and Larry Tisch which includes brief discussion of their charitable giving interests.

368. Paley, William S. *As It Happened: A Memoir.* New York: Doubleday, 1979.

369. Parker, Franklin. *George Peabody, 1795-1869.* Austin, Tex.: University of Texas, [1957].

George Peabody (1815-1869) was one of a few nineteenth-century Americans who made great fortunes. This biography, Parker's dissertation submitted to the University of Texas, focuses on his philanthropies, made remarkable by several factors. Peabody was not motivated by religious considerations, like most of his contemporaries; he gave a considerable portion of his money away while living; he had a deep devotion to the communities in which he lived and worked; and he had a secular vision of the Puritan doctrine of stewardship. Parker examines the institutions and causes to which Peabody gave generously and illuminates the personal and cultural motivations and aspirations that led him to act as he did. Parker attempts to evaluate the long-term significance and influence of Peabody's donations, which ranged from museums of archaeology and anthropology at Yale and Harvard to low-income housing for the urban working class in England. Heavily footnoted, with genealogy and bibliography.

370. Payton, Robert L. *Major Challenges to Philanthropy.* Washington: Independent Sector, 1984.

Keynote presentation from Independent Sector's 1984 Annual Meeting. Written to provide a vehicle for discussion, the paper examines some assumptions about philanthropy and the independent sector. Chapters include a discussion of the varieties of philanthropic experience, philanthropy as a vocation, and philanthropy and its discontents. Payton's essay deliberately emphasizes "tension, contradiction, [and] paradox—the dialectical quality," offering intellectual and historical challenges to readers, and addressing some fundamental criticisms of the sector. "Professionals have a moral obligation," says Payton, "to understand what they do and why they do it, as well as how they might do it better." An expanded version of the book is forthcoming from Macmillan. Brief bibliography.

371. Payton, Robert L., Brian O'Connell, and Peter Dobkin Hall. *Philanthropy: Four Views.* Studies in Social Philosophy and Policy, no. 11. Bowling Green, Ohio: Social Philosophy and Policy Center, 1988.

The contributors to this volume address a variety of public policy issues that emerge from an examination of philanthropy and the role it plays in shaping American social institutions and in giving expression to the fundamental values of the culture. Robert Payton surveys philanthropic activities, and concludes that philanthropy should have a central place in the university curriculum because it raises important questions about the value, meaning, and purpose of virtually all human activity. Michael Novak and Brian O'Connell, in separate essays, argue that philanthropy is essential to the maintenance of a free society: philanthropy allows individuals and groups to accomplish what government cannot, and it contributes to the maintenance of "public-spiritedness." Peter Dobkin Hall provides a detailed historical account of the impact of philanthropy on the formation of public health policy, concluding that private voluntary organizations were decisive in identifying the need for and creating such policy. Thus all the essays are a contribution to the ongoing process of investigation, analysis, and evaluation of the principles and practices of philanthropy, and they all support the contention that the role of private voluntary organizations will continue to expand in scope and importance.

372. Payton, Robert L. *Philanthropy. Voluntary Action for the Public Good.* American Council on Education/Macmillan Series on Higher Education. New York: Macmillan, 1988.

The American philanthropic tradition of voluntary service, voluntary association, and voluntary giving is analyzed in this book designed to stimulate reflection and discussion. The first part of the volume, *Major Challenges to Philanthropy*, is an overview of that American philanthropic tradition. Part 2, *Essays and Reflections*, is a collection of writings within the philanthropic tradition intended to explore aspects of philanthropic theory and practice.

373. Penfield, Wilder. *The Difficult Art of Giving: The Epic of Alan Gregg.* Boston: Little, Brown, 1967.

374. Penney Company, J.C. *Fifty Years with the Golden Rule.* New York: Harper & Bros., 1950.

375. Perry, Lewis. *Intellectual Life in America.* New York: Franklin Watts, 1984.

376. Pessen, Edward. *Riches, Class, and Power before the Civil War.* Lexington, Mass.: D.C. Heath, 1944.

Pessen disputes the Tocquevillian egalitarian thesis of antebellum American society, largely accepted as "the era of the common man," with virtually no rich or elite classes. He focuses his study on New York City, Philadelphia, Boston, and Brooklyn, four of the most densely populated and wealthy cities of the time, and examines the factors of wealth, social mobility, class, and influence and power in antebellum. His finding is that there did indeed exist a wealthy class, which, at one percent of the population, owned fifty percent of the wealth by 1850. Attention is given to the origins of wealth in the New World, life histories of certain individuals, the roles of the wealthy in society, the social circles of the elite, and even the streets on which they lived. There is a chapter as well on the role of the rich and elite in voluntary associations. Comprehensive bibliographical essay.

377. Petersen, Eleanor P. "Blacks Give to Blacks: For 'Survival Causes'." *Forum* 1 (Summer 1983): 1-3.

378. Peyser, Ethel. *Carnegie Hall, the House That Music Built.* New York: Robert M. McBride & Co., 1935.

379. Phalen, Dale. *Samuel Fels of Philadelphia.* Philadelphia: Drake Press, 1969.

380. Phelps, Edmund S., ed. *Altruism, Morality and Economic Theory.* New York: Russell Sage Foundation, 1975.

This collection of ten papers written by economists, with commentary supplied by philosophers and lawyers, is the product of a 1972 conference on the roles of altruism and morality in shaping the behavior of human society and institutions. Phelps notes in his introduction that "thinking about the economics of altruism has contributed to the rethinking of economics," especially the popular self-interest model. Papers by Kenneth Arrow, Roland McKean, and William Baumol address, primarily, the scope for altruistic codes and conduct in economic life as a means of raising economic efficiency. James Buchanan, Edmund Phelps, Wilfried Pauwels, and Peter Hammond, in Part 2, explore the role that morals play in certain game situations, and in Part 3 William Vickrey, Burton Weisbrod, and Bruce Bolnick analyze the motives and mechanisms that underlie certain institutions of cooperative altruism. The editor asserts the need for greatly increased attention to the factors of altruism and morality on the part of economists.

381. "Philanthropic Index Projects Charitable Giving Will Double by 1990." *Fund Raising Review* (February 1984): 4.

382. "Philanthropy 1, 2, 3: The Past, Present, and Future of Philanthropy." *Forum* 4 (Summer 1986): 5.

Presents an edited excerpt from the introduction to Craig Smith's forthcoming book, *Philanthropy 3: The Next Wave of Social Action in America.* Discusses the effect philanthropy has had on American history during the years 1910-1960 (Philanthropy 1), and 1960-1980 (Philanthropy 2). 1980 to the present (Philanthropy 3), refers to a new mode of giving funds by foundations and corporations and a new way of getting them by nonprofit organizations.

383. Philpott, Gordon M. *Daring Venture: The Story of William H. Danforth.* New York: Random House, 1960.

384. Pierson, John. "Double Identity: Several Churches and Synagogues Operate Grantmaking Programs Exactly like Private Foundations." *Foundation News* 25 (September-October 1984): 44-50.

385. Pifer, Alan. *Final Thoughts.* New York: Carnegie Corporation of New York, 1982.

386. Pifer, Alan. *Philanthropy in an Age of Transition: The Essays of Alan Pifer.* New York: Foundation Center, 1984.

This collection of essays by Alan Pifer, originally published in the annual reports of the Carnegie Corporation of New York during his tenure as president, addresses several important issues in philanthropy. His 1966 essay, *The Nongovernmental Organization at Bay,* asks what is the proper role of the federal government in financing nonprofit activity. In 1967 he turns his attention to *The Quasi Nongovernmental Organization,* an agency or association created and financed by government, yet acting independently of it. 1968 has Pifer ruminating in *Foundations at the Service of the Public* on the responsibility of foundations to promote social change both monetarily and intellectually. In *The Jeopardy of Private Institutions,* Pifer's 1970 essay, he assails financial difficulties and an erosion of public confidence, among other things, as grave threats to the future of private service institutions. Finally, his 1974 essay, *Foundations and Public Policy Formation,* explores the legitimacy of foundation involvement in public policy formation and argues chiefly that critics of this development are overestimating its impact and underestimating its potential benefits.

387. Plawin, Paul. "Sweet Charities." *Changing Times* 42 (May 1988): 95+.

Table lists forty-six national charities, showing income and expenditures for administration, fundraising, and programs. Nine of the charities are cited for not fully meeting standards set by the National Charities Information Bureau and/or the Philanthropic Advisory Service of the Council of Better Business Bureaus.

388. Plinio, Alex J. "Individual, Corporate Giving Depends on a Healthy Economy." *Fund Raising Management* 15 (May 1984): 94-5.

389. Powell, Horace B. *The Original Has This Signature, W.K. Kellogg.* Englewood Cliffs, N.J.: Prentice-Hall, 1956.

390. Pratt, Jon. *Minnesota Philanthropic Support for the Disadvantaged: A Report on Who Benefits from Grantmaking.* Minneapolis, Minn.: Philanthropy Project, 1985.

391. Pratt, Jon. *Minnesota Philanthropy and Disadvantaged People: A Report on Who Benefits from Grantmaking.* Minneapolis, Minn.: Philanthropy Project, 1986.

Report examines to what extent Minnesota foundations applied their resources to the needs of women, racial minorities and other disadvantaged people. An analysis of more than 10,000 grants totalling $145,965,363 made in 1985 by forty foundations shows that $55,623,346 or 38.1 percent, was intended to benefit disadvantaged people. The 38.1 percent funding for the disadvantaged is further broken down into 11.1 percent for racial minorities, 6.5 percent for women, and 20.5 percent for other disadvantaged people such as senior citizens, handicapped people and people with low incomes.

392. Prideaux, Tom. "What Makes a Rich Man Happy?" *People* 9 (5 June 1978): 92-6.

393. Prochaska, F.K. *Women and Philanthropy in Nineteenth Century England.* New York: Oxford University Press, 1980.

This is a broad history of women and philanthropy, encompassing a variety of forms of charitable activity on the part of English women in the nineteenth century. The author concludes that the profession of charity—paid or unpaid—did more to enlarge the horizons of women in this period than any other development. It was a way to serve and be useful and a way to escape boredom. Conversely, women exhibited a genius for fundraising and organization that fundamentally altered the shape and course of philanthropy as they expanded their benevolent activities to form societies, put on bazaars, and more. Prochaska claims that women engaged in charity were drawn from all levels of society. She explores some of the tensions between growing female contributions to public life through philanthropy and common perceptions of female nature on the parts of both women and men. Extremely extensive bibliography.

394. Prussing, Eugene E. *The Estate of George Washington, Deceased.* Boston: Little, Brown, 1927.

395. Public Relations Society of America. *Special Report.* New York: Public Relations Society of America, 1981.

396. Quinn, Jane Bryant. "The Charities Come Up Short." *Newsweek* 101 (3 January 1982).

397. Rankin, Watson S. *James Buchanan Duke.* New York: Newcomen Society, 1952.

398. Reckard, Edgar C. "The Philanthropy of Organized Religion: What It Is, What It Does, and How It Relates to the Work Being Done by Private Foundations and Corporate Grantmakers." *Foundation News* 25 (September-October 1984): 18-9.

399. "Religious Groups Lead in Philanthropy." *Covenant Companion* (April 1985).

Talks about Council on Foundations' study on giving by religious groups.

400. Remsen, Daniel S. *Post-Mortem Use of Wealth.* New York: G.P. Putnam, 1911.

401. Rhees, William J. *James Smithson and His Bequest.* Washington: Smithsonian Institution, 1880.

402. "The Rich List of 1845." *Forbes 400* (1 October 1984): 44-9.

Describes the wealthiest people in New York City in 1845.

403. Richmond, Mary E. *Friendly Visiting among the Poor: A Handbook for Charity Workers.* Montclair, N.J.: Patterson Smith, 1969.

This reprint of an 1899 treatise contains a helpful introduction by Max Siporin. Mary Richmond wrote the book when she was general secretary of the Charity Organization Society in Baltimore. The book was widely read during the next decade and helped influence public opinion toward the enactment of extensive social legislation and reforms. It also marked a major early development in theory and practice of the new profession of social work. Richmond uses the term "friendly visiting" in the sense that the Charity Organization Societies used it, to mean charitable work in the homes of the poor with an aim to not only improve the condition of the poor but also to become a real friend. The book is a practical guide to the effective exercise of charity and covers a wide range of topics from health and recreation to children and the church. It goes into surprising detail at times—for example, how to construct a makeshift ventilator for a poor person's room. Richmond lists a variety of collateral sources after each chapter.

404. Richmond, Mary E. *Social Diagnosis.* New York: Russell Sage Foundation, 1928.

This widely reprinted volume was written by the director of the Russell Sage Foundation's Charity Organization Department. The book represents an attempt on the part of the author to begin the process of standardizing and recording the theories and practices of social case work. It also attempts to create an underlying body of knowledge for the field. Richmond and her colleagues identified "the best social practice that could be found" in five cities, consulted extensively with colleagues and written material, and reported the results of their extensive research in the book. The volume includes discussion of case diagnosis in different fields and presents sample questionnaires, definitions, charts, comparisons, and other items of interest to social workers. The publication of *Social Diagnosis* was clearly an important step in the professionalization of social work. Brief bibliography.

405. Rimor, Mordechai, and Gary A. Tobin. *Is a Good Jew a Contributing Jew? The Relationship between Jewish Identity and Philanthropy.* Unpublished, 1988.

Statistical tables for several aspects of giving by Jewish philanthropists, including: contribution and basic background; factors of contribution behavior; correlation of contribution and amount contributed with religious practices, synagogue attendance, and visiting Israel; factors of Jewish identity; correlation of years of Jewish education with philanthropic variables; contribution to Jewish charities by number of Jewish friends; and reasons for giving.

406. Robb, Christina. "Charity Falls on Hard Times." *Boston Globe Magazine* (5 December 1982): 15, 41, 44-50, 61.

407. Rockefeller, David. *Giving: America's Greatest National Resource.* Fort Worth, Tex.: Sid W. Richardson Foundation, 1985.

Mr. Rockefeller talks about the motives of philanthropists and proposes several incentives to induce greater philanthropy including a citizen involvement campaign and the creation of a *Nobel Prize for Philanthropy.* He also comments on the adverse impact on philanthropy of pending Treasury Department tax reform proposals.

408. Rockefeller, John D. *Random Reminiscences of Men and Events.* New York: Doubleday, 1933.

The seven articles contained in this volume were originally published in consecutive issues of the monthly magazine *The World's Work* between 1908 and 1909. This collection includes the photographs that were published with the articles. Written when Rockefeller was almost seventy, the articles provide interesting insights into the character of one of the country's greatest industrialists and philanthropists. Of special interest are *The Difficult Art of Getting, The Benevolent Trust,* and *The Difficult Art of Giving.* The last is especially important in that it outlines Rockefeller's philosophy of giving. He eschews charity in its common sense for philanthropy dedicated to "employing people at a remunerative wage, to expand and develop the resources at hand, and to give opportunity for progress and healthful labor where it did not exist before. No mere money-giving is comparable to this in its lasting and beneficial results."

409. Rockefeller, John D., Jr. *John Davison Rockefeller, 1839-1937. A Memorial.* Privately Printed, 1937.

410. Rockefeller, John D., III. "The Third Sector." *Across the Board* 15 (March 1978): 13-8.

In this article addressed to leaders in the business community, Rockefeller warns that the third sector is weakening and that no one seems to be noticing. He suggests that one reason awareness of the sector is so dim is because so much of it "is individual, personal and local in nature," so it has "not been conceptualized as the important national phenomenon it is. Another reason is the sheer diversity of it." He highlights the role of the sector in shaping our national history, noting that "virtually every significant step forward in social progress sprang originally from the third sector." He cites care of the mentally ill, women's rights, conservation, and the abolitionist movement as examples. He attributes the erosion of the sector to a growing mood of alienation from massive social problems and a failure of leadership in all three sectors—private nonprofit, government, and business.

411. Rockwell, John. "He's First a Music Lover, Then a Philanthropist." *New York Times* (10 November 1976).

412. Rose-Ackerman, Susan. *The Charity Market: Paying Customers and Quality Control.* Program on Non-Profit Organizations, no. 19. New Haven, Conn.: Institution for Social and Policy Studies, 1980.

413. Ross, Irwin. "Tales of Sonnenberg." *Fortune* (23 April 1979): 118-20, 124.

414. Ross, Percy. "Thanks a Million." *Detroit News* (28 May 1983).

415. Rothman, David J., ed. *The Charitable Impulse in Eighteenth Century America: Collected Papers.* Reprint. Poverty, U.S.A.: the Historical Record. New York: Arno Press, 1971.

This collection of historical documents is part of a series entitled *Poverty, U.S.A.: The Historical Record.* It contains sermons on charitable duty by Jonathan Ashley, Charles Chauncy, and Benjamin Colman; legal acts incorporating charitable societies such as the German Society in Pennsylvania, the Fellowship Society in South Carolina, and the Society of St. George in New York; and other items of historical interest, including Cotton Mather's *Orphanotrophium*, or *Orphans Well-Provided For*. The documents are reprinted in their original form, which makes the quality of the print quite poor and virtually unreadable in photocopy.

416. Rothman, David J. *Conscience and Convenience: The Asylum and Its Alternatives in Progressive America.* Boston: Little, Brown, 1980.

This historical analysis of programs for the criminal, the delinquent, and the insane in the twentieth century addresses these larger questions: "How does each generation arrive at its reform program? What elements come together to earn a proposed innovation the title of reform? Who makes up the cadre of reformers?...Where do they find their constituents? How do their programs win enactment?...What difference do the programs make?...Why is it that reforms so often turn out to be in need of reform?" The Progressives, unlike their Jacksonian forbearers, sought to understand and cure crime, delinquency, and insanity on a case-by-case basis. They welcomed the necessary expansion of a state role this process would entail. But for reforms to be adopted, they had to win the support of the administrators of criminal justice and mental helath, whose priorities often rested on convenience and efficiency—resulting in modified institutions eventually deemed successes by the administrators and failures by the reformers. Rothman explores these kinds of dialectics throughout the book.

417. Rottenberg, Dan. "The Education of a Philanthropist." *Town & Country* 138 (December 1984): 202+.

Profiles Edwin C. Whitehead, who endowed the Whitehead Institute for Biomedical Research, the largest gift ever to a medical or scientific facility.

418. Rottenberg, Dan. "The Most Generous Living Americans." *Town & Country* 137 (December 1983): 197+.

419. Rottenberg, Dan. "The Most Generous Living Americans." *Town & Country* 140 (December 1986): 153-61.

Presents a survey of America's leading individual givers who have given more than $5 million to charities during their lifetimes. The names of the givers (about 100) are accompanied with a brief personal profile, and description of past philanthropic giving and interests. Lists are organized by total giving amounts ($5 million, $10 million, $20 million, $50 million, $75 million, $100 million, and $300 million). Also includes a list of over seventy-five major individual contributions and bequests to art, science, scholarships and the humanities.

420. Rottenberg, Dan. "The Triumph of a Prodigal Son." *Town & Country* 133 (February 1979): 114-7, 138-40, 144.

421. Rottenberg, Dan. "The Wealthiest Americans." *Town & Country* 132 (May 1978): 103-9.

422. Rudney, Gabriel, and Murray S. Weitzman. "Philanthropic Employment Growth from 1972 to 1982." *Fund Raising Management* 15 (May 1984): 20+.

423. Rule, Sheila. "Black Charities Face Opposition." *New York Times* (26 December 1982): 24.

424. Russell, Bertrand. *A History of Western Philosophy, and Its Connection with Political and Social Circumstances from the Earliest Times to the Present Day.* New York: Simon & Schuster, 1945.

425. Russell, Charles A. *Edward Warriner Hazen, 1860-1929: A Biographical Sketch.* New Haven, Conn.: Edward W. Hazen Foundation, 1954.

426. Ryan, Pat. "A Man of Arts and Letters." *Sports Illustrated* (16 March 1970): 58-68.

427. Sage Foundation, Russell. *Report of the Princeton Conference on the History of Philanthropy in the United States.* New York: Russell Sage Foundation, 1956.

428. Saltzman, Jack, ed. *Philanthropy and American Society: Selected Papers.* New York: Center for American Culture Studies, 1987.

Scholarly collection of selected papers on a wide range of topics concerning philanthropy and American culture. The papers are the result of a 1986 Center for American Culture Studies conference. Works included are *The Girard Will Case: Charity and Inheritance in the City of Brotherly Love*, the story of the case which historians generally agree is the source of modern American charity law; *Reflections on the Nonprofit Sector in the Post-Liberal Era*, an examination of the impact on the sector of public policy, nonprofits management, and scholarly perception; *College Lives and College Giving*, an essay on alumni gifts; *The Unintended Logic of the Philanthropic Foundation: Foundations and Ruling Class Elites*, a Gramscian analysis of the philanthropic elite's motives; *Women's Culture: The Decorative Arts Movement and the Rise of Feminine Cultural Philanthropy*, a reassessment of the theory that women historically dominated the artistic arena and the impact the decorative arts movement had on women's involvement in the arts; *The Selfish as Well as the Disinterested Affections of the Heart: The Case of the American Colonization Society*, a look at the black charitable enterprise; *Philanthropic Consciousness and Institution-Building in the American South: The Formative Years, 1867-1920*, a discussion of how Reconstruction, controlled by the federal government, was changed from a political-economic to a socio-cultural reconstruction controlled by Southerners and helped by wealthy Northerners; and *International Philanthropy in a Large Foundation*, a case study of the Ford Foundation's international activities. Contains bibliography.

429. Samuel, Sigmond. *In Return: The Autobiography of Sigmund Samuel.* Toronto, Canada: University of Toronto Press, [1963].

430. Sarnoff, Paul. *Russell Sage: The Money King.* New York: I. Obolensky, 1965.

431. Satterlee, Herbert. *J. Pierpont Morgan: An Intimate Portrait.* New York: Macmillan, 1940.

432. Schruers, Fred. "A Mother's Trust." *Manhattan, Inc.* 4 (January 1987): 82-92.

Comprehensive examination of the turmoil surrounding the estate of Margaret Strong de Cuevas de Larrain as well as a glimpse at her largely non-public life. Margaret was the granddaughter of John D. Rockefeller Sr. and when she died at the Palace Hotel in Madrid on December 2, 1985 she left her fortune to her younger second husband Raymundo de Larrain. With Margaret's death, the legal contest began over the series of wills and codicils. One will, the original 1968 will, was revoked three times, torn up, and replaced by a 1980 version which was then amended by two codicils. Author Fred Schruers writes not only of the current legal battle surrounding Margaret's fortune, but of her life. This short biography is a sensitive look at a wealthy woman's rather private life in a by-gone era. As the author puts it, "She was the girl-child of one of three surviving daughters of John D., which made her nearly inconsequential...the women were the ghosts of the family tree—generally well-off, but voiceless and unseen."

433. Schwartz, John J. *The Current Climate and Major Trends in American Philanthropy.* New York: Community Counselling Service Co., 1988.

John Schwartz, a prominent figure in the nonprofit community, discusses eight trends which show great promise for the future of philanthropy despite many negative aspects of the current climate. These trends are: a lessening of dependence on government support; a measurable improvement in the management of nonprofit organizations; a recognition of the importance of fundraising to the survival of the nonprofit by trustees, directors and key administrators; an increasing cooperation between donors and donees; attempts to discover alternate sources of funding in addition to straight fundraising campaigns (although Schwartz does warn against cause-related marketing, which he fears could seriously endanger the future of philanthropy); a measurable growth in professionalism in fundraising management; an increased effort towards cooperation and enhanced results in the philanthropic world, as evidenced by the programs of Independent Sector and other similar organizations (which are profiled here); and a recognition of the importance of philanthropy by academia (including a comprehensive program recently established at Indiana University which will conduct research and provide interdisciplinary programs in resource development, fundraising management and cultural aspects of philanthropy).

434. *Search for Security: A Guide to Grantmaking in International Security and the Prevention of Nuclear War.* Washington: Forum Institute, 1985.

Directory of seventy-seven foundations funding in the field of international security and the prevention of nuclear war. The guide is organized in four parts. Part 1 is an analysis of foundations active in international security, containing many explanatory tables and graphs. Part 2 explains eleven categories of support of nearly 2,000 foundation grants. Part 3 profiles seventy-seven foundations, including summary data on each foundation, its procedures, future plans, an annotated list of its 1984 grants, and grant summary data for 1982-84. Part 4 includes information on national and local organizations working in the field of international security and prevention of nuclear war, looking at their sources of funding and views about future support.

435. *Search for Security: A Study of Philanthropy in International Security and the Prevention of Nuclear War.* Washington: Forum Institute, 1985.

436. Sears, Jesse Brundage. *Philanthropy in the History of American Higher Education.* Bulletin, no. 26. Washington: Government Printing Office, 1922.

437. Seay, J. David. "Making a Stronger Case for Health Care Philanthropy." *Fund Raising Management* 15 (October 1984): 34+.

438. Seeley, John R. *Community Chest: A Case Study in Philanthropy.* Toronto, Canada: University of Toronto Press, 1957.

439. Shapiro, Harold T. *Philanthropy: Tradition and Change.* Grand Haven, Mich.: Council of Michigan Foundations, 1982.

440. Sharpe, Robert F. *Before You Give Another Dime.* Nashville, Tenn.: Thomas Nelson Publishers, 1979.

441. Silberstein, Richard. *Giving to Jewish Philanthropic Causes: A Preliminary Reconnaissance.* Reprint. North American Jewish Data Bank. Reprint Series, no. 2. Washington: Independent Sector, 1987.

442. Silha, Stephen. "The Media and Philanthropy." *Forum* 5 (Summer 1987): 1-2, 10.

How does a group gain access to the media? At a Chicago symposium, philanthropists who believe that their stories go untold learned that information is not news. Traditionally, foundation philanthropists shunned the media spotlight. Today they realize that media exposure multiplies their philanthropic clout and corporate givers say media exposure is the best way to increase corporate giving. Publicity means survival to nonprofits; it enables them to attract both funds and volunteers. Suggestions for gaining media visibility include such actions as writing articles on the media and philanthropy for specialized publications; providing the local media with a resource list of organizations and individuals; holding local issue-oriented meetings with people from both sectors; framing issues in more controversial, less boring, terms; and generally developing ways to spark dialogue between media and philanthropic leaders on local issues. The symposium was a success, if only for the fact that a dialogue was begun between the communications and philanthropic trade associations.

443. Slade, Margot. "On Giving: To Whom and Why." *New York Times* (19 December 1983): B-16.

444. Smith, S.L. *Builders of Goodwill: The Story of the State Agents of Negro Education in the South, 1910-1950.* Nashville, Tenn.: Tennessee Book Co., 1950.

445. Stanfield, John H. *Philanthropy and Jim Crow in American Social Science.* Westport, Conn.: Greenwood Press, 1985.

This book is composed of several inter-related case studies that illustrate the development of pre-World War II social science research on race relations. Such research was a product of the world views, consciousness, and organizational resources of philanthropists and foundation administrators interested in using social science to reinforce or modify the Jim Crow social order forged in the late nineteenth century. In presenting these cases, Stanfield shows the importance of studying societal and funding factors in the development of the social sciences, particularly in shaping the social scientific interest in race relations. He states, "Such an analysis cannot help but lead to the conclusion that, historically, the sponsorship of social scientific and especially sociological research on the Afro-American experience has evolved more from questions of socio-political control than from a search for empirical truth." The book examines the related activities of Robert E. Pack of Tuskegee, the Laura Spelman Rockefeller Memorial, the Julius Rosenwald Fund, Charles Spurgeon Johnson, and others. Bibliography.

446. Stanley, Edmund A., Jr. *Of Men and Dreams.* New York: Bowne & Co., 1975.

447. "State Eyes Fund Drive for Cancer." *New York Times* (7 June 1983).

448. Stehle, Vince. "Of $41.4-Billion Donated to Churches, Almost Half Goes to Charitable Work." *Chronicle of Philanthropy* 1 (20 December 1988): 1, 18.

An Independent Sector-sponsored study of 4,205 congregations finds that almost half of collected donations ($41.4-billion in 1986) is spent on charitable activities, proving that "America's religious institutions practice what they preach" about generosity, service to others, and caring. The findings also require re-interpretations of earlier reports on individual philanthropy; the 1988 edition of *Giving USA* reports that religious groups received fifty-eight percent of contributions by individuals, but this new study finds that many of those funds are then redistributed to other causes. Factoring in donations by religous congregations to other services, estimates of giving to education increase by forty percent, giving to health care by thirteen percent, and giving to other human services by twenty-seven percent. The study does not assemble financial data on the basis of denomination, but divides churches into four groups (liberal, moderate, conservative, and very conservative) based on responses by congregations. Congregations considering themselves to be liberal were more than twice as likely as very conservative congregations to provide housing for the elderly and the homeless, to support health programs abroad, and to give money for environmental-quality programs. However, anti-abortion programs were the only activities listed in which very conservative congregations would be more likely than liberal congregations to participate.

449. Sterne, Larry. "Helen O'Rourke-McClary: She Helped Make Charities Accountable." *NonProfit Times* 1 (May 1987): 16, 19.

450. Sterne, Larry. "Total Giving Continues to Climb, But Corporate Donations Are Flat: Giving USA Report." *NonProfit Times* 2 (July 1988): 1, 7-9, 14-15.

Presents the findings of *Giving USA*, the annual report of the American Association of Fund-Raising Counsel Trust for Philanthropy, concerning charitable giving trends and statistics for 1987. Some believe the estimated $93.68 billion charitable giving total may signal the victory of philanthropy over the negative impact of tax law changes and October's stock market plunge, though others warn that the actual growth rate (6.5 percent) is the lowest in twelve years and the money must be spread among more groups. Perhaps the "most ominous sign" in the report is the failure of corporate donations to increase (business donations, including corporate foundations, represent 4.8 percent of all 1987 U.S. contributions, down from 5.1 percent a year earlier); three main factors for the decline are cited: an inevitable "running out of steam" after great increases during previous years, economic difficulties experienced by key industrial sectors, and "the frenetic reconfiguration of U.S. industry," including mergers and divestments. Other findings: a modest 4.6 percent rise in giving to religion, though its $43.6 billion accounts for 46.6 percent of all giving; the breakdown for other areas: health up 11.3 percent with $13.65 billion, education up 7.5 percent with $10.84 billion, human services up 7.8 percent with $9.84 billion, arts, culture and humanities up 10 percent with $6.41 billion, and public society benefit up 2.5 percent with $2.44 billion.

451. Stidley, Leonard Albert. *Sectarian Welfare Federation among Protestants.* New York: Association Press, 1944.

452. Stinnett, Lee. "Philanthropy As News: Let the Media Be the Judge." *NonProfit Times* 1 (August 1987): 23-4.

A brief article by Lee Stinnett, executive director of the American Society of Newspaper Editors, on the Chicago meeting between the media and philanthropists. Examples of media-philanthropic "partnerships" which were cited by philanthropists at the symposium as models of media responsiveness and harbingers of a new kind of press/philanthropy cooperativeness to be emulated in the future were meet with discomfort by the media. Communications representatives rejected "partnership," saying a more accurate term is "relationship." It was argued by the media that private philanthropy ought to be subjected to the same standards of objective and critical journalism as other activities and that nonprofits should compete in a free market with other material seeking publication. The community will be better served if the journalists stick to their profession and leave the crusading to others.

453. "Strategies for Individuals Contributing to Charitable Organizations under the Old Tax Law As Compared to New Law in 1987." *Fund Raising Review* (October 1986): 5-8.

An analysis for charitable giving presented by the AAFRC Trust for Philanthropy, New York, New York, October 1986. The new law allows charitable gifts to be deducted for itemizers and allows gifts of appreciated property to be deducted at full market value when given to public charities. However, it disallows deductions for gifts by people who do not itemize which currently consists of sixty-two percent of the taxpayers. The analysis views the future impact on these taxpayers and those who may become non-itemizers under the new law.

454. Suhrke, Henry C. "The Liberal-Conservative Spectrum in Philanthropy." *Philanthropy Monthly* 20 (September 1987): 25-7.

Covers the Institute for Educational Affairs' Philanthropic Round Table discussion of whether left and right matter in philanthropy. Using a scholarly paper presented by Michael Joyce, executive director of the Lynde and Harry Bradley Foundation, Suhrke argues that liberal and conservative perspectives reflect the basic outlook of man upon his own potential and upon the potential of his social organizations, and that consciously or unconsciously they certainly exist as ideological factors in philanthropy. He reprints the president's statement of the Alfred P. Sloan Foundation to show that a few organizations have already confronted some implications of philosophical and ideological factors, and that improved awareness of its environment can only add to a greater understanding of philanthropy.

455. Suhrke, Henry C. "The Story of the Charles E. Merrill Trust: A Marxist Account of the Disposition of a Capitalist Fortune." *Philanthropy Monthly* 20 (January 1987): 5-15.

Critical review of *The Checkbook: The Politics and Ethics of Foundation Philanthropy* by Charles E. Merrill [See: PHILANTHROPY/PHILANTHROPISTS. Merrill, Charles E. *The Checkbook: The Politics...* .] In addition to copious criticisms, the author psychoanalyzes the "true" meanings of Charles E. Merrill's statements and quotes numerous sections of the book.

456. Suhrke, Henry C. "What Is the Economic Outlook for Philanthropy?" *Philanthropy Monthly* 16 (December 1983): 5-14.

457. Suhrke, Henry C. "Who Speaks for Philanthropy?" *Philanthropy Monthly* 17 (October 1984): 13-7.

458. Sullivan, Walter. "Einstein Revealed As Brillant in Youth." *New York Times* (14 February 1984): C-1.

459. "Super Santas of '84." *Town & Country* 138 (December 1984): 204-5.

Lists individuals and foundations making major contributions to art, science, scholarship and the humanities during 1984.

460. Szigethy, Zoltan. "Finally, a Beginning? Philanthropy and the American Indian." *Chronicle of Non Profit Enterprise* 7 (July 1988): 1-3, 13-6.

Considers the present-day opportunities for philanthropic efforts to aid Native Americans by first reviewing the opportunities lost in the past. In the eighteenth and early nineteenth centuries "the philanthropic plan required that the Indian abandon the hunter-warrior culture, the tribal order, and the communal ownership of land;" what was proposed was in essence the extinction of an entire race. But the Indians have survived, despite our best intentions, and the challenge today is to maintain the cultural differences, "while overcoming them for the purpose of helping reservations achieve economic self-sufficiency." This challenge, involving such thorny issues as the paradox between communal decision-making and individual enterprise, offers fertile ground for philanthropy to exercise its role as a pathfinder, experimenting for the creation of "fragile new solutions to old problems." Indeed, the author believes that the process involved in aiding Native Americans may develop solutions to our own civilization's troubles, with interdependent thinking and consensus models of decision-making benefiting from Indian cultures.

461. Talese, Gay. *The Kingdom and the Power.* New York: World Publishing Co., [1969].

462. Taylor, Bernard P. *Guide to Creative Giving.* South Plainfield, N.J.: Groupwork Today, 1980.

463. Tebbel, John. *The Inheritors: A Study of America's Great Fortunes and What Happened to Them.* New York: G.P. Putnam, 1962.

464. Teltsch, Kathleen. "'82 Gifts to Charity a Record, But Rate of Increase Slowed." *New York Times* (14 March 1983): A-1.

465. Teltsch, Kathleen. "New Jewish Philanthropy Aiming at Non-Sectarian Aid for All Poor." *New York Times* (13 August 1985): A-13.

Describes Jewish Fund for Justice.

466. Teltsch, Kathleen. "New Style Philanthropy." *Foundation News* 24 (January-February 1983): 32-3.

467. "The Ten Wealthiest People in the USA." *USA Today* (18 September 1984): A-1+.

468. Thom, Helen Hopkins. *Johns Hopkins: A Silhouette.* Baltimore, Md.: Johns Hopkins University Press, 1929.

469. Thompson, Jacqueline. *The Very Rich Book. America's Super-Millionaires and Their Money: Where They Got It, How They Spend It.* New York: William Morrow, 1981.

470. Thompson, Kenneth W., ed. *Philanthropy: Private Means, Public Ends.* Exxon Education Foundation Series on Rhetoric and Political Discourse, vol. 4. Lanham, Md.: University Press of America, 1987.

Examines the central values, origins, problems, and criticisms of philanthropy. Robert Payton, president of the Exxon Education Foundation, addresses the issue of values and philanthropy, including an exploration of the historical, philosophical, and theological thought that forms the root values of modern philanthropic efforts. David Robinson discusses the founder, origins, and evolving program of the Carnegie Corporation, of which he is executive vice president. Professor John G. Simon, organizer of Yale University's program of study and research on philanthropy, examines the independent sector, which he believes to be the most unique feature of American society. He also traces the problems and dilemmas associated with researching and studying this sector. Criticisms are supplied by Mark Rozell, who focuses on corporate philanthropy's influence on the dissemination of ideas in the academic community and within nonprofit policy research organizations, and by Theodore Lowi, who raises the issue of ethical responsibility in the field of political science, which provides a broad background for philanthropy. Includes bibliography.

471. Throndike, Joseph J., Jr. *The Very Rich: A History of Wealth.* New York: American Heritage Publishing Co., 1976.

472. "Throw Away Berlitz! Just Memorize These Terms." *Corporate Philanthropy Report* 2 (December 1986): 4+.

Lists sixteen terms and definitions used in communication with Japanese corporate philanthropy.

473. Tileston, Mary Wilder. *A Memorial of the Life and Benefactions of Mary Hemenway, 1820-1894.* Privately Printed, 1927.

474. Titmuss, Richard M. *The Gift Relationship: From Human Blood to Social Policy.* New York: Pantheon Books, 1971.

Titmuss examines blood donation to explore how voluntary and paid giving of blood not only create different qualities of blood for the recipients but also promote different cultural tendencies of market relationships and ethically influenced social relationships. Much of the book is devoted to a surprisingly interesting comparison of American and British systems of blood donation; in the United States blood is donated through a mixed system of purchased, credited, and unpaid donations, while in the United Kingdom all blood donation is made voluntarily through the National Health Service. Titmuss suggests that certain social institutions, such as those that encourage voluntary participation, can provide opportunities for moral action and human connection that are not possible under commercial relationships.

475. Tobias, Andrew. *Fire and Ice. The Story of Charles Revson: The Man Who Built the Revlon Empire.* New York: William Morrow, 1976.

476. Tonai, Rosalyn Miyoko. *Asian American Charitable Giving.* Working Papers, no. 4. San Francisco: Institute for Nonprofit Organization Management, 1988.

Results of a survey study of 321 Asian American donors in the San Francisco-Oakland area, testing key demographic, attitudinal, and situational factors affecting their charitable giving. Primary reasons for the study were to determine: a profile of donors in the sample; whether significant relationships exist between relevant factors and charitable giving; effective solicitation techniques; and reasons for giving and not giving. Among the findings: respondents were well educated, with 82.8 percent possessing at least a bachelor's degree; their median gross personal income was $34,279 (median gross household income was $52,638), and they gave an average of $1,325.15 to charitable causes in 1986 (averaging at 2.7 percent of their household income, the Asian American respondents classify as substantial givers); significant correlation was established for several of the factors involved; and in-person solicitations were rated most effective. Individuals at lower income levels gave significantly greater proportions of their incomes than those in higher income levels (persons with personal incomes under $10,000 donated an average 6.6 percent, while those making between $20,000 and $60,000 donated an average 2.2 percent), and volunteers were also found to give substantially more than non-volunteers.

477. "Total Giving, 1955-84. The Growth of Philanthropy, 1968-84." *Fund Raising Management* 16 (May 1985): 85.

478. Trattner, Walter I. *Homer Folks: Pioneer in Social Welfare.* New York: Columbia University Press, 1968.

This is a biography of a very important figure in the evolution of social welfare, Homer Folks (1867-1963). Folks' early work with dependent, neglected, and delinquent children convinced him that health and welfare were inseparable. He realized the social wellbeing of children depended on the preservation of the family and community and recognized how important it is to mobilize the entire community against illness and insecurity. Folks expanded his interest in the protection of needy children through foster homes (as opposed to institutional care) to a larger concern for maintaining the family and the home in its totality. He raised public awareness of practical aid to the distressed and helped draft and promote public health, mental health, and social welare legislation. The biography deals with his impressive achievements and the social context out of which they grew. Bibliographical essay.

479. Turgel, Stuart C. "The Generosity Factor: A New Index of Philanthropy." *NAHD Journal* (Winter-Spring 1983): 59-64.

480. *Two Perspectives on Our Future.* Special Report, PRSA Social Services Section. New York: Public Relations Society of America, 1981.

481. Tyler, Alice Felt. *Freedom's Ferment.* Philadelphia: Ayer Press, 1944.

Tyler's monumental social history of "the fundamentals of faith, crusades, reforms and reformers whose effect on American civilization was profound and permanent" covers in great detail a much broader topic than the history of philanthropy, but insofar as it explicates the national mood, character, or ethic at given moments in the country's history, it provides a valuable backdrop. The most directly relevant section and the largest, is Part 3, *Humanitarian Crusades*, which treats education, criminal reform, relief for the poor and infirm, the temperance movement, the slavery debate, the rights of women, the peace crusade, and anti-Catholicism. Tyler describes, in a word, "a period of social ferment...when Americans were superbly conscious of the fact that it was their duty and their privilege to lead the way in reforms that brought better care to the unfortunate, hope to the poor and downtrodden, and realization of their highest ambitions to the aspiring." Comprehensive bibliography.

482–499 PHILANTHROPY AND PHILANTHROPISTS

482. Unger, Craig. *Blue Blood.* New York: William Morrow, 1988.

Biography of Rebekah Harkness, the Standard Oil heiress whose enormous wealth and eccentricity dazzled New York in the sixties and seventies. She spent millions on medicine and the arts, especially through her own dance company, the Harkness Ballet. Explores the various facets of her personality: the wild debutante, the demure society matron, the world-famous arts patroness, the eccentric, capricious, decadent heiress; and traces the effect Rebekah had upon her children, to whom she left a legacy of abandonment and neglect.

483. United Way of America. *Some Aspects of Philanthropy in the United States, Scope and Trends.* Alexandria, Va.: United Way of America, 1981.

484. United Way of America. *What Lies Ahead: Looking toward the 90's.* Alexandria, Va.: United Way of America, 1987.

United Way of America's Environmental Scan Committee uses information drawn from print and broadcast media to forecast the most probable scenario for social, economic, political, and technological trends. In addition, a special section provides summary analyses of issues that have received much public attention and have generated increased demands for response, including generational equity, teenage pregnancy, the AIDS epidemic, drug abuse, corporate restructuring, and competition between nonprofits and for-profits.

485. University of Pennsylvania. School of Public and Urban Policy. *The Metropolitan Philadelphia Philanthropy Study.* Philadelphia: University of Pennsylvania, 1980.

486. University of Pennsylvania. School of Public and Urban Policy. *The Metropolitan Philadelphia Philanthropy Study. Final Report.* Philadelphia: University of Pennsylvania, 1980.

487. Urell, Emmet J. *Banking and Private Philanthropy.* Unpublished, 1952.

488. Wall, Joseph Frazier. *Andrew Carnegie.* New York: Oxford University Press, 1970.

This immense, detailed biography of Andrew Carnegie is testament to the tendency Carnegie had to write proliferously and to insist on notes, minutes, and records as an employer. Part 3 is especially germaine to philanthropy and covers the period 1899 to 1919, the year of Carnegie's death; it discusses his philanthropic activities in detail. There is an interesting discussion of the various reviews, both critical and not, that greeted *The Gospel of Wealth,* written in 1899, and Wall's examination of the inner doubts and questions that plagued Carnegie about being a millionaire is enlightening. Carnegie's philanthropy represented an effort to reconcile his immense wealth with the ideals of democracy—an effort not entirely successful. Wall's account of the formation and expansion of Carnegie's philanthropies is insightful and places in it the context of his entire life.

489. Wall, Joseph Frazier. *Skibo.* New York: Oxford University Press, 1984.

490. Warner, Amos G. *American Charities: A Study in Philanthropy and Economics.* New York: Thomas Y. Crowell Co., [1984].

491. Watson, Frank Dekker. *The Charity Organization Movement in the United States: A Study in American Philanthropy.* 1922. Edited by David J. Rothman. Reprint. Poverty, U.S.A.: the Historical Record. New York: Arno Press, 1971.

Watson traces the history of the American charity organization movement (a term used to describe the formation of societies for charitable purposes) to 1921. He touches on its antecedents in the United States and abroad, as well as the functions, principles, and methods of the charity organization society, and the various manifestations of the movement over time. He also devotes three chapters to discussion of the efficiency (or lack thereof) of the societies, prejudices, and criticisms against them; the philosophy of charity organization; and the relation of family case work to movements for improving social conditions. Watson calls his method "not only historical but philosophical and critical as well....An effort has been made...to indicate the economic and social forces that have shaped [the movement's] growth." Includes a bibliography.

492. *Wealth Holders of America.* San Francisco: Biodata, 1988.

Provides brief profiles of the wealthiest persons in America (those whose net worth is at least one million dollars). Each entry contains, when available, information about the person's address (home and/or work), education, date and place of birth, compensation (including salary, bonuses, stock options, etc.), business and position, insider holdings, and charitable and political contributions. Indexed by geographical location, city and state of birth, college or university, corporation, philanthropic and political contributions, and foundation and nonprofit affiliation.

493. Weaver, Warren. *Alfred P. Sloan Jr., Philanthropist.* New York: Alfred P. Sloan Foundation, 1975.

494. Weaver, Warren. *Scene of Change: A Lifetime in American Science.* New York: Charles Scribner's Sons, 1970.

495. Weigel, George. "Religious Philanthropy's Distinctive Mission." *Philanthropy* 6 (July-August 1988): 1, 5, 7.

George Weigel, a Roman Catholic theologian and president of the James Madison Foundation in Washington, DC, examines the relationship between religious philanthropy and the American democratic faith, which he believes is an extension of religious faith, and calls for a recreation of civil and moral debate concerning issues of public policy.

496. Weiman, Liz M. "Charity in Texas. Part 2: Hearts of Gold." *Ultra* 3 (February 1984): 80+.

497. Weiss, Philip. "How about Franklin Thomas for Mayor?" *Manhattan, Inc.* 5 (January 1988): 37-45.

498. Weymouth, Lally. "The Princess of Playboy." *New York* 15 (21 June 1982): 32-41.

499. Wheeler, Sessions S. *Gentleman in the Outdoors: A Portrait of Max C. Fleischmann.* Reno, Nev.: University of Nevada Press, 1985.

500. Whitaker, Ben. *The Philanthropoids: Foundations and Society.* New York: William Morrow, 1974.

An often critical examination of the aims, politics, economics, and achievements of U.S. private foundations by a British scholar. Chapter 9 presents Whitaker's views on *How Not to Get a Grant.*

501. White, Arthur H. *The Charitable Behavior of Americans: Management Summary.* New York: Rockefeller Brothers Fund, 1986.

Presents a comprehensive summary of the results from the national survey.

502. Whittemore, Henry. *History of the Sage and Slocum Families of England and America, Including the Allied Families of Montague, Wanton, Brown, Josselyn, Standish, Doty, Carver, Jermain or Germain, Pierson, and Howell.* Privately Printed, 1908.

503. *Who's Who in American Public-Private Partnerships.* Washington: Partnerships Dataline USA, 1983.

504. Wiebe, Robert H. *The Search for Order, 1877-1920.* Westport, Conn.: Greenwood Press, 1980.

Wiebe describes what he sees as a fundamental shift in American values from those of the small town, largely autonomous, in the 1880s, to those of a new, bureaucratic-minded middle class by 1920. It was largely this new class of urban professionals that transformed economic life, social structure, political behavior, and patterns of ideas, moving consciously toward values of rational administration and management of societal problems and ushering in a more pronounced, continuous role for government in the lives of people. "By contrast to the personal, informal ways of the community," Wiebe writes, "the new scheme was derived from the regulative hierarchical needs of urban-industrial life. Through rules with impersonal sanctions, it sought continuity and predictability in a world of endless change." The analysis is a useful backdrop for considering the expansion of philanthropic activity witnessed by this period, and in particular, the rise of modern foundations. The bibliographical essay is usefully divided by subject and methodology.

505. Williams, E. Morgan. "Community Partnerships at Home and Abroad." *Community Action* 1 (1982): 17+.

506. Williams, Edward F. *The Life of Dr. D.K. Pearsons, Friend of the Small College and of Missions.* New York: Pilgrim Press, 1911.

507. Williams, Roger M. "An American Abroad." *Foundation News* 28 (May-June 1987): 26-31.

J. Paul Getty Jr. has greatly enhanced British philanthropy with both the J. Paul Getty Jr. Charitable Trust and his personal largesse. Getty has combined his great wealth and diverse interests to become one of the world's outstanding philanthropists. He makes awesomely huge gifts and has stated that he intends over the long run to give his entire fortune to charity. It appears, however, that American charities will not share in that fortune; all the gifts have been to British causes. Getty's personal contacts are limited—he is considered a recluse, but his interests reflect that the contacts he does maintain keep him involved with both public affairs and current events. Getty's personal grants have gone to art and museums, film and its history, the disabled, the Imperial War Museum, the World Wildlife Fund, medical charities, assistance to striking miners' families, and a grandstand for a cricket stadium. The trust started with no priorities, but the trustees built on and expanded upon Getty's interests, including a chair in "addiction behavior" at the University of London, an AIDS residential and day-care center, historic preservation, art and museums, youth programs, and services-provided housing for aged and mental health.

508. Williams, Roger M. "Philanthropy Considered." *Foundation News* 27 (July-August 1986): 32-5.

Describes the proceedings of the first session on philanthropy sponsored by the Salzburg Seminar, which was attended by forty-five fellows from eighteen countries.

509. Wilson, Philip Whitwell. *George Peabody, Esq.* N.p.: Bruce R. Payne, 1926.

510. Wilson, Winthrop B. "Trends in Hospital Philanthropy: Reacting to Current Changes." *Fund Raising Management* 15 (October 1984): 28+.

511. Wing, William G. *Philanthropy and the Environment: A Report on Nature and Extent of Philanthropic Activity in the Environmental Field.* Washington: Conservation Foundation, 1973.

512. Winkler, John K. *John D.: A Portrait in Oils.* New York: Blue Ribbon Books, 1929.

513. Winkler, John K. *Morgan the Magnificent: The Life of J. Pierpont Morgan, 1837-1913.* New York: Vanguard Press, 1930.

514. WNET/Thirteen. *Charity in the USA.* New York: WNET/Thirteen, 1986.

Trancript from a public television show which examines how Americans respond to government cutbacks in social services and new tax laws that undercut charitable deductions during the Reagan years.

515. Woodroofe, Kathleen. *From Charity to Social Work in England and the United States.* London: Routledge & Kegan Paul, 1962.

Woodroofe traces the evolution of social work from a so-called pastime for the wealthy and leisured in Victorian England—the Charity Organization Society—to the efforts of group work and community organizations to release human potentialities imprisoned by fear, poverty, and ignorance in modern social work. The author begins with the origins of case work, group work, and community organization in nineteenth-century England. She follows the process by which ideas and concepts practiced in the Old World were transplanted to the New World, where, subject to different circumstances and interpretations, they were transformed. Thus altered, many of these concepts in social work have found their way back to England to continue the process of change. There is discussion of Mary E. Richmond and *Social Diagnosis.* 200-item bibliography.

516. Wooster, James W., Jr. *Edward Stephen Harkness, 1874-1940.* New York: Commonwealth Fund, 1949.

517. Wyllie, Irvin G. *Motives in Educational Philanthropy.* New York: American Public Relations Association, 1965.

518. Wyllie, Irvin G. *The Search for an American Law of Charity.* Reprint. Cedar Rapids, Iowa: Torch Press, 1959.

Wyllie's theme is the development in the new republic of policy on charity and philanthropy, which was largely influenced by local conditions. Massachusetts had a long, favorable history of philanthropy, as did the Pennsylvania Quakers. Policies in Virginia and Maryland were less favorable to philanthropy. In the absence of clear federal guidelines, each state set up policies in its constitution to either encourage or restrict charity or in some cases to allow it to function without any constitutional recognition. The first Supreme Court decisions having to do with charitable policy, handed down in 1819, illustrate the government's uncertainty, since they contradict each other with regard to two different "dead hand" issues. Wyllie traces the subsequent court decisions on both the state and federal levels and the role of Henry Baldwin, a little-known Supreme Court justice, in reversing the restrictive trend of charity policy with the *Magill vs. Brown* case of 1833. The reliance of Americans on English law is clearly evident in this account of legal development.

519. Wyllie, Irvin G. *The Self-Made Man in America: The Myth of Rags to Riches.* New York: Free Press, 1966.

Its preface states that this book attempts "to explore the story of the rags-to-riches idea in terms of its practical relation to our business civilization...to explain the origin, nature, and content of the idea; something of its relation to religion, education, and general movements of thought; something of its propagation, and its social uses; and something of the men who loved and despised the idea. The doctrine of self-help is simple and unsophisticated, more at home with ordinary men than with philosophers. Its history is not the history of a great abstraction, but the saga of an idea that had power among the people." This intellectual and practical history of the concept of success explores motivations and manifestations lost in the popular equation of success with material wealth. Wyllie's engaging analysis provides good background on the cult of successful business that generated and influenced some of our most famous philanthropists. Note on the sources.

520. Yankelovich, Skelly and White. *The Charitable Behavior of Americans: A National Survey.* New York: Rockefeller Brothers Fund, 1986.

The first major study to examine American charitable behavior since a 1974 study was conducted by the Filer Commission. Presents the results of telephone interviews conducted with 1,151 Americans, eighteen years of age and older, regarding their charitable behavior. The study highlights such topics as the attitudes of Americans toward charitable giving and volunteering, the effect of perceived discretionary income on giving, which charitable causes are supported by generous donors and why they receive support. Also examined are relationships between giving and volunteer time, religious giving, demographic characteristics, giving methods and amounts. The study gives special attention to the giving behavior of Americans under thirty-five years of age to determine if generation differences in giving exist. Contains detailed tables, graphs, and charts.

521. Young, Clarence H., and William A. Quinn. *Foundation for Living: The Story of Charles Stewart Mott and Flint.* New York: McGraw-Hill, 1963.

522. Zilg, Gerard Colby. *Du Pont: Behind the Nylon Curtain.* Englewood Cliffs, N.J.: Prentice-Hall, 1974.

2

FOUNDATIONS

523. *AIDS: An Update for Grantmakers.* Unpublished, 1987.

Summaries of speeches given at the September 29, 1987 meeting of Funders Concerned About AIDS, sponsored by the Health Services Improvement Fund. David E. Rogers, chairman of the New York Governor's AIDS Advisory Council speaks about the special regional problems of the epidemic; selected AIDS issues are addressed: *The Intravenous Drug Abuse Aspect, Adolescents—A Generation at Risk, The Impact of AIDS on Minorities,* and *Ethical Dimensions.* Update reports are given on federal, regional, state, and city funding efforts, and Michael Seltzer gives an overview of grantmaking to date, with brief presentations by people involved in programs that provide services or funds for AIDS-related projects.

524. Alchon, Guy. *The Invisible Hand of Planning: Capitalism, Social Science, and the State in the 1920s.* Princeton, N.J.: Princeton University Press, 1985.

This is a study of collaboration between social science and managerial institutions in the 1920s, which, according to Alchon, sought to promote capitalism by allowing for private yet "scientized" managerial authority in the economy. The major foundations played an important role in this process. Alchon contends that the 1920s saw the development of a "techno-corporatist" state in which national management would be achieved through the creation of public roles for technically informed private authorities. The rising social sciences conferred legitimacy on this apparatus by finding that capitalist ills were "curable" through better organization and management. Philanthropic foundations began to fund social and economic surveys, establish research institutions, and otherwise promote the social sciences—thus, in Alchon's view, becoming "financial sponsor, organizer and protector of technocratic institutions," a role he says they continue to play. These trends resulted in greatly increased professionalization of economics, management, and social work, and the emergence of a new kind of business leader with expanded claims to social authority.

525. Alexander, Marjorie. *Members and Library Partners Directory.* Chicago: Donors Forum of Chicago, 1988.

526. Allen, Herb, and Sam Sternberg, eds. *Small Change from Big Bucks: A Report and Recommendations on Bay Area Foundations and Social Change.* San Francisco: Bay Area Committee for Responsive Philanthropy, 1979.

Based primarily on 1976 990-AR returns filed with the IRS, CT-2 forms filed with California, annual reports, and interviews with forty-five Bay Area foundations. Main section arranged alphabetically by foundation—entries include statement of purpose and contact person, but no sample grants. Also sections on the Bay Area Committee for Responsive Philanthropy, foundations and social change, the study methodology, the committee's findings, and the committee's recommendations. No indexes. Appendixes of: Bay Area resources for technical assistance, bibliography, nonprofit organizations in law and fact, and glossary.

527. Allison, Dwight. "Much More Than Bricks and Mortar." *Foundation News* 28 (January-February 1987): 57-9.

Excerpt from a speech delivered by Boston Foundation Chairman, Dwight Allison. Allison discusses the real role of the community foundation in our society. He views community not just as a geographic area—a city, a county, or a state—but as a state of mind. Thus, the community foundation exists to nurture the community, a community which sees itself as part of a group. Allison in his discussion of priority of values states that he believes the most important duty of a community foundation is to concern itself with social and civic values. Allison feels that the community foundation is the natural institution to speak out on what makes a community work. For the future he sees the community foundation as an institution which will "sustain and disseminate those social and civic virtues that make community life feasible and fulfilling."

528–549 FOUNDATIONS

528. Alu Like. *A Guide to Charitable Trusts and Foundations in the State of Hawaii.* Honolulu, Hawaii: Alu Like, 1984.

529. American Association of Junior Colleges. *The Foundation and the Junior College: A Workshop for Junior College Institutional Teams.* Washington: American Association of Junior Colleges, 1966.

530. American Bankers Association. *Community Trusts in the United States and Canada: A Survey of Existing Trusts with Suggestions for Organizing and Developing New Foundations.* New York: American Bankers Association, 1931.

531. American Society of Association Executives. *Starting a Foundation.* Washington: American Society of Association Executives, [198?].

532. Anderson, Mary. "Foundations." *Presstime* 9 (April 1987): 6-9.

Examines the grantmaking practices of foundations born of newspaper fortunes and finds that communities in which affiliated newspapers are published benefit from research and educational projects and nationwide grants support journalistic interests more than any other cause. As independent private foundations such as those of Gannett, Hearst, Knight and McCormick grow in asset value, they tend to expand their giving focus; unlike public foundations formed by newspaper organizations (and which are primarily grantseekers, not grantmakers), private foundations do not have to concentrate on the interest of a sponsoring organization. Still, there is little consensus between newspaper-related foundations concerning the need for a clearinghouse or forum to coordinate grant-making activities.

533. Anderson, Shirley. *Grants and Fellowships.* Newark, Del.: American Philosophical Association, 1988.

Listings for grants and fellowships offered by fifty-six foundations, institutions and societies of interest to humanities scholars. (Majority of the grants are for doctorate and post-doctorate level research and study.).

534. Andrews, Frank Emerson. "Applications for Foundation Grants." *AAFRC Bulletin* 2 (26 January 1956): 1-4.

535. Andrews, Frank Emerson. *Foundation Reports to Internal Revenue Service: An Analysis and Evaluation.* New York: Foundation Center, 1970.

536. Andrews, Frank Emerson. *Foundation Watcher.* Lancaster, Pa.: Franklin and Marshall College, 1973.

This autobiographical look at foundations between approximately 1930 and 1970 arose out of a speech Andrews was asked to make approaching his retirement. In Andrews' words, "I have had the world's most fascinating job: foundation watcher. Indeed, for forty years I have been privileged to sit on the fifty-yard line of all of philanthropy." From his modest beginnings as a free-lance writer for the then twenty-year-old Russell Sage Foundation, to the establishment in 1956 of the Foundation Center, of which he was the first director, Andrews recounts in personal terms the evolution of some of philanthropy's most important institutions, the significant events, and the interplay of individuals that shaped the course of foundation development over those forty years and for many to come.

537. Andrews, Frank Emerson. "Foundations and Community Trusts." *Social Work Year Book* (1945): 1-5.

538. Andrews, Frank Emerson, ed. *Foundations: Twenty Viewpoints.* New York: Russell Sage Foundation, 1965.

539. Andrews, Frank Emerson. *Legal Instruments of Foundations.* New York: Russell Sage Foundation, 1958.

540. Andrews, Frank Emerson. *Patman and Foundations: Review and Assessment.* Foundation Center Occasional Papers, no. 3. New York: Foundation Center, 1968.

541. Andrews, Frank Emerson. *Philanthropic Foundations.* New York: Russell Sage Foundation, 1956.

Based on extensive interviews, correspondence, questionnaires, and Andrews' long experience with foundations, this study encompasses the situation of foundations in the 1950s: their types, organization, boards of trustees, finances, professional staff, methods of operation, grant programs, areas of interest, reporting and publicity, legal problems, and current trends. While the study was intended as a tool for foundations themselves, to further understanding and communication on issues of common concern, its thorough investigation of the principles of foundation operation are of interest to wider audiences. The first and last chapters, *Foundations Today* and *Trends and Prospects*, are of the greatest general interest, although they are naturally somewhat dated. This book is a complement to Andrews' *Corporation Giving* (1952), and contains a thirty-page bibliography.

542. Andrews, Frank Emerson. *Philanthropy in the United States: History and Structure.* New York: Foundation Center, 1978.

543. Andrews, Frank Emerson. *Scientific Research Expenditures by the Larger Private Foundations.* Washington: National Science Foundation, 1956.

544. "Annenberg/CPB Will Give $10 Million to Telecommunications Projects." *Foundation Giving Watch* 5 (June 1985): 1.

545. "Annual Report Survey. Part 1." *Channels* 36 (February 1984): 8.

546. "Annual Reports Often Reveal Giving Priorities." *Corporate Giving Watch* 4 (March 1985): 4.

Tells what to look for in corporate annual reports.

547. Anthony, Alfred Williams, ed. *Cooperation in Fiduciary Service.* Wise Public Giving Series, no. 14. New York: Abbot Press, 1927.

548. Arbuthnot, Thomas S. *Heroes of Peace: A History of the Carnegie Hero Fund Commission.* New York: Carnegie Hero Fund Commission, 1935.

549. Archabal, John. "Inspecting the Damage." *Foundation News* 25 (March-April 1984): 58-9.

550. "Are Unrestricted Funds Truly without Strings?" *Foundation News* 26 (May-June 1985): 53+.

551. Arnold, Alvin L. "Ford (Foundation) Has a Better Way." *Real Estate Review* 4 (Fall 1974): 72-6.

552. Arnove, Robert F., ed. *Philanthropy and Cultural Imperialism: The Foundations at Home and Abroad.* Boston: G.K. Hall & Co., 1980.

This collection of fourteen essays based on original research presents a critical analysis of the activities of foundations—principally Carnegie, Rockefeller, and Ford—in the production of culture and the formation of public policy. In Arnove's words, "A central thesis is that foundations like Carnegie, Rockefeller and Ford have a corrosive influence on a democratic society; they represent relatively unregulated and unaccountable concentrations of power and wealth which buy talent, promote causes, and, in effect, establish an agenda of what merits society's attention...They help maintain an economic and political order, international in scope, which benefits the ruling-class interests of philanthropists and philanthropoids—a system which, as the various chapters document, has worked against the interests of minorities, the working class, and Third World peoples." The essays are by Barbara Howe, Sheila Slaughter and Edward Silva, Russell Marks, E. Richard Brown, James Anderson, Edward Berman, Donald Fisher, Peter Seybold, Robert Arnove, Dennis Buss, David Weischadle, Frank Darknell, and Mary Anna Culleton Colwell.

553. Artists Foundation. *Money Business: Grants and Awards for Creative Artists.* Rev. ed. Boston: Artists Foundation, 1982.

Directory of ogranizations that offer financial assistance to poets, fiction writers, playwriters, filmmakers, video artists, composers, choreographers, painters, printmakers, sculptors, craftsmen and photographers. Aid is for both independent artists and students for special projects.

554. Ascoli, Lucy B. *Building Your Own Philanthropic Foundation.* Chicago: Donors Forum of Chicago, 1985.

Useful booklet written as a primer on setting up a foundation. Covers such topics as: advantages of a foundation, what you can accomplish with a foundation, getting started, and other funding vehicles. Although written to serve as a guide in the Chicago area, the information is applicable to any city.

555. Asher, Thomas R. "Why Foundations Should Support Advocacy Groups." *Foundation News* 24 (May-June 1983): 56+.

556. Associated Grantmakers of Massachusetts. *Massachusetts Foundation Directory.* Boston: Associated Grantmakers of Massachusetts, 1983.

557. Associated Grantmakers of Massachusetts. *Massachusetts Foundation Directory Supplement: Sources of Private Support for Individuals.* Boston: Associated Grantmakers of Massachusetts, 1984.

558. Associated Grantmakers of Massachusetts. *Massachusetts Grantmakers.* Boston: Associated Grantmakers of Massachusetts, 1986.

Published at the request of the Massachusetts attorney general, this directory contains descriptions of 385 foundations and corporate grantmakers in Massachusetts. Entries indicate type of foundation, funding sources which support nonprofit organizations and/or individuals, grantmaking philosophy/program emphasis, program interests, geographic focus, financial information, application procedures, trustees, and contact person. A reference chart indexing grantmaking organizations according to program areas and population groups is included. Contains indexes by corporate grantmaker and geographic location in Massachusetts. Appendixes list recently terminated foundations, and members of the Regional Associations of Grantmakers.

559. Association of Black Foundation Executives. *Membership Directory.* Washington: Association of Black Foundation Executives, 1986.

The first published directory of ABFE, listing seventy-six members and two honorary members for the year of 1985. Arranged alphabetically by state, the profiles give the areas of responsibility, professional and organizational affiliations, and other pertinent information about the members to facilitate networking.

560. Ballantine, Elizabeth. "Cedar Rapids Hall Foundation: Pot of Gold for Charities." *Des Moines Register* (27 July 1981): A-3.

561. Ballantine, Elizabeth. "Foundations Spread $10.5 Million through Iowa in '79." *Des Moines Sunday Register* (26 July 1981): B-1, B-4.

562. Barron, Deborah Durfee. "Setting Priorities for the 1980's." *Foundation News* (November-December 1980): 22-4, 46.

563. Barron, Lewis W. "Advise and Invest." *Currents* 13 (September 1987): 44-7.

Guide to investment policy for the institution-related foundation written by Lewis W. Barron, vice-president and senior consultant at the University of Illinois Foundation. Barron identifies the establishment of an investment philosophy, the setting of objectives, and the involvement of the right personnel as major aspects of a responsible investment program. An investment philosophy includes social, political and moral considerations as well as the desired rate of return. To meet your objectives divide the revenues into categories and establish a target for each of the classifications such as funds for current expenditure, quasi-endowments for designated uses, permanent endowments for designated uses, unrestricted monies, and life income trusts. In addition to the staff, personnel involved in policy-making should include an investment policy committee, investment counsel, and the custodian whether it is a person or an organization.

564. Beckman, Margaret, Stephen Langmead, and John Black. *The Best Gift: A Record of the Carnegie Libraries in Ontario.* Toronto, Canada: Dundurn Press, 1984.

565. Beckwith, Edward J., and Jana S. DeSirgh. *Private and Community Foundation Grants for Local Community Economic Development.* Resources for Grantmakers. Washington: Council on Foundations, [1987].

Provides advice for private and community foundations contemplating making grants to local community organizations in support of community economic development programs, including housing development and rehabilitation; technical job-training; assistance to small businesses; and other projects intended to benefit low-income, elderly, handicapped or other disadvantaged individuals; or to combat community deterioration. In light of the requirement that private and community foundations must operate exclusively in furtherance of their exempt purposes, this paper examines the limitations of section 501(c)(3) of the Internal Revenue Code and reviews IRS rulings and court decisions concerning business development in depressed areas, employment and job-assistance, self-help programs, and housing. Before making grants to community economic development programs, a foundation should consider whether its governing document permits such distributions to be made (if the purposes clause is stated in sufficiently broad terms, there should be no problem). Choose projects which provide comprehensive assistance aimed at rehabilitating and developing disadvantaged areas and which assist business as only a portion of their community economic development activities. Also consider requesting that restrictive contractual provisions be inserted which require the donor's consent before the grantee takes certain actions.

566. Beinecke, Richard H. *Foundations and Health: Opportunities in a Time of Rapid Change.* Cambridge, Mass.: Center for Effective Philanthropy.

567. Bencivenga, Jim. "Foundations: Private Giving for Public Schools." *Christian Science Monitor* (10 December 1982): B-1.

568. Bencivenga, Jim. "How at One Foundation a Grant Went from Idea to Reality." *Christian Science Monitor* (10 December 1982): B-10.

569. Bennett, James T. "Foundation Grants for Social Science Research." *Grants Magazine* 10 (June 1987): 85-90.

There was a time when American foundations made block grants to university social science departments with the belief that they were supporting eventual solutions to social problems. Today foundations are much more likely to support research that is applied rather than basic, with a significance clearly related to the public problems a particular foundation is trying to solve. Social scientists must learn to articulate the value of their research to something other than research—that is, they must convince society it will benefit by their research of it—especially when writing a grant proposal.

570. Berger, Judith D. "Foundation Funding: Information and Resource Guide." *Hospital Forum* (January-February 1982): 27-38.

571. Berliner, Howard S. *A System of Scientific Medicine: Philanthropic Foundations in the Flexner Era.* New York: Methuen, 1985.

Traces the development of the American medical education system from the late nineteenth century to the mid-twentieth. Using archival materials, diaries, letters, and other autobiographical data, Berliner documents the role of the great philanthropic foundations—the Rockefeller General Education Board and the Carnegie Foundation—in bringing scientific medicine and medical education centered around research into the forefront in the United States. 1985 saw the 75th anniversary of the Flexner Report on Medical Education in the United States and Canada, the document widely held to be the catalyst for the reorientation of the system of medical education in America. The struggle of the physicians against the ideas of the philanthropic foundations is vividly revealed, as is the battle of the institutions—Carnegie versus Rockefeller. The book shows the great philanthropic institutions granting and withholding their gifts and thereby determining the future path of U.S. medicine. Includes bibliography.

572. Berman, Edward H. *The Influence of the Carnegie, Ford and Rockefeller Foundations on American Foreign Policy: The Ideology of Philanthropy.* Albany, N.Y.: State University of New York Press, 1983.

Berman claims that, despite rhetoric to the contrary by foundation officers and trustees, internal foundation memoranda, letters, policy statements, and reminiscences left by them "indicate unequivocally how foundation programs were designed to further the foreign policy interests of the United States." These interests are essentially the furtherance of state capitalism, according to Berman. The way foundations promote ideological support for capitalism abroad is to encourage certain ideas congruent with their objectives and to support the educational institutions that produce and disseminate those ideas. Over the years, says Berman, the foundations "have perfected methods whereby their educational and cultural programs would complement the cruder and more overt forms of economic and military imperialism that are so easily definable." Berman draws on Italian cultural Marxist Antonio Gramsci's theory of cultural hegemony to make his case.

573. Birmingham Public Library. *Alabama Foundation Directory.* Birmingham, Ala.: Birmingham Public Library, 1983.

Based primarily on 1982 and 1983 990-PF returns filed with the IRS by 184 foundations. Main section arranged alphabetically by foundation—entries include areas of interest and officers, but no sample grants. Indexes of geographic areas and major areas of interest.

574. Blount, Lawanna Lease. *Contributions of Selected Private Philanthropic Foundations for Higher Education Administration, 1966-1975.* Unpublished, 1978.

575. Blum, D. Steven. "Good Works and Self-Help." *Grantsmanship Center News* 11 (July-August 1983): 4-7.

576. Blumenthal, Larry. "Getty Trust Goes National with Push for Art Education." *NonProfit Times* 1 (May 1987): 8.

577. Blumenthal, Larry. "Study Details Rise in New Foundations." *NonProfit Times* 1 (December 1987): 3, 13-4.

Data from the 11th edition of the *Foundation Directory* shows that 446 major foundations were established between 1980 and 1986 (five with assets of over $100 million), an average of seventy-four new foundations a year. This is up from an average of nearly sixty-three a year in the 1970s. The directory also documents solid growth in foundation assets and giving, attributed to record gains in the stock market, lower inflation, improved investment strategies, and recent legislative changes. Among other findings: more than twenty-six percent of giving by foundations was concentrated in general welfare funding, which includes community affairs, consumer interests, urban and rural development and other related areas; total giving by independent foundations rose to $3.7 billion between 1983 and 1985, the greatest two-year increase in nearly a decade; and the most rapid growth in assets in 1985 came in the East North Central states (Illinois, Indiana, Michigan, Ohio and Wisconsin).

578. Bolling, Landrum R. "Foundation Funding for Environmental Programs." *Catalyst* 7 (n.d.): 29-31.

579. Bolling, Landrum R., George W. Bonham, and McGeorge Bundy. *The Future of Foundations: Some Reconsiderations.* New Rochelle, N.Y.: Change Magazine Press, 1978.

This volume consists of an introduction by George Bonham, a paper by James Douglas and Aaron Wildavsky, and the transcript of a discussion of the paper by those above with Landrum Bolling, McGeorge Bundy, Fred Hechinger, John Knowles, Waldemar Nielsen, B.J. Stiles and Paul Ylvisaker—foundation executives and foundation watchers. Bonham outlines the disappointment of many critics with the "limited imagination" and "arthritic structure" of the large modern foundations. Douglas and Wildavsky, after tracing the trends in foundation development over the century, suggest a new intellectual rationale for them: a change to sociopolitical (as opposed to socioeconomic) emphasis—namely, coping with government failures, especially those occasioned by the "near-sighted time horizon" of public officials. According to the authors, foundations' freedom from political or market criteria makes them uniquely capable to find alternative solutions to problems with which government is not coping very well. The panel discussion is extremely interesting and very valuable.

580. Boniface, Zoe E., and Rebecca W. Rimel. *U.S. Funding for Biomedical Research.* Philadelphia: Pew Charitable Trusts, 1987.

581. Bothwell, Robert O., and Timothy Saasta. "Learning to Listen." *Grantsmanship Center News* 11 (January-February 1983): 86-8.

582. Boyer, Ernest L. "Why Should the Private Sector Support Public Education?" *Foundation News* 23 (November-December 1982): 4+.

583. Brickley, Peg, and Fred Powledge. *The Buck Bequest: A Case Study in Philanthropy.* New York: Nation Institute, 1983.

584. Broce, Thomas Edward. *A Study of Oklahoma-Based Private Philanthropic Foundations and Their Impact on Higher Education.* Unpublished, 1970.

585. Brody, Deborah. "More Than a Salary Survey." *Foundation News* 28 (September-October 1987): 61-2.

Article analyzes results of the *1987 Foundation Compensation Report*, which reveals more women holding CEO positions in foundations, although their average salary is only between fifty-two and fifty-eight percent of that earned by their male counterparts. However, the gap is decreasing for program officers, where women tend to earn about seventy-eight percent of what men in the same position earn. Ninety-three percent of all support staff positions are held by women, but minority representation is otherwise low, raising the question of whether foundation employment practices are as socially responsible as their grantmaking practices. General salary information shows salary increases declining steadily since 1982, though most average or mean salaries increase each year.

586. Broman, John. *Grantsmanship Resources for the Arts and Humanities.* Los Angeles: Grantsmanship Center, 1980.

587. Brown, E. Richard. *Rockefeller Medicine Men: Medicine and Capitalism in America.* Berkeley, Calif.: University of California Press, 1980.

Brown charges that the cost, inflation, and inaccessibility of medical care in the United States is "rooted in the interwoven history of modern medicine and corporate capitalism." He states that members of the corporate class, through philanthropic foundations, articulated a strategy for developing a medical system to meet the needs of capitalist society and to ensure their own positions in the social structure. As the major external influence on American medicine between 1900 and 1930, Brown argues, foundations, followed closely by the federal government, sought to rationalize medical care and to make it more universally accessible at the least cost to society's resources. He traces the role of Frederick T. Gates and the Rockefeller medical philanthropies in financing medical education, examining how they assumed control over policy and determined the direction medical practice would take professionally, technologically, and ideologically for years to come.

588. "The Buck Trust Petition: A Bid for Philanthropic Self-Regulation." *Nonprofit Executive* 3 (June 1984): 6.

589. Buckman, Thomas R. *Testimony of Thomas R. Buckman, President, the Foundation Center before the Commerce, Consumer, and Monetary Affairs Subcommittee of the Committee on Government Operations.* Unpublished, 1983.

590. Bulmer, Martin. "Philanthropic Foundations and the Development of the Social Sciences in the Early Twentieth Century: A Reply to Donald Fisher." *Sociology* 18 (1984): 572-87.

Bulmer attempts to refute Fisher's argument in "The Role of Philanthropic Foundations in the Reproduction and Production of Hegemony" (17*Sociology*: 206-33), having consulted the same archival sources. He offers an alternative interpretation of the social and intellectual role of foundations in the development of the social sciences and comments on the relationship between historical evidence and sociological evidence and hypotheses. He suggests that theories of behavior which incorporate "class interest" are not sound. Fisher, in an impassioned rebuttal of Bulmer's criticisms ("A Response to Martin Bulmer," same issue), accuses Bulmer of being content to accept and describe the facts without any theoretical framework at all and defends an analysis of foundations based on class. Fisher writes, "The concept directs our attention to the ways in which social groups consciously attempt to serve their own interest. Nowhere would we expect that to be more the case than with the ruling class...I believe the study of philanthropy provides one of the best opportunities for such research."

591. Bulmer, Martin, and Joan Bulmer. "Philanthropy and Social Science in the 1920s: Beardsley Ruml and the Laura Spelman Rockefeller Memorial, 1922-29." *Minerva* 19 (1981): 347-407.

This article presents a close look at the central role foundation philanthropy played early in this century in the development of research in such academic disciplines as economics, political science, and sociology, by examining one very important foundation's activities during a brief period. The authors discuss the career of Beardsley Ruml, the Laura Spelman Rockefeller Memorial's director from 1922-1929, almost its entire lifespan. Ruml was responsible for directing the fund's resources toward social science research—helping universities develop a body of fact and principle for the solution of social problems. The Bulmers' analysis of these developments, which quotes extensively from foundation documents, is quite thorough. There are detailed descriptions of the Memorial's work and its contributions to such institutions as the Social Science Research Council, the National Bureau of Economic Research, the University of Chicago, and more. When the Memorial was absorbed into the Rockefeller Foundation in 1929, many of its broader goals were retained.

592. Bundy, McGeorge, and George Brakeley. *Alma Mater.* Reprints. Washington: American Alumni Council, 1973.

593. Burns, Michael E., ed. *Connecticut Foundation Directory.* Hartford, Conn.: D.A.T.A., 1987.

Based on 1986 and 1987 990-PF forms filed with the Connecticut Attorney General's Office and completed questionnaires from a December 1987 survey of over 900 foundations. Main section arranged alphabetically by foundation—entries include selected grants list, principal officer, and statements of purpose. Index of foundations by city and an alphabetical index.

594. Burns, Michael E., ed. *Guide to Corporate Giving in New Hampshire.* New Haven, Conn.: OUA/DATA, 1984.

Based on questionnaires answered by 239 corporations. Main section arranged alphabetically by corporation—entries include contact person, product, plants and giving interests. List of corporations by city.

595. Butler, Francis J., and Catherine E. Farrell, eds. *Foundation Guide for Religious Grant Seekers.* 3rd ed. Scholars Press Handbook Series. Decatur, Ga.: Scholars Press, 1987.

Guide provides introductory essays for the religious grant-seeker and minimal information about 407 foundations with a history of religious grantmaking. Appendixes list the locations of *Foundation Center* reference libraries and cooperating collections, and provide a guide to reference books for further information on the foundations.

596. Butt, Martha G. "Getting to Know You: Post-Grant Evaluation." *Foundation News* 26 (July-August 1985): 26+.

597. Cahan, Emily Davis. *The William T. Grant Foundation: The First Fifty Years, 1936-1986.* New York: William T. Grant Foundation, [1986].

598. Calhoun, Susan. "A Helpful Look Inward." *Foundation News* 28 (January-February 1987): 63-4.

Description of a self-study program developed by the Association of Governing Boards of Colleges and Universities for their trustees and rewritten for use by foundation trustees. The program enables foundation trustees to evaluate and improve their performance. The self-study guide is available in three versions tailored to family, non-family and community foundations. The project is overseen by the Council on Foundations' Director of Information, Carol Hooper.

599. Calhoun, Susan. "Moving Target." *Foundation News* 29 (March-April 1988): 76-7.

Profiles the controversy surrounding *Foundations: the People and the Money*, a film intended to give novice grant-seekers and the interested citizen an inside view and better understanding of the foundation world. The film generated criticism not among its targeted audience but among foundation grantmakers, who claim it perpetuates stereotypes which foundations have striven to overcome such as white elitism, foundation arrogance, and the superficiality of funding decisions. However, Calhoun reports that "no one charges that the movie gives a false view of foundations. On the contrary, the film's authenticity has grantmakers squirming." Thomas Buckman, chair of the film's steering committee, suggests that grantmakers use the film as a catalyst for changing any negative aspects still existing within foundations. The film now comes with an introductory study guide, designed to explain the film's purpose, intended audience, the broader foundation world and the filmmaker's unusual techniques (utilizing a method of "direct art" which has cameras eavesdropping on board meetings, site visits and grantwriting sessions), in addition to providing questions for discussion.

600. Calhoun, Susan. "New Ways to Lead." *Foundation News* 28 (November-December 1987): 24—9.

601. Calhoun, Susan. "Pooling Lending Resources." *Foundation News* 28 (March-April 1987): 58-60.

Concise article which explains the current status of loan funds. Loan funds have come of age. Historically an emergency measure, they are now a major program which allows for the "leveraging [of] available funds to serve a larger, and often more varied, audience." This recycled pool of money is used for cash-flow loans, working capital loans, venture loans, fixed-asset loans for the purchase of equipment or to improve property, and occasionally for mortgage financing by providing a down payment. The loan funds have a record of success as a way to bridge loans for nonprofits and to extend the limited capital of foundations.

602. California State University and Colleges. *Federal and Private Foundation Programs Conference.* San Francisco: California State University and Colleges, 1972.

603. Calkins, Robert D., Wilmer Shields Rich, and L.K. Tunks. *The Impact of Foundations on Higher Education.* Chicago: North Central Association of Colleges and Secondary Schools, 1954.

604. Campisi, Dominic J. "Estate of Buck: Frustration of a Charitable Purpose." *Trusts & Estates* 124 (January 1985): 70-6.

605. Cantrell, Karen. *Funding for Anthropological Research.* Phoenix, Ariz.: Oryx Press, 1986.

Compiled to assist professional anthropologists and graduate anthropology students in locating funding sources. Lists 700 sponsored research programs alphabetically by sponsors. Includes programs offered by private and corporate foundations, government agencies, associations, institutes, museums, libraries and professional societies in the United States. Profiles include address, telephone number, purpose and activities, eligibility and limitations, deadlines, fiscal information, subject index terms and the Catalog of Federal Domestic Assistance

Program Number for federal programs. Contains indexes by subject, sponsor type and sponsor name. An annotated bibliography of over forty funding-related print materials and fourteen online databases is also included.

606. Carnegie Corporation of New York. *Fifty Years in Review.* New York: Carnegie Corporation of New York, 1961.

607. Carnegie Endowment for International Peace. *The Legacy Today, Andrew Carnegie's Peace Endowment: The Nineteen-Eighties.* Washington: Carnegie Endowment for International Peace, 1985.

608. Center for Research and Advanced Study. *Directory of Maine Foundations.* 7th ed. Portland, Maine: University of Southern Maine, 1986.

Based on information compiled from foundations, the Foundation Center, and primarily 1984-1985 990-PF returns filed with the IRS. Main section arranged in four parts: Section 1 is mainly an alphabetical listing of 412 Michigan foundations having assets of $200,000 or making annual grants of at least $25,000 with entries including statement of purpose and officers, geographic priority, limitations, application procedures, and grant analysis; Section 1 also provides brief information on 398 foundations making grants of less than $25,000 annually, geographical listing of foundations and special purpose foundations. Section 2 is a listing of sixty-four corporate giving programs and corporate foundations. Section 3 is a survey of Michigan foundation philanthropy. And section 4 provides information on seeking grants. Indexes of subjects/areas of interest; donors, trustees, officers; and foundation names.

609. Chamber of Commerce. *Community Foundations.* Washington: Chamber of Commerce of the United States, 1921.

610. Chambers, Merritt Madison. *Charters of Philanthropies: A Study of Selected Trust Instruments, Charters, By-Laws and Court Decisions.* New York: Carnegie Foundation for the Advancement of Teaching, 1948.

611. Chance, Ruth Clouse. *Bay Area Foundation History.* Madison, Wis.: University of Wisconsin-Madison, 1976.

612. *Charitable Foundations Conference.* Boston: Charitable Foundations Conference, 1969.

613. Chirhart, Edward F. *Today's Planning, Creating, Operating and Reporting for Foundations.* Unpublished, 1957.

614. Chumney, Candes P., ed. *The Hooper Directory of Texas Foundations: Supplement.* 9th ed. San Antonio, Tex.: Funding Information Center of Texas, 1987.

This directory contains updated financial information on Texas foundations. The *New and Revised* section includes complete information on 200 new foundations and on those foundations which have changed in either contact name, funding deadline, grantmaking interests or application procedures. Includes tables of Texas foundations by 1986 assets and grants, the top 100 Texas foundations in descending order by assets and by grants, and a 1986 grant distribution of larger Texas foundations. Indexed by areas of giving, city, trustees and officers, and foundation name.

615. Ciba Foundation. *The Future of Philanthropic Foundations.* Ciba Foundation Symposium, no. 30. New York: Ciba Foundation, 1975.

616. Clague, Ewan. *Charitable Trusts.* Philadelphia: Pennsylvania School of Social Work, 1935.

617. Clark, Dennis. "If Kids Can't Get Summer Jobs, What Can They Do?" *Foundation News* 25 (July-August 1984): 34-41.

618. Clearinghouse for Midcontinent Foundations, comp. *The Directory of Greater Kansas City Foundations.* Kansas City, Mo.: Clearinghouse for Midcontinent Foundations, 1986.

This directory provides detailed profiles on 281 foundations and trusts in the eight-county Greater Kansas City (Missouri) metropolitan area. These foundations have estimated market assets of $610.5 million and estimated annual contributions of $37 million. The foundation listings, arranged alphabetically by foundation name, are indexed by broad fields of interest. The foundation profile contains the foundation name, address, telephone number, contact person, officers and directors, administrators, assets, fiscal year date, recipient information, range, limitations, purpose, and other information. Indexes included in the directory are *Top Twenty Grantmaking Foundations*, based on assets; *Top Twenty Grantmaking Foundations*, based on charitable payout; *Foundations with Designated Recipients*; and *Foundations Making Grants in* (specific subject areas such as arts, health, etc.) .

619. Clearinghouse for Midcontinent Foundations. *A Grantmaker's Guide.* Unpublished, 1977.

620. Cleland, Robert Glass. *The Irvine Ranch.* San Marino, Calif.: Huntington Library, 1966.

621. Clinton, John, ed. *AIDS Funding: A Guide to Giving by Foundations and Charitable Organizations.* New York: Foundation Center, 1988.

Provides information on over 130 foundations (including public foundations, charitable organizations and international funders) with AIDS-related programs and services. These funders account for over 500 AIDS-related grants. Entries contain information on the grantmakers' primary interests, purposes, and limitations, along with detailed information on the hundreds of AIDS grants awarded, including those for women, children born with AIDS, racial minorities, and intravenous drug abusers.

622. Clinton, John, ed. *National Guide to Foundation Funding in Health.* New York: Foundation Center, 1988.

A directory containing facts on approximately 2,000 foundations which have a history of awarding grant dollars to hospitals, universities, research institutes, community-based agencies and national health associations for a broad range of health-related programs and projects. The guide is intended as a starting point for grantseekers looking for foundation support for health-related programs, services or research. Included are 742 national foundations and 1,857 local foundations that hold assets of $1 million or more or whose annual giving totals at least $100,000 and that have expressed a substantial interest in the field of health as part of their stated purpose or through the actual grants they reported to the Foundation Center in 1987. In 1987, America's 25,000 active private and community foundations awarded an estimated $6 billion in grants to nonprofit organizations across the country. Studies of foundation grantmaking patterns by the Foundation Center indicate that roughly twenty-three percent of these grants dollars are directed towards programs related to health.

623. Coffman, Harold Coe. *American Foundations: A Study of Their Role in the Child Welfare Movement.* New York: YMCA, 1936.

624. Coleman, William Emmet. *Grants in the Humanities: A Scholar's Guide to Funding Sources.* 2nd ed. New York: Neal-Schuman Publishers, 1984.

Informative guide for the humanist scholar seeking grant support for research. Begins with introductions to the art of grantsmanship and proposal writing (with a sample proposal and sample budget). Appendixes list 197 grant programs (including listings of many foreign study centers for scholars doing research abroad), providing the name of the program and type of aid (financial or facilities), the purpose of the program, the number of awards bestowed, the amount of support (or types of facilities) offered, eligibility conditions, duration, deadline, and address and telephone number for inquiries.

625. Colorado Committee for Responsive Philanthropy. *What Kinds of Groups Receive Colorado's Foundation Grants? A Study of the Grants of the Twenty-Five Largest Private Foundations from 1974-1976.* Denver, Colo.: Colorado Committee for Responsive Philanthropy, 1979.

626. *Colorado Foundation Directory.* 6th ed. Denver, Colo.: Junior League of Denver, 1988.

Information on more than 170 foundations, covering fiscal years from 1984 through 1987; entries include purpose statement/field of interest, sample grants, and contacts. Also includes an excellent guide to program planning and proposal writing. Indexed by areas of foundation interest.

627. Colwell, Mary Anna Culleton. *Philanthropic Foundations and Public Policy: The Political Role of Foundations.* Berkeley, Calif.: University of California Press, 1980.

628. Commission on Foundations and Private Philanthropy, comp. *Collected Newspaper Clippings and Newsreleases.* 1969. Unpublished, [1969].

629. Commission on Foundations and Private Philanthropy. *Foundations, Private Giving and Public Policy. Report and Recommendations of the Commission on Foundations and Private Philanthropy.* Chicago: University of Chicago Press, 1970.

Final report of the fifteen-member Commission, chaired by Peter G. Peterson, which was formed in 1969 to study American philanthropy and private foundations.

630. Commission on Private Philanthropy and Public Needs. *Guide to Sponsored Research of the Commission on Private Philanthropy and Public Needs.* Washington: Commission on Private Philanthropy and Public Needs, 1976.

631. Commission on Private Philanthropy and Public Needs. *Private Philanthropy: Vital and Innovative or Passive and Irrelevant?* Washington: Commission on Private Philanthropy and Public Needs, 1975.

632. Commission on Private Philanthropy and Public Needs. *Research Papers.* 5 Vols. Washington: U.S. Department of the Treasury, 1977.

633. Commonwealth Fund. *Directory of International Fellows, 1925-1965.* London: Hugh Evelyn, 1965.

634. Community Foundation of Greater Washington. *Directory of Foundations of the Greater Washington Area.* Washington: Community Foundation of Greater Washington, 1988.

Biennial directory of public and private foundations and trusts as well as some corporate foundations in the greater Washington area. Directory is divided into two sections. Section 1 contains the larger foundations with assets of $1 million or more, or which make grants of $100,000 or more in the reported years and Section 2 lists the smaller foundations which have below $1 million in assets, or award grants of less than $100,000. Section 2 comprises the largest number of foundations. Four indexes include: an alphabetical index of foundations; an alphabetical index of trustees, directors and managers; an index of foundations in order of the size of their assets; and an index grouped by the specific area of interest. Information on each foundation includes: name and address; telephone number; contact, trustees, directors and managers; areas of interest; application guidelines; financial and grant data; total assets; number of grants; amount of grants; grant range; and the five largest grants. Preceding the directory are helpful statistical tables and lists for distribution of giving by foundation assest size and by amount of grants awarded, largest independent/family foundations by total giving, largest company-sponsored foundations by total giving, community foundations by total giving, fifteen largest grants, foundations not included in directory, and foundations that do not accept proposals. Also included is a brief adaptation of F. Lee and Barbara L. Jacquette, "What makes a good proposal?"

635. *The Complete Guide to Florida Foundations.* Miami, Fla.: John L. Adams and Co., 1988.

Based primarily on information contained in 990-PF returns for over 1,000 foundations. Main section arranged alphabetically by foundation name; entries include officers, assets, total grants amount, high, low and average grants, funding priorities and geographic preferences. Included is an index of foundations excluded from the *Guide*. Appendix of foundations and their subject and geographic preferences.

636. *Conference of Foundations.* Unpublished, 1957.

637. *Conference of Foundations.* Unpublished, 1960.

638. Conrad, Chris. "The ABC's of Educational Foundations." *Grantsmanship Center News* 12 (January-February 1984): 8-15.

639. Conyngton, Hugh R. *Great Philanthropic Foundations.* 5 Vols. Unpublished, [1940].

640. Coon, Horace. *Money to Burn. What the Great American Philanthropic Foundations Do with Their Money.* New York: Longmans, Green & Co., 1938.

641. Cooperative Assistance Fund. *Information Brochure.* Washington: Cooperative Assistance Fund, 1980.

642. Cort, Doris M., ed. *Edwin Gould: The Man and His Legacy.* New York: Edwin Gould Foundation for Children, 1986.

643. Council for Community Services. *Directory of Grant-Making Foundations in Rhode Island.* Providence, R.I.: Council for Community Services, 1983.

Based on 1980 and 1981 990-PF and 990-AR returns filed with the IRS, information from the Rhode Island Attorney General's Office and information from the ninety-one foundations listed. Main section arranged alphabetically by foundation; entries include officers and trustees, assets, total dollar amount of grants and total number of grants, statement of purpose, geographic restrictions, application information and sample grants. Includes *Introduction to Foundations*; indexes of foundations by total dollar amount of grants made, foundations by location and by area of interest.

644. Council of Michigan Foundations. *Developing Good Will.* Grand Haven, Mich.: Council of Michigan Foundations, 1980.

645. Council of Michigan Foundations. *The Grantmaking Process: Setting Priorities, Assessing, Evaluating.* Council of Michigan Foundations Reports, no. 5. Grand Haven, Mich.: Council of Michigan Foundations, 1987.

Report on the distinct phases of the grantmaking process outlined during the 14th Conference of the Council of Michigan Foundations. The report summarizes both the formal conference presentations by experienced grantmakers and the informal conference discussions on setting priorities, assessing grant proposals and evaluating results. Some of the highlights cited for setting priorities or focus and goals included a mission statement, strategic planning, input from local consultants, brainstorming sessions, and staff retreats. The basics for assessing a grant proposal include the grantseeker's budget, nonprofit status, institution history, proposed program, and project personnel. In addition, site visitations, mid-project audits, and dispensing funds on a periodic basis and only after receipt of status reports are effective assessment tools. Evaluation is most effective when done at the project's beginning and end. For the impact evaluation, the funder must select instruments for the collection of information; the data collection itself should be meticulous. Quantified comparisons and direct project evaluations can be obtained from the use of IRS Form 990 ratios. Three to five percent of the total grant should go to post-grant evaluations.

646. Council of Michigan Foundations. *Survey of Michigan Foundation Philanthropy, 1988.* Grand Haven, Mich.: Council of Michigan Foundations, 1988.

This survey originally appeared as part of the *Michigan Foundation Directory*, sixth edition. The 936 private and community foundations located in Michigan have total assets of $8,447,162,856 and made charitable expenditures in their last reporting year totalling $429,439,373. Tables list the seventy-seven largest Michigan private foundations with assets over $3 million and/or making charitable expenditures in excess of $300,000; the fourteen Michigan community foundations with assets over $1 million; and the eighteen company-sponsored foundations with assets over $1 million. Includes a study of grantmaking patterns of 284 foundations making grants in excess of $50,000, and a comparative analysis of grantmaking from 1975 to 1988. The final table lists the 284 foundations alphabetically, showing their total number and dollar amount of grants; and a breakdown by field of endeavor (i.e., education, health, culture, human services, economic, and other).

647. Council on Foundations. *Alternative Investment Strategies for Institutions. Conference Proceedings.* Washington: Council on Foundations, 1985.

Based on a conference designed to provide grantmakers with current information on various forms of social investing, the legal issues related to social investment criteria, and recent developments in alternative investment approaches. Provides information about the use of investments to promote the development of affordable housing, small businesses, and diverse communities. Although intended for grantmakers, the book may also give ideas to grantseekers looking for funding for socially-oriented economic development projects.

648. Council on Foundations. *Annual Conference.* Washington: Council on Foundations, 1964.

649. Council on Foundations. *Community Foundation Resource Manual.* Washington: Council on Foundations, [1985].

650. Council on Foundations. *Concepts of Funding for Community Foundations.* Washington: Council on Foundations, 1981.

Special report gives twelve papers by community foundation staff on deferred giving techniques.

651. Council on Foundations. *Cooperation among Grantmakers: A Guide to Cooperative Associations of Foundations and Corporate Contributors.* Washington: Council on Foundations, 1974.

652. Council on Foundations. "Council to Develop Community Foundations Technical Assistance Program with Support of Charles Stewart Mott Foundation." *Council on Foundations Newsletter* 16 (18 October 1982): 1-2.

653. Council on Foundations. *Directory of Grantmakers Interested in Precollegiate Education.* Washington: Council on Foundations, [1987].

Alphabetical compilation of survey forms filled out by eighty-five organizations interested in or with a history of granting to precollegiate education. Information includes address, type of organization, market value of assets as of 12/31/86, amount of grants in 1986, names of program officers or trustees responsible for precollegiate programs, limitations (geographic, type/duration of grants, etc.), and sample grants.

654. Council on Foundations. *Foundation Compensation Report.* Washington: Council on Foundations, 1987.

Provides timely staff compensation data to grantmakers in the year between the biennial Foundation Management Reports. Details the low, high, mean, and median salaries for thirty-four of the most commonly employed foundation staff positions in independent, corporate, and private operating foundations; community and public foundations; and corporate foundations/giving programs. Special salary breakdowns for foundations with assets of $100-$299.9 million and for foundations with assets of $300 million and over; and total salary increases for 1986 and 1987. Findings in the overview section include: sixty-nine percent of foundation employees are women; they hold virtually all support/clerical positions as well as many of the assistant executive, program officer, and "other" professional positions such as communications officer and accountant. In contrast, men hold sixty-four percent of CEO positions (down from seventy percent in 1985) and sixty-six percent of executive staff positions. These findings are consistent with a recent Census Bureau report that the actual number of women in the highest paying jobs remains relatively small. Salaries were found to be higher not only in the larger foundations and in private foundations, but also in the Northeast and Mid-Atlantic states, with the lowest salaries in the South, reflecting, the report suggests, differences in the cost of living. Total salary increases for employees in early 1987 averaged between six and seven percent, slightly lower than increases in 1986 (which averaged between seven and eight percent), continuing a trend of lower salary increases over the past several years.

655. Council on Foundations. *Foundation Management Report.* Washington: Council on Foundations, 1984.

Results of the 1986 Foundation Management Survey, in which over 500 foundations participated. Contains information on compensation, benefits, and administrative issues relating to private and public grantmaking foundations. Divided into four sections: Overview contains a discussion of foundation board practices, staffing patterns, trustee and staff demographics, directors and officers liability insurance, use of consultants, and other issues; Compensation section provides information on salary increases, board fees, and staff salaries listed by position; Benefits and Personnel Policies sections contain discussions of retirement programs, health plans, life insurance and other employee benefits as well as vacation, sick, maternity, and other leave practices. Useful reference for foundation trustees and staff managers reviewing their administrative policies.

656. Council on Foundations. *Foundations and Computer Technology.* Resources for Grantmakers Series. Washington: Council on Foundations, 1985.

657. Council on Foundations. *Foundations and Public Policy.* Resources for Grantmakers Series. Washington: Council on Foundations, 1985.

Handbook that discusses what foundations are allowed to do in the area of public policy. Includes articles which explain foundations' interest in influencing public policy and clarify the legal limits. Section on case examples provides descriptions of over twenty recent foundation grants in the area of public policy.

658. Council on Foundations, comp. *The Grantmaking Process.* Washington: Council on Foundations, 1983.

One of a series of *Resources for Grantmakers*, this kit features articles, guidelines, and other materials on grantmaking procedures and practices.

659. Council on Foundations. *Guidelines for Publishing a Minimum Annual Report.* Washington: Council on Foundations, 1982.

660. Council on Foundations. *Hispanics and Grantmakers.* Washington: Council on Foundations, 1981.

661. Council on Foundations. *How We Helped.* Washington: Council on Foundations, [1987].

Booklet which explains foundation philanthropy to those with little or no working knowledge of the foundation world. This report on the foundation community is the first in a planned series of educational reports for the general public by the Council on Foundations. It contains profiles of twenty-five projects funded by over forty foundations. The brief profiles which describe the grants include photographs and quotes from both foundation staff and grant recipients. The sampling of foundations and projects attests to the diversity of foundation type, size, interests, and geographic location. The grants profiled include funding for literacy; music; environmental causes; urban, economic, and community development; minority education; public health, and arts projects, to name a few. The report concludes with definitions of the four foundation types and a chart which shows their general characteristics. In addition, the Council on Foundations, the Independent Sector, and the Foundation Center are described (includes addresses and telephone numbers).

662. Council on Foundations. *Recommended Principles and Practices for Effective Grantmaking.* Washington: Council on Foundations, 1980.

663. Council on Foundations. *Regional Associations of Grantmakers: Program Primer.* Washington: Council on Foundations, 1987.

Primer for staff and volunteers of regional associations of grantmakers (RAG's) outlines the basics of program planning and provides examples of successful programs offered by RAG's in the last few years. Final section contains a resource list of program planners and checklists for programs. Also includes a Council on Foundations organizing tool entitled, *Seven Steps in Organizing a Regional Association of Grantmakers.*

664. Council on Foundations. *Selected Bibliographies.* Washington: Council on Foundations, 1975.

665. Council on Foundations. *Trends Document.* Unpublished, 1987.

666. Council on Foundations, comp. *Trustee Orientation Packet.* Unpublished, [1988].

667. Council on Foundations. *Working Papers of the Subcommittee on the Case Statement for Community Foundations.* Washington: Council on Foundations, 1982.

A compilation of essays, correspondence, and responses initiated by the Subcommittee on the Case Statement for Community Foundations, established by the Committee on Community Foundations of the Council on Foundations, concerning the future direction of community foundation activities.

668. "Counting the Cost of Giving." *Christianity Today* 20 (30 January 1976): 21-2.

669. Cox, Jo-Ann. "How to Interpret and Use Financial Information." *Fund Raising Management* 14 (June 1983): 1-20.

670. Crabtree, Penni. "Wealthy, Rightest Foundation Plans 24-Hour-a-Day Cable TV Network." *National Catholic Reporter* 20 (9 December 1983): 1+.

671. Cronin, Jerry. *Guide to Arkansas Funding Sources.* West Memphis, Ark.: Independent Community Consultants, 1986.

Contains information on ninety-three private Arkansas foundations, fifty-nine corporate foundations, thirty-three scholarship sources, twenty-six church funding sources, and seven neighboring foundations (foundations with Arkansas giving interests). Descriptions of the private and neighboring foundations include the name, address, phone number, employer ID number, principal, trustee(s), year end financial information, notes, summary of grantmaking by giving area with sample grants, total dollars granted, number of grants made and grant range. Descriptions for other giving programs include the organization's name, address, phone number, contact person, preferred method of contact, application deadline and notes. Also included is a listing of inactive foundations.

672. Crossland, Fred E. "The Push-Pull of Foundation Dollars." *College Board Review* 90 (Winter 1973-74): 2-4.

673. Csapo, Rita Marika, ed. *The Artists Resource Guide to New England: Galleries, Grants, Services.* Boston: Artists Foundation, 1988.

Includes gallery listings for all of New England and basic information on more than sixty foundations and grants supporting artists.

674. "'Cultivating Relationships' Attracts Foundation Support." *Foundation Giving Watch* 9 (July 1984): 2.

675. Cuninggim, Merrimon. "The Foundations: Sources of Educational Variety or Constraint?" *Liberal Education* 59 (May 1973): 166-75.

676. Cuninggim, Merrimon. *Letters to a Foundation Trustee: What We Need to Know about Foundations and Their Management.* Center for Effective Philanthropy Occasional Papers, no. 3. Cambridge, Mass.: Center for Effective Philanthropy, 1986.

Paper written in the format of a series of letters to a friend who is about to join a foundation board. The letters discuss the philosophy behind being a good trustee and issues such as accountability, communications and public relations as well as suggesting literature for background reading.

677. Cuninggim, Merrimon. *Philanthropy and the Individual.* Austin, Tex.: Hogg Foundation for Mental Health, 1987.

Dr. Merrimon Cuninggim addresses the roles and responsibilities of the three types of individuals central to the work of foundations—donors, managers and grant recipients. A thoughtful, stimulating, and sometimes humorous analysis of the importance of individuals to philanthropy, offering both prescriptions and proscriptions for strengthening the philanthropic enterprise.

678. Cuninggim, Merrimon. *Private Money and Public Service: The Role of Foundations in American Society.* New York: McGraw-Hill, 1972.

Cuninggim wrote this book after ten years on the staff of the Danforth Foundation. It largely represents an attempt to repudiate the frequent charges leveled against foundations in preceding years. In this text, Cuninggim answers these questions: What is America's present attitude toward philanthropy? What are the main charges being leveled against those engaged in large-scale benevolence? To what extent are these criticisms supported by the facts, and to what extent are they based on serious misunderstandings? Apart from the particular headline achievements of some of the larger and better known foundations, what is the overall record of accomplishment that foundations of all sorts and sizes have written? Does the present state of government regulation of foundations help or hinder in their performance of philanthropic purposes? What ought foundations themselves do in order to repair their public image? Cuninggim admits a pro-foundation bias but tries to objectively examine the opportunities for self-improvement of which foundations ought to take advantage.

679. Cunningham, Michael, and Michael Seltzer. "Endowments." *NYRAGTimes* (Fall 1988): 3-5, 7-8.

Third and final article in the series, *Grantmaking Strategies, Rx for the Future*, examining what "may represent the earliest signs of revived interest in endowment grants as a way of helping both grantee organizations and new foundations to become financially viable." Although grantmakers favor project-specific and general support grants over endowments (which comprised only 1.4 percent of the over 40,000 reported grants made in 1987), many nonprofits, suffering under the lack of long-term support, would benefit more from the financial security provided by endowments. But grantmakers, beginning with Julius Rosenwald in 1930, are reluctant to award endowment grants to nonprofits. Endowments mean giving more money to fewer organizations, and the managing of the funds tends to create bureaucratic "fat cats." Still, an endowment grant to an organization that has proven its competency will give it "flexibility in terms of planning for the future," allowing it to progress in its groundbreaking efforts, rather than having to scrabble for general support.

680. Damude, Earl F. *The First Ten Years: The Story of the Beginning and Achievements of the Physicians' Services Incorporated Foundation during the First Decade from 1970 to 1980.* Toronto, Canada: Physicians' Services Incorporated Foundation, 1980.

681. Darcy, Kathy, ed. *Wyoming Foundations Directory.* 3rd ed. Cheyenne, Wyoming: Laramie County Community College, 1985.

Based on 990-PF and 990-AR returns filed with the IRS and a survey of the more than seventy foundations listed in the directory. Main section arranged alphabetically by foundation; entries include statement of purpose and contact person when available. Also sections on foundations based out-of-state that award grants to Wyoming and a list of foundations awarding educational loans and scholarships. Index of foundations.

682. de Bettencourt, Francis G. *The Catholic Guide to Foundations.* 2nd ed. Bethedsa, Md.: F.G. Bettencourt, 1973.

683. De Pas, Penney. "Networking in Ohio: The Ohio Association of Grantmakers." *Grantsmanship Center News* 10 (November-December 1982): 48+.

684–705 FOUNDATIONS

684. Defty, Sally Bixby. "Foundation Wealth in St. Louis Not Creatively Utilized." *St. Louis Post Dispatch* (11 March 1975): B-8.

685. Denker, Henry. *The Experiment: A Novel.* New York: Simon & Schuster, 1976.

686. Dennis, Patrick. *How Firm a Foundation.* New York: Pocket Books, 1969.

687. Dermer, Joseph, ed. *Where America's Large Foundations Make Their Grants.* 5th ed. Washington: Public Service Materials Center, 1983.

Brief listings of grants awarded by 651 foundations arranged by state and foundation name, noting grant amount, name and location of the organization receiving the grant. *Additional Insights* section provides further information on 182 of the foundations.

688. Deschin, Jacob. "Want a Photographic Grant?" *35mm Photography* (Winter 1973): 36-9, 112-6.

689. Desruisseaux, Paul. "Better Coordination of Science and Math Programs Sought by Foundations." *Chronicle of Higher Education* 30 (3 July 1985): 14.

690. Desruisseaux, Paul. "Ford Foundation Plans Sixty Percent Increase in Support for Hispanic Programs." *Chronicle of Higher Education* 24 (5 September 1984): 4.

691. Desruisseaux, Paul. "A Foundation Grapples with the Problems of a 'Magnificent Gift'." *Chronicle of Higher Education* 30 (27 March 1985): 15-6.

692. Desruisseaux, Paul. "Foundation Role Seen Threatened by U.S. Aid Cuts." *Chronicle of Higher Education* 31 (4 September 1985): 52.

693. Desruisseaux, Paul. "Foundations Asked to Reaffirm Commitment to the Arts." *Chronicle of Higher Education* 30 (15 May 1985): 20-1.

694. Desruisseaux, Paul. "Foundations Urged to Be More Active on Public Policy Issues." *Chronicle of Higher Education* 30 (8 May 1985): 1+.

695. Desruisseaux, Paul. "New Fund to Make Grants Only to Individual Artists." *Chronicle of Higher Education* 30 (15 May 1985): 21.

696. Desruisseaux, Paul. "Nuclear-War Studies Get $1.4 Million from Carnegie." *Chronicle of Higher Education* 27 (4 January 1984): 3.

697. Desruisseaux, Paul. "Science and Engineering Academies Get Two Large Gifts for California Center." *Chronicle of Higher Education* 31 (13 November 1985): 25.

698. Desruisseaux, Paul. "With Most of Its Assets Missing, Swanson Fund Faces Uncertain Future." *Chronicle of Higher Education* 31 (February 1986): 28.

699. DiMaggio, Paul J. *Support for the Arts from Independent Foundations.* Program on Non-Profit Organizations, no. 105. New Haven, Conn.: Institution for Social and Policy Studies, 1986.

While praising the critical role played by independent foundations in supporting the arts, this report also questions the lack of variation, risk, and innovation in their grantmaking. Most foundation dollars go to established traditional institutions, while few grants are made to support access to and participation in the arts for the poor and working poor, or to provide assistance for innovative artists and arts organizations. In addition, few grants support organizations which promote the values of pluralism and diversity through presentation of genres that, like jazz performance and composition or ethnic dance, are associated with specific racial or nationality groups or, like performance art and video art, have emerged out of the hybridization of classic and commercial culture. The autonomy, flexibility, and diversity of independent foundations is constrained by the aesthetic conservatism of reciprocal networks among local foundation trustees, and by the high cost of reliable information and the strategies employed to contain these costs by many of the larger, national foundations.

700. *Directory of Idaho Foundations.* 4th ed. Caldwell, Idaho: Caldwell Public Library, 1988.

Based on 1986 990-PF returns filed with the IRS and questionnaires answered by 100 foundations. Arranged in four sections: 1) active foundations that accept applications, 2) scholarship-granting foundations, 3) foundations that do not accept applications or appear to be inactiveand, 4) national and corporate giving in Idaho. Entries vary in completeness—include assets, grants paid, range of grants, sample grants and application information.

701. *The Directory of Missouri Foundations.* St. Louis, Mo.: Swift Associates, 1985.

Based on 1983 and 1984 990-PF returns and questionnaires of 788 foundations. Sections on foundations making grants to organizations, foundations giving assistance to individuals, foundations with designated recipients, foundations which contribute scholarship funds to educational institutions, and inactive, operating and terminated foundations. Entries include contact person, assets, total grants amount, low and high grant amounts and funding priorities; alphabetical index of foundations and listing of foundations by city.

702. Doll, Henry C. "Why Foundations Should Support the Projects of Religious Organizations." *Foundation News* 25 (September-October 1984): 71-3.

703. Doll, William. "Cooperation in Cleveland." *Foundation News* 25 (September-October 1984): 66-71.

Describes partnerships between churches and foundations.

704. Doll, William. "Money Isn't Everything." *Foundation News* 24 (May-June 1983): 46-50.

705. Dolnick, Edward. "Money Out of the Blue Aiding Individual Thinkers." *Miami News* (1 August 1983): 5+.

706. Donors Forum of Chicago. *The Directory of Illinois Foundations.* Chicago: Donors Forum of Chicago, 1986.

Alphabetically arranged directory provides information on over 400 Illinois foundations and trusts. The directory is then arranged into four main sections: foundations, analysis section, subject index, and county index. The foundation listing gives: foundation name, telephone number, contact name, donor type, purpose, field of interest, program limitations, geographic limits, contact procedure, information available, funding cycle, application deadlines, paid staff, matching gifts, grants to government funded agencies or programs, total assets, total grants, number of grants, grant range, model grant, officers and directors. The analysis section contains a synthesis of the statistical data collected for the directory. Graphs and charts are included in addition to a break-down of the 400 foundations by type—family, corporate, community, independent, or operating. The volume contains both county and subject indexes. The *County Index* contains a foundation listing and a compilation of total assets and grants made for each county and city. The *Subject Index* contains foundation listings by broad subject categories.

707. Donors Forum of Chicago. *Donors Forum Members Grant List.* Chicago: Donors Forum of Chicago, 1985.

A collection of grants of $500 or more awarded by Donors Forum members to organizations within the Chicago Metropolitan Area. Grantmakers arranged alphabetically under ten subject categories; entries include name of donee, amount of grant and whether the grant is new or a renewal of a previous grant; no address, financial data or officers. Appendix of miscellaneous grants.

708. Donors Forum of Chicago. *Orientation Packet for the Newcomer to Philanthropy.* Chicago: Donors Forum of Chicago, 1981.

709. Dooley, Betty L. *Health Giving of Private Foundations, 1975 and 1980.* Washington: Georgetown University, 1984.

710. Dooley, Betty L. "Health Giving Patterns of Philanthropic Foundations." *Health Affairs* 6 (Summer 1987): 144-56.

Survey of foundation giving in the field of health from 1975 through 1983. (The analysis is based on data from samples of foundations for 1975, 1980, and 1983.) Research for the paper was conducted with support from the Robert Wood Johnson Foundation. The research revealed that although the percentage of foundation contributions was a small part of total health giving, the impact was disproportionately large. From 1980 to 1983, foundations reduced their health care giving from twenty-one to sixteen percent. Although foundations continue to support research, planning, construction, and education, the greatest emphasis was on basic services and innovations in health care delivery. Hospitals, universities, and other health care delivery organizations received over three-fourths of foundation health funds. Approximately one-half of the health grant funds came from foundations in the northeastern United States; thirty-five percent of the grant dollars went to the Northeast. Few foundations give nationally or internationally. The foundations gave one-third of health dollars to specific population groups and one-quarter of the health grants to specific diseases or health disorders.

711. Dooley, Betty L. *Health Giving Patterns of Philanthropic Foundations, 1975, 1980 and 1983.* Washington: Center for Health Policy Studies, 1988.

712. Dooley, Betty L. "How Do Private Foundations Spend Their Money? A Description of Health Giving." *Health Affairs* 2 (Fall 1983): 104-14.

Study provides a brief longitudinal picture of changes in foundation health giving between 1975 and 1980, and a more detailed examination of 1980 health giving. While health giving did not keep pace with overall inflation, specific areas of prime interest among foundations did receive increased funding. Funds for current service activities, which include grants for direct medical care and general operating support, actually declined, but funds for investment activities, which enhance and develop components of the health care system over the long term, increased eighty-three percent. In 1980, private foundations gave $657 million for health, most of which was also allocated for investment rather than for current services. The two most notable giving increases were for research and planning and development funds, with a dollar concentration on hospital construction, biomedical research, and physician education.

713. Dougherty, Nancy C., ed. *A Guide to Kentucky Grantmakers.* Louisville, Ky.: Louisville Foundation, 1982.

Based on questionnaires to 101 foundations, and their 1981 990-PF and 990-AR IRS returns. Arranged alphabetically by foundation; entries include assets, total grants paid, number of grants, smallest/largest grant, primary area of interest and contact person. No indexes.

714. Dressner, Howard R. *The Search for the Public Interest.* Reprint. New York: Ford Foundation, 1969.

715. Drew, Joseph S. "The Foundation Center: A Valuable Information Resource." *Grants Magazine* 6 (December 1983): 249-52.

716. Duca, Diane J. "How Foundations Undergo the Grantmaking Process." *Fund Raising Management* (August 1981): 50-1.

717. Duke Endowment. *Indenture of James B. Duke Establishing the Duke Endowment.* Charlotte, N.C.: Duke Endowment, 1932.

718. Duke Endowment, comp. *North Carolina and South Carolina Foundation Directory.* Charlotte, N.C.: Duke Endowment, 1983.

719. Ebbeling, Donald C. *Courtroom Crucible: The Smith Charities.* Northampton, Mass.: Trustees of the Smith Charities, 1976.

720. Ebert, Robert H. "Learning from Foundation Reports." *Philanthropy Monthly* 17 (December 1984): 22-5.

Provides reflections from retired president of Milbank Memorial Fund.

721. Edie, John A. *Congress and Private Foundations: An Historical Analysis.* Council on Foundations Occasional Paper, no. 4. Washington: Council on Foundations, 1987.

Chronicles the relationship between government and foundations with particular emphasis on efforts made by Congress over the years to regulate the grantmaking sector.

722. Edie, John A. "Council Bill Seeks to Remove Impediments to Foundation Gifts." *Foundation News* 24 (May-June 1983): 68+.

723. Edie, John A. *First Steps in Starting a Foundation.* Washington: Council on Foundations, 1987.

A paper written for the non-lawyer, the grantmaker, and the person seeking advice on establishing a foundation. Edie discusses in detail the numerous types of organizations which are all generally labeled as foundations by the public—independent, company-sponsored, pass-through, pooled common funds, operating, exempt operating, community, and public charity. The options of establishing a public versus a private foundation are examined as well as the basic tax regulations governing each category and type of foundation. Part 6 discusses the advantages and disadvantages of starting your foundation as a trust or nonprofit corporation; state and federal tax-exempt status; and other federal requirements. An annotated bibliography contains materials on foundations, tax-exempt law, IRS documents, a brief list of professional support organizations for nonprofits, and an unannotated selected source of information for fundraisers. The appendix includes samples of articles of incorporation, by-laws, trust agreement, IRS forms 1023, SS-4, 2848, and a list of principles and practices for effective grantmaking.

724. Edie, John A. "Influencing Public Policy: The Legal Limits." *Foundation News* 26 (March-April 1985): 62-4.

725. Edie, John A. "New GAO Study Sees Decline in Foundation Birthrate." *Foundation News* 25 (January-February 1984): 47.

726. Edie, John A. "Ways and Means Committee Votes to Eliminate Impediments to Foundation Gifts, Operations." *Foundation News* 24 (September-October 1983): 46+.

727. Elia, Charles J. "Endowment and Foundation Funds Did Better Than Market As Whole in First Half, Data Show." *Wall Street Journal* (27 August 1981).

728. Elliot, Charles. *Charters of Philanthropies: A Study of the Charters of Twenty-Nine American Philanthropic Foundations.* Privately Printed, 1939.

729. Elnicki, Susan E., ed. *Taft Foundation Reporter.* 20th ed. Washington: Taft Group, 1988.

Directory which covers the largest and most important private foundations. Profiles 506 foundations with combined assets of $61.4 billion, or seventy-five percent of all assets held by private foundations. Profiles contain foundation contact, fiscal summary, contributions summary, donor information, foundation philosophy, contributions analysis, typical recipients list, officers and directors (includes alma mater and affiliations information), application and review procedures, grants analysis, and recent grants list. Indexes are arranged by state, grant type, recipient type, individuals by name, by place of birth, and by alma mater.

730. Ely, David. *Poor Devils.* Boston: Houghton Mifflin, 1970.

731. Embree, Edwin R. "The Business of Giving Away Money." *Harper's Magazine* (August 1930): 320-29.

732. Embree, Edwin R., and Julia Waxman. *Investment in People: The Story of the Julius Rosenwald Fund.* New York: Harper & Bros., 1949.

733. Environmental Grantmakers Association. *The Environmental Grantmakers Association Directory.* Philadelphia: Environmental Grantmakers Association, 1989.

Outlines the environmental programs of participants of the Environmental Grantmakers Association. The directory contains profiles for sixty-eight foundations with environmental programs and interests. The entries show the primary contact for environmental grantmaking; other environmental staff; most appropriate way to approach the foundation; 1987 financial information; areas of environmental interest; grant limitations; and other program interests or thrusts. Includes an index to assist users in locating foundations by topical interests (i.e., regulatory and quality control; public policy and education; preservation and protection) and by geographic focus.

734. Esposito, Virginia. "Serving Better by Cooperating More." *Foundation News* 24 (July-August 1983): 31+.

735. "Establishing a Private Foundation." *CPA Journal* 65 (April 1984): 57-8.

736. Evans, Eli N. "Creativity As the Cornerstones of Philanthropy." *Foundation News* 24 (May-June 1983): 64+.

737. Fabian, Larry L. *Beginnings. Andrew Carnegie's Peace Endowment: The Tycoon, the President, and Their Bargain of 1910.* Washington: Carnegie Endowment for International Peace, 1985.

738. Fanning, Carol. *Guide to California Foundations.* 7th ed. San Francisco: Northern California Grantmakers, 1988.

This directory lists more than 800 foundations located in California which award grants totaling $40,000 or more annually. Based primarily on 990-PF returns filed with the IRS or records in the California Attorney General's Office; some additional data supplied by foundations completing questionnaires. Main section arranged alphabetically by foundation; entries include statement of purpose, sample grants and officers. Also section on applying for grants. Indexes of all foundations by name, subject and county location.

739. Farr, Sally, and Laurence C. Murray. "Analyzing the Applicant's Financial Statements: A Grantor's Introduction." *Philanthropist/Le Philanthrope* 4 (Winter 1987): 9-31.

Article developed from a presentation to the Canadian Centre for Philanthropy's Fourth Conference for Foundations on June 17, 1986, in Toronto. An introduction to the analysis of applicant's financial statements for those who seek monies from a grantor in connection with an activity or project. A basic outline of general information and ideas. Includes topics such as financial statements, statement of revenue of expenses analysis, balance sheet analysis, fund accounting, and auditor's report.

740. Farrell, Charles S. "Black Colleges and Foundations Try 'Hand-Holding'." *Chronicle of Higher Education* 27 (18 January 1984): 3.

741. Feiden, Karyn. *A Funder's Guide to AIDS Grantmaking: Action Strategies.* Washington: Council on Foundations, [1988].

Pamphlet brings together current statistics and information concerning the AIDS epidemic and the responses of the federal government, state legislatures, and organized philanthropy. Urges creative efforts and financial commitment in order to confront the intensifying crisis. Briefly describes the demographics of the disease and its social and economic consequences, lists helpful tips for grantmakers to highlight the keys to effective involvement, and focuses on specific grantmaking opportunities in the areas of planning and advocacy, education, supportive services, health care delivery, and research. Includes a directory of AIDS-related informational resources.

742. Ferguson, Mary E. *China Medical Board and Peking Union Medical College: A Chronicle of Fruitful Collaboration, 1914-1951.* New York: China Medical Board of New York, 1970.

743. Field Foundation. *Facts and Trends 1987: A Resource Guide to Conditions in the USA.* New York: Field Foundation, 1988.

Prepared for the annual conference of the National Network of Grantmakers to help develop funding strategies for the future, the facts and trends presented here cover a series of conditions in the United States: demographics; education; employment; wealth, income and poverty; health; federal spending and taxes; environment; and energy.

744. Field Foundation. *A Statement from the Field Foundation.* New York: Field Foundation, 1981.

745. Filer, John H. *Strengthening the Voluntary Sector.* Unpublished, 1975.

746. Fisch, Edith L. *The Cy Pres Doctrine in the United States.* New York: Matthew Bender & Co., 1950.

747. Fischer, Jeri L., ed. *The Michigan Foundation Directory.* 6th ed. Grand Haven, Mich.: Council of Michigan Foundations, 1988.

Identifies over 543 potential grantmaking sources in Michigan; this includes 475 foundations and sixty-eight corporate giving programs. Divided into five separate parts: 1) largest foundations with assets of $200,000 or grantmaking of $25,000; 2) special purpose foundations (those with a single purpose); 3) foundations with assets less than $200,000 or grantmaking less than $25,000; 4) a listing of foundations by city and; 5) a listing of terminated foundations. Information about the largest foundations, special purpose foundations, and corporate foundations/giving programs in Section 2 includes address, phone number, contact person, donors, purpose and activities, geographic priorities, assets, expenditures, grant amounts, grant ranges, officers and trustees. Also presented is a comparison of the total number of grants and grant amounts made against those made in Michigan. Section 3 contains an in-depth analysis of grantmaking in Michigan. Section 4 provides information on how to research a foundation and compose grant proposals. The directory has indexes by subject, trustees, and foundation name.

748. Fisher, Donald. "The Role of Philanthropic Foundations in the Reproduction and Production of Hegemony: Rockefeller Foundation and the Social Sciences." *Sociology* 17 (1983): 206-33.

In this analysis of the relationship between Rockefeller philanthropy and the development of the social sciences, 1910-1940, Fisher proposes that philanthropic foundations attempt to maintain the social order rather than alter it. He feels that, in the period studied, they were key institutions in the production and reproduction of cultural hegemony. He further proposes that a "critical-conflict" perspective has most value when one is attempting to understand the nature and sources of change in the systematic production of both knowledge and intellectuals, and he brings this approach to his study of the process by which Rockefeller policy on the social sciences emerged. He locates the ideological viewpoint of Rockefeller philanthropy, as identified in this process, in the wider political economy. Fisher asserts that hegemony, ideology, and social class are essential concepts when one is attempting to understand and explain the role of philanthropy in a capitalist society.

749. Fishman, Leo. "Avoiding Private Foundation Status." *Grantsmanship Center News* 2 (May-June 1983): 76-8.

750. Fleischmann Foundation, Max C. *Twenty-Eight Years: A Narrative Report of the Foundation's Activities, 1952-1980.* Reno, Nev.: Max C. Fleischmann Foundation, 1980.

751. Flexner, Abraham. *Funds and Foundations: Their Policies, Past and Present.* New York: Harper & Bros., 1952.

In this little book, Flexner, associated with foundations for over thirty years, describes some of the major foundations and what they have done. The institutions he writes about are the Freedmen's Bureau (as an example of a failure), the Peabody Fund, the General Education Board, the Rockefeller Foundation, the Carnegie Foundation for the Advancement of Teaching, and the Carnegie Corporation of New York. His concluding chapter praises the combined contributions of the foundations to higher education, but also calls attention to "the crying inadequacy of funds devoted to humanistic studies." He worries that the growing American infatuation with science, business, and engineering in the universities is causing the humanities—to which the foundations pay only lip service—to be left far behind, to our common detriment.

752. Foote, Joseph. "For RAGs' It's Riches." *Foundation News* 27 (July-August 1986): 22-7.

Discusses the reasons for the growth of regional grantmaker associations and their role as a regional distributor of grantmaking information. Contains list of regional associations of grantmakers in the U.S.

753. Foote, Joseph. "Service Unlimited." *Foundation News* 26 (July-August 1985): 10+.

754. Foote, Joseph, and Lilibet Ziller. "So Why Not Start a Foundation?" *Foundation News* 25 (May-June 1984): 50-8.

755. Foote, Joseph. "Stretching the Career Ladder." *Foundation News* 26 (January-February 1985): 24-8.
Offers advice on preparing foundation staff for life after grantmaking.

756. Foote, Joseph. "You Name It, They Do It." *Foundation News* 26 (September-October 1985): 14+.

757. Ford Foundation. *Ford Foundation Support for the Arts in the United States: A Discussion of New Emphasis in the Foundation's Arts Programs.* New York: Ford Foundation, 1986.

758. Ford Foundation. "New Fund for the Arts." *Ford Foundation Letter* 14 (October 1983): 1+.

759. Ford Foundation. "PRI's: An Anniversary." *Ford Foundation Letter* 14 (December 1983): 5-6.

760. Ford Foundation. *Program-Related Investments.* New York: Ford Foundation, 1974.

761. Ford Foundation. *Report of the Study of the Ford Foundation on Policy and Program.* New York: Ford Foundation, 1949.

762. Ford Foundation. *A Selected Chronology of the Ford Foundation.* New York: Ford Foundation, [1980].

763. "Ford Foundation Weighs New Venture in Puerto Rico." *Fund Raising Review* (July 1984): 2.

764. Forster, Arnold, and Benjamin R. Epstein. *Danger on the Right.* New York: Random House, 1964.

765. Fosdick, Raymond Blaine. *Adventure in Giving: The Story of the General Education Board.* New York: Harper & Row, 1962.

766. Fosdick, Raymond Blaine. *A Philosophy for a Foundation.* New York: Rockefeller Foundation, 1963.

767. Fosdick, Raymond Blaine. *The Story of the Rockefeller Foundation.* New York: Harper, 1952.

768. Foster Foundation, James. *Michigan Foundations Conference.* Unpublished, 1954.

769. Foundation Center. *The Foundation Directory.* 1960-1989. New York: Russell Sage Foundation, 19—.

The Foundation Directory is the standard reference work for information about private and community grantmaking foundations in the United States. Used by grantseekers, foundation and government officials, scholars, journalists, and others generally interested in foundation giving in this country, the *Directory* provides information on the finances, governance, and giving interests of the nation's largest grantmaking foundations—those with assets of $1 million or more which have annual giving of at least $100,000. The information in the entries is based on reports received from 5,148 foundations and the most current public records available. These foundations represent over twenty percent of all grantmaking foundations, and together they held $89.9 billion (approximately ninety-seven percent) of all private foundation assets and awarded $5.3 billion (nearly ninety-two percent) of total foundation giving in 1985. Five indexes to descriptive entries are provided to assist grantmakers and other users of this volume: *Index to Donors, Officers, Trustees*; *Geograhic Index*; *Types of Support Index*; *Subject Index*; and *Foundation Name Index*. The directory is published biennially, and is updated in alternate years by *The Foundation Directory Supplement*.

770. Foundation Center. *Foundations Indicating Program-Related Investments As One of Their Types of Support.* Unpublished, [1980].

771. Foundation Center, comp. *List of Organizations Filing As Private Foundations.* New York: Foundation Center, 1973.

772. Foundation Center. *National Data Book of Foundations.* 1972-1989. New York: Foundation Center, 19—.

The *National Data Book of Foundations* is the most comprehensive listing of currently active grantmaking foundations in the United States. Contains entries for over 29,000 grantmaking foundations that awarded grants of one dollar or more during the latest fiscal reporting period. Each entry features foundation name and address; name of principal officer or contact person; foundation assets at market value at year end; total grants paid during the year; total gifts received by the foundation; and IRS number to aid in locating tax returns. A unique coding system guides readers to foundations by type (independent, community or corporate), indicates which foundations publish annual reports, and lists Foundation Center publications containing more in-depth data on the foundation. Provides statistics on national funding for corporate foundations and the largest foundations which award over $250 million annually. In addition to an alphabetical index, includes an index to community foundations to aid grantseekers in funding local projects.

773. Foundation Center. *Source Book Profiles.* 1975-1989. New York: Foundation Center, 19—.

Source Book Profiles offers the most comprehensive and up-to-date analysis available of the 1,000 largest foundations in the United States. Provides grantseekers with the data necessary to identify, research, and contact appropriate funding sources among these top 1,000 foundations. These foundations account for approximately sixty percent of all foundation grant dollars awarded in a given year. However, they represent less than five percent of the total number of active grantmaking foundations in the U.S. and because they are among the most visible of all foundations, competition for their grants is especially keen. *Source Book Profiles* operates on a two-year publishing cycle. One-half of the 1,000 largest foundations (based on total giving) are analyzed during a single subscription year; these profiles are then completely revised and updated every two years. Profiles are compiled using a variety of sources: direct information from the foundations, published foundation reports, news releases, newspaper and periodical articles, and the 990 PF information return filed annually by each private foundation with the IRS. Includes four indexes that provide access to all foundation profiles published in the previous two years as well as foundations included in the present volume: *Index of Foundations*; *Index of Subjects*; *Index of Types of Support*; and *Geographic Index*.

774. Foundation Center, comp. *Ten Largest Foundations Ranked by Grants and Assets: New York City, Boston, Chicago, Cleveland, and San Francisco.* Unpublished, 1984.

775. "Foundation Center of Gravity Shifting to West?" *Foundation Giving Watch* 3 (August 1983): 1-2.

776. "Foundation Denounces U.S. Education Policy." *New York Times* (3 June 1985): B-10.

777. *Foundation 500: An Index to Foundation Giving Patterns.* New York: Foundation Research Service, 1975.

Guide to giving programs and geographical distribution of 500 U.S. foundations.

778. *Foundation Grants in Hawaii, 1970-1980.* Honolulu, Hawaii: University of Hawaii at Manoa Libraries, 1981.

779. "Foundation Work: The Who's and Hows." *Foundation News* 25 (November-December 1984): 50+.

Excerpts from a study on *Career Patterns of Women and Men in Foundations.*

780. "Foundations and Higher Education." *Foundation Giving Watch* 3 (January 1984): 1-2.

781. *Foundations and Public Information: A Selection of Articles Reflecting Improved Public Information Performance by Foundations.* Washington: Council on Foundations, 1974.

782. "Foundations and Voter Registration." *Funding Citizen Participation* (Fall 1987): 4-7.

Foundations are free to fund voter registration activities so long as they observe the fundamental rule of nonpartisanship. Article examines the Internal Revenue Code as it relates to grants by private foundations required by the grantor to be used for voter registration work, general purpose grants by private foundations to public charities engaged in voter registration work, and support of nonpartisan voter registration by charities that are not private foundations, such as community foundations.

783. "Foundations Face Growing Worry: Giving Away Money Fast Enough." *Wall Street Journal* (6 September 1986): 35.

According to this article in the *Wall Street Journal,* the stock market has been good to the top philanthropic foundations. "So good, in fact, that foundation staffers have been working overtime to help spend the windfall" because of tax law requirements that at least five percent of their assets be given away each year.

784. "Foundations Hear Invitation to Rejoin U.S. Policy Arena." *New York Times* (28 April 1985): 32.

785. "Foundations: How to Approach and Successfully Solicit Them." *Philanthropic Trends Digest* 5 (1 March 1988): 1+.

Stressing that research makes the difference when applying for grants from foundations, article recommends *Foundation Grants to Individuals* as a source of information for individuals seeking financial support, and two publications of great use to nonprofits seeking funding: *Foundation 500* and *The Foundation Directory.* Also recommends calling foundations to verify application procedures and requesting copies of recent annual reports, which will aid in determining the best approach to take in meeting the giving needs of a foundation. Finally, the article contends that a well-informed presentation given at the foundation will greatly increase the odds of receiving a grant over merely using written communication.

786. "Foundations Re-Examine Program-Related Investments." *Foundation Giving Watch* 3 (August 1983): 1-2.

787. *Foundations Serving the Hudson Valley.* Poughkeepsie, N.Y.: Adriance Memorial Library, 1980.

788. *Foundations Support for Puerto Ricans.* Washington: Office of the Commonwealth of Puerto Rico, 1974.

789. "Foundations: What Are They? What Do They Do and Why?" *Philanthropic Trends Digest* 5 (1 February 1988): 3-4.

Briefly describes the four different types of foundations: independent, company-sponsored, operating, and community; the reasons for establishing a foundation; the ways in which they grant their money (using the Lily Endowment in Indianapolis as an example); and the pros and cons of government regulation of foundations.

790. "The Fourteen-Year Itch." *Grantsmanship Center News* 11 (July-August 1983): 11-2.

791. Fox, Jeanne J. "Foundations Increase Giving for Voter Issues." *Foundation Giving Watch* 5 (June 1985): 4.

792. Frazer, David R. "Investing Your Foundation's Assets." *Foundation News* 26 (January-February 1985): 46-9.

793. Frazer, David R. "Of Lasting Duration." *Foundation News* 29 (January-February 1988): 24-9.

Frazer, a lawyer specializing in estate planning, exempt organization and tax litigation, explains the benefits of establishing a private foundation. If created during one's lifetime, it can provide tax, family and community benefits, while enabling the donor to set the agenda for giving and to enjoy the satisfaction of active participation in the charities. In addition, a foundation continually renews itself, which means the chosen charities will receive much more over time than they would from a single gift. Frazer also discusses alternatives to the establishment of a private foundation which provide tax and community benefits, such as community, private operating, and pass-through foundations; supporting organizations (similar to a private foundation, but operating under the auspices of a particular charity); split interest trusts; and donations of property. Briefly covers initial steps to take when creating a private foundation, estimating the cost of the process to be between $2,500 and $5,000.

794. Freeberg, Ellen M., and Ellen S. Miller. *The Role of Politicians in Public Charities.* Washington: Center for Responsive Politics, 1987.

795. Freeman, David F. *The Handbook on Private Foundations.* Washington: Seven Locks Press, 1981.

Although designed primarily for foundation officials and those interested in forming a foundation, this handbook provides useful insights into the rules and regulations affecting foundations, grantmaking policies and practices, and other aspects of foundation operations.

796. French, William J., and Geddes Smith. *The Commonwealth Activities in Austria, 1923-1929.* New York: Commonwealth Fund, 1929.

797. Friedman, John S. "Public TV's CIA Show." *Nation* (9-16 July 1980): 73-6.

798. Friedman, Martin. "Foundations: Learning to Give." *Cultural Affairs* (Summer 1970): 32-6.

799. "Funds for Peace Are on the Rise." *Foundation Giving Watch* 5 (September 1985): 2.

800. Gantenbein, Douglas. "Giving It Away." *Corner Stone* (October 1983): 2-8.

801. Gardner, Frederic P. "Analyzing Foundations' Leadership and Decision-Making." *Fund Raising Management* 15 (June 1984): 70+.

802. Gardner, John W., and Merrimon Cuninggim. *Report of the Committee on the Foundation Field.* Unpublished, 1970.

803. Garonzik, Elan, ed. *Public/Private Cooperation: Funding for Small and Emerging Arts Programs.* New York: Foundation Center, 1983.

804. Gee, Thomas H. *Public Interest Law in the Bay Area.* San Francisco: San Francisco Foundation, 1978.

805. General Education Board. *Directory of Fellowship Awards for the Years 1922-1950.* New York: General Education Board, 1951.

806. Gerber, Albert B. *Bashful Billionaire.* New York: Dell Publishing Co., 1967.

807. Getz, Barbara J. "The Kresge Foundation and Capital Grants." *Grants Magazine* 6 (March 1983): 4-5.

808. Gilman, Daniel C. "Five Great Gifts." *Outlook* (August 1907): 648-57.

809. Ginzberg, Eli. "Foundations and the Nation's Health Agenda." *Health Affairs* 6 (Winter 1987): 128-40.

Ginzberg, an economist and director of the Conservation of Human Resources program at Columbia University in New York, presents an overview and critical analysis of the relationship between foundations and the U.S. health care system from the beginning of the century to the present. He acknowledges the early leadership role of foundations when their program efforts were future oriented: transforming medical education and expanding basic and clinical research to improve the education and practice of physicians. But he is critical of foundation impact on health care expansion between 1945 and 1972, claiming that they "took relatively little initiative to study and evaluate any of the high-priority issues of the time in the interest of informing public policy." He reviews health program funding for 1986, finding that most are oriented more to the present than to the future. Noting that foundation funds amount to only 0.2 percent of all funds flowing into the health care system, he recommends that foundations exercise caution in their efforts to improve the delivery of health care, and favors instead partial reallocation of funds to the planning and policy arenas, where the focus would be on assessing the strengths and weaknesses of the existing system. He also identifies operational and strategic policy issues that could benefit from foundation consideration and support, and advocates a joint effort by foundations to make a long-term commitment to a limited number of important policy issues, thereby maximizing their impact and advancing the nation's health agenda.

810. Ginzberg, Eli. "Foundations' Role in Health Policy." *Health Affairs* 7 (Summer 1988): 209-15.

Thomas Moloney, senior vice-president of the Commonwealth Fund, Leighton Cluff, president of the Robert Wood Johnson Foundation, and Rebecca Rimel, executive director of the Pew Charitable Trusts, respond to Eli Ginzberg's article concerning the role of foundations in relation to the nation's health agenda.

811. "Giving in America." *Preservation News* (March 1974): 4.

812. Glenn, John M. "Foundations in the Twentieth Century." *Councillor* 3 (September 1938): 1-7.

813. Glenn, John M., Lilian Brandt, and Frank Emerson Andrews. *Russell Sage Foundation, 1907-1946.* 2 vols. New York: Russell Sage Foundation, 1947.

814. Goheen, Robert F. "The Future of Foundations: The Jeffersonian Potential." *Future of Philanthropic Foundations* (1975): 195-213.

815. Gold, Steven D., and Karl T. Kurtz. "The State Solution." *Foundation News* 24 (September-October 1983): 42-4.

816. Goodenough, Simon. *The Greatest Good Fortune.* Midlothian, Edinburgh, Scotland: Macdonald Printers, 1985.

817. Goodman, Wolfe D., and Howard Carr. *Establishing a Private Foundation.* Toronto, Ontario, Canada: Canadian Centre for Philanthropy, 1987.

Comprehensive layman's guide to setting up a private foundation in Canada, examining establishment, operation, and tax treatment.

818. Gorman, James. "Adding the Human Dimension." *Foundation News* 28 (May-June 1987): 32-7.

Hands-on paper which discusses the benefits of an on-site visit by foundations as part of the pre-grant evaluation process. The visit should be a people-gauging and fact-finding mission. A grant proposal, like a resume, is not always the most accurate picture of the applicant. The essay states that grantmaking without site visits can become a competition between skilled proposal writers. The smaller nonprofits and grassroots organizations are at a disadvantage if they are rejected only because of a less than perfect proposal. Gorman suggests that prior to the visit the foundation do its homework. Re-read the group's grant proposal; be sure you have the group's IRS determination letter as well as a general background on the organization and its history, a copy of its budget, a project outline, and profiles of staff and directors. The visit can be summed up as a chance to observe, learn and question. The paper concludes with suggestions on what to look for during the on-site visit including a sense of the administration, the staff and how it functions; what leadership qualities are evident or lacking; what is the Board's commitment; are there limitations or deficiencies of the premises or facilities; how is the program itself, its goals and objectives; and what are the long-range (three to five years) plans. Check financial considerations such the current operating budget and such items as expenses, income, and cash-flow problems.

819. Gorman, James. "A Congressional Call for More Accountability." *Foundation News* 24 (May-June 1983): 25+.

820. Gorman, James. "Traversing the Spectrum." *Foundation News* 24 (July-August 1983): 22-4.

821. Gorman, James. "Two Shots in the Arm." *Foundation News* 27 (July-August 1986): 50-2.

Article outlines two long-term programs established by the Council on Foundations and the Ford Foundation to strengthen the management, grantmaking and endowments of community foundations.

822. Goulden, Joseph C. *The Money Givers: An Examination of the Myths and Realities of Foundation Philanthropy in America.* New York: Random House, 1971.

Goulden takes a critical look at American foundation philanthropy by asking if the undeniable accomplishments that have been perpetuated by foundation dollars in the twentieth century are enough of a justification for the tax benefits to donors or the creation of a corps of professional philanthropoids with virtually unlimited power to determine where their money is spent. He asks, "What are the proper functions of foundations? How much freedom of action should they enjoy?" He explores why foundations are created, how they spend their money, who runs them and how, and other issues. Goulden's journalistic and skeptical approach differs from much of the literature on foundations and displays a side of foundation philanthropy that deserves as much consideration as any.

823. Gow, J. Steele. *Notes on the Policies and Practices of Foundations.* Reprint. Pittsburgh: Maurice and Laura Falk Foundation.

824. Graham, David V. "Stock Market Helps Mott Foundation Set Assets Record." *Flint Journal (Flint, MI)* (31 July 1983): A-11+.

825. Gramm, Hanns. *The Oberleander Trust, 1931-1953.* Philadelphia: Carl Schurz Memorial Foundation, 1956.

826. Grantmakers in Health. *Trends in Health Philanthropy: A Survey of Private or Independent Foundations, Corporations, and Community Foundations Engaged in Health Grantmaking.* New York: Grantmakers in Health, 1983.

827. Grants Resources Library. *Virginia Foundations.* Hampton, Va.: Grants Resources Library, 1981.

Based on 1980 990-PF returns and information provided by foundations. Main sections arranged alphabetically by foundation; entries include total net worth, largest and smallest grants, total amount granted and purpose of the foundation. No index.

828. *Grants to Higher Education Related to Minorities, 1986-87.* Unpublished, 1988.

829. Greenberg, Bernard H. "The Modern Philanthropic Foundation: A Critique and a Proposal." *Yale Law Journal* (February 1950): 477-509.

830. Greene, Wade. "A Farewell to Alms." *New York Times* (23 May 1976): 36-46.

831. Grossman, David A. *Patterns of Foundation Giving in the Criminal Justice Field.* New York: Nova Institute, 1982.

832. Guzzardi, Walter, Jr. *The Henry Luce Foundation: A History, 1936-1986.* Chapel Hill, N.C.: University of North Carolina Press, 1988.

An historical account of the establishment and prosperity of the Henry Luce Foundation commissioned by Henry Luce III and written by Walter Guzzardi Jr. Among other things, Guzzardi was once an assistant to Henry R. Luce, a foreign correspondent for *Time* and a writer and editor for *Fortune.* As an insider, the author recounts not only background information about the founder and the formation of the foundation but a detailed account of the programs within the foundation, what they supported and who they supported as well as an assessment of the impact of the grants. The Luce Foundation interests lay in education (Luce professors), in East Asia, in art (an encouragement to museum scholarship), in theology (improvement of faculties in theological seminaries and divinity schools), and in public affairs (especially leadership among minority groups). Of interest are the appendixes which detail and list such things as short biographies of past and present boards of directors, graphs of grant distribution, twenty largest grants made by the foundation from 1936 to 1986, the Henry R. Luce Professorships with date of original grant, the advisory committees for foundation programs, books supported by the Luce Fund for Asian Studies, and museum publications supported by the Luce Fund for Scholarship in American Art.

833. Haislip, Bryan. *A History of the Z. Smith Reynolds Foundation.* Winston-Salem, N.C.: J.F. Blair, 1967.

834. Hall, Peter Dobkin. *The Community Foundation and the Foundations of Community: The H.C. Trexler Estate of Allentown, Pennsylvania—a Preliminary Report.* Program on Non-Profit Organizations, no. 34. New Haven, Conn.: Institution for Social and Policy Studies, 1980.

835. Hallahan, Kathleen M. "The Great Numbers Debate: And Why It's Important." *Foundation News* 24 (July-August 1983): 21.

836. Hallahan, Kathleen M. "Twenty-Five Years' Worth." *Foundation News* 25 (November-December 1984): 22-5.

837. Hans, Patricia, and Wayne Cook. "A Proper Upbringing." *Foundation News* 29 (May-June 1988): 52-4.

Stresses the need for good follow-up by trustees after dispensing funds. Suggestions include writing clearly-defined grant resolutions, making installment grants, enforcing the reporting schedule, and visiting local grantee organizations.

838. Harrington-Kostur, Jill Frances. *A Comparison of Joint Efforts by Philanthropic Foundations in Three States.* Eugene, Oreg.: University of Oregon, 1982.

839. Harrison, Shelby Millard, and Frank Emerson Andrews. *American Foundations for Social Welfare.* New York: Russell Sage Foundation, 1946.

840. Hart, Elosie B., ed. *The Directory of Kansas Foundations.* Topeka, Kans.: Topeka Public Library, 1986.

More than 300 foundations and trusts are featured in this new edition. Information was gathered from public records, Kansas Attorney General files and questionnaire responses. Each profile notes the grantmaker's name; address; phone number; financial data (assets, total annual gifts, high/low gift, number of gifts, date of data, and board members); funding priority areas, including types of support and sample grants; limitations; application information; and additional information. Contains a bibliography of various materials designed to aid the grantseeker; the front matter of the directory discusses composing a proposal. Indexes are arranged alphabetically by foundation name, city and subject of giving area.

841. Harvey, A. McGehee, and Susan Abrams. *For the Welfare of Mankind: The Commonwealth Fund and American Medicine.* Baltimore, Md.: Johns Hopkins University Press, 1986.

Chronicles the history of the Commonwealth Fund from its founding in 1918 to the present, and examines how the role of one foundation has affected medical and social history in America. The authors, associated with the Johns Hopkins University School of Medicine, focus on the foundation's organizational structure, its relationships with grantees, and the performances of staff members and directors. Their research is based on published and internal reports, materials from the Fund's archives, interviews with present and former Fund personnel and grant recipients. Appendixes include lists of grants made from 1919 to 1984 and fellowship recipients from the fields of medicine, psychiatry, creative scholarship and medical schools.

842. Hayden Foundation, Charles. *The Story of the Charles Hayden Foundation.* New York: Charles Hayden Foundation, [1952].

843. Heald, Henry T. *In Common Cause: Relations between Higher Education and Foundations.* New York: Ford Foundation, 1963.

844. Healey, Judith K. "Listening and Learning: Developing Foundation Programs." *Philanthropy Monthly* 16 (June 1983): 34-6.

845. Healey, Judith K. "Not Yet a Profession." *Foundation News* 28 (July-August 1987): 26-9.

A critical examination by Judith K. Healey, president of the Minnesota Foundation, of the grantmaking "profession" and its need for standards or a code of ethics. In an attempt to stimulate dialogue within the philanthropic sector, Healey argues that grantmaking is not yet truly a profession. Those in the field have (with the exception of the Council on Foundations members) no code of conduct to profess. The author discusses the most commonly expressed roadblocks to the formulation of a code including the fear of government intervention and regulation, certification, the loss of autonomy, and the lack of a consensus on a code. Healey believes that the most effective means to ensuring autonomy is to begin a dialogue within the sector and to establish an individual code of conduct built upon basic honesty and candor, respect and modesty in the grantmakers' dealings with the nonprofit applicants.

846. Hector, Layton Dean. *The Private Charitable Foundation: Its Role in Federal Income Tax Planning.* Unpublished, 1958.

847. Heimann, Fritz, ed. *The Future of Foundations.* Englewood Cliffs, N.J.: Prentice-Hall, 1973.

Nine articles by foundation officials, tax specialists, and scholars examine the status and future roles for American foundations in light of the 1969 Tax Reform Act.

848. Herfurth, Sharon, and Karen Fagg, eds. *Directory of Dallas County Foundations.* Dallas, Tex.: Dallas Public Library, 1984.

Based on 1982 and 1983 990-PF returns and information provided by the Funding Information Library and the Foundation Center on 268 foundations. Main section arranged alphabetically by foundation; entries include contact person, interests, total assets, total amount and number of grants, and officers. Appendix of Dallas foundations ranked by assets; index of foundations by giving interests and index of trustees and officers.

849. Hill, Sidney B. "Charities, Charitable Trusts and Foundations." *Record of the Association of the Bar of the City of New York* 10 (February 1955): 83-8.

850. Hirschfield, Ira S. "Corporate-Community Foundations: The Tie That's Binding." *Foundation News* 25 (November-December 1984): 55-60.

Describes collaborations between corporate and community foundations.

851. Hobhouse, Arthur. *The Dead Hand: Addresses on the Subject of Endowments and Settlements of Property.* London: Chatto and Windus, 1880.

852. Hohri, Sasha, and Adisa Douglas. *Women of Color: Building Bridges between Resources and Needs.* Washington: National Network of Grantmakers, 1986.

Publication captures the words and concerns of ten women grassroots organizers at a 1985 conference sponsored by the National Network of Grantmakers. Lillie Allen, a staff member of the National Black Women's Health Project; Willie Fae Daniels, a founder of the Concerned Citizens for Calvary Arms in Dallas, Texas; Julie Hatta, administrator of the Asian Law Alliance; Wilma Mankiller, Chief of the Cherokee Nation in Oklahoma; Cecilia Rodriquez, director of La Mujer Obrera/The Woman Worker; Rose Sanders, a founder of Mothers of Many; Young Hai Shin, director of the Asian Immigrant Women Advocates; Nancy Shippentower, member of the Northwest Indian Women's Circle; Esther Vicente, staff attorney for the Instituto de Derechos Civiles; and Sima Wali, director of the Refugee Women in Development project speak about their organizing efforts, the barriers of racism and sexism, the necessary approach for good technical assistance, and leadership development. Articulate and insightful representations of programs committed to social and economic justice.

853. Hollis, Ernest Victor. "Evolution of the Philanthropic Foundation." *Educational Record* 20 (October 1939): 575.

854. Holm, Daniel H. *Iowa Directory of Foundations.* Dubuque, Iowa: Trumpet Associates, 1984.

Based primarily on returns filed with the IRS and information supplied by 247 foundations; date of information is 1982 in most cases, no date is given in other entries. Main section arranged alphabetically by foundation; most entries include address, telephone number, Employer Identification Number, total assets, total grants, purpose and activities, officers and trustees, and contact person. Appendix of cancelled foundations. Index by city.

855. Honsa, Vlasta, comp. *Nevada Foundation Directory.* Las Vegas, Nev.: Clark County Library District, 1984.

Based on 1982 and 1983 990-PF forms filed with the IRS and interviews with forty-one foundations. Main section arranged alphabetically by foundation; entries include contact person, financial data, funding interests and sample grants. Section on inactive and defunct Nevada foundations. Section on thirty national foundations that fund Nevada projects. Index of fields of interest and index by foundation location.

856. Hopkins, Bruce R. "A Different Way to Start a Nonprofit." *Nonprofit World* 6 (July-August 1988): 32-3.

Examines the National Foundation, an organization which bypasses the process of communicating with the IRS, accords automatic public charity status, facilitates contributions that are deductible to the greatest extent, avoids state and local tax considerations, and obviates the necessity of filing annual information returns for those founding a new charity. In a recent U.S. Claims Court decision, the Foundation was granted 501(c)(3) status despite objections from the IRS which characterized the Foundation as a commercial enterprise and expressed concern about its use of commission-based fundraisers.

857. Hopkins, Bruce R., Jerome P. Walsh Skelly, and Edward J. Beckwith. *A Guide to the Making of Grants to Individuals by Private Foundations.* Resources for Grantmakers. Washington: Council on Foundations, 1987.

Provides a summary of the federal tax law governing the granting of scholarships and similar payments to individuals by private foundations, in addition to practical guidance for the establishment and maintenance of a private foundation individual grant program that will "avoid the difficulties (and taxes) lurking in the compliance requirements." Includes a sample statement of procedures for awarding grants to individuals.

858. Hopwood, Susan H., ed. *Foundations in Wisconsin: A Directory.* Milwaukee, Wis.: Marquette University Memorial Library, 1988.

Contains information on 713 active grantmaking foundations. Entries include name of foundation, address, officers and directors, assets, grants paid, range, purpose, sample grants, and interests. (Lists the fifty largest foundations by grantmaking amount.) Also listed are over 250 unprofiled grantmakers which are rated as inactive, operating, restricted, or terminated foundations. Directory includes an area of interest index, Wisconsin county index of foundations, and an officer index.

859. Horr, A.R. *Embarrassing Dollars and Hints to Their Holders.* New York: Harper & Bros., 1935.

860. "How Big Foundations Spend Their Millions." *U.S. News and World Report* (19 September 1983).

861. "How Close Is Too Close?" *Foundation News* 25 (May-June 1984): 65.

862. Howard, Nathaniel R. *Trust for All Time: The Story of the Cleveland Foundation and the Community Trust Movement.* Cleveland: Cleveland Trust Co., 1963.

863. Howe, Barbara. *The Emergence of the Philanthropic Foundation As an American Social Institution, 1900-1920.* Unpublished, 1976.

864. Hull, Robert H. "The Rules and Reasons for Creating Private Foundations." *Trusts & Estates* 127 (July 1988): 10, 12, 16, 20, 22.

Informative article contends that the benefits of private foundations to donors and society outweigh the complexity of regulations surrounding them. Covers federal regulations governing the operation of private foundations and the deductibility of gifts, and discusses the actual process for establishing a private foundation.

865. Hull, Robert H. *Why Establish a Private Foundation?* Atlanta, Ga.: Southeastern Council of Foundations, 1980.

866. Hull, Robert H., Patricia Thomas, and Donna Bradley. *Why Establish a Private Foundation?* Rev. ed. Atlanta, Ga.: Southeastern Council of Foundations, 1987.

Concise primer on establishing a private foundation. This booklet has been prepared for the purpose of increasing philanthropy through the examination of issues and problems such as incorrect information which might discourage those who would like to establish a foundation. The booklet begins with a short historical review of philanthropy and the Tax Reform Act of 1969. The chapters discuss the different types of foundations, the legal climate in which private foundations operate, the tax benefits and limitations offered donors, foundation organization and its tax-exempt status, and choosing foundation managers. It also outlines the philanthropic grantmaking process including grantmaking policies, procedures, and reporting and record-keeping. Sources of assistance for grantmakers are cited, including the Foundation Center and local, state and national councils (with a directory of associations).

867. Hulseman, Bertha F., comp. *American Foundations for Social Welfare.* Rev. ed. New York: Russell Sage Foundation, 1930.

868. Hulseman, Bertha F., comp. *American Foundations for Social Welfare.* Rev. ed. New York: Russell Sage Foundation, 1938.

869. Hurwitz, Ani. "Grantmaking in Hard Times." *Neighborhood Works* 8 (December 1985): 1+.

870. Hutchins, Robert Maynard. *Freedom, Education and the Fund: Essays and Addresses, 1946-1956.* Utica, N.Y.: Meridian, 1956.

This collection of essays and addresses by Robert Maynard Hutchins, former president of the University of Chicago and director of the Fund for the Republic, comprehensively illustrates his philosophy of education and freedom as it evolved over a ten year period. Hutchins' accounts of his association with the controversial Fund for the Republic, created by the Ford Foundation to operate as a separate grantmaking agency concerned with civil liberties, nicely pull together the strands of his thought on this subject. In an era of rampant anti-Communism and intense pressure to conform to "patriotic" ideals, a foundation created to protect the rights of dissenters (by affirming the Bill of Rights) came under tremendous attack, not least because one of the first projects it funded in its brief history was a study undertaken by the American Bar Association on congressional investigations. All of the essays, especially Part 3, *Freedom and the Fund* are interesting.

871. Hutchinson, Peter C. "Managing Change: The Challenge for Giving." *Foundation News* 24 (May-June 1983): 70+.

872. Iglehart, John K. "The Changing World of Private Foundations: An Interview with Dr. David E. Rogers." *Health Affairs* 2 (Fall 1983): 5-22.

Dr. David E. Rogers, president of the Robert Wood Johnson Foundation and chairman of the board of the Council on Foundations, discusses the role of foundation investment in the health care system, with a special focus on proposed solutions to the problem of rising medical care costs. The public sector, he claims, spends almost eighty percent of its health dollars on the immediate health concerns of today, leaving only a small share to fund programs that are looking for answers to the health care needs of tomorrow. Foundation dollars, therefore, can support development and testing of new programs and ideas that might reduce future costs in health care or make it more effective; they can finance limited-scale experiments to improve medical care delivery, train health professionals, or provide more efficient organizational methods; and they are able to fund individualized, locally tailored initiatives that focus on the critical needs of groups that may represent small percentages of the total population, but which may include as many as several million people nationally. Dr. Rogers also comments on health care and public attitudes, the physician surplus issue, the increasingly entrepreneurial aspect of the medical profession, and the future concerns of academic medical centers.

873. Iglehart, John K. "The Public Thoughts of a Private Foundation Leader: A Conversation with Alvin Tarlov." *Health Affairs* 7 (Fall 1988): 142-156.

Question and answer session with Alvin Tarlov, president of the Henry J. Kaiser Family Foundation, covering such issues as physician specialty distribution; the agenda of the Kaiser Family Foundation; health promotion/disease prevention; the role of private foundations in the health care arena; grass-roots efforts; foundation partnerships; and the quality of medical care.

874. Imberman, Joseph C. *The Community Foundation: Its Historical Background, the Creation of the North Dakota Community Foundation, and a Developmental Framework for Beginning New Community Foundations.* Unpublished, 1978.

875. *Important 20th Century Paintings, Watercolors, and Drawings from the Soloman R. Guggenheim Foundation.* [Catalog]. New York: Parke-Bernet Galleries, 1971.

876. Independent Sector. *Public Policy and Its Impact on Giving and Volunteering.* [Cassette tape]. Washington: Independent Sector, 1985.

877. Indian Health Service. *Foundations That Provide Support for Health and Human Services.* Rockville, Md.: Indian Health Service, 1981.

878. "An Interview with Susan K. Kinoy, Chief Grants Officer of the Villers Foundation." *Philanthropy Resource Letter* 6 (January 1988): 5-6.

879. "Investments of Philanthropic Organizations and Social Responsibility." *Intellect* (March 1975): 352-53.

880. Ittleson Family Foundation. *Selective Giving: An Account of the Ittleson Family Foundation.* New York: Mental Health Materials Center, 1971.

881. Jackman, Frederic L.R. "Putting Your Case to the Family Foundation." *Philanthropist/Le Philanthrope* 5 (Summer 1985): 48+.

882. Jacobsen, Lynn Madera. *A Directory of Foundations in Utah.* Salt Lake City, Utah: University of Utah Press, 1985.

Based on 1980 through 1982 990-PF returns filed with the IRS by 163 foundations in Utah, with additional information supplied by questionnaire. Main section arranged alphabetically by foundation name; entries include officers and directors, financial data, area of interest, types of support, grant analysis and sample grants. Alphabetical index of foundations as well as index by area of interest and index of officers, directors, and advisors.

883. Jacobson, Judith S. *The Greatest Good: A History of the John A. Hartford Foundation.* New York: John A. Hartford Foundation, 1984.

884. Jacobson, Robert L. "Four Foundations Aid New Study of Retirement in Academe." *Chronicle of Higher Education* 28 (March 7 1984): 27+.

885. Jarrell, H. Judith. "The Foundation Stakes: It's No Horse Race." *Currents* (May 1980): 26-8.

886. JDR 3rd Fund. *The JDR 3rd Fund and Asia, 1963-1975.* New York: JDR 3rd Fund, 1977.

887. "JFS Aids Social Change for $2 Million Annually." *Foundation Giving Watch* 5 (June 1985): 2.

Describes the interests of Joint Foundation Support.

888. Johnson Foundation, Robert Wood. *AIDS Health Services Program.* Princeton, N.J.: Robert Wood Johnson Foundation, 1986.

Describes program to support the establishment of specialized comprehensive health and supportive services for victims of AIDS and AIDS-related disorders. Provides information on eligibility, selection criteria, and administration of the program.

889. Johnston, David. "Money to Battle AIDS Scarce Despite Recent Surge in Grants." *NonProfit Times* 2 (December 1988): 1+.

While the Foundation Center's latest report on AIDS-related foundation grants shows a nearly threefold increase in dollar amount, it also reveals that sixty of the one hundred largest grantmaking foundations have yet to credit themselves with a single AIDS grant. In fact, the Robert Wood Johnson Foundation is responsible for $26.9 or nearly fifty-three percent of the total $51.65 million in grants made to AIDS charities in the last five years (not including an estimated $30 million in contributions made by the American Foundation for AIDS Research, corporate giving programs and public foundations not documented by the Foundation Center). Paul Jellinek, a senior program officer at the R.W. Johnson Foundation and a leading authority on AIDS funding, announces that more and more foundations are beginning to respond, but "by and large the dollar commitments have not been that significant so far." Many of the funders who are holding back may be reluctant to associate with groups controlled by gays and lesbians, having had little contact with these groups in the past, and fearing that AIDS-related grants will draw them into controversies within the homosexual communities. United Ways also do not show much commitment to funding AIDS-related projects, yet the United Way of the (San Francisco) Bay Area has taken an unusual step by publicizing donor options, allowing givers to route their money directly to AIDS charities.

890. Johnston, David. "Stars Strew Megabucks." *Foundation Journal* 29 (May-June 1988): 16-23.

Examines the charitable giving and philanthropic activities of various celebrities, including singers and writers, actors and directors, and athletes.

891. Jones, David R. "Restoring the Faith." *Foundation News* 29 (July-August 1988): 35-8.

Profiles the Enterprise Foundation, which has as its goal nothing less than to see that all poor people in this country have decent, affordable housing within a generation. Since 1982, Enterprise has formed public/private sector partnerships in twenty-seven cities, provided technical assistance, small seed grants and low-interest loans to over 100 community development corporations, and has raised over $22 million to support its work. Three thousand dwellings exist mainly due to Enterprise's efforts, and the foundation has commitments for another three thousand units. Of particular note is the Enterprise Loan Fund (ELF), a financing effort to provide low-interest construction loans for nonprofit developers and permanent financing for rehabilitation or raw construction of low-income housing. Writing of ELF in January 1987, the *Wall Street Journal* announced, "Philanthropists who are long on goodwill but short on cash now have a way to help low-income people;" their deposits of at least $500 in one-year certificates will be matched by the Community Development Administration of Maryland. But Enterprise's vision is even more comprehensive, as it realizes the problem of housing does not exist on its own; thus Enterprise also seeks to tackle the related problems of unemployment, inadequate education, and lack of job training.

892. Jones, Sylvia W. *Foundations: Potential Funding Sources for Speech Pathology and Audiology.* Washington: American Speech and Hearing Association, [1973].

893. Joseph, James A. "The Community Foundation Movement: An Idea Whose Time Has Come." *Corner Stone* 10 (March 1983): 3-4.

894. Joseph, James A. "Foundation Management in Transition." *Philanthropist/Le Philanthrope* 4 (Winter 1987): 39-47.

James A. Joseph, president of the Council on Foundations, examines five major challenges to foundation management in a time of transition. The paper was developed from a presentation to the Canadian Centre for Philanthropy's Fourth Conference for Foundations on June 17, 1986, in Toronto. The five challenges are a concern with principles—the idea that the practices of foundations should reflect, retain and reaffirm values; a concern with professionalism—the need to retain the voluntary spirit which is the basic essence of philanthropy while at the same time exposing the charitable impulse to acquired skills and shared experience; a concern with performance—the periodic need to assess impact and to determine whether the foundation is achieving its desired objectives; a concern with public policy—the idea that a democratic society works best when it respects and reinforces the contribution of all three sectors of its social and economic life; and a concern with personnel—the board composition as well as management responsibility. A primary requisite for effective governance is to be sure that women and men responsible for the foundation's policy directions have the skills, commitment, knowledge and background necessary for effective decision-making.

895. Joseph, James A. *Private Philanthropy and the Making of Public Policy.* Washington: Council on Foundations, 1985.

896. Joseph, James A. "Six Trends Shaping Philanthropy's Future." *Foundation News* 24 (May-June 1983): 22+.

897. Joseph, Samuel. *History of the Baron de Hirsch Fund: The Americanization of the Jewish Immigrant.* New York: Jewish Publication Society, 1935.

898. *Nebraska Foundation Directory.* Omaha, Nebr.: Junior League of Omaha, 1985.

Based on mostly 1982 and 1983 990-PF returns filed with the IRS by approximately 200 foundations. Main section arranged alphabetically by foundation; entries include statement of purpose and officers. No sample grants or indexes.

899. Junior League of Phoenix, comp. *Arizona Foundation Directory.* 2nd ed. Phoenix, Ariz.: Junior League of Phoenix, 1989.

Information for over 150 private and community foundations are featured in this directory produced by the Junior League of Phoenix in cooperation with the Arizona Chapter of the National Society of Fund Raising Executives. Foundations which have assets over $5,000 and which have made at least a total of $500 in grants are included. Descriptions include name, address, telephone number, source of information, employer identification number, year established, donors, purpose/fields of interest, restrictions, trustees, contact person, application deadline, and preferred form of contact. A presentation of financial data notes the fiscal year, total assets, total grants, number of grants, highest/lowest grants, and selected sample grants of the foundation. The directory also includes a guide for program planning, proposal writing, and budget formulation. Indexed by foundation name.

900–917 FOUNDATIONS

900. Kalb, Werner. *Stiftungen und Bildungswesen in den USA.* (Foundations and matters of education in the U.S.A.). Studien und Berichte, no. 11. Berlin, Germany: Institut fur Bildungsforschung in der Max-Planck-Gesellschaft, 1968.

901. Kanaly, E. Deane. "Corporations Have Something to Offer Those Foundations." *Houston Post* (24 July 1985).

Recommends that foundations be required to have one corporate trustee.

902. Karel, Frank. "Foundations and Public Policy: Coming of Age in the 1980's." *Foundation News* 26 (March-April 1985): 58-60.

903. Karl, Barry D., and Stanley N. Katz. *The American Private Philanthropic Foundation and the Public Sphere, 1890-1930.* London: Minerva, 1981.

Karl and Katz's inquiry begins with the changing conceptions of the public sphere after the Civil War. Out of the nineteenth century tradition of federalism arose a peculiarly American combination of charity and technology in which private interests appropriated national social well-being as their domain. The modern foundation was thus born of society's need for national social policy, but also society's unwillingness to let the federal government control it. The authors argue that the role the federal government was ultimately forced to accept in social reform was shaped and continues to be shaped by the presence of private philanthropy. The article includes discussion of public attitudes toward foundations during their formative years, the convergence of the Progressive movement and foundation aspirations, the way in which foundation and government related to each other, foundations after the deaths of their founders, and their role in social science.

904. Katz, Milton. *The Modern Foundation: Its Dual Character, Public and Private.* Foundation Library Center Occasional Papers, no. 2. New York: Foundation Library Center, 1968.

905. Keele, Harold M., and Joseph C. Kiger, eds. *Foundations.* Greenwood Encyclopedia of American Institutions. Westport, Conn.: Greenwood Press, 1984.

Includes brief histories of the nation's 230 largest foundations (ca. 1981-82).

906. Keens, Martha R., and Josephine E. Case, comps. *International Philanthropy: A Compilation of Grants by U.S. Foundations.* New York: Foundation Center, 1977.

907. Keillor, Garrison. *Happy to Be Here.* New York: Penguin Books, 1983.

Collection of stories which previously appeared the *New Yorker*, providing a satiric portrait of the philanthropy of foundations and the nonprofit entrepreneur.

908. Kellogg Foundation, W.K. *The First Half-Century, 1930-1980: Private Approaches to Public Needs.* Battle Creek, Mich.: W.K. Kellogg Foundation, [1979].

909. Kellogg Foundation, W.K. *Increasing the Impact, 1980's.* 2nd ed. Battle Creek, Mich.: W.K. Kellogg Foundation, 1985.

Important collection of essays written by grantmakers on successful approaches to project dissemination and use. Provides how-to tips shared by more than two dozen successful communicators. Gives examples for both print and telecommunications-oriented dissemination, including video teleconferencing, radio programming, computer-based information sharing, community forums, and television.

910. Keppel, Frederick Paul. *The Foundation.* New York: Macmillan, 1930.

911. Kiger, Joseph C. *Historiographic Review of Foundation Literature: Motivations and Perceptions.* New York: Foundation Center, 1987.

Provides a chronological review of literature dealing with independent foundations, including book-length works such as histories and biographies, publications from pertinent government agencies (in particular the U.S. Congress and Treasury Department), and works published by privately organized bodies. Kiger concludes that very few condemnatory or harshly critical works have been published on the subject of foundations (those that do attack the institutions are either worked from a Marxist standpoint or are the direct or indirect result of two congressional investigations, the Walsh Commission and the Reece Committee), and that foundations have matured greatly during this century to the point where they not only can stand up under scrutiny, but are actually encouraging it. He notes that today's foundation officials are devoting increasing attention to both past and present criticisms, a necessary step if foundations hope to continue to grow and change within their *Zeitgeist*.

912. Kilbride, Zeke. "Getting Grants Independently: A Resource Guide." *Grants Magazine* 9 (March 1986): 45-58.

Discusses the individual grantseeker's options and contains an annotated bibliography of information sources on grants to individuals.

913. Kiser, Clyde V. *The Milbank Memorial Fund: Its Leaders and Its Work, 1905-1974.* New York: Milbank Memorial Fund, 1975.

914. Kitman, Jamie. "MacArthur Foundation. Part 1: The Chicago School of Philanthropy." *Nation* (7 December 1985): 615-19.

915. Kitman, Jamie. "MacArthur Foundation. Part 2: Selling off the Family Business." *Nation* (14 December 1985): 641-46.

916. Kitman, Jamie. "MacArthur Foundation. Part 3: The Gold-Plated Charity Machine." *Nation* (21 December 1985): 674-80.

917. Kletzien, S. Damon. *Directory of Pennsylvania Foundations.* 3rd ed. Springfield, Pa.: Triadvocates Associated, 1986.

Based primarily on 1984 990-PF returns filed with the IRS and information supplied by the more than 2,300 foundations listed in the directory. Organized in five geographical regions. Full profile entries for about 975 foundations with assets exceeding $75,000 or awarding grants totaling $5,000 or more on a discretionary basis; entries include a statement on geographical emphasis of giving, a descending listing of all grants down to $250, listing of major interest codes, application guidelines and/or statement on giving policy when available, and a list of directors, trustees, and donors. Other foundations not meeting above criteria listed by name, address and status code only. Appendix article on broadening the foundation search. Indexes of officers, directors, trustees and donors; major giving interests; and foundation names.

918. Knauft, E.B. "The Filer Commission Revisited." *Foundation News* 25 (January-February 1984): 12-5.

919. Kohler, Robert E. "A Policy for the Advancement of Science: The Rockefeller Foundation, 1924-29." *Minerva* 16 (1978): 480-515.

Kohler outlines developments within the Rockefeller foundations and in the educational system of the country that led to a heavy emphasis on supporting science research in the 1920s. The scientific research programs of the Rockefeller Foundation proper were all but dwarfed in the 1920s by those of the General Education Board, the International Education Board, and the Laura Spelman Rockefeller Memorial, under the leadership of Wycliff Rose and Beardsley Ruml. The development of Rockefeller Foundation policy toward scientific research is elaborated in the article, with many references to primary sources. Kohler reveals an interesting interplay between different personalities and existing institutional policies. An interesting account is also given of the reorganization of the various funds into one Rockefeller Foundation, and of the effects of this development on scientific research programs.

920. Kopetzky, Samuel J. *Foundations and Their Trends.* Privately Printed, 1931.

921. Koppel, Ted. *The MacArthur Foundation.* New York: American Broadcasting Co., 1986.

Transcript of television show *Nightline.* Ted Koppel interview with several MacArthur Foundation fellows.

922. Korman, Rochelle. *Private Foundations and the Requirement to Exercise Expenditure Responsibility.* New York: New York Regional Association of Grantmakers, 1983.

923. Koshland, Daniel E. *Bay Area Foundation History.* Berkeley, Calif.: University of California-Berkeley, 1976.

924. Kresge Foundation. *Capital Grant Survey Results.* Detroit: Kresge Foundation, [1982].

925. Kresge Foundation. *The First Thirty Years: A Report on the Activities of the Kresge Foundation, 1924-1953.* Detroit: Kresge Foundation, 1954.

926. Kunen, James L. *Foundations, Universities, and Social Change.* Urbana, Ill.: Institute of Government and Public Affairs, 1968.

927. Kurtz, Daniel L. "Foundations: Excess Business Holdings." *Philanthropy Monthly* 18 (February 1985): 17-9.

928. Kurzig, Carol M., ed. *Foundation Grants to Individuals.* New York: Foundation Center, 1977.

Profiles foundation programs that make grants to individuals. The foundations described have made grants to students, artists, scholars, foreign individuals, minorities, musicians, scientists, and writers. The book includes information on foundation sources of funds for scholarships, fellowships, internships, medical and emergency assistance, residences and travel programs.

929. LaFranchi, Howard. "A More Thoughtful Path to Preventing Nuclear War: Foundations Are Supporting Research That Goes Beyond Counting Missiles." *Christian Science Monitor* (9 March 1984).

930. Lagemann, Ellen Condliffe. "A Philanthropic Foundation at Work: Gunnar Myrdal's *American Dilemma* and the Carnegie Corporation." *Minerva* 25 (Winter 1987): 441-70.

Interesting and thoroughly researched account of the various aims and perspectives exhibited by those responsible for the writing and publication of *An American Dilemma: the Negro Problem and Modern Democracy*, a study that has had significant impact on public policy and public opinion. In 1935 a trustee of the Carnegie Corporation, Newton Baker, suggested that the foundation "give consideration to the general question of Negro education and Negro problems," in an effort to develop new grantmaking approaches. Frederick Keppel, president of the Corporation, chose the Swedish economist Gunnar Myrdal to conduct "a comprehensive study of the Negro in the United States to be undertaken in a wholly objective and dispassionate way as a social phenomenon;" and from there the project moved on a course different from what had been originally conceived by either Baker or Keppel. Little concerned with providing guidance for the Corporation's allocation of grants, Myrdal based his study in the intellectual style of sociology as it was developed at the University of Chicago. While this disappointed Baker, Keppel and the Carnegie Corporation, the irony of the situation is that the Chicagoan orientation of sociology developed and gained prominence in the United States in part because of grants made by foundations. Thus a study expected to illuminate questions of education became, due to Myrdal's intellectual sympathy with prominent American sociologists, a study that analyzed fundamental patterns of American society. Lagemann concludes that "even though foundations have played a critical role in the formulation of public policies in the United States, their capacity to shape, let alone to determine, such policies has been deeply affected by the traditions and achievements of the major universities to which, in their turn, they have contributed so much."

931. Lagemann, Ellen Condliffe. "The Politics of Knowledge: The Carnegie Corporation and the Formulation of Public Policy." *History of Education Quarterly* 27 (Summer 1987): 205-20.

932. Lagemann, Ellen Condliffe. *Private Power for the Public Good: A History of the Carnegie Foundation for the Advancement of Teaching.* Middleton, Conn.: Wesleyan University Press, 1983.

Established in 1905 as a pension fund for college professors, the Carnegie Foundation for the Advancement of Teaching serves as a subject for this historical study, which critically examines the notion of "private power for the public good."

Lagemann devotes considerable attention to the role of Henry Pritchett, the foundation's first president, in establishing the traditions and basic institutional design that have informed policy-making at the foundation ever since his tenure, and to the earlier years of the foundation in general. Lagemann considers the history of this foundation—its work defining paradigms of education through studies as well as establishing the Teachers Insurance and Annuity Association (TIAA)—in relation to the larger social issues of the past seventy-five years, including the growth of science and professionalism, the relationship between education and social stratification, and problems of community or politics.

933. Langevin, Thomas H., ed. *The Battelle Memorial Institute Foundation, 1975-1982: A History and Evaluation.* Columbus, Ohio: Ohio Historical Society, 1983.

934. Lankford, John E. *Congress and the Foundations in the Twentieth Century.* River Falls, Wis.: Wisconsin State University, 1964.

This book examines congressional investigations of foundation activity in the twentieth century, focusing on the methods by which Congress attempted to get information and the ways the foundations responded to their concerns. Lankford shows how the congressional climate, like the public climate, shifted between the Progressive era and the middle of the century from an attitude of wary indifference in which foundations were thought of as preservers of the status quo, irrelevant if not offensive to the public good, to one of active hostility on account of their ostensibly radical tendencies. The study discusses the Cox Committee investigation of 1952 and the Reece Committee investigation of 1953-1954, but unfortunately predates the investigations that led to the Tax Reform Act of 1969. The book illuminates the question of the relationship between foundation and government, as well as their accountability—or lack thereof—and the appropriateness of their activities in the eyes of Congress. Essay on sources.

935. Lansford, Henry. "A Mile High and Still Growing." *Foundation News* 25 (March-April 1984): 41+.

936. Laski, Harold J. "Foundations, Universities, and Research." *Harper's Magazine* (August 1928): 295-303.

Laski outlines some concerns with the evolution during the 1920s of foundation-sponsored research institutes and other vehicles for collaborative scholarship springing up on campuses across the country, predominantly in the social sciences. "I doubt," he states, "whether the results to be achieved are likely to be proportionate to the labor involved. I doubt, in the second place, whether the effect on university institutions is likely, in the long run, to be healthy; and I doubt, in the third place, whether the result of the policy will not be to give to the foundations a dominating control over university life which they quite emphatically ought not to have." With respect to the last, Laski is not attributing to foundations a calculated desire to control. Rather, he is warning that the mere existence of foundation largesse impels universities to gravitate in its direction and thus adopt courses of action they may not have independently pursued.

937. Latino Institute. *Responsiveness of the U.S. Foundations to Hispanic Needs and Concerns.* Reston, Va.: Latino Institute, 1980.

938. Latino Institute. *Strangers in the Philanthropic World: The Limited Latino Share of Chicago Grants.* Reston, Va.: Latino Institute, 1986.

Documents the Latino perspective on the world of Chicago grantmaking emphasizing the quantitative record on issues of policy and funding, outlining priorities for action, and advocating for a relationship of cooperative exchange. Among the key points: only 2.7 percent of the philanthropic dollar goes to Latinos; three donors (the Chicago Community Trust, the John D. and Catherine T. MacArthur Foundation, and the Joyce Foundation) provide more than half of this funding; United Way funds only twelve Latino agencies with 4.2 percent of its contributions; and Latino funding in all categories is significantly below the Latino representation in the Chicago population.

939. "The Law Limiting Foundation Grant Expenses." *Philanthropy Monthly* 18 (April 1985): 9-11.

940. "Learning from Foundation Annual Reports." *Philanthropy Monthly* 18 (May 1985): 13-9.

941. "Learning from Foundation Reports." *Philanthropy Monthly* 17 (June 1984): 25-30.

942. Lee, C. Herbert. *The Investment History of the Carnegie Corporation of New York.* Philadelphia: William F. Fell Co., 1943.

943. Lehrfeld, William J. "Lehrfeld on Foundations." *Philanthropy Monthly* 17 (February 1984): 8-10.

944. "Length of Stock Market Meltdown Holds Key to How Foundations Will Fair, But Crash Not Seen Curbing Grants, Assets, Soon." *Tax Exempt News* 9 (November 1987): 1-3.

Survey assesses the damage done to various foundations by the stock market crash, but maintains that most will come out in good shape due to their tendency toward conservative investment policies.

945. Lester, Robert M. *A Thirty Year Catalog of Grants, during the Period November 10, 1911 to September 30, 1941.* New York: Carnegie Corporation of New York, 1942.

946. Levitan, Donald. *The Top Fifty Grant Awarding Foundations in 1982.* Newton Centre, Mass.: Grants Advisory Service, 1983.

947. Lewis, Marianna O., ed. *Information Quarterly. 1972-1974.* 2 vols. New York: Foundation Center, 1972-4.

948. Lewis, Sinclair. *Arrowsmith.* New York: New American Library, 1961.

949. Lindeman, Eduard C. *Wealth and Culture: A Study of One Hundred Foundations and Community Trusts and Their Operations during the Decade, 1921-1930.* New York: Harcourt, Brace, 1936.

950. Lindquist, Jack. *Increasing the Impact of Social Innovations Funded by Grantmaking Organizations.* Battle Creek, Mich.: W.K. Kellogg Foundation, [1979].

951. Lippard, Vernon W., and Elizabeth F. Purcell, eds. *Case Histories of Ten New Medical Schools.* New York: Josiah Macy Jr. Foundation, 1972.

952. Lipton, David A. *Significant Private Foundations and the Need for Public Selection of Their Trustees.* Reprint. Charlottesville, Va.: Virginia Law Review Association, 1978.

953. Littman, Wendy P., ed. *The Mitchell Guide to Foundations, Corporations, and Their Managers. New Jersey.* Belle Mead, N.J.: Littman Associates, 1988.

The information in this edition is based primarily on 990-PF returns filed with the IRS from 1984 through 1987 and, in some cases, information supplied by 196 foundations; the data for the 558 companies on the corporation list was compiled from basic business references. The funder profiles are arranged alphabetically by foundation name; entries include sample grants and foundation managers, restrictions and program priorities. The corporate section is a list which includes address, telephone, and contact person. Contains indexes by county for both foundations and corporations.

954. Locke, Elizabeth H. "Five Self-Serving Reasons for Foundations to Communicate and a New Service to Help Them Do It." *Grants Magazine* 8 (December 1985): 215-8.

Assessment of five major gains to foundations through better and more complete communication as well as information on the Communications Assistance Service, an organization which provides technical assistance to foundations.

955. Logan, Sheridan A. *George F. Baker and His Bank, 1840-1955.* New York: George F. Baker Trust, 1981.

956. Logos Associates. *The Directory of the Major California Foundations.* Attleboro, Mass.: Logos Associates, 1986.

Based on 1983 and 1984 990-PF returns and annual reports for more than ninety-seven foundations. Main section arranged alphabetically by foundation; entries include contact person, activities, categories of giving, board meeting dates, officers and directors and grants. No indexes.

957. Logos Associates, comp. *Directory of the Major Connecticut Foundations.* Attleboro, Mass.: Logos Associates, 1982.

Based on 1979 through 1980 990-PF and 990-AR returns, foundation publications and information from the Office of the Attorney General in Hartford. Arranged alphabetically by foundation; entries include grant range, sample grants, geographic limitations, officers and directors. Index of subjects.

958. Logos Associates. *The Directory of the Major Florida Foundations.* Attleboro, Mass.: Logos Associates, 1987.

Profiles 107 major Florida foundations that made over $50,000 in grants during 1984. Entries include information on contact person, foundation activities, financial data, officers and directors, geographic range, and grants made. Address, telephone number, contact person and officers are given for 775 foundations making grants of less than $50,000. Includes subject index.

959. Logos Associates, comp. *Directory of the Major Greater Boston Foundations.* Attleboro, Mass.: Logos Associates, 1981.

Based on 1975 through 1980 990-PF and 990-AR returns filed with the IRS by fifty-six Boston area foundations. Main section arranged alphabetically by foundation; entries include statement of purpose, sample grants, and officers. Index of fields of interest.

960. Logos Associates. *The Directory of the Major New Jersey Foundations.* Attleboro, Mass.: Logos Associates, 1988.

Based on IRS financial data, annual reports and other public materials, offers profiles on approximately 110 foundations, all of which have given away a minimum of $50,000 in the year of record, have distributed the bulk of this within the state of New Jersey, and are a source of funding to the general nonprofit institutions in New Jersey. Arranged alphabetically by foundation; entries include corporate profile, charitable giving, contact person, and sample grants. Subject index.

961. Logos Associates. *The Directory of the Major Texas Foundations.* Attleboro, Mass.: Logos Associates, 1986.

Full profiles for seventy-three major foundations making grants above $400,000 in Texas, with address, telephone number, contact, foundation activities, categories of giving, financial data, application procedures, grant range and geographic area (some grants made out of state), and sample grants. Partial profiles for thirty-three additional foundations making under $400,000 in grants, listing address, financial data, number and/or amount of grants made; some entries have sample grants. Name, address and telephone numbers for thirty-four major Texas foundations granting $200,000 to $399,000. Includes subject index.

962. "A Look at Some Conservative-Oriented Foundations." *Foundation Giving Watch* 1 (March 1984): 1-2.

963. Lord, Benjamin, ed. *America's Newest Foundations.* 3rd ed. Washington: Taft Group, 1989.

Profiles 550 newly established foundations, with nearly seventy percent being new to this edition. Each foundation has either assets or total giving of at least $100,000, with preference given to those with broad charitable interests or that emphasize institutional support to nonprofit organizations rather than individual support to scholars or students. Each profile begins with data on the contact person, address, telephone number, the year the foundation was initiated, and the name of the foundation's donor; an analysis of charitable giving follows, including a statement of the foundation's principal charitable interest, geographic preferences, typical recipients, and grant types; lists names and titles of foundation officers and directors and gives a summary of application procedures when available; presents fiscal data concerning assets, total giving, gifts received, number of grants and highest grant; and ends with a list of up to ten of the largest grants made by the foundation. Indexes to foundations by state, by grant type, and by recipient type (subject area); to individuals by name; and to grant recipients by location.

964. Lucas, Marilyn. *Corporate and Foundation Research Sources.* Unpublished, 1985.

965. Luck, James I. "Taken under Advisement." *Foundation News* 28 (September-October 1987): 52-5.

Contends that donor-advised funds have enormous value for community foundations, and expands upon seven reasons for actively pursuing them: they provide an introduction to giving for families and individuals new to philanthropy; they serve as a vehicle for sustained community giving; they link the resources of a concerned donor with the needs of a community; they generate contributions to the operating costs of the community foundation; they can support the foundation's grantmaking by providing a portion of income from advised funds to be utilized for unrestricted giving; they are often the most effective route to unrestricted endowment; and by providing direct involvement for donors, they attract interest and more donors who want to participate in charitable activities.

966. Lyman, Richard W. "So You Want to Run a Foundation?" *Foundation News* 23 (November-December 1982): 26+.

967. MacDonald, Dwight. *The Ford Foundation: The Men and the Millions.* New York: Reynal, 1956.

This book was published at a time when the resources of the Ford Foundation outstripped those of Rockefeller and Carnegie. The book is entertainingly written and examines the trustees and staff who ran the foundation. Their roles in various decisions are detailed, and a history of the foundation in its first twenty years is outlined, although most emphasis is on the present. Two central chapters of the book, *What Hath Ford Wrought* and *The Philanthropoids*, consist of a detailed but interesting account of the foundation's spending in 1951-1954 and a fascinating description, both generic and personal, of the people who give out the money—even how they dress and the language they use in the office. This book is not broadly historical or very analytical, but it does provide insight into the inner workings of a huge, important foundation.

968. Maddox, David C., and David Hammack, eds. *The Russell Sage Foundation: Social Research and Social Action in America, 1907-1947. Guide to the Microfiche Collection.* Frederick, Md.: Congressional Information Service, 1988.

Reference bibliography to Russell Sage Foundation materials, department pamphlet series, archival documents, and minutes on microfilm. Includes an historical introduction that chronicles the achievements of the Foundation in the realms of social activism and social research, from 1907 to 1947. Indexed by names and titles.

969. Magarrell, Jack. "Fund Raisers' Aim." *Chronicle of Higher Education* 9 (22 September 1975): 3.

970. Magarrell, Jack. "U.S. Finds Foundations Failing to Comply with Disclosure Law." *Chronicle of Higher Education* 27 (26 October 1983): 1+.

971. Magat, Richard. "Agreeing to Disagree." *Foundation News* 24 (July-August 1983): 25-7.

972. Magat, Richard. *The Ford Foundation at Work: Philanthropic Choices, Methods, and Styles.* New York: Plenum, 1979.

973. Magat, Richard. "The Issue That Won't Go Away." *Foundation News* 24 (July-August 1983): 14-20.

974. Magat, Richard. "Out of the Shadows." *Foundation News* 25 (July-August 1984): 24-33.

975. Magat, Richard. *Pitfalls and Ideals in Communicating for Foundations.* Washington: Council on Foundations, 1982.

976. Magat, Richard, and Arlie Schardt. "Report from the People." *Foundation News* 24 (July-August 1983): 39-42.

977. Mahoney, Constance W., and Carroll L. Estes. *The Changing Role of Private Foundations: Business As Usual or Creative Innovation?* San Francisco: University of California, 1986.

Study undertaken to determine: the impact of public policy changes since 1981 on foundations; the response of foundations to nonprofit organizations and public agencies, particularly those serving the elderly; the involvement of foundations with public agencies and private nonprofit organizations; and the extent to which foundations achieved their self-described status as "innovators." In addition, the research seeks to understand the extent to which foundations are "filling in" for public sector funding cutbacks, and to what extent, in a time of fiscal austerity, foundations are conducting business as usual or are acting as innovators. Foundations report that the major effect of federal funding cutbacks was a marked increase in requests, often "desperate" and for survival (not for new initiatives), and that as a result of federal policy changes since 1981, the foundations had become more aware of the need for human services. Includes bibliography.

978. Malaspina, Rick. "Money-Starved Schools Get Help from Foundations." *San Francisco Examiner* (7 November 1983).

979. "Management and the Foundations." *Management Forum* 2 (October 1973): 1-3.

980. Mandeville, John. *Foundation Funding Resource Guide for Programs Serving North Carolina's Handicapped Population.* Draft. Raleigh, N.C.: North Carolina Department of Human Resources, 1982.

981. Margolin, Judith B. *About Foundations: How to Find the Facts You Need to Get a Grant.* Rev. ed. New York: Foundation Center, 1977.

Guide prepared for all grantseekers, from newcomers in the field to experienced fundraisers; also useful for concerned citizens, government officials, writers, and members of foundation staffs and boards of directors. Provides guidelines for researching the various sources of fooundation information based on the name of the institution, funding interests, or geographical proximity. Information sources, available in the Foundation Center's national and regional collections and in many public libraries, include: annual reports, Foundation Center publications (*Source Book Profiles, Grants Index,* and *The Foundation Directory*), Internal Revenue forms 990-AR and 990-PF, state foundation directories, and pamphlets and news releases.

982. Margolin, Judith B. *About Foundations: How to Find the Facts You Need to Get a Grant.* New York: Foundation Center, 1975.

983. Margolis, Richard J. "Hot for Safe Energy." *Foundation News* 24 (March-April 1983): 32-5.

984. Margolis, Richard J. "Just like Jonah Said." *Foundation News* 25 (January-February 1984): 32+.

985. Margolis, Richard J. "Small Wonders: Personifying the Playboy Philosophy." *Foundation News* 24 (May-June 1983): 28+.

986. Marlowe, Howard. "Due to Circumstances Beyond Our Control." *Grantsmanship Center News* 11 (September-October 1983): 80-3.

987. Marten, A.W. *The Cleveland Foundation.* Cleveland: Cleveland Trust Co., 1950.

988. Maryland. Attorney General's Office. *Annual Index of Foundation Reports and Appendix, 1985.* Baltimore, Md.: Attorney General's Office, 1987.

Index compiled from foundation's IRS forms filed with the Attorney General's office and an appendix which contains information on those which filed after December 22, 1986. The index and appendix are arranged alphabetically and give the foundation's name, address, and employer identification number; fair market value of the foundation; foundation managers and their addresses; purpose of contributions; contributions given during the fiscal year with the recipient and amount; total contributions given during fiscal year; and contributions approved for future payment and total contributions approved for future payment, if any.

989. Massachusetts. Department of the Attorney General. *Directory of Foundations in Massachusetts.* Boston: Massachusetts Department of the Attorney General, 1977.

990. Mathews, David. "Educating Communities." *Foundation News* 25 (July-August 1984): 68-9.

Community foundations help their communities solve problems.

991. May, John Rickard. *Bay Area Foundation History.* Berkeley, Calif.: University of California-Berkeley, 1976.

992. Mayer, Steven E. *Growth Factors in the Development of Community Foundations: A Study Guide for Technical Assistance.* Minneapolis, Minn.: Rainbow Research, 1988.

Knowledge and techniques culled from the experiences of Eugene Struckhoff, working on behalf of the Council on Foundations with grants by the Charles Stewart Mott Foundation, to provide direct, extended consultations to new or revitalizing community foundations. Taking as its starting point the experiences of the fifteen community foundations receiving Mr. Struckhoff's extended technical assistance through December 1985, this study guide explores important lessons about community foundation growth, organized around five major Growth Areas: self-understanding, intended to increase a community foundation's appreciation of what it is and what it can do; board commitment, which enables the community foundation to face the challenge of development; organizational capacity, including the basic tools necessary to begin and sustain operations; asset development; and the foundation's role in the community. For each growth factor the study guide presents a group of questions frequently asked of the consultant, a set of diagnostic checkpoints intended to generate discussion, inspire ideas, and present how things are done in successful community foundations, and a compilation of articles and handbooks written by Eugene Struckhoff specifically for emerging and revitalizing community foundations.

993. Mayhew, Lewis B. *The Carnegie Commission on Higher Education.* San Francisco: Jossey-Bass Publishers, 1973.

994. McCandless, Anthony. *The Burke Foundation.* Briarcliff Manor, N.Y.: Stein & Day Publishers, 1985.

995. McCarthy, Kathleen D. "Twenty-Five Years and Change." *Foundation News* 25 (November-December 1984): 14-21.

Reviews the foundation field over the last twenty-five years.

996. McCarthy, Mary. *The Groves of Academe.* New York: New American Library, 1963.

997. McGuire, William. *Bollingen: An Adventure in Collecting the Past.* Princeton, N.J.: Princeton University Press, 1982.

998. McIlhany, William H. *The Tax-Exempt Foundations.* Westport, Conn.: Arlington House, 1980.

999. McManis Associates. *How to Establish and Fund an Association Foundation.* Washington: American Society of Association Executives, 1985.

Offers specific recommendations and procedures for associations considering the foundation approach to their funding needs, and provides the reader with insights into the experiences of associations that have established foundations.

1000. McPherson, Craig, comp. *The Guide to Oregon Foundations.* Portland, Oreg.: United Way of Columbia-Willamette, 1987.

Based on 990-PF and 990-AR forms filed with the Oregon Attorney General's Charitable Trust Division and information supplied by over 350 foundations. Main section arranged alphabetically by foundation within five subdivisions: general purpose foundations, special purpose foundations, student aid or scholarship funds, service clubs, and national or regional foundations with an active interest in Oregon. Entries include statement of purpose, financial data, sample grants, officers, and contact person. Appendixes include foundations ranked by asset size, by grants awarded, and by geographic focus; index of foundation names with Attorney General index numbers.

1001. McRae, Kendall, and Kim Pederson, eds. *Directory of Montana and Wyoming Foundations.* 4th ed. Billings, Mont.: Grants Assistance Center, 1985.

Provides information on the location, limitations, eligibility requirements, history, and giving trends of seventy-nine foundations that fund individuals or organizations in Montana and Wyoming. Includes information on the Montana Arts Council and the Montana Committee for the Humanities, an outline for locating funding sources, basic principles of proposal writing, an explanation of the cover letter, and general writing tips. Subject index.

1002. McRae, Kendall, and Kim Pederson, eds. *The Montana and Wyoming Foundation Directory.* 4th ed. Billings, Mont.: Grants Assistance Center, 1986.

Based on 990-PF returns filed with the IRS, the *National Data Book*, and information supplied by sixty-five foundations in Montana and twenty in Wyoming. Main section arranged alphabetically by foundation; entries include areas of interest, geographic preference, application process and contact person; no sample grants. Indexes of foundation names and areas of interest.

1003. Meade, Edward J., Jr. *Philanthropy and Public Schools: One Foundation's Evolving Perspective.* New York: Ford Foundation, 1979.

1004. Meade, Edward J., Jr. "When a Foundation Goes to School." *Today's Education* 62 (March 1973): 22-4, 62.

1005. Mellon Educational and Charitable Trust, A.W. *The A.W. Mellon Educational and Charitable Trust: A Report of Its Work for the Fifty Years, 1930-1980.* Pittsburgh: A.W. Mellon Educational and Charitable Trust, 1981.

1006. Memphis Bureau of Intergovernmental Management. *The Tennessee Directory of Foundations and Corporate Philanthropy.* Memphis, Tenn.: Memphis Bureau of Intergovernmental Management, 1982.

1007. Menninger, Roy W. *Foundation Work May Be Hazardous to Your Mental Health.* Washington: Council on Foundations, 1981.

1008. Miletich, John J. *Foundations and Fund Raising: A Bibliography of Books to 1980.* Monticello, Ill.: Vance Bibliographies, 1981.

1009. Mills, David Bloss. *The Story of the Davella Mills Foundation, 1935-1955.* Montclair, N.J.: Davella Mills Foundation, 1957.

1010. Minnesota Council of Nonprofits. *Minnesota Foundations List.* Minneapolis, Minn.: Minnesota Council of Nonprofits, 1987.

1011. Minnesota Council on Foundations. *Guide to Minnesota Foundations and Corporate Giving Programs.* Minneapolis, Minn.: University of Minnesota Press, 1983.

Based primarily on 1981 and 1982 IRS 990-PF returns and a survey of grantmakers. Main section arranged alphabetically by foundation name; entries include program interests, officers and directors, assets, total grants, number of grants, range, and sample grants. Some entries include geographic orientation, types of organizations funded and types of support. Indexes of foundations, types of organizations funded by specific grantmakers, and grantmakers by size. Appendixes of inactive foundations, foundations with designated recipients, foundations making grants only outside of Minnesota and foundations not accepting applications. Also section on funding research in Minnesota.

1012. Mitchell, Rowland L., Jr., ed. *The Mitchell Guide to Foundations, Corporations and Their Managers: Central New York, Including Binghamton, Corning, Elmira, Geneva, Ithaca, Oswego, Syracuse, Utica.* 2nd ed. Scarsdale, N.Y.: Rowland L. Mitchell Jr., 1987.

Based on 990-PF returns filed with the IRS. Main sections arranged alphabetically by foundation and by corporation; entries include managers, financial data and sample grants. Alphabetical indexes of foundations and corporations and index to managers.

1013. Mitchell, Rowland L., Jr., ed. *The Mitchell Guide to Foundations, Corporations and Their Managers: Long Island, Including Nassau and Suffolk Counties.* 2nd ed. Scarsdale, N.Y.: Rowland L. Mitchell Jr., 1987.

Based on 990-PF returns filed with the IRS. Main sections arranged alphabetically by foundation and by corporation; entries include managers, financial data and sample grants. Alphabetical indexes of foundations and corporations and index to managers.

1014. Mitchell, Rowland L., Jr., ed. *The Mitchell Guide to Foundations, Corporations and Their Managers: Upper Hudson Valley Including Capital Area, Glens Falls, Newburgh, Plattsburgh, Poughkeepsie, Schenectady.* 2nd ed. Scarsdale, N.Y.: Rowland L. Mitchell Jr., 1987.

Based on 990-PF returns filed with the IRS. Main sections arranged alphabetically by foundation and by corporation; entries include managers, financial data and sample grants. Alphabetical indexes of foundations and corporations and index to managers.

1015. Mitchell, Rowland L., Jr., ed. *The Mitchell Guide to Foundations, Corporations and Their Managers: Westchester, Including Putnam, Rockland and Orange Counties.* 2nd ed. Scarsdale, N.Y.: Rowland L. Mitchell Jr., 1987.

Based on 990-PF returns filed with the IRS. Main sections arranged alphabetically by foundation and by corporation; entries include managers, financial data and sample grants. Alphabetical indexes of foundations and corporations and index to managers.

1016. Mitchell, Rowland L., Jr., ed. *The Mitchell Guide to Foundations, Corporations and Their Managers: Western New York, Including Buffalo, Jamestown, Niagara Falls, Rochester.* 2nd ed. Scarsdale, N.Y.: Rowland L. Mitchell Jr., 1987.

Based on 990-PF returns filed with the IRS. Main sections arranged alphabetically by foundations and by corporation; entries include managers, financial data and sample grants. Alphabetical index of foundations and corporations and index to managers.

1017. Moody Foundation. *Attorney General's Report on the Trustees of the Moody Foundation: An Investigation Report to Crawford C. Martin, Attorney General of Texas from Wilmer B. Hunt, Special Assistant Attorney General.* Unpublished, 1971.

1018. Moore, Louis. "There's $10 Million in Religious Foundations in Texas." *Houston Chronicle* (19 April 1975): 1.

1019. Morgan, Dan. "Conservatives: A Well-Financed Network." *Washington Post* (4 January 1981): A-1, A-14-5.

1020. Morison, Robert S. "Foundations and Universities." *Daedalus* 93 (Fall 1964): 1109-41.

1021. Mouat, Lucia. "Americans Giving More: Even If Not Enough." *Christian Science Monitor* (29 July 1975): 4.

1022. Muller, Charles G. *The John Jay and Eliza Jane Watson Foundation, 1949-1964.* New York: John Jay and Eliza Jane Watson Foundation, 1964.

1023. Muller, Leo C. *Understanding Foundation Support for Higher Education.* Washington: American College Public Relations Association, 1963.

1024. Murrell, William G., and William M. Miller. *New Mexico Private Foundations Directory.* Tijeras, Minn.: New Moon Consultants, 1982.

Main section arranged alphabetically by foundation; entries include contact person, program purpose, areas of interest, financial data, application procedure, meeting times and publications. Also sections on proposal writing, private and corporate grantsmanship and bibliography. No indexes.

1025. Naples, Nancy. *Survey of Philanthropy.* New York: Women and Foundations/Corporate Philanthropy, 1988.

Special project survey by Women and Foundations/Corporate Philanthropy, a Council on Foundations affinity group. The purpose of this quantitative survey was to find out who is funding what adolescent pregnancy programs and to discern funding patterns and trends. Statistical data is supplied for the grants awarded, geographic range, gender and race of grantees, types of organizations funded, and fields of interest. The findings reveal that prevention is now the primary funding priority; the second is life options/self-esteem education; the third is counseling for teenage parents. Recently, some foundations have moved into broader areas, seeing young people who become pregnant and parents as one aspect of the larger problem of risk-taking behaviors on the part of children and youth. Appendixes include a survey sample and lists of participating foundations, geographic areas and the steering committee.

1026. Nason, John W. *Trustees and the Future of Foundations.* Washington: Council on Foundations, 1977.

Analysis of the role of foundation trustees in today's society, covering such topics as public accountability, professional staffs, and the 1969 Tax Reform Act.

1027. National Committee for Responsive Philanthropy. *Foundations and Public Information: Sunshine or Shadow?* Washington: National Committee for Responsive Philanthropy, 1980.

1028. National Committee for Responsive Philanthropy, comp. *An Inside Look at Foundations and United Ways.* Washington: National Committee for Responsive Philanthropy, [1985].

Compilation of articles provides perspectives on major grantmakers to aid fundraising strategists and encourage reform measure initiatives. While most of the articles originally appeared in the National Committee for Responsive Philanthropy's *Grantsmanship Center News*, several articles from other journals and newspapers have been added to more fully cover the important issues. Articles are grouped under topics such as: foundations, innovation, and changing the status quo; local foundations: are they different from national foundations in what they fund? how they give?; funding the women's movement; funding hispanics; foundations' accountability to the public: is it important?; the "brewing storm" of criticism against the United Way during the late 1970s; competition with United Ways: prospects, rationale and growth; and one reaction to competition—United Way donor option programs.

1029. National Committee for Responsive Philanthropy. *Introduction to Foundation and Public Information: Sunshine or Shadow? A Study of the Public Information Accountability of the Country's Largest Foundations.* Washington: National Committee for Responsive Philanthropy, 1980.

1030. National Committee on Community Foundations. *Community Trusts or Foundations: United States and Canada. Status of 1949.* New York: National Committee on Community Foundations, 1949.

1031. *National Community Foundations Mental Health Project: Final Report.* Chicago: National Community Foundations, 1981.

1032. National Council on Community Foundations. *National Council on Community Foundations Meeting.* Highland Park, Ill.: National Council on Community Foundations, 1959.

1033. National Council on Community Foundations. *National Council on Community Foundations Meeting.* Highland Park, Ill.: National Council on Community Foundations, 1960.

1034. "The National Grantmaker Networks. Part 1." *Corporate Philanthropy Report* 2 (July 1986): 4+.

1035. "The National Grantmaker Networks. Part 2." *Corporate Philanthropy Report* 2 (August 1986): 4-7.

Directory lists name, address, phone number and description of the topics which concern grantmaker affinity groups (e.g., Grantmakers in Health, Foundations in Film and Video).

1036. Nee, David M., and Dianne Metzger Bracco. *Grantmaking for the Elderly: An Analysis of Foundation Expenditures, 1978-1982.* New York: Florence V. Burden Foundation, 1986.

Prepared by the Florence V. Burden Foundation, this report provides timely information on the field of foundation expenditures for the elderly, including a detailed overview of grant monies in eight program areas (health care; social services; non-medical housing; education and recreation; volunteer programs; employment and retirement programs; public policy,

1037. Nelson, Ralph L. "Economic Research Sponsored by Private Foundations." *American Economic Review* 106 (May 1966): 519-29.

1038. Nelson, Ralph L. *The Investment Policies of Foundations.* New York: Russell Sage Foundation, 1967.

1039. Nelson, Ralph L. *The Investment Policies of Foundations.* Japanese ed. New York: Russell Sage Foundation, 1967.

1040. Neuhoff, Klaus. *Amerikanische Stiftungen; Organisation, Kapitalverhaltnisse und Arbeitsweise.* (American foundations; their organization, financial relations, and modes of operation). Baden-Baden, West Germany: Nomos Verlagsgesellschaft, 1968.

1041. "New Aging Foundation Emphasizes Senior-Led Groups." *Foundation Giving Watch* 9 (July 1984): 4.

1042. New Hampshire. Office of the Attorney General. *Directory of Charitable Funds in New Hampshire.* 3rd ed. Concord, N.H.: New Hampshire Office of the Attorney General, 1976.

Based on 1974 and 1975 records in the New Hampshire Attorney General's Office. Updated with cumulative, annual supplement published in June. Main section arranged alphabetically by foundation; entries include statement of purpose and officers; no sample grants. Indexes of geographical areas when restricted, and of purposes when not geographically restricted.

1043. New World Foundation. *Democracy in America: Towards Greater Participation.* New York: New World Foundation.

Presents a compendium of viewpoints from a 1983 conference on the future of voter participation efforts.

1044. New York Regional Association of Grantmakers, and Grantmakers in Health. *The AIDS Crisis: Challenges and Opportunities for Grantmakers.* New York: Health Services Improvement Fund, 1985.

1045. New York Regional Association of Grantmakers. *Membership Roster.* New York: New York Regional Association of Grantmakers, 1988.

Directory of New York Regional Association of Grantmakers member organizations. Member organization profile includes grantmaker name, address, telephone number, principal funding areas, and staff listing with titles. Also contains NYRAG Board of Directors list with names, titles, addresses and telephone numbers; NYRAG Committees list with names, titles, addresses and telephone numbers; Regional Associations of Grantmakers list with association name, address, contact person and telephone number; Professional Organizations and Affinity Groups list with organization name, address, contact person and telephone number. The indexes contained in the directory are: *List of Principal Funding Areas, Index of Principal Funding Areas* and *Index of Names of Individuals.*

1046. New York University School of Continuing Education and Extension Services. *Charitable Foundations Conference.* New York: New York University School of Continuing Education and Extension Services, 1965.

1047. New York University School of Continuing Education and Extension Services. *Charitable Foundations Conference.* New York: New York University School of Continuing Education and Extension Services, 1971.

1048. New York University School of Continuing Education and Extension Services. *Charitable Foundations Conference.* New York: New York University School of Continuing Education and Extension Services, 1973.

1049. New York University School of Continuing Education and Extension Services. *Charitable Foundations Conference.* New York: New York University School of Continuing Education and Extension Services, 1969.

1050. Nielsen, Waldemar A. *The Big Foundations.* Twentieth Century Fund Study. New York: Columbia University Press, 1972.

The "big foundations" are those with assets in excess of $100 million in 1972, and there are thirty-three of them in this book. Nielsen is impatient with the tone of most literature about foundations—"the self-congratulatory output of foundations themselves; and the ill-informed screeds of the Old Right on one extreme, the New Left on the other, and the neo-Know-Nothings like George Wallace in between." His book is an attempt at "plain honest talk" about foundations. In addition to turning his irreverent and critical eye on each of the big foundations, Nielsen discusses the setting and scope of foundation philanthropy, with attention to the then-recent Tax Reform Act of 1969, as well as a general look at patterns, processes, and performance. He also explores the interaction and relation of foundations to government and concludes with an exhortation for foundations to undertake self-reformation and self-renewal in response to growing and legitimate criticisms of their practices and policies.

1051. Nielsen, Waldemar A. *The Golden Donors: A New Anatomy of the Great Foundations.* New York: E.P. Dutton, 1985.

Nielsen examines the recent histories of America's thirty-six largest foundations, those with assets in excess of $250 million. After setting up the political and social context for their development and operation, Nielsen takes an often critical look at each foundation's programs and social impact. He usually focuses on the roles of institutional leaders in shaping them, for ill or good. He conveys strikingly the differences between the foundations and the forces of dominant personalities—whether of donor, board member, or chief executive—in determining foundation policy. After documenting some discernible patterns among the group, Nielsen calls on foundations to take advantage of their unique role by displaying greater initiative and creativity in recognizing and responding to critical social needs on a national and international level. He concludes with a set of recommendations. The book is engaging and easy to read, if not of traditional scholarly quality.

1052. Noe, Lee, ed. *The Foundation Grants Index.* 1970-1989. New York: Foundation Center, 19—.

The Foundation Grants Index provides access to the funding interests of major foundations by subject area, geographic focus, types of support, and the types of organizations which receive grants. It is one of the most valuable resources for grantseekers, grantmakers, and all others interested in identifying the current funding priorities of the nation's largest foundations, covering 43,032 grants of $5,000 or more awarded by 473 foundations. These grants have a total value of $2.58 billion, representing approximately forty-three percent of the total grant dollars awarded by private foundations in 1987. Designed as a current awareness service, both the bi-monthly issues and the annual volume of the *Foundation Grants Index* enable grantseekers and grantmakers to identify the current giving interests of foundations by subject and geographic focus, types of organizations funded, population groups served, and types of support awarded. The *Index* does not cover grants made directly to individuals, grants for projects managed directly by foundations, or grants awarded to other private or community foundations.

1053. Norris, Joan. "The Team Approach." *Foundation News* 25 (January-February 1984): 54-7.

1054. Northern California Grantmakers. *Buck Trust Trial: Copies of the Expert Witnesses Statements.* San Francisco: Northern California Grantmakers, 1986.

Contains statements of experts called by the San Francisco Foundation, Marin County, John E. Cook, California State Attorney General, and forty-six objector-beneficiaries.

1055. Northern California Grantmakers. *Buck Trust Trial: Copies of the Trial Briefs Submitted by Various Parties to the Suit.* San Francisco: Northern California Grantmakers, 1986.

Contains trial briefs submitted by John E. Cook; Wells Fargo, N.A.; forty-six objector-beneficiaries; California State Attorney General; Marin County; and San Francisco Foundation.

1056. Northern California Grantmakers. *Buck Trust Trial: Judgement and Statement of Decision in Buck Trust Case.* San Francisco: Northern California Grantmakers, 1986.

1057. Northern California Grantmakers. *Buck Trust Trial: Text of Agreement.* San Francisco: Northern California Grantmakers, 1986.

Complete transcript of the Buck agreement reprinted from the Marin Independent Journal, 26 July 1985. Orders granting petition of the San Francisco Foundation to resign as distributor trustee, for appointment of successor distributor trustee, and for appointment of special master.

1058. Odendahl, Teresa Jean, and Catherine Sullivan. "America's Wealth and the Future of Foundations." *Foundation News* 27 (March-April 1986): 22-9.

Study conducted by the Council on Foundations and the Yale University's Program on Nonprofit Organizations found that the formation rate of independent foundations has been falling in the 1980s. The authors suggest that complex legal guidelines and tax laws have made foundations an unfavorable choice for investment. The motivations of foundation donors, their views on philanthropy, and historical data on the establishment of foundations since 1910 is presented.

1059. Odendahl, Teresa Jean, ed. *America's Wealthy and the Future of Foundations.* New York: Foundation Center, 1987.

Co-sponsored by the Council on Foundations and the Yale University Program on Non-Profit Organizations, Odendahl and a team of multi-disciplinary scholars and researchers conducted surveys and interviews with foundation executives, advisors to the wealthy, and the wealthy themselves to determine whether America's wealthy are continuing to use the private foundation as a charitable vehicle in the 1980s. By bringing different perspectives to bear on the the issue of the apparent declining popularity of foundations among the wealthy, the research provides a greater understanding of foundation birth, development and death, examines historical trends in the formation and growth of foundations of all sizes (including legislation pertinent to the field), matches estate and income tax returns to understand how charitable giving patterns during donors' lifetimes compare with their bequests and in general throws light on the charitable decision-making by persons of wealth. Bibliography.

1060. Odendahl, Teresa Jean, and Elizabeth Trocolli Boris. "A Delicate Balance: Foundation Board-Staff Relations." *Foundation News* 24 (May-June 1983): 34+.

1061. Odendahl, Teresa Jean, Elizabeth Trocolli Boris, and Arlene Kaplan Daniels. *Working in Foundations: Career Patterns of Women and Men.* New York: Foundation Center, 1985.

Reports the results of a unique study on the career and employment patterns of foundation officers and trustees, by gender. The study includes relative salary information, an analysis of the structure of foundation employment, a look at recruitment and career paths, and a discussion of problems women face combining foundation work and personal life. In most instances, the study's findings reflect general societal trends—for instance, in foundation work as in many other occupations, women earn sixty to seventy percent of the salaries of men in comparable positions. Along with statistical data, the report is peppered with excerpts from extensive interviews of both women and men in the foundation world on such topics as job satisfaction, management style, relations with trustees, titles, and more. The book is a good source of information about working in foundations, as well as a comparative study of the roles, responsibilities, and rewards of women and men in the field. Brief bibliography.

1062. Odendahl, Teresa Jean, Elizabeth Trocolli Boris, and Arlene Kaplan Daniels. *Working in Foundations: Career Patterns of Women and Men.* Japanese ed. New York: Foundation Center, 1985.

Japanese edition.

1063. O'Donnell, Suzanna, and Kim Klein, eds. *A Guide to Funders in Central Appalachia and the Tennessee Valley.* Knoxville, Tenn.: Appalachian Community Fund, 1988.

Guide, funded by the Mary Reynolds Babcock Foundation, which lists nearly 500 funders which give grants in the geographical region that includes northern Alabama, northern Georgia, eastern Kentucky, western North Carolina, southeastern Virginia, and the entire states of Mississippi, Tennessee, and West Virginia. The directory begins with a section on *How to Write a Grant Proposal* which includes a sample proposal and a companion cassette tape. The audiotape *How to Write a Proposal* was produced by the Carpetbag Theatre. From the several thousand foundations operating in the region, the compilers included those which met the criteria of: 1) annual grantmaking of $25,000 or assets of $500,000, and 2) a willingness to consider proposals from organizations or groups not previously funded. (Businesses and corporations are not listed unless they have their own foundation.) In addition to these foundations, religious organizations as well as foundations outside Appalachia which make grants and revolving loan funds in the region are listed in Sections 3, 4, and 5. The guide is indexed alphabetically, by interest areas, and by funders grouped within interest areas. Also included is a bibliography and a listing of the Foundation Center research collections within the region.

1064. Ohio. Attorney General's Office. *Charitable Foundations Directory of Ohio.* 8th ed. Columbus, Ohio: Attorney General's Office, 1987.

Directory compiled from the registration forms and annual reports of the 1,800 grantmaking charitable organizations in Ohio which represent $3.4 billion in assets and $262 million in grants. The basic information in the directory includes name of foundation, address, contact person, and telephone number; restrictions; purpose (designated with a purpose code); total assets; year of latest Attorney General's report; total grants awarded for latest year; and the Ohio Attorney General's trust number. The directory contains both a purpose (subject areas) and a county index.

1065. Olson, Lynn. "Foundations Saying 'We All Have a Stake' in Schools." *Education Week* 7 (24 February 1988): 1+.

Examines the rising foundation interest in precollegiate education, providing examples of initiatives which show that the plight of public schools has found a place on the agenda of many foundations and corporations. Also discusses many of the factors that could ruin philanthropic initiatives in education, such as the difficulties involved in the evaluation process, which frustrates foundation officials and leads to the disruptive shifting of support priorities.

1066. Olson, Stan, ed. *Directory of New and Emerging Foundations.* New York: Foundation Center, 1988.

Provides descriptive entries for 768 foundations which have met the criteria for inclusion in the *Foundation Directory* since the eleventh edition was published in 1987. Thus, these foundations all have $1 million in assets and/or gave $100,000 or more in grants during the latest year of record. *New* foundations are those with establishment dates in the 1980s (comprising 299 of the 768 foundations described); data for new foundations has never before appeared in a Foundation Center publication. *Emerging* foundations, while established earlier, have only recently increased their assets or expanded their giving programs to meet the criteria for inclusion in future editions of the *Foundation Directory*. Entry descriptions contain the address and phone number of the foundation; principal donor(s); financial data on assets, gifts received, expenditures, and grants made; a statement of purpose and activities; application information; and the names and titles of officers, principal administrators, and trustees. Indexed by donors, officers and trustees; geographic location (with foundations awarding grants on a national or regional level indicated in bold type); types of support offered (such as consulting services, scholarship funds, and program-related investments); subject (broad categories of giving emphasis); and foundation name.

1067. Olson, Stan, and Natividad S.H. del Pilar, eds. *New York State Foundations: A Comprehensive Directory.* New York: Foundation Center, 1988.

Comprehensive directory of over 4,500 independent, company-sponsored, and community foundations which are currently active in New York State and which have awarded grants of one dollar or more in the latest fiscal year. Arranged alphabetically by New York counties (including the five boroughs of New York City). A separate section includes ninety-seven out-of-state foundations with funding interests in New York State. Each foundation entry includes information on address; telephone numbers; principal donor(s); assets; gifts received; expenditures, including dollar value and number of grants paid (with largest and smallest grant paid indicated); fields of interest; types of support; geographic preference; limitations; publications; application information; names of officers, principal administrators, trustees or directors; employer identification number (useful in ordering copies of the foundation's 990-PF); and a listing of sample grants, when available, to indicate the foundation's giving pattern. Indexed by donors, officers, and trustees; geographic location; types of support; broad giving interests; and foundation name.

1068. Ottinger, Richard. *The Role of Private Foundations in Our Society in the 1970's.* Unpublished, 1971.

1069. Paley, Martin A. "Learning from Foundation Reports: The San Francisco Foundation." *Philanthropy Monthly* 18 (January 1985): 38-9.

1070. Pattillo, Manning M., Jr. "Foundations and the Private College." *Liberal Education* 51 (December 1965): 1-8.

1071. Pattillo, Manning M., Jr. "The Role of Foundations in the Future Financing of Higher Education." *A.G.B. Reports* 10 (July-August 1968): 3-11.

1072. Penick, George. "Why Not a Program-Related Investment?" *Council on Foundations Newsletter* (June 1981): 17.

1073. Peterson, Peter G. *Statement of Peter G. Peterson, Chairman, Commission on Foundations and Private Philanthropy before the Senate Finance Committee.* Unpublished, 1969.

1074. "Philanthropy Goes to Congress." *Foundation News* 24 (May-June 1983): 12+.

1075. Pierson, John. "Creating the Right Match." *Foundation News* 27 (July-August 1986): 28-31.

Explanation of assistance given to the controversial Massachusetts Commonwealth Employment Forum by private and corporate foundations.

1076. Pifer, Alan. *The Foundation in the Year 2000.* Foundation Library Center Occasional Papers, no. 1. New York: Foundation Library Center, 1968.

1077. Pifer, Alan. *The Management of Carnegie Corporation.* Unpublished, 1977.

A paper focusing primarily on the organization, administration, and policies of Carnegie Corporation, from its founding early in the twentieth century to the present.

1078. Pifer, Alan. *Speaking Out: Reflections on Thirty Years of Foundation Work*. Washington: Council on Foundations, 1984.

Essay written by the former president of Carnegie Corporation of New York for the 35th Annual conference of the Council on Foundations.

1079. Pifer, Alan. *Summary. Senate Finance Committee's Subcommittee on Foundations*. Unpublished, [198?].

1080. Piton Foundation. *Program-Related Investments: A Primer*. Resources for Grantmakers Series. Washington: Council on Foundations, 1986.

Contains chapters on the elements of program-related investment (PRI) (e.g., income nature, legislative activities, safeguards, etc.); forms of investment; benefits of PRI; deciding to establish a PRI program; program management suggestions; and federal income tax implications. Appendixes contain a listing of foundations making PRI's, selected projects benefiting from PRI's, case studies of foundation PRI's, standardized documentation, a resource list, and bibliography.

1081. Playboy Foundation. *Network of Change-Oriented Foundations*. Chicago: Playboy Foundation, 1978.

1082. Plinio, Alex J. "Strategic Foundation Plan Requires Thoughtful Process." *Fund Raising Management* 15 (April 1984): 83.

1083. Powell, Daniel. *John Hay Whitney Foundation: The John Hay Fellows*. Vol. 2. New York: John Hay Whitney Foundation, 1972.

1084. Price, Don K. *Universities, Foundations, and Government*. Chicago: University of Chicago, 1957.

1085. Price Waterhouse. *A Survey of Financial Reporting and Accounting Practices of Private Foundations*. New York: Price Waterhouse & Co., 1983.

1086. "Principles and Practices Prescribed for Foundations." *Philanthropy Monthly* 19 (September 1986): 5-14.

Chronicles the development of the Council on Foundations' *Recommended Principles and Practices for Effective Grantmaking* (RP&P); insists that the standards impose a degree of orthodoxy which destroys the essential diversity of foundations; and questions the Council's requirement that all members subscribe to the RP&P, an approach considered to be as coercive as a loyalty oath, and one that gives birth to the paradox of mandatory recommendations. Includes a reproduction of the eleven-point statement as issued by the Council on Foundations.

1087. Pritchett, Henry Smith. *The First Twenty Years of Carnegie Corporation*. New York: Carnegie Corporation of New York, 1931.

1088. "The Problem of Being the Ford Foundation." *Institutional Investor* 2 (November 1968): 37-41.

1089. "A Progress Report on the Filer Commission." *Philanthropy Monthly* (July 1975): 31-2.

1090. *Public Information Reporting by Tax-Exempt Private Foundations Needs More Attention by IRS*. Gaithersburg, Md.: U.S. General Accounting Office, 1983.

1091. Public Media Center. *Index of Progressive Funders*. Rev. ed. San Francisco: Public Media Center, 1985.

Reference book on over 130 grantmakers that support social change, including a separate section on religious funding for progressive concerns. Entries generally give a brief description of funding interests followed by a listing of recent grants. Application guidelines are not given. Index is cross-referenced by subject matter.

1092. Public Service Materials Center, comp. *Foundations That Send Their Annual Report. Book 2*. Washington: Public Service Materials Center, 1984.

1093. Public Service Materials Center, comp. *Survey of Grant Making Foundations with Assets of over $1,000,000 or Grants of over $100,000, 1983-84*. Washington: Public Service Materials Center, 1982.

1094. Putt, S. Gorley, ed. *Cousins and Strangers. Comments on America by Commonwealth Fund Fellows from Britain, 1946-1952*. Cambridge, Mass.: Harvard University Press, 1956.

1095. Radford, Neil A. *The Carnegie Corporation and the Development of American College Libraries, 1928-1941*. Chicago: American Library Association, 1984.

1096. Radock, Michael. "College and Foundations: Partners or Antagonists?" *College Management* 9 (May 1974): 26-8.

1097. Ramey, Gaile. *Foundation Profiles: A Guide to Foundation Giving in the Health Field*. Health Care Fundraising Series, no. 2. San Francisco: Western Consortium for the Health Professions, 1982.

1098. Raushenbush, Esther. *John Hay Whitney Foundation: Opportunity Fellows, Fulbright and Visiting Professors*. Vol. 1. New York: John Hay Whitney Foundation, 1972.

1099. Read, Patricia E., ed. *Foundation Fundamentals: A Guide for Grantseekers*. 3rd ed. New York: Foundation Center, 1986.

A primer designed for readers interested in understanding the world of foundations and foundation funding. The work is in two sections: the first describes the various types of foundations, the regulations that govern their activities, the relationship of foundations to other funding sources, and who gets foundation grants. The second section describes the information resources available and how grantseekeers can use them to learn about the foundations most likely to be interested in their proposals. The work offers an extensive bibliography, and detailed appendixes focusing on foundations and foundation funding.

1100. Read, Patricia E. *Foundations Today: Current Facts and Figures on Private Foundations.* 1981-1988. New York: Foundation Center, 19—.

Foundations Today brings together data drawn from the Center's publishing databases to provide a brief overview of the foundation world. Data drawn from *The National Data Book*, which includes information drawn from the Internal Revenue Service's computer files of information returns by organizations classified as private foundations; *The Foundation Directory*, which provides fiscal and program information on the nation's largest grantmaking foundations; and *The Foundation Grants Index*, which includes descriptions of grants of $5,000 and more reported by foundations to the Center. More complete analyses of the statistical data are provided in each of these three publications.

1101. Read, W. Harold. "Accounting: The University View." *Philanthropy Monthly* (July 1975): 23-9.

1102. Reed, Edward Bliss, ed. *The Commonwealth Fund Fellows and Their Impressions of America.* New York: Commonwealth Fund, 1932.

1103. Reed, Susan K. "Nuclear Anonymity." *Foundation News* 24 (January-February 1983): 42-9.

1104. Reeves, Thomas C., ed. *Foundations under Fire.* Ithaca, N.Y.: Cornell University Press, 1970.

Anthology of twenty-four articles presents a wide variety of viewpoints on the role and the strengths and weaknesses of private foundations in America.

1105. Reeves, Thomas C. *Freedom and the Foundation: The Fund for the Republic in the Era of McCarthyism.* New York: Alfred A. Knopf, 1969.

Reeves analyzes the development and operation of the Fund for the Republic, created by the Ford Foundation in 1952 to assist the promotion of national security based on freedom and justice—or, to combat McCarthyism. This small but extremely controversial foundation, primarily under the leadership of Robert Maynard Hutchins, generated much public outcry and condemnation from the far right with even its smallest grants. Hutchins' key role in the life of the fund is prominently examined, as are the actions of the boards, congressional committees, columnists, journalists, staff, and consultants who participated in the drama of its relatively brief life. This window on the formation and operation of an unusual kind of foundation—one of the first, if not the first, to examine public policy—adds an important dimension to the study of foundations.

1106. Reid, Dee, ed. *Oklahoma Foundations Directory.* Norman, Oklahoma: Philanthropic Resource Associates, 1986.

Contains descriptive information of 159 Oklahoma foundations. Entries include foundation name, emphasis of giving interest, funding of specific population groups, restrictions, tax year of financial data, assets, income, total grants, range, application process, trustees, contact name, address and telephone number. Indexes arranged by excluded and terminated foundations, areas of interest, city and name.

1107. Reilly, Raymond R., and Donald H. Skadder. *Private Foundations: The Payout Requirement...* Ann Arbor, Mich.: University of Michigan Press, 1981.

1108. Reilly, Robert T. "Annual Reports, 1983: Cautious and Colorful." *Ragan Report* (1 July 1984): 1+.

1109. Rhodes, Catherine. *Directory of Tarrant County Foundations.* Fort Worth, Tex.: Texas Christian University, 1984.

Based on 1982 and 1983 990-PF forms filed with the IRS and foundation questionnaires answered by approximately 115 foundations. Main section arranged alphabetically by foundation; entries include financial data, background and program interest, officers and trustees, types of support and geographic focus. Indexes of foundations, trustees and officers, types of support and fields of interest. Appendixes of foundations by asset amount and foundations by total grants.

1110. Richardson, Carol, and Judy Tye. *Directory of Dayton Area Grantmakers.* Dayton, Ohio: Junior League of Dayton, Ohio, 1983.

Based on 1980 through 1982 data. Main section arranged alphabetically by foundation; most entries include contact person, fields of interest and limitations, and total assets, total and number of grants. Section on *Applying for a Grant* and glossary of grantmaker terms. Alphabetical index and index of interests.

1111. Richman, Saul. "Annual Reports Key to Foundation World View." *Fund Raising Management* 13 (January 1983): 60+.

1112. Richman, Saul. "Community Foundations Vary from Private in Many Ways." *Fund Raising Management* 15 (April 1984): 80-1.

1113. Richman, Saul. "Disappointed, Large Foundation Dumps Higher Education." *Fund Raising Management* 16 (September 1985): 162+.

Describes the grantmaking decisions of the Fred Meyer Charitable Trust.

1114. Richman, Saul. "Foundations Answer the Economic Distress Call." *Fund Raising Management* 14 (July 1983): 68-9.

1115. Richman, Saul. "Foundations May Gain from Sun Belt Religious Wealth." *Fund Raising Management* 14 (June 1983): 56+.

1116. Richman, Saul. "Foundations Now Provide Grantees with Seminar Help." *Fund Raising Management* 16 (October 1985): 132+.

1117. Richman, Saul. "Philanthropy in Support of Democracy and Its Institutions." *NonProfit Times* 1 (May 1987): 23, 29.

Reports briefly on Elizabeth Boris' presentation at the Spring Research Forum and on the revised and expanded second edition of Thomas E. Broce's *Fund Raising* to gain insight into the giving priorities of the wealthy and their foundations. Having used their own intelligence and initiative to rise within the system, writes author Richman, the wealthy would be most responsive to programs that foster individual effort. Thus, Ms. Boris suggests that fundseekers pay more attention to democratic and community values rather than economic values. Mr. Broce advocates using the vast body of information available about foundations, their interests and behavior, because "foundation money continues to go to the few institutions willing to do the work required to gain their support." The article ends with an observation concerning the future of foundations, focusing on the rise of community foundations.

1118. Richman, Saul. *Public Information Handbook for Foundations.* Washington: Council on Foundations, 1973.

1119. Richman, Saul. "Region Foundation Councils Still Growing, Learning." *Fund Raising Management* 15 (June 1984): 96.

1120. Richman, Saul. "Risk-Taking Grantmakers Make Commendable Efforts." *Fund Raising Management* 15 (October 1984): 96.

1121. Richman, Saul. "There's More Work in Making Grants to Individuals." *Fund Raising Management* 16 (June 1985): 108+.

1122. Richman, Saul. "Try Innovative Giving, Despite Government Cuts." *Fund Raising Management* 14 (June 1983): 74.

1123. Richman, Saul. "Varied Scherman Foundation: A Broad Philanthropic Model." *Fund Raising Management* 14 (February 1984): 80-1.

1124. Richman, Saul. "With Cutbacks in the Air, Grantee Health Monitored." *Fund Raising Management* 16 (August 1985): 92+.

1125. Riley, Margaret. "Private Foundation Information Returns, 1982." *Statistics of Income Bulletin* 5 (Fall 1985): 1-27.

IRS study in the annual Statistics of Income (SOI) series which examines trends/changes in grantmaking activities and reporting patterns. Information is derived from an analysis of income data, charitable distributions, and legislative activity. A summary of major legislative events which affect private foundations, and statistical tables based on income data are included in the appendix.

1126. Riley, Margaret. "A Private Foundation Profile for 1983." *Statistics of Income Bulletin* 6 (Winter 1986-87): 11-24.

Statistical analysis of private foundations based on a sample of 1983 IRS Form 990-PF's filed for periods ending December 1983 through November 1984. (Nonexempt charitable trusts and other taxable foundations were excluded.) The sample was stratified based on size of total book value of assets and selected at rates that ranged from 0.7 percent to 100 percent. The 1,374 returns in the sample were drawn from an estimated population of 29,863. The study shows, among other facts, that in 1983, private foundation revenue increased by seventy-eight percent, attributable mainly to a 138 percent increase in sales of capital assets. An estimated 29,863 foundations spent $5.2 billion for philanthropic purposes. Of this amount, $4.4 billion comprised grants to tax-exempt organizations engaging in philanthropic activities. The paper includes seven pages of statistical tables, charts, a selected glossary of terms, and endnotes.

1127. Robb, Christina. "The Foundation behind the 'Genius Grants'." *Boston Globe Magazine* (13 April 1986): 12.

1128. "Robert Wood Johnson Identifies Emerging Health Issues." *Foundation Giving Watch* 4 (July 1984): 1-2.

1129. Roberts, David R. *New Ideas for Foundation Investments: Program-Related Loans.* Atlanta, Ga.: Southeastern Council of Foundations, [1980].

1130. Robinson, Anthony L. *Foundations That Support Roman Catholic Activities.* Washington: Campaign for Human Development U.S. Catholic Conference, 1984.

Directory of eighty foundations whose grantmaking activities suggest some preference for supporting Roman Catholic activities. All eighty foundations either held assets of $1 million or awarded $100,000 or more in grants. Entries include address, phone, contact person, type of assistance, primary areas of interest, application procedures, and examples of funded projects.

1131. Robinson, Marshall. "Private Foundations and Social Science Research." *Society* 21 (May-June 1984): 76-80.

1132. Rockefeller Foundation. *Directory of Fellowship Awards for the Years 1917-1950.* New York: Rockefeller Foundation, [1951].

1133. Rockefeller Foundation. *Directory of Fellowship Awards for the Years 1917-1970.* New York: Rockefeller Foundation, 1972.

1134. Roelofs, Joan. "Foundations and the Supreme Court." *Telos: A Quarterly Journal of Critical Thought* 62 (Winter 1984-1985): 59-87.

In a critical and provocative article, Roelofs examines the relationship between two elite institutions: foundations (in this case, Ford, Rockefeller, Carnegie, Sage, and Twentieth Century Fund) and the Supreme Court. She concentrates in particular on the ways in which major foundations influenced or attempted to influence Supreme Court decision-making, especially during a period of intense judicial activism, 1952-1975. In an unflinchingly harsh indictment of foundations, Roelofs lays at the basis of her argument the idea that the goals of foundations are "to preserve the power and wealth of the present ownership class and to make whatever social and political changes are necessary to insure this." She contends that the way foundations do this is through shaping public opinion—especially elite public opinion. Avenues of influence include financing—and thus control—of social science research; creation or support of research institutes, think tanks, etc., which produce supporting material or enter litigation; new programs in legal education; law reviews; legal aid; and public interest law firms, as well as direct contact with Supreme Court justices.

1135. Rogers, David E. "On Building a Foundation." *Foundation News* 28 (July-August 1987): 48-51.

Essay which gives readers an insider's look at foundation decisions, policies and procedures. Rogers, who served for fifteen years as president of the Robert Wood Johnson Foundation, discusses seven significant decisions which shaped the foundation. Rogers explains that the foundation devoted its resources to health and medical care, building its agenda not from groups, but from the concerns of the American public. Its resources were focused on narrow priorities and on the desired human outcome, not on the process of getting to the desired end. In addition, the foundation decided that it would keep its staff small and use outside experts (senior program consultants) to manage large multi-site programs. The foundation frequently formed partnerships to share or co-sponsor health care programs on major problems. It also made the decision to have "independent objective evaluations as part of almost every...national program." The evaluation procedure, states Rogers, was "perhaps our most widely recognized contribution to modern philanthropy."

1136. Roisman, Lois. "Growing by Leaps and Towns." *Foundation News* 24 (November-December 1983): 50-3.

1137. Roisman, Lois. "The Other Bottom Line: One Central Question Determines Whether a Project Is Right for Your Foundation: Does It Build Community?" *Foundation News* 29 (May-June 1988): 68-69.

Author Roisman takes the psychological idea that certain conditions must be present in a therapeutic setting in order for a person to grow and thrive and applies it to the community foundation level to assess grantmaking. In this framework a grant is seen to be contributing to the necessary conditions for a thriving community if it creates trust (between disparate groups, for example), serves as an example for others to model, builds respect and understanding in the community, or actually assists individuals in becoming productive citizens, rather than merely alleviating the symptoms of their poverty.

1138. Roisman, Lois. "Philanthropic Entrepreneurs." *Foundation News* 55 (March-April 1984): 55-7.

1139. Rooks, Charles S. *Foundation Philanthropy in the Southeast.* Atlanta, Ga.: Southeastern Council of Foundations, [1977].

1140. Rosenwald, Julius. "Principles of Public Giving." *Atlantic Monthly* (May 1929): 599-606.

Rosenwald, a philanthropist, argues vehemently against the practice of perpetuating endowments, in which trustees of foundations, educational institutions, and other organizations are only able to spend income from endowments, and not principal, for purposes fixed by the donor. He cites well-intentioned but disastrous decisions by the likes of Benjamin Franklin and Alexander Hamilton, each of whom established funds in perpetuity for purposes that ceased to exist not long after their deaths. Rosenwald cautions that it is impossible for donors to predict the needs of the future, and too often their largesse ceases to do the good for which it was intended because circumstances change. He also argues against the policy of restricting expenditures to income from endowments, with the claim that many opportunities to do good are lost due to lack of faith in the trustee's ability to dispense portions of principal wisely.

1141. Rosenwald, Julius. "The Trend Away from Perpetuities." *Atlantic Monthly* 146 (December 1930): 741-49.

1142. *The Rotch Travelling Scholarship.* Cambridge, Mass.: Rotch Travelling Scholarship, 1980.

1143. Rothmeyer, Karen. "Citizen Scaife." *Columbia Journalism Review* (July-August 1981): 41+.

1144. Rudy, William H. *The Foundations: Their Use and Abuse.* Washington: Public Affairs Press, 1970.

1145. Rusk, Dean. *The Role of the Foundation in American Life.* Claremont, Calif.: Claremont University College, 1961.

1146. Russell, John M. *Giving and Taking: Across the Foundation Desk.* New York: Teachers College Press, 1977.

1147. Russell and Associates, Robert, comp. *J.M. Foundation. Final Report Evaluation.* Unpublished, 1986.

1148. Sabath, Donald. "Private Foundations Keep Secrecy Lid on Despite Law." *Cleveland Plain Dealer* (19 May 1974): B-1.

1149. Salamon, Lester M. *Managing Foundation Assets: An Analysis of Foundation Investment and Spending Policies and Performance.* Unpublished, 1987.

Results of a Council on Foundations project which presents for the first time an empirical examination of the way a cross-section of foundations manage their assets and expenditures over a reasonable period of time (a six year span, from 1979 to 1984). It is hoped that such a solid body of data on foundation investment management and on the relationship between investment performance and payout activity will prevent legislative enactments against the foundation community based, like the Tax Reform Act of 1969, on a handful of deplorable examples of misconduct or bad judgement. Organized into four chapters: Chapter 1 is the introduction; Chapter 2 focuses on the investment management process, examining the roles and responsibilities of the various participants involved in foundation investment activities, identifying the goals and strategies foundations seem to be pursuing, and seeking to determine whether these goals and strategies have changed as a consequence of the 1981 change in the payout requirement; Chapter 3 analyzes the actual investment performance of foundations, reporting rates of return achieved by the cross-section of foundations during the period of study, and assessing this against a "control fund;" and Chapter 4 addresses the relationship between payout rate and return rate. Among the conclusions: the data provide support for some of the arguments advanced on behalf of the change in the payout requirement in 1981, as the previous requirement produced a payout rate greater than could be sustained without cutting into the real value of foundation assets; smaller foundations were most heavily affected by these pressures, and they are the ones most likely to benefit from the 1981 change.

1150. Salkind, Milton. *Bay Area Foundation History.* Berkeley, Calif.: University of California-Berkeley, 1976.

1151. *San Diego County Foundation Directory.* San Diego, Calif.: San Diego Community Foundation, 1985.

Based on 990-PF returns filed with the IRS for sixty-seven foundations and fifty-six corporations. Main sections arranged alphabetically. Entries include contact person, type of support, range of grants, total amount and number of grants, application procedures and directors; no date of financial information indicated.

1152. Sanders, Lawrence. *The Sixth Commandment.* New York: G.P. Putnam, 1979.

1153. Sandler, Bernice Resnick. "How Impact Statements Can Help Foundations Assess Programs for Their Impact on Women and Girls: Or, How to Tell If You Are Really Being Fair to Women and Girls." *Women and Foundations/Corporate Philanthropy* 2 (Fall 1984): 1-4.

1154. Savage, Howard J. *Fruit of an Impulse: Forty-Five Years of the Carnegie Foundation, 1905-1950.* New York: Harcourt, Brace, 1953.

This is a history of the Carnegie Foundation for the Advancement of Teaching, founded by Andrew Carnegie, from the events that preceded its inception in 1905 to 1950. Carnegie established the foundation to provide a pension fund for professors in colleges, universities, and technical schools in the United States and Canada. The official text of his letter of gift stated: "I hope this Fund may do much for the cause of higher education and to remove a source of deep and constant anxiety to the poorest paid and yet one of the highest of all professions." He donated $10 million to this purpose. This detailed and thorough history is written by a member of the foundation's staff.

1155. Scanlan, Joanne B., and Eugene A. Scanlan, eds. *A Lexicon for Community Foundations.* Resources for Grantmakers. Washington: Council on Foundations, 1988.

Lexicon of terms commonly used by community foundations and the various sectors they relate to, including the legal and accounting professions and the nonprofit world, serves as a useful reference tool for new staff and governing board members of existing community foundations or those associated with newly-formed community foundations.

1156. Scanlan, Joanne B. *Status of Community Foundations in 1984.* Washington: Council on Foundations, 1986.

Study examines trends and prevalent issues relating to both community foundations and private philanthropy in general. Since the 1977 Council survey, community foundations became more diverse in their goals and abilities, with greatly increased assets and much more complex organizational structures.

1157. Schafran, Lynn Hecht. *Welcome to the Club! (No Women Need Apply). Removing Financial Support from Private Clubs That Discriminate against Women.* New York: Women and Foundations/Corporate Philanthropy, 1981.

1158. Schardt, Arlie. "The Problem That Knows No Boundaries." *Foundation News* 26 (July-August 1985): 44+.

1159. Schardt, Arlie. "A Unique Calling." *Foundation News* 26 (May-June 1985): 36+.

1160. Schlesinger, Bob. "Foundations: How Charity Molds Cleveland." *Cleveland Press* 104 (27 December 1981): A-1, A-10.

1161. Schlesinger, Bob. "Local Foundations: Their Dollar Power and Impact." *Cleveland Press* 104 (27 December 1981): A-10.

1162. Schrage, Michael. "Rockefeller's Magnificent Amateur: Peter Goldmark Mastered Budgets and Bridges on the Job. Now He's Going to Run the Rockefeller Foundation." *Manhattan, Inc.* 5 (August 1988): 60-5.

Traces the energetic public-service career of Peter Goldmark, recently named president of the Rockefeller Foundation, from his Harvard days to Massachusetts's secretary of Human Services to executive director of the Port Authority; analyzes the current position of the Foundation and intimates at what to expect from it under the leadership of Goldmark.

1163. Schwartz, John J. "Filer Commission Paved Philanthropic Road." *Fund Raising Management* (June 1980): 22-7.

1164. Scrivner, Gary N. "IRS Eases Foundation Rules for Pass through Foundations." *Philanthropy Monthly* (May 1970): 15-7.

1165. Scully, Malcolm G. "Foundations Urged to Help Colleges Cope with Financial Hard Times." *Chronicle of Higher Education* 26 (16 March 1983): 1+.

1166. *Selected Press Coverage: Philanthropy.* Unpublished, 1986.

1167. Seltzer, Michael. *Meeting the Challenge: Foundation Responses to Acquired Immune Deficiency Syndrome.* Ford Foundation Report. New York: Foundation Center, 1987.

Using information from interviews with over 100 foundation board and staff members who have awarded AIDS-related grants (amassed as part of a research project initiated by the Ford Foundation), Seltzer addresses the past, present, and future roles of philanthropic institutions during the epidemic. He examines early foundation response to the disease; the factors contributing to their participation or lack thereof; what efforts are currently underway; and the funding outlook for the future. Appendixes include a list of foundations with the number of grants and total amounts given to AIDS initiatives.

1168. Seybold, Peter J. *The Development of American Political Sociology: A Case Study of the Ford Foundation's Role in the Production of Knowledge.* Reprint. Ann Arbor, Mich.: United Microfilms International, 1978.

1169. Shakely, Jack. "Community Foundations." *Trusts & Estates* (February 1982): 30-2.

1170. Shanahan, Eileen. "Report by Philanthropic Group Proposes Ways to Spur Giving." *New York Times* (3 December 1975): 16.

1171. Shanahan, Eileen. "U.S. Seeks Curbs on Foundations." *New York Times* (9 February 1965): 1, 18.

1172. Shapiro, Harvey D. "Now Foundations Are Broadening Their Social Aims." *Institutional Investor* (August 1972): 69 80-1, 83-4.

1173. Shaplen, Ropert. *Toward the Well-Being of Mankind: Fifty Years of the Rockefeller Foundation.* New York: Doubleday, 1964.

1174. Shellow, Jill, ed. *Grantseekers Guide.* Mt. Kisco, N.Y.: Moyer Bell, 1985.

Directory of grantmakers which award grants to nonprofit organizations advocating social and economic justice programs. Describes, for the most part, foundation and corporate grantmakers with assets in excess of $1 million or grantmaking budgets of $100,000 or more per year. Entries include contact person, purpose, areas of interest, financial data, application procedures, grant limitations, and publications. In addition to directory listings, includes several chapters with useful how-to information.

1175. Shepard, Carla. *Proposal for a Study of the Role of Foundations in the Third Sector.* Unpublished.

1176. Shirley, Anita Gunn. *Grantseeking in North Carolina: A Guide to Foundation and Corporate Giving.* Raleigh, N.C.: North Carolina Center for Public Policy Research, 1985.

Based on 1981 through 1983 990-PF returns filed with the IRS and questionnaires answered by 589 foundations. Main sections arranged by type of foundation; entries include financial data, trustees, sample grants, limitations and application procedures. Alphabetical index of foundations and corporations; indexes by county, funding interest and index of officers, directors and trustees. Appendixes on proposal writing and corporate fundraising.

1177. "Shubert Foundation in Routine State Review." *New York Times* (1 August 1985): C18.

1178. Sillars, Edith E. "A Close Look at a RAG." *Grants Magazine* 6 (December 1983): 234-36.

1179. Simons, Gustave. "Start Your Own Medical Foundation." *Medical Economics* (18 November 1963): 213-242.

1180. Sloss, Frank. *Bay Area Foundation History.* Berkeley, Calif.: University of California-Berkeley, 1976.

1181. Smith, Craig. "A Modern Day Noah's Ark." *Foundation News* 26 (January-February 1985): 14-23. Profiles the Nature Conservancy.

1182. Smith, Craig. "Private Help for Public Schools." *Foundation News* 26 (September-October 1985): 42+.

1183. Smith, Datus C., Jr. *Foundations and Scholarly Publishing: A Working Paper for the National Enquiry into Scholarly Communication.* Unpublished, 1977.

1184. Smith, Nick L. "Foundation Support of Evaluation." *Evaluation Review* 9 (April 1985): 215-39.

1185. Smith, Norvel L. "Learning from Foundation Reports: The Rosenberg Foundation." *Philanthropy Monthly* 18 (January 1985): 38.

1186. Smollar, David. "Striving for Peace: Symbolic Doves at Hiroshima Strengthen Kroc's Resolve." *Los Angeles Times* (7 August 1985).

Describes Joan Kroc, head of Kroc Foundation, and her campaign against nuclear weapons.

1187. Social Service Planning Corporation. *Private Sector Giving, Greater Worcester Area: A Directory and Index.* Worcester, Mass.: Social Service Planning Corp., 1987.

Main section arranged alphabetically by foundation; entries include financial data, contact person, and a listing of award recipients with the dollar amount each received. Categorical index chart gives access to the foundation entries by their funding interest.

1188. Social Service Planning Corporation. *Private Sector Giving Report: Greater Worcester Area.* Worcester, Mass.: Social Service Planning Corp., 1983.

1189. Solow, Carol. *An Analysis of North Carolina Foundations.* Unpublished, 1982.

1190. *The Source: A Directory of Cincinnati Foundations.* Cincinnati, Ohio: Junior League of Cincinnati, 1985.

Based primarily on 1982 and 1983 990-PF returns filed with the IRS and questionnaires answered by 259 foundations. Main section arranged alphabetically by foundation; entries may include financial data, sample grants, area of interest, officers and trustees and application information. Index of areas of interest.

1191. South Dakota State Library, comp. *The South Dakota Grant Directory.* Pierre, S.Dak.: South Dakota State Library, 1989.

Directory produced by the South Dakota State Library contains information on over 300 grantmaking institutions in South Dakota, including foundations, state government programs, corporate giving programs, and South Dakota scholarships. Also list major foundations located outside the state which have shown an interest in South Dakota, and non-grantmaking foundations. Descriptions of grantmakers include name, address, and purpose statements, along with information on finances, application requirements, and eligibility/limitations. Indexed by subject and name, and appendixes contain definitions of foundation types, an annotated bibliography of materials relating to foundations, student funding, grant research and proposal writing.

1192. Southern California Association for Philanthropy, comp. *The Grantmaking Process: The Basics. Workshop Handbook.* Los Angeles: Southern California Association for Philanthropy, [1987].

Collection of materials compiled as a workshop handbook for grantmakers. The handbook contains basic information for grantmakers on a wide variety of topics such as regional associations, ethics, grant evaluations, financial analysis procedure, and two glossaries of terms. Although not produced for grantseekers, the materials provide invaluable information concerning grant requirements through the eyes of the grantmakers. Articles of particular note for the grantseeker include John Pierson's *A Little Focus Goes A Long Way*, on the focusing of giving; the Atlantic Richfield Foundation's *Application Procedures*; Teresa Odendahl and Elizabeth Boris' *The Grantmaking Process*, which relates the harsh reality of a proposal's review process; Richard Magat's *Decisions! Decisions!*, a hands-on article describing the grantmakers pre-grant assessment; *A Grant For Every Purpose* by Willard J. Hertz and Carol K. Kurzig is an overview of the diverse forms that grants can take; and *Getting To Know You* by Martha G. Butt, outlines the post-grant evaluation. Additional assistance to the grantseeker can be obtained from the listings of *Questions For Pre-Grant Evaluation; Materials Useful in Proposal Evaluation; Sample Proposal Evaluation Process;* and Michael Edwards' *Financial Statement Analysis for Foundations.* The handbook is unpaged, there is no index but the workshop items have been grouped in six sections listed in a table of contents.

1193. Southern Resource Center. *The Guide to Texas Foundations.* Dallas, Tex.: Dallas Public Library, 1980.

1194. Spear, Paula Reading, ed. *Indiana Foundations: A Directory.* Indianapolis, Ind.: Central Research Systems, 1985.

Based on 1983 and 1984 990-PF returns filed with the IRS and information supplied by 288 foundations. Main section arranged alphabetically by foundation; entries include officers, areas of interest, sample grants, high and low grants. Indexes of financial criteria, subjects, counties, and officers. Appendixes of restricted foundations, foundations for student assistance only, and foundations without funding.

1195. Spivack, Sydney Shepard. *Foundations and Accountability: A Preliminary Exploration of American Philanthropic Foundations and Their Attitudes with Respect to Accountability.* Unpublished, 1953.

1196. Staecker, Delmar. "The Beryl Buck Estate and the Future of Philanthropy." *Fund Raising Management* 16 (May 1985): 30+.

1197. Stamp, Tom. "Searching for Excellence." *Foundation News* 28 (July-August 1987): 36-9.

Profiles the 1986-1987 Wilmer Shields Rich Awards, founded to promote excellence in annual reports published by foundations of all types—community, corporate, independent, and operating—and to stress the importance of annual reports to grantmakers' public accountability. Reports are judged on six criteria with a point value ranging from ten to twenty-five points: provision of helpful information for grantseekers (25 points); provision of other helpful information for public accountability (25); readability (substance, style and language) (10); graphics and design (10); cost (10); and overall impression (20). Among the key factors in making an excellent report: easy access to information within the report; a concise statement of the foundation's goals and objectives; information about the character and quality of programs supported by the foundation; and a detailed description of the application process. Overall, an annual report should show a real desire to communicate with its constituency, and should accomplish the task with some flair while not becoming merely self-congratulatory.

1198. Stanford Center for Chicano Research. *A Study of Foundation Awards to Hispanic-Oriented Organizations in the U.S., 1981-1982. Preliminary Report.* Stanford, Calif.: Stanford University, 1984.

Preliminary study which identifies ninety-six foundations awarding grants to Hispanic-oriented organizations and projects. Includes numerous tables which show the geographic dispersal of awards, types of services supported, foundations making the most awards, the major recipients of foundation support, and the number of awards by subject categories.

1199. Staniforth, Sydney D. "Community Foundations Can Be Designed for Local Needs." *Municipality* (January 1988): 8, 23.

Briefly discusses the nature of a community foundation, which uses community funds for a flexible menu of services ultimately determined and controlled by the community itself.

1200. Starrett, Agnes Lynch. *Henry C. Frick Educational Commission, 1909-1974.* Pittsburgh: Henry C. Frick Foundation, [1975].

1201. Starrett, Agnes Lynch. *The Maurice and Laura Falk Foundation: A Private Fortune—a Public Trust.* Pittsburgh: Historical Society of Western Pennsylvania, 1966.

1202. Steiner, Robert O., Ellen Friedman, and Terry W. McAdam. *Balancing Quality and Equity: Toward a Grantmaking Program in Pre-Collegiate Public Education.* Occasional Paper Series. Los Angeles: Conrad N. Hilton Foundation, 1986.

Intended to develop a common knowledge base on the issue of pre-collegiate public education and design a meaningful grantmaking strategy in the field, this working paper provides a brief historical overview of public education in the United States, presents basic data on its current status, summarizes the findings, recommendations, and reactions to recent studies, explores some of the current trends in public school reform, outlines the crisis in the teaching profession, and examines specific leverage points for Conrad N. Hilton Foundation grantmaking. Aware of their limitations in terms of financial resources and the scale of problems which face public education today, the Foundation's directors have decided to focus on a single element of the public education system—the teachers. Seeking to attract intelligent, talented, and motivated people into the teaching profession and retain existing good teachers in the public schools, the Foundation will give priority to projects that develop peer networks for teachers to encourage their involvement in finding solutions for education problems, career development programs aimed at promising high school students, and programs that will strengthen public awareness of the positive aspects of the teaching profession. In addition, the Foundation wishes to support local literacy education programs that can be developed into large-scale efforts.

1203. Stephens, Barbara. *Private Funding for Rural Programs: Foundations and Other Private Sector Resources.* Washington: National Rural Center, 1978.

1204. Stiles, B.J. "AIDS: How a Problem Became a Priority." *Foundation News* 27 (March-April 1986): 48-56.

1205. Stone, Peter H. "The IEA: Teaching the 'Right' Stuff." *Nation* (19 September 1981): 231-35.

1206. Streich, Mary Deane, comp. and ed. *The Directory of Oklahoma Foundations.* Oklahoma City, Okla.: Foundation Research Project, 1988.

Based on information from the lastest IRS 990 forms on file at the Oklahoma Medical Research Foundation, directory provides basic information about most Oklahoma foundations. Includes funding emphasis, geographic area, restrictions, financial data (assets, income, total grants and total pledges), information on the application process and the name, address and phone number of the contact person. Indexed by foundation name, city location, areas of funding interest, and trustees.

1207. Struckhoff, Eugene C. *The Handbook for Community Foundations: Their Formation, Development and Operation.* 2 Vols. Washington: Council on Foundations, 1977.

Definitive guide to the history, governance, philosophy, and operations of community foundations.

1208. Struckhoff, Eugene C. "Seed Planting, Community Foundation Style." *Foundation News* 26 (January-February 1985): 36-42.

Describes programs of foundations and corporations to fund start-up and revitalization of community foundations.

1209. Suchman, Edward A., and Patricia P. Rieker. *Review and Evaluation of Maurice Falk Medical Fund.* Pittsburgh: Maurice Falk Medical Fund, 1969.

1210. Suhrke, Henry C. "Financial Reporting by Community Foundations." *Philanthropy Monthly* 20 (March 1987): 27-31.

Suhrke examines financial reports from several community foundations to make a case for full disclosure. Focuses on the New York Community Trust and the Cleveland Foundation.

1211. Suhrke, Henry C. "Foundations on Display: Money, Bias, and Brains." *Philanthropy Monthly* 17 (April 1984): 22-8.

1212. Suhrke, Henry C. "The Hearings Were Intended to Educate Ways and Means. What Happened?" *Philanthropy Monthly* 16 (June 1983): 6-11.

1213. Suhrke, Henry C. "Round Two: Waldemar Nielsen and the Large Foundations." *Philanthropy Monthly* 9 (February 1986): 5-16.

1214. Sutton, Francis X. *Foundations and Higher Education at Home and Abroad: A Tale of Heroic Efforts Abandoned.* Center for the Study of Philanthropy Working Papers. New York: Center for the Study of Philanthropy, 1986.

Examines the change in relations between universities and American foundations, both at home and abroad, from the "heroic" efforts of the 1960s to the abrupt decline of foundation enthusiasm for university development in the 1970s. Includes bibliography.

1215. Taft, J. Richard. *Understanding Foundations: Dimensions in Fund Raising.* New York: McGraw-Hill, [1967].

1216. "Taking the Lead with a Potential Grantee: How Much Is Too Much?" *Foundation News* 25 (March-April 1984): 62-3.

1217. Tarnacki, Duane L. *Establishing a Charitable Foundation in Michigan.* Grand Haven, Mich.: Council of Michigan Foundations, 1986.

How-to guide on establishing a foundation intended for lawyers, accountants and professional estate planners who have little or no experience with foundations. The practical three-ring binder format contains twelve chapters, a selected bibliography and fifteen appendixes. The chapters include *Reasons for Creating a Charitable Foundation, The Charitable Foundation As an Estate Planning Tool, Limitations on Deductibility of Contributions, Types of Charitable Foundations, Differences in Organizational Form, Organizational Documents, Taxes, Private Foundation Operating Restrictions, Fiduciary Duties and Indemnification, Internal Revenue Filing Requirements,* and *State Regulations and Filing Requirements.* The fifteen appendixes provide technical assistance and numerous document samples such as articles of incorporation, corporate by-laws, annual report, checklist for fundraisers, solicitation questionnaire, and required IRS Forms—1023, 2848, SS4, 990-PF, and 990.

1218. Taylor, Eleanor K. *Public Accountability of Foundations and Charitable Trusts.* New York: Russell Sage Foundation, 1953.

1219. Taylor, James H. *Foundation Profiles of the Southeast: Alabama, Arkansas, Louisiana, Mississippi.* Williamsburg, Ky.: James H. Taylor Associates, 1983.

Based on 1978 and 1979 990-PF and 990-AR returns filed with the IRS by 212 foundations. Main section arranged by state and alphabetically by foundation name; entries include principal officer, assets, total grants and sample grants. No indexes.

1220. Taylor, James H. *Foundation Profiles of the Southeast: Georgia.* Williamsburg, Ky.: James H. Taylor Associates, 1983.

Based on 1975 through 1977 990-PF and 990-AR returns filed with the IRS for 530 foundations. Main section arranged alphabetically by foundation; entries include statement of purpose, sample grants, and principal officer. Indexes of foundation names, cities, and program interests.

1221. Taylor, James H., and John L. Wilson. *Foundation Profiles of the Southeast: Kentucky, Tennessee, Virginia.* Williamsburg, Ky.: James H. Taylor Associates, 1981.

Based on 1978 and 1979 990-PF and 990-AR IRS returns for 117 foundations. Main section arranged alphabetically by foundation; entries include assets, total number and amount of grants, sample grants and officers. No indexes.

1222. Taylor, James H., and John L. Wilson. *Foundation Profiles of the Southeast: North Carolina, South Carolina.* Williamsburg, Ky.: James H. Taylor Associates, 1983.

Based on 1978 and 1979 990-PF and 990-AR returns filed by 492 foundations. Main sections arranged alphabetically by foundation name; entries include principal officer, assets, total grants and sample grants. No indexes.

1223. Taylor, John D. "Learning from Foundation Reports." *Philanthropy Monthly* 17 (September 1984): 30-2.

1224. Teltsch, Kathleen. "Community Trust Opens a Center to Study Aging." *New York Times* (17 March 1985): 48.

Describes New York Center on Aging policy, set up by New York Community Trust.

1225. Teltsch, Kathleen. "Conservative Unit Gains from Legacy: Olin Foundation Tells of Plans for Education Activity with Founder's $50 Million." *New York Times* (2 October 1983): 41.

1226. Teltsch, Kathleen. "Donations Increase to Groups Studying Prevention of War." *New York Times* (6 May 1985).

1227. Teltsch, Kathleen. "Filling Big Hopes with Small Grants." *New York Times* (1 May 1985): C-1.
Describes grants to emerging organizations.

1228. Teltsch, Kathleen. "Ford Foundation Leads Delayed Philanthropic Response to AIDS." *New York Times* (25 March 88): 26.

1229. Teltsch, Kathleen. "Foundation Plans Grants for Preventing War." *New York Times* (18 December 1983): L-13.

1230. Teltsch, Kathleen. "Foundations Seek Links to Congress." *New York Times* (5 May 1985): 39.

1231. Teltsch, Kathleen. "Foundations Seek Tax Changes." *New York Times* (27 June 1983): B-8.

1232. Teltsch, Kathleen. "Foundations Warned against Complacency." *New York Times* (29 April 1984): 30.

1233. Teltsch, Kathleen. "Philanthropies Focus Concern on Arms Race." *New York Times* (25 March 1984): 1.

1234. Teltsch, Kathleen. "Rockefellers Restyle Fund for the 1980's." *New York Times* (14 November 1983).

1235. Teltsch, Kathleen. "Study of Foundations Reveals Many Omit Critical Tax Data." *New York Times* (11 May 1983).

1236. *Tennessee Directory of Foundations and Corporate Philanthropy*. Memphis, Tenn.: City of Memphis. Bureau of Intergovernmental Management, 1982.
Based primarily on 990-PF returns filed with the IRS and questionnaires. Two main sections arranged alphabetically by foundation and alphabetically by corporation; entries include contact person, contact procedure, fields of interest, geographic limitations, financial data, officers and trustees and sample grants. Indexes of foundations and corporations by name, fields of interest and geographic area of giving. Appendixes of foundations giving less than $10,000 a year, and major corporations in Tennessee which employ more than 300 persons.

1237. "A Third Sector Headquarters." *Philanthropy Monthly* 9 (May 1976): 7-13.

1238. Tivnan, Edward. "Foundations: A Time for Review." *New York Times* (9 September 1984): 136+.

1239. Tjerandsen, Carl. *Education for Citizenship: A Foundation's Experience*. Santa Cruz, Calif.: Emil Schwarzhaupt Foundation, 1980.

1240. Townsend, Ted H. *Foundation Community Representation: An Analysis of the Representation of Community in Pennsylvania Foundation Grant Decisions*. Philadelphia: University of Pennsylvania, 1974.

1241. Traub, James. *Society's Stake in the Communications Future: What Can Grant-Makers Do?* New York: Aspen Institute for Humanistic Studies, 1982.

1242. Trench, Alan S. "Foundation Management Rewards." *Trusts & Estates* 126 (August 1987): 41-2.

1243. "Trendlines: Foundation Support of Higher Education." *Change* (February 1985).

1244. *Trends and Developments in Federal and Foundation Grants for Health*. Wall Township, N.J.: Health Funds Development Letter, 1982.

1245. Troyer, Thomas A., and Robert A. Boisture. "Can Foundations Support Voter Registration?" *Foundation News* 24 (November-December 1983): 22-3.

1246. United States. Department of Health and Human Services. *Private Foundations. Supporting Health Manpower Education and Training: An Inventory, 1971*. Washington: Government Printing Office, 1974.

1247. United States. Department of Health, Education and Welfare. *A Survey of Foundations Involved in U.S. Health R and D*. Washington: Government Printing Office, 1978.

1248. United States. Department of the Treasury. Internal Revenue Service. *Reporting Characteristics. Forms 990 and 990-PF: Returns of Organizations and Private Foundations Exempt from Income Tax for 1973*. Washington: U.S. Department of the Treasury. Internal Revenue Service, 1976.

1249. United States. Department of the Treasury. Internal Revenue Service. *Statistics of Income: Private Foundations, 1974-1978*. Washington: Government Printing Office, 1981.

1250. United States. General Accounting Office. *Statistical Analysis of the Operations and Activities of Private Foundations*. Gaithersburg, Md.: U.S. General Accounting Office, 1984.

1251. United States Human Resources Corporation. *U.S. Foundations and Minority Group Interests*. San Francisco: U.S. Human Resources Corporation, 1975.

1252. United Way of Delaware. *Delaware Foundations*. Wilmington, Del.: United Way of Delaware, 1983.
Based on 1979 through 1981 990-PF and 990-AR returns filed with the IRS, annual reports, and information supplied by 154 foundations. Main section arranged alphabetically by foundation; entries include statement of purpose and officers, grant analysis, type of recipient; no sample grants. Detailed information on 111 private foundations, a list of twenty-seven operating foundations and a sampling of out-of-state foundations with a pattern of giving in Delaware. Two indexes; alphabetical listing of all foundations, all trustees and officers.

1253. Vallance, Karla. "Small Foundation Tactic: Pooling for Grassroots Causes." *Christian Science Monitor* (10 December 1982): B-11.

1254. Vanguard Public Foundation. *Robin Hood Was Right: A Guide to Giving Your Money for Social Change.* Unpublished, 1978.

1255. Viscusi, Margo. "Annual Reports: Making a Good Idea Better." *Foundation News* 26 (January-February 1985): 30-5.

Gives guidelines for writing an annual report.

1256. Viscusi, Margo. "Coming of Age." *Foundation News* 26 (May-June 1985): 26+.

Discusses principles of effective grantmaking, telling how several foundations publicize their priorities.

1257. von Humboldt Foundation, Alexander. *Awards for Senior U.S. Scientists.* Bonn, West Germany: Alexander von Humboldt Foundation, 1983.

1258. Wadsworth, Homer C. "Vehicles for Urban Survival." *Foundation News* 25 (January-February 1984): 58-9.

1259. Wallen, Denise, and Karen Cantrell. *Funding for Museums, Archives and Special Collections.* Phoenix, Ariz.: Oryx Press, 1988.

This directory is designed to assist the search for financial support for museums and museum activities and programs as well as sources of individual support for work, study, training or research in museums or special collections. It lists over 500 sources of support available for disciplines from art history to zoology. The program profiles are arranged alphabetically and include subject, geographic restriction and sponsor type indexes. Includes bibliography.

1260. Walsh, Elsa. "From Family Fortune to Social Change." *Grantsmanship Center News* 13 (May-June 1985): 11+.

1261. Washington (State). Office of Attorney General. *Charitable Trust Directory.* Olympia, Wash.: Attorney General of Washington, 1987.

Based on the 1987 records in the files of the Attorney General of Washington. Includes information on all charitable organizations and trusts reporting to the Attorney General under the Washington Charitable Trust Act. Divided into two main sections: Grantmakers and Grantseekers. Grantmaker entries may include statement of purpose, officers, sample grants, and financial data. Alphabetical index of all organizations appearing in the directory, and another of grantmakers only, divided into purpose categories.

1262. Weaver, Glenn. *Hartford Foundation for Public Giving: The First Fifty Years.* West Hartford, Conn.: Hartford Foundation for Public Giving, 1975.

1263. Weaver, Warren, and George Wells Beadle. *U.S. Philanthropic Foundations: Their History, Structure, Management and Record.* New York: Harper & Row, [1967].

This book represents an inquiry into the question of whether foundations benefit society enough to warrant their continued existence. Weaver had over thirty-five years' experience on the staffs of large foundations when he wrote it. The first four chapters outline a brief history of foundations and their philanthropic antecedents, after which Weaver turns to modern foundations. He discusses their types, structure, staffing, resources, reasons for establishment, legal and financial aspects, chronological and geographic distribution, and more. In the second part of the book, eighteen contributors from diverse sectors such as education, physics, dance, law, international affairs, world health, and more comment on the value, or lack thereof, of foundation activities in their fields. Weaver concludes on the basis of these eighteen commentaries that foundations have been responsible for vastly more good than harm and enjoy more popular approval and gratitude than suspected.

1264. Webb, Missy, ed. *Directory of Texas Foundations.* 10th ed. San Antonio, Tex.: Funding Information Center of Texas, 1989.

A total of 1510 private foundations, corporate giving programs, government agencies and public charities are profiled. Directory is divided into 895 large foundations and 615 small foundations (with assets of less than $300,000 and grantmaking activity of less than $15,000). Entry information includes foundation name, emphasis (giving area), population group, restrictions, tax year of financial data, assets, total grants, grant range, application process, trustees, and contact person. Includes sections with top 100 Texas foundations in descending order by assets and by grants, excluded and terminated foundations, and a 1987 grant distribution of Texas foundations. Indexed by areas of giving, city, trustees and officers, and by foundation name.

1265. Weil, Henry. "Attorney General Probes Shubert Salaries." *New York City Business* 2 (29 July-9 August 1985): 1+.

Comments on the investigation of the Shubert Organization, which is owned by the Shubert Foundation.

1266. Weithorn, Stanley S. *Private Charitable Foundations.* Course Handbook Series, no. 2. New York: Practising Law Institute, 1968.

1267. Weithorn, Stanley S. *Private Charitable Foundations.* Transcript. New York: Practising Law Institute, 1968.

1268. Welles, Chris. "Foundations: The Quiet $20 Billion." *Institutional Investor* 2 (November 1968): 31-6.

1269. Wells, James A., Andrea Zuercher, and John Clinton. "Foundation Funding for AIDS Education." *Health Affairs* 7 (Winter 1988): 146-58.

Summarizes a Foundation Center study of support for AIDS-related programs, and reports on conversations with foundation representatives concerning evaluations of AIDS/HIV education, and why foundations do not fund enough of these evaluations. The article's premise is that if public education is our only recourse for altering the spread of AIDS (until a vaccine or cure is discovered), efforts should be taken to study scientifically the effects of educational interventions on different groups. A table ranks the top twenty-six foundations by amount of grants for AIDS programs, 1981-1988, with the Robert Wood Johnson Foundation in first place, providing roughly half of all private foundation dollars in this area. The article examines general foundation involvement, areas receiving support, target populations, and foundation-corporation coalitions, concluding that the groups targeted by foundation-funded programs (programs for women and children are especially popular) are not the groups at greatest risk, and that programs are readily implemented without a formal evaluation component to discover what works and what does not. The reasons cited for lack of evaluation include: the sophistication of research required for evaluations surpasses the abilities of foundations and especially many grantee organizations; they are too time-consuming; they are too expensive; they are not always applicable to other programs; and evaluations are often seen as unnecessary, or the responsibility of the public sector, not of foundations. The article emphasizes that all AIDS prevention programs are experimental, and without evaluation we risk losing the potential knowledge to be gained from experience. Recommends a series of simple manuals developed by Sage Publications entitled *The Program Evaluation Kit*, which are useful for those with few resources and little experience or formal training in evaluation.

1270. Wells, Joseph P. "Rewarding Innovation: The Beginnings of a Foundation's Awards Program." *Grants Magazine* 10 (June 1987): 72-78.

Profiles the Charles A. Dana Foundation's nationwide awards program for innovative ideas in health and higher education. The program began in 1986 and is authorized to bestow up to five awards every year of $50,000 each. The 1987 recipients include: Dr. F. Sherwood Rowland for his pioneering efforts in identifying the causes of the depletion of the earth's ozone layer and in bringing about international measures to prevent its further erosion; Dr. Alexander D. Langmuir for his achievements in the establishment of the Epidemiology Intelligence Service, which has critical relevance in efforts to cope with the AIDS epidemic; and Dr. Philip Uri Treisman for developing a program at the University of California, Berkeley, called the Mathematics Workshop Program, which has shown dramatic improvement in the academic performance of both black and Hispanic students in learning first-year calculus, and in their total performance and retention in undergraduate school. Special awards were given to Mrs. Albert Lasker and Dr. James R. Killian, Jr. for their lifelong achievements in health promotion and disease prevention.

1271. *West Virginia Foundation Directory.* 2nd ed. Charleston, W.Va.: Kanawha County Public Library, 1987.

Divided into two sections, the first half of the directory consists of profiles derived from survey data and 990-PF financial data. Each profile gives the foundation's name, address, contact person, and date established, and information on the foundation's giving interest, restrictions, and application procedures; lists trustees, when available, and provides a chronological list of assets and grants in dollars. The second half of the directory consists of foundations which did not return their surveys; provides the foundation's name, address, and contact person, if given in the tax form. Includes the assets and grants in dollars.

1272. Whelan, Sidney S., Jr. "Community Foundations Take off." *Trusts & Estates* 126 (August 1987): 10, 14, 16, 18.

Corporate executives, entrepreneurs and professionals control much of the private wealth in the United States. For those that are charitably inclined, the community foundation enables them to pool their funds to help others. Community foundations are public charities organized as a corporation or trust which administer charitable funds in accordance with the philanthropic objectives of the donor. Whelan states that, "Community foundations are the fastest growing sector of philanthropy in the United States." The donors use the community foundations because they are assisted by professionals who identify worthy charitable recipients, monitor the contributions, provide professional investment management, manage the funds as part of a general fund or maintain the donor's gift under the donor's name, and provide the maximum tax deductibility for charitable giving.

1273. "When a Grantee Seeks Money for Project A, and You Know It's Really for Project B." *Foundation News* 24 (March-April 1982): 56-8.

1274. *Where the Money Is: A Grantsmanship Handbook for Non-Profit Agencies and Organizations in Dutchess County.* Poughkeepsie, N.Y.: Junior League of Poughkeepsie, 1979.

1275. Whitaker, Ben. *The Foundations: An Anatomy of Philanthropic Societies.* New York: Pelican, 1979.

Whitaker analyzes the world's charitable trusts and the philanthropoids who run them in a critical but entertaining study. He reveals a substantial gap between their stated intentions and their cost-effectiveness and paints a disconcerting picture of a world in which foundation personnel and board directors are representative of an elite corps at the heart of the establishment. Whitaker thinks these factors may explain why foundations are treated with suspicion despite their seemingly altruistic endeavors. The book is also full of interesting trivia about foundations in the United States and abroad. 300-item bibliography.

1276. White, William S. "Building Community Partnerships: The Foundation Role." *Community Action* 1 (1982): 11+.

1277. Whitney, Thomas T. "Private Philanthropy and Public Needs." *Grantsmanship Center News* 2 (December-February 1975-1976): 9-19; 49-54.

1278. Wilding, Suzanne. "New York's Own Private Trust Fund." *Town & Country* 139 (September 1985): 220-23.

Describes the New York Community Trust.

1279. Williams, Guynell, ed. *South Carolina Foundation Directory.* 3rd ed. Columbia, S.C.: South Carolina State Library, 1987.

Based on 1984 through 1986 990-PF returns filed with the IRS. Main section arranged alphabetically by foundation; entries include areas of interest, principal officer, assets, total grants, number of grants, range and geographic limitations. Indexes of foundations alphabetically and by city, and of program interests.

1280. Williams, Robert R. *Williams-Waterman Fund for the Combat of Dietary Diseases: A History of the Period 1935 through 1955.* New York: Research Corp., 1956.

1281. Williams, Roger M. "All in the Family (Well, Mostly)." *Foundation News* 25 (July-August 1984): 42-9.

Alternative foundations become accepted segment of the philanthropic community.

1282. Williams, Roger M. "Gulling the Grantseeker." *Foundation News* 26 (July-August 1985): 20+.

Discusses publishers who misrepresent foundation grantmaking.

1283. Williams, Roger M. "Harder Than It Looked." *Foundation News* 30 (January-February 1989): 20-3.

Profiles the Marin Community Foundation (MCF) in California, which "inherited" the more than $400 million Buck Trust. In only two years the MCF has charted its future, conducted an unusual survey of its constituents' wishes and begun making grants, all while adjusting to a court-ordered "special master" (appointed as part of the settlement to end the Buck Trust litigation) and an array of formidable political pressures, such as a call for MCF's funds to be used in replacing lost government funds. At present MCF officials, including executive director Douglas X. Patino, the first Hispanic to head a large foundation, have decided to focus in seven program areas, with forty-four percent of available grant money going to human needs and twenty-six percent going to education and training; the remaining funds will be apportioned among arts and humanities, housing and community development, environment, religion, and integrative approaches that are meant to "cross over the traditional boundaries of program areas."

1284. Williams, Roger M. "An Interview with William E. Simon." *Foundation News* 24 (September-October 1983): 16-21.

1285. Williams, Roger M. "A Marriage of Convenience." *Foundation News* 25 (May-June 1984): 28-32.

1286. Williams, Roger M. "One More Try." *Foundation News* 25 (January-February 1984): 16-21.

1287. Williams, Roger M. "When the Buck Stopped." *Foundation News* 29 (November-December 1988): 24-9.

Traces the San Francisco Foundation's disastrous attempt to extend Buck Trust grantmaking beyond the narrow scope of Marin County, a move resulting in the removal of the Foundation as distribution trustee. Mrs. Beryl Buck had specified the original $11 million in proceeds from her estate be used "for exclusively nonprofit charitable...purposes...in Marin County;" but when the trust appreciated first to $260 million and then to $430 million, the Foundation's trustees felt a philosophical and ethical urge to divert at least a portion of the proceeds to other needy counties, especially as Marin is considered one of America's best-known affluent suburbs. The article examines several questionable aspects of the issue which include bringing the case to court witout unanimous committee backing (the vote was four to two with one member abstaining); allowing the Foundation's lawyers to put staff members on the stand to testify "against" the funding they had given to Marin County in order to demonstrate that such grants had been ill-advised and in effect wasted—a move that made the grantmakers look unprofessional; and the failure to thoroughly investigate innovative grantmaking possibilities that could be based in Marin County while engendering broader applications. The article concludes that the San Francisco Foundation revealed genuine concern, high principle and dedication in its efforts, but lacked the necessary sensitivity and creativity to solve its problem.

1288. Wilsnack, Dorie. "Four Months on the Road to Peace: A Fundraiser's Journey." *Grassroots Fundraising Journal* 2 (February 1983): 4+.

1289. Wilson, Emily Herring. *For the People of North Carolina: The Z. Smith Reynolds Foundation at Half-Century, 1936-1986.* Chapel Hill, N.C.: University of North Carolina Press, 1988.

Fifty-year history of the Z. Smith Reynolds Foundation, written in a highly readable journalistic style. Addresses both the history of the state of North Carolina and the changing values of three generations of the Reynolds family, spanning the rise of a worldwide tobacco fortune, the difficult years of the Great Depression, three American wars and the vast changes of a largely rural state struggling to adapt to the pressures of industrial growth and an evolving, technology-based economy. Examines how the Foundation has confronted issues of poverty, rural decline, illiteracy, racial discrimination, educational neglect, health crises and urban sprawl, and traces the internal struggle over process and the principles of giving and the evolution of a less reactive and more pro-active grantmaking board. Appendixes include a fifty-year chronology of grants approved by the Z. Smith Reynolds Foundation.

1290. Wisconsin (Milwaukee County) Circuit Court. *Court Decision: Erica P. John (DeRance, Inc.) vs. Harry G. John (DeRance, Inc.).* Unpublished, 1986.

1291. Wolling, Frank J. *Survey of Record Keeping Practices in Foundations.* Unpublished, 1977.

1292. Women and Foundations/Corporate Philanthropy. *New Ways to Lead.* New York: Women and Foundations/Corporate Philanthropy, 1987.

Transcript of panel discussion exploring women's leadership, with particular attention to grassroots women's leadership. Gloria Steinem leads the discussion which focuses on how grassroots women's leadership develops, what internal and external barriers to leadership exist, and how funders can best make use of grants and other forms of support. The four panel members represent the Native American Community Board in South Dakota; the National Black Women's Health Project in Georgia; the Dungannon Development Commission (conducting adult literacy programs in rural Virginia); and Ganados Del Valle, a community development project in New Mexico.

1293. Wormser, Rene A. *Foundations: Their Power and Influence.* New York: Devin-Adair Co., 1958.

1294. Wright, John M. "Salaries of the Top Officials at the Largest Foundations." *American Almanac of Salaries and Jobs* (1984): 735.

1295. Yung, Betty. "The Typewritten Request for the Grail: Grants in Fiction." *Grantsmanship Center News* 13 (March-April 1985): 36-9.

1296. Zuboff, Shoshanah. *A Study of the Demand for a Greater New York Association of Foundations.* Unpublished, 1979.

1297. Zwingle, J.L. *The Influence of Foundations on Education.* Ithaca, N.Y.: Cornell University Press, 1960.

3

CORPORATE PHILANTHROPY

1298. Ackerman, Robert W. "How Companies Respond to Social Demands." *Harvard Business Review* 51 (July-August 1973): 88-98.

1299. "Aetna's National Urban Revitalization Program Investments Reach $15 Million." *Response* (April 1983): 18, 20.

1300. Alexander, Anne S. "Understanding the Philanthropic Partnership." *Currents* 14 (March 1988): 12-6.

Alexander distinguishes between the two basic, but highly different, types of campus-corporate partnerships. One is very much a business agreement, where the university is sponsored to pay for faculty research and development that yields results for the company's future products and services. The other is a philanthropic partnership that works for more long-term benefits, ones from which society is likely to profit rather than simply the corporation. Alexander also points out that corporations are organized to strive for results; in a philanthropic partnership the results are evaluated in terms of the effects a corporation's grants have upon whatever social problem they're addressing.

1301. Allen, Kerry Kenn, Isolde Chapin, and Shirley Keller. *Volunteers from the Workplace.* Washington: National Center for Voluntary Action, 1979.

1302. Allen, Kerry Kenn. *The Wichita Experience. Mobilizing Corporate Resources to Meet Community Needs.* Washington: National Center for Voluntary Action, 1978.

1303. "American Corporations Contribute Record Amount to Charities." *Council on Foundations Newsletter* 2 (20 December 1983): 1.

1304. "American Express Expands 'Cause' Related Marketing Program." *Corporate Giving Watch* 4 (February 1985): 1-2.

1305. *American Firms in Foreign Countries.* New York: World Trade Academy Press, 1981.

1306. American Society of Corporate Secretaries. *Corporate Contributions Report.* New York: American Society of Corporate Secretaries, 1950.

1307. Andrews, Frank Emerson. *Corporation Giving.* New York: Russell Sage Foundation, 1952.

This volume, in three parts, is a practical source book for corporations interested or engaging in philanthropic activity. Andrews' interest in the topic grew out of his work on *Philanthropic Giving* (1950). The more recent work covers the statistical picture of corporate philanthropy at the time of writing, provides recommendations and guidance on questions of policy, choice of beneficiary, and more. It also explores legal and tax factors affecting corporate giving. The book includes a discussion of the historical development of corporate philanthropy in the second chapter. The findings presented in the book, though now outdated, at the time served to update data from the only extensive survey on the topic ever undertaken, published in 1930 by the National Bureau of Economic Research.

1308. Andrews, Kenneth R. "Can the Best Corporations Be Made Moral?" *Harvard Business Review* 51 (May-June 1973): 57-64.

1309. Andrews, Kenneth R. "Interview Guide for Review of Board Effectiveness." *Harvard Business Review* 57 (May-June 1979): 48.

1310. "Apple Computer Awards Equipment to Nonprofit Networks: Expansion of Donation Programs Planned." *Corporate Giving Watch* 3 (October 1983): 1-2.

1311. "Arts Focus on Business Surveys and New Programs." *Arts Management* (November-December 1983): 1+.

CORPORATE PHILANTHROPY

1312. Austin, Ann. "Talking to a Corporate Donor." *Philanthropy Monthly* 16 (February 1983): 12-3.

Austin notes that many companies are providing increased in-kind services to charitable organizations in an attempt to address what they see as their legitimate obligations and to ease their corporate consciences. Andrew J. Reinhart, executive vice president of Grolier Inc., outlines his firm's view of corporate contributions, which gives to charities that directly address human needs rather than to cause-oriented organizations.

1313. Austin, Robert W. "Responsibility for Social Change." *Harvard Business Review* 43 (July-August 1965): 45-52.

1314. Balz, Frank J., and Richard Bentley. *The Corporate Investment in Higher Education: State and National Trends in Gift and Tax Support.* Washington: National Institute of Independent Colleges and Universities, 1985.

1315. Bandow, Doug. "Misdirecting Corporate Philanthropy." *Journal of the Institute for Socioeconomic Studies* 8 (Spring 1983): 57+.

1316. Bank of America. *Bibliography: Corporate Responsibility for Social Problems.* San Francisco: Bank of America, 1973.

1317. Barach, Jeffrey. "Corporate Giving by Retail Department Stores." *Business and Society Review* 22 (Spring 1983): 49-52.

1318. Bertsch, Kenneth A. *Corporate Giving in the Reagan Years.* Washington: Investor Responsibility Research Center, 1985.

Report looks specifically at corporate giving since President Reagan came into office. Company reports section is based on an informal survey which provides a rough basis for comparing corporate philanthropic commitment. Provides giving information of 176 large companies, in most cases from 1980 to 1984, including each company's contributions total, contributions as percentage of pretax income, and contributions as percentage of domestic pretax income.

1319. Bertsch, Kenneth A. *Corporate Philanthropy.* Washington: Investor Responsibility Research Center, 1982.

Report on current issues and trends in corporate philanthropy, including a discussion of the motivations that guide corporate contributions officers.

1320. Blodgett, Timothy B. "The Corporation and Its Obligations: An Interview with C. Peter McColough of Xerox Corporation." *Harvard Business Review* 53 (May-June 1975): 127-38.

1321. Blomstrom, Robert L., Keith Davis, and William C. Frederick. *Business and Society: Concepts and Policy Issues.* 4th ed. New York: McGraw-Hill, 1980.

This textbook in the *McGraw-Hill Series in Management*, originally published as *Business and its Environment* (1966), seeks to relate business to the environment in which it operates. It discusses both socioeconomic concepts of business and society and policy applications in organizations. The book covers topics that include the following: 1) arguments for and against social involvement by business, 2) social power and social response, 3) pluralist society, 4) socioeconomic systems and cost-benefit analysis, 5) the managerial role and social issues, 6) technology and social change, 7) business ethics and values, 8) business involvement in community activities and cities, 9) multinational business and society, and much more. Each chapter includes study guides and problems. Brief bibliography.

1322. Blum, Joanne, ed. *Corporate 500: The Directory of Corporate Philanthropy.* 7th ed. San Francisco: Public Management Institute, 1988.

Reports on over 550 companies active in American philanthropy. Each entry includes a description of the company's principal business and its main subsidiaries, eligibility requirements, a funding analysis, subject interests, financial data, application procedures and sample grants. Indexing is by types of support, contact persons, contributions committee members, corporate boards of directors, corporate headquarters, funding areas, geographic areas of giving, grant recipients, main subsidiaries, principal businesses, and foundation names.

1323. Blumberg, Phillip I. *Corporate Responsibility in a Changing Society. Essays on Corporate Social Responsibility.* Boston: Boston University School of Law, 1972.

1324. Bohlen, Jeanne. *Non-Grant Fund Raising: Overall Fund Raising Campaign (Including Case Statement, Feasibility Study, Fund Raising Plan).* New York: Foundation Center, 1982.

1325. Bolman, Frederick. *Company-Sponsored Foundations in Education.* Reprint. New York: New York University, 1965.

1326. Boren, Jerry F. *Project Excellence. Perceptions of Corporate Social Involvement: A Survey of 64 Cities.* Chestnut Hill, Mass.: Center for Corporate Community Relations, 1987.

First in a series of research reports published by the Center for Corporate Community Relations. Focuses on the perceptions of local officials—a select group comprised of mayors, Chamber of Commerce executives, and United Way executives in cities with populations over 200,000—concerning the community relations performance of companies in their cities. The results list 194 companies singled out for special mention on the basis of eight criteria for excellence stipulated by the survey, including employee involvement, innovative programming, and general reputation. Table 1 alphabetically lists 186 corporations receiving multiple votes locally, and Table 2 ranks thirty-one corporations receiving votes from three or more cities (only eight of the thirty-one do not appear in Table 1). Study analysis shows three industrial sectors dominant in the field of community relations: manufacturing firms, the banking industry, and public utilities; also notes that although Forbes 500 companies receive high recognition by raters, small companies virtually unknown outside their local areas can have a reputation for strong community relations.

1327. Bradshaw, Thornton, and David Vogel, eds. *Corporations and Their Critics.* New York: McGraw-Hill, 1981.

In his article, *The Social Goals of a Corporation*, John H. Filer argues that corporations should revise a concept of corporate social responsibility as a separate pursuit, largely through charitable giving and community programs, into a commitment to meet the needs of society as well as one's customers through a corporation's basic business. To do this, he says, the chief executive officer of the corporation must set "social goals," which is much more difficult than setting corporate goals. This requires, generally, a genuine effort to understand the needs of the community in which the corporation is situated. Filer describes certain programs at Aetna Life and Casualty, where he was chairman, which sought to meet social goals. Other articles in the volume may also be of interest, especially Walter A. Haas Jr., on *Corporate Social Responsibility: A New Term for an Old Concept with New Significance.*

1328. Bragdon, Frances J. "Cause-Related Marketing: Case to Not Leave Home without It." *Fund Raising Management* 16 (March 1985): 42+.

Bragdon examines the cause-related marketing used by American Express to promote its products and services, and to benefit nonprofit organizations, through cash donations and extensive publicity.

1329. Breitstein, Joel M., and B. Terry Aidman. "Philanthropy May Benefit Corporations." *Tampa Bay Business* (3 July 1983).

1330. Brooks, Harvey, Lance Liebman, and Corinna S. Schelling, eds. *Public-Private Partnership: New Opportunities for Meeting Social Needs.* Cambridge, Mass.: Ballinger Publishing Co., 1984.

This is a collection of essays which examine the ways corporate partnerships with government have evolved and should continue to evolve in order to meet social needs. While the topic does not include nonprofit private organizations, it does treat corporate philanthropy in the broad sense of social responsibility. The essays are written from the perspectives of economic analysis, legal theory, history, management theory, public policy, social science, and business praxis. The authors generally agree that the public-private connection is constantly evolving and of great potential benefit to the public, but the editors caution that "for cultural and institutional reasons...realization of those benefits will be difficult and slow." In addition to analysis, the book includes recommendations for action.

1331. Brownrigg, W. Grant. *Effective Corporate Fundraising.* New York: American Council for the Arts, 1982.

Outlines a strategy for securing corporate funding for nonprofit activities, including sample calendar and budget for the campaign, introductory and appeal letters, etc.

1332. Brysh, Janet F., ed. *Maine Corporate Foundation Directory.* Portland, Maine: University of Southern Maine, 1984.

Based on information supplied by approximately seventy-five corporations. Main section arranged alphabetically by corporation; entries include contact person and, for a few corporations, the areas of interest.

1333. Burns, Michael E., ed. *Corporate Philanthropy in New England: Maine.* Vol. 3. Hartford, Conn.: D.A.T.A., 1987.

Describes over 180 corporate giving programs in Maine. Subject and geographic indexes.

1334. Burns, Michael E., ed. *Corporate Philanthropy in New England: New Hampshire.* Vol. 2. Hartford, Conn.: D.A.T.A., 1987.

Describes over 275 corporate giving programs in New Hampshire. Subject and geographic indexes.

1335. Burns, Michael E., ed. *Corporate Philanthropy in New England: Vermont.* Vol. 4. Hartford, Conn.: D.A.T.A., 1987.

Describes over 125 corporate giving programs in Vermont. Subject and geographic indexes.

1336. Burns, Michael E., ed. *Guide to Corporate Giving in Connecticut.* Hartford, Conn.: D.A.T.A., 1986.

The 3d edition of this guide features alphabetical and geographic listings of over 850 corporations; specific information for local Connecticut users; names, titles, and roles of charitable giving contacts; foundation information; non-cash giving policies; matching gift policies and priorities; and cash giving policies, procedures and priorities.

1337. Burns, Michael E., ed. *Guide to Corporate Giving in Massachusetts.* Hartford, Conn.: D.A.T.A., 1983.

Based on questionnaires and telephone interviews reaching 737 corporations. Main section arranged alphabetically by city and zip code; entries include product, amount given annually, frequency, area of interest and non-cash contributions. Index of corporations by city.

1338. Burns, Michael E., ed. *Guide to Corporate Giving in Rhode Island.* Hartford, Conn.: D.A.T.A., 1984.

Based on questionnaires and telephone interviews with 188 corporations. Main section arranged alphabetically; entries include product, plant location, giving interests and non-cash giving, where available. Index of corporations by city.

1339. Burns, Michael E. *Report on Corporate Giving.* Hartford, Conn.: D.A.T.A., 1982.

1340. Business Committee for the Arts. *Approaching Business for Support of the Arts.* [Leaflet]. New York: Business Committee for the Arts, 1976.

1341. Butcher, Willard C. *Total Corporate Responsibility in the 80's.* New York: Chase Manhattan Bank, [1981].

Speech given at University of North Carolina on October 16, 1981.

1342. Caesar, Patricia. "Cause-Related Marketing: The New Face of Corporate Philanthropy." *Business and Society Review* 59 (Fall 1986): 15-9.

Overview of the pros and cons on the controversial new approach to philanthropic giving—cause-related marketing—a fundraising program in which a nonprofit organization links up with a corporation to promote a particular cause. As an example, the fundraising for the Statue of Liberty restoration involved numerous corporate cause-related marketing programs.

1343. California Chamber of Commerce. *Five Percent and Two Percent Clubs in the United States.* Sacramento, Calif.: California Chamber of Commerce, 1982.

1344. California Community Foundation. *Other Than Grants: A Sampling of Southern California's Corporate Gift Matching, Volunteer, and in-Kind Giving Programs.* Los Angeles: California Community Foundation, 1984.

General advice on non-cash corporate philanthropy with brief profiles of thirty-one California corporations' giving programs.

1345. Carr, Elliott G. *Better Management of Business Giving.* New York: Hobbs, Dorman, 1966.

1346. "Cashing in on Noncash Corporate Support." *Nonprofit Executive* 3 (April 1984): 2.

1347. "Cause-Related Marketing: Blessing or Curse for Philanthropy?" *Philanthropic Trends Digest* 4 (1 May 1987): 3-4.

Thought-provoking article which queries the wisdom of cause-related marketing (a fundraising program which links a nonprofit organization with a corporation to promote a particular cause). Questions for debate are put forward to the philanthropic community. Has philanthropy become secondary to increased sales or a means of making a profit in the name of helping the needy? The article also questions the future role of cause-related marketing. Will it replace corporate philanthropy, and if it does, who will support causes which wouldn't be good for the corporate image or obtain media coverage? What are the consequences after the marketing campaign has concluded or the sales return is poor?

1348. "Cause-Related Marketing Does Not Fit All Corporations' Needs." *Corporate Giving Watch* 5 (December 1959): 8.

1349. "Cause-Related Marketing: The New Face of Corporate Philanthropy." *Nonprofit World* 5 (July-August 1987): 21, 24-6.

Based on interviews with leaders from the nonprofit and corporate sectors, this article explores the controversy surrounding cause-related marketing, focusing on the ethical implications (making a profit from altruism), the impact of cause-related marketing on traditional corporate giving (are cause-related funds supplementing or replacing the money traditionally designated for corporate philanthropy?), and the question of its impact on the goals and purposes of nonprofits (philanthropy becoming a business; nonprofits compromising their ideals in order to please the corporation providing the funds).

1350. Center for Arts Information. *Corporate Fundraising for the Arts.* New York: Center for Arts Information, 1981.

1351. Center for Corporate Community Relations. *Project Excellence. Supplement.* Chestnut Hill, Mass.: Center for Corporate Community Relations, 1987.

Complete list of the 647 companies recognized for excellence in community relations in the survey conducted by the Center for Corporate Community Relations. Includes the name of each city from which at least one official recommended a company.

1352. Center for Corporate Public Involvement. *Chief Executive Officer Conference on Corporate Social Responsibility. Report on Proceedings.* Washington: Center for Corporate Public Involvement, 1981.

1353. Center for Corporate Public Involvement. *Social Report of the Life and Health Insurance Business, 1986.* Washington: Center for Corporate Public Involvement, [1987].

Reveals a new high of 416 life and health insurance companies reporting public involvement activities and outlays. Gives statistics (over a five-year span) and examples of community projects, company contributions, equal employment opportunities, energy conservation and environmental concerns, voluntarism, social investments, and health and wellness programs. Appendixes contain list of reporting life and health insurance companies, and a sample copy of the reporting forms used.

1354. Chagy, Gideon, ed. *Business in the Arts '70.* Business Committee for the Arts. New York: Paul S. Eriksson, 1970.

1355. Chagy, Gideon, ed. *The State of the Arts and Corporate Support.* New York: Paul S. Eriksson, 1971.

1356. Chamberlain, Betty. "Corporations for Art." *Art & Artists* 12 (July 1983): 19.

1357. Chamberlain, Neil W. *The Limits of Corporate Responsibility.* New York: Basic Books, 1973.

1358. Chamberlain, Neil W. *Social Strategy and Corporate Structure.* New York: Macmillan, 1982.

1359. Chapman, Becky. "NAEIR: A Storehouse of Corporate Gifts." *Grantsmanship Center News* 10 (January-February 1984): 24-7.

1360. Charpie, Robert A. "Corporate Philanthropy Abroad: How's It Doing?" *Foundation News* 25 (March-April 1984): 52-4.

1361. Clark, Michael S. "EDI: Capital with a Conscience." *Grantsmanship Center News* 13 (January-February 1985): 35-42.

Profiles EDI, a capital venture firm.

1362. Clearinghouse on Corporate Social Responsibility. *Social Report of the Life and Health Insurance Business.* Washington: Clearinghouse on Corporate Social Responsibility, 1979.

1363. Clearinghouse on Corporate Social Responsibility. *Social Report of the Life and Health Insurance Business, 1981.* Washington: Clearinghouse on Corporate Social Responsibility, 1981.

1364. Close, Arthur C., and Gregory L. Bologna, eds. *National Directory of Corporate Public Affairs.* 6th ed. Washington: Columbia Books, 1988.

1365. Cmiel, Kenneth, and Susan M. Levy. *Corporate Giving in Chicago, 1980. A Study of the Giving Programs of 51 Major Chicago Corporations.* Chicago: Donors Forum of Chicago, 1980.

1366. Cohn, Jules. *The Conscience of the Corporations.* Baltimore, Md.: Johns Hopkins University Press, 1971.

1367. Collier, Abram T. "The Co-Corp: Big Business Can Re-Form Itself." *Harvard Business Review* 57 (November-December 1979): 121-34.

1368. Committee for Corporate Support of American Universities. *Private Universities in the Seventies: The Financial Crisis.* New York: Committee for Corporate Support of American Universities, 1970.

1369. Committee for Economic Development. Research and Policy Committee. *Investing in Our Children: Business and the Public Schools.* New York: Committee for Economic Development, 1985.

1370. Community Information Exchange. *Corporate Support for Community Development.* Washington: Community Information Exchange, 1984.

1371. Community Research and Publications Group. *Open the Books. How to Research a Corporation.* Boston: Urban Planning Aid, 1974.

Thorough how-to book about researching corporations. Chapters on researching multinational corporations, who controls large corporations, local subsidiaries, real estate companies, and small companies. Each chapter contains background information, sample case studies and materials to use to research corporations. Written primarily for organizers, but the research process is the same for fundraising.

1372. "Companies' Gifts to Colleges Up over 20% in 1982, Despite Sag in Profits, Survey Finds." *Chronicle of Higher Education* 27 (January 1984): 11.

1373. "Company Gifts Up 8.5%." *Chronicle of Higher Education* 11 (10 November 1975): 10.

1374. "Company Programs Illustrate Strong Commitment to the Arts." *Response* 13 (March 1984): 4+.

1375. "Computer Industry Shakeout Won't Affect Equipment Donations, Insiders Predict." *Corporate Giving Watch* 3 (October 1983): 1-2.

1376. "Computer Subsidy Divides Education." *New York Times* (26 December 1982): 30.

1377. Conference Board. *Company Contributions.* New York: Conference Board, 1971.

1378. Conference Board. *Company Contributions. Part 3: Policies and Procedures.* Studies in Business Policy, no. 89. New York: National Industrial Conference Board, 1958.

1379. Conference Board. *Company Policies on Donations.* Studies in Business Policy, no. 7. New York: National Industrial Conference Board, 1945.

1380. Conference Board. *Company Policies on Donations. Part 2: Written Statements of Policy.* Studies in Business Policy, no. 49. New York: National Industrial Conference Board, 1950.

1381. Conference Board. *Company-Sponsored Foundations.* Studies in Business Policy, no. 73. New York: National Industrial Conference Board, 1955.

1382. "Congress Debates More Liberal Equipment Donation Rules." *Corporate Giving Watch* 3 (July 1983): 1+.

1383. Connery, Robert H., ed. *The Corporation and the Campus.* New York: Academy of Political Science, Columbia University, 1970.

1384. Corderi, Victoria. "The New Need for Charity: Can Corporations Cover It?" *Miami News* (February 1982): 8, 13-5.

1385. Cordil, Lesta. "Budget Cuts, Tax Plan May Change Way Firms Contribute to Charities." *Gannett Westchester Newspapers* (24 February 1985): H1-2.

1386. "Corporate Clubs Can Stimulate Private Giving." *Michigan Scene* 9 (Spring 1983): 5.

1387. "Corporate Commitment to Philanthropy and Volunteerism." *KRC Letter* 14 (February 1984): 1-4.

1388. "Corporate Contributions of Goods and Services." *Volunteering* 1 (Fall 1982): 5-6.

1389. "Corporate Contributions of $100,000 or More in 1987 (Including Corporate Foundations)." *Philanthropic Digest* 34 (January 1988): 1-8.

1390. "Corporate Donation Clearinghouse Distributes $20 Million." *Corporate Giving Watch* 9 (June 1984): 8.

1391. "Corporate Foundations: A Charitable Alternative." *Response* 9 (March 1980): 3-4.

1392. "Corporate Giving." *Philanthropy Monthly* 15 (November 1982): 38-40.

1393. "Corporate Giving Clubs on the Rise." *Corporate Giving Watch* 3 (July 1983): 1+.

1394. "Corporate Giving in the United States, 1982." *Philanthropy Monthly* 16 (November 1983): 20+.

1395. "Corporate Giving Programs: Some Industries Stand Out." *Corporate Giving Watch* 4 (April 1984): 1-2.

1396. "Corporate Leaders Say They Have Obligation to Meet Needs of Their Communities." *Fund Raising Review* (June 1983): 3+.

1397. Corporate Special Projects Fund. *Report on Activities, 1977-78.* New York: New York Community Trust, 1979.

1398. Corporate Volunteer Coordinators Council. *Building a Corporate Volunteer Program.* New York: Corporate Volunteer Coordinators Council, 1980.

1399. Corporate Volunteerism Council of Minnesota. *Volunteerism Corporate Style.* 2nd ed. Minneapolis, Minn.: Corporate Volunteerism Council of Minnesota, 1984.

A collection of examples of corporate voluntarism in the Minneapolis/St. Paul Twin Cities area. Includes information on how to initiate, operate, and evaluate corporate volunteer programs, covering such diverse areas as how to recognize volunteers, set up a retiree volunteer program, and utilize computers. Shows many letters and brochures used by major corporations. Appendix gives names and addresses of volunteer resource and corporate resource organizations throughout the United States.

1400. "Corporations Increase Giving to Education in 1982 by Twenty Percent, to $1.3 Billion." *Fund Raising Review* (February 1984): 5.

1401. "Corporations with a Conscience." *Business and Society Review* 64 (Winter 1988): 58-9.

Describes the 1988 winners of America's Corporate Conscience Awards, established by the Council on Economic Priorities. The categories and winners are: Fair Employment for Minorities—Xerox Corporation, Fair Employment for Women—Gannett Co., Family Concerns—IBM, Charitable Giving—Ben and Jerry's Homemade, Opportunities for the Disabled—General Mills, Animal Rights—Procter & Gamble, Environment—3M Corporation, Community Action—Best Western International and South Shore Bank, Education—Gannett Co., and Most Improved Corporate Disclosure—Kellogg Company.

1402. Cott, Betty. *A Must for Effective Corporate Philanthropy: Good Communications.* New York: Ruder & Finn, 1979.

1403. Council for Aid to Education. *Corporate Handbook of Aid-to-Education Programs.* 14th ed. New York: Council for Aid to Education, 1987.

Describes nearly 200 corporate giving programs. Indexes list companies by size of program, by giving categories, by field of business, and by state.

1404. Council for Financial Aid to Education. *Aids to Corporate Support of Higher Education.* New York: Council for Financial Aid to Education, 1955.

1405. Council for Financial Aid to Education. *The CFAE Casebook. A Cross-Section of Corporate Aid-to-Education Programs.* New York: Council for Financial Aid to Education, 1980.

1406. Council for Financial Aid to Education. *Corporate Social Responsibility: Policies, Programs and Publications.* New York: Council for Financial Aid to Education, 1981.

1407. Council for Financial Aid to Education. *Corporate Support of Higher Education.* 1966-1985. New York: Council for Financial Aid to Education, 19—.

1408. Council for Financial Aid to Education. *Corporate Support of Higher Education.* 1972-1976. New York: Council for Financial Aid to Education, 1973-6.

1409. Council for Financial Aid to Education. *Guidelines: How to Develop an Effective Program of Corporate Support for Higher Education.* New York: Council for Financial Aid to Education, 1982.

Discusses the rationale for corporate support of higher education and the types of aid companies can provide to colleges and universities.

1410. Council for Financial Aid to Education. *How to Develop and Administer a Corporate Scholarship Program.* 2nd ed. New York: Council for Financial Aid to Education, 1981.

1411. Council for Financial Aid to Education. *Interface: Growing Initiatives between the Corporation and the Campus toward Greater Mutual Understanding.* New York: Council for Financial Aid to Education, 1977.

1412. Council for Financial Aid to Education. *New Goals for Corporate Giving to Higher Education.* New York: Council for Financial Aid to Education, 1975.

1413. Council for Financial Aid to Education, and Columbia University. Graduate School of Business. *Reference Book: Corporation Aid to American Higher Education.* New York: Council for Financial Aid to Education, 1955.

1414. Council of Better Business Bureaus. *Guidelines for Business Giving.* Arlington, Va.: Council of Better Business Bureaus, 1986.

Guidelines prepared by the Council of Better Business Bureaus to assist businesses in making more informed giving decisions. Basic suggestions include assigning one staff person to oversee all requests for charitable donations to save time and avoid the possibility of duplicate donations; making contributions by check, payable to the charity, not to the individual collecting the donation; keeping complete records of donations made to charitable organizations, especially for tax purposes; and checking the credentials of a local charity with the Better Business Bureau and local charitable registration office (usually a division of the state attorney general's office). Briefly mentions types of organizations which might ask for a donation, and whether or not a contribution would be tax deductible; advises asking the organization for a copy of its IRS determination letter if unsure of its tax exempt status. Provides questions to ask if presented with requests concerning benefit shows, coin canisters or display cards, advertising in charity publications, and fundraising dinners; also points to consider when confronted with telephone, mail, and door-to-door appeals.

1415. Council on Economic Priorities. *Guide to Corporations: A Social Perspective.* Chicago: Swallow Press, 1974.

1416. Council on Foundations. *Annual Survey of Corporate Contributions.* 1962-1987. New York: Conference Board, 19—.

Twentieth research report in the Conference Board's series on corporate contributions. This analysis of 1985 data on the giving practices of the largest U.S. corporations begins with highlights of the findings; sampling procedures and methodology; and an overview of the study—*Why This Report.* The analysis is written in three parts. *Reassessment and Change* examines the outlook for corporate contributions, cash and noncash giving and corporate assistance expenditures; *Setting Contributions Levels: Corporate Contributions and Pretax Income* analyzes foundation giving, industry patterns, 1985 ratios, employee size and contributions, geographic distribution of contributions, and overseas giving; and *Priorities In Corporate Giving* reviews giving in health and human services, education, culture and arts, civic and community activities, other organizations and regional differences. Supplementing the report are eighteen tables, nine charts and numerous statistical lists.

1417. Council on Foundations. *Corporate Giving: The Views of Chief Executive Officers of Major American Corporations.* Washington: Council on Foundations, 1982.

Report of a study of corporate CEOs that examined current giving practices and projections of future giving, with the major focus on cash giving. CEOs from companies with annual sales volumes of over $25 million were surveyed on their: current giving practices; general attitudes toward cash giving and the goals of giving; impression of factors influencing commitment and level of giving; and projection on future giving. Among the key findings, the study discovered that CEOs dominate giving decisions; that corporate giving is an expression of corporate self-interest; that many CEOs believe giving programs are underachieving; and that corporate giving is poorly understood in many corporations. The study recommends greater involvement by boards of directors, heightened professionalization of the giving function, refinement of mechanisms to ensure that both company goals and societal needs are met, and greater accountability from organizations receiving corporate dollars.

1418. Council on Foundations. *Corporate Philanthropy: Philosophy, Management, Trends, Future, Background.* Washington: Council on Foundations, 1982.

This report opens with major policy analysis papers by chief executive officers and others, focuses on cash giving, and offers a summary and analysis of the papers themselves by Nick Katz. In the four sections that follow, topics covered include the organization of corporate giving programs, current issues and trends in corporate philanthropy, a look at the future that includes the results of a major study by Yankelovich, Skelly, and White determining the perceptions of chief executive officers about factors influencing giving programs in their companies, and historical and background materials. In this last section, see especially Barry Karl's essay, which traces the evolution of corporate philanthropy from the days of the "direct benefit" doctrine to the present expanded notion of social responsibility. Karl concludes that, where once the power of corporations was feared as a power to do harm, society must now cope with their power to do good.

1419. Council on Foundations. *Corporate Public/Private Partnerships: Is It a New Time?* Occasional Paper, no. 1. Washington: Council on Foundations, 1986.

Examines the increasing popularity of public/private partnerships, where private and corporate grantmakers join government, nonprofit agencies, and business interests to bring about change or deliver social services in a neighborhood or municipality. While they can stimulate a local economy and attract the substantial resources necessary to provide housing and other high-cost services (as in the cases of Baltimore and Indianapolis), the report warns that public/private partnerships must be kept in perspective, as they are neither a complete substitute for government programs in some areas, nor a complete answer to social needs in other areas.

1420. Council on Foundations. *Managing Smaller Corporate Giving Programs.* Washington: Council on Foundations, 1983.

Primer sets out principles aimed to provide a sound base for smaller and medium-sized corporations seeking to start or manage a giving program. Discusses the case for giving, mentioning benefits to both corporation and communities, and stresses the importance of the chief executive officer's commitment to the program to insure successful startup and management. Advises the establishment of a contributions committee to oversee the giving program, a systematic approach to grantmaking, eligibility criteria for awarding grants, guidelines for nonprofit organizations that apply for grants, and a periodic evaluation of the program to ascertain its successes and remedy and learn from its failings. Includes addresses and phone numbers of further resources.

1421. Council on Foundations. *Memorandum on Corporate Giving: Including Compendium of Applicable Federal Tax Laws.* Washington: Council on Foundations, 1981.

1422. Council on Foundations. *Moral Obligation or Marketing Tool? Examining the Roles of Corporate Philanthropy.* Washington: Council on Foundations, 1985.

Based on discussions held by the Council on Foundations in April 1985, this book considers the pros and cons of cause-related marketing and discusses the placement of giving programs within the corporate structure. Profiles programs by B. Dalton Booksellers, which addresses illiteracy, and by United Technologies Corporation, which focuses on arts and culture.

1423. Council on Foundations. *Papers on Corporate Philanthropy.* Washington: Council on Foundations, [1986].

Three essays on corporate philanthropy. *Moral Obligation or Marketing Tool* examines the motives of corporations with giving programs and the tensions wrought by having a contributions program in a structure aimed at making money. *International Corporate Contributions* seeks to raise awareness about international social programs, show what many corporations are doing, and indicate what could and should be done to strengthen international corporate philanthropy. *Managing Smaller Corporate Giving Programs* offers sound advice to directors, chief executive officers, and managers concerned with starting and managing smaller corporate giving programs.

1424. "Credit Card Companies Embrace Cause Marketing." *NonProfit Times* 2 (December 1988): 27, 29, 30.

MasterCard International and Visa U.S.A. report sharp increases in revenue as a result of their involvement with cause-related marketing. American Express, after initiating the nation-wide high-profile campaign to restore the Statue of Liberty is now focusing on local promotions, such as a campaign to raise money for the Minnesota Zoo. American Express vice-president Warner Canto will not use cause-related marketing to raise money for charities fighting disease and human suffering because he believes such a link is "inappropriate." And although a member of the Red Cross in charge of cause marketing programs praises MasterCard for its sensitivity to the needs of nonprofits, he also warns charities to learn to be "hard-nosed and businesslike in negotiating such ventures. You can be a real pawn in the game."

1425. Crittenden, Ann. "Industry's Role in Academia." *New York Times* (22 July 1981): D-l, D-11.

1426. Cultural Assistance Center. *Partners: A Practical Guide to Corporate Support of the Arts.* New York: Cultural Assistance Center, 1982.

Designed as a guide for corporate officials, this report also suggests ways nonprofits, particularly arts groups, can improve and build corporate support.

1427. Demaris, Ovid. *Dirty Business: The Corporate-Political Money-Power Game.* New York: Harper's Magazine Press, 1974.

1428. Dermer, Joseph, and Stephen Wertheimer. *The Complete Guide to Corporate Fund Raising.* Washington: Public Service Materials Center, 1982.

Eleven articles offering advice and strategies on conducting corporate fundraising efforts.

1429. Desruisseaux, Paul. "Fund Uncovers Way for Companies to Use Frozen Overseas Assets: Give Them Away." *Chronicle of Higher Education* (29 October 1986): 31-2.

Discusses how corporations can take tax deductions by donating blocked foreign assets to charity.

1430. Desruisseaux, Paul. "Growth Is Explosive in Corporations' Gifts of Equipment." *Chronicle of Higher Education* 29 (21 November 1984): 1+.

1431. Dick, Ellen A. *Chicago's Corporate Foundations: A Directory of Chicago Area and Illinois Corporate Foundations.* Oak Park, Ill.: Ellen Dick, 1988.

Describes 122 corporate foundations in Illinois. Includes an index of in-kind contributions, a subject index of giving areas, and a matching gift index.

1432. Diebold, John. *The Role of Business in Society.* New York: Amacom, 1982.

1433. *Directory of Corporate Affiliations, 1989.* Wilmette, Ill.: National Register Publishing Co., 1988.

An annual guide to major U.S. corporations and their subsidiaries, divisions, and affiliates. Section 1 is an alphabetical index cross-referencing affiliates, divisions, and subsidiaries with their parent companies. Section 2 lists over 4,000 parent companies and their 40,000 subsidiaries, divisions and affiliates with assets, approximate sales, number of employees, type of business, and top corporate officers. The directory includes a geographical index to companies, a Standard Industrial Code (S.I.C.) index and a summary of mergers, acquisitions and name changes, dating back to 1976.

1434. *Directory of Directors in the City of New York and Tri-State Area.* Southport, Conn.: Directory of Directors Co., 1988.

This directory is arranged in two sections. The first section is an alphabetical list of important executives in New York City and State, New Jersey and Connecticut as well as names of the companies with which they are affiliated as officers, directors, trustees, or partners. It also includes individuals outside this area who sit on two or more corporate boards of sufficient importance within the geographical area. The second section includes important corporations or firms, and lists officers, directors or partners, address, telephone number, purchasing agent, and type of business. Also included are local directors who serve on boards of large corporations from outside the geographic area.

1435. Drake, Carl B., Jr. "Contributing to the Vitality of Our Community (St. Paul, MN)." *Response* 12 (July 1983): 8+.

1436. Duca Associates. *Colorado Corporate Contributions Survey.* Denver, Colo.: Duca Associates, [1979].

1437. Dun and Bradstreet. *Reference Book of Corporate Managements.* New York: Dun & Bradstreet, 1988.

1438. Dunkel, Tom. "Partnerships: Corporate Nonprofit Teamwork." *PSA/83* 2 (21 March 1983): 21-8.

1439. Dunkle, Margaret. *Cracking the Corporations: Finding Corporate Funding for Family Violence Programs.* Washington: Center for Women Policy Studies, 1981.

Offers tips for developing a corporate fundraising campaign, applicable to all types of nonprofits.

1440. Dunlop, Donna V. "Corporate Philanthropy: Alternate Funding Sources." *Bottom Line* 1 (Fall 1986): 35-7.

Concise article on corporate philanthropic sources. Includes explanations of the corporate forms of giving; research resources (The Foundation Center); and titles of available directories and monographs with brief content descriptions. Although the article is addressed to libraries and their funding needs, the information is general in nature and can readily assist with a wide variety of corporate funding queries.

1441. Earle, Benjamin. "Partnership: Lincoln Center's Consolidated Corporate Fund Drive Provides Business Support for the Arts." *Lincoln Center Stagebill* 12 (December 1984): 22+.

1442. Eckert, Ralph J. "Taking the Initiative for Corporate Public Involvement." *Response* 12 (March 1983): 8-9.

1443. "Education, a Capital Investment: Why Corporations Give Billions to Colleges and Universities." *Business Week* (June 22, 1987).

Explores corporate support for education as an investment decision and how the new relationship between universities and businesses is developing.

1444. Edwards, Thomas C. "Investor Involvement: Then and Now." *Response* 12 (January 1983): 8+.

1445. Eells, Richard. "Corporate Giving: Theory and Policy." *California Management Review* 1 (Fall 1958): 37-46.

1446. Eells, Richard. *The Corporation and the Arts.* New York: Macmillan, 1967.

1447. Eells, Richard. *Corporation Giving in a Free Society.* New York: Harper & Bros., 1956.

1448. Eells, Richard, ed. *International Business Philanthropy.* Studies of Model Corporations, Graduate School of Business, Columbia University. New York: Macmillan, 1979.

1449. "Exxon Increases Support for Nonprofit Management." *Corporate Giving Watch* 3 (October 1983): 2+.

1450. "Famous Amos Promotes Literacy Organization on Ice Cream Box." *Corporate Giving Watch* 3 (October 1983): 2.

1451. Fandel, Nancy A. *The National Directory of Arts and Education Support by Business Corporations.* 3rd ed. The Arts Patronage Series, no. 14. Des Moines, Iowa: Arts Letter, 1988.

One of a series of research publications in the Arts Patronage Series which updates listings and information published in the *Washington International Arts Letter.* This directory lists over 600 major businesses and corporations which contribute significantly to nonprofit arts organizations and educational institutions. Also in this edition, those who give direct financial support to individual artists are noted in the company profile. Profiles include name and address, contact, officers, types of arts and education support, recent grants list, and statistical information on percentage of arts support and dollar amounts for support.

1452. Farber, David R. *Corporate Philanthropy: An Annotated Bibliography.* Chicago: Donors Forum of Chicago, 1982.

1453. Fenwick, Dorothy C., ed. *Directory of Campus-Business Linkages: Education and Business Prospering Together.* Washington: American Council on Education, 1983.

1454. Ferguson, James L. *Cooperation: Key to the Future.* New York: Council for Financial Aid to Education, 1985.

Speech given at the 68th annual meeting of the American Council on Education.

1455. Ferguson, James L. *Why Corporations Need to Do More.* New York: Council for Financial Aid to Education, 1982.

1456. Fey, John T. *Why a New Goal for Corporate Giving to Higher Education?* New York: Council for Financial Aid to Education, [1981].

1457. Fiffer, Steve. "Suite Charity: The Big Business of Corporate Philanthropy in Chicago." *Chicago* 35 (October 1986): 165-212.

Examines the history, development and current trends of corporate philanthropy in Chicago as well as the views of nonprofit organizations on where this funding is spent.

1458. Finley, Michael. "The Benevolence of Businessmen." *Wisconsin Business Journal* (April 1984): 39-45.

1459. Fishman, Steve. "New Formulas for Philanthropy." *World* 22 (Summer 1988): 30-3.

Examines recent innovations in corporate philanthropy, including strategic giving (companies trying to maximize the impact of their gifts; making philanthropy "earn its keep"), cause-related marketing (donating a percentage of each purchase of goods or services to a worthy cause), and in-kind contributions (noncash contributions of company products, property and equipment). Includes several examples of programs that "make good social and business sense."

1460. "The Forbes Four Hundred." *Forbes* (13 September 1982): 99-108.

1461. Ford, Gerald. *An Examination of Bay Area Corporate Non-Cash Contributions.* San Francisco: Coro Foundation, 1981.

1462. Forrestal, Dan J. *Faith, Hope and $5,000. The Story of Monsanto: The Trials and Triumphs of the First 75 Years.* New York: Simon & Schuster, 1978.

1463. "Fortune 500 Directory: Geographic Breakdown, City." *Fortune* (27 April 1987): 1-43.

1464. "Fortune 500 Directory: Geographic Breakdown, State." *Fortune* (27 April 1987): 1-16.

1465. "The Fortune Service 500 Directory: Geographic Breakdown, City." *Fortune* (8 June 1987): 1-30.

1466. "The Fortune Service 500 Directory: Geographic Breakdown, State." *Fortune* (8 June 1987): 1-16.

1467. Foundation Center. *Corporate Foundation Profiles.* 1980-1988. New York: Foundation Center, 19—.

The 1988 edition provides detailed profiles of 239 major corporate foundations and brief descriptive listings of 771 smaller corporate foundations. Profile information includes name, address, purpose, limitations and contact for the major foundations; financial data concerning assets, gifts or contributions received by the foundation, expenditures including grants paid, high and low grant amount, employee matching gifts, grants to individuals, and loans and scholarships; sponsoring company and background; grant analysis, including types of support and listing of sample grants; policies and application guidelines; and funding cycle. Indexed by subject interest, type of support offered, and geographic location.

1468. "Foundations of a Better Society?" *Industry Week* (20 April 1981): 49-52.

1469. Freeman, Harry L. "The Media Don't Give Corporations Enough Credit." *NonProfit Times* 1 (August 1987): 23-4.

Freeman, executive vice-president of American Express Co., takes the media to task for not being responsible in its reporting of corporate philanthropy. The author cites examples such as the media not crediting corporate sponsors of events or covering philanthropic conferences. Also, the media does not cover "mundane giving"; they seek out only stories which are media events. Freeman believes that the lack of press coverage results in corporate funding support "of the sexy areas where media attention can be obtained." The dearth of print space and air time creates difficulties in obtaining philanthropic budgets within the corporation. Freeman notes that media credit could have a beneficial impact by tapping the natural competitive nature of companies. If company A, without a philanthropic program, sees company B obtaining media attention because of their philanthropic activity, company A may seek to emulate them.

1470. Fremont-Smith, Marion R. *Philanthropy and the Business Corporation.* New York: Russell Sage Foundation, 1972.

This study examines the legal and historical setting for corporate philanthropy, its current (1972) practice (scope, methods, and rationales), and the theory that underlies its practice, from shareholder ownership to the economic environment theories of Richard Eells. As Fremont-Smith puts it, the expansion of corporate philanthropy in recent decades into problems of poverty, race relations, urban renewal, pollution, education, and housing has necessitated a reappraisal of the philosophical and legal bases for corporate social action. While her analysis is often critical of current philanthropic practices, Fremont-Smith is careful to suggest that the practices can be improved, given commitment and imagination. Her summary of the legal and historical background of corporate philanthropy is helpful and concise.

1471. Galaskiewicz, Joseph. *Corporate-Nonprofit Linkages in Minneapolis-St. Paul. Preliminary Findings from Three Surveys.* Minneapolis, Minn.: University of Minnesota, 1982.

1472. Galaskiewicz, Joseph. *Social Organization of an Urban Grants Economy: A Study of Business Philanthropy and Nonprofit Organizations.* Orlando, Fla.: Academic Press, 1985.

This is a case study of the corporate philanthropic sector in Minneapolis-St. Paul, one of the nation's most generous corporate philanthropic communities, between 1979 and 1981. The study begins with a discussion of this question: "What are the social institutions that support an economy of donative transfers, and how do these institutions influence who gives, who gets, and who gives to whom?" It then examines the effect of the firm's market position and the executive's social position in the community on the volume of corporate contributions, before exploring the ideologies firms have offered to rationalize contributions (including the concept of enlightened self-interest). The roles of professional contributions staff on both the corporate donor and nonprofit donee side are considered, as well as those of professional fundraisers. Galaskiewicz sets forth an interesting analysis of who gives to whom by examining the theoretical literature on gift giving and exchanges, and assesses the Twin Cities experience in light of historical events. Substantial bibliography.

1473. Garvin, Clifton C., Jr. "Philanthropy: How Much Should Business Do?" *Enterprise* (July 1981): 8-9.

1474. General Electric Company. *Current Thought on Corporate Giving: A Survey and Analysis of the Literature.* Gainesville, Fla.: General Electric Co., 1956.

1475. "Getting 'Good Visibility'." *Corporate Philanthropy Report* 2 (May 1987): 1-3.

Brief article on the new era of corporate giving in which cost-cutting managers won't accept corporate giving budgets unless they build corporate image. Many corporations are engaged in efforts to "enhance public recognition of their company's good works." Profound implications could result from the changes. The article reviews six of the trends: the link between public relations and corporate giving is getting stronger; companies know they get less visibility for giving general purpose support than they can for programmatic support; companies want their grantees to mention where their grants came from; more companies are eager to boost their grantees' media relations capability; as companies take more initiative in their grantmaking, many are taking over more and more media relations functions themselves; and some companies have replaced press relations with arm-twisting to encourage other companies to contribute to the same project. The article concludes with a description of three trends nonprofits are using to meet the new corporate changes: 1) emphasizing their media saavy, 2) factoring press exposure efforts into their proposals, and 3) establishing media-nonprofit partnerships before going to companies.

1476. Gettinger, Steve. "New Horizons for Kids in the Middle." *Foundation News* 26 (March-April 1985): 42-7.

Describes New Horizons, one of nineteen foundation-sponsored programs that establish partnerships between businesses and schools to prevent youth unemployment.

1477. Gingrich, Arnold. *Business and the Arts.* New York: Paul S. Eriksson, [1969].

1478. Glynn, Jeannette E., Susan Huish, and Richard Kane. *Who Knows Who.* Berkeley, Calif.: Who Knows Who Publishers, 1987.

Traces the networks among the most influential people in America—the boards of directors of the Fortune 500 companies—to help fundraisers take practical action in approaching executives. Chapter 1 lists all directors of the 470 companies contained in this book, showing direct and indirect links between board members; Chapter 2 is an alphabetical listing of company-to-company links; Chapter 3 categorizes directors according to the number of boards to which they belong; Chapter 4 ranks each company by specifying the number of other companies linked to it; Chapter 5 contains an alphabetical listing of the names, addresses and telephone numbers of each company; and Chapter 6 lists each company's name with its individual directorate.

1479. Golden, L.L.L. *Only by Public Consent. American Corporations Search for Favorable Opinion.* New York: Hawthorn Books, 1968.

1480. Greater Cleveland Growth Association. *Matching Greater Cleveland's Corporate Philanthropy with Emerging Community Needs.* Cleveland: Greater Cleveland Growth Association.

1481. Greater Cleveland Growth Association. *Philanthropic Activity in the Greater Cleveland Area, 1979-1991.* Cleveland: Greater Cleveland Growth Association, 1985.

1482. Greater Minneapolis Chamber of Commerce. *Corporate Social Responsibility: Minnesota Strategies.* Minneapolis, Minn.: Greater Minneapolis Chamber of Commerce, 1981.

1483. Greenberg, Herb. "Soft Sheen Goes to the Top of Black Hair-Care Industry." *Chicago Tribune* (8 June 1983).

1484. Grohman, Robert. "As I See It: 'To Be a Good Citizen'." *Voluntary Action Leadership* (Summer 1983): 2+.

1485. Hagerty, Betty Lee. "How Small Businesses Can Be Big Contributors." *Fund Raising Management* 18 (August 1987): 54-8.

Examines the ways in which small businesses can benefit by becoming active in the community, including improvements in productivity, employee morale, community image, and the company's bottom line. Includes brief descriptions of involvement possibilities especially suited for small businesses.

1486. Haire, John R. "How Colleges Can Attract Corporate Funding." *Educational Record* (Fall 1981): 16-9.

1487. Hall, Elizabeth S., and Jerilyn D. Pope, comps. *Matching Gift Details: Guidebook to Corporate Matching Gift Programs.* Washington: Council for Advancement and Support of Education, 1988.

Provides information on corporations that match employee gifts to educational institutions. Also lists which of those companies match gifts to noneducational, nonprofit organizations. Entries include an indication of which organizations qualify for matching gifts, which employees are eligible, whether spouse's or retiree's gifts will be matched, the minimum and maximum amounts the company will match, how to obtain the matching gift, and how often the money is distributed. Appendixes include companies matching to institutions outside the United States, geographical listing of matching gift companies, parent companies listed with gift-matching divisions and subsidiaries, and an alphabetical listing of gift-matching divisions and subsidiaries shown with parent company.

1488. Hall, Mary S. "What Do They Think of Us?" *Foundation News* 29 (September-October 1988): 55-7.

Results of an informal survey to determine what employees outside of corporate contributions think of their corporation's giving programs and management personnel; focuses on the purpose of corporate philanthropy, the skills needed by those in corporate contributions programs, and the standing of the corporate contributions program among various stakeholders. The responses show that although corporate contributions programs are involved in more than simply "giving money away," most employees outside of the programs are unaware of the business-related goals of corporate philanthropy, such as supporting research and organizations that provide a base of knowledge for product and technology innovations, assisting programs and organizations that help create a favorable climate for the business, and using philanthropic strategies that will, in the long run, result in lower future expenses to the firms. The employees surveyed ranked leadership, technical management skills and general business knowledge as less important to a corporate contributions program than knowledge of the community and its organizations, which emphasizes the prevailing impression of the program as being an interface with the community's charitable activities. In the last issue of focus, the findings show that corporate contributions holds a relatively low standing with other employees, hypothesized as expressing the low value placed upon the notion of "giving money away" by the employees who believe this is the major function of the contributions programs. The article ends by identifying the "biggest challenge facing the corporate contributions profession: expanding the perceptions of our peers, first about the potential impact of corporate contributions on the long-term interests of the enterprise, and secondly, about the skills and qualifications of those entrusted to carry out that broader mission."

1489. Hall, Peter Dobkin. "The Forgotten Milestone." *Foundation News* 29 (March-April 1988): 44-7.

Reflections on the 50th anniversary of the corporate charitable deduction, examining pre- and post-deduction corporate activism in the area of social reform and the continuing link between doing well and doing good in business enterprise.

1490. Hall, Peter Dobkin. *The Organization of American Culture, 1700-1900: Private Institutions, Elites, and the Origins of American Nationality.* New York: New York University Press, 1982.

The introduction explains that the book's purpose is to examine "the ability of Americans to conduct their economic, political and cultural activities on a national scale...Because private for-profit and nonprofit corporate organizations operating first on a local, but ultimately on a national scale replaced the family and the local community as the primary instruments for implementing the fundamental tasks of production, distribution, communication, socialization, and social control, the book concentrates specifically on the rise of social groups whose outlook was national and who were able to translate their national ideals into institutional and operational reality." Hall defines culture as "a set of social institutions used by a people in organizing the entire range of their fundamental activities." He argues that it is the educated elite who direct these institutions in whom hope for a secure international world ultimately lies. Extensive notes.

1491. Harris, Louis. *The Welcome Mat Is Out.* New York: Council for Financial Aid to Education, 1978.

1492. Hawley, Karen. *New Haven: A Case Study of Corporate Philanthropy and the Federal Budget Cuts, 1980-1982.* Program on Non-Profit Organizations, no. 91. New Haven, Conn.: Institution for Social and Policy Studies, 1983.

1493. Hay, John Thomas. *How to Organize a Chamber of Commerce Two Percent Club, to Encourage Increased Private Sector Initiative in Your Community.* Sacramento, Calif.: California Chamber of Commerce, 1982.

1494. Heald, Morrell. *The Social Responsibilities of Business: Company and Community, 1900-1960.* Cleveland: Case Western Reserve University Press, 1970.

This is a study of the ideas and activities through which American businesses have attempted to define and respond to their relationship with the surrounding community. Heald points out that the idea of corporate social responsibility has developed over several decades, cresting in the 1920s with the notion of the "trusteeship" of corporate management for the interests of all parties to the enterprise, and again in the 1950s with the idea of the corporate "good citizen." By the 1960s it had become so broad as to escape definition. Heald concentrates on finding the meaning of corporate social responsibility through actual business policies. He examines the conditions and ideas that attracted business attention to a potential field of social action in which community-oriented programs were then implemented and picked up on a wider scale. His study is based mainly on top levels of management in the larger corporations, whose chiefs are seen as the most active and influential leaders. Especially intensive treatment is given to the community chest movement in the 1920s and 1930s. Bibliographical note.

1495. Henderson, Hazel. "Should Business Tackle Society's Problems." *Harvard Business Review* 46 (July-August 1968): 77-85.

1496. Herbers, John. "Starved Cities Hunger for Corporate Aid." *Business and Society Review* 45 (Spring 1983): 8-11.

1497. Heyne, Paul T. *Private Keepers of the Public Interest.* New York: McGraw-Hill, 1968.

1498. Hill, Donna. "NAEIR Members, Donors Both Benefit from Surplus Goods Supply." *Exchange Networks* (Summer 1984): 6-7.

Describes the National Association for the Exchange of Industrial Resources (NAEIR), which collects surplus items from businesses and distributes the goods to its nonprofit members.

1499. Hill, Kenneth D. "Two Executives Talk about the Reagan Cuts and One Company's Response." *NSFRE Journal* 8 (Spring 1983): 12+.

1500. Hillman, Howard, and Marjorie Chamberlain. *The Art of Winning Corporate Grants.* New York: Vanguard Press, 1980.

General guide to raising funds from corporations, including a section on questions most proposal evaluators ask, and a sample proposal.

1501. Hodnett, Edward. *Industry-College Relations.* New York: World Publishing Co., 1955.

1502. Hopkins, Bruce R., Edward J. Beckwith, and Jana S. DeSirgh. *Company Foundations and the Self-Dealing Rules.* Resources for Grantmakers. Washington: Council on Foundations, 1987.

Analysis examines the federal tax law prohibitions on self-dealing as they apply to the operations and relationships between a business entity and its related foundation. Consists of five parts, Part 1 being a general introduction to the concept of a company foundation and the inherent problem of self-dealing; Part 2 summarizes federal tax laws with respect to corporate foundations; Part 3 summarizes some of the applicable general tax law concepts; Part 4 reviews specific problem areas in this aspect of the self-dealing setting; and Part 5 summarizes the tax penalties underlying the self-dealing rules. Includes an appendix providing a technical summary of the federal tax self-dealing rules.

1503. Howarth, Shirley Reiff, ed. *International Directory of Corporate Art Collections.* New York: ARTnews Associates, 1988.

1504. Human Resources Network. *The Handbook of Corporate Social Responsibility: Profiles of Involvement.* 2nd ed. Radnor, Pa.: Human Resources Network, [1975].

1505. Hunt, Avery. "Strategic Philanthropy: New and More Imaginative Ways of Giving Away Money Are Paying off for Both Recipients and Corporate Donors." *Across the Board* (July-August 1986): 23-30.

Discusses the market-oriented approach that corporations are using in making donations. Examples of six alternative corporate giving programs are presented.

1506. Hunt, Freeman. *Worth and Wealth: A Collection of Maxims, Morals and Miscellanies for Merchants and Men of Business.* New York: Stringer and Townsend, 1856.

Hunt has collected in this volume approximately 300 short sayings, poems, readings, excerpts, etc., on business and trade, with an aim "to present illustrations rather than theories, examples rather than precepts." The organizing principle of the collection is the notion that there is a good and bad in trade. Hunt wishes to show the good through "the pithy maxim, the anecdotes" or "the happy illustration." Among the many snippets, usually no more than a page or two long, are some that deal with the social and charitable obligations of the business or trade entrepreneur.

1507. Hunter, Sam. *Art in Business: The Philip Morris Story.* New York: Harry N. Abrams, 1979.

1508. Hutchinson, Peter C. "Accountability: Ask Your Stakeholders." *Foundation News* 25 (September-October 1984): 81-3.

Dayton Hudson asked seven constituencies to evaluate its grantmaking.

1509. Hutchinson, Peter C. "Gaining Clarity in a Time of Change." *Foundation News* 28 (September-October 1987): 49-51.

Discusses the need to examine five basic issues in order to define the purpose or strategy of corporate giving and develop a grantmaking agenda. The corporate grantmaker must determine the highest common denominator of interests that unites, or could unite, his constituents; a point of balance between the interests of the constituents and those of the company; a focus for the giving program that is consistent with the focus of the company itself and its unique competence; the future of the giving program, or the long-term results that the program desires to achieve; and what actions can actually be taken today to start the process of achieving the results to which the program is committed. Recommends Peter Drucker's *Management: Tasks, Responsibilities, Practices* as a guide to understanding and dealing with these issues.

1510. Hutchison, Stanley P. "Corporate Responsibility and the American Dream." *Response* 14 (May 1985): 10-3.

1511. "IBM-Digital Pact at MIT." *New York Times* (1 June 1983): D-20.

1512. Independent Community Consultants. *Charitable Contributions by Arkansas Businesses.* Private Philanthropy in Arkansas Research Series, no. 1. West Memphis, Ark.: Independent Community Consultants, 1982.

Brief report of a study examining the size and scope of contributions to charities by Arkansas corporations.

1513. Independent Sector. *Corporate Philanthropy.* [Cassette tape]. Washington: Independent Sector, 1985.

1514. Independent Sector. *Valuation Guide for Donated Goods.* Washington: Independent Sector.

1515. "Industry Giving Spotlight: Oil Industry." *Corporate Giving Watch* 4 (April 1984): 5-6.

1516. "Insurance Industry Giving Reaches New High." *Corporate Giving Watch* 9 (June 1984): 2.

1517. "Insurance Industry Issues 11th Annual Social Report, Identifies Trends in Giving." *Channels* 36 (February 1984): 2-4.

11th Annual Social Report of the Life & Health Insurance Business.

1518. *International Directory of Corporate Affiliations.* Wilmette, Ill.: National Register Publishing Co., 1988.

Cross-references over 30,000 divisions, subsidiaries, affiliates, etc. with their parent companies. The listings for over 1,120 foreign parent companies and over 1,500 U.S. companies with foreign holdings give address, telephone number, international banking affiliates, approximate sales, number of employees, type of business and top corporate officers. Indexed by geographical location, type of business, and tradename. A useful resource for development officers seeking international support.

1519. International Paper Company Foundation. *A Venture in Industry Aid to Public Secondary Education.* New York: International Paper Company Foundation.

1520. Jacoby, Neil H. *Corporate Power and Social Responsibility: A Blueprint for the Future.* New York: Macmillan, 1973.

1521. Jaffee, Larry. "Corporate Support Key to United College Fund Growth." *Fund Raising Management* 15 (October 1984): 46+.

1522. Jaffee, Larry. "Gifts-in-Kind Organization Gives Something for Nothing." *Fund Raising Management* 15 (January 1985): 50+.

Describes the National Association for the Exchange of Industrial Resources (NAEIR), which distributes products to its nonprofit members.

1523. Jankowski, Katherine E., ed. *Corporate Giving Yellow Pages. Taft Guide to Corporate Giving Contacts.* 6th ed. Washington: Taft Group, 1989.

Revised and expanded edition contains over 2,650 alphabetically arranged corporate entries including both direct giving programs and corporate foundations. Each listing includes corporate name, contact person with their title and department, name of the giving program, address, telephone number, and codes (dg or fdn) to indicate if the program is direct giving or corporate foundation. The directory contains: *Index to Companies by Foundation Name, Index to Corporate Headquarters and Operating Locations,* and *Index to Publications on Corporate Charitable Giving Programs.*

1524. Jankowski, Katherine E., ed. *Directory of International Corporate Giving in America.* 1st ed. Washington: Taft Group, 1988.

Provides information on 245 internationally owned U.S. companies which support U.S. nonprofits. Entries give U.S. sponsoring company name; foundation name; financial information; number of employees; headquarters city and state; the company's major products or industry; foreign parent company name, address, and financial data; contact name, address, and phone number; types of grant support (total giving and average grant amounts, when available); types of nonmonetary support; geographic preference; a concise program description; typical recipients; names and titles of corporate officers and contributions program officers; application requirements; a section titled *Other Things You Should Know* offering information on restrictions, other U.S. subsidiaries of the foreign parent, and U.S. subsidiaries of the profiled company; and a list of recent grants by the company or foundation, when available. Appendix contains contact and background data for an additional sixty companies that support U.S. nonprofits but decline to release details of their giving pattern and application procedures. Comprehensively indexed by headquarters state, operating location, nonmonetary support type, recipient type, foreign parent compay, parent company country, corporate officers by name, and grant recipients by state.

1525. Jankowski, Katherine E., ed. *Taft Corporate Giving Directory.* 10th ed. Washington: Taft Group, 1988.

Over 550 corporate giving programs are profiled in this edition. Profiles are alphabetically arranged and include information on contact person, giving amounts, grant types, other support, giving priorities, typical recipients, geographic focus of giving, company locations, company and foundation directors, contact procedures and recent giving. Subject access to the profiles is provided through the table of contents. Indexes to the profiles are by headquarters state; operating location; nonmonetary support type; recipient type; individuals by name, birthplace, alma mater; and sponsoring company.

1526. Johnson, Donald J. "Trends in Corporate Giving." *KRC Letter* 14 (January 1984): 5-8.

1527. Johnston, David. "Charity Begins at the Pump: The Oil Companies As a Funding Source." *Grantsmanship Center News* (May-June 1981): 33-41.

1528. Joseph, James A. "The Case for Corporate Giving." *Foundation News* 27 (July-August 1986): 4.

Written by the president of the Council on Foundations, Mr. Joseph discusses the difficulty corporate givers have in maintaining generous contributions in light of increased market competition.

1529. Joseph, James A. *Issues and Trends in Corporate Philanthropy: The American Experience.* Washington: Council on Foundations, 1985.

1530. Karson, Stanley G. "Laying It on the Line." *Response* 12 (January 1983): 2.

1531. Kay, Jane Holtz. "A New Philanthropy: Patrons Single Out the Design Field for Support." *Christian Science Monitor* (27 May 1983).

1532. Kennedy, Roger. "How the Ford Foundation Deals with Social Issues." *Trusts & Estates* (April 1975).

1533. Kidd, Harry. "How American Can Came to Martin Luther King Junior High School: A Look at Corporate Responsibility in the USA." *Charity Supplement* 2 (November 1984): 3-9.

1534. Klein, Kim. "Profile of a Major Donor." *Grassroots Fundraising Journal* 3 (October-November 1984): 12.

Describes donor whose donations are all given as in-kind.

1535. Kleinfield, N.R. "Forbes's List of the Richest." *New York Times* (28 September 1983): 1.

1536. Klemesrud, Judy. "Corporate Planes Transport Cancer Victims." *New York Times* (6 June 1983): B-5.

1537. Klepper, Anne. *Corporate Contributions Outlook*. Research Bulletin, no. 204. New York: Conference Board, 1987.

Reports an all-time high of $4.4 billion in corporate contributions during 1985, but stresses that the future is highly volatile. Restructuring and reorganization of corporate chiefs, mergers and acquisitions, and the Tax Reform Act of 1986 promise to have a negative effect on corporate contributions. Pressures to justify contributions or to tie them to the marketing of the company's product (cause-related marketing) add to the cautionary outlook of the report.

1538. Klepper, Anne. *The Corporate Contributions Professional*. New York: Conference Board, 1981.

Klepper's report, based on a 1980 survey of Fortune 1300 companies (with 524 respondents), profiles the people responsible for corporate contributions activity. The data indicate that there are only a few hundred major corporate contributions programs (as opposed to casual or unplanned giving programs) in the United States. Predictably, these major programs are present in companies with net sales of over $1 billion. Each program is run by a professional holding major planning and budgeting responsibilities with a budget of over $1 million; to preserve confidentiality, the report does not identify specific companies by name.

1539. Klepper, Anne. *Corporate Social Programs: Nontraditional Assistance*. New York: Conference Board, 1983.

Report of the Conference Board's first survey of non-cash giving programs of corporations. Examples include loaned executive programs, employee assistance programs, and United Way employee-campaign costs.

1540. Klepper, Anne, and Selma Mackler. *Screening Requests for Corporate Contributions*. Conference Board Report, no. 887. New York: Conference Board, 1986.

Examines and analyzes the management techniques and systems contribution executives employ in sifting through grant proposals. Four corporate case studies present the range of corporate practices and diversity of programs in the contributions field. Includes exhibits of request forms, review guidelines, grantmaking policies and charts.

1541. Kletzien, S. Damon, ed. *The Corporate Funding Guide of Greater Philadelphia*. Philadelphia: Greater Philadelphia Cultural Alliance, 1984.

1542. Knauft, E.B. "A Case for Giving 2% of Pretax Income." *New York Times* (17 October 1982): F-2.

1543. Knauft, E.B. "Corporate Giving Clubs." *Foundation News* 24 (March-April 1983): 61-4.

1544. Knauft, E.B. "The End of Another Myth." *Foundation News* 24 (September-October 1983): 52-5.

1545. Knauft, E.B. *The Management of Corporate Giving Programs*. Program on Non-Profit Organizations, no. 114. New Haven, Conn.: Institution for Social and Policy Studies, 1986.

Describes an in-depth study of the operation of forty-eight corporate contributions programs to analyze the decision-making process and the impact of company management and culture on contributions decisions. Presents an analysis of quantitative data on a number of variables concerning each company's program, a subjective assessment by the author of features of each program and an analysis of that assessment against quantitative variables, a survey of opinions of a group of experienced contributions managers regarding factors important in the effectiveness of a program, and an integration of all findings of the study in an attempt to define characteristics of an effective contributions program. Key findings include, among others, the predominance of reactive grantmaking (in response to a wide range of unsolicited grant requests) over proactive grantmaking (the active seeking, encouraging, or structuring of grants by the company to meet its objectives and priorities); the CEO's involvement in decisions about individual grants is inversely related to the size of the company; and the existence of a corporate foundation was found to have no relationship on either the size of the contributions budget, contributions as a percent of pre-tax income, or the size of the professional contributions staff. Bibliography.

1546. Knauft, E.B. *Profiles of Effective Corporate Giving Programs*. Washington: Independent Sector, 1985.

New analysis of forty-eight corporate giving programs located across the country. Study collected two types of data: statistical information about the company and contributions program, and narrative information based on an interview with the contributions manager. Pamphlet is an important resource for describing how companies make their giving decisions.

1547. Knauft, E.B. "Should Business Give Money to Charity?" *Foundation News* 23 (November-December 1982): 44+.

1548. Koch, Frank. "Corporate Giving Is on Center Stage in the 1980's." *Grants Magazine* 4 (September 1981): 138-44.

1549. Koch, Frank. *The New Corporate Philanthropy: How Society and Business Can Profit.* New York: Plenum, 1979.

Directed primarily towards corporate executives, this book focuses on how philanthropy works within the corporation but also provides useful insights for the nonprofit seeking corporate support.

1550. Kristol, Irving. "Corporate Philanthropy: How Much, If at All? Charity and Business Shouldn't Mix." *New York Times* (17 October 1982): F-2.

1551. Kristol, Irving. *Two Cheers for Capitalism.* New York: Basic Books, 1978.

1552. Kuznik, Frank. "The Benefactory." *Cleveland Magazine* (August 1981): 51-5, 131-35.

1553. Lahn, Seth M. *Corporate Philanthropy: Issues in the Current Literature.* Program on Non-Profit Organizations, no. 29. New Haven, Conn.: Institution for Social and Policy Studies, 1980.

1554. Langton, Stuart. "Corporate Public Involvement: An Interview with John Filer." *Citizen Participation* 2 (May-June 1981): 3, 12-3.

1555. Lavin, Michael R. *Business Information: How to Find It, How to Use It.* Phoenix, Ariz.: Oryx Press, 1987.

Handbook offers in-depth descriptions of major business publications and discusses the basic concepts essential for using these publications effectively. Covers basic research skills, including how to begin a research project, where to look for needed information, and how to identify the best sources available. Text is organized into four sections. Part 1 introduces concepts and methods important to business research, including basic forms of published information, major sources of unpublished information, and guides to both. Part 2 surveys the task of researching companies, covering information sources from simple directory listings to detailed financial data. Part 3 covers statistical information of all types: demographic data, statistics on industries, and general economic indicators. Part 4 examines a number of specific areas: marketing, labor law, taxation, information for job hunters, and consumer research. Indexed by publication titles and by subject.

1556. Law-Yone, Wendy, and Donna M. Jablonski, eds. *Company Information: A Model Investigation.* Washington: Washington Researchers, 1980.

1557. "Leading Business Spokesmen Argue Strong Case for Corporate Public Involvement." *Response* 12 (January 1983): 8+.

1558. Lee, Thomas Graham, and Margaret Stewart Carr, eds. *Give-and-Take: The Complete Tax Incentive Guide and the Approved Methods for Donating or Accepting Corporate Gifts of Inventory.* 4th ed., rev. Ontonagon, Mich.: Electronic Classroom, 1986.

Concise and comprehensive guide to Section 170(e)(3) of the Internal Revenue Code, otherwise known as the Special Contribution Rule, which allows manufacturers and distributors to make donations of inventory to nonprofit, tax-exempt 501(c)(3) organizations and receive considerable tax advantages. Explains the law, regulations, mechanics and incentives involved, and presents examples of successful gifts-in-kind programs.

1559. Lefever, Ernest W., Raymond English, and Robert L. Schuettinger. *Scholars, Dollars, and Public Policy: New Frontiers in Corporate Giving.* Washington: Ethics and Policy Center, 1983.

1560. "Letters to the Editor: The Dangers of Research Partnerships with Industry." *Chronicle of Higher Education* 26 (18 May 1983): 32.

1561. Levine, Marsha, and Roberta Trachtman, eds. *American Business and the Public School: Case Studies of Corporate Involvement in Public Education.* New York: Teachers College Press, 1988.

Comprehensive examination of corporate America's commitment to and involvement with public education, with seven case studies and twenty-two mini-cases representing the full range of business/school collaboration in the 1980s. The cases are written by contributors from both the educational and corporate worlds, and are grouped under funding, programmatic participation, and policy making categories. In addition, the volume contains two appendixes, one discussing the impact of school/business partnerships on teachers in small urban and rural districts, and the other providing an update of a Committee for Economic Development survey of Fortune 500 companies, concerning the type and extent of their activity with the public schools. Although research-based, the book takes a practical view and suggests models for future collaborations. Includes a 107-item annotated bibliography.

1562. Levine, Marsha. "Schooled in Cooperation." *Foundation News* 29 (March-April 1988): 54-5, 57-8.

Examines how corporate-education partnerships reduce risks, enhance expertise and increase the impact of school programs. Corporate involvement is also influencing the new agenda for the school system, and insuring a broadened base of support for reforms that stress student success.

1563. Levy, Reynold. "Caught between Two Poles: Corporate Grantmakers Must Strike a Balance between Idealism and Institutional Self-Interest." *Foundation News* 26 (May-June 1985): 58+.

1564. Lewin, Tamar. "Corporate Giving Fails to Offset Cuts by U.S." *New York Times* (15 February 1985): 1.

1565. Lewis, Salim. "Do Corporations Give Enough?" *Challenge* 10 (March 1962): 17-9.

1566. Liedtke, Michael. "The Spirit of Corporate Giving." *Argus (Fremont, CA)* (11 December 1983).

1567. "Linking Philanthropy to Corporate Marketing." *Corporate Giving Watch* 3 (February 1984): 1-2.

1568. "Little-Known Funders Give Substantial Amounts." *Corporate Giving Watch* 6 (January 1987): 3-4.

Estimates the 1986 contributions for fourteen little-known yet significant corporate giving programs. Includes geographic giving areas, contact person, address, and telephone number. Recommends calling or sending for company guidelines and funding priorities.

1569. Longstreth, Bevis, and H. David Rosenbloom. *Corporate Social Responsibility and the Institutional Investor.* New York: Praeger, 1973.

1570. Lord, Benjamin, ed. *Corporate Philanthropy in America: New Perspectives for the Eighties.* Washington: Taft Group, 1984.

Special report which discusses the field of corporate philanthropy. Gives a comparison of corporate and foundation giving, analyzes the factors influencing corporate philanthropy, evaluates what subject areas corporate money supports, and looks at the future of corporate philanthropy. Includes a brief selected bibliography and six tables on corporate giving.

1571. Low, Murray B. "Farsighted Corporations Focus on Long-Term Gains." *Business and Society Review* 66 (Summer 1988): 61-4.

Presents a case for the "stakeholder concept" as the newest orientation in the evolution of the firm-society relationship. Stressing the inter-dependence between the firm and the overall system, the stakeholder perspective suggests it is time for firms to develop an active concern for the well-being of all constituent groups with which they interact. Three factors in the current American economy have produced a greater awareness of the inter-dependence among firms and between firms and the rest of society: the increasing emphasis on service, which demands attention to the concerns of customers and employees for success; the discovery that cooperation among firms helps to maintain global competiveness; and the uncertainty concerning government's ability to provide the physical and social infrastructure that supports the private sector. The author asserts that the stakeholder concept, while necessitating short-term sacrifices, will ultimately insure long-term prosperity. The end result will be a corporation that is both moral and efficient.

1572. Lydenberg, Steven D. *Minding the Corporate Conscience: Public Interest Groups and Corporate Social Accountability.* New York: Council on Economic Priorities, 1977.

1573. Lydenberg, Steven D., Alice Tepper Marlin, and Sean O'Brien Strub. *Rating America's Corporate Conscience: A Provocative Guide to the Companies behind the Products You Buy Every Day.* Reading, Mass.: Addison-Wesley, 1986.

Council on Economic Priorities' corporate guide which evaluates and ranks the social responsibility and performance of 130 American corporations. The book is arranged in two parts. Part 1 contains an explanation on how to use the book; an examination of the social issues; a section aimed at the consumer; and a chapter on social investing which contains a *Quick Guide to Some Socially Responsible Funds and Investment Advisors.* Part 2 contains corporate profiles and accompanying charts with information on current policies, past practices, and significant controversies on key social issues such as South Africa, nuclear and conventional weapons contracts, charitable contributions, representation of women and minorities in management, disclosure of social information, and the environment. In addition, specifics on corporate Political Action Committees (PACs) are included in the charts. The corporate profiles analyze in greater detail the issues presented in the charts. They also describe outstanding positive initiatives a company has taken as well as highly publicized controversies in which it has been involved. For a complete evaluation, readers must consult both charts and profiles. Another useful chart in the book is the *Corporate Product Charts* which presents hundreds of brand-name products in a handy checklist, comparing how the manufacturers rate on the issues. The appendixes contain information on the *Methodology and Sources of Information, References, Resources and Related Publications, Company Products and Services,* and *Chapter Notes.*

1574. Malkiel, Burton G. "Moral Issues in Investment Policy." *Harvard Business Review* 49 (March-April 1971): 37-47.

1575. Manne, Henry G., and Henry C. Wallich. *The Modern Corporation and Social Responsibility.* Washington: American Enterprise Institute, 1972.

1576. Matthews, Downs. "Giving to the College of Your Choice." *Exxon USA* (1982): 8-11.

1577. Mayberry, Debra J., Laura Gibbons, and David J. Hurvitz, eds. *The Corporate 1000: A Directory of Those Who Manage the Leading 1000 Listed U.S. Companies.* Washington: Monitor Publishing Co., 1989.

Lists board members, chief officers and management staff of 1000 corporations and their subsidiaries. Indexed by industry and personal names.

1578. McCall, David B. "Profit: Spur for Solving Social Ills." *Harvard Business Review* 51 (May-June 1973): 46-56.

1579. McKie, James W., ed. *Social Responsibility and the Business Predicament.* Studies in the Regulation of Economic Activity. Washington: Brookings Institution, 1974.

1580. McNamee, Mike. "Corporate Charity Is Still Spreading." *USA Today* (13 December 1982).

1581. Meadows, Doris. "Corporate Gifts Leveling off." *New York Times* (6 February 1983).

1582. Messier, Edward. "Corporate Restructuring with a Development Emphasis." *Fund Raising Management* 15 (October 1984): 18+.

Discusses the importance of development directors of nonprofit health care facilities involving themselves in corporate restructuring.

1583. Metropolitan Life Insurance Company. *Community Relations: Being a Good Neighbor.* New York: Metropolitan Life Insurance Co., 1949.

1584. Mettler, Ruben F. *Linking Corporate Philanthropy to Corporate Growth.* New York: Council for Financial Aid to Education, 1979.

1585. Miller, Jay. "Corporate Gift-Giving in Cleveland." *Crain's Cleveland Business* (22 June 1981): 12.

1586. Millsaps, Daniel. *National Directory of Arts Support by Business Corporations.* Des Moines, Iowa: Arts Letter, 1979.

1587. Mittenthal, Stephen. *Non-Cash Corporate Philanthropy: A Report on Current Practices with Annotated Bibliography.* Tacoma, Wash.: Weyerhaeuser Foundation, 1983.

Provides an overview of non-cash corporate philanthropy, arranged under four categories: donated products, donated services and facilities, employee voluntarism, and program-related investments. Also includes a short annotated bibliography of publications that address specific aspects of non-cash giving, such as voluntarism and program-related investments.

1588. Mittenthal, Stephen. "The Perfect Gift: Examples of Noncash Corporate Philanthropy." *Grantsmanship Center News* 11 (September-October 1983): 50-4.

Describes a variety of non-cash donations and other support given by businesses to nonprofits, including in-kind contributions of products, services and facilities, and loaned personnel, as well as matching gifts and program-related investments.

1589. Modic, Stanley J. "Movers and Shakers of Corporate Social Responsibility." *Business and Society Review* 65 (Spring 1988): 63-9.

Recognizes more than 500 "movers and shakers" (those considered to be among the "most concerned, involved, and active of the community-minded industrial and business leaders who make things happen") in more than 100 cities across the country.

1590. Morris, Dubois S., Jr. "Corporate Support: More Money and Involvement." *Currents* 5 (October 1979): 37-9.

1591. Morse, F. Bradford. *Private Responsibility for Public Management.* Boston: Harvard Business Review, 1967.

Reprinted from Harvard Business Review.

1592. Morton, Herbert C. "Minds, Money, and Markets." *Resources* 72 (February 1983): 20-1.

1593. Moseley, Jack. "USF and G: A Heritage of Giving." *Response* 14 (August 1985): 8+.

Provides an account of one insurance company's commitment to corporate public involvement.

1594. Moskal, Brian S. "Business Meets Its Social Responsibility." *Industry Week* (20 April 1981): 54-9.

1595. Moskowitz, Milton. *Everybody's Business, an Almanac: The Irreverent Guide to Corporate America.* New York: Harper & Row, 1980.

1596. Moskowitz, Milton. "The 1982 Annual Reports: A Potpourri for the Corporate Watchdog." *Business and Society Review* 46 (Summer 1983): 20-5.

1597. Mueller, Robert K. "Criteria for the Appraisal of Directors." *Harvard Business Review* 57 (May-June 1979): 47.

1598. "A Multi-Tiered Economy: Industry Outlooks 1981." *Business Week* (12 January 1981): 51-85.

1599. Murphy, Dennis J. *Asking Corporations for Money.* Port Chester, N.Y.: Gothic Press, 1982.

Analyzes the criteria and characteristics of the decision-making process in corporate contributions programs.

1600. Murphy, Dennis J. *Corporate Support Program Research Project.* Unpublished, 1981.

1601. Nader, Ann Marie. *A Special Report Summarizing Self-Study Methods for the Philanthropic Programs of Twelve Corporations.* Unpublished.

1602. National Chamber Foundation. *Corporate Philanthropy in the Eighties: Expert Advice for Those Who Give or Seek Funds.* Washington: National Chamber Foundation, 1980.

This brief booklet came out of a 1979 National Conference Focusing on a Changing Economy and Its Impact on Corporate Giving, cosponsored by the National Chamber Foundation and the California Chamber of Commerce. It includes remarks by corporate leaders such as A.W. Clausen, then president of Bank of America NT&SA; Council on Foundations chairman Landrum Bolling; Arthur White of Yankelovich, Skelly, and White; Leonard Silverstein, past executive director of the Commission on Private Philanthropy and Public Needs; and Earl Cheit, dean of the School of Business Administration at the University of California/Berkeley. Topics include giving more, and giving more effectively, the needs business ought to address, the impact of corporate philanthropy on public attitudes, and corporate support for higher education.

1603. National School Volunteer Program. *Partners for the 80's: Business and Education.* Alexandria, Va.: National School Volunteer Program, 1981.

1604. Nelson, Ralph L. *Economic Factors in the Growth of Corporation Giving.* National Bureau of Economic Research Occasional Paper, no. 3. New York: National Bureau of Economic Research, 1970.

1605. "New Service to Make Matches between Corporate Donors and Nonprofits." *Giving Forum* 7 (April 1984): 1.

1606. "New Study Shows Nearly All Major Corporations Give to Charity." *Fund Raising Review* (May 1983): 7.

1607. Noble, David F. "Corporatist Culture Ministries." *Nation* (21 March 1981): 335+.

1608. Nolan, Richard L. "Plight of the EDP Manager." *Harvard Business Review* 51 (May-June 1973): 143-52.

1609. Norton, Michael. *The Corporate Donor's Handbook.* London: Directory of Social Change, 1987.

It is one of the ironies of company charitable support that companies, the repositories of a wide range of management skills, seldom apply these skills effectively to the management of their charitable budgets. This book provides practical advice, examples and case studies, and technical information to help companies plan and implement a coherent and successful program of charitable activities. While written for British corporations, much of the advice is useful to companies in the

U.S. as well, including an examination of the reasons for corporate giving (based on the concept of enlightened self-interest); factors to consider when setting a charitable budget; determining policies and guidelines for giving; procedures for appeals administration, including assessment and response; making gifts in kind; employee involvement, community award and matching gift programs; promoting employee charitable giving; private-public sector collaboration and business-led initatives in environmental improvement and redevelopment projects; and an overview of superior corporate practices in the U.S.

1610. "Now That We're in an Age of Partnership, Let's Take a New Look at Those Five Phases of Grantsmanship." *Corporate Philanthropy Report* 1 (August 1987): 4-5.

Brief overview of the five steps nonprofits must take when seeking to forge an alliance with corporations: researching, gaining access to targeted companies, meeting with company officials, knowing what to ask for, and managing further requests. Subsequent issues will offer resources and practical tips to help nonprofits manage each stage.

1611. Oates, James F., Jr. *Business and Social Change.* McKinsey Foundation Lecture Series. New York: McGraw-Hill, 1968.

1612. Olasky, Marvin N. *Patterns of Corporate Philanthropy.* Studies in Philanthropy, no. 3. Washington: Capital Research Center, 1987.

Dr. Olasky compiles 101 company profiles (including ideological indicators), contributions data for seventy-eight corporate foundations and profiles of 100 recipient organizations for which a definite ideological component could be identified, and observes that the function of corporate contributions, as a subset of public relations, has moved from general community support to specific targeting, with an emphasis on placating groups that might be critical of some corporate policies. He is concerned to find that seven out of every ten public affairs dollars from the top twenty-five corporate contributors support establishment liberal—even outright radical—causes, including "litigious environmentalists, radical feminists, liberal racial establishmentarians, professional philanthropoids, and others who see the federal government as ally rather than usurper." He urges corporate contributions officers to reevaluate their giving in terms of short-term prudence, middle-range ethics, and long-term strategy, and remember that the foundation exists because of our economic system, and shouldn't have to apologize for being a "creature of capitalism" by funding organizations that seek to undermine our economic system in the name of "corporate social responsibility."

1613. Olasky, Marvin N. "Reagan's Second Thoughts on Corporate Giving." *Fortune* (20 September 1983): 130+.

1614. O'Neill, Joseph P. *Corporate Tuition Aid Programs.* Princeton, N.J.: Conference University Press, 1984.

Provides survey of 650 major companies on their employee tuition benefits. Directory describes the terms and limitations of each company's policy, covering which employees are eligible for tuition benefits, length of employment required for eligibility, limits on reimbursement, and timing of reimbursement. Useful publication for college career placement officers, directors of adult and continuing education, and those in business overseeing employment training and education.

1615. Palmieri, Victor H. "Corporate Responsibility and the Competent Board." *Harvard Business Review* 57 (May-June 1979): 46-47.

1616. Patrick, Kenneth G., and Richard Eells. *Education and the Business Dollar: A Study of Corporate Contributions Policy and American Education.* Studies of the Modern Corporation. New York: Macmillan, [1969].

1617. Payton, Robert L. *The Ethics of Corporate Grantmaking.* Occasional Paper, no. 5. Washington: Council on Foundations, 1987.

Payton examines the use of ethics in the field of corporate grantmaking, especially as opposed to the concept of enlightened self-interest, which he maintains is "ethically problematic in practice. It is an unreliable guide."

1618. Pellegrene, John E. "Corporations May Benefit from Promoting Nonprofits." *Corporate Giving Watch* 4 (March 1985): 8.

1619. Perry, Nancy J. "Saving the Schools: How Business Can Help." *Fortune* 118 (7 November 1988).

Imperiled by the dearth of skilled workers, companies are urgently looking for solutions to the problems of the public education system. An education summit sponsored by *Fortune* magazine brought together over 100 leaders from business, government, and academia to help plan the specific steps business could take to help the schools, and to discuss programs already in progress which can serve as models. A major issue is the call to completely restructure the system in order to develop problem-solving skills "necessary for today's globally competitive workplace;" the Exxon Education Foundation, for example, funds the Coalition of Essential Schools, which experiments with new approaches to teaching. To turn individual efforts into a national restructuring of public education, corporations can mobilize state-by-state to bring about legislative reform. A program in Minnesota to allow parents to choose which public school their children will attend is applauded as a free-market force for reform; full legislation takes effect over the next two years, but initial reactions appear promising. Efforts to lower the dropout rate, raise college enrollment, recruit better teachers, promote job training, support preschool programs and inspire students are also advocated; article cites examples of current programs, and provides their addresses and phone numbers as sources of information for other interested corporations.

1620. Perry, Suzanne. "Professors Can Land Corporate Sponsors for Research, If They Follow the Rules." *Chronicle of Higher Education* 26 (20 April 1983): 21-2.

1621. Pickslay, F. Frith, Jr. *Charitable Foundations for Business Corporations.* Unpublished, 1954.

1622. Platzer, Linda Cardillo. *Highlights from the Conference Board's Survey of Corporate Contributions.* New York: Conference Board, 1988.

Major findings of the 1986 Survey of Corporate Contributions: contributions by all U.S. corporations for 1986 are estimated to reach $4.5 billion, an increase over 1985 contributions of less than one percent in constant dollars and the smallest increase since 1975; the slow growth in corporate contributions reflects the ailing economic performance of reporting companies; and the share of giving to education surged from thirty-eight percent to forty-three percent of total contributions, the highest level in the history of the survey, while corporate giving to health and human services organizations and civic and community organizations declined.

1623. Plinio, Alex J. "Annual Report: A Necessity for Corporate Grant Programs." *Fund Raising Management* 15 (November 1984): 101.

1624. Plinio, Alex J. "Art Collections Can Showcase Non-Profits." *Fund Raising Management* 14 (June 1983): 76-7.

Plinio describes how a company may provide non-cash assistance to local nonprofit organizations as a way to promote its employees' volunteer involvement and to make its community relations position more visible.

1625. Plinio, Alex J. "Check If Non-Cash Gifts Deductible for Business." *Fund Raising Management* 14 (July 1983): 74-5.

1626. Plinio, Alex J. "Computer, Other Services Can Be Business-Donated." *Fund Raising Management* 13 (January 1983): 62+.

1627. Plinio, Alex J. "Corporate Donors Can Help Make Contracts." *Fund Raising Management* 14 (May 1983): 62-3.

1628. Plinio, Alex J. "In Non-Cash World, Barter Emerges As New Development." *Fund Raising Management* 14 (March 1983): 70-1.

1629. Plinio, Alex J. "Non-Traditional Corporate Assistance Under Study." *Fund Raising Management* 14 (November 1983): 82-3.

1630. Plinio, Alex J. "Resource Raising Calls for New Fund Raising Mind-Set." *Fund Raising Management* 13 (February 1983): 63.

1631. Plinio, Alex J. *Resource Raising: The Role of Non-Cash Assistance in Corporate Philanthropy.* Washington: Independent Sector, 1986.

Report on the ways that corporations can offer non-cash assistance to nonprofits, covering legal and tax considerations, new roles for corporate giving officers, brokerage services, and numerous examples of non-cash gifts.

1632. Plinio, Alex J., and Joanne B. Scanlan. *Resource Raising: The Role of Non-Cash Assistance in Corporate Philanthropy.* Washington: Independent Sector, 1986.

Practical guide to non-cash corporate giving, including gifts of products, human resources, and services. The authors hold that non-cash assistance provides the means for corporate-contributions officers to expand their companies' assistance to nonprofits while also extending their own influence within and outside the companies. Reviews current corporate activities, roles played by corporate-contributions officers, considerations in seeking non-cash gifts, domestic and international brokerage services, and legal and tax implications. Also includes many examples of non-cash giving, grouped within six categories: facilities and services; public-relations services; loaned talent; products, supplies, and equipment; program-related investments; and executive and employee volunteering. Bibliography.

1633. Plinio, Alex J. "Times Cause Exxon to Give More, Smaller Grants." *Fund Raising Management* 14 (October 1983): 90-1.

1634. Podesta, Aldo C. *Raising Funds from America's 2,000,000 Overlooked Corporations.* Washington: Public Service Materials Center, 1984.

1635. Pokrass, Richard J. "Corporate Giving to Two-Year Colleges." *Currents* 14 (January 1988): 38-9.

Author's survey of 400 corporations confirms they are less likely to give to two-year colleges than to any other type of higher education institution. However, he insists that a potential for significant corporate contributions to two-year colleges does exist, and offers advice on tapping that potential. Among his findings: a corporation is most likely to give to a two-year college that can show it is an integral part of the firm's own home community; corporations prefer to give to institutions whose programs relate to the company's interest; and most corporate donations to two-year colleges at present are matches of employee gifts. The findings suggest several strategies to increase corporate support: conducting more research on corporate giving to two-year colleges; approaching corporations close to the college to stress community; tailoring funding proposals to companies with similar interests; and making greater use of alumni to increase the amount of matching gifts.

1636. Polivy, Deborah K. *Increasing Giving Options in Corporate Charitable Payroll Deduction Programs: Who Benefits?* Program on Non-Profit Organizations, no. 83. New Haven, Conn.: Institution for Social and Policy Studies, 1985.

Study which looks at the expansion of corporate employee deduction programs beyond United Way. Examines six companies which have expanded their payroll deduction programs and offers alternative ways of designing such programs.

1637. Pollard, John A. "Emerging Pattern in Corporate Giving." *Harvard Business Review* 38 (May-June 1960): 103-12.

1638. Porter, Robert A., ed. *Guide to Corporate Giving in the Arts 4.* New York: American Council for the Arts, 1987.

1639. Porto, Linda. "Corporate Nonprofit Teamwork." *PSA/84* 3 (21 January 1984): 41.

1640. Powills, S. "Mergers Won't Slow Corporate Philanthropy." *Hospitals* 60 (20 January 1986): 52.

1641. President's Task Force on Private Sector Initiatives. *Building Partnerships.* Washington: Government Printing Office, 1982.

1642. President's Task Force on Private Sector Initiatives. *Corporate Community Involvement.* New York: Citizens Forum on Self-Government/National Municipal League, 1982.

Report reviews the range of strategies used by for-profit corporations to respond to community needs, including cash contributions, volunteering, in-kind donations of equipment and facilities, targeted business purchasing, hiring decisions, and investment strategies. Examples are given to illustrate elements of successful contributions programs, the changing role of the chief executive officer, and the importance of analyzing community needs. Report stresses the benefits of combining forms of involvement (e.g., volunteer participation tied to cash giving) in the community. Appendix contains a list of resources.

1643. President's Task Force on Private Sector Initiatives. *Investing in America: Initiatives for Community and Economic Development.* Washington: Government Printing Office, 1982.

1644. "Private Higher Education Focus of New Corporate/Private Foundation Effort." *Council on Foundations Newsletter* 2 (22 November 1983): 1.

1645. Project Share. *Corporate Philanthropy: A Human Services Bibliography.* Rockville, Md.: Project Share.

1646. "Proposed Tax Change Would Send High Tech Product Donations Soaring." *Corporate Philanthropy Report* 1 (July 1985): 3-6.

Enthusiastic report of the 1985 proposed change to the corporate tax code concerning product donation. Article reviews developments since the provision originally appeared in 1981, and predicts three indirect consequences applying to the next wave of giving: 1) a "spillover" effect benefiting non-science and non-educational nonprofits, 2) encouragement of voluntarism by technical employees to assist nonprofits with donated computers, and 3) increased gifts of cash to the same nonprofits receiving products. Includes useful information on how to get a donated high-tech product.

1647. Public Management Institute. "Golden Donor's Hidden Insight." *Corporate Philanthropy Report* 2 (August 1986): 5-7.

Critical review of Wally Nielsen's book, *Golden Donors*, written for those in corporate philanthropy. The book was written about the thirty-six largest endowed foundations, but ignored corporate philanthropy. The author of the article believes that the book provides insights into the subtle question of how foundations and corporations relate to each other and how that relationship has changed over time. *Golden Donors* discusses the historical link between the corporate and foundation worlds such as the evolution from the establishment of foundations with entrepreneurs' endowments through to the current policies which insulated them from the corporate culture. In the 1970's, the article points out, the gap between foundations and corporations was so great that many felt that foundation programs had begun to run counter to the interests of corporate America. The review cites questions that have been left unanswered in the volume's sweeping analysis, but notes the book reveals that the factors previously keeping the foundation and corporate worlds at arms' length have evaporated.

1648. Public Management Institute. *How to Get Corporate Grants.* San Francisco: Public Management Institute, 1980.

How-to workbook with numerous forms, worksheets, and checklists for use in corporate grantseeking.

1649. Public Management Institute. "The Pact Is Broken! Corporations Now Prefer Governmental Higher Ed." *Corporate Philanthropy Report* 2 (August 1986): 1-3.

Informational essay on the trend towards corporate giving to public colleges and universities. What was once thought of as impossible has happened—public higher education fundraisers are winning over the corporate world. According to the Council for the Advancement and Aid to Education, companies are donating more to public schools than to private ones. The privates are still showing annual gains, but public funding is increasing nearly three times faster. In dollar amounts, corporate support totaled $1.5 billion in 1985. Corporations give almost forty percent of their contribution's budget to higher education and that is in addition to hundreds of millions in research and development funding. Corporate support has been obtained by public fundraisers who have built a strong case for giving based on institution quality; local corporate support for local schools; the argument to corporations that their funds enhance the government monies and make the school top-notch; the fact that schools today are largely quasi-state related, not state run; the fact that local company support can be used as a leverage for national support; the placement of more corporate executives on public university boards; the fact that there is a natural economic development tie-in between universities and business; and the alumni tie-in (even if the public alumni give at lower levels, their numbers are so great that with a good computer tracking system, they still can give more support).

1650. Public Management Institute. *Seven Ways to Contact Corporate Funding Executives.* San Francisco: Public Management Institute, 1980.

1651. Public Management Institute. "When Nonprofits Fit into Marketing Strategy." *Corporate Philanthropy Report* 2 (October 1986): 5-6.

Comments by marketing executive Jerry Welsh who states that in 1981 he created a strategy to "generate superior business results, be newsworthy and be public spirited at the same time." The technique was cause-related marketing; in particular, American Express's Statue of Liberty campaign. The key, says Welsh, is that the project must excite the imagination, which "explains why cause-related marketing efforts have been able to garner positive press coverage—a factor that vastly increased the selling power of the marketing." Welsh's new challenge is to create cause-related marketing initiatives for higher education which "no marketer has ever defined...think of all the needs of that market. Think about how affluent that market is and is going to become."

1652. Public Service Materials Center. *The Corporate Fund Raising Directory.* Washington: Public Service Materials Center, 1987.

Describes the giving programs of over 600 corporations, including primary areas of interest, geographic preference, and application information. Indexed by headquarters state, geographic preference, contact persons, and corporations that issue guidelines.

1653. Public Service Materials Center. *Grant Making Corporations That Publish Guidelines.* Washington: Public Service Materials Center, 1984.

1654. Reinhold, Robert. "Stanford and Industry Forge New Research Link." *New York Times* (10 February 1984): A-22.

1655. Reiss, Alvin H. *Culture and Company: A Critical Study of an Improbable Alliance.* New York: Twayne Publishers, 1972.

1656. Reuter, Carol J. *Corporate Fundraising: Advice from an Expert.* Washington: League of Women Voters, [198?].

1657. Richards, Bill. "Berkshire Hathaway Pleases Shareholders by Letting Them Earmark Corporate Gifts." *Wall Street Journal* (26 April 1983): 37.

1658. Riggan, John. "Strategies for Leaner Times." *Foundation News* 29 (July-August 1988): 66-7.

With mergers, downsizing and declining earnings, corporate contributions programs are suffering under budget and staff cutbacks. Article recounts a successful funding partnership between the Pillsbury and Primerica foundations in order to achieve greater impact with limited funds by strategically targeting resources. Other approaches and techniques are suggested, including the adoption of tighter justification standards for the awarding of grants, avoiding multi-year commitments, and considering alternatives to cash grants, such as technical assistance or in-kind support.

1659. Rockefeller Foundation, Winthrop. *Responsible Choices in Taxation.* Little Rock, Ark.: Winthrop Rockefeller Foundation, 1984.

1660. Rockwell, John. "The Met Sings the Praise of Corporate Sponsorship." *New York Times* (29 September 1985).

1661. Roderick, David M. *Business and the Arts: From a Mutual Need, a Working Partnership.* Unpublished, 1981.

1662. Rosebush, James S. "Corporate Philanthropists Give Up on the 'Free Lunch'." *Business and Society Review* 66 (Summer 1988): 38-41.

Discusses expected trends in corporate philanthropy due to economic restructuring such as mergers and acquisitions. Many programs will suffer as new management policies seek to reduce costs; in order to increase effectiveness, contributions programs must develop clearly defined goals and be integrated with advertising, public relations, and government/international relations. Cause-related marketing and other creative, unconventional methods of corporate giving will be on the rise in the U.S., while many nonprofit organizations will be looking to foreign corporations as a growing new source of funding.

1663. Ruml, Beardsley, and Theodore Geiger. *The Manual of Corporate Giving.* Washington: National Planning Association, 1952.

1664. Rushton, William J., III. "Partners in Neighborhood Growth." *Response* 12 (May 1983): 8-13.

1665. Ryerson, Edward L. *A Businessman's Concept of Citizenship.* Privately Printed, 1960.

A series of lectures delivered in Australia during the Fall of 1958 under the auspices of the Fulbright Committee.

1666. Salewic, Marge. "Charities in the Marketplace: A Look at Joint-Venture Marketing. Part 1." *Insight* 2 (1987): 1-4.

Part 1 in a two-part series examining promotional partnerships between charities and corporations, also known as cause-related marketing. Describes the nature of the activity using recent examples of product sales that also benefit charities (such as the American Express-Statue of Liberty promotion). These promotions usually stipulate that a portion of the proceeds from sales will be used to help a designated charity; the exact amount contributed may be expressed as a flat amount, a percentage or a goal that depends upon quantities sold. One point of concern is that charities be careful not to endorse the products of a company with which it is joined, as this may lead to serious ethical problems for the nature of philanthropy.

1667. Salewic, Marge. "Charities in the Marketplace: A Look at Joint-Venture Marketing. Part 2." *Insight* 3 (1987): 1-4.

Results of an informal survey conducted by the Philanthropic Advisory Service in which 850 individuals commented on the circumstances under which they would support joint-venture marketing. About half indicated support for the concept, acknowledging that it provided needed income for worthy causes; an almost equal number expressed concern that promotional partnerships are saturating the market, and that "over-exploitation would eventually destroy effectiveness." In the end, of course, it is public perception of these promotions which will determine the success of charities in the marketplace. Includes points for charities and corporations to consider before participating in joint-venture marketing.

1668. Salmans, Sandra. "Big Business Tightens Its Arts Budget." *New York Times* (20 March 1983): H-1+.

1669. Schiller, Zachary. "Doing Well by Doing Good: Should Business Link Philanthropy to Promotional Schemes?" *Business Week* (5 December 1988): 53, 57.

Examines the continuing trend in cause-related campaigns, despite criticisms about ethics, the loss of traditional no-strings giving, and excessive support for established, uncontroversial charities. MasterCard's campaign has six charities for which it will try to raise money, selected in part through a popularity poll. Cause-related campaigns add as much as $100 million to charities annually, but that pales in comparison to the $4.6 billion in conventional corporate giving. Yet, corporations believe that promoting a cause makes their product stand out from the competitors, while charities facing government cutbacks see the commercial tie-ins as a welcome source of necessary funding. However, nonprofits do realize the need for standards when choosing a partner; it is unlikely, for instance, that the American Lung Association will link up with a tobacco company.

1670. "Service Companies Posting Record Profits May Give More." *Corporate Giving Watch* 5 (July 1985): 6.

A list of ten corporations that showed a profit increase from last year (1984 to 1985), garnered from a *Fortune* magazine special report. Corporations showing large increases in profits may represent best bets for increased giving.

1671. Seybold, Geneva. "Company Giving through Foundations." *Management Record* 14 (January 1952): 1-10.

1672. Shapiro, Leo J., and James C. Worthy. *Company Giving.* Chicago: Survey Press, 1960.

1673. Shuman, Philip Joel. *The Power of "Perceptual Marketing": An Analysis of Sponsorships As Components of Marketing-Support and Corporate Relations Programs.* New York: Burson-Marsteller, 1986.

Analyzes the power of cause-related marketing from four different perspectives: the sponsoring corporation; the organizations that seek and receive the funds; the trade audience which frequently serves as the intermediary in the relationship; and consumers. Examines a variety of contemporary sponsorship activities, including sports, music, public television, and community affairs, in order to document superior alternatives and procedures. The analysis indicates that firms benefit most when they fully integrate the sponsorship with the entire marketing communications field; extensive promotional support is required to make the investment truly cost effective. Advocates establishing specific objectives and choosing an event with significant publicity, motivation and sales incentives opportunities; most important is evaluating the event for its ability to be consistent with corporate, brand and product image.

1674. Simon, John G., Charles W. Powers, and Jon P. Gunnemann. *The Ethical Investor: Universities and Corporate Responsibility.* New Haven, Conn.: Yale University Press, 1972.

1675. Smith, Craig. "Gift Computers: Now's the Time." *Foundation News* 26 (March-April 1985): 31-7.

Provides strategies to follow in asking companies for gifts of computers. Smith holds that gifts of computers are "one of the fastest growing segments of the rapidly expanding grantmaking field," and also points out the increased employee voluntarism at companies that make in-kind gifts.

1676. Smith, Hayden W. "Business Sense." *Currents* 14 (March 1988): 6-10.

Smith, senior vice president of the Council for Aid to Education, examines the reasons behind the tremendous growth in corporate-campus relationships. The current philosophy of corporate management includes the concepts of enlightened self-interest and corporate social responsibility; these dictate that corporations may need to sacrifice some of their short-term profits in order to serve their long-term self-interest. Education, Smith points out, is an important investment for corporations, for businesses rely on colleges and universities for newly trained and intelligent employees, basic research that leads to better products and marketing techniques, and contributions to the overall quality of life, including the health of the economy and the state. Smith predicts a growth in the scope and intensity of corporate-campus cooperation, "for in the long run the quality, the extent, and the pervasiveness of corporate involvement in higher education will determine the flow of money from the corporate to the academic community."

1677. Smith, Hayden W. *A Profile of Corporate Contributions.* New York: Council for Financial Aid to Education, 1983.

A detailed research report on the development of corporate contributions from 1936 to 1981.

1678. Smith, Sally Bedell. "Corporate Ads on PBS Spark Debate." *New York Times* (1 April 1985): C-19.

1679. "Sponsoring PBS: Selling an Image, Tastefully." *Advertising Age* (24 January 1982): M-29-30.

1680. *Standard and Poor's Register of Corporations, Directors and Executives.* New York: Standard and Poor's Corp., 1988.

Volume 1 is an alphabetical list of over 50,000 corporations with address and telephone number; officers, directors and key staff; principal business and products and services; divisions and subsidiaries; annual sales and number of employees. Volume 2 is an alphabetical list of corporate officials. Volume 3 includes indexes by standard industrial classification, state and city location, "corporate family," with division and subsidiary cross-references, an obituary section and sections of new individual and company additions.

1681. *Standard and Poor's Register of Corporations, Directors and Executives. Cumulative October Supplement.* New York: Standard and Poor's Corp., 1987.

1682. Stern, Adam, and Mark Vermilion. *Corporate Social Investment: Portfolios for Social Wealth.* Menlo Park, Calif.: Steven P. Jobs Foundation, 1987.

1683. Stern, Phillip M. *The Rape of the Taxpayer.* New York: Random House, 1973.

1684. Sternberg, Sam. *National Directory of Corporate Charity.* San Francisco: Regional Young Adult Project, 1984.

Profiles the giving programs of 1600 companies with annual revenues in excess of $200 million. Entries include address, phone number, list of related companies and foundations, program interests, sample recipients, range of giving, application information, and contacts. In addition to the directory information, it includes several "how-to" essays, a bibliography, and indexes by areas of support and state.

1685. Sterne, Larry. "Clean Your Carpet and Help a Child: The Pros and Cons of Cause Marketing." *NonProfit Times* 1 (May 1987): 1, 14-5.

With a keen eye this article examines both sides of the cause-related marketing issue. Provides examples of successful fundraising events, and offers suggestions by Jay L. Vestal, vice president of development for the Osmond Foundation, on the proper way to submit proposals to corporations in order to gain support. The method works and many groups "have found the prospect of easy money to be an irresistible temptation," but there are deep concerns that linking charity to profit-making threatens the basic integrity of fundraising and philanthropy. A company involved in a cause-related program "uses marketing dollars to rent the good name of a likeable organization" in order to create a favorable public image and boost its sales, while such an association may weaken a voluntary organization's own case for public approval and philanthropic support. On the practical side, some corporations who give money to see their name widely publicized in a cause-related marketing event may feel no need to give further once they have achieved that goal, while the public recognition of supporters may dissuade competing businesses from giving when they know a rival has already done so.

1686. Stevenson, Richard. "Marketing Linked to Charity." *New York Times* (3 September 1985): D-12.

1687. Stickler, Robert. "Five Percent Clubs Channel Arts Donations." *Miami Herald* (31 May 1982): 9.

1688. Sturges, Kenneth. *Yardsticks for Corporation Gifts to Community Chests.* Washington: Community Chests and Councils of America, 1952.

1689. Sumariwalla, Russy D. "Corporate Caring: U.S. Business's Long (and Legal) Tradition." *Charity* 1 (May 1984): 8+.

1690. Sumariwalla, Russy D. "Tax Changes Swell the 'Products' Package." *Charity* 1 (June 1984): 8.

1691. "Survey Finds Significant Shift in Corporate Giving in 1982." *Fund Raising Review* (February 1984): 4.

1692. "Taft Survey Finds: Corporate Giving Could Go Up in 1983." *Nonprofit Executive* 2 (June 1983): 7+.

1693. Taylor, Karla. "How to Raise Money for Your Hispanic Students? Involve Your Alumni and Their Corporate Contacts." *Currents* 9 (April 1983): 18-21.

1694. Teltsch, Kathleen. "Lower Profits and Economic Uncertainty Threaten Corporate Philanthropy." *New York Times* (22 September 1982): A-20.

1695. Teltsch, Kathleen. "Noncash Giving on Rise to Needy Organizations." *New York Times* (27 December 1982): A-12.

1696. Teltsch, Kathleen. "Philanthropic Outlook Somber." *New York Times* (1 November 1982): D-4.

1697. Teltsch, Kathleen. "Survey Says Companies Gave Record Amount to Charities." *New York Times* (21 November 1983): B-16.

1698. "A Thing of Beauty Is a Profit Forever." *Newsweek* (5 June 1967): 76-8.

1699. Thomas, Ralph Lingo. *Policies Underlying Corporate Giving.* Englewood Cliffs, N.J.: Prentice-Hall, 1966.

1700. "Thoughts of a Corporate Gadfly: On Community Groups and Corporate Giving." *Donors Forum of Chicago* 2 (Winter 1984): 6-7.

1701. Timpane, Michael. "Increased Corporate Support for Urban Public Schools." *Foundation News* 23 (November-December 1982): 8+.

1702. Toland, Michelle R. *The Development of an Evaluation Procedure for Larger Grants.* Minneapolis, Minn.: Target Stores, 1983.

1703. "Top Consultants Tell All." *Corporate Philanthropy Report* 4 (August-September 1988): 7-9.

Chart of the fifteen leading consultants in corporate grant-making, listing their services, clients and brief comments. Includes a page of summarized responses to questions about methods of billing, most demanded services, and current trends in corporate grantmaking.

1704. Troy, Kathryn. *The Corporate Contributions Function.* New York: Conference Board, 1982.

1705. Troy, Kathryn. *Managing Corporate Contributions.* New York: Conference Board, 1980.

Written for the corporate executive, this report details how to establish and operate a contributions program.

1706. Troy, Kathryn. *Meeting Human Needs: Corporate Programs and Partnerships.* New York: Conference Board, 1986.

Report of a study of 331 corporate contributions and 512 human-resource executives. Examines trends in the funding of human service programs for employees and the broader community. Three communities (Danbury, Conn.; Seattle, Wash.; and Charlotte, N.C.) are profiled as bellwether indicators of community concerns, priorities, and initiatives. Over eighty percent of the companies surveyed offer counseling services to employees, and nearly forty percent offer child-care assistance. More than 100 of these companies have participated in a human-service needs assessment in their headquarters' communities.

1707. Troy, Kathryn. *Studying and Addressing Community Needs: A Corporate Case Book.* New York: Conference Board, 1985.

Study examines how companies identify community needs and use the results to adapt their contributions and community affairs practices. Through the use of several case studies, the report looks at why each company decided to study community needs, how it conducted the study, what it learned, and how it used the results. Shows many evaluation tools, including a checklist companies might use in a community needs assessment and sample questionnaire items.

1708. Turner, Judith Axler. "IBM, Digital to Give MIT $50-Million to Develop Computerized Curriculum." *Chronicle of Higher Education* 26 (8 June 1983): 1+.

1709. Turner, Judith Axler. "IBM Increased Its Support of Education More Than Fifty Percent in 1983." *Chronicle of Higher Education* 27 (25 January 1984): 9.

1710. United States Chamber of Commerce. *Staff Directory: State Chambers of Commerce and Associations of Commerce and Industry.* Washington: U.S. Chamber of Commerce, 1987.

Lists each broad-based statewide or regional business organization, its mailing address, telephone number and the key members of its executive staff. Includes partial listing of the U.S. Chamber's professional staff and a complete listing of the field operations staff who work closely with the state organizations.

1711. United States. Department of Commerce. *Business and Society: Strategies for the 1980's.* Washington: Government Printing Office, 1981.

1712. United States. Department of Commerce. *Corporate Social Reporting in the United States and Western Europe.* Washington: Government Printing Office, 1979.

1713. United Way of America. *Corporate Community Involvement: An Annotated Bibliography, 1980-1986.* Alexandria, Va.: United Way of America, 1986.

Provides a summary of over 200 books, journal articles, and research reports written about corporate philanthropy. All of the resources were published between 1980 and mid-1986, and are here organized under eleven categories: baseline information (definitions, issues, key players and institutions); case building; trends; research findings, model programming; employee involvement; cash giving; non-cash giving; accountability; educational initiatives; and strategic planning. Selected bibliography.

1714. United Way of America. *Corporate Contribution Programs: A Sampler of Policies and Statements.* Alexandria, Va.: United Way of America, 1983.

Presents an overview of the procedures which guide corporate decisions on contributions and includes guidelines for developing cases for United Way assistance. Samples of corporate contributions policies and statements drawn from twelve Fortune 500 companies.

1715. Urseny, Laura. "Businesses Urged Not to Forget Charity." *Chico Enterprise-Record* (29 September 1982).

1716. Useem, Michael, and Stephen I. Kutner. *Corporate Contributions to the Nonprofit Sector: The Organizations of Giving, and the Influence of the Chief Executive Officer and Other...* Program on Non-Profit Organizations, no. 94. New Haven, Conn.: Institution for Social and Policy Studies, 1984.

Examines three central features of the evolving internal organization of corporate giving: the bureaucratization of the contributions process, the critical role of the chief executive in guiding the giving program, and the mutually reinforcing influence of firms on one another's contributions levels. For pragmatic and conceptual reasons, the geographic focus was limited to the Commonwealth of Massachusetts. The survey provides information on such things as the number and percentage of companies maintaining a professional staff, written statement, company foundation, and matching-gift program to guide their allocation of gifts to nonprofit organizations, with the understanding that professionalization of company giving is accompanied by greater support to recognized cultural organizations rather than to experimental groups; the influence of the chief executive is especially critical in starting and sustaining the growth of contribution programs—when personal interest is strong, giving programs prosper; and the rise of more formal organizations is also accompanied by more openness to outside influence, i.e., companies with small contribution programs report that other firms have modest influence over their own decisions, while corporations with large contribution budgets are much more likely to make grants to organizations already "legitimized" by having received a grant from another major corporation. The authors expect substantial convergence in the structure, level, and distribution of major companies' philanthropic programs.

1717. Useem, Michael. "Corporate Funding: Who Gets It and Why." *501(c)(3) Monthly Letter* 8 (February 1988): 341-44.

Examines various forms of corporate giving such as direct funding, the use of corporate facilities and services and volunteering by top corporate officers. The major recipients of this giving are educational institutions, health and human services and cultural organizations. Companies prefer recipients that are prestigious, large, have personalized connections with corporate managers, and are located near headquarters or plants with large staffs.

1718. Useem, Michael. "Corporate Funding: Why You Did (or Didn't) Get That Grant." *501(c)(3) Monthly Letter* 8 (April 1988): 383-88.

Discusses the professionalization of corporate giving, its widespread formalization and its integration into general company planning at the highest level. Gift policies are usually developed at the top levels of management with the chairman and president playing a major role in setting goals, priorities, and budget levels for their contributions program. The leading factors in setting giving levels, following the discretion of the chief executive, are the size of the previous year's contribution budget and the company's earnings in the current year. Among the leading considerations when reviewing requests for gifts are the nonprofit organization's general reputation, the quality of the proposed program, and the likelihood of effective and successful completion. Article also discusses the determinants of corporate philanthropy and the role of corporate self-interest in accounting for the difference in socially responsible activities.

1719. Useem, Michael. "Tapping into the Power Base of Corporate Philanthropy." *501(c)(3) Monthly Letter* 8 (October 1988): 459-61.

Examines the influence of business culture on corporate giving. In the realm of management culture, chief executives are critical for starting and enlarging contributions programs, while widespread managerial commitment to public affairs is required if the programs are to flourish. In the wider scope of metropolitan and national business cultures, it is apparent that "peer company comparisons" are highly influential in establishing a company's contribution dollar levels to the point where a company will increase its giving when other firms in the same region increase their gifts. While a national business culture stressing social responsiveness does seem to be developing, it should never be forgotten that self-interest remains the primary reason for corporate giving. But while it is true that the most generous companies are esteemed within the business community as the most successful, thus accruing direct benefits from their giving, there is also a sense of "altruistic capitalism" at work, a concern for the business environment extending beyond the immediate interests of a single company. Many executives are willing to spend their own time and the resources of their company to "help create a better climate for the entire business community," thus creating benefits which can be shared by all large firms. The corporate culture appears to "encourage firms to support the nonprofit sectors at levels substantially above those dictated by corporate logic alone."

1720. Vanderleest, Henry W. "Corporate Funding: An Emerging Revenue Source for Nonprofit Organizations." *Nonprofit World Report* 2 (September-October 1984): 23-5.

1721. Verity, C. William, Jr. "The Role of Business in Community Service." *Community Action* 1 (1982): 5+.

1722. Volunteer-The National Center. *Report of Corporate Non-Cash Contributions.* Arlington, Va.: Volunteer-The National Center, 1985.

1723. Wall, Wendy L. "Helping Hands: Companies Change the Ways They Make Charitable Donations." *Wall Street Journal* (21 June 1984): 1+.

1724. Wallis, W. Allen. "Some Advice for Corporate Givers." *IEA Report*: 5.

1725. Washington Researchers. *How to Find Information about Companies: The Corporate Intelligence Source Book.* 5th ed. Washington: Washington Researchers, 1987.

Contains descriptions of various corporate information sources, the types of information they supply, and the means of accessing their information. Sources include federal and state governmental agencies, trade/professional organizations and unions, business and library information sources, business databases, fee-based information services, and obtaining information through stockholders meetings, plant tours, trade shows, etc.

1726. Washington Researchers. *Sources of State Information on Corporations.* Washington: Washington Researchers, 1981.

1727. Watkins, Beverly T. "Community Colleges and Industry Ally to Provide 'Customized' Job Training." *Chronicle of Higher Education* (27 October 1982): 4.

1728. Watson, John H., III. *Industry Support of Federated Appeals.* New York: National Industrial Conference Board, 1965.

1729. Watson, John H., III. "Report on Company Contributions." *Business Record* 18 (June 1961): 11-9.

1730. Watson, John H., III. *Twenty Company-Sponsored Foundations. Programs and Policies.* Studies in Public Affairs, no. 6. New York: National Industrial Conference Board, 1970.

1731. Webster, Philip J. "The Case for Cause-Related Marketing." *Foundation News* 30 (January-February 1989): 30-3.

Former president of the Scott Paper Company Foundation, Philip J. Webster writes in defense of cause-related marketing, calling it the latest step in the evolution of corporate social activism. This evolution, he claims, has come a long way from the "public be damned" attitude of the robber barons, through John D. Rockefeller's handing out of dimes to today's belief that corporations should give something back to the society that allowed them to prosper. Webster illustrates his argument with examples of successful cause-related marketing efforts, praising this form of philanthropy as the most "strategic," for its impact can be measured in dollars and cents, and it allows for joint efforts by corporate contributions and marketing departments. He predicts three significant developments for the future of the strategy: an expansion outside the packaged products industry, a broadened focus to include the business customer as well as the individual consumer, and a "title sponsorship" of one of the national telethons.

1732. Weisbrod, Burton A. *The Voluntary Nonprofit Sector: An Economic Analysis.* Lexington, Mass.: Lexington Books, 1977.

This book presents a theoretical model of a three-sector economy—public, private, and voluntary—supported by some empirical evidence. While certain sections will be difficult for non-economists to understand, most readers should be able to follow the main thesis. The author estimates the size of the voluntary nonprofit sector before developing a theory of the sector as a "quasi-governmental response to the forces that constrain the ability of democratic governments, as political institutions, to satisfy consumer demands for collective goods." Hypotheses arising out of this theory are then tested for hospitals and schools. While the hypothetical findings are not conclusive, Weisbrod states that "they do lend support to the view of the voluntary sector as being like the government sector—much involved in the provision of collective-consumptive good." Most chapters contain bibliographies.

1733. *What American Corporations Are Doing to Improve the Quality of Precollege Education: A CFAE Sampler.* New York: Council for Financial Aid to Education, 1985.

Brief sampler designed to tell interested companies about the extent and variety of corporate aid to pre-college education. Provides a cross-section of corporate efforts in this area to help companies decide if they should get involved in aid to pre-college education.

1734. "What Corporations Want to Know about You." *National Fund Raiser* 10 (May 1984): 3-4.

1735. White, Benjamin T. "Consequences of Corporate Giving." *Trusts & Estates* 126 (August 1987): 35-40.

Covers the substantial tax and non-tax incentives for establishing a company foundation, and also explains how a corporation can get a charitable deduction and avoid capital gain.

1736. White, Mike, and Jerry Cronin. *Managing a Business Contributions Program.* Private Philanthropy in Arkansas Research Series, no. 3. West Memphis, Ark.: Independent Community Consultants, 1983.

1737. Whitney, Barbara T. "Zoo Society Finds Corporate Partnership Easy to Charge." *Fund Raising Management* 16 (March 1985): 48+.

Interview with executive director of zoo society about cause-related marketing from American Express.

1738. Williams, Pierce, and Frederick E. Croxton. *Corporation Contributions to Organized Community Welfare Services.* New York: National Bureau of Economic Research, 1930.

1739. Wilson, Eugene R. "Finding the Real Bottom Line." *Foundation News* 25 (March-April 1984): 66+.

1740. Wilson, Eugene R. "Steering through Hard Times." *Foundation News* 27 (July-August 1986): 66-8.

Eugene Wilson's (President of the ARCO Foundation) speech to the Conference Board where he serves as vice-chair of the Contributions Council. Wilson presents his suggestions for corporate giving programs to cope with internal and external economic changes. His prescription calls for greater decentralization of contribution budgets and responsibility, and for tightly focused giving based on creditable research, a clear understanding of community problems which have an impact on long-term business interests, and accountable reporting of contributions and their allocation. Wilson offers six questions which test how well corporate community-involvement programs are positioned to respond to internal organization change.

1741. Wintner, Linda. *Business and the Cities: Programs and Practices.* Information Bulletin, no. 87. New York: Conference Board, 1981.

1742. Yankelovich Group, Daniel. *The Climate for Giving: The Outlook of Current and Future CEO's.* Corporate Leadership Project. Washington: Council on Foundations, 1988.

Follow-up to the 1982 corporate giving survey. According to this survey, corporate philanthropy is not in a state of decline. The highlights of this statistical study reveal that CEO commitment to corporate giving appears as strong in 1988 as it was in 1982. The CEO is an active participant in corporate giving and is so because of personal relevance, ethics or social responsibility, and company self-interest or tradition. Among the other findings were that community needs now play an important role in influencing CEO's orientation toward giving; they believe that community needs have grown in recent years.

The study also analyzed a group of what they identified as future CEO's and found that this group is also supportive of corporate giving, but are guided more by company tradition than by personal interest or ethics. This group singled out education as an area of community need which directly serves the interest of the company. The statistical findings for all aspects of the above highlights are enhanced with graphic representations, tables and quotes from survey interviewees.

1743. Yzaguirre, Raul. "Hispanic Corporate Partnerships: Some Observations and Examples." *KRC Letter* 13 (January 1983): 5-8.

1744. Zonana, Victor F. "Japanese Firms Learning Art of Image Polishing: Corporate Charity Is Alien Concept, But Companies Are Adapting to U.S. Rules." *Los Angeles Times* (28 December 1987).

Reports on attempts by Japanese companies in America to learn the art of corporate social responsibility. Briefly discusses the cultural differences that initially inhibited Japanese understanding of American philanthropy, and their recent efforts to develop corporate giving programs and charitable foundations. One example is the Matsushita Foundation, which has an American board of directors, earmarks only fifteen percent of grants toward Japanese studies, and goes to great lengths to avoid accusations of self-interest.

4

INTERNATIONAL PHILANTHROPY

1745. Accion en Colombia. *Directorio Nacional de Instituciones Privadas Filantropicas y de Desarrollo Social.* (National directory of private philanthropic institutions and social development). Bogota, Columbia: Accion en Colombia, 1974.

1746. Agency for International Development. *Voluntary Foreign Aid Programs.* Washington: Agency for International Development, 1985.

1747. Agnelli Foundation, Giovanni. *Guide to European Foundations.* 3rd ed. Torino, Italy: Giovanni Agnelli Foundation, 1978.

1748. Allen, Derek. "A Comparative Study of the Tax Treatment of Donors to Charity in Various Countries." *Philanthropy International* 23 (Spring 1987): 2-18.

Brief study which explains accepted charitable purposes in Austria, France, Germany (West), Great Britain, Hungary, Italy, Japan, Netherlands, Spain, Sweden, and United States of America. Information for each country includes a charitable purpose's statement or a definition of what is an accepted charity; an explanation of what the charitable bodies are, such as operating and non-operating foundations (U.S.A.); and a tax exemption summary for individuals, corporations, self-employed, or state organizations.

1749. Allen, Derek. *A Comparative Study of the Tax Treatment of Donors to Charity in Various Countries.* Tonbridge, Kent, England: Charities Aid Foundation, [1987].

1750. Arlett, Allan, Phelps Bell, and Robert W. Thompson. *Canada Gives: Trends and Attitudes Towards Charitable Giving and Voluntarism.* Toronto, Ontario, Canada: Canadian Centre for Philanthropy, 1988.

Statistical analysis of foundation, corporate and individual charitable giving in Canada from 1969 to 1985.

1751. Arlett, Allan, and Norah McClintock, eds. *Canadian Directory to Foundations.* 8th ed. Toronto, Ontario, Canada: Canadian Centre for Philanthropy, 1988.

Directory of 611 foundations prepared by the Canadian Centre for Philanthropy. Criteria for inclusion in the directory followed the narrowest definition developed by the Foundation Center (United States). (U.S. foundations with a record of giving in Canada are included.) A statistical analysis—*Profile of Canadian Foundations*—which contains ten tables of data precedes the foundation descriptions. Foundation listings are arranged alphabetically under the family or corporate name. Each foundation has a reference number which is used in the indexes for cross-referencing. The individual foundation profile includes foundation name and address, source of funds, year of establishment, statement of purpose and interests, geographic scope, receipted gifts (the dollar value of revenue for which the foundation distributed charitable donation receipts), total grants (an indication of grants to qualified charitable organizations only [is occasionally an inaccurate representation of the total grants awarded]), direct charitable (total amount expended on charitable activities carried out directly by the foundation), number of grants (based on the tally of the grants listing—may not always represent the total number of grants given as grants to individuals and others may not be included), grant range, officers and board of directors. The directory is indexed by foundation name, names of officers and board members, geographic location, and fields of interest.

1752. Arlett, Allan, and Ingrid van Rotterdam, eds. *Canadian Index to Foundation Grants.* Toronto, Ontario, Canada: Canadian Centre for Philanthropy, 1986.

Produced by the Canadian Centre for Philanthropy (a Foundation Center Cooperating collection), the index lists grants made by 493 Canadian foundations. The editors estimate the *Index* contains information on about seventy-eight percent of all monies paid by Canadian foundations in 1983. 8,730 grants of $500 or more are organized into eight sections: arts and culture, education, health and hospitals, international activities, religion, science and technology (including social sciences), social service and issues, and sports/recreation. Each entry notes the name of the foundation, recipient, organization, city and province, award amount, and the year of the award. Four indexes identify foundation interests by field of interest, recipient organizations, geographic location and foundation name. Coverage does not include grants made to individuals, or grants for projects managed directly by the foundation.

1753. Arlett, Allan. "The Power of Giving: What's What in Canada's World of Foundations." *Financial Post* (9 March 1987).

Focuses on the activities of Canada's top fifty foundations, including a table giving information on year established, headquarters, assets for fiscal year 1985, and grants in amount and number for 1985. The top fifty charitable foundations control more than $1.5 billion or eighty percent of all foundation assets and make more than $108 million or sixty-five percent of all foundation grants. Twenty-seven percent of foundation grants go to education, twenty-six percent to health-and-hospital activities, seventeen percent to social services, thirteen percent to arts and culture, eleven percent to religion, three percent to science and technology, two percent to sports and recreation, and one percent to international programs. Article describes the characteristics of the several types of foundations in Canada: family, community, corporate, special interest, and government.

1754. Aschrott, P.F. *The English Poor Law System.* London: Knight & Co., 1902.

1755. "Asian Invasion!: Japanese Corporate Philanthropy Zooms." *Corporate Philanthropy Report* 1 (January 1986): 1-4.

Discusses how factors such as the threat of protectionism, clever tax avoidance techniques, the hope of technology transfer, and the need for relationships advantageous to the transaction of business are paving the ground for greater growth in Japanese corporate philanthropy.

1756. "Aspects of Corporate Giving in Canada." *Philanthropy Monthly* 16 (December 1983): 25-32.

1757. Aubin, Pierre, and George Cotter. *Agencies for Project Assistance: Sources of Support for Small Church Sponsored Projects in Africa, Asia, Latin America and the Pacific.* 3rd ed. New York: Mission Project Service, 1988.

Directory of international organizations that provide socio-economic and pastoral development assistance to small church and/or lay sponsored projects in Africa, Asia, Latin America, and the Pacific. The types of assistance given include funds, conferences, training, information, research, marketing, materials, livestock, and personnel. Gives profiles of the supporting agencies which include address, telephone number, sources of income, financial data, fields of interest, geographical areas of interest, and application guidelines. The supporting agencies are private foundations, public charities, government agencies, and church agencies.

1758. Australian Council for Educational Research. *Philanthropic Trusts in Australia.* 3rd ed. Hawthorn, Victoria, Australia: Australian Council for Educational Research, 1981.

1759. Bartz, Carl. *Washington Embassies: A Guide for the Private Sector.* Washington: Washington Association Research Foundation, 1985.

1760. Beckmann, David M., Timothy J. Mitchell, and Linda L. Powers. *The Overseas List: Opportunities for Living and Working in Developing Countries.* Rev. and exp. ed. Minneapolis, Minn.: Augsburg Publishing House, 1985.

Handbook of how United States citizens can live, work and travel in developing countries. The authors wrote the book specifically for Christians seeking opportunities to serve in Asia, Africa, and Latin America. However, the book can assist anyone who is looking for a job or an out of the ordinary study and travel experience in the Third World. The handbook has divided opportunities into subject areas—private development assistance, church missions, study and tourism, teaching and journalism, international organizations, the U.S. government, and business. Chapters 1 and 2 contain general information on the book and the pros and cons of working in the Third World, respectively. Chapter 3, *Private Development Assistance* begins with a summary table of organizations—foundations, private groups, and general humanitarian groups among others—with staffing and budget information. These tables are accompanied by more detailed organization profiles. The remainder of the volume consists of organization profiles arranged in specific subject chapters and two short concluding chapters with comments on practical matters of living in the Third World and a Christian rationale for doing so. Contains an index.

1761. Bell, Peter D. "The Ford Foundation As a Transnational Actor." *International Organization* 25 (Summer 1971): 465-78.

This article, written by the Ford Foundation's then-representative to Chile, describes the international activities of the organization, one of the most influential American foundations abroad, as an example of the general role of foundations in influencing life in other countries. Bell describes the considerations that went into formulation of Ford's international programs and purposes; the decision-making process and the principal actors involved in it; and relations between the foundation and grantees, other aid donors, Ford Motor Company, the U.S. government, and the governments of countries in which Ford pursues philanthropic activities. Bell's thesis is that foundations are political no matter how neutral or independent they try to be. "When basically American foundations like the Ford and Rockefeller foundations venture beyond the United States," he says, "they are apt to become even more manifestly political not only as they are perceived by but also as they interact with other organizations."

1762. Berman, Edward H. "Foundations, United States Foreign Policy and African Education, 1945-1975." *Harvard Educational Review* 49 (1979): 145-79.

In an essentially Marxist analysis, Berman examines the rationale for foundation support of various educational programs and the ways in which foundation policy has been implemented in Africa since 1945. He suggests that the Ford, Carnegie, and Rockefeller foundations, in particular, were partially motivated by the need to promote a sympathetic view of American political and corporate activity—an activity that was necessary to ensure both continuing access to African mineral resources and the continued cultural dependence of the newly independent western nations. He equates current Chinese, Soviet, and Cuban policies in Africa—commonly thought of as detrimental to the creation of African-controlled models of development—with the previous activities of these foundations. Alan Pifer, Francis Sutton, and Laurence Stifel attempt to refute his thesis on behalf of the Carnegie, Ford, and Rockefeller foundations, respectively. Pifer's and Sutton's responses are especially worth reading.

1763. Beveridge, Lord. *Voluntary Action: A Report on Methods of Social Advance.* New York: Macmillan, 1948.

1764. Boba, Eleanor. "The Canadian Centre for Philanthropy: Building Resources North of the Border." *Grantsmanship Center News* 13 (March-April 1985): 40-4.

1765. Bolling, Landrum R., and Craig Smith. *Private Foreign Aid: U.S. Philanthropy for Relief and Development.* Boulder, Colo.: Westview Press, 1982.

Examines the issues related to past, present and future U.S. involvement in foreign assistance, recording the accomplishments of private groups and individuals as well as some of the problems, disappointments, and frustrations associated with foreign aid, both public and private. Provides fascinating descriptions of the various U.S. voluntary agencies, institutions and organizations along with the types of foreign relief and development they provide; discusses the method of funding these organizations and their accountability; whether efforts are being duplicated between private organizations and government agencies; whether the recipients of U.S. foreign aid prefer one form, public or private, over the other; practical methods of organizing foreign aid efforts to work together more effectively; and how much good U.S. assistance, from both government and private sources, actually does for those who receive it. Annotated bibliography.

1766. Boynes, Wynta, Florence M. Lowenstein, and Roger B. McClanahan, eds. *U.S. Nonprofit Organizations in Development Assistance Abroad: Directory.* 8th ed. New York: Technical Assistance Information Clearing House, 1983.

Primary source of information on the overseas development assistance programs of the nonprofit sector. Compiles basic data on a wide spectrum of organizations of varying sizes with diverse goals and program components, and serves as a useful indicator of the vitality and responsiveness of the sector's involvement in meeting the Third World's development needs. Profiles are arranged alphabetically by organization, and include information about the director(s) of overseas programs, objectives of the organizations, major program activities (listed under category headings), countries of assistance, total income (with a breakdown of sources), total expenditures in overseas development assistance, program personnel figures, and publications and/or audiovisuals. Indexed by program categories, countries, organizations, and by states.

1767. "Building Momentum in Japan." *Corporate Philanthropy Report* 2 (December 1986): 1+.

Discusses the Keidanren, the Japan Federation for Economic Organizations, which is firmly established as the broker of Japanese corporate philanthropy, and its role in bringing together U.S. nonprofit grantseekers and Japanese corporate grantmakers. Last year Keidanren directly arranged $55 million in corporate gifts, of which $20 million went to U.S. nonprofits. It is estimated that several million dollars more were received through the indirect help of Keidanren staffmembers who simply provided fundraisers with guidance and strategies. The article presents the process by which a nonprofit solicits the organization's help, and provides an address to get information in English about Keidanren and its perspective on U.S.-Japan relations in general.

1768. Bullock, Mary Brown. *An American Transplant: The Rockefeller Foundation and Peking Union Medical College.* Berkeley, Calif.: University of California Press, 1981.

This history explores the careers of graduates of Peking Union Medical College (PUMC), which was founded by the Rockefeller Foundation in 1921 in the People's Republic of China. The history is concerned conceptually with the appropriateness of the PUMC model of an American foundation's involvement in pre-Communist China. Bullock considers three components of the Rockefeller Foundation presence in China: ideology—that of American medicine; institutions—PUMC and the standards of medical training it embodied; and individuals, both Chinese and American, who brought the ideology and the institutions to life. Her primary concern is "whether and how an ideology and its institutions were adapted to China." She explores this issue through careful analysis of the acts and attitudes of key individuals associated with the establishment of the school, as well as the doctors who were educated there. 370-item bibliography.

1769. Business International. *Beyond Money: New Dimensions in International Corporate Giving.* New York: Business International, 1979.

1770. Butler, Nicholas Murray. "The Carnegie Endowment for International Peace." *The Independent* (November 27, 1913): 396-400.

At the time he wrote this article, Butler was director of the Carnegie Endowment's Division of Intercourse and Education. The article lays out the reasoning behind the establishment of the endowment and explains the development of the policies and programs of its first three years. Butler pays special attention to the work of the division that he led. One of the endowment's principal objectives was to educate the American public about the country's rights and responsibilities as a member of an international community—a task many would consider unfinished. Butler cites a legal doctrine whereby Congress is free to modify or abrogate international treaties without negotiating with the other countries affected. He uses the citation to call for public officials and private citizens to "look upon international obligations...as the upright man looks upon his personal relationships." It's his feeling that only thus will the peace of the world be secure.

1771. *The Canadian Book of Charities: The Guide to Intelligent Giving.* 3rd ed. Toronto, Canada: Mavora Publications, 1983.

1772. Centro de Fundaciones. *Directorio de las Fundaciones Espanolas.* (Directory of Spanish foundations). Madrid, Spain: Centro de Fundaciones, 1986.

Information on over 1,300 Spanish foundations which includes name, address, phone number, donor, directors, funding date, and information on annual grantmaking, when available. Has indexes by province and foundation names.

1773. Chadwick, John. *The Unofficial Commonwealth: The Story of the Commonwealth Foundation, 1965-1980.* London: George Allen & Unwin, 1982.

1774–1793 INTERNATIONAL PHILANTHROPY

1774. Chadwick, W. Edward. *The Church, the State, and the Poor.* London: Robert Scott, 1914.

1775. Charities Aid Foundation. *Directory of Grant-Making Trusts.* 10th ed. Tonbridge, Kent, England: Charities Aid Foundation, 1987.

Guide to British grantmaking resources for both the grantseeker and the grantmaker. Contains details on the location, objectives, policies and resources of over 2,450 grantmaking institutions. The contents include tables of trust statistics, guidelines for applicants on how to approach trusts, a list of charity information services, an explanation of the directory, how to use the directory, and a selected bibliography. The directory is divided into four parts. Part 1 lists the major fields supported by grantmaking trusts under main subject headings with detailed analysis within each category. Part 2 lists the trusts that have either given to a charity working within the area identified or where an entry indicates that the trustees may consider an appropriate application. In addition, there is a general illustration of the size of grants indicated by a code. Part 3 gives an alphabetical list of the grantmaking trusts providing the following information: title of trust, year established, and registration number; correspondent (contact); trustees, objectives; policy of trustees; restrictions; beneficial area; finances; type of grant; type of beneficiary; submission of applications; publications; and notes. Part 4 contains both a geographical index of trusts and an alphabetical index of subjects.

1776. Clark, Ronald W. *A Biography of the Nuffield Foundation.* London: Longram Group, 1972.

1777. Collins, Michael, ed. *Commonwealth African Directory of Aid Agencies.* New York: Commonwealth Fund, 1979.

1778. Contee, Christine E. *What Americans Think: Views on Development and U.S.-Third World Relations.* Washington: Overseas Development Council, 1987.

1779. "Corporate Giving in Canada." *Philanthropy Monthly* 16 (November 1983): 21-22.

1780. Council on Foundations. *Making Grants Overseas.* Washington: Council on Foundations, 1983.

1781. Council on Foundations. *The Status of Philanthropy in Latin America and the Caribbean.* Washington: Council on Foundations, [1988].

Among the conclusions of the symposium: an organized infrastructure for local philanthropy in Latin America and the Caribbean is needed to serve as a networking mechanism and clearinghouse for information about current projects and to enable organizations to combine their talents and financial assets; a system for collecting and disseminating data relating to the source of funding for Latin American and Caribbean nonprofits, including the extent of the funding and how it was utilized, is necessary, not only to identify potential funding sources, but also to teach other organizations about successful and innovative programs, as well as to indicate the mistakes made; nonprofits in Latin American and Caribbean countries should educate the local governments on the positive impact of the organizations' projects, including how the absence of those projects would harm the social welfare of the population, and indicate how the presence of legislation that rewards philanthropic activities helps to insure that such beneficial projects would continue; and foreign donors should accept some responsibility for teaching local organizations such technical skills as fundraising and funds management.

1782. Coutts, Jim. "The Role of Volunteers in Canadian Society." *Philanthropist/Le Philanthrope* 4 (Fall 1984): 23-8.

1783. Coutts, Rosemary J., and John E. Watson, comps. *A Directory of Philanthropic Trusts.* 2nd ed. Wellington, New Zealand: New Zealand Council for Educational Research, 1978.

1784. Cracknell, D.G. *Law Relating to Charities.* London: Oyez Publishing, 1973.

1785. Curti, Merle Eugene. *American Philanthropy Abroad: A History.* New Brunswick, N.J.: Rutgers University Press, 1963.

In this classic history, Curti examines the influence America has had on other nations through voluntary giving for the relief of suffering in catastrophe, the improvement of living standards, or the strengthening of cultural life. He explores the roots of international benevolence in human values throughout history and examines the religious motivations for missionary relief and other expressions of giving, but also discusses secular motivations such as guilt or political sympathy. Curti analyzes the changing methods of providing international aid over time and attempts to assess the successes of overseas philanthropic efforts. The volume contains a helpful bibliographical essay.

1786. Dalrymaple, Martha. *The AIA Story: Two Decades of International Cooperation.* New York: American International Association for Economic and Social Development, [1968].

1787. Daniel, Robert L. *American Philanthropy in the Near East, 1820-1960.* Athens, Ohio: Ohio University Press, 1970.

1788. Dayton, Edward R., ed. *Mission Handbook: North American Protestant Missionaries Overseas.* 11th ed. Monrovia, Calif.: Missions Advanced Research and Communication Center, 1976.

1789. de Lopez, Antonieta M. *Latin American Foundations.* Edited by Luisa E.M. de Pulido. Caracas, Venezuela: Eugenio Mendoza Foundation, 1974.

1790. Deeg, J.F. *How and What Canadians Contribute to Charity.* Toronto, Ontario, Canada: Canadian Centre for Philanthropy, 1982.

1791. *Development of the Activity of Foundations. International Field Conference.* Unpublished, 1964.

1792. Douglas, James. *English Charities. Part 1: Legal Definition, Taxation, and Regulation.* Program on Non-Profit Organizations, no. 15. New Haven, Conn.: Institution for Social and Policy Studies, 1980.

1793. Doyle, Denis P. "Socialist Sweden Tries to Reinvent Philanthropy." *Wall Street Journal* (17 April 1984).

1794. Finnish Cultural Foundation. *Saatiohakemisto.* (Finnish foundations). Helsinki, Finland: Finnish Cultural Foundation, 1977.

1795. Fisher, Donald. "The Rockefeller Foundation and the Development of Scientific Medicine in Great Britain." *Minerva* 16 (1978): 20-4.

This article examines the role of the Rockefeller Foundation in transforming the practice of medicine and medical education in Great Britain in the early years of the twentieth century. The prevailing system of medical education in England had been apprenticeship at voluntary hospitals in the nineteenth century. The consequent lack of scientific rigor was criticized by Abraham Flexner in *Medical Education in Europe* (1912). After World War I, the Rockefeller Foundation created a strategically placed university center of scientific medicine in London. Two foundation officials, Wycliffe Rose and Richard M. Pearce, were primarily responsible for the execution of Rockefeller's policy, and in July 1929 the London School of Hygiene and Tropical Medicine was created to integrate clinical research with scientific training of physicians. Rockefeller grants also made possible the integration of all medically relevant sciences at University College, London, in the early 1920s. In these actions and others, Rockefeller philanthropy far outweighted British philanthropy for medical education until 1936; it fundamentally changed the face of medical education and practice in Great Britain.

1796. *Fondation Europeenne de la Culture.* (European Cultural Foundation). Geneve, Switzerland: Fondation Europeenne de la Culture, 1957.

1797. *Le Fondazioni Italine. Con Un Saggio Sulle Fondazioni Private Nell 'Ordinamento Giurdico Di Dante Cosi.* Milan, Italy: Franco Angeli Editore, 1973.

1798. Ford Foundation. *Infrastructure Problems of the Cities of Developing Countries.* International Urbanization Survey, no. 1. New York: Ford Foundation, [1973].

1799. Ford Foundation. *Race and the Third World City.* International Urbanization Survey, no. 2. New York: Ford Foundation, [1973].

1800. Ford Foundation. *A Survey of European Programs: Education for Urbanization in the Developing Countries.* International Urbanization Survey, no. 3. New York: Ford Foundation, [1973].

1801. Ford Foundation. *Urbanization in Brazil.* International Urbanization Survey, no. 4. New York: Ford Foundation, [1973].

1802. Ford Foundation. *Urbanization in Chile.* International Urbanization Survey, no. 6. New York: Ford Foundation, [1973].

1803. Ford Foundation. *Urbanization in Colombia.* International Urbanization Survey, no. 5. New York: Ford Foundation, [1973].

1804. Ford Foundation. *Urbanization in India.* International Urbanization Survey, no. 8. New York: Ford Foundation, [1973].

1805. Ford Foundation. *Urbanization in Jamaica.* International Urbanization Survey, no. 9. New York: Ford Foundation, [1973].

1806. Ford Foundation. *Urbanization in Kenya.* International Urbanization Survey, no. 10. New York: Ford Foundation, [1973].

1807. Ford Foundation. *Urbanization in Morocco.* International Urbanization Survey, no. 11. New York: Ford Foundation, [1973].

1808. Ford Foundation. *Urbanization in Nigeria: A Planning Commentary.* International Urbanization Survey, no. 12. New York: Ford Foundation, [1973].

1809. Ford Foundation. *Urbanization in Peru.* International Urbanization Survey, no. 13. New York: Ford Foundation, [1973].

1810. Ford Foundation. *Urbanization in Thailand.* International Urbanization Survey, no. 14. New York: Ford Foundation, [1973].

1811. Ford Foundation. *Urbanization in the Developing Countries: The Response of International Assistance.* International Urbanization Survey, no. 7. New York: Ford Foundation, [1973].

1812. Ford Foundation. *Urbanization in Tropical Africa: A Demographic Introduction.* International Urbanization Survey, no. 15. New York: Ford Foundation, [1973].

1813. Ford Foundation. *Urbanization in Turkey.* International Urbanization Survey, no. 61. New York: Ford Foundation, [1973].

1814. Ford Foundation. *Urbanization in Venezuela.* International Urbanization Survey, no. 17. New York: Ford Foundation, [1973].

1815. Ford Foundation. *Urbanization in Zambia.* International Urbanization Survey, no. 18. New York: Ford Foundation, [1973].

1816. Foundation Library Center of Japan. *Directory of Grant-Making Foundations: Guide to Private Grant Sources.* Tokyo, Japan: Foundation Library Center of Japan, 1987.

1817. Fox, Tom. "Funding South of the Border." *Foundation News* 27 (July-August 1986): 58-60.

Describes the projects and interests of private, community and corporate foundations in Latin America.

1818. Fox, Tom. "Global Reach." *Foundation News* 24 (May-June 1983): 66+.

1819. Fox, Tom. "International Philanthropy at Ditchley Park." *Foundation News* 24 (September-October 1983): 56-7.

1820. Fox, Tom. "New Partnerships in International Corporate Philanthropy." *Foundation News* 24 (July-August 1983): 50-1.

1821–1839 INTERNATIONAL PHILANTHROPY

1821. Fox, Tom. "Private Grantmaking in Japan." *Foundation News* 26 (January-February 1985).

Discusses foundation and direct corporate giving in Japan.

1822. Fox, Tom. "A Rising Tide? International Grants Appear to Be Growing Steadily." *Foundation News* 26 (May-June 1985): 56+.

1823. Fox, Tom. "Understanding International Philanthropy." *Foundation News* 24 (January-February 1983): 65+.

1824. France. Ministre de l'Interieiur. *Fondations*. Paris, France: Journal Officiel de la Republique Francaise, 1980.

1825. Friedman, Ray. *The Role of Non-Profit Organizations in Foreign Aid: A Literature Survey*. Program on Non-Profit Organizations, no. 32. New Haven, Conn.: Institution for Social and Policy Studies, 1980.

1826. *Fundaciones Privadas de Venezuela*. Caracas, Venezuela: Eugenio Mendoza Foundation, 1973.

1827. Glamann, Kristof. *Carlsbergfondet*. Copenhagen, Denmark: Carlsbergfondet, 1976.

1828. Glaser, John S., and Jeanette J. Rainey. "The 1986 Finance Bill: Increasing Charitable Giving the U.K. Way—a Historical Perspective." *NSFRE Journal* (Spring 1989): 24-8, 31-2.

Examines how the United Kingdom's 1986 finance bill initiated broad reforms in the overall legality of the charity organization and established new tax incentives for private donors. Of particular interest is the introduction of a payroll deduction scheme which creates a personal tax-relief and could mean millions of dollars in charity funds.

1829. Godber, Joyce. *The Harpur Trust, 1552-1973*. Bedford, England: Harpur Trust, 1973.

1830. "Goodbye BBC, Hello NHK!" *Corporate Philanthropy Report* 2 (February-March 1987): 1-5.

Examines attempts by American public broadcasting stations to build long-term programmatic ties with NHK, Japan's well-funded (with a 1986 budget of $2.2 billion) and powerful public broadcasting network. Benefits of PBS-NHK relationships include increased funding capabilities, expanded projects (especially in the realm of documentaries, for which NHK has received much acclaim), and a redressing of the current cultural imbalance in which the Japanese know more about the United States than Americans know about Japan. However, several barriers must first be overcome before such relationships can be successful. The Japanese find American documentaries notoriously under-researched (most evident in films about Japan), and are frustrated when U.S. stations are unable to secure corporate funding for ambitious joint projects. The Americans, in turn, complain that NHK is overly bureaucratic and stifling to creativity, and that its programming never takes a critical look at Japan. The article examines several ongoing efforts to overcome these and other obstacles, where the hope is for joint multi-country programming within the near future.

1831. Goodman, Wolfe D. "The Impact of Taxation on Charitable Giving: Some Very Personal Views." *Philanthropist/Le Philanthrope* 4 (Fall 1984): 5-15.

1832. Gray, B. Kirkman. *A History of English Philanthropy*. London: P.S. King & Son, 1905.

1833. Gray, B. Kirkman. *Philanthropy and the State, or Social Politics*. London: P.S. King & Son, 1908.

1834. Gray, John F. "Charity Links with Commercial Enterprises in the U.K.: A Success Story." *NSFRE Journal* (Spring 1989): 12-5.

Profiles how the National Children's Home (NCH) in Great Britain joined forces with the video industry to raise funds for its "Children in Danger Campaign." These projects have not only raised large amounts of money for NCH (over $1,200,000 in all), but have also given them a great deal of publicity.

1835. Hague Club. *Foundation Profiles*. 4th ed. The Hague, Netherlands: Hague Club, 1988.

Profiles twenty-six large foundations in Europe. Entries include a summary of origin, nature, and purpose; information on the foundation's source of funds, annual expenditure, types of grants and restrictions, and application procedures; listings of trustees, staff and advisers, and chief executive; and a description of major activities, in-house facilities, and publications.

1836. Harrell-Bond, B.E. *Imposing Aid: Emergency Assistance to Refugees*. New York: Oxford University Press, 1986.

Critical examination of international agency assistance programs. The author questions the effects of emergency aid as humanitarian agencies proliferate in response to media appeals to save yet another population of starving, "helpless" refugees. What happens after the cameras leave? What is the effect of the large sums of money spent? What is the effect of the humanitarians and to whom are they accountable? Using a case study approach, the book examines international agency response to Ugandan refugees who fled into the Sudan beginning in early 1982. The methodology of the study is anthropological; 6,000 households were studied both in camps and among the large number who struggled to remain outside the aid umbrella. The book does not question the need for more aid. However, it does question the level of effectiveness of present approaches to assisting refugees. "The basic lesson which emerges...is that while human societies everywhere are able to adapt, and that migration and resettlement may be one method, the imposition of these solutions, denying as it does fundamental human rights, creates more problems than they solve."

1837. Hart, E.K., comp. *Directory of Philanthropic Trusts in Australia*. Hawthorn, Victoria, Australia: Australian Council for Educational Research, 1974.

1838. Hill, C.P. *A Guide for Charity Trustees*. London: Faber & Faber, [1966].

1839. Hodson, H.V., ed. *The International Foundation Directory*. 4th ed. Detroit: Gale Research Co., 1986.

130 entries have been added to this new edition bringing the total number of grantmaking organizations to 770. Arranged alphabetically by country, each entry notes the foundation's name in its native language followed by an English translation, year founded, founding person or organization, activities, publications, finance (assets and grantmaking expenditure in native country's currency), board of trustees, officers, address, and telephone number. Contains currency and exchange rate chart for British sterling and U.S. dollars, select bibliography,

alphabetical index and index of main activities. Introduction has an overview of the evolution of foundations in Europe from the Middle Ages through the present.

1840. Hollingsworth, Rogers, and Ellen Jane Hollingsworth. *Voluntary and Public Hospitals in England and Wales.* Program on Non-Profit Organizations, no. 75. New Haven, Conn.: Institution for Social and Policy Studies, 1983.

1841. Huntley, James Robert. *Private Initiatives and the Cohesion of the Western Democracies: Directory of Organizations.* Seattle, Wash.: Battelle Memorial Institute, 1983.

1842. Huntley, James Robert. *Private Initiatives and the Cohesion of the Western Democracies: Findings, Conclusions, Recommendations.* Seattle, Wash.: Battelle Memorial Institute, 1983.

1843. Huntley, James Robert. *Private Initiatives and the Cohesion of the Western Democracies: Notes and Documentation.* Seattle, Wash.: Battelle Memorial Institute, 1983.

1844. Institute of Donations and Public Affairs Research. *Report of the President.* Montreal, Canada: Institute of Donations and Public Affairs Research, 1985.

1845. Interphil. *Information Resources for the Non-Profit Sector. Interphil Conference.* Yalding, Kent, M E 18 6HU, England: Interphil, 1979.

1846. Interphil. *A World in Need, Opportunities and Changing Roles for Philanthropy.* Yalding, Kent, M E 18 6HU, England: Interphil, [1983].

1847. "Interphil Hosts First U.S. Philanthropy Confab." *Fund Raising Management* 14 (December 1983): 71-7.

1848. Jacobs, Brian D. "Why Britain Is Slow to Grasp Ethnic Needs." *Charity* 1 (October 1984): 6-7. Giving to minorities in Great Britain.

1849. Jaffee, Larry. "Musical Superstars Continue African Charity Relief Effort." *Fund Raising Management* 16 (September 1985): 30+.

1850. James, Estelle. *The Non-Profit Sector in International Perspective: The Case of Sri Lanka.* Program on Non-Profit Organizations, no. 28. New Haven, Conn.: Institution for Social and Policy Studies, 1980.

1851. James, Estelle. *Pre-Conditions, Benefits and Costs of Privatized Public Services: Lessons from the Dutch Educational System.* Program on Non-Profit Organizations, no. 47. New Haven, Conn.: Institution for Social and Policy Studies, 1982.

1852. James, Estelle. *The Private Provision of Public Services: A Comparison of Sweden and Holland.* Program on Non-Profit Organizations, no. 60. New Haven, Conn.: Institution for Social and Policy Studies, 1982.

1853. Janetatos, J.P., and Bertrand M. Harding, Jr. "Obtaining U.S. Financing to Support Foreign Charities." *Fund Raising Management* 16 (April 1985): 58+.

1854. Japan Center for International Exchange. *Activities of Japanese Nonprofit Organizations in Southeast Asia.* New York: Japan Center for International Exchange, 1977.

1855. Japan Center for International Exchange. *Japanese Philanthropy and International Cooperation.* New York: Japan Center for International Exchange, [1986].

Prepared as background material for *The Role of Philanthropy in International Cooperation,* an international symposium sponsored by the Japan Center for International Exchange, Part 1 of this report presents a summary of the international activities of Japan's private sector, discusses the background of greater expectations for Japan's role and examines future challenges for Japan's efforts in international philanthropy. Part 2 describes fifty-nine major Japanese grantmaking foundations engaged in international programs, each with a minimum asset of 100 million yen and annual contributions exceeding 10 million yen.

1856. Japan Center for International Exchange. *Philanthropy in Japan.* Rev. ed. New York: Japan Center for International Exchange, 1978.

1857. Japan Center for International Exchange. *Research Institutions in Japan.* New York: Japan Center for International Exchange, 1978.

1858. Japan Center for International Exchange. *The Role of Philanthropy in International Cooperation.* New York: Japan Center for International Exchange, [1986].

Transcripts of speeches given at the 1985 international conference on *The Role of Private Philanthropy in International Cooperation,* sponsored by the Japan Center for International Exchange. Discussion topics include: *Corporate Philanthropy—Present and Future,* with perspectives from both American and Japanese experiences; *Management of Corporate Philanthropy*; *Priorities of International Philanthropy,* with a focus on third world development; and *Prospects for International Philanthropic Cooperation.* Also includes discussion summaries for each topic section.

1859. Japan Hour Association. *Japanese-American Yellow Pages.* New York: Japan Hour Association, 1985.

1860. Japanese Association of Charitable Corporations. *The Japanese Present Condition of the Philanthropic Activities under Private Initiative.* Tokyo, Japan: Japan Association of Charitable Corporations, 1982.

1861. "Japanese Auto Manufacturers: The Quiet Philanthropists." *Corporate Giving Watch* 4 (April 1984): 1+.

1862–1881 INTERNATIONAL PHILANTHROPY

1862. "Japan's Rockefeller." *Corporate Philanthropy Report* 2 (December 1986): 5+.

Article discusses Ryoichi Sasakawa, the highest rolling philanthropist in the world, who has donated nearly $1.3 billion over the past fifteen years, and why his style of flamboyant grantmaking conflicts with the Japanese ethos of discrete giving. Also discusses his interest in international philanthropy and the Sasakawa Peace Foundation.

1863. Johnston, David. "Japanese Corporations Emerging As Key Players in Grantmaking." *NonProfit Times* 2 (October 1988): 1, 17-9.

Examines the emerging style of Japanese corporate giving in America. Because Americans are suspicious of the growing economic power of Japanese corporations, these donors "can't afford to to be seen as being even as self-serving in their philanthropy as the most enlightened U.S. corporations." Japanese corporate foundations often address themselves to social problems in America, "particularly the shortcomings of American public schools." In addition, they are developing ties to academic research centers and high technology complexes, insuring that the United States maintains enough economic power to offer a profitable market for Japanese high-tech products, while allowing Japanese firms access to state of the art American technology.

1864. Jordan, W.K. *Archaeologia Cantiana. Social Institutions in Kent, 1480-1660.* Kent, England: Kent Archaeological Society, 1961.

1865. Jordan, W.K. *The Charities of London, 1480-1660.* New York: Russell Sage Foundation, 1960.

This is a companion volume to Jordan's *Philanthropy in England, 1480-1660.* In this history, Jordan describes the great charitable contributions made by London, the aspirations and social philosophy of the controlling merchant aristocracy, and the "immense social dominance gained by London...as the flood of charitable generosity poured out across the face of the whole realm." Jordan observes that nearly a third of London's charitable benefactions (thirty-one percent) were made to meet the needs of other parts of the country. Furthermore, the merchant benefactors of London played an important role in this period by establishing a system of endowed education in London and beyond. Jordan chronicles the charitable achievements of the age in poor relief, social rehabilitations, public works, education, and religion. Like his earlier work, this volume is exhaustively researched and documented.

1866. Jordan, W.K. *The Charities of Rural England, 1480-1660.* New York: Russell Sage Foundation, 1962.

1867. Jordan, W.K. *The Forming of the Charitable Institutions of the West of England: A Study of the Changing Pattern of Social Aspirations on Bristol and Somerset, 1480-1660.* Philadelphia: American Philosophical Society, 1960.

1868. Jordan, W.K. *Philanthropy in England, 1480-1660.* New York: Russell Sage Foundation, 1959.

The purpose of this study is to trace "the changing aspirations of English society as reflected in the benefactions" of an age that witnessed "the collapse of the mediaeval society and the rise of the modern era, the triumph of a strong monarchy...the impact of...the Reformation, the emergence of a powerful and responsible gentry, and the swift rise of a principally Puritan urban aristocracy—the merchants—to the seats of economic power." Through a careful study of all the wills and benefactions made between 1480 and 1660 in ten representative English counties, Jordan documents the shift from primarily religious concerns to the secular attitudes that have shaped the intellectual and institutional character of the last three centuries. He traces the development of moral and social responsibility in English society from just after the Middle Ages, through the Tudor reign and the accession and rule of Queen Elizabeth, into the reign of the Stuarts. By that time, an outpouring of private secularized charitable dispositions was creating a new society that the monarchy was ill-equipped to administer.

1869. Jordan, W.K. *The Social Institutions of Lancashire: A Study of the Changing Patterns of Aspirations in Lancashire, 1480-1660.* Vol. 11. Manchester, England: Chetham Society, 1962.

1870. Keeton, George W. *The Modern Law of Charities.* London: Sir Isaac Pitman & Sons, 1962.

1871. Keeton, George W. *The Modern Law of Charities.* 3rd ed. Cardiff, Scotland: University College Cardiff Press, 1983.

1872. Kristof, Nicholas D. "Foreign Funding of Research." *New York Times* (5 August 1985): D-1.

Comments on foreign companies financing research at universities around the country.

1873. Landau, Thomas, ed. *Trusts and Foundations: A Select Guide to Organizations and Grant-Making Bodies Operating in Great Britain and the Commonwealth.* [Cambridge], England: Bowes & Bowes, [1953].

1874. Lehsmann, Kurt. *Kulturfonder I Sverige: Ett Urval Till Tjanst for Stipendiesokande.* Stockholm, Sweden: P.A. Norstedt & Soners forlag, 1980.

1875. Leonard, E.M. *The Early History of English Poor Relief.* Cambridge, England: University Press, 1900.

1876. Liermann, Hans. *Handbuch des Stiftungsrecht. Geschichte des Stiftungsrecht. Band 1.* (Handbook of foundation laws. History of foundation laws. Vol. 1). Tubingen, West Germany: J.C.B. Mohr, 1963.

1877. Lim, Narzalina Z., ed. *Philippine Directory of Foundations.* Manila, Philippines: SCC Development and Research Foundation, 1974.

1878. Lissner, Jorgen. *The Politics of Altruism: A Study of the Political Behaviour of Voluntary Development Agencies.* Geneva, Switzerland: Lutheran World Federation, 1979.

1879. Livingston-Booth, J.D. *A Global View on Philanthropy.* Washington: Independent Sector, 1983.

1880. Martin, Samuel A. *An Essential Grace: Funding Canada's Health Care, Education, Welfare, Religion and Culture.* Toronto, Canada: McClelland & Stewart, 1985.

1881. Martin, Samuel A. *Financing Humanistic Service.* Toronto, Canada: McClelland & Stewart, 1975.

1882. Mason, Todd. "Japan Digs Deep to Win the Hearts and Minds of America: A Growing Philanthropic Role Protects Its U.S. Investments and Improves Its Corporate Image." *Business Week* (11 July 1988): 73-5.

1883. Mauksch, Mary. *Corporate Voluntary Contributions in Europe.* New York: Conference Board, 1982.

1884. Mayer, Robert A. *Latin American Libraries and U.S. Foundation Philanthropy: An Historical Survey.* New York: Ford Foundation, [1971].

1885. Maynard, Rona. "Tightwads, Ltd." *Report on Business Magazine* (April 1987): 30, 32, 34, 36.

Canadian corporations are drowning in requests for money for worthy causes—and it's doling out less than ever before. Indeed, a McMaster University study revealed that ninety-four percent of corporations which made a profit in 1983 claimed no charitable donations. This despite the fact that Canadian corporations are subject to the lowest corporate tax rates of any industrialized country. Corporations which do have charitable giving programs have been met with an unprecedented rise in requests in recent years, states Maynard. After describing the current crisis in corporate charitable giving, the author describes what actions the Canadian charities and fundraisers have been forced to take. To further address the crisis, the Centre for Philanthropy has begun a multifaceted awareness campaign to convince more Canadians, both individuals and corporate decision-makers, that charities need their help.

1886. McCarthy, Kathleen D., ed. *Philanthropy and Culture: The International Foundation Perspective.* Philadelphia: University of Pennsylvania Press, 1984.

Provides the conference papers presented at a five-day conference on international humanities philanthropy, which was sponsored by the Rockefeller Foundation in Italy in 1981. These essays on international development review past work in the humanities in the United States and abroad and discuss the prospects for future efforts. Covering cultural support in the U.S., Europe, and the Third World, the book explores the importance of humanities support in a world still vexed by problems of basic human survival.

1887. McCarthy, Kathleen D. "U.S. Foundations and International Concerns." *Grants Magazine* 8 (March 1985): 28+.

1888. McCarthy, Kathleen D. *The Voluntary Sector Overseas: Notes from the Field.* Center for the Study of Philanthropy Working Papers. New York: Graduate School and University Center, [1988].

Examines the role of social activist and development organizations within Third World host countries (Singapore, Malaysia, Indonesia, India, Kenya, Egypt, Brazil and Argentina are studied here); particular attention is given to the risks of working with controversial issues that go against the desires of governments, the possibility of government support becoming governmental control, and the obstacles to generating or increasing indigenous funding. Bibliography.

1889. McCloy, Shelby T. *Government Assistance in Eighteenth-Century France.* Durham, N.C.: Duke University Press, 1946.

1890. McDougal, Dennis. "USA for Africa Decides to Disburse $17 Million." *Los Angeles Times* (7 August 1985).

1891. McGuire, E. Patrick. *Corporate Aid Programs in Twelve Less-Developed Countries.* New York: Conference Board, 1983.

1892. McLean, Sheila Avrin. *An Assessment for Grantmaking International.* Unpublished, 1982.

1893. McLean, Sheila Avrin, and Rona Kluger. *U.S. Foundation Giving to Enhance Educational Opportunities for Black South Africans: An Analysis of the Present State of Foundation Funding and a Foundation Inventory.* Information Exchange: Working Paper, no. 1. New York: Institute of International Education, 1987.

Provides a comprehensive picture of the present state of U.S. private foundation funding for South Africa-related problems, including observations on the legal considerations of such grantmaking; and a foundation inventory with specific information on the current South Africa-related policies and grants of twenty-five individual foundations.

1894. McLean, Sheila Avrin. *U.S. Philanthropy: Grantmaking for International Purposes.* Washington: Council on Foundations, 1982.

1895. McMullen, David H., Spencer G. Maurice, and David B. Parker. *Tudor on Charities.* London: Sweet & Maxwell, 1967.

1896. McQuillan, Judith. *Charity Statistics.* 9th ed. Tonbridge, Kent, England: Charities Aid Foundation, 1986.

A statistical survey of philanthropic giving in the United Kingdom. Tables, charts and graphs present breakdowns of giving by locality, and giving interest for corporate donors, charitable trusts, and individual givers. Includes lists of top 400 corporate donors, top 200 grantmaking trusts and top 200 grantseeking charities in the U.K.

1897. McQuillan, Judith, ed. *Charity Trends, 1986-87.* Tonbridge, Kent, England: Charities Aid Foundation, 1987.

This tenth edition of the formerly titled *Charity Statistics* interprets the data so that recent trends in the United Kingdom's charitable sector may be more readily understood. (Researchers may still obtain statistics from the editor.) Among the findings: the net income of registered charities in England and Wales increased thirty-two percent between the financial year of 1980/81 and 1985/86; statutory grants represent the fastest growing component of income; and the activities of modern charities appear remarkably traditional in scope, with relatively low priority given to the problems of youth, the aged, or the unemployed. In the area of health, however, resources are being directed to the provision of nursing and care facilities not available in the National Health Service. But even here charities appear to be smaller relative to those in the other dominant groups, and to receive a disproportionately low share of grant income.

1898. McQuillan, Judith, ed. *Charity Trends, 1987-88.* 11th ed. Tonbridge, Kent, England: Charities Aid Foundation, 1988.

1899–1916 INTERNATIONAL PHILANTHROPY

1899. Memo from Turner. *Misgivings*. Toronto, Ontario: Memo from Turner, 1972.

Reviews and evaluates the donation policies of certain corporations and foundations in Canada to identify those which are likely sources of funds for innovative and community services.

1900. Montias, J. Michael. *Public Support for the Performing Arts in Western Europe and the United States: History and Analysis*. Program on Non-Profit Organizations, no. 45. New Haven, Conn.: Institution for Social and Policy Studies, 1982.

1901. Murphy, E. Jefferson. *Creative Philanthropy: Carnegie Corporation and Africa, 1953-1973*. New York: Teachers College Press, 1976.

1902. Nebolsine, George. *Fiscal Aspects of Foundations and Charitable Donations in European Countries*. Amsterdam, Netherlands: European Cultural Foundation, 1963.

1903. Neuberger, Egon. *The de Facto Non-Profit Sector in Yugoslavia*. Program on Non-Profit Organizations, no. 41. New Haven, Conn.: Institution for Social and Policy Studies, 1982.

1904. Neuhoff, Klaus. *Die Bereitstellung von Unternehmenskapital fur Stiftungen*. (The preparation of business funds for foundations). Koln, West Germany: Universitat zu Koln, 1964.

1905. Neuhoff, Klaus, and Horst Vinken, comps. *Deutsche Stiftungen fur Wissenschaft, Bildung und Kultur*. (German foundations for science, education and culture). Baden-Baden, West Germany: Nomos Verlagsgesellschaft, 1969.

1906. Neuhoff, Klaus, and Uwe Pavel, eds. *Les Fondations En Europe: Une Etude Comparative*. Essen-Bredeney, West Germany: Stifterverband fur die deutsche Wissenschaft e. V., 1973.

1907. Neuhoff, Klaus. "Government and Private Roles in Activities for the Public Good." *Philanthropy Monthly* 16 (October 1983): 33-7.

1908. Neuhoff, Klaus. "Philanthropy in Germany." *Philanthropy Monthly* 20 (January 1987): 29-34.

Foundation Center/Donors' Association for the Promotion of Sciences and Humanities in Germany consultant Klaus Neuhoff's article is adapted from a talk to the European Donation Meeting of Hewlett Packard Corporation in 1986. In this article, Neuhoff describes the role of German philanthropic foundations, charitable giving, and corporate philanthropy in an economic/historical context.

1909. Neuhoff, Klaus, and Uwe Pavel, eds. *Trusts and Foundations in Europe: A Comparative Survey*. London: Bedford Square Press, [1972].

1910. Nightingale, Benedict. *Charities*. London: Allen Lane, 1973.

1911. Ninkovich, Frank A. *The Diplomacy of Ideas: U.S. Foreign Policy and Cultural Relations, 1938-1950*. New York: Cambridge University Press, 1981.

Ninkovich examines U.S. cultural diplomacy, including both private initiatives (beginning with the establishment of the Carnegie Endowment for International Peace in 1910) and public policies, concentrating on developments since 1938. He attempts to grasp the meaning of "cultural relations," to explore what is involved when a country like the United States tries to deal culturally with other countries, and to analyze how such relations tend to reflect prevailing anthropological and sociological thinking about culture. He asks whether there can be such a thing as cultural policy. Ninkovich argues that cultural programs were shaped fundamentally by institutional forces and by considerations of political power, not by the idealistic premises of cultural idealists. The first chapter, *Philanthropic Origins of Cultural Policy*, looks at the activities of not only Carnegie, but Rockefeller, the American Council of Learned Societies, and others. Extensive bibliography.

1912. Norton, Michael, ed. *Company Charitable Giving Statistics*. London: Directory of Social Change, 1987.

The latest (1987) statistics on charitable giving by the leading 1,000 British companies, listed by donations amount with information on turnover, pre-tax profits, and the number of employees; and an alphabetical listing with addresses, telephone numbers, and contact persons. Also provides information on the most recent trends in company giving and sponsorship in the U.K.; case studies of Community Links, a social sponsorship, and Water Aid, an industry initiative to help the Third World; and a report on trade union giving, including information on the charitable policies and practices of individual unions.

1913. Norton, Michael, ed. *A Guide to Company Giving*. London: Directory of Social Change, 1986.

Information on the donations of over 1,000 leading British companies listed alphabetically and by size of donation; detailed donations policies of the 155 largest companies; and case studies of the Shell Better Britain Campaign, the giving programs of Allied Dunbar and Rank Xerox, and the fundraising drive by John Laing, which raised over 600,000 in 1984.

1914. Norton, Michael. *Investment of Charity Funds*. London: Directory of Social Change, 1985.

Guide for charity trustees, investment advisors and those responsible for the day-to-day financial management of charities and nonprofit societies. Provides advice and guidance for the investment of a variety of different types of funds, including short-term cash balances, medium-term funds held pending the completion of an appeal or as a reserve for some future item of expenditure, and long-term investments and endowments. Written for charities in the United Kingdom, some of the information is specific to their institutions, though most of the advice is sound and transferable.

1915. O'Kelly, Elizabeth. *Aid and Self-Help: A General Guide to Overseas Aid*. London: Charles Knight & Co., 1973.

1916. Owen, David. *English Philanthropy, 1660-1960*. Cambridge, Mass.: Belknap Press, 1964.

"What is of primary concern here," states Owen, "is the benefactions (pecuniary) of Englishmen which went to create and support a network of services for the mitigation of poverty, disease, infirmity, and ignorance." Owen traces the evolution of private philanthropy in England from the eighteenth-century humanists (already inheritors of a tradition of social responsibility) to the twentieth-century individualists, whose faith in private answers to problems of destitution and public welfare was waning. While the history covers a 300-year period, it gives prolonged attention to the period between the economic revolution of the late eighteenth century to the First World War. An underlying theme of the history is "the dual importance of private charity"—its role as a pioneering force preceding and laying the groundwork for state action, and its ultimate inadequacy in dealing with the welfare requirements of an industrial-urban society.

1917. Patterson, Ben. "'Freedom' in France Means State Control." *Charity* 1 (June 1984): 9-10.

1918. Pederson, Johannes. *The Carlsberg Foundation.* Copenhagen, Denmark: Bianco Lunos Bogtrykkeri, 1956.

1919. Phillips, H.M. *Higher Education: Cooperation with Developing Countries.* Rev. ed. Rockefeller Foundation Working Papers. New York: Rockefeller Foundation, 1978.

1920. Pitman, Walter G. "The Role of the Charitable Foundation in a Changing Society." *Philanthropist/Le Philanthrope* 7 (Winter 1988): 33-9.

Provides an interesting analysis of the cultural, industrial and political qualities that have defined a uniquely Canadian pattern of philanthropic and public support for its social and educational services, and especially its arts. Reaffirms the role of philanthropy and foundations in promoting the well-being of all persons as well as developing a higher quality of life within society.

1921. Pomey, Michel. *Traite des Fondations D'utilite Publique.* Paris, France: Presses Universitaires de France, 1980.

1922. "Private Aid Keeps UK OK Abroad." *Charity* 1 (February 1984): 3.

1923. Public Management Institute. "Japanese Foundations That Support U.S. Nonprofits." *Corporate Philanthropy Report* 2 (February-March 1987): 8, 10.

Nine short selected profiles of Japanese foundations which fund American nonprofits. Most of the foundations promote science and technology research within Japan, but they are increasingly supportive of international activities. Sixty percent of these international budgets go to U.S. nonprofits. The information in the article was obtained from *Japanese Philanthropy and International Corporations* published by Japan Center for International Exchange (JCIE). JCIE is a beachhead for foreigners who are intent on building partnerships with Japanese foundations and corporations. Each profile includes the foundation's name, address, telephone number, and contact person as well as a short statement about the foundation's focus and assets.

1924. Public Management Institute. "Leaping the Cultural Barrier: A Roadmap to Japanese Corporate Philanthropy." *Corporate Philanthropy Report* 1 (January 1986): 3-4.

1925. Public Management Institute. "The Questions Nonprofits Ask." *Corporate Philanthropy Report* 2 (February-March 1987): 13-5.

Series of questions and answers regarding how an American nonprofit organization can gain access to Japanese corporate foundations. The article suggests that a relationship be built with the subsidaries and their executives. The foundations are likely to fund projects which build image, public relations, relationships, and transfer technology.

1926. Public Management Institute. "Want a Japanese Grant? Cultivate These Third Parties First." *Corporate Philanthropy Report* 2 (February-March 1987): 9-12.

An annotated list of nine organizations which, according to this article, American nonprofits must cultivate if they desire to obtain funding from Japanese corporations. When asked for contributions, Japanese companies tend to rely on advice from intermediary organizations which are already in close working relationships with the companies. The organizations detailed in the article include the Japan External Trade Organization (JETRO), Japanese consulates, Japanese Chambers of Commerce, Japan-America Societies, Japanese Industry Associations, Japanese Banks, Bilateral Business Councils, the Japan Foundation, and "Japan Desks" in U.S. government agencies. The annotations contain a brief informational profile on the group or agency and include the address and/or telephone number.

1927. Rainsbury, Colin. "Canadian Society of Fund Raising Executives Created." *Fund Raising Management* 15 (November 1984): 104.

1928. Reid, Alan, and William Kirk. *Royal Dunfermline. A Historical Guide to the City and Its Antiquities: With an Account of the Carnegie Benefactions.* Dunfermline, Scotland: A. Romanes & Son, [1906].

1929. *Report from His Majesty's Commissioners for Inquiry Into the Administration and Practical Operation of the Poor Laws.* London: B. Fellowes, 1834.

1930. *Report of the Charity Commissioners for England and Wales.* London: Her Majesty's Stationery Office, 1981.

1931. *Report of the Committee on the Law and Practice Relating to Charitable Trusts. (Nathan Report).* London: Her Majesty's Stationery Office, 1952.

1932. Robertson, William. *Welfare in Trust: A History of the Carnegie United Kingdom Trust, 1913-1963.* Dunfermline, Scotland: Carnegie United Kingdom Trust, 1964.

1933. Rowntree, Joseph. *One Man's Vision: The Story of the Joseph Rowntree Village Trust.* London: George Allen & Unwin, 1954.

1934. Ruof, Peter. *International Corporate Contributions.* Washington: Council on Foundations, 1983.

Looks at changes and developments in corporate social responsibility of U.S. corporations and foreign corporations.

1934–1944 INTERNATIONAL PHILANTHROPY

Summarizes a comparative overview of the present legislation regarding charitable contributions in different countries. Addresses the need to do more in international corporate philanthropy.

1935. Russell-Wood, A.J.R. *Fidalgos and Philanthropists. The Santa Casa Da Misericordia, 1550-1755.* Berkeley, Calif.: University of California Press, 1968.

Examines the Misericordia or Portuguese lay brotherhoods throughout the world and the branch in Bahia in particular. The brotherhood was a social organization established to give spiritual and material aid to all in need. The history of this institution and its social relief programs is set within a comprehensive social and economic history of the colonial capital of Portuguese America (Bahia) from 1549 to 1763. This scholarly work includes numerous quotes from archival documents on such topics as women in the Portuguese colonial empire, urban sanitation, prison aid and funeral services.

1936. Ryan, J. Patrick. "We Have Much to Learn from Our International Friends." *NSFRE Journal* (Spring 1989): 8-10.

Urges American fundraisers to investigate the possibilities of worldwide philanthropy. Ryan warns that Americans too often assume they are at the height of fundraising expertise and philanthropic sophistication, and therefore fail to learn from the experience of philanthropists in other countries. He concludes by speculating how the cooperation of charitable groups from various countries may add to the development of human understanding, and envisions a single-constituency world which works to improve the quality of life for all people everywhere.

1937. Schiller, Theo. *Stiftungen im Gesellschaftlichen Prozess.* (Foundations in the social process). Baden-Baden, West Germany: Nomos Verlagsgesellschaft, 1969.

1938. Schnabel, Teresa, Giselle Bricault, and Jennifer Carr, eds. *The International Corporate 1000: A Directory of Those Who Manage the World's Leading 1000 Corporations.* Washington: Monitor Publishing Co., 1989.

Directory of officers, management and boards of directors for approximately 1000 of the world's largest companies outside of the United States. Included are profiles of 675 companies located in Eupope, 237 in the Far East and Australia, fifty-four in Canada and Latin America and thirty-five in the Middle East and Africa. Profiles include company name, address, and telephone and telex numbers. Although little company data is given, the general nature of the business and/or products is given as well as an annual sales figure when available. For the company executives, name, title and the board of director's company affiliation are given. Reference aids include a list of world holidays, time zone chart, and telephone country codes. Indexed by company name, industry, and individuals.

1939. Schuster, J. Mark Davidson. *Supporting the Arts: An International Comparative Study.* Washington: Government Printing Office, 1985.

Focusing on eight countries (Canada, the Federal Republic of Germany, France, Italy, Great Britain, the Netherlands, Sweden and the United States), report describes the comparative context of arts support in each country, estimates national arts expenditures, compares the structure and levels of private support, including a description of the relevant tax incentives, and studies selected arts institutions to allow a micro-level view of the distribution of operating income.

1940. Schuster, J. Mark Davidson. *Tax Incentives for Charitable Donations: Deeds of Covenant and Charitable Contribution Deductions.* Program on Non-Profit Organizations, no. 71. New Haven, Conn.: Institution for Social and Policy Studies, 1983.

1941. Shea, Albert A., ed. *Corporate Giving in Canada.* Toronto, Canada: Clarke, Irwin & Co., 1953.

1942. Shorrock, John B. "Foreign Policy." *Currents* 14 (February 1988): 32-6.

Describes how the University of Akron tailored its standard corporate solicitation techniques to an international audience, bringing in over $300,000 from companies in seven countries ranging from France to Japan. Widely known for its expertise in the area of polymers, the University's development officers realized their program had an impact beyond U.S. boundaries; they researched the companies that gave to and benefited from polymer research, and traced their links to companies in other countries. Points to observe in appealing to international interests: focus on specific projects; research the field broadly and thoroughly; secure domestic gifts first (strengthen your case with the support of domestic companies that have international purchasing contracts or actual operations abroad); seek leaders from major domestic companies in the targeted industry; build on your faculty's connections; and time your campaign around industry gatherings, such as an international trade fair or conference. It may be that international philanthropic support is an integral part in the development of a global village.

1943. Simsar, Muhammed Ahmed. *The Waqfiyah of 'Ahmed Pasa.* Philadelphia: University of Pennsylvania Press, 1940.

1944. Sinclair, Michael R. *American Grantmaking in South Africa: A Conference Report.* Washington: Council on Foundations, 1988.

Proceedings of a conference jointly hosted by the Council on Foundations and the Henry J. Kaiser Family Foundation's Office for Health and Development in South Africa. The conference provided a forum for grantmakers from the foundation community, corporations, religious groups and the public sector to engage in discussion about the opportunities for, and obstacles to, effective grantmaking in South Africa. Among the key points that emerged from the deliberations: the eradication of apartheid is the primary motivation for grantmaking in South Africa; black empowerment and support for community-controlled grassroots initiatives should be the highest priority; constant consultation and social analysis is needed for all grantmaking in South Africa, as well as a long-term commitment; no grant is too small provided it is motivated by a desire to increase black self-sufficiency; and it must be recognized that it is impossible to be non-political when making grants in South Africa, and it is necessary to take risks.

1945. Sinclair, Michael R., and Julia Weinstein. *American Philanthropy: A Guide for South Africans.* Washington: Investor Responsibility Research Center, 1988.

In the wake of American firms' withdrawal from South Africa, many leaders of black community development are requesting more information about the motivations of American philanthropy and the mechanics of American assistance programs in order to obtain increased funding. The first part of this report examines political influences shaping U.S. foreign assistance programs, including the relationship between public attitudes and political action; the U.S. assistance program in South Africa, covering its initiation, its explicit and unwritten objectives, and South African suspicions of a hidden U.S. agenda; and the future of U.S. relations with South Africa, including current restrictions, the next administration's options in designing a new policy, the influence of public attitudes, interest groups and factions in Congress on U.S. policy, and the impact of these factors on U.S. assistance programs in South Africa. Also reviews the American philanthropic community and international grantmaking, including basic concepts of the foundation process; American grantmaking in South Africa, noting factors that influence foundation attitudes, along with both the obstacles to and opportunities for increased American foundation involvement in South Africa; and strategies to help South Africans mobilize American resources. The second part contains a list of foundations willing to at least consider funding South Africa-related projects, and a list of prospective corporate sources of funding, drawn from Investor Responsibility Research Center's *U. S. and Canadian Business in South Africa* and the *Eleventh Report on the Signatory Companies to the Statement of Principles for South Africa.*

1946. Sinclair, Michael R. *Community Development in South Africa: A Guide for American Donors.* Washington: Investor Responsibility Research Center, 1986.

Guide for American involvement in South African community development projects. The original report upon which this guide is based examined community development using extensive interviews with South Africans involved in community development projects, the church, trade unions and political organizations. In a short historical overview, the author examines both past and present political complexities of South Africa. Based upon the interviews, Sinclair pinpoints the interviewees' three major community development priorities—alleviating poverty, assisting the victims of apartheid and preparing for majority government. The book presents an analysis of the problem areas such as rural subsistence; education; job creation; urban housing; assisting victims of apartheid; refugee programs; developing internal institutions, organizations and management; regional considerations; and what resources are most needed. The last two chapters of the volume explore American involvement in community development in South Africa and black attitudes towards the involvement. The interviews attest to an "antipathy of most black South Africans toward the United States" which the author believes is "based as much on their perception of a characteristic American brusqueness and arrogance as any ideological aversion." The negative perception of America is contradicted by "a very high regard for the priority the U.S. attaches to human rights." The book concludes with a *Directory of Key Organizations* and pointers which might facilitate American access to black community development. The appendixes contain a map, *The Freedom Charter*, the *Manifesto of the Azanian People*, and the above mentioned directory.

1947. "Small Companies: Patterns and Attitudes of Charitable Giving." *Charity* 5 (November 1987): 2-3.

Findings and implications of a Charities Aid Foundation [CAF] research project focusing on the charitable giving patterns, preferences and disincentives of small businesses in Great Britain. Previous research by CAF revealed that larger companies give because they feel a responsibility to help provide for those needs considered to be deserving but which are not fully met by the welfare state; the study of small businesses reveals that the main reasons for a company's support policy are a feeling of involvement with and responsibility for the local area and social conscience to help those in need, while low-level profits were cited by the minority of small businesses which did not help charity. Finds that most financial donations tend to occcur as responses to specific requests and are therefore sporadic, and suggests that small businesses be encouraged to establish a regular commitment by setting an annual charitable budget, extending their charitable support into non-financial areas, and/or involving their employees in corporate charitable giving to a greater extent than exists at present.

1948. Smith, Brian H. *Churches As Development Institutions: The Case of Chile, 1973-1980.* Program on Non-Profit Organizations, no. 50. New Haven, Conn.: Institution for Social and Policy Studies, 1982.

1949. Smith, Brian H. *U.S. and Canadian Nonprofit Organizations (PVOs) As Transitional Development Institutions.* Program on Non-Profit Organizations, no. 70. New Haven, Conn.: Institution for Social and Policy Studies, 1983.

1950. Smith, Craig. "To Africa, with Love." *Foundation News* 26 (May-June 1985): 24+.

Reports on the recording *We are the World.*

1951. Somerville, Bill. "Foundations in the United Kingdom." *NonProfit Times* 1 (January 1988): 26+.

Examines various aspects of charitable giving and the recent growth of community foundations in the United Kingdom. The push for community foundations is occuring under the auspices of the London-based Charities Aid Foundation, the British equivalent of the Council on Foundations in Washington, DC. The British community foundations are only beginning to achieve stability, and the article concludes with an address for further information concerning partnership possibilities between U.S. and U.K. agencies.

1952. Soulis, Jean-Jacques. *Fondations: Reconnues D'utilite Publique En France.* Paris-Clichy-Sous-Bois, France: Vieux-Logis S.A., 1970.

1953. "South African Giving Gets a Voice." *Charity* 1 (June 1984): 3.

1954. Spear, Nathaniel, III. *A Handbook of Latin-American Foundations: Purposes and Activities.* New York: Foundation Center, 1974.

1955. Stifterverband fur die Deutsche Wissenschaft. *Foundations in Europe: A Comparative Survey.* Essen-Bredeney, West Germany: Stifterverband fur die deutsche Wissenschaft e. V., [1971].

1956–1967 INTERNATIONAL PHILANTHROPY

1956. *Stiftungen in Europa: Eine Vergleichende Ubersicht.* (Foundations in Europe: A comparative survey). Baden-Baden, West Germany: Nomos Verlagsgesellschaft, 1971.

1957. Stromberg, Ann, ed. *Philanthropic Foundations in Latin America.* New York: Russell Sage Foundation, 1968.

1958. Suhrke, Henry C. "Non-Profits and the U.N." *Philanthropy Monthly* 17 (March 1984): 4-19.

1959. Tanaka, Minoru. *Foundation(s) in Japan: Their Legal Provisions and Tax Regulations.* New York: Japan Center for International Exchange, 1975.

Discusses the difficulties associated with developing private philanthropic activities for the sake of public welfare in Japan, in terms of both a cultural and institutional context. Because human relations are based primarily on kinship and geographic affinity, donations in Japan are given on the basis of specific human relationships; there is simply no tradition of wide public support on which philanthropy can build. The prevailing belief that the government should administer and regulate social and educational institutions has led to special support in the form of funds and human resources being given to those organizations that are influenced by government policy and are judged to be useful in some way to the national purpose. This excessively close relationship—entailing both dependence and interference—with the government authorities is considered one of the most serious obstacles inhibiting the growth of private philanthropy in Japan. Suggestions for improvement also include the development of a more balanced tax policy to lessen the tax privileges gap between charitable corporations and charitable trusts; and a clearinghouse which collects and files theoretical and practical information concerning nonprofit, public-interest activites and makes it available upon request is recommended.

1960. Tanaka, Minoru, and Takako Amemiya. *Philanthropy in Japan '83: Private Nonprofit Activities in Japan.* Tokyo, Japan: Japan Association of Charitable Corporations, 1983.

This study follows up on a 1982 survey of nonprofit corporations and charitable trusts in Japan, most of which are governed by either central or local government offices, although they are considered private organizations. The book summarizes the history of nonprofit activity in Japan, with special attention to the legal environment in which such institutions became viable and began to be formed. It analyzes the functions of nonprofit and charitable institutions in Japanese society, with some reference to systems in the United States and Europe. After laying out the background, the authors examine trends in reform and the status of nonprofit activities at present, especially as they respond to certain revisions in Japanese legal codes. Part Two of the book consists of a directory of fifty foundations and three charitable trusts, with information about their budgets, purposes and activities, and dates of establishment.

1961. Task Force on Funding of the Arts. *Funding of the Arts in Canada to the Year 2000.* Ottawa, Ontario, Canada: Government of Canada, 1986.

Task Force report to the Canadian government which presents a strategic plan for the funding of the arts until the year 2000. The plan calls for a five percent annual increase in constant dollars in the funding of the arts. The success of the plan depends on the continued contributions and cooperation of the public sector, the private sector, the consumer, and the arts community. Selected bibliography.

1962. Technical Assistance Information Clearing House. *A Listing of U.S. Non-Profit Organizations in Small Industry Development Assistance Abroad.* New York: Technical Assistance Information Clearing House, 1976.

1963. Technical Assistance Information Clearing House. *Medicine and Public Health: Development Assistance Abroad.* New York: Technical Assistance Information Clearing House, 1979.

1964. Technical Assistance Information Clearing House. *U.S. Non-Profit Organizations, Voluntary Agencies, Missions, and Foundations Participating in Technical Assistance Abroad: A Directory.* New York: Technical Assistance Information Clearing House, 1964.

1965. Teltsch, Kathleen. "Finding Out about Foundations." *Sweden Now* 16 (1982): 19+.

1966. Teltsch, Kathleen. "From Perestroika to Philanthropy." *Foundation News* 29 (November-December 1988): 18-23.

Recounts the visit of Americans from fourteen U.S. foundations to the Soviet Union, where they witnessed the beginnings of a charitable sector. The visit's highpoint involved talking with Soviet organizers of the International Foundation for the Survival and Development of Mankind—the first philanthropy created in the Soviet Union to operate without government control or money, financed by private funds raised in that country and abroad. The foundation emphasizes collaborative efforts in researching global concerns, such as environmental pollution, arms control, energy efficiency and economic development. There were many obstacles to the foundation's independent legal and tax-free status in the beginning, and American supporters wanted assurances that the new philanthropy would be free of government pressure and from misuse as a funnel for government propaganda; however, the more Gorbachev pushes his reforms based on "glasnost" and "perestroika," the more willing Soviet leaders are to experiment with American-style foundations and other forms of nongovernmental activity. Another focus of the visit was meeting Gennady P. Alferenko, a correspondent for *Komsomolskaya Pravda* and a grassroots philanthropy fundraiser who invites his readers to submit proposals which deserve financial support. The ones he publishes not only raise money, but also help form public opinion, such as the proposal for a rehabilitation center for veterans of the Afghanistan war. The American visitors approved of his delegating decision-making to the people involved in the issues, stimulating them to give out of a true feeling of charity, not to receive a tax-deduction. One visitor stressed that for a country where philanthropy had never existed before, the Soviets "have as much to tell us as we them, and we must show mutual sensitivity."

1967. Tett, Norman, and Ronald McFarlane, eds. *Commonwealth Caribbean Directory of Aid Agencies.* London: Commonwealth Foundation, 1978.

1968. Thompson, Kenneth W. *Foreign Assistance: A View from the Private Sector.* Notre Dame, Ind.: University of Notre Dame Press, 1972.

1969. Thompson, Thomas Kirkland. *An Informal Inquiry into Philanthropy in Europe, 1961-1962.* New York: Russell Sage Foundation, 1962.

1970. Tsu, Yu-Yue. *The Spirit of Chinese Philanthropy.* New York: Columbia University, 1912.

1971. United Nations Fund for Population Activities. *Population Programmes and Projects.* 2 Vols. New York: United Nations, 1975.

1972. United States. Department of State. Agency for International Development. Advisory Committee on Voluntary Foreign Aid. *The Role of Voluntary Agencies in International Assistance.* Washington: U.S. Department of State, 1974.

1973. United States-Japan Foundation. *Japan-America Dialogue: A Survey of Organizational Activities.* New York: United States-Japan Foundation, 1981.

1974. Ural, Engin. *Foundations in Turkey.* Ankara, Turkey: Development Foundation of Turkey, 1978.

1975. van Hoorn, J., Jr. *Draft European Convention on the Tax Treatment in Respect of Certain Non-Profit Organizations.* Yalding, Kent, M E 18 6HU, England: Interphil, [1971].

1976. Waddilove, Lewis E. *Private Philanthropy and Public Welfare: The Joseph Rowntree Memorial Trust, 1954-1979.* London: George Allen & Unwin, 1983.

1977. Wall, David. *The Charity of Nations: The Political Economy of Foreign Aid.* New York: Basic Books, 1973.

1978. Watson, John H., III, and Douglas Monteath. *Company Contributions in Canada.* Montreal, Canada: National Industrial Conference Board, 1963.

1979. Webster, C.R. "Public and Private Philanthropy in the Eighties." *Philanthropist/Le Philanthrope* 4 (Winter 1984): 32-59.

1980. Weiner, Andrew. "Dollars to Donors: Revenue Canada Helps Those Who Help the Charities." *Financial Post* (March 1987): 24-9.

1981. West, Ruth. "These Phenomenally Orthodox Donors." *Charity* 1 (February 1984): 5-6.

1982. Wiederhold, Johannes. *Stiftung und Unternehmen im Spannungs-Verhaltnis.* (The relationship of the foundation and business). Bern, Switzerland: Verlag Herbert Lang & Cie AG, 1971.

1983. Williams, Roger M. "The Chocolate Soldiers." *Foundation News* 29 (January-February 1988): 36-40.

Profiles the Cadbury trusts, which address, among other things, the issues of racism and alienation in the West Midlands of Great Britain.

1984. Williams, Roger M. "Corporate Philanthropy Comes to Europe." *Foundation News* 26 (September-October 1985): 26+.

1985. Women's Technical Assistance Project. *Church Funding Sources for International Projects.* Washington: Center for Community Change, 1986.

Lists sixteen Protestant and Catholic religious funding organizations which support only international projects. Includes list of denominational sources and application deadlines; description of program objectives, purposes, goals; application guidelines; and sample application forms. Also included are a vocabulary sheet listing terminology for the major Protestant denominational statutes and a discussion of how to seek funds from church sources.

1986. Zimmerman, A.A. *Summary Guide to Educational Foundations: Europe (Excluding U.K.).* Vol. 1. Dagenham, Essex, England: Northeast London Polytechnic, 1976.

1987. Zimmerman, A.A. *Summary Guide to Educational Foundations: United Kingdom.* Vol. 2. Dagenham, Essex, England: Northeast London Polytechnic, 1978.

PART TWO

THE NONPROFIT SECTOR

NONPROFIT ORGANIZATIONS

1988. Access. *Opportunities in Non-Profit Organizations.* Cambridge, Mass.: Access: Networking in the Public Interest, 1988.

1989. Ad Hoc Committee on Voluntary Health and Welfare Agencies in the United States. *Voluntary Health and Welfare Agencies in the United States: An Exploratory Study.* New York: Schoolmasters Press, 1961.

The committee of private citizens that wrote this report came together at the invitation of the Rockefeller Foundation to examine a number of issues about voluntary agencies. The questions they explored include: To what degree are voluntary agencies responsive to public needs? Are so many agencies (100,000 at the time of the report) necessary? Have voluntary agencies adjusted to the increasing role of government? Should they be supervised, in the public interest? How efficient are they? Their findings prompted three principal recommendations: there should be established a new National Commission on Voluntary Health and Welfare Agencies to continue research, appraise performance, and strengthen interagency coordination; agencies owe the public full and frank disclosure of programs and their financing; and a system of uniform accounting should be developed by the American Institute of Certified Public Accountants to facilitate the work of budget-reviewing bodies, potential contributors, and voluntary agencies themselves.

1990. Adess, Nancy. "Looking Good. Part 2: Speaking the Language." *Grassroots Fundraising Journal* 7 (December 1988): 8-11.

Offers basic information about graphic designers, typesetters, and printers, along with suggestions for working with each of them to get the best finished product possible. Graphic designers make use of balance and positioning to maximize the effective visual presentation of ideas; however, they must understand what the actual message should be, lest the graphic elements be emphasized at the expense of the educational content. In addition, prior agreements about cost limitations will prevent problems later. Typesetters produce professional and easy to read materials usually well beyond the scope of most laser jet printers (although many basic materials may be attractively designed and printed in-house if the organization has the right computer programs and someone with enough talent). Learning some of the basics about the typesetter's language can save the expense of having a designer or typesetter translate specifications from inches. Printing prices depend upon many factors and may vary widely; thus it is best to contact several printers for comparison bids. Viewing paper samples and samples of their work is also an element in choosing a printer, as the lowest bidder may not provide the quality desired. When delivering a job to a printer, certain information should be supplied in writing, such as the number of pieces, the directions of the fold, the exact color(s) and paper, and the delivery date. The final consideration concerns factoring in enough time to get everything done well and when needed.

1991. Alliance of New York State Arts Councils. *The Alliance Handbook.* New York: Alliance of New York State Arts Councils, 1983.

1992. Alsop, Ronald. "More Nonprofit Groups Make Imaginative Aggressive Sales." *Wall Street Journal* (31 May 1984): 33.

1993. Alsop, Ronald. "On Nonprofits, Marketing, Competition and Sales." *Fundemensions* 8 (July 1984): 6.

1994. American Association of Fund-Raising Counsel. *The American Association of Fund-Raising Counsel, Inc.: Its First Thirty Years.* New York: American Association of Fund-Raising Counsel, 1966.

1995. American Association of Fund-Raising Counsel. *Symposium.* Unpublished, 1985.

1996. American Bar Association. *The Bar Foundation: Recognizing a Professional and Public Responsibility.* Chicago: American Bar Association, 1979.

1997. "American Business Provides $506 Million to Arts Organizations in 1982." *BCA News* (November-December 1983): 1.

1998. American Council for the Arts. *Americans and the Arts, 1984.* New York: American Council for the Arts, 1984.

1999. Anthony, Robert N. "How Nonprofits Can Beat the Depreciation Game." *Philanthropy Monthly* 21 (February 1988): 26-8.

Tongue-in-cheek article addresses the Financial Accounting Standards Board's (FASB) proposed Statement 93, which instructs all private colleges, universities, and other nongovernmental nonprofit organizations to report accumulated depreciation and depreciation expense on virtually all their buildings, equipment, and other long-lived assets. Professor Anthony suggests depreciating such things as buildings, books, and trees, with the major intent of generating as many pages of figures and graphs as possible. "The guiding principle," Anthony writes, "is that the benefits of any accounting procedure should exceed the cost of applying it—the FASB has said so. Since the benefit of reporting depreciation on contributed assets is zero, the cost of calculating depreciation should be the lowest that will satisfy the auditor."

2000. Aramony, William. *The United Way: The Next Hundred Years.* New York: Donald I. Fine, 1987.

Celebrates the one hundredth year of the United Way, and looks forward to the next hundred as "one of the nation's most important instruments for building community."

2001. Arts and Business Council. *Winterfare.* New York: Arts and Business Council, 1987.

An annual compendium listing more than three hundred arts organizations in the greater New York area with descriptions of specific projects. Divided into sections concerned with the performing arts (dance, music, opera, theatre), presenters, education and workshops, arts services, video and film, and visual arts, this compilation serves as a useful resource for corporations, foundations, arts organizations, government agencies, educational institutions and artists.

2002. Association of Information Systems Professionals. *Annual Salary Survey Results.* Willow Grove, Pa.: Association of Information Systems Professionals, 1983.

2003. Association of Research Libraries. *ARL Annual Salary Survey, 1981.* Washington: Association of Research Libraries, 1982.

2004. Backas, James. *The Regional Arts Organization Movement.* Washington: National Partnership Meeting, 1980.

2005. Backas, James. *The State Arts Council Movement.* Washington: National Partnership Meeting, 1980.

2006. Bailen, June. "Arts Stabilization Is Mission of New Fund." *Fund Raising Management* 15 (April 1984): 82+.

2007. Bailen, June. "New Arts Database Will Provide Information Leap." *Fund Raising Management* 14 (June 1983): 70-1.

2008. Barry, Bryan W. *Strategic Planning Workbook for Nonprofit Organizations.* St. Paul, Minn.: Amherst H. Wilder Foundation, 1986.

Clearly written workbook describes the step-by-step process for developing and effecting a strategic plan. Numerous worksheets and planning tips help both experienced nonprofit executives and volunteer leaders envision the future of their organization and construct the best path to reach that goal. Appendixes include a summary of a situation analysis, an example of a strategic plan, and removable strategic planning worksheets.

2009. Barsky, Robert. *A Review of the Literature on Non-Profit Organizations in Nursing Home Care for the Elderly.* Program on Non-Profit Organizations, no. 36. New Haven, Conn.: Institution for Social and Policy Studies, 1981.

2010. Bartlett, Dwight K., III. "Fringes Are Not Frills: Employee Benefits for Nonprofits." *Nonprofit World* 5 (September-October 1987): 18-21.

Evaluates the pluses and minuses of the options in employee retirement programs that are available to nonprofits: a basic pension plan (examining both the defined benefit and defined contribution plans), a tax deferred annuity program, and an individual retirement account.

2011. "Basic Standards in Philanthropy." *Wise Giving Guide* (January 1984): 1.

2012. Baumol, William J., and William G. Bowen. *Performing Arts, the Economic Dilemma: A Study of Problems Common to Theater, Opera, Music, and Dance.* New York: Twentieth Century Fund, 1966.

This study explains the financial problems of the performing arts and explores the implications of these problems for the future of the arts in the United States. The main research focus is the cost and revenue structure of the performing groups and the constitution of audiences. The study also deals with performer incomes, history and anatomy of cultural centers, grants and contributions, case studies, and the state of the arts in Great Britain. Part 3 is of special interest, as it is devoted to sources of funding, including individual, foundation, and corporate philanthropy. The authors conclude that the economic structure of live performance is the cause of its chronic financial difficulties, which is likely to worsen. While philanthropy is beginning to meet the ever-expanding needs of the more established groups, small, experimental, and less established organizations will find themselves in a progressively worsening state of financial crisis. Selected bibliography.

2013. Beals, Kathie. "Tax Plan Draws Jeers from Art World." *Gannett Westchester Newspapers* (24 February 1985): H1-2.

2014. Beeson, Peter G. "Improving Your Program through Evaluation: Besides Program Justification, Evaluation Research Can Provide Information to Help Improve Volunteer Programs." *Voluntary Action Leadership* (Spring 1983): 22-6.

2015. Ben-Horin, Daniel, and Fenton Johnson. "In the Public Interest." *San Francisco Examiner* (19 February 1984).

2016. Ben-Ner, Avner. *Nonprofit Organizations: Why Do They Exist in Market Economies?* Program on Non-Profit Organizations, no. 51. New Haven, Conn.: Institution for Social and Policy Studies, 1983.

2017. Bennett, James T., and Thomas J. DiLorenzo. "Are Nonprofits Wolves in Sheep's Clothing?" *Business and Society Review* 67 (Fall 1988): 40-4.

Commentary on the issue of nonprofits' unfair competition with small businesses. A small business cannot survive against a nonprofit receiving considerable tax and regulatory exemptions and subsidies from the government. Commercial nonprofit enterprises also pay lower postal rates, receive special treatment regarding unemployment insurance, minimum wages, securities regulation, bankruptcy, antitrust regulation, and copyright taxes; they can solicit tax-deductible contributions to finance their operations and growth, are often legally protected from litigation, and enjoy a generally favorable public image. Examples of unfair competition range from the lucrative operations of the Smithsonian Institution to the one-stop college bookstore selling everything from computers to razor blades. And *The Wall Street Journal* reports that many YMCAs are now "essentially health clubs for yuppies...in direct competition with private...clubs." Courts in at least two states have withheld tax exempt status from YMCAs because of such activities. The authors insist there is no objection to nonprofits starting up their own businesses; however, restoring fair competition without harming the legitimate charitable functions of the nonprofit sector is a critical issue. One recommendation involves requiring nonprofits to conduct commercial activities through a for-profit subsidiary subject to all the rules and regulations that govern all other for-profit businesses. As the authors point out, the U.S. Constitution requires that persons be treated equally under the law, and a business entity is a person for legal purposes.

2018. Bernick, Michael. "New Ventures for Antipoverty Agencies." *Grantsmanship Center News* 13 (March-April 1985): 48-53.

Describes five nonprofits that started businesses to become financially independent.

2019. Bistline, Susan Mitchell. "Service Corporations: The Profit Side of Nonprofits." *Association Management* (August 1982): 74-9.

2020. Blumenthal, Larry. "Low Pay, Long Hours." *NonProfit Times* 2 (October 1988): 30-2.

Examines the difficulties and benefits of working for grassroots activist and community organizing groups. While they are among the lowest paying jobs in the sector and demand long hours, recruiters for the groups find a great number of people interested in the positions, which offer "the occasional tangible reward of 'making a difference.'"

2021. Blumenthal, Larry. "Salary Wars." *NonProfit Times* 2 (October 1988): 25-9.

Reports that salaries and benefit packages for nonprofit executives, especially fundraisers, continue to rise dramatically, although the rest of the sector receives more moderate pay raises. In some cases, especially in smaller nonprofits located in depressed parts of the of country, the overall salaries are quite low, but throughout the sector the benefits packages, including medical, dental, and retirement plans, are improving; often a nonprofit's package is better than those offered by many small businesses. Article cites the continued gap in salaries between men and women despite the efforts to improve the situation, and gives information on where to get some recent nonprofit salary surveys.

2022. Blumenthal, Larry. "Salary Wars Boost Pay across Nonprofit Sector." *NonProfit Times* 1 (October 1987): 1, 4-6, 10.

Reports that a shortage of experienced professionals for executive nonprofit positions will drive salaries higher throughout the sector, although some experts warn that the less wealthy organizations can not afford to keep pace, and that the nonprofit sector may be losing sight of its mission in the scramble for prima donna fundraisers and top executives.

2023. Blumenthal, Larry. "United Way's President Talks about Restructuring, Alternative Funds." *NonProfit Times* 2 (January 1989): 11-4.

Interview with William Aramony, president of United Way of America since 1970. Discusses how United Ways are restructuring for the future; the United Way of San Francisco's failed affirmative action proposal; charges of United Way monopolies in the workplace; United Way's decision against cause-related marketing (identifying with one supplier will alienate others of similar products); and the Second Century Initiative.

2024. Bob, Murray L. "Confessions of a Grantsperson." *Grassroots Fundraising Journal* 7 (February 1988): 3-9.

Approaching grantsmanship as an art form, article employs "equal parts hyperbole and candor" to address thirteen astute questions, some hypothetical, with which the serious applicant should come to grips. Includes discussions on how to get the attention of a foundation and how long the letter of application should be, what to say to a foundation that believes you ought to charge clients (or raise the prices) for the services provided by your organization, and what happens if the foundation turns a simple request into a matching funds situation, or only offers half the sum requested.

2025. Boorman, Scott A., and Paul R. Levitt. *Network Matching: Nonprofit Structure and Public Policy. Chapter 1: Cultural Conflicts and the Roots of Nonprofit Social Structure.* Program on Non-Profit Organizations, no. 61. New Haven, Conn.: Institution for Social and Policy Studies, 1981.

2026. Boris, Elizabeth Trocolli. "Health Care for the Elderly: Turning from Coordinated Community-Based Services." *Foundation News* 25 (May-June 1984): 70-1.

2027. Borof, Irwin J. "Structuring a Nonprofit's Role in Real Estate Syndications." *Grantsmanship Center News* 5 (Spring-Summer 1984): 28-34.

Discusses the issues that can jeopardize a nonprofit's tax-exempt status.

2028. Bower, Margret, and Mary Durbin. "Making Choices: Issues Facing Charities and Donors. Part 1." *Insight* 1 (1988): 1-4.

This edition of *Insight* addresses the first two of four issues identified by the Philanthropic Advisory Service (PAS) as possible ethical dilemmas for the nonprofit sector, namely the effectiveness and worth of special events, duplication of services provided by nonprofit organizations, nonprofit salary levels, and the use of percentage-based versus flat-fee fundraising. Discussion of special events focuses on cost effectiveness and utility, as such events tend to be expensive, time consuming, and overused. Before holding an event, the goals should be decided upon; these may include objectives such as identifying qualified individuals for board members and finding good volunteers. PAS can see no clear consensus as to whether or not special events are worthwhile, but advocates careful consideration and the disclosure of certain information to aid the donor in making his or her own decision. The issue of duplication arises as a result of the sheer number of charitable, tax-exempt organizations in existence (over 400,000). While there are some benefits when more than one charity focuses on the same need (fresh approaches, raised public awareness), many would like to see a coordination of efforts as opposed to new charities springing up to take funds away from existing organizations. There is also a fear that donors will weary of appeals from different organizations doing the same thing. PAS believes that making the specific services of an organization publicly known will alleviate confusion, as it must be remembered that it is the donors who make the decisions about giving.

2029. Boyd, Thomas D. "Thinking the Unthinkable: Should We Go on?" *Grantsmanship Center News* 10 (November-December 1982): 24+.

2030. Boyd, Willard L. "The Funding Partnership: Public and Private Giving in the 80's." *Theatre Communications* (April 1982): 5-10.

2031. Brinkerhoff, Derick W., and Rosabeth Moss Kanter. *Formal Systems of Appraisal of Individual Performance: Some Considerations, Critical Issues, and Application to Non-Profit Organizations.* Program on Non-Profit Organizations, no. 9. New Haven, Conn.: Institution for Social and Policy Studies, 1979.

2032. Brinkerhoff, Derick W. *Review of Approaches to Productivity, Performance, and Organizational Effectiveness in the Public Sector: Applicability to Non-Profit Organizations.* Program on Non-Profit Organizations, no. 10. New Haven, Conn.: Institution for Social and Policy Studies, 1979.

2033. Bristow, Camille, Marian R. Cohn, and Tracy Huling. *Services for Sexually Active, Pregnant and Parenting Adolescents in New York City: Planning for the Future.* Vol. 1. New York: Center for Public Advocacy Research, 1982.

2034. Brownrigg, W. Grant. *Allocations: One Approach, Many Questions.* Hartford, Conn.: Greater Hartford Arts Council, [1980].

2035. Burnham, James R. "Heretic, Gadfly, or Prophet?" *Nonprofit World Report* 2 (May-June 1984): 33-5.

2036. Burns, Joan Simpson. *The Awkward Embrace: The Creative Artist and the Institution in America.* New York: Alfred A. Knopf, 1975.

2037. Cagnon, Charles. "Business Ventures of Citizen Groups." *NYRAG Papers* 4 (Summer 1982): 50.

Describes current efforts by twelve citizen groups to use commercial ventures for fundraising and analyzes the success of those efforts. Features guidelines for choosing appropriate ventures, an inventory of possibilities, and a discussion of some essential elements of success.

2038. Cagnon, Charles. "Nonprofits in the Business of Business: A Cautionary Look at Raising Money through For-Profit Ventures." *Community Jobs* 6 (February 1983): 7.

2039. Calhoun, Susan. "Balance-Sheet Strategy." *Foundation News* 29 (July-August 1988): 68-9.

Examines the methods of the National Arts Stabilization Fund (NASF), dedicated to reducing the vulnerability of arts organizations to economic pressures and proving that fiscal responsibility and artistic integrity are not mutually exclusive. NASF will often spend years providing technical assistance to a potential grantee to help it adopt a balance-sheet strategy and learn to withstand financial stresses. Only after an arts group has developed a comprehensive plan and demonstrated managerial competence will NASF consider giving it one of its five-year stabilization grants.

2040. Canter, MacKenzie, III. "Shifting Contributions from Corporation to Shareholder." *Fund Raising Management* 17 (October 1986): 64, 66, 69.

Article discusses techniques for solving the problem encountered when soliciting capital gifts from wealthy donors. The donor often changes his or her mind about giving when they realize that the corporation is the legal owner of the asset and receives the tax deduction for the charitable contribution. (IRS Section Code 170 recognizes the deduction for the corporation making the charitable contribution not for the donor.) The article, written by a tax specialist, reviews the options which the development officer can suggest for shifting the charitable contribution deduction for the gift of the corporate asset to the shareholder. The four options include making a gift of all stock of a corporation; sale of stock followed by property redemption; corporate liquidation; and using the S corporation or a pass-through entity similar to a partnership. Each strategy is briefly discussed and general examples are cited. The article is footnoted.

2041. Carter, Margaret, and Susan J. Ellis, comps. *Survey of Human Resource Policies and Practices among Non-Profit Organizations in New York City.* New York: Peat, Marwick, Mitchell & Co., [1986].

Results of a survey of forty-three New York City nonprofit organizations concerning their human resources policies and practices. Divided into seven major areas: pay practices, holidays/vacations, hiring practices, performance evaluation, general policies and practices (including breaks, employee assistance programs, complaints/grievances, and productivity improvement), tuition aid programs, and part-time employees' pay and privileges.

2042. Carter, Richard. *The Gentle Legions.* New York: Doubleday, 1961.

Carter cites health voluntarism as virtually the only means, next to the desegregation movement, whereby millions of Americans come together for direct action on national problems. He explores the role of voluntary health organizations in the United States "by means of historical and contemporary anecdote." He further examines public opinion and national policy directions bearing on the voluntary health movement. He also discusses ethical, political, and material questions about its continued operation or liquidation, given the current structure of the medical profession and the increasing scope of government support for scientific and medical purposes. Brief, discursive bibliography.

2043. Castells, Manuel. *The City and the Grassroots: A Cross-Cultural Theory of Urban Social Movements.* Berkeley, Calif.: University of California Press, 1983.

The introduction states, "This book intends to contribute to the development of [a new theory of urban change] by focusing on the study of urban social movements....Relying on a series of case studies in different socio-cultural contexts (Paris, San Francisco, Santiago de Chile and Madrid) we will try to understand how urban movements interact with urban forms and functions; how the movements develop; why they have different social and spatial effects; and what elements account for their internal structure and historical evolution." Castells' thesis is that urban social movements are successful grassroots efforts to change institutionalized socially dominant interests in a city. A theory of urban social change must account for the complete interaction between dominant and grassroots interests. It must also recognize sources of urban change other than class conflict, such as the autonomous role of the state, gender relationships, ethnic and national movements, and self-defined citizen movements. Urban protests, according to Castells, develop around demands for collective consumption, defense of cultural identity, and political mobilization, especially on a local level. 650-item bibliography.

2044. Cathcart, Jim, and Tony Alessandra. "Build the Organization You Would like to Have." *Nonprofit World Report* 2 (March-April 1984): 11-4.

2045. Center for Arts Information. *Bridge over Troubled Waters: Loan Fund for the Arts.* New York: Center for Arts Information, 1979.

2046. Center for Arts Information. *Jobs in the Arts and Arts Administration: A Guide to Placement/Referral Services, Career Counseling and Employment Listings.* New York: Center for Arts Information, 1984.

2047. Center for Community Change. *Organizing for Neighborhood Development: A Handbook for Citizen Groups.* Washington: Center for Community Change, 1985.

2048. Center for the Study of Social Policy. *A Collaborative Technical Assistance Strategy for Child Welfare Reform: Implementation Plan.* Washington: Center for the Study of Social Policy, 1986.

2049. Center for the Study of Social Policy. *New Futures Initiative: Strategic Planning Guide.* Rev. ed. Washington: Center for the Study of Social Policy, 1988.

Guide for those communities that have been invited to develop proposals under the Annie E. Casey Foundation's New Futures initiative, which aims at meeting the needs of at-risk youth, including such issues as the problems of dropouts, academic under-achievement, teen pregnancy and youth unemployment. The guide is organized into three general chapters, each divided into sub-sections, corresponding to the activities the Foundation expects candidate communities to follow as they develop their plans for a local New Futures initiative. The first chapter, *Describing and Analyzing the Problem*, covers important planning tasks that candidate sites must undertake before designing any new interventions, and includes an overview of America's at-risk youth problems with national statistics and trends; the necessity of describing and analyzing at-risk youth problems at the local level; and a conceptual look at conducting an inventory and critical assessment of current community responses to at-risk youth. The second chapter, *Designing More Effective Approaches*, describes the kinds of programmatic strategies that are likely to help at-risk youth mature into productive and successful adults, and includes the key functions of a case manager for youth; prerequisites for effective functioning of a case management system; and some of the challenges involved in implementing a comprehensive youth case management system. The third chapter, *The New Futures Process*, offers guidance on the planning process, administrative structures and information systems mechanisms needed to launch and sustain a successful local initiative. The appendixes contain descriptions of education reform and dropout prevention, teenage pregnancy prevention, youth employment, and youth case management programs.

2050. Chamber of Commerce. *Association Committees.* Washington: Chamber of Commerce of the United States, 1976.

2051. Chavers, Dean, ed. *Tribal Economic Development Directory.* Broken Arrow, Okla.: DCA Publishers, 1984.

Provides strategies for economic development on American Indian reservations. Tells how to develop a business plan and gives directory listings for various funding sources. Lists many types of funding sources, including federal programs, small business investment companies, minority corporate support, major insurance company lenders, state development agencies, and more.

2052. Citizens Committee for New York City. *Youthbook: Models and Resources for Neighborhood Use.* New York: Citizens Committee for New York City, 1980.

2053. City Harvest. *Food, Money and People. Seminar.* New York: City Harvest, 1985.

2054. Clark, Robert C. *Does the Nonprofit Form Fit the Hospital Industry?* Program on Non-Profit Organizations, no. 43. New Haven, Conn.: Institution for Social and Policy Studies, 1980.

2055. Clarkson, Kenneth W., and Philip E. Fixler, Jr. *The Role of Privatization in Florida's Growth.* Coral Gables, Fla.: Law and Economics Center, [1987].

Funded by the Florida Chamber of Commerce Foundation and the Florida Council of 100, this research project is designed to assist Florida's state and local public officials in undertaking privatization programs suitable to their own communities. The manual helps public officials identify privatization options, provides the means for estimating potential savings by type of service, and presents general guidelines for choosing a successful privatization program. Examines the major techniques for privatizing public services, including: contracting out; franchise agreements; grants and subsidies;

vouchers; self-help; volunteers; incentives; user fees; and service shedding. The manual also provides various decision tools and computer programs that enable local government officials to examine the feasibility of three major privatization options (contracting out, franchising, and divestiture) not only on purely financial grounds, but also on the basis of more subjective criteria such as availability of suppliers, ease of monitoring the performance of private providers, political interest, public service problems, legal authority, and acceptance by public employees.

2056. Coalition of National Voluntary Organizations. *To Preserve an Independent Sector. Organizing Committee Report.* Washington: Coalition of National Voluntary Organizations, 1979.

2057. "Coalition Says Nonprofits Have Unfair Business Edge." *Association Management* 36 (February 1984): 21-3.

2058. Coates, Matthew. "Money and the Board." *Foundation News* 29 (January-February 1988): 51-3.

Discusses the pros and cons of grassroots organizations enlisting trustees with financial clout. Involving someone with both substantial means and a strong commitment to the organization's mission adds valuable management skills and fundraising ability to the board. Difficulties are mostly social and psychological, including bruised egos and the barriers that class and racial unity raise against board diversity.

2059. Cole, Katherine W., ed. *Minority Organizations: A National Directory.* 2nd ed. Garrett Park, Md.: Garrett Park Press, 1982.

2060. Cole, Richard L. *Clientele Involvement in Non-Profit Organizations.* Washington: CRG Press, 1981.

2061. Cole, Richard L. *Constituent Involvement in Non-Profit Organizations: A Study of Twelve Participation Experiments.* Program on Non-Profit Organizations, no. 18. New Haven, Conn.: Institution for Social and Policy Studies, 1980.

2062. Conable, Barber. "Where Non-Profits Stand: Barber Conable Looks Back." *Fund Raising Management* 16 (March 1985): 72+.

2063. Conroy, Charles P. "Recent Challenges to Nonprofits: Some Questions." *Nonprofit World Report* 3 (March-April 1985): 22-3.

Discusses the need for competitive techniques in nonprofit management.

2064. Conroy, David J. "Proposed Model Act: Brave New World for Nonprofits?" *Nonprofit World* 5 (July-August 1987): 18-20.

Reviews the exposure draft of the American Bar Association's 1986 Revised Model Nonprofit Corporation Act. Discusses the reasons behind the revision and examines some of the new provisions, with emphasis on the proposed standards of conduct for directors, including duty of care, duty of loyalty, duty to act in good faith, and a standard of conduct for conflict-of-interest situations. The article questions whether the imposition of these relatively strict standards of care might not discourage qualified people from becoming charitable directors.

2065. Cook, Fay Lomax, Christopher Jencks, and Susan Mayer. *Stability and Change in Economic Hardship: Chicago, 1983-1985.* Hardship and Support Systems in Chicago, vol. 2. Chicago: Center for Urban Affairs and Policy Research, 1986.

Volume 2 in the study of Hardship and Support Systems in Chicago, this report examines changes from 1983 to 1985 in the extent and severity of economic hardship among Chicago families, focusing on the material needs of food, housing, and medical care and describing the support systems utilized by families in times of need. Among the major findings: while the economy of Chicago improved between 1983 and 1985, the number of hardships experienced by families in the area remained about the same. However, the kinds of hardships experienced changed in the time span studied: more families experienced difficulties in access to medical and dental care in 1985 than in 1983; fewer families experienced problems in affording needed food in 1985 than in 1983; but little change occurred in difficulties connected with housing.

2066. Cook, Jonathan B. "Can the Non-Profit Sector Work Better?" *NonProfit Times* 1 (May 1987): 33, 39.

2067. Council of Better Business Bureaus. *Standards for Charitable Solicitations.* Arlington, Va.: Council of Better Business Bureaus, 1982.

2068. Council of Better Business Bureaus. *Tips on Charitable Giving: How to Give But Give Wisely.* Arlington, Va.: Council of Better Business Bureaus, 1986.

Faced with ever-rising costs, the loss of government funding, and an increasing demand for their services, nonprofits are responding by soliciting more individual donors more often for greater gifts (individual donors account for over eighty percent of the money raised by charities in this country). The Council of Better Business Bureaus offers this pamphlet to help donors make wise giving decisions. Includes tips on the basics; mail appeals; and telephone, door-to-door, and street solicitations. Also examines the difference between tax exempt and tax deductible, offers a listing of publications by the Philanthropic Advisory Service, and provides information on how to evaluate the financial statements of a charity.

2069. Council of New York Law Associates. *Should You Incorporate?* New York: Council of New York Law Associates, 1977.

2070. Crimmins, James C., and Mary Keil. *Enterprise in the Nonprofit Sector.* Washington: Partners for Livable Places, 1983.

2071. Cultural Assistance Center. *The Arts As an Industry: Their Economic Importance to the New York-New Jersey Metropolitan Region.* New York: Cultural Assistance Center, 1983.

2072. Cunningham, James V., and Milton Kotler. *Building Neighborhood Organizations.* Notre Dame, Ind.: University of Notre Dame Press, 1983.

2073. Cunningham, Michael, and Michael Seltzer. "General Support vs. Project Support: A 75-Year-Old Philanthropic Debate." *NYRAGTimes* (Summer 1988): 3-6.

Second article in a series entitled *Grantmaking Strategies: Rx for the Future*, focusing on creative ways for grantmakers to meet the needs of nonprofits in the decades ahead. This article examines the increasing demand by nonprofits for unrestricted funds at a time when general support funding is decreasing, as evidenced by a review of the Foundation Center's *Grants Index*. Both sides of the issue are presented, in addition to a short list of measures some grantors are taking to offer general support where it is most needed.

2074. Davie, Ann R., ed. *Resource Directory*. Washington: American Council on Education, 1987.

Compiled to help answer questions from disabled persons, families, counselors, teachers, administrators, and others concerning postsecondary education for handicapped individuals, this directory provides a selection of resources in the major areas of interest in the field. The organizations included here can respond to questions about an individual's own situation and can provide published materials; in addition, each organization may be able to suggest further resources close to the caller's location. Includes a listing of toll-free telephone services.

2075. Davis, Nancy M. "Fighting the 'Chill Effect'." *Association Management* 39 (June 1987): 33-4.

Brief article which explores the independent sector's reaction to proposed Internal Revenue Service (IRS) rules that would jeopardize the tax-exempt status of many 50l(c)(3) organizations. The proposals severely restrict nonprofit research and grassroots lobbying activities and jeopardize the status of thousands of organizations now eligible to receive tax-deductible gifts. Communications that even mention legislation would become lobbying under the proposed changes. Organizations would be forced to decide between speaking out on issues and surviving. A coalition of nonprofit organizations was coordinated by Independent Sector to lobby for their right to promote public policy issues. They obtained bipartisan support from over forty congressmen and obtained some concessions on the proposed rules. The IRS will not make the rules on 50l(c)(3) lobbying retroactive and will involve nonprofit officials in the rule-making process.

2076. Davis, Pamela. *Nonprofit Organizations and Liability Insurance: Problems, Options and Prospects*. Conrad N. Hilton Foundation and California Community Foundation Occasional Paper. Los Angeles: California Community Foundation, 1987.

A report on the nonprofit sector's insurance liability crisis. (This report is one in a series of Occasional Papers issued periodically by both the Conrad N. Hilton Foundation and the California Community Foundation.) During the last decade the property/casualty insurance industry experienced periods of low profitability when they increased premiums and dropped or refused to renew the least profitable policies. This paper describes the basics of liability insurance and its cyclical nature, and reviews the impact of the insurance crisis on private nonprofit organizations. Short and long-term solutions to the problem are reviewed for the individual organization, including internal procedures, legislation, and collective efforts or risk sharing which includes such collective tools as a captive insurance company, a risk retention group, or a risk pool. These risk sharing mechanisms and how to establish them are reviewed as well as the criteria an organization should consider prior to joining such a venture. The appendixes contain copies of liability legislation. The paper also includes notes and bibliography.

2077. Dawes, Sharon S. *The State and the Voluntary Sector: A Report of New York State Project 2000*. New York State Project 2000 Series, no. 9. Albany, N.Y.: Nelson A. Rockefeller Institute of Government, 1988.

This report, one of a series commissioned by Governor Cuomo, explores the complex relationship between thousands of New York nonprofit organizations and the New York State government and identifies problems, benefits, and prospects. Begins with an historical overview of the political, economic and demographic forces which have shaped this relationship and goes on to explore its current status and dimensions, discussing possible future developments, and identifying key issues for public policymaking.

2078. Dawson, Margaret White. "The Path to Iona House." *NonProfit Times* 1 (August 1987): 35, 38-9, 43.

Profiles Iona House, a senior citizen service agency, and the changes which occurred during various stages of their long-range planning process. Contracting with a consultant, identifying potential competitors, and considering charging fees for certain services were all new and difficult activities for the Iona House board and director, but they now have strategies to carry them through the next five years of development. The consultant, John Boruff, notes that strategic planning allows a nonprofit to make current decisions based on the priorities of the future.

2079. Dawson, Margaret White. "What Lies Ahead: Looking toward the '90s." *NonProfit Times* 1 (May 1987): 34-6, 43.

To be used as a strategic planning tool, this article summarizes the trends and planning assumptions in the 1987 United Way of America's environmental scan. As in previous years, the report tracks the probable changes in four categories: social, economic, political, and technological, and added a new category—philanthropy. Also new is a special section which analyzes those trends. In the philanthropic sector, the trends are: corporate contributions of non-cash items are projected to increase; corporate support for basic human-care needs are expected to grow significantly; increased corporate support for human services not previously supported; increased corporate encouragement for voluntarism among employees; issue of competition between nonprofits and for-profits expected to intensify and demand resolution; and philanthropic sector will be reshaped as funding sources shift.

2080. Dean, Ruth. "The State of the Arts." *Foundation News* 24 (November-December 1983): 12-21.

2081. "Debate over For-Profit vs. Nonprofit Health Providers Heats Up." *Nonprofit Executive* 3 (May 1984): 1-2.

2082. Delfin, Stephen. "Accountability in Nonprofit Public Relations." *Channels* 36 (May 1984): 5-6.

2083. Desruisseaux, Paul. "Nonprofit Groups Want Academe to Help Train Their Administrators." *Chronicle of Higher Education* 23 (14 November 1984): 15.

2084. DiMaggio, Paul J., and Walter W. Powell. *The Iron Cage Revisited: Conformity and Diversity in Organizational Fields.* Program on Non-Profit Organizations, no. 52. New Haven, Conn.: Institution for Social and Policy Studies, 1982.

2085. Dingfelder, William M. "Your Financial Report: Fact and Fiction." *NAHD Journal* (Summer-Fall 1983): 76-7.

2086. "Directory of Hispanic Arts Organizations." *Hispanic Arts News* 78 (May 1988): 1-4.

Lists Hispanic dance, multi-arts, music, theatre, visual arts, and service organizations located in the New York area.

2087. *Directory of Religious Organizations in the United States of America.* Wilmington, Calif.: McGrath Publishing Co., 1977.

2088. *Directory of Women's Organizations.* Northbrook, Ill.: Allstate Group, 1985.

2089. Distelhorst, Garis F. "When Associations Become Entrepreneurs." *Association Management* 37 (February 1985): 109-11.

2090. Dorsey, Eugene C. "The 'Unseen' Sector." *Foundation News* 24 (March-April 1983): 52-5.

2091. Doss, Martha Merrill, ed. *Women's Organizations: A National Directory.* Garrett Park, Md.: Garrett Park Press, 1986.

A national women's organizations directory. The format is an alphabetically arranged listing by the organization name with address, telephone number and a brief annotation of organization programs and services. Preceding the indexes, the volume contains a listing of women's directories arranged alphabetically by state, then city within the state. The indexes are alphabetical by state and by general subject category such as associations, guidance and education.

2092. Douglas, James. *Towards a Rationale for Private Non-Profit Organizations: A Review of Current Theory.* Rev. ed. Program on Non-Profit Organizations, no. 7. New Haven, Conn.: Institution for Social and Policy Studies, 1980.

2093. Douglas, James. *Why Charity: Towards a Rationale for the Third Sector.* Program on Non-Profit Organizations, no. 7A. New Haven, Conn.: Institution for Social and Policy Studies, 1981.

2094. Dresser, Peter D., ed. *Research Centers Directory.* 2 Vols. 13th ed. Detroit: Gale Research Co., 1989.

Guide to approximately 10,300 university-related and other nonprofit research organizations in seventeen broad subject areas. An excellent guide to finding out what's being done where. Includes subject and master index—an index arranged by the names under which research units operate as well as by principal keyword and other important words in the name.

2095. Duncan, William A. *Looking at Income-Generating Businesses for Small Nonprofit Organizations.* Washington: Center for Community Change, 1982.

Useful pamphlet provides information to help small nonprofits decide whether or not to start a business and proposes an eleven-step process for seeking business opportunities.

2096. Dye, Susanne A. "Program-Related Investments." *Nonprofit World Report* 2 (November-December 1984): 19-21.

2097. Easton, Allan, ed. *Community Support of the Performing Arts: Selected Problems of Local and National Interest.* Hofstra University Yearbook of Business Series 7, no. 5. Hempstead, N.Y.: Hofstra University School of Business, 1970.

2098. Eby, Charles. *Performance Norms in Non-Market Organizations: An Exploratory Survey.* Program on Non-Profit Organizations, no. 56. New Haven, Conn.: Institution for Social and Policy Studies, 1982.

2099. Edie, John A. "Fiscal Agents Can Be Illegal." *Foundation News* 27 (May-June 1986): 62-3.

Examines the ways in which it is acceptable and unacceptable to utilize a fiscal agent to fund nonprofits lacking 501(c)(3) status. Improper use could lead to a penalty tax (in the case of private foundations) or a denial of the deduction (in the case of individual or corporate donations). The IRS is vehemently against the earmarking of funds, which they define as any agreement, oral or written, where a contributor causes the selection of a secondary grantee by the organization to which it has originally given the grant (the alleged fiscal agent).

2100. Egerton, John. "The Klan Basher." *Foundation News* 29 (May-June 1988): 38-43.

Chronicles the successful growth and legal history of the Southern Poverty Law Center (SPLC), focusing on enigmatic co-founder Morris Dees and the Center's most publicized venture, a program of anti-Ku Klux Klan litigation and education which more than doubled the SPLC's budget and endowment in just eight years. With the $7-million damage judgment by a federal court against the United Klans of America in 1987, the anti-Klan mission seems to be complete, and the SPLC is looking at some new areas, especially in education.

2101. Ellis, Arthur L., and E. Percil Stanford. "The Funding Crisis: Implications for the Survival of Human Service Institutions." *Grants Magazine* 5 (December 1982): 253-59.

2102. Elnicki, Susan E., ed. *Taft Directory of Nonprofit Organizations: Profiles of America's Major Charitable Institutions.* 1st ed. Washington: Taft Group, 1987.

Provides profiles of the programs, personnel, and finances of 1,125 major nonprofit organizations, each having assets of at least $5 million and a reputation as leaders in their respective areas of activity. Profiles include the organization's name, address and telephone number; a statement of purpose; a list of key executive staff, major donors and board of directors; a fiscal summary listing total assets and liabilities; and an analysis of revenues and expenses. An appendix lists summary data on more than 2,400 additional nonprofits categorized by ninety-five areas of interest, from academic publishing to zoos. Indexed by areas of activity, headquarters state, executive officers, board officers, and donors.

2103. *An Essential Bibliography for Grassroots Consumer Organizations.* Rosslyn, Va.: Consumer Education Resource Network, 1981.

2104. "An Expert Strategy for Saving the Non-Profit Postal Rate." *Philanthropy Monthly* 18 (February 1985): 5-15.

2105. Falleder, Arnold. "Construction Projects: A Source of Income for Nonprofits." *Nonprofit World Report* 3 (March-April 1985): 16-8.

2106. Federation Employment and Guidance Service. *Directory of Services.* New York: Federation Employment & Guidance Service, [198?].

Directory of educational/vocational and treatment services, including career development, skills training, criminal justice, vocational rehabilitation work centers, and mental health and developmental disabilities programs.

2107. "Feds Crack Down on Nonprofit Income." *Conserve Neighborhoods* (November-December 1983): 321.

2108. "Feeling Charitable? Find Out Where the Money Goes." *Business Week* 2973 (17 November 1986): 212-3.

Consumer-oriented article which advises givers on what to look for in a charity. As the director of the Better Business Bureau's Philanthropic Advisory Service is quoted as saying, "All charities are nonprofit, but not all nonprofit organizations are charities. If it's deductible, an organization's mailings definitely say so. Be wary of the fine print mentioning that 'your contribution may be deductible'." Rating services suggest that you contribute to charities which direct at least fifty to sixty percent of the funds to their program and no more than thirty to thirty-five percent to fundraising. Other things to be aware of are prestigious-sounding names, extremely rich charities that could live off endowment earnings, and redirected focus of charities. Examples of changed focus include CARE and Save the Children Federation: CARE's focus has changed from emergency food and clothing to development efforts such as small business loans in Peru, and the monthly donation to Save the Children Federation no longer sponsors a particular child, but instead goes toward community self-help projects, field office service operating costs, headquarters costs, management, and fundraising. The article lists several resources the donor can use to check on charitable organizations such as the Council of Better Business Bureaus, Philanthropic Advisory Service; the National Charities Information Bureau; your state attorney general or secretary of state; and the organization's IRS Form 990.

2109. *The Finances of the Performing Arts. Part 1: A Survey of 166 Professional Nonprofit Resident Theaters, Operas, Symphonies, Ballets, and Modern Dance Companies.* New York: Ford Foundation, 1974.

2110. Fiske, Edward B. "Private Groups Aid Budgets for Schools." *New York Times* (15 November 1983).

2111. "For-Profit Corporation Best Way to Make Money for Association, Provides 'Bottom-Line' Vehicle Needed." *Association Sales and Marketing* 24 (December 1982).

2112. Ford Foundation. *Social Investing through Program-Related Investments: A Report to the Ford Foundation.* New York: Ford Foundation, 1984.

Based on a survey of foundations making Program Related Investments (PRIs), the report describes PRI activities around the country, analyzes the pros and cons of PRIs, and offers suggestions to foundations interested in starting or expanding PRI programs. Includes five case studies of projects which could not have been undertaken without PRIs and also gives brief descriptions of twenty-four diverse projects to which PRIs have been made. Provides a brief bibliography.

2113. Forsythe, David P., and Susan Welch. *Citizen Support for Non-Profit Public Interest Groups.* Program on Non-Profit Organizations, no. 35. New Haven, Conn.: Institution for Social and Policy Studies, 1981.

2114. Forsythe, David P. *Humanizing American Foreign Policy: Non-Profit Lobbying and Human Rights.* Program on Non-Profit Organizations, no. 12. New Haven, Conn.: Institution for Social and Policy Studies, 1980.

2115. Foster, R. Scott. *Public-Private Partnership in American Cities.* Lexington, Mass.: Lexington Books, 1982.

2116. Friedman, John S. "Who Funds the Arts?" *Grantsmanship Center News* 10 (November-December 1982): 20+.

2117. Fruhling, Hugo. *Nonprofit Organizations As Opposition to Authoritarian Rule: The Case of Human Rights Organizations and Private Research Centers in Chile.* Program on Non-Profit Organizations, no. 96. New Haven, Conn.: Institution for Social and Policy Studies, 1985.

Examines the experience of Chilean nonprofit organizations (NPO's) as promoters of human rights and as alternative intellectual institutions in an authoritarian situation as experienced in Chile since 1973. Covers the emergence and consolidation of the Chilean authoritarian regime and the factors that contributed to the success of the NPO's in institutionalizing themselves, in devising adequate strategies to mobilize their resources, in gaining a non-partisan image and in forging international links. Fruhling cites the NPO's most important contributions to processes of transition to democracy: helping to integrate social and political forces that were fragmented by the authoritarian regime's policies; depriving the regime of some of its moral and political legitimacy; and giving a new relevance to human rights ideals to be taken into account by political parties and social organizations.

2118. Gardner, John W. "Effective Leadership." *Fundemensions* 8 (November 1984): 7-11.

Presents the patterns of leadership which are important.

2119. Gardner, John W. *The Nature of Leadership.* Leadership Papers, no. 1. Washington: Independent Sector, 1986.

2120. Gardner, John W. *Personal and Organizational Renewal.* Austin, Tex.: Hogg Foundation for Mental Health, 1984.

2121. Gartner, Alan, and Frank Riessman. *Help: A Working Guide to Self-Help Groups.* New York: New Viewpoints/Vision Books, 1980.

2122. Geiger, Roger L. *Private Sectors in Higher Education.* Ann Arbor, Mich.: University of Michigan Press, 1986.

In this volume, Geiger classifies, analyzes, and evaluates the experience of nongovernmental postsecondary education in seven selected countries. Then, using this comparative perspective, he examines the multifaceted private sector in the United States, analyzes the general issue of government financial support for private colleges and universities, and finally considers the inherent benefits and drawbacks associated with private higher education. From his case studies of Japan, the Philippines, Belgium, the Netherlands, France, Great Britain, and Sweden, Geiger identifies three structural paradigms, each representing quite different relationships between government, society, and higher education. Bibliography.

2123. "Generating Income for Nonprofit Programs." *Home Again* (Winter 1983): 16-8.

2124. Gershen, Howard. "A Consumer Guide to Charity: Where to Get More Balm for Your Buck." *Esquire* 108 (December 1987).

Chart profiles forty-eight charitable organizations, providing purpose statement, annual income, and total expenses (including overhead and fundraising costs, and expenditures on services).

2125. Giamatti, A. Bartlett. *Private Sector, Public Control and the Independent University.* Washington: Independent Sector, 1980.

2126. Gillingham, David W., and Louis R. Zanibbi. "Factors in the Success and Failure of Non-Profit Organizations." *Philanthropist/Le Philanthrope* 4 (Winter 1987): 39-47.

Scholarly paper quantitatively analyzes the relationship between various organizational attributes and measures of performance in thirty-two Canadian nonprofit associations and organizations. The research was conducted as part of a week-long workshop for the Canadian Institute for Organization Management in London, Ontario during June 1982. Participants from sixteen associations took part in the program and these individuals interviewed a further sixteen local nonprofit organizations. The groups were assessed with respect to overall goal achievement; strength of financial, human and physical resources; overall market performance; and any other specified criteria established as significant during the interview. Charts of the findings, sample questions and lists of positive and negative factors in rank accompany the text; the paper contains references.

2127. Godfrey, Howard. *Handbook on Tax-Exempt Organizations.* Englewood Cliffs, N.J.: Prentice-Hall, 1983.

Discusses exemption requirements for specific types of nonprofits and procedures for compliance, and offers practical advice on how to get and keep exempt status.

2128. Goldenhersh, Randy S. "Real Estate Essentials for Nonprofits." *Whole Nonprofit Catalog* 7 (Summer 1988): 24-5.

Highly informative article covers the basics of real estate development and finance for nonprofits, including the evaluation of property for development or redevelopment, joint venture development, accounting and tax issues, and a comparison of borrowing with sale-leaseback.

2129. Gollin, James. *Worldly Goods: The Wealth and Power of the American Catholic Church, the Vatican, and the Men Who Control the Money.* New York: Random House, 1971.

2130. Goodman, Walter. "Scholars Debate Need to Aid Arts." *New York Times* (2 May 1984): C-20.

2131. Goss, Helen. "Annual Reports Are 'Winning' Fund-Raising Technique." *Nonprofit Executive* 4 (June 1985): 5.

2132. Gould, Sara K. "Neighborhood: Enterprising Organizations." *Entrepreneurial Economy* 2 (September 1983): 6-7.

2133. Gould, Sara K. *Struggling through Tight Times: A Handbook for Women's and Other Nonprofits.* New York: Women's Action Alliance, 1984.

2134. Grant, Daniel. "The Museum As Employer." *Art & Artists* 12 (April 1983): 20.

2135. Grantsmanship Center. *Profit Making by Non-Profits.* Los Angeles: Grantsmanship Center, 1983.

Reprints of a series of articles originally published in the Grantsmanship Center News, including case studies, guidelines for setting up a profit-making subsidiary, and tax implications of profit-making ventures.

2136. Greater New York Fund/United Way. *Merger: Another Path Ahead: A Guide to the Merger Process for Voluntary Human Service Agencies.* New York: Greater New York Fund, 1981.

2137. Greater Washington Society of Association Executives. *Salary Survey Report, 1982.* Washington: Greater Washington Society of Association Executives, 1982.

2138. Green, Alan. *Communicating in the '80s: New Options for the Nonprofit Community.* Washington: Benton Foundation, 1983.

2139. Green, Alan. "Who's Watching the Watchdogs?" *Foundation News* 28 (March-April 1987): 18-23.

Critical examination of the two independent charitable watchdog organizations. The National Charities Information Bureau (NCIB) and the Council of Better Business Bureau's Philanthropic Advisory Service (PAS) help donors on a nationwide basis to make contributions based on an informed decision. Founded in 1918, NCIB researches a group by requesting data from the organization and using other public sources. It uses that data to determine whether a nonprofit meets NCIB's eight basic standards. In addition to detailed reports, NCIB publishes *Wise Giving Guide* bimonthly; it gives summaries of organization ratings. PAS evaluates charities after several inquiries and uses twenty-two criteria. Upon request two-page reports on specific organizations are available as well as PAS's bimonthly newsletter *Give But Give Wisely*. The article examines the strengths and weaknesses of both groups and their restructuring of standards and criteria to meet the changes in the nonprofit sector's competitive fundraising atmosphere.

2140. Grennon, Jacqueline, and Robert Barsky. *An Exploration of Entrepreneurship in the Field of Nursing Home Care for the Elderly: Case Studies.* Program on Non-Profit Organizations, no. 20. New Haven, Conn.: Institution for Social and Policy Studies, 1980.

2141. Gronbjerg, Kirsten A. *Responding to Community Needs: The Missions and Programs of Chicago Nonprofit Organizations.* Hardship and Support Systems in Chicago, vol. 1. Washington: Urban Institute Press, 1986.

Volume 1 in the study of Hardship and Support Systems in Chicago (part of the Urban Institute Nonprofit Sector Project), this report examines the missions, goals and program activities of a select group of nonprofit organizations directly involved in responding to changing human service needs in the Chicago-Cook County area. The report organizes its major findings under five headings: mission and service strategies, changes in targeting activities and service strategies, program growth, program decline, and organizational and funding constraints. An important theme throughout is the considerable gap between the unmet material needs of the city's low income population and the activities in which most nonprofit organizations are engaged.

2142. Gross, Susan. "Getting to the Source of Problems." *Grantsmanship Center News* 11 (March-April 1983): 38-42.

2143. *Guide to Black Organizations.* New York: Philip Morris USA, 1984.

2144. *The Guide to Gifts and Bequests: New York/Florida.* New York: Institutions Press, 1988.

Reference work designed to provide attorneys, accountants, bankers, foundation officers, and donors with basic information about the purposes, programs, and people of nonprofit institutions located in New York and Florida or serving the interests of their residents. Offers a range of information so that donors and legators can select charitable institutions best suited to their philanthropic objectives. Indexed by subjects and organizations, and by names of trustees, directors, officers, and staff.

2145. *A Guide to Hispanic Organizations.* New York: Philip Morris USA, 1983.

2146. Gunn, Selskar M., and Philip S. Platt. *Voluntary Health Agencies.* New York: Ronald Press, 1945.

2147. Haimes, Norma, comp. *Helping Others: A Guide to Selected Social Service Agencies and Occupations.* New York: John Day Co., 1974.

2148. Hallahan, Kathleen M. "Passing the Torch: John Gardner Steps Down As Chairman of Independent Sector." *Foundation News* 24 (November-December 1983): 32-3.

2149. Hample, Henry S., comp. *For More Information: A Guide to Arts Management Information Centers.* New York: Center for Arts Information, 1986.

Developed from the results of a survey conducted by the Center for Arts Information and the Arts Resources Corporation, contains information on eighty-seven domestic and four foreign arts management information centers. Profiles of 100 nonprofit, government and international organizations acting as information clearing houses for or about the nonprofit arts. Entries feature the following information: name; address; telephone number; contact person; geographic area served; disciplines covered by the information center; users; services provided (e.g., conference/workshops, artists' registry, employment referral, and space referral); information collection; periodicals; publications; and services. Also included are an alphabetical listing of organizations, geographical listing, guide to acronyms, and subject guide to directory listings. Appendixes contain a comprehensive listing of arts councils of the fifty states, six U.S. territories and regional arts agencies. Organizations which provide services to the arts field, such as film, writers and historical organizations, are also included.

2150. Handel, Beatrice. *The National Directory for the Performing Arts and Civic Centers.* 3rd ed. New York: John Wiley, 1978.

2151. Hansler, Daniel F. "Must Non-Profits Be Market Driven?" *Fund Raising Management* 17 (December 1986): 78-9.

"More non-profits are turning to marketing in their efforts to raise funds. But some key trends will affect marketing and how non-profit organizations use it." These key trends include the new federal tax law, a shrinking middle class, and increased competition among the growing number of nonprofit organization.

2152. Hansmann, Henry. *The Effect of Tax Exemption and Other Factors on Competition between Nonprofit and For-Profit Enterprise.* Program on Non-Profit Organizations, no. 65. New Haven, Conn.: Institution for Social and Policy Studies, 1982.

2153. Hansmann, Henry. *Externalities, Exclusivity, Stratification, and Cooperation: A Theory of Associative Organizations.* Rev. ed. Program on Non-Profit Organizations, no. 2. New Haven, Conn.: Institution for Social and Policy Studies, 1980.

2154. Hansmann, Henry. *Mutual Insurance Companies and the Theory of Nonprofit and Cooperative Enterprise.* Program on Non-Profit Organizations, no. 89. New Haven, Conn.: Institution for Social and Policy Studies, 1985.

Hansmann offers an explanation for the preponderance of the cooperative form (mutuals as opposed to investor-owned firms) in the insurance industry. Consumer cooperatives, Hansmann asserts, organize when two broad conditions are present: (1) there is a relatively severe market failure in the firm's product market, and (2) consumers are able to assume effective control without incurring excessive costs. He claims that the development of mutual companies in the life insurance industry is in large part a response to the difficulty in writing a long-term contract that provides adequate security to policyholders; like the patrons of a typical nonprofit, the policyholders in a mutual company derive protection not from the exercise of control over the firm, but rather from the fact that the management of the mutual, unlike the management of a stock company, does not have a pecuniary incentive to exploit its policyholders. In property and liability insurance, the role of the mutual is closer to that which is commonly performed elsewhere by consumer cooperatives: they provide a measure of protection against noncompetitive pricing.

2155. Hansmann, Henry. *The Role of Non-Profit Enterprise.* Program on Non-Profit Organizations, no. 1. New Haven, Conn.: Institution for Social and Policy Studies, 1980.

Hansmann develops a broad perspective on the economic role that nonprofit organizations perform. He notes that although large classes of nonprofits are accorded special treatment in almost all areas in which federal legislation impinges upon them significantly, the principles upon which this treatment is based are not clear. Hansmann explores some of the factors distinguishing the role of private nonprofits from that of government. He discusses the entire range of nonprofit organizations, but focuses primarily on those that provide goods and services—colleges, hospitals, day care centers, nursing homes, research institutes, publications, symphony orchestras, etc. Hansmann suggests that the nonprofit organization is a reasonable response to a relatively well-defined set of social needs that can be described in economic terms, and that the "hodgepodge of organizational and regulatory law applying to nonprofits should be revised and systematized in order to assist them in carrying out their function."

2156. Hansmann, Henry. *What Is the Appropriate Structure for Nonprofit Corporation Law? A Response to Ellman.* Program on Non-Profit Organizations, no. 100. New Haven, Conn.: Institution for Social and Policy Studies, 1985.

2157. Harrington, Howard, and Linda Sherman. *Five Evolving Strategies for Youth Services: A Resource Guide.* Chicago: Cook County Sheriff's Youth Services Department, 1979.

2158. Harris, Virginia, and Micki Jo Young. "A Nation of Groups." *Library Journal* 109 (May 1984): 944-47.

2159. Hart, Philip. *Orpheus in the New World: The Symphony Orchestra As an American Cultural Institution.* New York: W.W. Norton & Co., 1973.

2160. Hellwig, Henry. "Base Salary and Incentive Compensation Practices in Not-for-Profit Organizations." *Compensation Review* 10 (4th Quarter 1978): 34-48.

2161. "Help with Your Problems." *Nonprofit World* 5 (May-June 1987): 6-7.

Provides a listing of forty-four organizations that make loans to nonprofits, grouped under headings for national organizations, community foundations, and emergency loan funds.

2162. Hemmens, George, Charles Hoch, and Donna Hardina. *Changing Needs and Social Services in Three Chicago Communities.* Hardship and Support Systems in Chicago, vol. 4. Chicago: University of Illinois, 1986.

Volume 4 in the study of Hardship and Support Systems in Chicago investigates how people in three low income communities—South Austin, Little Village and East Side—are affected by economic conditions and how they are helped with problems. Interviews with households and with the public and nonprofit organizations which provide services in each of the three communities reveal that the overall economic status improved somewhat for families between 1983 and 1985 due to increased employment (rather than income assistance), and that households pool resources and rely upon help from relatives, friends and neighbors much more frequently than they turn to social service providers to get help with their problems. When households do contact a formal helping organization, the most common type of help received is food. Emergency help with a material crisis is the primary reason for seeking help from these agencies, with health care and counseling sharing second place.

2163. Herzlinger, Regina E., and William S. Krasker. "Who Profits from Nonprofits?" *Harvard Business Review* (January-February 1987): 93-106.

Study which uses the hospital industry as an indication that society would be well-advised to shift its investment from nonprofit hospitals to for-profit hospitals. The authors expand their for-profit theory by asserting that there are many other kinds of nonprofit organizations...whose services could also be offered by a for-profit. They cite colleges, universities and social service agencies.

2164. Hilgert, Cecelia. "Nonprofit Charitable Organizations, 1983." *Statistics of Income Bulletin* 6 (Spring 1987): 31-42.

Statistical analysis of nonprofit charitable organizations for 1983. The analysis, graphs and charts in this paper are based on a sample of Tax Year 1983 Forms 990 filed by organizations classified under Internal Revenue Code Section 501(c)(3) and having accounting periods ending December 1983 through November 1984. (Forms 990-PF filed by private foundations were excluded.) The sample was drawn from a multi-year sample frame of 105,391 organizations based on the latest return filed by each. Hilgert's findings show that nonprofit charitable organizations reported increases in all financial items for 1983. Asset holdings rose eighteen percent, from $279.6 billion to $331.2 billion. Organizations with assets of $10,000,000 or more accounted for three-fourths of total assets for all non-charitable organizations. Land, buildings and equipment represented thirty-eight percent of total assets. The article contains four pages of statistical tables on *Nonprofit Charitable Organizations—Selected Income and Balance Sheet Items by Total Assets.*

2165. Hodgkinson, Virginia A. "What Is a National Taxonomy for?" *Philanthropy Monthly* 20 (March 1987): 33-4.

Brief article on the newly created National Taxonomy of Exempt Entities (NTEE). The preliminary taxonomy was released in March 1987; a complete manual for the use of the system will be available in July 1987. The current National Center for Charitable Statistics (NCCS) emphasis is on implementation of the system in the government and the private sector. The project will translate current federal and state systems to the taxonomy. The IRS (which maintains the 990 and 990-PF collection) has no funds to change over to the classification system. NCCS has developed a two-year plan to classify and code all Section 501(c)(3) exempt organizations on the IRS master file to the taxonomy. In addition, the NCCS has a contractual agreement with the IRS Statistics of Income Division that they will use the system as soon as their samples are classified. The system will be tested and proposed changes to the system scheduled for 1989 will be based on user experience. In the private sector, the taxonomy will be implemented in major private organizations which collect or report on statistics for the nonprofit sector. The NCCS has commitments from the Foundation Center and the American Association of Fund-Raising Counsel to implement the new system and to report according to the major categories. (The Foundation Center has also promised technical assistance in the coding of private foundations by type.) The unified classification system should increase both national and local research.

2166. Holley, Robert. "Theatre Facts 86." *American Theatre* 4 (April 1987): 20-7.

2167. Holley, Robert. "'Unfair Competition': Business vs. Nonprofits." *American Theatre* 1 (May 1984): 24-5.

2168. Hollingsworth, Rogers, and Ellen Jane Hollingsworth. *A Comparison of Non-Profit, For-Profit and Public Hospitals in the United States, 1935 to the Present.* Program on Non-Profit Organizations, no. 113. New Haven, Conn.: Institution for Social and Policy Studies, 1986.

Discusses the extent to which nonprofit, for-profit, and public hospitals have varied in their behavior at various time points, and seeks to understand why hospitals in the three sectors have become more similar over time. Behavior is indicated here by a comparison of the concepts of financial arrangements, level of technological complexity, quality of medical services, bed size, level of utilization, and equality of access across social classes and income groups; the time points being studied are 1935, 1961, and 1979 to the present. The increased similarity, the authors contend, results from the change in the sources of funding over time. "When hospitals in the three sectors received their funding from quite distinct sources, they tended to be responsive to very different constituencies with quite different preferences." As the sources of revenue converged, so did the behavior of hospitals, "for reliance on similar funding sources has meant that hospitals have increasingly responded to the same constituencies with similar preferences. On the other hand...when hospitals vary substantially in their sources of funding, their behavior also tends to differ considerably;" these hospitals often experience chronic deficits and overcrowding, regardless of the sector to which they belong.

2169. Hopkins, Bruce R. "Appeals Courts Smash 'Commerciality Doctrine'." *Fund Raising Management* 15 (November 1984): 98-9.

Looks at Appeals Court's decision that advertising in an exempt organization's publication can be a related activity.

2170. Hopkins, Bruce R. "Buy Buildings through Partnerships." *Nonprofit Executive* 4 (May 1985): 1-2.

2171. Hopkins, Bruce R. "Fund Raising or Business?" *Fund Raising Management* 15 (May 1984): 96.

2172. Hopkins, Bruce R. "1987, the Year of Charity-Bashing." *American Theatre* 4 (December 1987): 42-3.

Examines the reasons behind the general antipathy toward charitable organizations in 1987, which manifested itself in House Subcommittee on Oversight hearings concerning questionable practices by charities, including lobbying, political campaign involvements, fundraising, private inurement, and commercial and competitive activities. An apparent alteration in the mindset of the political leadership towards nonprofit organizations is attributed to desperation (the alleged need for additional federal revenue), frustration (members of Congress opposed to charities engaged in lobbying), and resentment (anger with one nonprofit, the PTL, spills over onto other nonprofits), but the author raises a more profound possibility—that the politicians are merely responding to the general public's decline of respect for nonprofits. This loss of respect, the author maintains, results from the blurring of the socially necessary identity once ascribed to nonprofits; today nonprofits look too similar to any other business, and some of the resulting confusion is a product of actions by the nonprofits themselves. They are "changing in character and activities (but not purpose) faster than the ability of much of the general public to favorably perceive them." A redefining of the nonprofit sector's role in American society is needed, one that will satisfy the general public and in turn the legislators and regulators.

2173. Hopkins, Bruce R. "When Non-Profits Should Use Subsidiaries." *Fund Raising Management* 16 (June 1985): 114-15.

2174. Huntley, Kate. *Financial Trends in Organized Social Work in New York City.* New York: Columbia University Press, 1935.

2175. Hyndman, Noel. "Does Your Report Measure Up to the Objectives." *Charity* 1 (March 1984): 11-2.

2176. "Ideas in Print: Annual Report Review." *Channels* 35 (January 1983): 8.

2177. *Implementing Joint Urban Ventures: Community Organizations and Organized Philanthropy.* Chicago: Trust, 1982.

2178. Independent Sector. *The Constitution and the Independent Sector.* Spring Research Forum Working Papers. Washington: Independent Sector, [1987].

Collection of thirty-three working papers for Independent Sector's 1987 Spring Research Forum, centering on the relationship between the Constitution of the United States and the nonprofit sector. The papers are divided into twelve topical areas: (1) management issues; (2) economics of the nonprofit sector; (3) tax reform effects on giving and volunteering; (4) philanthropy abroad; (5) philanthropic activities of the wealthy; (6) philanthropic activities among minority groups; (7) legal issues affecting philanthropy; (8) voluntary organizations in an era of changing resources; (9) competition and the nonprofit sector; (10) history and values; (11) women in philanthropy; and (12) the Constitution and the independent sector. All of the papers are well-researched and interesting, providing entry points to the discussion of various aspects of the nonprofit sector.

2179. Independent Sector. *National Taxonomy of Exempt Entities (NTEE)*. Washington: Independent Sector, [1987].

One page fold-out poster of the National Taxonomy of Exempt Entities (NTEE). Information on the back of the poster includes Instructions/Users' Guide (with a statement of purpose and uses); Major Group Code Descriptions; Beneficiary Code Descriptions; and Taxonomy At A Glance. The purpose of the taxonomy is to standardize the description of tax-exempt organizations with a focus on the philanthropic [IRS 501(c)(3)] sector. It provides a system for classifying nongovernmental, nonbusiness tax-exempt organizations by broadly classifying all nongovernmental and nonbusiness organizations (but not the programs they conduct) in the United States. In particular, foundations and grantmaking institutions can use the system for classifying grants by purpose, field of service, or type of institution receiving the grant. The system is now in the implementation stage at both the state and federal level. The Foundation Center and the American Association of Fund-Raising Counsel have agreed to use the new taxonomy.

2180. Independent Sector. *Nonprofit Organizational Effectiveness Study*. Washington: Independent Sector, 1986.

2181. Independent Sector. *Program Plan*. Washington: Independent Sector, 1980.

2182. Independent Sector. *Research in Progress, 1985-1986. A National Compilation of Research Projects on Philanthropy, Voluntary Action, and Non-Profit Activity*. Washington: Independent Sector, 1987.

Reference volume designed to identify researchers and describe current research on giving, voluntary action, and nonprofit activities. Entries cover a wide range of fields, both disciplinary and interdisciplinary, such as economics, history, philosophy, labor, government and public policy. The 441 projects in this volume are arranged by research topic and by principal investigator or sponsoring agency. Specific topic headings and subheadings are accessed by using the table of contents. Within the topic headings, research projects are organized alphabetically, by principal investigator or sponsoring agency. (In addition, the projects are cross-referenced.) Each project profile includes researcher/sponsoring organization (with address), telephone number, project title, project description, and publications. The introduction contains a section on *Other Reference Works of Interest* and a request for other researchers to submit their research for the next volume by using the enclosed research summary sheets. The work also includes alphabetically arranged indexes for both project title and investigator and sponsoring agency.

2183. Independent Sector. *Strengthening Philanthropy and Voluntary Initiative. An Independent Sector Program for Candidates for National Office and for the New Administration and Congress*. Washington: Independent Sector, 1988.

Sets forth the policies that Independent Sector urges national leaders to adopt in order to support and strengthen nonprofit endeavors. Includes: broadening the charitable tax deduction to all taxpayers, not just the affluent; resisting efforts to limit the right and opportunities of voluntary organizations to be aggressive advocates of citizen needs and views; continuing the postal subsidies for nonprofits; supporting efforts to assure affordable liability insurance for volunteers; and maintaining current programs and strengthening federal recognition for outstanding voluntary effort.

2184. Information Service of Illinois. *How to Become a 501 (c)(3) Organization*. Chicago: Information Service of Illinois, 1980.

2185. Institution for Social and Policy Studies. *Program on Non-Profit Organizations Working Papers Series: Index, 1-25*. New Haven, Conn.: Institution for Social and Policy Studies, 1978.

2186. Istel, John, ed. *Theater Profiles 8*. New York: Theatre Communications Group, 1988.

2187. Jacquet, Constant H., Jr., ed. *Yearbook of American and Canadian Churches*. Nashville, Tenn.: Abingdon Press, 1986.

Contains a chapter, *Philanthropy of Organized Religion*, which briefly discusses the funding of religious group programs, and the relationship between philanthropy and organized religion. Also has statistical data on church finances, contributions, recipients of giving, and personal disposable income for U.S. and Canada.

2188. James, Estelle. *Cross Subsidization by Non-Profit Organizations: Theory, Evidence and Evaluation*. Program on Non-Profit Organizations, no. 30. New Haven, Conn.: Institution for Social and Policy Studies, 1982.

2189. James, Estelle, and Susan Rose-Ackerman. *The Nonprofit Enterprise in Market Economies*. Program on Non-Profit Organizations, no. 95. New Haven, Conn.: Institution for Social and Policy Studies, 1985.

Presents a realistic view of the strengths and weaknesses of nonprofit organizations (NPOs) relative to both for-profit firms and public agencies, based on theoretical models and on empirical tests. Affirms the continuing importance of nonprofits in many sectors of the economy but avoids exaggerated claims for their overriding value. The nonprofit, the authors point out, operates in a climate half-way between government agencies and profit-maximizing firms. Like the for-profit, the NPO must provide services that appeal to potential clients (donors and customers); but like the government, it lacks strong incentives for efficiency. However, unlike either government bureaus or for-profit corporations, NPOs undertake tasks that aim at ideological (religious) goals; this imbues their fundraising and products with an ideological dimension. Thus, "What one person views as inefficient, self-indulgent or divisive behavior by NPO managers, another views as socially beneficial, admirably generous or a reflection of the ideological diversity of the population." Includes bibliography.

2190. Jenkins, Thomas M. "The Party Line Returns." *Grantsmanship Center News* 11 (November-December 1983): 58-9.

2191. Johnson, Jim. *Spread the Word! A Publicity Handbook for Rhode Island Nonprofit Agencies*. Providence, R.I.: Providence Learning Connection, 1983.

2192. Johnson, Julian. "Can a Black Be Quarterback?" *NonProfit Times* 2 (January 1989): 21-3.

A 1988 survey by the National Society of Fund Raising Executives found that a mere 2.7 percent of the organization's members are from minority groups, and only 1.5 percent are blacks. Johnson points out that there is no lack of qualified minorities in the field; they are easily found in the major institutions that serve black life, including the United Negro College Fund, the Urban League, and leading black arts organizations. Unfortunately, prejudice (not necessarily vicious, but definitely blinding) excludes many talented individuals from the world of professional fundraising. Johnson recommends several options for improving the situation, including recognizing and then overcoming our prejudices; scheduling minorities to speak at fundraising symposia (and not having them discuss "minority subjects"); and adopting increased minority membership goals along with strategies to attain them. He refers to the nonprofit sector as the high road, which focuses on people instead of profits; this is the area where human beings can exhibit the courage and wisdom needed to overcome racial discrimination.

2193. Johnson, Kathryn E., and Judith D. Berger. "Creating the Nonprofit Entrepreneur." *Association Management* 37 (June 1985): 111-14.

2194. Johnson, Robert Matthews. "How to Evaluate a Neighborhood Organization." *Foundation News* 25 (May-June 1984): 33-7.

2195. Jones, David R. "Computing the Odds in Software." *Foundation News* 29 (March-April 1988): 60-5.

Provides clear and direct advice to help the nonprofit administrator choose a financial management computer package. Advocates evaluating your organization's needs; comparing and contrasting packages on the market which meet those needs; estimating investment cost, including staff training, trial and error, and maintenance; considering future adaptions or modifications that will suit long-term needs; and determining whether there are cost-effective alternatives to purchasing financial management software.

2196. Jones, Thomas. "Fitting the Business to the Non-Profit: Keeping in Control." *LRC-W Newsbriefs* (29 February 1984): 30.

2197. Kanter, Rosabeth Moss. *The Measurement of Organizational Effectiveness, Productivity, Performance, and Success: Issues and Dilemmas in Service and Non-Profit Organizations.* Program on Non-Profit Organizations, no. 8. New Haven, Conn.: Institution for Social and Policy Studies, 1979.

2198. Kennedy, Shawn G. "Nonprofit Groups' Answer to High Manhattan Rents." *New York Times* (9 October 1985): B-18.

2199. Kidder, Rushworth. "Non-Profit Sector Facing 'Tricky and Delicate' Times." *Houston Post* (20 February 1984).

2200. Kiger, Joseph C. *American Learned Societies.* Washington: Public Affairs Press, 1963.

2201. Kinkead, Gwen. "America's Best-Run Charities." *Fortune* 116 (9 November 1987): 145-46, 148, 150.

Presents brief profiles and chart of the fifteen largest social welfare and health charities in the United States which also manage to spend between sixty-seven and ninety-five percent of their revenue on programs. Chart ranks charities by 1986 revenues, showing amount in millions and percent of total annual revenues spent on programs and fundraising, public donations in millions and percent of change from 1977, government payments and other income in millions, and number of total paid staff and volunteers. Leaders in percent spent on programs are: CARE (ninety-five percent), Volunteers of America (ninety-one percent), the Salvation Army (eighty-six percent), and Unicef (eighty-five percent).

2202. Klein, Kim. "When Money Isn't the Problem." *Grassroots Fundraising Journal* 4 (October 1985): 9+.

Explores four of the most common organizational problems.

2203. Klinman, Debra G., and Joelle H. Sander. *The Teen Parent Collaboration: Reaching and Serving the Teenage Father.* New York: Bank Street College of Education, 1985.

Final report of the Teen Father Collaboration, a two-year national demonstration and research effort sponsored by the Ford Foundation, which encouraged agencies already working with teenage mothers and their children to extend services to teenage fathers and prospective fathers. Services included vocational training, job placement, assistance in education completion, individual counseling, parenting skills classes, pre-natal classes, group and couple's counseling and a grandparents' support group. Report describes the problem of adolescent fathers and its context, the Collaboration's goals and organizational participants, an overview of the documentation process, the myths of teen fathers and the critical ingredients of service programs for teen fathers. Documents and describes both the process of program development and the characteristics of the young men who participated in programs, including an assessment of the impact of programs in their lives.

2204. Klinman, Debra G., and Joelle H. Sander. *The Teen Parent Collaboration: Reaching and Serving the Teenage Father.* [Summary]. New York: Bank Street College of Education, [1985].

Executive summary of the Teen Father Collaboration, a two-year demonstration and research effort sponsored by the Ford Foundation that endeavored to bring a range of comprehensive services to teenage fathers. Among the findings: only thirty-five percent of the young men who availed themselves of the services said they were employed, with more than half of these working only part-time. Fifty-nine percent had dropped out of school between the ninth and eleventh grades. They also showed a surprising commitment to their female partners and children, frequently stating that they wanted "to be a better father than my father was to me. I want something different for my child from what I have." Towards this end a majority of the clients sought multiple services, which included vocational and personal counseling, educational services, job placement, and pre-natal and parenting skills classes.

2205. Knowles, Louis L. "Alternative Investments: Helping Communities the Old Fashioned Way." *Foundation News* 26 (May-June 1985): 18+.

Discusses the use of program-related investments, equity grants, and equity participation loans for community development.

2206. Kornblum, Carole Ritts, ed. *Guide for Charities*. Sacramento, Calif.: Attorney General's Office for Charities, 1988.

Prepared by the Office of the California Attorney General as a public service, this *Guide for Charities* provides comprehensive information about California laws that govern charities, and also about important federal laws. Includes a directory of resources available to charities, including government agencies, information services, technical assistance providers, and a bibliography of publications from government and private sources.

2207. Kramer, Ralph M. *From Voluntarism to Vendorism: An Organizational Perspective on Contracting*. Program on Non-Profit Organizations, no. 54. New Haven, Conn.: Institution for Social and Policy Studies, 1982.

2208. Kramer, Ralph M. *Voluntary Agencies in the Welfare State*. Berkeley, Calif.: University of California Press, 1981.

2209. Kramer, Ralph M. *The Voluntary Agency in a Mixed Economy: Dilemmas of Entrepreneurialism and Vendorism*. Program on Non-Profit Organizations, no. 85. New Haven, Conn.: Institution for Social and Policy Studies, 1985.

2210. Kusmer, Kenneth L. "The Functions of Organized Charity in the Progressive Era: Chicago As a Case Study." *The Journal of American History* 60 (1973): 657-78.

Kusmer focuses on the Charity Organization Movement (COS), which began with the founding of the Buffalo COS in 1877 and spread to more than 150 chapters by 1904. Kusmer uses the Chicago COS (founded 1883) as his model and seeks to determine why organized charity emerged so dramatically in the early years of the Progressive era. He also investigates who was involved in the formation and development of COS and why, and what functions charity organizations fulfilled for those in the movement and in society. He elaborates on the role of women in keeping the movement alive and expanding it, the motivations of Chicago philanthropists in supporting the COS, and more. He concludes that although it was ultimately unable to stop the fragmentation of a growing urban center (one of its underlying goals), the charity organization society became a distinctly urban service. It helped individuals to adjust to a complex industrial system while it also fulfilled rudimentary welfare functions.

2211. Lamm, Richard D. "Six Heresies and a New Reality." *Foundation News* 25 (May-June 1984): 24-7.

2212. Larson, Martin A., and C. Stanley Lowell. *The Churches: Their Riches, Revenues, and Immunities*. Washington: Robert B. Luce, 1969.

2213. Learmont, Carol L., and Stephen Van Houten. "Placements and Salaries, 1986: An Upswing." *Library Journal* 112 (15 October 1987): 27-34.

Results of the thirty-sixth annual survey of placements and salaries for graduates from ALA-accredited library school programs. Reveals improved salaries, a rising number of graduates, and more jobs than qualified people to fill them in major metropolitan areas.

2214. Leaver, Robert. "Is Starting a Nonprofit Business for You?" *Nonprofit Executive* 2 (December 1982): 7.

2215. Lecyn, Nancy, and William Paul Germano, eds. *Directory of Social and Health Agencies of New York City*. New York: Community Council of Greater New York, 1981.

2216. Lefferts, Robert B. "What Makes Projects Different?" *Grants Magazine* 6 (December 1983): 237-43.

2217. Leonard, Jennifer, and David Johnston. "The Payoff in Nonprofits." *Columbia Journalism Review* (May-June 1983): 51-4.

2218. Levitan, Peter A. "Serving God and Mammon: Financing Alternatives for Nonprofit Cultural Enterprises." *Art and the Law* 8 (1984): 403-25.

2219. Lewis, William, and Carol Milano. *Profitable Careers in Nonprofit*. New York: John Wiley, 1987.

Career guide for the nonprofit sector which examines all aspects of the not-for-profit field. The book begins with a general explanation of what a nonprofit is and how it differs from for-profits. Throughout the book, the authors use quoted statements of nonprofit personnel who relate their opinions and views on working within the nonprofit sector. This technique gives the reader the sense of getting insider information. Chapter 3 is an overview of the nonprofit workplace. It looks at nonprofit employee traits, workplace rewards and drawbacks, and the workplace itself. Included in the chapter are a values inventory and a personal checklist of key questions. The bulk of the book describes the functions of the executive director, administrative office, development office, program department, membership and publications, public relations, and government positions. The final chapter assists the reader with how to research, target, interview for and obtain a nonprofit job. Contains a list of professional associations, references, and an index.

2220. Lidoff, Lorraine, and Linda Zane Beaver. *Planning an Income-Generating Food Service Enterprise*. Program Innovations in Aging, no. 6. Washington: National Council on the Aging, 1983.

2221. Lofquist, William A. "Preventive Measures." *Grantsmanship Center News* 11 (November-December 1983): 30-7.

2222. Lyman, Richard W. *What Kind of Society Shall We Have?* Washington: Independent Sector, 1981.

2223. Magan, Geralyn Graf, ed. *How Do We Look? A Guide to Corporate Self Assessment and Ethical Reflection in Nonprofit Homes for the Aging*. Washington: American Association of Homes for the Aging, 1983.

2224. Majone, Giandomenico. *Professionalism and Non-Profit Organizations.* Program on Non-Profit Organizations, no. 24. New Haven, Conn.: Institution for Social and Policy Studies, 1980.

2225. Mangan, Michael. "New Health Care Strategy Outgrowth of Marketing Focus." *Fund Raising Management* 14 (January 1984): 46-9.

2226. Margolis, Richard J. "Native Profit." *Foundation News* 29 (January-February 1988): 18-23.

Profiles the First Nations Financial Project, an organization whose micro-enterprise approach is helping Native American tribes use an entrepreneurial path to self-sufficiency. Among their achievements: a $264,000 scholarship program for Indian graduate students at Yale University's School of Management, courtesy of the Carnegie Corporation; and the successful lobbying of Congress to keep the Bureau of Indian Affairs (BIA) from dispersing a $7 million compensation award to each resident of the reservation as the BIA has done with awards in the past. Instead, an investment fund, to be administered by the Saginaw-Chippewa tribe, was established to promote tribal development and self-determination.

2227. Marlowe, Howard. "Four More Years: What It Means to Non-Profits." *Grantsmanship Center News* 13 (January-February 1985): 18-24.

Discusses the impact of Ronald Reagan as president for four more years.

2228. Marlowe, Howard. "Profit-Making and Risk-Taking in the Nonprofit Sector." *Grantsmanship Center News* 12 (September-December 1984): 51-3.

2229. Martin, Andrew. "Charitable Giving and Financial Planning." *Nonprofit World Report* 3 (March-April 1985): 11+.

2230. Martinez, Arabella, and David B. Carlson. "Developing Leadership in Minority Communities." *Foundation News* 25 (November-December 1984): 40-5.

Describes community development corporations.

2231. Matthei, Chuck. "The Institute for Community Economics Where You Can Find Financial Aid, Technical Assistance, and a Firm Philosophical Footing." *Grantsmanship Center News* 13 (May-June 1985): 27+.

2232. Mayer, Martin. *Bricks, Mortar and the Performing Arts: Report of the Twentieth Century Fund Task Force on Performing Arts Centers.* New York: Twentieth Century Fund, 1970.

2233. Mayer, Robert A. *The Local Arts Council Movement.* Washington: National Partnership Meeting, 1980.

2234. Mayleas, Ruth. "Structure and Change: A Funder's Perspective on Multicultural Support." *Vantage Point* 19 (July-August 1988): 4-6.

Article analyzes the arts institutions of blacks, Hispanics, Asians, and other minority populations, aided in part by Ford Foundation studies of black and Hispanic art museums and Hispanic theaters. Among problems faced by these unique organizations is a lack of knowledgeable, affluent boards and adequately trained personnel. Development for minority arts organizations, the article asserts, can best be provided with carefully wrought programs offering technical assistance in marketing, fundraising, and management, backed by multi-year grants.

2235. McAdam, Terry W. *Careers in the Nonprofit Sector: Doing Well by Doing Good.* Washington: Taft Group, 1986.

A how-to and resource book for people wondering how to break into the sector, fundraisers seeking work changes, and volunteers who want to work professionally. First part of the book describes the distinguishing characteristics, economic and organizational views, functions, roles, values and nature of work in the nonprofit sector. Chapter 4 offers case histories of people with successful experiences in the field. Second part suggests job search strategies; appendix contains a sample list of the larger 501(c) organizations, a self test for compatibility of working in the nonprofit environment, listing of education and training opportunities, job change worksheet, bibliography, sample interview thank you letters, critique of job search paperwork, selected glossary of nonprofit terminology and compensation analysis worksheet.

2236. McDonald, Donna, ed. *Directory of Historical Societies and Agencies in the United States and Canada.* 11th ed. Nashville, Tenn.: American Association for State and Local History, 1978.

2237. McGrath, Glen. "Leadership and Voluntary Action." *Nonprofit World Report* 2 (May-June 1984): 23+.

2238. McGrath, Glen. "Obtaining Results for the Nonprofit Group." *Nonprofit World Report* 2 (September-October 1984): 21-2.

2239. McIlquham, John. "Urban Hospital's Rehab Efforts Lead Health Trend." *Fund Raising Management* 14 (December 1983): 28+.

2240. McMillen, Wayne. *Community Organization for Social Welfare.* Chicago: University of Chicago Press, 1945.

2241. Middleton, Melissa. *The Place and Power of Non-Profit Boards of Directors.* Program on Non-Profit Organizations, no. 78. New Haven, Conn.: Institution for Social and Policy Studies, 1983.

Reviews professional and theoretical literature on boards of directors in nonprofits, and explores their importance, their nature and roles, the concept of power, and board-management relations. Discusses two commonly-held assumptions about boards: 1) while nonprofit boards are assumed to be policy-making boards, they more often simply ratify policy presented by staff; and 2) the board-executive relationship is often a dynamic one, rather than a relationship built on mutual trust.

2242. Milofsky, Carl. *Not-for-Profit Organizations and Community: A Review of the Sociological Literature.* Program on Non-Profit Organizations, no. 6. New Haven, Conn.: Institution for Social and Policy Studies, 1979.

2243. Milofsky, Carl. *Scarcity and Community: A Resource Allocation Theory of Community and Mass Society Organizations.* Program on Non-Profit Organizations, no. 48. New Haven, Conn.: Institution for Social and Policy Studies, 1982.

2244. Milofsky, Carl. *Structure and Process in Self-Help Organizations.* Program on Non-Profit Organizations, no. 17. New Haven, Conn.: Institution for Social and Policy Studies, 1980.

2245. Milofsky, Carl, and Frank Romo. *The Structure of Funding Arenas for Community Self-Help Organizations.* Program on Non-Profit Organizations, no. 42. New Haven, Conn.: Institution for Social and Policy Studies, 1981.

2246. Mirvis, Philip H. "Work and Work Force Characteristics in the Nonprofit Sector." *Monthly Labor Review* (April 1983): 3-12.

2247. Molotsky, Irvin. "Federal Study Cites Slow Arts Growth." *New York Times* (8 March 1984): C-15.

2248. Moss, Jane. "Nonprofit Umbrella Group Offers New Services to Members." *Nonprofit Executive* 3 (May 1984): 5.

2249. "A Name for the Sector: Suggestions from the Accounting World." *Philanthropy Monthly* 16 (October 1983): 20-2.

2250. Natale, Samuel M. "Organizational Ethics, What Is It and What Does It Mean for Nonprofits?" *Nonprofit World Report* 2 (May-June 1984): 27-9.

2251. "National Arts Stabilization Fund Gets Underway." *Foundation Giving Watch* 3 (April 1984): 1-2.

2252. National Center for Charitable Statistics. *Non-Profit Service Organizations.* Washington: National Center for Charitable Statistics, 1985.

Assembles statistical information from the 1982 census of service industries conducted by the U.S. Bureau of the Census.

2253. National Center for Charitable Statistics. *Yearbook of New York State Charitable Organizations: Fund-Raising and Expense Information As Reported by Charitable, Civic, Health, Fraternal, and Other Organizations.* Washington: Independent Sector, 1987.

Directory lists the charities registered with the New York State Department of State, Office of Charities Registration as either raising or intending to raise contributions of at least $10,000 annually. The directory is arranged in three parts—an alphabetical master list, a cross-reference guide by type of organization, and a county cross-reference. The master list contains organization name and address; New York State registration number; a classification code which identifies the general organization type; date of information; and dollar amounts for direct public support, total support and revenue, payments to affiliates, program expense, management and general expense, fundraising expense and total expenses.

2254. National Charities Information Bureau. *Standards in Philanthropy.* New York: National Charities Information Bureau, 1988.

2255. National Clearinghouse for Primary Care Information. *Directory. Three Hundred-Thirty Funded Community Health Centers.* Arlington, Va.: National Clearinghouse for Primary Care Information, 1985.

2256. National Information Bureau. *NIB Standards in Philanthropy.* New York: National Information Bureau, 1982.

2257. National Information Bureau. *Service for Givers: The Story of the National Information Bureau, Inc.* New York: National Information Bureau, 1983.

2258. National Rural Center. *A Directory of Rural Organizations.* Washington: National Rural Center, 1977.

2259. National Trust for Historic Preservation. *Directory of Private, Nonprofit Preservation Organizations: State and Local Levels.* Washington: Preservation Press, 1980.

2260. Navaretta, Cynthia. *Guide to Women's Art Organizations and Directory for the Arts.* New York: Midmarch Arts Books, 1982.

Information on visual and performing arts, crafts, writing, film. The financial help and work opportunities section has information on emergency funds, artists' colonies and residences, studying abroad, and grants, awards, and fellowship resources.

2261. Navaretta, Cynthia. *Whole Arts Directory.* Midmarch Arts Directory Series. New York: Midmarch Arts Books, 1987.

With a primary focus on the visual arts (including intermedia, photography, performance art, film and video, and crafts), directory provides brief information on organizations, alternative spaces, cooperative galleries and special museums; artists' colonies, retreats and study centers; financial help, arts management, legal assistance, insurance; health hazards information, art therapy groups; arts advocacy and information services—federal, state and private agencies; and arts resources state by state in the United States and Canada.

2262. "NCIB's New Standards." *NonProfit Times* 2 (July 1988): 6, 16.

Reprint of the new standards from the National Charities Information Bureau, New York.

2263. Neighborhood Development Collaborative. *Entrepreneurship in the Non-Profit Sector: Preliminary Report.* Washington: Neighborhood Development Collaborative, [1982].

2264. New England Foundation for the Arts. *The Arts and the New England Economy.* Cambridge, Mass.: New England Foundation for the Arts, 1980.

2265. New York City. Commission on the Status of Women. *Women's Organizations: A New York City Directory.* New York: New York City Commission on the Status of Women, 1986.

Resource for women and men seeking services, information or a way to connect with groups addressing social, economic, or political issues as they relate to women. Entries are organized by categories reflecting the scope of the issues concerning women's organizations in New York City today, including arts and letters, child care, counseling/referral, education, employment, foundations, homeless women, legal rights, networking, parenting, teen pregnancy, and violence and physical safety. Also includes a listing of selected guides, handbooks and directories.

2266. New York Community Trust. *New York City Arts-in-Education Directory.* New York: New York Community Trust, [1979].

2267. New York Community Trust. *A Survey of Arts-in-Education in New York City.* New York: New York Community Trust, 1979.

2268. New York Public Library. *Directory of Community Services: The Bronx, Manhattan and Staten Island.* 9th ed. New York: New York Public Library, 1987.

An annotated bilingual (English/Spanish) guide to nonprofit organizations and groups which offer programs and services to the public, at the neighborhood level, in the Bronx, Manhattan and Staten Island. The directory is divided into two sections. Section 1 lists the organizations grouped by subject area. At the beginning of each subject heading there is a brief explanation of what areas are included under that heading. There are cross-references and directory references which cite other helpful directories in order of usefulness. Section 2 alphabetically lists the organizations. Organization profiles include agency name; address; telephone number; annotation of services and activities, etc.; New York Public Library (NYPL) branch code; date of verification; and zip code. The appendixes include NYPL information/addresses and zip code maps.

2269. New York University. *Conference on Charitable Organizations.* New York: Matthew Bender & Co., 1983.

2270. Nicholas, Ted. *Non-Profit Tax Exempt Corporations: The Alternative Tax Shelter.* Wilmington, Del.: Enterprise Publishing, 1982.

2271. "Nonprofit Agencies Are Turning to Fees to Balance Books." *New York Times* (12 September 1983).

2272. "The Nonprofit Economic Miracle." *Philanthropy Monthly* 16 (November 1983): 24-6.

2273. "Nonprofit Loan Funds Diversify Lending to Nonprofits." *Nonprofit Executive* 6 (July 1987): 1-2, 9, 10.

Brief article on nonprofit loan funds. Nonprofit loan funds are usually foundations which provide low or no-interest loans to nonprofit organizations. The funds are more numerous now than they were just two years ago and have begun to give loans for a wider variety of purposes. The article lists and describes the various types of loans which are made to nonprofits such as cash-flow, working-capital, venture, fixed asset, mortgage, and down payment for mortgage. Included in the same issue is a *Nonprofit Loan Fund Directory* of eighty-five funds in twenty-five states. The directory is arranged alphabetically by state and then by the loan fund within the state and includes the name, address and telephone number of the fund.

2274. "The Nonprofit Sector in the New York Area." *City Almanac* 19 (Winter-Spring 1985-86): 1-36.

This issue is dedicated to increasing the understanding of the nonprofit sector in the New York region. Articles include highlights of an empirical study of the New York nonprofits by David Grossman and the Nova Institute; perspectives on management, fundraising, and volunteers in the nonprofit sector; the challenge New York City poverty poses to the nonprofit sector; and a colloquium on the relationship between government and the nonprofit sector, sponsored by the Research Foundation of the City University of New York.

2275. O'Connell, Brian. "Charitable Giving at Crossroads: An Interview with Independent Sector's Brian O'Connell." *Trusts & Estates* 124 (September 1985): 8+.

2276. O'Connell, Brian. *Our Organization.* New York: Walker & Co., 1987.

Lampoons the world of volunteer organizations by presenting the minutes of a fictional nonprofit's board meetings. The speakers invariably hoist themselves with their own petards and foolish antics as they cling to Robert's Rules of Order and struggle to keep their organization above water.

2277. Odell, Richard. "Venture Capital Ideas for Schools and Other Nonprofits." *Nonprofit World Report* 2 (January-February 1984): 8+.

2278. Olcott, William. "Oxfam Leads the Way." *Fund Raising Management* 19 (October 1988).

Profiles Oxfam, the largest charity in the United Kingdom, covering its history, fundraising programs, public awareness efforts and Charity Shops.

2279. "Organizations That Make Loans to Nonprofits." *Nonprofit World* 5 (May-June 1987): 7.

2280. Orlans, Harold. *The Nonprofit Research Institute: Its Origins, Operations, Problems and Prospects.* Carnegie Commission on Higher Education Profile, no. 9. New York: McGraw-Hill, 1972.

2281. Palmer, Stacy E. "Nonprofit Groups Required to Join Social Security." *Chronicle of Higher Education* 27 (11 January 1984): 19-20.

2282. "Partnerships in Education: Executive Department/Agency Partnership Programs." *PSI Lights* (20 June 1984): 1.

2283. Paul, R. Dana, and Ken Stark. "The Mixmasters." *Currents* 9 (November-December 1983): 24-6.

2284. Peat, Marwick, Mitchell and Company. *Directors' and Officers' Liability: A Crisis in the Making.* New York: Peat, Marwick, Mitchell & Co., 1987.

Survey of 2,532 leaders of national not-for-profit voluntary organizations within the Washington, D.C. organization Independent Sector. Over eighty percent of the respondents believe that the directors' and officers' liability problem is damaging the quality of governance in American national volunteer organizations and has reached crisis proportions. The leaders responded that they believed the major impediments to resolving the problem included the legal profession, the insurance industry, the litigious nature of the society, inadequate legislation/lack of legislative understanding, high awards, and legal lobbies, respectively. The report recommends the draft of model legislation to aid states in implementing their own laws; adopting the English Rule, whereby the losing party assumes all court costs; reassessing the legal bases for the crisis; definition of the scope of directors' responsibilities to their boards, organizations, or companies, including the clarification of the limits of their responsibility; and establishing a task force to review directors' responsibilities.

2285. Peirce, Neal R., and Carol F. Steinbach. *Corrective Capitalism: The Rise of America's Community Development Corporations.* New York: Ford Foundation, 1987.

A Ford Foundation report on a survey of community development corporations (CDC's) which traces the evolution of CDC's over the past twenty years. The paper describes the CDC movement and its activities in detail and assesses their role in revitalizing urban slums and depressed rural areas. Few CDC's existed twenty-five years ago, now they number in the thousands. They build and rehabilitate housing using the local labor force and are advocates for the neighborhoods demanding better city services. CDC's provide services such as job training, credit unions, and day-care and senior centers. They finance and operate shopping centers, industrial parks, business incubators, and retail franchises. The report examines the evolution of CDC funding from the beginnings in the 1960's when the funds came from the government and foundations to the 1980's. During the 1980's, the CDC's broadened their funding base with a sophisticated combination of funding from state and local governments, churches, foundations, banks, private corporations, and in some cases, universities and hospitals. The report also presents a look at the human side of the CDC story with profiles and selected photographs of specific projects, programs and community leaders in Philadelphia, Brooklyn, the South Bronx, Los Angeles, Pittsburgh, Richmond, and Boston, among others.

2286. "Perspective on the Arts in GNP." *Philanthropy Monthly* 16 (October 1983): 29-32.

2287. Peterson, Eric. *Nonprofit Arts Organizations: Formation and Maintenance.* San Francisco: Bay Area Lawyers for the Arts, 1977.

2288. Peterson, Eric. *Nonprofit Arts Organizations: Formation and Maintenance. Supplement.* San Francisco: Bay Area Lawyers for the Arts, 1978.

2289. Pipines, Pamela, and Terence Ripmaster. *The Arts Catalogue of New Jersey.* Wayne, N.J.: Avery Publishing Group, 1978.

2290. Pires, Shelia A. *Competition between the Nonprofit and For-Profit Sectors.* Washington: National Assembly of National Voluntary Health and Social Welfare Organizations, 1985.

Special report based on a study of competition between the for-profit and nonprofit sectors, exploring the ramifications and implications of the competition issue. Compares and reviews the findings of this study with the U.S. Small Business Administration's report, *Unfair Competition by Nonprofit Organizations with Small Business...* Discusses the two sides of the competition issue, where on one side, nonprofits are becoming more entrepreneurial, and on the other, for-profits are increasingly entering traditionally nonprofit arenas.

2291. Plinio, Alex J. "Donor/Donee Relationship: Reciprocal Positive Influence." *Fund Raising Management* 14 (February 1984): 82-3.

2292. Plinio, Alex J. "Time for a Hard Look, at Ourselves." *Foundation News* 27 (July-August 1986): 48-9.

A call for both philanthropy and the nonprofit sector to promote research and development programs and to support the establishment of research and development funds.

2293. Polivy, Deborah K. *A Study of the Admissions Policies and Practices of Eight Local United Way Organizations.* Program on Non-Profit Organizations, no. 49. New Haven, Conn.: Institution for Social and Policy Studies, 1982.

2294. Portnoy, Fern C. "An Introduction to Program-Related Investments." *Whole Nonprofit Catalog* 2 (Fall 1986): 2-3.

Discusses the charitable purposes, income motive and legislative activities related to Program Related Investments (PRIs) by foundations. Also discusses forms of PRIs available to foundations, such as direct loans, equity investments, and guarantees. A list of foundations making PRIs follows the article.

2295. Potter, Roberto Hugh. "Back to the Future: Human Resource Planning for Nonprofits." *Nonprofit World* 4 (November-December 1986): 14-6.

Potter warns that as cheap well-educated labor disappears, nonprofits will lose an important resource. Using secondary research, the author explores the impact of the "baby bust" on certain industries and then reviews the possible impact on nonprofit organizations as well as suggestions for techniques to minimize the impact.

2296. Powell, Luther P. *Money and the Church.* New York: Association Press, 1962.

2297. Powell, Walter W., ed. *The Nonprofit Sector: A Research Handbook.* New Haven, Conn.: Yale University Press, 1987.

Scholarly handbook of multi-disciplinary studies examining the role, character, organization, and impact of the voluntary sector in the United States and abroad. The volume is divided into six sections which include an historical overview of the nonprofit sector; theoretical writings on economic and political science reasons for the existence of the nonprofit sector; an empirical survey of the nonprofit sector; the relationship of the voluntary sector to government and private enterprise; crucial organizational and management issues; the range of activities and services undertaken or offered by nonprofits in health care, private and public educational institutions, personal social services, community-based nonprofits, and social movements; fundamental issue of financing in the nonprofit sector; and the role played by the nonprofit sector in both industrialized nations and in developing countries. Volume includes bibliographic references with each of the twenty-four chapters, extensive tables, index, and notes on the contributors.

2298. Practising Law Institute. *Non-Profit Organizations: Current Issues and Developments.* New York: Practising Law Institute, 1984.

Published as a supplement to the Practising Law Institute's 1984 program, *Nonprofit Organizations: Current Issues and Developments.*

2299. Preston, Anne E. *Compensation Differentials in the Nonprofit Sector: An Application to the Day Care Industry*. Program on Non-Profit Organizations, no. 99. New Haven, Conn.: Institution for Social and Policy Studies, 1985.

Preston uses the day care industry as a subject with which to test the wage differential predictions of a labor donations model. The industry is comprised of nonprofit and for-profit centers competing against each other; there is also a division between federally subsidized and non-federally financed sectors. Because managers in the federally financed sector have the opportunity to channel excess profits into higher wages, the model predicts that stronger demand forces will create a greater nonprofit wage differential in this branch of the industry. Results from salary equations run on a cross-section of day-care centers support the predictions, with nonprofit salaries in the federally financed sector running five to nine percent higher than for-profit salaries. These high salaries contrast with the low nonprofit wages found in earlier economy-wide comparisons, suggesting the need for a more complete model of wage determination in the sector. Includes bibliography.

2300. Preston, Anne E. *Women in the White Collar Non-Profit Sector: The Best Option or the Only Option*. Program on Non-Profit Organizations, no. 101. New Haven, Conn.: Institution for Social and Policy Studies, 1985.

Examines possible reasons for the notably large number of women working in the nonprofit sector. Anne Preston employs data from three large economy-wide worker data sets to analyze wages, fringes, and non-pecuniary attributes of jobs offered to men and women in the nonprofit and for-profit sectors, finding that "opportunities for women in the nonprofit sector are comparable to those offered by the for-profit sector. In addition female wage discrimination in the sector is non-existent." Based on these findings, Preston claims that women may prefer the non-pecuniary compensations of the nonprofit sector over those offered by the for-profit market; these compensations include flexibility, autonomy, interesting and important work, and lack of wage discrimination. She does warn that while wage discrimination may not exist, the equality of occupational opportunities for men and women in the nonprofit sector needs to be addressed. Includes bibliography.

2301. *Prevention of Nuclear War: Funders' Guide to Non-Partisan Voter Education Activities*. Washington: Forum Institute, [1984].

Describes thirteen nonpartisan voter registration and citizen education programs dedicated to disseminating information and promoting discussions about the likelihood and consequences of nuclear war.

2302. *Program Related Investments*. New York: Ford Foundation, 1983.

2303. *Public Interest Public Relations. Promoting Issues and Ideas*. New York: Foundation Center, 1987.

An all-in-one guide to public relations for nonprofit organizations. Chapters include: *The Public Relations Plan, Advertising - A Primer, Speaking Before the Public, Evaluating a Public Relations Effort*, and others.

2304. Putsch, Henry E. *Issues and Opportunities Facing the Public-Sector Arts Support Network*. Washington: National Partnership Meeting, 1980.

2305. Reiner, Thomas A., and Julian Wolpert. "The Non-Profit Sector in the Metropolitan (Philadelphia) Economy." *Economic Geography* 57 (January 1981): 25-33.

While annual philanthropic giving is about two percent of the GNP, say the authors, no regional studies of the flow of philanthropic dollars had been attempted until their study and resulting article on the Philadelphia metropolitan area. They used empirical evidence and theoretical constructs to observe the relationship between philanthropy and metropolitan growth or decline. According to their study, the magnitude and targeting of funds to support nonprofit activity is directly related to behavior of immobile industries (banks, public utilities, real estate corporations, etc.) and footloose industries (less region-specific). They found that regional decline is paralleled by a disproportionately large share of philanthropy from immobile industries, whereas footloose industries respond to decline by reducing their philanthropic activities.

2306. Reiter, Susan. "In the Company of Choreographers." *American Arts* 14 (May 1983): 12+.

2307. Rickard, Al. "Saving the Postal Subsidy." *Association Management* 37 (June 1985): 62+.

2308. Rockefeller, John D., III. *The Second American Revolution: Some Personal Observations*. New York: Harper & Row, [1973].

2309. Rockefeller Brothers Fund. *The Performing Arts: Problems and Prospects*. New York: McGraw-Hill, [1965].

2310. Rose-Ackerman, Susan. *Do Government Grants to Charity Reduce Private Donations?* Program on Non-Profit Organizations, no. 13. New Haven, Conn.: Institution for Social and Policy Studies, 1980.

2311. Rose-Ackerman, Susan, ed. *The Economics of Nonprofit Institutions: Studies in Structure and Policy*. Yale Studies on Nonprofit Organizations. New York: Oxford University Press, 1986.

Both quantitative and nontechnical articles written by economists for noneconomists as well as for other economists comprise this volume, another in the series from the Yale Studies on Nonprofit Organizations. The collection is compiled in two parts. The first part, *Models of Nonprofit Firms*, includes eleven articles arranged in two sections—government failure and contract failure and information asymmetry. The articles outline different economic reasons for the existence of nonprofits such as to provide additional public services and to provide a vehicle for altruistic motives or objectives other than profit maximization. The second part, *Public Policy Toward Nonprofits*, presents policy issue essays arranged in four sections—the charitable deduction, government grants, fundraising, and corporate tax benefits. This second part examines tax deductibility of contributions, the link between government grants and private donations, the regulation of fundraising, and the exemption of nonprofits from corporate income tax. The articles include endnotes, some include references. The volume contains notes on contributors as well as author and subject indexes.

2312. Rose-Ackerman, Susan. *The Market for Loving Kindness: Day Care Centers and the Demand for Child Care.* Program on Non-Profit Organizations, no. 55. New Haven, Conn.: Institution for Social and Policy Studies, 1983.

2313. Rose-Ackerman, Susan. *Unfair Competition and Corporate Income Taxation.* Program on Non-Profit Organizations, no. 37. New Haven, Conn.: Institution for Social and Policy Studies, 1981.

2314. Rose-Ackerman, Susan. *United Charities: An Economic Analysis.* Program on Non-Profit Organizations, no. 11. New Haven, Conn.: Institution for Social and Policy Studies, 1980.

Although United Funds can be an efficient response to donor ignorance, they have also been charged with monopolizing the charity market, using unsophisticated allocation procedures, and failing to take into account government's growing role in social services. This paper assesses these criticisms, and emphasizes the limits imposed on United Fund power by the ability of donors to give elsewhere and the power of charities to leave the Fund. Given these constraints, as well as the real difficulties involved in monitoring social services, the Fund's allocations processes will inevitably be imperfect, Rose-Ackerman concedes. She concludes that even when these limits are taken into account, however, United Funds do have some limited monopoly power because of access to the payroll deduction, and most of them have failed to respond in a sophisticated way to the rise in government support of social services.

2315. Rosenbaum, Nelson. "The Competitive Market Model: Emerging Strategy for Nonprofits." *Nonprofit Executive* 3 (July 1984): 3-4.

2316. Rosenbaum, Nelson. *Entrepreneurial Approaches to Revenue Generation in the Voluntary Sector.* Washington: Center for Responsive Governance, 1983.

2317. Rosenbaum, Nelson, and Bruce L.R. Smith. *The Fiscal Capacity of the Voluntary Sector.* Washington: Center for Responsive Governance, 1981.

2318. Rudney, Gabriel. *A Quantitative Profile of the Nonprofit Sector.* Program on Non-Profit Organizations, no. 40. New Haven, Conn.: Institution for Social and Policy Studies, 1981.

2319. Rudney, Gabriel, and Murray S. Weitzman. *Significance of Employment and Earnings in the Philanthropic Sector, 1972-1982.* Program on Non-Profit Organizations, no. 77. New Haven, Conn.: Institution for Social and Policy Studies, 1983.

2320. Salamon, Lester M. "The Future of the Nonprofit Sector." *Grantsmanship Center News* 12 (September-December 1984): 54-61.

2321. Salamon, Lester M. *The New Federalism, the Federal Budget, and the Nonprofit Sector.* Washington: Urban Institute, 1983.

Testimony given before the Joint Economic Committee of the U.S. Congress in 1983 on the role and character of the private nonprofit sector, and on the impact that recent budget cuts and program reforms in public policy will have upon this sector. The four major points of Mr. Salamon's testimony are: that the nonprofit sector plays a far more important role in the nation's human service delivery system than is commonly acknowledged; that despite conservative theories viewing government and the nonprofit sector as adversaries, government has been a major factor in stimulating the growth of nonprofits, and has actually been involved in an elaborate and generally fruitful partnership with the sector; that the policy changes in the recent past and those proposed for the near future threaten to reduce significantly the effectiveness of this government-nonprofit partnership; and that an alternative course of action could be devised to build upon the strengths of existing government-nonprofit relationships while eliminating some of the difficulties past cooperation has sometimes entailed. Much of the information presented here can also be found in *Voluntary Organizations and the Crisis of the Welfare State.*

2322. Salamon, Lester M. "The Results Are Coming in." *Foundation News* 25 (July-August 1984): 16-23.

2323. Salamon, Lester M., James C. Musselwhite, Jr., and Alan J. Abramson. *Voluntary Organizations and the Crisis of the Welfare State.* Washington: Urban Institute, 1983.

Advocates a system of human service delivery that involves a partnership of government and voluntary organizations to resolve the crisis of the welfare state and thus effectively provide "public goods." The authors agree that despite impressive achievements, the welfare state has proven inadequate in coping with major problems in modern industrial society—urban distress, poverty, crime and unemployment—but argue that the conservative political challenge to governmental involvement in this area fails to consider the immense support which the welfare state has provided to voluntary associations. Government in the United States is a major funder of the sector, underwriting its operations and facilitating expansion of these operations. The document provides an overview of the nonprofit sector; traces the pattern of interaction between the sector and government, along with some the problems encountered by the partnership; explores the theoretical basis for continuing and strengthening the partnership, with suggestions for profit-making organizations to contribute to the system; and outlines how an improved partnership between these sectors, which the authors refer to as "rationalized welfare pluralism," might function in practice. In addition to financial support, government involvement would aid in an equitable distribution of the available resources to the areas and populations that need them, ensure a sufficient degree of diversity in the service delivery system, and would allow for public priority setting, a central tenet of our democratic society.

2324. *The Salary and Benefits Survey of National Voluntary Human Service Organizations, 1981.* Washington: National Assembly of National Voluntary Health and Social Welfare Organizations, 1981.

2325. Salvatore, Tony. "From Voluntary to para-Corporate: Today's Nonprofit Spectrum." *Nonprofit World Report* 3 (May-June 1985): 19+.

2326. Schiff, Jerald. *Expansion, Entry and Exit in the Nonprofit Sector: The Long and Short of It.* Program on Non-Profit Organizations, no. 111. New Haven, Conn.: Institution for Social and Policy Studies, 1986.

Contends that the nonprofit sector will respond to changes in demand or cost conditions via entry or exit, in addition to expansion or contraction of existing organizations, much as occurs in the proprietary sector.

2327. Schutzer, George J. *Prevalence of Nonprofit Organizations in the Broadcast Media.* Program on Non-Profit Organizations, no. 14. New Haven, Conn.: Institution for Social and Policy Studies, 1980.

2328. Schutzman, Harold, ed. *A Guide to Information Sources and Services for Voluntary Human Services Agencies.* Washington: National Assembly of National Voluntary Health and Social Welfare Organizations, 1979.

2329. Selby, Cecily Cannan. "Better Performance from 'Nonprofits'." *Harvard Business Review* 56 (September-October 1978): 92-8.

2330. *Self Help: Earned Income Opportunities for Cultural Organizations.* New York: New York Commission for Cultural Affairs, 1982.

2331. Shabecoff, Alice. "Bringing High-Tech to Neighborhoods: Here's How High Technology Created a Network That Really Works for Grassroots Organizations." *Nonprofit World* 6 (July-August 1988): 35-7.

Profiles the Community Information Exchange in Washington, D.C., an information network service that takes advantage of the information explosion to aid grassroots organizations. The service provides valuable information needed to plan, finance, and operate revitalization projects in urban neighborhoods and rural communities, in addition to in-depth case studies of exemplary projects which enable organizations to learn from each other's experiences.

2332. Shabecoff, Philip. "Earth, Wind and Loss of Momentum." *New York Times* (28 April 1984): A-9.

2333. Sherlock, John F. "Hospital Marketing Moves into Convenience Shopping Centers." *Fund Raising Management* 15 (October 1984): 98.

2334. Shore, Lys Ann. "The Turnaround." *Association Management* 37 (May 1985): 71+.

2335. Simmons, Nicole. "Rents Bedevil Arts Groups: Compromise Gained with City Eases Plight." *New York Times* (9 October 1983): 7, 14.

2336. Skloot, Edward. "Should Not-for-Profits Go into Business?" *Harvard Business Review* 61 (January-February 1982): 20-7.

2337. Skloot, Edward. "Survival Time for Nonprofits." *Foundation News* 28 (January-February 1987): 38-42.

A critical examination of the nonprofit sector's entry into competition with the market economy. Reductions in federal funds, changes in the tax code, privatization of former public sector services, for-profit corporations' search for new markets, and government deregulation have had and will continue to have a significant impact on the nonprofit sector. Beginning in the 60's and 70's, the private sector seized upon opportunities in areas which were previously dominated by nonprofits. Particularly in such areas as hospitals and the penal system where third party reimbursement was available. Services such as sanitation, ambulance, youth training, substance abuse and home health care have also increasingly become privatized. In an example of one maneuver in the attack against nonprofits, Skloot relates that in 1983 the Small Business Administration called for restricting the definition of substantially related income for nonprofits and possibly setting a limit nonprofits are allowed to earn as a percentage of their budget. The author believes that it is time for the nonprofit sector to assess their true demographic profile, address the sector's effectiveness, and "articulate the valuable, mutually enhancing, and necessarily interlocking relationships of the three sectors."

2338. Sladek, Frea E. "Profits." *Grants Magazine* 6 (March 1983): 2-3.

2339. Smith, Brian H. *Nonprofit Organizations and Socioeconomic Development in Columbia.* Program on Non-Profit Organizations, no. 93. New Haven, Conn.: Institution for Social and Policy Studies, 1985.

Focuses on results of investigation into the capacity of the indigenous private voluntary organizations (PVOs) of Columbia to reach the poorest sectors and promote sustainable development processes among them, facilitate their power to pressure larger social institutions that affect their livelihood, and stimulate through innovation and advocacy better public policies in service delivery to the poor. Working his Columbian findings into the multidimensional framework of his larger research project, Brian Smith states that "development-oriented PVOs in the third world are a parallel system of important but limited action on behalf of the poor, but are not likely to affect substantially the values or behavior of more significant institutions affecting the lives of their clientele."

2340. Smith, G. Stevenson. "Redefinition of Nonprofit Accounting." *Nonprofit World* 5 (July-August 1987): 27-9.

Outlines several of the changes expected to occur in nonprofit financial statement requirements as a result of the Financial Accounting Standards Board Concepts Statement No. 6. This concept statement redefines seven major elements of financial statements for nonprofits: assets, liabilities, net assets (fund balance), revenues, expenses, gains, and losses. Among other things, these redefinitions will significantly reduce the amount of liabilities recognized on a nonprofit's financial statements, and cause any decisions previously made and based on amounts in a nonprofit's assets (fund balance) to be reviewed in light of the redefinition of liabilities.

2341. Society for Nonprofit Organizations. *National Directory of Service and Product Providers to Nonprofit Organizations and Resource Center Catalog.* Madison, Wis.: Society for Nonprofit Organizations, 1988.

2342. *The Solicitation and Collection of Funds for Charitable Purposes: Article 7-A of the Executive Law.* Albany, N.Y.: New York State. Department of State, 1986.

2343. Solomon, Amy. "Non Profits in Business." *Chronicle of Non Profit Enterprise* 3 (May 1984): 4-7.

2344. Sommers, David. *Women in Organizations: An Analysis of the Role and Status of Women in American Voluntary Organizations.* Washington: B'nai B'rith International, 1983.

2345. Southern California Association for Philanthropy. *Private Resources and Public Needs: Los Angeles in the Twenty-First Century.* Southern California Association for Philanthropy Special Report. Los Angeles: Southern California Association for Philanthropy, 1988.

Summary report of meeting on the future of non-governmental organizations and their leadership. The program's purpose was to explore the challenges and opportunities being created by the rapid demographic changes in the region.

2346. Speeter, Greg. *Power: A Repossession Manual. Organizing Strategies for Citizens.* Amherst, Mass.: Citizen Involvement Training Project, 1978.

2347. Staecker, Delmar. "For-Profit Activities in the Nonprofit World: Where Do We Draw the Line?" *Nonprofit World* 5 (March-April 1987): 31-2.

Critical examination of nonprofits' increasing involvement with marketing and for-profit entrepreneurship. Many nonprofits view services as products and clients as customers. Today, profit is no longer considered a dirty word in the nonprofit sector. As might be expected, complaints have arisen from both big and small business alike. These complaints have been heard by the government—particularly by the GAO and the IRS. Indeed, the tax-exempt status of nonprofits is jeopardized by the commercialism; the very fabric of the nonprofit sector and its role in society is being questioned by the threatened for-profits, writes Staecker. The author believes acceptance of the "marketing mentality" and other important issues should be questioned by the nonprofit sector itself.

2348. Stagner, Matthew, and Harold Richman. *Help-Seeking and the Use of Social Service Providers by Welfare Families in Chicago.* Hardship and Support Systems in Chicago, vol. 3. Chicago: University of Chicago, 1986.

Volume 3 in the study of Hardship and Support Systems in Chicago, this report investigates the extent to which welfare families turn to social service providers for help, the nature of their experiences with social service providers, and the reasons why some families do not use social service providers. Interviews with 737 Chicago welfare households found that approximately half had not turned to social service providers for assistance during the year preceding the interview, but instead had made use of informal helping networks, such as friends, neighbors, and family members. The families who did make use of social service providers generally found their experiences with private agencies and with churches to be more positive than their experiences with government social service providers.

2349. Stein, Sharman. "A Roof and a Future." *Foundation News* 30 (January-February 1989): 24-9.

As the number of homeless families increases, foundations are placing more emphasis on programs that help families regain the road to independence rather than ones that merely provide a place for the night. With estimates of up to 735,000 homeless people on any given night in America (which includes 100,000 children within an "intact" family), service programs which aim to help the homeless learn the skills of living, from finishing their high school educations to mastering problems of saving money and budgeting, are receiving priority consideration. Legal aid and advocacy groups are filing suits to establish rights for homeless families, and efforts are being made to distill information about available services. Affordable housing for low-income families is, of course, the main issue, but the most difficult one to resolve. The Cleveland Housing Network offers an example of success: this coalition of nine neighborhood groups acquires vacant one-and two-family homes and sells them to families on a lease-purchase plan. The network keeps monthly rental fees to an average of $150 by encouraging corporations to invest in packages of houses, for which the corporations receive tax benefits.

2350. Steinberg, Richard. *Donations, Local Government Spending, and the "New Federalism."* Program on Non-Profit Organizations, no. 107. New Haven, Conn.: Institution for Social and Policy Studies, 1986.

Theoretically and empirically examines the tenet of "new federalism" which states that local governments and nonprofit organizations will increase their expenditures on social services in response to federal cutbacks. A number of studies, admittedly flawed, do suggest that when a local government reduces its provision of social service, some replacement by the nonprofit sector will occur, usually between 1/2 and 30 cents on the dollar. A specific study of the recreational services finds that if federal aid were to decrease, overall nonprofit and governmental expenditures on recreation would increase. The author warns that the data are badly flawed, and should be seen chiefly as an indication that better estimates may be produced in future studies.

2351. Sterne, Larry. "'Market Yourself' Becoming a Common Cry at Nonprofit Conferences." *NonProfit Times* 2 (January 1989): 5, 19.

Comments on the ever-increasing trend of cause-related marketing in the nonprofit sector. With more and more companies embracing the new method, fears grow that corporate philanthropy will never again be purely charitable. Present marketing efforts are focusing on arts groups and their events, as they provide a stimulating, non-controversial cause with an upscale audience. Nonprofits are warned, however, not to create an artistic event simply to receive funding, but rather to continue with socially responsible, long-term activities. The most important advice for nonprofits is to not underestimate the amount of time such cause-related marketing efforts take to plan (if they are to avoid serious problems); the article notes that some projects currently being discussed between corporations and nonprofits will not take shape until 1990.

2352. Stevenson, J. John. "Splitting the Profits of a Business: Nonprofit Joint Venture." *Philanthropy Monthly* 16 (December 1983): 33-4.

2353. *Stimulating Joint Urban Ventures: Community Organizations and Organized Philanthropy.* Chicago: Trust, 1980.

2354. Street, Wolcott D. *A Beacon for Philanthropy: The American Association of Fund-Raising Counsel through Fifty Years, 1935-1985.* New York: American Association of Fund-Raising Counsel, 1985.

2355. Suhrke, Henry C. "Depreciation Will Be Required for All Nonprofits: The Discussion in the FASB (Financial Accounting Standards Board)." *Philanthropy Monthly* 20 (March 1987): 5-19.

Presents responses to the Financial Accounting Standards Board requirement that all nonprofits recognize depreciation in their general purpose financial statements. Public accounting firms, government auditors, museums, religious organizations and institutions of higher education are represented. The majority of respondents oppose recognizing depreciation.

2356. Suhrke, Henry C. "A Future for the National Charities Information Bureau?" *Philanthropy Monthly* (December 1986): 14-6.

With a nod to its good intentions, author Suhrke campaigns against the National Charities Information Bureau (NCIB) and suggests they close their doors. Citing the admonition to "do no harm" as the minimum standard required of philanthropic organizations, he maintains the NCIB's emphasis on fundraising costs is wrong and cuts off needed funds, and holds the watchdog group responsible for new and more stringent legislation against philanthropy.

2357. Suhrke, Henry C. "Looking Ahead: The Future for Nonprofits." *Philanthropy Monthly* 16 (October 1983): 5-8.

2358. Suhrke, Henry C. "NCIB Standards Shift to Governance and Program: Less Emphasis on Fund Raising." *Philanthropy Monthly* 21 (April 1988): 23-30.

A commentary by Henry Suhrke on the new standards of the National Charities Information Bureau, followed by the full text of the standards. While admitting the final product is a "genuine improvement over the draft" version released in 1987, Suhrke protests the need for affirmative action policies, objects to what he calls a "counterproductive" requirement that prohibits "material conflicts of interest involving board or staff," and continues to advocate the self-regulation of nonprofits as opposed to the burden of regulations and legislation.

2359. Suhrke, Henry C. "Should For-Profit Go Non-Profit?" *Philanthropy Monthly* (October 1980): 5-14.

2360. Suhrke, Henry C. "Some Limitations of Standard Setting." *Philanthropy Monthly* 20 (October 1987): 5-16.

Claims that the National Charities Information Bureau's (NCIB) basic standards in philanthropy erroneously attempt to apply scientifically objective measurements to social science concepts such as governance and management; moreover, Suhrke points out that the thirty-six individuals on the NCIB Standards Review Project Advisory Panel are imposing subjective findings upon nonprofit organizations in the guise of "objective standards," determining specific measures of performance such as percentages of fundraising costs, ratios of resources devoted to program, and minimum numbers for board membership, without the benefit of study or analysis of actual practice among nonprofits. Includes a reproduction of the NCIB standards in draft together with NCIB staff commentary and commentary by Suhrke.

2361. Suhrke, Henry C. "What Does (or Should) Society Want from Non-Profits?" *Philanthropy Monthly* 21 (May 1988): 5-15.

Review of economist Burton A. Weisbrod's *The Nonprofit Economy*, a book that encourages debate about the economic role of nonprofits. Article briefly covers issues such as fundraising costs, the rising number of nonprofits, and the relation between publicness and public support, with major emphasis on Weisbrod's eight recommendations involving public policy toward nonprofits. Recommended: encouraging nonprofits to provide collective goods, and not otherwise; restrictions on "unrelated business activities" and a limited definition of the scope of exempt purposes; abolishing interlocking control of nonprofits and proprietary firms; eliminating tax deductibility as the primary public encouragement for contributions and adopting tax credits (a reduction of the donor's tax bill by a percentage of the donation) in its place; replacing postal subsidies for nonprofits with broader, less restrictive subsidies; replacing the IRS as the principal regulator of the nonprofit sector; and developing a comprehensive statistical program to provide data about the nonprofit sector—its size, composition, outputs, fundraising activities, and interactions with the private market economy.

2362. Sullivan, John. "IRS Commentary on Small Business Administration's 'Statistical Profile of the Nonprofit Sector'." *Philanthropy Monthly* 18 (July-August 1985): 13+.

2363. Sumariwalla, Russy D. "The American Way of Giving." *Charity* 1 (February 1984): 7-8.

2364. Sumariwalla, Russy D. "A Taxonomy of the Tax-Exempt." *Foundation News* 28 (May-June 1987): 66-7, 70.

Article adapted from a paper presented by Sumariwalla at the Spring 1987 Research Forum on the development of a National Taxonomy of Exempt Entities (NTEE). Taxonomy is the study of the general principles of scientific classification—the systematic distinguishing, ordering and naming of type-groups within a subject-group. A classification system is crucial to the dissemination and retrieval of information. The National Center for Charitable Statistics (NCCS), a program of Independent Sector, has developed a taxonomy of tax-exempt entities. The system enables the quantification of data, promotes uniformity, and provides quality data for research. The developmental steps of establishing the taxonomy are discussed in the article along with an explanation of the system. The system is designed as a 3-part, 4-digit code representing a major group code, a major activity or program focus code, and a beneficiary code. Also included is *Taxonomy at a Glance*, a table of suggested major group codes A-Z organized in nine categories. The classification system is in place. The next step is to ensure that it is adopted and used nationally.

2365. Taylor, Karla. "Ten Ways That Institutions Are Raising New Resources." *Currents* 9 (September 1983): 18-21.

2366. Taylor, Karla. "Why We Need Better Marketing." *Currents* 12 (July-August 1986): 44-50.

2367. Technical Assistance Center. *Colorado Non-Profit Wage and Benefits Survey, 1984.* Denver, Colo.: Technical Assistance Center, 1984.

2368. Teltsch, Kathleen. "Nonprofit Group Goes into Business." *New York Times* (6 March 1983): 53.

2369. Temme, Jim. "How's the Weather in Your Organization?" *Nonprofit World Report* 2 (January-February 1984): 12+.

2370. Theatre Communications Group. *Survey, 1979.* New York: Theatre Communications Group, 1980.

2371. "Time for the Annual Headache: The Annual Report." *Channels* 35 (January 1983): 2-3.

2372. Tolchin, Martin. "Nonprofit Hospitals Join to Offer Insurance." *New York Times* (6 August 1985): A-12.

2373. "Touring Rosters and Funding Support." *PARS Information Quarterly* 1 (Summer 1987): 3-7.

Focuses on Touring Rosters, which list groups and individual performers who have been "approved" by particular organizations. These organizations assist in funding performances by paying a portion of the fees (approximately twenty to fifty percent support). Provides a detailed example of the Tour Roster directed by the Western States Arts Foundation (WESTAF), one the six Regional Arts Agencies to have been established in the continental U.S., and one that will allow up to fifty percent of its Roster to be out-of-region performers. Also lists the fifty State Arts Agencies, noting whether they coordinate their own Touring Rosters and/or offer other assistance programs.

2374. "Toward Fairer Competition between For-Profit and Non-Profits." *Philanthropy Monthly* 17 (July-August 1984): 14-6.

2375. Troyer, Thomas A. *Charities and the Fiscal Crisis: Creative Approaches to Income Production.* Reprint. New York: Bender & Co., 1983.

2376. Turner, Judith Axler. "Computer Grants May Depend on Whom You Know." *Chronicle of Higher Education* 26 (15 June 1983): 25-6.

2377. Twin Cities Regenerative Funding Project. *In Search of Cash Cows: Exploring Money-Making Options for Nonprofit Agencies.* Minneapolis, Minn.: Peter C. Brown & Associates, 1983.

Describes nonprofits' experiences with revenue-generating programs, types and potential sources of money-making programs, financing and developing business plans, and implementing the programs.

2378. Twin Cities Regenerative Funding Project. *New Money for Nonprofits.* Minneapolis, Minn.: Peter C. Brown & Associates, 1982.

2379. United States Jaycees Foundation. *Uplift. What People Themselves Can Do.* Salt Lake City, Utah: Olympus Publishing Co., 1974.

2380. United States. Small Business Administration. *Unfair Competition by Nonprofit Organizations with Small Business: An Issue for the 1980's.* Washington: U.S. Small Business Administration, 1983.

2381. "Universities Come to the Aid of Neighboring Communities." *New York Times* (7 July 1985): 1+.

Describes universities embarking on projects to bolster their communities.

2382. Upshur, Carole C. *How to Set Up and Operate a Non-Profit Organization.* Englewood Cliffs, N.J.: Prentice-Hall, 1982.

Guidelines for incorporating, raising funds and writing grant proposals.

2383. Van Slyke, Judy K. "Position-by-Position Salary Data. Part 3." *Currents* (September 1982): 19-22.

2384. Vandegriff Research. *National Survey on Women in the Arts and Humanities.* Bethesda, Md.: Vandegriff Research, [1975].

2385. "Venture Censure." *Grantsmanship Center News* 11 (September-October 1983): 6-7.

2386. Ver Schave, Sally. "Assessing the Strengths and Challenges of Your Group." *Fund Raising Management* 15 (December 1984): 60-1.

Outlines the steps to meaningful self-assessment for the nonprofit.

2387. Volunteer Lawyers for the Arts. *To Be or Not to Be: An Artist's Guide to Not-for-Profit Incorporation.* New York: Volunteer Lawyers for the Arts, 1982.

Covers the critical questions you should ask yourself and your attorney about nonprofit incorporation.

2388. Volunteer-The National Center. *Building Partnerships with Business: A Guide for Nonprofits.* Arlington, Va.: Volunteer-The National Center, 1987.

2389. Walters, Jonathan. "Do Nonprofit Organizations Compete Unfairly with Business?" *Association Management* 36 (May 1984): 66-9.

2390. Ward, Haskell G. *A Matter of Vision: Community and Economic Development in the Philadelphia Area.* Philadelphia: Pew Charitable Trusts, 1987.

Study conducted for the Pew Charitable Trusts which chronicles the story of Philadelphia area neighborhood-based organizations. The Philadelphia area was a casualty of the nationwide economic displacement and population dislocation of the 1970's. During the period it was popular among the policy-makers to allow the neighborhoods to decline because the Northeast region, they claimed, was a victim of urban evolution. These opinions led to institutional obstacles when communities attempted development projects; they were "redlined" by the local banks and federal agencies refused monies until areas were cleaned up or obtained commitments from the city. This report shows how against economic, social, and political odds the communities fought for their neighborhoods. The story is told in the words of the grassroots leaders themselves and it is a unique view of neighborhood-based community development. The study is enhanced by profiles of four community development leaders done in an oral history format and includes photographs.

2391. Wark, John. "Faith, Hope, and Chicanery." *Washington Monthly* 18 (January 1987): 25-31.

Two reporters with *The Orlando Sentinel* expose charity frauds. The authors describe both fraudulent charities and grossly mismanaged charities. According to the authors, without disclosure laws and regulation, charity fraud and mismanagement have gone largely unchecked. This freedom allows charities to operate like someone on an open-ended expense account. The burden of searching for and obtaining financial information on charities is left to the public. The authors have made a particular study of the Shriners, one of the largest charities, which has "been misleading the public for years." "In 1984, the Shrine circuses reaped an estimated profit of $17.5 million. The charity's own records show the hospitals received only one percent...they spent more money in 1984 and earlier years on conventions and parties than on the hospital charity." "Even money the public contributed directly to the hospital endowment was not used to treat disabled or burned children." In addition to the Shriners, the article names other well-known charities that have a wide variety of questionable financial practices. Many do not meet, or even come close, to the minimum sixty percent program services payout guideline recommended by the National Charities Information Bureau. The out-and-out frauds, dishonest charities and professional fundraisers cited in the article by state regulators and assistant attorneys general from several states used dying children, missing children, multiple sclerosis research, Christa McAuliffe's death, and the record and video of the *Super Bowl Shuffle* to dishonestly raise funds from the public.

2392. Weber, William, and Suzanne Weber. "Long-Range Process Planning: The First Cut." *Grantsmanship Center News* 9 (July-August 1982): 24-35.

2393. Weitzman, Jerrold. "A Project to Assess the Effectiveness and Efficiency of Philanthropic Programs." *Philanthropy Monthly* 17 (May 1984): 12-4.

2394. Welch, Randy. "Lending Sources for Nonprofits." *Grantsmanship Center News* 13 (May-June 1985): 10+.

2395. Welles, Chris. *Conflicts of Interest: Nonprofit Organizations.* Twentieth Century Fund Report. New York: Twentieth Century Fund, 1977.

2396. "When Should the Profits of Nonprofits Be Taxed?" *Business Week* (5 December 1983): 191+.

2397. White, Michelle J., ed. *Nonprofit Firms in a Three Sector Economy.* Washington: Urban Institute Press, 1981.

2398. "Who Needs D and O Insurance?" *Foundation News* 29 (July-August 1988): 52-4.

Article poses and answers the most common questions by grantmakers concerning directors and officers liability insurance (D & O). As most claims against nonprofits are employment discrimination and wrongful termination cases, D & O earns its keep by paying the defense costs, even though most suits are dismissed or settled without the plaintiff winning. The Chubb Group's D & O policy, endorsed by the the Council on Foundations' board of directors, covers not only the directors and officers, but also all of the employees, the committee members, the volunteers and, most importantly, the foundation itself, which is often named as a party in any lawsuit. If an organization cannot afford insurance, the article advises having legal counsel review state law and bylaws to be certain directors and officers may be indemnified, and to "run a tight ship" by keeping careful minutes of all board meetings and alerting board members to the importance of attending board meetings, as frequent absences can weaken a case in the event of a lawsuit.

2399. Wilder Foundation, Amherst H. *Nonprofit Decline and Dissolution Project Report.* St. Paul, Minn.: Amherst H. Wilder Foundation, 1987.

Researched and prepared by Management Support Services, a program of the Amherst H. Wilder Foundation. Documents a year-long project that set out to discover how and why nonprofit organizations fall into existence-threatening situations, the methods they use to confront the issue of survival, and how they go out of business. Bibliography.

2400. Williams, Roger M. "Centering on the Underdog." *Foundation News* 28 (September-October 1987): 18-24.

Profiles the Center for Community Change, the largest free-of-charge provider of technical assistance, and its director Pablo Eisenberg, one of philanthropy's most successful fundraisers.

2401. Williams, Roger M. "For Fee or Charity?" *Foundation News* 24 (March-April 1983): 18-23.

2402. Williams, Roger M. "The Wave of Self-Help." *Foundation News* 29 (July-August 1988): 28-31.

Examines the rise of self-help groups, which recently received credibility when the Surgeon General, C. Everett Koop, told nearly 200 health-care providers at a national workshop, "I believe self-help is an effective way of dealing with problems, stress, hardship and pain." Discusses the funding sources and the history of some self-help programs, focusing on operations in California and New York, with inside views of actual sessions. Ends with an examination of the pros and cons of the self-help movement.

2403. Williams, Roger M. "Why Don't We Set Up a Profit-Making Subsidiary?" *Grantsmanship Center News* (January-February 1982): 14-23.

2404. Wilson, Jane. *New Information Technologies for the Nonprofit Sector.* New York: Foundation Center, 1982.

Examines the current and potential applications of information technologies in the nonprofit sector. Offers brief descriptions of how eight diverse nonprofit organizations have successfully used such technologies either to the direct benefit of those they serve or for the improvement of internal operations. Each of these case studies was originally presented at a 1981 conference, and was followed by a discussion session. Several broad themes arose from these discussions including: the need for basic information to ease consumers' confusion; the importance of planning in order to avoid unnecessary expense; and the difficulty of identifying a user's needs and finding a technology with characteristics to match.

2405. Wineman, Steven. *The Politics of Human Services: Radical Alternatives to the Welfare State.* Boston: South End Press, 1984.

2406. Winston Foundation for World Peace. *Financial Survey of Peace and International Security Organizations: A Preliminary Report.* Boston: Winston Foundation for World Peace, 1988.

The financial condition of arms control and disarmament organizations is a constant concern to funders, one heightened by events of the last year. The October 1987 stock market crash, changes in income taxes for wealthy individuals, and, perhaps most important, a new period of superpower detente may have an impact on the total amount of money available to the non-profit groups working for peace. With those trends in mind, the Winston Foundation surveyed the peace community to learn more about these organizations' current condition, their anticipated gains and losses, and their perceptions of needs. The Foundation sent surveys to 122 national groups and received seventy-seven completed surveys. The same survey was sent to a sampling of local groups, receiving twenty responses from thirty-one organizations.

2407. Wolpert, Julian, and Thomas A. Reiner. "The Philanthropy Marketplace." *Economic Geography* 60 (1984): 197-209.

Nonprofits rely in part on gifts for their revenues. However, the authors say the process by which donations are made to museums, educational institutions, charitable and welfare organizations, and other nonprofits is not well understood. In this paper, gifts are considered in the context of an interaction between donor and recipient; each has a range of possible motivations and expectations. For example, the donor may expect control, while the recipient may expect the widest latitude in use of funds with respect to targeting; there also may be divergence in clarity of agendas and intensity of preferences. According to Wolpert and Reiner, locational factors are important inasmuch as such donor-recipient markets generally function at a metropolitan or smaller scale.

2408. Wrolstad, Marwin. "Nonprofit Enterprise: Through the Eyes of For-Profit." *Nonprofit World Report* 2 (May-June 1984): 10.

2409. Wrolstad, Marwin. "The Unrelated Business: Concerns for Profits and Losses." *Nonprofit World Report* 2 (March-April 1984): 8.

2410. Wrolstad, Marwin. "The Unrelated Business: The Myth of 'Stare Decises'." *Nonprofit World Report* 2 (July-August 1984): 8+.

2411. Young, Dennis R. "Compensation in the Nonprofit Sector." *Nonprofit World* 5 (May-June 1987): 26-7.

Examines how nonprofits manage to do work of higher quality or prestige than competing institutions in the business and government sectors, yet pay less for the labor needed to do that work.

2412. Young, Dennis R. *If Not for Profit, for What?* Lexington, Mass.: D.C. Heath, 1983.

This is a study of entrepreneurship in the nonprofit sector and of what, in a world without conventional profit incentives, distinguishes entrepreneurs from those in government and business. Young's twenty-one case studies of nonprofit entrepreneurship serve as the basis for the development of a theory of the behavior of nonprofit organizations, which in turn underlies Young's analysis of policy implications for the sector. Among his conclusions are that the nonprofit sector is inherently flexible and diverse and accommodates a wide variety of entrepreneurial motivations. He also feels that the sector tends to exhibit mixes of entrepreneurial motivation that "offer assurances of trustworthy behavior but a slowness or response to societal demands for service." He suggests that the sector's qualities can only be understood in the context of its economic environment, especially those qualities related to performance.

2413. Young, Dennis R. *Incentives and the Nonprofit Sector.* Program on Non-Profit Organizations, no. 53. New Haven, Conn.: Institution for Social and Policy Studies, 1982.

2414. Young, Dennis R. *Motives, Models, and Men: An Exploration of Entrepreneurship in the Nonprofit Sector.* Program on Non-Profit Organizations, no. 4. New Haven, Conn.: Institution for Social and Policy Studies, 1978.

2415. Young, Dennis R. *Performance and Reward in Nonprofit Organizations: Evaluation, Compensation, and Personnel Incentives.* Program on Non-Profit Organizations, no. 79. New Haven, Conn.: Institution for Social and Policy Studies, 1984.

Looks at how personnel of nonprofit organizations are evaluated, selected, deployed, and compensated. Based on information gathered from literature review, report analysis, and interviews. Gives an industry by industry discussion of compensation levels, performance evaluations, and the relationship of performance to evaluation.

2416. Yunker, Katherine K. *The Market for the Development of Appalachian Kentucky: Government Demand and Nonprofit Supply.* Program on Non-Profit Organizations, no. 59. New Haven, Conn.: Institution for Social and Policy Studies, 1982.

2417. Zald, Mayer N. *Organizational Change: The Political Economy of the YMCA.* Chicago: University of Chicago Press, 1970.

This book presents an analysis from the standpoint of political economy of the history of the Young Men's Christian Association (YMCA) and a case study of one urban association, the YMCA of metropolitan Chicago. Zald was intrigued by the underlying complexity of YMCAs, commonly thought of as bland organizations serving the recreational needs of the middle class, which, he asserts, are in many cities directly linked with urban change and ferment. Through his study of the YMCA, an organization based in a changing urban environment and presenting an interesting amalgam of organizational characteristics, Zald develops an analytic framework that can be used to investigate and explain the directions of change in any large-scale organization. It takes into account the interaction between environment, internal organization, and political life.

2418. Zedlewski, Sheila, and Jack A. Meyer. *Toward Ending Poverty among the Elderly and Disabled: Policy and Financing Options.* Washington: Urban Institute Press, 1987.

Examines a set of public policy proposals for substantially reducing poverty among elderly and disabled persons in the United States, and suggests a variety of ways that the costs of achieving this objective could be met. Policy options to improve the Supplemental Security Income (SSI) program include: increasing the benefit guarantee to the aged poverty line; increasing the guarantee to the mid-point between current law and the aged poverty line; liberalizing the assets test; increasing the cash income disregard; reducing the age at which one can apply for benefits; and combining a higher benefit guarantee with the options that expand benefit eligibility. The study estimates how many persons would be affected by each option, what their characteristics are, and how program participation is likely to be affected by each change. Options for financing the improvements to SSI involve either broadening the tax base or reducing government expenditures. Both categories are fully explored, with the conclusion that the improvements would not only be effective in reducing poverty among the elderly and disabled, but the financing of these improvements would have a modest and equitable impact on the non-poor elderly and non-elderly population. Includes bibliography.

2419. Zesch, Lindy. "Theatre Facts 87." *American Theatre* 5 (April 1988): 24-33.

Reports on the mixture of positive and negative trends in the finances and productivity of America's nonprofit professional theaters during 1987. The Theatre Communications Group's survey reveals the smallest growth rate of private contributions from individual and corporate donors in the five-year period studied, while federal support dollars dropped sharply. Total operating costs rose only slightly, suggesting little expansion of activity, while compensation levels for artists and other administrative staff and production/technical personnel did not keep pace with the low-level inflation. However, the survey suggests that theaters are employing good management to control costs, resulting in a slightly improved bottom-line compared to the previous four years. Other good news: a rise in box office income, attendance, support from foundations and income from endowments and fundraising events.

6

NONPROFIT ORGANIZATION ADMINISTRATION

2420. Abrams, Susan. *Recommendations for Improving Trustee Selection in Private Colleges and Universities.* Washington: Association of Governing Boards of Universities and Colleges, 1980.

2421. Accounting Advisory Committee. *Report to the Commission on Private Philanthropy and Public Needs.* Washington: Commission on Private Philanthropy and Public Needs, 1974.

2422. *Accounting Principles and Reporting Practices for Certain Nonprofit Organizations: A Discussion of the More Important Provisions of the AICPA Statement of Position.* New York: Price Waterhouse & Co., 1978.

2423. Acker, David D. "Skill in Communication: A Vital Element in Effective Management." *501(c)(3) Monthly Letter* 7 (April 1987): 146-50.
Effective communication skills guidelines to assist the nonprofit executive with both the content and form of the presentation as well as the presentation itself.

2424. Adams, John D., ed. *Transforming Work: A Collection of Organizational Transformation Readings.* Alexandria, Va.: Miles River Press, 1984.

2425. Ader, Elaine R. *Impact Evaluation: A Field Manual.* Privately Printed, 1981.

2426. Adolph, Val. *Managing Crisis.* Vancouver, B.C., Canada: Voluntary Action Resource Centre, 1982.

2427. Ahlbrandt, Roger S., Jr. "Is Technical Assistance Worth Funding?" *Help For Nonprofits* 1 (March 1983): 7-8.

2428. Alkin, Marvin C., Robert O. Bothwell, and Marilyn W. Levy. *Conducting Evaluations: Three Perspectives.* New York: Foundation Center, 1980.

2429. Allen, Wendy. "Profit Making Subsidiaries, Are They for You?" *Board Letter* 28 (Winter 1988): 4-6.
Step-by-step assessment guide for determining the feasibility of entrepreneurial ventures by nonprofit organizations.

2430. Alley, Brian, and Jennifer Cargill. *Keeping Track of What You Spend: The Librarian's Guide to Simple Bookkeeping.* Phoenix, Ariz.: Oryx Press, 1982.

2431. Alliance of New York State Arts Councils. *Management Pamphlets. Series 1.* New York: Alliance of New York State Arts Councils, 1982.

2432. Alvey, Wendy, and Beth Kilss, eds. *American Statistical Meeting. Statistics of Income and Related Administrative Record Research: Selected Papers.* Detroit: American Statistical Association, 1981.

2433. Alvo, Stella, and Kate Shackford. *Funding for Social Change: How to Become an Employer and Gain Tax Exempt Status.* Vol. 1. New York: Funding for Social Change, 1977.

2434. American Accounting Association. *An Inventory of Data Sources for Governmental and Other Nonprofit Organizations.* Columbia, Mo.: University of Missouri-Columbia, 1985.

2435. American Bar Association. *Directory of Private Bar Involvement Programs.* Chicago: American Bar Association, 1988.
Provides descriptions of the Private Bar Involvement (PBI) programs in each state which offer legal assistance to low-income and poverty-level communities through the services of private attorneys. In addition to basic program contact information, the directory contains information regarding special service projects sponsored by PBI programs; technical

assistance which may be obtained from various organizations; training materials that are available through established programs; and a statistical analysis of PBI projects.

2436. American Council on Education. National Committee on Preparation of a Manual on College and University Business Administration, comp. *College and University Business Administration.* Washington: American Council on Education, 1952.

2437. American Institute of Certified Public Accountants. *Audits of Certain Nonprofit Organizations.* New York: American Institute of Certified Public Accountants, 1981.

2438. American Institute of Certified Public Accountants. *Exposure Draft: Proposed Guide: The Audits of Certain Nonprofit Organizations.* New York: American Institute of Certified Public Accountants, 1980.

2439. American Institute of Certified Public Accountants. *Hospital Audit Guide.* New York: American Institute of Certified Public Accountants, 1972.

2440. American Institute of Certified Public Accountants. *Statement of Position (on) Accounting Principles and Reporting Practices for Certain Nonprofit Organizations: A Proposed Recommendation to the Financial Accounting Standards Board.* New York: American Institute of Certified Public Accountants, 1978.

2441. American Planning Association. *Planning Consultant Roster.* Chicago: American Planning Association, 1987.

2442. American Stock Exchange. *Options for Institutions: Charitable Organizations.* New York: American Stock Exchange, 1981.

2443. "And What Would You Do about Mr. Gotrocks?" *Foundation News* 24 (January-February 1983): 62-4.

2444. Anosike, Benji O. *How to Form Your Own Profit/Non-profit Corporation without a Lawyer.* 2nd ed., rev. New York: Do-It-Yourself Legal Publishers, 1986.

Practical guide to incorporating while avoiding lawyers' fees. Includes information applicable to all fifty states, step-by-step procedures, sample illustrated forms, advice on writing the purpose clause on the certificate of incorporation (along with examples), and corporate tax-shelter methods. Assists in setting up business, professional and nonprofit corporations. Bibliography.

2445. Anthes, Earl W., Jerry Cronin, and Michael Jackson, eds. *The Nonprofit Board Book: Strategies for Organizational Success.* West Memphis, Ark.: Independent Community Consultants, 1983.

Provides an in-depth examination of the duties and responsibilities of the nonprofit board. Chapters address the issues of: productive board meetings, effective board committees, board recruitment and orientation, board and staff relations, finances and fundraising, public relations, and board liability. Includes numerous questionnaires, checklists, evaluation forms, and worksheets.

2446. Anthes, Earl W., and Jerry Cronin, eds. *Personnel Matters in the Nonprofit Organization.* West Memphis, Ark.: Independent Community Consultants, 1987.

Nineteen authors address personnel issues common to all nonprofits. The first section of the book is devoted to contextual issues including chapters on *Human Issues in the Rapidly Changing Nonprofit Organization, Legal Issues for the Nonprofit Employer,* and *Union-Management Issues in the Nonprofit Organization.* The second section of the book deals with functional issues: *Hiring—Screening and Selecting Staff for the Nonprofit Organization, Trauma in the Boardroom—Terminating and Hiring the CEO, Performance Appraisal—A Basic Tool for Employee Evaluation and Development.* Includes bibliography and index.

2447. Anthony, Robert N. *Financial Accounting in Nonbusiness Organizations: An Exploratory Study of Conceptual Issues.* Stamford, Conn.: Financial Accounting Standards Board, 1978.

2448. Anthony, Robert N., and Regina E. Herzlinger. *Management Control in Nonprofit Organizations.* Chicago: Richard D. Irwin, 1975.

2449. Anthony, William P. "Effective Strategic Planning in Nonprofit Organizations." *Nonprofit World Report* 2 (July-August 1984): 12-6.

2450. Apostolou, Nicholas G., Hartwell G. Herring, III, and Walter A. Robbins, Jr. "Are Changes Needed in Private Foundation Reporting Practices?" *Management Accounting* (November 1980): 39-41, 47.

2451. Arnett, Trevor. *College and University Finance.* New York: General Education Board, 1922.

2452. Ashfield, Jean A. *Friends of the Library Handbook: Organization, Administration, Public Relations, Fund Raising.* Somersworth, N.H.: New Hampshire Printers, 1980.

2453. Associated Grantmakers of Massachusetts. *The Clearinghouse for Technical Assistance.* Boston: Associated Grantmakers of Massachusetts.

2454. Association of Governing Boards of Universities and Colleges. *Composition of Governing Boards, 1985: A Survey of College and University Boards.* Washington: Association of Governing Boards of Universities and Colleges, 1986.

2455. *The Audit Committee: The Board of Trustees of Nonprofit Organizations and the Independent Accountant.* New York: Price Waterhouse & Co., [1978].

2456. Aufrecht, Steven E. "Protecting Personal Information: What Every Nonprofit Should Know." *Grantsmanship Center News* 12 (September-December 1984): 32-6.

2457. Auster, Ethel. *Managing Online Reference Services.* New York: Neal-Schuman Publishers, 1986.

2458. Bailen, June. "On-Line Databanks Provide Valuable Information Link." *Fund Raising Management* 14 (February 1984): 64-5.

2459. Ballenger, Bruce P. "By Itself, Media Isn't Enough." *Community Jobs* 6 (July-August 1983): 4.

2460. Barker, Robert R. *Managing Educational Endowments.* Educational Endowment Series. New York: Ford Foundation, [1969].

2461. Bates, Don. *Communicating and Moneymaking. A Guide for Using Public Relations to Improve Fund-Raising Success.* New York: Heladon Press, 1979.

2462. Bates, Don. "How to Be a Better Board Member: Guidelines for Trustees." *Voluntary Action Leadership* (Winter 1983): 19.

2463. Bates, Don. *Trends in Nonprofit Public Relations.* Unpublished, 1986.

Results of a questionnaire which asked respondents to rank twenty trends in public relations for nonprofit organizations. In descending order (with many tying for a place), the most important trends are: the increasing influence of traditional marketing concepts on the practice of public relations in nonprofits and the rising expectations of nonprofit CEOs regarding the value of public relations to their organizations; the increasing need to measure and evaluate the effectiveness of public relations; public concern about the credibility and accountability of nonprofits and competition among nonprofit organizations for the same audiences; the use of new technology as a means of speeding up and extending the reach of public relations activities, the use of these tools and techniques to support fundraising, and a growing number of nonprofits with paid public relations staff.

2464. Baughman, James C. *Trustees, Trusteeship, and the Public Good: Issues of Accountability for Hospitals, Museums, Universities and Libraries.* Westport, Conn.: Greenwood Press, 1987.

Incisive study of behind-closed-doors deeds and misdeeds in nonprofit boardrooms. The author provides a clear, concise, and informative discussion of modern nonprofit trusteeship, utilizing data from court records, newspapers, professional literature, and interviews. Trustees, Baughman claims, are generally not aware of their full accountability to the public; his exposition on the judicial status of the relationship between nonprofits and the public good offers a guide for trustees wishing to foster better trusteeships.

2465. Becker, Sarah, and Donna Glenn. *Off Your Duffs and Up the Assets: Common Sense for Non-Profit Managers.* Rockville, N.Y.: Farnsworth Publishing Co., 1985.

Primer for nonprofit managers that explains management and accounting principles in understandable and entertaining terms. Book covers four major areas: managerial skills, financial management, control of management, and management of change. Useful explanations for the novice as well as new ideas for the practiced manager.

2466. Bell and Howell Microcomputer Systems. *Funding Report for Microcomputers.* San Francisco: Photo & Sound Co., 1980.

2467. Benedict, Stephen, and Linda C. Coe. *Arts Management: An Annotated Bibliography.* Rev. ed. New York: Center for Arts Information, 1980.

2468. Bennett, Joseph. "Little Things Mean a Lot: The Care and Feeding of Speakers." *Currents* 10 (March 1984): 24-6.

2469. Bennett, Paul. *Up Your Account-Ability: How to Up Your Serviceability and Funding Credibility by Upping Your Accounting Ability.* Washington: Taft Products, 1973.

2470. Berner, Roberta. "Technical Assistance: What Role for Foundations and Corporations." *Help For Foundations* 1 (March 1983): 9-10.

2471. Biegel, Len, and Aileen Lubin. *Mediability: A Guide for Nonprofits.* Washington: Taft Products, 1975.

2472. Black, Ralph. "What Do You Do with a Do-Nothing Board Member?" *American Symphony Orchestra League* (1987).

After tossing around a few facetious punishments, the author acknowledges that leadership must effectively and specifically inform each trustee of his or her share of responsibility in order for them to meet the challenge. For those trustees who habitually fail to meet goals set for them, he advocates not re-electing them.

2473. Blumenthal, Larry. "Hired Guns: Tips on Finding and Using Consultants." *NonProfit Times* 2 (August 1988): 21-3.

Fundraising veterans offer hard-earned advice on the process of choosing and dealing with consultants, including tips on checking out the firm or individual before signing a contract, and the importance of remaining in control after a consultant has been hired, especially in relation to expenses, management and direction.

2474. *The Board of Directors.* Reprint. San Francisco: Grassroots Fundraising Journal, 1984.

Selected articles from issues printed in 1982 and 1983.

2475. Borst, Diane, and Patrick J. Montana, eds. *Managing Nonprofit Organizations.* New York: Amacom, 1977.

2476. Bortin, Virginia. *Publicity for Volunteers.* New York: Walker & Co., 1981.

2477. Boss, Richard W. *Telecommunications for Library Management.* Professional Librarian. White Plains, N.Y.: Knowledge Industry Publications, 1985.

The choices faced by the librarian of the 1990s will be far more complex than those of today. Not only will telecommunications play a bigger role, it will also involve more competing suppliers, and the librarian will have to choose among voice communications providers, primarily data communications providers, and primarily video communications providers. For this reason, a library's initial procurement decision should anticipate these trends and take them into consideration. This volume serves as an introduction to telecommunications for library management covering concepts, standards, short, medium and long-distance telecommunications, and transmission suppliers, equipment, and software products, all to help the librarian become telecommunications literate and insure against losing control of one of the major decision-making areas in the library of the rapidly-approaching future. Includes appendixes of selected telecommunications suppliers and a list of acronyms; a glossary; and bibliography.

2478. *The Bottom Line: Improved Management of Nonprofit Organizations. Proceedings.* Dallas, Tex.: Human Systems, 1979.

2479. Boyd, Thomas D., ed. *Annual Conference.* Minneapolis, Minn.: Nonprofit Management Association, 1984.

Provides six selected articles originally presented at the 1984 Annual Conference of the Nonprofit Management Association. The first three articles examine the ways in which nonprofit managers create and maintain the organization's sense of direction, purpose, and appropriateness. The articles in the second part of the journal characterize entrepreneurial thinking, offer a collaborative approach to computerization, and present issues and approaches for the assistance provider working outside his or her own culture.

2480. Brace, Paul K., Robert Elkin, and Daniel D. Robinson. *Reporting of Service Efforts and Accomplishments.* Stamford, Conn.: Financial Accounting Standards Board, 1980.

2481. Brakeley, John Price Jones. *The Brakeley Compensation Report: A Report on the Compensation of Chief Development Officers in Higher Education.* Stamford, Conn.: Brakeley, John Price Jones, 1986.

Presents initial compensation data for chief development officers (CDOs) at institutions of higher education in order to track career patterns with regard to the most significant factors affecting levels of compensation, to provide a reference for development professionals in career planning and compensation, and to provide colleges and universities with a sample of compensation data on mid-level development positions for use in developing plans and budgets. The profile for the average CDO is: a male, 47.4 years of age, working in current position for 5.7 years (out of 14.9 in the profession), earning $64,957 in salary at a university with an operating budget of $215 million, an endowment of $94 million, and a student enrollment of 18,136, where he is responsible for bringing in just over $18 million (at a cost of just under twelve cents on the dollar).

2482. Breen, George Edward, and A.B. Blankenship. *Do-It-Yourself Marketing Research.* 2nd ed. New York: McGraw-Hill, 1982.

2483. Brinckerhoff, Peter C., Leslie L. Wilson, and Judith L. Groves. *A Business Planning Guide for Not-for-Profit Organizations.* Management Strategies for Not-For-Profits Monograph Series, no. 3. Springfield, Ill.: Corporate Alternatives, 1987.

Designed to give nonprofits the basic tools and concepts necessary to decide whether entrepreneurial ideas can be developed into viable, profitable business ventures to support their mission. This step-by-step guide includes how to deal with the issue of related and unrelated income, a complete sample business plan, how to prepare the financial aspects of a plan (with sample forms to help organize the information), a business plan checklist, and a bibliography of resources.

2484. Brinckerhoff, Peter C. "Management Audit: A Key to Cost Control." *Nonprofit Executive* 3 (December 1983): 1-2.

2485. Brooklyn In Touch Information Center. *Building a Board of Directors.* Brooklyn, N.Y.: Brooklyn In Touch Information Center, 1984.

2486. Brooklyn In Touch Information Center. *How to Conduct a Meeting.* Fact Sheet for the Nonprofit Manager, no. 4. Brooklyn, N.Y.: Brooklyn In Touch Information Center, 1988.

Fourth in a series of one page fact sheets written for the nonprofit manager. This fact sheet contains the basic steps and functions for conducting a meeting.

2487. Brooklyn In Touch Information Center. *How to Conduct a Membership Drive.* Fact Sheet for the Nonprofit Manager, no. 5. Brooklyn, N.Y.: Brooklyn In Touch Information Center, 1988.

Fifth in a series of one page fact sheets written for the nonprofit manager. It reviews the purpose, preparation, recruitment, and assessment of the nonprofit organization's membership drive with a few comments on retention of new members, stressing that adequate attention be given them.

2488. Brooklyn In Touch Information Center. *How to Develop a Board of Directors.* Fact Sheet for the Nonprofit Manager, no. 1. Brooklyn, N.Y.: Brooklyn In Touch Information Center, 1988.

First in a series of useful one page fact sheets for nonprofit managers. It covers the nonprofit board's composition, qualifications, recruitment, selection process and orientation.

2489. Brooklyn In Touch Information Center. *How to Form and Operate a Nonprofit Corporation.* Fact Sheet for the Nonprofit Manager, no. 2. Brooklyn, N.Y.: Brooklyn In Touch Information Center, 1988.

Second in a series of one page fact sheets written for the nonprofit manager. This fact sheet reviews the steps, applicable form and results for the nonprofit organization's articles of incorporation, federal employer identification number, federal tax exemption, state registration and reporting, and reporting to the IRS.

2490. Brooklyn In Touch Information Center. *How to Prepare a Budget.* Fact Sheet for the Nonprofit Manager, no. 3. Brooklyn, N.Y.: Brooklyn In Touch Information Center, 1988.

Third in series of one page fact sheets written for the nonprofit manager. This fact sheet contains a sample proposed budget for a twelve month period.

2491. Brown, Kathleen M. *Applied Empirical Research on Nonprofit Organization Management: Survey and Recommendations.* Institute for Nonprofit Organization Management Working Paper, no. 1. San Francisco: Institute for Nonprofit Organization Management, 1986.

2492. Brown, Peter C. *The Complete Guide to Money-Making Ventures for Nonprofit Organizations.* Washington: Taft Group, 1986.

Handbook offers practical advice for any organization seeking to develop or expand earned income endeavors to supplement revenues secured from foundations, government grants, or membership fees. Covers organizational positioning, brain-storming money-making ideas, gaining board and staff support, minimizing risk in new ventures, market research and analysis, business plan development, and start-up funding.

2493. Bryce, Herrington J. *Financial and Strategic Management for Nonprofit Organizations.* Englewood Cliffs, N.J.: Prentice-Hall, 1987.

Intended for use as a college-level textbook, a training tool for managers and boards of directors of nonprofit organizations, and as a desk reference for these officials. The book challenges both those who believe that business techniques are readily transferable to nonprofits and those who believe they are totally inapplicable to them. Bryce views nonprofits as economic organizations with welfare missions rather than welfare organizations with welfare missions. Thus, making profits or surpluses is perfectly consistent with the legal authority of nonprofits. The text discusses how a nonprofit organization can increase its revenues including individual and corporate gifts, and the sale of goods and services which results in a positive cash flow; objectives of financial planning and strategic management; the role of budget and financial statements; setting and evaluating financial targets; and the severe legal penalties imposed on both management and organization for the abuse and violation of the principles and laws which govern nonprofit organizations. Tax reform and the impact it can have on the financial strategies of the nonprofit and its donors is examined, but is only analyzed in respect to the *Tax Reform Act of 1969.* Throughout the book, numerous organizations are used as illustrations. In addition, there are tables, lists, reprints of documents and newspaper articles, charts, and diagrams. Each chapter ends with a summary and conclusions, endnotes and/or references and an appendix.

2494. Buhl, Lance, and William Hoffman. *Indirect Costs.* Washington: Council on Foundations, 1986.

2495. *Building Networks: Cooperation As a Strategy for Success in a Changing World.* Dubuque, Iowa: Kendall/Hunt Publishing Co., 1984.

Provides step-by-step guidance to forming a network, from the basic beginnings to the administration needed to maintain its momentum. Includes resource materials to aid in transferring ideas into action, a bibliography listing publications that deal with networking and group dynamics, as well as a directory of organizations offering technical assistance and helpful information.

2496. Bushnell, Shirley W. "On Using Professional Fund-Raising Counsel." *Chronicle of Non Profit Enterprise* 3 (Summer 1984): 6-7.

2497. Business Volunteers for the Arts/Seattle. *A Buyer's Guide to Microcomputers for Non-Profit Arts Organizations.* Seattle, Wash.: Greater Seattle Chamber of Commerce, 1983.

2498. Center for Arts Administration. *Survey of Arts Administration Training.* New York: American Council for the Arts, 1987.

Provides current information about graduate level arts administration and management training programs in the United States and Canada. Recognizing that highly skilled, professional administrators are vital to the arts, these programs emphasize the technical, analytical, human and conceptual skills necessary for successful management. Appendixes include information on select seminars, workshops, and institutes geared toward a broad range of subjects and issues in arts administration, and a listing of job placement services.

2499. Center for Arts Information. *Management Assistance for the Arts: A Survey of Programs.* New York: Center for Arts Information, 1980.

2500. Center for Board and Administrator Relations. *Board Member Manual.* Sioux City, Iowa: Center for Board and Administrator Relations, 1988.

Manual written to assist the board member understand their role on the board and to maximize their efforts for the organization or institution. In twenty-two pages the manual reviews the board member's responsibilities and roles including planning, policy setting, and finances. Personal commitment, relationships with administrators and staff are explored as well as evaluating your board, required training for board members and how to keep board meetings running smoothly. Forms are included for meeting evaluation, evaluating the board, and expenses.

2501. Center for Community Change. *The Community Reinvestment Act: A Citizen's Action Guide.* Washington: Center for Community Change, 1981.

2502. Center for Management Systems. *How to Manage Cutbacks and Develop Local Funding Sources.* Sioux City, Iowa: Center for Management Systems, 1981.

2503. Center for Urban Economic Development. *Business Spinoffs: Planning the Organizational Structure of Business Activities.* Chicago: Center for Urban Economic Development, 1982.

Result of a technical assistance project of the University of Illinois Center for Urban Economic Development, manual discusses legal, taxation, and managerial matters associated with nonprofits setting up and controlling for-profit businesses without threatening their tax-exempt status; under what conditions for-profit status is preferable to nonprofit status; and whether a business can be operated in-house or has to be spun off.

2504. Chapman, Terry S., Mary L. Lai, and Elmer L. Steinbock. *Am I Covered for? A Guide to Insurance for Nonprofit Organizations.* San Jose, Calif.: Consortium for Human Resources, 1984.

2505. Churchman, David. "Negotiating the Terms of a Grant." *Grants Magazine* 6 (March 1983): 9-15.

2506. Cleveland Foundation. *Staff Reference Manual.* 2nd ed., rev. Cleveland: Cleveland Foundation, 1981.

2507. Cleveland Foundation. *Staff Reference Manual.* Cleveland: Cleveland Foundation, 1973.

2508. Clifton, Roger L., Richard L. Reinert, and Louise K. Stevens. *The Road Map to Success: A Unique Development Guide for Small Arts Groups.* Boston: Massachusetts Cultural Alliance, 1988.

Manual helps managers and trustees of small cultural organizations to assess their own organization by comparing its development against the examples offered. Presents three ways in which small cultural organizations develop: artist/founder-led; community-based; and collectively-run. Each section covers stages of development (existence, transition, and dynamic stability) for artistic product; leadership and board model; organizational structure and systems; financial management and planning; fundraising; and marketing and earned income. There is also a section of review questions concerned with each area of development, a reference bibliography, and a separately-bound assessment kit.

2509. Cloud, Deborah A., ed. *The Volunteer Leader: Essays on the Role of Trustees of Nonprofit Facilities and Services for the Aging.* Washington: American Association of Homes for the Aging, 1985.

Examines the role and responsibilities of trustees in nonprofit organizations and presents guidelines which trustees and directors can use to evaluate their performance and identify areas for improvement. Composed of essays by authors who have direct knowledge of and experience with organizations serving the elderly, but much of the information can be applied generally to any voluntary board. Topics include organizational mission and values; board powers, responsibilities, and liabilities; board composition and education; organizing and conducting board meetings; hiring and evaluating the administrator; board-staff relations; board members' role in strategic planning, fundraising, and financial accountability; assuring quality of life; and assessing corporate behavior.

2510. Coe, Linda C., and Stephen Benedict. *Arts Management: An Annotated Bibliography.* Washington: National Endowment for the Arts, 1978.

2511. Cok, Mary Van Someren. *All in Order: Information Systems for the Arts.* Washington: National Assembly of State Arts Agencies, 1981.

2512. Collins, Chuck. *Directory of Socially Responsible Investments.* 2nd ed. New York: Funding Exchange, 1986.

Listings for forty-six community organizations, advisors and brokers offering assistance to investors who want to make socially responsible investments. Grouped into three major categories: community investment (loan funds, credit unions, banks and advisors); socially screened investment (mutual and money market funds, advisors and brokers); and research and resources. All entries are selected on the basis of a proven record of quality and investor safety; a policy of providing information and opportunities to individual investors; a national operational ability; and a demonstrated broad interest in socially responsible investment issues, including peace, environmental impact, affirmative action, employee ownership, fair labor policies, worker health and safety, human rights, and the nature of foreign investment.

2513. Committee on College and University Accounting and Auditing. *Audits of Colleges and Universities.* New York: American Institute of Certified Public Accountants, 1975.

2514. Committee on Voluntary Health and Welfare Organizations. *Audits of Voluntary Health and Welfare Organizations.* New York: American Institute of Certified Public Accountants, 1974.

2515. Committee to Defend Reproductive Rights of the Coalition for the Medical Rights of Women. *The Media Book: Making the Media Work for Your Grassroots Group.* San Francisco: Committee to Defend Reproductive Rights, 1981.

2516. *Community Resources Directory.* 2nd ed. Detroit: Gale Research Co., 1984.

Basic guide provides information on over 2,000 U.S. volunteer organizations and other resource groups, services, training events, and local program models. The directory is divided into the following three sections: resource groups and publications, training programs, and local volunteer programs. The programs cover subject areas such as the arts, business assistance, civic affairs, consumer services, education, social services, the physical environment, and transportation. The entries provide basic information on each organization, including name, address, and description. Indexes are provided by organization name and program emphasis.

2517. Community Service Society. *Technical Assistance Guide (TAG). A Directory of Resources for New York Non-Profit Organizations.* New York: Community Service Society, 1986.

Directory of selected resources for technical assistance services for organizations in the City of New York. Sixty-seven organizations are alphabetically listed. Organization profile includes organization name, address, telephone number, contact person, and additional comments. Contents include a brief article on *Working Successfully With Consultants* and a subject index.

2518. Connors, Tracy Daniel, and Christopher T. Callaghan, eds. *Financial Management for Nonprofit Organizations.* New York: Amacom, 1982.

2519. Connors, Tracy Daniel. *The Nonprofit Organization Handbook.* 2nd ed. New York: McGraw-Hill, 1988.

Anthology of articles by thirty-four experts provides practical advice and guidelines on all aspects of nonprofit management, including securing tax-exemption, program planning and fundraising, public relations, and financial management. Index contains reproduction of IRS Form 990 and instructions.

2520. Conrad, William R., Jr., and William E. Glenn. *The Effective Voluntary Board of Directors: What Is It and How It Works.* Rev. ed. Chicago: Swallow Press, 1983.

Provides basic ground rules for effective nonprofit board action and explains many important board issues, including definitions of policy, legal concerns, role of board and staff, recruitment and evaluation of board members, the function of committees, and the conducting of successful meetings. Includes practical applications, numerous worksheets, exhibits, bibliography, and a comprehensive series of appendixes.

2521. Conrad, William R., Jr. *Guide to Public Relations for Voluntary Organizations.* Downers Grove, Ill.: Voluntary Management Press, 1983.

2522. Cook, Jonathan B. "Defining Purpose. Part 2: Writing the Statement of Purpose." *NonProfit Times* 1 (March 1988): 36, 38-42.

Examines the issues and problems that arise when choosing a statement of purpose for a nonprofit organization, from distinguishing between results and methods (methods for achieving a desired outcome should not appear in the purpose statement), to choosing between a broad statement and a narrow focus, and the advantages of each.

2523. Corbin, John. *Managing the Library Automation Project.* Phoenix, Ariz.: Oryx Press, 1985.

2524. Corder, Robert E. "Trustees' Role in a Major Campaign." *Board Letter* (8 December 1982): 3+.

2525. Council for Advancement and Support of Education. *Guidelines for the Administration of Matching Gift Programs.* Washington: Council for Advancement and Support of Education, 1983.

2526. Council of Better Business Bureaus' Foundation. "Understanding Nonprofit Financial Statements. Part 1." *Insight* 5 (1984): 1-4.

Guidelines to help donors, board members, volunteers, and staff extract and understand the most important elements of nonprofit financial statements. Part 1 covers the auditor's opinion, the balance sheet, fund accounting, the statement of income and expenses, and the notes. Part 2 offers advice on interpreting expenses, evaluating extenuating circumstances, and assessing the statement of functional expenses.

2527. Council of Better Business Bureaus' Foundation. "Understanding Nonprofit Financial Statements. Part 2." *Insight* 6 (1984): 1-4.

2528. Council on Foundations. *Communications and Public Affairs Guide.* Washington: Council on Foundations, 1984.

2529. Council on Foundations. *Directors and Officers Liability Insurance.* Resources for Grantmakers Series. Washington: Council on Foundations, 1983.

2530. Crawford, Robert W. *In Art We Trust: The Board of Trustees in the Performing Arts.* Columbus, Ohio: Ohio State University, 1981.

2531. Croake, Elizabeth A. *How to Raise Money for Your Organization.* Mattituck, N.Y.: TFL Press, 1977.

2532. Cronbach, Lee J. *Toward Reform of Program Evaluation: Aims, Methods, and Institutional Arrangements.* San Francisco: Jossey-Bass Publishers, 1980.

2533. Cronin, Jerry. "Ethics and the NMA." *Grantsmanship Center News* 2 (May-June 1983): 62-3.

2534. Cronk, Thomas. "Keep Board Members Motivated and Working." *Nonprofit Executive* 2 (June 1983): 3+.

2535. Cross, Sally S. "Examining the Role of a Hospital Trustee." *Fund Raising Management* 14 (November 1983): 58+.

2536. Cultural Assistance Center. *Spacesearch: A Guide to Cultural Facilities in New York City.* New York: Cultural Assistance Center, 1984.

2537. Dade Council of Arts and Sciences. *The Starter Kit: A Resource Program for New Community Cultural Organizations.* Miami, Fla.: Dade County Council of Arts and Sciences, [1981].

2538. D'Amico, Philip, and George Epstein. "Computers for Nonprofits. Computer Equipment: How to Know What You Want." *Grantsmanship Center News* 13 (March-April 1985): 20-7.

2539. D'Amico, Philip. "How a Computer Thinks (and How It Doesn't)." *Grantsmanship Center News* 12 (September-December 1984): 25-31.

2540. Daniels, Raymond D. *University-Connected Research Foundations.* Norman, Okla.: University of Oklahoma, 1977.

2541. Daughtrey, William H., Jr., and Malvern J. Gross, Jr. *Museum Accounting Handbook.* Washington: American Association of Museums, 1978.

2542. Davis, Barbara H. "How and Why to Hire a Consultant." *Whole Nonprofit Catalog* 5 (Winter 1987-88): 7-9.

Extremely helpful article discusses the type of work consultants do (urgent, specific tasks; ones that require objectivity; the design of systems, structures, or processes; brokering; and the implementation of unpleasant and often radical changes); where to look for a consultant; how to select and hire a consultant, including advice on interviewing and preparing a comprehensive contract; and what to do to make the consultancy as productive as possible, including the etiquette of using a consultant; establishing internal agreement before hiring a consultant; appointing a staff member as "heir" to the consultant; and having a consultant help implement his or her own recommendations, emphasizing action and results over words.

2543. Davis, Kenneth A. "How Your Agency Can Organize a Conference." *Grantsmanship Center News* 13 (March-April 1985): 20-7.

2544. Davis, Larry Nolan, and Earl McCallon. *Planning, Conducting, and Evaluating Workshops: A Practitioner's Guide to Adult Education.* Austin, Tex.: Learning Concepts, 1974.

2545. Dayton, Kenneth N. "Define Your Roles: Nonprofits Must Have Clearly Understood Responsibilities for Their CEO's and Trustees." *Foundation News* 26 (May-June 1985): 68+.

2546. Dayton, Kenneth N. *Governance Is Governance.* Washington: Independent Sector, 1987.

Speech given at Independent Sector's Second Professional Forum on May 7, 1985 by Ken Dayton. Examines appropriate roles and responsibilities in governing and managing nonprofit organizations, emphasizing the distinction between the two. Provides position descriptions of the president and CEO, and of the board of trustees and the chairman of the board, stressing that the chairman of the board should not be the CEO. In addition, Dayton advocates a strict rotation policy for board members, including the chairman of the board.

2547. de Oliveira, Fred H. "Management Accounting Techniques for Not-for-Profit Enterprises." *Management Accounting* (November 1980): 30-4.

2548. De Thomasis, Brother Louis. "Churches That Face Peril Need Marketing Skills." *Fund Raising Management* 13 (January 1983): 32-43.

2549. Debatin, June B. "Guiding Charitable Funds." *Trusts & Estates* 127 (July 1988): 24, 26, 28, 30.

Guide for trustees setting the investment objectives and strategies for medium and smaller size funds, with an aim to including assets likely to provide a return in excess of the inflation rate. Objectives should include providing an ever increasing stream of cash flow, maintaining the purchasing power of the assets over time, and developing investment goals and objectives for the management of the assets with a high probability of achieving the fund's spending and rate of return objectives within the risk tolerance of the trustees. Recommends separate investment pools to provide flexibility and allow specific objectives to be obtained and offers advice on selecting a manager. Analyzes the impact of the rates of return, investment risk, and liquidity with divestment in companies who do business in South Africa as an example of social investing constraints. Spending and gifting activity and an acceptable risk tolerance should be foremost in mind when trustees review their fund's asset strategy.

2550. Dewan, Bradford N. "Operation of a Business by Non-Profit, Tax Exempt Organizations." *Economic Development and Law Center* 10 (March-April 1980): 14-6.

2551. Dewey, Barbara I. *Library Jobs: How to Fill Them, How to Find Them.* Phoenix, Ariz.: Oryx Press, 1987.

Guide for both library administrators seeking to hire and librarians looking for professional positions at all levels in libraries. Reviews the job market and educational considerations for professional library positions; discusses the planning process for developing job descriptions using proven techniques from the business and public management fields; the relationship between legal requirements in the hiring process and the activities of recruitment and job announcement posting procedures; the creation and use of resumes, cover letters, and references; interviewing guidelines and techniques; procedures for making and accepting job offers; the initial period of organizational entry; unique factors for the hiring and placement of middle to advanced-level library professionals; and motivation for advancement. Extensive bibliography on topics from orientation of a new library employee to burn out.

2552. Dickson, John P., and Sarah S. Dickson. "How to Conduct a Marketing Research Project." *Nonprofit World Report* 3 (May-June 1985): 14+.

2553. Dickson, John P., and Sarah S. Dickson. "How to Plan a Marketing Research Project." *Nonprofit World Report* 3 (January-February 1985): 14+.

2554. Dickson, John P., and Sarah S. Dickson. "The Importance of Marketing Research to the Nonprofit Organization." *Nonprofit World Report* 2 (November-December 1984): 12-4.

2555. DiGregorio, Beverly J. "Establishing a Nonprofit Corporation: A Case Study." *Grants Magazine* 10 (March 1987): 7-12.

DiGregorio utilizes both her experience in creating the Crime Victims Fund and Peter Drucker's principles of planning to explore the reality of starting a nonprofit organization. Provides examples for the parts of a concept paper, a tool useful in enlisting support for a cause, including a statement of the mission and goals of the organization, documentation of data establishing need for the services being proposed, a definition of a course of action, and a listing of objectives. The concept paper aids in gaining the commitment of people with the prestige and resources needed to create a charitable corporation, from serving on a founding board of directors to obtaining that important first donation. The initial two or three years of fundraising serve the dual purpose of securing funds and promoting name recognition; releasing information on the accomplishments of the nonprofit can greatly stimulate contributions. The successful creation of a nonprofit corporation, DiGregorio insists, results from a vision based on a genuine need and much hard work by people with enduring commitment to the organization's mission.

2556. DiMaggio, Paul J. *Managers of the Arts.* Research Division Report [National Endowment for the Arts. Research Division], no. 20. Washington: Seven Locks Press, 1988.

Examines the backgrounds, education, and career experiences of top managers in arts agencies. The managers evaluate the preparation they had prior to taking their positions in the art field; the rewards and satisfactions they receive from their jobs; and their expectations for future employment. They also offer opinions on a range of policy and management issues, many of which relate to their organizations' missions, thus providing useful insights for all managers in the nonprofit sector.

2557. DiMaggio, Paul J., ed. *Nonprofit Enterprise in the Arts: Studies in Mission and Constraint.* Yale Studies on Nonprofit Organizations. New York: Oxford University Press, 1986.

Part of the Yale Studies on Nonprofit Organizations' series, this volume is a collection of scholarly articles by economists, lawyers, sociologists, and management specialists which inquire into the production and distribution of art in the United States. Because nonprofit organizations, rather than proprietary firms or government agencies, play a predominant role in American artistic life it is essential that their crucial part is understood. The essays examine the ways in which certain artistic enterprises are organized as nonprofit firms rather than as for-profits or public agencies; the problems caused within arts management and policy; the ways cultural institutions are changing, or are likely to change; and the policy alternatives that we all face. The volume is arranged in five sections: *Why Are So Many Arts Organizations Nonprofit?*, *Between the Market and the Public Purse*, *Management and Mission*, *Nonprofit Enterprise in Commerical Cultural Industries*, and *European Perspectives*. The text contains endnotes, index and brief notes on contributors.

2558. Direct Mail/Marketing Association. *Membership Roster.* Washington: Direct Mail/Marketing Association, 1978.

2559. Dodson, Jerome, and Michael Kieschnik. "Cash Management for Smaller Non-Profit Organizations." *Grassroots Fundraising Journal* 3 (February-March 1984): 3-7.

2560. "Does Your System Get in the Way of Your Mission?" *Nonprofit Executive* 3 (November 1983): 3-4.

2561. "Donald Young: Unique Loan Finances Modernization Projects." *Nonprofit Executive* 3 (March 1984): 2-3.

2562. Donaldson, Lufkin and Jenrette. *Managing Endowment Capital. The Endowment Conference.* New York: Donaldson, Lufkin & Jenrette, 1972.

2563. Donaldson, Lufkin and Jenrette. *Managing Endowment Capital. The Endowment Conference.* New York: Donaldson, Lufkin & Jenrette, 1970.

2564. Donaldson, Lufkin and Jenrette. *Managing Endowment Capital. The Endowment Conference.* New York: Donaldson, Lufkin & Jenrette, 1969.

2565. Donaldson, Lufkin and Jenrette. *Managing Endowment Capital. The Endowment Conference.* New York: Donaldson, Lufkin & Jenrette, 1971.

2566. Donors Forum Emergency Loan Fund, ed. *A Fiscal Management Handbook for Small Nonprofit Organizations.* 1986 ed., rev. Chicago: Donors Forum Emergency Loan Fund, 1986.

Resource guide designed to enhance the understanding and skills of small nonprofits' managers in fiscal management. Includes chapters on fiduciary responsibility; finance management; cash flow management ("the critical chapter"); setting up a bookkeeping system, a chart of accounts, and internal controls; reading, understanding and utilizing financial and audit statements; the audit process; and tax and other required reports. Includes tips on hiring and managing financial staff and reconciling bank statements, as well as a fiscal management audit for use as an assessment tool and for sensitizing the board of directors to their fiduciary responsibilities. Glossary of fiscal terms.

2567. Donors Forum of Chicago. *Can Do 2.* 2nd ed. Chicago: Donors Forum of Chicago, 1980.

2568. Drago, John, Alan Andolsen, and Richard Levitz. "Assessing the Future Needs of Nonprofit Management." *Fund Raising Management* 15 (August 1984): 22+.

2569. Drucker, Peter F. *Innovation and Entrepreneurship.* New York: Harper & Row, 1985.

Analyzes the entrepreneurial economy. Part 1 tells where and how the entrepreneur searches for innovative opportunities. Part 2 looks at established businesses, public-service institutions, and new ventures, explaining the problems and importance of innovation in each area. Part 3 gives entrepreneurial strategies.

2570. Duca, Diane J. "The Independent Sector Can Be Strengthened If Boards Assume Their Proper Responsibilities." *Board Letter* 10 (July 1983): 7+.

2571. Duca, Diane J. "Keeping the Board on a Roll: Interview with Amy Harwell." *Board Letter* 11 (September 1983): 1-2.

2572. Duca, Diane J. "Most Boards Are Still Operating in the 19th Century. Interview with Harvey Newman." *Board Letter* 10 (July 1983): 1+.

2573. Duca, Diane J. *Nonprofit Boards: A Practical Guide to Roles, Responsibilities, and Performance.* Phoenix, Ariz.: Oryx Press, 1986.

Examines the legal responsibilities of the board, methods of organizing for maximum effectiveness, policy management and planning, recruiting and sustaining board membership, orientation and training of board members, the board's fiscal responsibilities, how to hold effective board meetings, the board's evaluation responsibilities, and ways to build working relationships. Appendixes include a board member job description and a board self-evaluation instrument. Annotated bibliography.

2574. Edie, John A. "Calling All Directors: Have You Checked Your Insurance Policy Lately?" *Foundation News* 25 (May-June 1984): 61.

2575. Eldon, Elder, comp. *Will It Make a Theatre.* New York: Drama Book Specialists, 1979.

2576. Elkin, Robert, and Mark Molitor. *Management Indicators in Nonprofit Organizations: Guidelines to Selection and Implementation.* Baltimore, Md.: University of Maryland, 1984.

2577. Elliott, Eleanor. "On Being a Trustee." *Foundation News* 25 (May-June 1984): 38-41.

2578. Epstein, George, and Philip D'Amico. "Understanding Software." *Grantsmanship Center News* 13 (May-June 1985): 37+.

2579. Ewald, William. "The Board Is Key in Strengthening Nonprofit Corporations." *Nonprofit Executive* 2 (May 1983): 3.

2580. *Executive Session: The Best of the Nonprofit Executive.* Washington: Taft Group, [1984].

2581. Fear, Richard A. *The Evaluation Interview.* New York: McGraw-Hill, 1984.

2582. Financial Accounting Standards Board. *Conceptual Framework for Financial Accounting and Reporting: Objectives of Financial Reporting by Nonbusiness Organizations.* Stamford, Conn.: Financial Accounting Standards Board, 1978.

2583. Financial Accounting Standards Board. *Financial Accounting in Nonbusiness Organizations: An Overview of the Research Report by Robert N. Anthony.* Stamford, Conn.: Financial Accounting Standards Board, 1978.

2584. Financial Accounting Standards Board. *Objectives of Financial Reporting by Nonbusiness Organizations.* Stamford, Conn.: Financial Accounting Standards Board, 1980.

2585. Financial Accounting Standards Board. *Statement of Financial Accounting Concepts. No. 2: Qualitative Characteristics of Accounting Information.* Stamford, Conn.: Financial Accounting Standards Board, 1980.

2586. Financial Accounting Standards Board. *Statement of Financial Accounting Concepts. No. 3: Elements of Financial Statements of Business Enterprises.* Stamford, Conn.: Financial Accounting Standards Board, 1980.

2587. Financial Accounting Standards Board. *Statement of Financial Accounting Concepts. No. 4: Objectives of Financial Reporting by Nonbusiness Organizations.* Stamford, Conn.: Financial Accounting Standards Board, 1980.

2588. Firstenberg, Paul B. *Managing for Profit in the Nonprofit World.* New York: Foundation Center, 1986.

Primer focusing on the process of managing tax-exempt, nonprofit organizations. In six sections, the work demonstrates how current management techniques can be applied to nonprofit organizations through a discussion of: the nature of nonprofit organizations—legal, tax and economic considerations; financing growth—fundraising, commercial income, and endowments; marketing; managerial tools; board relations; and entrepreneurial management. Includes profiles of Ruth Maxwell and McGeorge Bundy.

2589. Fisher, John. *How to Manage a Nonprofit Organization.* Toronto, Canada: Management and Fund Raising Centre, 1978.

2590. Fisher, John. *Money Isn't Everything: A Survival Manual for Nonprofit Organizations.* Toronto, Canada: Management and Fund Raising Centre, 1977.

2591. Flanagan, Joan. "Members, Committees, and the Board of Directors." *Grantsmanship Center News* 12 (January-February 1984): 34-43.

2592. Foote, Joseph. "Grantees' Overhead Costs: Should Foundations Pay?" *Foundation News* 24 (May-June 1983): 51+.

2593. "For a Price, Free Advice: Some Thoughts on the Role of Consultants." *Grassroots Fundraising Journal* 3 (February-March 1984): 10-2.

2594. Foundation for American Communications. *Media Resource Guide.* Los Angeles: Foundation for American Communications, 1981.

2595. Foundation for the Extension and Development of the American Professional Theatre. *Investigation Guidelines for Setting Up a Not-for-Profit Tax-Exempt Regional Theatre.* New York: Foundation for the Extension and Development of the American Professional Theatre, 1979.

Contains investigation guidelines for establishing a theater; management resource list; suggested bibliography; guidelines for audience development and audience surveys (an essential element of a theater's market research); a sample development campaign schedule; guidelines for an effective foundation proposal; compilation of direct mail principles resulting from a study by the National Research Bureau; accounting principles and reporting practices of nonprofit organizations; sample budget worksheets for physical production, performance, administration, advertising and promotion, theater/house, returnable bonds and deposits, and totals; a managerial analysis of boards of directors in the performing arts; a general outline of equipment and supplies recommended for a new theater; and a listing of volunteer lawyers and opportunity resources for the arts.

2596. Fox, Harold W. "Planning: The Key to Nonprofit Success." *Nonprofit World Report* 2 (January-February 1984): 15-6.

2597. Fram, Eugene H. "Nonprofit Boards: They're Going Corporate." *Nonprofit World* 4 (November-December 1986): 20-3, 36.

Fram relates his experiences as a board member and consultant. He states that some nonprofit boards have made the radical change to a corporate model and provides a pattern for other nonprofit organizations to follow in setting up a more workable board structure.

2598. Frantzreb, Arthur C. "Governing Boards: A Governing Board Membership Audit for Nonprofits." *NonProfit Times* 2 (January 1989): 30-1.

Questionnaire allows trustees to assess their commitment, perceptions, experiences, and functions as members of a governing board.

2599. Frantzreb, Arthur C. "Selective Selectivity." *Board Letter* (December 1983): 3-4.

2600. Frantzreb, Arthur C. "Six Questions to Ask before Becoming a Trustee." *NonProfit Times* (July 1987): 30, 32.

Stressing the importance of a trustee as an interpreter of the mission, role and status of an organization, and lamenting nominations just to fill a chair, author Frantzreb offers several key questions a potential board candidate should ask, including: why me, who is the board, what is the board's role, and how does the board function?

2601. Freedman, Marc R. *The Elusive Promise of Management Cooperation in the Performing Arts.* Program on Non-Profit Organizations, no. 98. New Haven, Conn.: Institution for Social and Policy Studies, 1985.

Investigates the disparity between cooperative rhetoric and actual cooperation efforts among performing arts organizations by focusing on the attempt to provide central management services to the resident groups of performing arts centers. "The legacy of this examination," Freedman writes, "is a robust appreciation of the strategic, economic, and political factors that impede, and commonly cripple, well-intentioned cooperative initiatives."

2602. Gaby, Patricia V., and Daniel M. Gaby. *Nonprofit Organization Handbook: A Guide to Fundraising, Grants, Lobbying, Membership Building, Publicity and Public Relations.* Englewood Cliffs, N.J.: Prentice-Hall, 1979.

2603. Galer, Donna. "Achieving Quality in Nonprofits." *Nonprofit World* 6 (May-June 1988): 22-4.

Offers guidelines for achieving quality in a nonprofit organization, including advice on establishing and enunciating a commitment to quality along with clear, objectively measurable standards; discusses pitfalls to avoid (such as shortcomings in orientation and training, lack of delegation, lack of procedures, and poor communication); and stresses evaluation to insure proper management and documentation to show donors, funders, and other interested parties that quality has been achieved.

2604. Gallagher, Richard. *Managing Voluntary Organizations: A Manual for Community Development and Management of Voluntary Organizations.* Buffalo, N.Y.: New York State Association of Councils on Alcoholism, 1979.

2605. Gambino, Anthony J., and Thomas J. Reardon. *Financial Planning and Evaluation for the Nonprofit Organization.* New York: National Association of Accountants, 1981.

2606. Gardner, John W. *Attributes and Context.* Leadership Papers, no. 6. Washington: Independent Sector, 1987.

Gardner develops two related themes here: he first examines how the combination of a particular context or situation and an individual with the appropriate attributes becomes a leader in that situation; and he offers an admittedly incomplete list of qualities or attributes that, in one combination or another, often turn up in all leaders: physical vitality and stamina; intelligence and judgement-in-action; willingness (eagerness) to accept responsibility; task competence; understanding of followers/constituents and their needs; skill in dealing with people; need to achieve; capacity to motivate; courage/resolution/steadiness; capacity to win and hold trust; capacity to manage, decide, and set priorities; confidence; ascendance/dominance/assertiveness; and adaptability, flexibility of approach.

2607. Gardner, John W. *The Heart of the Matter: Leader-Constituent Interaction.* Leadership Papers, no. 3. Washington: Independent Sector, 1986.

Third in a series of papers prepared for *Independent Sector's Leadership Studies Program*, examines the relationship between leaders and followers in its reciprocal aspect of leader-constituent interaction. Gardner explains that, "Good constituents produce good leaders. They not only select good ones, they make them better by holding them to standards of performance. Good leaders, for their part, are not blindly reactive. They select what they will react to, drawing impulses from various parts of their constituency and then charting a course that bears the stamp of their own perceptions and judgment." Considers the degrees of structure and control between leaders and followers, the methods of communication, psychoanalytic interpretations of the relationship, the problems of heterogeneous constituencies and pluralistic pressures, the importance of a leader winning the trust of his followers, and the concept of the "transforming leader," who responds to "fundamental human needs and wants, hopes and expectations, and who may transcend and even seek to reconstruct the political system rather than simply operate within it."

2608. Gardner, John W. *Leadership and Power.* Leadership Papers, no. 4. Washington: Independent Sector, 1986.

Discusses the aspects of power: how it enables leaders to bring about certain intended consequences in the behavior of others, and how many mistrust its placement in the hands of a few. Briefly examines various sources of power, including custom, beliefs, organizations and institutions, public opinion, and economic strength, and constructs an argument for the necessity of leaders in our pluralistic society. Provides examples of leaders uncorrupted by the allure of power, and asserts the need for accountability and the avoidance of abuse.

2609. Gardner, John W. *The Moral Aspect of Leadership.* Leadership Papers, no. 5. Washington: Independent Sector, 1987.

Gardner points out that being an effective leader is not enough; without moral considerations a leader is in danger of falling into the belief that the end justifies the means. He examines the American framework of values in which we judge our leaders and the relationship between leaders and constituents. He develops and illustrates the moral goals of leadership: the release of human potential; the balancing of mutual dependence between the individual and the group; commitment to keeping alive fundamental and traditional human values; and ensuring individual initiative and responsibility.

2610. Gardner, John W. *Renewing: The Leader's Creative Task.* Leadership Papers, no. 10. Washington: Independent Sector, 1988.

Examines the role of leaders in ensuring the continuous renewal of the systems over which they preside. Discusses some of the commonly observed changes that occur in any human system, be it an organization, corporation, or society, as it moves from infancy to maturity; the concerned leader, Gardner avows, will want to keep the energy, flexibility, and openness to new solutions which are associated with young systems while avoiding their disorder, and benefit from the orderliness of maturity while staving off rigidity. Among the measures leaders can take to combat the rigidities of age and enhance the possibility of renewal: nurturing human potential (stressing the promising—and often neglected—strategy of reassignment); encouraging a measure of diversity and dissent; maintaining first-hand contact with reality (original purpose as opposed to procedures and routines); restoring open communication; and remaining sensitive to the currents of change, attuned to emerging trends. Also describes the leader's need for personal renewal, focusing on the problem of stress and methods for relieving and preventing it.

2611. Gardner, John W. *The Tasks of Leadership.* Leadership Papers, no. 2. Washington: Independent Sector, 1986.

Discusses some of the significant functions of leadership including goals, affirming values, motivating, managing, achieving a workable level of unity, explaining, serving as a symbol and representing the group externally.

2612. Geldzahler, Henry. "Managing the Arts." *Wharton Magazine* (Spring 1981): 66-71.

2613. Georgi, Charlotte. *The Arts and the World of Business.* 2nd ed. Metuchen, N.J.: Scarecrow Press, 1979.

2614. "Getting Management Support to Nonprofits." *Nonprofit Executive* 3 (March 1984): 5.

2615. Gilbert, Michael A. "What's Your Organizational Posture?" *Nonprofit World* 6 (July-August 1988): 18-20.

Analyzes the posture of an organization, or the way in which it approaches the goals it wishes to achieve. Beginning with a brief summary of motivation, the article examines four basic ways an organization can go about its mission: as an independent; as a team player, closely aligned with others of similar activity or proximity; corporate merger (a rare alternative); and corporate dissolution. Considers the impact of factors of motivation (especially the desire for status and recognition) on organizational posture, and stresses the need for planning and controlling posture, rather than just letting it happen.

2616. Gilman, Kenneth L. *Computers for Nonprofits*. San Francisco: Public Management Institute, 1981.

Workbook to assist nonprofit organizations considering either computerizing or upgrading their current computer capabilities. Covers the following areas of computer planning: feasibility study, request for proposal, selecting a vendor, contract negotiations, conversion/implementation, service bureaus, and use of consultants. Includes numerous checklists, forms and worksheets to guide the way. For the novice, a glossary of computer jargon is also provided.

2617. Girl Scouts of the U.S.A. *Corporate Planning in Girl Scouting*. New York: Girl Scouts of the U.S.A., 1978.

2618. Goldberg, Gary. "A Model for Pre-Award Grant Information Management Using a Word Processor: In the Move to Bring Technology to Pre-Award Grant Management, a Word Processor May Be More Cost and Time Effective Than a Computer." *Grants Magazine* 7 (December 1984): 235-40.

2619. Golden, Joseph. *Help! A Guide to Seeking, Selecting and Surviving an Arts Consultant*. Syracuse, N.Y.: Cultural Resources Council of Syracuse & Onondaga County, 1983.

2620. Golden, Joseph. *Olympus on Main Street: A Process for Planning a Community Arts Facility*. Syracuse, N.Y.: Syracuse University Press, 1980.

2621. Grace, Kay Sprinkel. "Team Building May Enhance Development Effectiveness." *Fund Raising Management* 14 (July 1983): 30+.

2622. Gray, Sandra Trice. *An Independent Sector Resource Directory of Education and Training Opportunities and Other Services*. 2nd ed. Washington: Independent Sector, 1987.

Identifies existing educational efforts to strengthen the leadership and management of nonprofit organizations. Directory is divided into five sections: profiles of careers in the independent sector (new to this edition, tracing the career paths of successful leaders in a variety of nonprofit organizations); campus-based education and training programs; internships, fellowships and grants to individuals; consultants, executive search firms and other services; and training facilities. Includes information on program concentrations, objectives, duration and fees; entrance and exit requirements; courses; workshops and seminars; and whether scholarships and fellowships are available.

2623. Greenman, D.H. "Record Keeping Is Important." *Philanthropy Monthly* 13 (January 1980): 28-9.

2624. Gross, Malvern J., Jr., and William Warshauer, Jr. *Financial and Accounting Guide for Nonprofit Organizations*. 3rd ed., rev. New York: John Wiley, 1983.

Provides practical and knowledgeable advice for handling the special problems that financial reporting, accounting and control, and federal and state reporting requirements present to nonprofit organizations. The guide blends theory and practical application to assist managers in effectively communicating their organization's financial activities and conditions to constituents and to the public; provides board members and staff with the essentials needed to interpret periodic financial statements; and presents step-by-step section on setting up and keeping the necessary books for a small organization.

2625. Gross, Malvern J., Jr. *The New Accounting Standards for Charitable Organizations and Their Importance to Regulatory Bodies*. New York: Price Waterhouse & Co., 1974.

2626. Gross, Malvern J., Jr. "Nonprofit Accounting: A Revolution in Process." *Price Waterhouse Review* 3 (1973): 1-8.

2627. Gross, Malvern J., Jr. "Nonprofit Accounting: The Continuing Revolution." *Journal of Accountancy* (June 1977): 66-74.

2628. Gross, Malvern J., Jr. "Report on Nonprofit Accounting." *Journal of Accountancy* (June 1975): 55-9.

2629. Gross, Susan. "The Power of Purpose." *Conserve Neighborhoods* 30 (May-June 1983): 291+.

2630. Gross, Susan. "The Ten Most Common Organizational Problems: Getting to Their Source." *Foundation News* 24 (January-February 1983): 25-6.

2631. Gross, Susan. "The Truth about Nonprofit Managers." *Foundation News* 29 (September-October 1988): 48-51.

Offers ten common pitfalls for managers of nonprofit organizations and some suggestions on how to avoid them. Among the pitfalls: thinking there is one right way to manage people, when in reality different kinds of people need to be managed differently; not communicating openly and honestly with your staff; not delegating enough responsibility to others—or delegating it without commensurate authority; and not taking responsibility for the fact that the tone and style of the organization are probably a reflection of your own.

2632. *The Guide to Software for Nonprofits*. New York: NPO Resource Review, 1984.

2633. Guyette, Susan. "Documenting Needs for the Program Plan." *Grants Magazine* 5 (September 1982): 188-95.

2634. Hackett, Edward J. "Managers Should Protect the Unique Strengths of the Nonprofit Workplace." *Nonprofit Executive* 3 (July 1984): 5-6.

2635. Haller, Leon. *Financial Resource Management for Nonprofit Organizations.* Englewood Cliffs, N.J.: Prentice-Hall, 1982.

2636. Haller, Leon. "Nonprofit Organizations: Management, Not Charity." *Grants Magazine* 7 (December 1984): 251-52.

2637. Hansmann, Henry. *Non-Profit Enterprise in the Performing Arts.* Program on Non-Profit Organizations, no. 3. New Haven, Conn.: Institution for Social and Policy Studies, 1978.

2638. Hardy, James M. *Managing for Impact in Nonprofit Organizations: Corporate Planning Techniques and Applications.* Erwin, Tenn.: Essex Press, 1984.

Describes how corporate planning techniques can be applied in nonprofit organizations for both strategic and operational planning.

2639. Harrison, Randall P. *How to Have a Successful Career in Fund Raising.* Washington: Public Service Materials Center, 1985.

2640. Hartogs, Nelly, and Joseph Weber. *Impact of Government Funding on the Management of Voluntary Agencies.* New York: Greater New York Fund, 1978.

2641. Haycock, Nancy. *Dare to Chair.* New York: Community Resource Exchange, [1988].

Directly addresses the role and art of the volunteer board chairperson, providing twenty case examples which share the experiences of other nonprofit organizations in dealing with the most common procedural and developmental problems. Includes discussions on the problem of attendance, recording board meetings, keeping by-laws current and simple, planning and running a meeting, rotating chairpeople, chairing the board of a coalition, fiscal responsibility, dealing with fundraising, defining the organization's mission, expectations for new staff, replacing a founder/director, expanding the board, and reacting to changes in funding. Appendixes include an annotated agenda, a simplified minute taking format, and a board questionnaire.

2642. Heilbron, Louis H. *The College and University Trustee: A View from the Board Room.* San Francisco: Jossey-Bass Publishers, 1973.

2643. Henderson, Albert. "Refine Your Approach to Fundraising." *Association Management* 36 (December 1984): 165-67.

How to use a microcomputer in fundraising.

2644. Henderson, Lyman. *The Ten Lost Commandments of Fund Raising.* Don Mills, Ontario: Davis & Henderson, 1985.

2645. Henke, Emerson O. *Introduction to Nonprofit Organization Accounting.* Boston: Kent Publishing Co., 1980.

Comprehensive guide to nonprofit accounting, book presumes college-level introductory accounting background. Develops logical framework for understanding and solving accounting-related problems of nonprofit organizations through explanatory text and problem-and-exercise sections.

2646. Hennessey, Paul. *Managing Nonprofit Agencies for Results: A Systems Approach to Long-Range Planning.* San Francisco: Institute for Fund Raising, 1978.

Loose-leaf handbook describes a seven-step process for organizational planning with many forms, worksheets, and checklists.

2647. Heywood, Ann M., comp. *The Resource Directory for Funding and Managing Nonprofit Organizations.* New York: Edna McConnell Clark Foundation, 1982.

2648. Hodgson, Richard S. *Direct Mail and Mail Order Handbook.* 2nd ed. Chicago: Dartnell, 1977.

2649. Holder, William W. *The Not-for-Profit Organization Reporting Entity: An Exploratory Study of Current Practice.* New Nilford, Conn.: Philanthropy Monthly Press, 1986.

Reports the results of a study commissioned by the Financial Accounting Standards Board to address the issues of the financial reporting entity for not-for-profit organizations. The financial reporting practices of six types of nonprofit organizations are examined: colleges and universities, hospitals, professional/trade organizations, voluntary health and welfare organizations, philanthropic organizations, and religious organizations. Two basic concepts of the financial reporting entity for nonprofit organizations were revealed by the study: the legal entity and control concepts.

2650. Holtz, Herman. *How to Succeed As an Independent Consultant.* New York: John Wiley, 1983.

Gives guidelines on how to set up, manage, and operate a consulting practice. Chapters cover a wide range of skills needed by the consultant, including sales, marketing, proposal writing, negotiations, fees, contracts, and handling business ethics. The "nuts and bolts" approach might be instructive to an organization contemplating hiring a consultant.

2651. Honig, Lisa. "Developing a Membership Base." *Grassroots Fundraising Journal* 3 (December 1984): 3-5.

2652. Honig, Lisa. "Expanding Your Board of Directors." *Grassroots Fundraising Journal* 2 (June 1983): 8-9.

2653. Honig, Lisa. "Membership Development: Part 2, Attracting New Members." *Grassroots Fundraising Journal* 4 (February 1985): 3-8.

2654. Honig, Lisa. "Record-Keeping for Membership Campaigns." *Grassroots Fundraising Journal* 4 (June 1985): 3-6.

2655. Honig, Lisa. "So, You Want Your Board to Raise Money." *Grassroots Fundraising Journal* 7 (April 1988): 6-8.

Insists that motivation is the essential ingredient in involving the board in fundraising efforts; motivation, in turn, is generated by "sharing ownership" of the organization with the board, allowing them to take part in the decision-making process. It is also important that the board be familiar enough with the organization's activities and finances to answer whatever questions might be raised in a fundraising meeting.

2656. Honig, Lisa. "So, You Want Your Board to Raise Money." *Grassroots Fundraising Journal* 2 (February 1982): 14.

2657. Horwitz, Tem. *Arts Administration: How to Set Up and Run Successful Nonprofit Arts Organizations.* Chicago: Chicago Review Press, 1978.

2658. Houle, Cyril O. *The Effective Board. 1960.* Reprint. New York: Association Press, [1980].

2659. *How to Make Big Improvements in the Small PR Shop.* Washington: Council for Advancement and Support of Education, 1985.

2660. Howe, Fisher. "Trustees and the Fund-Raising Role: Facing the Hard Truth." *AGB Reports* 25 (September-October 1983): 19-23.

2661. Huenefeld, John. *Developing a Mass Promotion for Books: How to Use Ads and Direct Mail to Increase Your Sales.* Bedford, Mass.: Huenefeld Co., 1979.

2662. Hummel, Joan. *Starting and Running a Nonprofit Organization.* Minneapolis, Minn.: University of Minnesota Press, 1980.

Handbook explains the steps involved in setting up a nonprofit organization—how to define goals and plan programs, put together a board of directors, incorporate, become tax exempt, develop a budget, raise funds, set up a bookkeeping system, hire staff, and plan a program of community relations. Includes worksheets and sample budgets which can be easily adapted to the specific needs of individual organizations.

2663. Independent Sector. *Formal Education of Nonprofit Organization Leaders/Managers.* Effective Sector Leadership/Management Program. Washington: Independent Sector, [1988].

Participants in the Academic Focus Group include foundation and corporate giving officers, college and university professors, and nonprofit executives and consultants. They meet to explore existing and potential alternatives for educating nonprofit leaders and managers; make recommendations regarding: curriculum, experiential components, financial resources, coalitions, role of librarians, placement, principles and approaches for the future; identify strategies for implementing these recommendations; exchange information and materials; and expand the network of persons who have a vested interest in nonprofit leadership/management education (appendix includes names and addresses of those attending the Academic Focus Group meeting).

2664. Independent Sector. *Professional Forum Conference. Proceedings.* Washington: Independent Sector, 1985.

Proceedings of a conference covering two themes, governance and board development. Leaders in the nonprofit field discuss what governance is, tell how to develop an effective board, and identify the strategy for assessing a board's performance.

2665. Institute for Nonprofit Organizations. *Organizing Your Way to Dollars.* Toronto, Canada: Management and Fund Raising Centre, [1977].

2666. Institute for Voluntary Organizations. *How to Use Consultants Once You Have Retained Them.* Chicago: Institute for Voluntary Organizations, 1974.

2667. Interface. *Short-Staffed! The Personnel Crisis in New York City's Voluntary Human Service Agencies.* New York: Interface, 1987.

Study of the personnel needs of voluntary agencies in New York City intended to serve as an initial step in understanding some of the key issues confronting this sector. Survey concentrates on employment trends, the extent of personnel recruitment and retention problems, comparable salary levels, employee turnover rates, vacancies, causes of and possible solutions to personnel recruitment and retention problems, and current responses to personnel problems. Findings, in summary, confirm serious personnel recruitment and retention problems in nonprofit human service agencies, especially relating to social workers and direct service positions; a decreasing pool of potential college-educated employees; and non-competitive salary levels as the prime cause of personnel shortages. Preliminary recommendations include: increasing salaries; addressing deficiencies in pensions, health care, and other fringe benefits; further research into certification and licensing requirements for human services postions; changing contracting procedures; methods for increasing the supply of college-educated workers coming into the field; and conducting research into the training of agency clients to fill staff positions in human service programs.

2668. "Interview: Budgeting and Financial Reporting in the Not-for-Profit Sector." *Board Letter* 25 (Spring 1987): 1-4.

Robert J. Fleming, CPA, is a partner with a Seattle, Washington firm which provides audit, tax and management advisory services. In addition, he is the editor of the *Non-Profit Organization Newsletter*. This article was prepared from an article and interview with Fleming in which he discusses critical issues in the financial management of nonprofit organizations. Budgeting is the most important part of the financial management process, states Fleming. The organization must associate its costs with plans for achieving its goals and objectives. Problems can arise because there are limitations in applying traditional budgetary processes to nonprofit organizations. Effectiveness may be measured in social benefits, not dollars. Thus, the usual cost-benefit analysis may not be the most effective way to evaluate the organization. Often budgets are prepared as a necessary evil or as part of funding requirements. After citing the limitations inherent in nonprofit organizations, Fleming discusses the essential components of an effective budget, the necessary financial records and reports, nonprofit audits, and where nonprofits can obtain assistance in developing sound accounting procedures and practices. Fleming also advises board members that they must use relevant guidelines in assessing not-for-profits. Net income, return on investment and earnings per share have less relevance in the nonprofit sector, as nonprofit success is measured by the degree to which it accomplishes its stated purpose. Fleming recommends that board members not only review financial results of the organization but especially relate those results to non-financial information such as number of people served and accomplishments achieved.

2669. Jacob, M.E.L., ed. *Telecommunications Networks: Issues and Trends*. White Plains, N.Y.: Knowledge Industry Publications, 1986.

Telecommunications networks enable institutions and individuals to interact in providing effective information services. The papers in this book offer librarians and information systems' designers a perspective on where the science has been and where it may be going. In most cases the papers assume some familiarity with and understanding of telecommunications terminology and concepts, and so is not casual reading for the novice. The first part supplies a context for looking at telecommunication issues and technology, including an historical overview on policy and related issues, and an expert's view of some of the capabilities wideband networks will provide in the future. Part 2 examines open systems and the Linked Systems Project (LSP) in detail, covering the open systems interconnection (OSI) model, and the practical use of OSI/LSP computer protocols. Part 3 contains specific network perspectives, and Part 4 discusses the possibilities for future trends and options in telecommunications.

2670. Jeffri, Joan. *The Emerging Arts: Management Survival and Growth*. New York: Praeger, 1980.

2671. Jevnikar, Jana, comp. *Video Service Profiles: A Guide to Services for the New York State Video Community*. New York: Center for Arts Information, 1983.

2672. Johnson, Eugene M. "Situation Analysis for Nonprofit Marketing Planning." *Nonprofit World* 4 (July-August 1986): 26-9.

Presents guide to assessing an organization's present position in its current environment in order to develop a marketing plan.

2673. Johnson, R. Bradley. *Risk Management Guide for Nonprofits*. Alexandria, Va.: United Way of America, 1987.

Produced by the United Way of America in association with the Public Risk and Insurance Management Association, this guide provides a comprehensive system to identify loss exposures and assess risk potential in nonprofit organizations and offers advice on how to avoid or reduce those risks that threaten continued operations. Demonstrates that in a time of rapidly inflating premium costs and restricted or even unavailable coverage, commercial insurance is one of the most expensive options for protecting a nonprofit against loss; even when insurance is readily available, purchasing it often leads to serious managerial oversight, and often undermines sound management practice. Thus this guide seeks to make risk management a critical component of any sound management structure and to increase the nonprofit organization's control over the task of protecting against loss.

2674. Johnson, Richard R., ed. *Directory of Evaluation Consultants*. New York: Foundation Center, 1981.

Useful for locating potential evaluators (organizations and individuals), former clients of potential evaluators who could supply information about their performance, and documents generated by evaluators which might be examined before contacting either clients or evaluators to assess the quality of work. Indexed alphabetically by name, geographic location, and by subject.

2675. Joseph, James A. "Attracting and Retaining Talented People." *Foundation News* 26 (May-June 1985): 64+.

Gives six propositions to attract and keep good managers.

2676. Josephson, Michael. "How Ethical Is Creative Accounting?" *Nonprofit World* 2 (May 1988): 38-9.

Discusses the ethical aspects of using creative accounting to circumvent the requirements of a grantor, and insists that those in the nonprofit world have a higher duty to be more objective and circumspect.

2677. Karn, G. Neil. "The Business of Boards Is Serious Business." *Voluntary Action Leadership* (Winter 1983): 14-9.

2678. Karn, G. Neil. "The No-Apologies Budget: How to Justify the Financial Support a Volunteer Program Deserves." *Voluntary Action Leadership* (Spring 1984): 29-31.

2679. Kauffman, Joseph F. "Strengthening Chair, CEO Relationships." *AGB Reports* 25 (March-April 1983): 17-21.

2680. Keens Company, ed. *The Challenge of Change*. New York: Foundation for the Extension and Development of the American Professional Theatre, 1987.

Contains twenty-two edited presentations and position papers from the Foundation for the Extension and Development of the American Professional Theatre's 1986 fifteenth annual national conference. Speakers from a wide range of fields—the arts, management, religion, political science, sociology, education and technology—offer their views about the changes we are currently undergoing, the opportunities and dangers that may lie ahead, and ways in which arts management leaders can not only better understand the nature of change, but can also apply these insights to their work and effect changes that are favorable to their interests.

2681. Kelley, Stephen M. "Nonprofits, Meet the Computer, Computer, Meet the Nonprofits." *Exchange Networks* (Fall 1982): 1+.

2682. Kennedy, Dan S. "Staff and Volunteer Motivation: Helping People Overcome Discouragement." *Nonprofit World Report* 3 (January-February 1985): 12+.

2683. Kiger, Joseph C. *Operating Principles of Larger Foundations*. New York: Russell Sage Foundation, 1954.

2684. King, Richard. "Trustee Leadership Succession: The Key to Long-Term Stability." *Nonprofit World* 6 (May-June 1988): 16-7.

2685. Kinnick, Mary K. "Eleven Criteria for Evaluating the Executive Director." *Board Letter* 16 (Winter 1985): 3-5.

2686. Kirk, Donald J. "FASB's Proposals for 'Nonbusiness' Accounting: Comments from Four Directions." *Philanthropy Monthly* 16 (October 1983): 17-8.

2687. Kirk, W. Astor. *Nonprofit Organization Governance: A Challenge in Turbulent Times.* New York: Carlton Press, 1986.

W. Astor Kirk, management consultant and president of Policy Management Services, defines governance as "those decisions and actions by which the overall performance of an organization is led, guided, directed, and controlled with respect to carrying out the mission that justifies the organization's existence." This book, written primarily for governing board members and executive managers of community-based, public-serving nonprofit organizations, proposes that the tasks to be accomplished are the same in both commercial and non-commercial organizations. Indeed, the book attempts to redefine the roles and responsibilities of governing leaders of nonprofits in the public sector. His approach to nonprofit governance is one of strategic analysis and problem solving techniques which allow the administrators to make conscious choices prior to the stage of crisis management. An index and endnotes are included.

2688. Kirschner, Leo, and Ellen Zisholtz-Herzog. *A Study of Financial Management Issues and Reporting Requirements of South Bronx Community Organizations.* New York: Community Service Society, 1981.

2689. Klein, Kim. "Advisory Boards: No Miracle Solution." *Grassroots Fundraising Journal* 1 (October 1982): 6-8.

2690. Klein, Kim. "Earth to Board Members: Are We All Clear?" *Grassroots Fundraising Journal* 1 (December 1982): 6-7.

2691. Klein, Kim. "Twenty-Nine Ways That Board Members (and Other Volunteers) Can Raise about $500 without Very Much Effort." *Grassroots Fundraising Journal* 2 (December 1983): 7-9.

2692. "Knock, Knock, Who's There: Evaluating Your Board of Directors." *Grassroots Fundraising Journal* 2 (April 1983): 5-8.

2693. Koestler, Frances A. *Planning and Setting Objectives.* New York: Foundation for Public Relations Research and Education, 1977.

2694. Kotler, Philip, O.C. Ferrell, and Charles Lamb. *Case Readings for Marketing for Nonprofit Organizations.* Englewood Cliffs, N.J.: Prentice-Hall, 1983.

2695. Kotler, Philip. *Marketing for Nonprofit Organizations.* 2nd ed. Englewood Cliffs, N.J.: Prentice-Hall, 1982.

2696. Kotler, Philip, and Alan R. Andreasen. *Strategic Marketing for Nonprofit Organizations.* 3rd ed., rev. Englewood Cliffs, N.J.: Prentice-Hall, 1987.

2697. Kramer, Ralph M. *Toward a Contingency Model of Board-Executive Relations in Nonprofit Organizations.* Program on Non-Profit Organizations, no. 86. New Haven, Conn.: Institution for Social and Policy Studies, 1985.

2698. Krashinsky, Michael. *Transactions Costs and a Theory of the Non-Profit Organization.* Program on Non-Profit Organizations, no. 84. New Haven, Conn.: Institution for Social and Policy Studies, 1984.

Argues that the search for a single simple explanation of the nonprofit sector cannot be successful. Krashinsky works through the idea that market failure is responsible for the rise of nonprofit firms by examining the relative advantages of nonprofit and for-profit organizations in overcoming transactions costs, those factors which make contractual arrangements among elements of production and consumers unwieldy. He also points to the critical role of government in the development of the nonprofit sector, and examines the properties of nonprofits which lead governments to subsidize them. Thus, in his paper Krashinsky discusses various transactions costs which give rise to nonprofit firms, and considers when nonprofits might effectively supplement the activities of various public agencies. He concludes that nonprofit organizations overcome one set of transactions costs only to create another, with the relative sizes of those costs depending on the details of each sector.

2699. Kruger, Myra. "Evaluating Public Relations Effectiveness: A Necessary Function." *Channels* 36 (February 1984): 5-6.

2700. Kurtz, Daniel L. *Board Liability: Guide for Nonprofit Directors.* Mt. Kisco, N.Y.: Moyer Bell, 1988.

Prepared under the auspices of the Committee on Non-Profit Organizations of the Association of the Bar of the City of New York. Well-written, well-organized and non-technical in its approach, book describes the legal principles that govern liability of directors and officers of nonprofit organizations. Introductory chapter offers an overview of the nonprofit sector; subsequent chapters describe the composition and structure of nonprofit boards, what nonprofit boards do, the responsibilities of directors, why directors get sued, and indemnification and insurance.

2701. Lampton, William. "Ten Significant Questions You Might Have to Answer." *Fund Raising Management* 18 (December 1987): 80-2.

Reminder to answer the easy questions when fundraising rather than merely preparing for the tough ones. Advises specificity when describing one's organization (tell which services are included and which ones are excluded), knowing the competition (how another organization's services differ from one's own), and being able to defend the organization's staffing (no one wants to support inefficiency).

2702. Landy, Laura. *Something Ventured, Something Gained: A Business Development Guide for Non-Profit Organizations.* Trenton, N.J.: Center for Non-Profit Corporations, 1987.

Because of decreased governmental support and increased competition for charitable contributions, nonprofits are more and more looking to income-generating ventures as a means of supporting their operations. This manual provides a realistic introduction to venturing, details the potential risks and repercussions, and examines the philosophical and practical issues involved. A step-by-step process helps nonprofits: assess their suitability for venturing; evaluate the environment's receptivity to their entrepreneurial bid; research business ideas; and develop a detailed business plan. Appendixes include material on business packaging and a short bibliography.

2703. Lane, Frederick S. "Book Reviews: Managing Not-for-Profit Organizations." *Public Administration Review* (September-October 1980): 526-30.

2704. Lant, Jeffrey L. "Getting the Most from a Consultant." *Nonprofit World* 6 (May-June 1988): 28-30.

Examines the situations in which a nonprofit could benefit from hiring a consultant; methods for finding the right one; and ways to structure the client-consultant relationship. Discusses the usefulness of consultants as supplemental staff; as scapegoats for unpopular decisions; as trainers; as pathfinders in defining or redefining a nonprofit's mission; as decoys in diverting attention from troublesome issues; and as experienced organizational travellers, bringing varied perspectives to any problem. Recommends contacting peer organizations to ask about consultants who have proven useful to them; following articles written by consultants in professional publications; and checking the *Encyclopedia of Associations* and the *Consulting Opportunities Journal* to find a consultant with the skills you need. The protocols of the client-consultant relationship should be specified in the contract, along with a guarantee of at least two return visits after the conclusion of the formal relationship, thus insuring a proper evaluation of the newly implemented systems.

2705. Lant, Jeffrey L. *Money Making Marketing.* Cambridge, Mass.: JLA Publications, 1987.

Lant's philosophy is, "If you have a product or service that makes people's lives better, then it is your responsibility to do whatever is necessary to get it into their hands, as quickly as possible, and so make this a better world." Covers a multitude of creative marketing techniques, from direct mail and telephone promotions to the use of premiums, co-op advertising, and direct-response card decks. Includes listing of resources and specialists who aid in a wide range of marketing areas.

2706. Larkin, Richard F. "Certain Nonprofit Organizations: Proposed Audit Guide." *CPA Journal* (November 1980): 45-8.

2707. Larkin, Richard F. "Effective Budgeting." *American Arts* 14 (January 1982): 27.

2708. Larkin, Richard F. "Financial Management of Nonprofit Organizations: Selected Topics." *American Arts* (January 1983): 1-4.

2709. Larkin, Richard F. "How to Maximize the Return from Your Operational Budget." *Fund Raising Management* 14 (November 1983): 34-8.

2710. Larochelle, Wayne. "Take Custody of Your Assets." *Foundation News* 27 (July-August 1986): 61-3, 76.

Larochelle, vice-president at United Virginia Bank in Richmond, discusses the automation and centralization of nonprofit organization and foundation investments through the use of a custodian. In the article he explains what a custodian is, what they do, and how to select one for an organization.

2711. Lauffer, Armand. *Strategic Marketing for Not-for-Profit Organizations.* New York: Free Press, 1984.

Strategic marketing is a comprehensive approach to the management of internal and external environmental variables that often seem to control the behavior of our organizations. With this definition, the author begins Chapter 1 in which he continues to define marketing terminology including throughput—staff, volunteers and members; input—providers of resources and legitimacy; and output—consumers. Lauffer examines how to establish and maintain productive exchange relationships; use a strategic marketing approach to assess, design, locate, price, budget, schedule, and evaluate a program; raise money; increase grants, contracts, and allocations; and spotlight programs and services through the media as well as through personal appearances and presentations. The book contains numerous tables, diagrams, and exercises which require the reader to question, analyze and review his or her own organization. The appendix contains a role-playing game called *Compacts II* (Collaborative Marketing, Planning, and Action Simulation). The volume also contains a bibliography and an index.

2712. Laundy, Peter, and Massimo Vignelli. *Graphic Design for Non-Profit Organizations.* New York: American Institute of Graphic Arts, 1980.

2713. Leaver, Robert, and Bob Metz. *Artswork: A System for Program Planning and Design (of an Arts Employment Program).* Resource Package, no. 2. Braintree, Mass.: A.L. Nellum & Associates, 1981.

2714. LeBarron, Suzanne, ed. *Directory of Humanities Resource People in New York State.* Albany, N.Y.: New York State Library, 1981.

2715. Lee, James C. *Do or Die: Survival for Nonprofits.* Washington: Taft Products, 1974.

2716. Leerburger, Benedict A. *Marketing the Library.* White Plains, N.Y.: Knowledge Industry Publications, [1981].

2717. Lefkowitz, Rochelle. "Fitting the Pieces Together." *Community Jobs* 6 (July-August 1983): 6-7.

2718. Levene, Victoria E. *A Bibliography on Arts Administration.* Binghamton, N.Y.: State University of New York, 1977.

2719. Levinson, David. "Selecting the Right Management Training Program." *Nonprofit World* 5 (March-April 1987): 28-9.

Guidelines for assessing and choosing a management training program to fit the individual needs of the organization. The author prepared a series of checklists with questions concerning the organization, the proposed training program, degree programs, and in-house training programs. With this self-evaluation the organization can custom-design a training program or select from a prepared training program to best suit the organization's specific needs.

2720. Levis, Wilson C. "Questions Donors Ask and How They Can Be Answered by the Financial Statements of Not-for-Profit Organizations." *Philanthropy Monthly* 16 (September 1983): 21-9.

2721. Lidstone, Herrick K., and R.J. Ruble. *Exempt Organizations and the Arts.* New York: Volunteer Lawyers for the Arts, 1976.

2722. Lindsey, Jonathan A. *Performance Evaluation: A Management Basic for Librarians.* Phoenix, Ariz.: Oryx Press, 1986.

2723. Linkow, Peter R. "Implementing a Long-Range Plan." *Grantsmanship Center News* 11 (January-February 1983): 18-27.

2724. Lipnack, Jessica, and Jeffrey Stamps. *Networking: The First Report and Directory.* New York: Doubleday, 1982.

2725. Listro, John P. "The AICPA Discussion Draft for Nonprofit Organizations." *CPA Journal* 47 (June 1978): 25-8.

2726. Lohmann, Roger A. *Breaking Even: Financial Management in Human Service Organizations.* Philadelphia: Temple University Press, 1980.

2727. Loo, Shirley, ed. *Management by Design: Library Management.* Vol. 2. Washington: Special Libraries Association, 1982.

2728. "Look Carefully at That Contract before You Sign Up with a Fund-Raising Consultant." *FRI Bulletin* 23 (February 1984): 1-2.

2729. Lynn, Edward S., and Joan W. Thompson. *Introduction to Fund Accounting.* Reston, Va.: Reston Publishing Co., 1974.

2730. Lyons, Morgan. "Unlocking the Power of Computers: Statistics for Nonprofits." *Nonprofit World* 6 (July-August 1988): 12-4.

Covers the basics in statistical analysis software while making a case of its value for nonprofit organizations. Points out the usefulness in an improved ability to produce frequencies, descriptive statistics, cross-tabulation, and measures of significance and association. Offers examples of several tasks (a simple distribution of data, simple and complex cross-tabulations, graphs and statistical testing), with special attention given to the *Reflex* software package by Borland.

2731. Maas, Jane. *Better Brochures, Catalogs and Mailing Pieces.* New York: St. Martin's Press, 1981.

2732. MacBride, Marie. *Step by Step. Management of the Volunteer Program in Agencies.* Hackensack, N.J.: Volunteer Bureau of Bergen County, 1979.

2733. MacIntyre, Kate. *Sold Out: A Publicity and Marketing Guide.* New York: Theatre Development Fund, 1980.

2734. Macpherson, David. "Planning: Essential Ingredient of Time Management Formula." *Fund Raising Management* 15 (December 1984): 50+.

2735. Maddalena, Lucille A. *A Communications Manual for Nonprofit Organizations.* New York: Amacom, 1981.

Explains practical methods for implementing, evaluating, and updating organizational communications, an element critical to the health and growth of nonprofits. Contains publicity strategies designed to address the unique needs of nonprofit organizations in communicating their purpose, goals, and significance. Includes sample forms for job descriptions, news releases, volunteer orientations, program checklists, media contact sheets, press invitations, and more.

2736. Mahaffey, J.C. "New Breed, Meet the Old Creed. The Trend to Be like For-Profit Executives May Have Violated a Basic Rule about Who's in Charge." *Association Management* (April 1987): 12.

Observations on what the drive towards professionalism is doing to a basic premise of volunteer organizations—allowing volunteer members to hold the sole decision-making power in the organization. The author believes that professional association executives should follow the principle which states that "committees recommend, boards decide, and staff implements."

2737. Malinconico, S. Michael. "The Use and Misuse of Consultants." *Library Journal* 108 (15 March 1983): 558-60.

2738. *The Management and Financing of Colleges.* New York: Committee for Economic Development, 1973.

2739. Management Assistance Center. *Manual for Board Members of Not-for-Profit Organizations.* Denver, Colo.: Technical Assistance Center, 1987.

Succinct and helpful introduction to the functions and responsibilities of a not-for-profit board.

2740. Management Assistance Group. *Steering Nonprofits.* Washington: National Trust for Historic Preservation, 1984.

2741. "Management Corporations: The New Trend in Human Services." *Executive Administration* (July 1984): 3.

2742. Management Research Center. *Executive Development for Foundation Management: The Results of a National Survey.* Milwaukee, Wis.: Management Research Center, 1986.

Survey undertaken to determine the perceived need among foundation administrators for formal education designed to prepare persons for a career in the field and/or programs designed to facilitate professional development for administrators and their staffs during their careers. The survey reveals little evidence of a demand for foundation administration educational programs, particularly lengthy or formal programs. Contains summary of interviews with foundation administrators, reviews of selected university and internship programs, description of survey methodology, and statistical tabulations and cross-tabulations.

2743. Mancuso, Anthony. *The California Non-Profit Corporation Handbook.* Berkeley, Calif.: Nolo Press, 1984.

Guide to preparing articles and bylaws, obtaining exempt status, keeping legal records, choosing a lawyer, etc.

2744. Margolis, Richard J. "The New Mexican Umbrella." *Foundation News* 25 (May-June 1984): 46-9.

2745. Markoff, John. "Apples for Nonprofits." *NPO Resource Review* 1 (May-June 1983): 1+.

2746. Marlowe, Howard. "Making Your Voice Heard." *Grantsmanship Center News* 11 (January-February 1983): 75-7.

2747. "MAS Program Places Retired Corporate Execs with Nonprofits." *Nonprofit Executive* 3 (April 1984): 6.

2748. Masaoka, Jan. "Computers and Accounting 2: Accounting Software for Nonprofits." *NonProfit Times* 1 (May 1987): 31, 38-9.

Provides a list of factors to consider, such as the accounting expertise of the responsible person, the number of income and expense accounts required, and the number of programs and/or funds that must be tracked, before investigating accounting software packages for nonprofits. Discusses two broad categories of accounting software: integrated software that can be used for both business and fund accounting, and "low end" or simple accounting software. Integrated software with general ledger, payroll, and accounts payable modules can handle the entire accounting system of a nonprofit, including income and expense reports for various programs within the agency. Although developed first for commercial business, recent entries in the field of integrated software are written specifically for organizations on a fund accounting basis. "Low end" accounting software packages are often good choices for the organization with only one fund, but the article warns against attempting to substitute them for bookkeeping or accounting expertise. As a final option, an organization may consider partial computerization of its accounting functions while keeping other books manually. Includes a sample list of a few low end programs and some integrated systems for business use, in addition to a more extensive list of fund accounting programs, noting operating systems, cost per module and total system cost, and the address and phone number of the publisher.

2749. Mason, David E. "The Distinctive Nature of the Voluntary Organization Management." *Voluntary Action Leadership* (Spring 1979): 2, 40-2.

2750. Mason, David E. *Voluntary Nonprofit Enterprise Management.* New York: Plenum, 1984.

2751. McAdam, Terry W., and David L. Gies. *Managing Expectations: What Effective Board Members Ought to Expect from Nonprofit Organizations.* Unpublished.

2752. McAdam, Terry W. "Ten Questions for the Thinking Board Member." *Board Letter* 16 (Winter 1985): 6-8.

2753. McCaskey, Cynthia Gelhard, and John A. Dunn, Jr. "Look into My Crystal Cathode Ray Tube: Computer Models Make Annual Giving Predictions Easy." *Currents* 9 (March 1983): 38-42.

2754. McConkey, Dale D. *MBO for Nonprofit Organizations.* New York: Amacom, 1975.

2755. McCurdy, William B. *Program Evaluation. A Conceptual Tool Kit for Human Service Delivery Managers.* New York: Family Service Association of America, 1979.

2756. McCurley, Stephen H. "Memo to Nonprofit Board Members. Re:: What You Should Know about Legal Liability." *Voluntary Action Leadership* (Winter 1983): 16-8.

2757. McCurley, Stephen H., and Sue Vineyard. "Three Checklists: Marketing Your Volunteer Program to Recruit Volunteers." *Voluntary Action Leadership* (Summer 1986): 26-7.

Excerpt from *101 Ideas for Volunteer Programs*. Short article which consists of three checklists: 1) *Checklist Prior to Recruitment Campaign*, 2) *Motivations to Appeal to in Recruitment Campaigns*, and 3) *Recruitment Ideas*. The first list assists in the assessment of an organization's recruitment and management style by suggesting twenty no-nonsense questions about the organization's volunteer program. List number two cites thirty-six reasons why people volunteer. Included are a wide range of social, personal and psychological motivations which managers and administrators can use in recruitment. The third list consists of thirty-six recruitment ideas which include suggestions for administrators such as—tell the truth about the work or time needed; break large jobs down into smaller components; be careful about titles; diagram the position in the overall organization; always offer a job design; and don't recruit until you know what you are doing.

2758. McGrath, Glen. "Know Your Goals and How to Achieve Them." *Nonprofit World Report* 2 (January-February 1984): 17-8.

2759. McGrath, Glen. "Organizational Momentum." *Nonprofit World Report* 2 (March-April 1984): 17+.

2760. McMorrow, Michael J. "Preparing an Annual Report: Your Creative Calling Card." *Fund Raising Management* 7 (November-December 1975): 20-1.

2761. McNamee, Mike. "The Divestment Dilemma: The South African Divestment Issue's Impact on Fund Raising, PR, and Alumni Relations." *Currents* 11 (September 1985): 20+.

2762. Megna, Ralph J. "Computer Basics for Nonprofit Organizations." *Grantsmanship Center News* 11 (July-August 1983): 15-29.

2763. Melillo, Joseph V., ed. *Market the Arts!* New York: Foundation for the Extension and Development of the American Professional Theatre, 1983.

2764. Mellon Bank Corporation. *Discover Total Resources: A Guide for Nonprofits.* Pittsburgh: Mellon Bank Corp., 1985.

Guide written for board members, staff and volunteers to help them evaluate their use of community resources—money, people, goods and services. Provides a checklist of resources and techniques to use in organization assessment and to offer resource ideas. Based primarily on Mellon Bank's work within the Pittsburgh nonprofit community, but has broad applicability to other communities. Focus is on making use of total community resources rather than just looking at support from foundations or corporations or volunteers.

2765. Metropolitan Cultural Alliance. *Accounting for Culture: A Primer for Non-Accountants.* Boston: Metropolitan Cultural Alliance, 1980.

2766. Metzger, Eric L. *Too Many Clients, Too Little Time: A Guide to Planning and Managing a Legal Services Program.* New York: National Legal Aid and Defender Association, 1974.

2767. Mico, Paul R. *Developing Your Community-Based Organization: With Special Emphasis on Economic Development Organizations and Community Action Agencies.* Oakland, Calif.: Third Party Publishing Co., 1981.

2768. Middleton, Melissa. *Nonprofit Management: A Report on Current Research and Areas for Development.* Program on Non-Profit Organizations, no. 108. New Haven, Conn.: Institution for Social and Policy Studies, 1986.

Describes the current status of research on nonprofit management, focusing on those areas with potential for theory-development or theory-testing. Because of the growing complexity of multiple funding sources and diverse constituencies, nonprofit management roles and skills are developing amidst great interest and activity. This report describes recently completed research, work in progress, and potential research questions in four major areas of management concern: operating management, strategic management, interorganization and cross-sectoral relations, and nonprofit management education. A particularly important theme in the report concerns the types of nonprofits that would benefit by adopting for-profit models, and the conditions under which these models are most likely to be successful.

2769. Milano, Carol. "How to Start a Low-Budget Publicity Program." *Fund Raising Management* 19 (April 1988): 40+.

Covers basic methods of publicity, such as press releases, business connections, and public service announcements. Includes examples and practical suggestions.

2770. Milter, John R. "Management: A Missing Function?" *NAHD Journal* (Winter-Spring 1983): 43-7.

2771. Mittenthal, Richard A., and Brooke W. Mahoney. "Getting Management Help to the Nonprofit Sector." *Harvard Business Review* 55 (September-October 1977): 95-103.

2772. Mokwa, Michael P., William M. Dawson, and E. Arthur Prieve, eds. *Marketing the Arts.* New York: Praeger, 1980.

2773. Moore, Harry E., and David F. Long, eds. *Money: Raising and Managing Funds for Human Services.* South Plainfield, N.J.: Groupwork Today, 1984.

2774. Moore, R. Keith. "Advice and Consent: Before You Hire a PR Consultant, Learn Whether You Need One, Where to Look for One, and What You Can Expect One to Do." *Currents* 10 (April 1984): 32-4.

2775. Morris, Lynn Lyons, and Carol Taylor Fitz-Gibbon. *Evaluator's Handbook.* Beverly Hills, Calif.: Sage Publications, 1978.

2776. Morris, Lynn Lyons, and Carol Taylor Fitz-Gibbon. *How to Deal with Goals and Objectives.* Beverly Hills, Calif.: Sage Publications, 1978.

2777. Morris, Lynn Lyons, and Carol Taylor Fitz-Gibbon. *How to Present an Evaluation Report.* Beverly Hills, Calif.: Sage Publications, 1981.

2778. Murray, Dennis J. *How to Evaluate Your Fund-Raising Program: A Performance Audit System.* Boston: American Institute of Management, 1985.

Murray has researched organizational conditions which have led to successful fundraising programs, and has developed a set of standards against which to measure such programs. Part 1 presents a guide to performance auditing, reviews the evaluation methodologies currently being used on nonprofit fundraising programs and explains the steps in a performance audit. Part 2 lists the performance audit standards that should be used in evaluating nonprofit fundraising programs.

2779. Murray, Sheila L. *How to Organize and Manage a Seminar: What to Do and When to Do It.* Englewood Cliffs, N.J.: Prentice-Hall, 1983.

Offers a chronological outline for the essential details needed to plan and lead a successful seminar, including: creating a master plan, budget, and schedule for the seminar; obtaining a speaker or trainer and designing an effective presentation; audio-visual techniques and equipment; food, refreshments, and facilities—including fire protection; the ins and outs of registering participants; holding the actual seminer; and obtaining objective feedback. Interviews with successful seminar leaders appear throughout the book to offer inside advice and experience, and help avoid the stresses of trial-and-error learning.

2780. Myers, Helen. *The Business for Seminars.* Las Vegas, Nev.: Center of Seminar Management, 1982.

2781. "Myths and Maxims about Boards of Directors." *Conserve Neighborhoods* 27 (November-December 1982): 256-59.

2782. Nash, Edward L. *Direct Marketing: Strategy, Planning, Execution.* New York: McGraw-Hill, 1982.

2783. Nash, John. "Getting Your Board Unstuck." *Nonprofit Executive* 3 (June 1984): 3-4.

2784. Nason, John W. *The Nature of Trusteeship: The Role and Responsibilities of College and University Boards.* Washington: Association of Governing Boards of Universities and Colleges, 1982.

Nason examines the expanding roles and responsibilities of college and university trustees over the last twenty-five years, citing the changes in higher education as an opportunity for boards to rethink their structure and purpose and reshape the future of their institutions. Describes thirteen responsibilities of trustees and their collective activities. Appendexes include characteristics of the governing boards surveyed and a bibliography.

2785. Nass, Elyse. *Queens Arts Manager's Survival Guide: A Directory of Services, Arts Resources, and Publicity Outlets.* Edited by Mark J. Schuyler. Jamaica, N.Y.: Queens Council on the Arts, 1988.

Designed to assist Queens (NY) arts managers and artists strengthen their organizations, manage their creative work, and establish collaborative efforts, this guide highlights useful services offered by borough arts councils, Queens arts and cultural organizations, and national and regional membership and service organizations. Also includes a listing of grants and entries for media outlets.

2786. National Catholic Development Conference. *A Guide for Preparing a Statement of Accountability.* Rockville Centre, N.Y.: National Catholic Development Conference, 1982.

2787. National Council of Welfare. *Bookkeeping Handbook for Low-Income Citizens Groups.* Ottawa, Ontario: National Council of Welfare, 1973.

2788. National Council on Philanthropy. *Donors and Donees: Sharing Philanthropic Responsibilities.* Cleveland: National Council on Philanthropy, 1974.

2789. National Health Council. *Standards of Accounting and Financial Reporting for Voluntary Health and Welfare Organizations.* 3rd ed., rev. New York: National Health Council, 1988.

The third revised edition reflects current authoritative literature for acccounting and financial reporting for voluntary health and welfare agencies. Among the significant developments since the 1974 edition: the creation of the Financial Accounting Standards Board and its initiatives in the nonprofit accounting arena; the 1981 release of the American Institute of Certified Public Accountants' (AICPA) *Audits of Certain Nonprofit Organizations*; and a number of issues which have arisen concerning reporting practices that need clarification, including AICPA's formulation of Statement of Position 87-2, "Accounting for Joint Costs of Informational Materials and Activities of Not-for-Profit Organizations that Include a Fund-Raising Appeal," issued in 1987. This edition of *Standards* continues the quest to attain uniform accounting and external financial reporting in compliance with generally accepted accounting principles by all voluntary health and welfare organizations. Includes illustrative financial statements and informative appendixes.

2790. National Information Bureau. *The Volunteer Board Member in Philanthropy: Responsibilities, Achievements, Special Problems.* New York: National Information Bureau, 1979.

Highlights the basic principles of trusteeship and identifies problems common to nonprofits. Brief sections on the importance and scope of the voluntary sector; what happens when the volunteer board fails; characteristics of good board members; misconceptions of contemporary philanthropy; and board self-evaluation.

2791. Neddermeyer, Dorothy M., and Kevin Montgomery. "Stress: A Fact of Life." *Nonprofit World Report* 2 (November-December 1984): 24-5.

2792. "'Network Call' Helps Nonprofits Save Money Talking to Each Other." *NonProfit Times* 1 (May 1987): 4, 13.

2793. Neuber, Keith A. *Needs Assessment: A Model for Community Planning.* Beverly Hills, Calif.: Sage Publications, 1980.

2794. Nickerson, Anne. "The Board's Job Is to Hire the Executive Director in a Responsible Manner." *Board Letter* (Spr 1984): 3-4.

2795. "Non-Profit Software Package Directory." *Fund Raising Management* 18 (September 1987): 28+.

2796. Nonprofit Management Association. *Board Management Tapes.* [Sound recording]. Los Angeles: Southern California Center for Nonprofit Management, 1985.

2797. Nonprofit Management Association. *Directory of Members.* Minneapolis, Minn.: Nonprofit Management Association, 1985.

2798. Nonprofit Management Association. *Financial Management of Nonprofit Organizations: Reference Material.* Minneapolis, Minn.: Nonprofit Management Association, 1984.

2799. Nonprofit Management Association. *National Conference on Nonprofit Management and Technical Assistance.* Minneapolis, Minn.: Nonprofit Management Association, 1983.

2800. Nonprofit Management Association. *Toward the Future. National Conference Report.* Minneapolis, Minn.: Nonprofit Management Association, [1988].

Papers from the Nonprofit Management Association's 1987 Annual Conference cover: *Major Trends and Social Issues: Implications for the Management of Nonprofits*; *Preparing the Work Force of the 21st Century*; *The Ethics Crisis and Nonprofit Management*; *An Alternative to the Liability Crisis*; *Nonprofit vs. Profit Business*; *Operations Planning and Control in Social Services Agencies*; *Techniques for Organizational Inertia: Barriers to the Future*; *Communications Planning and Management*; *Career Planning and Development in Human Service Organizations*; *A Resource File for Proactive Managerial Leadership*; *Executive Development: Five Critical Factors for a Future of Excellence*; and papers on resource development, including: *Non-cash Contributions*; *Discover Total Resources, A Model for Fundraising Training*, *Joint Venturing with a For-Profit: A Successful Example*; and *Communicating with a Laser*.

2801. "Nonprofit Memberships of Corporate Board Influence Grants." *Corporate Giving Watch* 5 (July 1985): 2+.

2802. Nordhoff, Nancy S. *Fundamental Practices for Success with Volunteer Board of Non-Profit Organizations: A Self-Assessment and Planning Guide.* Seattle, Wash.: FunPrax Associates, 1982.

2803. Norton, Alice. *Measuring Potential and Evaluating Results.* New York: Foundation for Public Relations Research and Education, 1977.

2804. Norton, Michael, ed. *Legacies: A Practical Guide for Charities.* London: Directory of Social Change, 1983.

Comprehensive guide for charity administrators to all elements of raising money through legacies. Covers the importance of legacy income; how to increase a charity's legacy income, including how to advertise for it and the aspects of memorials as a source of income; legal aspects of leaving money to charity; tax issues; and suggested wording for legacies and codicils.

2805. O'Connell, Brian. *The Board Member's Book: Making a Difference in Voluntary Organizations.* New York: Foundation Center, 1985.

Practical guide to the essential functions of voluntary boards, covering such areas as: the legal responsibilities of board members; finding, developing, and recognizing good board members; the role of the board president; working with committees; the board's role in fundraising; and evaluating the results. Includes an extensive reading list.

2806. O'Connell, Brian. *Budgeting and Financial Accountability.* Nonprofit Management Series, no. 8. Washington: Independent Sector, 1988.

This paper is drawn from material in the books, *Effective Leadership in Voluntary Organizations* and *The Board Member's Book* by Brian O'Connell.

2807. O'Connell, Brian. *Conducting Good Meetings.* Nonprofit Management Series, no. 4. Washington: Independent Sector, 1988.

This paper is drawn from material in the books, *Effective Leadership in Voluntary Organizations* and *The Board Member's Book* by Brian O'Connell.

2808. O'Connell, Brian. *Effective Leadership in Voluntary Organizations.* New York: Walker & Co., 1981.

Practical resource guide for nonprofit managers. The effective organization has the ability to acquire resources, attend to participants, maintain strong morale, involve the participation and involvement of the community, and adapt to new demands. It also keeps its decisions congruent with its goals and plans for the future, including constructive planning and fundraising.

2809. O'Connell, Brian. *Evaluating Results.* Nonprofit Management Series. Washington: Independent Sector, 1988.

This paper is drawn from material in the books, *Effective Leadership in Voluntary Organizations* and *The Board Member's Book* by Brian O'Connell.

2810. O'Connell, Brian. *Finding, Developing and Rewarding Good Board Members.* Nonprofit Management Series, no. 2. Washington: Independent Sector, 1988.

This paper is drawn from material in the books, *Effective Leadership in Voluntary Organizations* and *The Board Member's Book* by Brian O'Connell.

2811. O'Connell, Brian. *Fund Raising.* Nonprofit Management Series, no. 7. Washington: Independent Sector, 1987.

This paper is drawn from material in the books, *Effective Leadership in Voluntary Organizations* and *The Board Member's Book* by Brian O'Connell.

2812. O'Connell, Brian. *Operating Effective Committees.* Nonprofit Management Series, no. 3. Washington: Independent Sector, 1988.

This paper is drawn from material in the books, *Effective Leadership in Voluntary Organizations* and *The Board Member's Book* by Brian O'Connell.

2813. O'Connell, Brian. *Recruiting, Encouraging and Evaluating the Chief Staff Officer.* Nonprofit Management Series, no. 6. Washington: Independent Sector, 1988.

This paper is drawn from material in the books, *Effective Leadership in Voluntary Organizations* and *The Board Member's Book* by Brian O'Connell. Offers eight essential criteria to help search committees with the task of recruiting new chief executive officers.

2814. O'Connell, Brian. *The Role of the Board and Board Members.* Nonprofit Management Series, no. 1. Washington: Independent Sector, 1988.

This paper is drawn from material in the books, *Effective Leadership in Voluntary Organizations* and *The Board Member's Book* by Brian O'Connell.

2815. O'Connell, Brian. *The Roles and Relationships of the Chief Volunteer and Chief Staff Officers, Board, and Staff: Who Does What?* Nonprofit Management Series, no. 5. Washington: Independent Sector, 1988.

This paper is drawn from material in the books, *Effective Leadership in Voluntary Organizations* and *The Board Member's Book* by Brian O'Connell.

2816. Olenick, Arnold J., and Philip R. Olenick. *Making the Non-Profit Organization Work: A Financial, Legal and Tax Guide for Administrators.* Englewood Cliffs, N.J.: Institute for Business Planning, 1983.

Provides detailed explanations of how to obtain and keep tax-exempt status, set up budgets, and maintain financial records.

2817. Olenick, Arnold J. "Simple Financial Ratios Can Show You Not Only How Your Organization Is Doing: But Also Where You're Heading." *Nonprofit Executive* 3 (June 1984): 5-6.

2818. Olenick, Arnold J. "Straight Talk about a Nagging Problem: How to Improve Nonprofit Management." *Nonprofit World* 6 (May-June 1988): 31-3.

Proposes an integrated approach between funding agencies, technical assistance service providers, and nonprofit organizations in order to improve nonprofit management and assure that the most innovative and needed programs are funded. Grantors avoid risk by funding well-managed and reliable organizations to the detriment of many nonprofits offering worthy and original proposals but lacking sound resource management or accountability. Nonprofits tend to respond to the problems of financial management by over-emphasizing fundraising activities, leaping into risky profit-making ventures, or limiting their perspective to stress safe programs at the expense of those that are most needed and most innovative. Consultants often compound problems by hesitating to reveal the real problems of a nonprofit when hired to cure a symptom of a much worse disease. Thus, grantors could minimize risk by offering small technical assistance grants for nonprofits to acquire needed management skills, and by training their own officers in the area of financial analysis of grant applications. Technical assistance providers must use multi-disciplinary skills to diagnose the true problems of a nonprofit, and establish meaningful professional standards or a team approach for conducting a diagnosis. Nonprofits, in their turn, must recognize that financial management is an essential investment, not a luxury, which will promote their own well-being and allow for innovative programs that minimize risk and maximize accountability.

2819. Olsen, Thomas L. "Can Do, Can Do: What a Computer Can Do for Independent Schools." *Currents* 9 (March 1983): 28-30.

2820. Olson, Paul M. "Straight Talk about Our Future." *Foundation News* 29 (September-October 1988): 40-4.

Working from the thesis that foundations are no better than the people who run them, this article challenges staff members to grow personally and professionally. Three occupational hazards are cited: 1) a lack of training to deal with such great financial resources; 2) the paradox of power, where a few succumb to the intoxication of making God-like decisions about who receives the funds, while all must deal with the public misconception of foundation staff arrogance; and, 3) the lure of the call, which drives staff to overcommitment resulting in exhaustion and a lack of focus with "no time for reflection that can yield real depth and expertise." Offers three responses: 1) personal development plans to increase an individual's capacity to learn, change and prepare for the future; 2) the development of professional institutes for foundation staff, which would offer perspectives on the human side of philanthropy and a more reflective approach for those who have gained experience and are concerned about their future contributions; and, 3) exchanges within the foundation community to prevent stagnation and to expose staff to new ideas, styles and perspectives. Presents ground rules for an exchange program and discusses the benefits to the author, who participated in an exchange, to his foundation, and to the field of philanthropy as a whole.

2821. *On Technical Assistance Programs. A Directory of Resources for New York City Nonprofit Organizations.* New York: Public Interest Public Relations, 1979.

2822. O'Neill, Michael, Dennis R. Young, and Terry W. McAdam. *Educating Managers of Nonprofit Organizations.* New York: Praeger, 1988.

Collection of eleven essays addressing the topic of manager education in the nonprofit sector. Programs of training for nonprofit management (especially university-based programs that combine theory and research with practice) will help the sector to identify, recruit, train, and continuously develop the degree of competence and sophistication required to make the entire constellation of nonprofit organizations an effective and efficient instrument of American society.

2823. Ott, J. Steven, and Jay M. Shafritz. *The Facts On File Dictionary of Nonprofit Organization Management.* New York: Facts On File, 1986.

Designed for the field of philanthropy, a dictionary dedicated to the codification of nonprofit organization language. It is a comprehensive work of definitions for terms and phrases related to the purposes, structures, functions, processes, laws, codes, ethics, court cases, and financing (especially fundraising) of nonprofit organizations. In addition, it focuses on the laws, practices, and tax limitations of giving and bequesting. The dictionary includes a selected listing of organizations and resources which provide services to nonprofit organizations, but not specific foundations. Only selected regional associations, newsletters, and journals are included; authors and books are cited only if terms or concepts are credited or attributed to them. An extremely useful book for nonprofit organization acronyms. Includes charts, samples, data tables, and a bibliography of definitive nonprofit organization management related monographs.

2824. "Overcompensating." *Grantsmanship Center News* 11 (January-February 1983): 6-12.

2825. Pallenik, Michael. "Evaluation, Media Style." *Foundation News* 28 (March-April 1987): 48-50.

Guidelines for funders are beginning to emerge for film and television project evaluation, but common sense remains the key ingredient. It is recommended that formal tests be utilized only when the project budget is large enough to warrant the expense of testing, and when the goals of the project are detailed and explicit enough to expect that a formal test would validly measure intended or possible effects relevant to those goals.

2826. Parson, Mary Jean. *Back to Basics: Planning.* New York: Facts On File, 1985.

2827. Pearson, Henry G. "Interviewing Volunteer Applicants for Skills." *Voluntary Action Leadership* (Summer 1986): 15-8.

Career consultant and former corporate trainer, Henry Pearson, presents a technique for choosing the proper candidate for a volunteer position. He writes that the mismatching of volunteers stems principally from the lack of effective interviewing techniques; he believes that the techniques used for paid jobs are inappropriate. Since most agencies provide on-the-job training, lack of experience is not an issue. Indeed, Pearson claims that the identification of transferable skills is the key to finding good volunteers. With the assistance of the *Transkills Finder* the interviewer can identify those skills which become one's personal transferable skills. The only requirement is that the activity must be one which the person enjoys. According to the author, this technique by-passes fruitless questions and answers about irrelevant education and work.

2828. Peat, Marwick, Mitchell and Company. *Ratio Analysis in Libraries.* New York: Peat, Marwick, Mitchell & Co., [1987].

2829. Peat, Marwick, Mitchell and Company. *Ratio Analysis in Voluntary Health and Welfare Organizations.* New York: Peat, Marwick, Mitchell & Co., [198?].

2830. Peebles, Marvin L. *Directory of Management Resources for Community Organizations.* 3rd ed. San Francisco: MLP Enterprises, 1981.

2831. Peterson, Virginia M. "Determining Cost of Services, Break-Even Analysis and Pricing." *Fund Raising Management* 14 (December 1983): 54-7.

2832. Peterson, Virginia M. "Financial Analysis and Planning: Tools for Non-Profit Organizations." *Fund Raising Management* 14 (November 1983): 24-30.

2833. Peterson, Virginia M. "Monitoring Financial Health." *Help for Nonprofits* 1 (March 1983): 5-6.

2834. "Planning Is Key to Public Relations Efforts in 1984." *Nonprofit Executive* 3 (January 1984): 3-4.

2835. Posch, Robert J., Jr. "Contractual Protection of Agency's Confidential Data." *Fund Raising Management* 14 (February 1984): 58-63.

2836. Poutas, Bernice J. "Building the Case for Solid Gift Support." *Fund Raising Management* 14 (February 1984): 66-8.

2837. Powers, Charles W. *People/Profits: The Ethics of Investment.* New York: Council on Religion and International Affairs, 1972.

2838. Practising Law Institute. *Representing Artists, Collectors, and Dealers.* New York: Practising Law Institute, 1985.

2839. Price Waterhouse. *Effective Internal Accounting Control for Nonprofit Organizations: A Guide for Directors and Management.* New York: Price Waterhouse & Co., 1982.

2840. Price Waterhouse. *Effective Internal Accounting Control for Nonprofit Organizations: A Guide for Directors and Management.* New York: Price Waterhouse & Co., 1982.

2841. Price Waterhouse. *Survey of Financial Reporting and Accounting Practices of Private Foundations.* New York: Price Waterhouse & Co., 1983.

2842. "Professionalizing Technical Assistance: The Nonprofit Management Association." *Grantsmanship Center News* 11 (January-February 1983): 32-5.

2843. Public Management Institute. *Bookkeeping for Nonprofits.* San Francisco: Public Management Institute, 1979.

2844. Public Management Institute. *Budgeting for Nonprofits.* San Francisco: Public Management Institute, 1980.

2845. Public Management Institute. *The Effective Nonprofit Executive Handbook.* San Francisco: Public Management Institute, 1982.

2846. Public Management Institute. *Evaluation Handbook.* San Francisco: Public Management Institute, 1980.

Practical handbook in loose-leaf format discusses how to use evaluation as a tool for organizational planning, program management, and grants planning.

2847. Public Management Institute. *How to Be an Effective Board Member.* San Francisco: Public Management Institute, 1980.

2848. Public Management Institute. *How to Find Funds to Attend Conferences.* San Francisco: Public Management Institute, 1979.

2849. Public Management Institute. *Managing Volunteers for Results.* San Francisco: Public Management Institute, 1979.

2850. Public Management Institute. *Nonprofit Financial Management.* San Francisco: Public Management Institute, 1979.

2851. Public Management Institute. *Successful Public Relations Techniques.* San Francisco: Public Management Institute, 1980.

Step-by-step Public Management Institute manual on public relations for nonprofits and public agencies. The guide, divided into four parts, is presented in a three-ring binder format. Section 1, *Public Relations Planning*, contains a series of six steps beginning with *Auditing Your P.R.: What is Your P.R. Accomplishing?* The other five steps are *Public Relations Goals and Objectives, Audiences, Messages, Media*, and *Public Relations Action Plan and Budget*. Section 2 examines *Getting Organized* and Section 3 concentrates on *Tools for Public Relations* and includes items on news angles, the press, brochures and publications, and slide shows. All three sections conclude with endnotes. The final section is a resources section with suggestions on such actions as choosing an ad agency or consultant and obtaining free advertising. The manual contains numerous tables, checklists, worksheets, and examples; it also includes a brief selected bibliography.

2852. Public Management Institute. *Successful Seminars, Conferences and Workshops.* San Francisco: Public Management Institute, 1980.

How-to book on planning and managing conferences, seminars and workshops. Designed around a program planning system, it focuses on the following areas critical to successful program planning: how to create, design and administer a program; organize a publicity campaign; direct a mail campaign; manage finance; and choose audio-visual aids.

2853. Rabby, Rami. *Locating, Recruiting and Hiring the Disabled.* New York: Pilot Books, 1981.

2854. Radock, Michael, and Herman B. Smith. "Wanted: More Trustees with Certain Wallop." *Fund Raising Management* 14 (September 1983): 66-8.

2855. Rados, David L. *Marketing for Non-Profit Organizations.* Boston: Auburn House Publishing Co., 1981.

Guide to help nonprofit managers analyze and devise solutions to marketing problems that arise in their organizations. Frequent examples and case studies illustrate sound marketing analysis and describe the development of successful nonprofit marketing.

2856. Rand Corporation. *Indirect Costs: A Guide for Foundations and Nonprofit Organizations.* Santa Monica, Calif.: Rand Corp., 1986.

2857. Rath, Frederick L., Jr., and Merrilyn Rogers O'Connell. *A Bibliography on Historical Organization Practices.* Nashville, Tenn.: American Association for State and Local History, 1980.

2858. Rathmell, John M. *Marketing in the Service Sector.* Cambridge, Mass.: Winthrop Publishers, 1974.

2859. Raymond, Thomas J.C., and Stephen A. Greyser. "The Business of Managing the Arts." *Harvard Business Review* 56 (July-August 1978): 123-32.

2860. Rees, David Morgan. *Getting Publicity.* North Pomfret, Vt.: David & Charles, 1984.

2861. Reisig, Edwin. "Hardware and Software Needs to Improve Staff Efficiency." *Fund Raising Management* 14 (February 1984): 50-2.

2862. Reiss, Alvin H., ed. *The Arts Management Reader.* New York: Marcel Dekker, 1979.

2863. Robinson, Daniel D. "The Continuing Struggle toward a Conceptual Accounting Framework." *Philanthropy Monthly* 17 (September 1984): 25-9.
Reports on the work of the Financial Accounting Standards Board.

2864. Robinson, Daniel D. "Non-Profit Accounting Concepts Take a Step Forward." *Philanthropy Monthly* 18 (February 1985): 27-8.

2865. Robinson, Daniel D. "Progress toward Change in Financial Reporting by Nonbusiness Organizations." *Philanthropy Monthly* 17 (December 1984): 12-5.
Reports on work of the Financial Accounting Standards Board.

2866. Ronen, Simcha. *Alternative Work Schedules: Selecting, Implementing, and Evaluating.* Homewood, Ill.: Dow Jones-Irwin, 1984.

2867. Rotenberg, Marc. "Computers for Non-Profits? Part 2." *Grassroots Fundraising Journal* 3 (June-July 1984): 9-12.

2868. Ruffner, Robert H. *Handbook of Publicity and Public Relations for the Nonprofit Organization.* Englewood Cliffs, N.J.: Prentice-Hall, 1984.
Examines the major issues that are affecting the nonprofit manager and tells how to deal with those issues while building effective public relations. Chapters include a blueprint for the public relations program, communicating with different constituencies, generating favorable publicity and how to position your nonprofit. Provides case studies and numerous examples of publicity used by well-known nonprofits.

2869. Runquist, Lisa A. "Sixteen Questions Every Nonprofit Director Should Ask." *Grantsmanship Center News* 13 (May-June 1985): 54+.

2870. Saccomandi, Patrick. "Using the Buddy System to Survive Computerization." *Exchange Networks* (Spring 1984): 1-3.

2871. Sager, Don. "Managing Public Library Investments." *Library Journal* 110 (15 June 1985): 27-8.

2872. Sakayue, Beverly, and William R. Conrad, Jr. *How to Analyze and Report Annual Giving Campaign Progress.* Downers Grove, Ill.: Voluntary Management Press, 1983.

2873. Sander, John R. "Zero Based Budgeting Gives You the Big Picture." *Nonprofit Executive* 4 (December 1984): 3-4.
Gives the principles of zero-based budgeting.

2874. Sanders, Joseph. "Go, Team, Go!" *Currents* 9 (September 1983): 36-8.

2875. Savage, Thomas J. *The Cheswick Process: Seven Steps to a More Effective Board.* Boston: Cheswick Center, 1982.
Booklet written for governing bodies of seminaries and schools of theology, but ideas can be adapted to fit the needs of other nonprofits. Provides information on planning a board retreat, including sample purposes, agendas, and questionnaires for board self-evaluation.

2876. Savage, Thomas J. *Rating Board Performance.* Boston: Cheswick Center, 1985.

2877. Schardt, Arlie. "To Be a Better Trustee." *Foundation News* 25 (May-June 1984): 42-5.

2878. Scheir, Wendy, ed. *National VLA Directory.* New York: Volunteer Lawyers for the Arts, 1986.
Describes thirty-nine Volunteer Lawyers for the Arts programs throughout the United States, and one in Canada, which have been organized to assist artists and arts organizations with the legal system. The directory, alphabetically arranged by state, provides basic information about the groups such as name, address, telephone number, contact person, area served, income eligibility requirements, administrative fee, legal services, educational programs, publications, university affiliation, resource library, and other services.

2879. Schilling, Barbara H. *Glossary of Tools and Concepts for Nonprofit Managers.* 2nd ed. San Francisco: Management Center, 1981.

2880. Schindler-Rainman, Eva. "Effective Boards in a Time of Transition." *Voluntary Action Leadership* (Winter 1983): 12-4.

2881. Schmidt, Frances. *Using Publicity to Best Advantage.* New York: Foundation for Public Relations Research and Education, 1977.

2882. Schneider, Robert F. "Computerized Information Management Systems for Research Administration: General Issues Affecting Their Implementation." *Grants Magazine* 7 (September 1984): 171-78.

2883. "School Advertises for New Trustees." *New York Times* (14 June 1982).

2884. Schooler, Dean. "The Preoccupations of Boards." *Board Letter* 12 (December 1982): 6+.

2885. Schreiner, Samuel Jonathan. *An Introduction to the Art of Leadership of Commuity Service Organizations.* New York: Vantage Press, 1970.

2886. Schroder, Spense. "Communication Is a Board's Job Too. Part 1: Internal Communication." *Board Letter* 10 (July 1983): 5+.

2887. Schultz, Whitt N. "What Makes a Good Nonprofit Manager?" *Nonprofit World Report* 2 (May-June 1984): 32.

2888. Schwartz, John B. *New Telecommunications Technologies and Programming.* Unpublished, 1982.

2889. Setterberg, Fred, and Kary Schulman. *Beyond Profit: The Complete Guide to Managing the Nonprofit Organization.* New York: Harper & Row, 1985.

Covers essential aspects of nonprofit organization management, from hiring staff, establishing goals, and keeping accurate financial records, to writing a fundraising plan and achieving public visibility. Includes diagrams, appendixes, and complete bibliographic notes.

2890. Shabecoff, Alice. *Alternative Investing in Community Development.* Technical Bulletin. Washington: Community Information Exchange, 1987.

Alternative investments, also known as social investments, are made by foundations, insurance companies, corporations, churches and pension funds, as well as by individuals, in non-traditional areas outside of their customary lending practices. While considerations of positive social impact influence the investor's decisions, these investments are not charity, and repayment, preferably with a return, is expected. This bulletin is intended to assist community-based organizations tap into this wellspring of financing, offering ideas, strategies, and examples, as well as a brief look at the history of alternative investments, to help these groups understand barriers that have arisen in the past and thereby learn to frame new arguments and techniques. Describes the activites of the major sources of alternative investment dollars in community economic development, and includes a resource bibliography, a list of further contacts, and samples of alternative investment information available from the Community Information Exchange.

2891. Shay, Philip W. *How to Get the Best Results from Management Consultants.* New York: Acme, 1981.

2892. Shore, Harvey. "Arts Administration: Managing the Resources of Arts Organizations." *Business Quarterly* 47 (August 1982): 53+.

2893. Sidler, Mark P. "Okay, We Need One. Now What?" *Nonprofit World Report* 2 (May-June 1984): 11+.

2894. Sidler, Mark P. "What Is My Database?" *Nonprofit World Report* 2 (July-August 1984): 9+.

2895. Simonse, Arnold B. "Nonprofit Accounting: The Search for a Solution." *Nonprofit World Report* 3 (January-February 1985): 23+.

2896. Sirkin, Michael S. "Compensation and Benefits." *Philanthropy Monthly* 19 (November 1986): 17-8.

2897. Skloot, Edward, ed. *The Nonprofit Entrepreneur: Creating Ventures to Earn Income.* New York: Foundation Center, 1988.

This guide demonstrates how nonprofits can launch successful earned income enterprises without compromising their missions. According to the Urban Institute's Nonprofit Sector Project, approximately fifteen percent of nonprofits actually engage in commerce, but more than seventy percent now earn some money through fees and service charges. It is this larger cluster of organizations for which this book is relevant. This guide shows how many nonprofit organizations have transformed themselves into entrepreneurial organizations in order to deal with sharply rising costs, diminishing government dollars, increased competition for funding, and real marketing opportunity. Includes bibliography.

2898. Sladek, Frea E., and Eugene L. Stein. *Grant Budgeting and Finance: Getting the Most Out of Your Grant Dollar.* New York: Plenum, 1981.

2899. Smith, Craig. "Matching Your Needs with Computer Capability." *Foundation News* 26 (March-April 1985): 26-30.

2900. Snydle, Carol L. "Some ABC's of Indirect Cost for the Uninitiated: Philosophies and Development of University Indirect Cost." *Grants Magazine* 7 (September 1984): 181-7.

2901. Special Libraries Association. *Triennial Salary Survey.* Washington: Special Libraries Association, 1988.

2902. Stevens, Susan Kenny. "Measuring Financial Health: Hands-on." *Foundation News* 29 (September-October 1988): 23-5.

Thirteenth in a series of hands on articles designed to help improve the management and performance of organizations in the philanthropic sector, this article assists grantmakers in interpreting the financial statements of nonprofits. These statements—the balance sheet, income and expense statements, budget, and cash flow information—provide an objective way to measure an organization's financial health and future. Advises looking at the balance sheet to determine the "healthy" organizations with enough cash to pay off current liabilities, and the "ill" ones with mounting payroll taxes; examining income and expense statements for deficits and surpluses ("Deficits kill organizations. Surpluses can contribute to stability."); using the budget to provide answers to questions concerning community benefit versus organization building, total project cost compared to similar projects in other organizations, and whether or not the organization knows how much it will cost to deliver a unit of service; and studying cash flow statements as an indicator of a nonprofit's attitude about responsible cash management.

2903. Stevenson, J. John. "Keeping Up with the States." *Philanthropy Monthly* 17 (April 1984): 39-40.

2904. Stringer, G.E., and K.B. Arsem. *The Board Manual Workbook.* Arlington, Va.: Volunteer Consultants, 1982.

Novel approach to training and orienting board members, designed to allow each board member have his or her own workbook for completion and use as a personal orientation tool. Focuses on topics such as bylaws, annual reports, job descriptions, financial tools, board-staff relations, parliamentary procedures, and personal records.

2905. "Suggestions for Future Accounting Treatment of Non-Profit..." *Philanthropy Monthly* (8 February 1985): 1-44.

2906. Suhrke, Henry C. "When May Conditional Pledges of Support Become 'Receivables' on Your Books?" *Philanthropy Monthly* 21 (February 1988): 23-5.

Examines the discussion of alternatives and the implications of terms employed by the Financial Accounting Standards Board in determining that conditional pledges may not be recognized as receivables until the stipulated condition has been substantially fulfilled. Until then, information about conditional pledges should be disclosed in the notes to the financial statements.

2907. Suhrke, Henry C. "Why Has the Cost of Directors and Officers Liability Insurance Gone through the Ceiling?" *Philanthropy Monthly* 18 (September 1985): 5+.

2908. Swanson, Andrew P. "The Board and Its Executive Director: A Supervisory Checklist." *Exchange Networks* (Winter 1984): 4.

2909. Swanson, Andrew P. *The Board President and the Board of Directors: A Guide.* Providence, R.I.: Community Services Consultants, 1982.

2910. Taft, J. Richard. *When Development Directors Fail.* Washington: Taft Group, 1982.

2911. Taft Group. *Ten for the Eighties: What Every Nonprofit Executive Should Know.* Washington: Taft Group, 1982.

2912. *Taking Charge: Management and Marketing for the Media Arts.* New York: Media Alliance, 1986.

2913. Talley, Olive. "Mattox Offers Guidelines for Foundation Trustees." *Houston Post* (17 August 1985).

2914. Taylor, James B. *Using Microcomputers in Social Agencies.* Beverly Hills, Calif.: Sage Publications, 1981.

2915. Technical Assistance Study Group. *Recommendation to Foundations Regarding Technical Assistance.* Chicago: Technical Assistance Study Group.

2916. "Technical Assistance: Tea and Sympathy?" *CCFlash* 12 (1 April 1984): 1-2.

2917. Thennes, Mark A. *Creating Neighborhood Enterprise: A Primer for Nonprofits.* Washington: National Center for Neighborhood Enterprise, 1984.

Drawing heavily from the experiences and techniques of community agencies that have already added economic development to their services, manual discusses various aspects related to economic development projects, including opportunities, organizational issues, required skills and resources, tax related issues, and methods of obtaining funding. Also reviews available printed and technical assistance resources.

2918. Third Sector Press. *The Development Consultant Program: Kit of Guidelines and Samples.* Cleveland: Third Sector Press, 1985.

2919. Thomas, Susan. "Team Building within Your Organization." *Grantsmanship Center News* 2 (May-June 1983): 34-7.

2920. Thompson, Lynn Stanley. "System Selection: Staff Input Assures Best Computer Output." *Foundation News* 30 (January-February 1989): 38, 46.

A thoroughly undertaken needs assessment will enable a nonprofit to understand exactly what it wants in a computer system, how the system will be used most efficiently in daily operations, and which system will not only meet the needs of today, but also has the capacity to expand for future needs. A group meeting to determine overall goals and priorities for the new system is a good first step. The person assigned to needs assessment will interview each staff member and examine all aspects of current procedures, in order to put together a detailed requirements checklist. This checklist is broken down into four parts: functionality; data elements; report options; and budget. The final checklist is used to compare vendors and their software packages; often vendor support is the deciding factor when purchasing.

2921. Timm, Paul R. *Supervision.* St. Paul, Minn.: West Publishing Co., 1984.

2922. Topor, Robert S. *Your Personal Guide to Marketing a Nonprofit Organization.* Washington: Council for Advancement and Support of Education, 1988.

Offers practical advice for applying marketing concepts and techniques to the often intangible services offered by nonprofits. Organized in sections that cover basic but important ideas about marketing, including marketing planning, strategy development, and implementation, this guide contains models, checklists, worksheets and reference lists to help readers understand their organization's political environment and define its mission, identify and aim for target markets, use research to achieve marketing results and use competition and competitive forces to understand the strengths and weaknesses of their own organization. Discusses the techniques of promotion, advertising, and sales, and provides a complete marketing blueprint to help nonprofits achieve their organizational goals and meet the needs of its market. Includes bibliography.

2923. Totten, Jeff. "Using a Consumer-Oriented Approach: A Personal and Professional Perspective." *Voluntary Action Leadership* (Summer 1986): 25.

Brief article by marketing specialist who suggests that nonprofits can meet their volunteer needs by becoming more consumer/volunteer-oriented. Totten believes that nonprofits must become more flexible with their hours and schedules; permit off-site work; and demand shorter periods of involvement from the volunteers. The consumer-oriented approach will enable agencies to entice more people to volunteer, especially those who have never been a volunteer.

2924. Touche Ross and Company. *The Touche Ross Survey of Business Executives on Non-Profit Boards.* New York: Touche Ross, 1979.

A 1979 opinion study based on interviews with 308 business executives commissioned by Touche Ross. The study reveals what the executives feel are the major issues confronting nonprofit board members, what they consider the board's functions and responsibilities to be, and their view of the evaluation function.

2925. Traub, James. *Accounting and Reporting Practices of Private Fundations: A Critical Evaluation.* New York: Praeger, 1977.

2926. Trenbeth, Richard P. *The Membership Mystique: How to Create Income and Influence with Membership Programs.* Ambler, Pa.: Fund Raising Institute, 1986.

Reveals how the development and use of a membership program can produce substantial advantages for any nonprofit organization. Discusses all aspects of such a program, from creation to administration to evaluation and improvement, including illustrations of all the essential materials: recruitment letters, mailing packages, sample benefits, renewal and upgrading forms and procedures. Provides case studies of various nonprofits that have implemented successful supportive membership programs.

2927. Tricarico, MaryAnn. "The Quest for Funds: Dialing for Data and Dollars." *Grants Magazine* 9 (March 1986): 27-9.

The author's suggestion for grantsmanship success is the online computer database search using the Foundation Center's databases at a convenient location such as one's local library.

2928. Trost, Arty, and Judy Rauner. *Gaining Momentum for Board Action.* San Diego, Calif.: Marlborough Publications, 1983.

Presents the basics of boards and board development with practical examples and worksheets to help the reader apply ideas to his or her specific situation. Logical and direct presentation of information will benefit new board members while offering new approaches and a comprehensive review to experienced board members.

2929. Troyer, Thomas A. *Divestment of South Africa Investments: A Legal Analysis for Foundations, Other Charitable Institutions and Pension Funds.* New York: New World Foundation, 1985.

Report analyzes the laws within which charitable and pension plan decisions on divestment of South African holdings must be made. Includes information on how to assess the cost of divestment, the relationship of divestment to the nonprofit's purposes, and how to divest prudently.

2930. Turk, Frederick J., and Robert P. Gallo. *Financial Management Strategies for Arts Organizations.* New York: American Council for the Arts, 1984.

Translates financial management strategies into practical applications for arts organizations, providing sophisticated management tools for systems' planning, budgeting, controlling, and evaluating. Reveals how management can effectively and efficiently combine and adjust resources (the people, facilities, equipment and finances available to the arts organization) to produce programs and provide services; helps management identify chronic financial problems that plague arts groups, understand why they occur, and formulate possible solutions. A case study of an arts center is referred to throughout the book to illustrate the key elements in the financial management process: a clearly defined organizational structure; financial policies appropriate to an arts organization; a financial management information system; and a detailed definition of financial activities.

2931. *Twelve Tips on Use of Consultants.* Tacoma, Wash.: Weyerhaeuser Foundation, 1981.

2932. Udvarhelyi, Elspeth. "Your Board Members Will Raise Funds Effectively, But They Do Need Your Help." *Nonprofit Executive* 2 (March 1983): 3-4.

2933. United States. Congress. Senate. Committee on the Judiciary. *Hearings before the Subcommittee on Federal Charters, Holidays and Celebrations.* Washington: Government Printing Office, 1972.

2934. United States. Department of Health and Human Services. *Making PSAs Work. TV, Radio: A Handbook for Health Communication Professionals.* Bethedsa, Md.: National Cancer Institute, 1984.

2935. United Way of America. *Accounting and Financial Reporting: A Guide for United Ways and Not-for-Profit Human Service Organizations.* Alexandria, Va.: United Way of America, 1974.

2936. United Way of America. *Competitive Marketing: A Guide for United Ways and Other Nonprofits.* Alexandria, Va.: United Way of America, 1988.

Produced by the United Way of America's Strategic Planning and Market Management Division, guide covers basic marketing concepts as they apply to United Ways and other nonprofits, and explores strategy development in a competitive nonprofit marketplace. Contains sections on gathering and utilizing marketing information; communication planning and implementation; customer service and contact; and organizational structures and systems for marketing. Appendixes include United Way of America marketing support materials, such as demographic and economic data, market research data and tools, strategic management tools, and consultation and technical assistance; a summary of the research undertaken by the United Way's marketing committee focus group; and recommendations for target markets.

2937. United Way of America. *Creating a Media Resource Guide: Communication Resource Handbook Five.* Alexandria, Va.: United Way of America, 1982.

2938. United Way of America. *Needs Assessment: A Guide for Planners, Managers, and Funders of Health and Human Care Services.* Alexandria, Va.: United Way of America, 1982.

2939. Upshur, Carole C. "Life after a Grant: Now the Hard Work Begins for Grantee." *Fund Raising Management* 14 (September 1983): 26-30.

2940. Villarejo, Don. *Research for Action: A Guidebook to Public Records Investigation for Community Activists.* Davis, Calif.: California Institute for Rural Studies, 1980.

2941. Vinter, Robert D., and Rhea K. Kish. *Budgeting for Not-for-Profit Organizations.* New York: Free Press, 1984.

Provides how-to budget information for small and midsize nonprofit organizations. Guide is written for program managers rather than financial managers. Uses an illustrative service program to show the key elements of budgeting and how to solve fiscal tasks/problems. Provides a chapter on planning a budget for a new program and submitting it to a prospective funder. Includes numerous exhibits of fiscal forms and regulations.

2942. Vogel, Frederic B., ed. *No Quick Fix (Planning)*. New York: Foundation for the Extension and Development of the American Professional Theatre, 1985.

Although prepared primarily for theater groups, this handbook describes a process and tools for planning that can be used by all nonprofits.

2943. Vogel, Lynn Harold. "Automating Your Management Information System." *Nonprofit Executive* 3 (October 1983): 3-4.

2944. Vogel, Lynn Harold, and Robert Borden. *Documenting Your Organization's Information System: A Manual*. Chicago: University of Chicago, 1983.

2945. Vogt, Jay W. *Successful Resources Fairs: Guidelines for Planning*. Boston: Associated Grantmakers of Massachusetts, 1983.

2946. Volkmann, M. Fredric. "It's about Time: How to Make It and Manage It." *Currents* 9 (October 1983): 14-7.

2947. Volunteer-The National Center. *Basic Computer Knowledge for Nonprofits*. Washington: Taft Group, 1985.

2948. Wacht, Richard F. *Financial Management in Nonprofit Organizations*. Atlanta, Ga.: Georgia State University, 1984.

Book examines the role of the financial manager in the nonprofit context and explains how it is different from the for-profit role, providing in-depth information on the theory and practice of financial management. Among the many topics covered are sections on endowment policy and management, short-term and long-term financing, management of receivables and inventory, and resources allocation principles. Text is accompanied by many instructive examples and tables.

2949. Wachtell, Ester, comp. and ed. *Stretch: A Resource Directory of Technical Assistance Providers*. Los Angeles: California Community Foundation, [1981].

2950. Waldo, Charles N. *A Working Guide for Directors of Not-for-Profit Organizations*. Westport, Conn.: Greenwood Press, 1986.

Guide to help new and even experienced nonprofit board members find their way through the maze of responsibilities, legalities, and financial reports in which they find themselves. Provides a direct and easily accessible overview of the essential factors inherent to board meetings, financial statements, committee responsibilities, tax and legal matters, marketing, commercial ventures, grantsmanship, board-staff relations and more. Contains bibliography.

2951. Walko, Donald R., and Mary L. Farnsworth. *Accounting for Nonprofit Organizations*. Pittsburgh: Community Technical Assistance Center, 1981.

2952. Ward, Sue. *Socially Responsible Investment*. London: Directory of Social Change, 1986.

A handbook for those concerned with the ethical and social implications of their investments who wish to apply non-financial or ethical criteria as well as the more usual financial criteria when deciding whether to make a particular investment or planning an investment strategy for their own or their organization's funds. Although the specific information (organizations and legislation) apply to the United Kingdom, much of the general information on investments and investment strategies and decisions are applicable to the United States. The appendixes include company facts and figures for such categories as charitable donations, political contributors, involvement in South Africa, animal experimentation, the environment, and defense contractors; a review of company reports and accounts; obtaining publicity; and a resource bibliography.

2953. Warshauer, William, Jr. *Keeping Nonprofit Organizations Out of Trouble*. New York: Price Waterhouse & Co.

2954. Weber, John. "The Building Better Boards Project." *Voluntary Action Leadership* (Winter 1983): 20-1.

2955. Webster, Frederick E., Jr. *Social Aspects of Marketing*. Englewood Cliffs, N.J.: Prentice-Hall, 1974.

2956. Weiss, Nancy. "Cheaper by the Dozen." *NPO Resource Review* 1 (July-August 1983): 1+.

2957. Whisler, Thomas, and Gregory Nigosian. "The Business Executive As Nonprofit Trustee: A Fish Out of Water?" *Board Letter* (Spring 1984): 5+.

2958. Whitaker, Fred A. *How to Form Your Own Non-Profit Corporation in One Day*. Oakland, Calif.: Minority Management Institute, 1979.

2959. Whitney, Elizabeth. "Computers for Non-Profits? Part 1." *Grassroots Fundraising Journal* 3 (April-May 1984): 7+.

2960. Wiehe, Vernon R. *Management by Objectives in Mental Health Services*. Rev. ed. Ann Arbor, Mich.: Masterco Press, 1974.

2961. Williams, J.M. *Publicity Guidelines for Fundraisers*. Mattituck, N.Y.: Training for Living, 1981.

2962. Williamson, Jim. "Should I Buy a Personal Computer?" *Nonprofit World Report* 2 (January-February 1984): 9+.

2963. Willis, Jerry, and Merl Miller. *Computers for Everybody*. 3rd ed. Beaverton, Oreg.: Dilithium Press, 1984.

2964. Willmer, Wesley Kenneth. *The Small College Advancement Program: Managing for Results*. Washington: Council for Advancement and Support of Education, 1981.

2965. Wilson, Leslie L. "Is It Feasible? The Prime Question in Venture Planning: A Case Study Shows How One Nonprofit Found Its Own Answer." *Nonprofit World* 6 (September-October 1988): 10-2.

For the nonprofit considering entering into a money-making venture or expanding an existing one, this article offers a step-by-step guide through a feasibility study. Includes a case study to clarify the procedure.

2966. Wilson, Marlene. *The Effective Management of Volunteer Programs.* Boulder, Colo.: Johnson Publishing Co., 1979.

2967. Wolf, Thomas. *The Nonprofit Organization: An Operating Manual.* Englewood Cliffs, N.J.: Prentice-Hall, 1984.

Primer based on the author's course at Radcliffe College teaches the administrative skills crucial to the effectiveness of any nonprofit organization. Focuses on such important areas as: financial management and accounting, which planning process works best, fundraising basics, and what computers can do to make the organization easier to run.

2968. Wolf, Thomas. *Presenting Performances: A Handbook for Sponsors.* 3rd ed. Cambridge, Mass.: New England Foundation for the Arts, 1979.

2969. Wolfers, Elsie E., and Virginia B. Evansen. *Organizations, Clubs, Action Groups: How to Start Them, How to Run Them.* New York: St. Martin's Press, 1980.

2970. Wood, Struthers and Company. *Trusteeship of American Endowments.* New York: Macmillan, 1932.

2971. Woolf, Burton I. *Mission Accomplished: Automating Your Tax-Exempt Organizations.* Brookline, Mass.: Burt Woolf Management, 1983.

2972. Yanowitz, Alan J. "'Take Care': The Legal Duties of Board Members." *Grantsmanship Center News* 2 (March-April 1983): 84-6.

2973. Young, David W. "'Nonprofits' Need Surplus Too." *Harvard Business Review* 60 (January-February 1982): 124+.

2974. Young, Donald R., and Wilbert E. Moore. *Trusteeship and the Management of Foundations.* New York: Russell Sage Foundation, 1969.

2975. Youth Project. *Technical Assistance Pamphlet (TAP).* Atlanta, Ga.: Youth Project/Southern Office, 1977.

2976. Zaltman, Gerald, ed. *Management Principles for Nonprofit Agencies and Organizations.* New York: Amacom, 1979.

2977. Zehring, John William. *How to Work Smarter, Not Harder: A Manual for Development Officers.* Cleveland: Third Sector Press, 1986.

2978. Zurcher, Arnold. *The Foundation Administrator: A Study of Those Who Manage America's Foundations.* New York: Russell Sage Foundation, 1972.

Results of a 1970 study of the people who manage American foundations and determine their policies. Provides detailed information on employment patterns and policies and examines the pros and cons of increased professionalization of foundation service.

2979. Zurcher, Arnold. *Management of American Foundations: Administration, Policies, and Social Role.* New York: New York University Press, 1972.

2980. Zwingle, J.L. *Effective Trusteeship: Guidelines for Board Members.* Washington: Association of Governing Boards of Universities and Colleges, 1975.

7

FUNDRAISING

2981. Adams-Chu, Lynda Lee. *The Professionals' Guide to Fund-Raising, Corporate Giving, and Philanthropy: People Give to People.* Westport, Conn.: Greenwood Press, 1988.

An in-depth introduction to philanthropic activities in the United States, with a focus on understanding the fundraising process in relation to nonprofit organizations (this chapter offers descriptions of national organizations which help stimulate philanthropy and assure professionalism, such as Independent Sector, the National Committee for Responsive Philanthropy, Women and Foundations/Corporate Philanthropy, and the National Society of Fund Raising Executives); individuals; corporations; foundations; United Way; and religious institutions. The final chapter briefly covers important points associated with writing and evaluating grant proposals, and the appendix lists women's funds in the United States. Includes bibliography.

2982. Aetna Life and Casualty. *A Neighborhood Reinvestment Partnership.* Hartford, Conn.: Aetna Life & Casualty, 1982.

2983. Alberger, Patti. *Winning Techniques for Athletic Fund Raising.* Washington: Council for Advancement and Support of Education, 1981.

2984. Alberto, Charles E., George S. Macko, and Nike B. Whitcomb. *Money-Makers: A Systematic Approach to Special Events Fund Raising.* Evanston, Ill.: Nike B. Whitcomb Associates, 1982.

2985. Aldige, James G., III. "Supplement Your Fund Raising with a Direct Mail Campaign." *Association Management* 35 (June 1983): 91+.

2986. Allen, Stewart E. *Private Financing in Public Parks: A Handbook.* Washington: Hawkins and Associates, 1979.

2987. Allen, Thomas W., and K. Scott Hughes. *Fund Raising in California School Districts: A Discussion Paper.* New York: Peat, Marwick, Mitchell & Co., 1982.

2988. "Alternative Funds Emerge As Force in Charitable Campaigns." *Nonprofit Executive* 4 (July 1985): 1+.

2989. Altman, D. "More Effective and Less Costly AIDS Health Services." *Caring* 5 (June 1986): 52-5.

2990. American Alumni Council. *Educational Fund Raising Manual.* 1956-1960. Washington: American Alumni Council, 19—.

2991. American Association of Fund-Raising Counsel. *East-West Philanthropy Conference.* New York: American Association of Fund-Raising Counsel, 1968.

2992. American Association of Fund-Raising Counsel. *East-West Philanthropy Conference. Philanthropy in the Seventies.* New York: American Association of Fund-Raising Counsel, 1970.

2993. American Association of Fund-Raising Counsel. *An Introduction to the American Association of Fund-Raising Counsel, Inc. and AAFRC Trust for Philanthropy.* New York: American Association of Fund-Raising Counsel, 1987.

Explains the aims and purposes of the American Association of Fund-Raising Counsel, Inc. (AAFRC) and the AAFRC Trust for Philanthropy. AAFRC, originally founded by nine professional fundraising counseling firms, seeks to maintain high standards of ethics in fundraising counseling, to study and identify trends in American philanthropy and share this information with the general public, and to foster and encourage professional training in fundraising techniques through strict adherence to AAFRC's Fair Practice Code. The 1987 revision of the Fair Practice Code and the requirements for applying for membership in AAFRC are included. The AAFRC Trust for Philanthropy addresses the need for more extensive research and education about philanthropy and its role in American society. To this end the Trust serves as a grantmaking foundation, as an operating foundation (conducting projects and studies), and as a catalytic agent—initiating programs and studies and encouraging other associations and agencies to conduct them. It is also responsible for the publication of *Giving USA*, an authoritative annual report on charitable giving, and the bi-monthly *Fund-Raising Review*. Lists the Trust's current programs and projects and its officers and board members. Also includes a listing of thirty AAFRC member firms, outlining the varied services of each.

2994. American Association of Fund-Raising Counsel Trust for Philanthropy. *An Analysis of Charitable Contributions by Upper-Income Households for 1986 and 1987*. New York: American Association of Fund-Raising Counsel Trust for Philanthropy, [1988].

Study proposes to determine the amount contributed to charitable organizations by upper-income households in 1986; to identify the proportion of cash gifts versus the proportion given as gifts in the form of securities or property; to identify the extent to which federal tax reform influenced contributors to give more in 1986 to take advantage of a more favorable deduction under the old tax laws; to determine how contributions are distributed among ten areas of giving (religion, health, education, human services, arts/culture/humanities, public society benefit, environment (including animals), international/foreign aid, youth development, and other charities); and to measure the extent to which contributors anticipate a change in their level of giving for 1987 compared with 1986 as a result of the Tax Reform Act. Eighty percent of respondents report they intend to contribute the same amount or more in 1987 as in 1986.

2995. American Association of State Colleges and Universities. Office of Urban Affairs. *The Urban Funding Guide: Sources of Funds for Urban Programs at Colleges and Universities*. Washington: American Association of State Colleges and Universities, 1983.

2996. American Council for the Arts. *Raising Money for the Arts. Conference Report*. New York: American Council for the Arts, 1979.

2997. American Council on Education. Committee on Institutional Research Policy. *Sponsored Research Policy of Colleges and Universities*. Washington: American Council on Education, [1954].

2998. *American Giving in the Field of Higher Education*. New York: John Price Jones Co., 1955.

2999. American Library Association. *Facilities Funding Finesse. Proceedings. ALA Conference*. Edited by Richard B. Hall. Chicago: American Library Association, 1982.

3000. Ames, Seth N. "The Twelve Best Things You Can Do to Strengthen Your Development Program: In a World of Priorities." *NSFRE Journal* (Spring 1989): 38-41.

Twelve recommendations to maximize development efforts and results: create a strong identity for the development office and program, one that clearly establishes your intent and earnestness; coordinate all fundraising activities through the development office to avoid conflicts, inappropriate timing, dual solicitations, and potential damage to public relations; maintain a proper staffing level and hire people with strong intelligence and personality; have a five-year plan that is published and available to prospects; involve development personnel in senior management and board of director proceedings, or at least provide special project briefings so that no opportunities for major gifts will slip past; cooperate and have open communication with the institution's public relations department, thus avoiding conflicts and insuring proper corporate identity and good press relations; have an easily understood and unified recognition system for donors; protect all charitable contributions and bequests from infringement, and keep a balance between immediate fundraising activities and those activities that encourage restricted and unrestricted endowment giving; protect your tax-exempt status; always keep the primary mission of raising funds for your organization in mind and don't become too involved in committees; recognize the side benefits of fundraising, especially in terms of public relations for your organization; and encourage professional growth for yourself and all member of the development office.

3001. Andres, Susan. "A Primer on Mailing Lists." *Grantsmanship Center News* 9 (September-October 1982): 15-30.

3002. Andresky, Jill. "Psst, Wanna Make a Donation?" *Forbes* 133 (7 May 1984): 100.

3003. Andrews, Frank Emerson. "Bounty from Beyond, How to Give the Most Good with Your Bequests." *Harper's Magazine* 225 (August 1962): 65-6

3004. "Another Way: A Look at Alternative Funds." *Conserve Neighborhoods* 37 (April 1984): 359+.

3005. Anthony, Alfred Williams, ed. *More and Better Wills: Testamentary Benefactions*. Wise Public Giving Series, no. 41. New York: Federal Council of the Churches of Christ in America, 1933.

3006. Aramony, William. "Voluntary Agencies and Community Partnerships." *Community Action* 1 (1982): 8+.

3007. Ardman, Perri, and Harvey Ardman. *Woman's Day Book of Fund Raising*. New York: St. Martin's Press, 1980.

3008. Armstrong, Richard. "How to Turn Humble Public Service Ad into a Moneymaker." *Fund Raising Management* 13 (January 1983): 20+.

3009. Arnett, Trevor. *Recent Trends in Higher Education in the United States: With Special Reference to Financial Support for Private Colleges and Universities*. Occasional Papers, no. 13. New York: General Education Board, 1940.

3010. "The Art of Soliciting a Prospective Donor in Person. Part 1." *Donor Briefing* 3 (11 May 1988): 1, 80.

3011. Artists Foundation. *Open Studio Event: An Artist's Planning Guide.* Boston: Artists Foundation, 1980.

3012. Arts and Business Council. *Highlights 3: Arts and Business Council Seminar Series for Small Community Arts Organizations.* New York: Arts and Business Council, 1979.

3013. Artz, Robert M. *Guide to New Approaches to Financing Parks and Recreation.* Washington: Acropolis Books, 1974.

3014. Ashton, Debra. *The Complete Guide to Planned Giving.* Cambridge, Mass.: JLA Publications, 1988.

Practical handbook on fundraising through bequests, charitable remainder trusts, gift annuities, life insurance, and many other innovative planned giving means, providing all the information necessary to start a successful planned giving program. Includes sample documents essential to both donors and charities.

3015. Ashton, Debra. "If You Do Not Have a Planned Giving Program: Use These Guidelines to Gain the Planned Giving Support You Need." *Nonprofit World* 6 (September-October 1988): 15-6, 18.

Part of a series on planned giving, article presents methods to gain the approval of the board to hire a director of planned giving and a secretary to the director. Includes possible objections to consider before attending the board meeting.

3016. Ashton, Debra. "Planned Giving in a One Person Shop." *Chronicle of Non Profit Enterprise* 6 (February 1988): 5-6.

Strongly advises hiring a full-time director of planned giving, but realizes that sometimes an administrator or director of development must enhance the organization's fundraising capabilities alone. Discusses how one person can initiate a non-comprehensive planned giving program (a comprehensive program requires a full-time director and a full-time secretary to the director) by concentrating on those things which require little or no maintenance, and which produce the best results for the limited amount of time one person has to spend. Advice includes selecting an experienced law firm for tax counsel on gift-related matters; promoting awareness about gifts of appreciated stock in the annual giving program and establishing a visibility campaign for bequests; studying the general benefits and operation of charitable remainder trusts; and acquiring planned giving software, which would save time on tax calculations, and which could be received as a gift of inventory from a computer company.

3017. Ashton, Debra. "Planned Giving Success Starts with Your Board." *Nonprofit World* 5 (November-December 1987): 15-7.

The degree of board commitment determines the success or failure of a planned giving program; article offers rationale behind this premise and a strategy for winning the board's support.

3018. Ashton, Debra. "Screen Your Prospects for Major Giving." *Nonprofit World* 5 (September-October 1987): 14-7.

Explores the steps and benefits involved in prospect screening, a meeting in which individuals (usually those who have already contributed at leadership levels to your organization) come together to discuss a select group of prospects, providing information and rating them according to the potential size of their gift. The benefits from the process are thus twofold: it identifies prospects with significant gift potential and develops appropriate solicitation strategies, and it heightens the awareness of those already committed to your organization about their own role in the fundraising effort.

3019. Audio Independents. *Foundation Radio Funding Guide.* San Francisco: Audio Independents, 1982.

Lists and describes those foundations which have given grants to radio-related projects, and includes contact data, brief guidelines, criteria and a sample listing of grants.

3020. *Ayer Fund-Raising Dinner Guide.* Philadelphia: Ayer Press, 1974.

3021. Ayres, Edward B., ed. *Educational Fund Raising Manual.* Washington: American Alumni Council, 1973.

3022. Baglia, Joseph R. "Planned Giving." *Philanthropy Monthly* 17 (October 1984): 25-6.

3023. Baglia, Joseph R. "Planned Giving: Untapped Sources." *Philanthropy Monthly* 18 (April 1985): 23-4.

Reports on Robert Sharpe's ideas on soliciting life insurance and retirement plans for charity.

3024. Bailen, June. "Electronic Funds Transfer Ideal for Monthly Giving." *Fund Raising Management* 14 (October 1983): 87+.

3025. Bailey, Anne Lowrey. "So You Want to Get a Grant: Some Advice from the Experts." *Change* (February 1985).

3026. Bailey, Willard. "Cause-Related Marketing: Savior or Devil for Hospital Fund Raising?" *Fund Raising Management* 18 (August 1987): 80-1.

3027. Baird, John A., Jr. "Carry on: Making Careful Promises to Donors, Prospects." *Fund Raising Management* 14 (January 1984): 44-5.

3028. Baird, John A., Jr. "How to Handle Personal Gifts." *Fund Raising Management* 19 (April 1988): 28+.

Explores the tensions involved when a charitable fundraiser is offered a personal gift, and discriminates between the suitable and permissible in contrast to the awkward or even unlawful offer.

3029. Baird, John A., Jr. "How to Use Flowers for Fund Raising." *Fund Raising Management* 17 (August 1986): 45-6, 48.

3030. Baird, John A., Jr. "Truth Telling Pays off in Development Game Plan." *Fund Raising Management* 15 (January 1985): 36+.

Discusses the importance of telling the truth to a potential donor.

3031. Baird, Nina, and Ruth Glazer. *Grantsmanship and Fundraising.* Madison, Wis.: Association of College, University and Community Arts Administrators, 1977.

3032. Baldwin, Pamela. *How Small Grants Make a Difference.* 2nd ed. Washington: National Endowment for the Arts, 1980.

3033. Balthaser, William F. *Call for Help: How to Raise Philanthropic Funds with Phonothons.* Ambler, Pa.: Fund Raising Institute, 1983.

For nonprofits seeking a new fundraising frontier, the phonothon may provide the necessary dollars. A phonothon usually raises more gift-money per contact than mail; it is less expensive per contact than in-person solicitation, and it invariably increases giving when other techniques have plateaued. Helpfully illustrated book instructs organizers in putting together a phonothon with minimum trouble and maximum income. Topics covered include: how to recruit, train, and motivate callers; how to design the message; when to call; how to estimate costs; and how to follow up and transform promises into gifts.

3034. "Baltimore's Responses to Difficult Times." *KRC Letter* 15 (May 1984): 1-5.

3035. Bargerstock, Charles T. *Educational Fund Raising and the Law.* Washington: Council for Advancement and Support of Education, 1984.

3036. Barkas, J.L. *The Help Book.* New York: Charles Scribner's Sons, 1979.

3037. Barnes, Bill L. *Planning for the Planned Gift.* Indianapolis, Ind.: Lilly Endowment, 1987.

While the purpose of this study is to provide a current "snapshot" of existing planned giving programs among seminaries and comprehensive data regarding funding patterns in support of theological education, it also provides clearly written and useful information for any organization wishing to initiate or strengthen a planned giving program. Covers the nature and impact of planned giving; the pivotal role and profile of leadership; a view of current planned giving programs at 155 theological institutions; and a comprehensive overview, including planned giving as a catalyst for other funding, marketing programs, costs, breadth of support, and benchmarks of successful programs.

3038. Barnes, W. David, and Sharon A. MacLatchie. *Meeting Today's Fund Raising Challenges.* Roseville, Calif.: Barnes Associates, 1982.

3039. Barnes, W. David. "What Are Your Responsibilities As a Professional Fund Raiser?" *Fund Raising Management* 16 (June 1985): 18+.

3040. Barr, Rhoda. "Developing a Fundraising Strategy." *NonProfit Times* 2 (June 1988): 33-5.

Offering sound advice for increasing revenue, article advocates having a realistic picture of the amount needed for current and projected activities and an analysis of past efforts when developing fundraising strategies. Includes a checklist for development planning.

3041. "Basic Grantsmanship Library." *Whole Nonprofit Catalog* 6 (Spring 1988): 10-2.

3042. Bates, Don. "The Electronic Tonic." *KRC Letter* 13 (March 1983): 1-4.

3043. Bauer, David G. *The Complete Grants Sourcebook for Higher Education.* 2nd ed. American Council on Education/Macmillan Series in Higher Education. New York: Macmillan, 1985.

Comprehensive and practical guide to staging a grant-seeking campaign for higher educational institutions. Part 1 contains a step-by-step methodology for developing and implementing a grants search with checklists, worksheets and references to other information sources to aid in the search. Parts 2, 3 and 4 profile about 500 private foundations, corporate grantmakers and government agencies which have regularly contributed to higher education. Includes subject and geographic indexes to funding programs.

3044. Bauer, David G. *The How to Grants Manual.* New York: Macmillan, 1984.

Basic how-to manual for the novice grantseeker. Explains the methods to develop a systematic approach to needs assessment, identify the best sources of funds, and work with government, foundation, and corporate funders. Includes helpful tips on dealing with the decisions of funding sources and ways to follow-up after a decision has been made.

3045. Bayley, Ted D. *The Fund Raiser's Guide to Successful Campaigns.* New York: McGraw-Hill, 1988.

A general guide for the initiate fundraiser, including how to organize and motivate volunteers. Divided into four parts, Part 1 examines the psychology of charitable giving, the leadership characteristics needed to raise money, and general principles for successful fundraising; Part 2 presents basic organizational concepts for conducting an annual campaign, including such aspects as the audit function, records and progress reports, and receipts and acknowledgments; Part 3 offers insights on soliciting corporations, foundations, and individuals; and Part 4 provides an overview of special fundraising methods beyond the annual fund drive, such as direct mail, planned giving, and capital campaigns, along with a layman's guide to the implications of the Tax Reform Act of 1986. Examples of materials used in successful fundraising drives are included throughout the book.

3046. Beach, Cecil. "Local Funding of Public Libraries." *Library Journal* 10 (15 June 1985): 23-6.

3047. Beatty, Betsy, and Libby Kirkpatrick. *The Auction Book: A Comprehensive Fund-Raising Resource for Nonprofit Organizations.* Denver, Colo.: Auction Press, 1985.

Step-by-step guide for running a charity auction is valuable for the novice and the experienced auction chairperson.

Addresses every aspect of putting together a successful event, from time lines to budgets, contracts, job descriptions, volunteers, and clean-up.

3048. Beaumont, Constance, ed. *Equity Syndication: How Does It Work? How Can Cities, Nonprofits Use It?* Washington: Preservations Reports, 1982.

3049. Bell, Herb. "Strategic Income Unit Indicators Identify Most Profitable Paths." *Fund Raising Management* 14 (January 1984): 32-5.

3050. Bendixen, Mary Anne. "Accurate, Thorough Research Nets Bigger Prospect Dollars: Effective Research Is a Key to More Effective Fund Raising." *Fund Raising Management* 16 (April 1985): 28+.

3051. Bendixen, Mary Anne. "Grantsmanship Provides Gains." *Volunteer Leader* 27 (Summer 1986): 4-5.

3052. Bendixen, Mary Anne. "Increasing Contributions through Effective Writing." *Fund Raising Management* 15 (May 1984): 76-9.

3053. "Benefit by Bids: The Gavel Rises." *New York Times* (16 May 1982): H-1.

3054. Berendt, Robert J., and J. Richard Taft. "Budgeting for Development." *Nonprofit Executive* 2 (August 1983): 5-6.

3055. Berendt, Robert J., and J. Richard Taft. *How to Rate Your Development Office: A Fund-Raising Primer for the Chief Executive.* Washington: Taft Group, 1983.

3056. Berney, Albert. "Financing Private Colleges: The Picture Has Changed." *Education Digest* 40 (September 1974): 44-6.

3057. Betts, Francis M., III. "The Successful Fund Raiser: Born or Made?" *Grants Magazine* 6 (December 1983): 255-56.

3058. Big Brothers/Big Sisters of America. *Fund Raising Review.* Philadelphia: Big Brothers/Big Sisters of America, 1979.

3059. "Black Fund Raising." *Black Scholar* 7 (March 1976): 1-64.

3060. Blanshard, Paul, Jr. *KRC Fund Raiser's Manual: A Guide to Personalized Fund Raising.* New Canaan, Conn.: KRC Development Council, 1974.

3061. Blum, Robert, and Joan Blum. "A Case for Constituency Building As a Direct Program Expense." *Philanthropy Monthly* 16 (October 1983): 13-6.

3062. Blumenthal, Larry. "Most Big United Ways Shield Executive Salaries from Public." *NonProfit Times* 1 (February 1988): 1, 12-3, 18, 22.

Article examines the salaries of top executives at the twenty-five largest United Ways, focusing on the issues of public disclosure (only five United Ways provided salary information on request) and salary justification. While the most frequently occuring reason for non-disclosure is confidentiality, and the strongest justification of salary levels is competition for high-caliber managers, the article suggests that non-disclosure only incites public mistrust and suspicion of charitable institutions, and that the best course would be to educate the public to the business realities which require such competitive salaries. A chart shows salaries for top United Way executives; data for the organizations that refused to supply salary information upon request was obtained from state agencies and the IRS.

3063. Blumenthal, Larry. "Wanted: More Minorities for Top Fundraising Jobs." *NonProfit Times* 1 (December 1987): 1, 4, 9.

Although the entry and mid-management levels of the nonprofit sector have opened up to minorities, top fundraising positions remain a white male dominated field. Among the reasons cited for low minority representation: a shortage of experienced, qualified applicants due to a lack of training programs which would attract minorities to the field or help them advance their careers; "cultural assumptions" and prejudices; little pressure on nonprofits to hire minorities and lack of awareness by board members of the situation; and competition from the better paying for-profit sector for the few available candidates.

3064. Blumenthal, Ralph. "Catholic Relief Services Involved in Dispute over Spending of Ethiopia Aid." *New York Times* (7 August 1985): A-8.

3065. Boba, Eleanor. "Cataloging Urban Needs: Gifts Catalogs Encourage Private Giving to Cities." *Grantsmanship Center News* 10 (January-February 1984): 16-20.

3066. Boitano, David. "Filling the School Funding Gap." *Argus* (15 May 1983).

3067. Bornstein, Rita. "Adding It Up." *Currents* 15 (January 1989): 12-7.

Investigates differences in capital campaign reporting for educational institutions. Survey responses confirm that campaigns have diverse purposes and structures, making results hard to compare, but some of the general findings are as follows: institutions allowing a longer period for collecting their nucleus fund can announce a higher percentage of the goal achieved when going public, and thus have an advantage when starting off; the average pre-public phase in the campaigns surveyed lasted twenty-two months; the average length of the public phase was four-and-a-half years, with the lowest being two years and nine months, and the highest being seven years; seventy-two percent of the twenty-nine reporting institutions used fundraising counsel to help plan and/or conduct the campaign, suggesting a question about the role of consultants in establishing guidelines for accounting and reporting; and the three areas that can have a significant impact on campaign results in terms of whether or not the institutions choose to include them in their reports are: gifts for medical purposes; planned gifts and bequest expectancies; and government support. Asks if each institution should establish accounting guidelines for their campaigns or if a series of general principles should be developed to guide college and university officers in their planning. In any case, the recommended first step toward consistency in reporting comprehensive campaigns is documentation of each institution's policies and guidelines.

3068. Borr, Ernest B. "Deferred Gift Derring-Do." *Currents* 9 (July-August 1983): 21.

3069. Borton, Georgina L. "Names and Numbers: A Survey Shows How Major Universities Go about Prospect Research." *Currents* 13 (October 1987): 34-6.

Survey of senior development officers at fifty-six member institutions of the Association of American Universities reveals the scope of prospect research programs, some common approaches, and the information resources most frequently consulted. Research programs were found to be operating full-time, investigating at least four major types of donors: alumni, nonalumni individuals, corporations, and foundations. Basic profiles for individuals included at least the following data: educational, personal, and family background; professional title and affiliation; social, philanthropic, civic, and professional activities; past giving to the institution and other organizations; personal and professional achievements and awards; financial information; and connections to other donors. Corporate and foundation profiles focus on shared interests between the prospect and university, and on relationships of alumni and other donors with the corporation or foundation. Preferred research sources for individuals: *Who's Who, Standard & Poor's Directors and Executives, Biographical and Genealogical Master Index*, and *Dun & Bradstreet's Reference Book on Corporation Management*. For corporations: *Standard & Poor's Register of Corporations, Taft Corporate Giving Directory, Million Dollar Directory, Moody's Manuals*, and *Directory of Corporation Affiliates*. For foundations: *Source Book Profiles, Foundation Directory*, and *Taft Foundation Reporter*.

3070. Boss, Richard W. *Grant Money and How to Get It: A Handbook for Librarians.* New York: R.R. Bowker Co., 1980.

A guide to funding sources for libraries with advice on proposal writing and approaching funders.

3071. Bothwell, Robert O., and Timothy Saasta. "Reagan Administration Does It Again." *Grantsmanship Center News* 12 (January-February 1984): 62-4.

3072. Braddy, Glen J. "Good Professional Contacts: Tapping Your Hidden Resource." *Fund Raising Management* 14 (October 1983): 74-5.

3073. Bradley, William L. "Reversing the Old Order." *Foundation News* 25 (September-October 1984): 42-3.

Explains how foundation indifference to the work of religious agencies has given way to respect.

3074. Brakeley, George A., Jr. *Tested Ways to Successful Fund Raising.* New York: Amacom, 1980.

3075. Brakeley, John Price Jones. *Voluntary Support for Public Higher Education.* Stamford, Conn.: Brakeley, John Price Jones, 1972.

3076. "Breaking Ground: Private Interest in Public Job Training." *Emergings* (November 1983): 4.

3077. Breiteneicher, Joseph C.K. *Quest for Funds: Insider's Guide to Corporate and Foundation Funding.* Washington: National Trust for Historic Preservation, 1983.

Special issue of the bimonthly newsletter, *Conserve Neighborhoods*, this brief guide presents an overview of private fundraising with an emphasis on the planning process.

3078. Breivik, Patricia Senn, and E. Burr Gibson, eds. *Funding Alternatives for Libraries.* Chicago: American Library Association, 1979.

3079. "Bridging the Cash Flow Gap." *NPO Resource Review* 2 (September-October 1983): 1+.

3080. Brilakis, Antony A. "Computerized Spreadsheets Offer Objective Mail Analysis." *Fund Raising Management* 16 (October 1985): 38+.

3081. Brinckerhoff, Peter C. "Tax-Induced Fund Raising: New Techniques to Prosperity." *Fund Raising Management* 15 (April 1984): 58+.

3082. Broce, Thomas Edward. *Fund Raising. The Guide to Raising Money from Private Sources.* Norman, Okla.: University of Oklahoma, 1986.

3083. Brody, Ralph, and Marcie Goodman. *Fund-Raising Events: Strategies and Programs for Success.* New York: Human Sciences Press, 1988.

Focuses on fundraising activities designed to provide contributors with something in return for their financial support. Part 1 describes generic principles and concepts to guide strategic thinking involving all of a nonprofit's events; part 2 describes actual fundraising events in detail. Includes bibliography.

3084. Broman, John. *Grantsmanship Resources for Problems in Aging.* Los Angeles: Grantsmanship Center, 1979.

3085. Broman, John. *Grantsmanship Resources for Rehabilitation Programs.* Reprint. Los Angeles: Grantsmanship Center, 1980.

3086. Bromley, E. Blake. "Planned Giving Instruments: The Great Circle Route." *Philanthropist/Le Philanthrope* 5 (Summer 1985): 3+.

3087. Brooklyn In Touch Information Center. *Grass-Roots Fundraising.* Brooklyn, N.Y.: Brooklyn In Touch Information Center, 1982.

3088. Brotman, M. "The Reluctant Fund-Raisers: Getting Physicians into the Act." *Trustee* 40 (February 1987): 21-3.

Offers practical suggestions for enlisting the support of the medical staff for donations or fundraising activities.

3089. Brown, Jack H. "Planning and Marketing Development Programs in the Future." *NAHD Journal* (Winter-Spring 1984): 69-71.

3090. Brown, Kathleen M. "Marketing Demystified: Even Small Nonprofit Organizations Can Use Marketing Tools in Fund Raising." *Grassroots Fundraising Journal* 3 (October-November 1984): 3-7.

3091. Bruce, Bob. "New Relief for Tired Fund-Raising Messages." *Fund Raising Management* 16 (June 1985): 36+.

3092. Bryant, David S. "Private Funding and Public Libraries." *Library Journal* 109 (1 February 1984): 145-48.

3093. "Building on Experience: Improving Organizational Capacity to Handle Development Projects." *Conserve Neighborhoods* 52 (October 1985): 1-15.

3094. Builta, Jeanine, ed. *The Campaign Manuals.* 2 Vols. Cleveland: Third Sector Press, 1984.

Provides consultant's forms, samples, checklists, schedules, and plans for conducting a fundraising campaign.

3095. Burkhart, Patrick J. "Partnerships with Industry and Government Propel an Engineering School toward Its Goal." *Fund Raising Management* 16 (July 1985): 34+.

3096. Burnett, Ed. "How to Avoid Pitfalls in Fund Raising Direct (Mail) Response." *Fund Raising Management* 14 (March 1983): 18-9.

3097. Burns, Michael E., ed. *Religious Philanthropy in New England: A Sourcebook.* Hartford, Conn.: D.A.T.A., 1987.

Describes grantmaking and other philanthropic activities of more than thirty-five religious denominations in New England. Designed to help researchers identify potential sources of funding for their organizations, entries provide address, phone number, contact person, application procedures, eligibility, forms of assistance/support, types of projects considered, and special population or program priorities.

3098. Burzynski, T. "A Method for Hospice Economic Survival." *American Journal of Hospital Care* 4 (November-December 1987): 15-20.

3099. Business Committee for the Arts. *Directory of Matching Gift Programs for the Arts.* New York: Business Committee for the Arts, 1984.

Describes matching gift programs for the arts of 255 companies. Each entry gives contact information, defines who may make a matching gift, describes eligible recipients, details the type of match, and states the minimum/maximum match.

3100. Butners, Marite M. "Pooled Income Funds." *Chronicle of Non Profit Enterprise* 3 (March 1984): 6-7.

3101. California Community Foundation. *Funding Information Center Handbook.* Los Angeles: California Community Foundation, 1987.

Provides essential information about grantmaking sources in both the private and public sector, with emphasis on the private sector, especially foundations. Includes information on the research process, proposal writing, meeting with the representative of a potential funding source, and resources for the individual grantseeker.

3102. California. Office of Appropriate Technology. *Funding for Renewable Energy and Conservation Projects.* Rev. ed. Sacramento, Calif.: California Office of Appropriate Technology, 1981.

3103. Caming, H.W. William. "Solicitation by Telephone: A Constitutional Perspective." *Philanthropy Monthly* 15 (November 1982): 19-21.

3104. Campbell, Craig. "Marketplace Only Real Way to Get True Response Results." *Fund Raising Management* 16 (April 1985): 48+.

Basic fundraising tips on direct mail.

3105. Campbell, D.A. "Philanthropy: Shareholders and Capital Formation for Hospitals." *Hospital Capital Finance* 3 (2nd Quarter 1986): 7-8.

3106. "Capital Campaigns: Knowing When You're Ready." *National Fund Raiser* 10 (August 1984): 1.

3107. Carbone, Robert F. *An Agenda for Research on Fund Raising.* College Park, Md.: Clearinghouse for Research on Fund Raising, 1986.

3108. Carbone, Robert F. "Class Act: More and More Institutions Offer Development Training." *Currents* 11 (July-August 1985): 40-1.

3109. Carbone, Robert F. *Fund Raisers of Academe.* College Park, Md.: Clearinghouse for Research on Fund Raising, 1987.

Brief summary of a study of academic fundraisers. The study questioned the sample group about their academic backgrounds, their current positions, how they became fundraisers, what career paths they followed and their attitudes toward professionalism. Among the author's findings were the facts that the fundraisers of academe are young, white, well educated, and increasingly more equally divided between female and male. Members of this group have little tenure in their positions and change their jobs frequently in search of greater responsibility and higher pay. The training in the field is informal, "even accidental." Their view of professionalism is narrow, limited to a question of competence when what is needed is a broad-based view that includes competence as well as a sense of moral and intellectual values and accomplishments.

3110. Carestia, Elizabeth. *Aide de Fondations aux Universites Americaines.* (Foundation aid to American universities). Privately Printed, 1981.

3111. Carmichael, Stephen J. "Finding Funds for Youth Shelters." *Grants Magazine* 9 (September 1986): 158-62.

Checklist of potential sources for funding youth shelters which provide a safe haven for juvenile runaways. The article cites two needed types of support—base funding for establishing the shelter and enhancement funds for the betterment of the existing program. Following a brief discussion of these two funding types, Carmichael identifies funding sources using an annotated checklist which covers government, foundation, charity, business and industry, and agency fundraising.

3112. Carroll, Margaret. "The $25 Billion Giveaway: America Perfects the Fine Art of Fund Raising." *Chicago Tribune* (20-23 October 1975).

3113. Carson, Emmett D. *The Attitudes, Accessibility, and Participation of Blacks and Whites in Work-Site Charitable Payroll Deduction Plans.* Unpublished, 1988.

Examines the extent to which blacks and whites participate in workplace charitable payroll deduction plans. While the survey data has several shortcomings, several findings are clear:

a substantial percentage of both blacks and whites from diverse socio-economic backgrounds believe it is important to be able to choose the organizations which would benefit from their payroll-deducted contributions; blacks and whites in the same occupational grouping have dramatically different views about the issues to which charitable organizations should give priority (the report suggests that the number of charitable contributors and the level of their giving may be increased if organizations to which an employee wished to give had access to payroll deduction plans); and while blacks are somewhat less likely than whites to have access to a workplace charitable payroll deduction plan, blacks are more likely to participate in such plans than whites. By right of their high level of participation, black employees should possess the leverage to choose charities to which they wish to contribute and to influence the charities which receive their contributions to allocate those funds for the provision of services that interest them the most. Otherwise, the report states, the continued black support of organizations which do not adequately represent their philanthropic interests amounts to participation without representation.

3114. Carter, Lindy Keane. "Family Secrets." *Currents* 15 (January 1989): 42-5.

Interviews with members of five families involved in fundraising reveal important lessons and insights they have gained from each other.

3115. Caswell, G.M. "How to Market Planned Giving." *Fund Raising Management* 17 (February 1987): 56-61.

3116. Cawley, Rebecca, comp. *Guide to Funding Sources for American Indian Library and Information Services.* Washington: U.S. Department of the Interior. Office of Library Services, 1974.

3117. Center for Arts Information. *New York City Arts Funding Guide.* New York: Center for Arts Information, 1985.

3118. Center for Community Change. *Rural Development Programs: A Citizen's Action Guide.* Washington: Center for Community Change, 1979.

3119. Center for Third World Organizing. *Church Funders List.* Oakland, Calif.: Center for Third World Organizing, 1986.

Chart lists over sixty Protestant and Catholic religious funding organizations. Information includes names and address, contact person, key dates, application form, grant size, restrictions, and funding interests.

3120. Chambers, Merritt Madison. *Higher Education: Who Pays? Who Gains? Financing Education Beyond the High School.* Danville, Ill.: Interstate Printers & Publishers, [1968].

3121. "Charity Begins at Work." *KRC Letter* 17 (September 1986): 1-4.

3122. "Charity on Their Lips and Larceny in Their Hearts: A Study of New York State's Professional Fund Raisers." *Philanthropy Monthly* 16 (July-August 1983): 10-30.

3123. Chavers, Dean. *Basic Fund Raising.* Broken Arrow, Okla.: DCA Publishers, [198?].

3124. Chavers, Dean. *Funding Guide for Native Americans.* Broken Arrow, Okla.: DCA Publishers, 1983.

Loose-leaf handbook and directory of foundation, corporate, and religious funders that support Native American programs and organizations.

3125. Chegwidden, Daniel. "Helpful Hints and Observations for Fund Raising Neophytes." *Fund Raising Management* 15 (March 1984): 66-9.

3126. Cherner, Beverly. "Setting Up a Canvass." *Grassroots Fundraising Journal* 3 (April-May 1984): 9-12.

3127. Chernikoff, Larry. "President Asks $125 Million for Arts in '84." *Cultural Post* 8 (March-April 1983): 5.

3128. Chetkovich, Michael N. *The Crisis in Higher Education: A Shared Responsibility and a Major Opportunity.* New York: Haskins & Sells, 1978.

3129. "Choosing the Right Capital Campaign Consulting Firm." *National Fund Raiser* 13 (March 1987): 2-3.

Brief article relating to the capital campaign of over one million dollars. The author believes that the keys to the success of the capital campaign are the leadership provided by the board and the competency of the professional consulting firm retained. In interviewing the consulting firm the most important questions that can be asked are who will be your resident director and does the consulting firm have the computer software to eliminate time-consuming, costly, manual record keeping chores? Other important considerations include: have you interviewed a wide selection of firms; what are their track records with institutions similar to yours; do the firms have reputations for conducting and presenting feasibility studies accurately; have you obtained frank assessments from former clients; do the firms know your region, audience and program; has the firm outlined their general plan of attack; and what obligatory provisions have been included in your contract?

3130. Christensen, Robert. "Arts Groups Can Obtain Non-Arts Dollars Too." *Fund Raising Management* 14 (March 1983): 4.

3131. Church, David M. *Philanthropic Fund Raising As a Profession.* Vocational and Professional Monographs, no. 88. Bethesda, Md.: Bellman Publishing Co., 1957.

3132. Church, Susan, and Tracey Shafroth. *Capital Campaigns for Community Organizations.* Chicago: United Way of Chicago, 1987.

Guide to aid community organizations implement a capital campaign, based on the authors' experience with such projects. Among their observations, all of which are fully discussed: a thorough plan that considers the space needs of the agency for the next five years is always the best first step; it is important to involve staff members in capital projects from the outset; organizations are more likely to raise money if they have a project design; a good relationship with the right architect is essential (includes a description of the architect's services); a fundraising feasibility study can greatly reduce the chances of disaster (especially when trying to raise more than $100,000); dedicated board members are crucial, not only to fundraising, but also to the committees that plan the different fundraising activities (includes descriptions of various subcommittees); and the board of directors should make its financial contribution before the campaign gets underway (with individual pledges kept confidential; only the total amount pledged by the board need be announced).

3133. Cialdini, Robert B. "What Leads to Yes: Applying the Psychology of Influence to Fund Raising, Alumni Relations, and PR." *Currents* 13 (January 1987): 48-50.

Describes six psychological principles and applications of compliance (the process of getting other people to say yes to your requests) in fundraising, public relations and alumni administration. The principles discussed are: reciprocity, authority, commitment, consensus, scarcity, and friendship/liking.

3134. Clark, William J. "Public-Private Partnerships: Helping to Achieve Common Goals." *Response* 12 (September 1983): 8+.

3135. Clay, Edwin S., III. "Fund Raising by Strategic Design." *Bottom Line* 1 (1987): 25-7.

Addresses the importance of strategic planning in determining why and when a public library will turn to the private sector for support. Provides essential considerations before taking the first step towards fundraising, such as examining your organization's history and role in the community, establishing commitment to the fundraising campaign, assigning roles and responsibilities, and setting the campaign's chronology.

3136. Cobb, Leyland M. "Fund Raising's Revolving Door: How It Can Be Stopped." *Fund Raising Management* 16 (March 1985): 40-1.

3137. Cobb, Leyland M. "More Helpful Cues for a New Position." *Fund Raising Management* 15 (December 1984): 66-7.

Suggestions on adjusting to a new development position.

3138. Cockerill, Adrian B., Jr. "Economics of Planned Gifts: Myths Destroy Programs." *Fund Raising Management* 14 (October 1983): 44+.

3139. Cockerill, Adrian B., Jr. "Fund Raising Management of the Feasibility Deficient." *Fund Raising Management* 15 (August 1984): 46+.

3140. Coe, Linda C. *Funding Sources for Cultural Facilities: Private and Federal Support for Capital Projects.* Salem, Oreg.: Oregon Arts Commission, 1980.

3141. Cohen, Lilly, ed. *Funding in Aging: Public, Private and Voluntary.* 2nd ed. Garden City, N.Y.: Adelphi University Press, 1979.

3142. Coldren, Sharon L. *The Constant Quest: Raising Billions through Capital Campaigns.* Washington: American Council on Education, 1982.

3143. Colvard, Richard, and Andre M. Bennett. *Patterns of Concentration in Large Foundations' Grants to U.S. Colleges and Universities.* ACT Research Report, no. 63. Iowa City, Iowa: American College Testing Program, 1974.

3144. Colwell, Phoebe T. "The Use of Charts: A Tool for Management." *Fund Raising Management* 15 (August 1984): 52+.

3145. "The Combined Federal Campaign: Let's Make It Work Better." *Philanthropy Monthly* 16 (September 1983): 10-4.

3146. Combs, Stephen M. *This Old Neighborhood: A Business and Community Guide to Neighborhood Revitalization.* Chicago: Catholic Charities of Chicago, 1982.

3147. "Computers in Alumni and Development." *Currents* 9 (March 1983): 30+.

3148. "Conducting a Major Gifts Campaign." *Grassroots Fundraising Journal* 5 (June 1986): 7-13.

3149. Cone, Arthur Lambert, Jr. *How to Create and Use Solid Gold Fund-Raising Letters.* Ambler, Pa.: Fund Raising Institute, 1987.

Guidelines and examples for writing effective fundraising letters. Advice on finding prospects and testing their reactions; points to consider before beginning to write; methods for mastering an easy writing style; seven steps to a profitable letter, including how to explain why you're writing, how to make it believable, how to ask for money, and ways to make your P.S. pay off; profitable packaging ideas; and how to raise maximum dollars.

3150. Conference on Alternative State and Local Policies. *Community Energy Cooperatives: How to Organize, Manage and Finance Them.* Rev. ed. Washington: Conference on Alternative State and Local Policies, 1982.

3151. Conrad, Daniel Lynn. *The Grants Planner.* San Francisco: Institute for Fund Raising, 1976.

3152. Conrad, Daniel Lynn. *How to Solicit Big Gifts.* San Francisco: Public Management Institute, 1985.

A step-by-step how-to manual for an organization's big gift fundraising. The manual divides big gift solicitation into six phases. The process begins with *Getting Ready for Big Gifts*, *Prospect Researching*, and *Finding and Training Solicitors* (includes a course outline for a solicitor training program). The guide then proceeds with the actual preparation and solicitation phases with *Preparing for Solicitation, Face-to-Face: The Six Skills of Solicitation* and *Follow Up After the Big Gifts*. Each section is filled with worksheets, checklists, tables, charts, graphs, diagrams, and lists of suggestions. Section 7 contains case studies of fictitious big gifts prospects; a questionnaire to be completed and used by the reader and his/her organization; a *Solicitation Skills Inventory* and *Solicitation Preparation Packet*. Section 1 concludes with an eight page bibliography of fundraising monographs and articles.

3153. Conroy, Tom. "The Celebrity Auction." *Grassroots Fundraising Journal* 6 (June 1987): 9-13.

3154. Converse, Philip Ray. "Federal Reserve Board Survey Suggests Bright Future for Planned Giving." *NonProfit Times* 1 (May 1987): 30.

3155. Conyngton, Hugh R. "I Have a Million Dollars to Leave." *[Source Unknown]* (1935): 5.

3156. Coolbirth, Alison G. "The Increased Competition for Private Contributions and Grants." *Grants Magazine* 7 (March 1984): 34-7.

3157. Cooley, Charles A. *Fund-Raising for the Private School: The Alumni Fund.* Boston: Independent School Consultants, 1962.

3158. Cooley, Charles A. *Fund-Raising for the Private School: The Capital Gifts Campaign.* Boston: Independent School Consultants, 1968.

3159. Cooley, Charles A. *Fund-Raising for the Private School: The Foundation Approach.* 3 Vols. Boston: Independent School Consultants, 1964.

3160. Corbally, John E. "In the Money: A Foundation President's Advice on Foundation Solicitation." *Currents* 10 (July-August 1984): 14-6.

3161. Corey, Kenneth E. *Neighborhood Grantsmanship: An Approach for Grassroots Self-Reliance in the 1980's.* Cincinnati, Ohio: University of Cincinnati, 1979.

3162. Cornesky, R.A. "Fund-Raising Strategies for the Allied Health Professions." *Journal of Allied Health* 16 (May 1987): 155-66.

Describes a development model for raising private contributions which emphasizes allied health academic units (e.g., schools and colleges of allied health), including the roles of the academic department, development advisory committee, and faculty in developing the mission statement, needs, objectives, and case statement for the department. Explores interactions between the development office staff and the department chairperson, faculty, dean, and advisory committee members in identifying, cultivating, and soliciting private support.

3163. Cornwell, Jim L. "Planned Giving: A Look at the Eighties." *NAHD Journal* (Winter-Spring 1984): 52-7.

3164. Corry, Emmett. *Grants for Libraries.* 2nd ed. Littleton, Colo.: Libraries Unlimited, 1986.

Discusses various funding programs for school, academic and public libraries. Contains chapters on: federal programs for libraries serving children; college/university libraries; public libraries; library/information science education programs; and ways librarians and patrons can persuade legislators that libraries should be adequately supported and financed. Includes an updated chapter on private foundation funding, composing a grant proposal, and planning a development campaign.

3165. Coughlin, Ellen K. "Gifts to Education Down 3.5% in 1975." *Chronicle of Higher Education* 12 (17 May 1976): 9.

3166. Council for Advancement and Support of Education. *Mindpower Match/Double Your Dollar.* [Leaflet]. Washington: Council for Advancement and Support of Education, 1981.

3167. Council for Advancement and Support of Education. *Special Events Survival Kit.* Washington: Council for Advancement and Support of Education, 1977.

3168. Council for Financial Aid to Education. *Handbook of Aid to Higher Education by Corporations, Major Foundations and the Federal Government.* New York: Council for Financial Aid to Education, 1972.

3169. Council for Financial Aid to Education. *Voluntary Support of America's Colleges and Universities.* 1956-1986. New York: Council for Financial Aid to Education, 19—.

Annual report of giving to 1118 colleges and universities, and 415 independent secondary and elementary schools from voluntary sources. Voluntary support includes donations from individuals, foundations, corporations, religious organizations, and other nongovernmental givers. Provides detailed analysis of survey results and numerous tables. For each of the survey participants, totals are given for educational expenditures, support for capital purposes, voluntary sources of support, market value of endowment, and other vital statistics. Historical tables recap annual giving support back to 1949-50.

3170. Council for Financial Aid to Education. *Working Conference on Financial Aid to Education.* New York: Council for Financial Aid to Education, 1954.

3171. Cover, Nelson, comp. *A Guide to Successful Phonathons.* Washington: Council for Advancement and Support of Education, 1980.

3172. Crawford, Jean A., and Judith A. Potts. "How to Survive a Capital Campaign: Ways and Means of Using Consultants to Maximize Your Organization's Major Efforts." *Fund Raising Management* 17 (July 1986): 39-46.

3173. Crohn, Richard J. "Direct Mail Fund Raising: Where Do I Begin?" *KRC Letter* 14 (February 1984): 5-6.

3174. Crohn, Richard J., and Mitchell Keller, comps. and eds. *KRC Portfolio of Fund Raising Letters.* New Canaan, Conn.: KRC Development Council, 1973.

3175. Crouch, David C. "A Phenomenal Phonathon." *Currents* 9 (July-August 1983): 26.

3176. Crovetti, F. Urbon. "Repositioning a Non-Profit Requires Prospect Strategy." *Fund Raising Management* 15 (December 1984): 40+.

3177. Crowell, Chester T. "Giving Away Money." *Saturday Evening Post* (20 March 1926): 10-11, 194, 197-98.

3178. Cruickshank, Joseph H. "Good Management Requires a Director of Planning and Development." *Philanthropy Monthly* 27 (September 1984): 16-8.

3179. Cumerford, William R. *Fund Raising: A Professional Guide.* Fort Lauderdale, Fla.: Ferguson E. Peters Co., 1978.

3180. Cunneen, Frank J. *Best Techniques*. Yalesville, Conn.: Resources, [198?].

3181. Cunningham, Robert M., Jr. *Asking and Giving: A Report on Hospital Philanthropy*. Chicago: American Hospital Association, 1980.

3182. Curtis, Charlotte. "A First for the Cathedral: St. John the Divine Hopes to Emulate the Fund-Raising Successes of the Public Library and the Zoo." *New York Times* (10 September 1985): C-15.

3183. Cushman, Charles P. "Don't Call It Fund Raising." *NAHD Journal* (Winter-Spring 1983): 22-4.

3184. Cutlip, Scott M. *Fund Raising in the United States: Its Role in America's Philanthropy*. New Brunswick, N.J.: Rutgers University Press, [1965].

This is the only comprehensive history of American fundraising. Cutlip examines fundraising's functional relationships to our changing social structure, especially the shift of philanthropy from an elite to a mass base, from predominantly religious to predominantly secular appeals for funds, from amateur volunteers to professional fundraisers, and from the original agencies of media, church, and benefit to the YMCA, Community Chest, United Ways and Appeals, and the onset of large fundraising firms. He traces fundraising from its inception among the struggling colleges of colonial states, through the advent of large-scale philanthropy and the fantastic explosion of giving during World War I, and on to the rise of professional fundraisers and public relations experts who organize campaigns to net vast sums from the population. The study's discussion of the evolution of fundraising reflects many changes in American culture, including the trend from activist donors to activist recipients, and the increasing anonymity of personal relationships in which donor and recipient are becoming more and more remote from one another. Brief bibliography.

3185. Dalgliesh, J. "Deferred Giving: It's Never Too Late." *Hospital Trustee* 11 (September-October 1987): 15-6, 21.

3186. Daniels, Arlene Kaplan. *Grantsmanship*. Evanston, Ill.: Northwestern University, 1980.

3187. Daniels, Ellen Stodolsky, ed. *How to Raise Money: Special Events for Arts Organizations*. New York: Associated Councils of the Arts, 1977.

3188. Dannelley, Paul. *Fund Raising and Public Relations: A Critical Guide to Literature and Resources*. Norman, Okla.: University of Oklahoma, 1986.

3189. Davidson, Alice H. "Secrets of Success in Special Events." *Fund Raising Management* 18 (April 1987): 66, 68, 70, 73, 87.

According to Alice Davidson, the special event is essentially a clever marketing device. It can establish a permanent link between the donor and the organization. A strong, well-defined fundraising program should always include special events. However, an organization would not depend on special events for most of its income because they are not the most efficient fundraising method. The article discusses cost efficiency, frequency of the events, the pros and cons of the special event, and the essential factors necessary to produce a successful event. The essentials are listed and discussed, including the product, the leadership, the volunteers, the constituency, and the plan. Also included are the *Ten Commandments* for producing a successful special event. Remember, the writer warns, the process is not over when the event has come to a conclusion. Davidson concludes with suggestions for what to do after the ball is over which she refers to as "the wrap."

3190. Davis, Frampton. "Show Prospective Donors the Way and They Can Provide the Will for Deferred Gifts and Bequests." *College and University Business* 51 (December 1971): 28-9, 31, 33.

3191. Davis, King E. *Fund Raising in the Black Community: History, Feasibility, and Conflict*. Metuchen, N.J.: Scarecrow Press, 1975.

3192. Davis, Margaret Bergan. "The Untapped Resource: Corporate Matching Gifts." *Fund Raising Management* 14 (May 1983): 20-4.

3193. Dawson, Judith M. "Carnival Time in Hawaii: The Punahou School in Hawaii Has One of the Most Successful of All Special Events." *Fund Raising Management* 18 (April 1987): 50-2, 54.

Profiles the annual Punahou School Carnival fundraising event in Hawaii, a two-day affair that has been called the "King of School Carnivals." The 1986 Punahou Carnival grossed $885,000 with a net of $322,000, an increase of $86,000 over the previous year's event. Among the reasons cited for the Carnival's success: fifty-five years of tradition, the fulfillment of community need, expectation and reputation of excellence, and the generous school support of volunteer involvement.

3194. Day, Heather F. *Seeking Foundation Funds: A Brief Guide for Nonprofit Groups in Indiana*. Indianapolis, Ind.: Central Research Systems, 1982.

3195. "Day Care: A New Alliance." *New York Times* (1 August 1985): C-6.

Discusses collaboration between corporations and government on child care.

3196. de Groot, Jane, ed. *Education for All People: A Grassroots Primer*. Boston: Institute for Responsive Education, 1979.

3197. De Rea, Philip. "Getting a Star to Help Your Cause." *NonProfit Times* 1 (May 1987): 17-9.

Advice on employing celebrities for special events and image building. Stresses the importance of good ideas, careful planning and meticulous execution to insure success, and suggests contacting promotion directors, especially for local celebrities, as a source of assistance. Celebrities can add glamor to a fundraising event and offer media exposure and credibility to your organization, but thoughtful consideration must be given to choosing a celebrity whose public image is appropriate to your cause.

3198. Deabler, L. "Advantages of a Community Foundation." *Hospital Topics* 57 (September-October 1987): 24-7.

3199. Deckoff, Marvin J. "The Volunteer Key to Successful Fund Raising." *Philanthropy Monthly* 15 (November 1982): 29-37.

FUNDRAISING

3200. Delgado, Gary. *Activists Guide to Religious Funders: Leveraging God's Resources from Her Representatives on Earth. A Working Model.* Oakland, Calif.: Center for Third World Organizing, [1987].

Lists names and addresses of major religious denominations. Describes some of the projects they have funded and offers advice on how to approach them.

3201. Delgado, Gary. "Raising Money from Churches." *Grassroots Fundraising Journal* 5 (February 1986): 5-11.

3202. Dennis, Barry, and Gabriel Rudney. *Charitable Contributions: The Discretionary Income Hypothesis.* Program on Non-Profit Organizations, no. 63. New Haven, Conn.: Institution for Social and Policy Studies, 1983.

3203. DeNunzio, Michael A. "Case Statements, Feasibility Studies, and Action Plans." *NAHD Journal* (Winter-Spring 1984): 62-5.

3204. Dermer, Joseph, ed. *America's Most Successful Fund Raising Letters.* Washington: Public Service Materials Center, 1976.

3205. Dermer, Joseph. *A Guide to Foundation Fund Raising under the Reagan Administration.* Washington: Public Service Materials Center, 1982.

3206. Dermer, Joseph. *The New How to Raise Funds from Foundations.* Washington: Public Service Materials Center, 1979.

Practical advice on submitting funding requests to foundations.

3207. Dermer, Joseph, ed. *A Treasury of Successful Appeal Letters.* Washington: Public Service Materials Center, 1985.

Shows successful fundraising letters written by diverse organizations, ranging from large universities to small community-based agencies. The letters, which include requests for money, equipment, and membership, are divided into seven chapters: social welfare agencies, hospitals and health groups, higher education, schools, cultural organizations, environmental agencies, and religious and international agencies. Preceding each letter is the author's comments on what made the letter successful.

3208. Desmond, Richard L., and John S. Ryan. "Serving People Needs." *Currents* 11 (March 1985): 42-4.

Tells how to strike the correct balance between centralized fundraising and raising money by school and college.

3209. DeSoto, Carole. *For Fun and Funds: Creative Fund-Raising Ideas for Your Organization.* West Nyack, N.Y.: Parker Publishing Co., 1983.

3210. Desruisseaux, Paul. "Abuse and Fraud Said to Threaten Matching Gifts: Companies Accuse Colleges of Laundering Contributions." *Chronicle of Higher Education* 30 (24 July 1985): 1+.

3211. Desruisseaux, Paul. "Consortium Provides Grants to Help Small Colleges Help Themselves." *Chronicle of Higher Education* 32 (2 April 1986): 1+.

3212. Desruisseaux, Paul. "Fierce Competition among Colleges Predicted As Many Gear Up to Seek More Private Money." *Chronicle of Higher Education* 31 (4 September 1985): 52.

3213. Desruisseaux, Paul. "Gifts to Higher Education Reach Record $5.6-Billion: Businesses, Foundations, Individuals All Increase Aid." *Chronicle of Higher Education* 30 (17 July 1985): 1+.

3214. Detmold, John Hunter, ed. *Papers in Educational Fund Raising.* Washington: American Alumni Council, 1972.

3215. Devlin, A. "How to Capitalize on a Strong Endowment Fund." *Trustee* 39 (May 1986): 24, 27, 31.

3216. DeVries, R.A. "Private Philanthropy in Support of Health Service Demonstrations and Research." *Health Services Research* 16 (Spring 1981): 7-10.

3217. "Dialing for Dollars: Using Phone-a-Thons for Renewals." *Grassroots Fundraising Journal* 3 (February-March 1984): 8-9.

3218. Dickson, John P., and Sarah S. Dickson. "Collecting Marketing Research Data." *Nonprofit World Report* 3 (March-April 1985): 19+.

3219. Diehl, Richard J., and Christine D. Weger, comps. *Alcoholism Funding Service: A Directory of Federal, State and Foundation Grants for Alcohol Education, Prevention and Treatment Services.* Honolulu, Hawaii: Program Information Associates, 1987.

Directory of alcoholism program funding sources. The directory is divided into four sections: *The Alcoholism Grants Register, The Grants Register Alternate Funding Sources, The Foundation Register,* and *The Law Register.* The *Alcoholism Grants Register* contains primary funding sources for education, prevention, research, and treatment programs and alternate funding sources rarely used by eligible programs. The *Grants Register Alternate Funding Sources* contains a detailed description of each of the major federal block grants. The *Foundation Register* contains foundations which have a demonstrated history of giving for or have expressed an interest in alcoholism, drug abuse, mental health and general health/community agencies. The giving patterns of the foundations are reflected by their division into *National Foundations* and *State and Local Foundations.* The *Law Register* is a compilation of both federal and state laws and federal regulations which pertain to various aspects of alcohol abuse and alcoholism programs.

3220. Diehl, Richard J., and Christine D. Weger. *Drug Abuse Funding Service: A Directory of Federal, State and Foundation Grants for Drug Abuse Education, Prevention and Treatment Services.* Honolulu, Hawaii: Program Information Associates, 1987.

Directory of drug abuse program funding sources. [For content arrangement See also: FUNDRAISING. Program Information Associates. *Alcoholism Funding Service.*].

3221. Diehl, Richard J., and Christine D. Weger. *Mental Health Funding: A Directory of Federal, State and Foundation Grants for Mental Health Education, Prevention and Treatment Services.* Honolulu, Hawaii: Program Information Associates, 1987.

Directory of mental health program funding sources. [For content arrangement See also: FUNDRAISING. Program Information Associates. *Alcoholism Funding Service.*].

3222. DiMaggio, Paul J. *Can Culture Survive the Marketplace?* Program on Non-Profit Organizations, no. 62. New Haven, Conn.: Institution for Social and Policy Studies, 1983.

3223. Dimino, E.R. "Acquiring Foundation Funds for Health-Related Projects." *Pediatric Nursing* 13 (September-October 1987): 363-4.

3224. Dingfelder, William M. "Non-Profits Must Consider Ethics in Soliciting Gifts." *Fund Raising Management* 13 (December 1982): 36-7.

3225. *Direct Mail: A Preliminary View.* Winchester, Mass.: Divoky & Associates, 1981.

3226. "Direct Mail Expectations, Great and Small." *KRC Letter* 14 (April 1983): 5-6.

3227. Direct Mail/Marketing Association. *List Brokers.* Washington: Direct Mail/Marketing Association, [1975].

3228. *Directory of Biomedical and Health Care Grants.* Phoenix, Ariz.: Oryx Press, 1988.

Contains 2,316 health-related funding programs which are designed to study the needs of society in health care delivery. Areas covered include clinical and programmatic studies in gerontology and mental health; clinical studies of the cause, detection and elimination of cancer; health care delivery and maintenance; and epidemological studies of infectious diseases. Describes the focuses and goals of each program's requirements listing eligibility statements; restrictions listing exclusions; contact; deadlines; and funding amounts. Has sponsoring organizations index by subject and type.

3229. *Directory of Grants in the Physical Sciences.* Phoenix, Ariz.: Oryx Press, 1986.

1,561 programs which fund laboratory research, undergraduate education, scholarships and fellowships for graduate and postgraduate students, internships and conferences in the physical sciences. Descriptions of each program include focuses and goals, requirements listing eligibility statements, restrictions listing exclusions, contacts, deadlines and funding amounts. Indexed by subject, and by organization name and type (foundation, corporation, business and professional organizations, and state and federal governmental agencies).

3230. *Donors and Dollars: Investing in Direct Mail Fund Raising.* Burlington, Mass.: Epsilon Data Management, 1978.

3231. Donors Forum of Chicago. "Facing Emergency Needs: Foundations in Other Cities Have Created Emergency Structures." *Forum* 1 (Winter 1983): 3.

3232. Donors Forum of Chicago. "Not Passing the Bucks: Study Finds Arts Are Relatively Unscathed by Funding Cuts." *Forum* 1 (Winter 1983): 1+.

3233. "Donors Must Be Cultivated to Become Major Donors." *FRM Weekly* (October 1986): 1-2.

3234. Dorsey, Eugene C. "International Conference on Fund Raising Keynote Address." 1987. *Fundemensions* 11 (May 1987): 5-8.

Eugene C. Dorsey, president of the Gannett Foundation, discusses the findings of the Independent Sector Task Force on Measurable Growth in Giving and Volunteering and outlines the program that challenges all Americans to double charitable giving and increase volunteer activity by fifty percent by 1991.

3235. Douty, Christopher M. "Disasters and Charity: Some Aspects of Cooperative Economic Behavior." *American Economic Review* 62 (September 1973): 580-90.

3236. Dove, Kent E. "Audit Your Development Office for Results." *Currents* 11 (September 1985): 28+.

3237. Dove, Kent E. *Conducting a Successful Capital Campaign: A Comprehensive Fundraising Guide for Nonprofit Organizations.* Jossey-Bass Management Series/Jossey-Bass Higher Education Series. San Francisco: Jossey-Bass Publishers, 1988.

Written for the executives and staff of a wide range of nonprofit organizations, this book can be used by seasoned practitioners as a review of and guide to the fundamental issues and challenges of capital campaigns; by newcomers, volunteers, and professionals without campaign experience as an introduction to the principles of campaigning; and by philanthropic agencies as a resource for assessing the caliber of programs they are asked to fund. The principles discussed throughout the book are relevant to arts-related, religious, educational, community, and health care organizations that are either contemplating or conducting a capital campaign. Chapters cover global considerations; preparatory assessments; the roles of leaders and volunteers in the campaign; how to recruit, educate, and mobilize volunteers; the characteristics of a case statement; the usefulness of a gifts table; how to establish the campaign structure and solicitation process; how to identify, research, and rate prospects; methods for cultivating and soliciting major gift prospects; how to manage campaign logistics and day-to-day operations; successful publications, promotion, and public relations; how to conclude the campaign, including the recognition of donors and volunteers, writing final reports, and auditing the productivity of the campaign; and the emerging trends affecting the future of capital campaigns. Resource sections contain samples of communications materials, case statements, a program brochure, a question-and-answer sheet, a plan of action/volunteer handbook, pledge cards, newsletters, and stationary and envelopes. Also includes a reference bibliography.

3238. Dow, Adele. "Secrets to a Successful Major Gift Program." *Nonprofit World* 5 (July-August 1987): 14-5, 29.

Especially strong major gift programs are highlighted to stress the three keys of success: developing a sense of ownership by involving donors in the organization in ways other than giving money; developing a feeling of group spirit by providing

3239. Downes, Michael. "Corporate Matching Gift Program for Schools Underway." *Fund Raising Management* 15 (June 1984): 102.

3240. Downes, Michael. "The Curse of Assumptions." *NSFRE Journal* (Spring 1989): 17-20, 22.

Downes argues against ten common assumptions about fundraisers and fundraising in general. Fundraising is not begging, he insists, and until those in the field become convinced that one has to train and be fully committed to fundraising as a marketing discipline in the nonprofit sector, no one else will believe it either. To those who insist government should fund nonprofits, Downes points to the evidence that all governments today are financially incapable of providing adequate funding. In addition, he notes differences in the way governments and the nonprofit sector operate, and cautions that government funding could result in institutionalized compassion. Downes also rebukes claims that fundraising has reached a saturation point; that a donor can be asked too often; that there is such a thing as average giving (instead, he refers to evidence suggesting that over forty percent of a goal is received from one or two donors); that major gifts can be received by mail (they can only be obtained by identifying and educating prospects, and then personally asking them for such a gift); that bequests must be offered, not solicitated; that basic fundraising principles won't work at *your* agency; that little or no money should be spent on fundraising, because it takes away from the programs; and that those who give time to a cause need not give financial support as well.

3241. Downes, Michael. "The Growth of Schuller's Television Ministry in Australia." *Fund Raising Management* 16 (August 1985): 90+.

Reviews the fundraising history of *The Hour of Power* in Australia.

3242. Drotning, Phillip T. *Putting the Fun in Fund Raising: 500 Ways to Raise Money for Charity.* Chicago: Contemporary Books, 1979.

3243. du Pont, Pierre S., IV. "State Government and Community Partnerships." *Community Action* 1 (1982): 15+.

3244. Duguay, Lois. "Copy Makes Difference in This Salvation Army Appeal." *Fund Raising Management* 14 (November 1983): 52-6.

3245. Dunkel, Tom. "The Olympics Are Coming! The Olympics Are Coming!" *PSA/84* 3 (21 January 1984): 36-40.

3246. Dunkel, Tom. "Telethons and Radiothons: Tales from the Toteboard." *PSA/83* 2 (21 March 1983): 2-6.

3247. Dunlop, David R. "The Ultimate Gift: The Biggest Gifts of All Take a Special Kind of Fund Raising." *Currents* 13 (May 1987): 8-13.

Dunlop, Director of Capital Projects for Cornell University, explains what he calls the third type of giving—the ultimate gift. Different from the annual and special gifts, the ultimate gift demands time, talent and financial resources of the volunteers and staff. The most important concept is to change the prospect's views from they and them to we and us. "Once that change occurs," states Dunlop, "you'll get not only financial commitments, but personal, moral, and spiritual support as well." In order to reach this level of bonding, the institution or organization must develop awareness, knowledge, interest, involvement, and sense of commitment which leads to expressions of that commitment. The article examines the players, the necessary initiatives and management of the moves in such a campaign. The author gives encouragement to large and small organizations alike. Regardless of size, both can tend to the needs and interests of the giver because the heart of the business is "human values and human purposes...those are the things people will commit themselves to."

3248. Dunlop, Donna V. "Fundraising Network." *Library Journal* 109 (1 September 1984): 1576.

Describes The Foundation Center's network of reference collections.

3249. Dunlop, Donna V. "Solving the Funding Puzzle." *International Musician* (March 1982): 1, 14.

3250. Dunn, Thomas G. *How to Shake the New Money Tree.* New York: Penguin Books, 1988.

Describes alternative methods of fundraising—such as theater parties, street fairs, commercial tie-ins, auctions, program advertising, fashion shows, baseball games, sponsorships, and memberships—which are epitomized by Bob Geldof's *Live Aid* effort and referred to as the "show me" approach. These methods offer donors something tangible in return for their donations, while increasing their social awareness and establishing their ongoing support. Presents step-by-step guide to setting goals, selecting methods, planning events, troubleshooting, and follow-up.

3251. Dunten, Kathleen, comp. *Grants Resources Directory.* Washington: Grants Management Advisory Service, 1982.

3252. Ecclesine, Joseph A., ed. *The KRC Handbook of Fund Raising Strategy and Tactics.* New Canaan, Conn.: KRC Development Council, 1972.

3253. Eckstein, Burton J., ed. *Handicapped Funding Directory.* 6th ed. Margate, Fla.: Research Grant Guides, 1988.

Describes foundations, corporations, associations, and agencies that provide funding for programs and services for the emotionally, mentally, or physically handicapped. Includes sections on proposal writing basics, why proposals fail, and ways to improve the chances of getting a grant.

3254. Eckstein, Richard M. *Directory of Building and Equipment Grants.* 1st ed. Margate, Fla.: Research Grant Guides, 1988.

Basic directory of 538 sources which give grants or non-cash donations for equipment and building. The directory lists federal programs as well as foundations and corporations. Also included are six short essays on non-cash or in-kind gifts and raising funds for capital spending. Includes indexes.

3255. "Education Gifts Forecast to Rise Nine Percent a Year." *Chronicle of Higher Education* 27 (14 December 1983): 2.

3256. Edwards, A.H. "Hit the Ground Running: How the Chief Advancement Officer Can Start a Job and a Capital Campaign in 60 Working Days." *Currents* 10 (April 1984): 26-30.

3257. "Eight Months of Good Intentions, But No Grants to Schools." *Breeze (Torrance, CA)* (20 May 1983).

3258. *Elderly Private/Public Partnerships.* Allentown, Pa.: Pennsylvania. Department of Aging, 1981.

3259. *Eleven Ways Associations Can Increase Income.* Bethesda, Md.: B. Zadek & Associates, 1982.

3260. Elnicki, Susan E., ed. *Fund Raiser's Guide to Human Service Funding.* Washington: Taft Group, 1989.

Profiles more than 875 corporations and foundations that provide grant-level support (at least $50,000 in the latest disclosure period) to human service agencies and causes. Each entry provides concise information on the institution's contact person, human service interests, geographic preferences, typical recipients, and grant types. Lists influential officers and directors, provides a summary of formal application procedures, if available, and lists up to ten of the largest grants awarded in the human service field. Indexed by grant recipients (state); institutions by headquarters state, grant type, and recipient type; and by officers and directors. In addition, provides data on more than 125 important human service nonprofits (including major donors, when available) to help fundraisers develop networks, professional support, and joint-venture programs, and to help new organizations understand the competitive aspects of grant seeking for their cause.

3261. "Emergency Loan Funds: Help for Cash Flow Crisis." *Nonprofit Executive* 3 (March 1984): 1-2.

3262. Engel, James F. "What Motivates Giving to Christian Organizations?" *Fund Raising Management* 18 (July 1987): 48, 50, 52.

Examines the ways giving decisions are made and the implications for organizational marketing strategy. The decision to give as well as donor loyalty are linked to involvement—the degree of pertinence and relevance of the cause to the individual. When involvement is high, the donor acts as a rational problem solver and is likely to continue giving as long as the cause is perceived as having relevance and the organization as having credibility; but when involvement is low, decisions to give are a result of passive reasoning, and continued support cannot be counted upon. In both cases, immediate personalized follow up based on an understanding of donor interests and motivations is advocated to earn donor loyalty.

3263. Engelberg, M. "Procuring Incentives for Community Health Promotion Programs." *Journal of Community Health* 12 (Spring 1987): 56-65.

Investigates various solicitation methods employed by community health promotion programs when approaching community merchants as a source of incentives. The effect of setting (i.e., level of urban development) and the type of business are also analyzed in terms of procurement rates. Among the findings: telemarketing and face-to-face contact had similar procurement rates; restaurants were by far the type of business most likely to donate; and rural merchants provided incentives significantly more often than urban merchants, while developing urban area merchants' donation rates were midway in between. Telemarketing proved the most cost effective method of solicitation.

3264. Ensman, Richard G., Jr. "The Art and Science of Direct Mail Copywriting." *Grassroots Fundraising Journal* 6 (April 1987): 3-6.

Covers the basics of mass direct mail planning and the preparation of the appeal letter. Offers copywriting techniques to enhance the quality of personal communication in the appeal letter, such as: using short sentences, writing warmly and casually without being trite, and underscoring important words or points.

3265. Ensman, Richard G., Jr. "The Art of Friendship Entices Unsolicited Donors." *Fund Raising Management* 15 (April 1984): 78-9.

3266. Ensman, Richard G., Jr. "Building a Mailing List: An Introduction." *Grantsmanship Center News* 2 (May-June 1983): 10-21.

3267. Ensman, Richard G., Jr. "Database Creation Helps This School Build Income, Friends." *Fund Raising Management* 14 (June 1983): 36+.

3268. Ensman, Richard G., Jr. "Organizational Tools for a Small Development Office." *Fund Raising Management* 14 (January 1984): 78-9.

3269. Enters, Carol. "Primer on Tried and True List Testing Techniques." *Fund Raising Management* 14 (October 1983): 69-73.

3270. Eves, Margaret. *Guidelines to Fund Raising: Annual Support.* Rev. ed. Chicago: United Way of Chicago, 1987.

Originally prepared for United Way member agencies, this manual identifies basic fundraising principles and practices useful to all nonprofit organizations. Focuses on fundraising for annual support and program funding, which provides a basis for all other types of fundraising. Reviews the essential components of fundraising planning, including a discussion of program policy, organizational leadership, administration, and agency image; describes the elements of the annual fundraising plan, including sources of support, goal setting, scheduling, volunteer organization, solicitation materials, and recognition of volunteers and donors; and describes various methods of seeking contributions (personal solicitation, project funding proposals, direct-mailings, and benefits and events) along with practical advice for implementing them. Appendixes provide information regarding ethical standards in fundraising as established by the National Society of Fund-Raising Executives and samples of records and other fundraising materials.

3271. "Exploratorium Shares Research: Corporations Match Employee Gifts." *ASTC Newsletter* (January-February 1981): 10.

3272. Faust, Paula J. *An Introduction to Fund Raising: The Newcomers' Guide to Development.* Washington: Council for Advancement and Support of Education, 1983.

3273. Federal Resources Advisory Service. *Grants: Views from the Campus.* Washington: Association of American Colleges, 1979.

3274. Ferrell, O.C. "Strategic Planning for Nonprofit Health Care Organization Funding." *Journal of Healthcare Marketing* 6 (March 1986): 13-21.

3275. Fillingham, E. "Fundraising: A Marketing Perspective." *Hospital Trustee* 10 (July-August 1986): 26, 28-9.

3276. "Financing Arts Organizations: The Charity As the General Partner in a Limited Partnership." *Philanthropy Monthly* 17 (May 1984): 24-38.

3277. Fincher, Beatrice, comp. *Funds for Hispanics.* Austin, Tex.: Spanish Publicity, 1981.

3278. Fink, Norman S., and Howard C. Metzler. *The Costs and Benefits of Deferred Giving.* New York: Columbia University Press, 1982.

3279. Fink, Norman S. "Finally: A Study on Costs, Benefits of Deferred Gifts." *Fund Raising Management* 13 (January 1983): 26-30.

3280. Finn, Matia. *Fundraising for Early Childhood Programs: Getting Started and Getting Results.* Washington: National Association for the Education of Young Children, 1982.

3281. Fischer, Howard E. *How to Collect Triple Profits from Your Hobbies, Skills or Interests!* New York: Venture Publishing, 1978.

3282. Fishman, Arnold. "Database Marketing Propels Non-Profits into New Age." *Fund Raising Management* 15 (August 1984): 62+.

3283. Fishman, Arnold. "Mail Order Influence on Giving Grows According to New Study." *Fund Raising Management* 14 (September 1983): 54-65.

3284. "Five-Page Letter Raises $546,116 from 2,400 Prospects." *Fund Raising Management* 14 (December 1983): 62-3.

3285. Flanagan, Joan. *The Grass Roots Fundraising Book.* 2nd ed. Chicago: Contemporary Books, 1982.

Basic guide on how to set up a fundraising program, choose the right strategy for your group, and raise money through a variety of approaches.

3286. Flanagan, Joan. "Raising Money from Members: Who Needs What You Do?" *Grantsmanship Center News* 12 (September-December 1984): 10—22.

3287. Fleischman, Ellen. "Fundraising in Rural Communities." *Grassroots Fundraising Journal* 1 (October 1982): 1, 3-5, 13.

3288. Fojtik, Kathleen M. *The Bucks Start Here: How to Fund Social Service Projects.* Ann Arbor, Mich.: Michigan Domestic Violence Project, 1978.

3289. Ford Foundation. *Survey of Foundation and Government Grants for Women's Rights and Opportunities, 1971-75.* Unpublished, 1975.

3290. "Foundation and Corporate Funding: Effecting the Possible." *CCFlash* 15 (September 1987): 1-2.

Advises small nonprofits, such as arts groups, to concentrate on one or two major foundations or corporations a year in their fundraising efforts, rather than inefficiently scattering generic proposals in a mass mailing that only produces more rejections (due to the higher chances of the nonprofit and the potential funder having no common goals) and a deflation of morale and esteem. Stresses the importance of cultivating small and local businesses as a form of corporate support, the efficacy of in-kind contributions (the nonprofit not only has access to useful and/or necessary equipment, but it is also establishing a corporate track record), and the value of creative thinking in the research process.

3291. *Foundation Grants Guide for Schools, Museums and Libraries: Grants with a Slice for Communications Technology Products.* Fairfax, Va.: International Communications Industries Association, 1984.

Provides very brief entries on 161 foundations which fund media and materials.

3292. Foundations-Corporations Emergency Fund Committee. *Annual Report.* San Francisco: Foundations-Corporations Emergency Fund Committee, 1981.

3293. Foxwell, Elizabeth. "Winning Tickets: Capital Campaign Strategies That Helped Rally Support for Seven Community Colleges." *Currents* 12 (June 1986): 40-5.

3294. Frank, Curtiss E. *The Vital Margin of Voluntary Support.* Ann Arbor, Mich.: University of Michigan Press, 1972.

3295. Freeman, Douglas. "Concepts in Planned Giving: Or, How Property Is like Celery." *Whole Nonprofit Catalog* 8 (Winter 1988/1989): 23-5.

Sound introduction to the principles of planned giving, including the different methods of giving, tax considerations, legal concepts concerning property, and two case studies.

3296. Freiser, Leonard H. "Fundraising and the Meaning of Public Support." *Library Journal* 110 (15 June 1985): 29-31.

3297. Freyd, William. "Improving the Direct Mail Program in a Small Development Office." *KRC Letter* 16 (April 1985): 5-8.

3298. Froomkin, Joseph. *Aspirations, Enrollments, and Resources: The Challenge to Higher Education in the Seventies.* Washington: Government Printing Office, 1970.

3299. Fulton, William. "Indian Bingo: High Stakes Fundraising." *Grantsmanship Center News* 13 (March-April 1985): 13-9.

3300. "Fund-Raisers Are Invited to 'Lend a Hand' with Ad Council Campaign." *FRI Monthly Portfolio* 23 (June 1984): 1-2.

3301. *Fund Raising Handbook.* New York: Sperry & Hutchinson Co., 1980.

3302. Fund Raising Institute. *The FRI Idea Pack.* Ambler, Pa.: Fund Raising Institute, [198?].

3303. "Fund Raising Questions from the Supreme Court." *Philanthropy Monthly* 16 (November 1983): 5-19.

3304. "Fund-Raising Software Package Review." *Fund Raising Management* 16 (May 1985): 49-52.

3305. "Fundraising Events. Part 3: Budgeting." *Grassroots Fundraising Journal* (August 1982): 8-11.

3306. *Fundraising Terminology: A Glossary.* Unpublished.

Compilation of philanthropic glossaries from various sources, covering terms related to foundations, fundraising, grants, planned giving, and technical assistance. Sources include the American Association of Fund-Raising Counsel, the *Directory of Special Programs for Minority Group Members*, *Planned Giving Idea Book*, and *Fund Raising Management* magazine.

3307. Galella, Armando. "Word Processing May Promote Better Donor Record Use." *Fund Raising Management* 13 (February 1983): 32+.

3308. Garonzik, Elan. "Planning a Funding Search: How to Identify a Foundation That Could Fund Your Project." *Voluntary Action Leadership* (Summer 1983): 29-31.

3309. Gearhart, S.C. "The Grant Development Process: A Nursing Solution for a Community Health Need." *Health Care Supervisor* 6 (April 1988): 19-26.

3310. Geary, G.F., Jr. "The 'Now' Value of Deferred Gifts." *Fund Raising Management* 17 (February 1987): 62-6, 83.

3311. Geier, Ted. *Make Your Events Special: How to Produce Successful Events for Nonprofit Organizations.* New York: Folkworks, 1986.

Step-by-step guide to planning and implementing special events. Chapters on how to design a special events program, prepare a budget, recruit and coordinate personnel, handle technical, on-site and logistical operations, and promote, market, and evaluate the program. Each chapter ends with worksheets to help develop ideas and clarify plans.

3312. Geiger, Aryeh. "Teaching Doctors to Fund Raise." *Grants Magazine* 9 (December 1986): 242-45.

Emphasizes the benefits to be realized when physicians learn to raise funds for their own projects. Doctors will learn to describe their own mission, values, treatment, and various projects in an articulate and concise manner, while at the same time forcing them to appraise their own work and needs and to begin to plan for the future.

3313. Geller, Robert E. *Plain Talk about Grants. A Basic Handbook.* Sacramento, Calif.: California State Library Foundation, 1988.

Of special interest, chapter 4 contains a framework for developing and composing a proposal, and a sample proposal is contained in chapter 5.

3314. Georgi, Charlotte, and Terry Fate. *Fund-Raising, Grants, and Foundations: A Comprehensive Bibliography.* Littleton, Colo.: Libraries Unlimited, 1985.

Lists 1500 titles which are, for the most part, from 1970 on. The bibliography is divided into two main sections, the first arranged by general reference sources, which include associations, national, state, and local directories, journals, and online databases; the second section is divided by subject areas, including accounting, management, corporate responsibility, philanthropy, and proposal writing. Includes a chapter on *A Basic Fund-raising Library* which gives twenty-five titles of primary interest to fundraisers and an index of the materials which provides access by author, title, and organization.

3315. Gertzog, Alice. "Gathering Grants: Financial Boon or Bust?" *Bottom Line* (Fall 1986): 17-20.

Discusses how receiving a grant could endanger a public library's regular municipal funding allocation.

3316. *Gifts and Bequests to Colleges and Universities in Good Times and Bad Times.* New York: John Price Jones Co., 1938.

3317. "Gifts to Education Rose 7.1% in 1983, Study Finds." *Chronicle of Higher Education* 28 (June 1984): 9.

3318. Gilman, Kenneth L., Robert Munson, and K. Scott Sheldon. "Guide to Eliminate Confusion of Software Technology Options." *Fund Raising Management* 15 (October 1984): 90-3.

3319. "Giving in 1982: Colleges Got $8.59 Billion." *Chronicle of Higher Education* 26 (29 June 1983): 8.

3320. "Giving Rises in 1986, But Future Is in Doubt." *FRI Monthly Portfolio* 26 (January 1987): 1-4.

3321. *Giving with Interest: A Guide to Enlightened Charitable Giving.* Rockville, Md.: Bissell, Gorochow & Associates.

3322. Glueck, Grace. "Met Museum Seeks Endowed Chairs." *New York Times* (15 March 1983): C-11.

3323. Goldberg, Richard M. "Getting Your Message on Television News." *Nonprofit World Report* 2 (May-June 1984): 20+.

3324. Goldberg, Richard M. "How Nonprofits Can Use Television Talk Shows." *Nonprofit World Report* 2 (July-August 1984): 22+.

3325. Goldberg, Richard M. "Improve Communications with Local TV News People." *Fund Raising Management* 14 (Marchch 1983): 31.

3326. Goldberg, Richard M. "Local TV News: De-Mystifying the Medium and Getting Your Stories on the Air." *Channels* 35 (June 1983): 5+.

3327. Golden, Hall. *The Grant Seekers: The Foundation Fund Raising Manual.* Dobbs Ferry, N.Y.: Oceana Publications, 1976.

3328. Gonzales, Rosy B., ed. *Bibliography for Fund Raising and Philanthropy.* 2nd ed. Rockville Centre, N.Y.: National Catholic Development Conference, 1982.

3329. Gonzales, Rosy B. *Bibliography of Fund Raising and Philanthropy.* 2nd ed. Rockville Centre, N.Y.: National Catholic Development Conference, 1982.

3330. Goodale, Toni K. "Teaching Volunteers the Art of Asking." *Fund Raising Management* 17 (January 1987): 32, 35-6, 38.

Consultant Goodale calls for formalized fundraising training of volunteers. Includes a workshop training agenda which stresses an explanation of why people give and solicitation role-playing combined with critiques of the sessions.

3331. Goodban, Nicholas. "Opportunity or Imposition?" *Foundation News* 24 (March-April 1983): 36-9.

3332. Gordon, Les. "Soliciting Patients: The Best New Source of Prospects." *Fund Raising Management* 15 (October 1984): 60-1.

3333. Gotthelf, Nicole. "A Case Study in Federated Fundraising: Aid to Wisconsin Organizations." *Grassroots Fundraising Journal* 2 (August 1983): 5-8.

3334. Gottschalk, Sister Mary Therese. "A CEO Views Philanthropy and the Fund Raiser." *NAHD Journal* (Winter-Spring 1983): 12-7.

3335. Graham, V.L. "Is Planned Giving Dead?" *Fund Raising Management* 17 (February 1987): 48, 50, 52.

3336. Graham, V.L. "What Fund Raisers Should Know about Planned Giving." *Fund Raising Management* 16 (February 1986): 28, 31-2.

3337. Grant, Andrew J., and Emily S. Berkowitz. "Knowledge Is Power: Learn about Prospective Donors before You Write Your Proposals." *Currents* 14 (October 1988): 6-9.

Stresses the importance of the research process in successful proposal writing. A development officer must first learn about his or her own institution, especially concerning knowledge that cannot be directly discerned in the written material and statistical charts, such as institutional priorities and the organizational culture. Then the research for prospects begins, which is basically a process of elimination that removes inappropriate funders and identifies the most viable options. Advises calling other institutions that have been funded by your prospect to gain insight into the foundation or corporation's idiosyncrasies, and weighs the pros and cons of establishing contacts between your institution's trustees and the donor organization's trustees.

3338. Grantsmanship Center. *Grantsmanship Bibliography.* Los Angeles: Grantsmanship Center, 1973.

3339. Grantsmanship Center. *The Grantsmanship Book.* Los Angeles: Grantsmanship Center, 1976.

Loose-leaf collection of reprints from the *Grantsmanship Center News* provides a wealth of practical advice and information on program planning and proposal writing, funding strategies, and other areas of interest to nonprofit managers.

3340. Grasty, William K., and Kenneth G. Sheinkopf. "The Annual Fund." *Grantsmanship Center News* 11 (September-October 1983): 8-29.

3341. Grasty, William K., and Kenneth G. Sheinkopf. *Successful Fundraising: A Handbook of Proven Strategies and Techniques.* New York: Charles Scribner's Sons, 1982.

3342. Greater Minneapolis Council of Churches. *Church Funds for Social Justice: A Directory.* Minneapolis, Minn.: Greater Minneapolis Council of Churches, [198?].

Directory provides information on church funding sources at the local, regional, and national levels for social change organizations. Entries include the following information, when available: church name, address, phone number, contact person, type of assistance provided, financial data, areas of interest, application procedures, restrictions, and sample grants.

3343. Greeley, Tamara, ed. *The Housing Handbook: A Guide to Financing for Non-Profit Organizations.* New York: Federation of Jewish Philanthropies of New York, 1986.

3344. Greenhouse, Linda. "U.S. Is Upheld in Charity Drive Curb." *New York Times* (2 July 1985): B-20.

3345. Greenwood, Linda. "Publisher Tries New Twist in Fund Raising." *Fund Raising Management* 17 (October 1986): 46-7, 50.

Description of how Yankee Publishing Incorporated funded an intern program to provide jobs in historic preservation for college students in a creative subscriber-based fundraising drive.

3346. Grenzebach, John. "Tales Out of School: A Wry Look at How Not to Succeed in Fund Raising." *Currents* 10 (January 1984): 28-30.

3347. Gribble, Roger. "No Strings on Gifts to Universities." *Journal (Madison, Wisconsin)* (2 December 1973).

3348. Griffin, Moira. *Funding for Women's Programs.* Los Angeles: Grantsmanship Center, 1980.

3349. Groman, John E. "Good Telemarketers Have Good Databases." *NonProfit Times* 1 (May 1987): 26.

3350. Groman, John E. "New Strategy: 'Databased' Donor Personalization." *Fund Raising Management* 18 (May 1987): 36-40.

3351. Groman, John E. "New Techniques for Upgrading Donors." *Nonprofit World Report* 2 (May-June 1984): 12+.

3352. Groman, John E. "The Theory of a Positive Crisis." *Epsilon* 8 (1983): 4+.

3353. Grubb, David L., and David R. Zwick. *Fund Raising in the Public Interest: A Citizen's Guide to Direct Mail Fund Raising.* Washington: Public Citizen, 1977.

3354. Gurin, Maurice G. "The Compelling Case for Fund Raising by Objective." *Fund Raising Management* 14 (October 1983): 22+.

3355. Gurin, Maurice G. *Confessions of a Fund Raiser: Lessons of an Instructive Career.* Washington: Taft Group, 1985.

Chronicles the career of Maurice Gurin in the fundraising profession. Provides advice and ideas for those involved in nonprofit development, covering such topics as what motivates giving, how to recognize priorities, and how to implement fundraising techniques.

3356. Gurin, Maurice G. "Is Marketing Dangerous for Fund Raising?" *Fund Raising Management* 17 (January 1987): 72-6.

Gurin, a veteran fundraiser, believes marketing offers slick jargon, sweeping claims and serious dangers for the non-profit sector. Unchecked, marketing could adversely affect fundraisers and the philanthropic causes they serve.

3357. Gurin, Maurice G. "What Fund Raisers Should Know about TV Talk Shows." *Fund Raising Review* (31 December 1982): 2.

3358. Gurin, Maurice G. *What Volunteers Should Know for Successful Fund Raising.* Briarcliff Manor, N.Y.: Stein & Day Publishers, 1981.

3359. Gutenberg, Jeffrey S. "Fund Raising Efforts Really Produce Management Strategies." *Fund Raising Management* 14 (August 1983): 22-4.

3360. Guzman, Carol. *Semillas de Prosperidad or How to Cultivate Resources from the Private Sector.* Albuquerque, N.Mex.: Neighborhood Housing Services of Albuquerque, 1982.

Useful guide to organizing and conducting the funding search, with an emphasis on community-based organizations.

3361. Hale, Alice M. "Sweet Charity: Building an Approach to Foundation Money." *Theatre Crafts* (August-September 1986): 4.

3362. Hale, Jim, Richard Gorman, Bob Blashak, et al. "The Use of Sweepstakes and Other Donor Promotions." *Fund Raising Management* 16 (June 1985): 70+.

3363. Hall, Margarete R. "Breaking into Foundation Big Time: A Strategy for Seeking Grants from Major Foundations." *Currents* 10 (July-August 1984): 18-22.

3364. Hallock, Duane D. "The Relationship between Marketing and Development." *NAHD Journal* (Summer-Fall 1983): 21-2.

3365. Hammond, Laurie. "Fundraising Is a Song and Dance." *Grassroots Fundraising Journal* (December 1986): 7-9.

Guide on how to use a musical production to raise funds. The author stresses the fact that quality is the key to a successful show. Quality extends to all personnel involved in the production. Do not cut corners on the people who work on the show. Expert people who know what they are doing are very important. As an example, a non-union band was hired one year to save money. The non-union players "did not learn the music as quickly and were not as responsible and as a result the opening night orchestra was not one which the dancers or audience could keep time with." Besides quality, the other important factor is a strong board of directors who will sell the program advertisements, tickets, and publicity. If possible, get donated publicity—media people are more willing to get involved with a volunteer board member. In fact, most media people are willing to give more than asked for. Another important detail in a successful show is the obtaining of underwriting for big ticket items needed to produce the event.

3366. Hannah, Jacki K. *Fundraising for Independent Living Centers.* Edited by Susan R. Elkins. Lawrence, Kans.: Research and Training Center on Independent Living, 1986.

A how-to fundraising guidebook prepared for program directors and board members of independent living centers (ILCs). However, the guide is general in content and is applicable to most nonprofit organizations. Before the manual examines fundraising basics, it provides the reader with step-by-step procedures for setting up basic management systems, incorporating the nonprofit organization, and acquiring tax-exempt status. The fundraising portion of the manual includes developing the feasibility study and its presentation to the board, a summary of fundraising methods, five alternative organizational structures for fundraising, putting policy into words—the fundraising plan and the case statement—and how to find and work with consultants. Throughout the book there are charts, tables and references. Also included is a fundraising bibliography and appendixes which provide sample by-laws and a reprint of the Support Center's *Board of Directors Assessment of Roles and Responsibilities* with information on reasons for the board; the board's role, structure, and duties and responsibilities; suggestions for a board manual; and a board checklist and worksheets.

3367. Hansler, Daniel F. "American Cancer Society's Market Planning Process." *Fund Raising Management* 14 (August 1983): 32+.

3368. Hansler, Daniel F. "Information Systems for Fund Raising Development Phase." *Fund Raising Management* 16 (August 1985): 88+.

3369. Hansler, Daniel F. "Secondary Market Research: A First Step in the Process." *Fund Raising Management* 17 (October 1986): 90-1.

Brief overview of secondary market research for the fundraiser.

3370. Hansler, Daniel F. "Use Good Marketing for Fund Raising Success." *NSFRE Journal* (Spring 1984): 11-3.

3371. Hansmann, Henry. *Why Do Universities Have Endowments?* Program on Non-Profit Organizations, no. 109. New Haven, Conn.: Institution for Social and Policy Studies, 1986.

Suggests and assesses a number of possible theories to explain the accumulation of endowments by universities, finding that the most convincing arguments relate to protecting the institution's intellectual freedom, which could be infringed by a strong reliance upon any single source of current income. Also discusses the need to link the rate of accumulation and the pattern of income spending to the overall objectives of the institution which holds an endowment.

FUNDRAISING

3372. Hanson, Abel A. *Guides to Successful Fund Raising.* New York: Teachers College Press, [1961].

3373. Hanson, Ranae, and John McNamara. *Partners.* Minneapolis, Minn.: Dayton Hudson Foundation, 1981.

3374. Hardin, Paul. "How I Learned to Love Fund Raising." *Currents* 10 (January 1984): 14-8.

3375. Harnik, Tema Greenleaf. *Wherewithal: A Guide to Resources for Museums and Historical Societies in New York State.* New York: Clearinghouse for Arts Information, 1981.

3376. Harris, April L. *Special Events: Planning for Success.* Washington: Council for Advancement and Support of Education, 1988.

Step-by-step guide to a successful special event, from initial planning to invitations and publicity to paying the bills when the party's over. Harris has thirteen years experience in advancement for educational institutions, and she defines a special event as both the best and the most exasperating part of her job. They offer, however, a unique opportunity to showcase an institution in interesting, time-effective, and creative ways that at the same time allow for personal contact. They help to educate, make a point, build friendships, enable constituents to feel like insiders, and foster a sense of community. But special events do not exist in isolation, Harris cautions; instead, they should be integrated into your institution's total advancement program. Concluding chapter contains sample checklists. Bibliography.

3377. Harris, Virgil M. *Wills and Willmakers.* Minneapolis, Minn.: Trust Officers' Association of Minnesota, 1921.

3378. Harrison, Randall P. *Fund Raising by Formula: Steps to Make People Give.* Washington: Public Service Materials Center, 1984.

3379. Hartman, Hedy A. *Fund Raising for Museums: The Essential Book for Staff and Trustees.* 2nd ed. Bellevue, Wash.: Hartman Planning and Development Group, 1987.

Looseleaf directory is a how-to book designed for all types of museums—aquariums, arboretums, botanical gardens, historical museums, zoos, and so on, which have similar needs. Through case studies, the reader is shown examples of programs and given strategies to identify foundations, corporations, government agencies, and individuals for support. The bulk of the material is a directory of foundations, corporations, and government agencies which have supported museums in the past. The entries include organization name, address, telephone number, financial data, application guidelines, and sample grants, in some cases. Provides several indexes to the foundation and corporate sections, including geographic and types of museums funded.

3380. Hartman, Hedy A., comp. *Funding Sources and Technical Assistance for Museums and Historical Agencies: A Guide to Public Programs.* Nashville, Tenn.: American Association for State and Local History, 1979.

3381. Hauman, David J. *The Capital Campaign Handbook: How to Maximize Your Fund Raising Campaign.* Washington: Taft Group, 1988.

Integrates the theory and practice of managing a capital campaign, explaining not only what needs to happen, but why it is necessary to the success of the campaign. Provides information on campaigns in general; feasibility; creating a prospect pool; prospect evaluation; organizational structure; volunteer orientation; tracking and records; and wrap-up procedures. Appendixes include samples of a campaign plan, feasibility study, questionnaires and interviews, agendas and orientation sheets, job descriptions, acknowledgement procedure and final report.

3382. Hay, John Thomas. *Five Hundred Thirty-Four Ways to Raise Money.* New York: Simon & Schuster, 1983.

3383. Hayes, Susan W. "How to Package and Market Major Donor Club Benefits." *Fund Raising Management* 16 (October 1985): 58+.

3384. Heaton, William E., Jr. "Skills Called for in Managing Prospect Research." *Fund Raising Management* 14 (October 1983): 60-3.

3385. Hellige, J.R. "An Overall Look at Planned Giving." *Fund Raising Management* 16 (February 1986): 74-82, 128-9.

3386. Helmer, Michael K., and David Collver. "How to Survive Success or Coping with Rapid Growth." *Fund Raising Management* 16 (July 1985): 72+.

3387. Henderson, Emily Pfizenmaier. "Proactive Prospecting." *Currents* 13 (March 1987): 28-9.

Henderson, a prospect researcher and information manager, sets forth a proposal for a new approach to the role of prospect research specialist—proactive prospecting. In addition to the standard methods of researching prospects, Henderson's proactive prospecting demands active research on a broad scale within the whole community to seek out wealth. Including the local chamber of commerce, the investigation of property records, and the regional planners office.

3388. Hennix, Kenneth L. "Lessons Learned from the New Century Campaign." *Fund Raising Management* 16 (July 1985): 54+.

Reflections on a four year capital campaign.

3389. Henry, Yvette, ed. *Fund Raiser's Guide to Capital Grants.* Washington: Taft Group, 1988.

Describes 589 corporations and foundations that have given grants for buildings and equipment. Indexes list grantmakers by the state in which they are headquartered, by the types of capital grants they give, and by their specific charitable preferences. Also includes an index of officers and directors and an index of recent grant recipients by state.

3390. Henry, Yvette. *Fund Raiser's Guide to Religious Philanthropy: A Source for Nonprofits Seeking Aid from Religiously Oriented Donors and Organizations.* Washington: Taft Group, 1987.

Profiles over 250 major foundations that provide grant-level support to organized religion and religiously affiliated charities. Each foundation has assets over $100,000 and has awarded over $50,000 to religious charities in the most recent disclosure period. Each profile includes information on denominational and geographic preferences, types of grants awarded, when and by whom the foundation was established, a narrative summary of how religious charities figure in the foundation's philanthropic program, and a list of recipient types typically receiving foundation support for religiously affiliated activities. Also includes a list of foundation officers and directors; a statement of special application procedures if any; whether the foundation publishes any descriptive, policy, or application materials of its own; and a fiscal analysis of the foundation's activity in its latest available disclosure period, including dollar amounts for assets, total contributions, the typical range of grant sizes awarded, and a listing of sample grants. A second section contains summary information on over 100 important religious organizations which, while not providing direct financial support, maintain active service programs to community organizations, offering professional support, joint-venture service programs, and networking opportunities. Indexed to foundations by headquarters state, denominational preference, type of support, type of activities supported, and foundation officers. Indexed to organizations by headquarters state, denominational preference/affiliation, type of support, and type of activities supported.

3391. Herbers, John. "As U.S. Aid to Cities Withers, Private Money Gets Bigger Role." *New York Times* (17 August 1982): A-18.

3392. Herold, Patricia. "Funding Cutbacks Have Nonprofit Groups Scrambling for $$$." *Daily News* (18 November 1984): 4.

3393. Hertz, Willard J., and Carol M. Kurzig. "A Grant for Every Purpose." *Foundation News* 24 (January-February 1983): 26-31.

3394. Hickey, James K. *Prospecting: Searching Out the Philanthropic Dollar.* 2nd ed. Washington: Taft Group, 1984.

Basic how-to book for the novice grantseeker on researching and organizing information on prospective grantmakers. Includes many sample forms for research and recordkeeping and an annotated bibliography.

3395. Hicks, M.E. "Donor Pyramid Explained." *Texas Hospitals* 42 (February 1987): 36-7.

3396. "Higher Education Receives Lion's Share of Corporate Matching Gifts..." *CFAE Newsletter* (April 1984): 1-4.

3397. Hobson, R.L. "Deferred Giving: Accent on Planning." *Fund Raising Management* 16 (February 1986): 58-62.

3398. Hodges, Leo C., and Marc L. Carmichael. "Charity Life Insurance Gifts: Installments and No Probate." *Fund Raising Management* 16 (May 1985): 22+.

3399. Hodgkinson, Virginia A., Murray S. Weitzman, and Arthur D. Kirsch. *From Belief to Commitment: The Activities and Finances of Religious Congregations in the United States.* Washington: Independent Sector, 1988.

Results of a study undertaken to investigate the connection and contribution of religious institutions to the independent sector. Explores the influence of these institutions on the services provided to communities, the nation, and other countries, and examines the ways religious values motivate people to give and volunteer both to the religious institutions and to other organizations. Among the highlights of the study: in 1986 the total revenues of the estimated 294,000 religious congregations in the U.S. were $49.6 billion, of which eighty-two percent came from individual donations. Total expenditures for 1986 were estimated at $48.8 billion, of which $35.7 billion was for paid expenditures and $13.1 billion was for the assigned value of volunteer time. Of the $48.8 billion, $28.5 billion was for religious activities, including religious education; $7.0 billion for education; $4.6 billion for human services, $2.8 billion on health and hospitals; $1.6 billion for public and societal benefit programs (human justice and community development); $1.6 billion for arts and culture; $1.5 billion for international activities; and $0.7 billion on environmental quality. The report also documents religious congregations as the primary voluntary service providers for neighborhoods, with nine out of ten congregations reporting their facilities were available for groups within their congregations, and six out of ten reporting their facilities were available to other groups in the community.

3400. Hodsoll, Frank. "Prospects for Private Arts Support." *Cultural Post* 8 (March-April 1983): 2.

3401. Hoelterhoff, Manuela. "The Fine Art of Funding." *Elle* (August 1987): 110, 112.

With the new tax code cutting deductions on charitable gifts to twenty-eight percent, the future of the arts may depend on funding from corporations, which view the support of cultural activities as a vital marketing expense.

3402. Holck, Manfred, Jr. *Money and Your Church: How to Raise More, How to Manage It Better.* New Canaan, Conn.: Keats Publishing, 1974.

3403. Honig, Lisa. "Fund Raising Events. Part 4: Starting at Home." *Grassroots Fundraising Journal* 1 (December 1982): 10-2.

3404. Honig, Lisa. "Membership Development: Part 3, the Brochure." *Grassroots Fundraising Journal* 4 (April 1985): 10-3.

3405. Honig, Lisa. "Personalizing Fundraising Appeals." *Grassroots Fundraising Journal* 3 (April-May 1984): 3-6.

3406. Honig, Lisa. "Summer in the Non-Profit World." *Grassroots Fundraising Journal* 2 (June 1983): 7, 11.

3407. Honig, Lisa. "Think before You Plunge: Advance Planning for Fundraisers." *Grassroots Fundraising Journal* 2 (December 1983): 10-1.

3408. Hooper, Carol A. "The Building Bloc: Kresge Survey Reveals Who's Doing What in Capital Grantmaking." *Foundation News* 24 (November-December 1983): 62-3.

3409. Hooper, Carol A. "Should Your Foundation (or Nonprofit) Go Hi-Tech?" *Foundation News* 25 (November-December 1984): 33-9.

3410. Hopkins, Bruce R. "Association-Related Foundation: A Fund-Raising Vehicle." *Fund Raising Management* 18 (August 1987): 84-5.

Examines various aspects of the association-related foundation, which can be established by organizations that are tax-exempt but non-charitable (as in the case of a 501(c)(6) entity—a trade, business, or professional association). The purpose of a related foundation is to raise funds which will support programs of interest and possible benefit to the association and its members. The foundation's programs must primarily be those that qualify as charitable, educational, scientific, or similar undertakings, and they may be initiated by the foundation's leadership and/or may be spun off from the association. Control of the related foundation is maintained by means of interlocking directorates, with a majority overlap to achieve formal control. Identical boards between association and foundation are to be avoided, as this limits fundraising potential, reduces the credibility of the foundation, and possibly endangers the tax-exempt status of the foundation in the eyes of the IRS. Several methods for structuring the control mechanisms are discussed, including empowering the association's board to appoint a majority of the foundation's board, or to form the foundation in a state permitting non-profit corporations with stock. This allows the association to become the sole stockholder of the foundation. As the association-related foundation is a separate legal entity, consideration must be given to annual information returns with the IRS, state laws requiring an annual filing, the legal form of the foundation, and state laws concerning registration and annual reporting by charities that solicit contributions from the general public. This especially illustrates the underlying principle of association-related foundations—bifurcation—which allows charitable activities to be housed in a charitable organization, thus utilizing the charitable deduction and attracting grants.

3411. Hopkins, Bruce R. "Fund Raising by Phone Comes under Court Attack." *Fund Raising Management* 14 (November 1983): 76-7.

3412. Hopkins, Bruce R. "New York Adopts Revised Fund-Raising Regulation Law." *Fund Raising Management* (October 1986): 80-1.

Hopkins, a specialist in tax-exempt law outlines the basic requirements of and changes in the New York State legislation governing the state's Charitable Solicitation Act effective July 1, 1987.

3413. Hopkins, Bruce R. "Planned Giving: It's for Everyone." *Nonprofit World* 4 (July-August 1986): 30-1, 38.

Proposal for a far wider use of planned giving by charitable organizations. Includes ten easy steps to implementation of a planned giving program.

3414. Hopkins, Bruce R. "The Professional Fund Raiser's Contract." *Fund Raising Management* 16 (July 1985): 102+.

3415. Hopkins, Bruce R. "Revenue Enhancement Part of Wider Look at Fund Raising." *Fund Raising Management* 15 (June 1984): 100-01.

3416. Hopkins, Ellen. "Our Ladies of Charity." *New York* (13 October 1986): 48-53.

3417. Horan, Jerome C. "Repositioning Development in a Corporate Reorganization." *Fund Raising Management* 15 (April 1984): 54+.

3418. Hornfischer, David R. "Computer Technology and the Connecticut Junior Republic." *KRC Letter* 13 (January 1983): 1-4.

3419. Horowitz, David. "Billion Dollar Brains: How Wealth Puts Knowledge in Its Pocket." *Ramparts* (May 1969): 36-44.

3420. Horsley, Carter B. "An Evening at the Theater to Help AIDS Research." *New York Times* (20 May 1985): C-12.

3421. Hostetter, D. Ray. *The Challenge Grant and Higher Education.* Washington: American College Public Relations Association, 1966.

3422. "How Colleges Cope with the Red Ink." *Business Week* (21 November 1970): 56-8.

3423. "How Many Legitimate Prospects Do You Have?" *National Fund Raiser* 13 (October 1987): 2-6.

Tips on planning and implementing a successful personal call program, including a sample prospect analysis form and personal call solicitation form.

3424. "How Software Helped Humanize the Chore of Statistic Gathering." *Fund Raising Management* 16 (May 1985): 44+.

3425. "How to Approach Foundations." *National Fund Raiser* 10 (February 1984): 2-3.

3426. *How to Approach the Corporate Donor: A Guide for Fund Raisers.* Summit, N.J.: Chamber of Commerce of Summit, 1982.

3427. "How to Convince Your Prospects to Become Donors." *National Fund Raiser* 14 (April 1988): 1-3.

3428. "How to Design a Great Major-Gifts Club: Benefits Are the Key, As Mt. Sinai Courts the Big Donors." *FRI Monthly Portfolio* 22 (April 1983): 3+.

3429. "How to Develop Your Own Donor Profile." *National Fund Raiser* 14 (June 1988): 1-5.

Matching the demographic and psychographic characteristics of your organization's most loyal and ideal donors with those on a new-donor acquisition list may increase the percentage of response and average gift, according to the results of a special, one year project for the American Cancer Society, California Division. Article includes a sample questionnaire to aid in developing your organization's own donor profile.

3430. "How to Guarantee Success of a Large Gift Club." *National Fund Raiser* 10 (April 1984): 3-4.

3431. "How to Organize a Memorial Giving Program." *National Fund Raiser* 14 (May 1988): 1-2.

Concise appraisal of memorial or tribute giving programs, including the basics necessary for success and a suggestion list of places to distribute tribute giving materials.

3432. *How to Raise Money for Community Action.* New York: Scholarship, Education and Defense Fund for Racial Equality, 1970.

3433. "How to Raise Money from Churches." *Nonprofit Executive* 6 (January 1987): 1-2.

Local churches and their national organizations are the third largest funder of nonprofit organizations. Council on Foundations' latest available figures (1983) show that American churches gave about $8.5 billion, or twenty percent of the donations they received to nonprofit organizations. This short article serves as a guide to tapping the resource. The Council of Churches is suggested as a good starting point. The contact, continues the source, should be through a letter asking for a meeting where the fundseeker can establish the basis of a relationship—not ask for money. The process of convincing the contact person to become an advocate of your nonprofit is discussed as well as the follow-up, proposals and applications. A directory of religious institutions (with addresses and telephone numbers) which fund nonprofit organizations is included.

3434. "How to Reinstate Your Lapsed Donors." *National Fund Raiser* 13 (September 1987): 1-2.

Donors may stop giving if they feel unappreciated, are asked to give too much too soon, or are asked to give too often. Article suggests planning to reinstate at least twenty to twenty-five percent of total lapsed donors through a direct mailing and telephone campaign; respondents should be thanked immediately and renewal efforts should avoid upgrading until they have given for two consecutive years. Among those who did not respond, clear the files of all those who have not given in the past four years.

3435. *How to Start and Manage Your Direct Mail Annual Appeal.* Burlington, Mass.: Epsilon Data Management, 1977.

3436. "How to Use the Media: Getting on the Air." *Community Jobs* 6 (July-August 1983): 5-6.

3437. Hoyt, Marilyn. "Testing: A Conduit to Solid Development Growth." *Fund Raising Management* 16 (April 1985): 88+.

3438. Hruby, Norbert J. *A Survival Kit for Invisible Colleges, or What to Do until Federal Aid Arrives.* Washington: Academy for Educational Development, 1973.

3439. Hughes, Thomas M. "Phonathon Spurs Parents' Fund, Increasing Donors from 19 to 140." *Fund Raising Management* 16 (November 1985): 30+.

3440. Human Resources Corporation. *Profiles of Involvement.* 3 Vols. Philadelphia: Human Resources Corp., 1972.

3441. Human Resources Network. *How to Get Money for: Arts and Humanities, Drug and Alcohol Abuse, and Health.* Radnor, Pa.: Chilton Book Co., 1975.

3442. Human Resources Network. *How to Get Money for: Conservation and Community Development.* Radnor, Pa.: Chilton Book Co., 1975.

3443. Human Resources Network. *How to Get Money for: Youth, the Elderly, the Handicapped, Women and Civil Liberties.* Radnor, Pa.: Chilton Book Co., 1975.

3444. Hunt, Susan, ed. *New Sources of Revenue: An Ideabook.* Washington: Council for Advancement and Support of Education, 1984.

Examines entrepreneurial and unrelated business enterprises for educational institutions, with case studies of several successful enterprises.

3445. Huntsinger, Jerald E. "Ethics and Fund Raising Letters: Ten Suggestions." *Fund Raising Management* 16 (May 1985): 106-07.

3446. Huntsinger, Jerald E. *Fund Raising Letters: A Comprehensive Study Guide to Raising Money by Direct Response Marketing.* Richmond, Va.: Emerson Publishers, 1982.

3447. Huntsinger, Jerald E. "Prediction for 1987: A Year of Intense Change." *Fund Raising Management* 17 (December 1986): 52+.

The author predicts fourteen changes in the way nonprofit organizations conduct their direct mail fundraising campaigns, including a significant increase in fundraising costs, increased personalization and segmentation of mailings, and how the new tax bill may possibly confuse major gift donors who contribute by mail.

3448. Huntsinger, Jerald E. "Predictions for 1988: The Worst Is Yet to Come!" *Fund Raising Management* 18 (December 1987): 46, 48, 50-1.

Huntsinger predicts that: higher costs for direct mail fundraising in 1988 will reduce return income unless the packages get better (i.e., more creative); lack of public confidence in nonprofits will continue, affecting international organizations most, but increasing donor support of regional charities where results can be seen; religious fundraising will continue to meet with skepticism, affecting all nonprofits unless they practice complete financial disclosure and develop an attitude of public trust in all decision making; and telemarketing will die out as consumers and donors criticize it for being a high-pressure marketing technique, though limited telemarketing can be effective in certain situations (renewing lapsed donors). He insists, however, "there is absolutely no shortage of money for your organization, there is only a shortage of creative ideas to raise that money."

3449. Huntsinger, Jerald E. "Twelve Suggestions about Fund-Raising Packages." *NonProfit Times* 1 (May 1987): 27-8.

Jerry Huntsinger, a direct mail fundraising consultant, offers twelve suggestions for executive directors preparing for their next appeal, including: keeping your donors off balance by introducing an element of surprise into each fundraising package; relating more incidents of actual people being helped by your organization; and putting more of your ego into the letter.

3450. Huntsinger, Jerald E. "Twenty-Two Predictions on the Future of Direct Mail Fund Raising." *Fund Raising Management* 15 (May 1984): 68+.

3451. Huntsinger, Jerald E. "What Do You Do after All Your Donors Are Dead?" *Fund Raising Management* 18 (September 1987): 82+.

Presents profiles for three categories of direct mail donors: those seventy years of age and over; those sixty-five and over; and those fifty-five and older. Advocates further research of the people in these groups, especially the last, which in a few years will be substantially stronger than any other population segment in terms of economic standards—financial assets, net worth and income. Nonprofits, Huntsinger claims, will have to invest large amounts of money into making their direct mail programs more appealing and relevant to these categories of donors.

3452. "Ideas for Expanding Your Mailing List." *Grassroots Fundraising Journal* 2 (April 1983): 9-10.

3453. "In Peapack, Moroccan Fantasy Benefits Channel 13." *New York Times* (27 June 1983): B-5.

3454. Independent Sector. *Fund-Raising*. [Cassette tape]. Washington: Independent Sector, 1985.

3455. Independent Sector. *Secretary of State of Maryland v. Joseph H. Munson Co., Inc.* Washington: Independent Sector, [1984].

3456. "Independent Sector Outlines Plan to Double Giving." *Fund Raising Management* 17 (December 86): 93.

3457. "Individual Contributions Expected to Rise by 10% for 1982." *Fund Raising Review* (31 December 1982): 1+.

3458. Ingerson, Marshall. "Parents Chip in to Keep School Programs Afloat." *Christian Science Monitor* (22 June 1983).

3459. "The Inside Story on Hopkin's Billet-Doux." *FRI Monthly Portfolio* 22 (April 1983): 5-6.

3460. Institute for Educational Affairs. "Give Me Your Money and We'll Be Partners." *IEA Report* (1983): 1+.

3461. Institute for Urban Design. *Funding Urban Design*. Reprint. Purchase, N.Y.: Institute for Urban Design, 1981.

3462. "Interest in Endowment Campaigns for Arts Growing." *Arts Management* (January-February 1984): 1+.

3463. Jackson, Bruce, and Diane Christian. *Get the Money and Shoot*. Buffalo, N.Y.: Documentary Research, 1986.

A practical manual designed to help documentary filmmakers find grant money. Contains information on sources which provide current status of grant availability; how to locate corporate support for projects; how to establish a working relationship with a nonprofit sponsor; composing a proposal; formulating a budget; and descriptions of proposal evaluation by government, private and corporate grantmakers. Presents a hypothetical example of how an idea for a film is developed into a grant porposal. Sample budget, letters, proposal submission guidelines, are included with discussion. Appendix lists addresses of state arts and humanities agencies and councils.

3464. Jaffee, Larry. "Agent Requires Voluntary Responsibility from Athletes." *Fund Raising Management* 16 (September 1985): 34+.

Describes Leigh Steinberg's efforts to instill consciousness of charity in professional athletes.

3465. Jaffee, Larry. "Black United Funds Battle over Workplace Solicitation." *Fund Raising Management* (September 1984): 89-90.

3466. Jaffee, Larry. "Democrats' Direct Mail Efforts Segment the Issues." *Fund Raising Management* 15 (October 1984): 62+.

3467. Jeffri, Joan. *Artsmoney: Raising It, Saving It, and Earning It*. New York: Neal-Schuman Publishers, 1983.

A general guide to fundraising techniques and strategies for arts organizations. In addition to the traditional forms of grantsmanship in the private, public, and corporate sectors, discusses earned-income activities including bank interest and real estate, and methods of saving money by sharing costs and activities with other organizations.

3468. Joachim, Robert. "A Charity Ball: A Nuts and Bolts Approach." *NAHD Journal* (Winter-Spring 1984): 85-9.

3469. John Price Jones Company. *Giving to Higher Education Maintains Its Upward Curve. Report for 1954-55*. New York: John Price Jones Co., 1956.

3470. Johnsen, Robert, David Tobin, and Jessie Bond. *Organizing for Local Fundraising: Self-Sufficiency for the 80s*. Boulder, Colo.: Volunteer: The National Center for Citizen Involvement, 1982.

3471. Johnson, Bill. "To Some Celebrities, Stints for Charities Are Strictly Business." *Wall Street Journal* (1 June 1984): 1.

3472. Johnson, Julian. "Emotion, Right Price, Prizes Spark Employee Contributions." *Fund Raising Management* 16 (June 1985): 56+.

3473. Johnson, Verne, and Ted Kolderie. "Public/Private Partnerships: Useful But Sterile." *Foundation News* 25 (March-April 1984): 29-33.

3474. Jordan, Richard G. *Bequests*. New York: American Association of Fund-Raising Counsel, 1966.

3475. Kaiser, Leland. "Fund Raising's Future Lies with Creative Visionaries." *Fund Raising Management* 16 (March 1985): 34+.

3476. Kanel, David L. "The Role of Viewpoint Neutrality in Nonpublic Fora Access Restrictions: Cornelius v. NAACP Legal Defense and Educational Fund." *University of San Francisco Law Review* 20 (Summer 1986): 851-75.

3477. Kansas City Resource Institute. *Steps and Strategies of Good Grantsmanship*. Kansas City, Mo.: Kansas City Resource Institute, 1977.

3478. Kantonen, T.A. *A Theology for Christian Stewardship*. Philadelphia: Muhlenberg Press, 1956.

3479. Kashian, Miriam Lynch. "How to Get On-Line with Database Software Programs." *Fund Raising Management* 14 (February 1984): 54-7.

3480. Kassman, Deborah N. "Handle with Care: Thirteen Steps to Better Stewardship Reports." *Currents* 9 (September 1983): 26-8.

3481. Katz, Wendy. "Analysis and Testing of Acquisition Mailings." *Fund Raising Management* 16 (April 1985): 52-3.

Ten tips on testing and analysis offered by a direct-mail professional.

3482. Keezer, Dexter M., ed. *Financing Higher Education, 1969-70*. Study of the Economics of Higher Education. New York: McGraw-Hill, 1959.

3483. Keller, Mitchell. *The KRC Aide and Advisor to Fund Raising Copywriters*. New Canaan, Conn.: KRC Development Council, 1981.

3484. Keller, Mitchell, ed. *The KRC Guide to Direct Mail Fund Raising*. New Canaan, Conn.: KRC Development Council, 1977.

3485. Kelley, B.F., Jr. "The Donor Process: Solicitation and Recognition." *Fund Raising Management* 17 (November 1986): 38-42.

3486. Kemeny, John G. "The Mystique of University Endowments." *AGB Reports* 25 (March-April 1983): 11-5.

3487. Kempf, Beverly. "Obtaining Pledges through Electronic Funds Transfer." *Nonprofit World Report* 2 (July-August 1984): 10-1.

3488. Kennedy, N. Brent. "Here's How Simple Research Tool Audits Communication." *Fund Raising Management* 14 (November 1983): 40-2.

3489. Kennedy, N. Brent. "Improve Your Mail Solicitation Using Tested Testing Techniques." *NSFRE Journal* 8 (Spring 1983): 9+.

3490. Kennedy, Sam J. "Cultivating the Big Gift." *KRC Letter* 15 (January 1985): 1-5.

3491. Ketchum, Carlton G. "Unforgettable Characters in Fund Raising: Charles R. Hook, William Allen White." *Fund Raising Review* (November 1984): 3-5.

3492. "Key Fund-Raising Statistics." *Fund Raising Management* 18 (November 1987): 30,32-4,36-8,40-2.

3493. "Key Fund-Raising Statistics." *Fund Raising Management* 19 (August 1988).

Key fundraising statistics useful for reference, including data on contributions and distribution for 1987 philanthropy, total giving amounts from 1955 to 1987, comparison of 1987 estimates to revised 1986 estimates, donors' contributions and recipients from 1955 to 1987, and state laws regulating charitable solicitations (as of December 31, 1987). Includes information from Arnold Fishman's Guide to Mail Order Sales, which examines the size and characteristics of religion, education, health and hospitals, human services, arts and humanities, and public society benefit.

3494. Kim, D. "Foundation Funding and Psychiatric Research." *American Journal of Psychiatry* 145 (July 1988): 830-5.

Describes the role and structure of foundations, the historical trends in foundation support for research in mental illness, and the results of a study of the extent to which foundations support mental health research. The study results confirm the dearth of foundation support for psychiatric research but reveal important differences and similarities among the foundations that support such research.

3495. Kisselgoff, Anna. "Art and Money in a Ballet Conflict." *New York Times* (22 May 1985): C-17.

3496. Klein, Kim. "Asking Current Donors for Extra Gifts: Why, How and How Often." *Grassroots Fundraising Journal* 2 (August 1983): 9-11.

3497. Klein, Kim. "Federated Fundraising." *Grassroots Fundraising Journal* 2 (August 1983): 4.

3498. Klein, Kim. "The Four Basic Principles of Fundraising." *Grassroots Fundraising Journal* 7 (April 1988): 9-10.

Discusses four simple but profound ground rules of grassroots fundraising, both to instruct the novice and to remind the experienced. They are: people give out of self-interest, and a fundraiser must address a potential donor's concerns; fundraising is a long term process; personal contact is the most effective; and funding sources should be diversified. In addition, a successful fundraising program needs an active and large number of people working on it, whether they be paid or volunteer. When developing new fundraising techniques, the ones that are built upon these principles will be more effective and will allow the organization to work smarter, not harder.

3499. Klein, Kim. *Fundraising for Social Change*. 2nd ed., rev. and exp. Inverness, Calif.: Chardon Press, 1988.

Primer which explains community-based fundraising techniques for small nonprofit groups with budgets under $500,000. Recommends fundraising strategies that have been successful for low-budget groups. Divided into four major sections: overview and planning, methods and mechanics of fundraising, campaigns and special events, and fundraising management. Contains a glossary, a bibliography, and several appendixes, including examples of successful fundraising plans and mail appeal formats.

3500. Klein, Kim. "Fundraising in the Late 80s: Survival May Be the Best Goal." *Grassroots Fundraising Journal* 7 (December 1988): 3-4, 6.

Summarizes charitable giving by the private sector in 1987 and provides an overview of the economy in order to discuss suggestions for the survival of social change organizations. Klein points out that even though giving amounts have increased every year of the Reagan administration (eight to eleven percent per year until 1987), it would take increases of forty percent per year to keep pace with federal cutbacks. In addition, we are now faced with a vastly increased set of needs: the hungry and homeless, AIDS treatment and research, programs addressing drug abuse and crime, and solutions to hazardous waste dumping, to name a few. In the economy, Klein contends the distribution of wealth has shifted markedly in favor of the wealthy, so that the top one-half of one percent of the United States population now controls thirty-five percent of the nation's wealth, owning more than all those in the bottom ninety percent put together. Deteriorating infrastructures (such as roads and sewers, public hospitals and schools), a national debt of over $1 trillion, and a lack of public faith in institutions (as a result of scandals in television ministries and the military) all contribute to the feeling that people will be less likely to give to nonprofits. Klein insists that grassroots nonprofits, to ensure their own survival, must thoroughly plan their fundraising strategies, giving particular attention to personal solicitation; involve their boards in fundraising efforts and remove those who will not participate; spend most of their energies in raising money from individuals, as that is where most of the money comes from; determine to "hang in for the long haul," instead of hoping to enact social justice in this lifetime; and face the fact that without doing the dirty work of raising funds, the goals of the organization will never be fulfilled.

3501. Klein, Kim. "Getting over the Fear of Asking. Part 1." *Grassroots Fundraising Journal* 2 (April 1983): 1+.

3502. Klein, Kim. "Getting over the Fear of Asking. Part 2." *Grassroots Fundraising Journal* 2 (June 1983): 1+.

3503. Klein, Kim. "Going Back to Major Donors." *Grassroots Fundraising Journal* 7 (June 1988): 3-6.

Focuses on strategies useful for the "tired solicitor" when going back to major donors for repeat and upgraded gifts, including how best to renew one's own enthusiasm for the work, when to ask a donor to upgrade a gift, and commonsense factors to consider prior to making the request.

3504. Klein, Kim. "Hiring a Development Director." *Grassroots Fundraising Journal* 4 (August 1985): 8+.

3505. Klein, Kim. "Keeping in Touch with Major Donors." *Grassroots Fundraising Journal* 6 (October 1987): 3-5.

Stresses the importance of a carefully planned system for frequent contact with major donors, which not only shows appreciation but also develops donor loyalty.

3506. Klein, Kim. "Mail Appeals: But Will They Open the Envelope?" *Grassroots Fundraising Journal* 3 (December 1984): 12-4.

3507. Klein, Kim. "Major Donor Prospecting: 'I Don't Know Anyone with Money'." *Grassroots Fundraising Journal* 4 (August 1985): 6+.

3508. Klein, Kim. "Profile of a Major Donor." *Grassroots Fundraising Journal* 2 (December 1983): 12-3.

3509. Klein, Kim. "Profile of a Major Donor. No. 2." *Grassroots Fundraising Journal* 2 (February 1983): 12.

3510. Klein, Kim. "Profile of a Small Donor." *Grassroots Fundraising Journal* 4 (June 1985): 12-3.

3511. Klein, Kim. "Record Keeping for Fundraisers: How to Get Lost in the Shuffle." *Grassroots Fundraising Journal* 1 (December 1982): 1+.

3512. Klein, Kim. "Research Is the Bane of My Existence." *Grassroots Fundraising Journal* 2 (February 1983): 6-10.

3513. Kleinhenz, Frank. "Establishing Endowment: A Small College's Survival Kit." *Fund Raising Management* 16 (July 1985): 44+.

3514. Klinenberg, Edward L. "Audiovisuals: They Can Add Punch to Your Pitch." *Grantsmanship Center News* 13 (January-February 1985): 30-5.

3515. Knudsen, Raymond B. *New Models for Financing the Local Church*. 2nd ed. Wilton, Conn.: Morehouse-Barlow Co., 1985.

3516. Kobs, Jim. *Twenty-Four Ways to Improve Your Direct Mail Results: A Dartnell Report for Direct Mail and Mail Order Advertising Executives*. Chicago: Dartnell, 1974.

3517. Koochoo, Elizabeth. *Prospecting: Searching Out the Philanthropic Dollar*. Washington: Taft Group, 1979.

3518. Kotler, John D., and Debrah L. Wallace. *Ways to Find Private Sector Funding for Schools*. Arlington, Va.: Education Funding Research Council, 1984.

3519. Kotler, Milton. *Community Service Partnerships*. Washington: Center for Responsive Governance, 1983.

Fully examines the various aspects associated with community partnerships formed between local government and neighborhood organizations that are capable of delivering public services. Funding cutbacks and declining revenues have made this alternative means of service delivery very attractive: from the city's point of view, partnerships produce more service out of the same, or fewer, dollars; from the neighborhood perspective, community partnerships promise better service delivery and a steady source of annual revenue for local organizations. Discusses the history of public service delivery by neighborhood organizations; impediments and potential benefits; appropriate services for neighborhood capacities, and those considered beyond their scope; general factors characterizing appropriate neighborhood organizations (general management capability, a mission suited to the delivery of services, strong and decisive governance, and operational and fiscal management capabilities); organizational structure; external relationships; standard operating procedure; and strategies of control—examples of three distinct "partnership models." Includes case studies on community service partnerships from thirteen cities and counties.

3520. KRC Development Council. *The KRC Handbook of Fund Raising Principles and Practices: With Sample Forms and Records*. New Canaan, Conn.: KRC Development Council, 1982.

3521. Krummel, D.W., ed. *Organizing the Library's Support: Donors, Volunteers, Friends*. Allerton Park Institute, no. 25. Champaign-Urbana, Ill.: University of Illinois, 1980.

3522. Kuhn, Donald M. "How to Achieve Real Donor Base Growth." *Fund Raising Management* 17 (June 1986): 33-40.

3523. Kuniholm, Roland. "Getting Started in Direct Mail." *Interlit* 20 (March 1983): 16-9.

3524. Kurzig, Carol M. *New Directions for Institutional Advancement. Understanding and Increasing Foundation Support.* San Francisco: Jossey-Bass Publishers, 1981.

3525. La Rose, Ronald W., and Carol E. Cohen. "Lose Art, Jobs, Treasure Revived with Cathedral Plan." *Fund Raising Management* (August 1981): 28-35.

3526. Lambremont, Jane A. *The Grant-Seeker's Guide.* Baltimore, Md.: Southeastern Atlantic Regional Medical Library Services, 1986.

Designed to acquaint and guide the health sciences librarian new to the grantmaking process. Contains chapters on locating and contacting grant sources, the institutional grants program, developing and submitting a proposal, the grant review process, administering grant-funded projects, and NLM Extra Mural Program Grants. Appendix contains a suggested reading list, sample entries from grantseeking reference tools, sample DHHS grant application, sample compliance forms, and an example of a NLM grant proposal review.

3527. Lampton, William. "Development Trends at Selected Hospitals." *Fund Raising Management* 19 (September 1988): 43-6.

Results of an informal survey of hospitals in the southeastern United States concerning board sizes, gift club levels, naming opportunities, and the method of supporting development programs. Among the conclusions: a larger board of trustees means a wider network of ties with prospects, broader perspectives in decision making, and more total gift dollars; the cumulative approach is suggested for giving club memberships, though in most cases the naming of facilities is linked to one-time gifts; most hospital gifts appear to average seventy-five percent restricted and twenty-five percent unrestricted. Donors want to be able to see what they're supporting, not just visualize a concept. In addition, only a small number of development programs attempt to support themselves solely through contributions, as most subscribe to the belief that few people want to give generously to fund an office, but rather prefer their gifts to provide surgical supplies, continuing education for health-care professionals, or the latest technology for laboratories. Statistical tables are included for both board size and gift recognition policies, and unrestricted giving and support of foundation.

3528. Lampton, William. "Flexibility: Essential Trait for Successful Fund Raising." *Fund Raising Management* 15 (August 1984): 90-1.

3529. Lant, Jeffrey L. *Development Today: A Fund Raising Guide for Nonprofit Organizations.* 3rd ed., rev. Nonprofit Technical Assistance. Cambridge, Mass.: JLA Publications, 1986.

Guide for those who find fundraising a frustrating process. Lant's guide of technical assistance provides practical information as well as techniques for overcoming fundraising fears. The author guides the would-be fundraiser through a series of basic steps such as the planning process; the documents required; the key people involved and how to work with them; the function of the coordinating committee; corporate, federal and foundation fundraising; the capital campaign; special events; and direct mail and other fundraising. The chapters each contain practical lists of things to be done; typical problems and questions and answers. The final section provides information on what the author labels *Fifteen Fatal Flaws* of fundraising and thirty-nine samples including such things as sample cover letter, precis, questionnaires, and pledge cards. Contains no indexes, only table of contents and sample content listings. Bibliography.

3530. Lant, Jeffrey L. "An Introduction to Capital Campaigns." *Grantsmanship Center News* 11 (March-April 1983): 18-25.

3531. Lant, Jeffrey L. "Secrets to a Successful Special Event." *Nonprofit World* 5 (March-April 1987): 13-4, 16.

Tips for every stage in the planning of a special event, from appointing a chairperson to obtaining funding. Advises having all organizers keep detailed reports to serve as a blueprint for next year's event.

3532. Lant, Jeffrey L. "Your Worst Fears Realized, or What to Do When the Corporation or Foundation Declines Your Proposal." *Nonprofit World* 5 (January-February 1987): 18-9.

Brief guide for successful fundraising which concentrates on steps to follow after your request has been declined.

3533. Larose, R. "Fundraising: As Dollars Shrink, Campaigns Grow." *Dimensions in Health Service* 61 (May 1984): 29-31.

3534. Lauffer, Armand. *Grantsmanship.* Beverly Hills, Calif.: Sage Publications, 1977.

Practical workbook for developing a fundraising/marketing strategy, identifying funding sources, and developing a budget and proposal.

3535. Lautman, Kay Partney, and Henry Goldstein. "Credibility Critical in Celebrity Mail Packages." *Fund Raising Management* 15 (October 1984): 56-9.

3536. Lautman, Kay Partney, and Henry Goldstein. *Dear Friend. Mastering the Art of Direct Mail Fund Raising.* Washington: Taft Group, 1984.

Step-by-step manual on direct mail fundraising, written on a track system to provide techniques for the novice as well as the experienced fundraiser. Advice on identifying the proper market, finding and testing mailing lists, projecting renewal costs and income, creating the direct mail package, testing and analyzing mail results, hiring and working with with a consultant, getting renewals, and more. Numerous illustrations show some of the most successful direct mail campaigns in the nonprofit field.

3537. Lautman, Kay Partney, and Henry Goldstein. "Elements to Test in Direct Mail Packages." *Fund Raising Management* 15 (November 1984): 70-6.

3538. Lawson, Charles E. "Brakeley President Spots Trends in Major-Gift Fund Raising." *FRI Monthly Portfolio* 24 (March 1985): 3-4.

3539. Lawson, Charles E. "Why Do People Make Gifts? Here Are the Main Reasons." *FRI Bulletin* (August 1986): 1-2.

3540–3560 FUNDRAISING

3540. Leat, Diana. "The Minus and Plus of Partial Funding." *Charity* 4 (October 1987): 8-9.

Partial funding—giving grant applicants half of what they ask and expecting them to raise the rest—is viewed by grantmakers as a means of making their money spread a long way while underlining the character building effects of suffering and struggle for the charity (with the assumption, of course, that partial funding also has the effect of encouraging funding from other sources, thus bringing the suffering and struggling to a happy ending). In considering the effects of partial funding on acquisition of other funding, however, it may be important to take into account not only the source of funding but also the perception of that source by other funders and the amount given relative to the total sought.

3541. Leavitt, Robert Keith. *Common Sense about Fund Raising.* Privately Printed, 1949.

3542. Leduc, Robert F. "Beyond Coping with Crisis: Cooperation for Survival." *Fund Raising Management* 14 (October 1983): 88-9.

3543. Lee, Lawrence. *The Grants Game: How to Get Free Money.* San Francisco: Harbor Publishing, 1981.

Basic introduction and handbook for identifying funding prospects, preparing a proposal, and following-up on funding requests.

3544. Leed, Jean. "Beyond the Ask: Ten Other Ways to Involve Faculty in Fund Raising." *Currents* 13 (September 1987): 14-8.

Offers ten ways for university faculty to help with the fundraising process without putting undue constraints on their time or comprising their integrity by having them ask for money. Among the suggestions: faculty can help determine the fundraising priorities, articulate the substance and importance of the goals to prospective donors and other faculty, and thank donors for gifts received. Includes methods for increasing cooperation between faculty and the development office.

3545. Lemish, Donald L. *The Foundation Handbook: A Private Foundation Approach to Fundraising at State Colleges and Universities.* Washington: American Association of State Colleges and Universities, 1981.

3546. Lenz, Frank B. *It's Fun to Raise Money for World Service.* New York: Association Press, 1953.

3547. Lenz, Kurt, and Peter Wahl. "On-Line Database System Raises ALA's Fund Raising Capabilities." *Fund Raising Management* 15 (May 1984): 52+.

3548. Leonard, Jennifer. "Cooperation or Collusion?" *Grantsmanship Center News* 9 (July-August 1982): 13+.

3549. Leslie, John W. *Seeking the Competitive Dollar: College Management in the Seventies.* Washington: American College Public Relations Association, 1971.

3550. Leslie, Larry L. "What Appeals to Whom?" *Currents* 11 (July-August 1985): 34-7.

Analyzes which institutional variables influence certain donor groups.

3551. Leslie, Larry L., and Garey W. Ramey. "When Donors Give: How Giving Changes in Good and Bad Economic Times." *Currents* 11 (October 1985): 25+.

3552. Levi, Julian H., and Fred S. Vorsanger. *Patterns of Giving to Higher Education: An Analysis of Contributions and Their Relation to Tax Policy.* Washington: American Council on Education, 1968.

3553. Levi, Julian H., and Sheldon Elliott Steinbach. *Patterns of Giving to Higher Education. Part 2: Analysis of Voluntary Support of American Colleges and Universities, 1970-71.* Washington: American Council on Education, 1972.

3554. Levi, Julian H., and Sheldon Elliott Steinbach. *Patterns of Giving to Higher Education. Part 3: An Analysis of Voluntary Support of American Colleges and Universities, 1973-74.* Washington: American Council on Education, 1976.

3555. Levin, Donald. "Adding Creativity to Public Relations: You Can Do It!" *Channels* 36 (January 1984): 5-6.

3556. Levin, Nora Jean, and Janet Dempsey Steigler. *To Light One Candle: A Handbook for Organizing, Funding and Maintaining Public Service Activities.* Chicago: American Bar Association, 1978.

3557. Levis, Wilson C. "The Average Gift Size Factor." *Philanthropy Monthly* (July-August 1981): 6-14.

3558. Levitan, Donald. "For All It's Worth: Analyzing Revenue, Assets, and Fundraising Costs." *501(c)(3) Monthly Letter* 8 (September 1988): 448-9.

Analyzing data based on information from the 1983 IRS Statistics of Income Bulletin, article finds, among other things, that a majority of the nonprofit organizations in the U.S. have fundraising costs of less than one percent of their total revenue. Other findings: a nineteen percent increase in program service revenue from 1982 to 1983 indicates that tax-exempt organizations were generating more revenue from their own programs instead of relying on contributions and grants, and total revenue increased by $28 billion during the time span, with the larger organizations, ones with assets of $10 million, receiving seventy-five percent of the money. Also includes ratings of the top ten nonprofit organizations ranked by total assets and by revenue for 1983.

3559. Levitan, Donald, and Daniel F. Donahue. *Grants Resource Manual.* Newton Centre, Mass.: Government Research Publications, 1980.

3560. Levitan, Donald. *A Guide to Grants: Governmental and Nongovernmental.* 2nd ed. Newton Centre, Mass.: Government Research Publications, 1985.

Combination reference and workbook assists grantseekers find and secure support from governmental and nongovernmental sources. Provides details on the grantor mix; grant preparation and writing; and grant management—an often overlooked component in the quest for funding. Also includes samples of federal assistance application forms, a useful glossary, and grant preparation checklists.

3561. Levitan, Donald. *Selected Bibliography on Grantsmanship*. Edited by Mary Vance. Exchange Bibliography, no. 641. Monticello, Ill.: Council of Planning Librarians, 1974.

3562. Levitan, Donald. *Selected Bibliography on Grantsmanship*. Monticello, Ill.: Council of Planning Librarians, 1974.

3563. Levy, David. "Telephone Fundraising Strategies." *Whole Nonprofit Catalog* 7 (Summer 1988): 6-7.

3564. Lewin, Ann W. "The Six R's of Fund Raising: The Toil of Getting Grants." *Fund Raising Management* 14 (December 1983): 44-8.

3565. Lewis, Herschell Gordon. "Don't Make the Creative Mistakes That Cut Response." *Fund Raising Management* 14 (June 1983): 52-5.

3566. Lewis, Herschell Gordon. "Verisimilitude, Benefit and Clarity: Your Copy Umbrella." *Fund Raising Management* 16 (August 1985): 64+.

3567. Lewis, Herschell Gordon. "What Worked in 1970 Won't Work Anymore in 1990." *Fund Raising Management* 16 (July 1985): 64+.

3568. Lewis, Jim. "Composing Effective Letters with Word Processing Features." *Fund Raising Management* 16 (September 1985): 86+.

3569. Libbey, Theodore W., Jr. "Notes: The Philharmonic Reaches Out." *New York Times* (18 April 1982): D-21.

3570. *Libraries: Getting into the Philanthropic Thick of Things*. Washington: Taft Group, 1988.

Compilation of articles to help libraries realize the enormous fundraising potential they have from non-governmental sources, primarily foundations, corporations and individual donors.

3571. Liebold, Louise Condak. *Fireworks, Brass Bands and Elephants: Promotional Events with Flair for Libraries and Other Nonprofit Organizations*. Phoenix, Ariz.: Oryx Press, 1986.

Describes the staging of successful promotional events by some libraries and nonprofit organizations. Case studies of various promotional events and techniques are presented with comments and additional ideas. Chapters include special events and celebrations, cooperative ventures, thematic programming, games/contests, and festivals/fairs. Also discusses publicity and the media, and 100 additional ideas.

3572. Lilley, Robert D. "The LISC Public-Private Partnership." *Response* 12 (May 1983): 19-20.

3573. Lind, Norman G. "The Function of Lists: A Fund Raising Primer." *Fund Raising Management* 15 (May 1984): 42+.

3574. Linehan, Jean Dinwoodey, ed. *Some Aspects of Educational Fund Raising*. Washington: American Alumni Council, [1961].

3575. Liner, Fran. "Selecting a Special Event." *Fund Raising Management* 18 (April 1987): 56, 58-61, 2.

Step-by-step guide for organizing the special event which Fran Liner recommends most frequently—the tribute dinner. All special events have certain advantages, including the involvement of new supporters; an additional chance for giving by regular donors; opportunities for publicity; a chance to recognize people who have made important contributions; special appeal to different population segments; and a chance to present your message personally. The tribute dinner does all of the above, providing opportunities for giving awards, making multi-media presentations, and group participation, and is inexpensive as well. In addition, it can become an annual affair with tables of ten to provide the possibility of selling more tickets. Essentials for the tribute dinner include four to six months planning time; chairperson and guest of honor; dinner committee; dinner mailing list; and the letters. Effective letters are described in detail as well as the reservation application form. Throughout the article the author provides solid hints to the event organizer such as: keep the dinner program brief and stimulating and make every effort to get as much donated and underwritten as possible. It is suggested that the ticket price not appear in the first letter to see what kind of a committee can be attracted before fixing the price. In conclusion, the article notes that groups should not overlook special events other than the tribute dinner which highlight their particular organization. The tribute dinner may not be appropriate for every organization, but aspects of the dinner can effectively be added to benefits, balls and dinner dances.

3576. Lione, Henry V. "The Fund Raising Profession." *NAHD Journal* (Winter-Spring 1983): 39-42.

3577. Lione, Henry V. "The Future of Fund Raising: An Endangered Species." *NAHD Journal* (Winter-Spring 1984): 9-15.

3578. Lipman, Samuel. "Why Give to the Arts." *Artsreview* 4 (Summer 1987): 12-4.

Criticizes fundraising efforts in the arts and humanities which will use any argument to bring in the necessary dollars. Emphasizes the arts and the humanities as the great repository of the best that has been thought and known throughout history, the inheritance of all human beings, and the structure which binds us together as a people in the past, the present, and the future. These are the arguments, Lipman avers, which should be put forth when fundraising for the arts and humanities, for these arguments enhance rather than diminish their integrity.

3579. Littman, C. Arthur. "Premiums: An Innovative Way to Increased Gift Giving." *Fund Raising Management* 15 (June 1984): 50.

3580. Loessin, Bruce A., Margaret A. Duronio, and Georgina L. Borton. "Questioning the Conventional Wisdom." *Currents* 14 (September 1988): 33-6.

Study examines private and public research, doctoral and comprehensive universities, and baccalaureate and two-year colleges to test the fundraising assumption that the rich always get richer, while those institutions lacking high levels of wealth, size, and prestige rarely achieve fundraising success. While the results indicate that conventional wisdom is true for only a limited number of institutions, these happen to be the ones that are best-known (major research and doctoral universities), and thus ones to which most fundraisers look as being models and standards of successful practice. The researchers warn against using these institutions in this way, as it may be misleading and even harmful to design fundraising programs and allocate resources in imitation of an organization that is unlike your own; instead, fundraising comparisons should be made on peer institutions, as factors related to voluntary support differ by type of institution and donor. Article includes tables on ranges and medians for fundraising results, correlation coefficients for total voluntary support for all institutions and types, and correlation coefficients for all institutions for total voluntary support and separate donor groups.

3581. Lord, James Gregory. "Going for the Gold: A Training Manual for Volunteer Fund Raisers." *Currents* 10 (November-December 1984): 36-7.

3582. Lord, James Gregory. *Philanthropy and Marketing: New Strategies for Fund Raising*. Cleveland: Third Sector Press, 1981.

3583. Lord, James Gregory. *The Raising of Money: Thirty-Five Essentials Every Trustee Should Know*. Cleveland: Third Sector Press, 1983.

Discusses the importance of listening to donor needs and concerns; how to involve people in development; how to set the pace for giving; the need for structure in the campaign process; how to ask for contributions; stewardship; kindling the philanthropic spirit; and the role of fundraising consultants.

3584. Love, Jay B. "Evaluating Fund-Raising Software." *Fund Raising Management* 19 (October 1988): 46, 48, 50.

Offers practical advice on choosing a fundraising software package. Most important is maintaining control by developing a complete and reasonable set of objectives; this establishes the course you will want to take when dealing with vendors. A set of guidelines should be prepared to use when reviewing vendor presentations, proposals, or promotional material, including a checklist to enquire as to what fields of information are necessary to fulfill your objectives, what information about each function or transaction performed is kept and for how long, how information is entered and checked, what type of help and prompting is available, and what interfaces to other systems or departments are needed. These preparations should all be done before entering into demonstrations with vendors so that control will be maintained. Points to consider after the demonstration: the vendor's support and training policy, the handling of software updates, the type of user's manual provided, and the specific pricing and equipment configurations.

3585. Lovelock, Christopher H., and Charles B. Weinberg. "Marketing for Public and Nonprofit Managers." *Philanthropy Monthly* 18 (January 1985): 20-32.

Reprint of first chapter of a new book about marketing for nonprofits.

3586. Luehrs, Karen. *Funding Sources and Financial Aid Techniques for Historic Preservation*. Atlanta, Ga.: Georgia Department of Natural Resources, Historic Preservation Section, 1983.

3587. Lukac, George J. "Continuity Yields Turnaround for Rio Grande College." *Fund Raising Management* 16 (October 1985): 26+.

3588. Luther, Judith. *For the Working Artist: A Survival Guide for Performing, Visual and Media Artists Who Choose to Manage Their Own Careers*. Valencia, Calif.: California Institute of the Arts, 1986.

This book is designed for those artists who wish to manage their art and their business beyond that fundamental food-and-rent subsistence stage. Chapters discuss first-time proposal writing, terminology, sample summaries, budgets, project descriptions from successful grant proposals, and affiliation of a nonprofit organization.

3589. Lyman, Richard W. "International Conference on Fund Raising Keynote Address." *Fundemensions* 9 (April 1987): 4-8.

Keynote address given at the 1987 International Conference on Fund Raising by Richard W. Lyman, president of the Rockefeller Foundation. Lyman cites several of the most outstanding problems facing the private not-for-profit organizations and institutions. Specifically, the political problems of the sector such as the 1986 Tax Act; the tax act's impact on non-itemizers; OMB Circular 122 which would have made it impossible for most nonprofits to do any lobbying; the battle between the for-profits and the Small Business Administration against nonprofits over alleged unfair competition; the "model law" for the regulation of charities developed by the National Association of Attorneys General; and the Pennsylvania proposal to limit nonprofit tax-exempt status to only those organizations that serve the disadvantaged. Lyman believes that the problems in the political arena demand that the American public and their representatives, who are by and large unaware of the part played by voluntary effort, must be educated to the important role played by the Third Sector.

3590. Lynch, Mary Jo. *Financing Online Search Services in Publicly Supported Libraries*. Chicago: American Library Association, 1981.

3591. Lynn, Joyce, ed. *A Guide to Organizations, Agencies, and Federal Programs for Children*. Washington: Day Care and Child Development Reports, 1978.

3592. Lynn, Robert J. "The Questionable Testamentary Gift to Charity: A Suggested Approach to Judicial Decision." *University of Chicago Law Review* 30 (Spring 1963): 450-68.

3593. MacKinnon, G. "Hospitals 'Buy' the Future through Fundraising Efforts." *Health Care* 28 (October 1986): 16, 18.

3594. Macnab, Alexander G. "Telemarketing Fund Raising Can Have Giving Drawbacks." *Fund Raising Management* 16 (August 1985): 48+.

3595. Magarrell, Jack. "College Endowments Return a Record 42% in One Year." *Chronicle of Higher Education* 27 (16 November 1983): 1+.

3596. Mai, Charles F. "Learning the Magic of Asking Via Walt Disney and Joyce Hall." *Fund Raising Management* 16 (May 1985): 108.

3597. Makar, Arthur. "Challenges for the Manager of the One-Person Shop." *NSFRE Journal* (Spring 1989): 34-6.

Strategies for having a successful one-person development office. Begin by examining current and projected bases of financial support and dividing donors into three categories: consistent donors; irregular donors; and long shot prospects. Planning for the coming year involves decisions about upgrading present donors and cultivating prospects. Identify your own strengths and weaknesses and seek help to fill in the weak spots. Suggested resources when asking for help: board members; student interns; retired persons willing to volunteer; people willing to work part-time if you cannot afford a full-time staff; and consultants, when they really can fill a gap for you. These steps are all part of the organization process; also necessary for success is communication with volunteers, staff and consultants. Be certain everyone knows what is expected of them, and involve them in the planning process whenever possible. Evaluate each component of the development program as well as the broader picture to be aware of what works and what doesn't. And remember to recognize work that is well done by personal compliments, letters to administrators, and recommendations to other organizations (in the case of consultants).

3598. "Making Endowments Greener." *Business Week* (13 September 1969): 66-8.

3599. Marks, Linda J. "Improving Our Prospects." *Currents* 13 (November-December 1987): 38, 40, 42, 44.

Profiles Stanford University's National Resources Program, a comprehensive study of alumni and donors. Volunteers and development staff joined efforts in prospect screening sessions that identified new donor prospects and reviewed perceptions of existing donors. Provides structure of their session scenario and useful suggestions for the prospect research process.

3600. Marks, Linda J. "Rating Gift Capacity through Screening Sessions." *Fund Raising Management* 16 (July 1985): 26+.

3601. Mason, Bryant S. "How to Raise Funds for a Cause." *Black Enterprise* (May 1982): 51-6.

3602. *Matching Gifts: Patterns and Practices in Corporate Matching-Gift Programs.* New York: Council for Financial Aid to Education, 1986.

3603. Matthews, Fred A. "The Politics of Planned Giving: Alligators in the Swimming Pool." *Fund Raising Management* 16 (April 1985): 54-6.

3604. Mayrand, Lionel E., Jr., ed. *A Grantsman's Bibliography.* Durham, N.H.: New England Gerontology Center, [1975].

3605. McBrearty, Bruce R. "Scripting for Successful Telemarketing Campaigns." *Fund Raising Management* 16 (September 1985): 150+.

3606. McBrearty, Bruce R. "Testing Increases Contributions in Telemarketing Campaigns." *Fund Raising Management* 15 (November 1984): 106-07.

3607. McBrearty, Bruce R. "Testing Telemarketing Reveals Donor Efficiencies." *Fund Raising Management* 15 (November 1984): 50+.

3608. McCants, Calvin. "Funders Who Are Serious about Self-Sufficiency for Nonprofits Have to Start Thinking Endowment." *Nonprofit Executive* 3 (December 1983): 3-4.

3609. McCarthy, Thomas R. *A Guide to Community Fundraising for Runaway Centers and Other Community-Based Youth Programs.* Washington: 70001 Ltd., [198?].

3610. McClain, Austin V. *Stock Market Trends: Their Effects upon Fund Raising for Education.* New York: Marts & Lundy, 1962.

3611. McCormick, John L., Bruce R. McClintock, and Russell R. Picton. "Major Gifts: Three Perspectives." *Counsel* (May 1988): 3-5.

Covers basic fundraising concepts and techniques, beginning with the cultivation of prospects. Offers general tips on solicitation and five standard and important ways of expressing gratitude. Stresses the importance of maintaining and advancing relationships between the institution and those "at the top of the pyramid." The general fundraising rule of thumb is that one percent of the donors to a campaign account for fifty percent of the dollars raised. Also offers practical advice towards building life-long relationships. Ends with a discussion of the staff's role in a major gifts campaign, including the important activities of identification, research and tracking.

3612. McEvilly, C.C. "Honor Thy Donors." *Fund Raising Management* 18 (June 1987): 69-71.

3613. McGill, Douglas C. "Met Given $1 Million for Armor." *New York Times* (15 May 1985): C-16.

Tells about gift from Dr. Armand Hammer.

3614. McGovern, Gail. "The Inside Track: What the Experts Say about Seeking Alternative Funding." *Bottom Line* 1 (1987): 30-1.

Compiles philosophical and practical hints about the basic approach towards fundraising, as written by experts in various magazines devoted to the nonprofit sector.

3615. McGovern, Gail. "Local Fund Raising: Demonstrating the Value of Libraries." *Bottom Line* 1 (1987): 32-3.

3616. McGowan, Andrew. "What TV Stations Want in Public Service Announcements." *Fund Raising Management* 16 (October 1985): 96+.

3617. McGuire, Jack. "Let's Clear the Air about Public Service Announcements." *Association Management* 35 (December 1983): 143-47.

3618. McIlquham, John. "Public/Private Partnerships Bring a Building to Harlem." *Fund Raising Management* (April 1982): 16-23.

3619. McIntyre, E.J. "Establishing a Nursing Education Fund." *Focus on Critical Care* 12 (February 1985): 52-3.

3620. McKallip, Jonathan. "Funding Opportunities for Fighting Illiteracy." *Grants Magazine* 7 (March 1984): 25-31.

3621. McKee, David T. "Are You Ready for Fund Raising?" *NAHD Journal* (Summer-Fall 1983): 3+.

3622. McLaughlin, David. "The President's Role in the Capital Campaign." *Currents* 10 (January 1984): 6-8.

3623. McLaughlin, Jeff. "Community Spirit Lives in Local Arts." *Boston Globe* (6 June 1983).

3624. McNamee, Mike. "Fund Raising after Tax Reform." *Currents* 13 (January 1987): 44-7.

"CASE fund-raising professionals predict that the new law will require more effort, more knowledge, and better communication than ever before from development officers. It will speed fundraising's shift in emphasis toward planned giving and estate planning....And it will wipe out the one-size-fits-all contribution program... ." The author presents several fundraising strategies for overcoming obstacles created by the new tax law.

3625. Meeker-Lowry, Susan. *Catalyst's Guide to Social Change Revolving Loan Funds.* Rev. ed. Worcester, Vt.: Catalyst, 1987.

Describes the purposes and current projects of thirty-five revolving loan funds (RLFs). RLFs make loans at below-market rates to projects without access to traditional sources of capital, financing low-income housing, cooperative businesses, worker-owned businesses, the projects of community development corporations, community land trusts, limited equity co-ops and housing, and appropriate agricultural development. All of the RLFs listed provide technical assistance to borrowers, ranging from business plan development guidance to locating the best contractors for a job, as well as providing on-going accounting and planning services. RLFs provide the ideal opportunity for investors willing to accept lower interest payments because they believe the social goals are so valuable; most allow investors to set their preferred rate of return, from zero percent to six or seven percent, depending on the prime. Several of the funds allow lenders to target their money towards a specific area or even a particular project. In addition, all loans up to $250,000 to a nonprofit organization (including community development loan funds) are exempt from the rules regarding imputed interest, allowing a deduction of the difference between the interest received and the prevailing T-bill market rate.

3626. Menchin, Robert S. "The Last Caprice: A Collection of Unusual Wills, Proving That People's Bequests Are Almost As Fascinating As People." *McCall's* (September 1963): 126-7, 177.

3627. Merrill, J.C. "The Changing Health Care System: A Challenge for Foundations." *Inquiry* 23 (Fall 1986): 316-21.

3628. Messina, William J. "Join the Club: More and More Institutions Use Mega-Gift Clubs to Get Bigger Slice of the Pie." *Currents* 12 (July-August 1986): 12-5.

3629. Meyer, Dennis. "Cultivating Major Donors As Greatest Untapped Source." *Fund Raising Management* 16 (April 1985): 64+.

3630. Miller-Leposky, Rosalie, and George Leposky. "Rx for Getting a Grant." *Journal of Energy Medicine* ([198?]).

Solid introduction to the game of grantsmanship in general, with a focus on securing health-related grants. Warns that getting a grant involves a great deal of time and effort, and results can only be attained if the work is taken seriously. Discusses methods of research, basics of proposal writing, and what to expect from a foundation or government agency in terms of on-site evaluations and reporting requirements. Includes a listing of resources, a glossary of grant-related terms, and a brief listing of foundations particularly interested in funding holistic health programs.

3631. Millett, John D. *Financing Higher Education in the United States.* New York: Columbia University, 1952.

3632. "Million Dollar and Up Donors." *Philanthropic Trends Digest* 21 (15 February 1987): 3-6.

3633. Millsaps, Daniel. *National Directory of Arts Support by Private Foundations.* Vol. 5. Des Moines, Iowa: Arts Letter, 1983.

3634. Mirkin, Howard R. *The Complete Fund Raising Guide.* Washington: Public Service Materials Center, 1981.

Discusses the planning and financing of a fundraising campaign, with advice on specific funding sources and fundraising techniques.

3635. Mitchell, Rob. "Hospital Development Is Growing Up." *Fund Raising Management* 19 (September 1988): 49, 50, 52, 54, 62.

While for many years patient revenues were more than adequate for maintaining a quality health care institution, hospitals are now setting up foundations to handle fundraising for their expanding and more sophisticated programs. The National Association of Hospital Development (NAHD) reports increased membership, with the most requested information from the organization being a packet on how to start a development program. Existing development programs are expanding and hospital fundraising methods are becoming more sophisticated, the article reports, with computerization, planned giving, telemarketing, and endowment campaigns increasing financial success. Sixty percent of NAHD members report they are conducting their development effort through a foundation whose sole purpose is to raise and manage charitable gifts for the benefit of the hospital they represent; this allows for more flexibility in fundraising emphasis and for the financial reporting of gifts, which donors are interested in seeing, while maintaining privacy for the hospital's privileged financial data.

3636. Molotsky, Irvin. "Private Contributions to the Arts Increase." *New York Times* (22 April 1985).

3637. Mones, Wayne. "A Planned Giving Program for the Small Development Office." *Fund Raising Management* (September 1984): 66+.

3638. Mooney, Charles D., and Susan Regan Henry. "Charitable Giving Techniques for Business Owners." *Trusts & Estates* 123 (December 1984): 25-8.

3639. Moreau, Arthur J. *Funding: How to Get Your Fair Share of the $47.74 Billion Given in the U.S. Today.* Peoria, Ill.: Continuing Education Programs of America, 1981.

3640. Morrisey, M.A. "Hospital Philanthropy in the Future." *Business and Health* 3 (June 1986): 11-4.

3641. Moskin, William P. *Beyond the Bake Sale: A Fund Raising Handbook for Public Agencies.* Sacramento, Calif.: City of Sacramento, 1988.

Handbook of private sector fundraising for government agencies based upon the success of the Department of Parks and Community Services, City of Sacramento. The handbook begins with a sensible analysis of the pros and cons of beginning such a fundraising program. It enumerates the internal issues to be looked at such as financial goals, program goals, staff capabilities and training, and understanding your community. Setting up a development program, hiring skilled staff, and training the staff are explained as well as the legal and fiscal options available for each specific agency. The basics of grants and contributions are discussed along with deferred and memorial giving, gifts catalogs, special events, and earned income. An appendix includes information on fundraising basics such as a list of standard books and periodicals, organizations, and conferences and workshops.

3642. *Motivations for Charitable Giving: A Reference Guide.* Washington: 501(c)(3) Group, 1973.

3643. "Mott Advisor Recommends Fund-Raising Strategies." *Foundation Giving Watch* 4 (July 1984): 1-2.

3644. Mudry, Michael. "Higher Rates for Charitable Annuities: How Charitable Annuities 'Work'." *Philanthropy Monthly* 16 (September 1983): 30-40.

3645. Mulford, Carolyn. *Guide to Student Fundraising.* Reston, Va.: Future Homemakers of America, 1984.

Tells the basic guidelines followed by a youth organization in raising funds.

3646. Muller, Steven. "Marketing Imagination." *Currents* 14 (May 1988): 6-10, 12.

Explores the application of imagination to marketing, or cultivation, in higher education fundraising. Muller, president of Johns Hopkins University for the past sixteen years, advises keeping four things in mind: the reality of the institution should match the image being promoted; the image should be kept as simple as possible so that people can remember what they read or hear about it; an external relations program should be tailored to meet the needs of diverse audiences; and the message must be consistent and repeated often in order for it to sink in.

3647. Mulligan, Thomas J. "There's More to Special Events Than Raising Money." *Fund Raising Management* 18 (April 1987): 36,38,40,43.

Article based on a presentation at the 17th Annual Conference on Support of Independent Schools. Mulligan, a development officer in the field of education for thirty years, examines the special event. Special events, states the author, can be great for any institution or organization because they raise substantial amounts of money, involve great numbers of people, and provide opportunities for good public relations. Mulligan discusses the elements to be considered before holding a special event—dollar potential, audience, appropriateness, timeliness, and attractiveness to volunteer leaders. In addition, the components of a successful event are considered including leadership—a person with clout; ownership—all constituents have a sense of ownership; enjoyment—the event as well as the preparation must be fun; quality—first-class, not necessarily expensive, but tasteful; appreciation—clearly demonstrated appreciation throughout the preparation in addition to the usual form letter when the event is over; and finally, analysis—what worked and what didn't.

3648. Munson, Robert. "Information: The Key to Making Your Mid-Sized Donors Act Big." *Fund Raising Management* 16 (May 1985): 40+.

3649. Murphy, J. Prentice. "Crazy about Families." *Survey (Philadelphia)* (15 June 1959): 3.

3650. Murphy, Mary Kay. "Reach Out and Touch Someone." *Currents* 10 (July-August 1984): 29.

3651. Murray, George B. "New Technologies Media for Fund Raising Are on the Way." *Fund Raising Management* 13 (February 1983): 26+.

3652. Nagel, Stuart, and Marian Neef, eds. *Policy Grants Directory: A Directory Describing Governmental and Private Funding Sources for Policy Studies Research.* Urbana, Ill.: Policy Studies Organization, 1977.

3653. National Association for Hospital Development. *Bibliography for Hospital Resource Development: A Useful Tool for Fund Raisers and Resource Development Teams.* Falls Church, Va.: National Association for Hospital Development, 1984.

Covers fifteen subject areas, including books published from 1979 through 1983 and articles from periodicals published from 1982 through 1983.

3654. National Association of Broadcasters. *If You Want Air Time.* Washington: National Association of Broadcasters, 1977.

3655. National Catholic Development Conference. *Bibliography of Fund Raising and Philanthropy.* Rockville Centre, N.Y.: National Catholic Development Conference, 1975.

3656. National Center for Neighborhood Enterprise. *Information Brochure.* Washington: National Center for Neighborhood Enterprise.

3657. National Center for the Control of Rape. *Public and Private Sources of Funding for Sexual Assault Treatment Programs.* Rockville, Md.: U.S. Department of Health and Human Services, 1981.

3658. National Committee for Responsive Philanthropy. *Charity Begins at Work: Alternatives to United Way Dramatically Change the Billion Dollar World of Workplace Fundraising.* Washington: National Committee for Responsive Philanthropy, 1986.

3659. National Committee for Responsive Philanthropy. *New Approaches to Increase Private Funds for Neighborhood Organization Development.* Washington: National Committee for Responsive Philanthropy, 1978.

Report by the National Committee for Responsive Philanthropy examines the factors which limit private philanthropic funding of neighborhood groups, particularly for organizational purposes; new mechanisms adopted by the traditional funding institutions and new developments in the world of philanthropy that could increase funding of resident-based neighborhood groups; and actions that neighborhood leaders could take to open new revenues and promote possibilities for increased private sector support for development of neighborhood organizations (as opposed to funding for neighborhood programs). In partial summary, recommendations to increase funding from private individuals includes: repealing United Way policies which insist on a monopoly of workplace solicitation; organizing alternative fundraising federations at the local level; and creating foundations or endowed funds at the national level which focus on neighborhood revitalization in each metropolitan area. To increase funding from corporations: establishing a Businessmen's Committee for Neighborhood Revitalization; requiring disclosure of basic information about all corporate contributions and other payments to nonprofit organizations. From foundations: eliminating structural and operational aspects which reduce the likelihood of personal communication between foundation decision-makers and grassroots organizations of all types; establishing quick release, small grants programs to provide easier access by newer, smaller neighborhood organizations and for emergency needs of more established groups. And from United Ways: establishing special allocation committees for neighborhood development; reinstituting or continuing special funds for grants to non-member agencies; boycotting United Way fundraising campaigns which deny access to legitimate, deserving organizations.

3660. National Conference on Solicitations. *Proceedings.* Cleveland: National Conference on Solicitations, 1954.

3661. National Council for Resource Development. *Energy Resource Guide.* Washington: National Council for Resource Development, [1980].

3662. National Council of the Churches of Christ in the U.S.A. *Conference on Philanthropy in Action.* New York: National Council of the Churches of Christ in the U.S.A., 1966.

3663. National Council of the Churches of Christ in the U.S.A. *Conference on Voluntary Giving for American Christian Institutions.* New York: National Council of the Churches of Christ in the U.S.A., 1964.

3664. National Council of the Churches of Christ in the U.S.A. *Conferences on Wills, Annuities, and Special Gifts.* New York: National Council of the Churches of Christ in the U.S.A., 1958.

3665. National Exchange Club. *Money Raising Ideas for Exchange Clubs.* Toledo, Ohio: National Exchange Club, 1975.

3666. National Society of Fund Raising Executives. *Glossary of Fund-Raising Terms.* Alexandria, Va.: National Society of Fund Raising Executives, 1986.

Contains 935 definitions and terms used within the field of fundraising.

3667. National Society of Fund Raising Executives. *Program for Certification of Fund Raising Executives: Study Guide Outline.* Alexandria, Va.: National Society of Fund Raising Executives, [198?].

3668. National Society of Fund Raising Executives. *So Now You're a Fund Raiser.* Glen Ellyn, Ill.: Chicago Society of Fund Raising Executives, 1976.

3669. National Society of Fund Raising Executives. *Who's Who in Fund-Raising.* Alexandria, Va.: National Society of Fund Raising Executives, 1988.

National Society of Fund Raising Executives' membership directory with an alphabetical listing of approximately 8,000 members as of May 1988.

3670. National Wildlife Federation. *Conservation Directory.* 32nd ed. Washington: National Wildlife Federation, 1987.

List of organizations, agencies, and officials concerned with natural resource use and management.

3671. Negovetic, Neal. "Non-Profit Software Package Review: Part 4." *Fund Raising Management* 17 (July 1986): 22-7.

3672. "Neighborhood Revitalization Partnerships." *Community Action* 1 (1982): 24+.

3673. Netzel, Paul A. *YMCA Capital Development. Key Planning Steps Leading to a Capital Campaign.* Los Angeles: YMCA of Metropolitan Los Angeles, 1977.

3674. "Never Mind the Project Just Give Us a Grant." *Charity* 1 (April 1984): 14-5.

3675. New School for Social Research. Center for New York City Affairs. *Priorities in Social Services: A Guide for Philanthropic Funding.* Praeger Special Studies in U.S. Economic and Social Development. New York: Praeger, 1971.

3676. "New United Fund Cut Charity Drives." *Nation's Business* (September 1955): 36-73, 80-3.

3677. New York. Department of Social Welfare. *Fund Raising in New York State. Second Report: An Analysis of Charitable Organizations Registered in New York State, 1956-57.* New York: New York State. Department of Social Welfare, 1958.

3678. Newlin, Larry, ed. *Resource Guide for Rural Development: Handbook for Accessing Government and Private Funding Sources.* Washington: National Rural Center, 1978.

3679. Newman, Danny. *Subscribe Now: Building Arts Audiences through Dynamic Subscription Promotion.* New York: Theatre Communications Group, 1977.

3680. Newton, Walter L. *The Use of the Mail in Philanthropic Finance: A Compilation of the Theory and Practice of the Use of the Mail in Fund Raising for the Use of Philanthropic and Social Service Organizations Accompanied by a Collection of Successful Fund Raising Letters.* 2 Vols. Los Angeles: Walter L. Newton, 1924.

3681. Nicholas, Ted. *Where the Money Is and How to Get It.* Wilmington, Del.: Enterprise Publishing, 1980.

3682. Nichols, David A. "Applying the Theory Z Method to the Development Office." *Fund Raising Management* 15 (March 1984): 26-31.

3683. Nichols, Judith E. "Personality Type Theory Weds Programs, Motivation." *Fund Raising Management* 17 (October 1986): 58, 60, 62.

Wayne State University's executive director of university development poses the question "Is fund raising an art or a science?" According to Nichols, it is both. The author goes beyond the use of traditional marketing studies and psychological profiling for obtaining action from prospects. She combines these methods with classic personality type theory which enables the fundraiser to do more than set the scene and wait. Personality types of both individuals and organizations are reviewed as well as a plan of action for their specific development as donors.

3684. Nichols, Susan K., comp. and ed. *Fund Raising: A Basic Reader*. Resource Report, no. 1. Washington: American Association of Museums, 1987.

Intended as a sourcebook introduction to the topic of fundraising for use by small and moderate-size museums with and without a principal fundraiser. Offers advice on assessing mission, needs, and goals; considering the resources of the community; and the various fundraising options. Provides many articles describing the fundraising experiences of seasoned professionals, and stresses the need to remember, however obvious it may appear, that fundraising is first and foremost a human endeavor.

3685. Nielson, Richard P. "Cost Squeeze, Budget Ax Prods Market Piggybacking Trend." *Fund Raising Management* 15 (April 1984): 20+.

3686. "Non-Profit Software Package Directory." *Fund Raising Management* 18 (September 1987): 28-30, 32-3, 36.

3687. "Non-Profit Software Package Directory: Fall '88 Update." *Fund Raising Management* 19 (October 1988).

Profiles various software packages, from accounting to donor management to fundraising and more. Each profile includes description of functions, technical specifications, training and services, address and telephone number for the vendor with brief background information and most common users, and the price.

3688. "Nonprofit Loan Funds Emerge with Cash for Crises." *Nonprofit Executive* 4 (June 1985): 1-2.

3689. Norback, Judith, and Patricia Weitz, eds. *Sourcebook of Aid for the Mentally and Physically Handicapped*. New York: Van Nostrand Reinhold Co., 1983.

Describes a variety of services and funding programs offered by public and private agencies for the mentally annd physically handicapped.

3690. North, Halsey. *Ten Prerequisites for Successful Fund Raising*. Madison, Wis.: Association of College, University and Community Arts Administrators, 1979.

3691. Nygren, Terry. "Go Ye into All the World: Doane College Used Church Connections to Bring Its Message to Corporations." *Currents* 11 (November-December 1985): 20+.

3692. Odendahl, Teresa Jean, and Elizabeth Trocolli Boris. "The Grantmaking Process." *Foundation News* 24 (September-October 1983): 22-31.

3693. Olenick, Arnold J. "The Bottom Line in Fundraising." *Grantsmanship Center News* 13 (January-February 1985): 48-53.

Discusses importance of demonstrating good program and fiscal management.

3694. Olson, Jon B. "Marketing: A Development Opportunity." *NAHD Journal* (Winter-Spring 1984): 21-7.

3695. "On Target: The Anatomy of an Effective Direct-Mail Appeal." *Currents* 14 (May 1988): 14-7.

Detailed examination of a seven-piece annual appeal from the Wharton Center for Performing Arts at Michigan State University, a recent direct mail winner in the CASE Recognition program. Each facet of the package is reproduced with comments about its strengths and suggestions for improvement by Patti Absher of Absher Direct Marketing in Washington, DC. The seven pieces are: the mailing envelope, the appeal letter, a testimonial, a brochure, list of past givers, the response device, and the return envelope.

3696. O'Neill, June A. *Sources of Funds to Colleges and Universities: A Technical Report*. Hightstown, N.J.: Carnegie Commission on Higher Education, 1973.

3697. O'Rourke, Helen L. "Direct Mail Fund Raising: Sweepstakes and Other Trends." *Fund Raising Management* 16 (August 1985): 56+.

3698. Outlaw, Bill. "Maryland Approves Private Fund Raising for Schools." *Washington Times* (1 September 1983).

3699. Owen, Virginia Lee. *Public vs. Private Arts Subsidies: Are They Equivalent?* Unpublished, 1981.

3700. Padberg, Ann M. "Successful Involvement of Volunteers Uses Phone." *Fund Raising Management* 14 (December 1983): 40-3.

3701. Panas, Jerold. *Born to Raise. What Makes a Great Fundraiser; What Makes a Fundraiser Great*. Chicago: Pluribus Press, 1988.

Panas identifies and interviews many of those fundraisers who, he contends, deserve to be called great. They share the lessons they have learned, their skills and talents, and what it takes to be the best. Includes a list of sixty-three fundraising maxims and a self-appraisal form that will help fundraisers assess their strengths and weaknesses.

3702. Panas, Jerold. *Mega Gifts: Who Gives Them, Who Gets Them?* Chicago: Pluribus Press, 1984.

"This book is a treatise on motivation," Panas writes, the motivation associated with giving and getting gifts of $1 million or more. Interviews with major givers such as W. Clement Stone, Virginia Piper, James Gamble, and Arthur Rubloff present the reasons these people gave and are giving during their lives rather than postmortem through their wills. Towards the end of the book Panas compiles sixty-four rules for success in major gift fundraising; while few of these are new, they illuminate the importance of the board in the process; the strong impact of women, as individuals, as decision-makers in husband and wife teams, and as solicitors; and the great significance of a history of giving in the securing of large gifts. Appendix contains a series of charts listing Panas' research findings on the reasons people give, with separate charts for health, education, religious, the YMCA, the Salvation Army, and cultural organizations; a chart listing responses from seventy-seven expert fundraisers; and a chart averaging all of the above. Top priority in the motivation of a megadonor is belief in the mission of the institution; the wealthy also give importance to community responsibility and civic pride, regard for volunteer and professional leadership of the agency, involvement, fiscal stability, and respect for the institution locally.

3703. Parker, Gary. *Survey of Giving Report, Fiscal Year 1985.* Falls Church, Va.: National Association for Hospital Development, 1986.

The Association's second annual report on giving to health care. The survey examines funds raised, population and bedsize, budgets, age of development program, size of staff, structure, means of fundraising, sources of funds raised, how funds were spent, concerns of development officers, and capital campaigns. Each of the above twelve categories contains a summary of the statistical data gathered in the survey as well as a chart (with the exception of captial campaigns). In 1985, NAHD members raised $1.2 billion in donations, or 10.6 percent of the total of $11.25 billion given to health and hospitals. The most important types of fundraising, according to members, remain major gifts, planned giving, and direct mail. Individuals remain the largest source of gifts. The bulk of funds raised came from members in medical centers followed by teaching hospitals, then community hospitals. Fifty-six percent of members conduct their fundraising through a foundation. In addition, twenty-five percent of the respondents said they plan to establish a foundation.

3704. Paton, G. Jeffery. "Research about Development: Reasons for It, Obstacles to It." *Fund Raising Management* 16 (October 1985): 42+.

3705. Pavoni, M.M. "Obtaining a Grant: A Collaborative Effort." *Journal of American Medical Record Association* 58 (July 1987): 18-20.

Describes the step-by-step process of obtaining funds from a foundation in order to purchase capital equipment, based on the authors' experience in seeking grant support for a medical record department at a 503-bed nonprofit hospital in Chicago.

3706. Pendleton, Niel. *Fund Raising: A Guide for Non-Profit Organizations.* Englewood Cliffs, N.J.: Prentice-Hall, 1981.

3707. "Percentage Fundraising: Is an Ethical Code Giving Way to Expediency?" *Chronicle of Non Profit Enterprise* 7 (July 1988): 4, 8.

Examines the rising trend toward percentage fundraising, the practice of rewarding fundraisers by linking pay to performance by including incentive levels, commissions and bonuses within the terms of agreement. While some see performance-based compensation as a way to increase income level, many oppose the method on an ethical basis, seeing it as diametrically opposed to the spirit of philanthropy. Voluntarism, visionary ideals and the goal of contributing to the quality of life may succumb to the mercenary tactics of the commercial business world, and many in the nonprofit sector fear that "inappropriate pressures" will be placed on donors in order to bring in the extra dollars, leading to disillusionment and the end of long term cultivation.

3708. *The Perfect Development Officer: From Harvard Business Review.* Vol. 2. Cleveland: Third Sector Press, 1986.

3709. *The Perfect Development Officer: Skills and Characteristics for Success.* Vol. 1. Cleveland: Third Sector Press, 1986.

3710. Performing Arts Referral Service. "Focus on: Grant Funding." *Information Quarterly* 1 (Summer 87): 1, 2, 8, 15-6.

Article highlights the Foundation Center, founded and supported by foundations to provide an authoritative source of information on foundation giving, and to serve as a valuable resource for arts-related organizations and individuals needing outside funding for their projects. Includes an informative interview with Ann Caviness, Foundation Center Library Director, and a guide to useful publications available at the Center that deal specifically with grantseeking.

3711. *Perspectives on Collaborative Funding: A Resource for Grantmakers.* San Francisco: Northern California Grantmakers, 1985.

Written by California grantmakers, the book is a collection of different perspectives on collaborative funding. The authors give various examples of how grantmakers can increase their impact through joint effort while still preserving their individual priorities. Although written primarily for foundation trustees and staff members, the book could also help grantseekers looking for models on collaboration.

3712. Petranek, Jan G. "Breaking Down the Barriers: Ten Ways to Promote Partnerships between Alumni Officers and Fund Raisers." *Currents* 9 (November-December 1983): 66.

3713. Pfizenmaier, Emily. "A Software Primer: What the Chief Development Officer Needs to Know." *Currents* 9 (March 1983): 12-6.

3714. Phariss, Bruce. "Putting the Fun in Fund-Raising." *Theatre Communications* 5 (June 1983): 14-7.

3715. Phelps-Stokes Fund. *DC Directory of Native American Federal and Private Programs.* Washington: Phelps-Stokes Fund, 1982.

3716. Phillips, Ken. "The Thoughtful Marketing of Foster Parents Plan." *Fund Raising Management* 16 (June 1985): 40+.

3717. Phillips, Michael. *The Seven Laws of Money.* Menlo Park, Calif.: Word Wheel, 1974.

3718. Phillips, Stephanie. "How to Get a Celebrity to Attend Your Special Event." *Fund Raising Management* 16 (September 1985): 58+.

3719. Pierce, Catherine. *Troubled Youth and the Arts: A Resource Guide.* Silver Spring, Md.: Read, 1979.

3720. Pierce, Lyman L. *How to Raise Money.* New York: Harper & Bros., 1932.

3721. Pierce, Milt. "The Seven Sins of Direct Mail Fund Raising." *Fund Raising Management* 18 (August 1987): 88-9.

3722. "The Plain Fact Is Our Colleges and Universities Are Facing What Might Easily Become a Crisis." *Alma Mater* 26 (March-April 1968): 1-52.

3723. *Planned Gift Fund Raising: A Programmed Instructional Text.* Indianapolis, Ind.: Pictorial Publishers, 1981.

3724. Plinio, Alex J. "Getting the Employee into the Corporate Giving Act: The Growth of Matching Gifts." *Philanthropy Monthly* (March 1982): 17-21.

3725. Polivy, Deborah K. "The United Way and the Issue of Admissions." *Grants Magazine* 6 (June 1983): 91-7.

3726. Pollard, John A. *Fund-Raising for Higher Education.* New York: Harper & Bros., [1958].

3727. Poole, Mary D. "Policies Clear Up Confusion for Board, Staff, Committees." *Fund Raising Management* 15 (March 1984): 18+.

3728. Porter, Robert A., ed. *United Arts Fundraising.* New York: American Council for the Arts, 1986.

3729. Porter, Robert A., ed. *United Arts Fundraising. Campaign Analysis, 1980.* New York: American Council for the Arts, 1981.

3730. Porter, Robert A., ed. *United Arts Fundraising Manual.* New York: American Council for the Arts, 1980.

3731. Porter, Robert A., ed. *United Arts Fundraising Policybook.* New York: American Council for the Arts, [1980].

3732. Posch, Robert J., Jr. "Cable Watch Out!" *Fund Raising Management* 14 (July 1983): 48-50.

3733. Posch, Robert J., Jr. "Direct Marketers' Battle Tactic Good Strategy for Fund Raisers." *Fund Raising Management* 15 (June 1984): 22+.

3734. "The Postal Rate Wars." *Philanthropy Monthly* 15 (December 1982): 6-11.

3735. Poummit, Morris R. "Who Took the Fun Out of Fundraising?" *Nonprofit World Report* 2 (March-April 1984): 10.

3736. Pratt, George. "Make an Average Investment, Get an Average Return." *Fund Raising Management* 16 (October 1985): 74+.

3737. Pray, Francis C., ed. *Handbook for Educational Fundraising.* San Francisco: Jossey-Bass Publishers, 1981.

Collection of seventy-one articles discusses philosophical and practical approaches to every aspect of fundraising for higher education institutions.

3738. "Preservation and the Neighborhoods." *Response* 12 (January 1983): 19-20.

3739. Pritchard, J. Harris. *There's Plenty of Money for Nonprofit Groups Willing to Earn Their Shares: How to Do It Successfully.* Phoenix, Ariz.: Cornucopia Publications, 1984.

Tells how to conduct numerous fundraising events and sell products to earn income. Chapters on fundraising events discuss advantages, disadvantages, typical costs, and average time frame for events. Includes extensive information on planning and execution of the ideas.

3740. Pritchett, Henry Smith. "The Use and Abuse of Endowments." *Atlantic Monthly* (October 1929): 1-10.

3741. "The Problem Proposal." *Currents* 14 (October 1988): 18-22.

Development officers from various universities and colleges provide their answers to three hypothetical dilemmas that make the drafting of a grant proposal problematic. The dilemmas are: a tempting invitation from a corporation whose aims do not match those of your institution; a request for specific information (enrollment and finances) that will reveal problems in your organization; and what type of proposal to write to a foundation with which one of your organization's trustees has a tenuous connection, though the foundation itself has no obvious interest in education. The answers are thoughtful and well-developed, indicative of the various approaches and amount of resources available to the developer of grant proposals.

3742. Procter, Arthur W., and Arthur A. Schuck. *The Financing of Social Work.* New York: A.W. Shaw, 1926.

3743. Proffitt, Stuart. "Methods of Evaluating Computer Software Systems." *Fund Raising Management* 16 (May 1985): 54+.

3744. "Profile of a Major Donor." *Grassroots Fundraising Journal* 2 (April 1983): 11.

3745. Program Information Associates. *Federal Alcohol and Drug Abuse Initiatives: A Special Report.* Honolulu, Hawaii: Program Information Associates, 1987.

A brief guide to block grants and other federal monies for both drug and alcohol abuse programs. Contains information on funds available from the Office of Substance Abuse Prevention, ADTR Block Grants to the States, New Research Priorities Under Anti-Drug Abuse Act, Department of Education Funding Under the Drug-Free Schools and Communities Act of 1986, U.S. Department of Labor, ACTION—Demonstration Grants for Drug Abuse Prevention and Education, and the Bureau of Justice Assistance.

3746–3767 FUNDRAISING

3746. Public Management Institute. *Capital Campaign Resource Guide.* San Francisco: Public Management Institute, 1984.

Resource book on capital campaigns which includes a campaign workbook, a capital grants directory, a consultants directory, a client directory, and state laws. The capital grants directory covers nearly 250 foundations and corporations that make grants for capital purposes. Provides several indexes, including funding areas, geographic areas of giving, grant recipients, and principal business.

3747. Public Management Institute. *Computer Resource Guide for Nonprofits.* 2 vols. 3rd ed. San Francisco: Public Management Institute, 1985.

Directory provides information on two types of computer resources. First volume describes computer software packages which provide special services to nonprofits, such as accounts receivable, donor history, mailing list/labels, and solicitation. The second volume is a directory of foundations, corporations, and federal agencies which have made computer-related grants, loans, and/or in-kind donations. Several indexes, including types of support, contributions committee members, computer software, contact person, corporate headquarters, geographic focus, and sample grant recipients.

3748. Public Management Institute. *Direct Mail Fund Raising.* San Francisco: Public Management Institute, 1980.

3749. Public Management Institute. *How to Build a Big Endowment.* 2nd ed., rev. San Francisco: Public Management Institute, 1982.

3750. Public Management Institute. *The New Grants Planner: A Systems Approach to Grantsmanship.* San Francisco: Public Management Institute, 1980.

3751. "Public Schools Emerge As Fund Raisers." *Nonprofit Executive* 4 (April 1985): 1-2.

Interview with Beverly Meinhart of the Columbus, Ohio Public Schools system, who talks about the school's corporate solicitations program.

3752. Pulling, Lisa. *The KRC Desk Book for Fund Raisers.* New Canaan, Conn.: KRC Development Council, 1980.

3753. Purcell, David. "Spinning the Web of Partnership: Binding Public and Private Sectors." *Christian Science Monitor* (29 September 1983).

3754. *A Quick Guide to Loans and Emergency Funds.* New York: Center for Arts Information, 1982.

3755. Quigg, H. Gerald, ed. *The Successful Capital Campaign: From Planning to Victory Celebration.* Washington: Council for Advancement and Support of Education, 1986.

Collection of papers on the capital campaign for both professionals and newcomers to the fundraising field. The book is a comprehensive and in-depth examination of a most important type of fundraising which has changed significantly over the years and has reached new thresholds in both frequency and larger and larger goals. Included in the book are over twenty essays written by experienced development and fundraising professionals who represent some of the major American educational institutions. The volume performs three functions—it is a directory which provides technical assistance, an encyclopedia on the capital campaign, and it documents in one volume the current thinking in the field on the capital campaign. Aspects of the capital campaign in today's world which are explored include its values and purposes; long-range planning process; the internal audit; consultants; the feasibility study and the case statement; prospect research, screening and evaluation; the president's and the trustees' role; major gifts success; the campaign's plan, mechanics, budget, goals, and calendar; solicitation methods and training; public relations; and the public university perspective.

3756. Radcliffe, R.L. "Encourage Donors to Consider Living Trusts." *Trustee* 40 (June 1987): 11, 26.

3757. *Raising Funds with Souvenir Journals.* Brooklyn, N.Y.: Bay Ridge Press, 1976.

3758. Ramey, Gaile, and Kim Klein. *Fundraising Resource Guide: Annotated Bibliography and Resource List.* San Francisco: Western Consortium for the Health Professions, 1982.

3759. Rankin, Deborah. "Capital Drives Prosper." *New York Times* (13 November 1977).

3760. "Rapidly Growing Women's Funds." *Grassroots Fundraising Journal* 4 (August 1985): 11+.

3761. Raybin, Arthur D. *How to Hire the Right Fund Raising Consultant.* Washington: Taft Group, 1985.

Basic book on selecting and working with a fundraising firm or independent consultant. Includes interview checklists, sample contract, fair practice codes from professional fundraising associations, sample letters, and forms for interviewing potential donors.

3762. Raymond, Louis. "For a Mere Song." *Manhattan, Inc.* 4 (July 1987): 110-11.

3763. "The Rebuttable Presumption Is a Key Issue: The Munson Case Attracts Friends of the Court." *Philanthropy Monthly* 16 (March 1983): 28-32.

3764. Reed, Steve. "Selecting a Computer System for Fund Raising." *Fund Raising Management* 16 (May 1985): 34+.

3765. "Regional Film Grants." *Reel World* 2 (August 1982): 1, 3.

3766. Reilly, Timothy A., ed. *Raising Money through an Institutionally Related Foundation.* Washington: Council for Advancement and Support of Education, 1985.

Looks at university and college foundations and their relationship with the institutions they serve. Discusses how university foundations meet their objectives, their policies, their general operation patterns, and legal and financial responsibilities. Written for institutions considering the establishment of a foundation and officers of existing college and university foundations.

3767. Reiss, Alvin H. "Arts Groups Try New Approaches to Win Corporate Sponsorship." *Fund Raising Management* 18 (April 1987): 88-9.

In the face of corporations becoming more bottom-line oriented in their sponsorship of the arts (seeking highly visible projects that meet their business objectives), Reiss profiles smaller institutions that lack the glitter yet still gain support through their relentless pursuit and imaginative methods. One particularly ingenious sponsorship concept is the creative match initiated by the GeVa Theatre in Rochester, New York. To sponsor its production of *Inherit the Wind*, a courtroom drama based on the famed Scopes trial of the 1920s, the theater turned to local law firms. In addition to the usual benefits, including performance tickets, printed program and lobby listings, GeVa also allowed ten lawyers from each firm that donated $1,000 to sponsor one performance to appear on stage during the performance in the role of non-speaking jurors. Examples of linking sales to arts groups are also mentioned, including Lord & Taylor's annual "Focus: America" series, which spotlights a different American city or area each year. Previews for the series benefit one or more nonprofit institutions from the host city.

3768. Reiss, Alvin H. "At Your Place or Mine? Special Events Are the Sine Qua Non of Arts Fund Raising." *Fund Raising Management* 18 (April 1987): 26, 28, 30-2, 35.

Special events in the world of arts fundraising are the glue that helps hold members and volunteers close to an organization, and the magnet that attracts audiences—and celebrities—who might never otherwise get involved. Special events bring recognition and media coverage to the arts, according to Reiss. Of course, the bottom line to the special event is money. Indeed, the ideal event should gross three times its cost. Competition among nonprofits has made it especially important that the event be attractive and unique. The author pinpoints what can be done to make the event successful while still being cost effective. Reiss includes tips such as: relate the event to the organization's artistic program, obtain a top-drawer chairperson and high-level committee, announce that a major celebrity will attend, be creative—choose an unusual site and event theme. (The article contains numerous examples of creative, successful benefits.) The successful special event needs predetermined goals; focus; suitable site and date; a plan of action which includes timetable, budget, spending controls, an accountability chart; and coordinated direct mail and publicity effort.

3769. Reiss, Alvin H. *Cash In! Funding and Promoting the Arts.* New York: Theatre Communications Group, 1986.

Describes imaginative concepts, tested ideas and case histories of programs and promotions that have made money for nonprofit arts organizations. Includes an annotated bibliography of books and periodicals dealing with various aspects of fundraising.

3770. Reiss, Alvin H. "Creative Financing for Nonprofits." *Nonprofit World Report* 2 (May-June 1984): 21+.

3771. Reiss, Alvin H. *How to Win Friends and Influence Audiences: Expert Tips in Financing and Promoting Your Session.* Port Chester, N.Y.: Rosco, [198?].

3772. Reiss, Alvin H. "On-Target Marketing Programs Key to Successful Arts Funding." *Fund Raising Management* 19 (August 1988): 68-9.

Focuses on the aggressive and professional "new look" marketing campaigns of the Brooklyn Academy of Music (now popularly known as BAM), the Colden Center for the Performing Arts at Queen College (whose 1987-1988 season launched the slogan "The Queen of Arts in the Heart of Queens"), and the Quincy Society for Fine Arts in Quincy, Illinois (which dramatically generated $3 million in support for Quincy arts organizations and activities in only five years, with new initiatives still being planned). As Reiss writes, "Marketing, a term once virtually unknown in the arts, has become one of the essential ingredients of arts management," allowing arts organizations to communicate their vision and achievements to both their audiences and their funding sources.

3773. Renfroe, Elton. "Donor Motivation." *Philanthropy Monthly* 18 (January 1985): 33-5.

Analyzes donor motivation from the fundraiser's perspective.

3774. "Return of the Givers: Happy Surprise for Colleges." *U.S. News and World Report* (31 July 1972): 45-6.

3775. Robbins, Williams. "Delaware Museum Seeks Funds to Support a Du Pont Legacy." *New York Times* (27 June 1983): A-10.

3776. Robinson, Daniel D. "Guidelines to Deal with Corporate Matching Gift Problems." *Philanthropy Monthly* 17 (October 1984): 29-31.

3777. Rockefeller, John D., Jr. "The Technique of Soliciting." *Currents* 10 (November-December 1984): 38-9.

3778. Roel, Raymond. "The Future of Telethons: Cutting through the Clutter." *Fund Raising Management* 15 (April 1984): 42+.

3779. Roel, Raymond. "How to Create a Film to Increase Fund Raising." *Fund Raising Management* 14 (October 1983): 50+.

3780. Roel, Raymond. "Increasing Dollar Levels by Building Relationships." *Fund Raising Management* 15 (October 1984): 67-72.

Describes direct mail successes of the National Republican Senatorial Committee.

3781. Rose-Ackerman, Susan. *Charitable Giving and "Excessive" Fundraising.* Program on Non-Profit Organizations, no. 26. New Haven, Conn.: Institution for Social and Policy Studies, 1980.

3782. Rosen, Michael. "The Evolution of Telephone Fund Raising: 5 Case Studies." *Fund Raising Management* 16 (August 1985): 24+.

3783. Rosso, Hank. "If Only We Had an Endowment Fund." *Grassroots Fundraising Journal* 4 (June 1985): 7.

3784. Rothman, Iris, and Marc Rotenberg. "Hardware and Software: Panic or Panacea." *Community Jobs* 7 (April 1984): 1+.

3785. Rothschild, Michael L. "Marketing Communications in Nonbusiness Situations or Why It's So Hard to Sell Brotherhood like Soap." *Journal of Marketing* 43 (Spring 1979): 11.

3786. Rowland, A. Westley, ed. *Handbook of Institutional Advancement.* San Francisco: Jossey-Bass Publishers, 1977.

3787. Rubacky, Tricia. "Essential Ingredients for Fundraising Planning. Part 2." *Grassroots Fundraising Journal* 7 (October 1988): 3-6.

Covers the essential steps of developing income projections and income cash flow projections, which enable an organization to continuously evaluate its fundraising progress, monitor its successes and appraise its program accordingly, and to correct for disappointment in a timely manner. A sample annual plan serves as an example of probability-based planning, which allows for realistic income expectations. The income cash flow projection can reveal high-income and low-income months, and is recommended to help an organization plan its expenses and avoid over-extending its cash flow.

3788. Rubin, Mary. *How to Get Money for Research.* Westbury, N.Y.: Feminist Press, 1983.

A guide to research funding opportunities for and about women at the pre- and post-doctoral levels. Compiled for women scholars, researchers, and others pursuing research questions about women.

3789. Rust, Brian. "Five Steps to Progressive Fundraising." *Nonprofit World Report* 3 (January-February 1985): 11+.

3790. Ryan, D. "Identifying and Nurturing Core Donors." *Fund Raising Management* 16 (February 1986): 20-4, 32.

3791. Ryan, John S. "Converting an Estate Donor into a Substantial Annual Giver." *Fund Raising Management* 15 (April 1984): 62+.

3792. Ryan, John S. "The Donor Connection: How to Make It Click." *Currents* 10 (March 1984): 56.

3793. Ryan, John S. "Keep It Simple: Overcoming Call Reluctance." *Fund Raising Management* 15 (November 1984): 64-9.

Advises fundraisers on talking person-to-person with donors.

3794. Saasta, Timothy. "United Way: Who Are Its Critics?" *Grantsmanship Center News* 11 (November-December 1983): 53-4.

3795. Salzman, Ruth, and Robin Balding. "How Lockboxes Can Unlock the Fund Raising Gridlock." *Fund Raising Management* 14 (December 1983): 36-9.

3796. Sammer, Joanne M., ed. *The Health Funds Grants Resource Yearbook.* Wall Township, N.J.: Health Resources Publishing, 1987.

Reference volume for the professional health grantseeker which analyzes trends and statistics and describes federal, corporate and foundation health grants programs. The material is arranged in broad subject categories and contains descriptive profiles of grants for elderly health services, child and maternal health, AIDS, adolescent health and pregnancy prevention, health professions training, alcohol and drug abuse, home health care services, cancer research, health care for the uninsured, community health centers, and native American and refugee health programs. The book includes a reference and resource bibliography which lists literature in the field. The appendixes list twenty-seven major foundations which make health care grants; forty sources of federal and foundation information; planning charts, guides and worksheets. The reference work also contains three indexes—subject, alphabetical order, and chronological order by the date in which the material was published in the *Health Funds Development Letter*.

3797. Sandberg, J. Robert. "Organizing Your Operation." *Currents* 11 (March 1985): 46+.

Provides four models which explain how to increase constituency fundraising.

3798. Sanders, Ralph W. "The Donor Profile Survey: A Way to Determine Priorities." *Fund Raising Management* 16 (April 1985): 18+.

3799. Santoro, Elaine. "Fund Raising Direct Mail Peaks in December, February." *Fund Raising Management* 15 (June 1984): 78+.

3800. Sasek, Joseph A. "Fourteen Rather Rocky Reasons for a Capital Campaign." *Fund Raising Management* 16 (October 1985): 50+.

3801. Savage, Joseph G. "Building the Tiers of Your Resource Development Program." *Fund Raising Management* 16 (March 1985): 54+.

3802. Sawyer, Willits H. "Raise More Money, Easier with EFT." *NSFRE Journal* 8 (Spring 1983): 11+.

3803. Schneiter, Paul H. *The Art of Asking: How to Solicit Philanthropic Gifts.* 2nd ed. Ambler, Pa.: Fund Raising Institute, 1985.

Tells how to ask for a gift, with emphasis on asking an individual for a gift in person. Covers four asking techniques (in person solicitation, soliciting groups of prospects at one time, soliciting by phone, and soliciting by direct mail) and provides detailed model approaches to individuals, foundations, and corporations. Relates three case histories of large gifts given by individuals to nonprofit organizations and also includes rationale for giving by twelve donors and advice from several veteran fundraisers.

3804. Schneiter, Paul H., and Donald T. Nelson. *The Thirteen Most Common Fund-Raising Mistakes and How to Avoid Them.* Washington: Taft Group, 1982.

3805. "School Initiative." *Indianapolis Star* (14 May 1983).

3806. Schreyer, R. Blair. "Three Common Problems Faced in Capital Campaigns." *Fund Raising Management* 16 (July 1985): 22-4.

3807. Schulte, Linda S. "Combined Federal Campaign: Philanthropy and Politics on the Potomac." *PSA/83* 2 (21 October 1983): 43-6.

3808. Schultz, Louis Arthur. *Telepledge: The Complete Guide to Mailphone Fund Raising.* Washington: Taft Group, 1986.

Describes the steps necessary to design, implement, and manage an ongoing mail/telephone solicitation program. Appendix contains sample request letters, and a cassette tape of sample telephone solicitations accompanies the book.

3809. Scribner, Susan, and Florence Green. "Asking for Money." *Grantsmanship Center News* 2 (March-April 1983): 8-17.

3810. Scully, Malcolm G. "Voluntary Support of Colleges Drops $80 Million in Year." *Chronicle of Higher Education* 12 (29 March 1976): 4-5.

3811. "Seasonality Study Category: Fund Raising." *KRC Letter* 16 (October 1985): 8.

3812. Seltzer, Michael. *Securing Your Organization's Future: A Complete Guide to Fundraising Strategies.* New York: Foundation Center, 1987.

A step-by-step approach to creating and sustaining a network of funding sources. Discusses major organizational tasks to address before applying for funding; the world of money available to nonprofits; new, emerging funding opportunities from religious groups and other organizations; a blueprint for designing and implementing fundraising strategies; and how to capitalize on the uniqueness of your organization to secure funding. Case studies and worksheets accompany discussions. Appendixes include a compilation of state laws regulating charitable organizations, list of resource organizations, list of regional associations of grantmakers, and participating libraries in the Foundation Center National Library Network.

3813. Semple, Robert F. "Gift Rating Donors: An Important First Step." *Fund Raising Management* 16 (March 1985): 78+.

3814. "The Serious Problem of State and Local Barriers to Fund Raising: Are We Creating Walled States?" *Philanthropy Monthly* 20 (July-August 1987): 5-18.

Examines trends in new state laws regulating fundraising and details specific provisions of some state laws to illustrate the restrictions and difficulties encountered by charities.

3815. Seymour, Harold James. *Campanas para Obtencion de Fondos.* Mexico City, Mexico: Editorial Limusa, 1970.

3816. Seymour, Harold James. *Designs for Fund-Raising: Principles, Patterns and Techniques.* New York: McGraw-Hill, 1966.

3817. Sharpe, Robert F. "The Perils and Promise of Life Insurance Policies." *Fund Raising Management* (September 1984): 38+.

Offers ways for donors to give life insurance gifts to nonprofits.

3818. Sharpe, Robert F. *The Planned Giving Idea Book.* Nashville, Tenn.: Thomas Nelson Publishers, 1978.

3819. Sharpe, Robert F. "Planned Giving: Key to Prosperity, Professionalism." *Fund Raising Management* 17 (February 1987): 69-73.

3820. Sheerin, Mira J. "Special Events Face New Challenge in 1987." *Fund Raising Management* 17 (December 1986): 58.

"The economy, tax reform, and competition have all put pressure on special events. But the 'right' event growing out of innovative thinking will always have a place." Among the events Sheerin expects to survive are established annual events, fashion shows, theater benefits, sports events, and events with small fundraising potential (e.g., garage sales, cocktail parties, etc.).

3821. Sheerin, Mira J. "Telemarketing: The Key to Successful Fund Raising." *Fund Raising Management* 16 (September 1985): 154+.

3822. Sheldon, K. Scott. "Exploring New Developments in Computerized Fund Raising." *Fund Raising Management* 15 (May 1984): 36+.

3823. Sheldon, K. Scott. "Fund Raising Information Is Analyzed by Costs, Benefits." *Fund Raising Management* 14 (February 1984): 18-23.

3824. Sheppard, William E., comp. *Fund Raising Letter Collection.* Ambler, Pa.: Fund Raising Institute, [1976].

3825. Sheridan, Philip G. *Fund Raising for the Small Organization.* New York: M. Evans & Co., 1968.

3826. Shimer, John C. "Your Introduction to Endowments." *National Fund Raiser* (June 1984): 4.

3827. Shirley, Bill. "Some Athletes Build on Solid Foundations." *Grantsmanship Center News* 13 (January-February 1985): 8-10.

Describes the philanthropic giving of several famous athletes.

3828. Shreckengast, Earl K. "Cultivating Your Computer: A Botanical Garden Case Study." *Fund Raising Management* 14 (February 1984): 38+.

3829. Silverman, Paul H. "Universities and High Technology Industry." *Grants Magazine* 5 (September 1982): 157-67.

3830. Simons, Robin, Peter Lengsfelder, and Lisa Farber Miller. *Nonprofit Piggy Goes to Market: How the Denver Children's Museum Earns $600,000 Annually.* Denver, Colo.: Children's Museum of Denver, 1984.

"Market driven philanthropy" is a concept attracting a lot of attention in nonprofit circles. As one of the most successful practitioners of this new trend, the Children's Museum of Denver offers the fruits of its own experience to nonprofit organizations interested in achieving a higher degree of financial self-sufficiency. Although the presentation is often humorous, it asks the hard questions of effective business practices while making an effort to expose the pitfalls associated with this new type of funding strategy. Essential reading for any organization considering projects and programs aimed at creating new unrestricted and diversified income streams.

3831. Simpson, Carol. "No Bow and Arrow." *Grassroots Fundraising Journal* 3 (October-November 1984): 8-9.

A special fundraising event planned around Valentine's Day.

3832. Skovgard, Robert O. "Public Speaking As a Fund Raising Tool." *KRC Letter* 13 (February 1983): 1-6.

3833. Sladek, Frea E., and Eugene L. Stein. "Funding Agency Contacts: Letting Them Help." *Grants Magazine* 6 (March 1983): 19-31.

3834. Smith, Becky. *How to: Fund Raising Manual.* Utica, N.Y.: Bauer Associates, 1983.

3835. Smith, Craig. "Deferred Giving: Letting the Donor Have His Cake While You Eat It Too." *Foundation News* 25 (January-February 1984): 22-31.

3836. Smith, Craig. *How to Increase Corporate Giving to Your Organization.* San Francisco: Public Management Institute, 1984.

Provides advice on how to identify prospective corporate donors and when and how to ask for cash and non-cash gifts.

3837. Smith, David Horton. "The Philanthropy Business." *Society* 15 (1978): 8-15.

Examines how United Way charities, or other community-wide fundraising campaigns, raise and allocate their funds, to whom the funds are given, with what effect, to whom they are accountable, and what philosophy of operation is used. The author's conclusions are based on extensive personal interviews and a review of the literature on federated community giving in the United States. Smith argues for a breakup of the United Way monopoly on charitable fundraising for health, welfare, and recreation, especially at the workplace. He concludes, "unless the United Way and similar federated fundraising and allocation organizations can...increase their overall responsiveness to the public interest, they should be legislated out of existence on public interest grounds, much in the same way that business cartels, trusts, and the like were legislated out of existence earlier in this century, even though they—like the United Way—were very efficient and effective."

3838. Smith, Virginia Carter. "Getting in Gear." *Currents* 9 (June 1983): 40-3.

3839. Snedcof, Harold F. *Cultural Facilities in Mixed-Use Development.* Washington: Urban Land Institute, 1985.

3840. "Soliciting Mega Gifts from the Wealthy." *Cost Containment Newsletter* 8 (11 February 1986): 3-6.

3841. "Solicitor's Guide: Prepared for the Volunteer Fund Raiser." *Fundemensions* 8 (March 1984): 6-8.

3842. Solomon, Stephen L. "New York: A New Charitable Solicitation Statute." *Philanthropy Monthly* 19 (September 1986): 23-8.

Analysis of the New York State House Bill 6931-E. The amendment, effective July 1, 1987, makes changes in the law relating to charitable solicitation, including expanded registration requirements, disclosure requirements, prohibited activities and enforcement methods.

3843. Solyn, Paul, and Mary Durling. "Anniversaries: Celebrating a Big Birthday for Love and Money." *Currents* 10 (June 1984): 9-12.

3844. Sontag, Sherry. "Assessing How Gifts to Charity Are Used." *New York Times* (29 June 1985): 52.

3845. Soroker, Gerald S. *Fund Raising for Philanthropy.* Pittsburgh: Pittsburgh Jewish Publication and Education Foundation, 1974.

3846. Soukup, David J. "Successful Fund Raising Using Simple Engineering." *Fund Raising Management* 15 (December 1984): 30+.

Presents a model which helps the fundraiser calculate which of several fundraising options will yield the greatest income.

3847. Southern Regional Education Board. *Proceedings: A Symposium on Financing Higher Education.* Atlanta, Ga.: Southern Regional Education Board, 1969.

3848. Sparks, D. Martin, and William R. George. "Marketing for Volunteer Service Organizations: A Case Study." *Nonprofit World Report* 2 (March-April 1984): 24+.

3849. "Special Conference Report: Independent Sector Explores Giving Trends and Structures." *Fund Raising Management* 16 (June 1985): 96+.

3850. Spinney, William R. *Estate Planning: Quick Reference Outline.* 20th ed. Chicago: Commerce Clearing House, 1973.

3851. Squires, C. "Secrets of Computer-Based Direct Mail Fund Raising." *Fund Raising Management* 17 (June 1986): 48-58.

3852. Stanford, Sheila. "International Disaster: Fund Raiser's Dream or Nightmare?" *Fund Raising Management* 16 (October 1985): 84+.

Tells how CARE's direct marketing efforts were focused to handle the drought in Africa.

3853. "State Campaigns Open Up to Broader Range of Charities." *Responsive Philanthropy* (Winter 1985): 1+.

3854. "State-Imposed Fund Raising Limitations Struck Down by Supreme Court." *Fund Raising Management* (27 June 1984): 1.

3855. "The State of Fundraising in 1985." *FRI Monthly Portfolio* 25 (January 1986): 1-2.

3856. Stein, Marilyn A. "A View from Both Sides of the Fence." *Grants Magazine* 6 (September 1983): 148-50.

3857. Steinberg, Richard. *Economic and Empiric Analysis of Fund-Raising Behavior by Nonprofit Firms.* Program on Non-Profit Organizations, no. 76. New Haven, Conn.: Institution for Social and Policy Studies, 1983.

3858. Stephan, George N. "Packaged Goods Techniques Work in Fund Raising As Well." *Fund Raising Management* 15 (June 1984): 28+.

3859. Sterne, Larry. "Debate Grows over Fundraising Bonuses." *NonProfit Times* 1 (October 1987): 8, 20.

Presents both sides of the argument concerning percentage fundraising and other types of performance incentives for development staff. While some critics suggest that bonus packages can destroy a nonprofit's standing with donors and volunteers, others argue such plans are needed to keep good people in a field where relatively low salaries produce almost constant turnover.

3860. Stevenson, J. John. "Combined Federal Campaign, Broad Changes: Will Radical Surgery Cure the CFC or Kill It?" *Philanthropy Monthly* 17 (April 1984): 5-21.

3861. Stevenson, J. John. "Combined Federal Campaign: New, Final Rules Will Govern 1984 Campaign." *Philanthropy Monthly* 17 (July-August 1984): 23-32.

3862. Stevenson, J. John. "The Munson Case." *Philanthropy Monthly* 17 (May 1984): 20-3.

3863. Stevenson, J. John. "Political Advocacy Again: Revamping the Combined Federal Campaign." *Philanthropy Monthly* 16 (June 1983): 26-33.

3864. Stevenson, J. John. "The Thrift Shop Dilemma: Fund Raising or Business Venture?" *Philanthropy Monthly* 15 (November 1982): 22-7.

3865. Steward, Edwin E. "Planned Giving: A Training Aid to Help Volunteers Qualify Gift Leads." *Philanthropy Monthly* 17 (April 1984): 33-6.

3866. Steward, Edwin E. "Planned Giving: How to Qualify Planned Gift Leads Promptly." *Philanthropy Monthly* 17 (March 1984): 33-4.

3867. Steward, Edwin E. "What's on Your Prospective Planned Gift Donor's Mind?" *Fund Raising Management* (September 1984): 74+.

3868. "Stewardship/Fund Raising Topic in Christian Conference." *Fund Raising Management* 15 (August 1984): 76+.

3869. Stinchcomb, Lawrence S. "Building Strength from Weakness." *Foundation News* 24 (January-February 1983): 68-70.

3870. Stone, Gregory B., and John Carroll. "A Remarkable Rally." *Currents* 9 (July-August 1983): 23-4.

3871. Stopp, G. Harry, Jr. "IRIS and SPIN: Using Computers to Identify Funding Sources." *Grants Magazine* 8 (December 1985): 235-9.

Comprehensive summary of two national computerized grant search programs available—IRIS, the Illinois Researcher Information System from the University of Illinois and SPIN, the Sponsored Programs Information Network housed in the Research Foundation of the State University of New York. As of the 1985 data, Spin had over 2,500 funding opportunities and IRIS 4,000 funding opportunities on file.

3872. Strand, Bobbie J. *Bibliography: Development Research Materials.* Detroit: Bentz, Whaley, Flessner & Associates, 1986.

3873. Strand, Bobbie J., and Susan Hunt, eds. *Prospect Research: A How-to Guide.* Washington: Council for Advancement and Support of Education, 1986.

Presents a step-by-step method for locating and uncovering information on prospective donors (foundation, corporate, individual). Includes charts which illustrate the process of compiling, evaluating, and organizing data on a prospect; annotated bibliography of information sources and glossary of terms.

3874. "Strategies for Giving: Developed by the Contributions Strategies Committee." *Voluntary Action Leadership* (Winter 1983): 27-9.

3875. Strawhecker, Paul. "The Process of Developing Innovation and Leadership." *Fund Raising Management* 16 (March 1985): 26+.

3876. Suhrke, Henry C. "Interested and Knowledgeable Individuals Say No on Cost Allocation Proposal." *Philanthropy Monthly* 18 (January 1985): 5-18.

3877. Suhrke, Henry C. "Joint Costs Accounting a Key Issue in the Supreme Court's Munson Decision." *Philanthropy Monthly* 18 (April 1985): 25-7.

3878. Suhrke, Henry C. "Understanding Fund Raising: The Media Obstacle." *Philanthropy Monthly* 15 (October 1982): 23-6.

3879. Suhrke, Henry C. "United Way Results for 1982." *Philanthropy Monthly* 16 (March 1983): 20-5.

3880. Suhrke, Henry C. "United Way Results for 1983." *Philanthropy Monthly* 17 (March 1984): 20-31.

3881. Suhrke, Henry C. "United Way Results, 1984." *Philanthropy Monthly* 18 (April 1985): 17-22.

3882. Suhrke, Henry C. "What's at Stake in Government Regulation of Fund Raising: A Story in Five Parts." *Philanthropy Monthly* 19 (October 1986): 5-24.

Full text of a "model" law to regulate charitable fundraising by state governments; resolution of a private sector advisory group which urges support with specific reservations; memorandum from Adam Yarmolinsky pointing out serious deficiencies; ten specific aspects which render the model unsatisfactory in the opinion of the editors of *Philanthropy Monthly*; and a general critique with the view that the statute is not one which charitable organizations should support.

3883. Sullivan, Daniel J. "Stewardship: A Future Direction for Catholic Fund Raising?" *Fund Raising Management* 18 (July 1987): 76, 78-81.

Examines the theological and philosophical framework as well as the difficulties and benefits associated with a program of Christian stewardship. While the challenge of stewardship to the American individual is demanding, it is capable of deepening faith and commitment. Stereotypical views of fundraising are also seen as an obstacle to the message of stewardship, but they can be overcome by educational efforts explaining the fundraising community's concern for ethics and by the personal commitment of the individual professional working within the church. Analysis of parishes with stewardship programs reveals an impressive response rate, for these programs are seen as a manifestation of faith and as a community-building service rather than as a solution to financial problems.

3884. Sumariwalla, Russy D. "Giving and Volunteering in America: Findings of a Major National Survey." *Charity* 3 (June 1986): 11-3.

3885. "Supporters Finding New Ways to Assist the Arts." *Arts Management* (March-April 1984): 1+.

3886. "Survey Indicates Fund Raising Continues on Upward Swing." *Fund Raising Management* 15 (April 1984): 76.

3887. "Survey: Rapidly Growing Alternative Funds Raise $13.7 Million. Supplement." *Responsive Philanthropy* (Winter 1985).

3888. Sweeney, Tim, and Michael Seltzer. *Fundraising Strategies for Grassroots Organizations.* Reprint. Community Jobs, no. 1. Washington: Community Careers Resource Center, 1982.

3889. Taft, J. Richard, and Robert J. Berendt. "Perfecting Your 'Case' Statement." *Nonprofit Executive* 2 (March 1983): 7.

3890. Taft, J. Richard. "Public Libraries: Getting into the Philanthropic Thick of Things." *Nonprofit Executive* 3 (November 1983): 5-6.

3891. Taft, J. Richard. *Secrets of Foundation Fund Raising.* Washington: Taft Group, [198?].

3892. Tatum, Liston. "How to Select a Fund Raising Software Package." *KRC Letter* 17 (September 1986): 5-8.

3893. Tatum, Liston. *KRC Computer Book for Fund Raisers.* New Canaan, Conn.: KRC Development Council, 1975.

3894. Taylor, Bernard P. *Guide to Successful Fund Raising.* Rev. ed. South Plainfield, N.J.: Groupwork Today, 1980.

3895. Taylor, Lauren. "Turn on the Light." *Community Jobs* 6 (July-August 1983): 3-4.

3896. Taylor, Martha A. "Making Beautiful Music." *Currents* 11 (March 1985): 50-2.

Tells how to coordinate and centralize fundraising at universities.

3897. Technical Assistance Center. *Community Cash Flow Fund Program: Guidelines, Application, and Sample Cash Flow Application Forms.* Denver, Colo.: Technical Assistance Center, 1981.

3898. Teitell, Conrad. "The ABC's of Making a Will." *U.S. News and World Report* (7 May 1984).

3899. Teltsch, Kathleen. "Changing Patterns in Donations Challenges United Way Methods." *New York Times* (8 March 1985): B-6.

3900. Teltsch, Kathleen. "Charity Appeals Sharply on Rise." *New York Times* (13 December 1982): 48.

3901. Teltsch, Kathleen. "Cornell Medical Unit Given $50 Million: Donor Anonymous." *New York Times* (9 December 1983): B-1+.

3902. Teltsch, Kathleen. "Gifts to Universities Rise 6.2%, Survey Finds." *New York Times* (6 May 1984).

3903. Teltsch, Kathleen. "Social Welfare Agencies Survive Cuts in U.S. Aid." *New York Times* (11 March 1983).

3904. Tempkin, Terrie. "Use Persuasion Theory to Raise More Money." *NSFRE Journal* 7 (Fall 1982): 15-7+.

3905. "The Ten Cardinal Rules of Writing Fund Raising Copy." *KRC Letter* 15 (June 1984): 1-3.

3906. Tenbrunsel, Thomas W. *The Fund Raising Resource Manual.* A Spectrum Book. Englewood Cliffs, N.J.: Prentice-Hall, 1982.

Designed to serve as a self-learning tool, guide includes numerous checklists and worksheets for organizational planning and building a diversified funding strategy.

3907. Thompson, Hugh L. "The Team Approach Leads to Better Fund Raising." *Fund Raising Management* 15 (March 1984): 38+.

3908. Thompson, Robert L. "The Capital Campaign." *NAHD Journal* (Winter-Spring 1984): 66-8.

3909. Thompson, Robert L. "Fund-Raising in Difficult Times." *Trustee* 40 (December 1987): 14.

3910. Tivnan, Edward. "Bittersweet Charity: The High Cost of Fund-Raising." *New York* 16 (15 August 1983): 25-8.

3911. Tolan, David J. "Immortality on the Installment Plan." *Milwaukee Foundation Newsletter* (Spring 1983): 1-2.

3912. "Total for United Way in 1983 Was $15.5 Million, a 12% Rise." *New York Times* (15 January 1984).

3913. Traska, M R "Philanthropy: A Much Underused Hospital Resource." *Hospitals* 60 (20 January 1986): 67.

3914. Traska, M.R. "Philanthropy Provides Fiscal Edge, Leverage." *Hospitals* 60 (5 May 1986): 108-10.

3915. Tromble, William W. "Two Surefire Ways to Increase Annual Giving." *Fund Raising Management* 14 (September 1983): 46+.

3916. Tschop, Carol A. "Make Crisis Work for You: Wilson College Case History." *Fund Raising Management* 14 (December 1983): 20-7.

3917. Tueller, Alden B. "Planned Giving: An Introduction." *Whole Nonprofit Catalog* 6 (Spring 1988): 24-5.

Provides twenty-five guidelines to keep in mind in order to set up a successful planned gift program, from educating yourself and your board about the basic forms of planned giving and its benefits, to drawing up gift acceptance policies and the correct organizational structure, to developing a comprehensive marketing plan, one-on-one presentation skills, and a program evaluation plan.

3918. Turner, Toni, Bowman Burr, and Jay Hogue. "Whose Move Is It? A Computer Program Helps SMU Win at the Game of Donor Cultivation." *Currents* 10 (April 1984): 20-4.

3919. Twentieth Century Fund. *Funds for the Future.* New York: McGraw-Hill, 1975.

3920. *Twenty Master Keys to Increase Giving.* New York: Douglas M. Lawson Associates, [1979].

3921. United States. Congress. Senate. Committee on Labor and Public Welfare. Subcommittee on Children and Youth. *Children's Charities. Part 4: Voluntary Foreign Aid Agencies Serving Children and Youth, 93rd Congress, 2nd Session, October 10, 1974.* Washington: Government Printing Office, 1974.

3922. United States. Department of Agriculture. Office of Rural Development Policy. *Rural Resources Guide: A Directory of Public and Private Assistance for Small Communities.* Washington: Government Printing Office, 1984.

Catalog of about 400 public and private national level organizations offering resources to small communities. Describes organizations providing technical as well as financial assistance. Entries include information on the resource provider, eligibility requirements, and special conditions. Includes a subject index.

3923. United States. Department of Housing and Urban Development. *Funding Sources for Neighborhood Groups.* Washington: Government Printing Office, 1980.

3924. Upshur, Carole C. "Developing a Sensible Fund Raising Strategy." *Fund Raising Management* 14 (July 1983): 39-41, 79.

3925. Upshur, Carole C. "Getting Started: What to Do before You Ask for Money." *Fund Raising Management* 13 (February 1983): 16+.

3926. "Using Your Donor Surveys to Find New Donors." *Grassroots Fundraising Journal* (December 1986): 4,6.

Brief article on using demographic and psychographic surveys as part of your organization's fundraising strategy. The survey can be used to find new donors who are like the ones you already have. The organization can focus its attention on people of the same age, income bracket, occupation, education, neighborhood, and religious and political identifications.

3927. Valentine, Michael J. "Spelling for Dollars: An Educational Way to Raise Funds for School Programs." *Grassroots Fundraising Journal* 6 (April 1987): 7-9.

3928. "Value of 202 Endowments on June 30, 1983." *Chronicle of Higher Education* 28 (May 1984): 16.

3929. van Patten, Betty. "Small Can Be Beautiful: Tips on How to Win Grants from Regional, Community and Family Foundations." *Currents* 10 (July-August 1984): 24-6.

3930. Vecchitto, Daniel W., ed. *An Introduction to Planned Giving Fund Raising through Bequests, Charitable Remainder Trusts, Gift Annuities and Life Insurance.* Nonprofit Technical Assistance Series, no. 2. Cambridge, Mass.: JLA Publications, 1982.

3931. Vecchitto, Daniel W. "People First: A Requirement for the Success of Any Planned Giving Program." *NSFRE Journal* 7 (Fall 1982): 8+.

3932. Verdery, John D. *Dear Chris: Advice to a Volunteer Fund Raiser.* Washington: Taft Group, 1986.

3933. Verhoven, Peter J., and Donald E. Hawkins. *Obtaining Funds for Therapeutic Recreation and the Creative Art Therapies.* Washington: Hawkins and Associates, 1981.

3934. Vidal, David. "Gifts to Colleges Down $80 Million." *New York Times* (April 1976).

3935. Vineyard, Sue, and Stephen H. McCurley. *One Hundred and One Ways to Raise Resources.* Brainstorm Series. Downers Grove, Ill.: Heritage Arts, 1987.

More than 900 creative fundraising ideas divided into forty-five different categories. Covers an array of subjects, including: general fundraising advice, solicitation of individuals, support from corporations and foundations, utilization of volunteers, noncash resource raising, special events, and publicity.

3936. Vinson, Elizabeth A. *For the Soul and the Pocketbook: A Resource Guide for the Arts in Rural and Small Communities.* Washington: National Rural Center, 1981.

3937. "Volunteers Try to Raise Sports Funds." *New York Times* (17 February 1982): B-9, 10.

3938. Wagner, Ken. "The Personal Experience of a Canvasser: Through Rain, Sleet and Snow." *Grassroots Fundraising Journal* 4 (August 1985): 3+.

3939. Walker, Robert L., and Drew A. Bennett. "Major Gifts: Building an Effective Program." *Nonprofit World* 6 (July-August 1988): 15-7.

Sound principles and basic development formula for establishing a people-oriented approach to major gift campaigns. Stresses the importance of having a worthwhile project, one that promotes involvement and commitment, and the proper method of presenting it to prospective donors. A useful overview of the process for improving effectiveness.

3940. Walsh, Lee G. "Zero-Based Goal-Setting for Your Community Campaign." *Fund Raising Management* 16 (July 1985): 30+.

3941. Warner, Irving R. *The Art of Fund Raising.* New York: Harper & Row, 1975.

3942. Warren, Paul B. *The Dynamics of Funding.* Boston: Allyn & Bacon, 1980.

3943. Waters, R.C., and Janet Sanfilippo. "New Life Insurance Plan Boon to Endowment Fund." *Fund Raising Management* 15 (April 1984): 36+.

3944. Watkins, Clyde P. "Major Gift Volunteers: A Balanced View." *Fund Raising Management* 17 (January 1987): 48, 50, 52, 54.

This article, based on a presentation to the International Conference of the National Society of Fund-Raising Executives (NSFRE), discusses identifying a volunteer's innate ability and the additional training necessary, even for the ideal volunteer, to be successful on a major gifts campaign.

3945. Wattenberger, James L., and Bob N. Cage. *More Money for More Opportunity. Financial Support of Community College Systems.* San Francisco: Jossey-Bass Publishers, 1974.

3946. Webb, Charles H. "Test Yourself!" *Currents* 9 (May 1983): 34-6.

3947. Weinberger, Jane. *Please Buy My Violets: Or How to Raise Money for Your Causes.* Mount Desert, Maine: Windswept House Publishers, 1986.

Jane Weinberger, a fundraising veteran of forty years, discusses numerous projects she has engineered or taken part in, from the one-woman fund drive, to cake sales, arts and crafts shows, raffles and picnics, up to dinners and gala balls. Includes reproductions of various programs, tickets and committee lists. A detailed how-to and how-it-was-done book.

3948. Weiner, Harold N. *Making the Most of Special Events.* Managing Your Public Relations: Guidelines for Nonprofit Organizations. New York: Foundation for Public Relations Research and Education, 1977.

One of a series of six management guides published by the Foundation for Public Relations Research and Education designed to help administrators and board members of nonprofit organizations understand the principles and practices of sound public relations. As a category of public relations tactics, special events defy easy definition: they comprise a widely diversified assortment of activities designed for a variety of occasions, resources, and targets; they possess, however, the unique capacity to "cast a bright light on an organization's human side," revealing its personality and vitality. Discusses the need for nonprofit organizations to conduct their business in the public spotlight in order to build confidence and support, and examines examples of classic special events which illuminate the value of tailoring the event to the purpose.

3949. Weinhold, Dick. "Telemarketing Variables Work Together for Campaign Success." *Fund Raising Management* 16 (November 1985): 22+.

3950. Weiss, David M., and Diane E. Mahlmann, comps. and eds. *National Guide to Funding in Aging.* New York: Foundation Center, 1987.

The result of a unique collaborative effort between the Nassau County (NY) Department of Senior Citizens Affairs, the Foundation Center, and Long Island University, this guide provides essential information on public and private sources of support for programs and services for the older adult, including detailed descriptions of ninety-nine federal funding programs, arranged in fifteen areas of service, with listings of the government agencies and their local and regional offices that administer these critical funding programs; all state government agencies responsible for coordinating or providing services and funding for the aging with the eligibility and application requirements for specific state funding programs; eighty-four national foundations and 285 local foundations that have stated or demonstrated an interest in funding services and programs for the aging with information about their program interests and restrictions, application procedures, officers and directors, and the actual grants awarded in the field of aging by 226 foundations; seventy-eight private organizations offering funding, technical assistance, or other support for programs in aging, including gerontological institutions, religious groups, professional organizations, and academic and research center.

3951. Weiss, Nancy. "The United Way." *NPO Resource Review* 2 (July-August 1984): 1+.

Describes the United Way and how it operates.

3952. Wellisz, Christopher. "Raffle of a Co-Op Is Planned." *New York Times* (11 October 1981): H-16.

3953. Wellisz, Christopher. "Raffles: A Chancy Thing for Homeowners." *New York Times*: R-14.

3954. Wells, James A. "Foundation Funding for AIDS Programs." *Health Affairs* 6 (Fall 1987): 113-36.

3955. Western States Shelter Network. *Dollars and Sense: A Community Fundraising Manual for Women's Shelters and Other Non-Profit Organizations.* San Francisco: Western States Shelter Network, 1982.

3956. Whelan, Donald J. *Handbook for Development Officers at Independent Schools.* Washington: Council for Advancement and Support of Education, 1979.

3957. White, Virginia P. *Grants for the Arts.* New York: Plenum, 1979.

Comprehensive guide to resources for fundraisers seeking grant support for all types of artistic activities. Includes descriptions of federal funding programs and advice on approaching funders.

3958. White, Virginia P. *Grants: How to Find Out about Them and What to Do Next.* New York: Plenum, [1975].

Designed for the novice, this guide explains government, foundation, and corporate funding sources; how to find the right funder; and how to submit a proposal.

3959. Whitehead, Ralph, Jr. "Catalyst for Dollars and Issues Is Role of Mail." *Fund Raising Management* 14 (July 1983): 52-3.

3960. Whitley, Frank V. "Raising Funds for Women's Causes: The New Frontier." *Fund Raising Management* 17 (July 1986): 84-94.

3961. Whitney, J.J. "Hospital Philanthropy: Strengthening the Financial Base of Nonprofit Hospitals." *Health Care Management Review* 6 (Spring 1981): 19-33.

3962. Wieboldt, Linda D. "The Craft of Research Foundations and Corporations." *Fund Raising Management* 15 (March 1984): 56+.

3963. Wilker, Lawrence J. *Fund Raising.* Madison, Wis.: Association of College, University and Community Arts Administrators, 1979.

3964. Willard, Timothy J. "What Makes a Successful Chief Development Officer?" *Currents* 11 (July-August 1985): 38-9.

3965. Williams, M. Jane, ed. *Capital Ideas. Step by Step: How to Solicit Major Gifts from Private Sources.* 2nd ed. Ambler, Pa.: Fund Raising Institute, 1979.

3966. Williams, M. Jane, ed. *Capital Ideas: The Elements and Techniques of a Systematic Approach to Capital Fund Raising.* 3 Vols. Ambler, Pa.: Fund Raising Institute, 1975.

3967. Williams, M. Jane. *Foundation Primer.* 4th ed. Ambler, Pa.: Fund Raising Institute, 1981.

Basic handbook on how to start and run a foundation solicitation program, including several examples of forms, internal procedures, appeal letters and proposal formats to help guide the program toward its full potential. Research section describes numerous foundation reference sources, along with details on how to obtain and use each one.

3968. Williams, M. Jane. *The FRI Annual Giving Book.* Ambler, Pa.: Fund Raising Institute, 1981.

3969. Williams, M. Jane. *Fund-Raising by Computer: Basic Techniques.* 3rd ed. Ambler, Pa.: Fund Raising Institute, 1977.

3970. Williams, Roger M. "The Readiest Reference: When It Comes to Providing the Facts about Foundations, No One Can Match the Foundation Center." *Foundation News* 25 (November-December 1984): 26-32.

3971. Williams, Roger M. "What Hath Geldof Wrought?" *Foundation News* 28 (January-February 87): 31-7.

Examines the "Geldof Factor" and its short and long term impact on the fundraising field. The keys to the success of Geldof and Band Aid/Live Aid included many factors. The staff's lack of permanency allowed them the freedom an agency does not have; they could be brash and they could appeal to "crude emotionalism." Geldof's contacts in the music industry gave him access to entertainers; he "relentlessly and shamelessly exploited his position." The news media did the major portion of the fundraising for the group; Band Aid needed only a "channel for the money to flow in." The greatest single impact of Band Aid/Live Aid on fundraising was the "remaking" of fundraising's image into fundraising as fun. The author believes that agencies can apply some of the strategies of Band Aid/Live Aid. They can be more market-oriented—use advertising and a sense of humor; motivate population groups to raise funds within their field; apply pressure to governments, if necessary, to goad them into responsible behavior; and cut overhead by using volunteers. [See: PHILANTHROPY/PHILANTHROPISTS. Bob Geldof. *Is That It?*].

3972. Williamson, Jim. "Do You Need a Computer?" *Fund Raising Management* 16 (September 1985): 66+.

3973. Willmer, Wesley Kenneth. "Preventing the No. How to Spot, and Work with, a Donor's Mental Anchors." *Currents* 13 (January 1984): 52-4.

Offers explanation of prospective donor's judgement process by examining how donors listen, process, and act on information received in a presentation.

3974. Wilson, C. "Fund Raising: The Search for Discretionary Income." *Dimensions in Health Service* 60 (July 1983): 11-2.

3975. *Winning the Money Game: A Guide to Community-Based Library Fundraising.* New York: Baker & Taylor Co., 1979.

3976. Witt, J.A. "Is It Time to Start Acting like a Corporation?" *Health Care* 30 (January-February 1987): 65.

3977. Wogan, Thomas F. "Successful Small Shop Approaches to Foundations." *Fund Raising Management* 16 (June 1985): 26-7.

3978. "Women's Funds: A Growing Response to Poverty, Abuse, and Discrimination." *Grantsmanship Center News* 13 (May-June 1985): 7+.

3979. "Women's Funds: A New Movement." *KRC Letter* 17 (December 1986): 1-4.

Essay on the growth of the Women's Funds Movement. There are many reasons for their dramatic growth including the historical neglect of women's needs by traditional philanthropy and the explosion in the womanization of poverty. Judy Austermiller, a founding member of the National Network of Women's Funds, says that it is also a "reflection of women's decision to take control of resources that in the past they either had no control over or let others control." Currently, most women's funds are public foundations which make grants to local nonprofits, but some are involved in statewide, regional, and nationwide funding and several are private foundations. Although there are funds which back specific social agendas or service-oriented projects, almost all the funds are directing their support to low-income women and those without access to resources. The article discusses several different women's funds programs across the United States. The comments by those involved and their projects illustrate the diversity of both the goals and projects which have been undertaken. The Women's Funds have grown despite the fact that they have not been created by millionaires; they must raise all their grant monies as well as their operating expenses. The broad-based support for the Women's Funds Movement is reflected in the fact that almost all of the monies are coming from individuals obtained face-to-face, by telephone or through the mail. Other techniques used for fundraising include special events, endowments, foundations and corporations, and workplace payroll deductions.

3980. "Women's Funds in the U.S." *Responsive Philanthropy* (Spring 1986): 8-9.

Contains descriptions of federations, and public, private, and recently formed foundations which provide funding for projects/issues affecting women.

3981. Women's Technical Assistance Project. *Church Funding Sources. Resource Guide.* 5th ed. Washington: Women's Technical Assistance Project, 1988.

Information on twenty-nine Protestant, Catholic and Jewish religious funding organizations. Lists addresses and telephone numbers, describes organization's purpose, project criteria and application procedures. Also included is a sheet listing application deadlines, and a discussion on seeking funds from church sources.

3982. Wood, J.B. "Grantmanship: Winning Foundation Funding." *Nursing Economics* 4 (March-April 1986): 80-2, 88.

3983. Wood, Leonard A. "Graying Population Means Rosier Fund Raising Ahead." *Fund Raising Management* 14 (November 1983): 18-22.

3984. Woodroof, Bob. "World's Fastest Fund Raisers." *Currents* 9 (July-August 1983): 17-8.

3985. Worth, Janice M. "Giving More and like It More." *Foundation News* 24 (May-June 1983): 58+.

3986. Worth, Michael J., ed. *Public College and University Development.* Washington: Council for Advancement and Support of Education, 1985.

Provides a discussion of how public and private sector fundraising differs, and how fundraising procedures for the public institution are different from those of the private college or university. Book covers three main areas: the public institution's organizational role, strategies for fundraising, and special types of support.

3987. Wunderman, Lester. "Ad Agency Helps Non-Profit Become Self-Sufficient." *Direct Marketing* 47 (May 1984): 36+.

3988. Yanowitz, Alan J. "Investment Partnerships Can Finance Charitable Activity." *Nonprofit World Report* 3 (January-February 1985): 19-20.

3989. Yengst, Nancy L. "Employee Annual Giving." *NAHD Journal* (Winter-Spring 1984): 74-5.

3990. Young, Joyce. *Fundraising for Non-Profit Groups: How to Get Money from Corporations, Foundations and Government.* 2nd ed. Vancouver, BC: International Self-Counsel Press, 1981.

Step-by-step guide for nonprofit groups needing to raise between $3,000 and $1 million annually. Explains all aspects of fundraising, from developing the budget to approaching corporation presidents and other possible funders. Also includes advice on hiring a professional fundraiser.

3991. Zalkind, Ronald. *How to Raise Money for Anything.* New York: Simon & Schuster, 1981.

3992. Zien, Laurel. "Tao House Calendar." *Grassroots Fundraising Journal* 4 (February 1985): 10-2.

Describes one organization's venture into product sales.

3993. Zuer, Robert J. "Endowment. Key Ingredient for Non-Profit Hospitals." *Fund Raising Management* 19 (September 1988): 60-2.

Examines the benefits of endowments in general and advocates increasing their number specifically within the nonprofit hospital sector. Breaks down the myths that raising endowment funds for hospitals and medical centers lacks urgency and that endowments cannot be planned but must simply happen; cites examples of successful campaigns and reiterates the benefits of a planned gift for endowment.

8

PROPOSAL DEVELOPMENT

3994. Allen, Herb, ed. *The Bread Game.* Rev. and exp. ed. San Francisco: Regional Young Adult Project, 1981.

A humorous yet helpful look at the "nature and feeding habits of the beast known as foundations." Includes bibliography.

3995. Ammon-Wexler, Jill, and Catherine Carmel. *How to Create a Winning Proposal.* Santa Cruz, Calif.: Mercury Communications Corp., 1978.

3996. Bailey, Anne Lowrey. "Writing Proposals Grows More Exacting As the Competition for Grants Heats Up." *Chronicle of Higher Education* 33 (11 January 1987): 33-5.

3997. Barlett, Debbie, and Tom Martin. *All Aboard the Grantsmanship: A Bibliography on Government and Proposal Writing.* Freehold, N.J.: Monmouth County Board of Social Services, 1977.

3998. Bauer, David G. "The Chicago Opera Youth Program: Proposal Writing Exercises." *Grants Magazine* 6 (March 1983): 71-84.

3999. Bauer, David G. "Successful Grant-Seeking Techniques for Obtaining Private Grants: How to Contact a Private Funding Source." *Grants Magazine* 10 (March 1987): 60-8.

Emphasizes that contacting a funding source before writing a proposal will increase your chances of success. Discusses the best ways to write a letter of inquiry, an appointment letter, and a letter proposal (or concept paper); includes sample formats for each. Also describes steps to cover when discussing a project over the phone, best methods for obtaining an appointment by phone, and how to get the most useful information from the actual visit to the funding source.

4000. Belcher, Jane C., Julia M. Jacobsen, and Richard Rossi. *A Process for Development of Ideas.* 3rd ed. Washington: Association for Affiliated College and University Offices, 1984.

Unusual handbook uses the proposal format to explain a process for developing new program ideas.

4001. Biles, Bert R., and John P. Murray. *Tips for Proposal Writers.* Manhattan, Kans.: Graduate Services and Publications, 1980.

4002. Brooklyn In Touch Information Center. *Fundraising through Proposal Writing.* Brooklyn, N.Y.: Brooklyn In Touch Information Center, 1982.

4003. Carpetbag Theatre. *How to Write a Proposal.* [Cassette tape]. Knoxville, Tenn.: Appalachian Community Fund, 1988.

Tape produced by the Carpetbag Theatre with actors Jeff Cody and Linda Parris-Bailey is the audio companion to Section 1, *How to Write a Grant Proposal* in the book *A Guide to Funders in Central Appalachia and the Tennessee Valley.*

4004. Chavers, Dean. "Learning to Think like Proposal Readers." *Nonprofit Executive* 3 (December 1983): 5-6.

4005. Coleman, William Emmet, David Keller, and Arthur Pfeffer. *A Casebook of Grant Proposals in the Humanities.* New York: Neal-Schuman Publishers, 1982.

Presents examples of fifteen proposals that resulted in individual or group research grants or program grants to institutions. Includes annotated comments from the editors.

4006. Conrad, Daniel Lynn. *The Grant Writer's Handbook. 2 Vols.* San Francisco: Public Management Institute, 1978.

4007–4021 PROPOSAL DEVELOPMENT

4007. Conrad, Daniel Lynn. *The Quick Proposal Workbook.* San Francisco: Public Management Institute, 1980.

A workbook on project planning, proposal writing, and evaluation techniques.

4008. Contact Center. *Getting Yours: A Publicity and Funding Primer for Nonprofit and Voluntary Organizations.* Lincoln, Nebr.: Contact Center, 1984.

4009. Council of Michigan Foundations. *Information for Seeking Foundation and Corporate Grants: How to Research, How to Prepare a Proposal, Where to Get More Information.* Grand Haven, Mich.: Council of Michigan Foundations, [1989].

4010. Daniels, Craig E. *A Budget Primer and Worksheets for Proposal Writers.* Washington: Association of American Colleges, 1979.

4011. Decker, Virginia A., and Larry E. Decker. *The Funding Process: Grantsmanship and Proposal Development.* Charlottesville, Va.: Community Collaborators, 1978.

4012. Dermer, Joseph. *How to Write Successful Foundation Presentations.* Washington: Public Service Materials Center, 1984.

4013. Drew, Joseph S., and Anne O. Hughes. "Firing Up for Funding: A Model Faculty Proseminar in Grants and Contracts." *Grants Magazine* 6 (June 1983): 101-07.

4014. Duca, Diane J. "Twelve Tips Will Help When Compiling Proposals." *Fund Raising Management* 13 (January 1982): 63.

4015. Eaves, George N. "Preparation of the Research-Grant Application: Opportunities and Pitfalls." *Grants Magazine* 7 (September 1984): 151-57.

4016. Gold, Joel J. "Ingenuity and the Grant Application." *Chronicle of Higher Education* 27 (7 September 1983): 32.

4017. Gooch, Judith Mirick. *Writing Winning Proposals.* Washington: Council for Advancement and Support of Education, 1987.

Based on her experience as director of development in the Massachusetts Institute of Technology School of Science, Judith Gooch prepared a basic book on proposal writing. Gooch's text focuses primarily on college and university proposal writing, but provides general information useful to all grantseekers. She admits there's no such thing as a perfect proposal or the perfect way to write a proposal, but stresses the importance of doing your homework before writing one. Doing homework will assist the writer in finding the proper fit between the fundseeker and the fundraiser. Gooch's first chapter explains the research method in stages. Chapter 2 begins with seven fundamental research questions and concentrates on the organization of information obtained during your research. The third chapter on the budget is detailed and includes a case study and samples. Chapter 4 follows a structured outline and takes the writer through the actual writing process. The follow-up procedure is discussed in Chapter 5. The concluding chapter, *Tools of the Trade*, provides some technical assistance including a location list of the Foundation Center's library network. The volume contains a bibliography on funding, noting general and research materials as well as those for proposal development.

4018. Grantsmanship Center. *Grantsmanship Training Program.* Los Angeles: Grantsmanship Center, 1978.

4019. Hall, Mary S. *Getting Funded: A Complete Guide to Proposal Writing.* 3rd ed. Portland, Oreg.: Continuing Education Publications, 1988.

Guidebook to proposal writing is organized along a logical pattern of planning, beginning with a discussion of ideas for projects and ending with considerations about submissions, negotiation and project renewal. The planning and information collection section emphasizes such significant skills as assessing the capability to compete and selecting appropriate funding sources, including details on foundations and corporations. Focuses on the considerations which must be given to planning applications submitted in response to *Requests for Proposals* (RFPs)—formal solicitations for specified services desired by a funding source. Each chapter of the section dealing with the actual writing of a proposal focuses on a specific component, from title pages, abstracts and accompanying forms, to purpose statements, statements of need, dissemination, qualifications and budget. Includes strategies based on winning proposals from science, the arts, education, health, social services, and other fields, in addition to resource lists, cases, models, checklists, and sample formats.

4020. Hans, Patricia. "The Foundation Game: Unwritten Rules." *Nonprofit World* 5 (March-April 1987): 20-1.

Management consultant Patricia Hans provides a brief guide to what she calls the unwritten rules of grantsmanship. "The rules are simple, but, because they are unwritten, many grantseekers break them." Hans suggests that you make your requests as short as possible; make your request simple and straightforward; give the foundation everything it wants the first time; show your appreciation when you receive a grant; know when to quit; be a good loser; and avoid the six deadly sins of grantsmanship—acronyms, professional jargon, small type, fat proposals held together with a rubber band or paper clip, irrelevant appendix material, and complex proposals with many component parts.

4021. Hayes, Christopher L. "Confessions of a Grant Writer: The Development of the PREP Project." *Grants Magazine* 10 (June 1987): 91-4.

Hayes discusses the work behind the development of a proposal which was awarded a $300,000 two-year grant by the Department of Health and Human Services, Administration on Aging. Realizing the needs of the potential funding agency (in this case, the federal government, which was stressing that individuals will have to address their own needs after retirement), the project was developed to satisfy the current administration's agenda; realizing that his organization was not in the best position to implement the applied aspects of the project, a collaborative cosponsorship was established to increase the proposal's chances of success; and being able to admit that the project was not exactly revolutionary (the "nothing new under the sun" syndrome) led to long hours of researching previous work to bolster an argument concerning the uniqueness of this effort compared to others and to substantiate their knowledge of the current state of the art. This case study for the novice grant writer captures the strategies, emotions, and grueling work involved in proposal development.

4022. Heathington, Betty S., and Gerald V. Teague. "The Review Process: From the Viewpoint of the Unsuccessful Grant Applicant." *Journal of the Society of Research Administrators* 12 (Summer 1980): 31-4.

4023. Hill, William J. *Grant Writing Made Easy.* Steamboat Springs, Colo.: Grant Development Institute, 1980.

4024. Hillman, Howard, and Karen Abarbanel. *The Art of Winning Foundation Grants.* New York: Vanguard Press, 1975.

4025. Hillman, Howard. *The Art of Writing Business Reports and Proposals.* New York: Vanguard Press, 1981.

4026. Holtz, Herman. *The Consultant's Guide to Proposal Writing.* New York: John Wiley, 1986.

4027. Honig, Lisa. "Grammar for Grantseekers." *Grassroots Fundraising Journal* 2 (August 1983): 1+.

4028. Kalish, Susan Ezell, ed. *The Proposal Writer's Swipe File.* 3rd ed. Washington: Taft Group, 1984.

Contains fifteen sample proposals, written by education, science, and arts and humanities organizations to foundations or corporate giving programs. Each example provides insights into how fundraising proposals should be constructed, organized, styled and presented. Each sample complete from title page to budget layout.

4029. Kennicott, Patrick C. "Developing a Grant Proposal: Some Basic Principles." *Grants Magazine* 6 (March 1983): 36-41.

4030. Kiritz, Norton J. "Guidelines for the Selection of Training Programs." *Whole Nonprofit Catalog* 1 (Winter 84-85): 12-3.

4031. Kiritz, Norton J. *Program Planning and Proposal Writing.* Reprint. Los Angeles: Grantsmanship Center, 1979.

4032. Kiritz, Norton J., and Jerry Mundel. "Program Planning and Proposal Writing: Introductory Version." *Whole Nonprofit Catalog* 7 (Summer 1988): 13-8.

A shortened version of Mr. Kiritz' 1979 article, providing an excellent step-by-step guide to grant proposal format. Discusses the thrust of the proposal summary; how to establish credibility in the introduction; the need for a clearly defined problem in the problem statement (while stressing the difference between problems or needs and methods of solving problems or satisfying needs); the importance of distinguishing between methods and objectives for your program; the methods, evaluation, and future funding sections; an exercise for developing a realistic program budget (including personnel, non-personnel, and indirect costs); and a list of items routinely requested by funding sources which are to be included in the appendix.

4033. Knight, Lucy. "Write on the Money: The Basics of Effective Proposal Writing, from Content to Structure to Length." *Currents* 14 (October 1988): 10-2, 14-7.

Working from the premise that the objective of a proposal is to persuade, article provides advice on the basics of effective proposal writing. Like the classic newspaper story, a grant proposal must always answer certain key questions: who, what, where, when, and why. Specific to fundraising proposals is the additional question: how much? A concise summary answering these questions is highly recommended for the beginning of any proposal, since "the human mind has a need to know these answers quickly before it's receptive to greater detail." Examples of good summary paragraphs are included in the article. After the summary should come an introduction, often a somewhat philosophical discussion of the problem or issue the proposal is addressing; then a description of the problem; a description of the proposed solution; a focused treatment of your institution's qualifications (which should never come at the beginning of a grant proposal); a detailed account of the methods that will be employed; information on additional items such as evaluation plans and future funding; a budget breakdown; and appendixes. Final tasks include preparing a table of contents and cover letter. Perhaps most important to preparing an effective proposal is simply allowing enough time to do a good job: "You can fix most of the imperfections in your proposal if you allow yourself and your colleagues enough time to discover them."

4034. Krathwohl, David R. *How to Prepare a Research Proposal: Guidelines for Funding and Dissertations in the Social and Behavioral Sciences.* 3rd ed. Syracuse, N.Y.: Syracuse University Press, 1988.

While the major emphasis is on proposal writing for research (with the aim of increasing the chances for early recognition of good ideas), this book provides the important principles and basic logic necessary to construct a proposal that communicates ideas in the framework of a shared decision-making situation between writer and reviewer. Step-by-step proposal development process, including illustrations of the chain of reasoning; information on submission, review, and negotiation procedures in federal programs; summary of results of research on disapproved proposals; a checklist for critiquing proposals; guides to resources for federal and foundation funding; suggestions and insights for beginners; an annotated bibliography; glossary; and copies of federal forms. Useful for both the novice and experienced writer of proposals, theses and dissertations.

4035. Lefferts, Robert B. *Getting a Grant: How to Write Successful Grant Proposals.* Englewood Cliffs, N.J.: Prentice-Hall, 1978.

4036. Lefferts, Robert B. *Getting a Grant in the 1980s: How to Write Successful Grant Proposals.* 2nd ed. Englewood Cliffs, N.J.: Prentice-Hall, 1982.

Manual which provides guidelines for preparing, writing, and presenting proposals to foundations and government funding agencies for the user who has basic writing skills and an understanding of the field in which they are writing. The author "oriented the book to program proposals that account for the majority of grants in fields such as physical and mental health, education, welfare, employment and training, and social services." However, the methodology and many of the principles are applicable to research proposals. This edition includes a special chapter specifically geared to the preparation of applied research proposals. Includes bibliography.

4037. Lucas, Robert A. "Indirect Costs: The Wonder of Never Having to Say Anything." *Grants Magazine* 10 (June 1987): 95-7.

Entertaining article describes the frustrations of justifying indirect costs to faculty and sponsors at a university grants administration office.

4038. Lucas, Robert A., and Thomas R. Harvey. "Successful Strategies for Institutionalizing Grants." *Grants Magazine* 7 (March 1984): 19-24.

Ideas on program continuation after financial assistance ends.

4039. Mager, Robert F. *Preparing Instructional Objectives.* Belmont, Calif.: Fearon Publishers, [1962].

4040. McAdam, Robert E., Michael Maher, and John F. McAteer. *Research and Project Funding for the Uninitiated.* Springfield, Ill.: Charles C. Thomas, 1982.

Designed for the novice, this brief handbook focuses on proposal writing and submission of grant requests to funders.

4041. McIlnay, Dennis P. "Proposalese Spoken Here: How to Survive in the Wonderful World of Grants." *Currents* 10 (July-August 1984): 64.

4042. Meador, Roy. *Guidelines for Preparing Proposals.* Chelsea, Mich.: Lewis Publishers, 1985.

A manual on how to organize proposals for grants, venture capital, and research and development projects, among others. The book relies heavily on the author's experience specializing in technical and scientific projects for government clients and corporations. Meador's *Elements of a Proposal* contains the usual guidelines for a proposal but with the additional items necessary for use in a highly technical format including such things as PERT and GANTT charts, appendixes and support materials, bibliographies and references. After discussing the how, the author examines *The Value of Debriefing* or the follow-up procedure and specific do's and don'ts for specific government departments. Numerous examples appear throughout the manual as well as a sample grant proposal, references and an index.

4043. Mills, Miriam K. "Proposal Preparation in a Dry Season." *Grants Magazine* 6 (June 1983): 111-14.

4044. Mitiguy, Nancy. *The Rich Get Richer and the Poor Write Proposals.* Amherst, Mass.: Citizen Involvement Training Project, 1978.

The basics of fundraising made easy and enjoyable. Step-by-step guide to designing and implementing a fundraising strategy, including long- and short-term planning, setting up an appropriate organizational structure, researching and prioritizing possible funding sources, and writing and editing proposals. Contains several exercises, an interview role-playing scenario, and a case study of the Women's Campaign Fund as an example of a good direct mail approach.

4045. Moran, Irene E. "Writing a Winning Grant Proposal." *Bottom Line* 1 (1987): 13-7.

Although geared towards library developers, article contains sound, practical information that is beneficial to any novice grantseeker.

4046. Morrow, John C. *A Basic Guide to Proposal Development.* 3rd ed. Silver Spring, Md.: Business Publishers, 1977.

4047. Mullins, Carolyn J. *The Complete Writing Guide to Preparing Reports, Proposals, Memos, Etc.* Englewood Cliffs, N.J.: Prentice-Hall, 1980.

4048. Mundel, Jerry. "Anybody Need a Good Proposal Writer?" *Grants Magazine* 7 (March 1984): 7-12.

4049. Ohio. Department of Mental Health and Mental Retardation. *Oh No, Not Another Proposal!* Columbus, Ohio: Ohio Department of Mental Health and Mental Retardation.

4050. Ricci, Carla W. "Know Who Will Be Reading Your Proposal." *Grants Magazine* 5 (September 1982): 186-87.

4051. Scanlan, Eugene A. *Researching Foundations: A to $.* Reprint. Englewood Cliffs, N.J.: Prentice-Hall, 1985.

A brief, clearly written guide on basic research techniques with a step-by-step approach for identifying foundations with the best funding potential. Topics include: before you start—knowing who you are, getting started, checking the competition, building a primary list, using foundation directories and other foundation information, and visiting foundations. Useful source for novice grantseekers.

4052. Schell, John, and John Stratton. *Writing on the Job: A Handbook for Business and Government.* New York: New American Library, 1984.

4053. Shapek, Raymond A. "Dos and Don'ts in Proposal Writing: How to Increase Your Probability of Obtaining Federal Funding." *Grants Magazine* 7 (March 1984): 51-8.

4054. Shapek, Raymond A. "Understanding Evaluation of Research Proposals: The First Step toward More Effective Writing." *Grants Magazine* 7 (September 1984): 198-208.

4055. Sinclair, James P. *How to Write Successful Corporate Appeals.* Washington: Public Service Materials Center, 1982.

Provides samples of initial requests, renewal letters, and other fundraising letters with commentary.

4056. Somerville, Bill. "Where Proposals Fail: A Foundation Executive's Basic List of What to Do and Not Do When Requesting Funding." *Whole Nonprofit Catalog* 2 (Fall 1986): 9.

4057. Somerville, Bill. "Writing a Proposal: A Conceptual Framework." *NonProfit Times* 1 (July 1987): 23.

4058. Stein, Eugene L. "The Grants Clinic." *Grants Magazine* 6 (December 1983): 262-82.

4059. Stein, Eugene L. "The Grants Clinic." *Grants Magazine* 10 (June 1987): 106-129.

Presents a clearly written proposal developed within the constraints of questions posed by the sponsor (in this case, the Henry J. Kaiser Family Foundation). While some applicants find this approach stifling and disconcerting, others find it sensible and prefer knowing precisely what the sponsor wants and whether or not they can provide it. Many of the Foundation's questions ask for information that might have been omitted in an open-ended proposal format, and the questions are narrowly focused so that a weak proposal will be easily weeded out. This proposal (which includes the original questions asked by the Kaiser Foundation), serves as an example of excellence to all proposal writers.

4060. Steiner, Richard. *Total Proposal Building*. 2nd ed. Albany, N.Y.: Trestletree Publications, 1988.

Basic guide to obtaining government, corporate and foundation funding. The book attempts to assist the grantseeker with all aspects of proposal development, everything from evaluating funding options and assessing your competition to selecting probable funders and writing winning proposals. The guide also explains the review process and what to do after the project has been funded. The guide has scant material pertaining to foundation funding; some of the included information is basic at best. The sample proposals both concern government funding.

4061. Stewart, Rodney D., and Ann L. Stewart. *Proposal Preparation.* New York: John Wiley, 1984.

4062. Taylor, Alfred H., Jr. "A Foundation's Observations about Its Selection Process." *NAHD Journal* (Winter-Spring 1983): 35-8.

4063. Volunteers in Technical Assistance. *Manual of Practical Fund Raising.* 3rd ed. Boston: Volunteers in Technical Assistance, 1975.

4064. Westenberg, Robert W. "Only Crazy People Write Fund-Raising Copy." *Interlit* (December 1981): 20-1.

9

TAX AND LEGAL IMPLICATIONS FOR NONPROFITS

4065. Ad Hoc Funders' Committee for Voter Registration and Education. *Funders' Guide to Voter Registration and Education: How Funders Can Support Non-Partisan Efforts to Increase Citizen Participation in America.* New York: Ad Hoc Funders' Committee for Voter Registration and Education, [1988].

Designed for staff and trustees of private foundations, corporations and corporate foundations, community foundations and public charities as well as for individual donors, this brochure answers general questions and explains the reasons why the members of the Ad Hoc Committee support nonprofit organizations engaged in non-partisan voter registration and education programs. Also provides a list of organizations active in the field and a partial list of the funders who have supported their activities.

4066. Adams, Roy M. "Here Comes the Earthquake: Preliminary Analysis of the Conference Agreement for the 1986 Tax Reform Bill." *Trusts & Estates* 125 (October 1986): 10-12+.

Discusses the impact of the 1986 *Tax Reform Act* on trusts and estates, as taken from the preliminary House-Senate Conference Committee report.

4067. Adams, Roy M. "Reassessing the Earthquake." *Trusts & Estates* 125 (November 1986): 36-45.

Discusses the effects of the new tax law as taken from the Act's statutory report, in relation to trust and estate planning.

4068. "Administration Rejects Overhaul of 1969 Tax Act." *Dallas Morning News* (28 June 1983).

4069. American Association of Fund-Raising Counsel. "Improving New York's Fund Raising Law." *Philanthropy Monthly* 16 (December 1983): 17-9.

4070. American Association of Fund-Raising Counsel Trust for Philanthropy. "State Laws Regulating Charitable Solicitations (As of December 1, 1986)." *Fund Raising Review* (January 1987): 2-6.

State-by-state listing of regulatory agencies, cost limitations, annual financial reporting requirements, monetary exemption ceilings, charitable solicitation disclosure and registration/licensing and bonding requirements.

4071. American Association of Fund-Raising Counsel Trust for Philanthropy. *Strategies for Individuals under the Old Tax Law As Compared to New Law in 1987.* New York: American Association of Fund-Raising Counsel Trust for Philanthropy, 1986.

4072. American Bar Association. *Revised Model Nonprofit Corporation Act. Exposure Draft.* Chicago: American Bar Association, 1986.

Exposure draft distributed for study, criticism, and comment in 1986. See: *Revised Model Nonprofit Corporation Act* as adopted by the Subcommittee on the Model Nonprofit Corporation Law of the Business Law Section, American Bar Association, Summer of 1987.

4073. American Bar Association. Commission on the Mentally Disabled. *Mental and Developmental Disabilities Directory of Legal Advocates.* Washington: American Bar Foundation, 1981.

4074. American Bar Association. Subcommittee on the Model Nonprofit Corporation Law of the Business Law Section. *Revised Model Nonprofit Corporation Act: Official Text with Official Comments and Statutory Cross-References.* Clifton, N.J.: Prentice Hall Law & Business, 1988.

Comprehensive revision of the *Model Nonprofit Corporation Act(Revised Act)*, completed in 1987. Over 300 major and minor changes have been made in the final version of the Revised Act to address numerous questions unanticipated by the old *Model Act of 1964*. Examples of the new concerns: standards of care or loyalty for directors and officers; statutory immunity or protection for directors who acted with due care and did not breach their duty of loyalty; rules covering conflict of interest; derivative suits; transfer and purchase of membership; the resignation or termination of members; self-perpetuating boards of directors; and the delegation of authority by directors.

4075. American Law Institute. *Restatement of the Law of Trusts As Adopted and Promulgated by the American Law Institute.* Philadelphia: American Law Institute, 1935.

4076. *Analysis and Text of the Tax Reform Act of 1976. 2 Vols.* New York: Matthew Bender & Co., 1976.

4077. Anderson, John B. "Tax Reform and the Foundations." *Congressional Record* (21 April 1972): E4065-66.

4078. Andresky, Jill. "Taxation 101." *Forbes* (28 February 1983): 43+.

4079. Andrews, Frank Emerson. *Foundation Reports to Internal Revenue Service: An Analysis and Evaluation.* New York: Foundation Center, 1970.

4080. "Are You Feeling Pressure to Take Your Charity 'into Business'? The Museum Experience." *Philanthropy Monthly* 16 (April 1987): 13-6.

The unrelated-business income tax and its legal and non-legal application for museums is analyzed in view of an Internal Revenue Service (IRS) technical advice memorandum. (According to the article, knowledgeable sources confirm that the memo concerned the Smithsonian Institute.) The tax code provides that gross income for organizations subject to the tax is includable in computing unrelated business income tax if it is income from a trade or business, the trade or business is regularly carried on by the organization, and the conduct of the trade or business is not substantially related to the organization's performance of its exempt functions. The memorandum and other IRS rulings are discussed in detail explaining procedures for determining relatedness, determining the primary purpose of selling an article, casual sales, the inclusion of descriptive literature with the items, educational utilitarianism, and the *de minimis* application, among other issues.

4081. Arenson, Karen W. "Tax Law Spurs Giving in '81." *New York Times* (16 November 1981): D-1, 4.

4082. Arthur Andersen and Company. *Charitable Giving: A Tax Guide for Individual Donors.* New York: Arthur Andersen & Co., 1987.

Provides donors with basic tax rules for the most common charitable gifts made by individuals. Discusses limitations on giving, present and deferred giving, gifts of income and other gifts, and the methods and importance of substantiating the deduction. Comments and examples are based on federal tax rules and reflect rulings pertinent as of August 1, 1987, including relevant provisions of the *Tax Reform Act of 1986.*

4083. Arthur Andersen and Company. *Tax Considerations in Charitable Giving.* 8th ed. Chicago: Arthur Andersen & Co., 1981.

4084. Arthur Andersen and Company. *Tax Economics of Charitable Giving.* 10th ed. New York: Arthur Andersen & Co., 1987.

Outlines the tax considerations involved with the more important methods of making charitable gifts by individuals. Major emphasis is on income tax, although estate and gift taxes and the generation-skipping transfer tax rules are also considered. Comments and examples based on the applicable tax rules as of August 1, 1987, including relevant provisions of the Tax Reform Act of 1986.

4085. Auten, Gerald, and Gabriel Rudney. *Charitable Deductions and Tax Reform: New Evidence on Giving Behavior.* Reprint. Program on Non-Profit Organizations, no. 102. New Haven, Conn.: Institution for Social and Policy Studies, 1986.

Presents preliminary results of a longer term study of tax reform and giving behavior sponsored by Yale University's Program on Non-Profit Organizations with support from the Ford Foundation and the U.S. Treasury. Examines how the Bradley-Gephardt and Kemp-Kasten tax reform proposals would affect the deduction of charitable contributions, and provides new evidence on the sensitivity of giving to price and income effects and the efficiency of the charitable deduction. The analysis reveals a substantial impact on charitable giving as a result of the bills, especially among high income households, with the beneficiaries favored by high income givers, such as universities, cultural institutions, hospitals and foundations, suffering the most. Modifications to the Bradley-Gephardt bill are suggested to reduce its severe impact on charitable giving.

4086. Auten, Gerald, and Gabriel Rudney. *Tax Reform and Individual Giving to Higher Education.* Program on Non-Profit Organizations, no. 110. New Haven, Conn.: Institution for Social and Policy Studies, 1986.

Examines the effects of tax deductibility of charitable contributions to higher education and provides quantitative estimates of the impacts certain tax reform proposals will have on individual giving. The authors contend that while individual giving is a relatively small source of income for higher education, it is often the margin needed to employ first-rate faculty and provide quality education. Lower tax rates will affect higher education because the incentives for giving will be reduced, but it must be noted that tax reform decisions cannot be made solely on the impact they will have on higher education giving.

4087. Baglia, Joseph R. "Dramatic Changes in New Planned Giving Tables: New IRS Tables for Charitable Gift Annuities." *Philanthropy Monthly* 17 (December 1984): 5-11.

4088. Balk, Alfred. *The Free List: Property without Taxes.* New York: Russell Sage Foundation, 1971.

4089. Bandy, Dale. "Avoiding Limits on Private Foundation Business Holdings: Planning Possibilities." *Journal of Taxation* 38 (March 1973): 136-40.

4090. Bartlett, Richard. *Predictions on the Effect of a Value-Added Tax on Charitable Contributions.* Program on Non-Profit Organizations, no. 25. New Haven, Conn.: Institution for Social and Policy Studies, 1980.

4091. Bass, Gary D., Shannon Ferguson, and David Plocher. *Living with A-122: A Handbook for Nonprofit Organizations.* 3 Vols. Washington: OMB Watch, 1984.

Manual for nonprofit organizations on how to deal with the new anti-lobbying rules from the White House Office of Management and Budget (OMB). The guide is written in three parts. Titles for the three booklets are: Part 1, *Technical Analysis of Lobbying Rules*; Part 2, *Coping with Lobbying Rules*; and Part 3, *Comparisons with Other Lobbying Rules, Text of A-122 Lobbying Rules.*

4092. Beveridge, John Wendell. *Transfers to Charities under the Tax Reform Act of 1969.* Chicago: Callaghan & Co., 1971.

4093. Biscoe, Patricia P. "Easing the Bite from Unrelated Business Income Tax." *Nonprofit Executive* 4 (September 1984).

4094. Bliss, Anthony A. "Proposed Tax Changes Prompt Giving in 1985." *Trusts & Estates* 124 (September 1985): 15+.

4095. Boris, Elizabeth Trocolli. "Paying for Keeps." *Foundation News* 29 (March-April 1988): 69-71.

4096. Borof, Irwin J. "The Private Foundation Question: Problems and Solutions for CBOS." *Grantsmanship Center News* 11 (September-October 1983): 32-6.

4097. Bothwell, Robert O. *Testimony of Robert O. Bothwell. Miscellaneous Revisions to Improve Federal Tax Laws Especially Regarding Elimination of Certain Overlapping Reporting Requirements in the Case of Private Foundations and Generally Increasing Public Access.* Washington: National Committee for Responsive Philanthropy, 1978.

4098. Brandt, Sanford F. *Tax-Exempt Organizations' Lobbying and Political Activities Accountability Act of 1987: A Guide for Volunteers and Staff of Nonprofit Organizations.* Washington: Independent Sector, 1988.

Summarizes relevant provisions of the *Lobbying and Political Activities Accountability Act* for volunteers and staff of nonprofit organizations. The provisions are grouped under three categories: 1) disclosure requirements, 2) lobbying and political activities, and 3) miscellaneous. Appendixes list suggested further reading and set forth an extract from the Conference Report on the legislation.

4099. Brinckerhoff, Peter C. "Tax Breaks for Not-for-Profits." *Grantsmanship Center News* 11 (January-February 1983): 14-7.

4100. Brodhead, William M. *Foundation Tax Law: History, Problems and Prospects.* Grand Haven, Mich.: Council of Michigan Foundations, 1983.

4101. Bromberg, Robert S. "Non-Profit Homes for the Aged: How to Avoid Private Foundation Status." *Journal of Taxation* 38 (February 1973): 120-24.

4102. Bromberg, Robert S., and Norman A. Sugarman. "Termination of Private Foundations." *Taxes* (July 1972): 388-419.

4103. Brooklyn In Touch Information Center. *Forming and Operating a Nonprofit Organization.* Brooklyn, N.Y.: Brooklyn In Touch Information Center, 1982.

4104. Brooklyn In Touch Information Center. *How to Assess Board Liability.* Fact Sheet for the Nonprofit Manager, no. 6. Brooklyn, N.Y.: Brooklyn In Touch Information Center, 1988.

Sixth in a series of one page fact sheets written for the nonprofit manager. Board liability reviews the basic types of lawsuits and discusses how often derivative suits are brought against board members as well as the provisions made to protect directors. It also discusses the possibility of negligence suits, and examines who is covered under directors and officers liability insurance policies.

4105. Brophy, Beth. "Foundations under IRS Scrutiny." *USA Today* (11 October 1983).

4106. Buie, James A. *The 1986 Tax Reform Act: Bad News for Nonprofits.* Alexandria, Va.: Tax Exempt News, 1986.

This review of the 1986 *Tax Reform Act*, opens with a quote from Washington, DC attorney Bruce Hopkins, "It's about as bad as could be expected...philanthropy really lost out." The booklet continues with more unfootnoted quotes from secondary sources to present information on the history of the act, the provisions of the bill, the serious impact of the act on nonprofits, and a page reviewing the possibility for future changes of the act.

4107. *Bulletin on Public Relations and Development for Colleges and Universities.* Chicago: Gonser, Gerber, Tinker & Stuhr, 1970.

4108. Bush, Barbara, and Daniel Yohalem. "Lobbying and Political Activity for Nonprofits: What You Can and Can't Do under Federal Law." *KRC Letter* 14 (December 1983): 1-6.

4109. "Business Groups Join in Fight on Lobbying Rules." *New York Times* (25 February 1983): A-16.

4110. Cammack, Charles W., III. "The Charitable Nonprofit Institution and the Highly Compensated Employee." *Philanthropy Monthly* 20 (September 1987): 17-8.

The *Tax Reform Act of 1986* defines a highly compensated employee as: a five percent owner (this may be applicable if the 501(c)(3) organization has satellite for-profit divisions); a person earning over $75,000 a year in either the current or preceding year; a person earning over $50,000 a year in either the current or preceding year who is or was in the top twenty percent of all active employees for such year; or an officer earning over 150 percent of the dollar limit for annual additions to a defined contribution plan in either the current or preceding year. Article examines various questions concerning the tax treatment of highly compensated exployees working for nonprofit organizations.

4111. Canter, MacKenzie, III. "Federal Tax on Unrelated Debt-Financed Income." *Philanthropy Monthly* 16 (October 1983): 9-12.

4112. Canter, MacKenzie, III. "Federal Tax Update." *Philanthropy Monthly* 17 (September 1984): 33-5.

4113. Canter, MacKenzie, III. "Federal Tax Update." *Philanthropy Monthly* 16 (November 1983): 37-9.

4114. Canter, MacKenzie, III. "The 1982 Tax Act and the 'New' Minimum Tax: Its Impact on Charitable Contribution Deductions." *Fund Raising Review* (August 1983): 2+.

4115. Canter, MacKenzie, III. "When a Donor Asks 'Will the Charity's Re-Sale Price Undermine My Appraisal?' What Do You Tell Him?" *Philanthropy Monthly* 18 (September 1985): 9+.

4116. Caplin and Drysdale. *Impact of the Omnibus Budget Reconciliation Act of 1987 on Tax-Exempt Organizations.* Unpublished, [1988].

Describes in detail the most significant provisions of the *Omnibus Budget Reconciliation Act of 1987* as they concern exempt organizations, and shows the effective dates of each provision. In partial summary, the new legislation requires public access to annual returns and exemption applications; authorizes the IRS to require charitable organizations to disclose transactions and relationships with non-charitable exempt organizations and with political organizations in their annual returns; requires complete and "correct" annual returns; requires exempt organizations not qualified for deductible charitable contributions to disclose that fact clearly in all fundraising solicitations; requires exempt organizations selling certain services or information that may be obtained free from the Federal government to disclose that fact; and imposes substantial penalties for failure to comply with these disclosure requirements.

4117. Caplin and Drysdale. *Revised OMB Proposal to Amend Circular A-122 Treatment of Lobbying Expenditures.* Washington: Caplin & Drysdale, 1983.

4118. Cary, William L., and Craig B. Bright. *The Developing Law of Endowment Funds.* New York: Ford Foundation, 1974.

4119. Cary, William L., and Craig B. Bright. *The Law and the Lore of Endowment Funds.* Educational Endowment Series. New York: Ford Foundation, [1969].

4120. Casey, William J., J.K. Lasser, and Walter Lord. *Tax Planning for Foundations and Charitable Giving.* Roslyn, N.Y.: Business Reports, 1953.

4121. Cleveland Associated Foundation. *Philanthropy in the Seventies. The Tax Reform Act of 1969 As It Affects Foundations and Charitable Contributions.* Cleveland: Greater Cleveland Associated Foundation, 1970.

4122. Cline, Edward. *Charity Deductions Aren't Subsidies.* Unpublished, 1985.

4123. Clotfelter, Charles T., and Lester M. Salamon. *The Federal Government and the Nonprofit Sector: The Impact of the 1981 Tax Act on Individual Charitable Giving.* Washington: Urban Institute Press, 1981.

4124. Clotfelter, Charles T. *Federal Tax Policy and Charitable Giving.* National Bureau of Economic Research. Chicago: University of Chicago Press, 1985.

Clotfelter presents and discusses econometric evidence on the relationship of federal taxes and charitable giving, analyzing four sets of data and adding results based on computer simulations of charitable giving. Although the topic at times necessitates a highly technical presentation, there are more general discussions for those not conversant with statistical and economic methods. Clotfelter divides the book into two general chapters—an overview of tax policy and support for the nonprofit sector, and an evaluation of tax policy in regard to charitable giving behavior—and six topical chapters, which deal with contributions by individuals, volunteer effort, corporate contributions, charitable bequests, and foundations. There are, in addition, numerous appendixes.

4125. Clotfelter, Charles T. "Life after Tax Reform." *Change* (July-August 1987): 12, 14-8.

Assesses the impact of the *Tax Reform Act of 1986* upon higher education. Anticipated are: a reduction in donations to colleges and universities; increased tuition costs; and increased operating costs for institutions of higher education. Also notes some of the relatively bright spots in the tax reform, which are: the retaining of favorable treatment for gifts of appreciated property; an incentive for colleges and universities to alter the way they compensate faculty; and the belief that the new tax law is both fairer and more efficient, likely to benefit the economy as a whole.

4126. Collier, Charles W. "The Charitable Lead Trust: An Update on the Tax Savings Available to Donors." *Currents* 9 (April 1983): 30-2.

4127. Commerce Clearing House. *Exempt Organizations Reporter.* 1971-1982. Chicago: Commerce Clearing House, 19—.

4128. Commerce Clearing House. *An Explanation Selected from CCH Tax Reform Action of 1976 Law and Explanation.* Chicago: Commerce Clearing House, 1976.

4129. Commerce Clearing House. *Tax Reform Act of 1969.* Chicago: Commerce Clearing House, 1969.

4130. Committee to Study the Laws of Rhode Island Charitable Trusts. *Report of Special Committee to Study the Laws of This State (Rhode Island) with Respect to and Governing Charitable-Trusts.* Providence, R.I.: Committee to Study the Laws of Rhode Island, 1950.

4131. "A Compilation of State Laws Regulating Charitable Solicitations." *Fund Raising Review* (December 1985): 5+.

Entire issue presents a compilation of state laws affecting philanthropy, as of 1 Dec 1985. Includes a chart of state laws regulating charitable solicitation for thirty states and notes each state's regulatory agency.

4132. Conservation Foundation. *Law and Taxation: A Guide for Conservation and Other Nonprofit Organizations.* Washington: Conservation Foundation, 1970.

4133. Council of New York Law Associates. *Getting Organized: Incorporation and Tax-Exemption for Non-Profit Organizations in New York.* New York: Council of New York Law Associates, 1987.

Introductory manual for attorneys representing organizations that wish to incorporate and to secure recognition of tax-exempt status. This manual is adapted from a 1978 joint-publication of the Council of New York Law Associates, Volunteer Lawyers for the Arts and Community Law Offices, thus the forms and instructions are geared towards securing tax-exempt status in New York.

4134. Council on Foundations. *Government Tax and Expenditure Limitations: Analyses and Impacts.* Washington: Council on Foundations, 1980.

4135. Council on Foundations. *Summary of Provisions of the Tax Reform Act of 1969 and 1976 Relating to Private Foundations.* Washington: Council on Foundations, 1976.

4136. Council on Foundations. *Technical Memorandum on Corporate Giving. Corporate Foundations vs. Corporate Giving Programs: Compendium of Applicable Federal Tax Laws.* Washington: Council on Foundations, 1983.

Gives an overview of corporate giving through a company-sponsored foundation or direct giving, explaining the advantages and disadvantages of each type, and provides a review of relevant federal laws.

4137. "The Day Trust: The High Cost of a $2,801 Foundation Excise Tax Refund." *Philanthropy Monthly* 18 (May 1985): 8-12.

4138. Debnam, Robert J. *Handbook of Legal Liabilities for Nonprofit Executives.* Washington: Rural America.

4139. Deja, Sandy. "Nonprofit Organizations, Business Ventures, and the IRS: Your Guide to the Unrelated Business Income Tax Law." *Whole Nonprofit Catalog* 6 (Spring 1988): 7-9.

Informative article offers five basic steps to aid entrepreneurial nonprofits assess whether or not their profits will be subject to taxation. Step 1: determine whether the business activity results in unrelated business income (defined as income from the conduct of a trade or business regularly carried on which is not related to the excercise or performance of the organization's exempt purpose). Step 2: determine whether any Internal Revenue Code (IRC) Code section 513(a) exceptions apply to the business activity. Step 3: determine whether one of the IRC section 512(b) modifications applies. Step 4: determine whether a miscellaneous exclusion applies. Step 5: compute the unrelated business income tax liability. In conclusion, the article stresses the importance of consulting a professional with specific experience in the unrelated business income tax field if your organization is considering a business venture.

4140. Desruisseaux, Paul. "Philanthropy under Attack, Foundation Head Charges." *Chronicle of Higher Education* 30 (29 May 1985): 15-6.

4141. Dressner, Howard R., and Sheila Avrin McLean. "Tax Reform Act: Public Charities, Lobbying." *New York Law Journal* (14 December 1976).

4142. Edie, John A. "New Tax Bill Creates Crucial Changes in Tax Return: Revisions in 990-PF Call for Greater Detail on Administrative Costs." *Foundation News* 25 (November-December 1984): 48-9.

4143. Edie, John A. "Streamlining Foundation Tax Forms: Recent Changes Make Form 990-PF Easier to Complete, More Information for Grantseekers." *Foundation News* 24 (January-February 1983): 66-7.

4144. *Explanation of Tax Reform Act of 1969.* Chicago: Commerce Clearing House, 1969.

4145. "Federal Office of Management and Budget Proposes More Stringent Rules on Advocacy by Nonprofit Groups Receiving Federal Funds." *For Your Information* 4 (28 February 1983): 1+.

4146. "Federal Restrictions on Foundations." *Social Science Review* 44 (June 1970): 196-98.

4147. "Federal Tax Plan Called Devastating to Charitable World." *Fund Raising Review* (February 1985): 1+.

4148. Finch, Johnny C. "Where Is IRS Likely to Look in 'Unrelated Business Income' Audits?" *Philanthropy Monthly* 18 (September 1985): 13+.

4149. Finehout, Raymond L. *Taxation and Education.* Washington: American Alumni Council, 1966.

4150. Fiore, Ernest D., Jr., and Paul E. Klein. *(Analysis of) the Tax Reform Act of 1969.* New York: Matthew Bender & Co., 1970.

4151. Fisch, Edith L., Doris J. Freed, and Esther R. Schachter. *Charities and Charitable Foundations.* Pomona, N.Y.: Lond Publications, 1974.

Brings together the law, and to a lesser extent, the history pertaining to the creation, management and regulation of charities and charitable foundations in three organizational forms—as trusts, corporations or associations. Considers laws applicable to contributions and dispositions made to such entities; the creation of charitable trusts, charitable corporations and unincorporated associations; the operation and management of the charitable entity; its powers and duties; liability; termination; charitable solicitation; state and federal tax treatment; and unrelated business income tax. Updated with supplements.

4152. Fisch, Edith L., Doris J. Freed, and Esther R. Schachter. *Charities and Charitable Foundations. Cumulative Supplement.* Pomona, N.Y.: Lond Publications, 1988.

4153. Fischer, Howard E. *Nonprofit Organizations: Laws and Regulations Affecting Establishment and Operation.* New York: Center for Nonprofit Organizations, 1982.

4154. "For Nonprofits: What Is Permissible Activity during a Political Campaign." *Exchange Networks* (Spring 1984): 7-8.

4155–4176 TAX AND LEGAL IMPLICATIONS FOR NONPROFITS

4155. "Form 990 for 1984." *Philanthropy Monthly* 17 (October 1984): 18-24.

4156. Foundation Center. *Foundations and the Tax Bill: Testimony on Title I of the Tax Reform Act of 1969 Submitted by Witnesses Appearing before the United States Senate Finance Committee, October 1969.* New York: Foundation Center, 1969.

4157. Foundation Center. *Foundations and the Tax Reform Act of 1969.* New York: Foundation Center, 1970.

4158. Foundation Center. *Press Comment on Foundation Proposals in the Tax Reform Bill.* New York: Foundation Center, 1969.

4159. *Foundations, Charities and the Law: The Interaction of External Controls and Internal Policies.* Los Angeles: UCLA Law Review, 1966.

4160. Fremont-Smith, Marion R. *Foundations and Government: State and Federal Law and Supervision.* New York: Russell Sage Foundation, 1965.

4161. Funding Exchange. *Gift Giving Guide: Methods and Tax Implications of Giving Money Away.* New York: Funding Exchange, 1981.

4162. Galloway, Joseph M. *The Unrelated Business Income Tax.* New York: John Wiley, 1982.

4163. Gary, Susan N. *A Lawyer's Guide to Private Foundations. Supplement.* Chicago: Donors Forum of Chicago, 1987.
Handbook originally published in 1985 with a 1987 supplement to assist attorneys in their work with clients setting up private grantmaking foundations and charitable trusts. Emphasis is on the laws and by-laws of Illinois, though some of the information is general enough to apply to all states, and the bibliography should serve as a starting point for further research. Covers organizational form and documents, taxes, prohibited activities, fiduciary duties, and required filings. Includes sample copies of IRS Form 1023, application for recognition of exemption; IRS Form SS-4, application for employer identification number; Form 2848, power of attorney and declaration of representative; IRS Form 990-PF, federal return of private foundation; and Illinois registration statement and Form AG-990-PF, state return of private foundation.

4164. Glen, Maxwell. "The Looming Battle: Partisan Activities of Tax-Exempt Organizations." *Grantsmanship Center News* 13 (January-February 1985): 25-9.

4165. Goldberg, Stephen S. *Taxation of Charitable Giving.* New York: Practising Law Institute, 1973.

4166. Goodwin, Michael. "A Court Approves City's Right to Tax Nonprofit Group." *New York Times* (3 March 1983): 1.

4167. Gould, Carole. "Making the Most of Charitable Impulses: An Outright Gift to Your Alma Mater Cuts Your Taxes." *New York Times* (7 April 1985): F-11.

4168. Grange, George R., II, and Nancy S. Oliver. "No Longer a Free Ride: New Regulations on below-Market Loans Are Restrictive." *Foundation News* 27 (July-August 1986): 56-7.
Review of current regulations governing below-market loans. The regulations—IRS Code Section 7872—became effective 1 January 1985. The code section described below-market loans as arm's length transactions in which the lender is deemed to have made a loan to the borrower at a statutory interest rate, and the borrower is deemed to have paid the interest to the lender. This deemed-interest must be accounted for by the lender as income, and may be deductible by the borrower as a nonbusiness deduction. Five types of below-market interest loans are subject to the new rules: gift loans, compensation-related loans, corporation/shareholder loans, tax avoidance loans, and any loan in which the interest arrangement has a significant effect on the federal tax liability of the lender, borrower or both. Code section changes went into effect as of 10 July 1986. Among the changes—the $10,000 limitation now applies to loans made by a single lender to each charitable organization and a new exemption on any loan of $250,000 or less made to a charitable organization. In addition, below-market interest rules do not apply if a foundation or charitable organization classified within IRS Code Section 170(c) makes a loan that primarily furthers its tax-exempt purpose. Exempted purposes include religious, charitable, scientific, literary, educational, or fostering national or international sports competition or for the prevention of cruelty to children or animals.

4169. Gray, David Ross. *Nonprivate Foundations: A Tax Guide for Charitable Organizations.* Colorado Springs, Colo.: Shepard's, 1977.

4170. Gray, Phil. "Using the Charitable Remainder Unitrust." *Nonprofit Executive* 3 (February 1984): 3-4.

4171. Greisman, Bernard, ed. *J.K. Lasser's 53 New Plans for Saving Estate and Gift Taxes.* 5th ed., rev. New York: Doubleday, 1969.

4172. Gruppenhoff, John T., and James T. Murphy. *Nonprofits' Handbook on Lobbying: The History and Impact of the New 1976 Lobbying Regulations of the Activities of Nonprofit Organizations.* Washington: Taft Group, 1977.

4173. Haberek, Judy. "Getting H.R. 911 Passed: How the Process Works and What You Can Do." *Voluntary Action Leadership* (Spring-Summer 1987): 15-7.

4174. Hansmann, Henry. *The Rationale for Exempting Nonprofit Organizations from Corporate Income Taxation.* Program on Non-Profit Organizations, no. 23A. New Haven, Conn.: Institution for Social and Policy Studies, 1981.

4175. Hansmann, Henry. *Rationalizing Non-Profit Corporation Law.* Program on Non-Profit Organizations, no. 22. New Haven, Conn.: Institution for Social and Policy Studies, 1981.

4176. Hansmann, Henry. *Reforming Nonprofit Corporation Law.* Program on Non-Profit Organizations, no. 22A. New Haven, Conn.: Institution for Social and Policy Studies, 1981.

4177. Hansmann, Henry. *Why Are Non-Profit Organizations Exempted from Corporate Income Taxation?* Program on Non-Profit Organizations, no. 23. New Haven, Conn.: Institution for Social and Policy Studies, 1980.

4178. Harmon, Gail, and Andrea Ferster. "Dealing with the IRS." *NonProfit Times* 2 (May 1988): 26-9.

Briefly examines legal issues and court decisions involving the IRS and/or tax exempt status. Among the topics covered: a nonprofit operated to raise and distribute funds to other nonprofits qualifies as a 501(c)(3) exempt organization; a retirement benefit association does not qualify as a volunteer employees' beneficiary association (VEBA), and thus the IRS may revoke its tax exemption.

4179. Hasson, James K., Jr. *Private Foundations and the Problem of "Tipping": A Description of the Problem and Some Practical Suggestions for Use in Grantmaking.* Council of Michigan Foundations Reports, no. 4. Grand Haven, Mich.: Council of Michigan Foundations, 1987.

A paper which discusses the problem of *tipping*. Tipping may occur if a foundation makes grants or loans to any publicly supported charity (which generally means a charitable organization other than a church, college, hospital, medical research institute, or a section 509(a)(3) supporting organization). If a small or newly organized charitable organization receives a large grant or series of grants from one or more private foundations and the grantee ceases to have one-third of its financial support derived from public sources the status of the grantee would *tip* from being publicly supported to being privately supported. Thus, the grantee would no longer qualify as a public charity. Also, if the foundation's grant created the *tipping* problem, the grantor foundation may not be entitled to count the grant against its minimum payout requirement and it may have to exercise expenditure responsibility in order to prevent the imposition of a penalty tax on the grantor foundation. In addition, the paper summarizes the pertinent IRS regulations and documentation necessary to protect the foundation and the grantee and contains examples of documents which can be used during the application procedure to protect the foundation.

4180. Hauser, Crane C. "How Infirm a Foundation." *Taxes* 49 (December 1971): 750-67.

4181. Hochberg, Lester, and Malcolm L. Stein. "Private Foundations: A Tour through the Labyrinth Created by the '69 Act." *Journal of Taxation* 37 (July 1972): 49-54.

4182. Hopkins, Bruce R. *Charitable Giving and Tax-Exempt Organizations: The Impact of the 1981 Tax Act.* New York: John Wiley, 1982.

4183. Hopkins, Bruce R. *Charity under Siege: Government Regulation of Fund-Raising.* New York: John Wiley, 1980.

4184. Hopkins, Bruce R. "A Disturbing New Wrinkle from IRS: Exchange of Mailing Lists Is Now Considered Taxable Income." *Foundation News* 23 (November-December 1982): 32+.

4185. Hopkins, Bruce R. "Fund Raising and Taxes: When Is a 'Gift' Not a Gift?" *Fund Raising Management* 14 (December 1983): 80-1.

4186. Hopkins, Bruce R. "Fund Raising and the Law: What's Ahead in 1988." *Fund Raising Management* 18 (December 1987): 52+.

Recent developments in the legislative and regulatory environment concerning nonprofits and fundraising are conducive to more "charity bashing" in 1988, writes Hopkins. He discusses legislative recommendations resulting from the House Oversight Subcommittee hearings on competition and unrelated business; restrictions on the lobbying and political campaign activities of nonprofits; state enactment of various types of legislation, all of it stringent, to regulate fundraising and solicitation; the formation and use by the IRS of the Exempt Organization Advisory Group; recent legislative proposals to reduce the federal deficit at the expense of nonprofits and their donors; and the new IRS regulations that must follow in the wake of the 1986 tax reform.

4187. Hopkins, Bruce R. "Hearings on Nonprofit 'Competition'." *Nonprofit World* 5 (September-October 1987): 31, 34.

Outlines some of the recent testimony on the matter of nonprofit competition as given before the House Subcommittee on Oversight. Both the IRS and the Treasury stressed the need for additional information about the nonprofit sector in general and unrelated business income in particular before specific proposals can be put forward; both departments also rejected the idea that competition should be a factor in deciding whether an activity is related or unrelated to an organization's tax-exempt status. Initial observations and recommendations by the Treasury include: more detailed reporting to improve enforcement and compliance; increasing the specific deduction from unrelated income from $1,000 to $5,000; and examining the matter of tax-exempt organizations participating in partnerships. Groups representing small business offered a variety of proposals, such as the recommendation by the National Federation of Independent Business to limit the amount of income tax-exempt organizations could receive from for-profit subsidiaries.

4188. Hopkins, Bruce R. "IRS Strikes Out at Two Property Acquisition Tacts." *Fund Raising Management* 16 (October 1985): 122+.

4189. Hopkins, Bruce R. "Is New Regulation Really Needed?" *Fund Raising Management* 17 (October 1986): 52-4, 56.

Discusses current efforts to write a uniform charitable solicitation act.

4190. Hopkins, Bruce R. *The Law of Tax-Exempt Organizations.* 5th ed. New York: John Wiley, 1987.

Based on materials developed for Hopkins' course in tax-exempt organizations at the George Washington University National Law Center. The footnoted book is a general text which can be used as a resource to gain access to more specific information. It includes documentation of regulations, rulings, cases, and literature in the field. Hopkins believes that the volume can be useful to fundraising executives, managers, accountants, and lawyers as well as tax-practitioners and others interested in tax-exempt organizations. This new edition has delegated the Internal Revenue Code citations and the Internal Revenue Service references to footnotes and the appendix to make the text more readable. The contents are divided into seven parts, beginning with an introduction to tax-exempt organizations. Other sections include charitable organizations; other tax-exempt organizations; private foundations; qualification of exempt organizations—substance and procedure; feeder organizations and unrelated income taxation; and inter-organizational structures and operational forms. The appendix contains *Internal Revenue Code Sections*; *Table of Cases*; *Table of IRS Revenue Rulings and Revenue Procedures*; *Table of IRS Private Letter Rulings and Other Items*; *Table of IRS Private Determinations Cited in Text*; and *IRS Key District Offices*. Also contains an index.

4191. Hopkins, Bruce R. *The Law of Tax-Exempt Organizations. Cumulative Supplement.* 5th ed. New York: John Wiley, 1988.

Hopkins writes that hostility against charitable organizations was widespread and generally indiscriminate in 1987, causing great changes in the law regulating these groups. He summarizes the events of the year as they concern nonprofits and other tax-exempt organizations, including the unrelated income hearings, revenue-raising options, lobbying and political activities hearings, and the first meeting of the Exempt Organization Advisory Group. He suggests that even more law changes—by Congress, the courts, and the Treasury and the IRS—are on the way.

4192. Hopkins, Bruce R. *Legal Issues Involving Competition by Nonprofits with Small Business.* Unpublished, 1987.

4193. Hopkins, Bruce R. "Nonprofits and Free Speech: Where Are the Boundaries?" *Foundation News* 25 (September-October 1984): 84-5.

4194. Hopkins, Bruce R. "Tax-Exempt Status Threatened by Fund Raising?" *Fund Raising Management* 14 (October 1983): 94-5.

4195. Hopkins, Bruce R. "Tax Reform Act of 1984 Begets Many Changes for Non-Profits: Part 1." *Fund Raising Management* 15 (September 1984): 104.

4196. Hopkins, Bruce R. "Tax Reform Act of 1984 Begets Many Changes for Non-Profits: Part 2." *Fund Raising Management* 15 (October 1984): 86+.

4197. Hopkins, Bruce R. "Treasury Tax-Reform Proposal." *Fundemensions* 10 (January 1985): 6-8.

Reviews the 1984 proposal to revise the federal tax laws, focusing on those recommendations which would impact nonprofits.

4198. Hopkins, Bruce R. "What, When, How Much Primer on the Reagan Tax-Reform Plan." *Fund Raising Management* 16 (August 1985): 94+.

4199. Hunter, T. Willard. *The Tax Climate for Philanthropy.* Washington: American College Public Relations Association, 1968.

4200. "Implications for Accounting in the Munson Decision." *Philanthropy Monthly* 27 (September 1984): 36-8.

4201. Independent Sector. *Advocacy Is Sometimes an Agency's Best Service: Opportunities and Limits within Federal Law.* Washington: Independent Sector, 1984.

4202. Independent Sector. *The Grass Is Greener: Fund Raising Opportunities under the 1981 Tax Act.* Washington: Independent Sector, 1982.

4203. Independent Sector. *Interim Appraisal of the Economic Recovery Program's Impact on Philanthropic and Voluntary Organizations and the People They Serve.* Washington: Independent Sector, 1982.

4204. Independent Sector. *The Permanent Charitable Contributions Legislation.* Washington: Independent Sector, 1983.

4205. Independent Sector. "Questions and Answers Regarding the Impact of the U.S. Treasury's Tax Plan on Charitable Giving." *Memo to Members* (8 February 1985): 4.

4206. Independent Sector, comp. *The Taxation of Nonprofits: A State-by-State Summary.* Washington: Independent Sector, 1988.

Nationwide summary of recent legislation, revenue department decisions, and court opinions concerning unfair competition practices and the tax exempt status of nonprofits. Arranged alphabetically by state, information is identified by type of proposal, type of nonprofits affected, and government branch involved.

4207. Independent Sector. "Testimony of Brian O'Connell, President, Independent Sector, on the Impact of the President's Tax Proposals on Charities." *Memo to Members* (12 July 1985): 1-10.

4208. *Internal Revenue Code.* 1939-1988. Washington: Government Printing Office, 19—.

4209. "IRS Plans Major Research on Tax-Exempt Organizations." *Philanthropy Monthly* 18 (July-August 1985): 14+.

4210. *IRS Revenue Procedures on Tipping.* Unpublished, 1981.

4211. "IRS' Special Emphases for Nonprofits in 1988." *Philanthropy Monthly* 20 (December 1987): 5-14.

Reprint of the Official IRS Manual Statement of its *Program Objectives for Fiscal Year 1988* for its EP/EO (Employee Plans/Exempt Organizations) area. The Statement is in three parts: 1) the program to examine the returns of exempt organizations; 2) the program to process determination letter applications from exempt organizations, and 3) overall EP/EO Program Objectives.

4212. Joblove, Leonard. *Special Treatment of Churches under the Internal Revenue Code.* Program on Non-Profit Organizations, no. 21. New Haven, Conn.: Institution for Social and Policy Studies, 1980.

4213. Johnston, William E., Jr. "Taxing Educational Gifts." *Commonweal* 102 (10 October 1975): 468-70.

4214. Joyce, Fay S. "IRS's Crackdown on Art Gifts Gains." *New York Times* (2 May 1983): D-1,4.

4215. Kahn, C. Harry. *Personal Deductions in the Federal Income Tax.* Princeton, N.J.: Princeton University Press, 1960.

4216. Kaye, Jude. "Reference Guide 1989: Tax and Reporting Compliance for Nonprofit Organizations." *NonProfit Times* 2 (January 1989): 32-3.

Annotated list of forms that the federal government requires a nonprofit to file. Lists those forms necessary for incorporation, as well as annual information returns and payroll-related reports. Describes the purpose of each form, and indicates due date along with penalties for failure to file.

4217. Kucharsky, David. "Churches Await Impact of Tax Reform." *Christianity Today* 14 (16 January 1970): 31.

4218. Kutner, Luis. *Legal Aspects of Charitable Trusts and Foundations: A Guide for Philanthropoids.* Chicago: Commerce Clearing House, 1970.

4219. Labovitz, John R. *The Impact of the Foundation Provisions of the Tax Reform Act of 1969: Early Empirical Measurements.* Washington: American Bar Foundation, 1973.

An early attempt to assess the impact of the private foundation provisions of the Tax Reform Act of 1969, centered around two empirical components: a comparative analysis of data from information tax returns filed by a sample of foundations (stratified by asset size) in 1967, before the new provisions were under consideration in Congress, and in 1970, the first year they went into effect; and impressionistic and anecdotal material from a series of interviews conducted with foundation personnel in the spring of 1972. This report is not intended to pass judgement on the wisdom or folly of various foundation provisions, but merely seeks to develop a method and baseline data for assessing the impact of the provisions and to make an initial assessment of the effects of the Tax Reform Act of 1969. Benchmark data and worksheets for compiling later comparative data are included in the appendixes.

4220. Lane, Marc J. *Legal Handbook for Nonprofit Organizations.* New York: Amacom, 1980.

Nontechnical legal guide provides advice for making legal decisions. Examples illustrate the opportunities and pitfalls that one is likely to encounter in organizing and operating any type of nonprofit. Explains legal fundamentals and the various aspects of the tax-exempt process, including unrelated business taxable income, charitable fundraising regulations, and a look towards future trends concerning nonprofits—all to help avoid risk and error.

4221. Larson, Martin A., and C. Stanley Lowell. *Praise the Lord for Tax Exemption.* Washington: Robert B. Luce, 1969.

4222. Laskin, William A., and Michael T. Boland. "The Charitable Lead Trust in the Ten Percent World." *Fund Raising Management* 15 (September 1984): 22+.

4223. Lasser, J.K. *How Tax Laws Make Giving to Charity Easy.* New York: Funk & Wagnalls Co., 1948.

4224. Lehrfeld, William J. *Federal Tax Treatment of Unrelated Business Income.* Washington: Chamber of Commerce of the United States, 1977.

4225. Lehrfeld, William J. "More Paperwork on Gifts of Property Worth $5,000." *Philanthropy Monthly* 18 (February 1985): 29-36.

Relates how to substantiate major gifts of property.

4226. Lehrfeld, William J. "More Unrelated Business Tax Issues." *Philanthropy Monthly* 17 (October 1984): 33-9.

4227. Lehrfeld, William J. "Private Foundations in the Post-69 Era: Have Controls Spawned a Trend to Orthodoxy?" *Journal of Taxation* 36 (May 1972): 292-97.

4228. Lichter, Jonathan M. "The Effects of the Proposed Regulations on Charitable Remainder Trusts." *Trusts & Estates* 123 (June 1984): 41-50.

4229. Lichter, Jonathan M. "Profiles in Philanthropy: Opportunities for Gifts." *Trusts & Estates* 124 (September 1985): 22+.

Modern estate planning techniques with charitable remainder trusts and charitable lead trusts.

4230. Lidstone, Herrick K., ed. *A Tax Guide for Artists and Arts Organizations.* Lexington, Mass.: Lexington Books, 1979.

4231. Lutheran Church Foundation. "Important Information for Persons with 'Private' or 'Family' Foundations." *Lutheran Church Foundations Bulletin.*

4232. Luttrell, Jordan. "The Effect of the Private Foundations Provisions of the Tax Reform Act of 1969 on Community Development Corporations." *Law and Contemporary Problems* 36 (Spring 1971): 238-76.

4233. Mackay-Smith, Anne, and Alexandra Peers. "Schools Using Tax Bill to Prod Donors to Give." *Wall Street Journal* (8 August 1985): 25.

4234. Madlin, Nancy. "Legal Advice." *NPO Resource Review* 2 (May-June 1984): 1+.

4235. Magarrell, Jack. "Bill to Cut Excise Tax on Foundations Could Yield $50-Million to Charities." *Chronicle of Higher Education* 27 (9 November 1983): 23-4.

4236. Manchester, Jay A. "IRS Form 990: An Analytical Tool for Donors." *Philanthropy Monthly* 15 (November 1982): 10-3.

4237. Mandel Center for Nonprofit Organizations. *Legal Issues in Nonprofit Organizations.* Mandel Center for Nonprofit Organizations Discussion Paper Series. Cleveland: Case Western Reserve University, 1988.

Conference notes from six of the ten speakers at a national conference on *Legal Issues in Nonprofit Organizations* sponsored by the Mandel Center for Nonprofit Organizations and the Law School, Case Western Reserve University, November 5, 1988. Included are outlines on liability by Daniel L. Kurtz and Robert S. Bromberg, an outline by A.L. Spitzer and Howard Schoenfeld on unrelated business income tax with appendixes of the *Draft Report of Oversight Subcommittee to Ways and Means Committee* and the testimony of Adelbert L. Spitzer before the House Committee on Small Business. Malvin E. Bank's outline on nonprofit advocacy is included as well as the outline of Peter Swords' talk on private foundation status and his short informative piece *Introduction to Taxes* which clearly explains the implications of Sections 501(c)(3) and 509(a) of the Internal Revenue Code for nonprofit organizations and the various tests for exemption.

4238. Mann, Jim. "Two Standards for Charities' Lobbying OKd." *Chicago Sun-Times* (24 May 1983).

4239. Marlowe, Howard. "Give and Take." *Grantsmanship Center News* 2 (May-June 1983): 58-60.

4240. Maymudes, Carol S., and Ellen Weiss, eds. *Tax-Exempt Organizations*. 2 Vols. Englewood Cliffs, N.J.: Prentice-Hall, 1988.

Loose-leaf reports contain up-to-date information on all aspects of taxation, regulations and procedures, and legal and operating policies affecting nonprofit organizations. Sections include articles by experts in the field—accountants, attorneys, and management experts of major foundations—discussing possible solutions to problems faced by exempt organizations and foundations; applicable provisions of the Internal Revenue Code, followed by Committee Report explanations, final regulations (including temporary regulations under the law), and proposed regulations involving exempt organizations, charitable contributions, unrelated business income tax, private foundation excises, returns and penalties, and IRS procedures (Part 601 of the Code of Federal Regulations); current rulings, releases, pertinent announcements, and cases relating to exempt organizations and charitable contributions; legislative proposals relating to exempt organizations and charitable contributions as they move through the Congress, including tax bills and important Committee Reports; and current forms and specimen filled-in forms by the IRS for use by exempt organizations and new and revised forms as they are released. Includes finding lists for current rulings and releases, a table of cases, and a subject matter index. Updated by monthly reports.

4241. McDowell, Edwin. "Tax Laws Aiding Arts Faulted by Foundation." *New York Times* (28 July 1983).

4242. *McKinney's Consolidated Laws on New York Annotated*. St. Paul, Minn.: West Publishing Co., 1984.

4243. Mental Health Association. *A Layman's Guide to Lobbying without Losing Your Tax-Exempt Status*. Roslyn, Va.: Mental Health Association, 1976.

4244. Metropolitan Life Foundation. *Guide to Using the Form 990*. New York: Metropolitan Life Foundation, [198?].

4245. Migdail, Rhonda G. "Lobbying and Political Activities: What Every Nonprofit Should Know." *Nonprofit World Report* 3 (May-June 1985): 21+.

4246. Milford, Dale. "Arguments Regarding Tax Reform." *Congressional Record* (19 September 1974): E-5895, 5896.

4247. Miller, Howard S. *The Legal Foundations of American Philanthropy, 1776-1844*. Madison, Wis.: State Historical Society of Wisconsin, 1961.

Concise legal history of philanthropy during the colonial era outlines the English foundations of American attitudes and laws about charity, and traces the initial development of laws governing charitable gifts and bequests in the new Republic. It also describes the Supreme Court case, *Philadelphia Baptist Association vs. Hart's Executors* (1819), which contributed to the ultimate creation of an American law of charity, and others which followed, up to the Girard Will case in 1844, which established permissive public policy toward philanthropy in American legal tradition. Miller's analysis incorporates discussion of social, political, and religious factors that affected the evolution of American laws governing philanthropy. Notes and list of sources.

4248. Moskowitz, Daniel D. "Going into Business Can Be 'Taxing' Experience for Nonprofits." *Exchange Networks* (Summer 1984): 1-2.

4249. Moskowitz, Daniel D. "Nonprofits Find Going into Business Can Be Taxing Experience." *Washington Post* (22 August 1983).

4250. Munro, J. Richard. *Remarks*. Unpublished, 1981.

4251. "Munson: The Supreme Court Disposes of the Rebuttable Presumption." *Philanthropy Monthly* 17 (June 1984): 5-13.

The full text of the decision is presented with a discussion of the impact on private agencies.

4252. "NAHD Sees Threat to Charitable Contributions Law in Analysis of Philanthropic Issues." *Fund Raising Review* (November 1984): 1+.

4253. National Association of Attorneys General. "NAAG Seeks Model Law for Charities." *Fund Raising Review* (July 1984): 1-2.

4254. National Association of Attorneys General. *Regulation of Charitable Trusts and Solicitations: Summary of the Special Meeting of the Subcommittee on Charitable Trusts and Solicitations*. Atlanta, Ga.: National Association of Attorneys General, 1974.

4255. *National Association of Attorneys General Conference*. Atlanta, Ga.: National Association of Attorneys General, 1947.

4256. National Information Bureau. *A Grantmaker's Guide to a New Tool for Philanthropy: Form 990*. New York: National Information Bureau, 1983.

4257. Needham, Roger A., ed. *Tax Aspects of Charitable Giving and Receiving*. New York: Practising Law Institute, 1971.

4258. Nemy, Enid. "How Artists Don't Just Sing for Their Supper." *New York Times* (25 April 1985).

Comments on lobbying techniques for the arts in Washington, DC.

4259. "New Ball Game for the Foundations." *Forbes* (15 June 1972): 65-6.

4260. New York City. Task Force on the Exemption of Non-Profit Organizations from Real Property Tax. *Report of New York City Task Force on the Exemption of Non-Profit Organizations from Real Property Tax*. New York: Office of the Mayor, 1982.

4261. New York University Institute on Federal Taxation. *Problems of the Charitable Foundation. New York Institute on Federal Taxation Conference.* New York: New York University Institute on Federal Taxation Conference, 1953.

4262. Nielson, Richard P. "How Market Piggybacking Affects Your Exempt Status." *Fund Raising Management* 15 (June 1984): 32+.

4263. "The 1982 Form 990." *Philanthropy Monthly* 15 (November 1982): 5.

4264. Nixon, Hargrave, Devans and Doyle. *Admissibility in Evidence of Microfilm Records*. New York: Eastman Kodak Co., 1971.

4265. Nixon, Hargrave, Devans and Doyle. *The Tax Reform Act of 1986*. Philadelphia: American Law Institute, 1986.

Report on the *Tax Reform Act of 1986*. Prepared as a survey of the Act, it does not offer technical analysis. Although this is not a detailed study, it gives a general explanation of the changes for both individuals and corporations. The report is divided into fifteen sections dealing with specific issues and groups, including *Charitable Giving and Tax-Exempt Organizations* and *Trusts and Estates*.

4266. Oberdorfer, Louis F. *Tax Reform and the Crisis of Financing Higher Education: A Report of the Association of American Universities*. Washington: Association of American Universities, 1973.

4267. O'Connell, Brian. "Discouraging Charity." *Washington Post* (4 February 1985).

Discusses the Treasury Department's proposal to change the tax laws as they relate to charitable contributions.

4268. O'Connell, Brian. *Public Statement on OMB Circular A-122*. Washington: Independent Sector, 1983.

4269. Oleck, Howard. *Nonprofit Corporations, Organizations, and Associations*. 5th ed. Englewood Cliffs, N.J.: Prentice-Hall, 1988.

Widely regarded as the definitive authority on the law and operation of nonprofit enterprises of all kinds, this book offers practical information concerning every aspect of organization, administration, regulation, taxation, mergers and dissolutions. Includes details on qualifying for nonprofit status, protecting tax-exempt status, utilizing powers and purposes clauses, conducting directors' meetings, forming committees, removing or suspending nonprofit directors, drafting bylaws, recognizing unauthorized and improper acts, dealing with lawsuits or bankruptcy, when and how donations can be solicited, new limits on charitable deductions, standards for nonprofit accounting, federal and state lobbying laws, management techniques, mixing profit and nonprofit activities, handling unrelated business income, and parliamentary law. Provides model business and tax forms, such as the annual report, resolution on salaries, appointment of an agent, ballot for election, articles to amend charter, bylaws of large and small nonprofits, and applicable IRS documentation. 200-item bibliography.

4270. Oleck, Howard. *Parliamentary Law for Nonprofit Organizations*. Philadelphia: American Law Institute, 1979.

4271. "On Complying with the 1987 Tax Act: Even the IRS Has As Many Questions As Answers." *Philanthropy Monthly* 21 (January 1988): 15-9.

Lists the enforcement problems of the exempt organization provisions contained in the revenue act of 1987, citing code section/provision/effective date, the issues and IRS enforcement problems, and the proposed IRS actions.

4272. Organization Management. *Washington Non-Profit Tax Conference*. Washington: Organization Management, 1977.

4273. Organization Management. *Washington Non-Profit Tax Conference*. Washington: Organization Management, 1978.

4274. Organization Management. *Washington Non-Profit Tax Conference*. Washington: Organization Management, 1979.

4275. Organization Management. *Washington Non-Profit Tax Conference*. Washington: Organization Management, 1981.

4276. Organization Management. *Washington Non-Profit Tax Conference*. Washington: Organization Management, 1982.

4277. Organization Management. *Washington Non-Profit Tax Conference*. Washington: Organization Management, 1983.

4278. Organization Management. *Washington Non-Profit Tax Conference*. Washington: Organization Management, 1984.

4279. Organization Management. *Washington Non-Profit Tax Conference*. Washington: Organization Management, 1985.

4280. Organization Management. *Washington Non-Profit Tax Conference*. Washington: Organization Management, 1980.

4281. Pasquariello, Ronald D. *Religious and Ethical Issues on Tax Policy*. Shalom Paper, no. 14. Washington: Center for Theology and Public Policy, 1985.

4282. Peat, Marwick, Mitchell and Company. *Tax Equity and Fiscal Responsibility Act of 1982*. New York: Peat, Marwick, Mitchell & Co., 1982.

4283. Peat, Marwick, Mitchell and Company. *Tax Reform Act of 1976: Tax Considerations for Individuals.* New York: Peat, Marwick, Mitchell & Co., 1976.

4284. "Permissible Activities of 501(c)(3) Organizations during a Political Campaign." *Memo to Members* (17 February 1984): 1-5.

4285. Peterson, Peter G. "A Report on American Philanthropy." *Fund Raising Management* (January-February 1970): 12-6.

4286. Philadelphia Volunteer Lawyers for the Arts. *Guide to Forming a Non-Profit, Tax-Exempt Organization.* Philadelphia: Philadelphia Volunteer Lawyers for the Arts, 1980.

4287. Practising Law Institute. *Non-Profit Cultural Organizations.* Patents, Copyrights, Trademarks and Literary Property Course Handbook Series, no. 113. New York: Practising Law Institute, 1979.

4288. Price Waterhouse. *Tax Aspects of Individual Charitable Giving.* Tax Information Planning Series. New York: Price Waterhouse & Co., 1982.

4289. Price Waterhouse. *Tax Aspects of Individual Charitable Giving.* New York: Price Waterhouse & Co., 1982.

4290. *The Private Foundation and the Tax Reform Act.* Chicago: Commerce Clearing House, 1970.

4291. "Private Foundations and the Tax Reform Act." *Columbia Journal of Law and Social Problems* 7 (Spring 1971): 240-77.

4292. "Projected 1985 Levels of Charitable Giving." *FRM Weekly* (19 December 1984): 1-2.

4293. "The Question of Revising the Tax Status of Foundations: Pro and Con." *Congressional Digest* 48 (May 1969): 130-60.

4294. Rankin, Deborah. "Charitable Trusts and the Taxman." *New York Times* (27 November 1983): F-11.

4295. "Reagan Hatches Plan to Gag Nonprofit Groups." *New Directions for Women* 12 (March-April 1983): 1+.

4296. "Reagan Restricts Lobbying by Charities with Federal Grants." *Responsive Philanthropy* (Winter 1985): 3+.

4297. Register, Levon C., and David E. Gormanous. "Private Foundations and the Tax Reform Act of 1969." *Taxes* 48 (May 1970): 283-91.

4298. "Regulating Religion." *Philanthropy Monthly* 16 (March 1983): 5-9.

4299. "Regulating the Political Activity of Foundations." *Harvard Law Review* 83 (June 1970): 1843-69.

4300. "Research on the Impact on Charitable Giving of the U.S. Treasury's November 1984 Tax Reform Proposal." *Government Relations Info and Action* 7 (17 April 1985).

4301. Riecker, Ranny. "New Law Called 'a Victory'." *Michigan Scene* 11 (Summer 1984): 1+.

Summarizes the legislation in the 1984 tax bill which affects private foundations.

4302. Robertson, Mark. "Can Two Heads Be Better Than One? Collaborations among Not-for-Profit Corporations." *CCFlash* 17 (January 1989): 1-2.

Examines legal aspects of a collaboration between nonprofit arts organizations. The purpose clause of each organization's certificate of incorporation must be examined to determine whether the proposed collaborative activity will compromise nonprofit and tax exempt status; a broad purpose statement alleviates such difficulties. Rights and responsibilities should be allocated to the organizations and set in writing before the project is launched; and the handling of the project's financial aspects should be determined in advance, including setting up a system for controlling expenditures. One individual from each group should be designated as the official representative of that group in all areas where communication is critical and conflicts may occur. Additional areas of concern include: dividing day-to-day work; arranging deadlines and assigning them to individuals; the manner of sharing proceeds, if any; methods for resolving disputes; and the future of any property created by a collaboration (who will own the copyright?). The final consideration is to provide for the termination of the collaboration in both good and bad circumstances.

4303. Robinson, James D., III. "James D. Robinson III on Tax Incentives for Charitable Giving." *Brookings Review* 3 (Spring 1985): 28-9.

4304. Rubinstein, Gwen. "The Tax Man Cometh." *Association Management* 39 (June 1987): 26-9.

The unrelated-business income tax (UBIT) is the subject of this essay and interview with House Ways and Means Committee Chairman Dan Rostenkowski. There is a perception that tax-exempt organizations compete unfairly with for-profit companies. "For-profit businesses have complained that tax-exempt organizations are provided an unfair competitive advantage under the present tax law," stated Rostenkowski. The article questions the chairman of the Oversight Committee on the tax-exempt organizations and UBIT and assesses the possible short and long-range ramifications of the hearings. When queried about the Pennsylvania plan to require nonprofit disclosure of business ventures, the chairman responded, "Any government that allows an organization to escape taxes...has a right...to regulate nonprofit activity." "The issue is a general one of whether any level of government has a right to impose regulation in return for special benefits that are granted. From my perspective, it clearly does."

4305. Rudney, Gabriel. "Second Thoughts on the Felstein Findings." *Philanthropy Monthly* 13 (January 1980): 10-2.

4306. Salamon, Lester M., and Charles T. Clotfelter. "Will the Tax Act Hurt Giving?" *Trusts & Estates* (December 1981): 8-14.

4307. Sanden, B. Kenneth. "Charitable Giving and the Tax Bill." *Price Waterhouse Review* 14 (Autumn 1969): 34-9.

4308. Sanders, Michael I. "Final Regs on Section 4945: Working with the New Rules Restricting Foundations' Activities." *Journal of Taxation* 38 (March 1973): 130-35.

4309. Sanderson, Glen R. "Tax Reform Act of 1969: An Overview." *Business and Economic Review* 15 (March 1970): 2-7.

4310. Sandison, Hamish R., and Jennifer Williams. *Tax Policy and Private Support for the Arts in the U.S., Canada and Great Britain.* Washington: British American Arts Association, 1981.

4311. Schatz, Barbara A., and Wendy P. Seligson, eds. *By-Laws a Guide for New York Not-for-Profit Organizations and Their Lawyers.* New York: Council of New York Law Associates, 1983.

Presented in two parts, the first half of the booklet is directed to new nonprofits and features a questionnaire designed to focus attention on decisions that need to be made in the by-laws. The second half is addressed to lawyers representing nonprofits and deals with the requirements of the New York Not-for-Profit Corporation Law.

4312. Schiff, Jerald, and Burton A. Weisbrod. "State Income Tax Reform and Charitable Giving: The Case of Wisconsin." *Philanthropy Monthly* 18 (July-August 1985): 17+.

4313. Schwartz, John J. "Problems with Matching-Grant Charity." *New York Times* (16 March 1985): 18.

4314. Scott, Austin Wakeman. *The Law of Trusts.* 2nd ed. Boston: Little, Brown, 1956.

4315. "The Search for New Tax Revenues." *Philanthropy Monthly* 17 (October 1984): 5-12.

4316. "A Search for Scandal Boomerangs in House Foundation Hearings." *Philanthropy Monthly* 16 (April 1987): 7-10.

Brief essay on Congressional hearings convened to investigate foundation non-compliance with Internal Revenue Service (IRS) requirements. The General Accounting Office (GAO) report to the hearings detailed those areas in which the foundations did not report required information—those managing the foundation, descriptions of all securities and other assets, complete grant descriptions, and grant recipient addresses. The article suggests that non-compliance be put into perspective because the GAO report also states that about ninety-two percent of the 990 PF returns sampled reported all the return information that IRS had identified as being necessary. The article mentions the impact of Robert Bothwell (National Committee for Responsive Philanthropy) on the hearings and the GAO report. The essay also cites Thomas Buckman, president of the Foundation Center as "one of the most informative witnesses at the hearings." He presented evidence of the Foundation Center's efforts to make free information on foundations available to the public.

4317. Shorrock, John B. "Free Advice: IRS Publications Fill You in on the Rules for Charitable Giving and Getting." *Currents* 11 (February 1985): 32-3.

4318. Shribman, David. "To Get Grants, Universities Use Applied Political Science." *New York Times* (11 September 1983): E-7.

4319. Simes, Lewis M. *Public Policy and the Dead Hand: The Thomas Cooley Lectures.* Ann Arbor, Mich.: University of Michigan Law School, 1955.

4320. Simon, John G. *Charity and Dynasty under the Federal Tax System.* Program on Non-Profit Organizations, no. 5. New Haven, Conn.: Institution for Social and Policy Studies, 1978.

4321. Simpson, Janice C. "If Starting a Private Foundation Incurs Legal Headaches, Here Are Alternatives." *Wall Street Journal* (1 July 1987): 25.

Briefly examines supporting organizations and pass-through foundations, alternatives to private foundations that give donors more generous tax deductions and sometimes even avoid the extra restrictions.

4322. "Sixty-Six Nonprofit Groups Assail Lobbying Curbs." *New York Times* (6 October 1983): A23.

4323. Skousen, Mark. *Tax Free.* Merrifield, Va.: Mark Skousen, 1982.

4324. Sligar, James S. "Constitutionality of the Tax on Lobbying by Private Foundations under Section 4945(d)(1) of the Internal Revenue Code." *Taxes* (May 1983): 306-18.

4325. Sloane, Leonard. "Your Money: Rules of I.R.S. on Donations." *New York Times* (25 May 1985).

4326. Smith, Thomas M. "Trust vs. Corporate Form." *Trusts & Estates* 126 (August 1987): 20-2, 24.

Provides relevant information to help advisors determine which legal form—a trust or a not-for-profit corporation—best meets the tax needs and altruistic interests of a donor wishing to establish a private foundation. Discusses the similarities and differences of the two forms, the laws and regulations governing their formation and management, the nature of their governance structures, and the procedures for their creation.

4327. Smith, William H., and Carolyn P. Chiechi. *Private Foundations: Before and after the Tax Reform Act of 1969.* Washington: American Enterprise Institute, 1974.

4328. Smolar, Boris. "The Tax-Deduction Issue." *Sentinel* (21 February 1985).

Comments on the possible effects of the tax reform proposals on nonprofit organizations.

4329. Speeter, Greg. *Playing Their Game Our Way. Using the Political Process to Meet Community Needs.* Citizen Involvement Training Project. Amherst, Mass.: University of Massachusetts, 1978.

Manual disusses ways to use governmental processes to plan solutions for social problems, and how to develop the influence necessary to hold elected and appointed officials accountable to implement those plans. Outlines traditional and not so traditional strategies to push important issues, including: holding agencies accountable; compiling report cards on officials and agencies; lobbying; developing initiative and referendum campaigns; and promoting voter registration drives. Each chapter contains models of successful actions, a planning guide, and/or role playing preparation aids. Includes resource guide.

4330. "State Laws Regulating Charitable Solicitations: As of December 31, 1987." *Giving USA Update* (January-February 1988): 4-10.

Lists registration or licensing requirements, limitations on use of funds raised, reporting dates, monetary exemptions, and solicitation disclosure requirements for charitable organizations by state; includes registration/licensing and bonding requirements for fundraisers, and gives the address and phone number of each state/regulatory agency.

4331. Steinmann, Frederick, and Jacques T. Schlenger. "Tax Reform Act of 1969 and the Treatment of Accumulation Trusts." *Taxes* 48 (May 1970): 273-82.

4332. Steinwurtzel, Samuel L. "First Meeting: The Form 990 Advisory Committee." *Philanthropy Monthly* 17 (February 1984): 29-38.

4333. Steinwurtzel, Samuel L. "The New 990." *Philanthropy Monthly* (May 1980): 31-40.

4334. Stern, Sue S., Jon L. Schumacher, and Patrick D. Martin, eds. *Charitable Giving and Solicitation.* Englewood Cliffs, N.J.: Prentice-Hall, 1988.

Provides an in-depth explanation of the federal tax aspects of charitable giving and a series of analyses, written by experts, describing successful and practical professional fundraising techniques and methods. In addition, there are summaries of state laws regulating charitable solicitations and charitable gift annuities. A *Cross Reference Table* coordinates all the material throughout the volume, and monthly *Report Bulletins* update all current developments in the charitable giving area.

4335. Stevenson, J. John. "More on Munson: State Laws Unconstitutional." *Philanthropy Monthly* 17 (July-August 1984): 17-9.

State-by-state discussion of charitable solicitation laws affected by the Munson case.

4336. Stevenson, J. John. "Munson and the Watchdogs." *Philanthropy Monthly* 17 (June 1984): 22-4.

Discusses different standards the CBBB and NCIB have when reviewing a charitable organization's activities.

4337. Stewart, Susan Stern. "Major Tax Changes Affect Property Gifts." *Fund Raising Management* 17 (November 1986): 30, 32, 35-6.

First installment in a two part series describing the effects of the 1986 Tax Reform Act on property gifts deductions.

4338. Stratton, Debra J. "A Guide to Dealing with the IRS." *Association Management* 31 (August 1979): 45-52.

4339. Sugarman, Norman A., and Paul H. Feinberg. *Charitable Giving in Light of the Economic Recovery Tax Act of 1981.* New York: Council of Jewish Federations, 1981.

4340. Sugarman, Norman A. "Conduct of the 'Business' of a Private Foundation under the Tax Reform Act of 1969." *Business Lawyer* 26 (July 1971): 1493-1503.

4341. Sugarman, Norman A. "Foundation Operations under the Tax Reform Act." *Taxes* (December 1970): 767-86.

4342. *Suggested Clauses for Wills and Trust Agreements.* Atlanta, Ga.: Trust Company of Georgia, [195?].

4343. "Suggestions to Change Form 990." *Philanthropy Monthly* 17 (June 1984): 38-40.

4344. Suhrke, Henry C. "Discussions of the Form 990 Advisory Committee: Problems of a Multi-Purpose Form." *Philanthropy Monthly* 17 (May 1984): 5-11.

4345. Suhrke, Henry C. "A 1984 Tax Bill after All: Extensive Provisions Affecting Charitable Nonprofit Organizations." *Philanthropy Monthly* 17 (February 1984): 5-7.

4346. Suhrke, Henry C. "'Political' Advocacy by Non-Profits." *Philanthropy Monthly* 16 (February 1983): 5+.

4347. Suhrke, Henry C. "Why Is Munson a Liberal-Conservative Issue?" *Philanthropy Monthly* 17 (June 1984): 20-1.

Discusses the liberal-conservative line-up on the Munson decision.

4348. *Survey of State Laws Regulating Charitable Solicitation.* New Milford, Conn.: Nonprofit Report, 1977.

4349. Swords, Peter. *Charitable Real Property Tax Exemptions in New York State: Menace or Measure of Social Progress?* New York: Association of the Bar of the City of New York, 1981.

Examines the real property tax exemption accorded to nonprofit charitable organizations in New York State as of 1981. Contains chapters on the NYS real property tax system; an explanation of the real property tax system with focus upon charitable exemptions; surveys prior studies which evaluated the charitable property tax exemption; analysis of the amount of exempt property by type in NY; an analysis of the New York decisional law interpreting the purposes for which property can be granted a charitable exemption; and examines theoretical justifications for the charitable real property tax exemption.

4350. "Tax Deductions for Volunteers." *Volunteering* 1 (Spring 1982): 7.

4351. Tax Institute of America. *Tax Impacts on Philanthropy. Tax Institute of America Conference.* Washington: Tax Institute of America, 1971.

4352. *Tax Reform Act of 1969. News Clippings and Press Comment.* Unpublished, 1969.

4353. *Tax Reform Act of 1986. Conference Committee Bill and Report.* 2 Vols. Englewood Cliffs, N.J.: Prentice-Hall, 1986.

4354. *Tax Reform in Review. Selected Articles.* Chicago: Commerce Clearing House, 1970.

4355. "Taxation and Private Foundations: Special Issues." *Tax Letter* 7 (September 1985): 1-4.

4356. "Taxing Charitable Giving Undermine Our Worthiest Institutions." *Swarthmore College Bulletin* (August 1985): 8-9.

4357. Teitell, Conrad. *The All Givers Charitable Deduction.* Old Greenwich, Conn.: Taxwise Giving, 1982.

4358. Teitell, Conrad. *The Charitable Lead Trust: A Wise Way to Be a Philanthropist and Pass Wealth to Family Members Free of Gift and Estate Taxes.* Old Greenwich, Conn.: Taxwise Giving, 1984.

4359. Teitell, Conrad. *Counsellor's Tax Guide to Charitable Contributions.* White Plains, N.Y.: Conrad Teitell, 1983.

4360. Teitell, Conrad. *New 1986 Tax Law: Explanation, Year-End Strategies and Charitable Gifts.* White Plains, N.Y.: Conrad Teitell, 1986.

4361. Teitell, Conrad. "Philanthropy and Estate Planning." *Trusts & Estates* 127 (July 1988): 59-60.

The Internal Revenue Service (IRS) has discussed the tax consequences associated with donating fractional portions or the entire retained income interest from a charitable remainder trust to the charitable remainderman. In nearly all cases the beneficiaries are entitled to income and gift tax charitable deductions, but a problem revolves around the right to revoke a unitrust by Will when a spouse (B) is the sole survivor beneficiary after the donor (A). In this case B is not entitled to a charitable deduction as her life interest is contingent upon two factors: B must survive A and A must not exercise his testamentary power to revoke B's survivorship interest. Thus, with "no ascertainable assurance that B's contingent interest will ever pass to charity," B's contribution of interest does not qualify for tax deduction. IRS also ruled that when the governing instrument of a trust does not provide for charitable payments or set-asides, the trust may not deduct charitable payments made by assignment.

4362. Teitell, Conrad. "A Tale of Two Donors: Claiming Charitable Deductions." *Trusts & Estates* 124 (September 1985): 57+.

4363. Teitell, Conrad. "A Tax Guide to Contributions." *Trusts & Estates* 126 (August 1987): 25-32.

Provides the tax benefits of charitable contributions of a wide variety of gifts to schools, churches, hospitals and other public charities by those who itemize their deductions, together with the relevant Internal Revenue Code sections, Treasury regulations, revenue rulings and court cases. Examines deductibles for gifts made by individuals, enhanced deductions for gifts of inventory made by corporations, fair market value, volunteer expenses, charitable remainder trusts, pooled income funds, charitable gift annuities, and charitable lead trusts.

4364. Teitell, Conrad. "Tax Reform Act of 1976: Effects on Charitable Giving." *Trusts & Estates* 116 (January 1977): 46-50.

4365. Teitell, Conrad. *Tax Techniques in Fund-Raising.* New York: Philanthropy Tax Institute, 1968.

4366. Teitell, Conrad. "TRA '84 Provisions Affecting Charities and Donors." *Trusts & Estates* 15 (October 1984): 15-8.

4367. Teitell, Conrad. *You Can Be a Philanthropist: Ten Painless Ways.* White Plains, N.Y.: Conrad Teitell, 1983.

4368. Teltsch, Kathleen. "Charities Gear Up for a Fight over the Treasury's Tax Plan." *New York Times* (24 January 1985).

4369. Teltsch, Kathleen. "Nonprofit Groups Said to Face Big Cuts in U.S. Aid." *New York Times* (21 April 1985): 28.

4370. Thompson, Robert L. "Why Philanthropy Will Overcome Tax Reform." *Fund Raising Management* 19 (April 1988): 44, 46, 48.

Predicts that philanthropy will not only survive the Tax Reform Act of 1986, but that it should thrive under it. Survival of philanthropy is based on the assertion that tax considerations have never been the primary motivation of either large or small donors, while the thriving of charitable of giving is attributed to human nature, philanthropic history, the unity of purpose demonstrated by fundraisers and others related to philanthropy, and to the positive aspects of the tax law itself: with many long-standing deductions having been eliminated, the charitable gift remains one of the few voluntary ways for itemizers to reduce income tax; deferred giving vehicles offer donors opportunities to avoid the high taxation on capital gains and the reduction on tax subsidized savings for retirement income; gifts of appreciated property to charities are still deductible at fair market value, thus avoiding the new twenty-eight percent capital gains taxes; and the new tax law will create more disposable income for Americans, which appears to be the key factor in giving by individuals.

4371. Tidd, Jonathan G. "Impact of TRA '84 on Nonprofits." *Trusts & Estates* 15 (October 1984): 22-6.

4372. Tidd, Jonathan G. "Tax Act May Hurt Charitable Giving." *Trusts & Estates* (December 1981): 16-8.

4373. Topinka, James E., Carolyn Mar, and Barbara H. Schilling. *A Guide to the California Nonprofit Public Benefit Corporation Law.* 1st ed. San Francisco: Management Center, 1981.

4374. Treusch, Paul E., and Norman A. Sugarman. *Tax-Exempt Charitable Organizations.* 2nd ed. Philadelphia: American Law Institute, 1983.

Basic text on tax law and charitable organizations discusses the pros and cons of operating as a tax-exempt organization, the categories under which exemption may be obtained, the tax consequences of unrelated business income, and other relevant legal information.

4375. Trompeter, Jean E. "Formation and Qualification of a Charitable Organization." *Milwaukee Lawyer* 7 (Fall 1983): 5+.

4376. Troyer, Thomas A., Walter B. Slocombe, and Robert A. Boisture. *The New Tax Law: A Guide for Child Welfare Organizations*. New York: Child Welfare League of America, [1982].

4377. United States Conference of Mayors. *The Taxpayers' Revolt and the Arts: A U.S. Conference of Mayors' Position Paper*. Washington: U.S. Conference of Mayors, 1978.

4378. United States. Congress. House. *Additional Views of Angier L. Goodwin*. Washington: Government Printing Office, 1954.

4379. United States. Congress. House. *Hearing before the Select Committee to Investigate Foundations and Other Organizations, 82nd Congress, 2nd Session*. Washington: Government Printing Office, 1952.

4380. United States. Congress. House. *Hearings before a Subcommittee of the Committee on Government Operations. (Federal Agencies and Philanthropies.) 85th Congress, 2nd Session*. Washington: Government Printing Office, 1958.

4381. United States. Congress. House. *Hearings before the Select Committee to Investigate Tax-Exempt Foundations and Comparable Organizations, 82nd Congress, 2nd Session*. Washington: Government Printing Office, 1952.

4382. United States. Congress. House. *Hearings before the Special Committee to Investigate Tax-Exempt Foundations and Comparable Organizations, 83rd Congress, 2nd Session. 2 Vols*. Washington: Government Printing Office, 1954.

4383. United States. Congress. House. *Patman Report*. 1962-1964. Washington: Government Printing Office, 19—.

4384. United States. Congress. House. *Public Law 91-172, 91st Congress, H.R. 13270, December 30, 1969: An Act to Reform the Income Tax Laws*. Washington: Government Printing Office, 1969.

4385. United States. Congress. House. *Tax-Exempt Foundations and Charitable Trusts: Their Impact on Our Economy*. 4th installment. Washington: Government Printing Office, 1966.

4386. United States. Congress. House. *Tax-Exempt Foundations and Charitable Trusts: Their Impact on Our Economy*. 5th installment. Washington: Government Printing Office, 1967.

4387. United States. Congress. House. *Tax-Exempt Foundations and Charitable Trusts: Their Impact on Our Economy*. 7th installment. Washington: Government Printing Office, 1969.

4388. United States. Congress. House. *Tax Reform Act of 1983. H.R. 4170, Title III, 98th Congress, 1st Session*. Washington: Government Printing Office, 1983.

4389. United States. Congress. House. Committee of Conference. *Tax Reform Act of 1969. Conference Report (to Accompany H.R. 13270) 91st Congress, 1st Session, December 21, 1969*. Washington: Government Printing Office, [1970].

4390. United States. Congress. House. Committee on Banking and Currency. Subcommittee on Domestic Finance. *The Fifteen Largest United States Foundations: Financial Structure and the Impact of the Tax Reform Act of 1969*. Washington: Government Printing Office, 1971.

4391. United States. Congress. House. Committee on Banking and Currency. *Hearings before the Subcommittee on Domestic Finance of the Committee on Banking and Currency. Tax-Exempt Foundations and Charitable Trusts: Their Compliance with the Provisions of the Tax Reform Act of 1969*. Washington: Government Printing Office, 1973.

4392. United States. Congress. House. Committee on Banking and Currency. *Tax-Exempt Foundations and Charitable Trusts: Their Impact on Our Economy*. 8th installment. Washington: Government Printing Office, 1972.

4393. United States. Congress. House. Committee on Finance. *Hearing before the Committee on Finance, U.S. Senate, 91st Congress. 1st Session. Improper Payments by Private Foundations to Government Officials*. Washington: Government Printing Office, 1969.

4394. United States. Congress. House. Committee on Government Operations. Subcommittee on Commerce, Consumer and Monetary Affairs. *IRS Oversight of Tax-Exempt Foundations, 98th Congress, 1st Session, May 11, 1983*. Washington: Government Printing Office, 1983.

4395. United States. Congress. House. Committee on Ways and Means. *Charitable Distribution Requirements for Private Foundations*. Washington: Government Printing Office, 1972.

4396. United States. Congress. House. Committee on Ways and Means. *Hearings before the Committee on Ways and Means, House of Representatives, on the Subject of Tax Reform, 91st Congress, 1st Session. 6 Vols*. Washington: Government Printing Office, 1969.

4397. United States. Congress. House. Committee on Ways and Means. *Hearings before the Committee on Ways and Means, House of Representatives. Part 2: On the Subject of Tax Reform, 91st Congress, 1st Session*. Washington: Government Printing Office, 1969.

4398. United States. Congress. House. Committee on Ways and Means. *Hearings on the Subject of General Tax Reform, 93rd Congress, 1st Session. 3 Vols.* Washington: Government Printing Office, 1973.

4399. United States. Congress. House. Committee on Ways and Means. *Legislative Activity by Certain Types of Exempt Organizations. Hearings on H.R. 13720, May 3, 4 and 5, to Amend the Internal Revenue Code of 1954 with Respect to Lobbying by Certain Types of Exempt Organizations, 92nd Congress, 2nd Session.* Washington: Government Printing Office, 1972.

4400. United States. Congress. House. Committee on Ways and Means. *Press Release Announcing Tentative Decisions to Date on Tax Reform Subjects As Announced by Chairman Wilbur D. Mills on May 27, 1969, 91st Congress, 1st Session.* Washington: Government Printing Office, 1969.

4401. United States. Congress. House. Committee on Ways and Means. *Tax Reform Act of 1969: Report of the Committee on Ways and Means to Accompany H.R. 13270, a Bill to Reform the Income Tax Laws with Separate and Supplemental Views, 91st Congress, 1st Session. 2 Vols.* Washington: Government Printing Office, 1969.

4402. United States. Congress. House. Committee on Ways and Means. *Tax Reform Proposals Contained in the Message from the President on April 21, 1969 and Presented by Representatives of the Treasury Department to the Committee on Ways and Means, April 22, 1969, 91st Congress, 1st Session.* Washington: Government Printing Office, 1969.

4403. United States. Congress. House. Committee on Ways and Means. *Tax Rules Governing Foundations. 98th Congress, 1st Session. 2 Vols.* Washington: Government Printing Office, 1984.

Transcripts of the hearings to examine the impact of the *Tax Reform Act of 1969* on the vitality of private foundations. Includes testimony from private tax practitioners, legal scholars, private foundation managers, and recipients of private foundation grants.

4404. United States. Congress. House. Committee on Ways and Means. *Treasury Department Report on Private Foundations. 89th Congress, 1st Session.* Washington: Government Printing Office, 1965.

4405. United States. Congress. House. Committee on Ways and Means. *Written Statements by Interested Individuals and Organizations on Treasury Department Report on Private Foundations Issued on February 2, 1964, Submitted to Committee on Ways and Means, 89th Congress, 1st Session.* Washington: Government Printing Office, 1965.

4406. United States. Congress. House. Committee on Ways and Means. *Written Statements Submitted by Witnesses Scheduled to Appear before the Committee on Ways and Means at Hearings on the Subject of Tax Reform on February 18-24, 1969, 91st Congress, 1st Session. 5 Vols.* Washington: Government Printing Office, 1969.

4407. United States. Congress. House. Committee on Ways and Means. Subcommittee on Oversight. *Development of the Law and Continuing Legal Issues in the Tax Treatment of Private Foundations, 98th Congress, 1st Session, June 17, 1983.* Washington: Government Printing Office, 1983.

4408. United States. Congress. House. Committee on Ways and Means. Subcommittee on Oversight. *Honorable Richard Shelby before the Subcommittee on Oversight, June 28, 1983, 98th Congress, 1st Session.* Washington: Government Printing Office, 1983.

4409. United States. Congress. House. Committee on Ways and Means. Subcommittee on Oversight. *Outline of Testimony of Malcolm L. Stein before the Subcommittee on Oversight, June 28, 1983, 98th Congress, 1st Session.* Washington: Government Printing Office, 1983.

4410. United States. Congress. House. Committee on Ways and Means. Subcommittee on Oversight. *Remarks of David E. Rogers, M.D., President, the Robert Wood Johnson Foundation before the Subcommittee on Oversight, June 28, 1983, 98th Congress, 1st Session.* Washington: Government Printing Office, 1983.

4411. United States. Congress. House. Committee on Ways and Means. Subcommittee on Oversight. *Report and Recommendations Concerning Federal and Tax Rules Governing Private Foundations, 98th Congress, 1st Session, September 28, 1983.* Washington: Government Printing Office, 1983.

4412. United States. Congress. House. Committee on Ways and Means. Subcommittee on Oversight. *Report of the Committee on Ways and Means, U.S. House of Representatives on H.R. 4170, Title III, 98th Congress, 1st Session.* Washington: Government Printing Office, 1983.

4413. United States. Congress. House. Committee on Ways and Means. Subcommittee on Oversight. *Statement by Congressman Mickey Leland, Hearings of the Subcommittee on Oversight, June 28, 1983, 98th Congress, 1st Session.* Washington: Government Printing Office, 1983.

4414. United States. Congress. House. Committee on Ways and Means. Subcommittee on Oversight. *Statement of Johnny C. Finch, Associate Director, U.S. General Accounting Office before the Subcommittee on Oversight, June 28, 1983, 98th Congress, 1st Session.* Washington: Government Printing Office, 1983.

4415. United States. Congress. House. Committee on Ways and Means. Subcommittee on Oversight. *Statement of Joseph J. DioGuirdi, C.P.A., Tax Partner Arthur Andersen and Co. before the Subcommittee on Oversight, Committee on Ways and Means. Hearings, June 28, 1983, 98th Congress, 1st Session.* Washington: Government Printing Office, 1983.

4416. United States. Congress. House. Committee on Ways and Means. Subcommittee on Oversight. *Statement of Millie Torres before the Subcommittee on Oversight, June 15, 1983, 98th Congress, 1st Session.* Washington: Government Printing Office, 1983.

4417. United States. Congress. House. Committee on Ways and Means. Subcommittee on Oversight. *Statement of the Honorable James P. Shannon before the Subcommittee on Oversight, June 28, 1983, 98th Congress, 1st Session.* Washington: Government Printing Office, 1983.

4418. United States. Congress. House. Committee on Ways and Means. Subcommittee on Oversight. *Tax Administration: Information on Lobbying and Political Activities of Tax-Exempt Organizations.* Gaithersburg, Md.: U.S. General Accounting Office, 1987.
Report of the General Accounting Office to the Committee on Ways and Means provides a brief description of relevant statutes which address political and lobbying activities by tax-exempt organizations; statistics on the number and type of tax-exempt organizations which engage in political and lobbying activities; and general information on the Internal Revenue Service's program(s) designed to monitor lobbying and political activities of tax-exempt organizations.

4419. United States. Congress. House. Committee on Ways and Means. Subcommittee on Oversight. *Testimony of Brian O'Connell, President, Independent Sector, before the Subcommittee on Oversight, June 27, 1983, 98th Congress, 1st Session.* Washington: Government Printing Office, 1983.

4420. United States. Congress. House. Committee on Ways and Means. Subcommittee on Oversight. *Testimony of Dorothy A. Johnson, Executive Director, Council of Michigan Foundations, Hearings before Subcommittee on Oversight, 98th Congress, 1st Session, June 28, 1983.* Washington: Government Printing Office, 1983.

4421. United States. Congress. House. Committee on Ways and Means. Subcommittee on Oversight. *Testimony of J. Stoddard Hayes, Jr. on Behalf of the American Bankers Association before the Subcommittee on Oversight, June 28, 1983, 98th Congress, 1st Session.* Washington: Government Printing Office, 1983.

4422. United States. Congress. House. Committee on Ways and Means. Subcommittee on Oversight. *Testimony of James P. Shannon, Executive Director of General Mills Foundation before Subcommittee on Oversight, 98th Congress, 1st Session, June 28, 1983.* Washington: Government Printing Office, 1983.

4423. United States. Congress. House. Committee on Ways and Means. Subcommittee on Oversight. *Testimony of Janet C. Taylor, Executive Director, Associated Grantmakers of Massachusetts before the Subcommittee on Oversight, 98th Congress, 1st Session, June 28, 1983.* Washington: Government Printing Office, 1983.

4424. United States. Congress. House. Committee on Ways and Means. Subcommittee on Oversight. *Testimony of John L. Currin, Counselor and Secretary on Behalf of Richard F. Schubert, President, the American Red Cross, before the House Subcommittee on Oversight of the Committee on Ways and Means, 98th Congress, 1st Session.* Washington: Government Printing Office, 1983.

4425. United States. Congress. House. Committee on Ways and Means. Subcommittee on Oversight. *Testimony of Marjorie P. Allen, President of the Powell Family Foundation. Hearings before the House Subcommittee on Oversight, Committee on Ways and Means, 98th Congress, 1st Session.* Washington: Government Printing Office, 1983.

4426. United States. Congress. House. Committee on Ways and Means. Subcommittee on Oversight. *Testimony of Norman B. Ture, Chairman, Institute for Research on the Economics of Taxation before the Subcommittee on Oversight, June 28, 1983, 98th Congress, 1st Session.* Washington: Government Printing Office, 1983.

4427. United States. Congress. House. Committee on Ways and Means. Subcommittee on Oversight. *Testimony of Pablo Eisenberg, President, Center for Community Change, before the Subcommittee on Oversight, June 28, 1983, 98th Congress, 1st Session.* Washington: Government Printing Office, 1983.

4428. United States. Congress. House. Committee on Ways and Means. Subcommittee on Oversight. *Testimony of Wilbur D. Mills, Counsel, Shea and Gould before the Oversight Subcommittee, 98th Congress, 1st Session.* Washington: Government Printing Office, 1983.

4429. United States. Congress. House. Committee on Ways and Means. Subcommittee on Oversight. *Testimony of William L. Bondurant before the Oversight Subcommittee, June 28, 1983, 98th Congress, 1st Session.* Washington: Government Printing Office, 1983.

4430. United States. Congress. House. Committee on Ways and Means. Subcommittee on Oversight. *Testimony Presented before the Oversight Subcommittee of the House Ways and Means Committee by Christopher F. Edley, Presented on Behalf of the United Negro College Fund, 98th Congress, 1st Session.* Washington: Government Printing Office, 1983.

4431. United States. Congress. House. Select Committee on Small Business. *Tax-Exempt Foundations and Charitable Trusts: Their Impact on Our Economy.* Washington: Government Printing Office, 1964.

4432. United States. Congress. House. Select Committee on Small Business. Subcommittee No. 1. *Tax-Exempt Foundations: Their Impact on Small Business.* Washington: Government Printing Office, 1967.

4433. United States. Congress. Joint Committee on Internal Revenue Taxation. *General Explanation of the Tax Reform Act of 1969, H.R. 13270, 91st Congress, Public Law 91-172.* Washington: Government Printing Office, 1970.

4434. United States. Congress. Joint Committee on Taxation. *Description of Income Tax Provisions Relating to Private Foundations. Scheduled for Hearings before the Subcommittee on Oversight of the Committee on Ways and Means on June 27, 28, and 30, 1983.* Washington: Government Printing Office, 1983.

4435. United States. Congress. Joint Committee on Taxation. *Tax Policy: Competition between Taxable Businesses and Tax-Exempt Organizations.* Gaithersburg, Md.: U.S. General Accounting Office, 1987.

Report of the General Accounting Office to the Joint Committee on Taxation provides available information relating to the issue of competition between taxable businesses and tax-exempt organizations. Examines the evolution and growth of the tax-exempt community; various legislative and administrative efforts that address the competition issue; and concerns voiced by representatives of selected taxable businesses and tax-exempt organizations about the issue.

4436. United States. Congress. Senate. *Intelligence Activities and the Rights of Americans. Book 2: Final Report of the Select Committee to Study Governmental Activities, 94th Congress.* Washington: Government Printing Office, 1976.

4437. United States. Congress. Senate. Committee on Finance. *Committee Amendment (in the Nature of a Substitute) Reported by Mr. Long, from the Committee on Finance, to H.R. 13270, an Act to Reform the Income Tax Laws, Calender No. 547, 91st Congress, 1st Session.* Washington: Government Printing Office, 1969.

4438. United States. Congress. Senate. Committee on Finance. *Hearings before the Committee on Finance, United States Senate, 91st Congress, 1st Session, on H.R. 13270 to Reform the Income Tax Laws. 3 Vols.* Washington: Government Printing Office, 1969.

4439. United States. Congress. Senate. Committee on Finance. *Hearings before the Subcommittee on Foundations of the Committee on Finance. The Role of Private Foundations in Today's Society and a Review of the Impact of Charitable Provisions of the Tax Reform Act of 1969..., 93rd Congress, 1st Session.* Washington: Government Printing Office, 1973.

4440. United States. Congress. Senate. Committee on Finance. *H.R. 13270. An Act to Reform the Income Tax Laws, 91st Congress, 1st Session.* Washington: Government Printing Office, 1969.

4441. United States. Congress. Senate. Committee on Finance. *Impact of Current Economic Crisis on Foundations and Recipients of Foundation Money. Hearings, 93rd Congress, 2nd Session, November 25-26, 1974.* Washington: Government Printing Office, 1974.

4442. United States. Congress. Senate. Committee on Finance. *Improper Payments by Private Foundations to Government Officials. Hearings before the Committee on Finance, United States Senate, 91st Congress, 1st Session on S. 2075, June 4, 1969.* Washington: Government Printing Office, 1969.

4443. United States. Congress. Senate. Committee on Finance. *Public Inspection of IRS Private Letter Rulings. Hearing before the Subcommittee on Administration of the Internal Revenue Code, 94th Congress.* Washington: Government Printing Office, 1975.

4444. United States. Congress. Senate. Committee on Finance. *Role of Private Foundations in Today's Society and a Review of the Impact of the Tax Reform Act of 1969. Hearings.* Washington: Government Printing Office, 1974.

4445. United States. Congress. Senate. Committee on Finance. *Summary of H.R. 13270 Tax Reform Act of 1969. As Reported by the Committee on Finance, Russell B. Long, Chairman, 91st Congress, 1st Session.* Washington: Government Printing Office, 1969.

4446. United States. Congress. Senate. Committee on Finance. *Summary of H.R. 13270, the Tax Reform Act of 1969 (As Passed by the House of Representatives), 91st Congress, 1st Session.* Washington: Government Printing Office, 1969.

4447. United States. Congress. Senate. Committee on Finance. *Tax Reform Act of 1969. Compilation of Decisions Reached in Executive Session.* Washington: Government Printing Office, 1969.

4448. United States. Congress. Senate. Committee on Finance. *Tax Reform Act of 1969. H.R. 13270. Part A: Testimony to Be Received Tuesday, September 9, 1969. Part B: Additional Statements (Topic: Foundations), 91st Congress, 1st Session.* Washington: Government Printing Office, 1969.

4449. United States. Congress. Senate. Committee on Finance. *Tax Reform Act of 1969. H.R. 13270: Testimony to Be Received Wednesday, October 22, 1969 (Topic: Foundations), 91st Congress, 1st Session.* Washington: Government Printing Office, 1969.

4450. United States. Congress. Senate. Committee on Finance. *Tax Reform Act of 1976. Supplemental Report.* Washington: Government Printing Office, 1976.

4451. United States. Congress. Senate. Committee on Finance. Subcommittee on Foundations. *The Role of Foundations Today and the Effect of the Tax Reform Act of 1969 upon Foundations. Testimony Presented October 1-2, 1973, 93rd Congress, 1st Session.* Washington: Government Printing Office, 1973.

4452. United States. Congress. Senate. Committee on Finance. Subcommittee on Foundations. *Role of Private Foundations in Public Broadcasting. Hearings before the Subcommittee on Foundations, 93rd Congress, 2nd Session.* Washington: Government Printing Office, 1974.

4453. United States. Congress. Senate. Committee on Interstate and Foreign Commerce. *Hearings before Subcommittee on the Committee on Interstate and Foreign Commerce, Senate, 80th Congress, 2nd Session. 2 Vols.* Washington: Government Printing Office, 1948-9.

4454. United States. Congress. Senate. Committee on Labor and Public Welfare. Subcommittee on Employment, Manpower, and Poverty. *Tax Exemptions for Charitable Organizations Affecting Poverty Programs: Examination of Internal Revenue Service Decision to Deny Tax-Exempt Status to Charitable Organizations Which Engage in Litigation Affecting Poverty Programs. Hearings, 91st Congress, 2nd Session, November 16-17, 1970.* Washington: Government Printing Office, 1970.

4455. United States. Department of the Treasury. *Tax Reform Studies and Proposals U.S. Treasury Department: Joint Publication Committee on Ways and Means of the House and Committee on Finance of the Senate, February 5, 1969, 91st Congress, 1st Session. 3 Vols.* Washington: Government Printing Office, 1969.

4456. United States. Department of the Treasury. Internal Revenue Service. *Highlights of 1969 Changes in the Tax Law.* Washington: Government Printing Office, 1970.

4457. United States. Department of the Treasury. Internal Revenue Service. *Instructions for Form 990-PF. Return of Private Foundation or Section 4947(a)(1) Trust Treated As a Private Foundation.* Washington: Government Printing Office, 1987.

4458. United States. Department of the Treasury. Internal Revenue Service. *IRS Rulings Re: Tax Reform Act of 1969.* Washington: Government Printing Office, 1970.

4459. United States. Department of the Treasury. Internal Revenue Service. *IRS Rulings Re: Tax Reform Act of 1969.* Washington: Government Printing Office, 1971.

4460. United States. Department of the Treasury. Internal Revenue Service. *IRS Rulings Re: Tax Reform Act of 1969. April 1971-October 1971.* Washington: Government Printing Office, 1971.

4461. United States. Department of the Treasury. Internal Revenue Service. *Projections. Calendar Years 1985-1992: Number of Returns to Be Filed.* Washington: U.S. Department of the Treasury. Internal Revenue Service, 1985.

4462. United States. Department of the Treasury. Internal Revenue Service. *Return of Organizations Exempt from Income Tax.* Washington: Government Printing Office, 1988.

4463. United States. Department of the Treasury. Internal Revenue Service. *Returns for Private Foundations Exempt from Income Tax, 1973.* Washington: Government Printing Office, [1974].

4464. United States. Department of the Treasury. Internal Revenue Service. *Statistics of Income: Exempt Organization Studies. 1982-1988.* Washington: U.S. Department of the Treasury. Internal Revenue Service, 19—.
Contains final report on private foundations, preliminary estimates for selected Form 990 data, and a discussion of the SBA report, *Statistical Profile of the Nonprofit Sector*.

4465. United Way of America. *The 1981 Tax Act and Charitable Organizations.* Alexandria, Va.: United Way of America, 1982.

4466. United Way of America. *Tax Policies and United Ways.* Alexandria, Va.: United Way of America, 1983.

4467. Urban Institute. "The Economic Recovery Program and the Non-Profit Sector." *Urban Institute Policy and Research Report* 2 (Fall 1981): 5+.

4468. Urrows, Henry. "TRA '69: Coming Up on 10 Years." *Foundation News* (May-June 1979): 23-8.

4469. Volunteer Lawyers for the Arts. *New York Not-for-Profit Organization Manual.* New York: Volunteer Lawyers for the Arts, 1982.
An attorney's guide to incorporating in New York State and gaining tax-exempt status.

4470. Walker, Tom. "Foundations Face Uncertainty." *Journal Constitution* (1 October 1972).

4471. *The Washington Lobby.* Washington: Congressional Quarterly, 1971.

4472. "Ways and Means Subcommittee Releases UBIT Options." *NonProfit Times* 2 (May 1988): 27-9.

Reprint of the House Ways and Means Subcommittee on Oversight's press release of March 31 detailing what it calls "preliminary discussion options regarding the unrelated business income tax." Includes such options as repealing the substantially related test and replacing it with a directly related test, or retaining the "substantially related test and imposing Unrelated Business Income Tax (UBIT) on specified activities, which are listed, whose nature and scope are inherently commercial rather than charitable; a suggested modification of the definition of control in the case of exempt organizations having taxable subsidiaries; and expansion of tax information reporting and IRS administration.

4473. Webster, George D., and Frederick J. Krebs. *Associations and Lobbying. A Guide for Non-Profit Organizations.* Washington: Chamber of Commerce of the United States, 1979.

4474. Weithorn, Stanley S. *Tax Techniques for Foundations and Other Exempt Organizations.* 5 Vols. New York: Matthew Bender & Co., 1972.

4475. Wellford, Harrison, and Janne C. Gallagher. *The Myth of Unfair Competition by Nonprofit Organizations: A Review of Government Assistance to Small Business.* New York: Family Service Association of America, 1985.

Report presents the results of an analysis of the federal tax treatment of small business and nonprofit organizations which provide human services. Outlines the assistance available to small businesses under the federal tax code and through various federal programs. Concludes that nonprofit organizations do not enjoy a substantial competitive advantage over small business and that further restrictions are not warranted.

4476. "Why College Donors Are Uptight: House-Passed Tax Bill Would Change Rules on Donations and Could Reduce Gifts." *Business Week* (November 8 1969): 126-8.

4477. Williamson, J. Peter. *Foundation Investment Strategies: New Possibilities in the 1981 Tax Law.* Mt. Kisco, N.Y.: Seven Springs Center, 1981.

4478. Wormser, Rene A. *Your Will and What Not to Do about It.* New York: Simon & Schuster, 1937.

4479. "Your Family's Financial Future. Impact of New Tax Law: An Interview with Conrad Teitell." *U.S. News and World Report* (21 September 1981).

4480. Zimmerman, Dennis. "1985 Tax Reform Options and Charitable Contributions." *Philanthropy Monthly* 18 (May 1985): 23-31.

10

VOLUNTARISM

4481. Adams, James Luther. *Voluntary Associations: Socio-Cultural Analyses and Theological Interpretation.* Chicago: Exploration Press, 1986.

Collection of essays by James Luther Adams which concerns itself with the history, theology, ethics, sociology, and politics of voluntary associations. Covering a period of forty years, the essays are grouped chronologically within three major sections. The first introduces the theological and cultural analyses that inform Adams' approach. The second scrutinizes the role of voluntary associations in the promotion of democratic values. In the third, Adams brings a multidisciplinary theology of voluntary associations to bear on the wide range of personal, professional, political, and economic issues in contemporary society, and explores the possibilities of new avenues of human fulfillment. The editor writes, "Interpreting and undergirding each of these essays is Adams' central conviction that human beings are made for the life of free association, and that divine reality, the Holy Spirit, is manifest in all associations committed to the democratic pursuit of justice in the common life."

4482. Adams, Katherine. "Investing in Volunteers: A Guide to Effective Volunteer Management." *Conserve Neighborhoods* 47 (1985): 1-16.

4483. Allen, Kerry Kenn. "National Conference Sharpens Focus of Volunteer Community." *Volunteering* (September-October 1984): 3-5.

Reports on Volunteer's 1984 National Conference on Citizen Involvement.

4484. Allen, Kerry Kenn. "Volunteering in America." *Voluntary Action Leadership* (Winter 1982): 18-333.

4485. Allen, Kerry Kenn. "Volunteering in America, 1982-83." *Voluntary Action Leadership* (Winter 1983): 22-5.

4486. Beattie, L. Elizabeth. "Business Voluntarism Means Giving People As Well As Money." *Fund Raising Management* 16 (September 1985): 110+.

4487. Bentley-Kasman, Jeremy. *Volunteer to Career: A Study of Student Volunteerism and Employability and a Directory of Employers Recognizing the Volunteer Experience of Recent College Graduates.* New York: Mayor's Voluntary Action Center, 1983.

4488. Berg, Barbara J. *The Remembered Gate. Origins of American Feminism: The Woman and the City, 1800-1860.* New York: Oxford University Press, 1978.

Berg's thesis is that the roots of feminism, as we understand it today and as distinct from "women's rights," lie in the benevolent aspirations and activities of early nineteenth-century women. It is in the growing cities, Berg argues, that women first began to resist the "woman-belle" ideal that arose with the increasingly circumscribed role for women in post-colonial society. Through their work in voluntary societies, women began to find outlets for fuller and expanding expressions of their abilities and sensibilities. Berg asserts that, unlike their male counterparts in charitable activity, women developed a geniune affection for and identification with their poor sisters, which transcended class boundaries. This nascent feminism was mitigated by the concern of the women's movement with abolition and the franchise in subsequent years, and has only begun to flower in our time. 450-item bibliography.

4489. Berger, Peter L., and Richard John Neuhaus. *To Empower People: The Role of Mediating Structures in Public Policy.* Washington: American Enterprise Institute, 1977.

The authors' contention is that we need a new paradigm for pluralism in social policy. They focus on the "mediating structures" of family, neighborhood, church, voluntary associations, and ethnic and racial subcultures—the institutions closest to the control and aspirations of most Americans. These are "those institutions standing between the individual in his private life and the large institutions of public life," or megastructures. To empower people in the areas of education, child care, law enforcement, housing, social services, and health care, they recommend first that public policies be devised so that they do not weaken or undercut mediating structures, and second that public policy should, where feasible, use mediating structures to advance legitimate social goals. The chapter on voluntary associations includes a discussion of foundations.

4490. Berkowitz, Bill. *Local Heroes.* Lexington, Mass.: Lexington Books, 1987.

Series of twenty interviews with "ordinary people," nonprofessional human beings of dimension and flaw, who have worked hard, reaped some rewards, and accepted some costs, all because they were committed to making community life stronger, closer, happier and more prosperous. Their accomplishments, Berkowitz contends, should inspire us all to help build a sense of community, which may be the most neglected need on the domestic scene today.

4491. Boyte, Harry C. *The Backyard Revolution: Understanding the New Citizen Movement.* Philadelphia: Temple University Press, 1980.

Boyte had originally planned to write a book about the threat to democracy in the 1970s by new forms of corporate organization and the general domination of society by corporate goals of higher profits. But he became more and more fascinated with grassroots resistance to this "corporate offensive." He asks, "How were the massive forms of grassroots activism to be explained and what did they represent—the more than 20 million Americans who had become active in some form of neighborhood group; the farmers' protests; the growing consumer activism; the new forms of workplace organizing; the social justice trends in apparently conservative religious institutions?" Puzzled as well by the relative disinterest of the Left in such developments, he searched for and found clues to the roots of this activism in the "citizen advocacy" tradition pioneered by Saul Alinsky, Fred Rose, Ralph Nader, and others. He concludes that the citizen movement represents "an alternative popular democratic thread of insurgency in modern society" and that it grows out of "different spaces" in society than the Left. This last idea became the topic of Boyte's later book, with Sara Evans, *Free Spaces* (1986).

4492. Brooks, Andree. "Among Volunteers, Change in the Suburbs." *New York Times* (28 October 1983).

4493. Brown, Kathleen M. *Keys to Making a Volunteer Program Work.* Richmond, Calif.: Arden Publications, 1982.

4494. Brown, Kathleen M. "Thoughts on the Supervision of Volunteers." *Voluntary Action Leadership* (Spring 1984): 14-6.

4495. Brown, Kathleen M. "Training Volunteers: The Trainer As Teacher, a Personal Perspective." *Voluntary Action Leadership* (Spring 1983): 31-2.

4496. Buratto, Bill. "Think Youth: The Challenge of Youth Volunteerism." *Nonprofit World Report* 2 (May-June 1984): 16-9.

4497. Butterfield, Fox. "Universities Take Lead in New Volunteer Efforts." *New York Times* (17 October 1985).

4498. Carter, Novia. *Volunteers: The Untapped Potential.* Ottawa, Canada: Canadian Council on Social Development, [1975].

4499. Casey, Susan B. *Developing Successful Volunteer Programs: A Guide for Local Government.* Durham, N.H.: New England Municipal Center, 1982.

4500. Chambre, Susan Maizel. *Good Deeds in Old Age. Volunteering by the New Leisure Class.* Lexington, Mass.: Lexington Books, 1987.

With estimates projecting that seventeen percent of the U.S. population will be over the age of sixty-five in the year 2020, this book addresses an important issue facing American society and older people themselves: how people can construct lives with meaning in the absence of significant work and family involvements. While volunteering has been described as an important way to fashion a meaningful lifestyle in old age, Dr. ChambrB finds that it is actually a part of a more general pattern of adjustment to old age, and one which is practiced by a small segment of the older population: those with high life satisfaction and a history of successful involvement as volunteers over the course of their lives. Her recommendations for increasing the numbers and types of volunteers involves recruiting new volunteers; redirecting volunteers as they grow old; and showing sensitivity to the fact that the retention of older volunteers is closely linked to their levels of job satisfaction. Certain demographic trends do suggest that the number and proportion of older people engaged in volunteering should continue to increase: in the future, the older population will be a better-educated group, and more of it will be composed of women who are retired (as opposed to homemakers), a group who tend to be especially likely to volunteer.

4501. Clark, A. "Computers Calculate Volunteer's Future." *Volunteer Leader* 27 (Spring 1986): 1-5.

4502. Cohen, Nathan E., ed. *The Citizen Volunteer: His Responsibility, Role, and Opportunity in Modern Society.* New York: Harper & Bros., 1960.

Written primarily for the volunteer, but also germane for professionals who work with volunteers, this anthology of nineteen previously published essays touching on every aspect of voluntarism was published by the National Council of Jewish Women to commemorate their sixty-fifth year. Topics covered include why people volunteer, where and how they can do so, whether their work is important, and what the future holds for the volunteer—and vice versa. Citizen volunteers, in the words of Moise S. Cohn, who wrote the foreword, are those individuals who voluntarily accept the responsibilities as well as the rights of citizenship. Cohen, additionally, sees voluntary associations as necessary vehicles for nourishing a democracy composed of free, intelligent, and responsible citizens. Brief bibliography.

4503. Conrad, Daniel Lynn, and Diane Hedin. *Youth Service: A Guidebook for Developing and Operating Effective Programs.* Washington: Independent Sector, 1987.

Provides assistance to persons wishing to begin, expand, or promote programs of youth community service. Illustrates a number of ways in which youth can and do help in working with a variety of problems and populations; outlines ways in which community service can be integrated into the organizational structure of youth agencies and schools; examines the nuts-and-bolts issues of starting a program and keeping it operating smoothly; and offers practical suggestions for helping young people maximize the learning opportunities in their service experiences. Appendixes contain sample administrative forms, a short bibliography, and a listing of youth service resources.

4504. Conyngton, Mary. *How to Help.* New York: Ronald Press, 1906.

4505. Cott, Nancy F. *The Bonds of Womanhood: "Woman's Sphere" in New England, 1780-1835.* New Haven, Conn.: Yale University Press, 1977.

Cott examines the forces of change in women's lives prior to the 1830s, when the "cult of domesticity"—an ethic glorifying the role of woman as wife and mother—became fully evident in the writings of the time. The 1930s also became a turning point in women's economic participation, public activities, and social visibility, despite the cult of domesticity. Women entered reform movements, created societies, and became active in the anti-slavery movement, where some of them became early feminists. Cott uses a sample of 100 New England women of various ages, backgrounds, and stages of life to focus on the relationship between change in the material circumstances of women's lives and their outlook on their place as women. She shows what laid the groundwork for the events of the 1830s, including women's activity in religious and charitable associations, which comprised virtually the only public sphere available to them.

4506. Council for Financial Aid to Education. *Voluntarism, Tax Reform, and Higher Education.* New York: Council for Financial Aid to Education, 1973.

4507. Coyne, Kevin. "Volunteerism in the '80's: Takes Steps to Erase 'Miss Goody Two Shoes' Image." *Amesbury News* (16 March 1983): 1b+.

4508. de Harven, Gerry Ann. "Fostering the Voluntary Spirit: Motivating People to Serve." *Fund Raising Management* 15 (March 1984): 62-4.

4509. DeCarlo, Mary. "Performance-Based Certification: An Avenue for Professional Development and Recognition." *Voluntary Action Leadership* (Fall 1983): 25-7.

4510. Dewey, Richard E., ed. *Federal Policy and the Voluntary Sector: A Bibliography.* Washington: Coalition of National Voluntary Organizations, 1977.

4511. Dick, Alice. "Volunteers Bank Their Skills." *Exchange Networks* (Fall 1983): 6-7.

4512. Dodd, Ruth M. *Volunteer Values.* New York: Family Welfare Association of America, 1934.

This brief booklet is concerned mainly with practical suggestions for recruiting and training volunteers, but it does contain a discussion of the "unique contribution of the volunteer." Interestingly, Dodd uses feminine pronouns throughout the booklet when referring to both volunteers and professionals, and cites articles and publications written almost exclusively by women. This in itself is certainly a manifestation of the common perception of volunteering as women's work, but also implies a subtle early feminism in its tacit affirmation of territorial boundaries.

4513. Dorsey, Eugene C. "A Standard for Citizenship." *Foundation News* 28 (January-February 1987): 70-2.

Eugene Dorsey, Gannett Foundation president and chairman of the new Independent Sector initiative to double charitable giving and increase volunteering by fifty percent over the next five years outlines the campaign—*Daring Goals for a Caring Society.* The project began with an analysis of current giving levels. The study found that people with low and moderate incomes tend to give a much higher percentage of their income than the affluent. Nine out of ten Americans give money to the causes of their choice. Their total donations comprise ninety percent of all that is contributed and about half of individual contributions come from people earning less than $40,000 a year. The next campaign phase is to increase public awareness that giving is essential to maintaining and strengthening a free and caring society. With foundations and communities playing a leadership role, Dorsey believes that "organized philanthropy can help a caring society achieve its daring goals."

4514. Duca, Diane J. "Matching Executives and Nonprofits: Interview with Aetna Life and Casualty." *Board Letter* (Spring 1984): 1-2.

4515. Ellis, Susan J., and Katherine H. Noyes. *By the People. A History of Americans As Volunteers.* Philadelphia: Energize Assoc., 1978.

The intent of this book is to provide "a companion volume" for all the histories of the United States that take as their subject matter individuals with extraordinary political power, literacy, artistic or scientific genius, willingness to take unusual risks, or ability to create large and lasting empires. It focuses instead on the involvement of volunteers in "every area of American life" and traces their effect on institutions, professions, and social events in an attempt to provide "the between-the-lines material necessary to a more complete appreciation of our democratic heritage." The book also seeks to dispel certain negative stereotypical assumptions about volunteers and pays special attention to reformulating the debate about women volunteering in light of present-day and historical circumstances. After a historical account of volunteering from 1620 to the 1970s, the authors conclude with some thoughts about the future. Extensive footnotes.

4516. Ellis, Susan J. *From the Top Down: The Executive Role in Volunteer Program Success.* Philadelphia: Energize Assoc., 1986.

4517. Evans, Sara M., and Harry C. Boyte. *Free Spaces: The Sources of Democratic Change in America.* New York: Harper & Row, 1986.

Evans and Boyte seek to call attention to "that vast middle ground of communal activity between private life and large-scale institutions, as the arenas in which notions of civic virtue and a sense of responsibility for the common good are nourished, and democracy is given living meaning." These are "free spaces." The authors dispute the notion of citizenship as derived solely from politics and public life and contend that true citizenship is being expressed through voluntary activities—be they national civil rights movements or neighborhood block associations—in which the public participates. They seek thereby to redefine democratic values. The book's discussion of these issues takes place in the context of the underground activities of black slaves, the women's movement, the emergence of labor struggles, and other important social developments which had lasting effects on the evolution of American democratic society.

4518. "Everyone Benefits When Families Volunteer: A Preview of Volunteer's New Workbook for Involving Families." *Voluntary Action Leadership* (Spring 1983): 15-21.

4519. Federation of Protestant Welfare Agencies. *Funding Volunteer Services: Potential Sources of Dollars to Expand Agency Programs.* New York: Federation of Protestant Welfare Agencies, 1981.

4520. Flanagan, Joan. "The Changing Aspirations of Men and Women Volunteers." *Nonprofit Executive* 2 (December 1982): 5.

4521. Flanagan, Joan. *The Successful Volunteer Organization: Getting Started and Getting Results in Nonprofit, Charitable, Grass Roots and Community Groups.* Chicago: Contemporary Books, 1981.

Handbook offers practical advice on planning, fundraising, and managing nonprofits.

4522. Fottler, Myron D., and Carol A. Fottler. "The Management of Volunteers in Nonprofit Organizations: Theory and Practice." *Nonprofit World Report* 2 (September-October 1984): 18+.

4523. Gamwell, Franklin I. *Beyond Preference: Liberal Theories of Independent Association.* Chicago: University of Chicago Press, 1984.

Gamwell brings political theory to bear on the question of independent associations, defined as nongovernmental and noncommercial organizations. He examines the theories of Milton Friedman (nineteenth-century established liberalism), Alan Gewirth (twentieth-century established liberalism), and John Dewey (reformed liberalism) for their implications for a theory of independent associations and offers an assessment of each position. He criticizes the established liberalism of Friedman and Gewirth for internal incoherence and disagrees with the established liberal view of happiness (or self-interest) as a matter solely of preference, lacking an ethical or moral criterion. Gamwell believes that insofar as Dewey lays a moral foundation for human behavior, his is the superior theory. In the end, going beyond Dewey to posit his own theory, Gamwell outlines a metaphysical position onto which he grafts Dewey's theory of independent associations. His conclusion is that independent associations "constitute the most important class of associations in our public life."

4524. Geraghty, Laura Lee M. "The Changing Profession of Volunteer Administration." *Voluntary Action Leadership* (Spring 1984): 11+.

4525. Gorman, Paul, and Ram Dass. *How Can I Help? Stories and Reflections on Service.* New York: Alfred A. Knopf, 1985.

This book for a general audience explores a number of issues related to the concept of service as it applies to our everyday lives. The authors try to consider what is common to all forms of helping, from organized volunteering to "common courtesies, thoughtful gestures, the simplest moments of human affirmation." Some of their questions include: What exactly is the nature of conscious service? What are the challenges posed by present conditions? What are the important issues being encountered by people active in service and social action in America? The authors interviewed widely and researched the files of voluntary action centers across the country. They have included first-hand accounts liberally in the book in a seemingly endless illustration of the forms that helping takes, the feeling it inspires, and the effects it achieves.

4526. Gowen, George W. *A Willingness of Heart: Volunteerism and the Non-Profit Organization in the American Society.* Privately Printed, 1983.

Essays originally prepared to introduce students at the New York University Graduate School of Business Administration to nonprofit organizations. The majority of essays address a selection of the many operational, legal and economic concerns confronted by nonprofits, while the opening and closing chapters reflect the philosophical basis of the American experience from which voluntarism draws its strength.

4527. Graff, Linda L. "Considering the Many Facets of Volunteer/Union Relations." *Voluntary Action Leadership* (Summer 1984): 16-20.

4528. *A Guide for Youth Participation and Youth Programs.* Washington: Sister Cities International.

4529. Hamann, Joan. "Volunteerism." *Voluntary World Report* 2 (November-December 1984): 15-7.

4530. Harman, John D., ed. *Volunteerism in the Eighties: Fundamental Issues in Voluntary Action.* Lanham, Md.: University Press of America, 1982.

This is a collection of fourteen essays and responses. Of particular interest are Kerry Kenn Allen, *Social Responsibility: the Growing Partnership of Business and Voluntary Organizations*; Nelson Rosenbaum, *Government Funding and the Voluntary Sector: Impacts and Options*; David Horton Smith, *Altruism, Volunteers and Volunteerism*; and Jon Van Til, *Volunteering and Democratic Theory.* These essays, and the others with them, address both conceptual and practical issues. Smith challenges the common assumption that altruism is a primary motivation for volunteering, drawing on the perspectives and findings of different disciplines. His own conclusions are then challenged by Harlan Miller. Jon Van Til's discussion of the part voluntary action plays in defining democracy also poses some conceptual difficulties for respondent Deborah Mayo. And Allen's appraisal of the benefits and problems of corporate support for volunteer efforts prompts some comments from Richard Wokutch and Alex DeNoble, representing the business view.

4531. Hausknecht, Murray. *The Joiners: A Sociological Description of Voluntary Association Membership in the United States.* New York: Bedminster Press, 1962.

Hausknecht seeks to find out if voluntary associations do, in fact, play the critical role in contemporary democratic society ascribed to them by social theory. He bases his conclusions on empirical evidence—the statistics of two mid-1950s national surveys—about the extent of voluntary association membership in the United States. He examines the correlation between socioeconomic status and "life cycle," religious preference, and other factors. There is discussion of different types of voluntary associations. The author finally uses the data to test certain hypotheses about the functions of voluntary membership for the individual and for society as a whole. Brief bibliography.

4532. Hayes, Helen, and Larry Jaffee. "First Lady of Theater Always a Pushover for a Good Cause." *Fund Raising Management* 16 (September 1985): 54+.

Helen Hayes talks about her volunteer efforts.

4533. Henderson, Charles R. "The Place and Functions of Voluntary Associations." *The American Journal of Sociology* 1 (1895-1896): 327-34.

This article represents an attempt to systematically define and categorize the kinds of voluntary associations that "ask the time and funds of thinkers and philanthropists." Henderson defines the voluntary association as "that form of social cooperation in which the conscious choice of each member determines his membership." He does not consider family, state, or, notably, church, to number among voluntary associations. Voluntary associations are seen to satisfy transitory needs of society or the wants of a particular or limited group, to develop and apply criticism of established customs and institutions, to experiment locally with methods that may later be exported to a larger audience, and to supply personal service where the bureaucracy of church or state cannot. While he recognizes that there may be too many voluntary associations and some bad ones, Henderson endorses the principle of voluntary associations.

4534. Hodgkins, R.C., Jr. "Your Program Is Worth More Than You Think: An Introduction to Volunteer Program Cost Accountability." *Voluntary Action Leadership* (Spring 1983): 27-30.

4535. Hofstader, Richard. *The Age of Reform: From Bryan to F.D.R.* New York: Alfred A. Knopf, 1965.

Hofstader analyses the reform movements of 1890 through the Second World War, dividing them into three main episodes: "the agrarian uprising that found its most intense expression in the Populism of the 1890s and the Bryan campaign of 1896; the Progressive movement, which extended from about 1900-1914; and the New Deal, whose dynamic phase was concentrated in a few years of the 1930s." He focuses throughout on the ideas of the participants in these movements: "the most characteristic thinking...the middlebrow writers...the issues as they were presented in the popular magazines, the muckraking articles, the campaign speeches, and the essays of the representative journalists and influential publicists." While he does not deal with charitable or social reform separately from larger political movements, the book provides a useful, analytical background for other works that examine aspects of social and charitable reform more systematically.

4536. "How to Recruit Good Corporate Volunteers." *FRI Monthly Portfolio* 22 (April 1983): 8.

4537. Hunter, Bill. "The New Face of Volunteerism." *American Way* 17 (May 1984): 130+.

4538. Independent Sector. *Americans Volunteer, 1981.* Washington: Independent Sector, 1982.

4539. Independent Sector. *Individual Giving and Volunteering.* [Cassette tape]. Washington: Independent Sector, 1985.

4540. Kaminer, Wendy. *Women Volunteering: The Pleasure, Pain, and Politics of Unpaid Work from 1830 to the Present.* Garden City, N.Y.: Anchor Press, 1984.

Based on extensive interviews with women of all ages, this book examines the attitudes of women toward volunteering as they contrast it to paid work and other options now available to them. There is a brief overview of the recent history of volunteering and women's role in it from the 1830s through the 1920s. Kaminer also analyzes the effects of the women's movement on attitudes of today's younger women. Kaminer concludes, "To suggest that there may still be a place for volunteering in the lives of women today, not just as a form of career advancement but for its own sake, along with paid work and family, is not to suggest that women were born to serve. The impulse to volunteer is a simply human one—that's been sexualized by our culture."

4541. Kimball, Emily Kittle. *How to Get the Most Out of Being a Volunteer: Skills for Leadership.* Phoenix, Ariz.: Jordan Press, 1980.

4542. Kipps, Harriet L., ed. *Green Sheets.* Annandale, Va.: Four-One-One, 1980.

4543. Knoke, David, and James R. Wood. *Organized for Action: Commitment in Voluntary Associations.* New Brunswick, N.J.: Rutgers University Press, 1981.

The authors draw upon data collected from thirty-two local chapters of a wide variety of "social influence associations"—voluntary citizen groups—in order to answer two basic questions: What organizational conditions enable some groups to generate high levels of membership commitment to the collective enterprise? What organizational characteristics are most effective in helping associations to attain their goals of influencing public policies in their areas of interest? They found three types of organizational control structures at work in generating high levels of membership: emphasis on purposive incentives, widespread opportunities for decision-making and influence, and formal legitimacy of leaders. In addition, a professionalized formal structure correlated with stronger financial resources. They also found that members are more likely to evaluate their association in terms of its ability to produce large financial resources and generate membership commitment, rather than on its performance in attaining stated goals. Bibliography.

4544. Lauffer, Armand, and Sarah Gorodezky. *Volunteers.* Beverly Hills, Calif.: Sage Publications, 1977.

4545. Lewthwaite, Gilbert A. "Charity May Be Stretched Thin over Gulf in Services Dug Out by Reagan." *Baltimore Sun* (12 October 1981): A-8.

4546. Loeser, Herta. *Women, Work, and Volunteering.* Boston: Beacon Press, 1974.

4547. London, Mark. "Effective Use of Volunteers: Who, Why, When and How." *Fund Raising Management* 16 (August 1985): 18+.

4548. Lynch, Richard. "Designing Volunteer Jobs for Results." *Voluntary Action Leadership* (Summer 1983): 20-3.

4549. Manser, Gordon, and Rosemary Higgins Cass. *Voluntarism at the Crossroads.* New York: Family Service Association of America, 1976.

The authors assert that voluntarism in the United States is in a crucial period of transition, buffeted by forces that, although incremental and cumulative, are changing the face of voluntarism radically. Among these forces, they cite a money crunch compounded by inflation, changing relationships with government, the changing role and status of the volunteer, and lack of public understanding. Also cited are changing demographics, increased access of minorities and underprivileged classes to political and social power, growing national and international interdependence, and the questioning of traditional values and institutions. To help readers understand the juncture at which voluntarism finds itself today, the authors delve into its history and roots, examine the internal and external forces affecting it, and speculate on its future. The book is in no small way a call to action on the part of voluntary leaders (both professional and volunteer) to respond and adapt to these changes.

4550. Massey, Mary Elizabeth. *Bonnet Brigades.* New York: Alfred A. Knopf, 1966.

The author delved into the records and diaries of more than a hundred persons of the Civil War era in an attempt to show how the Civil War affected American women. Massey shows that the war compelled women to become more active, self-reliant, and resourceful, and that this ultimately contributed to their economic, social, and intellectual advancement. Among her conclusions is that the women of the North and South were really very similar in their wartime pursuits and aspirations, which naturally included charitable and voluntary activities of every kind.

4551. Maves, Paul B. *Older Volunteers in Church and Community.* Valley Forge, Pa.: Judson Press, 1981.

4552. McCurley, Stephen H. "How Much Are Volunteers Worth?" *Voluntary Action Leadership* (Spring 1984): 12-3.

4553. McCurley, Stephen H. "Protecting Volunteers from Suit: A Look at State Legislation." *Voluntary Action Leadership* (Spring-Summer 1987): 17-9.

An examination of volunteer liability legislation at the state level. The article analyzes legislation already passed and reviews the options for coverage. Volunteers can be held liable for any negligence on their part while performing their duties. McCurley demonstrates the continuum of fault which represents an increasing degree of legal seriousness. Beginning with 1) accident, 2) simple negligence, 3) wanton/gross negligence, and 4) intentional/willful misconduct. The state legislation enacted has made it harder for a potential plaintiff to demonstrate that a volunteer is legally at fault by raising the definition of legal fault. It must be demonstrated that a volunteer's actions were more than a mistake; he or she must have made a major mistake constituting gross negligence or willful misconduct. The article discusses what organizations are covered, the extent to which a volunteer is protected, and what is not done by the legislation. Legislation does not prevent volunteers from being sued nor does it eliminate the need for insurance or the need for good volunteer management.

4554. Meister, Albert. *Participation, Associations, Development, and Change.* New Brunswick, N.J.: Transaction Publishers, 1984.

This volume contains excerpts from three of Albert Meister's works: *Vers une Sociologie des associations* (1972), *La Participation dans les associations* (1974), and *La Participation pour le developpement* (1977). The excerpts chosen by the translator, Jack C. Ross, treat the relationship of social participation to types of societies (from a sociological standpoint); historical accounts of associations in France and the United States; sociological studies of development and change with respect to members; member roles; association types and types of participation in different societies; development associations in Africa and Latin America; and, finally, the future of democratic participation in a postindustrial society. In his introduction, Ross highlights some of the differences between Meister's French view of associations and traditions and the American view. It is a discussion that helpfully outlines the influences of national perspectives. Brief bibliography.

4555. Melder, Kenneth E. *Beginnings of Sisterhood: The American Woman's Rights Movement, 1800-1850.* New York: Schocken Books, 1977.

This analysis of the development of early American feminism includes attention to women's roles in reform and in creating societies as well as the eventual onset of activism on their own behalf. Melder considers the bond that formed between women engaged in voluntary benevolent works one of six categories of sisterhood that developed in the early nineteenth century. It paved the way for the reform societies women later organized more formally. Women saw the care of the poor, destitute, and otherwise deprived as firmly in their province, limited as that was, and they were encouraged by religious organizations to involve themselves in charity. When their efforts focused on helping other women, they began to transcend class boundaries and identify as a group—an attitude that naturally fostered growing feminist tendencies (a theory Berg [1978] develops in considerable detail). Bibliography.

4556. Mock, Richard. "Twenty Recipients of President's Volunteer Action Awards Honored." *Voluntary Action Leadership* (Spring 1983): 5-6.

4557. Mutual Benefit Life. *The Mutual Benefit Life Report. Corporate Commitment to Volunteerism.* Newark, N.J.: Mutual Benefit Life, 1984.

4558. Mutual Benefit Life. *The Mutual Benefit Life Report 2. Small Business Commitment to Volunteerism and Community Development.* Newark, N.J.: Mutual Benefit Life, 1984.

4559. National Forum on Volunteerism. *Shaping the Future.* Appleton, Wis.: Aid Association for Lutherans, 1982.

4560. O'Connell, Brian, ed. *America's Voluntary Spirit: A Book of Readings.* New York: Foundation Center, 1983.

Anthology of forty-five selections presents a diverse picture of the history, philosophy, and impact of private philanthropy and voluntary action in America, ranging from tracts of historical importance such as John Winthrop's *Model of Christian Charity* and historical analyses by Warren Weaver, Robert Bremner, Daniel Boorstin, and others, to more contemporary selections representing the writings and views of figures such as Lewis Thomas, John Filer, John D. Rockefeller 3rd, John Gardner, Erma Bombeck, and more. Many of the articles or excerpts annotated in this bibliography appear in *America's Voluntary Spirit*. It is the only existing anthology of classic writings about philanthropy and voluntarism and contains an extensive bibliography. Other authors represented include Cotton Mather, Ralph Waldo Emerson, Alexis de Tocqueville, Booker T. Washington, Jane Addams, Andrew Carnegie, Julius Rosenwald, David Riesman, John Hope Franklin, Inez Haynes Irwin, Walter A. Haas, Jr., Waldemar Nielsen, David Horton Smith, Adam Yarmolinsky, Alan Pifer, and others. 600-item bibliography.

4561. O'Connell, Brian. *Origins, Dimensions and Impact of America's Voluntary Spirit.* Washington: Independent Sector, 1984.

4562. Owen, Barbara L. *Volunteerism: A Directory of Special Collections.* Blacksburg, Va.: Center for Volunteer Development, 1988.

Directory lists existing public, university, government and special libraries, in addition to nonprofit organizations and agencies in the United States, Canada and England which maintain collections of materials on voluntarism. Arranged alphabetically by state or county, each entry contains the name, address, contact person and phone number of the organization, the largest geographic area it serves, the specific publics served, methods available to acquire materials, possible fees, quantitative data on holdings related to voluntarism, key subjects covered, special focus, classification scheme employed, forms of catalogs maintained, computer hardware/software used, holdings lists available, additional materials produced, and services available.

4563. Park, Jane Mallory. *Meaning Well Is Not Enough.* South Plainfield, N.J.: Groupwork Today, 1983.

4564. Pennock, J. Roland, and John W. Chapman, eds. *Voluntary Associations, Nomos XI.* New York: Atherton Press, 1969.

This collection of fifteen essays explores the nature and theory of voluntary associations, historical perspectives on them, and pluralism. The collection contains contributions by philosophers, political scientists, and lawyers. Some of the papers were written as commentary on others. Arthur Selwyn Miller's essay, *The Constitution and the Voluntary Association: Some Notes Toward a Theory,* is of particular note. It sets forth a number of propositions that concern the rise of voluntary associations to prominence and the emergence of the "positive state," characterized by a proliferating government with positive duties to perform. Miller focuses on the super-corporation, seen as both "voluntary" and "private," to elucidate some of his points. He asserts that provisions must be made for the corporation and other pluralistic social groups in constitutional theory.

4565. Plinio, Alex J. "Volunteerism, Third Sector Are Indeed Alive and Growing." *Fund Raising Management* 16 (July 1985): 100+.

4566. President's Task Force on Private Sector Initiatives. *Project Bank Information Form.* Washington: Government Printing Office, [1982].

4567. "Report of the Marshalling Human Resources Committee." *Voluntary Action Leadership* (Winter 1983): 28-9.

4568. Rexnord Resource Center. *Citizen Volunteer Program.* Brookfield, Wis.: Rexnord Resource Center, 1983.

4569. Rich, Richard C. "Interaction of the Voluntary and Government Sectors: Toward an Understanding of the Coproduction of Municipal Services." *Administration and Society* 13 (1981): 59-76.

According to Rich, fiscal strain and the demand for more responsive service delivery have combined to create an interest in new ways of involving citizens in municipal service delivery systems and of increasing the effectiveness and efficiency of public service delivery. He suggests that a clear understanding of the relationship between the governmental and voluntary sectors of our society offers a means of accomplishing both ends. Rich explores the logic of the processes by which public services are coproduced by the actions of public employees and citizen consumers. He attempts to discover ways in which government structures and policies can facilitate or inhibit voluntary, collective effort at community betterment, and looks at ways in which voluntary efforts can affect the need for and cost of government subsidies.

4570. Robertson, D.B., ed. *Voluntary Associations: A Study of Groups in Free Societies.* Richmond, Va.: John Knox Press, 1966.

This volume of essays in tribute to James Luther Adams, the great scholar of associations, represents an attempt to understand "the myriad groups—clubs, organizations, and associations—alternately muddling and clarifying the spaces between the state and the family and the state and the individual." The book includes essays by professors of sociology, religion, history, and ethics in four sections: *Sociological Theory, Associations in History: Theory and Practice, The Voluntary Church and Other Associations Today,* and *James Luther Adams.* Not surprisingly, most of the essays deal with the role of religion in the nature and formation of associations, and many treat the intersection of religious reflections and political action, with which Adams has been concerned all his life. There is a bibliography of Adams' writings.

4571. Ryan, Mary P. *Cradle of the Middle Class: The Family in Oneida County, New York. 1790-1865.* New York: Cambridge University Press, 1981.

This social history of the family and gender in antebellum America is based on Oneida County, part of the "Burned Over District"—a region rocked by evangelical religion and reforming zeal. The area was representative of the large-scale changes sweeping the nation as a result of increased commercial capitalism and the beginnings of industrialization. Ryan calls the maternal associations of Utica, funded in the 1820s to cultivate grace in young children, "the keystone to the transformation of family and gender" in this period. The major historical process that was discernible through Ryan's local investigations was the emergence of a middle class. Ryan spends considerable time exploring the patterns of association and voluntary activity that emerged during the period she studies, with special attention to how these activities transformed the lives of women and vice-versa. 300-item select bibliography.

4572. Saccomandi, Patrick. *The Volunteer Skillsbank: An Innovative Way to Connect Individual Talents to Community Needs.* Boulder, Colo.: Volunteer: The National Center for Citizen Involvement, 1980.

4573. Scheier, Ivan H. *Exploring Volunteer Space: The Recruiting of a Nation.* Boulder, Colo.: National Center for Citizen Involvement, 1982.

This book is written in an informal, personal style. It looks at volunteering and tries to explain its place in human society. One of Scheier's underlying themes is that volunteering is an expression of "inclusive and integrating" values, which are healthy and humanizing. He vigorously promotes the notion that volunteering, although already a powerful force in society, is occurring at only a fraction of its potential and could be expanded greatly to everyone's benefit. Scheier defines "volunteer space" in different ways—for instance, in relation to other activities such as paid work or play—often using spatial analogies. He breaks the space down into many categories in an attempt to demonstrate the immense variety of volunteer activities, arguing that organized volunteering accounts for very little of the total. He also touches on motivations, styles of leadership, and possibilities for the future.

4574. Schindler-Rainman, Eva. "Looking Ahead: Mobilizing Sources and Resources for the Future." *Voluntary Action Leadership* (Summer 1986): 28-30.

Guidelines for the human resources administrator on marketing their service organization to recruit volunteers and suggestions on the skills needed by the administrator to keep them with the organization.

4575. Schindler-Rainman, Eva. "Voluntarism Challenges." *NAHD Journal* (Summer-Fall 1983): 32-6.

4576. Schlesinger, Arthur M. *The American As Reformer.* 2nd ed. New York: Atheneum, 1971.

This volume grew out of a series of lectures Schlesinger gave at Pomona College in 1950. Although the book is small, it is a broad history of a large topic, divided into three parts: the historical climate of reform, the reform impulse in action, and opposition to reform. Schlesinger analyzes the reasons that reform has proceeded at a generally faster pace in the United States than elsewhere and cites a lighter burden of tradition in a new country and the character of an immigrant nation, composed of people who consciously rebelled against unsupportable conditions. This rebellious mentality, he later demonstrates, contributed not only to the zeal with which American reformers pursue justice, but also to the schisms that develop among them. His discussion of resistance to reform is especially salient, and amusing as well. Brief narrative bibliography; chapter notes.

4577. Scott, Anne Firor. *To Cast Our Mite on the Altar of Benevolence: Women Begin to Organize.* Center for the Study of Philanthropy and Voluntarism Working Papers. Durham, N.C.: Center for the Study of Philanthropy and Voluntarism, 1988.

In this working paper, the first chapter of a book tentatively entitled *Women's Voluntary Associations in the Shaping of American Society*, Anne Firor Scott seeks to devise a framework for a comprehensive historical analysis of the part these institutions have played. She has guided her research with four broad questions: What vital functions do women's associations perform for society? What have been their social, political and economic consequences? Are there characteristics of women's organizational behavior which are unique to them and which differentiate them from all-male associations or those which include both men and women? How has associational activity affected the status of American women and the social definition of woman's sphere? In addition, the records of women's organizations provide a rare view into nineteenth century "middle class" culture, revealing the values, aspirations, anxieties and self-images of women bound together to effect social change and improvement.

4578. Seipp, Catherine R. "Keeping Track of Volunteers with Micro-Computer." *Nonprofit Executive* 3 (April 1984): 5.

4579. Shanahan, Thomazine. *Volunteers: A Valuable Resource.* Washington: Government Printing Office, 1982.

4580. Shenon, Philip. "Volunteer Executives Find Jobs Make Tough Demands." *New York Times* (19 September 1983): B-1+.

4581. Silverman, Myrna, Betty Hepner, and Edmund Ricci. "The Importance of Staff Involvement in Volunteer Program Planning." *Voluntary Action Leadership* (Summer 1984): 25-9.

4582. Smith, Constance, and Anne Freedman. *Voluntary Associations: Perspectives on the Literature.* Cambridge, Mass.: Harvard University Press, 1972.

This is a thorough survey of the literature on voluntary associations. The authors first sketch major theories on the origin, growth, and functions of voluntary associations. They discuss the place of associations in political theory and challenge the unproven assumption that voluntary associations are beneficial to a democratic society. They then survey the findings of the role of voluntary associations in the political and social structure in the United States and abroad. General surveys on participations are enumerated, as well as studies that focus on such variables as social class, race, ethnic origins, sex, and age. The specific organizations themselves are also covered, and the last chapter reviews volunteers in government service, such as the Peace Corps. The final section of each chapter is an annotated bibliography of works cited in the text or related to its subject. Over 600 items are listed.

4583. Smith, David Horton, ed. *Voluntary Action Research.* Lexington, Mass.: Lexington Books, 1974.

This volume is the third in a series of books which contain individual essays. The books review major themes and aspects of voluntary action and citizen participation. (The 1972 volume deals with problems of definition and typology and participation in voluntary action. The 1973 volume is about historical dimensions and trends in voluntary action and its impact at different levels, from individual to societal.) This, the 1974 volume describes, discusses, and assesses voluntary action and citizen participation around the world. The essays come from a variety of disciplinary perspectives, with social science playing a dominant role. Many of the essays have helpful bibliographies.

4584. Smith, David Horton. *Voluntary Sector Policy Research Needs.* Washington: Center for a Voluntary Society, 1974.

An outgrowth of a conference, this report addresses the problem of supporting and increasing the effectiveness of the American voluntary sector by defining the scope and specifying the range of policy-relevant research needed. The report identifies nineteen "high-priority" concerns of voluntary action. Those with the highest ranking (representing the greatest degree of consensus among the project's seventy participants) include 1) increasing citizen participation in policy decision-making, 2) promoting and experimenting with innovation, 3) achieving a balanced distribution of power between the voluntary sector, business, and government, and 4) promoting equitable distribution of the opportunities and services of society through the voluntary sector. The policy implications and research needs of the nineteen priorities, grouped into six broad categories, are each explored in the course of the report, which concludes with a chapter on implications for the future. Bibliography.

4585. Sterling, John C. *Volunteers As Managers: A Philosophy and Plan for Involvement and Leadership.* Unpublished, 1986.

Focuses on the ways in which key volunteers as managers helped revitalize the Alumni Association for the N.Y.S. College of Agriculture and Life Sciences at Cornell University. The strategy chosen to reverse the failing alumni membership was to build a solid volunteer alumni leadership base in districts, closer to alumni. These volunteer managers would be responsible for initiating alumni leadership involvement in alumni activities and programs; a regular, personalized membership process; an organized membership effort; and local alumni activity. Sterling's paper details the concepts used to establish the new responsibilities for volunteers as managers; the strategy involved in developing volunteer alumni leadership (including commitment, a sense of ownership, specifically written job descriptions for volunteer positions, and organizational structure); nurturing and support of key volunteer alumni; and a philosophy of organizational success. Sterling's theory proposes that interested, enthusiastic people will determine an organization's structure and program; the salaried staff's primary effort is directed toward the leadership and membership base (and less on program and organizational structure), allowing volunteer leadership to share in the organization's growth, management, and success.

4586. Stokes, Bruce. *Helping Ourselves: Local Solutions to Global Problems.* New York: W.W. Norton & Co., 1981.

Stokes argues that it is increasingly necessary for individuals and local groups to act on their own behalf to confront social and economic problems that a bureaucratic state and professionalized private sector are ill-equipped to handle. It is necessary not only to get the job done, but also because "state and corporate dominance of problem solving engenders a sense of dependency and helplessness that undermines people's capacity to be active, informed citizens," according to Stokes. Through self-help activities, he contends, this psychology of dependence can be transformed into a sense of self-reliance and help create a sense of community. He adds that an appropriate vehicle for such efforts already exists in voluntary associations. Stokes argues that self-empowerment of this nature will help the nation and pave the way toward true democracy. He examines self-help possibilities in the workplace, energy, health, housing, family planning, and more.

4587. Stone, Julita Martinez. *How to Work with Groups: Guidelines for Volunteers.* Springfield, Ill.: Charles C. Thomas, 1983.

4588. "Tax Deductions for Volunteers." *Exchange Networks* (Spring-Summer 1983): 9-10.

4589. Taylor, Shirley H., and Peggy Wild. "How to Match Volunteer Motivation with Job Demands." *Voluntary Action Leadership* (Summer 1984): 30-1.

4590. Tobin, Gary A., ed. *Social Planning and Human Service Delivery in the Voluntary Sector.* Westport, Conn.: Greenwood Press, 1985.

The twelve essays in this anthology, with an introduction by David Horton Smith, focus on the planning and human service delivery aspect of the voluntary sector. Clarke Chambers describes the historical development of the modern system. Jennifer Wolch explores the sector's relationship to an urban economy. Orval Westby describes the sector's religious groups and institutions. Child care and day-care are put into the context of the whole system by Frances Hoffmann, and E. Terrence and William Schaefer discuss the relationship of public and private sectors; the latter deals with local governments. Essays by Russy Sumariwalla and George Wilkinson discuss needs identification and strategic planning as specific techniques for more efficient delivery of voluntary sector services. The planning process as it relates to the interaction of clients, lay leaders, committees, volunteers, and staff is the subject of John Forester and David Horton Smith's essays, with Gary Tobin adding a discussion of ethical concerns in planning. 300-item bibliography.

4591. Treasch, Harold T. "The Role of the Volunteer." *NSFRE Journal* 9 (Spring 1984): 8+.

4592. Van Til, Jon. *Mapping the Third Sector: Voluntarism in a Changing Social Economy.* New York: Foundation Center, 1988.

Extremely interesting and coherent scholarly view of voluntary action, the "human endeavor not motivated by private gain or compulsion of law." Author Van Til analyzes the terms and concepts of voluntarism, volunteering, voluntary action, and voluntary association, seeking to "clarify broader aspects of the role we ourselves and our institutions may play in this field." Reviews the variety of perspectives used to examine voluntary action throughout American history, all the while stating the need of a social/economic climate in which principles of voluntarism are widely practiced and voluntary associations thrive. Examines the traditions and practices of voluntarism in other countries and stresses the need for a new conception of how to preserve, extend, and experience community within the interactive web of modern society. Includes criteria for desirable voluntary action goals, such as enhanced social justice, clarified societal understanding, and a blending of good leadership and effective management. Contains reference bibliography.

4593. Verity, C. William, Jr., and Frank Pace, Jr. "Volunteering: The Policy-Maker's Role." *Voluntary Action Leadership* (Winter 1983): 30-4.

4594. Vizza, Cynthia. *A New Competitive Edge: Volunteers from the Workplace.* Arlington, Va.: Volunteer-The National Center, 1986.

Presents information on the rationale for and benefits of employee volunteer programs. Profiles fifteen corporations which have developed employee volunteer programs. Chapters include information on the structure, administration, and programs developed by businesses; partnerships between the private sector and the community; organized labor's role in voluntary community involvement; and volunteering in small business.

4595. Volunteer-The National Center. *New Challenges for Employee Volunteering.* Arlington, Va.: Volunteer-The National Center, 1982.

4596. "Volunteering and Unemployment: The Flint Conference." *Voluntary Action Leadership* (Summer 1984): 21-4.

4597. Warner, Alice Sizer. *Volunteers in Libraries: 2.* New York: R.R. Bowker Co., 1983.

4598. Warren, David L. "Some Thoughts on Voluntarism in the 80's." *NAHD Journal* (Summer-Fall 1983): 37+.

4599. Watkins, Roger. "Good for the Company: Good for the Community." *Charity* 1 (February 1984): 8-10.

4600. Wattel, Harold L., ed. *Voluntarism and the Business Community.* Hofstra University Yearbook of Business, no. 8. New York: Hofstra University, 1971.

4601. "Why Corporations Support Employee Volunteering." *Voluntary Action Leadership* (Summer-Fall 1987): 21-4.

Voluntary organizations will be better able to compete for corporate volunteer resources if they understand and can respond to the concerns expressed by the corporate rationale for employee volunteering. Businesses support employee volunteer programs because they are a way for corporations to respond to workers' concerns about the quality of life in their working and living environments; to increase and reinforce workers' skills, particularly in leadership and participatory decision-making; to respond affirmatively to the public's expectation of its involvement in community problem-solving; and to demonstrate moral leadership, which provides ultimate benefit to the company by building public respect and enhancing the marketing of products and services.

4602. Wishik, Debra Englander. "Corporate Volunteer Programs." *NPO Resource Review* 2 (March-April 1984): 3-4.

11

GOVERNMENT FUNDING AND THE NONPROFIT SECTOR

4603. Abramson, Alan J., and Lester M. Salamon. *The Nonprofit Sector and the New Federal Budget.* Washington: Urban Institute Press, 1986.

Report analyzes the impact of recent federal budget decisions on the nonprofit sector, and considers the proposed changes for the next three years. The volume makes no attempt to evaluate the merits or drawbacks of budget proposals. It reviews the nonprofit sector's problems in relation to the budget reductions of the 1980s and provides an overview of the nonprofit sector. Then, it examines the impact of federal budget decisions on the need for nonprofit services as reflected in overall changes in the levels of federal spending in fields where nonprofits are active as well as the effect of the budget cuts on the revenues of nonprofit agencies. The work is footnoted, includes twenty-one tables, nine figures of budget information, twenty-three pages of appendixes, and a bibliography. It also includes a guide to budget concepts and procedures; statistical data on target deficits; and outlays by program in 1980 and current dollars.

4604. American Council for the Arts. *Arts Advocacy: A Citizen Action Manual.* New York: American Council for the Arts, 1980.

4605. Ammon-Wexler, Jill, and Catherine Carmel. *Getting Your Share of the R and D Funds.* Santa Cruz, Calif.: Mercury Communications Corp., 1978.

4606. Andrews, J. David. "Kicking the Federal Habit." *Foundation News* 24 (January-February 1983): 40-1.

4607. Arey, June Batten. *State Arts Agencies in Transition: Purpose, Program, and Personnel.* Wayzata, Minn.: Spring Hill Conference Center, 1975.

4608. Art Resources International. *Money to Work: Grants for Visual Artists.* Washington: Art Resources International, 1988.

Result of an extensive research project conducted by the Center for Arts Information (CAI) to identify and describe sources of direct fellowship support for visual artists in the U.S. and to analyze the nature and structure of these activities. Sources are divided into three categories: national, regional, and state and local. The introduction assesses the nature of fellowship awards, the application process, and the selection process. Includes a bibliography of books and peridicals listing grants to visual artists, in addition to a resource list of organizations. Extensively indexed by geographical eligibility; alphabetical/media; national grants; grants available by nomination; financial need; emergency grants; acronyms of organizations; and common award names.

4609. Artsreview. *Portrait of the Artist, 1987. Who Supports Him/Her?* Washington: Government Printing Office, [1987].

4610. Associated Councils of the Arts. *The Public Service Budget of Arts and Cultural Organizations: A Better Measure of Full Financial Need.* New York: Associated Councils of the Arts, 1976.

4611. Baker, Earl M. *Federal Grants. The National Interest and State Response: A Review of Theory and Research.* Philadelphia: Center for the Study of Federalism, [197?].

4612. Baker, John A. *A Guide to Federal Programs for Rural Development.* 4th ed. Washington: U.S. Department of Agriculture. Rural Development Service, [1975].

4613. Battaglia, Carmen L. "How to Ask for Federal Funding." *American Education* (July 1977): 1-4.

4614. Bennett, James T., and Thomas J. DiLorenzo. *Destroying Democracy: How Government Funds Partisan Politics*. Washington: Cato Institute, 1985.

4615. Bond, Kathleen, comp. *Federal Funding Programs for Social Scientists*. Washington: American Sociological Association, [1980].

4616. Bush, Vannevar. *Science: The Endless Frontier*. Reprint. Washington: National Science Foundation, 1945.

4617. Cappalli, Richard B. "Grants As a Matter of Law." *Grants Magazine* 7 (December 1984): 241-44.

Discusses perspectives on the use of legal counsel in the federal financial assistance process.

4618. Cappalli, Richard B. "In Defense of the Federal Grant." *Grantsmanship Center News* 11 (July-August 1983): 46-51.

4619. Cappalli, Richard B. *Rights and Remedies under Federal Grants*. Washington: Bureau of National Affairs, 1979.

4620. Center for Community Change. *Community Development Block Grant: A Basic Guidebook for Community Groups*. Washington: Center for Community Change, 1986.

4621. Ciavarella, Michael A. *Community Education Funding Guide*. Shippensburg, Pa.: Commonwealth Center for Community Education, 1977.

4622. Clack, George. "How to Keep the Grant Money Flowing: Some Answers to the Most Commonly Asked Questions about Filling Out the Endowment's Application Forms." *Cultural Post* 8 (March-April 1983): 4-5.

4623. Clark Foundation, Edna McConnell. *Review of Federal Programs to Alleviate Rural Deprivation*. Santa Monica, Calif.: Rand Corp., 1974.

4624. Coe, Linda C., comp. *Folklife and the Federal Government: A Guide to Activities, Resources, Funds and Services*. Publications of the American Folklife Center, no. 1. Washington: American Folklife Center, 1977.

4625. Cohen, Vicki L. "International Programs at the Department of Education." *Grants Magazine* 7 (September 1984): 158-61.

4626. Collender, Stanley E. *The Guide to the Federal Budget*. Washington: Urban Institute Press, 1984.

4627. Congressional Quarterly. *Washington Information Directory*. Washington: Congressional Quarterly, 1988.

Facilitates access to information sources in Washington, D.C., including all federal government offices and agencies, congressional committees, and private, nonprofit organizations. Arranged by subject, covering communications and the media, economics and business, education and culture, employment and labor, energy, advocacy, government personnel and services, health, housing and urban affairs, individual assistance programs, international affairs, law and justice, national security, agriculture, environment and natural resources, science and space, transportation, and Congress and politics. Indexed by name and subject.

4628. Cook, Betsy, ed. *Federal Yellow Book: A Directory of the Federal Departments and Agencies*. Washington: Monitor Publishing Co., 1987.

Direct petition or inquiry access to more than 31,000 top people in the executive branch of the federal government, arranged organizationally and by position title. Divided into Executive Office of the President/Office of the Vice President, the thirteen executive departments, sixty-three independent agencies (from ACTION to the Veterans Administration), and regional offices. Each section's entries indicate address and phone numbers.

4629. Cook, Constance Ewing. "A Guide to Grants." *Currents* 14 (May 1988): 38-42, 44, 46.

Directory of federal support for institutions of higher education, offered by the U.S. Department of Education, the National Endowment for the Humanities, and the National Science Foundation. The twenty-two grants listed here are for learner-centered, action-oriented institutional improvement projects; each listing includes: *Catalog of Federal Domestic Assistance* title and number, fiscal year 1988 appropriation, average size of grants awarded in fiscal year 1987, brief description of the competition, and contact address and phone number.

4630. *Cultural Directory 2: Federal Funds and Services for the Arts and Humanities*. Washington: Smithsonian Institution Press, 1980.

Describes many federal funding programs for the arts and the humanities which are included in the *Catalog of Federal Domestic Assistance*.

4631. Des Marais, Philip. *How to Get Government Grants*. Washington: Public Service Materials Center, 1975.

4632. DiMaggio, Paul J. *The Impact of Public Funding on Organizations in the Arts*. Program on Non-Profit Organizations, no. 31. New Haven, Conn.: Institution for Social and Policy Studies, 1981.

4633. *Directory of Federal Aid for Education*. Santa Monica, Calif.: Ready Reference Press, 1982.

4634. Disney, Diane M., Madeleine H. Kimmich, and James C. Musselwhite, Jr. *Partners in Public Service: Government and the Nonprofit Sector in Rhode Island*. Washington: Urban Institute Press, 1984.

4635. DuChez, JoAnne. *The National Directory of State Agencies*. Bethesda, Md.: Cambridge Information Group, 1988.

Comprehensive U.S. directory of the states, possessions, territories and 105 state agency functions. Divided into two main sections, first section lists state agencies alphabetically by state and second section lists state agency functions alphabetically by subject area, such as aging, child welfare, environmental affairs, historic preservation, etc. For each state agency, entry includes the contact person, address and telephone number. Useful source for identifying contacts on the state level.

4636. Dumouchel, J. Robert. *Government Assistance Almanac.* Washington: Regnery Gateway, 1988.

4637. Dupree, A. Hunter. *Science in the Federal Government: A History of Policies and Activities to 1940.* Cambridge, Mass.: Belknap Press, 1957.

4638. Eddy, Junius. *A Review of Federal Programs Supporting the Arts in Education.* New York: Ford Foundation, 1970.

4639. Eddy, Junius. *A Review of Projects in the Arts.* New York: Ford Foundation, 1970.

4640. *Factbook: Guide to National Science Foundation Programs and Activities.* 2nd ed. Chicago: Marquis Academic Media, 1975.

4641. Falleder, Arnold. "New Job Training Act: What Does It Mean for Nonprofits?" *Nonprofit World Report* 2 (January-February 1984): 19-20.

4642. Falleder, Arnold. "Obtaining Grants in the Electronic Age: The Impact of the Federal Program Information Act." *Nonprofit World Report* 2 (March-April 1984): 26.

4643. Falleder, Arnold. *Understanding and Obtaining Federal Grants.* New York: New York Management Center, 1977.

4644. Farley, Pamela J. *The Medicare Hospital Insurance System: An Illustration of Non-Profit Participation in a Federal Government Program.* Program on Non-Profit Organizations, no. 33. New Haven, Conn.: Institution for Social and Policy Studies, 1979.

4645. Feron, James. *Arts Endowment Starts New Grant Program.* New York: New York Times, 1983.

4646. Finn, Chester E., Jr. *Federal Patronage of Universities: A Rose by Many Other Names?* Brookings General Series Reprint, no. 330. Washington: Brookings Institution, 1977.

4647. Fox, Tom. "Government Foundations: Worthy But Threatened." *Foundation News* 25 (May-June 1984): 62-4.

4648. Friedman, John S. "The Battle for the NEH." *Nation* (19 December 1981): 662-63.

4649. Gibans, Nina Freedlander. *The Community Arts Council Movement: History, Opinions, Issues.* New York: Praeger, 1982.

4650. Gingold, Diane J. *The Challenge Grant Experience: Planning, Development, and Fundraising.* Washington: National Endowment for the Arts, 1980.

4651. Godfrey, Nancy. *Federal Grants for Library and Information Services.* Chicago: American Library Association, 1986.

4652. Goetcheus, Vernon M. "Voluntarism and Reagan." *Journal of the Institute for Socioeconomic Studies* 9 (Summer 1984): 36-48.

4653. Government Information Services. *Federal Funding Guide. 2 Vols.* Arlington, Va.: Government Information Services, 1986.

Guide for federal dollars. Arranged by chapter according to general topic areas such as community development, economic development, energy and energy impact, housing, jobs/personnel, transportation, health, environment and ecology, social services, law enforcement, senior citizens, arts and cultural affairs, Native American programs, and disaster/fire/emergency. Each chapter begins with an overview of the programs contained in the chapter as well as recent, or pending legislative and regulatory actions. Individual program descriptions begin with a brief summary in a format called *Quick Check*. This boxed-in summary includes facts such as eligibility, type of aid provided, and requirements. To the right of the *Quick Check* box is another brief summary of important facts and figures concerning the program. The profile itself provides sections on *What the Program Does, Contacts, Are We Eligible?, Uses of the Funds, Any Restrictions?, Deadline, Funding Potential, How to Apply, Approval Time, Guidelines/Restrictions,* and *Legislative Authority*. The volume contains an index and appendixes with lists of comparative appropriations and program deadlines at a glance.

4654. *The Green Book. The Official Directory of the City of New York.* New York: Citybooks, 1988.

4655. Greenly, Robert B. *How to Win Government Contracts.* New York: Van Nostrand Reinhold Co., 1983.

Practical guide to the government contracting system covering how to get on qualified bidders' lists, determine a budget, organize and write a proposal, etc.

4656. Grisham, Roy A., Jr., and Paul D. McConaughey, eds. *The Encyclopedia of U.S. Government Benefits.* 2nd ed. Union City, N.J.: William H. Wise & Co., 1978.

Provides background information on over 5,000 government services, including the contact person, funding programs, and publications of each service agency.

4657. Gronbjerg, Kirsten A., Madeleine H. Kimmich, and Lester M. Salamon. *The Chicago Nonprofit Sector in a Time of Government Retrenchment.* Washington: Urban Institute Press, 1985.

4658. Gronbjerg, Kirsten A., James C. Musselwhite, Jr., and Lester M. Salamon. *Government Spending and the Nonprofit Sector in Cook County/Chicago.* Washington: Urban Institute Press, 1984.

4659. Gross, Ronald, and Beatrice Gross. "Government Adopts Foundation Mode." *Christian Science Monitor* (10 December 1982): B-7.

4660. Grossman, David A., Lester M. Salamon, and David M. Altschuler. *The New York Nonprofit Sector in a Time of Government Retrenchment.* Washington: Urban Institute Press, 1986.

Presents the results of a mail survey of New York area nonprofit human service agencies carried out in late 1982 and early 1983 to determine the size and scope of the nonprofit sector in the New York metropolitan area, its sources of funding and the ways in which it has been affected by recent changes in government support. Also discusses the search for alternative revenue sources and changes in agency staffing patterns, management practices and service levels. Contains statistical tables based on figures from the 1982 mail survey.

4661. *A Guide for Colleges and Universities Cost Principles and Procedures for Establishing Indirect Cost Rates for Grants and Contracts with the Department of Health, Education, and Welfare.* Washington: Government Printing Office, 1971.

4662. Gutowski, Michael, Lester M. Salamon, and Karen Pittman. *The Pittsburgh Nonprofit Sector in a Time of Government Retrenchment.* Washington: Urban Institute Press, 1984.

4663. Harder, Paul, James C. Musselwhite, Jr., and Lester M. Salamon. *Government Spending and the Nonprofit Sector in San Francisco.* Washington: Urban Institute Press, 1984.

4664. Harder, Paul, Madeleine H. Kimmich, and Lester M. Salamon. *The San Francisco Bay Area Nonprofit Sector in a Time of Government Retrenchment.* Washington: Urban Institute Press, 1985.

4665. Hensley, Oliver, Beverly Gulley, and Jacquie Eddleman. "Evaluating Development Costs for a Proposal to a Federal Agency." *Journal of the Society of Research Administrators* 12 (Summer 1980): 35-9.

4666. Hillman, Howard, and Kathryn Natale. *The Art of Winning Government Grants.* New York: Vanguard Press, 1977.

Although much of the information on federal agencies is now dated, Hillman's basic introduction to the six grant-seeking phases still contains relevant, practical advice for the government grantseeker.

4667. Hoffman, Donald, and James J. Marshall. *Education Resource Directory.* Arlington, Va.: Education Funding Research Council, 1986.

4668. Holtz, Herman. *Government Contracts: Proposalmanship and Winning Strategies.* New York: Plenum, 1979.

Reviews the workings of the government contract market and presents strategies for learning about and obtaining contracts.

4669. Independent Sector. *Accountability with Independence: Toward a Balance in Government/Independent Sector Financial Partnerships.* Washington: Independent Sector, 1983.

4670. Johnson, Huey D. "Bears and Beggars." *Foundation News* 28 (March-April 1987): 36-9.

Huey D. Johnson, former secretary of the California Resources Agency, presents an argument against the private sector funding government agencies which have been the victims of budget cuts. According to the author, government-foundation coalitions are increasing. Now, nonprofit and grassroots organizations must compete for limited grant funds not only with other nonprofits but with government lobbyists paid with taxpayer dollars. Monies that could be used by the nonprofit sector for experimental and innovative projects are swallowed into the massive government budget where its impact, if any, is dissipated on safe, established programs. The process also harms the government agencies; their time is spent seeking handouts rather than building a strong agency with a broad base of public support. In addition, the chances of restoring the budget cuts after once having gone to the private sector are extremely low. Citing John D. Rockefeller's words of caution to the philanthropic world about government involvement, the author believes that foundations must draw the line—no matter how difficult—on giving to government operations.

4671. Keller, Anthony S. *Contemporary European Arts Support Systems: Precedents for Intergovernmental Development in the United States.* Washington: National Partnership Meeting, 1980.

4672. Kidd, Charles V. *American Universities and Federal Research.* Cambridge, Mass.: Harvard University Press, 1959.

4673. Larson, Gary O. *The Reluctant Patron: The United States Government and the Arts, 1943-1965.* Philadelphia: University of Pennsylvania Press, 1983.

4674. Lawrence, William, and Stephen Leeds. *An Inventory of Federal Income Transfer Programs, Fiscal Year 1977.* White Plains, N.Y.: Institute for Socioeconomic Studies, 1978.

4675. "Leave the Left Alone." *New York Times* (9 December 1983).

4676. Lesko, Matthew. *Getting Yours: The Complete Guide to Government Money.* 3rd ed. New York: Viking Penguin, 1987.

Directory of government funding based mainly on the *Catalog of Federal Domestic Assistance*. Programs arranged by relevant agency with access to grants by subject index. Each entry includes current addresses, phone numbers, ranges of assistance, and eligibility requirements for all existing grant, direct payment, loan, and loan guarantee programs. Section of examples to stimulate the imagination and direct the reader to sources of money for similar aims. The third edition has a new section with complete information on state-sponsored programs to aid businesses.

4677. Levy, Daniel C. *Private Versus Public Financing of Higher Education: U.S. Policy in Comparative Perspective.* Program on Non-Profit Organizations, no. 38. New Haven, Conn.: Institution for Social and Policy Studies, 1981.

4678. Lippert, Paul G., Michael Gutowski, and Lester M. Salamon. *The Atlanta Nonprofit Sector in a Time of Government Retrenchment.* Washington: Urban Institute Press, 1984.

4679. Lomask, Milton. *A Minor Miracle: An Informal History of the National Science Foundation.* Washington: National Science Foundation, 1976.

4680. Lukermann, Barbara, Madeleine H. Kimmich, and Lester M. Salamon. *The Twin Cities Nonprofit Sector in a Time of Government Retrenchment.* Washington: Urban Institute Press, 1984.

4681. McGuigan, Catherine, ed. *Cities, Counties and the Arts*. New York: Associated Councils of the Arts, 1976.

4682. Merkowitz, David, and Sarah E. Walzer, eds. *Guide to Government Resources for Economic Development: A Handbook for Nonprofit Agencies and Municipalities*. Washington: Northeast-Midwest Institute, 1982.

4683. Morrison, Anne S. *The Reagan Economic Program: A Working Paper for Grantmakers*. Washington: Council on Foundations, 1981.

4684. *Museum Guide to Federal Programs*. Washington: Association of Science-Technology Centers, 1975.

4685. Musselwhite, James C., Jr., Winsome Hawkins, and Lester M. Salamon. *Government Spending and the Nonprofit Sector in Atlanta/Fulton County*. Washington: Urban Institute Press, 1985.

4686. Musselwhite, James C., Jr., Rosalyn B. Katz, and Lester M. Salamon. *Government Spending and the Nonprofit Sector in Pittsburgh/Allegheny County*. Washington: Urban Institute Press, 1985.

4687. Musselwhite, James C., Jr., and Lauren K. Saunders. *Government Spending and the Nonprofit Sector in Two Michigan Communities: Flint/Genesee County and Tuscola County*. Washington: Urban Institute Press, 1984.

4688. National Clearinghouse on Domestic Violence. *Funding Family Violence Programs: Sources and Potential Sources for Federal Monies*. Rockville, Md.: National Clearinghouse on Domestic Violence, 1979.

4689. National Endowment for the Arts. *Annual Report*. Washington: National Endowment for the Arts, [1987].

Report lists 4,553 grants totaling $146.6 million arranged by program areas, including: dance, design arts, expansion arts, folk arts, inter-arts, literature, media arts (film/radio/television), museum, music, opera-musical theater, theater, and visual arts. Within each program area information on grants appears alphabetically by recipient name and includes recipient's name, city and state; amount of grant; and short explanation of support given. Other information included in the report are the chairman's statement; the agency and its functions, the membership list of the National Arts Council; statement of mission; advisory panel lists; financial summary; and history of authorizations and appropriations.

4690. National Endowment for the Arts. *Artists in Education Application Guidelines*. Washington: National Endowment for the Arts, 1981.

4691. National Endowment for the Arts. *The Arts and 504: A 504 Handbook for Accessible Arts Programming*. Washington: Government Printing Office, [1985].

4692. National Endowment for the Arts. *Dance: Application Guidelines*. Washington: National Endowment for the Arts, 1981.

4693. National Endowment for the Arts. *Expansion Arts: Application Guidelines*. Washington: National Endowment for the Arts, 1982.

4694. National Endowment for the Arts. *Guide to the National Endowment for the Arts*. Washington: Government Printing Office, 19—.

Describes the overall purpose of each of the Endowment's programs and outlines the types of support available in each of their funding categories (dance, design arts, expansion arts, folk arts, inter-arts, literature, media arts, museums, music, opera-musical theater, theater, visual arts, and international), to assist individuals and organizations determine whether their artistic projects might be eligible for grants from the National Endowment for the Arts. Appendixes include listings for state and regional arts organizations, selected publications, and telephone directory of Endowment offices.

4695. National Endowment for the Arts. *Museum Program*. Washington: National Endowment for the Arts, 1981.

4696. National Endowment for the Arts. *Theater Program: Application Guidelines*. Washington: National Endowment for the Arts, 1984.

4697. National Endowment for the Arts. Research Division. *Conditions and Needs of the Professional American Theatre*. National Endowment for the Arts Research Division Reports, no. 11. Washington: National Endowment for the Arts, 1981.

4698. National Endowment for the Humanities. *Guidelines and Application Instructions for the United States Newspaper Projects*. Washington: National Endowment for the Humanities, 1982.

4699. National Endowment for the Humanities. *Overview of Endowment Programs*. Washington: National Endowment for the Humanities, [1988].

Provides information about the history, purposes, policies, and organization of the National Endowment for the Humanities to help individuals and organizations determine whether proposed projects and activities in the humanities may be eligible for Endowment support. Discusses the activities supported by the Endowment's grantmaking programs, provides a current schedule of application deadlines for these programs, and includes a directory of Endowment telephone numbers, names and addresses of the state humanities councils, and a list of members of the National Council on the Humanities.

4700. National Endowment for the Humanities. *Report*. Washington: National Endowment for the Humanities, 1987.

Annual report of the National Endowment for the Humanities, including grants made in the divisions of Fellowships and Seminars, Education, General, Research, and State Programs, Preservation, Challenge Grants, and the National Capital Arts and Cultural Affairs. Financial report and summary of grants and awards for fiscal year 1987, and an index of grants arranged alphabetically by state.

4701. National Endowment for the Humanities. *Support for Museums and Historical Organizations.* Washington: National Endowment for the Humanities, [198?].

4702. National Health Council. *Congress and Health: An Introduction to the Legislative Process and Its Key Participants.* 6th ed. New York: National Health Council, 1985.

4703. National Institute of Mental Health. *U.S. Facilities and Programs for Children with Severe Mental Illness: A Directory.* Rockville, Md.: National Institute of Mental Health, 1974.

4704. National Science Foundation. *Announcement of Research Programs in the Division of Information Science and Technology.* Washington: National Science Foundation, 1982.

4705. National Science Foundation. *Development in Science Education: Guide for the Preparation of Proposals.* Washington: National Science Foundation, 1980.

4706. National Science Foundation. *Federal Funds for Research and Development, Fiscal Years 1977, 1978 and 1979. Surveys of Science Resources Studies.* Washington: Government Printing Office, 1979.

4707. National Science Foundation. *Guide to Programs.* Washington: National Science Foundation, 1982.

Lists foundation programs in various areas of scientific research. Describes NSF criteria for selection of research projects.

4708. National Science Foundation. *Research in Undergraduate Institutions.* Washington: National Science Foundation, [1985].

4709. National Science Foundation. *Research Opportunities for Minority Scientists and Engineers.* Washington: National Science Foundation, 1987.

4710. National Science Foundation. *Research Opportunities for Women.* Washington: National Science Foundation, 1987.

4711. National Science Foundation. *University/Industry Research Relationships: Myths, Realities and Potentials.* 14th ed. Washington: National Science Foundation, 1982.

4712. National Science Foundation. *Visiting Professorships for Women.* Washington: National Science Foundation, [1985].

4713. National Youth Work Alliance. *Stalking the Large Green Grant.* 3rd ed. Washington: National Youth Work Alliance, 1980.

4714. Netzer, Dick. *The Subsidized Muse: Public Support for the Arts in the United States.* New York: Cambridge University Press, 1978.

4715. New Jersey. Committee for the Humanities. *Guidelines and Application.* New Brunswick, N.J.: New Jersey Committee for the Humanities, [198?].

4716. New Jersey. Committee for the Humanities. *Program Information.* New Brunswick, N.J.: New Jersey Committee for the Humanities, [198?].

4717. New Jersey. Committee for the Humanities. *The Report of the New Jersey Committee for the Humanities, 1980-1983.* New Brunswick, N.J.: New Jersey Committee for the Humanities, [198?].

4718. New Jersey. Department of Community Affairs. *New Jersey State Aid Catalog for Local Governments.* Trenton, N.J.: New Jersey Department of Community Affairs, 1985.

4719. New York City. Mayor's Advisory Commission for Cultural Affairs. *Funding for Culture: The Cultural Policy of the City of New York.* New York: Mayor's Advisory Commission for Cultural Affairs, 1983.

4720. New York. Council for the Humanities. *Annual Report.* New York: New York Council for the Humanities, 1985.

4721. New York. Council for the Humanities. *Guidelines.* New York: New York Council for the Humanities, [1985].

4722. New York. Council for the Humanities. *Speakers in the Humanities: A Free Resource.* New York: New York Council for the Humanities, [1985].

4723. New York. Council on the Arts. *Funding Report.* New York: New York State Council on the Arts, 1988.

Lists grants made by New York State Council on the Arts programs for architecture, planning and design; arts; dance; decentralization; film; folk arts; individual artists; literature; local arts organizations/service organizations; media; museum aid; music; presenting organizations; special arts services; theatre; and visual artists.

4724. New York. Council on the Arts. *Program Guidelines. Supplement.* New York: New York State Council on the Arts, [1985].

4725. New York. Department of Education. *Resources for Adult Learning Services.* Albany, N.Y.: New York State Education Department, 1980.

4726. New York. Senate. Special Committee on the Culture Industry. *Decentralization: A Program for the Arts in New York State.* Albany, N.Y.: New York. Senate. Special Committee on the Culture Industry, 1981.

4727. Nichols, Vera, comp. *Catalog of California State Grants Assistance.* Sacramento, Calif.: California State Library Foundation, 1987.

Contains information on various kinds of financial assistance offered through California governmental agencies, which are either funded by state or federal "pass-through" funds. Ninety-two departments or programs are described noting their purpose, limitations, authorization, type of assistance, funding and range, who may apply, deadline, contact person and phone number.

4728. "1984 in Philanthropy." *Philanthropy Monthly* 16 (July-August 1983): 5-9.

4729. Northeast-Midwest Institute. *Guide to Federal Energy Development and Assistance Programs.* Washington: Northeast-Midwest Institute, 1981.

4730. Orfield, Gary, and William L. Taylor. *Racial Segregation: Two Policy Views.* New York: Ford Foundation, 1979.

Gary Orfield and William L. Taylor outline plans for a concerted federal attack on urban segregation.

4731. Palmer, John L., and Isabel V. Sawhill, eds. *The Reagan Experiment: An Examination of Economic and Social Policies under the Reagan Administration.* Washington: Urban Institute Press, 1982.

4732. *Power in the States: The Changing Face of Politics across America.* Washington: Congressional Quarterly, 1984.

4733. Presidential Task Force on the Arts and Humanities. *Report to the President.* Washington: Government Printing Office, 1981.

4734. Project Share. *Block Grants: A Human Services Bibliography.* Rockville, Md.: Project Share, [198?].

4735. Rich, Abby D., and Charles J. Edwards, eds. *Guide to Federal Funding for Education.* 2 Vols. Arlington, Va.: Education Funding Research Council, 1987.

4736. Ruder, William, and Raymond Nathan. *The Businessman's Guide to Washington.* New York: Collier Books, [1975].

4737. Salamon, Lester M., and Alan J. Abramson. *The Federal Budget and the Nonprofit Sector.* Washington: Urban Institute Press, 1982.

Examines the scope and structure of the nonprofit sector, its relationships with government, and the impact of reduced federal funding proposals on the sector.

4738. Salamon, Lester M., and Alan J. Abramson. *The Federal Government and the Nonprofit Sector: Implications of the Reagan Budget Proposals.* Washington: Urban Institute Press, 1981.

4739. Salamon, Lester M. *The Nonprofit Sector and the Rise of Third-Party Government: The Scope, Character, and Consequences of Government Support of Nonprofit Organizations.* Washington: Urban Institute Press, 1983.

Looks at the relationship between government and the nonprofit sector and identifies the principles that might guide this relationship in the future. Reviews the past history of government-nonprofit interaction, assesses the current status, and suggests a framework for evaluating the evolution of government-nonprofit relationships in the future.

4740. Salamon, Lester M., and Alan J. Abramson. "Nonprofits and the Federal Budget: Deeper Cuts Ahead." *Foundation News* 26 (March-April 1985): 48-54.

4741. Scheiber, Jodie, ed. *Congressional Yellow Book: A Directory of Members of Congress, Including Their Committees and Key Staff Aides.* Washington: Monitor Publishing Co., 1987.

Entries for senators and representatives include information on political party and state represented, office location, major area(s) of career concentration prior to election to current office, key staff aides, legislative responsibility, other leadership positions and membership in informal groups, and addresses and phone numbers for state or district offices. Information on *Senate, House and Joint Committees* includes address and phone number, jurisdiction, majority and minority members, key staff aides, and subcommittees. Section on *Leadership, Party and Member* indicates address, phone number, description of intent, chairmen and staff contacts for senate and house leadership and party-related organizations, informal caucuses, task forces, coalitions, and bicameral groups. Also includes maps for state delegations and districts, listing senators by seniority and representatives by district.

4742. Siegel, Barry. "When It's Cutback Time at NIH." *Grantsmanship Center News* 13 (May-June 1985): 43+.

4743. Smith, Bruce L.R., ed. *The New Political Economy: The Public Use of the Private Sector.* New York: John Wiley, 1975.

This book, says Smith, "ultimately an exercise in political theory, explores the complex interrelationships between government and other institutions participating in the policy process—universities, health care providers, corporations, voluntary societies, multinational firms, and others. We seek a formulation that will help answer the question: how, in a policy process strongly influenced if not dominated by professionals, is government responsible to the people and their traditional representatives, to be made workable?" Twelve essays by political scientists, professionals in the voluntary sector, professors of law and public policy, and government officers seek to address this question. The term "new political economy" here signifies the increasingly large role of nongovernmental organizations in conducting the public's business. It is interesting to note that this is a reversal of the formulation used by several other studies dealing with a similar question: the increasing role of government in public domains previously attended to by private bodies (e.g., welfare).

4744. Straight, Michael. *Twigs for an Eagle's Nest. Government and the Arts, 1965-1978.* In Great Decades, no. 4. Berkely, Calif.: Devon Press, 1979.

4745. Suhrke, Henry C. *The Federal Government and the Nonprofit Sector: Philanthropy Monthly Reviews.* New Nilford, Conn.: Philanthropy Monthly Press, 1981.

4746. Tapper, Donna. *Coping with Cutbacks: A Study of the Differential Impact and Response by Voluntary Social Agencies in New York City to Government Funding Reductions.* New York: Community Council of Greater New York, 1982.

4747. Tober, James A. *Wildlife and the Public Interest: Nonprofit Organizations and Federal Wildlife Policy.* Program on Non-Profit Organizations, no. 80. New Haven, Conn.: Institution for Social and Policy Studies, 1984.

GOVERNMENT FUNDING AND THE NONPROFIT SECTOR

4748. Troxler, G. William, and H. Judith Jarrell. "Capital Ideas: How an Independent College Got State Government Aid." *Currents* 10 (March 1984): 46-8.

4749. United States. Congress. House. Committee of Foreign Aid. *Final Report on Foreign Aid Submitted to Congress by the Select Committee on Foreign Aid, 80th Congress, 2nd Session.* Washington: Government Printing Office, 1948.

4750. United States. Congress. Senate. Committee on Industrial Relations. *Final Report and Testimony Submitted to Congress by the Commission on Industrial Relations, 64th Congress, 1st Session.* Washington: Government Printing Office, 1916.

4751. United States. Congress. Senate. Committee on Industrial Relations. *Final Report. 64th Congress, 1st Session.* Washington: Government Printing Office, 1915.

4752. United States. Congress. Senate. Committee on Labor and Public Welfare. Special Subcommittee on Arts and Humanities. *National Arts and Humanities Foundations.* 2 vols. Washington: Government Printing Office, 1965.

4753. United States. Congress. Senate. Committee on Labor and Public Welfare. Special Subcommittee on Arts and Humanities. *Survey of United States and Foreign Government Support for Cultural Activities.* Washington: Government Printing Office, 1971.

4754. United States. Department of Education. *The Arts and the U.S. Department of Education: A List of Funded Projects and Activities, 1979.* Washington: U.S. Department of Education, 1979.

4755. United States. Department of Education. *Guide to Programs: Administered by Office of Higher Education Programs and Fund for Improvement of Post-Secondary Education.* Washington: U.S. Department of Education, 1987.

Provides essential information on programs administered by the Fund for the Improvement of Postsecondary Education and the Office of Higher Education Programs, including student support services, institutional development, incentive, and international education programs. Each entry describes the program, its authorizing legislation, eligibility requirements, funding cycle, closing date notice, appropriation for fiscal year 1986 and 1987, the number of awards granted, the average and range of grant amounts, and the contact address. Thirty-one programs in all, seven of which are new.

4756. United States. Department of Health and Human Services. Administration on Aging. *Education and Training Program Plans and Guidelines.* Rockville, Md.: U.S. Department of Health and Human Services, 1980.

4757. United States. Department of Health, Education and Welfare. *A Manual on State Mental Health Planning.* Rockville, Md.: U.S. Department of Health, Education and Welfare, 1977.

4758. United States. Department of Health, Education and Welfare. *National Institute of Mental Health Research Support Programs and Activities.* Rev. ed. Washington: Government Printing Office, 1980.

4759. United States. Department of Health, Education and Welfare. *Profiles of Financial Assistance Programs.* Rev. ed. Rockville, Md.: U.S. Department of Health, Education and Welfare, 1978.

Describes the financial assistance programs administered by the various agencies of the Public Health Service (Alchohol, Drug Abuse, and Mental Health Administration; Center for Disease Control; Food and Drug Administration; Health Resources Administration; Health Services Administration; National Institutes of Health; and the Office of the Assistant Secretary for Health). Profiles describe the purpose, legal basis, eligibility, special requirements, and application procedures for each grant.

4760. United States. Joint Economic Committee. *The Economics and Financing of Higher Education in the United States.* Washington: Government Printing Office, 1969.

4761. United States. Office of Management and Budget. *Catalog of Federal Domestic Assistance.* Washington: Government Printing Office, 1988.

Essential guide to financial and non-financial federal assistance available to state and local governments, private profit and nonprofit agencies, and individuals. Includes suggestions for proposal writing and following grant application procedures. Indexed by agency (with a summary of functions and activities), agency program (coded to show type(s) of assistance available), applicant eligibility (also coded), deadlines, functional summaries (amplification of the twenty functional categories under which all domestic assistance programs have been grouped), function (listing each program number and title under the appropriate basic category and subcategory), and subject. Each program entry includes information about the objectives of the program, the types of assistance available, uses and use restrictions, eligibility requirements, the application and award process, assistance considerations, post assistance requirements, financial information, program accomplishments, contact(s), related programs, examples of funded projects and the criteria for selecting proposals.

4762. United States. Office of Management and Budget. *Cost Principles for Nonprofit Organizations.* Washington: Government Printing Office, [198?].

4763. Urban Institute. *Serving Community Needs: The Nonprofit Sector in an Era of Governmental Retrenchment.* Progress Report, no. 3. Washington: Urban Institute Press, 1983.

4764. Weinstein, Amy, ed. *Public Welfare Directory.* Washington: American Public Welfare Association, 1987.

Guide to public human service programs offered by federal, state, territorial, county, and major municipal agencies in the United States and Canada. Descriptions of federal agencies include those most likely to have contact with state and local welfare agencies, and personnel listings indicating organizational structure and names, addresses, and direct-dial phone numbers for key personnel.

PART THREE

RELATED AND REFERENCE WORKS

12

GENERAL WORKS RELATED TO PHILANTHROPY

4765. Abels, Michael L. "Social Change in a 'Conservative' Setting." *Grantsmanship Center News* 11 (January-February 1983): 28-31.

4766. Academy for Educational Development. *The Energy Conservation Idea Handbook.* Washington: Academy for Educational Development, 1980.

4767. Academy for Educational Development. *The Idea Book for Colleges and Universities.* Washington: Academy for Educational Development, 1979.

4768. "AIDS: Giving Soars for Medical Care, Public Health; Foundation in Lead." *Giving USA Update* (March-April 1988): 1, 6.

Foundation grants directly related to AIDS increased from $216,000 in 1983 to more than $18 million by the middle of 1987, according to *AIDS: A Status Report on Foundation Funding*, a Foundation Center survey. Over half of the grant money went for direct medical care (58.8%), with the next two highest percentages being received by public health (20.5%) and research (17.8%). Examples of business giving to AIDS are also cited.

4769. Allen, Anne. "Award Winning Performers." *Foundation News* 25 (March-April 1984): 34.

4770. Allen, Anne. "The Problem That Won't Go Away." *Foundation News* 25 (July-August 1984): 54-9.

4771. Alperovitz, Gar, and Jeff Faux. *Rebuilding America: A Blueprint for the New Economy.* New York: Pantheon Books, 1984.

Frustrated by what they perceive as a gap between political economic theory and reality, the authors set out to address this central question: "What kind of economic policies meet the needs of the new economic era while reinforcing certain values—especially community and fairness—essential to support the kind of economic policies we need?" They begin by describing how the economic system is breaking down and examining "the disjuncture between an obsolete ideology and the new economic era." They then propose an integrated series of solutions for the "so-called" trade-off between stable prices and full employment. Finally they consider some of the institutional and political requirements for democratic planning, stressing the importance of locality and asserting that the absence of community is the central problem of our economy. The theme of the book is that building community ought to and can be the focus of economic planning.

4772. "America Responds to AIDS." *Fundemensions* 12 (March 1988): 4-8.

Describes the efforts undertaken by various sectors to confront the AIDS epidemic. The federal government is expected to approve a budget of more than $1.1 billion for AIDS research and services for fiscal 1989, while the Center for Disease Control is conducting a national AIDS awareness campaign that is linked to various state and local activities. Major U.S. corporations endorsed a set of principles which protect the rights of employees with the disease and bar employer-testing for the AIDS virus. In addition, many corporations have taken an early lead in AIDS education and research programs. The number of AIDS-related foundation grants is growing rapidly, with funds being awarded in several fields and across a broad geographic base. The Robert Wood Johnson Foundation has announced the nation's largest AIDS-related grant program, expected to award $19.6 million over four years, supporting projects that develop coordinated systems of health care for AIDS patients. Individual efforts, particularly by entertainers, publicize the need for AIDS funding, and singer Dionne Warwick has created a foundation to make grants to community-based or national organizations with effective local outreach programs which provide AIDS education and health care. While the initial response to the AIDS crisis was slow, funding for research, education, care and policy is now a priority on the national agenda.

4773. American Council of Learned Societies. *Scholarly Communication: The Report of the National Enquiry.* Baltimore, Md.: Johns Hopkins University Press, 1979.

4774. "Apple Plants Seeds for Community Networking." *Conserve Neighborhoods* (January 1984): 324.

4775. Arnett, Trevor. *Observations in the Financial Conditions of Colleges and Universities.* Occasional Papers, no. 9. New York: General Education Board, 1937.

4776. *Arts and the People. A Survey of Public Attitudes and Participation in the Arts Culture in New York State.* New York: National Research Center of the Arts, 1973.

4777. "Attitudes That Shape the Fight against AIDS." *New York Times* (2 June 1985): E-6.

4778. Badger, Henry G. *Statistics of Higher Education: Faculty, Students and Degrees, 1951-52.* Washington: Government Printing Office, [1955].

4779. Badger, Henry G. *Statistics of Higher Education: Receipts, Expenditures, and Property, 1951-52.* Washington: Government Printing Office, 1955.

4780. Barber, Virginia, and Rick Mathews. *Starting a Local Conservation and Passive Solar Retrofit Program: An Energy Planning Sourcebook.* Los Alamos, N.Mex.: Los Alamos National Laboratory, 1982.

4781. Barney, Gerald O., ed. *The Unfinished Agenda: The Citizen's Guide to the Environmental Issues.* Task Force Report sponsored by the Rockefeller Brothers Fund. New York: Thomas Y. Crowell Co., 1977.

4782. Bayer, Ronald. "AIDS, Power, and Reason." *Milbank Quarterly* 64 (September 1986): 168-82.

4783. Berger, Margaret A. *Litigation on Behalf of Women.* New York: Ford Foundation, 1980.

4784. Bloom, Kathryn, Junius Eddy, and Charles Fowler. *An Arts in Education Source Book: A View from the JDR 3rd Fund.* New York: JDR 3rd Fund, 1980.

4785. Boyer, Ernest L. *College: The Undergraduate Experience in America.* New York: Harper & Row, 1987.

Ernest Boyer and the Carnegie Foundation for the Advancement of Teaching undertake a study of the undergraduate experience in America, with particular attention given to the way the structures and procedures of colleges affect the lives of students. The report focuses on eight points of tension—conflicting priorities and competing interests that diminish the intellectual and social quality of the undergraduate experience and restrict the capacity of the college to effectively serve its students. The focus points are: the lack of continuity between school and higher education, the confusion concerning direction and purpose on the part of the colleges, conflicting loyalties and competing career concerns among the faculty, too much conformity and not enough creativity in the classroom, the gulf between academic and social life on campus, the complexities of campus governance, the methods of assessing the quality of education, and the connection between the campus and the world.

4786. Branscomb, Anne W. *Who Owns Information.* Occasional Paper, no. 2. New York: Gannett Center for Media Studies, 1986.

4787. Brecher, Charles, and Susan Nesbitt. *A Commonwealth Fund Paper: The Financial Condition of New York City Voluntary Hospitals.* New York: Commonwealth Fund, 1983.

4788. Cafferty, Pastora San Juan, and Gail Spangenberg. *Backs against the Wall: Urban-Oriented Colleges and Universities and the Urban Poor and Disadvantaged.* New York: Ford Foundation, 1983.

4789. Canter, MacKenzie, III. "What Is Fair Market Value?" *Philanthropy Monthly* 16 (April 1987): 25-9.

Brief but detailed explanation of the methods used to determine the value of a charitable contribution of property. Canter defines fair market value as the price at which the property would change hands between a willing buyer and a willing seller, neither being under any compulsion to buy or sell, and both having reasonable knowledge of relevant facts. The Internal Revenue Service (IRS) regards the determination of fair market value as a question of fact, not a legal issue. The burden of substantiating the claimed fair market value of the property is placed squarely on the taxpayer. The author describes the pitfalls of the methods of valuation, the appraisal of the property, IRS approved appraisal standards and format, and the new overvaluation penalties added by the 1981 Economic Recovery Tax Act and applicable to post-1981 returns.

4790. Carmody, Deirdre. "Public Library under Gregorian Celebrating a Good Year." *New York Times* (8 July 1982): B-1,B-6.

4791. Carnegie Commission on Higher Education. *The Campus and the City: Maximizing Assets and Reducing Liabilities.* Report and Recommendations by the Carnegie Commission on Higher Education. Hightstown, N.J.: Carnegie Commission on Higher Education, 1972.

4792. Carnegie Commission on Higher Education. *College Graduates and Jobs: Adjusting to a New Labor Market Situation.* Report and Recommendations by the Carnegie Commission on Higher Education. New York: McGraw-Hill, 1973.

4793. Carnegie Commission on Higher Education. *Continuity and Discontinuity: Higher Education and the Schools.* Report and Recommendations by the Carnegie Commission on Higher Education. New York: McGraw-Hill, 1973.

4794. Carnegie Commission on Higher Education. *A Digest of Reports of the Carnegie Commission on Higher Education with an Index of Recommendations and Suggested Assignments of Responsibility for Action.* New York: McGraw-Hill, 1974.

4795. Carnegie Commission on Higher Education. *Governance of Higher Education: Six Priority Problems.* Report and Recommendations by the Carnegie Commission on Higher Education. New York: McGraw-Hill, 1973.

4796. Carnegie Commission on Higher Education. *Higher Education: Who Pays? Who Benefits? Who Should Pay?* Report and Recommendations by the Carnegie Commission on Higher Education. New York: McGraw-Hill, 1975.

4797. Carnegie Commission on Higher Education. *Institutional Aid, Federal Support to Colleges and Universities.* Report and Recommendations by the Carnegie Commission on Higher Education. New York: McGraw-Hill, 1972.

4798. Carnegie Commission on Higher Education. *The More Effective Use of Resources, an Imperative for Higher Education.* Report and Recommendations by the Carnegie Commission on Higher Education. New York: McGraw-Hill, 1972.

4799. Carnegie Commission on Higher Education. *Opportunities for Women in Higher Education: Their Current Participation Prospects for the Future, and Recommendations for Action.* Report and Recommendations by the Carnegie Commission on Higher Education. New York: McGraw-Hill, 1973.

4800. Carnegie Commission on Higher Education. *Priorities for Action.* Hightstown, N.J.: Carnegie Commission on Higher Education, 1973.

4801. Carnegie Commission on Higher Education. *The Purposes and the Performances of Higher Education in the United States: Approaching the Year 2000.* Report and Recommendations by the Carnegie Commission on Higher Education. New York: McGraw-Hill, 1973.

4802. Carnegie Commission on Higher Education. *Reform on Campus, Changing Students, Changing Academic Programs.* Report and Recommendations by the Carnegie Commission on Higher Education. New York: McGraw-Hill, 1972.

4803. Carnegie Commission on Higher Education. *Sponsored Research of the Carnegie Commission on Higher Education.* New York: McGraw-Hill, 1975.

4804. Carnegie Commission on Higher Education. *Toward a Learning Society: Alternative Channels to Life, Work, and Service.* Report and Recommendations by the Carnegie Commission on Higher Education. New York: McGraw-Hill, 1973.

4805. Carnegie Commission on Higher Education. *Tuition.* Hightstown, N.J.: Carnegie Commission on Higher Education, 1974.

4806. Carnegie Commission on the Future of Public Broadcasting. *A Public Trust.* Report of the Carnegie Commission on the Future of Public Broadcasting. New York: Bantam, 1979.

4807. Carnegie Corporation of New York. *Keeping Pace with the New Television: Public Television and Changing Technology.* New York: VNU Books International, 1980.

4808. Carnegie Council on Policy Studies in Higher Education. *The Federal Role in Postsecondary Education: Unfinished Business, 1975-1980.* Report of the Carnegie Council on Policy Studies in Higher Education. San Francisco: Jossey-Bass Publishers, 1975.

4809. Carnegie Council on Policy Studies in Higher Education. *Progress and Problems in Medical and Dental Education: Federal Support Versus Federal Control.* San Francisco: Jossey-Bass Publishers, 1976.

4810. Carnegie Forum on Education and the Economy. *A Nation Prepared: Teachers for the 21st Century.* New York: Carnegie Forum, 1986.

The Carnegie Forum, "created to draw America's attention to the link between economic growth and the skills and abilities of the people who contribute to that growth, and to help develop education policies to meet the economic challenges ahead," recommends establishing higher standards for the teaching profession, such as an improved professional curriculum for graduate schools of education, the creation of a national board to review professional standards, and upgraded salaries and career opportunities to be competitive with those in other professions.

4811. Carnegie Foundation for the Advancement of Teaching. *More Than Survival: Prospects for Higher Education in a Period of Uncertainty.* San Francisco: Jossey-Bass Publishers, 1975.

4812. *Centers for Community Education Development and Other Resources.* Flint, Mich.: Charles Stewart Mott Foundation.

4813. Central Hanover Bank and Trust Company. *The Mental Hygiene Movement.* New York: Central Hanover Bank and Trust Co., 1937.

4814. Coleman, John R. "Diary of a Homeless Man." *New York* 16 (26 February 1983): 26-35.

4815. Coleman, Laurence Vail. *Historic House Museums.* Washington: American Association of Museums, 1933.

4816. Commission on the Humanities. *The Humanities in American Life.* Berkeley, Calif.: University of California Press, 1980.

4817. Commonwealth Fund. Commission on Elderly People Living Alone. *Medicare's Poor: Filling the Gaps in Medical Coverage for Low-Income Elderly Americans.* Baltimore, Md.: Commonwealth Fund, 1987.

4818. Council on Fine Arts. *A Survey of Arts and Cultural Activities in Chicago, 1977.* Chicago: Council on Fine Arts, [1979].

4819. Creager, John A. *The American Graduate Student: A Normative Description.* Research Reports, no. 5. Washington: American Council on Education, 1971.

4820. Crossland, Fred E. *Minority Access to College.* Ford Foundation Report. New York: Schocken Books, 1971.

4821. Culliton, Barbara, and Wallace Waterfall. *Prescription for Change.* Report of the Task Force on Academic Affairs. New York: Commonwealth Fund, 1985.

4822. Demkovich, Linda E. "FRAC: A Lean, Mean Hunger Machine." *Grantsmanship Center News* 10 (January-February 1984): 28-33.

4823. Desruisseaux, Paul. "Afro-American Studies Here to Stay, Ford Foundation Report Says." *Chronicle of Higher Education* 31 (18 September 1985): 30.

4824. Dewey, John. *The Public and Its Problems.* New York: Henry Holt & Co., 1927.

This volume grew out of a series of lectures Dewey delivered in 1926 at Kenyon College. Dewey's conception of the public is as an association which has added to itself political organization: the state. He examines the form and function of the state in democratic society and its growing difficulty in being responsive to a "public" that has been "lost" or "eclipsed," by which Dewey means has grown inchoate, pluralistic, and largely apathetic. He asserts that democratic ideals will not be realized in a world of rapidly advancing technology until communication and free social inquiry furnish us with intellectual symbols and ideals fit for our age. In presenting a method of achieving this goal, Dewey considers factors such as the relationship of the individual to society and the roles of community and associated activity.

4825. *Digest of Statistics on Higher Education in the United States, 1969-1970, 1973-74.* New York: TIAA-CREF, 1974.

4826. Donahey, Isabelle. "Where to Find Money in New York." *Voice of Experience* (June 1988): 18, 20, 22.

Brief summaries of forty-eight New York State agencies and programs that can help entrepreneurs and corporations get services and financial support. The programs are organized into six functions: financial assistance, infrastructure, research and development, tax incentives, business assistance, and training. Each listing includes contact person and phone number.

4827. Dooley, Betty L. "A Healthy Sign." *Foundation News* 25 (March-April 1984): 59.

4828. Ellman, Ira M. *Driven from the Tribunal: Judicial Resolution of Internal Church Disputes.* Reprint. Program on Non-Profit Organizations, no. 44. New Haven, Conn.: Institution for Social and Policy Studies, 1981.

4829. Etheredge, Lynn. "Private Foundations, Government, and Social Change: Home and Community-Based Care for the Elderly." *Health Affairs* 6 (Spring 1987): 176-89.

Beginning with this essay, *Health Affairs* introduces a new section concerning trends in health philanthropy. The first essay analyzes public policy surrounding the issue of home and community-based care for the elderly. It reviews the recent work of the most active foundations engaged in implementing social policy changes through improved home and community-based care for the elderly. It also reports on both the broad strategies and major projects by which these private foundations seek to influence public policy. The essay is based on interviews with foundation officials and researchers as well as foundation reports. The urgency for the creation of home and community-based care lies in the projections of the demographics of American society. In the next fifty years, the population of people sixty-five and over will increase from 27 million to 51 million in the year 2020 and to 67 million in 2040. Those eighty-five and older who demand the greatest care will be the fastest growing part of American society. This rapidly increasing and aging population will strain an already burdened health care system. Currently the government long-term care policies have financed a nursing home-based service system rather than home and community-based care. In addition, federal Medicaid funds have been allocated on the basis of state spending and per capita income without regard to the number of poor or elderly persons in need of assistance. This health care crisis, writes Etheredge, has been addressed by foundations through six broad strategies. They have sought to increase national learning by funding research studies, develop the current system's capacity, create new institutions to manage care, upgrade educational capacity for key personnel, assist users of long-term care, and support prevention and model care programs. The article reviews the government's policies on elder health care and compares government and foundation funding differences.

4830. "Excerpts from Newman's Report on Higher Education Policy." *Chronicle of Higher Education* 31 (18 September 1985): 17+.

4831. Fadiman, Mark. "Break a Leg, Cleveland." *Forbes* 134 (July 1984): 74+.

4832. Feld, Alan L., Michael O'Hare, and J. Mark Davidson Schuster. *Patrons Despite Themselves: Taxpayers and Arts Policy.* New York: New York University Press, 1983.

4833. Feshbach, Norma. *Early Schooling in England and Israel.* New York: McGraw-Hill, 1973.

4834. Fisher, Robert. *Let the People Decide: Neighborhood Organizing in America.* New York: Twayne Publishers, 1984.

Provides a general history of the dominant strategies for neighborhood organizing since 1880. Fisher's goal was to write a social history that did not isolate the neighborhood from its national economic and political situation. To do this, he divides the past century into five blocks that represent major differences in the national political economy and changes in the dominant form of political organizing. He analyzes the most crucial local organizing movement of each period. Fisher characterizes the history of neighborhood organizing by three distinct approaches: social work, political activism, and neighborhood maintenance. Included are studies of the Cincinnati Social Unit Plan, the Back of the Yards Neighborhood Council (led by Saul Alinsky), some of the Communist party's organization efforts, and the Houston Civic Clubs. Fisher says that current efforts at neighborhood organizing lack a sense of its past, with most people thinking the movement is at most twenty years old. In fact, as he shows, it has its roots in the late nineteenth century. Bibliographical essay.

4835. Fitzgibbons, Ruth Miller. "Vintage Victorian: Swiss Avenue's Wilson Block Is Restored to New Life." *D [Dallas Magazine]* 9 (November 1982): 118-21.

4836. Ford Foundation. *Civil Rights, Social Justice, and Black America.* Working Paper from the Ford Foundation. New York: Ford Foundation, 1984.

4837. Ford Foundation. *Created Equal.* Report on Ford Foundation Women's Programs. New York: Ford Foundation, 1986.

4838. Ford Foundation. *Hispanics: Challenges and Opportunities.* Working Paper from the Ford Foundation. New York: Ford Foundation, 1984.

4839. Ford Foundation. *Research Universities and the National Interest. A Report from Fifteen University Presidents.* New York: Ford Foundation, 1978.

4840. Ford Foundation. *Toward Greatness in Higher Education.* New York: Ford Foundation, 1964.

4841. Ford Foundation. *Women, Children, and Poverty in America.* Working Paper from the Ford Foundation. New York: Ford Foundation, 1985.

4842. Ford Foundation. *Women in the World.* Ford Foundation position paper. New York: Ford Foundation, 1980.

4843. Fox, Daniel M. "AIDS and the American Health Polity: The History and Prospects of a Crisis of Authority." *Milbank Quarterly* 64 (September 1986): 7-33.

4844. Gardner, John W. *Excellence: Can We Be Equal and Excellent Too?* Rev. ed. New York: W.W. Norton & Co., 1984.

4845. Garfield, Robert. "Patent Fight: Inventor's Battle for Cable Cements His Fame, Fortune." *USA Today* (3 August 1983).

4846. Gaylin, Willard, Ira Glasser, Steven Marcus, et al. *Doing Good: The Limits of Benevolence.* New York: Pantheon Books, 1978.

The four essays in this volume, *In the Beginning: Helpless and Dependent, Their Brother's Keepers: An Episode from English History, The State As Parent: Social Policy in the Progressive Era,* and *Prisoners of Benevolence: Power versus Liberty in the Welfare State,* written by a psychoanalyst, a humanist, a historian, and a social worker, respectively, represent "an attempt to clarify how it is that, particularly in the United States, dependency and benevolence have become such problematic subjects." The authors examine the concept of "paternalism"—social policy derived from the biological model of the caring parent, the history of benevolence in England and the United States as evidenced by "reforms" in English poor laws and twentieth-century progressive "reforms" in America, and implications for modern social policy that seeks to be "decent and caring without being coercive." Certain essays include mention of further reading in the subject.

4847. Gehrig, Cynthia. "Portrait of the Producer As Artist." *Foundation News* 28 (January-February 1987): 76-8.

Cynthia Gehrig, president of the Jerome Foundation, discusses the funding of film and video art which operates ahead and outside of the mainstream of American art. There are a few private funding agencies that recognize the value of film and video art forms and lend them support, writes Gehrig. Specifically, she cites the Jerome Foundation and Art Matters, Inc. In addition to direct giving, there are creative funding methods such as the Pioneer Fund which supports individuals through sponsoring nonprofit organizations; and the Hewlett Foundation which worked with the Film Arts Foundation to establish a re-granting program (a partnership in which private funding supplements or attracts public support). Other foundation examples are discussed including the Rockefeller Foundation media arts program which dates back to the mid-1960's and the impact of the multi-faceted program in media arts by the National Endowment for the Arts.

4848. Geiger, Roger L. *After the Emergence: Voluntary Support and the Building of American Research Universities.* Program on Non-Profit Organizations, no. 87. New Haven, Conn.: Institution for Social and Policy Studies, 1985.

4849. Geiger, Roger L. *American Private Higher Education in Comparative Perspective.* Program on Non-Profit Organizations, no. 39. New Haven, Conn.: Institution for Social and Policy Studies, 1981.

4850. Geiger, Roger L. *Creating Private Alternatives in Higher Education.* Program on Non-Profit Organizations, no. 97. New Haven, Conn.: Institution for Social and Policy Studies, 1985.

Argues that private universities can complement state institutions in some socially beneficial ways, serving as outlets for groups in society that feel themselves ill-served by the majority-oriented state-run system, and as vehicles for increasing pluralism, innovation and the input of private resources to higher education.

4851. Goodlad, John I. *The Dynamics of Educational Change: Toward Responsive Schools.* New York: McGraw-Hill, [1975].

4852. Goodlad, John I., M. Frances Klein, and Jerrold M. Novotney. *Early Schooling in the United States.* IDEA Reports on Schooling. Early Schooling Series. New York: McGraw-Hill, 1973.

4853. Goodman, Charles, and Wolf von Eckhardt. *Life for Dead Spaces: The Development of the Lavanburg Commons.* New York: Harcourt, Brace & World, 1963.

4854. Gostin, Larry. "The Future of Communicable Disease Control: Toward a New Concept in Public Health Law." *Milbank Quarterly* 64 (September 1986): 79-96.

4855. Gross, Ronald. "Budget-KO'd Scholars Come Back Fighting." *New York Times* (21 August 1983): 31-2.

4856. Hallett, Stanley. "The Limits of a Model Community Bank." *Grantsmanship Center News* 12 (January-February 1984): 46-50.

4857. Halperin, Samuel. *The Forgotten Half: Pathways to Success for America's Youth and Young Families. Youth and America's Future Final Report.* Washington: William T. Grant Foundation Commission on Work, Family and Citizenship, 1988.

Final report by the William T. Grant Foundation Commission on Work, Family and Citizenship. The report features not only diagnoses for treating youth in trouble but prescriptions to foster the healthy development of all youth and to prevent trouble from occuring. It describes pathways to success that families and communities with adequate help from both the public and private sector including employers can offer to young people. Conclusions of the study include the fact there is a tendency to view youth mainly as problems to be solved; we invest much more in college-bound youth than in those seeking work after high school; changes in the economy and American life-styles have eroded the family's ability to serve youth; and there is more than enough evidence available to justify major additional public and private investments in youth. The Commission's major recommendations require additional long-term investments by all levels of government; other recommendations are directed at employers, nonprofit organizations and private philanthropy.

4858. Halstead, D. Kent. *College and University Endowment.* Washington: Government Printing Office, 1965.

4859. Halstead, D. Kent. *Higher Education Prices and Price Indexes.* Washington: Government Printing Office, 1975.

4860. Hamburg, David M. "Investing in Children." *Response* 12 (March 1983): 19-20.

4861. Hammond, J.D., and Arnold F. Shapiro. "AIDS and the Limits of Insurability." *Milbank Quarterly* 64 (September 1986): 143-67.

4862. Harari, Maurice. *Internationalizing the Curriculum and the Campus: Guidelines for AASCU Institutions.* Washington: American Association of State Colleges and Universities, 1981.

4863. Harrar, J. George. *Strategy for the Conquest of Hunger.* New York: Rockefeller Foundation, 1963.

4864. Harrington, Michael. *The Other America: Poverty in the United States.* Reprint. New York: Penguin Books, 1971.

This book, widely recognized as the impetus for Lyndon Johnson's "War on Poverty," describes the 40-50 million citizens of the United States (in 1962) who live in poverty as an invisible part of our society. Harrington maintains that the increasingly segmented development of American society is creating a new blindness about the poor, who are slipping out of the consciousness of the nation. The poor live in parts of the city or the country where others do not venture; they are relatively well-clothed even if they are hungry, homeless, or ill; many of them are over sixty-five or under eighteen and more likely to remain within the confines of a room or neighborhood; and they are politically invisible and mute. Harrington argues that the creation of the welfare state helped the poor less than any other class—that they were left behind by the rest of society. He also points out that the debilitating psychological effect of poverty—the loss of aspiration—is a consequence of the new invisibility of today's poor and characterizes the poor as "immune to progress." His concluding chapter, *The Two Nations*, outlines some recommendations for reform, which he argues must be undertaken by the federal government to be effective.

4865. Harris and Associates, Louis. *A Catalyst for Action: A National Survey to Mobilize Leadership and Resources for the Prevention of Alcohol and Other Drug Problems among American Youth.* Louis Harris Study, no. 874007. New York: Louis Harris & Associates, 1988.

4866. *Helping Minority Students Succeed.* Washington: Association of American Colleges, 1985.

4867. Hesburgh, Theodore M., Paul A. Miller, and Clifton R. Wharton, Jr. *Patterns for Lifelong Learning: A Report of Explorations Supported by the W.K. Kellogg Foundation.* San Francisco: Jossey-Bass Publishers, 1973.

4868. Hodgkinson, Harold L. "Putting Your Campus Assets to Work Full Time." *Currents* 9 (September 1983): 14-7.

4869. Holloway, George T. "Accountability and Ethics: A Priority for All Fund Raisers." *Fund Raising Management* 18 (July 1987): 82, 84-5.

Article on the accountability of religious fundraisers. The recent Jim and Tammy Bakker scandal and Oral Roberts' questionable fundraising methods on broadcast television have caused a plunge in religious contributions. The lack of public confidence and dollars has begun a dialogue on accountability and ethics in the religious community. Holloway, executive director of the National Catholic Development Conference (NCDC), addresses Catholic fundraising, the United States Catholic Bishops' *Principles and Guidelines for Fund Raising in the U.S.* and NCDC's code of ethics, nationwide seminars and *A Guide for Preparing a Statement of Accountability.*

4870. Hosmer, Charles Bridgham. *Presence of the Past: A History of the Preservation Movement in the United States before Williamsburg.* New York: Putnam, [1965].

4871. "Hospice Letter." *Hospice Letter* 9 (February 1983): 1-6.

4872. Housing Assistance Council. *Taking Stock: Rural People and Poverty from 1970 to 1983.* Washington: Housing Assistance Council, 1984.

4873. Hunter, Marjorie. "Budget Cuts Threaten Historic Houses." *New York Times* (5 January 1984): C-12+.

4874. Jellema, William W. *Higher Education Finance: A Comparative Study of Matched Samples of Black and White Private Institutions.* Atlanta, Ga.: Southern Regional Education Board, 1972.

4875. Johnson, Robert Matthews. "What's Happening to the Neighborhood Movement?" *Foundation News* 25 (January-February 1984): 36+.

4876. Johnson Foundation, Robert Wood. *The School-Based Adolescent Health Care Program.* Princeton, N.J.: Robert Wood Johnson Foundation, 1986.

4877. Jones, David R. "Coming of Age." *Foundation News* 28 (July-August 1987): 16-21.

An article on ethically or socially responsible investment. The author traces the historic development of ethically and socially responsible investing (SRI) beginning in the 1960's, citing such influences as Saul Alinsky's 1967 strategy in Rochester, New York, of obtaining Kodak stock proxies for the group called FIGHT to obtain jobs for the black community; Ralph Nader's 1970 campaign against General Motors; and the South Africa disinvestment movement. The article reviews the growth, acceptance and success of SRI's including Lyndon Comstock's Bank for Socially Responsible Lending (BSRL). BSRL will combine traditional banking with a social goal to "stimulate the growth of a socially responsible business sector whose activities will provide for community-based economic development." The bank provides all the usual services, but also provides construction and mortgage loans, lines of credit and standby commitments. The socially invested funds appear competitive with traditional funds. "People don't have to give up return to do ethical investing," states Social Investment Forum's Gordon Davidson.

4878. Jones, Gareth Stedman. *Outcast London: A Study in the Relationship between Classes in Victorian Society.* New York: Pantheon Books, 1984.

Gareth Stedman Jones argues that London experienced a crisis of social and industrial development in the last quarter of the nineteenth century, primarily involving the problem of casual labor, the first generation of unemployed workers in England. He argues that the existence of certain endemic forms of poverty associated with casual labor aroused fear in various classes in a city which symbolized national and imperial power. As Jones puts it, "The presence of an unknown number of the casual poor, indistinguishable to many contemporaries from criminals, apparently divorced from all forms of established religion, or ties with their social superiors, inhabiting unknown cities within the capital, constituted a disquieting alien presence in the midst of mid-Victorian plenty...so London, impregnable from without, might become vulnerable to an even more potent and volatile threat from within." The book studies the efforts—charitable, reformist, and others—of middle and upper class London to deal with this poor underclass of casual laborers. Extensive bibliography.

4879. Jones, Lawrence N. "Serving 'the Least of These'." *Foundation News* 25 (September-October 1984): 58-61.

Profiles social service programs of black churches.

4880. Joseph, James A. "Private-Religious Collaboration: Asking the Right Questions Together." *Foundation News* 25 (September-October 1984): 51-3.

4881. Judge, Harry. *American Graduate Schools of Education: A View from Abroad.* New York: Ford Foundation, 1982.

4882. Kanter, Rosabeth Moss. *Commitment and Community: Communes and Utopias in Sociological Perspective.* Cambridge, Mass.: Harvard University Press, 1972.

Kanter examines the ideas and values underlying utopian communities and communal living in the nineteenth century and the present. Her focus is on how groups are built and maintained. To skeptics of communes, she demonstrates that a number of such communities have in fact been successful. She also warns, however, that important organizational considerations need to be taken into account for a community to be viable. Kanter hopes that her historical and sociological account of communes and utopian communities in America will help readers understand social life in general by exposing challenges to common assumptions about human social nature. In this vein, she explores the issue of whether such communities can solve contemporary social problems and speculates as to the possibilities for new social institutions, from consumer cooperatives to community development corporations. 350-item bibliography.

4883. Kass, Stephen L., Judith M. LaBelle, and David A. Hansell. *Rehabilitating Older and Historic Buildings: Law, Taxation, Strategies.* New York: John Wiley, 1985.

Guide to the legal, financial, and regulatory processes involved in the rehabilitation of historic and older buildings. Covers federal income tax and state and local incentives, historic preservation certifications and federal and state statutory protection for historic buildings, private and public financing opportunities, and descriptions of four preservation projects that illustrate both the common elements and the extraordinary diversity of the rehabilitation process; the examples cover the range from a small residential building to a low-income housing project to the comprehensive Forty-second Street development project in New York City. Appendixes contain copies of numerous pertinent documents.

4884. Kass, Stephen L., Judith M. LaBelle, and David A. Hansell. *Rehabilitating Older and Historic Buildings. Supplement.* New York: John Wiley, 1988.

Updates the 1985 edition, containing detailed coverage of statutory, regulatory, and business developments, including the ongoing effects of the 1986 tax reform upon the legal, real estate, and preservation communities.

4885. Kellogg Foundation, W.K. *Rural Development and Higher Education: The Linking of Community and Method.* Battle Creek, Mich.: W.K. Kellogg Foundation, [197?].

4886. Kendall, Elizabeth. *Dancing.* Report of the Ford Foundation. New York: Ford Foundation, 1983.

4887. Klineberg, Otto. *Mental Health: An Interdisciplinary and International Perspective.* Austin, Tex.: Hogg Foundation for Mental Health, 1981.

4888. Knowles, Louis L. "Religion Gives As Well As It Gets." *Fund Raising Management* 18 (July 1987): 54, 56-8, 114.

Short paper on religious giving by Louis L. Knowles, director of the religious philanthropy program at the Council on Foundations. The article contains data from a 1984 Council on Foundations survey of philanthropic activity by non-parish religious organizations. The survey shows that the churches and synagogues have been in the forefront of assisting Americans who have fallen through the government's "safety nets." It also reveals that religious philanthropy on the local level includes cash and non-cash support of human needs. Emergency food and refugee assistance topped the list of most frequently mentioned activities in a survey. As an example, the paper cites a 1986 estimate by Trinity Church that religious organizations provided eighty-five percent of emergency food and meals in New York City. The article also reviews national religious grantmaking programs which are free from governmental restrictions and can thus fund small, grassroots groups and organizations that generate controversy, and mentions evangelical and new age religious philanthropic activity.

4889. Kotz, Nick. *Hunger in America: The Federal Response.* New York: Field Foundation, 1979.

4890. Kozol, Jonathan. *Alternative Schools.* Rev. ed. New York: Continuum Publishing Co., 1982.

4891. Kuller, Lewis H., and Lawrence A. Kingsley. "The Epidemic of AIDS: A Failure of Public Health Policy." *Milbank Quarterly* 64 (September 1986): 56-78.

4892. Lansford, Henry. "Resurrecting Denver's Lost Neighborhood." *Foundation News* 25 (July-August 1984): 50-3.

Denver foundations support redevelopment of city land.

4893. Lape, Esther Everett. *Medical Research: A Mid-Century Survey.* 2 Vols. Boston: Little, Brown, 1955.

4894. Learmont, Carol L., and Stephen Van Houten. "Placements and Salaries, 1982." *Library Journal* 108 (15 September 1983): 1760-766.

4895. Levy, Daniel C., ed. *Private Education: Studies in Choice and Public Policy.* Yale Studies on Nonprofit Organizations. New York: Oxford University Press, 1986.

Part of the Yale Studies on Nonprofit Organizations, this scholarly collection of papers focuses on one of the largest fields of American private nonprofit activity—education. Elementary and secondary as well as higher education are examined. In an era of heated debate over the use of federal funds for education in private schools and the conversion of compensatory education funds into vouchers, this interdisciplinary volume does not expound either a pro-private or a pro-public stance. The authors, Daniel C. Levy, Mary-Michelle Upson Hirschoff, Mark A. Kutner, Joel D. Sherman, Mary F. Williams, Donald A. Erickson, Estelles James, Richard J. Murname, and Roger L. Geiger suggest ways which they believe that one sector or the other may be preferable for certain groups or goals. The essays discuss public policy and private choice as they affect the quality, finance, governance, mission, and division of labor; as well as the impact of public funding on institutional autonomy, private choice, and client satisfaction. Each paper contains endnotes. The book includes notes on the contributors, a selected bibliography and an index.

4896. Lyons, Gene M. *The Uneasy Partnership: Social Science and the Federal Government in the Twentieth Century.* New York: Russell Sage Foundation, 1969.

4897. Margolis, Richard J. "One Worthwhile Coffee Klatch." *Foundation News* 23 (November-December 1982): 12+.

4898. Margolis, Richard J. "To Live on This Earth." *Foundation News* 25 (March-April 1984): 18-28.

4899. Margolis, Richard J. "Will the Patient Live?" *Foundation News* 26 (September-October 1985): 33+.

4900. "Matching Business Resources with Neighborhood Needs." *Home Again* (Winter 1983): 13.

4901. May, William F. "Christian Charity: Its Roots, Its Forms, Its Critics." *Foundation News* 25 (September-October 1984): 32-6.

4902. McAndrew, Alice. "Common Ground: The Marriage of America's Rural and Corporate Workplace." *American City* (August 1985): 42-9.

4903. McBeath Foundation, Faye. *White Paper on Self-Care.* Milwaukee, Wis.: Consumer Health Consultants, 1979.

4904. McDonald, Jean A. "Survey Finds Religious Groups Strongly Favor More Collaboration." *Foundation News* 25 (September-October 1984): 20-4.

Looks at philanthropic giving by religious groups and discusses their interest in cooperative efforts with other philanthropic entities.

4905. Miles, Matthew B., ed. *Innovation in Education.* New York: Columbia University, 1964.

4906. Morrison, Jack. *The Rise of the Arts on the American Campus.* New York: McGraw-Hill, 1973.

4907. Mueller, Daniel P., and Paul S. Higgins. *Funders' Guide Manual. A Guide to Prevention Programs in Human Services: Focus on Children and Adolescents.* 1st ed. St. Paul, Minn.: Amherst H. Wilder Foundation, 1988.

Result of an eighteen-month project designed to gather and analyze information on prevention programming in human services of use to funders. The project is part of a larger Prevention Planning Initiative at the Amherst H. Wilder Foundation. This guide reviews and analyzes available research literature on prevention effectiveness in four problem areas affecting youth: child abuse and neglect; poor school performance and school failure; teenage pregnancy; and teenage substance abuse. It is hoped the findings will help funders to assess the merits of specific prevention program proposals, and presents key questions funders should ask about such proposals: What impact will the program have on its targeted problem, if successful? Is the proposed program truly aimed at prevention? Is it soundly conceived, based on current knowledge of effectiveness? Is the timing of the preventive intervention consistent with achieving maximum program effectiveness? And does the program have an adequate evaluation component? Discusses factors associated with prevention program effectiveness; identifies common patterns across the problem areas; and recommends future directions for prevention efforts. Also includes a list of key persons and organizations to contact in the prevention field, indicating their area(s) of expertise.

4908. Murnane, Richard J., and Stuart Newstead. *Comparing Public and Private Schools: The Puzzling Role of Selectivity Bias.* Program on Non-Profit Organizations, no. 68. New Haven, Conn.: Institution for Social and Policy Studies, 1983.

4909. Murnane, Richard J. *Comparisons of Public and Private Schools: Lessons from the Uproar.* Program on Non-Profit Organizations, no. 73. New Haven, Conn.: Institution for Social and Policy Studies, 1983.

4910. Murnane, Richard J. *The Uncertain Consequences of Tuition Tax Credits: An Analysis of Student Achievement and Economic Incentives.* Program on Non-Profit Organizations, no. 46. New Haven, Conn.: Institution for Social and Policy Studies, 1982.

4911. Musto, David F. "Quarantine and the Problem of AIDS." *Milbank Quarterly* 64 (September 1986): 97-117.

4912. Naisbitt, John. *Megatrends: Ten New Directions Transforming Our Lives.* New York: Warner Books, 1982.

4913. National Association of Small Business Investment Companies. *Venture Capital, Where to Find It. Membership Directory.* Washington: National Association of Small Business Investment Companies, 1985.

4914. National Commission of the Reform of Secondary Education. *The Reform of Secondary Education.* New York: McGraw-Hill, 1973.

4915. National Science Foundation. *Research and Development and Its Impact on the Economy.* Washington: National Science Foundation, 1958.

4916. National Trust for Historic Preservation. *Bibliography for Neighborhood Leaders.* Washington: National Trust for Historic Preservation, 1980.

4917. Nelkin, Dorothy, and Stephen Hilgartner. "Disrupted Dimensions of Risk: A Public School Controversy over AIDS." *Milbank Quarterly* 64 (September 1986): 118-42.

4918. Nevin, David. *Left-Handed Fastballers: Scouting and Training America's Grass-Roots Leaders, 1966-1977.* New York: Ford Foundation, 1981.

4919. Nichols, Dan. "How to Get Cash without Compromising Ethics." *Fund Raising Management* 18 (July 1987): 30-4, 81.

Religious ethics essay. Dan Nichols, former news and information director for National Religious Broadcasters and associate editor of *Religious Broadcasting* magazine explains that the PTL scandal and the Oral Roberts "cash-or-death" television threat has led to distrust of broadcast ministries and the loss of public confidence and contributions. The recent occurrences have dealt "a serious blow to the credibility of TV evangelists" resulting in contribution losses. Robert Schuller's donations are down 2.7 percent, Pat Robertson's CBN has lost approximately $10 million in donations, and Jimmy Swaggart's donations are down $8 million. Nichols proposes guidelines for accountability and ethics which he calls *The Ten Commandments of Religious Fund Raising.* With the proposals, this religious broadcast insider relates examples of behavior in religious fundraising which necessitate an ethical code, stating that some televangelists spend as much as half their program seeking donations like "sanctified Tupperware salesmen."

4920. "NOPEC Works to Conserve Energy Costs." *Nonprofit Executive* 3 (June 1984): 1-7.

4921. Ogg, Frederic Austin. *Research in the Humanistic and Social Sciences.* New York: Century Co., 1928.

4922. Pace, C. Robert. *The Demise of Diversity? A Comparative Profile of Eight Types of Institutions.* Hightstown, N.J.: Carnegie Commission on Higher Education, 1974.

4923. Pattillo, Manning M., Jr., and Donald Mackenzie. *Church-Sponsored Higher Education in the United States.* Report of the Danforth Commission. Washington: American Council on Education, 1966.

4924. Pear, Robert. "$20 Million Private Project to Aid Homeless." *New York Times* (4 December 1983): 1.

4925. Pifer, Alan. *Women Working: Toward a New Society.* Reprint. New York: Carnegie Corporation of New York, 1976.

4926. Piven, Frances Fox, and Richard A. Cloward. *Regulating the Poor: The Functions of Public Welfare.* New York: Vintage, 1972.

Piven and Cloward advance the provocative argument that relief policies—public welfare—are designed "to mute civil disorder, and restrictive ones to reinforce work norms." After introducing this theory with reference to other countries and other historical periods, the authors focus on the rise of mass disorder and the initiation of national relief programs during the Great Depression. They also look at the consequences that giving relief had for the control of disorder. Next, they demonstrate that in the more stable 1940s and 1950s relief arrangements were designed to reinforce work norms. Finally, Piven and Cloward examine the economic sources of the outbreak of civil disorder in the 1960s, which resulted in a great upsurge in the welfare rolls. They use history, political interpretation, and sociological analysis to argue that what lies at the crux of the welfare system is not the spirit of philanthropy, but a desire to maintain social and economic inequities necessary for the functioning of a market economy.

4927. Porto, Linda. "What Is the Ad Council and How Does It Work?" *NPO Resource Review* 2 (July-August 1984): 2.

4928. Pottlitzer, Joanne. *Hispanic Theater in the United States and Puerto Rico.* New York: Ford Foundation, 1988.

This report on Hispanic theater in the United States was originally prepared to acquaint the Ford Foundation with the scope of Hispanic theater activity and to place it in a broader historical and cultural context. In the course of her two-year research throughout the country in 1984-85, Ms. Pottlitzer uncovered so much interesting material, both historical and current, that the Ford Foundation decided to make the report available to the public. The report discusses Hispanic theater within its complex cultural context. Chapters 2 and 3 present a brief history of Hispanic theater activity throughout the northern hemisphere—emphasizing regional differences and the variety of genres. Chapter 4 surveys current theater activity in the United States. Chapter 5 presents recommendations for increasing the stability and fostering the growth of this art form. In the course of this study Ms. Pottlitzer surveyed some 150 institutions and interviewed more than 200 people connected with Hispanic theatre.

4929. *Poverty in America: The Impact of Changing Attitudes and Public Policies on the Poor. Proceedings of the Conference of the National Assembly and the National Conference on Social Welfare.* Washington: National Assembly of National Voluntary Health and Social Welfare Organizations, 1984.

4930. Pyle, Kathryn, and Carol G. Simonetti. *The Teen Parent Collaboration: A Cooperative Venture between National and Community Foundations.* Washington. Council on Foundations, 1985.

Reports on various aspects of the collaborative effort between the Ford Foundation, a private foundation, and a group of community foundations, which produced the Teen Parent Collaboration. Issues include roles and responsibilities; expectations compared with outcome; interaction with other participants; assessment of the three phases of the project; impact on the participants and their foundations; and the cost of the collaboration in dollars and staff time. Examines the current position of collaboration in the philanthropic field; the Teen Parent Collaboration background; the historical role of community foundations; and examples of two other major efforts to develop skills in collaboration on a national scale. Describes the Collaboration, the perspective of the community foundations, the Ford Foundation, and the intermediaries on the Collaboration, and offers recommendations developed from their joint experience. Among these: all parties should participate in the planning and implementation to facilitate both equality and networking; written agreements are important for the clarification of goals, objectives, responsibilities, and roles; and the effort must allow for sufficient planning time if the collaboration is to be organized and coordinated.

4931. Pyle, Kathryn, and Carol G. Simonetti. *The Teen Parent Collaboration: A Cooperative Venture between National and Community Foundations.* [Summary]. Washington: Council on Foundations, 1985.

Executive summary of the Teen Parent Collaboration, a two-year national project benefiting teenage mothers and fathers. This report, as issued by the Council on Foundations, is concerned with evaluating the collaborative effort as a whole, determining the benefits and problems involved with such a project. The difficulties included securing funds and/or appropriate staff, which could have been anticipated; a lack of clarity among community foundation staff as to the Ford Foundation's role in program support; and insufficient interaction among many of the participants, which was a result of too much focus being placed upon the programs without realizing that the collaboration itself required attention. The full report develops on these and many more aspects of the Teen Parent Collaboration in particular, as well as the addressing the general issue of collaboration as a grantmaking option.

4932. Raley, Nancy. "A Medley of Radio Winners." *Currents* 10 (March 1984): 18-23.

4933. Riccio, James A., and Delia L. Council. *The Teen Parent Collaboration: Strengthening Services for Teen Mothers.* New York: Manpower Demonstration Research Corporation, 1985.

4934. Riccio, James A., and Delia L. Council. *The Teen Parent Collaboration: Strengthening Services for Teen Mothers.* [Summary]. New York: Manpower Demonstration Research Corporation, [1985].

4935. Richards, Charles R. *The Industrial Museum.* New York: Macmillan, 1925.

4936. Robertson, Gail. "A Community United." *Grassroots Fundraising Journal* 4 (June 1985): 9-11.
Describes a successful grassroots fundraising project.

4937. Robinson, Marshall. "Social Science Research: Shifting Infatuation with a Critical Resource." *Foundation News* 24 (September-October 1983): 58+.

4938. Rockefeller Foundation. *Symposium on Strategy for the Conquest of Hunger. Proceedings.* New York: Rockefeller University, 1968.

4939. Roel, Raymond. "The Challenge and Rewards of Promoting the Bible." *Fund Raising Management* 15 (November 1984): 34-46.
Interview discusses the use of executive volunteers.

4940. Rogers, James F. *Staffing American Colleges and Universities.* Washington: Government Printing Office, 1967.

4941. Rose-Ackerman, Susan. *Mental Retardation and Society: The Ethics and Politics of Normalization.* Program on Non-Profit Organizations, no. 27. New Haven, Conn.: Institution for Social and Policy Studies, 1980.

4942. Rose-Ackerman, Susan. *Unintended Consequences: Regulating the Quality of Subsidized Day Care.* Program on Non-Profit Organizations, no. 69. New Haven, Conn.: Institution for Social and Policy Studies, 1983.

4943. Rosenberg, Charles E. "Disease and Social Order in America: Perceptions and Expectations." *Milbank Quarterly* 64 (September 1986): 34-55.

4944. Rothman, David J. *The Discovery of the Asylum: Social Order and Disorder in the New Republic.* Boston: Little, Brown, 1981.

Rothman is concerned with the revolution in social practice after 1820, in which Americans suddenly began to construct and support institutions—penitentiaries, asylums, reformatories, and almshouses—for the deviant and dependent members of the community. His primary question is: Why were these institutions considered "reforms"—or steps forward—in the usual sense of the word? The creation of these institutions, Rothman argues, represented an attempt to insure the cohesion and stability of the community in new and changing circumstances. By the 1820s, the causes of poverty, crime, and insanity were perceived to lie in the faulty organization of the community, a viewpoint which naturally led to the development of a community-based solution: the asylum. Throughout the study, Rothman relates ideas and developments closely to the social context from which they sprung. Bibliographical note.

4945. Salamon, Lester M., and Fred Teitelbaum. "Religious Congregations As Social Service Agencies: How Extensive Are They?" *Foundation News* 25 (September-October 1984): 62-5.

4946. Scanlan, Eugene A. "Some Considerations on Funding Policy Research." *Philanthropy Monthly* 18 (April 1985): 13-6.

4947. Schick, Frank L., ed. *Statistical Handbook on Aging Americans.* Phoenix, Ariz.: Oryx Press, 1986.

Provides recent statistical data about the aging population in the United States. Includes demographics, social characteristics, health aspects, employment conditions, economic status, and public and private expenditures for the elderly. Studies of the aging population are receiving increased attention as we move closer to the year 2000, when one in every five Americans will be in the over sixty-five age group.

4948. Schlabach, Theron F. *Pensions for Professors.* Madison, Wis.: University of Wisconsin-Madison, 1963.

4949. Seltzer, Michael, and John E. Gallagher. "Funding the AIDS Fight." *Foundation News* 29 (May-June 1988): 24-31.

Reports on the key issues stemming from the AIDS crisis (education efforts, social services, medical care, mental health, medical and social-science research, housing, civil rights, public policy, criminal justice, international concerns, and the arts) and offers examples of responses by nonprofit organizations. The article stresses that even small acts in confronting the epidemic can be heroic; in the words of Edmund Burke, "Nobody made a greater mistake than he who did nothing because he could only do a little."

4950. Sennett, Richard. *The Fall of Public Man.* New York: Alfred A. Knopf, 1977.

This book, by a sociologist, examines the balance between public and private life. The author contends that public life has become a matter of formal obligation, not only in political life but also in all social interactions involving people not intimately associated. Using an interplay of history and theory, Sennett analyzes the erosion of public life and its implications for human social relations in general. The "intimate" vision of society that has replaced the public—by which we only care about institutions and events when we can discern personalities at work in them or embodying them—is a confused one, says Sennett, which has been fostered by modern psychology. He contends that individuals in western societies are becoming self-absorbed. "As a result, confusion has arisen between public and intimate life; people are working out in terms of personal feelings public matters which properly can be dealt with only through codes of impersonal meaning." The source of this confusion lies in broad changes in capitalism and religious belief, and has yielded two "tyrannies of intimacy": an inability to act politically, and "retribalization" away from that vast sum of impersonal experiences, the city.

4951. Shakely, Jack. "Lesson from a Community Organizer." *Foundation News* 25 (March-April 1984): 60-1.

4952. Shatzkin, Leonard. *In Cold Type: Overcoming the Book Crisis.* Boston: Houghton Mifflin, 1982.

4953. Shepard, David S. *How to Fund Media.* Washington: Council on Foundations, 1984.

Companion handbook to the Council on Foundations videotape, *We Don't Fund Media.* Looks at the issues and questions involved in media funding. Written as a resource for grantmakers but is also instructional to grantseekers. May be used independently or with the videotape.

4954. Shiman, David A., ed. *Teachers on Individualism: The Way We Do It.* New York: McGraw-Hill, 1974.

4955. Simmons, Adele. *Exploitation from 9 to 5.* Report of the Task Force on Women and Employment. New York: Twentieth Century Fund, 1975.

4956. Simonetti, Carol G. *The Chronically Mentally Ill: Improving the Knowledge Base through Research.* Washington: Council on Social Work Education, 1985.

4957. Sloan Commission on Government and Higher Education. *A Program for Renewed Partnership. The Report of the Sloan Commission on Government and Higher Education.* Cambridge, Mass.: Ballinger Publishing Co., 1980.

4958. Sloan Commission on Government and Higher Education. *A Program for Renewed Partnerships. The Report of the Sloan Commission on Government and Higher Education: An Overview.* Cambridge, Mass.: Ballinger Publishing Co., 1980.

4959. Smith, Craig. "Winds of Change from the West." *Foundation News* 22 (May-June 1985): 46+.

4960. Smith, R.C., and Carol A. Lincoln. *America's Shame, America's Hope: Twelve Million Youth at Risk.* Chapel Hill, N.C.: MDC, 1988.

Funded by the Charles Stewart Mott Foundation, this study is an inquiry into the education reform movement which began roughly with the publication of the National Commission on Excellence in Education's report *A Nation At Risk* in 1983. Focusing on at-risk youth (so called because they are at risk of emerging from school unprepared for further education or for adequate employment), the study lists its findings, which include: an increasing awareness by the educational and political leadership of the states that the problems of at-risk youth cannot be solved by measures designed to assist advantaged youth; funding for programs targeted to at-risk youth rarely exceeds five percent of state education expenditures or affects more than ten percent of the at-risk population; no state has a comprehensive policy addressed to at-risk youth; lack of public concern remains a barrier to building such policies; the at-risk problem exists in both urban and rural areas; and evidence mounts that certain features of the Excellence-in-Education movement are contributing to the dropout problem. Recommends a comprehensive program involving political authorities (especially Congress, the Department of Education, and state governors) to confront the problem of at-risk youth and raise the educational attainment level for all children.

4961. Smith, Virginia Carter, and Weslie S. Stubbs, eds. *Currents Index, 1975-1984.* Washington: Council for Advancement and Support of Education, 1985.

4962. Sosin, Michael R., Paul Colson, and Susan Grossman. *Homelessness in Chicago: Poverty and Pathology, Social Institutions and Social Change.* Chicago: University of Chicago, 1988.

Report of the University of Chicago's School of Social Service Administration Scholar-in-Residence project examining the problem of homelessness in Chicago. Explores the traits of the very poor to determine whether the homeless have unique traits compared to other members of this group, and examines social institutions in Chicago concerned with homelessness and poverty as well as the general social and economic conditions. Among the findings: despite prevailing theories supposing a high degree of voluntary alienation from society among the homeless, they "do not currently seem to completely lack an interest in improving themselves nor do they withdraw from society;" still, the presently homeless appear to have had fewer important ties to others, whether they be to family or friends, before becoming homeless, and are more likely than others in the sample to live alone. The currently increasing population of homeless people is younger, and there are more homeless women with children, and more members of minorities, many of whom do not have obvious pathologies. Homelessness is particularly likely to occur when individuals either do not have or exhaust ties with relatives on which to rely, pay a high rent, are in the lowest part of their cycle of earnings, or run into trouble with the welfare system. Report suggests policy implications ranging from prevention to reversal of homelessness, from focusing on special groups to considering the general nature of extreme poverty.

4963. Southwest Foundations Conference. *Alternative Futures and Human Development: Challenges for the Southwest.* Juares, Mexico: Southwest Foundations Conference, 1978.

4964. Spiegel, Hans B.C. *New Tools for Neighborhood Development: A Look at Some Information Providers and Users.* New York: Hunter College of the City of New York, 1987.

Of central concern to this inquiry, which was sponsored by the Ford Foundation, is the availability and use of information that will strengthen public and private community organizations so they may effectively engage in local community development. Presents an overview of five national community development data providers and a cross-section of community development data users before making recommendations to improve the provision and use of information in community development. Especially thought-provoking and critical for the future shape of communities are the issues of equitable public access to information and the capacity of individuals and organizations to actually translate data and information into tangible, positive community change. Recommendations include: increasing local organizations' capacity to gather and use information by means of training (which is discussed conceptually) and by facilitating access to information sources (making systems more user-friendly; providing clearly indexed directories to data-providing agencies); strengthening city-wide and regional information access, use and exchange by designating or creating a local institution as the focal point for collecting and maintaining development data and for responding to local inquiries; strengthening the role of national data providers by encouraging specialization and jointly conducted marketing (to make their existence more widely known), and by establishing a national clearinghouse of community development databanks and information networks; widely distributing straightforward, user-oriented materials about conduct of and participation in local community development projects (the report focuses on handbooks, pointing out that many are already available—they simply haven't been put into the hands of key actors in community improvement activities); and by improving government's ability to collect, store, and finally disseminate useable information to the public. Bibliography.

4965. Suhrke, Henry C. "The Humanities' Message to Grantmakers." *Philanthropy Monthly* 18 (May 1985): 5-12.

4966. Taper, Bernard. *The Arts of Boston.* Cambridge, Mass.: Harvard University Press, 1970.

4967. Task Force on Community-Based Development. *Community-Based Development: Investing in Renewal.* Washington: National Congress for Community Economic Development, 1987.

4968. Teltsch, Kathleen. "Analysts Say Cuts in Aid Hurt Young." *New York Times* (1 September 1985): 37.

4969. Teltsch, Kathleen. "How Sale Helps the Institute." *New York Times* (6 June 1985): D-19.

4970. Theatre Communications Group. *National Working Conference of Nonprofit Professional Theatres.* New York: Theatre Communications Group, 1976.

4971. Theatre Communications Group. *Theatre Directory.* 13th ed. New York: Theatre Communications Group, 1986.

4972. Threatt, Jane R. "Rethinking Development: Women As Catalysts for Change." *Grants Magazine* 8 (March 1985): 41+.

4973. Thurston, Henry W. *The Dependent Child: A Story of Changing Aims and Methods in the Care of Dependent Children.* Reprint. Salem, N.H.: Ayer Co. Publishers, 1974.

This is a critical analysis of child welfare in its many forms from the days of Queen Elizabeth to the early twentieth century, although it is arranged topically, not chronologically. Thurston asks why different social solutions to the problem of dependent children (those whose parents are unable to care for them in whole or part) came about at different times. He also investigates the aims and methods of the solutions through liberal use of primary historical sources. He likewise assesses their impact and success largely in terms of contemporary children and observers, through the use of autobiographical material. The scope of his treatment includes the almshouse, the orphan asylum, foster care, the State Children's Home Societies, and much more. The book is also a call to action; Thurston enlists the reader to join in reforming present-day institutions for the good of all children. Brief bibliography.

4974. Trattner, Walter I. *From Poor Law to Welfare State: A History of Social Welfare in America.* 3rd ed. New York: Free Press, 1984.

This is a review of American social welfare policies and practices from colonial times to the present, set against a background of social and intellectual trends in the United States and Britain. By "social welfare" Trattner means "those social security, social service, and health programs, activities and organizations, public and private, intended primarily to promote the wellbeing of individuals who society felt needed and deserved help." He describes the evolution of this concept from simply caring for those in need, to attempting to attack underlying roots of their problems, to creating constructive programs aimed at bettering everyone's lives—from a "residual" role to an "institutional" one. A chapter is devoted to each of the major movements and developments in social welfare history—child welfare, settlement houses, mental health, and the like—and a brief bibliography is provided for each chapter.

4975. Tye, Kenneth A., and Jerrold M. Novotney. *Schools in Transition: The Practitioner As Change Agent.* Series on Educational Change. New York: McGraw-Hill, 1975.

Designed to assist educational practitioners in defining their roles as agents of change, understand the school as a structure undergoing change, and to provide some perspective and guidance as changes are considered. This book provides an overview of the factors involved in educational change and suggests strategies useful in overcoming obstacles to change in schools. Appendix contains guidelines for applying for grant funds, both to help clarify the thought process and aid in writing the final proposal for submission. Bibliography.

4976. Unger, Walter J. "Taming the Cost of Health Care." *Foundation News* 23 (November-December 1983): 16+.

4977. Vidich, Arthur J. *American Sociology.* New Haven, Conn.: Yale University Press, 1985.

4978. Ward, F. Champion, ed. *Education and Development Reconsidered.* New York: Praeger, [1974].

4979. Warren, Donald I. *Helping Networks: How People Cope with Problems in the Urban Community.* Notre Dame, Ind.: University of Notre Dame Press, 1981.

By "helping networks" Warren means the many individuals to whom each of us turn in coping with both mundane and serious problems in our lives—spouses, friends, colleagues, neighbors, and so on. Warren argues that these [naturally formed] networks are being eroded because of increased social and geographic mobility, family dissolution, the generation gap, loss of trust in neighbors, professional overspecialization, and community segregation by race, sex, class, and social attitudes. This results, he says, in social alienation, isolation, and increasing public agency workloads. It is argued that understanding these informal networks will help more formal problem-solving agencies, volunteer or otherwise, provide critical services to those in need, and that the preservation of helping networks is important to the health of our society.

4980. Weber, Nathan. *Banks, Neighborhoods and the Community Reinvestment Act.* Conference Board Information Bulletin, no. 85. New York: Conference Board, 1981.

4981. "What Is a Church?" *Philanthropy Monthly* 18 (July-August 1985): 29+.

4982. White House Conference on Aging. *New Direction in Funding and Program Priorities for the Aging: The Interrelationship of Government, Private Foundations, Corporate Grantmakers and Unions.* Washington: White House Conference of Aging, 1981.

4983. Williams, Richard C. *Effecting Organizational Renewal in Schools: A Social Systems Perspective.* New York: McGraw-Hill, 1974.

4984. Wilson, John F. "Metaphor Carried Too Far." *Foundation News* 25 (September-October 1984): 25-7.

4985. Withey, Stephen B. *A Degree and What Else? Correlates and Consequences of a College Education.* Report for the Carnegie Commission on Higher Education. Hightstown, N.J.: Carnegie Commission on Higher Education, 1972.

4986. Women and Foundations/Corporate Philanthropy. *Inequality of Sacrifice: The Impact of the Reagan Budget on Women.* New York: Women and Foundations/Corporate Philanthropy, 1982.

4987. Women and Foundations/Corporate Philanthropy. *Women and Economic Independence Conference.* New York: Women and Foundations/Corporate Philanthropy, 1981.

4988. Women and Foundations/Corporate Philanthropy. "Women in the Eighties: The Future." *Women and Foundations/Corporate Philanthropy* 7 (Spring-Summer 1984): 1+.

PART FOUR

INDEXES

SUBJECT INDEX

Citations refer to entry number, not page number. Numbers in
bold type indicate abstracted bibliographic entries.

AAFRC. *See* American Association of Fund-Raising Counsel
Accounting. *See* Foundations, accounting; Nonprofit organizations, accounting
Ad Council, 4927
Adams, James Luther, **4570**
Addams, Jane, **5**, **7**, **51**, **118**, **149**, 293
Administration. *See* Foundations, administration; Nonprofit organizations, administration
Adult education, 4725
Aetna Life and Casualty, 4514
African-Americans. *See* Blacks
Afro-Americans. *See* Blacks
Aged. *See* Aging
Agency for International Development, 1891
Aging, 977, **1036**, 1041, **1224**, 2009, 2026, 2140, 2220, 2223, **2418**, 3084, 3141, 3258, 3443, **3950**, 4551, 4756, 4770, 4817, **4947**, 4982
   statistics, **4947**
AICPA. *See* American Institute of Certified Public Accountants
AID. *See* Agency for International Development
AIDS (Disease), **523**, **621**, **741**, **888**, **889**, 1044, **1167**, 1228, **1269**, 2989, 3954, **4768**, **4772**, 4782, 4843, 4854, 4861, 4891, 4911, 4917, 4943, **4949**
AIDS funding. *See* AIDS (Disease)
Air pollution. *See* Environment
Alcoholism, 3219, **3745**. *See also* Substance abuse
   directories, 3219
Alexander, Will, 140
Alternative resources. *See* Energy conservation
American Association of Fund-Raising Counsel, 125, **2993**
American Council of Learned Societies, **1911**
American Express, 1567
American Indians. *See* Native Americans
American Institute of Certified Public Accountants, 2725
American International Association for Economic and Social Development, 1786
American Negroes. *See* Blacks

Amoco Foundation, 1700
Andrews, Frank Emerson, 15, **536**
Annual reports, 545, **546**, 659, 669, **720**, 940, 941, 1069, 1092, 1108, 1111, 1185, **1197**, 1223, **1255**, 1596, 1623, 2085, 2131, 2175, 2176, 2371
Anthropology, **605**. *See also* Social sciences
Apple Computer, 1310, 2745
Aramony, William, **2023**
Architecture
   conservation and restoration, 3586, 4870, **4883**, **4884**
Archives, **1259**
Art, 875
   study and teaching, 576
Arts, **699**, 757, 1350, **1961**, 1998, **2001**, 2006, 2013, 2030, 2034, 2036, 2045, 2080, 2116, 2130, 2218, **2234**, 2251, 2264, 2286, 2330, 2335, 2384, **2387**, 2499, 2537, **2557**, **2601**, 2612, 2637, 2713, 2718, 2721, 2763, 2772, 2838, 2859, 2892, 2996, 3011, 3127, **3578**, 3623, 3771, 3839, 3963, 4214, **4258**, 4310, 4639, 4649, 4733, 4769, 4776, 4784, 4818, 4832, 4906, 4966, 4970
   administration, **2039**, 2046, 2497, **2498**, 2511, **2556**, **2785**, **2878**, **3467**
   analysis, **1939**, **1961**, **2012**, 2071, 2097, 2109, **2261**, 2264, 2309, 2575, 3222, 4609, 4671, 4776, 4818
   bibliographies, 2467, 2510, 2613, 2718
   Canada, surveys, **1961**
   corporate giving, 1311, **1331**, 1340, 1354, 1355, 1356, 1374, **1426**, 1441, 1446, **1451**, 1477, 1507, 1531, 1586, 1638, 1655, 1660, 1661, 1668, 1698, 1997, **3099**, **3767**, **3957**. *See also* Arts, grants
   directories, **553**, **673**, 2007, **2086**, **2149**, 2150, **2260**, **2261**, 2266, 2267, 2289, **2373**, 2536, **2785**, **3099**, 3633, 3936
   festivals. *See* Arts, grants
   finance, 2109, 2232, 3679, 4609
   fundraising, 803, **1451**, 3011, 3117, 3130, 3140, 3187, 3276, 3400, **3401**, 3441, 3462, **3467**, 3495, **3578**, 3633, 3679, 3719, 3728, 3729, 3730, 3731, **3769**, 3770, 3772
   government policy, **1939**, 2004, 2005, 2233, 2304, 2575, **3957**, 4604, 4607, 4610, 4624, **4630**, 4638, 4645, 4650, 4671, 4673, **4689**, 4690, 4691, 4692, 4693, **4694**, 4696, 4697, 4714, 4719, 4725, 4726, 4744, 4752, 4753, 4754
   grants, 129, 180, 358, **553**, 586, **673**, 693, 695, 758, 803, **2039**, 3117, 3127, **3463**, **3467**, 3633, 3885, **3957**, **4608**, **4700**, 4716, **4723**, 4724, 4754
   handbooks, manuals, etc., 1991
   management, **2149**, **2261**, 2431, 2467, 2499, 2530, 2541, **2557**, **2601**, 2613, 2620, 2637, 2657, 2670, 2721, 2772, **2785**, 2862, 2912, **2930**, 2968, **3588**, **3772**, 4230
   management, study and teaching, **2498**
   marketing, 2071, **3588**
   studies, **2234**, 4241
   study and teaching, **2001**
   surveys, 249, 798, 1503, 1900, 1998, 2247, **2556**, 3232, 3636, 3699, 4377, 4632, 4832
Arts and education. *See* Arts, study and teaching
Arts and government. *See* Arts councils; Government funding
   federal. *See* Government funding, arts and humanities, federal
   international. *See* Government funding, arts and humanities, international
   state. *See* Government funding, arts and humanities, state
Arts councils, 2004, 2005, 2034, 2233, 2304, 3936, 4649, 4681
   New York (State), 1991, 4726
Asian-Americans, **476**
Association
   foundation. *See* Association-related foundations
Association of Black Foundation Executives, **559**
Association-related foundations, **999**, **3410**
Associations of foundations, 525, 612, 648, **663**, 683, **752**, 768, 838, 1119, 1178, 1296, 3548
   directories, 651, **1045**

301

SUBJECT INDEX

Astor family, 22
Astor Foundation, Vincent, 23
Athletics. *See* Recreation and athletics
Auctions. *See* Fundraising, special events
Awards and prizes, 1257, **1270**
Awards dinners. *See* Fundraising, special events
Baker Trust, George F., 955
Baker, George F., 955
Balls. *See* Fundraising, special events
Barrier Free Environments, 4691
Battelle Memorial Institute Foundation, 933
Beckman Foundation, Arnold and Mabel, 697
Beckman, Arnold O., 147
Benefit Trust Life Insurance Company, 1442
Benefits. *See* Fundraising, special events
Bequests. *See* Planned giving
Bertram, James, 219
Better Business Bureaus, **2068**
Blacks, 87, 88, **89**, 170, **301**, 377, 423, **445**, **559**, 740, **930**, **938**, 1521, **1848**, 2059, 2143, 3059, **3063**, **3113**, 3191, 3465, 3601, 4866, **4879**
Blind. *See* Handicapped
Block grants. *See* Government funding
Board members, 547, 666, **676**, **837**, 952, **1026**, 1838, **2241**, 2420, **2445**, 2454, 2462, **2464**, **2472**, **2474**, 2485, **2488**, **2500**, **2509**, **2520**, 2524, 2530, 2534, 2535, 2545, **2549**, 2570, 2571, 2572, **2573**, 2577, 2579, **2598**, 2599, **2600**, **2641**, 2642, 2652, **2655**, 2656, 2658, 2660, **2664**, 2665, 2677, 2679, **2680**, 2684, 2685, 2690, 2691, 2692, **2739**, 2740, 2751, 2752, 2756, 2781, 2783, **2784**, **2790**, 2796, 2801, 2802, **2805**, **2810**, **2814**, **2815**, 2847, 2854, 2869, **2875**, 2876, 2877, 2880, 2884, 2886, **2904**, 2907, 2908, 2909, 2913, **2924**, **2928**, 2932, 2954, 2957, 2970, 2972, 2974, **2978**, 2980, 3583, **4104**
Bollingen Foundation, 997
Bookkeeping. *See* Foundations, accounting; Nonprofit organizations, accounting
Bowen, Louise Hadduck, **51**
Brakeley, John Price Jones, 381
Broadcasting, 368, 797, 1079, 2327, 2515, 2934, **3019**, 3453, 4452, 4806, 4932
Brochures. *See* Nonprofit organizations, public relations
Bronfman, Samuel, 355
Buck Trust, 583, 588, 604, 691, **1054**, **1055**, 1056, **1057**, 1196, **1283**, **1287**
Budget Deficit Reduction Act. *See* Tax Reform Act of 1984
Budgeting. *See* Foundations, accounting; Nonprofit organizations, accounting

Budgets
  nonprofit organizations. *See* Nonprofit organizations, accounting
Bundy, McGeorge, 193, 3722
Burden Foundation, Florence V., 831
Burdett-Coutts, Angela, 206
Busch family, **70**
Business
  small. *See* Small business
Business Advisory Service, **1414**
Business Committee for the Arts, 1507
Butler, Nicholas Murray, 71
Cadbury Schweppes PLC, **1983**
California
  directories. *See* State directories of foundations, California
Canada. *See* Corporate philanthropy, Canada; Foundations, Canada; Philanthropy, Canada
Candler, Asa Griggs, 76
Capital campaigns, 924, **3067**, **3094**, 3106, **3129**, **3132**, 3140, 3142, 3158, 3172, **3237**, 3256, 3293, **3381**, **3388**, **3389**, 3408, 3673, **3746**, **3755**, 3800, 3806, 3908, 3965, 3966, 4748. *See also* Fundraising
CARE, 3852
Career and adult education. *See* Adult education
Carlsberg Foundation, 1918
Carnegie Commission on Higher Education, 993
Carnegie Corporation of New York, 153, 250, **552**, 564, **572**, 606, 640, **930**, 931, 942, 945, 998, **1077**, **1078**, 1087, **1154**, 1901
Carnegie Endowment for International Peace, 251, **552**, 607, 696, 737, **1762**, **1770**, **1911**
Carnegie family, 210, 489
Carnegie Foundation for the Advancement of Teaching, **571**, 582, 776, **932**, 1243, 4948
Carnegie Hero Fund Commission, 548
Carnegie Steel Company, 62
Carnegie United Kingdom Trust, 1932
Carnegie, Andrew, 9, 62, 72, 79, 83, **84**, 85, 123, 128, 151, 192, 209, 250, 251, 271, 286, 298, 315, 378, **488**, 489, 548, 564, 737, 816, **1077**, 1928
Carnegie, Louise Whitfield, 210
CASE. *See* Council for Advancement and Support of Education
Cause-related marketing, **433**, 1304, **1328**, **1342**, **1347**, 1348, **1349**, **1422**, **1424**, **1459**, **1537**, **1651**, **1662**, **1666**, **1667**, **1669**, **1673**, **1685**, **1731**, **1737**, **1834**, **2351**, 3026, 3245. *See also* Corporations, marketing
CBS. *See* Columbia Broadcasting System
Center for Community Change, **2400**
Center for Corporate Public Involvement, 1530
CFAE. *See* Council for Financial Aid to Education

Challenge grants, 3331, 3421. *See also* Fundraising
Charitable giving. *See* Fundraising
Charitable solicitation. *See* Fundraising
Charities Aid Foundation, **1947**
Charity rackets, 269, **2068**, **2391**
Chemical Bank, 2431
Chicano Education Project, 4897
Child welfare. *See* Children
Children, **157**, **478**, 623, 1286, 2048, **2049**, 2136, **2299**, 2312, **3111**, **3195**, 3280, 3591, 3609, 3657, 4376, 4841, 4860, 4942, **4960**, **4973**
China Medical Board of New York, 742
Church charities. *See* Religion
Churches. *See* Religion
CIA. *See* Government and philanthropy
Citizens groups. *See* Public interest groups
Clark Foundation, Edna McConnell, 831, 4814
Cleveland Foundation, 684, 704, 862, 987, 1258
College foundations. *See* Education, public charities
Colleges and universities. *See* Higher education
Columbia Broadcasting System, 368
Columbus Foundation, 874
Combined federal campaigns. *See* Fundraising, federated
Commission on Foundation and Private Philanthropy, 1073
Commonwealth Foundation, 1773
Commonwealth Fund, 633, 796, **841**, 1094
Communications, 544, 975, 1241, 2138, 2190, 2515, 2528, 2594, 2792, 4912
Community Chests and Councils of America, 1688
Community development, **252**, **364**, **565**, 617, **891**, 984, **1137**, 1276, 1370, **1531**, **1593**, **1642**, 1700, **1707**, 1741, **2037**, 2047, 2052, 2072, 2177, **2205**, **2230**, 2231, 2240, 2243, 2245, 2263, **2285**, **2331**, 2353, 2379, **2381**, **2390**, **2516**, 2767, **2917**, 2982, 3032, 3150, **3360**, 3373, 3432, 3442, 3461, **3519**, 3618, **3659**, **3922**, 3923, 4232, **4490**, 4558, 4620, 4682, **4771**, 4780, 4835, 4853, 4856, 4875, **4882**, **4892**, 4899, **4936**, **4964**, 4967, 4980
  South Africa, **1944**, **1946**
Community development corporations, 2263, **2285**, 4232
Community Foundation of Greater Washington, 3869
Community foundations, **527**, 530, 550, 609, 649, **650**, 652, **667**, 691, 800, **821**, 826, 834, **850**, 874, 893, **965**, **990**, **992**, 1030, 1031, 1032, 1033, 1053, 1112, 1136, **1137**, 1138, **1155**, **1156**, 1169, **1199**, **1207**, **1208**, **1210**, 1240, 1258, 1262, **1272**, **1278**, **1283**, 2506, 2507, 3198. *See also* Foundations

SUBJECT INDEX

Community Foundations Technical Assistance Program, 652
Community Information Exchange, **2331**
Community organizing. *See* Community development
Community planning. *See* Community development
Community Reinvestment Act, 4980
Community Trust Movement, 862
Companies. *See* Corporations
Compensation. *See* Nonprofit organizations, wages
Competitions. *See* Awards and prizes
Computer technology, 656, 1241, 1310, 1375, 1382, 1511, **1646, 1675, 2195, 2331,** 2376, 2458, 2466, **2477,** 2497, 2511, 2538, 2539, 2578, **2616,** 2618, 2632, **2643, 2669,** 2681, **2730,** 2745, **2748,** 2753, 2762, 2795, 2819, 2861, 2867, 2870, 2874, 2882, 2888, 2893, 2894, 2899, 2914, **2920, 2927,** 2943, 2944, 2947, 2959, 2962, 2963, 2971, 3147, 3282, 3307, 3318, 3409, 3418, 3424, 3479, 3568, **3584,** 3590, 3651, 3671, 3686, **3687,** 3713, 3743, 3764, 3784, 3822, 3828, 3892, 3918, 4501, 4578, 4774
  fundraising. *See* Fundraising, computer aided
Computers. *See* Computer technology
Conable, Barber, 2062
Concerts. *See* Fundraising, special events
Conduit organizations. *See* Sponsors
Conference Board, 1671, 1729
Conferences, 18, 19, 107, 336, 349, 360, 427, 602, 612, 636, 637, 644, 648, 768, 1032, 1033, 1046, 1047, 1048, 1049, 1159, 1352, 1791, 1796, 1845, **2345,** 2468, 2543, 2780, 2788, 2799, **2800,** 2848, **2852,** 2945, 2991, 2992, 3005, 3170, **3234,** 3574, 3662, 3663, 3664, 3668, 4254, 4255, 4261, 4272, 4273, 4274, 4275, 4276, 4277, 4278, 4279, 4280, 4722, 4915, 4929, 4963, 4970, 4987
Connecticut Junior Republic, 3418
Conservation. *See* Environment; Energy conservation
Conservative foundations. *See* Grantmakers, social issues
Consultants, **1703,** 2441, **2473,** 2496, 2533, **2542,** 2593, 2614, 2619, **2622, 2650,** 2666, **2674, 2704,** 2714, 2728, 2737, 2774, 2824, 2891, 2903, 2918, 2931, **2993,** 3172, 3227, **3669, 3707, 3761, 3990**
Contests. *See* Awards and prizes
Controversial activities. *See* Foundations, controversial activities
Cooley, Thomas, 4319
Cooper, Peter, **319,** 352
Cooperative funding, 335, 503, 505, 617, **850,** 1276, **1330, 1418,** 1480, 1496, 1641, 1643, 2115, 2353, 2982, 3004, 3006, 3048, 3076, 3095, 3134, 3146, **3195,** 3235, 3243, 3258, 3391, 3460, 3473, **3519,** 3542, 3548, 3572, 3618, **3711,** 3738, 3753, 3839, 3869, 4902
Corporate foundations, **106,** 1381, 1391, 1468, 1621, 1633, **1647, 1652,** 1671, 1700, 1704, **1716,** 1730, **1735**
  administration, 1377, **1420, 1488, 1502, 1540, 1609, 1658,** 1663, 1736
  Arkansas, 1736
  directories, **594,** 651, **953, 1322, 1332, 1337, 1338, 1431, 1467, 1524, 1525,** 1541, 1638
  evaluations, 1702
Corporate giving programs, 1306, **1319,** 1355, 1365, 1379, 1380, 1395, 1402, 1410, **1417, 1420, 1423,** 1425, **1428,** 1435, **1443,** 1446, 1447, 1477, **1485, 1487, 1500,** 1507, **1523,** 1526, 1527, **1528, 1538, 1545,** 1548, 1585, 1586, **1614,** 1634, 1637, **1648,** 1650, 1653, 1655, **1658,** 1664, 1672, **1677, 1684,** 1700, 1704, **1706, 1714,** 1722, 1729, 1741, 1769, 1861, 1883, 2053, 2801, **2981, 3290,** 3440, 3724, **3747, 4055**
  administration, **1705,** 1736
  analysis, 1682, **1742**
  directories, **594,** 747, **953, 1011, 1322, 1336, 1337, 1338, 1431, 1524, 1525,** 1541, 1638, **3254**
  evaluations, 1481, **1508, 1540,** 1702
  statistics, **1416, 1546, 1742**
Corporate philanthropy, 200, 300, 483, 564, 826, **850,** 1301, 1302, 1303, 1306, **1307, 1312,** 1314, 1315, 1317, **1319,** 1323, **1327,** 1329, **1331,** 1340, **1342,** 1343, **1344,** 1345, 1350, 1355, 1357, 1358, 1360, 1363, 1366, 1370, 1373, 1377, 1378, 1379, 1380, 1381, 1384, 1385, 1386, 1388, 1388, 1389, 1393, 1394, 1398, **1399,** 1400, 1402, 1406, 1407, 1408, **1409,** 1410, 1411, 1413, **1414,** 1415, **1416, 1417, 1418, 1419,** 1421, **1423, 1426, 1428, 1429,** 1438, **1439,** 1442, 1446, 1447, 1448, 1449, 1450, 1456, **1457, 1459, 1469, 1470,** 1471, **1472,** 1473, 1474, **1475,** 1477, 1482, **1488, 1489,** 1491, 1492, 1493, 1499, **1500,** 1504, **1505, 1506,** 1507, **1509,** 1513, 1515, 1516, **1517,** 1526, 1529, **1537, 1539,** 1542, 1543, 1544, **1545, 1546,** 1547, 1548, **1549,** 1550, 1553, **1558,** 1559, 1563, 1564, 1567, **1568, 1570,** 1580, 1581, 1584, 1586, **1587, 1593, 1599,** 1600, 1601, **1602,** 1604, 1606, **1610,** 1613, 1616, 1621, 1626, 1628, 1629, 1630, **1631, 1632,** 1633, 1634, **1636, 1639,** 1640, **1642,** 1643, **1648, 1649,** 1650, 1655, 1656, 1657, 1661, **1662,** 1663, 1668, 1672, **1677,** 1678, 1679, 1683, **1684,** 1687, 1690, 1691, 1692, 1694, 1695, 1696, 1697, 1699, 1701, **1706, 1707,** 1708, 1709, **1713, 1714,** 1715, **1716, 1717, 1718, 1719,** 1720, 1722, 1723, 1724, 1728, 1730, **1733,** 1734, 1738, 1739, **1740,** 1743, 1756, 1779, 1780, 1844, 1883, 1891, **1934,** 1941, 1978, 1984, 2053, 2801, **3044,** 3077, 3128, 3134, 3170, 3548, 3602, 3738, **3836,** 3885, **4055,** 4078, **4136,** 4530, 4595
  administration, **1307,** 1345, 1378, 1379, 1380, **1420, 1540, 1705,** 1736
  alternatives, **106, 1440, 1459, 1505, 1731**
  analysis, 350, 1318, 1339, 1397, **1419,** 1427, 1436, **1512, 1512, 1537, 1546, 1570, 1602,** 1604, **1612,** 1659, **1677,** 1682, 1699, **1732, 1742**
  bibliographies, 664, 1316, 1452, 1474, 1645
  California, directories, 1461
  Canada, **1750, 1885**
  Canada, analysis, 1756, 1941, 1978
  Canada, directories, **1899**
  case studies, 1492, **1561**
  Connecticut, directories, **1336**
  directories, **492,** 747, **1305, 1333, 1334, 1335, 1403, 1612**
  ethics, **1617**
  Europe, 1982
  Great Britain, **1609, 1912, 1913, 1947, 1983**
  handbooks, manuals, etc., **1609**
  Illinois, directories, **1431**
  Japan, **242,** 243, **1744, 1755, 1830, 1855, 1858, 1863,** 1882, **1923,** 1924, **1925, 1926**
  Maine, directories, **1332, 1333**
  Massachusetts, directories, **1337**
  Minnesota, analysis, 1471, 1482
  New Hampshire, directories, **1334**
  Ohio, 1480, 1585
  Rhode Island, directories, **1338**
  statistics, **450,** 1397, **1416,** 1436, **1622, 1912**
  Vermont, directories, **1335**
Corporations, **1326, 1351, 1353,** 1362, 1364, 1432, 1462, 1463, 1464, 1465, 1466, 1479, **1490,** 1497, 1503, 1513, 1520, 1556, **1571, 1573,** 1575, 1579, 1596, 1598, 1611, **1665,** 1711, 1712, **1725, 1938,** 2154, 2388
  bibliographies, **1555**
  directories, 1364, 1415, **1433, 1434,** 1437, 1463, 1464, 1465, 1466, **1478,** 1503, **1518, 1523, 1577,**

303

SUBJECT INDEX

Corporations
   directories (*continued*)
      1595, **1614**, **1652**, 1653, **1680**, 1681, **1684**, **1710**, **1725**, 1726, **1938**, **3746**
   marketing, 1304, **1328**, **1342**, **1347**, 1348, **1349**, **1422**, **1424**, 1618, **1651**, **1666**, **1667**, **1669**, **1673**, **1685**, 1686, **1731**, **1737**, **2351**
   research, 964, **1371**, 1556, 1726
   research support, 1369, **1403**, **1539**, 1560, 1592, 1620, 1654, **1872**, 3829
   research, handbooks, manuals, etc., **1555**
   social responsibility, **106**, 207, 1298, 1301, 1302, 1308, 1309, 1313, 1316, 1320, **1321**, **1323**, **1326**, **1327**, **1330**, **1341**, **1351**, 1352, **1353**, 1354, 1357, 1358, 1362, 1364, 1366, 1367, 1383, 1384, 1387, 1396, 1398, **1399**, **1401**, 1402, 1406, 1412, 1415, **1422**, **1423**, 1432, 1444, 1445, 1448, 1455, 1458, 1462, 1468, **1470**, 1473, 1479, 1482, 1484, **1494**, 1495, 1497, 1504, **1506**, 1510, 1520, 1527, 1530, 1532, 1533, **1539**, 1542, **1549**, 1550, 1551, 1552, 1553, 1554, 1557, 1565, 1566, 1569, **1571**, 1572, **1573**, 1574, 1575, 1578, 1579, 1583, **1589**, **1591**, 1594, 1597, **1599**, **1602**, 1608, 1611, **1612**, 1615, **1617**, 1641, **1642**, 1643, **1665**, 1674, 1682, 1683, 1688, 1689, 1711, 1712, **1713**, **1719**, 1721, **1732**, 4250, **4530**, 4557, 4558, 4595, 4600
   surveys, **1555**

Cottrell, Frederick Gardner, 75
Council for Advancement and Support of Education, 3524
Council for Financial Aid to Education, 1400, 1576
Council on Foundations, **366**, **399**, 814, 836, 1159
Covenant House, 1286
Cox Committee, **934**, 4379, 4381
Crime, **416**, 4688
Criminal justice, 831
Cullen, Roy Hugh, 275
Cummins Engine Company, 339
Dana Foundation, Charles A., **1270**
Dance, 2306, 4886
Danforth, William H., 383
Daring Goals for a Caring Society, **231**, **4513**
Davella Mills Foundation, 1009
Davison, Henry P., 291
Day Trust, 4137
Daycare. *See* Children
Dayton Hudson Corporation, 871, 1482, **1508**, 1618
de Hirsch Fund, Baron, 897
Dees, Morris, **2100**
Deferred gifts. *See* Planned giving
DeRance Foundation, 1290

Development officers. *See* Fundraising, administration
Dinner dances. *See* Fundraising, special events
Direct mail, 2558, 2661, 2782, 2985, 3001, 3052, 3080, 3096, **3104**, 3173, 3174, 3204, **3207**, 3225, 3226, 3227, 3230, 3244, 3252, **3264**, 3266, 3269, 3283, 3284, 3297, 3353, 3362, 3435, 3446, **3449**, 3450, **3451**, 3452, 3466, **3481**, 3484, 3489, 3506, 3516, 3523, 3535, **3536**, 3537, 3547, 3565, 3566, 3567, 3573, 3680, **3695**, 3697, 3721, 3733, 3748, **3780**, 3799, **3808**, 3824, 3834, 3851, **3852**, 3959, 3987
Disabled. *See* Handicapped
Disaster relief. *See* Social welfare
Divestiture. *See* Foundations, divestiture
Donors Forum of Chicago, **29**
Drug abuse, 3220, **3745**. *See also* Substance abuse
   directories, 3220
du Pont family, 86, 135, 138, 241, 421, 522
du Pont, Alfred I., 241
Duke Endowment, 397, 717
Duke, James B., 248, 397, 717
Earned income. *See* Nonprofit organizations, entrepreneurship
Eastman, George, 3
Ecology. *See* Environment
Economic assistance, **565**, 1746, 1798, 1799, 1800, 1962, 1972, **4676**
   Africa, 1806, 1807, 1808, 1812, 1815, **1893**, **1944**, **1945**, **1946**, **3852**
   Latin America, 1801, 1802, 1803, 1809, 1814, **2339**
   Third World, **1766**, 1778, 1804, 1805, 1810, 1811, 1813
Economic conditions, 665, 1037, 1598, **2349**, **4771**, 4915
Economic Recovery Act of 1981. *See* Tax Reform Act of 1981
Economics. *See* Philanthropy, economic aspects
Education, 273, **870**, 951, **1065**, **1202**, 1425, 1584, **1619**, 1851, 2277, 2365, 2544, 2990, 3021, 3035, 3120, 3196, 3214, **3291**, 3518, 3574, 3620, 3724, **3737**, 3829, 3956, 4233, 4476, 4639, 4705, 4711, 4784, **4810**, 4812, 4833, 4844, 4851, 4852, 4867, 4890, 4905, 4954, **4975**, 4983
   corporate giving, **1300**, 1314, 1369, 1372, 1373, 1383, 1392, 1400, **1403**, 1404, 1405, 1407, 1408, **1409**, 1410, 1411, 1412, 1413, **1443**, 1453, **1454**, **1476**, 1486, 1491, 1501, 1519, **1561**, **1562**, 1576, 1590, 1603, **1614**, 1616, **1619**, **1635**, 1674, **1676**, 1727, **1942**, 2525, 3095, 3168, 3518, 4961
   directories, **653**

   finance, **3069**, 3157, 3158, 3159, **3544**, **3645**, **3766**, 3786, **3986**, 4621
   government funding, 2995, 3168, 4318, 4633, 4638, 4667
   public charities, 638, 978, 1182, 3066, 3257, 3458, 3698, **3766**, 3805
   statistics, **3169**
Eisenberg, Pablo, **2400**
Elderly. *See* Aging
Electronic funds transfer. *See* Fundraising, computer aided
Elementary and secondary education, 142, 567, 582, 603, **653**, 1003, **1202**, 1369, **1476**, 1519, **1561**, 1701, **1733**, 2110, 2282, 2987, 3267, **3645**, **3751**, 3927, 4667, **4810**, 4851, 4876, 4890, **4895**, 4908, 4909, 4910, 4914
Emergency funding, **1174**, 3079, 3231, 3261, 3292, 3352, 3688, 3754, 3897
Employment, **1061**, **1062**, **2219**, 2319, **2551**, 2581, 2853, **3109**, **3137**, 3576, 4487, 4837, 4940, 4955
   directories, 2046, **2235**
Endowments, **287**, 607, **679**, **1140**, 2442, 2460, 2562, 2563, 2564, 2565, 2871, **3043**, 3322, **3371**, 3462, 3486, 3513, 3595, 3598, 3608, 3722, 3740, 3749, 3783, 3826, 3919, 3928, 3943, **3993**, 4118, 4119, 4858. *See also* Fundraising
Energy conservation, 3102, 3150, 3661, 4729, 4766, 4780, 4920
Engineering, 4709
Enterprise Foundation, **891**
Entrepreneurs, 2414, 4254, **4826**
Entrepreneurship. *See* Nonprofit organizations, entrepreneurship
Environment, 511, 578, **733**, **1181**, 2332, 2986, 3013, 3102, 3150, 3442, **3670**, 4729, 4780, 4781
Equity syndication. *See* Fundraising, alternatives
Estate planning. *See* Planned giving
Ethics. *See* Corporate philanthropy, ethics; Foundations, ethics; Fundraising, ethics; Nonprofit organizations, ethics
Ethnic/racial matters. *See* Minorities
Evaluations. *See* Corporate foundations, evaluations; Foundations, evaluations; Fundraising, evaluations; Nonprofit organizations, evaluations
Excess business holdings. *See* Foundations, divestiture
Exxon Corporation, 1449
Exxon Education Foundation, 1633
Falk Medical Fund, Maurice, 1201, 1209
Family planning, 2033
FASB. *See* Financial Accounting Standards Board
Federal aid, 4636
Federal Program Information Act, 4642
Federal programs. *See* Government funding

SUBJECT INDEX

Federated fund raising. *See* Fundraising, federated
Fellowships. *See* Scholarships, fellowships and loans
Fels, Samuel S., 379
Field, Marshall, III, 34
Filer Commission, **102**, 630, 631, 632, 668, 745, 811, 830, 918, 969, 1021, 1089, 1101, 1163, 1170, 1237, 1277
Films and video, 2671, **2825**, **3463**, 3514, 3765, 3779, **4847**, **4953**
Financial Accounting Standards Board, **1999**, 2440, **2649**, 2686, **2863**, **2865**, **2906**
Financial aid. *See* Emergency funding; Loan funds; Loans; Scholarships, fellowships and loans
First Nations Financial Project, **2226**
Fisher, Avery, 411
Fleischmann Foundation, Max C., 750
Fleischmann, Max C., 499
Flexner, Abraham, **154**
Folks, Homer, **478**
Food and hunger. *See* Social welfare
Ford family, 100
Ford Foundation, 193, 551, **552**, **572**, 575, 690, 757, 762, 763, **967**, 972, 998, 1088, 1168, 1228, **1761**, **1762**, **1765**, 4823
Ford, Edsel, **187**
Ford, Henry, **187**
Ford, Henry, II, 761
Foreign foundations. *See* International philanthropy
Fosdick, Raymond Blaine, 160, 199
Foundation Center, 715, **3248**, **3710**, 3970
Foundation funding, **605**, 1968, **3494**
 analysis, 3289
Foundation funding trends. *See* Funding trends
Foundations, 538, **541**, 560, 561, **599**, 602, 616, 627, 636, 637, 644, 648, **661**, **699**, **729**, 744, 768, **783**, **789**, **817**, 836, 876, 904, **919**, 920, **921**, 935, **954**, 1040, **1050**, 1068, **1104**, **1140**, 1141, 1144, 1160, 1161, 1171, 1253, 4231, 4378, 4379, 4381, 4382, 4383, 4385, 4386, 4387, 4391, 4392, 4415, 4424, 4430, 4439, 4441, 4452
 accounting, 1085, 2450, 2841, **2906**, 4256
 administration, 19, 207, 531, 538, 539, **541**, 547, **585**, **598**, 610, 613, 619, **645**, **654**, **655**, 656, **658**, 659, 662, 666, **676**, 708, **723**, 727, 728, **739**, **755**, 779, **795**, 801, **817**, **818**, 823, 844, 846, 865, **866**, 871, **894**, **901**, 922, 924, 939, 966, 972, 975, **1026**, 1038, 1039, 1046, 1047, 1048, 1049, 1060, **1078**, 1082, 1085, 1088, 1092, 1114, 1118, 1121, 1123, 1127, **1135**, 1146, **1149**, **1156**, **1162**, **1192**, **1207**, 1209, **1217**, 1218, 1242, 1250, 1254, **1256**, 1268, 1285, 1291, 1294, 1904, **2284**, **2398**, 2443, 2506, 2507, 2528, 2529, 2562, 2563, 2564, 2565, 2658, 2683, **2742**, 2760, 2788, 2837, 2974, **2978**, 2979, 2980, 3409, 4130, 4160, **4163**, **4179**, 4256, 4264, 4395, 4457
 analysis, 11, **84**, **261**, 330, 331, **342**, 343, **350**, **366**, **386**, 390, **391**, **455**, **500**, 530, **532**, 535, **536**, 540, 542, **552**, 562, **565**, **571**, **572**, 575, **579**, 615, 625, 627, 628, **629**, 632, 640, **677**, **678**, 684, 692, **710**, 711, **721**, 725, 736, **748**, 775, **777**, 794, **795**, 802, 814, 816, **822**, 829, 836, 838, **847**, **852**, 860, **873**, 878, 896, **909**, **911**, 920, 924, 937, **938**, 943, **944**, 950, 952, 973, **995**, 998, 1007, 1027, **1028**, 1029, **1036**, 1040, **1050**, **1051**, **1058**, 1076, **1086**, **1100**, **1104**, 1115, **1117**, **1134**, **1137**, 1139, 1144, 1147, **1149**, 1153, **1167**, 1168, 1175, 1188, 1189, 1195, **1198**, 1209, 1211, 1213, 1235, 1238, 1240, 1248, 1249, 1250, 1251, **1263**, 1266, 1267, **1275**, **1287**, 1293, 1296, 1884, **2820**, **2978**, 2979, 3874, 4079, 4105, 4121, 4156, 4157, **4219**, 4290, 4320, 4327, 4378, 4379, 4381, 4382, 4383, 4385, 4386, 4387, 4392, 4393, 4408, 4409, 4410, 4413, 4414, 4416, 4417, 4419, 4420, 4421, 4422, 4423, 4424, 4425, 4426, 4427, 4428, 4431, 4432, 4434, 4437, 4441, 4442
 Arizona, **899**
 Australia, directories, 1758, 1837
 bibliographies, 247, 664, 849, **911**, 1008, 3559
 birth and death. *See* Foundations, establishment and termination
 California, 611, 923, **956**, 991, 1150, 1180
 Canada, **1753**, **1920**
 Canada, directories, **1751**, **1752**, **1899**
 case studies, **536**, 574, 584, **921**, 930, 931, 972, **1051**, **1077**
 Colombia, directories, 1745
 Congressional hearings, 1983, 722, 726, 734, 790, 819, 820, 971, 976, 986, 1074, 1212, 1231, 4394, **4403**, 4407, 4408, 4409, 4410, 4411, 4412, 4413, 4414, 4415, 4416, 4417, 4419, 4420, 4421, 4422, 4423, 4424, 4425, 4426, 4427, 4428, 4429, 4429, 4430, 4434
 conservative. *See* Grantmakers, social issues
 controversial activities, 698, 764, **870**, 1081, **1105**, 4385
 directories, **622**, **643**, 651, 682, **687**, **729**, **733**, **769**, 771, 772, 773, 803, 839, 867, 868, 906, 946, 947, **963**, **1052**, **1066**, **1067**, 1081, **1091**, 1093, **1130**, **1174**, 1215, **1219**, **1236**, **1282**, **1467**, **1893**, **1945**, **3260**, **3746**
 divestiture, 550, 927, 973
 establishment and termination, 531, **554**, **723**, 735, 749, 754, **793**, **817**, **864**, 865, **866**, **999**, 1179, **1217**, **4163**, **4321**, **4326**, 4355
 ethics, **177**, **845**, 861, 914, 915, 916, 952, 1216, 1273, **2929**
 Europe, directories, 1747, **1772**, **1775**, 1797, 1824, **1835**, **1839**, 1873, 1905, 1952, 1986
 evaluations, 549, 581, 596, **645**, 1177, 1183, 1184, **1192**, 1232, **1265**, **1508**, 2428, **2820**
 fiction, 685, 686, 730, 806, **907**, 948, 994, 996, 1152, 1295
 Finland, directories, 1794
 Florida, **958**
 foreign. *See* International philanthropy
 Form 990. *See* Tax returns
 France, directories, 1824, 1952
 future. *See* Foundations, analysis
 Germany, directories, 1905
 grantmaking, 534, 619, 625, 662, **679**, 716, **785**, **857**, **889**, 982, 1121, **1167**, **1192**, 1240, **1269**, **2073**, **2902**, **4953**
 grants, 580, **621**, **658**, **687**, 704, 705, **773**, **777**, 804, 807, 815, 831, 860, 869, 877, 881, 885, 892, **928**, 946, 1116, 1124, 1146, 1157, **1227**, 1234, 2026, **2981**, 3078, 3159, 3165, 3223, **3290**, 3308, 3348, 3393, 3692, 3810, 3954, 3962, 4024
 Great Britain, directories, **1775**, 1873, 1987
 history, **136**, 198, **267**, 320, **524**, 537, 542, **552**, **571**, 587, 590, 591, 609, 623, 639, 640, 642, **678**, 731, 737, **751**, 808, 812, 816, **832**, 853, 863, 900, **903**, **905**, 910, **911**, **919**, 931, **932**, 949, **967**, **968**, **1051**, 1076, **1077**, 1098, **1104**, **1105**, 1145, 1147, **1200**, 1215, **1263**, **1283**, **1289**
 individual histories, 23, **334**, 548, 568, 583, 597, 606, 611, 620, 633, 639, 680, 717, 719, 732, 742, 750, 761, 762, 765, 766, 767, 796, 805, 813, 825, 833, **841**, 842, 862, 874, 875, 880, 883, 886, 897, **905**, 908, 913, 923, 925, 933, 945, 955, 987, 991, 997, 1005, 1009, 1017, 1022, **1054**, **1055**, 1056, **1057**, 1083, 1087, 1094, 1095, 1102, 1132, 1133, 1142, 1150, **1154**, 1168, 1173, 1180, 1196, 1201, 1209, 1239, 1262, 1280, 1901, 1976. *See also* Foundations, history
 international, directories, 1747, **1751**, **1752**, 1758, 1783, 1794, 1816, 1837, **1839**, 1873, 1874, 1877, 1954, 1974, 1986, 1987

305

SUBJECT INDEX

Foundations (*continued*)
  investigations, 540, 589, **629**, 632, **856**, 918, 998, **1054**, **1055**, 1056, **1057**, 1073, 1079, 1090, 1250, **4316**, 4379, 4381, 4383, 4386, 4387, 4392, **4403**, 4408, 4409, 4410, 4413, 4414, 4415, 4416, 4417, 4419, 4420, 4421, 4422, 4423, 4425, 4426, 4427, 4428, 4429, 4430, 4441, 4444
  investments, 551, 641, 649, 759, 792, 824, 942, **944**, 1017, 1038, 1039, **1080**, 1107, **1149**, 2442, 2837, **2929**, **2952**, 4120, 4477, **4877**
  Iowa, 560, 561
  Italy, directories, 1797
  Japan, directories, 1816
  Latin America, directories, 1745, 1789, 1826, 1954, 1957
  law and legislation, 1876
  legal instruments, 400, 539, 588, 604, 610, 717, 728, 746, 851, 859, 3850, **4163**, 4171, 4314, 4319, 4342, 4478
  liberal. *See* Grantmakers, social issues
  loans. *See* Loans
  management, 2683
  Michigan, **646**
  Nebraska, **898**
  New Jersey, **960**
  New Zealand, directories, 1783
  Ohio, 1161
  Oregon, **1000**
  Philippines, directories, 1877
  political activity, **4065**
  project reports, 804, **909**, 950, **968**, 993, 1037, 1801, 1802, 1803, 1804, 1805, 1806, 1807, 1808, 1809, 1810, 1811, 1812, 1813, 1814, 1815, 4674, 4766, 4767, 4781, 4783, 4787, 4791, 4792, 4793, 4794, 4795, 4796, 4797, 4798, 4799, 4800, 4801, 4802, 4803, 4804, 4805, 4806, 4807, 4808, 4809, 4811, 4819, 4821, 4832, 4833, 4836, 4837, 4839, 4841, 4842, 4851, 4852, 4853, 4863, 4867, 4881, 4885, 4886, 4887, 4889, 4896, 4903, 4906, 4914, 4918, 4922, 4923, 4938, 4954, 4955, 4957, 4958, 4966, **4975**, 4978, 4983, 4985, 4990
  proposals to. *See* Proposal development
  public policy, 627, **657**, 694, 724, 784, 876, 895, 902, 931, 1027, 1230
  public responsibility, **434**, 435, 714, 781, 814, 879, 970, 974, **977**, 1027, 1090, 1111, 1118, 1122, 1148, 1195, 1218, 1235
  reasons for creating. *See* Foundations, establishment and termination
  research, **591**, **919**, **936**, 964, **981**, 982, **1099**, **3337**
  Rhode Island, **643**, 4130
  social justice. *See* Grantmakers, social issues
  South Dakota, **1191**

Spain, directories, **1772**
statistics, 23, **330**, 331, 543, 561, **577**, **646**, 774, 835, **1099**, **1100**, **1125**, **1126**, 1248, 1249, 2116
surveys, 530, 535, **646**, 1018, 1029, **1061**, **1062**, 1093, 1183, 1188, **1198**, **2742**
Texas, **614**, **961**, 1018, **1264**
Turkey, directories, 1974
Venezuela, directories, 1826
Washington, D.C., **634**
Wisconsin, **858**
Foundations in fiction. *See* Foundations, fiction
Franklin, Benjamin, 225
Freedom of Information Act, 4443
Freeman, Gaylord, 229
French-American Foundation, 1158
Frick Educational Commission, Henry C., 1200
Frick, Henry Clay, 201, 1200
Fund for the Republic, **870**, **1105**
Fund raising. *See* Fundraising
Fund-raising. *See* Fundraising
Funding. *See* Fundraising
Funding sources. *See* Fundraising
Funding trends, **433**, **1025**, 1790, **1897**, 1898, 3049, 3320, 3462, **3527**, 3538, 3658, **3703**, 3849, 3855, 3879, 3880, 3884, 3886, **3979**
Fundraising, 26, **134**, 360, 440, 479, **650**, 892, 1007, **1117**, **1227**, 1302, **1331**, 1343, 1350, 1386, 1393, **1439**, **1451**, 1493, 1543, 1634, 1640, **1648**, 1650, 1656, 1687, 1715, 1880, 1994, 2138, 2229, 2256, **2508**, 2524, 2531, 2590, 2621, 2639, **2643**, 2656, 2660, 2677, 2689, 2690, 2691, 2692, 2761, **2811**, 2883, 2893, 2894, 2961, 2983, 2984, 2985, 2986, 2989, 2991, 2992, 2996, 2999, 3001, 3007, 3010, 3012, **3014**, **3015**, **3018**, 3020, **3023**, 3026, **3028**, 3029, **3030**, 3035, 3038, 3039, 3041, **3045**, 3046, **3047**, 3050, 3051, 3052, 3057, 3058, 3059, 3060, 3065, 3068, **3069**, **3070**, 3074, **3077**, 3080, 3082, **3083**, 3085, 3087, **3088**, 3091, **3094**, 3096, 3098, **3104**, 3105, 3107, 3108, 3112, **3114**, 3118, 3125, 3126, 3130, 3131, **3132**, **3133**, **3135**, 3136, 3142, 3145, **3152**, 3153, 3154, **3162**, **3164**, 3167, 3171, 3173, 3174, 3175, 3179, 3180, 3181, 3183, 3185, 3186, 3187, 3188, **3189**, 3196, 3198, 3199, 3201, 3203, 3204, 3205, **3206**, **3207**, 3209, 3212, 3215, 3216, 3223, 3225, 3226, 3230, 3233, **3234**, **3238**, **3240**, 3242, 3244, 3245, **3247**, **3250**, 3252, 3259, **3262**, **3263**, 3266, 3269, **3270**, 3272, 3273, 3274, 3275, 3276, 3277, 3278, 3279, 3280, 3281, 3284, **3285**, 3286,

3287, **3290**, 3293, **3295**, 3296, 3297, 3298, 3299, 3301, 3302, 3305, **3306**, 3309, 3310, **3311**, **3312**, **3313**, 3320, 3321, 3327, 3333, 3335, 3336, **3337**, **3339**, 3340, 3341, **3345**, 3348, 3350, 3352, 3353, 3354, **3355**, **3356**, 3358, **3360**, 3362, 3364, **3366**, **3369**, 3372, 3374, **3376**, 3378, **3381**, 3382, 3383, 3384, 3385, 3392, **3394**, 3395, 3397, **3401**, 3402, 3403, 3405, **3412**, 3416, 3418, 3421, **3423**, 3426, 3427, 3428, **3429**, 3432, **3434**, 3435, **3444**, 3446, **3447**, **3448**, **3449**, 3450, 3452, 3453, 3454, 3456, 3459, **3463**, 3466, 3468, 3472, 3475, 3476, 3477, **3481**, 3483, 3484, 3485, 3489, 3491, 3492, 3495, 3496, **3498**, 3501, 3502, **3503**, **3505**, 3506, 3507, 3515, 3516, 3520, 3521, 3522, 3523, 3524, 3525, **3526**, 3528, **3529**, 3530, **3532**, 3533, 3535, **3536**, 3537, 3539, 3541, **3544**, 3546, 3547, **3560**, 3563, 3564, 3565, 3566, 3567, 3573, 3574, **3575**, 3576, 3577, 3579, 3581, 3582, **3583**, **3589**, 3590, 3593, 3596, **3599**, 3601, 3612, 3615, 3619, 3622, **3624**, **3625**, 3627, 3628, **3634**, **3635**, 3639, 3640, **3641**, 3642, 3643, **3645**, **3646**, 3648, 3650, 3655, 3660, 3662, 3663, 3664, 3665, **3666**, 3667, 3668, 3673, 3676, 3680, 3681, **3683**, **3684**, 3690, 3697, **3701**, **3705**, 3706, 3712, 3714, 3717, 3720, 3723, 3726, 3730, 3731, 3733, 3735, **3739**, 3742, 3748, 3750, 3752, **3755**, 3756, **3761**, **3771**, 3777, **3780**, 3786, 3790, 3792, **3796**, 3799, **3803**, 3804, 3809, 3815, 3816, 3818, 3824, 3825, 3834, 3835, 3840, 3841, **3842**, 3845, **3846**, **3859**, 3867, 3870, **3871**, **3873**, 3878, **3882**, **3883**, 3888, 3889, 3891, 3893, 3894, 3900, 3904, 3905, **3906**, 3909, 3912, 3913, 3914, 3915, 3920, 3924, 3930, 3931, 3932, 3937, 3938, 3941, **3947**, 3955, **3958**, 3959, 3960, 3961, 3963, 3965, 3966, 3968, 3969, 3970, **3973**, 3974, 3975, 3976, 3977, 3982, 3984, **3986**, 3987, 3988, **3990**, 3991, **3992**, 4002, 4006, 4018, 4026, 4064, 4069, 4183, 4202, 4606, 4643, **4666**
administration, 2461, **2473**, **2481**, 2496, 2558, **2638**, 2639, 2644, **2655**, 2665, 2728, 2753, **2764**, 2770, 2773, **2778**, **2804**, 2835, 2836, 2848, 2872, 2918, **2926**, 2977, **3000**, **3015**, **3018**, 3027, **3028**, **3040**, **3045**, 3049, 3054, 3055, 3074, **3083**, 3093, 3115,

Fundraising
administration (*continued*)
3123, 3125, **3129**, **3137**, 3139, 3144, 3148, **3149**, **3152**, 3176, 3178, 3179, 3203, **3208**, 3224, 3236, **3240**, 3256, 3268, 3275, 3304, 3307, **3330**, 3334, 3343, 3346, 3351, **3355**, 3357, 3359, **3365**, 3367, 3368, 3386, **3394**, 3395, 3406, 3407, 3414, 3427, **3429**, 3430, **3434**, 3437, 3445, 3470, 3471, 3480, 3485, 3488, 3490, 3504, **3505**, 3511, 3512, 3522, **3529**, 3563, 3577, **3583**, **3584**, 3587, **3597**, **3599**, 3600, **3611**, 3612, 3621, 3629, **3634**, 3651, 3668, 3671, 3682, **3683**, **3687**, 3694, **3701**, 3708, 3709, 3713, 3727, **3739**, 3752, **3761**, 3764, **3787**, 3789, 3790, 3795, **3797**, 3798, 3801, **3812**, 3813, 3819, 3823, 3838, 3845, 3856, 3875, 3888, 3892, 3894, **3896**, 3907, 3908, 3918, 3925, **3926**, **3939**, 3940, **3944**, 3946, **3947**, 3964, 3969, 3972, 3977

alternatives, 1628, 1630, **1685**, 2401, 2515, 2988, 3008, 3024, 3029, **3033**, 3042, 3048, 3065, 3078, 3081, 3121, 3148, 3209, **3250**, **3312**, 3325, **3345**, 3382, **3410**, 3487, 3616, 3617, 3628, **3641**, 3658, 3665, 3732, **3739**, 3748, 3757, 3770, 3779, 3802, **3812**, 3828, 3832, 3864, 3887, 3925, 3952, 3953

analysis, 27, 279, 388, **1636**, **2192**, 2293, **2701**, **2994**, **3062**, 3071, **3109**, **3113**, **3114**, **3133**, 3202, 3205, 3222, **3234**, **3240**, 3283, 3320, 3344, **3399**, **3448**, **3500**, **3503**, 3524, 3539, **3578**, **3580**, 3610, **3624**, 3632, 3642, 3658, 3677, **3701**, **3702**, 3704, 3725, 3729, 3781, 3794, 3811, **3837**, 3849, 3853, 3855, 3857, **3859**, 3860, 3863, 3879, 3880, 3881, 3886, 3887, 3899, 3921, **3951**, 3983, **4086**, **4964**

bibliographies, 2103, 3041, **3314**, 3328, 3329, 3338, 3561, 3604, **3653**, 3655, 3872

computer aided, **2643**, 2753, 2893, 2894, **2927**, 3304, 3349, 3350, 3487, **3584**, 3686, **3687**, 3851, **3871**, 3893, 3969, 3972, 4501

costs, 2824, **3040**, 3061, **3062**, 3064, 3303, 3454, 3455, 3471, 3557, **3558**, **3707**, 3736, 3763, 3781, 3844, 3854, 3862, 3876, 3877, 3910

dictionaries, **3306**, **3666**

directories, **595**, 682, **1710**, **1985**, **3200**, 3227, **3253**, **3260**, **3389**, 3586, 3591, 3652, **3669**, **3689**, 3715, **3922**

ethics, **2068**, **2139**, 2761, **3062**, 3122, 3344, 3445, 3465, **3707**, 3725, 3794, 3861, 3863, **4869**

evaluations, **2356**, **2778**, 2872, 3055, 3064, **3067**, 3071, 3122, 3145, 3236, 3445, **3481**, **3558**, 3704, **3787**, **3837**, 3849

federated, 2988, 3004, 3121, 3145, 3333, 3344, 3465, 3497, 3676, 3725, 3794, 3807, 3853, 3860, 3861, 3863, 3880, 3881, 3887, 3899, **3951**

handbooks, manuals, etc., **981**, 982, **1099**, **1428**, 2328, 2452, **2492**, 2647, 2918, **2981**, 2986, 2990, 3013, **3014**, 3021, **3045**, 3060, **3070**, 3074, 3082, **3094**, **3101**, 3123, **3124**, **3149**, 3157, 3158, 3159, 3171, 3179, 3204, **3207**, 3214, **3237**, **3250**, 3252, **3270**, 3272, **3285**, **3311**, **3313**, 3327, **3339**, 3341, **3376**, 3378, **3379**, 3380, **3381**, 3446, 3483, **3499**, 3517, 3518, 3520, **3526**, **3529**, **3536**, 3545, 3556, **3634**, **3641**, 3675, 3678, 3681, **3684**, 3706, 3720, 3723, 3730, 3731, **3737**, 3750, 3752, **3769**, **3803**, 3804, **3808**, **3812**, 3816, 3824, 3834, **3836**, **3873**, 3894, **3906**, **3935**, 3941, 3955, 3956, **3990**, 3991, 4035, 4621, 4631

history, 326, 2354, **2993**, **3184**, 3191

law and legislation, **4186**

professional ethics. *See* Fundraising, ethics

special events, 2984, 3020, **3033**, 3034, **3047**, 3053, **3083**, 3112, 3153, 3167, 3171, 3187, **3189**, **3193**, **3197**, 3209, 3242, **3311**, 3353, **3376**, 3382, 3416, **3431**, 3432, 3453, 3468, 3470, **3531**, **3571**, **3575**, **3647**, 3654, 3665, 3700, 3714, 3718, 3757, **3768**, **3820**, **3831**, 3843, 3927, **3948**, 3952, 3953, **3971**

standards, **2068**, **2356**

statistics, **3492**, **3493**, 3728

studies, 125, 3131, **3580**

surveys, 2245, 2293, 3059, **3067**, 3107, **3113**, 3283, **3527**, 3538, 3610, 3632, 3677, **3703**, 3729, 3811, 3855, 3879, 3884, 3886, 3983

telemarketing, 1165, **3033**, 3349, 3563, **3808**

women, **3979**

Fundraising techniques, **2487**. *See also* Fundraising

Future of foundations. *See* Foundations, analysis

Gannett Foundation, 4786

Garage sales. *See* Fundraising, special events

Gardner, John W., 2148, 3722

Gates, Frederick Taylor, **171**, 172, **587**

Geldof, Bob, **173**

General Education Board, 409, **571**, 765, 805

General Foods Corporation, 1455

General Mills, 1557

Getty family, 297, 340

Getty Trust, J. Paul, 129, 148, 576

Getty, J. Paul, 148, 297, 340

Getty, J. Paul Jr., **507**

Girard, Stephen, 213

Golden Donors, 1213

Gould Foundation for Children, Edwin, 642

Gould, Edwin, 642

Government, 794, 4255, 4436, 4613, **4627**, 4683, **4743**

directories, 1759, 3440, **4627**, **4628**, **4635**, 4654, **4656**, 4732, 4736, **4741**

Government and nonprofit sector, 480, **903**, 1641, 1852, **2055**, 2207, 2310, **2321**, 2322, **2323**, **2350**, 2416, 4203, 4606, 4614, 4634, 4644, 4657, 4658, **4660**, 4662, 4663, 4664, 4669, **4670**, 4675, 4678, 4680, 4685, 4686, 4687, **4737**, 4738, **4739**, **4743**, 4745, 4747, 4763, 4929

Government and philanthropy, 3205, 3807, 4183, 4606, 4763

Government funding, **605**, 1244, 1247, **2350**, **3044**, 3141, **3228**, 3559, **3560**, 3591, 3661, 3678, 3719, **4040**, 4134, **4475**, 4605, 4609, 4611, 4612, 4615, **4617**, 4618, 4619, 4620, 4623, 4624, 4626, **4629**, 4631, 4633, 4636, 4637, 4640, 4641, 4642, 4643, 4647, 4651, 4652, **4653**, **4655**, 4661, 4665, **4666**, **4668**, 4672, **4676**, 4679, 4682, 4684, 4688, 4695, 4706, **4707**, 4713, 4729, **4730**, 4735, 4738, 4742, 4746, 4748, **4755**, 4756, **4759**, 4760, **4761**, 4762, 4958

analysis, 346, 2640, 3289, 4611, 4614, 4619, 4731

arts and humanities, federal, 1900, 3140, 4604, 4610, 4622, 4624, **4630**, 4632, 4638, 4639, 4645, 4650, 4673, 4684, **4689**, 4690, 4691, 4692, 4693, **4694**, 4695, 4696, 4698, **4699**, **4700**, 4701, 4714, 4733, 4744, 4752, 4753, 4754

arts and humanities, international, 1900, 4753

arts and humanities, state, 4607, **4608**, 4610, 4649, 4650, 4681, 4715, 4716, 4717, 4719, 4720, 4721, 4722, **4723**, 4724, 4725, 4726

bibliographies, 4734

California, directories, **4727**

directories, 3254, 4676, 4718, **4727**, **4761**

education, 4633, 4646, 4659, 4667, 4677, 4735

government policy, 4614, 4731

handbooks, manuals, etc., 4621, 4626, **4629**, 4631, 4643, **4653**, **4655**, **4668**, 4682, 4729

SUBJECT INDEX

307

SUBJECT INDEX

Government funding (*continued*)
    surveys, 4634, 4657, 4658, **4660**, 4662, 4663, 4664, 4674, 4678, 4680, 4685, 4686, 4687, **4737**, **4739**, 4740, 4745

Government grants. *See* Government funding

Government regulation of philanthropy
    bibliographies, 4134
    federal, **102**, **721**, **2183**, **4074**, 4096, 4100, **4116**, **4469**, 4728
    state and local, **2064**, 3122, **3493**, **3842**, 4069, **4070**, **4074**, 4130, **4131**, **4206**, 4253, 4254, 4255, 4348, **4469**, 4728

Graduate Medical Education National Advisory Committee, **873**

Grammercy Park Foundation, 413

Grant Foundation, William T., 597, **4857**

Grantmakers, **663**, **1192**, 3856
    conservative. *See* Grantmakers, social issues
    directories, 733, 1034, **1035**
    liberal. *See* Grantmakers, social issues
    social issues, 203, **323**, **434**, 435, **465**, 555, 670, 696, 791, 797, 799, **887**, 929, 962, 983, 984, 985, 1019, **1043**, **1075**, **1091**, 1103, 1120, 1143, 1158, **1174**, **1186**, 1205, 1225, 1226, 1229, 1233, 1245, 1254, 1260, **1281**, 1284, 1288, 1607, **2349**, **3981**, 4648, 4814

Grantsmanship. *See* Nonprofit organizations, grantsmanship

Grassroots fundraising. *See* Fundraising, alternatives

Great Britain
    directories. *See* Foundations, Great Britain, directories

Gregg, Alan, 373

Grolier, Inc., **1312**

Guggenheim family, 120, 302, 316

Guggenheim Foundation, Solomon R., 875

Gulbenkian, Calouste, 216

Hall Foundation, 560

Hammer, Armand, **194**

Handicapped, 892, 980, **2074**, **2418**, 2853, 3085, **3253**, **3366**, **3689**, 3933, 4073, 4691, 4941

Hariri, Rafiq, **63**

Harkness, Edward Stephen, 516

Harkness, Rebekah Hale, **482**

Hartford Foundation, John A., 883, 1262

Hartke Subcommittee, 4441

Hayden Foundation, Charles, 842

Hayes, Helen, **4532**

Hazen Foundation, Edward W., 425

Hazen, Edward Warriner, 425

Health, 566, **587**, **621**, **622**, 709, **710**, 711, **712**, **809**, **810**, 826, **872**, **873**, 877, 951, 1128, 1244, 1246, 1247, **1269**, **1582**, 1640, **2042**, 2081, 2146, 2225, 2372, 2439, 2829, 2938, 2989, 3026, 3029, 3051, 3085, **3088**, 3098, 3105, 3115, **3162**, 3172, 3181, 3185, 3198, 3215, 3216, 3223, **3263**, 3274, 3275, 3309, 3310, **3312**, 3335, 3336, 3350, 3385, 3395, 3397, 3441, 3485, **3494**, 3522, 3533, 3576, 3593, 3612, 3619, 3627, **3630**, 3640, **3705**, 3756, 3790, **3796**, 3819, 3840, 3851, 3908, 3909, 3913, 3914, 3954, 3961, 3974, 3976, 3982, 4501, 4702, **4759**, 4769, 4821, 4827, **4829**, 4871, 4903, 4976, 4989
    bibliographies, 3758
    directories, 1097, **1989**, 2121, 2215, 2255, **3228**, **3689**, 3796

Health Resource Center, **2074**

Hearst family, **30**, 93

Hearst, William Randolph, 93

Hefner, Christie, 498

Hemenway, Mary, 473

Heritage Foundation, 943

Hewitt, Abram S., 352

Higher education, **54**, **63**, **114**, 117, 224, **287**, **301**, **319**, 327, 436, 517, 529, 574, 584, 592, 603, 672, 675, 740, 776, 780, 843, 884, 885, 926, **936**, 969, 979, 993, 1004, 1020, 1023, 1070, 1071, 1084, 1096, 1098, **1113**, 1297, 1314, 1325, 1368, 1372, 1373, 1392, 1400, 1404, 1405, 1408, **1409**, 1411, 1412, 1453, 1456, **1487**, 1491, 1501, 1521, 1576, 1590, 1644, 1727, 1919, **2074**, **2122**, 2125, 2283, 2366, 2420, 2436, 2451, 2460, 2513, 2540, 2642, 2738, **2784**, 2883, 2964, 2970, 2995, 2997, 3009, 3056, 3095, 3110, 3120, 3128, 3142, 3167, 3168, **3169**, 3170, 3210, 3211, 3212, 3213, 3256, 3272, 3273, 3293, 3294, 3298, 3347, **3371**, 3372, 3396, 3419, 3422, 3438, **3444**, 3482, 3486, 3545, **3550**, 3551, 3595, 3598, 3602, 3631, 3722, 3726, 3759, 3774, 3829, 3843, 3901, 3907, 3916, 3919, 3928, 3945, 4013, 4107, 4118, 4119, 4149, 4213, 4266, 4318, 4646, 4661, 4672, 4677, 4708, 4712, **4755**, 4760, 4767, 4775, 4778, **4785**, 4788, 4791, 4792, 4793, 4794, 4795, 4796, 4797, 4798, 4799, 4800, 4801, 4802, 4803, 4804, 4805, 4808, **4810**, 4811, 4819, 4820, 4823, 4830, 4839, 4840, 4844, 4848, 4849, **4850**, 4859, 4866, 4868, 4881, 4885, 4906, 4922, 4923, 4932, 4940, 4948, 4957, 4958, 4961, 4978, 4985
    directories, 828, **3043**
    finance, **54**, **114**, 224, 1383, 1405, 1407, 1453, 1501, 1616, 1674, **2481**, **3069**, 3110, 3120, **3169**, 3273, 3421, 3482, **3544**, 3610, 3631, 3726, **3766**, 3786, 3945, **3986**, **4086**, **4125**, 4760, 4859
    indexes, 4961
    philanthropy. *See* Higher education
    studies, 1243, **2122**, 2454, 2998, 3075, 3143, 3165, 3255, 3316, 3317, 3319, 3469, 3549, 3552, 3553, 3554, **3580**, 3696, 3810, 3847, 3902, 3934, 4506, 4779, **4785**, 4825, 4858, 4874

Hispanics, **350**, 660, 690, 788, 937, **938**, **1198**, 1693, 1743, **2086**, 2145, 3277, 4838, 4897, **4928**. *See also* Minorities

Historic buildings
    preservation, 3525, 4835, 4870, 4873, **4883**, **4884**
    preservation, directories, 2259, 3375, 3586

Historical projects. *See* Historic buildings, preservation

History, 2236, 2857, 4815

Hogg Foundation for Mental Hygiene, 303

Hogg, Will, 303

Hollis, Thomas, **287**

Homelessness, **282**, **4962**

Hook, Charles R., 3491

Hopkins, Johns, 468

Hospitals, 437, 510, 570, 1840, 2054, 2085, **2163**, **2168**, 2239, 2333, 2535, 3089, 3181, 3203, 3332, 3417, **3527**, 3621, **3635**, 3640, **3653**, 3913, 3961, 3989, **3993**, 4644, 4787, 4989

Housing, **282**, **311**, 466, **891**, 2223, **2349**, 3343, 3373, 4765, 4967

Human services, 1645
    directories, 2033, **2106**, **4764**

Humanities, **1886**, **2149**, 2384, 4701, 4816, 4921, 4965
    directories, 2714
    grants, 586, **4005**, 4698, **4699**, **4700**, 4715, 4717, 4720, 4721, 4722
    grants, directories, **624**

Hutchins, Robert Maynard, **1105**

Illegal operations. *See* Charity rackets

Immigration and emigration, 1158

In-kind contributions, 1310, 1324, **1344**, 1346, 1359, 1375, 1376, 1382, 1388, 1390, 1430, 1438, 1461, **1498**, 1511, 1514, **1522**, **1534**, 1536, **1558**, **1587**, **1588**, 1605, **1624**, 1625, 1626, 1627, 1628, 1629, 1630, **1631**, **1632**, **1646**, **1675**, 1691, 1695, 1708, 1722, **3254**, **3747**, **3935**, 4078, **4363**, 4486, 4602. *See also* Corporate philanthropy

Income generating businesses. *See* Nonprofit organizations, entrepreneurship

Independent Sector, 457, 2148, 3849, 4109, 4300

Indians. *See* Native Americans

Individual giving, **24**, 33, 35, **68**, 97, **104**, **105**, 137, 142, 147, 150, 158, 168, 169, 179, **185**, 202, **212**, 220, 263, **304**, 305, **306**, 351, 356, **364**, **402**, 414, **417**, **419**, **453**, 458, **459**, 467, **476**, 479, 890, 1460, 1483, 1535, 3005, 3278, 3322, 3454, 3457,

SUBJECT INDEX

Individual giving (*continued*)
　　3508, 3509, 3510, **3613**, 3623,
　　3744, 3792, 3840, 3884, 4071,
　　4082, 4204, 4236, 4288, 4294,
　　4363, 4367, 4539, 4845. *See also*
　　　Fundraising
Individual grantseekers, **624**, 695, **912**, **928**,
　　1121
Individuals. *See* Individual grantseekers
Information science, 2466, **2669**, 4704
Inland Steel Ryerson Foundation, **1665**
Institute for Community Economics, 2231
Insurance. *See* Liability insurance
Insurance companies. *See* Corporate
　　philanthropy
Internal Revenue Service, 535, **856**, **1125**,
　　2432, 4105, 4112, 4153, **4178**,
　　4184, 4185, 4208, 4209, **4225**,
　　4236, 4317, 4333, 4338, **4361**,
　　4394, 4436, 4443, 4458, 4460,
　　4461, 4463, **4464**
International activities, **63**, **434**, 435, 505,
　　552, **572**, 607, 796, 886, 906,
　　1448, **1518**, **1757**, 1759, **1760**,
　　1761, **1762**, 1764, **1765**, **1766**,
　　1771, 1777, 1778, **1785**, 1786,
　　1787, 1788, 1791, **1795**, 1798,
　　1799, 1800, 1801, 1802, 1803,
　　1804, 1805, 1806, 1807, 1808,
　　1809, 1810, 1811, 1812, 1813,
　　1814, 1815, 1825, **1836**, 1840,
　　1841, 1842, 1843, 1844, 1845,
　　1846, 1847, 1851, 1852, 1854,
　　1857, 1878, 1879, 1881, 1883,
　　1888, 1891, **1893**, 1903, **1911**,
　　1915, 1927, **1934**, **1939**, **1944**,
　　1945, **1946**, 1949, 1958, 1962,
　　1963, 1964, 1967, 1968, 1971,
　　1972, 1977, **1985**, 2114, **2117**,
　　2339, **2406**, 4647, 4671, 4862
International education, **1762**, **1768**, **1770**,
　　1795, 1919, 4625
International philanthropy, **63**, **66**, **323**,
　　572, 615, 763, 1360, 1746, **1748**,
　　1749, **1757**, **1765**, 1769, 1773,
　　1776, 1777, 1780, **1781**, **1785**,
　　1786, 1787, 1791, 1792, 1796,
　　1817, 1818, 1819, 1820, 1822,
　　1823, 1827, 1829, 1841, 1842,
　　1843, 1845, 1846, 1850, 1853,
　　1855, 1856, 1857, **1858**, 1860,
　　1867, **1868**, 1870, 1871, 1875,
　　1876, 1879, **1886**, 1887, **1888**,
　　1889, 1891, 1892, 1894, **1896**,
　　1901, 1902, 1904, 1906, 1909,
　　1910, 1915, **1916**, 1918, 1921,
　　1928, 1929, 1932, 1933, **1934**,
　　1935, 1937, 1943, 1955, 1956,
　　1960, 1965, **1966**, 1967, 1969,
　　1970, 1973, 1975, 1977, 1979,
　　1984, **2278**, **3241**
　　directories, 1305, 1745, **1751**, **1752**,
　　　1758, **1772**, **1775**, 1777, 1783,
　　　1789, 1794, 1797, 1816, 1824,
　　　1826, 1837, **1839**, 1874, 1877,
　　　1905, 1952, 1954, 1957, 1967,
　　　1974, 1986, 1987
　　Europe, directories, 1747, **1835**

　　taxation, 1749, 1902, 1975
Investments, **647**, 727, 1299, 1569, **2549**,
　　2952, 2970, 3919
Iona House, **2078**
IRS. *See* Internal Revenue Service
Irvine Foundation, James, 620
Ittleson Family Foundation, 880
J.M. Foundation, 1147
Jackman Foundation, 881
JDR 3rd Fund, 886, 4784
Jeanes Fund, 55
Jerome Foundation, **4847**
Job Training Partnership Act, 4641
Jobs. *See* Employment
Johnson Foundation, Robert Wood, **872**,
　　888, 1128
Joint Foundation Support, **887**
Jones, John Price, 139
Jones, Thomas, 2035
Journalism. *See* Journalism and mass
　　communications
Journalism and mass communications, **532**,
　　4786
Judicial. *See* Law and justice
Kaiser Family Foundation, Henry J., **873**,
　　4059
Kellogg Foundation, W.K., 270, 908, 4867
Kellogg, W.K., 389
Keppel, Frederick Paul, 21, 272
Kettering, Charles F., 274
Kidd, James, 167
Koestler Foundation, 1981
Kresge Foundation, 807, 925, 3408, 4062
Kroc Foundation, Joan B., **1186**
Kunstadter Foundation, Albert, 323
Kunstadter, Albert, 323
Lasker, Albert D., 190
Lavanburg Foundation, 4853
Law and justice, **2100**, 2156, 2766, 4270,
　　4959
Laws regulating philanthropy, **134**, **518**,
　　856, 857, 864, 970, 1164, 1267,
　　1502, 1940, **2183**, **2206**, **2489**,
　　2972, 3035, **4072**, **4074**, 4111,
　　4118, 4119, **4124**, 4127, **4136**,
　　4154, 4169, 4185, **4189**, **4190**,
　　4191, 4208, 4215, 4218, **4237**,
　　4256, 4260, 4310, 4314, **4335**,
　　4348, **4349**, 4351, 4355, **4374**,
　　4440, 4466, 4474
　　(1900-1939), 4075, 4750, 4751
　　(1940-1949), 4223, 4453, 4749
　　(1950-1959), 4380
　　(1960-1969), 4121, 4129, 4144, 4150,
　　　4156, 4157, 4158, 4159, **4219**,
　　　4264, 4290, 4327, 4352, 4354,
　　　4384, 4391, 4393, 4395, 4396,
　　　4397, 4399, 4400, 4401, 4402,
　　　4404, 4405, 4406, 4433, 4437,
　　　4438, 4439, 4442, 4445, 4446,
　　　4447, 4448, 4449, 4455, 4458,
　　　4459, 4460
　　(1970-1979), 830, 4076, **4151**, 4165,
　　　4398, 4444, 4450, 4451, 4452
　　(1980-1989), 447, **657**, 735, 749, **1828**,
　　　2013, 2269, **2906**, 3476, **4065**,
　　　4080, 4095, **4098**, 4123, **4139**,

　　　4152, **4179**, 4182, 4183, 4200,
　　　4210, 4235, 4239, **4251**, **4265**,
　　　4304, 4305, **4316**, **4334**, **4336**,
　　　4345, **4347**, 4373, 4388, 4394,
　　　4403, 4407, 4411, 4412, 4434
　　Great Britain, 1784, 1895, 1929, 1931
　　history, **934**, **1207**, 4160, 4218
　　state and local. *See* State laws
　　　regulating philanthropy
Lawyers
　　directories, **2878**
Leadership. *See* Nonprofit organizations,
　　administration
Learning disabilities. *See* Handicapped
Legal instruments. *See* Foundations, legal
　　instruments
Legal issues. *See* Laws regulating
　　philanthropy
Legal responsibilities. *See* Laws regulating
　　philanthropy
Levi Strauss Foundation, 1484
Levinson Foundation, Max and Anna, 983
Liability insurance, **2076**, **2284**, **2398**, 2504,
　　2529, 2574, **2673**, 2756, 2907,
　　4104, 4173, **4237**, **4553**
Liberal foundations. *See* Grantmakers,
　　social issues
Libraries, 564, 1095, 1884, 2003, **2213**,
　　2430, 2716, 2871, 2999, 3046,
　　3070, 3092, **3135**, **3164**, **3248**,
　　3291, 3296, **3315**, 3521, 3615,
　　3890, 3970, 3975, 4597, 4651,
　　4773, 4790, 4894
　　administration, 2452, 2457, **2477**,
　　　2523, **2551**, 2722, 2727, 2828,
　　　2901, **3570**, 3590
　　automation, 2457, **2477**, 2523
　　directories, 525, 2434, **4562**
　　grants, 2452, 2999, 3078, 3116, **3164**,
　　　3315, 3521, **3570**, **3614**, 3975
　　wages, 2901
Library programs. *See* Libraries
Loan funds, 2045, **2161**, **2273**, 2279, 2501,
　　2512, **2890**, 3261, **3625**, 3688
Loans, 466, **601**, **647**, 2045, **2161**, **2273**,
　　2279, 2394, 2501, 2561, **2890**,
　　3079, 3231, 3261, 3292, **3625**,
　　3688, 3754, 3897, 4161, 4980
Lobbying, 555, 1273, **2075**, 2114, **2298**,
　　2602, 2746, **4091**, **4098**, 4108,
　　4109, 4117, 4145, 4154, 4172,
　　4201, 4238, 4243, 4245, **4258**,
　　4268, 4284, 4295, 4296, 4318,
　　4322, 4324, **4329**, 4346, 4399,
　　4418, 4471, 4473, 4604, 4702
Local Initiatives Support Corporation, 3572
Luce, Clare Boothe, **60**
Luce, Henry R., **832**
Luce, Henry R., III, **832**
Lundy, George, 325
MacArthur Foundation, John D. and
　　Catherine T., 705, 914, 915, 916,
　　921, 1127
Major gifts campaigns, 3238, 3538, **3611**,
　　3939, **3944**. *See also* Fundraising
Management, **524**, 2119, 2436, **2479**, **2546**,
　　2607, **2608**, **2631**, **2663**, 2679,

SUBJECT INDEX

Management (*continued*)
    2727, 2754, **2779**, **2822**, **2823**, 2866, 2921, **3137**
    handbooks, manuals, etc., **2446**, 2775, 2776, 2777, **2779**, 2826, 2830, **2889**, 2960, **2967**, 2976, 2977
Management Institute for New Hampshire, 1053
Marin Community Foundation, **1283**
Marketing. *See* Nonprofit organizations, marketing
Marts, Arnaud Cartwright, 90
Massachusetts Mutual Life Insurance Company, 3134
Matching gifts, **1487**, 2525, **3099**, 3166, 3192, 3210, 3239, 3271, 3396, **3540**, 3602, 3724, 3776, 3985. *See also* Fundraising
Mathematics, 689
Mather, Cotton, **39**
McBeath Foundation, Faye, 38
Meadows Foundation, 4835
Media. *See* Journalism and mass communications
Medical research. *See* Medicine, research
Medicine
    research, 124, 580, 685, **841**, **888**, 1204, 3420, 4777, 4782, 4843, 4854, 4861, 4891, 4893, 4911, 4917, 4943, 4969, 4989
    study and teaching, **571**, **587**, **1768**, **1795**, 4809
Mellon Educational and Charitable Trust, A.W., 1005
Mellon family, 214, 288, 421
Mellon, Andrew W., 363
Mellon, Paul, 99, 215, 392, 426
Membership. *See* Nonprofit organizations, administration
Membership drives, **2487**
Mental health, **841**, 1031, 2960, 4073, 4757, 4758, 4813, 4887, 4941, 4956
    directories, **3221**, 4703
Mental retardation. *See* Handicapped
Mergers. *See* Nonprofit organizations, administration
Merrill Trust, Charles E., **334**, **455**
Meyer Charitable Trust, Fred, **1113**
Milbank Memorial Fund, **720**, 913
Millionaires. *See* Individual giving
Minorities, **465**, 788, 937, 1251, **1848**, 2059, 2143, 2145, **2192**, **2230**, **2234**, 3116, 3191, 3277, 3715, 4709, 4788, 4820, 4836, 4838, 4866, 4874
Minority groups. *See* Minorities
Misericordia, Santa Casa da, **1935**
Model Nonprofit Corporation Act, **4072**, **4074**
Monsanto, 1462
Moody Foundation, 1017
Morgan, J. Pierpont, 431, 513
Motion pictures. *See* Films and video
Motives of givers. *See* Philanthropists
Mott Foundation, Charles Stewart, 265, 521, 652, 824, 3985
Mott, Charles Stewart, 94, 521
Mott, Stewart Rawlings, 265, 420

Munson Case, 3455, 3763, 3862, 3877, 4193, 4200, **4251**, **4335**, **4336**, **4347**
Museums, 148, **1259**, 2134, 2236, 2541, **3291**, 3322, 3375, **3379**, 3380, **3684**, 3775, **3830**, 4166, 4684, 4695, 4701, 4815, 4935
Music, 2159, 3249, 3569, 3762. *See also* Performing arts
NAEIR. *See* National Association for the Exchange of Industrial Resources
Nathan Report, 1931
National Arts Stabilization Fund, 758, 2006, **2039**, 2251
National Association for the Exchange of Industrial Resources, 1359, **1498**
National Black United Fund, 423
National Center for Charitable Statistics, **2165**, **2179**, **2364**
National Charities Information Bureau, 2011, **2124**, **2139**, **2356**, **2358**, **2360**
National Committee for Responsive Philanthropy, 581
National Endowment for the Arts, **1939**, 2247, 3127, 3400, 4622, 4645
National Endowment for the Humanities, 4050, 4648
National Executive Service Corps, 2747
National Foundation, **856**
National Industrial Conference Board. *See* Conference Board
National Institutes of Health, 4050, 4742
National Science Foundation, 4640, 4679
National Society of Fund Raising Executives, 3669
National Taxonomy of Exempt Entities, **2165**, **2364**
National Trust for Historic Preservation, 3738
National Urban Coalition, 1370
Native Americans, **460**, **2051**, **2226**, 3116, **3124**, 3299, 3715, 4898
Nature Conservancy, **1181**
NCIB. *See* National Charities Information Bureau
NEA. *See* National Endowment for the Arts
NEH. *See* Carnegie Endowment for International Peace
Neighborhoods, 1664, 2072, 2177, 2194, **2285**, 2353, **2390**, **2917**, 2982, 3032, 3146, 3161, 3373, 3656, **3659**, 3672, 3738, 3923, **4834**, 4875, 4900, 4916, 4959, 4967
Networking. *See* Nonprofit organizations, administration
Networks. *See* Nonprofit organizations, administration; Associations of foundations
New Mexico Research Education Enrichment Foundation, 2744
New York (City)
    directories, 2821, 4654

New York (State)
    directories, 787, **1012**, **1013**, **1014**, **1015**, **1016**, 1274, 4242, 4654, **4723**
New York Community Trust, **1224**, **1278**
New York Regional Association of Grantmakers, 1296
New York Times Company, 461
Newman, Harvey, 2572
Newman, Paul, **240**, 356
Newsletters. *See* Nonprofit organizations, public relations
Nielsen, Waldemar, 1213
NIH. *See* National Institutes of Health
NMA. *See* Nonprofit Management Association
Non-cash contributions. *See* In-kind contributions
Nonprofit loan funds. *See* Loan funds
Nonprofit Management Association, 2533, 2842
Nonprofit organizations, **289**, 612, **1472**, 1880, **1990**, 2015, **2020**, **2043**, 2050, 2056, 2090, **2102**, **2117**, 2140, 2148, 2153, **2155**, 2158, **2179**, **2182**, 2185, **2189**, 2199, 2200, **2219**, 2222, 2239, 2242, 2249, 2254, 2257, 2275, **2292**, **2303**, 2325, **2326**, 2363, 2388, 2395, **2399**, **2402**, 2414, **2479**, **2606**, **2610**, **2698**, **2739**, 2787, **2806**, **2807**, **2809**, **2812**, **2813**, **2897**, 4090, **4133**, 4138, 4172, 4192, **4302**, **4311**, 4471, 4473, **4490**, **4491**, **4523**, **4560**, **4964**
    accounting, 1164, **1999**, 2034, 2085, **2340**, **2355**, 2421, 2422, 2430, 2437, 2438, 2439, 2440, 2447, 2448, 2450, 2451, 2455, **2465**, 2469, 2480, **2483**, **2490**, **2493**, 2494, 2513, 2514, 2518, **2519**, **2526**, 2527, 2541, 2547, 2576, 2582, 2583, 2584, 2585, 2586, 2587, 2592, 2605, 2623, **2624**, 2625, 2626, 2627, 2628, 2635, **2645**, **2649**, **2668**, 2676, 2678, 2686, 2688, 2706, 2707, 2709, 2720, 2725, 2726, 2729, 2740, **2748**, 2765, 2786, **2789**, 2796, 2798, **2816**, 2817, 2829, 2831, 2832, 2833, 2839, 2840, 2841, 2843, 2844, 2845, 2850, 2856, **2863**, 2864, **2865**, 2872, **2873**, 2895, 2898, 2900, 2905, 2925, **2930**, 2935, **2941**, **2948**, 2951, 2953, 2956, 2973, 3012, 3236, 3305, 3426, **4007**, 4010, **4133**, 4148, 4162, **4216**, 4224, 4230, 4333
    administration, 683, 1449, **1990**, 1996, **1999**, **2008**, **2010**, 2019, **2021**, **2023**, 2029, **2041**, 2044, **2049**, 2050, 2056, **2063**, 2066, 2070, **2073**, **2076**, 2083, 2107, 2113, **2118**, 2119, 2120, **2127**, 2131, 2136, 2138, 2142, 2160, 2170, 2175, 2176, 2180, 2181, 2184,

310

Nonprofit organizations
administration (continued)
2188, 2198, **2202**, **2206**, 2216, **2219**, 2229, 2237, 2238, **2241**, 2250, 2271, 2272, 2281, **2284**, 2286, **2295**, 2307, 2329, 2334, 2341, 2346, **2355**, **2358**, 2359, 2367, 2369, 2371, **2382**, 2383, 2388, 2392, **2398**, 2401, **2404**, **2407**, 2413, **2415**, 2420, 2422, **2423**, 2424, 2425, 2426, 2431, 2433, **2435**, 2436, 2441, **2444**, **2445**, **2446**, 2447, 2448, 2449, 2451, 2455, 2456, 2458, 2460, 2461, 2462, **2463**, **2464**, **2465**, 2467, 2469, 2471, **2472**, **2474**, 2475, 2476, 2478, 2480, 2484, 2485, **2486**, **2487**, **2488**, **2489**, **2490**, 2491, **2493**, 2494, **2495**, 2497, 2499, **2500**, 2502, 2504, 2505, **2508**, **2509**, **2517**, 2518, **2519**, **2520**, **2522**, 2524, 2525, 2529, 2530, 2531, 2532, 2533, 2534, 2535, 2536, 2537, 2540, 2544, 2545, **2546**, **2549**, 2553, 2554, **2555**, **2557**, 2559, 2560, 2562, 2563, 2564, 2565, **2566**, 2568, **2569**, 2570, 2571, 2572, **2573**, 2574, 2576, 2577, 2579, 2580, 2581, 2582, 2583, 2585, 2586, 2587, **2588**, 2589, 2590, 2591, 2592, 2593, 2594, **2595**, 2596, **2597**, **2598**, 2599, **2600**, 2602, 2603, 2604, 2605, **2606**, **2607**, **2608**, **2609**, **2610**, **2611**, 2612, 2614, **2615**, **2616**, 2617, 2620, 2621, **2624**, 2627, 2629, 2630, **2631**, 2632, 2633, 2634, 2635, 2636, **2638**, 2640, **2641**, 2642, 2644, **2645**, **2646**, 2647, **2649**, 2651, 2652, 2653, 2654, **2655**, 2656, 2657, 2658, 2659, 2660, **2662**, **2663**, **2664**, 2665, **2667**, 2670, **2673**, **2674**, **2675**, 2677, 2679, **2680**, 2682, 2684, 2685, **2687**, 2688, 2689, 2690, 2691, 2692, 2693, 2696, 2697, 2699, **2700**, **2702**, 2703, **2705**, 2708, 2712, 2713, 2715, **2719**, 2723, 2724, 2726, 2728, 2729, **2730**, 2732, 2733, 2734, **2735**, **2736**, 2738, **2739**, 2740, **2743**, 2749, 2750, 2751, 2752, 2754, 2755, 2756, **2757**, 2758, 2759, **2764**, 2766, 2767, **2768**, 2771, 2773, 2775, 2776, 2777, **2778**, **2779**, 2780, 2781, 2783, **2784**, 2786, 2787, 2788, **2789**, **2790**, 2791, 2793, 2794, 2795, 2796, 2798, 2799, **2800**, 2802, 2803, **2805**, **2806**, **2807**, **2808**, **2809**, **2810**, **2811**, **2812**, **2813**, **2814**, **2815**, **2816**, **2818**, **2822**, **2823**, 2826, **2827**, 2829, 2830, 2835, 2836, 2838, 2839, 2841, 2843, 2844, 2845, **2846**, 2847, 2848, 2849, 2850, **2851**, **2852**, 2853, 2854, **2855**, 2856, 2857, 2859, 2860, 2861, 2866, **2868**, 2869,
2875, 2876, 2879, 2880, 2881, 2883, 2884, 2885, 2886, 2887, **2889**, 2892, 2896, **2897**, 2898, **2902**, **2904**, 2907, 2908, 2909, 2910, 2911, 2912, 2914, 2915, 2919, **2920**, **2922**, **2923**, **2924**, 2925, **2926**, **2928**, **2930**, 2932, 2933, 2934, 2935, **2936**, 2937, 2938, 2939, **2941**, **2942**, 2944, 2945, 2946, 2947, **2948**, **2950**, 2951, 2953, 2954, 2956, 2957, 2958, 2960, 2961, 2963, 2964, **2965**, 2966, **2967**, 2969, 2971, 2972, 2973, 2975, 2976, 2977, 2980, 3012, **3028**, 3055, 3061, 3093, **3101**, 3151, 3268, 3274, 3281, 3286, 3288, **3330**, 3386, **3387**, **3394**, 3409, 3479, **3499**, **3500**, 3524, 3557, 3617, 3685, 3700, 3706, 3708, 3709, **3741**, **3747**, 3750, 3823, 3825, **3830**, **3836**, **3944**, 3972, **4032**, **4033**, **4091**, **4098**, **4104**, **4106**, 4120, 4138, 4154, 4169, **4178**, 4188, 4193, **4220**, 4224, 4230, 4234, **4240**, 4261, 4264, **4269**, 4270, **4311**, 4323, **4329**, 4338, 4365, **4374**, 4462, 4493, 4498, 4516, **4521**, 4534, **4543**, **4574**, **4585**, **4592**, 4683, 4757, 4774, 4868, 4963
administration, bibliographies, 2103
analysis, **221**, **222**, 230, **234**, **1028**, 1825, 1852, 1903, 1995, 2009, 2011, 2014, 2016, 2025, **2028**, 2029, 2031, 2032, 2054, **2055**, 2062, **2065**, **2077**, **2079**, 2081, 2084, 2090, 2092, 2093, 2098, **2100**, **2108**, 2113, **2117**, **2124**, **2126**, **2141**, 2152, **2154**, 2156, 2157, **2162**, **2163**, **2168**, **2172**, 2174, 2197, 2188, **2189**, **2192**, 2194, 2197, 2201, 2208, 2209, 2211, 2217, 2221, 2223, 2224, **2227**, **2241**, 2243, 2244, 2245, 2256, **2262**, 2269, **2276**, **2278**, **2297**, **2298**, **2299**, **2300**, **2311**, 2312, **2314**, 2315, 2317, 2318, 2319, 2320, **2323**, **2326**, 2337, 2344, **2345**, **2347**, 2357, **2360**, **2361**, **2386**, **2391**, 2393, 2395, 2397, **2399**, 2413, **2415**, 2425, **2479**, 2491, 2576, **2606**, **2610**, 2633, 2697, **2698**, **2701**, 3558, 3844, 3921, 4174, 4175, 4176, 4177, **4187**, **4269**, 4534, **4603**
budgeting. See Nonprofit organizations, accounting
business. See Nonprofit organizations, entrepreneurship
case studies, 2078, **2400**, **2404**
directories, **1766**, 1771, 1962, 1963, 1964, 2059, **2074**, 2088, **2091**, **2094**, **2102**, 2143, **2144**, 2145, 2147, 2150, 2236, 2240, 2258, 2259, **2265**, **2268**, **2301**, 2328, 2341, **2435**, 2536, 2797, 3440

SUBJECT INDEX

economic aspects, 2208, **4269**
employment, 2246
employment, directories, 1988, 2046, **2235**
entrepreneurship, 1992, 1993, **2017**, **2018**, 2019, **2027**, 2035, **2037**, 2038, 2070, 2089, **2095**, 2105, 2107, 2111, 2123, 2133, **2135**, **2169**, 2173, 2193, 2196, 2209, 2214, 2218, 2220, 2263, 2277, **2290**, **2298**, 2316, 2330, 2336, 2338, 2343, 2352, 2365, 2368, 2374, 2375, **2377**, 2378, 2380, 2396, 2403, 2408, 2409, 2410, **2412**, **2429**, **2483**, **2492**, **2503**, 2550, **2569**, **2702**, **2897**, **2936**, **2965**, 3415, **3444**, 4093, **4187**, 4226, 4248, 4249, 4262, **4472**
establishment and termination, **856**, 2270, 2287, 2288, **2382**, **2444**, **2489**, **2662**, 2958, 2969
ethics, **2028**, 2067
evaluations, 2254, 2393, 2428, 2532
finance, **2058**, **2128**, **2206**, 2229, **2273**, 2279, **2406**, **2483**, **2492**, **2508**, 2531, **2566**, 2590, 2602, **2638**, 2647, **2680**, 2688, 2738, **2789**, **2811**, **2902**, **2926**, **2948**, 3040, 3077, 3098, 3105, **3237**, 3556, 3708, 3709, 3825, **3939**, 3974, 3988, **4269**, 4603
future. See Nonprofit organizations, analysis
government regulations, **357**, 1266, 1267, **1999**, **2064**, 2069, 2104, **2127**, **2139**, **2183**, 2269, 2270, 2281, **2311**, 2313, 2380, **2387**, 2433, **2444**, **2519**, **2700**, 2721, 2933, 2958, 3476, 3734, **3814**, **4072**, 4100, 4103, 4109, 4123, 4127, **4133**, **4139**, **4145**, **4151**, 4152, 4153, 4169, 4175, 4176, 4184, **4190**, **4191**, 4194, **4216**, **4220**, **4225**, **4240**, 4242, 4245, 4268, **4269**, **4271**, 4284, 4286, 4287, **4311**, **4334**, 4346, 4348, 4365, 4373, 4375, **4418**, **4435**, 4454, **4469**, 4474, 4683, 4762
grantsmanship, 674, 715, 1734, **2024**, **2049**, 2291, 2505, 2898, **2927**, 2939, 2940, 3025, 3031, **3044**, 3082, **3101**, 3151, **3152**, 3156, 3160, 3161, 3186, 3194, **3206**, 3288, 3308, **3313**, **3314**, 3327, 3328, 3338, **3339**, 3363, 3393, 3425, 3477, 3517, **3526**, **3534**, **3543**, **3630**, 3639, 3650, **3653**, 3674, 3692, **3693**, **3710**, 3833, 3891, 3929, 3942, **3958**, 3962, **3967**, 3982, **3994**, **4000**, 4006, 4008, 4011, 4012, 4018, 4026, 4030, **4051**, **4057**, **4668**
grantsmanship, bibliographies, 3251, 3562, 3997
history, **136**, **362**, 1994, **2000**, 2280, 2354, **2417**, **2993**

311

SUBJECT INDEX

Nonprofit organizations (*continued*)
  investigations, 449, **2028**, 2067, **2139**, **2172**, 2254, **2262**, **2356**, **2358**, **4080**, **4304**
  investments, **1914**, **2128**, 2442, **2512**, 2559, **2673**, **2710**, 2761, **2890**, **2952**, 3988, **4877**
  legal issues. *See* Laws regulating philanthropy; Nonprofit organizations, administration
  management, **2008**
  marketing, 1438, 1567, **1651**, **2151**, **2347**, 2366, 2482, 2548, 2552, 2648, 2661, **2672**, 2694, 2695, 2696, **2702**, **2705**, **2711**, 2716, 2731, 2733, **2757**, 2763, 2782, **2855**, 2858, 2912, **2922**, **2936**, 2955, 3090, 3180, 3188, 3218, 3282, **3356**, 3359, 3364, 3367, 3370, 3555, 3582, **3585**, **3646**, 3694, 3716, 3785, **3830**, 3848, 3858, **3926**
  memberships. *See* Nonprofit organizations
  New York, **2077**, **2274**, 4746
  New York, directories, **2144**, 2215, **2253**
  political activity, 1878, 3476, **4065**
  public relations, **1990**, 2082, 2191, **2303**, 2366, 2459, 2461, **2463**, 2471, 2476, 2521, 2594, 2659, 2693, 2699, 2712, 2717, 2733, **2735**, 2746, **2769**, 2803, 2834, 2845, **2851**, **2852**, 2860, **2868**, 2881, 2934, 2937, 2961, 3042, 3180, 3188, 3265, 3300, 3323, 3324, 3325, 3326, 3404, 3436, 3555, **3571**, **3769**, **3772**, **3895**, **3948**, 4008, 4927
  regulations. *See* Nonprofit organizations, government regulations
  research, **2065**, **2141**, **2162**, **2182**, **2311**, **2348**
  salaries. *See* Nonprofit organizations, wages
  statistics, **2164**, **2174**, **2252**, 2362, 2432
  studies, 2060, **2361**, **2399**, 4209, 4652
  surveys, 2002, **2041**, 2061, 2098, 2180, **2252**, 2317, 2318, 2319, 2322, 2397, **2924**, 4634, 4657, 4658, **4660**, 4662, 4663, 4664, 4678, 4680, 4685, 4686, 4687, **4737**, **4739**, 4740, 4745
  wages, **585**, **654**, **655**, **655**, 1294, 2002, 2003, **2021**, **2022**, 2137, 2160, 2272, **2299**, 2324, 2367, 2383, **2411**, **2481**
Nonprofit sector. *See* Nonprofit organizations
North Dakota Foundation, 874
Northwest Area Foundation, 1223
NSFRE. *See* National Society of Fund Raising Executives
NTEE. *See* National Taxonomy of Exempt Entities
Nuclear disarmament. *See* Grantmakers, social issues

Nuffield Foundation, 1776
NYRAG. *See* New York Regional Association of Grantmakers
Oberleander Trust, 825
Olin Foundation, 1225, 1284
Operating foundations, 148, **563**, 753, 756, **999**, 2540
Orientals. *See* Asian-Americans
Overhead costs. *See* Nonprofit organizations, accounting; Nonprofit organizations, administration
Paley, William S., 368
Parks. *See* Environment
Partnership Project, **1476**
PAS. *See* Philanthropic Advisory Service
Patman Report, 540, 1266, 4385, 4386, 4387, 4392
Patman, Wright, 540
Pavlevsky, Joan, 361
Peabody Education Fund, 509
Peabody, George, **369**, 509
Pearsons, D.K., 506
Peking Union Medical College, 742, **1768**
Penny Company, J.C., 374
Percent clubs, 1343, 1386, 1393, 1543, 1687, 1715. *See also* Fundraising
Performing arts, 1493, **2001**, **2012**, 2097, 2109, 2150, 2232, 2309, 2370, 2637, 2763, 2968, 3679
Permanent Charity Fund, 4966
Personnel. *See* Personnel management
Personnel management, **2041**, **2446**, **2667**, 2921
Petersen, Eleanor, **29**
Peterson Commission, 628, **629**, 632, 1073
Peterson, Peter G., 628
Phelps-Dodge family, **133**
Philanthropic Advisory Service, 449, **2028**, **2124**, **2139**, 3697
Philanthropists, 2, 3, 3, 9, **10**, **14**, 21, 22, 24, **29**, **30**, 31, 32, 33, 34, 35, **36**, 38, 40, 42, **43**, **49**, **51**, 53, 55, **60**, **61**, 62, **70**, 71, 72, 75, 76, 77, 78, 79, 80, **81**, 83, 85, 86, 90, 93, 94, 97, 98, 99, 100, **101**, **105**, 115, **116**, **118**, 120, 121, 123, 126, 128, **133**, 135, 138, 139, 140, 143, 145, 146, **149**, 151, 153, **154**, 155, 156, 160, 161, 162, 164, 167, **171**, 172, **173**, 179, 184, **187**, 190, 192, 193, **194**, 198, 199, 201, 203, 206, 208, 209, 210, **212**, 213, 214, 215, 216, 217, 218, 219, 223, 225, 228, 229, **240**, 241, 244, 245, 248, 250, 251, 257, 262, 264, 265, 266, 270, 272, 274, 275, **278**, 284, 285, 286, 288, 290, 291, **293**, 297, 298, 300, 302, 303, **304**, 305, **306**, 307, 308, 312, 313, 314, 315, 316, 317, **319**, 320, 321, 325, **333**, 340, 345, 352, **353**, 355, 361, 363, **367**, 368, **369**, 373, 374, 378, 379, 383, 389, 392, 394, 397, 401, **402**, **408**, 409, 411, 413, 418, 420, 421, 425, 426, 429, 430, 431, **432**, 443, 444, 446, 449, 461, 463, 468, 469, 471, 473, **474**, 475,

478, 479, **482**, **488**, 489, 493, 494, 497, 498, 499, **500**, 502, 506, **507**, 509, 512, 513, 516, 517, 521, 522, 642, 731, 737, **822**, **832**, **890**, **905**, 955, **1862**, **3702**
  biographical directories, **212**, **304**, 305, **306**, **492**, **492**, 503, **559**, **1434**, 1437, **1478**, **1577**, **1680**, 1681
  motives of givers. *See* Philanthropists
Philanthropy, **16**, **17**, 25, 26, 41, **49**, **57**, 69, 82, **87**, **89**, **111**, **112**, **113**, 122, **132**, **134**, 175, 180, 181, **183**, 186, **188**, **189**, 195, **226**, **235**, 237, 271, 280, 284, 292, **294**, 296, **328**, 335, 336, 337, 344, 349, 360, **382**, 396, 406, 412, 424, 439, 440, 457, **460**, 462, **470**, **474**, 487, **495**, **519**, 631, **677**, 737, 811, **1059**, 1244, **1888**, 3856
  abroad. *See* International philanthropy
  Africa, 1849, 1890, **1950**, 1953
  analysis, 11, **12**, **13**, 37, 48, 50, **54**, 64, 67, **68**, 73, **84**, 88, **91**, 95, 96, **102**, 103, 110, 117, 127, **131**, **141**, **152**, 159, **170**, 176, 178, 218, **221**, **222**, **227**, 230, **231**, 232, 233, **234**, **235**, 236, **253**, 254, 255, 256, 258, 259, 260, **261**, **267**, 269, 271, 277, 279, 281, **283**, 296, **330**, 331, 332, **342**, 343, **346**, **347**, 348, 351, **364**, 366, **370**, **371**, **372**, **380**, 381, 385, **386**, 388, 390, **391**, 395, **410**, **428**, 438, **450**, **454**, 456, 464, **470**, **476**, 477, 483, **484**, **484**, 485, 486, **501**, **520**, 540, **579**, **743**, 802, 816, **822**, **847**, 895, **934**, 998, **1059**, 1293, 1385, **1886**, **1936**, 1937, 2011, **2178**, **2297**, **2345**, **2820**, 3202, 3255, 4199, 4285, 4380
  assessment and review. *See* Philanthropy, analysis
  bibliographies, 4, 15, 247, 276, **294**, 3329
  Canada, **1750**, 1756, 1779, 1782, 1790, 1790, 1831, 1844, 1880, 1881, 1949, 1979, 1980
  case studies, 277, 438
  Chile, 1948
  China, 1970
  CIA involvement. *See* Government and philanthropy
  Denmark, 1827, 1918
  economic aspects, **24**, **39**, **49**, 50, 65, 67, 95, 96, 103, **104**, **131**, 168, 175, 186, 195, 239, **253**, 269, 271, 351, **370**, **380**, 388, **419**, 422, **484**, 490, **501**, **520**, 1551, **2305**, **2407**, 4088, 4094, **4603**
  Europe, 1906, 1909, 1955, 1956, 1969, 1982
  finance, 50, 65, 239, 1551
  France, 1889, 1917, 1921
  future. *See* Philanthropy, analysis
  Germany, 1876, 1904, 1907, **1908**, 1937
  Great Britain, 249, **359**, **393**, 1754, 1763, 1773, 1774, 1776, 1784,

312

Philanthropy
- Great Britian (*continued*)
  - 1792, **1828**, 1829, 1832, 1833, **1834**, 1838, **1848**, 1864, **1865**, 1866, **1868**, 1869, **1896**, **1897**, 1898, 1910, **1914**, 1922, 1930, 1931, 1932, 1933, 1940, **1951**, 1976, 1981, **2804**, **4878**
- Great Britain, history, **515**, 1832, 1833, **1865**, 1866, 1867, **1868**, 1870, 1871, 1875, 1895, **1916**, 1928, 1929
- history, **5**, **6**, **7**, **11**, **17**, 18, 19, **28**, **39**, **44**, 45, 46, **58**, **59**, **91**, **92**, 107, **112**, **113**, **114**, **119**, 130, **136**, **157**, 165, **174**, **182**, **183**, **196**, **204**, **205**, 224, 246, 254, 255, 256, **267**, 268, 273, **293**, **309**, **310**, **311**, **322**, 324, 326, **328**, **333**, **338**, **357**, **362**, 365, 375, **376**, **393**, **415**, **416**, 427, **428**, 451, **481**, 487, 490, **491**, **504**, 616, **751**, 839, 867, 868, 949, 1145, **1214**, 1738, 1754, 1763, **1765**, 1774, **1785**, 1832, 1833, 1864, **1865**, 1866, 1869, 1889, **1935**, **2000**, **2210**, 2257, **4247**, **4571**, 4679, **4878**
- international cooperation, **1936**
- Japan, **74**, **242**, 243, **472**, **1744**, **1755**, **1767**, **1821**, **1830**, 1854, **1855**, 1856, 1857, **1858**, 1859, 1860, 1861, **1862**, **1863**, **1923**, **1926**, **1959**, **1960**, 1973
- Japan, directories, **1960**, 1973
- Latin America, **1781**, **1817**, **1884**, **1935**
- Latin America, analysis, **1781**
- law and legislation, 1977
- New England, **3097**
- New York, analysis, **12**, 3122, 3677
- Pennsylvania, 485, 486, **2305**, **2390**
- philosophy, 8, **14**, 18, 33, 53, 77, 80, **81**, 162, **166**, **177**, 179, **196**, **197**, **252**, 259, **318**, 339, 354, **407**, 743, **1059**, **1117**, **3702**, **4846**
- press treatment, 109, **211**, **442**, **452**, 464, 1166, **1469**
- public policy, **234**
- research, **66**, 159, **362**
- Rhode Island, 2191
- seminars, **508**, **508**
- statistics, **176**, **221**, **222**, **347**, **1896**
- studies, 73, 125, **152**, **191**, 348, **448**, **508**, **1214**
- study and teaching, 295, **470**
- surveys, 332, 1188, 1746, 3983
- Sweden, directories, 1793, 1874
- Texas, 200, 496
- Turkey, 1943
- United States, 7, 26, **56**, **58**, **59**, **92**, **112**, **113**, **118**, **119**, 130, **131**, **144**, 165, **176**, **183**, **204**, **205**, **231**, 246, **253**, 277, 279, **309**, **319**, **322**, 324, **333**, **341**, **347**, 365, **371**, **372**, 375, 381, **387**, 395, **428**, **433**, 440, 451, 480, 490, **491**, **500**, **514**, **536**, 542, **661**, **678**, **743**, **751**, 863, 900, 949, 1145, **1263**, **2210**, **2994**, **3184**, **4247**, **4526**

United States, analysis, **27**. *See also* Philanthropy, United States
United States, history, **52**, **56**, 227, **371**, **382**, **415**, **515**, **3184**, **4564**, **4577**
United States, statistics, **27**. *See also* Philanthropy, United States
Philanthropy and government. *See* Government and philanthropy
Philip Morris, 1507
Philosophy, **252**, **318**
Phonathons. *See* Telemarketing
Photography, 688
Physicians' Services Incorporated Foundation, 680
Planned giving, 263, 284, **359**, 400, **419**, 649, **650**, 746, 851, **2804**, 2838, 3002, 3003, 3005, **3014**, **3015**, **3016**, **3017**, 3022, **3023**, **3037**, 3049, 3068, 3072, 3086, 3100, 3115, 3138, 3154, 3155, 3163, 3177, 3185, 3190, 3278, 3279, **3295**, 3310, 3321, 3335, 3336, 3377, 3385, 3397, 3398, **3413**, **3431**, 3474, 3592, 3603, 3626, 3637, 3638, 3644, 3649, 3723, 3749, 3756, **3773**, 3791, 3798, **3817**, 3818, 3819, 3834, 3835, 3850, 3865, 3866, 3867, 3898, 3911, **3917**, 3920, 3930, 3931, **3993**, 4083, 4087, 4126, 4137, 4161, 4167, 4170, 4171, 4222, 4223, 4228, **4229**, 4257, 4289, 4294, 4319, 4358, **4361**, 4478, 4479. *See also* Fundraising
Planning. *See* Nonprofit organizations, administration
Playboy Foundation, 498, 985
Political activity. *See* Nonprofit organizations, political activity; Foundations, political activity
Pollack-Krasner Foundation, 695
Pooled income funds. *See* Planned giving
Population control. *See* Social welfare
Precollegiate education. *See* Elementary and secondary education
Preservation
- historic. *See* Historic buildings, preservation

President's Task Force on Private Sector Initiatives, 406, 1315, 1721, 4566, 4579
Primary education. *See* Elementary and secondary education
Princess Grace Foundation, 496
PRIs. *See* Program-related investments
Pritchett, Henry S., 153
Program development. *See* Nonprofit organizations, administration; Nonprofit organizations, grantsmanship
Program on Non-Profit Organizations, 422
Program on Studying Philanthropy, 295
Program-related investments, **647**, 759, 760, 770, 786, 1072, **1080**, 1129, 1172, 1299, 1444, 2096, **2112**, **2205**, **2294**, 2302, 4477

SUBJECT INDEX

Proposal development, 534, **624**, 716, 2392, **3337**, **3534**, **3543**, 3561, **3588**, 3604, **3741**, 3942, **3958**, **3967**, **3994**, 3995, 3996, 3997, 3998, **3999**, **4000**, 4001, 4002, **4003**, 4004, **4005**, 4006, **4007**, 4008, 4009, 4010, 4011, 4012, 4013, 4014, 4015, 4016, **4017**, 4018, **4020**, **4021**, 4022, 4023, 4024, 4025, 4026, 4027, **4028**, 4029, 4031, **4032**, **4033**, 4035, **4036**, **4037**, **4038**, 4039, **4040**, 4041, **4042**, 4043, **4044**, **4045**, 4046, 4047, 4048, 4049, 4050, 4052, 4053, 4054, **4055**, 4056, 4057, 4058, **4059**, **4060**, 4061, 4062, 4063, 4064, 4613, **4655**, **4666**, **4668**, 4713
- handbooks, manuals, etc., **4019**, **4034**, **4036**, 4046, **4060**. *See also* Proposal development

Proposal writing. *See* Proposal development
Proposed foundations. *See* Foundations, establishment and termination
Provident Life Insurance Company, 1664
Prudential Foundation, 1082
Psychiatry, **3494**
Psychology, **166**, **4950**
Public charities, 794
Public health, 1963, 2140, **3263**, **4759**, 4817, 4821, 4865, 4876
Public interest groups, 1559, 1572, **2020**, 2113, 2346, 4946
Public relations. *See* Nonprofit organizations, public relations
Public service announcements. *See* Fundraising, alternatives
Public/private partnerships. *See* Cooperative funding
Publishing, 2661, 4773, 4952
Puerto Ricans. *See* Hispanics
Racial discrimination
- government policy, **4730**

Rackets. *See* Charity rackets
Radiothon. *See* Fundraising, special events
Raffles. *See* Fundraising, special events
Rangel Hearings, 734, 790, 819, 820, 971, 973, 976, 986, 1074, 1212, 1231
Reader's Digest Association, 36
Recreation and athletics, 2983, 3245, **3464**, 3827, 3933, 3937
Reece Committee, **934**, 1293, 4382
Refugees
- Uganda, **1836**

Religion, 77, **108**, 165, 237, **238**, 283, 365, 384, 398, **399**, **405**, 441, **448**, 495, 668, 670, 702, **703**, 1018, 1115, **1757**, **1760**, 1948, **1985**, 2129, 2212, 2296, 2548, **3037**, **3073**, 3182, 3201, **3241**, **3262**, 3267, **3342**, **3399**, 3402, **3433**, 3478, 3515, 3525, 3655, 3662, 3663, 3664, 3691, 3868, **3883**, **3981**, 4212, 4217, 4221, 4281, 4298, **4481**, 4551, 4828, **4869**, **4879**, 4880, **4888**, 4901, **4904**, **4919**,

313

SUBJECT INDEX

Religion (continued)
    4923, **4939**, 4945, 4977, 4981, 4984
  directories, **595**, 682, **1130**, 1788, 2087, **2187**, **3097**, **3119**, **3200**, **3390**
Research, **338**, 543, **605**, 665, 1131, 1247, **1259**, 1425, 2280, **2292**, 2882, 2940, 2997, **3228**, **3229**, 3652, **4034**, **4040**, 4672, 4704, 4706, **4707**, 4708, 4709, 4710, 4711, 4758, 4773, 4848, 4855, 4912, 4915, 4921, 4937, 4946
  directories, **2094**, 2434, **3788**
Research Health Services, 2225
Revson Foundation, 736
Revson, Charles, 475
Reynolds Foundation, Z. Smith, 833, **1289**
RFPs. See Proposal development
Rich, Wilmer Shields, 320
Riley Foundation, 4899
Rockefeller Brothers Fund, 1234
Rockefeller family, 2, **101**, 150, 290, 313, 345
Rockefeller Foundation, 2, 160, **171**, 172, 199, 345, 409, 494, **572**, **587**, 640, **748**, 766, 767, 805, **919**, 1132, 1133, 1173, **1762**, **1765**, **1768**, **1795**, **1886**, **1911**, 2222, 2888
Rockefeller Memorial, Laura Spelman, **591**
Rockefeller, David, 223, 266, 317
Rockefeller, John D., 2, 156, **353**, **408**, 409, 512
Rockefeller, John D., Jr., 161
Rosenberg Foundation, 611, 1124, 1185
Rosenwald Fund, 732
Rosenwald, Julius, 245
Rowntree Memorial Trust, Joseph, 1976
Rowntree Village Trust, Joseph, 1933
Ruml, Beardsley, **591**
Rural development, 1203, 2258, 2416, 3118, 3287, 3678, **3922**, 3936, 4612, 4623, 4872, 4885, 4902
Ryerson, Edward L., **1665**
Sage family, 502
Sage Foundation, Russell, 430, 813, **968**
Sage, Russell, 430
Salaries. See Nonprofit organizations, wages
Salvation Army, 3244
Samuel, Sigmund, 429
San Francisco Foundation, 583, 588, 691, 923, 991, **1054**, **1055**, **1057**, 1069, 1150, 1180, 1196, **1287**
Sasakawa, Ryoichi, **1862**
Scherman Foundation, 1123
Scholarships, fellowships and loans, 857, **921**
  directories, 557, **673**, 805, **912**, 1132, 1133, 1142, **2622**, **3229**, **4608**
  graduate and professional study, directories, **533**
  research. See Research
  travel and study abroad. See Travel and study abroad
School foundations. See Education, public charities
Schwarzhaupt Foundation, Emil, 1239

Science, **338**, 543, 689, 697, 1257, 3102, **3229**, 3271, 4616, 4637, 4640, 4704, 4705, 4706, **4707**, 4708, 4709, 4710, 4711, 4712
Scrivner, Winston, **116**
Seagram's, 355
Secondary education. See Elementary and secondary education
Seed money, **837**
Seminars. See Conferences
Senior citizens. See Aging
Seniors. See Aging
Shubert Foundation, 1177, **1265**
Simon, Norton, 321
Sloan Foundation, Alfred P., 493, 494, 568
Sloan, Alfred P., Jr., 493
Slocum family, 502
Small business, **1361**, **1485**, **2017**, 2051, 2569, 4432, **4475**, 4558, **4826**, 4913
Smith Charities, 719
Smithson, James, 78, 401
Smithsonian Institution, 78, 401, 4637
Social issues. See Grantmakers, social issues
Social sciences, **445**, 524, 569, 590, 605, 1131, 3652, **4034**, 4035, 4896, 4921
Social services. See Social welfare
Social welfare, 1, 5, 6, 7, 47, 51, 52, 57, 58, 82, **92**, 119, 122, **157**, 163, **174**, **182**, **188**, **189**, 204, 205, 282, 299, **309**, **310**, **311**, **322**, **342**, 385, 390, **391**, **403**, **404**, 416, 451, 478, **515**, **526**, 623, **873**, **903**, **968**, 1664, 1738, 1971, **2042**, 2053, **2210**, 2308, **2348**, **2402**, 2405, **2418**, 2726, 2793, 2938, 3280, **3342**, 3343, **3366**, 3443, **3499**, **3519**, 4454, 4504, 4542, **4569**, **4590**, 4623, 4814, 4822, **4846**, **4857**, 4863, **4864**, 4889, **4907**, 4924, **4926**, 4929, 4937, 4938, **4944**, 4951, **4960**, **4962**, 4963, **4973**, **4974**
  bibliographies, 276, 4734
  directories, 839, 867, 868, **1989**, 2121, 2147, 2215, 2240, **2268**, 2328, 2379, 2724, 3036, **3260**, **4764**
  funding, 877, **1036**, 2101, 2174, **2203**, **2204**, 2401, 2773, 3084, 3141, **3360**, 3556, 3609, 3657, **3659**, 3675, 3742, 3903, 3933, **3950**, 4615, 4688, 4746, 4756, **4907**, **4930**, **4931**, 4933, 4934
Socially responsible investments, 1569, 2837, **2929**, 4877
Sociology, 6, 28, 37, 39, 166, 170, 197, 289, 299, 329, 376, 504, 519, **748**, **1472**, **1490**, 2405, 2607, 2608, **4481**, **4517**, **4531**, **4533**, **4554**, **4824**, **4878**, **4882**, 4912, **4926**, **4950**, **4962**, 4977, **4979**, 4991
Sonnenberg, Benjamin, 413
Southern Poverty Law Center, **2100**
Special events. See Fundraising, special events

Sponsors, **2099**, **3588**
Sports. See Recreation and athletics
Stanford, Jane Lathrop, 257
State directories of charitable organizations
  New York, **2253**
State directories of foundations
  Alabama, 573, **1219**
  Arizona, **899**
  Arkansas, **671**, **1219**
  California, **526**, **738**, **956**, 1461
  California (San Diego), **1151**
  Colorado, **626**
  Connecticut, **593**, 957, **1336**
  Delaware, **1252**
  District of Columbia. See State directories of foundations, Washington, D.C.
  Florida, **635**, **958**
  Georgia, **1220**
  Hawaii, 528, 778
  Idaho, **700**
  Illinois, 525, 706, 707
  Indiana, **1194**
  Iowa, **854**
  Kansas, **840**
  Kentucky, 713, **1063**, **1221**
  Maine, **608**, **1332**
  Maryland, **988**
  Massachusetts, 556, 557, **558**, **959**, 989, **1187**
  Massachusetts (Boston), **959**
  Massachusetts (Greater Worcester), **1187**
  Michigan, **747**
  Minnesota, 1010, **1011**
  Missouri, **701**
  Missouri (Greater Kansas City), **618**
  Montana, **1001**, **1002**
  Nebraska, **898**
  Nevada, **855**
  New Hampshire, **594**, **1042**
  New Jersey, **953**, **960**
  New Mexico, **1024**
  New York, 787, **1012**, **1013**, **1014**, **1015**, **1016**, **1045**, **1067**, 1274, **2253**
  North Carolina, 718, 980, **1176**, **1222**
  Ohio, **1064**, **1110**, **1190**
  Oklahoma, **1106**, **1206**
  Oregon, **1000**
  Pennsylvania, **917**, 1541
  Rhode Island, **643**
  South Carolina, 718, **1222**, **1279**
  South Dakota, **1191**
  Tennessee, 1006, **1063**, **1221**, **1236**, **4003**
  Texas, **614**, 848, **961**, **1109**, 1193, **1264**
  Utah, **882**
  Virginia, 827, **1221**
  Washington (State), **1261**
  Washington, D.C., **634**
  West Virginia, **1063**, **1271**, **4003**
  Wisconsin, **858**
  Wyoming, **681**, **1001**, **1002**
State laws regulating charitable solicitation, 2342, **3493**, **3814**, 4069, **4070**, **4131**, **4151**, 4152

SUBJECT INDEX

State laws regulating foundations, **4070, 4206, 4330,** 4373
State laws regulating philanthropy, **4131,** 4153
Statistics, 2432, **2730, 4464**
    directories. *See* Foundations, statistics; Nonprofit organizations, statistics
Stiemke Foundation, Walter and Olive, 38
Strong de Cuevas de Larrain, Margaret, **432**
Study abroad. *See* Travel and study abroad
Substance abuse, **3219, 3220,** 3441, **3745,** 4865
Sulzberger family, 461
Sun Company, 1499
Sunshine Foundation, **4490**
Support Centers of America, **2748**
Swanson Foundation, 698
Tarlov, Alvin, **873**
Tax deduction, 722, **1558,** 1683, 1940, **2040, 2108, 4066, 4067,** 4078, **4082,** 4083, **4084, 4085,** 4090, 4114, 4115, 4122, **4124,** 4149, 4161, 4162, 4170, 4182, 4185, 4199, 4204, 4214, 4215, 4223, 4257, 4281, 4288, 4289, 4294, 4305, 4306, 4325, **4337,** 4350, 4357, 4359, **4361,** 4362, **4363,** 4367, 4372, **4789.** *See also* Laws regulating philanthropy
Tax exemption, 749, 846, **2075, 2127,** 2152, 2212, 2287, 2288, 2313, **2387,** 4088, 4096, 4099, 4111, 4159, 4162, 4164, 4166, **4168,** 4174, 4177, **4178,** 4194, 4212, 4221, 4249, 4260, **4269,** 4287, **4316,** 4323, 4338, **4349,** 4359, 4365, 4375, 4399, **4418, 4435,** 4454, 4466. *See also* Laws regulating philanthropy
    advantages and disadvantages, 1659, **4271,** 4320, 4355, 4359
    history, 4407
    procedures, 2270, 2433, 2657, **2743,** 4103, **4216,** 4242, 4286, 4375
    types. *See* Tax exemption
Tax reform, 876, **1646, 4085, 4086,** 4090, 4094, 4113, 4122, 4140, 4147, 4159, 4172, **4197,** 4198, 4199, 4205, 4207, 4233, 4235, 4252, **4267,** 4272, 4273, 4274, 4275, 4276, 4277, 4278, 4279, 4280, 4282, 4292, 4300, 4303, 4312, 4313, 4315, 4324, **4328,** 4351, 4353, 4356, 4368, 4369, **4370,** 4377, 4398, 4466, 4480, 4506
Tax Reform Act of 1969, **1502,** 4068, 4077, 4089, 4092, 4101, 4102, 4107, 4121, 4129, 4132, 4135, 4144, 4146, 4150, 4156, 4157, 4158, 4165, 4180, 4181, 4217, **4219,** 4227, 4231, 4232, 4246, 4259, 4266, 4285, 4290, 4291, 4293, 4297, 4299, 4307, 4308, 4309, 4327, 4331, 4340, 4341, 4352, 4354, 4384, 4389, 4390, 4391, 4393, 4396, 4397, 4400, 4401, 4402, 4406, 4433, 4437, 4438, 4439, 4440, 4442, 4444, 4445, 4446, 4447, 4448, 4449, 4451, 4455, 4456, 4458, 4459, 4460, 4468, 4470, 4476
Tax Reform Act of 1976, 4076, 4097, 4128, 4135, 4141, 4283, 4364, 4450
Tax Reform Act of 1981, 230, 744, **1418,** 3903, 4081, 4099, 4123, 4182, 4202, 4203, 4250, 4306, 4339, 4357, 4372, 4376, 4465, 4467, 4477, 4479
Tax Reform Act of 1982, 4114
Tax Reform Act of 1983, 1238, 4388, 4412
Tax Reform Act of 1984, 4195, 4196, **4301,** 4366, 4371
Tax Reform Act of 1986, 453, 3624, **4066, 4067, 4071, 4106, 4110, 4125, 4265, 4337,** 4353, 4360
Tax regulation. *See* Laws regulating philanthropy; Tax deduction; Tax exemption; Tax reform; Taxation
Tax returns, 939, 1090, 4079, 4105, 4142, 4143, 4155, **4211,** 4236, 4244, 4263, 4332, 4343, 4344, 4367, 4457, 4461, 4462, 4463
Taxation, **4084, 4124,** 4150, 4165, **4206, 4240,** 4261, 4272, 4273, 4274, 4275, 4276, 4277, 4278, 4279, 4280, **4334, 4349,** 4360, 4411, 4443, 4461
Taxonomy, **66, 2165, 2179, 2364**
Teacher's Insurance and Annuity Association, 1444
Technical assistance, **954, 992,** 1603, **1632,** 1771, 1964, 2231, **2331,** 2341, 2427, **2435,** 2453, 2470, **2517,** 2567, 2575, **2622,** 2671, 2741, 2744, 2747, 2771, 2792, 2799, 2821, 2830, 2842, **2878,** 2915, 2916, 2945, 2949, 2975, 3380, **3981,** 4073, 4542
Technology information. *See* Computer technology
Telecommunications, **2404, 2669,** 2888. *See also* Communications
Telefunds. *See* Telemarketing
Telemarketing, 3103, 3217, 3246, 3411, 3439, 3569, 3594, 3605, 3606, 3607, 3778, 3782, **3793,** 3821, 3949
Telephone solicitation. *See* Telemarketing
Telethons. *See* Fundraising, special events; Telemarketing
Television and radio. *See* Arts, grants; Broadcasting; Communications
Television broadcasting, 368, **1830,** 3325, 3654, 4807
Theater, 2166, 2186, 2248, **2419, 2595,** 3361, 4696, 4697, 4831, **4928, 4971.** *See also* Performing arts
Third sector. *See* Nonprofit organizations
Thomas, Franklin, 497
Thrift shops. *See* Fundraising, alternatives
TIAA-CREF. *See* Teacher's Insurance and Annuity Association
Tiffany, Louis Comfort, 285
Tipping, **4179,** 4210
Toyota Foundation, **1821**
Travel and study abroad, **533,** 1142, **1760,** 4625
Trexler Estate, H.C., 834
Tribute dinners. *See* Fundraising, special events
Trusts, 20, 1909, 4075, 4257, 4288, 4314, 4342. *See also* Planned giving
Twentieth Century Fund, 628, 4241, 4714, 4832
UBIT. *See* Unrelated business income tax
Umbrella organizations. *See* Sponsors
Unfair competition, 1496, **2017,** 2057, 2152, 2167, 2171, 2228, 2313, **2361,** 2374, 2380, 2385, 2389, 4174, 4192, **4435, 4472, 4475.** *See also* Nonprofit organizations, entrepreneurship
UNICEF. *See* United Nations Children's Fund
Union-sponsored programs. *See* Scholarships, fellowships and loans
United Nations, 1958
United Nations Children's Fund, 169
United Nations International Children's Emergency Fund. *See* United Nations Children's Fund
United Negro College Fund, 1521
United States-Japan Foundation, **242**
United Way of America, **1028, 2000, 2023, 2079,** 2293, **3062,** 3121, 3725, 3794, **3837,** 3879, 3880, 3881, **3951**
Universities. *See* Higher education
University foundations. *See* Education, public charities
Unrelated business income tax, **4080, 4139, 4186, 4187, 4190, 4191,** 4237, **4304, 4374, 4472**
Urban development, 1299, 1798, 1799, 1800, **2043,** 2115, 2995, 3034, 3048, 3461, 3618, 3839, 4788, 4853
USA for Africa Foundation, 1849, 1890, **1950**
Villers Foundation, 878, 1041
Voluntarism, 41, **64,** 207, **231,** 232, **235,** 236, **289, 294,** 480, 1301, **1344,** 1387, **1399,** 1484, 1603, 2014, **2042, 2043,** 2072, **2077,** 2113, **2178,** 2207, 2208, 2209, **2276,** 2282, 2344, 2476, **2509, 2516, 2520,** 2604, **2615, 2664, 2667,** 2732, **2736,** 2750, **2757,** 2802, **2805, 2808,** 2827, 2849, 2885, **2904,** 2909, **2923,** 2966, 2969, 3007, 3199, 3358, 3700, 3865, **3935,** 3937, **3944,** 4173, 4350, **4481, 4482, 4483,** 4484, 4485, 4486, 4487, **4488, 4489, 4490, 4491,** 4492, 4493, 4494, 4495, 4496, 4497, 4498, 4499, **4500,**

315

SUBJECT INDEX

Voluntarism (*continued*)
    4502, **4503**, 4504, 4507, 4508, 4509, 4511, **4512**, **4513**, 4514, **4515**, 4516, **4517**, 4518, 4519, 4520, **4521**, 4522, **4523**, 4524, **4525**, **4526**, 4527, 4528, 4529, **4530**, **4531**, **4532**, **4533**, 4534, **4535**, 4536, 4537, 4538, 4539, **4540**, 4541, 4542, **4543**, 4544, 4545, 4546, 4547, 4548, **4549**, **4550**, 4551, 4552, **4553**, **4554**, **4555**, 4556, 4557, 4558, 4559, **4560**, 4561, **4562**, 4563, **4564**, 4565, 4566, 4567, 4568, **4569**, **4570**, **4571**, 4572, **4573**, **4574**, 4575, **4576**, 4578, 4579, 4580, 4581, **4582**, **4583**, **4584**, **4586**, 4587, 4588, 4589, **4590**, 4591, **4592**, 4593, **4594**, 4595, 4596, 4597, 4598, 4599, 4600, **4601**, 4602, **4939**
  analysis, **346**, 372, **3399**, **4500**, **4585**
  bibliographies, 4510
  directories, **4562**. *See also* Voluntarism
  history, **56**, **4515**, **4560**, **4577**
  management. *See* Nonprofit organizations, administration
  New York, analysis, **12**
Volunteerism. *See* Voluntarism
Volunteers. *See* Voluntarism
Voter registration, **782**, **2301**
Wages. *See* Nonprofit organizations, wages
Wallace, Dewitt, **36**
Ward Foundation, Marcus L., 198
Washington, George, 208, 394
Welch, Foundation, Robert A., 98
Welch, Robert Alonzo, 98
Welch, William Henry, 155
Wexner Foundation, 115
White Burkett Miller Center of Public Affairs, **470**
White, William Allen, 3491
Whitehead Institute for Biomedical Research, **417**
Whitehead, Edwin C., **417**
Whitney Foundation, John Hay, 264
Whitney, Gertrude Vanderbilt, 164
Whitney, John Hay, 264
Wilder Foundation, Amherst H., 244
Wilder, Amherst H., 244
Wildlife conservation, **3670**, 4747
Willard, Emma, 314
Williams-Waterman Fund, 1280
Wills. *See* Planned giving
Wilson, Woodrow, 307
Windom Fund, 984

Women, 51, 91, 118, 149, 163, 182, 293, 393, 585, 600, 852, 984, **1025**, **1061**, **1062**, 1153, 1157, **1292**, **1439**, 2132, 2133, **2300**, 2344, 2384, 3186, 3289, 3348, 3443, 3657, 3760, 3955, 3960, 3978, **3980**, **4488**, **4505**, **4540**, 4546, **4550**, **4555**, **4577**, 4710, 4712, 4783, 4837, 4841, 4842, 4925, 4933, 4934, 4955, 4972, 4986, 4987, 4988, **4992**
  directories, 2088, **2091**, **2260**, **2265**, **3788**
Women and Foundations/Corporate Philanthropy, **29**, 600
Woodruff, Robert W., 143
Worker's compensation, **2673**
Writing, **553**, 4047, 4052
YMCA, **2417**
Youth, **1025**, 1286, 2033, **2049**, 2052, 2157, **2203**, **2204**, 2617, **3111**, 3609, 3673, 3675, 3719, 3921, **4503**, 4528, 4713, **4857**, 4865, **4907**, **4930**, **4931**, 4933, 4934, **4960**, 4968, 4990

AUTHOR INDEX

Citations refer to entry number, not page number. Numbers in
bold type indicate abstracted bibliographic entries.

Abarbanel, Karen, 4024
Abbott, Edith, **1**
Abels, Jules, 2
Abels, Michael L., 4765
Abrams, Susan, **841**, 2420
Abramson, Alan J., **2323**, **4603**, **4737**, 4738, 4740
Academy for Educational Development, 4766, 4767
Access, 1988
Accion en Colombia, 1745
Accounting Advisory Committee, 2421
Acker, David D., **2423**
Ackerman, Carl William, 3
Ackerman, Robert W., 1298
Ad Hoc Committee on Voluntary Health and Welfare Agencies in the United States, **1989**
Ad Hoc Funders' Committee for Voter Registration and Education, **4065**
Adams, Herbert, 4
Adams, James Luther, **4481**
Adams, John D., 2424
Adams, Katherine, **4482**
Adams, Roy M., **4066**, **4067**
Adams-Chu, Lynda Lee, **2981**
Addams, Jane, **5, 6, 7**
Ader, Elaine R., 2425
Adess, Nancy, **1990**
Adolph, Val, 2426
Adventist World Headquarters, 8
Aetna Life and Casualty, 2982
Agency for International Development, 1746
Agnelli Foundation, Giovanni, 1747
Ahlbrandt, Roger S., Jr., 2427
Aidman, B. Terry, 1329
Alberger, Patti, 2983
Alberto, Charles E., 2984
Alchon, Guy, **524**
Alderson, Barnard, 9
Aldige, James G., III, 2985
Alessandra, Tony, 2044
Alexander, Anne S., **1300**
Alexander, Marjorie, 525
Alkin, Marvin C., 2428
Allen, Anne, 4769, 4770
Allen, Derek, **1748**, 1749
Allen, Herb, **526**, **3994**
Allen, Kerry Kenn, 1301, 1302, **4483**, 4484, 4485
Allen, Marjorie P., 4425
Allen, Michael Patrick, **10**
Allen, Stewert E., 2986
Allen, Thomas W., 2987

Allen, Wendy, **2429**
Allen, William Harvey, 11
Alley, Brian, 2430
Alliance of New York State Arts Councils, 1991, 2431
Allison, Dwight, **527**
Alper, Sirota and Pfau, **12**
Alperovitz, Gar, **4771**
Alsop, Ronald, 1992, 1993
Altman, D., **2989**
Altschuler, David M., **4660**
Alu Like, 528
Alvey, Wendy, 2432
Alvo, Stella, 2433
Amemiya, Takako, **1960**
American Accounting Association, 2434
American Alumni Council, 2990, 3021, 3574
American Association for State and Local History, 2236, 3380
American Association of Fund-Raising Counsel, **453**, 1994, 1995, 2991, 2992, **2993**, 4069, **4131**
American Association of Fund-Raising Counsel Trust for Philanthropy, **2994**, **4070**, 4071
American Association of Junior Colleges, 529
American Association of Museums, 2541, **3684**
American Association of State Colleges and Universities. Office of Urban Affairs, 2995
American Bankers Association, 530, 4421
American Bar Association, 1996, **2435**, **4072**, **4219**, **4374**
American Bar Association. Commission on the Mentally Disabled, 4073
American Bar Association. Subcommittee on the Model Nonprofit Corporation Law of the Business Law Section, **4074**
American Bar Foundation, 4073
American Can Company, 1533
American College Public Relations Association, 1023, 3574
American Council for the Arts, 1638, 1998, 2996, 3728, 3729, 3730, 3731, **4604**
American Council of Learned Societies, 4773
American Council on Education, **372**, 1453, **2074**, 3142, 3214, 3552, 4923
American Council on Education. Committee on Institutional Research Policy, 2997

American Council on Education. National Committee on Preparation of a Manual on College and University Business Administration, 2436
American Institute of Certified Public Accountants, 2437, 2438, 2439, 2440, 2513, 2514
American Institute of Management, **2778**
American Law Institute, 4075, **4374**
American Library Association, 2999, 3590, 4651
American Management Association, 2754
American Philosophical Association, **533**
American Philosophical Society, 1867
American Planning Association, 2441
American Public Welfare Association, **4764**
American Red Cross, 4424
American Society for Information Science, **2669**
American Society of Association Executives, 531, **999**
American Society of Corporate Secretaries, 1306
American Speech and Hearing Association, 892
American Stock Exchange, 2442
Ames, Seth N., **3000**
Ammon-Wexler, Jill, 3995, 4605
Anderson, John B., 4077
Anderson, Mary, 532
Anderson, Shirley, **533**
Andolsen, Alan, 2568
Andreasen, Alan R., 2696
Andres, Susan, 3001
Andresky, Jill, 3002, 4078
Andrews, Frank Emerson, **14, 15, 16, 17,** 534, 535, **536**, 537, 538, 539, 540, **541**, 542, 543, 813, 839, **1307**, 3003, 4079
Andrews, J. David, 4606
Andrews, Kenneth R., 1308, 1309
Anosike, Benji O., **2444**
Anthes, Earl W., **2445, 2446**
Anthony, Alfred Williams, 18, 19, 20, 547, 3005
Anthony, Robert N., **1999**, 2447, 2448, 2583
Anthony, William P., 2449
Apostolou, Nicholas G., 2450
Appalachian Community Fund, **1063**, **4003**
Aramony, William, **2000**, **2023**, 3006
Arbuthnot, Thomas S., 548
Archabal, John, 549
Ardman, Harvey, 3007
Ardman, Perri, 3007
Arenson, Karen W., 4081

AUTHOR INDEX

Arey, June Batten, 4607
Arlett, Allan, **1750, 1751, 1752, 1753**
Armstrong, Richard, 3008
Arnett, Trevor, 2451, 3009, 4775
Arnold, Alvin L., 551
Arnove, Robert F., **552**
Arsem, K.B., **2904**
Art Resources International, **4608**
Arthur Andersen and Company, **4082, 4083, 4084**
Artists Foundation, **553, 673,** 3011
Artnews Associates, 1503
Arts and Business Council, **2001,** 3012
Artsreview, 4609
Artz, Robert M., 3013
Aschrott, P.F., **1754**
Ascoli, Lucy B., **554**
Asher, Thomas R., 555
Ashfield, Jean A., 2452
Ashton, Debra, **3014, 3015, 3016, 3017, 3018**
Aspen Institute, 1241, **2404**
Associated Councils of the Arts, 3187, 4610, 4681
Associated Grantmakers of Massachusetts, 556, 557, **558,** 2453, 4423
Association of Arts Administration Educators, **2498, 2498**
Association of Black Foundation Executives, **559**
Association of Governing Boards of Universities and Colleges, 2454
Association of Information Systems Professionals, 2002
Association of Management Consulting Firms, 2891
Association of Research Libraries, 2003
Astor, Brooke, 22, 23
Aubin, Pierre, **1757**
Audio Independents, **3019**
Aufrecht, Steven E., 2456
Auster, Ethel, 2457
Austin, Ann, **1312**
Austin, Robert W., 1313
Australian Council for Educational Research, 1758
Auten, Gerald, 24, **4085, 4086**
Ayres, Edward B., 3021
Backas, James, 2004, 2005
Badger, Henry G., 4778, 4779
Baglia, Joseph R., 3022, **3023,** 4087
Bailen, June, 2006, 2007, 2458, 3024
Bailey, Anne Lowrey, 3025, 3996
Bailey, Willard, 3026
Bailward, William Amias, 25
Baird, John A., Jr., 3027, **3028, 3029, 3030**
Baird, Nina, 3031
Bakal, Carl, 26, **27**
Baker, Earl M., **4611**
Baker, John A., **4612**
Balding, Robin, 332, 3795
Baldwin, Pamela, 3032
Balk, Alfred, 4088
Ballantine, Elizabeth, 560, 561
Ballenger, Bruce P., **2459**
Balthaser, William F., **3033**
Baltzell, E. Digby, **28**

Balz, Frank J., 1314
Bandow, Doug, 1315
Bandy, Dale, 4089
Bank of America, 1316
Bank Street College of Education, **2203, 2204**
Barach, Jeffrey, 1317
Barber, Virginia, 4780
Bargerstock, Charles T., 3035
Barkas, J.L., 3036
Barker, Robert R., 2460
Barlett, Debbie, 3997
Barnes, Bill L., **3037**
Barnes, W. David, 3038, 3039
Barney, Gerald O., 4781
Barr, Rhoda, **3040**
Barrett, Nina, **29**
Barrett, William P., **30**
Barron, Clarence W., 31, 32
Barron, Deborah Durfee, 562
Barron, Lewis W., **563**
Barry, Bryan W., **2008**
Barsky, Robert, 2009, 2140
Bartlett, Dwight K., III, **2010**
Bartlett, Richard, 4090
Bartz, Carl, 1759
Barzun, Jacques, 33
Bass, Gary D., **4091**
Bates, Don, 2461, 2462, **2463,** 3042
Battaglia, Carmen L., 4613
Battelle Memorial Institute, 1841, 1842, 1843
Bauer, David G., **3043, 3044,** 3998, **3999**
Baughman, James C., **2464**
Baumol, William J., **2012**
Bay Area Committee for Responsive Philanthropy, **526**
Bay Area Lawyers for the Arts, 2287, 2288
Bayer, Ronald, 4782
Bayley, Ted D., **3045**
Beach, Cecil, 3046
Beadle, George Wells, **1263**
Beals, Kathie, 2013
Beattie, L. Elizabeth, 4486
Beatty, Betsy, **3047**
Beaumont, Constance, 3048
Beaver, Linda Zane, 2220
Becker, Sarah, **2465**
Becker, Stephen, 34
Beckman, Margaret, 564
Beckmann, David M., **1760**
Beckwith, Edward J., **565,** 857, **1502**
Beeson, Peter G., 2014
Behar, Richard, 35, **36**
Beinecke, Richard H., 566
Belcher, Jane C., **4000**
Bell, Herb, 3049
Bell, Peter D., **1761**
Bell, Phelps, **1750**
Bell and Howell Microcomputer Systems, 2466
Bellah, Robert N., **37**
Ben-Horin, Daniel, 2015
Ben-Ner, Avner, 2016
Bencivenga, Jim, 567, 568
Bender, Marylin, 38
Bendixen, Mary Anne, 3050, 3051, 3052

Benedict, Stephen, 2467, 2510
Benedum Foundation, Claude Worthington, 4767
Bennett, Andre M., 3143
Bennett, Drew A., **3939**
Bennett, James T., **569, 2017,** 4614
Bennett, Joseph, 2468
Bennett, Paul, 2469
Bentley, Richard, 1314
Bentley-Kasman, Jeremy, 4487
Benton Foundation, 2138
Berendt, Robert J., 3054, 3055, 3889
Berg, Barbara J., **4488**
Berger, Judith D., 570, 2193
Berger, Margaret A., 4783
Berger, Peter L., **4489**
Berkowitz, Bill, **4490**
Berkowitz, Emily S., **3337**
Berliner, Howard S., **571**
Berman, Edward H., **572, 1762**
Berner, Roberta, 2470
Berney, Albert, 3056
Bernhard, Virginia, **39**
Bernick, Michael, **2018**
Bertsch, Kenneth A., **1318, 1319**
Betts, Francis M., III, 3057
Beveridge, John Wendell, 4092
Beveridge, Lord, 1763
Biegel, Len, 2471
Big Brothers/Big Sisters of America, 3058
Biles, Bert R., 4001
Birmingham, Stephen, 40
Birmingham Public Library, 573
Biscoe, Patricia P., 4093
Bistline, Susan Mitchell, 2019
Black, John, 564
Black, Ralph, **2472**
Black Political Scientists, 88
Blankenship, A.B., 2482
Blanshard, Paul, Jr., 3060
Blashak, Bob, 3362
Bliss, Anthony A., 4094
Blitz, Mark, 41
Blodgett, Timothy B., 1320
Blomstrom, Robert L., **1321**
Bloom, Kathryn, 4784
Blount, Lawanna Lease, 574
Blum, D. Steven, 575
Blum, Joan, 3061
Blum, Joanne, **1322**
Blum, Robert, 3061
Blumberg, Phillip I., 1323
Blumenthal, Larry, 576, **577, 2020, 2021, 2022, 2023, 2473, 3062, 3063**
Blumenthal, Ralph, 3064
Board and Administrator Newsletter, **2500**
Bob, Murray L., 42, **2024**
Boba, Eleanor, 1764, 3065
Bohlen, Jeanne, 1324
Boisture, Robert A., 1245, 4376
Boitano, David, 3066
Boland, Michael T., 4222
Bolling, Landrum R., 578, **579, 1765**
Bolman, Frederick, 1325
Bologna, Gregory L., 1364
Bolton, Sarah Knowles, **43**
Bond, Jessie, 3470

AUTHOR INDEX

Bond, Kathleen, 4615
Bondurant, William L., 4429
Bonham, George W., **579**
Boniface, Zoe E., 580
Boorman, Scott A., 2025
Boorstin, Daniel J., 44, 45
Borden, Robert, 2944
Boren, Jerry F., **1326**
Boris, Elizabeth Trocolli, 46, 1060, **1061**, **1062**, 2026, 3692, 4095
Bornet, Vaughn Davis, 47
Bornstein, Rita, **3067**
Borof, Irwin J., **2027**, 4096
Borr, Ernest B., 3068
Borst, Diane, 2475
Bortin, Virginia, 2476
Borton, Georgina L., **3069**, **3580**
Bosanquet, Bernard, 6
Boss, Richard W., **2477**, **3070**
Bothwell, Robert O., 48, 581, 2428, 3071, 4097
Boulding, Kenneth E., **49**, 50
Bowen, Louise Hadduck, 51
Bowen, William G., **2012**
Bower, Margret, **2028**
Boyd, T.A., 274
Boyd, Thomas D., 2029, **2479**
Boyd, Willard L., 2030
Boyer, Ernest L., 582, **4785**
Boynes, Wynta, **1766**
Boyte, Harry C., **4491**, **4517**
Bracco, Dianne Metzger, **1036**
Brace, Charles Loring, **52**
Brace, Paul K., 2480
Braddy, Glen J., 3072
Bradley, Donna, **866**
Bradley, William L., **3073**
Bradshaw, Thornton, **1327**
Bragdon, Frances J., **1328**
Brakeley, George, 592
Brakeley, George A., Jr., 53, 3074
Brakeley, John Price Jones, **54**, **2481**, 3075
Brandt, Lilian, 813
Brandt, Sanford F., **4098**
Branscomb, Anne W., **4786**
Brawley, Benjamin, 55
Brecher, Charles, **4787**
Breen, George Edward, 2482
Breiteneicher, Joseph C.K., **3077**
Breitstein, Joel M., 1329
Breivik, Patricia Senn, 3078
Bremner, Robert Hamlett, **56**, **57**, **58**, **59**
Brenner, Marie, **60**
Breunig, Robert, **61**
Bricault, Giselle, **1938**
Brickley, Peg, 583
Bridge, James H., 62
Bright, Craig B., 4118, 4119
Brilakis, Antony A., 3080
Brinckerhoff, Peter C., **2483**, 2484, 3081, 4099
Brinkerhoff, Derick W., 2031, 2032
Bristow, Camille, 2033
Broaddus, Will, **63**, **64**
Broce, Thomas Edward, 584, 3082
Brodhead, William M., 4100
Brody, Deborah, **585**

Brody, Ralph, **3083**
Broman, John, 586, 3084, 3085
Bromberg, Robert S., 4101, 4102
Bromley, E. Blake, 3086
Brookings Institution, 65
Brooklyn In Touch Information Center, 2485, **2486**, **2487**, **2488**, **2489**, **2490**, 3087, **4002**, 4103, **4104**
Brooks, Andree, 4492
Brooks, Elizabeth, **66**
Brooks, Harvey, **1330**
Brophy, Beth, 4105
Brotman, M., **3088**
Brown, E. Richard, **587**
Brown, Jack H., 3089
Brown, Kathleen M., 2491, 3090, **4493**, 4494, 4495
Brown, Peter C., **2492**
Brown, Susan Love, 67
Brownrigg, W. Grant, **1331**, 2034
Bruce, Bob, 3091
Bryant, David S., 3092
Bryce, Herrington J., **2493**
Brysh, Janet F., **1332**
Bubnic, Anne M., **68**
Buckley, William F., Jr., 69
Buckman, Thomas R., 589, 3078, **4403**
Buhl, Lance, 2494
Buie, James A., **4106**
Builta, Jeanine, **3094**
Bullock, Mary Brown, **1768**
Bulmer, Joan, **591**
Bulmer, Martin, **590**, **591**
Bundy, McGeorge, **579**, 592
Buratto, Bill, 4496
Burden Foundation, Florence V., **1036**
Burdett-Coutts, Angela, 206
Bureau of National Affairs, 4619
Burkhart, Patrick J., 3095
Burnett, Ed, 3096
Burnham, James R., 2035
Burns, Joan Simpson, 2036
Burns, Michael E., **593**, **594**, **1333**, **1334**, **1335**, **1336**, **1337**, **1338**, 1339, **3097**
Burr, Bowman, 3918
Burzynski, T., 3098
Bush, Barbara, 4108
Bush, Bernard, 251
Bush, Vannevar, 4616
Bushnell, Shirley W., 2496
Business and Professional Women's Foundation, **3788**
Business Committee for the Arts, 1340, **3099**
Business International, 1769
Business Volunteers for the Arts/Seattle, 2497
Butcher, Willard C., **1341**
Butler, Francis J., **595**
Butler, Nicholas Murray, 71, 72, **1770**
Butler, Stuart M., 73
Butners, Marite M., 3100
Butt, Martha G., 596
Butterfield, Fox, 4497
Caesar, Patricia, **1342**
Cafferty, Pastora San Juan, 4788
Cage, Bob N., 3945

Cagney, Penelope, **74**
Cagnon, Charles, **2037**, 2038
Cahan, Emily Davis, 597
Caldwell Public Library, **700**
Calhoun, Susan, **598**, **599**, 600, **601**, **2039**
California. Attorney General's Office, **2206**
California Chamber of Commerce, 1343
California Community Foundation, **1344**, **2076**, 2949, **3101**
California. Office of Appropriate Technology, 3102
California State University and Colleges, 602
Calkins, Robert D., 603
Callaghan, Christopher T., 2518
Cameron, Frank, 75
Caming, H.W. William, 3103
Cammack, Charles W., III, **4110**
Campbell, Craig, **3104**
Campbell, D.A., 3105
Campisi, Dominic J., 604
Canadian Centre for Philanthropy, **817**, **1750**, 1790, **4562**
Candler, Charles Howard, 76
Canter, MacKenzie, III, **2040**, 4111, 4112, 4113, 4114, 4115, **4789**
Cantrell, Karen, **605**, **1259**
Caplin and Drysdale, 4116, 4117
Cappalli, Richard B., **4617**, 4618, 4619
Carbone, Robert F., 3107, 3108, **3109**
Carestia, Elizabeth, 3110
Cargill, Jennifer, 2430
Carlson, David B., **2230**
Carlson, Martin E., 77
Carmel, Catherine, 3995, 4605
Carmichael, Leonard, 78
Carmichael, Marc L., 3398
Carmichael, Stephen J., **3111**
Carmody, Deirdre, 4790
Carnegie, Andrew, 79, 80, **81**, 82
Carnegie Commission on Higher Education, 2280, 3696, 4791, 4792, 4793, 4794, 4795, 4796, 4797, 4798, 4799, 4800, 4801, 4802, 4803, 4804, 4805, 4811, 4906, 4922, 4985
Carnegie Commission on the Future of Public Broadcasting, 4806
Carnegie Corporation of New York, 83, 219, 385, **386**, 606, 945, 1087, 1095, **1945**, 4807, 4839, 4925
Carnegie Council on Policy Studies in Higher Education, 4808, 4809
Carnegie Dunfermline Trust, **84**
Carnegie Endowment for International Peace, 85, 607
Carnegie Forum on Education and the Economy, **4810**
Carnegie Foundation for the Advancement of Teaching, **932**, **4785**, 4792, 4793, 4794, 4795, 4797, 4799, 4800, 4801, 4802, 4804, 4811, 4830, 4906, 4985
Carpetbag Theatre, **4003**
Carr, Elliott G., 1345
Carr, Howard, 817
Carr, Jennifer, **1938**
Carr, Margaret Stewart, **1558**
Carr, William H., 86

319

AUTHOR INDEX

Carroll, John, 3870
Carroll, Margaret, 3112
Carson, Emmett D., 87, 88, **89**, **3113**
Carter, Lindy Keane, **3114**
Carter, Margaret, **2041**
Carter, Novia, 4498
Carter, Paul C., 90
Carter, Richard, **2042**
Cary, William L., 4118, 4119
Case, Josephine E., 906
Case Western Reserve University, **4237**
Casey, Susan B., 4499
Casey, William J., 4120
Casey Foundation, Annie E., **2049**
Cass, Rosemary Higgins, **4549**
Castells, Manuel, **2043**
Caswell, G.M., 3115
Catalyst, **3625**
Cathcart, Jim, 2044
Catholic Charities of Chicago, 3146
Catholic Relief Services, 3064
Cato Institute, 4614
Cawley, Rebecca, 3116
Center for American Culture Studies, **428**
Center for Applied Social Research, 122
Center for Arts Administration, **2498**
Center for Arts Information, 1350, 2045, 2046, **2149**, 2499, 3117, **4608**
Center for Board and Administrator Relations, **2500**
Center for Community Change, 2047, **2501**, 3118, **3981**, 4427, **4620**
Center for Corporate Community Relations, **1326**, **1351**
Center for Corporate Public Involvement, 1352, **1353**
Center for Effective Philanthropy, 566, **676**
Center for Health Policy Studies, 709, 711
Center for Management Systems, **2502**
Center for Non-Profit Corporations, **2702**
Center for Public Advocacy Research, 2033
Center for Research and Advanced Study, 608, 1332
Center for Responsive Politics, 794
Center for the Study of Federalism, **4611**
Center for the Study of Philanthropy, **91**, **170**, **1214**
Center for the Study of Philanthropy and Voluntarism, **4577**
Center for the Study of Social Policy, 2048, **2049**
Center for Third World Organizing, **3119**, **3200**
Center for Urban Affairs and Policy Research, **2065**
Center for Urban Economic Development, **2503**
Center for Women Policy Studies, **1439**
Central Hanover Bank and Trust Company, 4813
Centro de Fundaciones, **1772**
Chadwick, John, 1773
Chadwick, W. Edward, 1774
Chagy, Gideon, 1354, 1355
Chamber of Commerce, 609, 2050, 4224, 4473
Chamberlain, Betty, 1356

Chamberlain, Marjorie, **1500**
Chamberlain, Neil W., 1357, 1358
Chambers, Clarke A., **92**
Chambers, Merritt Madison, 610, 728, 3120
Chambre, Susan Maizel, **4500**
Chance, Ruth Clouse, 611
Chaney, Lindsay, 93
Chapin, Isolde, 1301
Chapman, Becky, 1359
Chapman, John W., **4564**
Chapman, Terry S., **2504**
Charities Aid Foundation, **1775**, **1896**, **1897**, 1898
Charpie, Robert A., 1360
Chavers, Dean, **2051**, 3123, **3124**, 4004
Chegwidden, Daniel, 3125
Chemical Bank, 95, 96, 332
Cherner, Beverly, 3126
Chernikoff, Larry, 3127
Chetkovich, Michael N., 3128
Chicago Council on Fine Arts, 4818
Chiechi, Carolyn P., 4327
Chirhart, Edward F., 613
Christensen, Robert, 3130
Christian, Diane, **3463**
Chumney, Candes P., **614**
Church, David M., 3131
Church, Susan, **3132**
Churcher, Sharon, 97
Churchman, David, 2505
Cialdini, Robert B., **3133**
Ciavarella, Michael A., 4621
Ciba Foundation, 615
Cieply, Michael, 93
Citizen Involvement Training Project, 2346, **4329**
Citizens Committee for New York City, 2052
City Harvest, 2053
Clack, George, 4622
Clague, Ewan, 616
Clark, A., 4501
Clark, Dennis, 617
Clark, James A., 98
Clark, Michael S., **1361**
Clark, Robert C., 2054
Clark, Ronald W., 1776
Clark, William J., 3134
Clark Foundation, 2667
Clark Foundation, Edna McConnell, 1296, 4623
Clarke, Gerald, 99
Clarkson, Kenneth W., **2055**
Clay, Edwin S., III, **3135**
Clearinghouse for Midcontinent Foundations, **618**, 619
Clearinghouse for Research on Fund Raising, 3107, **3109**
Clearinghouse on Corporate Social Responsibility, 1362, 1363
Cleland, Robert Glass, 620
Cleveland Associated Foundation, 4121
Cleveland Foundation, 2506, 2507
Clifton, Roger L., **2508**
Cline, Edward, 4122
Clinton, John, **621**, **622**, **1269**

Close, Arthur C., 1364
Clotfelter, Charles T., 4123, **4124**, **4125**, 4306
Cloud, Deborah A., **2509**
Cloward, Richard A., **4926**
Cmiel, Kenneth, 1365
Coalition of National Voluntary Organizations, 2056, **4510**
Coates, Matthew, **2058**
Cobb, Leyland M., 3136, **3137**
Cockerill, Adrian B., Jr., 3138, 3139
Coe, Linda C., 2467, 2510, 3140, 4624
Coffman, Harold Coe, 623
Cohen, Carol E., 3525
Cohen, Lilly, 3141
Cohen, Nathan E., **4502**
Cohen, Vicki L., 4625
Cohn, Jules, 1366
Cohn, Marian R., 2033
Cok, Mary Van Someren, 2511
Coldren, Sharon L., 3142
Cole, Katherine W., 2059
Cole, Richard L., 2060, 2061
Coleman, John R., 4814
Coleman, Laurence Vail, 4815
Coleman, William Emmet, **624**, **4005**
Collender, Stanley E., 4626
Collier, Abram T., 1367
Collier, Charles W., 4126
Collier, Peter, 100, **101**
Collins, Chuck, **2512**
Collins, Michael, 1777
Collver, David, 3386
Colorado Committee for Responsive Philanthropy, 625
Colson, Paul, **4962**
Columbia University. Graduate School of Business, 1413
Colvard, Richard, 3143
Colwell, Mary Anna Culleton, 627
Colwell, Phoebe T., 3144
Combs, Stephen M., 3146
Commerce Clearing House, 4127, 4128, 4129
Commission on Financing Higher Education, 3631
Commission on Foundations and Private Philanthropy, 628, **629**
Commission on Private Philanthropy and Public Needs, **102**, 110, 630, 631, 632
Commission on the Humanities, 4816
Committee for Corporate Support of American Universities, 1368
Committee for Economic Development, **1561**
Committee for Economic Development. Research and Policy Committee, 1369
Committee on College and University Accounting and Auditing, 2513
Committee on Community Foundations, **1155**
Committee on Voluntary Health and Welfare Organizations, 2514
Committee to Defend Reproductive Rights of the Coalition for the Medical Rights of Women, 2515

AUTHOR INDEX

Committee to Study the Laws of Rhode Island Charitable Trusts, 4130
Commonwealth Center for Community Education, 4621
Commonwealth Foundation, 1967
Commonwealth Fund, 516, 633, 796, 1102, 4787, 4817
Commonwealth Fund. Commission on Elderly People Living Alone, 4817
Community Council of Greater New York, 2215
Community Foundation of Greater Washington, **634**
Community Information Exchange, 1370
Community Research and Publications Group, **1371**
Community Service Society, **2517**
Conable, Barber, 2062
Cone, Arthur Lambert, Jr., **3149**
Conference Board, 1377, 1378, 1379, 1380, 1381, **1537, 1538, 1540,** 1704, **1705, 1706, 1707,** 1730, 1741, 1883, 1891, 4980
Conference Board Corporate Relations Program, **1706**
Conference of Southwest Foundations, 613
Conference on Alternative State and Local Policies, 3150
Congressional Quarterly, **4627**
Connery, Robert H., 1383
Connors, Tracy Daniel, 2518, **2519**
Conrad, Chris, 638
Conrad, Daniel Lynn, 3151, **3152,** 4006, **4007, 4503**
Conrad, William R., Jr., **2520,** 2521, 2872
Conroy, Charles P., **2063**
Conroy, David J., **2064**
Conroy, Tom, 3153
Conservation Foundation, 511, 4132
Consumer Education Resource Network, 2103
Contact Center, 4008
Contee, Christine E., 1778
Converse, Philip Ray, 3154
Conyngton, Hugh R., 639, 3155
Conyngton, Mary, **4504**
Cook, Betsy, **4628**
Cook, Constance Ewing, **4629**
Cook, Fay Lomax, **2065**
Cook, Jonathan B., 2066, **2522**
Cook, Wayne, 837
Coolbirth, Alison G., 3156
Cooley, Charles A., 3157, 3158, 3159
Coon, Horace, 640
Cooperative Assistance Fund, 641
Corbally, John E., 3160
Corbin, John, 2523
Corder, Robert E., 2524
Corderi, Victoria, 1384
Cordil, Lesta, 1385
Corey, Kenneth E., 3161
Cornesky, R.A., **3162**
Cornuelle, Richard, 103
Cornwell, Jim L., 3163
Coro Foundation, 1461
Corporate Special Projects Fund, 1397
Corporate Volunteer Coordinators Council, 1398

Corporate Volunteerism Council of Minnesota, **1399**
Corry, Emmett, **3164**
Cort, Doris M., 642
Cott, Betty, 1402
Cott, Nancy F., **4505**
Cotter, George, **1757**
Coughlin, Ellen K., 3165
Council, Delia L., 4933, 4934
Council for Advancement and Support of Education, 2525, 3035, 3166, 3167, 3171, 3272, **3376, 3737, 3755,** 3786, **3873,** 3956, **3986, 4017,** 4961
Council for Aid to Education, **1403,** 3169, 3396
Council for Business and the Arts in Canada, 2644
Council for Community Services, **643**
Council for Financial Aid to Education, **104,** 1404, 1405, 1406, 1407, 1408, **1409,** 1410, 1411, 1412, 1413, **1454,** 1491, **1677,** 3168, **3169,** 3170, 3602, **4506**
Council of Better Business Bureaus, **134, 1414,** 2067, **2068**
Council of Better Business Bureaus' Foundation, **2526,** 2527
Council of Michigan Foundations, **105,** 439, 644, **645, 646, 747, 1217,** 4009, **4179,** 4420
Council of New York Law Associates, 2069, **4133, 4311**
Council on Economic Priorities, 1415, 1572, **1573**
Council on Fine Arts, 4818
Council on Foundations, 69, **106,** 107, **108,** 109, 110, **647,** 648, 649, **650,** 651, 652, **653, 654, 655,** 656, **657, 658,** 659, 660, **661,** 662, **663,** 664, 665, 666, **667, 721, 723,** 975, 1007, **1026,** 1030, **1059, 1078, 1080,** 1149, **1155, 1156, 1192, 1416, 1417, 1418, 1419,** 1420, 1421, **1422, 1423,** 1529, **1617, 1742,** 1780, **1781,** 1894, **1934, 1944,** 2494, 2528, 2529, 4134, 4135, **4136,** 4210, **4930, 4931**
Coutts, Jim, 1782
Coutts, Rosemary J., 1783
Cover, Nelson, 3171
Cox, Jo-Ann, 669
Coyne, Kevin, **4507**
Crabtree, Penni, 670
Cracknell, D.G., 1784
Crawford, Jean A., 3172
Crawford, Robert W., 2530
Creager, John A., 4819
Crimmins, James C., 2070
Crittenden, Ann, 1425
Croake, Elizabeth A., 2531
Crohn, Richard J., 3173, 3174
Cronbach, Lee J., 2532
Cronin, Jerry, **671,** 1736, **2445, 2446,** 2533
Cronk, Thomas, 2534
Crook, William W., **2464**
Cross, Sally S., 2535
Crossland, Fred E., 672, 4820
Crouch, David C., 3175
Crovetti, F. Urbon, 3176
Crowell, Chester T., 3177

Croxton, Frederick E., 1738
Cruickshank, Joseph H., 3178
Csapo, Rita Marika, **673**
Culliton, Barbara, 4821
Cultural Assistance Center, **1426,** 2071, 2536
Cumerford, William R., 3179
Cuninggim, Merrimon, 675, **676, 677, 678,** 802
Cunneen, Frank J., 3180
Cunningham, James V., 2072
Cunningham, Michael, **679, 2073**
Cunningham, Robert M., Jr., 3181
Currin, John L., 4424
Curti, Merle Eugene, **111, 112, 113, 114, 1785,** 3184
Curtis, Charlotte, 115, 3182
Curtis, Jody, **116**
Cushman, Charles P., 3183
Cutlip, Scott M., **3184**
D'Amico, Philip, 2538, 2539, 2578
Dade Council of Arts and Sciences, 2537
Dalgliesh, J., 3185
Dalrymple, Martha, 1786
Damude, Earl F., 680
Dane, John Hunter, 117
Danforth Foundation, 4923
Daniel, Robert L., 1787
Daniels, Arlene Kaplan, **1061, 1062,** 3186
Daniels, Craig E., **4010**
Daniels, Ellen Stodolsky, 3187
Daniels, Raymond D., 2540
Dannelley, Paul, 3188
Darcy, Kathy, **681**
Daring Goals for a Caring New York, **12**
Dass, Ram, **4525**
Daughtrey, William H., Jr., 2541
Davidson, Alice H., **3189**
Davie, Ann R., **2074**
Davis, Allen F., **118,** 119
Davis, Barbara H., **2542**
Davis, Frampton, 3190
Davis, John H., 120
Davis, Keith, **1321**
Davis, Kenneth A., 2543
Davis, King E., 3191
Davis, Larry Nolan, 2544
Davis, Margaret Bergan, 3192
Davis, Nancy M., **2075**
Davis, Pamela, **2076**
Davis, William, 121
Dawes, Sharon S., **2077**
Dawson, Judith M., **3193**
Dawson, Margaret White, **2078, 2079**
Dawson, William M., 2772
Day, Heather F., 3194
Dayton, Edward R., 1788
Dayton, Kenneth N., 2545, **2546**
Dayton Hudson Foundation, 3373
de Bettencourt, Francis G., 682
De Grazia, Alfred, 122
de Groot, Jane, 3196
de Harven, Gerry Ann, 4508
de Lopez, Antonieta M., 1789
de Oliveira, Fred H., 2547
De Pas, Penney, 683
de Pulido, Luisa E.M., 1789

AUTHOR INDEX

De Rea, Philip, **3197**
De Thomasis, Brother Louis, 2548
Deabler, L., 3198
Dean, Ruth, 2080
Debatin, June B., **2549**
Debnam, Robert J., 4138
DeCarlo, Mary, 4509
Decker, Larry E., 4011
Decker, Virginia A., 4011
Deckoff, Marvin J., 3199
Deeg, J.F., 1790
Defty, Sally Bixby, 684
Deja, Sandy, **4139**
del Pilar, Natividad S.H., **1067**
Delfin, Stephen, 2082
Delgado, Gary, **3200**, 3201
Demaris, Ovid, 1427
Demkovich, Linda E., 4822
Denker, Henry, 685
Dennis, Barry, 3202
Dennis, Patrick, 686
DeNunzio, Michael A., 3203
Dermer, Joseph, **687**, **1428**, 3204, 3205, **3206**, **3207**, 4012
Des Marais, Philip, 4631
Deschin, Jacob, 688
DeSirgh, Jana S., **565**, **1502**
Desmond, Richard L., **3208**
DeSoto, Carole, 3209
Desruisseaux, Paul, 123, 124, 125, 126, 127, 128, 129, 689, 690, 691, 692, 693, 694, 695, 696, 697, 698, **1429**, 1430, 2083, 3210, 3211, 3212, 3213, 4140, 4823
Detmold, John Hunter, 3214
Devine, Edward T., 130
Devlin, A., 3215
DeVries, R.A., 3216
Dewan, Bradford N., 2550
Dewey, Barbara I., **2551**
Dewey, John, **4824**
Dewey, Richard E., 4510
Dick, Alice, 4511
Dick, Ellen A., **1431**
Dickinson, Frank G., **131**, **132**
Dickson, John P., 2552, 2553, 2554, 3218
Dickson, Sarah S., 2552, 2553, 2554, 3218
Diebold, John, 1432
Diehl, Richard J., **3219**, **3220**, **3221**
DiGregorio, Beverly J., **2555**
DiLorenzo, Thomas J., **2017**, 4614
DiMaggio, Paul J., **699**, 2084, **2556**, **2557**, 3222, 4632
Dimino, E.R., 3223
Dingfelder, William M., 2085, 3224
Direct Mail/Marketing Association, 2558, 3227
Directory of Social Change, **2952**
Disney, Diane M., 4634
Distelhorst, Garis F., 2089
Dodd, Ruth M., **4512**
Dodge, Phyllis B., **133**
Dodson, Jerome, 2559
Doherty, Elizabeth M., **134**
Doll, Henry C., 702
Doll, William, **703**, 704
Dolnick, Edward, 705
Donahey, Isabelle, **4826**

Donahue, Daniel F., 3559
Donaldson, Lufkin and Jenrette, 2562, 2563, 2564, 2565
Donors Forum Emergency Loan Fund, **2566**
Donors Forum of Chicago, 525, **554**, **706**, **707**, 708, 1365, 1452, 2567, 3231, 3232, **4163**
Dooley, Betty L., 709, **710**, 711, **712**, 4827
Dorian, Max, 135
Dorsey, Eugene C., 2090, **3234**, 4513
Doss, Martha Merrill, **2091**
Dougherty, Nancy C., **713**
Douglas, Adisa, **852**
Douglas, James, **136**, 1792, 2092, 2093
Douty, Christopher M., 3235
Dove, Kent E., 3236, **3237**
Dow, Adele, **3238**
Downes, Michael, 3239, **3240**, **3241**
Doyle, Denis P., 1793
Drago, John, 2568
Drake, Carl B., Jr, 1435
Dresser, Peter D., **2094**
Dressner, Howard R., 714, 4141
Drew, Joseph S., 715, 4013
Drotning, Phillip T., 3242
Drucker, Peter F., **2569**
du Pont, Pierre S., IV, 3243
Duca, Diane J., 716, 2570, 2571, 2572, **2573**, 4014, 4514
Duca Associates, 1436
DuChez, JoAnne, **4635**
Dufour, F. Philip, 3829
Duguay, Lois, 3244
Duke, Marc, 138
Duke Endowment, 717, 718
Dumouchel, J. Robert, 4636
Dun and Bradstreet, 1437
Duncan, Robert F., 139
Duncan, William A., **2095**
Dunkel, Tom, 1438, 3245, 3246
Dunkle, Margaret, **1439**
Dunlop, David R., **3247**
Dunlop, Donna V., **1440**, **3248**, 3249
Dunn, John A., Jr., 2753
Dunn, Thomas G., **3250**
Dunten, Kathleen, 3251
Dupree, A. Hunter, 4637
Durbin, Mary, **2028**
Durling, Mary, 3843
Duronio, Margaret A., **3580**
Dye, Susanne A., 2096
Dykeman, Wilma, 140
Earle, Benjamin, 1441
Easton, Allan, 2097
Eaves, George N., 4015
Ebbeling, Donald C., 719
Ebert, Robert H., **720**
Eby, Charles, 2098
Ecclesine, Joseph A., 3252
Eckert, Ralph J., 1442
Eckstein, Burton J., **3253**
Eckstein, Richard M., **3254**
Eddleman, Jacquie, 4665
Eddy, Junius, 4638, 4639, 4784
Edie, John A., **721**, 722, **723**, 724, 725, 726, **2099**, 2574, 4142, 4143

Edley, Christopher F., 4430
Education Funding Research Council, 3518
Edwards, A.H., 3256
Edwards, Charles J., 4735
Edwards, Thomas C., 1444
Eells, Richard, 1445, 1446, 1447, 1448, 1616
Effective Sector Leadership/Management Program, 2180
Egerton, John, **2100**
Eisenberg, Pablo, **141**, 4427
Eldon, Elder, 2575
Elia, Charles J., 727
Elkin, Robert, 2480, 2576
Elkins, Ken, 142
Elkins, Susan R., **3366**
Elliot, Charles, 143, 728
Elliott, Eleanor, 2577
Ellis, Arthur L., 2101
Ellis, Susan J., **2041**, **4515**, 4516
Ellman, Ira M., 4828
Elnicki, Susan E., **729**, **2102**, **3260**
Ely, David, 730
Embree, Edwin R., 731, 732
Energize Associates, **4562**
Engel, James F., **3262**
Engelberg, M., **3263**
England, Robert, **144**
English, Raymond, 1559
Ensman, Richard G., Jr., **3264**, 3265, 3266, 3267, 3268
Enters, Carol, 3269
Environmental Grantmakers Association, **733**
Epstein, Benjamin R., 764
Epstein, George, 2538, 2578
Epstein, Joseph, 145
Esposito, Virginia, 734
Estes, Carroll L., **977**
Etheredge, Lynn, **4829**
European Cultural Foundation, 1902
Evangelauf, Jean, 147
Evans, Eli N., 736
Evans, Sara M., **4517**
Evansen, Virginia B., 2969
Eves, Margaret, **3270**
Ewald, William, 2579
Exxon Corporation, 2796
Exxon Education Foundation, **470**, **2674**
Fabian, Larry L., 737
Fadiman, Mark, 4831
Fagg, Karen, **848**
Failing, Patricia, 148
Falk Medical Fund, Maurice, 1209
Falleder, Arnold, 2105, 4641, 4642, 4643
Fandel, Nancy A., **1451**
Fanning, Carol, **738**
Farber, David R., 1452
Farley, Pamela J., 4644
Farnsworth, Mary L., 2951
Farr, Sally, **739**
Farrell, Catherine E., **595**
Farrell, Charles S., 740
Farrell, John C., **149**
Fate, Terry, **3314**
Faust, Paula J., 3272
Faux, Jeff, **4771**

AUTHOR INDEX

Fear, Richard A., 2581
Federal Resources Advisory Service, 3273
Federation Employment and Guidance Service, **2106**
Federation of Jewish Philanthropies, 3343
Federation of Protestant Welfare Agencies, 4519
Feiden, Karyn, **741**
Feinberg, Paul H., 4339
Feld, Alan L., 4832
Fenwick, Dorothy C., 1453
Ferguson, James L., **1454**, 1455
Ferguson, Mary E., 742
Ferguson, Shannon, **4091**
Feron, James, 150, 4645
Ferrell, O.C., 2694, 3274
Ferster, Andrea, **4178**
Feshbach, Norma, 4833
Fey, John T., 1456
Fidler, Kathleen, 151
Field Foundation, **743**, 744, 4889
Fiffer, Steve, **1457**
Filer, John H., 745
Fillingham, E., 3275
Financial Accounting Standards Board, 2447, 2480, 2582, 2583, 2584, 2585, 2586, 2587, 2905
Finch, Johnny C., 4148
Fincher, Beatrice, 3277
Finehout, Raymond L., 4149
Fink, Norman S., 3278, 3279
Finley, Michael, 1458
Finn, Chester E., Jr., 4646
Finn, Matia, 3280
Finnish Cultural Foundation, 1794
Fiore, Ernest D., Jr., 4150
Firstenberg, Paul B., **2588**
Fisch, Edith L., 746, **4151**, **4152**
Fischer, Howard E., 3281, 4153
Fischer, Jeri L., **747**
Fisher, Donald **748**, **1795**
Fisher, James L., **152**
Fisher, John, 2589, 2590
Fisher, Robert, **4834**
Fishman, Arnold, 3282, 3283
Fishman, Leo, 749
Fishman, Steve, **1459**
Fiske, Edward B., 2110
Fitz-Gibbon, Carol Taylor, 2775, 2776, 2777
Fitzgibbons, Ruth Miller, 4835
Fixler, Philip E., Jr., **2055**
Flanagan, Joan, 2591, **3285**, 3286, 4520, **4521**
Fleischman, Ellen, 3287
Fleischmann Foundation, Max C., 750
Fleming, Robert J., **2668**
Flexner, Abraham, 153, **154**, **751**
Flexner, Simon, 155
Flynn, John T., 156
Fojtik, Kathleen M., 3288
Folks, Homer, **157**
Foote, Joseph, **752**, 753, 754, **755**, 756, 2592
Ford, David S., 159
Ford, Gerald, 1461

Ford Foundation, 551, 757, 758, 759, 760, 761, 762, 843, 1003, **1167**, 1569, 1798, 1799, 1800, 1801, 1802, 1803, 1804, 1805, 1806, 1807, 1808, 1809, 1810, 1811, 1812, 1813, 1814, 1815, 1884, **2112**, **2203**, **2204**, **2285**, 2302, 2460, 3289, 4118, 4119, 4638, 4639, **4730**, 4783, 4788, 4820, 4836, 4837, 4838, 4839, 4840, 4841, 4842, 4886, 4918, **4928**, **4930**, **4931**, 4933, 4934, 4978
Forrestal, Dan J., 1462
Forster, Arnold, 764
Forsythe, David P., 2113, 2114
Fosdick, Raymond Blaine, 160, 161, 765, 766, 767
Foster, R. Scott, 2115
Foster Foundation, James, 768
Fottler, Carol A., 4522
Fottler, Myron D., 4522
Foundation Center, 247, **294**, **362**, **386**, **536**, 540, 542, 589, **621**, **622**, 769, 770, 771, **772**, **773**, 774, 803, 906, **911**, 928, 947, **981**, 982, **1052**, **1059**, **1061**, **1062**, **1066**, **1067**, 1076, **1099**, **1100**, **1167**, **1282**, **1467**, **1684**, 1954, 2077, **2303**, **2404**, 2428, **2588**, **2674**, **2805**, **2897**, **3812**, **3950**, 4156, 4157, 4158, **4403**, **4560**, **4562**, **4592**
Foundation for American Communications, 2594
Foundation for the Extension and Development of the American Professional Theatre, **2595**, **2680**
Foundation Library Center of Japan, 1816
Foundation News, 660
Foundation Research Project, **1206**
Foundations-Corporations Emergency Fund Committee, 3292
Fowler, Charles, 4784
Fox, Daniel M., 4843
Fox, Harold W., 2596
Fox, Jeanne J., 791
Fox, Tom, **1817**, 1818, 1819, 1820, **1821**, 1822, 1823, 4647
Foxwell, Elizabeth, 3293
Fram, Eugene H., **2597**
France. Ministre de l'Interieiur, 1824
Frank, Curtiss E., 3294
Frantzreb, Arthur C., 162, **2598**, 2599, **2600**
Frazer, David R., 792, **793**
Frederick, William C., **1321**
Freeberg, Ellen M., 794
Freed, Doris J., **4151**, **4152**
Freedman, Anne, **4582**
Freedman, Estelle B., **163**
Freedman, Marc R., **2601**
Freeman, David F., **795**
Freeman, Douglas, **3295**
Freeman, Harry L., **1469**
Freiser, Leonard H., 3296
Fremont-Smith, Marion R., **1470**, 4160
French, William J., 796
Freyd, William, 3297
Frick Foundation, Henry C., 1200
Friedman, B.H., 164
Friedman, Ellen, **1202**

Friedman, John S., 797, 2116, 4648
Friedman, Martin, 798
Friedman, Ray, 1825
Frisch, Ephraim, 165
Fromm, Erich, **166**
Froomkin, Joseph, 3298
Fruhling, Hugo, **2117**
Fuller, John G., 167
Fulton, William, 3299
Fund Raising Institute, **2926**, **3033**, **3149**, 3302, **3803**, 3824, 3965, 3966, 3968, 3969
Funding Exchange, 203, 4161
Funding Information Center of Texas, **614**, **1264**
Future Homemakers of America, 3645
Gaby, Daniel M., 2602
Gaby, Patricia V., 2602
Galaskiewicz, Joseph, 1471, **1472**
Galella, Armando, 3307
Galer, Donna, **2603**
Gallagher, Janne C., **4475**
Gallagher, John E., **4949**
Gallagher, Richard, 2604
Gallo, Robert P., **2930**
Galloway, Joseph M., 4162
Gallup Omnibus, 168
Gamarekian, Barbara, 169
Gambino, Anthony J., 2605
Gamwell, Franklin I., **4523**
Gannett Center for Media Studies, 4786
Gantenbein, Douglas, 800
Gardner, Frederic P., 801
Gardner, John W., 802, **2118**, 2119, 2120, **2606**, **2607**, **2608**, **2609**, **2610**, **2611**, 4844
Garfield, Robert, 4845
Garonzik, Elan, 803, 3308
Garrow, David J., **170**
Garside, Edward B., 135
Gartner, Alan, 2121
Garvin, Clifton C., Jr., 1473
Gary, Susan N., **4163**
Gates, Frederick Taylor, **171**, 172
Gaylin, Willard, **4846**
Gearhart, S.C., 3309
Geary, G.F., Jr., 3310
Gee, Thomas H., 804
Gehrig, Cynthia, **4847**
Geier, Ted, **3311**
Geiger, Aryeh, **3312**
Geiger, Roger L., **2122**, 4848, 4849, **4850**
Geiger, Theodore, 1663
Geldof, Bob, **173**
Geldzahler, Henry, 2612
Geller, Robert E., **3313**
General Education Board, 805
General Electric Company, 1474
General Mills Foundation, 4417, 4422
George, William R., 3848
Georgi, Charlotte, 2613, **3314**
Geraghty, Laura Lee M., 4524
Gerber, Albert B., 806
Germano, William Paul, 2215
Gershen, Howard, **2124**
Gertzog, Alice, **3315**
Gettinger, Steve, **1476**
Gettleman, Marvin E., **174**
Getz, Barbara J., 807

323

AUTHOR INDEX

Giamatti, A. Bartlett, 2125
Gibans, Nina Freedlander, 4649
Gibbons, Laura, **1577**
Gibson, E. Burr, 3078
Giddings, Franklin, **6**
Gies, David L., 2751
Gilbert, Michael A., **2615**
Gillin, John Lewis, 175
Gillingham, David W., **2126**
Gilman, Daniel C., 808
Gilman, Kenneth L., **2616**, 3318
Gingold, Diane J., 4650
Gingrich, Arnold, 1477
Ginzberg, Eli, **809**, **810**
Girl Scouts of the U.S.A., 2617
Gladden, Washington, **177**
Glamann, Kristof, 1827
Glaser, John S., **1828**
Glasser, Ira, **4846**
Glazer, Ruth, 3031
Glen, Maxwell, 4164
Glenn, Donna, **2465**
Glenn, John M., 812, 813
Glenn, William E., **2520**
Glueck, Grace, 3322
Glynn, Jeannette E., **1478**
Godber, Joyce, 1829
Godfrey, Howard, **2127**
Godfrey, Nancy, 4651
Goetcheus, Vernon M., 4652
Goheen, Robert F., 814, **1026**
Gold, Joel J., 4016
Gold, Steven D., 815
Goldberg, Gary, 2618
Goldberg, Richard M., 3323, 3324, 3325, 3326
Goldberg, Stephen S., 4165
Golden, Hall, 3327
Golden, Joseph, 2619, 2620
Golden, L.L.L., 1479
Goldenhersh, Randy S., **2128**
Goldin, Milton, 178, 179
Goldstein, Henry, 3535, **3536**, 3537
Goldstein, Richard, 180
Goldstein, Sherry, 3078
Gollin, James, 2129
Gonzales, Rosy B., 3328, 3329
Gonzalez, A. Miren, 181
Gooch, Judith Mirick, **4017**
Goodale, Frances A., **182**
Goodale, Toni K., **3330**
Goodban, Nicholas, 3331
Goodenough, Simon, 816
Goodlad, John I., 4851, 4852
Goodman, Charles, 4853
Goodman, Marcie, **3083**
Goodman, Paul, **183**
Goodman, Walter, 2130
Goodman, Wolfe D., **817**, 1831
Goodspeed, Thomas Wakefield, 184
Goodwin, Angier L., 4378
Goodwin, Michael, 4166
Gordon, Les, 3332
Gorman, James, **818**, 819, 820, **821**
Gorman, Paul, **4525**
Gorman, Richard, 3362
Gormanous, David E., 4297

Gorodezky, Sarah, 4544
Goss, Helen, 2131
Gostin, Larry, 4854
Gotthelf, Nicole, 3333
Gottschalk, Sister Mary Therese, 3334
Gould, Carole, 4167
Gould, Sara K., 2132, 2133
Gould Foundation for Children, Edwin, 642
Goulden, Joseph C., **822**
Government Information Services, **4653**
Gow, J. Steele, 823
Gowen, George W., **4526**
Grace, Kay Sprinkel, 2621
Graff, Linda L., 4527
Graham, David V., 824
Graham, V.L., 3335, 3336
Gramm, Hanns, 825
Grange, George R., II, **4168**
Grant, Andrew J., **3337**
Grant, Daniel, 2134
Grant Foundation, William T., 597
Grantmakers Concerned with Adolescent Pregnancy, **1025**
Grantmakers in Health, 826, 1044
Grants Assistance Center, **1001**
Grants Management Advisory Service, 3251
Grants Resources Library, **827**
Grantsmanship Center, **2135**, 3338, **3339**, 4018, 4031
Grasty, William K., 3340, 3341
Gray, B. Kirkman, 1832, 1833
Gray, David Ross, 4169
Gray, John F., **1834**
Gray, Phil, 4170
Gray, Sandra Trice, **2622**
Greater Cleveland Associated Foundation, 2507
Greater Cleveland Growth Association, 1480, 1480, 1481
Greater Minneapolis Chamber of Commerce, 1482
Greater Minneapolis Council of Churches, **3342**
Greater New York Fund/United Way, 2136, 2640, **2667**
Greater Washington Society of Association Executives, 2137
Greeley, Tamara, 3343
Green, Alan, 2138, **2139**
Green, Florence, 3809
Green, Judith, **112**
Greenberg, Bernard H., 829
Greenberg, Herb, 1483
Greene, Bert, 186
Greene, Wade, 830
Greenhouse, Linda, 3344
Greenleaf, William, **187**
Greenly, Robert B., **4655**
Greenman, D.H., 2623
Greenwood, Linda, **3345**
Greisman, Bernard, 4171
Grennon, Jacqueline, 2140
Grenzebach, John, 3346
Greyser, Stephen A., 2859
Gribble, Roger, 3347

Griffin, Moira, 3348
Grisham, Roy A., Jr., **4656**
Grohman, Robert, 1484
Groman, John E., 3349, 3350, 3351, 3352
Gronbjerg, Kirsten A., **188**, **189**, **2141**, 4657, 4658
Gross, Beatrice, 4659
Gross, Malvern J., Jr., 2541, **2624**, 2625, 2626, 2627, 2628
Gross, Ronald, 4659, 4855
Gross, Susan, 2142, 2629, 2630, **2631**
Grossman, David A., 831, **4660**
Grossman, Susan, **4962**
Groves, Judith L., **2483**
Grubb, David L., 3353
Gruppenhoff, John T., 4172
Gulley, Beverly, 4665
Gunn, Selskar M., 2146
Gunnemann, Jon P., 1674
Gunther, John, 190
Gurin, Maurice G., **191**, 3354, **3355**, **3356**, 3357, 3358
Gurr, Ted, 122
Gutenberg, Jeffrey S., 3359
Gutowski, Michael, 4662, 4678
Guyette, Susan, 2633
Guzman, Carol, **3360**
Guzzardi, Walter, Jr., **832**
Haberek, Judy, 4173
Hacker, Louis Morton, 192
Hackett, Edward J., 2634
Hagerty, Betty Lee, **1485**
Hague Club, **1835**
Haimes, Norma, 2147
Haire, John R., 1486
Haislip, Bryan, 833
Halberstam, David, 193
Hale, Alice M., 3361
Hale, Jim, 3362
Hall, Elizabeth S., **1487**
Hall, Margarete R., 3363
Hall, Mary S., **1488**, **4019**
Hall, Peter Dobkin, **371**, 834, **1489**, **1490**
Hall, Richard B., 2999
Hallahan, Kathleen M., 835, 836, 2148
Haller, Leon, 2635, 2636
Hallett, Stanley, 4856
Hallock, Duane D., 3364
Halperin, Samuel, **4857**
Halstead, D. Kent, 4858, 4859
Hamann, Joan, 4529
Hamburg, David M., 4860
Hamlin, Robert H., **1989**
Hammack, David, **968**
Hammer, Armand, **194**, **3613**
Hammond, J.D., 4861
Hammond, Laurie, **3365**
Hample, Henry S., **2149**
Handel, Beatrice, 2150
Handlin, Mary F., 195
Handlin, Oscar, 195
Hands, A.R., **196**
Hannah, Jacki K., **3366**
Hans, Patricia, **837**, **4020**
Hansell, David A., **4883**, **4884**
Hansler, Daniel F., **2151**, 3367, 3368, **3369**, 3370

AUTHOR INDEX

Hansmann, Henry, 2152, 2153, **2154**, **2155**, 2156, 2637, **3371**, 4174, 4175, 4176, 4177
Hanson, Abel A., 3372
Hanson, Ranae, 3373
Harari, Maurice, 4862
Harder, Paul, 4663, 4664
Hardin, Garrett, **197**
Hardin, John R., 198
Hardin, Paul, 3374
Hardina, Donna, **2162**
Harding, Bertrand M., Jr., 1853
Hardy, James M., **2638**
Harman, John D., **4530**
Harmon, Gail, **4178**
Harnik, Tema Greenleaf, 3375
Harrar, J. George, 199, 4863
Harrell-Bond, B.E., **1836**
Harrington, Howard, 2157
Harrington, Michael, **4864**
Harrington-Kostur, Jill Frances, 838
Harris, April L., **3376**
Harris, Leon, 200
Harris, Louis, 1491
Harris, Virgil M., **3377**
Harris, Virginia, 2158
Harris and Associates, Louis, 4865
Harrison, Randall P., 2639, 3378
Harrison, Shelby Millard, 839
Hart, E.K., 1837
Hart, Elosie B., **840**
Hart, Philip, 2159
Hartford Foundation, John A., 883
Hartford Foundation for Public Giving, 1262
Hartman, Hedy A., **3379**, 3380
Hartogs, Nelly, 2640
Harvey, A. McGehee, **841**
Harvey, George, 201
Harvey, Thomas R., **4038**
Hasson, James K., Jr., **4179**
Hauman, David J., **3381**
Hauser, Crane C., 4180
Hausknecht, Murray, **4531**
Hawkins, Donald E., 3933
Hawkins, Winsome, 4685
Hawley, Karen, 1492
Hay, John Thomas, 1493, 3382
Haycock, Nancy, **2641**
Hayden Foundation, Charles, 842
Hayes, Christopher L., **4021**
Hayes, Helen, **4532**
Hayes, J. Stoddard, Jr., **4421**
Hayes, Susan W., 3383
Haymarket Peoples Fund, 203
Hazen Foundation, Edward W., 425
Heald, Henry T., 843
Heald, Morrell, **1494**
Heale, M.J., **204**, **205**
Healey, Edna, 206
Healey, Judith K., 844, **845**
Heathington, Betty S., 4022
Heaton, William E., Jr., 3384
Hector, Layton Dean, 846
Hedin, Diane, **4503**
Heilbron, Louis H., 2642
Heimann, Fritz, 847

Held, Walter J., 207
Helderman, Leonard C., 208
Hellige, J.R., 3385
Hellwig, Henry, 2160
Helmer, Michael K., 3386
Hemmens, George, **2162**
Henderson, Albert, **2643**
Henderson, Charles R., **4533**
Henderson, Daniel, 210
Henderson, Emily Pfizenmaier, **3387**
Henderson, Hazel, 1495
Henderson, Lyman, 2644
Hendrick, Burton J., 209, 210
Henke, Emerson O., **2645**
Hennessey, Paul, 2646
Hennix, Kenneth L., **3388**
Henry, Susan Regan, 3638
Henry, William A., III, **211**
Henry, Yvette, **212**, **3389**, **3390**
Hensley, Oliver, 4665
Hepner, Betty, 4581
Herbers, John, 1496, 3391
Herfurth, Sharon, **848**
Herold, Patricia, 3392
Herrick, Cheesman A., 213
Herring, Hartwell G., III, 2450
Hersh, Burton, 214, 215
Hertz, Willard J., 3393
Herzlinger, Regina E., **2163**, 2448
Hesburgh, Theodore M., 4867
Hewins, Ralph, 216
Hewitt, Edward Ringwood, 217
Hewlett Foundation, William and Flora, 4839
Heyne, Paul T., 1497
Heyns, Roger W., 218
Heywood, Ann M., 2647
Hickey, James K., **3394**
Hicks, M.E., 3395
Higgins, Paul S., **4907**
Hilgartner, Stephen, 4917
Hilgert, Cecelia, **2164**
Hill, C.P., 1838
Hill, Donna, **1498**
Hill, Frank Pierce, 219
Hill, Kenneth D., 1499
Hill, Sidney B., 849
Hill, William J., 4023
Hillman, Howard, **1500**, 4024, 4025, **4666**
Hilton Foundation, Conrad N., **1202**, 2076
Hirschfield, Ira S., **850**
Hobhouse, Arthur, 851
Hobson, R.L., 3397
Hoch, Charles, **2162**
Hochberg, Lester, 4181
Hodge, Paul, 220
Hodges, Leo C., 3398
Hodgkins, R.C., Jr., 4534
Hodgkinson, Harold L., 4868
Hodgkinson, Virginia A., **221**, **222**, **2165**, **3399**
Hodgson, Richard S., 2648
Hodnett, Edward, 1501
Hodsoll, Frank, 3400
Hodson, H.V., **1839**
Hoelterhoff, Manuela, **3401**
Hoffman, Donald, 4667

Hoffman, William, 223, 2494
Hofstader, Richard, **4535**
Hogg Foundation for Mental Health, 4887
Hogue, Jay, 3918
Hohri, Sasha, **852**
Holck, Manfred, Jr., 3402
Holder, William W., **2649**
Holley, Robert, 2166, 2167
Hollingsworth, Ellen Jane, 1840, **2168**
Hollingsworth, Rogers, 1840, **2168**
Hollis, Ernest Victor, 224, 853
Holloway, George T., **4869**
Holm, Daniel H., **854**
Holman, Louis A., 225
Holton, Felicia Antonelli, **226**
Holtz, Herman, **2650**, 4026, **4668**
Honig, Lisa, 2651, 2652, 2653, 2654, **2655**, 2656, 3403, 3404, 3405, 3406, 3407, 4027
Honsa, Vlasta, **855**
Hooper, Carol A., 3408, 3409
Hopkins, Bruce R., **856**, **857**, **1502**, 2169, 2170, 2171, **2172**, 2173, **3410**, 3411, **3412**, **3413**, 3414, 3415, 4182, 4183, 4184, 4185, **4186**, **4187**, 4188, **4189**, **4190**, **4191**, 4192, 4193, 4194, 4195, 4196, **4197**, 4198
Hopkins, Ellen, 3416
Hopwood, Susan H., **858**
Horan, Jerome C., 3417
Hornfischer, David R., 3418
Horowitz, Daniel, **227**
Horowitz, David, 100, **101**, 3419
Horr, A.R., 859
Horsley, Carter B., 3420
Horwitz, Tem, 2657
Hosmer, Charles Bridgham, 4870
Hostetter, D. Ray, 3421
Houle, Cyril O., 2658
Housing Assistance Council, 4872
Howard, Nathaniel R., 862
Howarth, Shirley Reiff, 1503
Howe, Barbara, 863
Howe, Fisher, 2660
Hoyt, Marilyn, 3437
Hruby, Norbert J., 3438
Huenefeld, John, 2661
Hughes, Anne O., 4013
Hughes, K. Scott, 2987
Hughes, Thomas M., 3439
Huish, Susan, **1478**
Huling, Tracy, 2033
Hull, Robert H., **864**, 865, 866
Hulseman, Bertha F., 867, 868
Human Resources Corporation, 3440
Human Resources Network, 1504, 3441, 3442, 3443
Hummel, Joan, **2662**
Hunt, Avery, **1505**
Hunt, Freeman, **1506**
Hunt, Susan, **3444**, **3873**
Hunter, Bill, 4537
Hunter, Marjorie, 4873
Hunter, Sam, 1507
Hunter, T. Willard, 4199
Huntington, James O.S., 6
Huntley, James Robert, 1841, 1842, 1843
Huntley, Kate, 2174

AUTHOR INDEX

Huntsinger, Jerald E., 3445, 3446, **3447**, **3448**, **3449**, 3450, **3451**
Hurvitz, David J., **1577**
Hurwitz, Ani, 869
Hutchins, Robert Maynard, **870**
Hutchinson, Peter C., 871, **1508**, **1509**
Hutchison, Stanley P., 1510
Hyman, Sidney, 229
Hyndman, Noel, 2175
Iglehart, John K., **872**, **873**
Illinois Neighborhood Development Corporation, 4856
Imberman, Joseph C., 874
Independent Community Consultants, **1512**, 1736
Independent Schools Forum, 3021
Independent Sector, 218, **221**, **222**, 230, **231**, 232, 233, **234**, **235**, 236, 237, **238**, 268, **370**, **501**, **520**, 876, 1513, 1514, **1546**, 1879, 2119, **2178**, **2179**, 2180, 2181, **2182**, **2183**, 2222, **2253**, 2275, **2546**, **2606**, **2607**, **2608**, **2609**, **2610**, **2622**, **2663**, **2664**, **2806**, **2807**, **2809**, **2810**, **2811**, **2812**, **2813**, **2814**, **2815**, **2994**, **3399**, 3454, 3455, 4098, 4123, 4201, 4202, 4203, 4204, 4205, **4206**, 4207, 4419, **4503**, 4538, 4539, **4562**, 4669
Indian Health Service, 877
Information Service of Illinois, 2184
Ingerson, Marshall, 3458
Institute for Educational Affairs, 41, 300, 3460
Institute for Fund Raising, **2646**
Institute for Nonprofit Organization Management, **68**, **476**, 2491
Institute for Nonprofit Organizations, 2665
Institute for Research on the Economics of Taxation, 4426
Institute for Urban Design, 3461
Institute for Voluntary Organizations, 2666
Institute of Donations and Public Affairs Research, 1844
Institute of Policy and Public Affairs, **4577**
Institution for Social and Policy Studies, **24**, 181, 412, **699**, 834, 1492, **1545**, 1553, **1636**, **1716**, 1792, 1825, 1840, 1850, 1851, 1852, 1900, 1903, 1940, 1948, 1949, 2009, 2016, 2025, 2031, 2032, 2054, 2061, 2084, 2092, 2093, 2098, 2113, 2114, **2117**, 2140, 2152, 2153, **2154**, **2155**, 2156, **2168**, 2185, 2188, **2189**, 2197, 2207, 2209, 2224, **2241**, 2242, 2243, 2244, 2245, 2293, **2299**, **2300**, 2310, 2312, 2313, **2314**, 2318, 2319, **2326**, 2327, **2339**, **2350**, 2413, 2414, **2415**, 2416, **2601**, 2637, 2697, **2698**, **2768**, 3202, 3222, **3371**, 3781, 3857, **4085**, **4086**, 4090, 4174, 4175, 4176, 4177, 4212, 4320, 4632, 4644, 4677, 4747, 4828, 4848, 4849, **4850**, 4908, 4909, 4910, 4941, 4942
Interface, **2667**
Internal Revenue Service, 1248, 1249
International Art Alliance, 1503
International Paper Company Foundation, 1519
Interphil, 1845, 1846, 1975

Ireland, Thomas R., 239
Istel, John, 2186
Ittleson Family Foundation, 880
Jablonski, Donna M., 1556
Jackman, Frederic L.R., 881
Jackson, Bruce, **3463**
Jackson, Michael, **2445**
Jacob, M.E.L., **2669**
Jacobs, Brian D., **1848**
Jacobsen, Julia M., **4000**
Jacobsen, Lynn Madera, **882**
Jacobson, Judith S., 883
Jacobson, Robert L., 884
Jacoby, Neil H., 1520
Jacquet, Constant H., Jr., 2187
Jaffee, Larry, **240**, 1521, **1522**, 1849, **3464**, 3465, 3466, **4532**
James, Estelle, 1850, 1851, 1852, 2188, **2189**
James, Marquis, 241
Janetatos, J.P., 1853
Jankowski, Katherine E., **1523**, **1524**, **1525**
Japan Association of Charitable Corporations, **1960**
Japan Center for International Exchange, **1423**, 1529, 1854, **1855**, 1856, 1857, **1858**, **1959**
Japan Hour Association, 1859
Japanese Association of Charitable Corporations, 1860
Jarchow, Merrill E., 244
Jarrell, H. Judith, 885, 4748
Jarrette, Alfred Q., 245
JDR 3rd Fund, 886
Jeffri, Joan, 2670, **3467**
Jellema, William W., 4874
Jencks, Christopher, **2065**
Jenkins, Edward C., 246
Jenkins, Frederick Warren, 247
Jenkins, John Wilbur, 248
Jenkins, Simon, 249
Jenkins, Thomas M., 2190
Jevnikar, Jana, 2671
Joachim, Robert, 3468
Joblove, Leonard, 4212
Jobs Foundation, Steven P., 1682
John Price Jones Company, **54**, 3469
Johnsen, Robert, 3470
Johnson, Alvin, 250
Johnson, Bill, 3471
Johnson, David B., 239
Johnson, Donald J., 1526
Johnson, Dorothy A., 4420
Johnson, Eugene M., **2672**
Johnson, Fenton, 2015
Johnson, Huey D., **4670**
Johnson, Jim, 2191
Johnson, Joseph E., 251
Johnson, Julian, **2192**, 3472
Johnson, Kathryn E., 2193
Johnson, R. Bradley, **2673**
Johnson, Richard R., **2674**
Johnson, Robert Matthews, 252, **253**, 2194, 4875
Johnson, Verne, 3473
Johnson Foundation, Robert Wood, **888**, 4410, 4876

Johnston, David, **889**, **890**, 1527, **1863**, 2217
Johnston, William E., Jr., 4213
Jones, David R., **891**, **2195**, **4877**
Jones, Gareth Stedman, **4878**
Jones, John Price, 254, 255, 256
Jones, Lawrence N., **4879**
Jones, Sylvia W., 892
Jones, Thomas, 2196
Jordan, David Starr, 257
Jordan, Richard G., 3474
Jordan, W.K., 1864, **1865**, 1866, 1867, **1868**, 1869
Joseph, James A., 258, 259, 260, **261**, 893, **894**, 895, 896, **1528**, 1529, **2675**, 4880
Joseph, Samuel, 897
Josephson, Matthew, 262
Josephson, Michael, **2676**
Joyce, Fay S., 4214
Judge, Harry, 4881
Junior League of Fort Worth, **1109**
Junior League of Omaha, 898
Junior League of Phoenix, 899
Kahn, Arnold D., 263
Kahn, C. Harry, 4215
Kahn, E.J., Jr., 264, 265, 266
Kaiser, Leland, 3475
Kaiser Family Foundation, Henry J., **1944**
Kalas, John W., 267
Kalb, Werner, 900
Kalish, Susan Ezell, **4028**
Kaminer, Wendy, **4540**
Kammen, Michael, 268
Kanaly, E. Deane, **901**
Kane, Richard, **1478**
Kanel, David L., 3476
Kansas City Resource Institute, 3477
Kanter, Rosabeth Moss, 2031, 2197, **4882**
Kantonen, T.A., 3478
Karel, Frank, 902
Karl, Barry D., **903**
Karn, G. Neil, 2677, 2678
Karson, Stanley G., 1530
Kashian, Miriam Lynch, 3479
Kass, Stephen L., **4883**, **4884**
Kassman, Deborah N., 3480
Katz, Harvey, 269
Katz, Milton, 904
Katz, Rosalyn B., 4686
Katz, Stanley N., **903**
Katz, Wendy, **3481**
Kauffman, Joseph F., 2679
Kay, Jane Holtz, 1531
Kaye, Jude, **4216**
Keele, Harold M., **905**
Keeling, Guy W., 1873
Keens, Martha R., 906
Keens Company, **2680**
Keeton, George W., 1870, 1871
Keezer, Dexter M., 3482
Keil, Mary, 2070
Keillor, Garrison, **907**
Keller, Anthony S., 4671
Keller, David, **4005**
Keller, Mitchell, 3174, 3483, 3484
Keller, Shirley, 1301
Kelley, B.F., Jr., 3485

AUTHOR INDEX

Kelley, Stephen M., 2681
Kellogg Foundation, W.K., 270, 908, **909**, 950, 4885
Kemeny, John G., 3486
Kempf, Beverly, 3487
Kendall, Elizabeth, 4886
Kennedy, Dan S., 2682
Kennedy, Gail, 271
Kennedy, N. Brent, 3488, 3489
Kennedy, Roger, 1532
Kennedy, Sam J., 3490
Kennedy, Shawn G., 2198
Kennicott, Patrick C., 4029
Kent Archaeological Society, 1864
Keppel, David, 272
Keppel, Frederick Paul, 273, 910
Ketchum, Carlton G., 3491
Kettering, Charles F., 274
Kettering Foundation, Charles F., 4914, 4954, **4975**, 4983
Kidd, Charles V., 4672
Kidd, Harry, 1533
Kidder, Rushworth, 2199
Kieschnik, Michael, 2559
Kiger, Joseph C., **905**, **911**, 2200, 2683
Kilbride, Zeke, **912**
Kilman, Ed, 275
Kilss, Beth, 2432
Kim, D., **3494**
Kimball, Emily Kittle, 4541
Kimmich, Madeleine H., 4634, 4657, 4664, 4680
King, Cornelia S., 276
King, Richard, 2684
King, Willford Isbell, 277
Kingsley, Lawrence A., 4891
Kinkead, Gwen, **2201**
Kinnick, Mary K., 2685
Kipps, Harriet L., 4542
Kiritz, Norton J., 4030, 4031, **4032**
Kirk, Donald J., 2686
Kirk, W. Astor, **2687**
Kirk, William, 1928
Kirkland, Edward C., **81**
Kirkland, Richard I., Jr., **278**
Kirkpatrick, Libby, **3047**
Kirsch, Arthur D., **3399**
Kirschner, Leo, 2688
Kirstein, George G., 279, 280
Kiser, Clyde V., 913
Kish, Rhea K., **2941**
Kisselgoff, Anna, 3495
Kitman, Jamie, 914, 915, 916
Klein, Kim, **1063**, **1534**, **2202**, 2689, 2690, 2691, 3496, 3497, **3498**, **3499**, **3500**, 3501, 3502, **3503**, 3504, **3505**, 3506, 3507, 3508, 3509, 3510, 3511, 3512, 3758
Klein, M. Frances, 4852
Klein, Paul E., 4150
Kleinfield, N.R., 1535
Kleinhenz, Frank, 3513
Klemesrud, Judy, 1536
Klepper, Anne, **1537**, **1538**, **1539**, **1540**
Kletzien, S. Damon, **917**, 1541
Klineberg, Otto, 4887
Klinenberg, Edward L., 3514
Klinman, Debra G., **2203**, **2204**

Kluger, Rona, **1893**
Knauft, E.B., 281, 918, 1542, 1543, 1544, **1545**, **1546**, 1547
Kneerim, Jill, **282**
Knight, Lucy, **4033**
Knoke, David, **4543**
Knowles, Louis L., **283**, 2205, **4888**
Knudsen, Raymond B., 284, 3515
Kobs, Jim, 3516
Koch, Frank, 1548, **1549**
Koch, Robert, 285
Koch, Theodore Wesley, 286
Koestler, Frances A., 2693
Kohler, Robert E., **919**
Kohr, Russell Vernon, 287
Kolderie, Ted, 3473
Koochoo, Elizabeth, 3517
Kopetzky, Samuel J., 920
Koppel, Ted, **921**
Korman, Rochelle, 922
Kornblum, Carole Ritts, **2206**
Koshland, Daniel E., 923
Koskoff, David E., 288
Kotler, John D., 3518
Kotler, Milton, 2072, **3519**
Kotler, Philip, 2694, 2695, 2696
Kotz, Nick, 4889
Kozol, Jonathan, 4890
Kramer, Ralph M., **289**, 2207, 2208, 2209, 2697
Krashinsky, Michael, **2698**
Krasker, William S., **2163**
Krathwohl, David R., **4034**
KRC Development Council, 3060, 3173, 3174, 3226, 3252, 3483, 3484, 3520, 3752, 3893
Krebs, Frederick J., 4473
Kresge Foundation, 924, 925
Kristof, Nicholas D., **1872**
Kristol, Irving, 1550, 1551
Kruger, Myra, 2699
Krummel, D.W., 3521
Kucharsky, David, 4217
Kuhn, Donald M., 3522
Kuller, Lewis H., 4891
Kunen, James L., 926
Kuniholm, Roland, 3523
Kurtz, Daniel L., 927, **2700**, **4237**
Kurtz, Karl T., 815
Kurzig, Carol M., **928**, 3393, 3524
Kusmer, Kenneth L., **2210**
Kutner, Luis, 4218
Kutner, Stephen I., **1716**
Kutz, Myer, 290
Kuznik, Frank, 1552
La Rose, Ronald W., 3525
LaBelle, Judith M., **4883**, **4884**
Labovitz, John R., **4219**
LaFranchi, Howard, 929
Lagemann, Ellen Condliffe, **930**, 931, **932**
Lahn, Seth M., 1553
Lai, Mary L., 2504
Lamb, Charles, 2694
Lambremont, Jane A., **3526**
Lamm, Richard D., 2211
Lamont, Thomas W., 291
Lampman, Robert J., 292

Lampton, William, **2701**, **3527**, 3528
Landau, Thomas, 1873
Landy, Laura, **2702**
Lane, Frederick S., 2703
Lane, Marc J., **4220**
Langevin, Thomas H., 933
Langmead, Stephen, 564
Langton, Stuart, 1554
Lankford, John E., **934**
Lansford, Henry, 935, **4892**
Lant, Jeffrey L., **2704**, **2705**, **3529**, 3530, **3531**, **3532**
Lape, Esther Everett, 4893
Larkin, Richard F., 2706, 2707, 2708, 2709
Larochelle, Wayne, **2710**
Larose, R., 3533
Larson, Gary O., 4673
Larson, Martin A., 2212, 4221
Lasch, Christopher, **293**
Laski, Harold J., **936**
Laskin, William A., 4222
Lasser, J.K., 4120, 4223
Latino Institute, 937, **938**
Lauffer, Armand, **2711**, **3534**, 4544
Laundy, Peter, 2712
Lautman, Kay Partney, 3535, **3536**, 3537
Lavin, Michael R., **1555**
Law and Economics Center, **2055**
Law-Yone, Wendy, 1556
Lawrence, William, 4674
Lawson, Charles E., 3538, 3539
Layton, Daphne Niobe, **294**, 295
Leadership Studies Program, **2607**
Learmont, Carol L., **2213**, 4894
Leat, Diana, **3540**
Leaver, Robert, 2214, 2713
Leavitt, Robert Keith, 3541
LeBarron, Suzanne, 2714
Lecyn, Nancy, 2215
Leduc, Robert F., 3542
Lee, C. Herbert, 942
Lee, James C., 2715
Lee, Lawrence, **3543**
Lee, Thomas Graham, **1558**
Leed, Jean, **3544**
Leeds, Stephen, 4674
Leerburger, Benedict A., 2716
Lefever, Ernest W., 1559
Lefferts, Robert B., 2216, 4035, **4036**
Lefkowitz, Rochelle, 2717
Lehrfeld, William J., 943, 4224, **4225**, 4226, 4227
Lehsmann, Kurt, 1874
Leland, Mickey, 4413
Lemish, Donald L., 3545
Lengsfelder, Peter, **3830**
Lenz, Frank B., 3546
Lenz, Kurt, 3547
Lenzner, Robert, 297
Leonard, E.M., 1875
Leonard, Jennifer, 2217, 3548
Leposky, George, **3630**
Lesko, Matthew, **4676**
Leslie, John W., 3549
Leslie, Larry L., **3550**, 3551
Lester, Robert M., 298, 945
Levene, Victoria E., 2718

AUTHOR INDEX

Levi, Julian H., 3552, 3553, 3554
Levin, Donald, 3555
Levin, Nora Jean, 3556
Levine, Marsha, **1561**, **1562**
Levinson, David, **2719**
Levis, Wilson C., 2720, 3557
Levitan, Donald, 946, **3558**, 3559, **3560**, 3561, 3562
Levitan, Peter A., 2218
Levitt, Paul R., 2025
Levitt, Theodore, **299**
Levitz, Richard, 2568
Levy, Daniel C., 4677, **4895**
Levy, David, 3563
Levy, Marilyn W., 2428
Levy, Reynold, 1563
Levy, Susan M., 1365
Lewin, Ann W., 3564
Lewin, Tamar, 1564
Lewis, Herschell Gordon, 3565, 3566, 3567
Lewis, Jim, 3568
Lewis, Marianna O., 947
Lewis, Salim, 1565
Lewis, Sinclair, 948
Lewis, William, **2219**
Lewthwaite, Gilbert A., 4545
Libbey, Theodore W., Jr., 3569
Lichter, Jonathan M., 4228, **4229**
Lidoff, Lorraine, 2220
Lidstone, Herrick K., 2721, 4230
Liebman, Lance, **1330**
Liebold, Louise Condak, **3571**
Liedtke, Michael, 1566
Liermann, Hans, 1876
Lilley, Robert D., 3572
Lilly Endowment, 4839
Lim, Narzalina Z., 1877
Lincoln, Carol A., **4960**
Lind, Norman G., 3573
Lindeman, Eduard C., 949
Lindquist, Jack, 950
Lindsey, Jonathan A., 2722
Linehan, Jean Dinwoodey, 3574
Liner, Fran, **3575**
Linkow, Peter R., 2723
Lione, Henry V., 3576, 3577
Lipman, Samuel, **3578**
Lipnack, Jessica, 2724
Lippard, Vernon W., 951
Lippert, Paul G., 4678
Lipton, David A., 952
Lissner, Jorgen, 1878
Listro, John P., 2725
Littlejohn, Edward, 300
Littman, C. Arthur, 3579
Littman, Wendy P., **953**
Livingston-Booth, J.D., 1879
Locke, Elizabeth H., **954**
Lockhart-Moss, Eunice J., **301**
Loeser, Herta, 4546
Loessin, Bruce A., **3580**
Lofquist, William A., 2221
Logan, Sheridan A., 955
Logos Associates, **956**, **957**, **958**, **959**, **960**, **961**
Lohmann, Roger A., 2726
Lomask, Milton, 302, 4679

Lomax, John A., 303
London, Mark, 4547
Long, David F., 2773
Long, John Cuthbert, 78
Long, Russell B., 4437
Longstreth, Bevis, 1569
Loo, Shirley, 2727
Lord, Benjamin, **304**, 305, **306**, **963**, **1570**
Lord, James Gregory, 3581, 3582, **3583**
Lord, Walter, 4120
Loth, David, 307
Louis, Arthur M., 308
Love, Jay B., **3584**
Lovelock, Christopher H., **3585**
Low, Murray B., **1571**
Lowell, C. Stanley, 2212, 4221
Lowell, Josephine Shaw, **309**
Lowenstein, Florence M., **1766**
Lubin, Aileen, 2471
Lubove, Roy, **310**, **311**
Lucas, Marilyn, 964
Lucas, Robert A., **4037**, **4038**
Luck, James I., **965**
Luehrs, Karen, 3586
Lukermann, Barbara, 4680
Lukac, George J., 3587
Lundberg, Ferdinand, 312, 313
Luther, Judith, **3588**
Lutheran Church Foundation, 4231
Luttrell, Jordan, 4232
Lutz, Alma, 314
Lydenberg, Steven D., 1572, **1573**
Lyman, Richard W., 966, 2222, **3589**, 4140
Lynch, Frederick, 315
Lynch, Mary Jo, 3590
Lynch, Richard, 4548
Lyndon, Neil, **194**
Lynn, Edward S., 2729
Lynn, Joyce, 3591
Lynn, Robert J., 3592
Lyon, Peter, 316, 317
Lyons, Gene M., **4896**
Lyons, Morgan, **2730**
Maas, Jane, 2731
MacBride, Marie, 2732
MacDonald, Dwight, **967**
MacIntyre, Alasdair, 318
MacIntyre, Kate, 2733
Mack, Edward C., **319**
Mackay-Smith, Anne, 4233
Mackenzie, Donald, 4923
MacKinnon, G., 3593
Mackler, Selma, **1540**
Macko, George S., 2984
MacLatchie, Sharon A., 3038
Macnab, Alexander G., 3594
Macpherson, David, 2734
Maddalena, Lucille A., **2735**
Maddox, David C., **968**
Madlin, Nancy, 4234
Magan, Geralyn Graf, 2223
Magarrell, Jack, 969, 970, 3595, 4235
Magat, Richard, 320, 971, 972, 973, 974, 975, 976
Mager, Robert F., 4039
Mahaffey, J.C., **2736**
Maher, Michael, **4040**

Mahlmann, Diane E., **3950**
Mahoney, Brooke W., 2771
Mahoney, Constance W., **977**
Mai, Charles F., 3596
Majone, Giandomenico, 2224
Makar, Arthur, **3597**
Malaspina, Rick, 978
Malinconico, S. Michael, 2737
Malkiel, Burton G., 1574
Management Assistance Center, **2739**
Management Assistance Group, 2740
Management Research Center, **2742**
Manchester, Jay A., 4236
Mancuso, Anthony, **2743**
Mandel Center for Nonprofit Organizations, **4237**
Mandeville, John, 980
Mangan, Michael, 2225
Mann, Arthur, **322**
Mann, Jim, 4238
Manne, Henry G., 1575
Manpower Demonstration Research Corporation, 4933, 4934
Manser, Gordon, **4549**
Mar, Carolyn, 4373
Marcus, Steven, **4846**
Margolin, Judith B., **981**, 982
Margolis, Richard J., **323**, 983, 984, 985, **2226**, 2744, **4897**, **4898**, 4899
Markoff, John, 2745
Marks, Linda J., **3599**, 3600
Marlin, Alice Tepper, **1573**
Marlowe, Howard, 986, **2227**, 2228, 2746, 4239
Marshall, James J., 4667
Marten, A.W., 987
Martin, Andrew, 2229
Martin, Patrick D., **4334**
Martin, Samuel A., 1880, 1881
Martin, Tom, 3997
Martinez, Arabella, **2230**
Marts, Arnaud Cartwright, 324, 325, 326, 327, **328**
Maryland. Attorney General's Office, **988**
Masaoka, Jan, **2748**
Mason, Bryant S., 3601
Mason, David E., 2749, 2750
Mason, Todd, 1882
Massachusetts. Department of the Attorney General, 989
Massey, Mary Elizabeth, **4550**
Mathews, David, **990**
Mathews, Rick, 4780
Matthei, Chuck, 2231
Matthews, Downs, 1576
Matthews, Fred A., 3603
Mauksch, Mary, 1883
Maurice, Spencer G., 1895
Mauss, Marcel, **329**
Maves, Paul B., 4551
Maxwell, Joan, **330**, 331
May, John Rickard, 991
May, William F., **4901**
Mayberry, Debra J., **1577**
Mayer, Martin, 2232
Mayer, Robert A., 1884, 2233
Mayer, Steven E., **992**

AUTHOR INDEX

Mayer, Susan, **2065**
Mayhew, Lewis B., 993
Mayleas, Ruth, **2234**
Maymudes, Carol S., **4240**
Maynard, Rona, **1885**
Mayrand, Lionel E., Jr., 3604
McAdam, Robert E., **4040**
McAdam, Terry W., **1202, 2235,** 2751, 2752, **2822**
McAndrew, Alice, 4902
McAteer, John F., **4040**
McAuley, John J., 332
McBeath Foundation, Faye, 4903
McBrearty, Bruce R., 3605, 3606, 3607
McCall, David B., 1578
McCallon, Earl, 2544
McCandless, Anthony, 994
McCants, Calvin, 3608
McCarthy, Kathleen D., **333,** 995, **1886, 1887, 1888**
McCarthy, Mary, 996
McCarthy, Thomas R., 3609
McCaskey, Cynthia Gelhard, 2753
McClain, Austin V., 3610
McClanahan, Roger B., **1766**
McClintock, Bruce R., **3611**
McClintock, Norah, **1751**
McCloy, Shelby T., 1889
McConaughey, Paul D., **4656**
McConkey, Dale D., 2754
McCormick, John L., **3611**
McCurdy, William B., 2755
McCurley, Stephen H., 2756, **2757, 3935,** 4552, **4553**
McDonald, Donna, 2236
McDonald, Jean A., **4904**
McDougal, Dennis, 1890
McDowell, Edwin, 4241
McEvilly, C.C., 3612
McFarlane, Ronald, 1967
McGill, Douglas C., **3613**
McGovern, Gail, **3614,** 3615
McGowan, Andrew, 3616
McGrath, Glen, 2237, 2238, 2758, 2759
McGuigan, Catherine, 4681
McGuire, E. Patrick, 1891
McGuire, Jack, 3617
McGuire, William, 997
McIlhany, William H., 998
McIlnay, Dennis P., 4041
McIlquham, John, 2239, 3618
McIntyre, E.J., 3619
McKallip, Jonathan, 3620
McKee, David T., 3621
McKie, James W., 1579
McKinsey Foundation for Management Research, 1611
McLaughlin, David, 3622
McLaughlin, Jeff, 3623
McLean, Sheila Avrin, 1892, **1893,** 1894, 4141
McManis Associates, **999**
McMillen, Wayne, 2240
McMorrow, Michael J., 2760
McMullen, David H., 1895
McNamara, John, 3373
McNamee, Mike, 1580, 2761, **3624**

McPherson, Craig, **1000**
McQuillan, Judith, **1896, 1897,** 1898
McRae, Kendall, **1001, 1002**
Meade, Edward J., Jr., 1003, 1004
Meador, Roy, **4042**
Meadows, Doris, 1581
Medgyesi-Mitschang, Suzanne, **330,** 331
Meeker-Lowry, Susan, **3625**
Megna, Ralph J., 2762
Meister, Albert, **4554**
Melder, Kenneth E., **4555**
Melillo, Joseph V., 2763
Mellon Bank Corporation, **2764**
Mellon Educational and Charitable Trust, A.W., 1005
Memo from Turner, **1899**
Memphis Bureau of Intergovernmental Management, 1006
Menchin, Robert S., 3626
Menninger, Roy W., 1007
Mental Health Association, 4243
Merkowitz, David, 4682
Merrill, Charles E., **334**
Merrill, J.C., 3627
Messier, Edward, **1582**
Messina, William J., 3628
Metropolitan Cultural Alliance, 2765
Metropolitan Life Foundation, 4244
Metropolitan Life Insurance Company, 1583
Mettler, Ruben F., 1584
Metz, Bob, 2713
Metzger, Eric L., 2766
Metzler, Howard C., 3278
Meyer, Dennis, 3629
Meyer, Jack A., 335, **2418**
Mico, Paul R., 2767
Middleton, Melissa, **2241, 2768**
Migdail, Rhonda G., 4245
Milano, Carol, **2219, 2769**
Milbank Memorial Fund, 913
Miles, Matthew B., 4905
Miletich, John J., 1008
Milford, Dale, 4246
Mill, John Stuart, 337
Miller, Ellen S., 794
Miller, Howard S., **338, 4247**
Miller, J. Irwin, 339
Miller, Jay, 1585
Miller, Lisa Farber, **3830**
Miller, Merl, 2963
Miller, Paul A., 4867
Miller, Russell, 340
Miller, William M., **1024**
Miller-Leposky, Rosalie, **3630**
Millett, John D., 3631
Mills, David Bloss, 1009
Mills, Miriam K., 4043
Mills, Wilbur D., 4428
Millsaps, Daniel, 1586, 3633
Milofsky, Carl, 2242, 2243, 2244, 2245
Milter, John R., 2770
Minnesota Council of Nonprofits, **342,** 1010
Minnesota Council on Foundations, 343, 344, **1011**
Mirkin, Howard R., **3634**

Mirvis, Philip H., 2246
Mitchell, Rob, **3635**
Mitchell, Rowland L., Jr., **1012, 1013, 1014, 1015, 1016**
Mitchell, Timothy J., **1760**
Mitiguy, Nancy, **4044**
Mittenthal, Richard A., 2771
Mittenthal, Stephen, **1587, 1588**
Mock, Richard, 4556
Modic, Stanley J., **1589**
Mokwa, Michael P., **2772**
Molitor, Mark, 2576
Molotsky, Irvin, 2247, 3636
Mones, Wayne, 3637
Montana, Patrick J., 2475
Monteath, Douglas, 1978
Montgomery, Kevin, 2791
Montias, J. Michael, 1900
Moody Foundation, 1017
Mooney, Charles D., 3638
Moore, Harry E., **2773**
Moore, Louis, 1018
Moore, R. Keith, **2774**
Moore, Samuel Taylor, 31, 32
Moore, Wilbert E., **2974**
Moran, Irene E., **4045**
Moreau, Arthur J., 3639
Morgan, Dan, 1019
Morison, Robert S., 1020
Morris, Dubois S., Jr., 1590
Morris, Lynn Lyons, 2775, 2776, 2777
Morrisey, M.A., 3640
Morrison, Anne S., 4683
Morrison, Jack, 4906
Morrow, John C., 4046
Morse, F. Bradford, **1591**
Morton, Herbert C., 1592
Moscow, Alvin, 345
Moseley, Jack, **1593**
Moskal, Brian S., 1594
Moskin, William P., **3641**
Moskowitz, Daniel D., 4248, 4249
Moskowitz, Milton, 1595, 1596
Moss, Jane, 2248
Mott Foundation, Charles Stewart, 4621
Mouat, Lucia, 1021
Mudry, Michael, 3644
Mueller, Daniel P., **4907**
Mueller, Robert K., 1597
Mulford, Carolyn, **3645**
Muller, Charles G., 1022
Muller, Leo C., 1023
Muller, Steven, **3646**
Mulligan, Thomas J., **3647**
Mullins, Carolyn J., 4047
Mulloy, Teresa, 4510
Mundel, Jerry, **4032,** 4048
Munro, J. Richard, 4250
Munson, Robert, 3318, 3648
Murnane, Richard J., 4908, 4909, 4910
Murphy, Dennis J., **1599,** 1600
Murphy, E. Jefferson, 1901
Murphy, J. Prentice, 3649
Murphy, James T., 4172
Murphy, Mary Kay, 3650
Murray, Charles A., **346**
Murray, Dennis J., **2778**

AUTHOR INDEX

Murray, George B., 3651
Murray, John P., 4001
Murray, Laurence C., **739**
Murray, Sheila L., **2779**
Murrell, William G., **1024**
Musselwhite, James C., Jr., **2323**, 4634, 4658, 4663, 4685, 4686, 4687
Musto, David F., 4911
Mutual Benefit Life, 4557, 4558
Myers, Helen, 2780
Nader, Ann Marie, 1601
Nagel, Stuart, 3652
Naisbitt, John, 4912
Naples, Nancy, **1025**
Nash, Edward L., 2782
Nash, John, 2783
Nash, Roderick, **112**, **114**
Nason, John W., **1026**, **2784**
Nass, Elyse, **2785**
Natale, Kathryn, **4666**
Natale, Samuel M., 2250
Nathan, Raymond, 4736
National Assembly of National Voluntary Health and Social Welfare Organizations, **2290**, 2324, **2789**
National Association for Hospital Development, 3653
National Association of Accountants, 2605
National Association of Attorneys General, 4253, 4254
National Association of Broadcasters, 3654
National Association of Small Business Investment Companies, 4913
National Bureau of Economic Research, **131**, 292, 1604
National Catholic Development Conference, 2786, 3328, 3329, 3655
National Center for Charitable Statistics, **2252**, **2253**
National Center for Neighborhood Development, **2917**
National Center for Neighborhood Enterprise, 3656
National Center for the Control of Rape, 3657
National Center for Voluntary Action, 1302
National Chamber Foundation, **1602**
National Charities Information Bureau, **347**, 2254
National Clearinghouse for Primary Care Information, 2255
National Clearinghouse on Domestic Violence, 4688
National Commission of the Reform of Secondary Education, 4914
National Committee for Responsive Philanthropy, 348, 1027, **1028**, 1029, 3658, **3659**, 4097
National Committee on Community Foundations, 1030
National Conference on Solicitations, 3660
National Council for Resource Development, 3661
National Council of the Churches of Christ in the U.S.A., 3662, 3663, 3664
National Council of Welfare, 2787

National Council on Community Foundations, 1030, 1032, 1033
National Council on Philanthropy, 349, 1448, 2056, 2788, 4285
National Council on Social Service, 1909
National Endowment for the Arts, **1939**, **2508**, **2556**, 3032, **4608**, 4609, 4650, **4689**, 4690, 4691, 4692, 4693, **4694**, 4695, 4696, 4744
National Endowment for the Arts. Research Division, 4697
National Endowment for the Humanities, 4698, **4699**, **4700**, 4701
National Exchange Club, 3665
National Forum on Volunteerism, 4559
National Health Council, **2789**, 4702
National Industrial Conference Board, 1728, 1978
National Information Bureau, 2256, 2257, **2790**, 4256
National Institute of Mental Health, 4703
National Institutes of Health, 1247
National Network of Grantmakers, **852**
National Puerto Rican Coalition, **350**, 4416
National Recreation and Park Association, 3013
National Rural Center, 1203, 2258
National School Volunteer Program, 1603
National Science Foundation, 4704, 4705, 4706, **4707**, 4708, 4709, 4709, 4710, 4711, 4712, 4915
National Society of Fund Raising Executives, **3666**, 3667, 3668, **3669**
National Trust for Historic Preservation, 2259, 4916
National Wildlife Federation, **3670**
National Youth Work Alliance, 4713
Navaretta, Cynthia, **2260**, **2261**
Nebolsine, George, 1902
Neddermeyer, Dorothy M., 2791
Nee, David M., **1036**
Needham, Roger A., 4257
Neef, Marian, 3652
Negovetic, Neal, 3671
Neighborhood Development Collaborative, 2263
Nelkin, Dorothy, 4917
Nelson, Donald T., 3804
Nelson, Ralph L., 351, 1037, 1038, 1039, 1604
Nemy, Enid, **4258**
Nesbitt, Susan, 4787
Netzel, Paul A., 3673
Netzer, Dick, 4714
Neuber, Keith A., 2793
Neuberger, Egon, 1903
Neuhaus, Richard John, **4489**
Neuhoff, Klaus, 1040, 1904, 1905, 1906, 1907, **1908**, 1909
Nevin, David, 4918
Nevins, Allan, 352, **353**
New England Foundation for the Arts, 2264
New Hampshire. Office of the Attorney General, **1042**
New Jersey. Committee for the Humanities, 4715, 4716, 4717

New Jersey. Department of Community Affairs, 4718
New School for Social Research. Center for New York City Affairs, 3675
New World Foundation, **1043**
New York City. Commission on the Status of Women, **2265**
New York City. Mayor's Advisory Commission for Cultural Affairs, 4719
New York City. Task Force on the Exemption of Non-Profit Organizations from Real Property Tax, 4260
New York Community Trust, 1397, 2266, 2267
New York. Council for the Humanities, 4720, 4721, 4722
New York. Council on the Arts, **4723**, 4724
New York. Department of Education, 4725
New York. Department of Social Welfare, 3677
New York Management Center, 4643
New York Public Library, **2268**
New York Regional Association of Grantmakers, 1044, **1045**
New York. Senate. Special Committee on the Culture Industry, 4726
New York University, 1325, 2269, 2375
New York University. Department of Government, 122
New York University Institute on Federal Taxation, 4261
New York University School of Continuing Education and Extension Services, 1046, 1047, 1048, 1049
Newberry, J.O., 354
Newlin, Larry, 3678
Newman, Danny, 3679
Newman, Peter C., 355
Newstead, Stuart, 4908
Newton, Walter L., 3680
Nicholas, Ted, 2270, 3681
Nichols, Dan, **4919**
Nichols, David A., 3682
Nichols, Judith E., **3683**
Nichols, Susan K., **3684**
Nichols, Vera, **4727**
Nickerson, Anne, 2794
Nielsen, Waldemar A., **357**, 358, **1050**, **1051**
Nielson, Richard P., 3685, 4262
Nightingale, Benedict, 1910
Nigosian, Gregory, 2957
Ninkovich, Frank A., **1911**
Nixon, Hargrave, Devans and Doyle, 4264, **4265**
Noble, David F., 1607
Noe, Lee, **1052**
Nolan, Richard L., 1608
Nonprofit Management Association, **2479**, 2796, 2797, 2798, 2799, **2800**
Nonprofit Sector Project, 2322, 4657, **4660**, 4664, 4680, 4685, 4686, 4687, 4763
Norback, Judith, **3689**
Nordhoff, Nancy S., 2802
Norris, Joan, 1053
North, Halsey, 3690

AUTHOR INDEX

Northeast-Midwest Institute, 4682, 4729
Northern California Grantmakers, 738, **1054**, **1055**, 1056, **1057**
Norton, Alice, 2803
Norton, Michael, 359, **1609**, **1912**, **1913**, **1914**, **2804**
Nova Institute, 831
Novotney, Jerrold M., 4852, **4975**
Noyes, Katherine H., **4515**
Nygren, Terry, 3691
O'Connell, Brian, **362**, **371**, 2275, 2275, **2276**, **2805**, **2806**, **2807**, **2808**, **2809**, **2810**, **2811**, **2812**, **2813**, **2814**, **2815**, 4207, **4267**, 4268, 4419, **4560**, 4561
O'Connell, Merrilyn Rogers, 2857
O'Connor, Harvey, 363
O'Donnell, Suzanna, **1063**
O'Grady, John, 365
O'Hare, Michael, 4832
O'Kelly, Elizabeth, 1915
O'Neill, Joseph P., **1614**
O'Neill, June A., 3696
O'Neill, Michael, **2822**
O'Rourke, Helen L., 3697
O'Toole, Patricia, 367
Oates, James F., Jr., 1611
Oates, Marylouise, 361
Oberdorfer, Louis F., 4266
Odell, Richard, 2277
Odendahl, Teresa Jean, **1058**, **1059**, 1060, **1061**, **1062**, 3692
Ogg, Frederic Austin, 4921
Ohio. Attorney General's Office, **1064**
Ohio. Department of Mental Health and Mental Retardation, 4049
Olasky, Marvin N., **366**, **1612**, 1613
Olcott, William, **2278**
Oleck, Howard, **4269**, **4270**
Olenick, Arnold J., **2816**, 2817, **2818**, **3693**
Olenick, Philip R., **2816**
Oliver, Nancy S., **4168**
Olsen, Thomas L., 2819
Olson, Jon B., 3694
Olson, Lynn, **1065**
Olson, Paul M., **2820**
Olson, Stan, **1066**, **1067**
Orfield, Gary, **4730**
Organization Management, 4272, 4273, 4274, 4275, 4276, 4277, 4278, 4279, 4280
Orlans, Harold, 2280
Ott, J. Steven, **2823**
Ottinger, Richard, 1068
Outlaw, Bill, 3698
Owen, Barbara L., **4562**
Owen, David, **1916**
Owen, Virginia Lee, 3699
Pace, C. Robert, 4922
Pace, Frank, Jr., 4593
Padberg, Ann M., 3700
Paley, Martin A., 1069
Paley, William S., 368
Pallenik, Michael, **2825**
Palmer, John L., 4731
Palmer, Stacy E., 2281
Palmieri, Victor H., 1615
Panas, Jerold, **3701**, **3702**
Park, Jane Mallory, 4563

Parker, David B., 1895
Parker, Franklin, **369**
Parker, Gary, **3703**
Parson, Mary Jean, 2826
Pasquariello, Ronald D., 4281
Pate Poste, **673**
Paton, G. Jeffery, 3704
Patrick, Kenneth G., 1616
Patterson, Ben, 1917
Pattillo, Manning M., Jr., 1070, 1071, 4923
Paul, R. Dana, 2283
Pavel, Uwe, 1906, 1909
Pavoni, M.M., **3705**
Payton, Robert L., **370**, **371**, **372**, **1617**
Peale, Norman Vincent, 324
Pear, Robert, 4924
Pearson, Henry G., **2827**
Peat, Marwick, Mitchell and Company, **2041**, **2284**, 2828, 2829, 4282, 4283
Pederson, Johannes, 1918
Pederson, Kim, **1001**, **1002**
Peebles, Marvin L., 2830
Peers, Alexandra, 4233
Peirce, Neal R., **2285**
Pellegrene, John E., 1618
Pendleton, Niel, 3706
Penfield, Wilder, 373
Penick, George, 1072
Penney Company, J.C., 374
Pennock, J. Roland, **4564**
Performing Arts Referral Service, **3710**
Perry, Lewis, 375
Perry, Nancy J., **1619**
Perry, Suzanne, 1620
Pessen, Edward, **376**
Petersen, Eleanor P., 377
Peterson, Eric, 2287, 2288
Peterson, Peter G., 1073, 4285
Peterson, Virginia M., 2831, 2832, 2833
Petranek, Jan G., **3712**
Pew Charitable Trusts, 580, **733**, **2390**
Peyser, Ethel, 378
Pfeffer, Arthur, **4005**
Pfizenmaier, Emily, 3713
Phalen, Dale, 379
Phariss, Brother, 3714
Phelps, Edmund S., **380**
Phelps-Stokes Fund, 3715
Philadelphia Volunteer Lawyers for the Arts, 4286
Philanthropic Resource Associates, **1106**
Philanthropy Project, **342**, **390**, **391**
Phillips, H.M., 1919
Phillips, Ken, 3716
Phillips, Michael, 3717
Phillips, Stephanie, 3718
Philpott, Gordon M., 383
Physicians' Services Incorporated Foundation, 680
Pickslay, F. Frith, Jr., 1621
Picton, Russell R., **3611**
Pierce, Catherine, 3719
Pierce, Lyman L., 3720
Pierce, Milt, 3721
Pierson, John, 384, **1075**
Pifer, Alan, 385, **386**, 692, 1076, **1077**, **1078**, 1079, 4925

Pipines, Pamela, 2289
Pires, Shelia A., **2290**
Pitman, Walter G., **1920**
Piton Foundation, **1080**
Pittman, Karen, 4662
Piven, Frances Fox, **4926**
Platt, Philip S., 2146
Platzer, Linda Cardillo, **1622**
Plawin, Paul, 387
Playboy Foundation, 1081
Plinio, Alex J., 388, 1082, 1623, **1624**, 1625, 1626, 1627, 1628, 1629, 1630, **1631**, **1632**, 1633, 2291, **2292**, 3724, 4565
Plocher, David, **4091**
Podesta, Aldo C., 1634
Pokrass, Richard J., **1635**
Polivy, Deborah K., **1636**, 2293, 3725
Pollard, John A., 1637, 3726
Pomey, Michel, 1921
Poole, Mary D., 3727
Pope, Jerilyn D., **1487**
Porter, Robert A., 1638, 3728, 3729, 3730, 3731
Portnoy, Fern C., **2294**
Porto, Linda, 1639, 4927
Posch, Robert J., Jr., **2835**, 3732, 3733
Potter, Roberto Hugh, **2295**
Pottlitzer, Joanne, **4928**
Potts, Judith A., 3172
Poummit, Morris R., 3735
Pound, Arthur, 31, 32
Poutas, Bernice J., 2836
Powell, Daniel, 1083
Powell, Horace B., 389
Powell, Luther P., 2296
Powell, Walter W., 2084, **2297**
Powell Family Foundation, 4425
Powers, Charles W., 1674, 2837
Powers, Linda L., **1760**
Powills, S., 1640
Powledge, Fred, 583
Practising Law Institute, 1266, 1267, **2298**, 2838, 4257, 4287
Pratt, George, 3736
Pratt, Jon, 390, **391**
Pray, Francis C., **3737**
President's Task Force on Private Sector Initiatives, 1641, **1642**, 1643, 4566
Presidential Task Force on the Arts and Humanities, 4733
Preston, Anne E., **2299**, **2300**
Price, Don K., 1084
Price Waterhouse, 1085, 2839, 2840, 2841, 4288, 4289
Prideaux, Tom, 392
Prieve, E. Arthur, 2772
Pritchard, J. Harris, **3739**
Pritchett, Henry Smith, 1087, 3740
Prochaska, F.K., **393**
Procter, Arthur W., 3742
Proffitt, Stuart, 3743
Program Information Associates, **3745**
Program on Non-Profit Organizations, 24, 181, 412, **699**, 834, 1492, **1545**, 1553, **1636**, **1716**, 1792, 1825, 1840, 1850, 1851, 1852, 1900, 1903, 1940, 1948, 1949, 2009, 2016, 2025, 2031, 2032,

AUTHOR INDEX

2054, 2061, 2084, 2092, 2093, 2098, 2113, 2114, **2117**, 2140, 2152, 2153, **2154**, **2155**, 2156, **2168**, 2185, 2188, **2189**, 2197, 2207, 2209, 2224, **2241**, 2242, 2243, 2244, 2245, 2272, 2293, **2299**, **2300**, 2310, 2312, 2313, **2314**, 2318, 2319, **2326**, 2327, **2339**, **2350**, 2413, 2414, **2415**, 2416, **2601**, 2637, 2697, **2698**, **2768**, 3202, 3222, **3371**, 3781, 3857, **4085**, **4086**, 4090, 4174, 4175, 4176, 4177, 4212, 4320, 4632, 4644, 4677, 4747, 4828, 4848, 4849, **4850**, 4908, 4909, 4910, 4941, 4942
Project Share, 1645, 4734
Prussing, Eugene E., 394
Public Interest Public Relations, **2303**
Public Management Institute, **1322**, **1647**, **1648**, **1649**, 1650, **1651**, **1923**, 1924, **1925**, **1926**, **2616**, 2843, 2844, 2845, **2846**, **2847**, 2848, 2849, 2850, **2851**, **2852**, **3152**, **3746**, **3747**, 3748, 3749, 3750, **3836**, 4006
Public Media Center, **1091**
Public Relations Society of America, 395
Public Service Materials Center, 1092, 1093, **1428**, 1634, **1652**, 1653, 3204, **3206**, **3207**, 3378, **3634**, 4012, 4631
Pulling, Lisa, 3752
Purcell, David, 3753
Purcell, Elizabeth F., 951
Putsch, Henry E., 2304
Putt, S. Gorley, 1094
Pyle, Kathryn, **4930**, **4931**
Quigg, H. Gerald, **3755**
Quinn, Jane Bryant, 396
Quinn, William A., 521
Rabby, Rami, 2853
Radcliffe, R.L., 3756
Radford, Neil A., 1095
Radock, Michael, 1096, 2854
Rados, David L., **2855**
Rainey, Jeanette J., **1828**
Rainsbury, Colin, 1927
Raley, Nancy, 4932
Ramey, Gaile, 1097, 3758
Ramey, Garey W., 3551
Rand Corporation, 2856, 4623
Rankin, Deborah, 3759, 4294
Rankin, Watson S., 397
Rath, Frederick L., Jr., 2857
Rathmell, John M., 2858
Rauner, Judy, **2928**
Raushenbush, Esther, 1098
Raybin, Arthur D., **3761**
Raymond, Louis, 3762
Raymond, Thomas J.C., 2859
Read, Patricia E., **1099**, **1100**
Read, W. Harold, 1101
Reardon, Thomas J., 2605
Reckard, Edgar C., 398
Reed, Edward Bliss, 1102
Reed, Steve, 3764
Reed, Susan K., 1103
Rees, David Morgan, 2860
Reeves, Thomas C., **1104**, **1105**
Regional Young Adult Project, **1684**
Register, Levon C., 4297

Reid, Alan, 1928
Reid, Dee, **1106**
Reilly, Raymond R., 1107
Reilly, Robert T., 1108
Reilly, Timothy A., **3766**
Reiner, Thomas A., 2305, **2407**
Reinert, Richard L., **2508**
Reinhold, Robert, 1654
Reisig, Edwin, 2861
Reiss, Alvin H., 1655, 2862, **3767**, **3768**, **3769**, 3770, 3771, **3772**
Reiter, Susan, 2306
Remsen, Daniel S., 400
Renfroe, Elton, **3773**
Reuter, Carol J., 1656
Revlon Foundation, 475
Revson, Charles, 475
Rexnord Resource Center, 4568
Rhees, William J., 401
Rhodes, Catherine, **1109**
Ricci, Carla W., 4050
Ricci, Edmund, 4581
Riccio, James A., 4933, 4934
Rich, Abby D., 4735
Rich, Richard C., **4569**
Rich, Wilmer Shields, 603
Richards, Bill, 1657
Richards, Charles R., 4935
Richardson, Carol, **1110**
Richardson Foundation, Sid W., **407**
Richman, Harold, **2348**
Richman, Saul, 1111, 1112, **1113**, 1114, 1115, 1116, **1117**, 1118, 1119, 1120, 1121, 1122, 1123, 1124
Richmond, Mary E., **403**, **404**
Rickard, Al, 2307
Riecker, Ranny, **4301**
Rieker, Patricia P., 1209
Riessman, Frank, 2121
Riggan, John, **1658**
Riley, Margaret, **1125**, **1126**
Rimel, Rebecca W., 580
Rimor, Mordechai, **405**
Ripmaster, Terence, 2289
Robb, Christina, 406, 1127
Robbins, Walter A., Jr., 2450
Robbins, Williams, 3775
Roberts, David R., 1129
Robertson, D.B., **4570**
Robertson, Gail, **4936**
Robertson, Mark, **4302**
Robertson, William, 1932
Robinson, Anthony L., **1130**
Robinson, Daniel D., 2480, **2863**, 2864, **2865**, 3776
Robinson, James D., III, 4303
Robinson, Marshall, 1131, 4937
Rockefeller, David, **407**, 1477
Rockefeller, John D., **408**
Rockefeller, John D., Jr., 409, 3777
Rockefeller, John D., III, **410**, 2308
Rockefeller Brothers Fund, **520**, 2309, 4781
Rockefeller Foundation, 766, 1132, 1133, 1919, 4863, 4938
Rockefeller Foundation, Winthrop, 1659
Rockwell, John, 411, 1660
Roderick, David M., 1661

Roel, Raymond, 3778, 3779, **3780**, **4939**
Roelofs, Joan, **1134**
Rogers, David E., **1135**, 4410
Rogers, James F., 4940
Roisman, Lois, 1136, **1137**, 1138
Romo, Frank, 2245
Ronen, Simcha, 2866
Rooks, Charles S., 1139
Roper Organization, **347**
Rose-Ackerman, Susan, 412, **2189**, 2310, **2311**, 2312, 2313, **2314**, 3781, 4941, 4942
Rosebush, James S., **1662**
Rosen, Michael, 3782
Rosenbaum, Nelson, 2315, 2316, 2317
Rosenberg, Charles E., 4943
Rosenbloom, H. David, 1569
Rosenwald, Julius, **1140**, 1141
Ross, Irwin, 413
Ross, Percy, 414
Rossi, Richard, **4000**
Rosso, Hank, 3783
Rotenberg, Marc, 2867, 3784
Rothman, David J., **309**, **415**, **416**, **491**, **4846**, **4944**
Rothman, Iris, 3784
Rothmeyer, Karen, 1143
Rothschild, Michael L., 3785
Rottenberg, Dan, **417**, 418, **419**, 420, 421
Rowland, A. Westley, 3786
Rowntree, Joseph, 1933
Rubacky, Tricia, **3787**
Rubin, Mary, **3788**
Rubinstein, Gwen, **4304**
Ruble, R.J., 2721
Ruder, William, 4736
Rudney, Gabriel, **24**, 422, 2318, 2319, 3202, **4085**, **4086**, 4305
Rudy, William H., 1144
Ruffner, Robert H., **2868**
Rule, Sheila, 423
Ruml, Beardsley, 1663
Runquist, Lisa A., 2869
Ruof, Peter, **1934**
Rushton, William J., III, 1664
Rusk, Dean, 1145
Russell, Bertrand, 424
Russell, Charles A., 425
Russell, John M., 1146
Russell and Associates, Robert, 1147
Russell-Wood, A.J.R., **1935**
Rust, Brian, 3789
Ryan, D., 3790
Ryan, J. Patrick, **1936**
Ryan, John S., **3208**, 3791, 3792, **3793**
Ryan, Mary P., **4571**
Ryan, Pat, 426
Ryerson, Edward L., **1665**
Saasta, Timothy, 48, 581, 3071, 3794
Sabath, Donald, 1148
Saccomandi, Patrick, 2870, 4572
Sage Foundation, Russell, 247, **380**, 427, 538, **541**, 839, 867, 868, **1470**, 1604, 2683, 4088, 4896
Sager, Don, 2871
Sakayue, Beverly, 2872
Salamon, Lester M., **1149**, 2320, **2321**, 2322, **2323**, 4123, 4306, **4603**, 4657,

4658, **4660**, 4662, 4663, 4664, 4678, 4680, 4685, 4686, **4737**, 4738, **4739**, 4740, 4945
Salewic, Marge, **1666**, **1667**
Salkind, Milton, 1150
Salmans, Sandra, 1668
Saltzman, Jack, **428**
Salvatore, Tony, 2325
Salzman, Ruth, 3795
Sammer, Joanne M., **3796**
Samuel, Sigmond, 429
San Francisco Foundation, 804
Sandberg, J. Robert, **3797**
Sanden, B. Kenneth, 4307
Sander, Joelle H., **2203**, **2204**
Sander, John R., **2873**
Sanders, Joseph, 2874
Sanders, Lawrence, 1152
Sanders, Michael I., 4308
Sanders, Ralph W., 3798
Sanderson, Glen R., 4309
Sandison, Hamish R., 4310
Sandler, Bernice Resnick, 1153
Sanfilippo, Janet, 3943
Santoro, Elaine, 3799
Sarnoff, Paul, 430
Sasek, Joseph A., 3800
Satterlee, Herbert, 431
Saunders, Lauren K., 4687
Savage, Howard J., **1154**
Savage, Joseph G., 3801
Savage, Thomas J., **2875**, 2876
Sawhill, Isabel V., 4731
Sawyer, Willits H., 3802
Scanlan, Eugene A., **1155**, **4051**, 4946
Scanlan, Joanne B., **1155**, **1156**, **1632**
Schachter, Esther R., **4151**, 4152
Schafran, Lynn Hecht, 1157
Schardt, Arlie, 976, 1158, 1159, 2877
Schatz, Barbara A., **4311**
Scheiber, Jodie, **4741**
Scheier, Ivan H., **4573**
Scheir, Wendy, **2878**
Schell, John, 4052
Schelling, Corinna S., **1330**
Schick, Frank L., **4947**
Schiff, Jerald, **2326**, 4312
Schiller, Theo, 1937
Schiller, Zachary, **1669**
Schilling, Barbara H., **2879**, 4373
Schindler-Rainman, Eva, 2880, **4574**, 4575
Schlabach, Theron F., **4948**
Schlenger, Jacques T., **4331**
Schlesinger, Arthur M., **4576**
Schlesinger, Bob, 1160, 1161
Schmidt, Frances, 2881
Schnabel, Teresa, **1938**
Schneider, Robert F., 2882
Schneiter, Paul H., **3803**, 3804
Schooler, Dean, 2884
Schrage, Michael, **1162**
Schreiner, Samuel Jonathan, 2885
Schreyer, R. Blair, 3806
Schroder, Spense, 2886
Schruers, Fred, **432**
Schubert, Richard F., 4424
Schuck, Arthur A., 3742

Schuettinger, Robert L., 1559
Schulman, Kary, **2889**
Schulte, Linda S., 3807
Schultz, Louis Arthur, **3808**
Schultz, Phillip Stephen, 186
Schultz, Whitt N., 2887
Schumacher, Jon L., **4334**
Schurz Memorial Foundation, Carl, 825
Schuster, J. Mark Davidson, **1939**, 1940, 4832
Schutzer, George J., 2327
Schutzman, Harold, 2328
Schuyler, Mark J., **2785**
Schwartz, John B., 2888
Schwartz, John J., **433**, 1163, 4313
Schwartz and Associates, Robert, 344
Schwarzhaupt Foundation, Emil, 1239
Scott, Anne Firor, **4577**
Scott, Austin Wakeman, 4314
Scribner, Susan, 3809
Scrivner, Gary N., 1164
Scully, Malcolm G., 1165, 3810
Sears, Jesse Brundage, 436
Seay, J. David, 437
Seeley, John R., 438
Seipp, Catherine R., 4578
Selby, Cecily Cannan, 2329
Seligson, Wendy P., **4311**
Seltzer, Michael, 679, **1167**, 2073, **3812**, 3888, **4949**
Semple, Robert F., 3813
Sennett, Richard, **4950**
Setterberg, Fred, **2889**
Seybold, Geneva, 1671
Seybold, Peter J., 1168
Seymour, Harold James, 3815, 3816
Shabecoff, Alice, **2331**, **2890**
Shabecoff, Philip, 2332
Shackford, Kate, 2433
Shafritz, Jay M., **2823**
Shafroth, Tracey, **3132**
Shakely, Jack, 1169, 4951
Shanahan, Eileen, 1170, 1171
Shanahan, Thomazine, 4579
Shannon, James P., 4417, 4422
Shapek, Raymond A., 4053, 4054
Shapiro, Arnold F., **4861**
Shapiro, Harold T., 439
Shapiro, Harvey D., 1172
Shapiro, Leo J., 1672
Shaplen, Ropert, 1173
Sharpe, Robert F., 440, **3817**, 3818, 3819
Shatzkin, Leonard, 4952
Shay, Philip W., 2891
Shea, Albert A., 1941
Sheerin, Mira J., **3820**, 3821
Sheinkopf, Kenneth G., 3340, 3341
Shelby, Richard, 4408
Sheldon, K. Scott, 3318, 3822, 3823
Shellow, Jill, **1174**
Shenon, Philip, 4580
Shepard, Carla, 1175
Shepard, David S., **4953**
Sheppard, William E., 3824
Sheridan, Philip G., 3825
Sherlock, John F., 2333
Sherman, Linda, 2157

Shiman, David A., 4954
Shimer, John C., 3826
Shirley, Anita Gunn, **1176**
Shirley, Bill, **3827**
Shore, Harvey, 2892
Shore, Lys Ann, 2334
Shorrock, John B., **1942**, 4317
Shreckengast, Earl K., 3828
Shribman, David, 4318
Shuman, Philip Joel, **1673**
Sidler, Mark P., 2893, 2894
Siegel, Barry, 4742
Silberstein, Richard, 441
Silha, Stephen, **442**
Sillars, Edith E., 1178
Silverman, Myrna, 4581
Silverman, Paul H., 3829
Simes, Lewis M., 4319
Simmons, Adele, 4955
Simmons, Nicole, 2335
Simon, John G., 1674, 4320
Simonetti, Carol G., **4930**, **4931**, 4956
Simons, Gustave, 1179
Simons, Robin, **3830**
Simonse, Arnold B., 2895
Simpson, Carol, **3831**
Simpson, Janice C., **4321**
Simsar, Muhammed Ahmed, 1943
Sinclair, James P., **4055**
Sinclair, Michael R., **1944**, **1945**, **1946**
Sirkin, Michael S., 2896
Skadder, Donald H., 1107
Skelly, Jerome P. Walsh, **857**
Skloot, Edward, 2336, **2337**, **2897**
Skousen, Mark, 4323
Skovgard, Robert O., 3832
Slade, Margot, 443
Sladek, Frea E., 2338, 2898, 3833
Sligar, James S., 4324
Sloan Commission on Government and Higher Education, 4957, 4958
Sloan Foundation, Alfred P., **2822**, 4839, 4957, 4958
Sloane, Leonard, 4325
Slocombe, Walter B., 4376
Sloss, Frank, 1180
Smith, Becky, 3834
Smith, Brian H., 1948, 1949, **2339**
Smith, Bruce L.R., 2317, **4743**
Smith, Constance, **4582**
Smith, Craig, **1181**, **1182**, **1675**, **1765**, **1950**, 2899, 3835, **3836**, 4959
Smith, Datus C., Jr., 1183
Smith, David Horton, 3837, **4583**, 4584
Smith, G. Stevenson, **2340**
Smith, Geddes, 796
Smith, Hayden W., **1676**, **1677**
Smith, Herman B., 2854
Smith, Nick L., 1184
Smith, Norvel L., 1185
Smith, R.C., **4960**
Smith, S.L., 444
Smith, Sally Bedell, 1678
Smith, Thomas M., **4326**
Smith, Virginia Carter, 3838, 4961
Smith, William H., 4327
Smith Charities, 719

AUTHOR INDEX

Smolar, Boris, **4328**
Smollar, David, **1186**
Snedcof, Harold F., 3839
Snydle, Carol L., 2900
Social Service Planning Corporation, **1187**, 1188
Society for Nonprofit Organizations, 2341
Solomon, Amy, 2343
Solomon, Stephen L., **3842**
Solow, Carol, 1189
Solyn, Paul, 3843
Somerville, Bill, **1951**, 4056, 4057
Sommers, David, 2344
Sontag, Sherry, 3844
Soroker, Gerald S., 3845
Sosin, Michael R., **4962**
Soukup, David J., **3846**
Soulis, Jean-Jacques, 1952
South Dakota State Library, **1191**
Southeastern Council of Foundations, 865, **866**, 1139, **4179**
Southeastern/Atlantic Regional Medical Library Services, **3526**
Southern California Association for Philanthropy, **1192**, **2345**
Southern Educational Communications Association, 69
Southern Regional Education Board, 3847, 4874
Southern Resource Center, 1193
Southwest Foundations Conference, 4963
Spangenberg, Gail, 4788
Sparks, D. Martin, 3848
Spear, Nathaniel, III, 1954
Spear, Paula Reading, **1194**
Special Libraries Association, 2901
Speeter, Greg, 2346, **4329**
Spiegel, Hans B.C., **4964**
Spinney, William R., 3850
Spivack, Sydney Shepard, 1195
Squires, C., 3851
Staecker, Delmar, **1196**, **2347**
Stagner, Matthew, **2348**
Stamp, Tom, **1197**
Stamps, Jeffrey, 2724
Stanfield, John H., **445**
Stanford, E. Percil, 2101
Stanford, Sheila, **3852**
Stanford Center for Chicano Research, **1198**
Staniforth, Sydney D., **1199**
Stanley, Edmund A., Jr., 446
Stark, Ken, 2283
Starrett, Agnes Lynch, 1200, 1201
Stehle, Vince, **448**
Steigler, Janet Dempsey, 3556
Stein, Eugene L., 2898, 3833, 4058, **4059**
Stein, Malcolm L., 4181, 4409
Stein, Marilyn A., 3856
Stein, Sharman, **2349**
Steinbach, Carol F., **2285**
Steinbach, Sheldon Elliott, 3553, 3554
Steinberg, Richard, **2350**, 3857
Steinbock, Elmer L., 2504
Steiner, Richard, **4060**
Steiner, Robert O., **1202**
Steinmann, Frederick, 4331

Steinwurtzel, Samuel L., 4332, 4333
Stephan, George N., 3858
Stephens, Barbara, 1203
Sterling, John C., **4585**
Stern, Adam, 1682
Stern, Phillip M., 1683
Stern, Sue S., **4334**
Sternberg, Sam, **526**, **1684**
Sterne, Larry, 449, **450**, **1685**, **2351**, **3859**
Stevens, Louise K., **2508**
Stevens, Susan Kenny, **2902**
Stevenson, J. John, 2352, 2903, 3860, 3861, 3862, 3863, 3864, **4335**, **4336**
Stevenson, Richard, 1686
Steward, Edwin E., 3865, 3866, 3867
Stewart, Ann L., 4061
Stewart, Rodney D., 4061
Stewart, Susan Stern, **4337**
Stickler, Robert, 1687
Stidley, Leonard Albert, 451
Stifterverband fur die Deutsche Wissenschaft, 1955
Stiles, B.J., 1204
Stinchcomb, Lawrence S., 3869
Stinnett, Lee, **452**
Stokes, Bruce, **4586**
Stokley, James, 140
Stone, Gregory B., 3870
Stone, Julita Martinez, 4587
Stone, Peter H., 1205
Stopp, G. Harry, Jr., **3871**
Straight, Michael, 4744
Strand, Bobbie J., 3872, **3873**
Stratton, Debra J., 4338
Stratton, John, 4052
Strawhecker, Paul, 3875
Street, Wolcott D., 2354
Streich, Mary Deane, **1206**
Stringer, G.E., **2904**
Stromberg, Ann, 1957
Strub, Sean O'Brien, **1573**
Struckhoff, Eugene C., **1207**, **1208**
Stubbs, Weslie S., 4961
Sturges, Kenneth, 1688
Suchman, Edward A., **1209**
Sugarman, Norman A., 4102, 4339, 4340, 4341, **4374**
Suhrke, Henry C., **454**, **455**, 456, 457, **1210**, 1211, 1212, 1213, 1958, **2355**, **2356**, 2357, **2358**, 2359, **2360**, **2361**, **2906**, 2907, 3876, 3877, 3878, 3879, 3880, 3881, **3882**, 4344, 4345, 4346, **4347**, 4745, 4965
Sullivan, Catherine, **1058**
Sullivan, Daniel J., **3883**
Sullivan, John, 2362
Sullivan, Walter, 458
Sumariwalla, Russy D., 1689, 1690, 2363, 2364, 3884
Sutton, Francis X., **1214**
Swanson, Andrew P., 2908, 2909
Sweeney, Tim, 3888
Swords, Peter, **4237**, **4349**
Szigethy, Zoltan, **460**
Taft, J. Richard, 1215, 2910, 3054, 3055, 3889, 3890, 3891

Taft Group, **2492**, 2911, 2947, **3260**, **3381**, **3389**, 3517
Talese, Gay, 461
Talley, Olive, 2913
Tanaka, Minoru **1959**, **1960**
Taper, Bernard, 4966
Tapper, Donna, 4746
Tarnacki, Duane L., **1217**
Task Force on Community-Based Development, 4967
Task Force on Funding of the Arts, **1961**
Tatum, Liston, 3892, 3893
Tax Institute of America, 4351
Taylor, Alfred H., Jr., 4062
Taylor, Bernard P., 462, 3894
Taylor, Eleanor K., 1218
Taylor, James B., 2914
Taylor, James H., **1219**, **1220**, **1221**, **1222**
Taylor, Janet C., **4423**
Taylor, John D., 1223
Taylor, Karla, 1693, 2365, 2366
Taylor, Lauren, 3895
Taylor, Martha A., **3896**
Taylor, Shirley H., 4589
Taylor, William L., **4730**
Teague, Gerald V., 4022
Tebbel, John, 463
Technical Assistance Center, 2367, 3897
Technical Assistance Information Clearing House, 1962, 1963, 1964
Technical Assistance Study Group, 2915
Teitelbaum, Fred, 4945
Teitell, Conrad, 3898, 4357, 4358, 4359, 4360, **4361**, 4362, **4363**, 4364, 4365, 4366, 4367, 4479
Teltsch, Kathleen, 464, **465**, 466, **1224**, 1225, 1226, **1227**, 1228, 1229, 1230, 1231, 1232, 1233, 1234, 1235, 1694, 1695, 1696, 1697, 1965, **1966**, 2368, 3899, 3900, 3901, 3902, 3903, 4368, 4369, 4968, 4969
Temme, Jim, 2369
Tempkin, Terrie, 3904
Tenbrunsel, Thomas W., **3906**
Tetlock, Philip, 181
Tett, Norman, 1967
Theatre Communications Group, 2370, 4970, **4971**
Theatre Development Fund, 2733
Thennes, Mark A., **2917**
Third Sector Press, 2918
Thom, Helen Hopkins, 468
Thomas, James, 155
Thomas, Patricia, **866**
Thomas, Ralph Lingo, 1699
Thomas, Susan, 2919
Thompson, Hugh L., 3907
Thompson, Jacqueline, 469
Thompson, Joan W., 2729
Thompson, Kenneth W., **470**, 1968
Thompson, Lynn Stanley, **2920**
Thompson, Robert L., 3908, 3909, **4370**
Thompson, Robert W., **1750**
Thompson, Thomas Kirkland, 1969
Threatt, Jane R., 4972
Throndike, Joseph J., Jr., 471
Thurston, Henry W., **4973**

AUTHOR INDEX

Tidd, Jonathan G., 4371, 4372
Tileston, Mary Wilder, 473
Timm, Paul R., 2921
Timpane, Michael, 1701
Titmuss, Richard M., **474**
Tivnan, Edward, 1238, 3910
Tjerandsen, Carl, 1239
Tober, James A., 4747
Tobias, Andrew, 475
Tobin, David, 3470
Tobin, Gary A., **405**, **4590**
Tolan, David J., 3911
Toland, Michelle R., 1702
Tolchin, Martin, 2372
Tonai, Rosalyn Miyoko, **476**
Topinka, James E., 4373
Topor, Robert S., **2922**
Torres, Millie, 4416
Totten, Jeff, **2923**
Touche Ross and Company, 2924
Townsend, Ted H., 1240
Trachtman, Roberta, **1561**
Traska, M.R., 3913, 3914
Trattner, Walter I., **478**, **4974**
Traub, James, 1241, 2925
Treasch, Harold T., 4591
Trenbeth, Richard P., **2926**
Trench, Alan S., 1242
Treusch, Paul E., **4374**
Tricarico, MaryAnn, **2927**
Tromble, William W., 3915
Trompeter, Jean E., 4375
Trost, Arty, **2928**
Troxler, G. William, 4748
Troy, Kathryn, 1704, **1705**, **1706**, **1707**
Troyer, Thomas A., 1245, 2375, **2929**, 4376
Tschop, Carol A., 3916
Tsu, Yu-Yue, 1970
Tueller, Alden B., **3917**
Tunks, L.K., 603
Ture, Norman B., 4426
Turgel, Stuart C., 479
Turk, Frederick J., **2930**
Turner, Judith Axler, 1708, 1709, 2376
Turner, Toni, 3918
Twentieth Century Fund, **1050**, **2012**, 2232, 2395, 3919, 4955
Twin Cities Regenerative Funding Project, **2377**, 2378
Tye, Judy, **1110**
Tye, Kenneth A., **4975**
Tyler, Alice Felt, **481**
UCLA Law Review, 4159
Udvarhelyi, Elspeth, 2932
Unger, Craig, **482**
Unger, Walter J., 4976
United Nations Fund for Population Activities, 1971
United Negro College Fund, 4430
United States Chamber of Commerce, **1710**
United States Conference of Mayors, 4377
United States. Congress. House, 4378, 4379, 4380, 4381, 4382, 4383, 4384, 4385, 4386, 4387, 4388
United States. Congress. House. Committee of Conference, 4389

United States. Congress. House. Committee of Foreign Aid, 4749
United States. Congress. House. Committee on Banking and Currency, 4391, 4392
United States. Congress. House. Committee on Banking and Currency. Subcommittee on Domestic Finance, 4390
United States. Congress. House. Committee on Finance, 4393
United States. Congress. House. Committee on Government Operations. Subcommittee on Commerce, Consumer and Monetary Affairs, 4394
United States. Congress. House. Committee on Ways and Means, 4097, 4395, 4396, 4397, 4398, 4399, 4400, 4401, 4402, **4403**, 4404, 4405, 4406
United States. Congress. House. Committee on Ways and Means. Subcommittee on Oversight, 4407, 4408, 4409, 4410, 4411, 4412, 4413, 4414, 4415, 4416, 4417, **4418**, 4419, 4420, 4421, 4422, 4423, 4424, 4425, 4426, 4427, 4428, 4429, 4430
United States. Congress. House. Select Committee on Small Business, 4431
United States. Congress. House. Select Committee on Small Business. Subcommittee No. 1, 4432
United States. Congress. Joint Committee on Internal Revenue Taxation, 4433
United States. Congress. Joint Committee on Taxation, 4434, **4435**
United States. Congress. Senate, 4436
United States. Congress. Senate. Committee on Finance, 4437, 4438, 4439, 4440, 4441, 4442, 4443, 4444, 4445, 4446, 4447, 4448, 4449, 4450
United States. Congress. Senate. Committee on Finance. Subcommittee on Foundations, 4451, 4452
United States. Congress. Senate. Committee on Industrial Relations, 4750, 4751
United States. Congress. Senate. Committee on Interstate and Foreign Commerce, 4453
United States. Congress. Senate. Committee on Labor and Public Welfare. Special Subcommittee on Arts and Humanities, 4752, 4753
United States. Congress. Senate. Committee on Labor and Public Welfare. Subcommittee on Children and Youth, 3921
United States. Congress. Senate. Committee on Labor and Public Welfare. Subcommittee on Employment, Manpower, and Poverty, 4454
United States. Congress. Senate. Committee on the Judiciary, 2933
United States. Department of Agriculture, 4612

United States. Department of Agriculture. Office of Rural Development Policy, **3922**
United States. Department of Commerce, 1711, 1712
United States. Department of Education, 4754, **4755**
United States. Department of Health and Human Services, 1246, 2934
United States. Department of Health and Human Services. Administration on Aging, 4756
United States. Department of Health, Education and Welfare, 1247, 4757, 4758, **4759**
United States. Department of Housing and Urban Development, 3923
United States. Department of State. Agency for International Development. Advisory Committee on Voluntary Foreign Aid, 1972
United States. Department of the Treasury, 4455
United States. Department of the Treasury. Internal Revenue Service, 1248, 1249, 4456, 4457, 4458, 4459, 4460, 4461, 4462, 4463, **4464**
United States. General Accounting Office, 1250
United States Human Resources Corporation, 1251
United States-Japan Foundation, 1973
United States Jaycees Foundation, 2379
United States. Joint Economic Committee, 4760
United States. Office of Management and Budget, **4761**, **4762**
United States. Small Business Administration, 2380
United Way Institute, **234**, 236, 351, **2178**
United Way of America, 351, 483, **484**, 1513, 1600, **1713**, **1714**, **2673**, **2789**, 2935, **2936**, 2937, 2938, 3658, 4465, 4466
United Way of Chicago, 3132, 3270
United Way of Delaware, **1252**
University of Pennsylvania. School of Public and Urban Policy, 485, 486
Upshur, Carole C., **2382**, 2939, 3924, 3925
Ural, Engin, 1974
Urban Institute, **2141**, 2321, 2322, **2323**, 2397, **2418**, 4123, 4467, **4603**, 4626, 4634, 4657, 4658, **4660**, 4662, 4663, 4664, 4678, 4680, 4685, 4686, 4687, 4731, **4737**, **4738**, **4739**, 4763
Urban Land Institute, 3839
Urell, Emmet J., 487
Urrows, Henry, 4468
Urseny, Laura, 1715
Useem, Michael, **1716**, **1717**, **1718**, **1719**
Valentine, Michael J., 3927
Vallance, Karla, 1253
Vallely, Paul, **173**
van Hoorn, J., Jr., 1975
Van Houten, Stephen, **2213**, 4894
van Patten, Betty, 3929
van Rotterdam, Ingrid, **1752**
Van Slyke, Judy K., 2383

AUTHOR INDEX

Van Til, Jon, **4592**
Vance, Mary, 3561
Vandegriff Research, 2384
Vanderleest, Henry W., 1720
Vanguard Public Foundation, 1254
Vecchitto, Daniel W., 3930, 3931
Ver Schave, Sally, **2386**
Verdery, John D., 3932
Verhoven, Peter J., 3933
Verity, C. William, Jr., 1721, 4593
Vermilion, Mark, 1682
Vidal, David, 3934
Vidich, Arthur J., 4977
Vignelli, Massimo, 2712
Villarejo, Don, 2940
Vineyard, Sue, **2757**, **3935**
Vinken, Horst, 1905
Vinson, Elizabeth A., 3936
Vinter, Robert D., **2941**
Virginia Law Review, 952
Viscusi, Margo, **1255**, **1256**
Vizza, Cynthia, **4594**
Vogel, David, **1327**
Vogel, Frederic B., **2942**
Vogel, Lynn Harold, 2943, 2944
Vogt, Jay W., 2945
Volkmann, M. Fredric, 2946
Volunteer Lawyers for the Arts, **2387**, 2721, **2878**, **4469**
Volunteer-The National Center, 1722, 2388, 2947, 4595
Volunteers in Technical Assistance, 4063
von Eckhardt, Wolf, 4853
von Humboldt Foundation, Alexander, 1257
Vorsanger, Fred S., 3552
Wacht, Richard F., **2948**
Wachtell, Ester, 2949
Waddilove, Lewis E., 1976
Wadsworth, Homer C., 1258
Wagner, Ken, 3938
Wahl, Peter, 3547
Waldo, Charles N., **2950**
Walker, Robert L., **3939**
Walker, Tom, 4470
Walko, Donald R., 2951
Wall, David, 1977
Wall, Joseph Frazier, **488**, 489
Wall, Wendy L., 1723
Wallace, Debrah L., 3518
Wallen, Denise, **1259**
Wallich, Henry C., 1575
Wallis, W. Allen, 1724
Walsh, Elsa, 1260
Walsh, Lee G., 3940
Walters, Jonathan, 2389
Walzer, Sarah E., 4682
Ward, F. Champion, 4978
Ward, Haskell G., **2390**
Ward, Sue, **2952**
Wark, John, **2391**
Warner, Alice Sizer, 4597
Warner, Amos G., 490
Warner, Irving R., 3941
Warren, David L., 4598
Warren, Donald I., **4979**
Warren, Paul B., 3942

Warshauer, William, Jr., **2624**, 2953
Washington Consulting Group, 2379
Washington International Arts Letter, **1451**
Washington Researchers, 1556, **1725**, 1726
Washington (State). Office of Attorney General, **1261**
Waterfall, Wallace, 4821
Waters, R.C., 3943
Watkins, Beverly T., 1727
Watkins, Clyde P., **3944**
Watkins, Roger, 4599
Watson, Frank Dekker, **491**
Watson, John E., 1783
Watson, John H., III, 1728, 1729, 1730, 1978
Wattel, Harold L., 4600
Wattenberger, James L., 3945
Waxman, Julia, 732
Weaver, Glenn, 1262
Weaver, Warren, 493, 494, **1263**
Webb, Charles H., 3946
Webb, Missy, **1264**
Weber, John, 2954
Weber, Joseph, 2640
Weber, Nathan, 4980
Weber, Suzanne, 2392
Weber, William, 2392
Webster, C.R., 1979
Webster, Frederick E., Jr., 2955
Webster, George D., 4473
Webster, Philip J., **1731**
Weger, Christine D., **3219**, **3220**, **3221**
Weigel, George, **495**
Weil, Henry, **1265**
Weiman, Liz M., 496
Weinberg, Charles B., **3585**
Weinberger, Jane, 3947
Weiner, Andrew, 1980
Weiner, Harold N., **3948**
Weinhold, Dick, 3949
Weinstein, Amy, **4764**
Weinstein, Julia, **1945**
Weisbrod, Burton A., **1732**, 4312
Weiss, David M., **3950**
Weiss, Ellen, **4240**
Weiss, Nancy, 2956, **3951**
Weiss, Philip, 497
Weithorn, Stanley S., 1266, 1267, 4474
Weitz, Patricia, **3689**
Weitzman, Jerrold, 2393
Weitzman, Murray S., 422, 2319, **3399**
Welch, Randy, 2394
Welch, Susan, 2113
Welles, Chris, 1268, 2395
Wellford, Harrison, **4475**
Wellisz, Christopher, 3952, 3953
Wells, James A., **1269**, 3954
Wells, Joseph P., **1270**
Wertheimer, Stephen, **1428**
West, Ruth, 1981
Westenberg, Robert W., 4064
Western States Shelter Network, 3955
Weyerhaeuser Foundation, **1587**, 1601, 2931
Weymouth, Lally, 498
Wharton, Clifton R., Jr., 4867
Wheeler, Sessions S., 499

Whelan, Donald J., 3956
Whelan, Sidney S., Jr., **1272**
Whisler, Thomas, 2957
Whitaker, Ben, **500**, **1275**
Whitaker, Fred A., 2958
Whitcomb, Nike B., 2984
White, Arthur H., **501**
White, Benjamin T., **1735**
White, Michelle J., 2397
White, Mike, 1736
White, Virginia P., **3957**, **3958**
White, William S., 1276
White House Conference on Aging, 4982
Whitehead, Ralph, Jr., 3959
Whitley, Frank V., 3960
Whitney, Barbara T., **1737**
Whitney, Elizabeth, 2959
Whitney, J.J., 3961
Whitney, Thomas T., 1277
Whitney Foundation, John Hay, 1083, 1098
Whittemore, Henry, 502
Wiebe, Robert H., **504**
Wieboldt, Linda D., 3962
Wiederhold, Johannes, 1982
Wiehe, Vernon R., 2960
Wild, Peggy, 4589
Wilder Foundation, Amherst H., 244, **2399**, **4907**
Wilding, Suzanne, **1278**
Wilker, Lawrence J., 3963
Willard, Timothy J., **3964**
Williams, E. Morgan, 505
Williams, Edward F., 506
Williams, Guynell, **1279**
Williams, J.M., 2961
Williams, Jennifer, 4310
Williams, M. Jane, 3965, 3966, **3967**, 3968, 3969
Williams, Pierce, 1738
Williams, Richard C., 4983
Williams, Robert R., 1280
Williams, Roger M., **507**, **508**, **1281**, **1282**, **1283**, 1284, 1285, 1286, **1287**, **1983**, 1984, **2400**, 2401, **2402**, 2403, 3970, **3971**
Williamson, J. Peter, 4477
Williamson, Jim, 2962, 3972
Willis, Jerry, 2963
Willmer, Wesley Kenneth, 2964, **3973**
Wilsnack, Dorie, 1288
Wilson, C., 3974
Wilson, Emily Herring, **1289**
Wilson, Eugene R., 1739, **1740**
Wilson, Jane, **2404**
Wilson, John F., 4984
Wilson, John L., **1221**, **1222**
Wilson, Leslie L., **2483**, **2965**
Wilson, Marlene, 2966
Wilson, Philip Whitwell, 509
Wilson, Thomas Frederick, 50
Wilson, Winthrop B., 510
Wilson Foundation, Woodrow, 307
Wineman, Steven, 2405
Wing, William G., 511
Winkler, John K., 512, 513
Winston Foundation for World Peace, **2406**
Wintner, Linda, 1741

AUTHOR INDEX

Wisconsin (Milwaukee County) Circuit Court, 1290
Wisconsin Corporate Philanthropy, 1458
Wishik, Debra Englander, 4602
Withey, Stephen B., 4985
Witt, J.A., 3976
WNET/Thirteen, **514**
Wogan, Thomas F., 3977
Wohlstetter, Charles, 300
Wolf, Thomas, **2967**, 2968
Wolfers, Elsie E., 2969
Wolling, Frank J., 1291
Wolpert, Julian, **2305**, **2407**
Women and Foundations/Corporate Philanthropy, **1025**, 1153, 1157, **1292**, 4986, 4987, 4988
Women's Action Alliance, 2133
Women's Technical Assistance Project, **1985**, **3981**
Wood, Carolyn R., 4989
Wood, J.B., 3982
Wood, James R., **4543**
Wood, Leonard A., 3983
Wood, Struthers and Company, 2970
Woodroof, Bob, 3984
Woodroofe, Kathleen, **515**
Woods, Robert A., **6**
Woolf, Burton I., 2971
Wooster, James W., Jr., 516
Wormser, Rene A., 1293, 4478
Worth, Janice M., 3985
Worth, Michael J., **3986**
Worthy, James C., 1672
Wright, John M., 1294
Wright, Theon, 275
Wrolstad, Marwin, 2408, 2409, 2410
Wunderman, Lester, 3987
Wyllie, Irvin G., 517, **518**, 519
Yale Studies on Nonprofit Organizations, **2557**, **4895**
Yale University, **24**, 181, 412, **699**, 834, 1448, 1492, **1545**, 1553, **1636**, **1716**, 1792, 1825, 1840, 1850, 1851, 1852, 1900, 1903, 1940, 1948, 1949, 2009, 2016, 2025, 2031, 2032, 2054, 2061, 2084, 2092, 2093, 2098, 2113, 2114, **2117**, 2140, 2152, 2153, **2154**, **2155**, 2156, **2168**, 2185, 2188, **2189**, 2197, 2207, 2209, 2224, **2241**, 2242, 2243, 2244, 2245, 2293, **2299**, **2300**, 2310, 2312, 2313, **2314**, 2318, 2319, **2326**, 2327, **2339**, **2350**, 2413, 2414, **2415**, 2416, **2601**, 2637, 2697, **2698**, **2768**, 3202, 3222, **3371**, 3781, 3857, **4085**, **4086**, 4090, 4174, 4175, 4176, 4177, 4212, 4320, 4632, 4644, 4677, 4747, 4828, 4848, 4849, **4850**, 4908, 4909, 4910, 4941, 4942
Yale University Press, **2297**
Yankelovich, Daniel, 4990, 4991
Yankelovich, Skelly and White, **501**, **520**
Yankelovich Group, Daniel, **1742**
Yanowitz, Alan J., 2972, 3988
Yengst, Nancy L., 3989
Yohalem, Daniel, 4108
Young, Clarence H., 521
Young, David W., 2973
Young, Dennis R., **2411**, **2412**, 2413, 2414, **2415**, **2822**
Young, Donald R., 2974
Young, Joyce, **3990**
Young, Micki Jo, 2158
Youth Project, 2975
Yung, Betty, 1295
Yunker, Katherine K., 2416
Yzaguirre, Raul, 1743
Zald, Mayer N., **2417**
Zalkind, Ronald, 3991
Zaltman, Gerald, 2976
Zanibbi, Louis R., **2126**
Zedlewski, Sheila, **2418**
Zehring, John William, 2977
Zesch, Lindy, **2419**
Zien, Laurel, **3992**
Zilg, Gerard Colby, 522
Ziller, Lilibet, 754
Zimmerman, A.A., 1986, 1987
Zimmerman, Caroline, 3362
Zimmerman, Dennis, 4480
Zisholtz-Herzog, Ellen, 2688
Zonana, Victor F., **1744**
Zuboff, Shoshanah, 1296
Zuer, Robert J., **3993**
Zuercher, Andrea, **1269**
Zurcher, Arnold, **2978**, 2979
Zwick, David R., 3353
Zwingle, J.L., 1297, 2980
392, 493, 1258, **2906**, 3880, 4835, 4899, 492

TITLE INDEX

Citations refer to entry number, not page number. Numbers in bold type indicate abstracted bibliographic entries.

"The ABC's of Educational Foundations", 638
"The ABC's of Making a Will", 3898
About Foundations: How to Find the Facts You Need to Get a Grant, **981**, 982
Abram S. Hewitt, with Some Account of Peter Cooper, 352
"Abuse and Fraud Said to Threaten Matching Gifts: Companies Accuse Colleges of Laundering Contributions", 3210
Accent on Philanthropy, 8
"Accountability and Ethics: A Priority for All Fund Raisers", **4869**
"Accountability: Ask Your Stakeholders", **1508**
"Accountability in Nonprofit Public Relations", 2082
Accountability with Independence: Toward a Balance in Government/Independent Sector Financial Partnerships, 4669
Accounting and Financial Reporting: A Guide for United Ways and Not-for-Profit Human Service Organizations, 2935
Accounting and Reporting Practices of Private Fundations: A Critical Evaluation, 2925
Accounting for Culture: A Primer for Non-Accountants, 2765
Accounting for Nonprofit Organizations, 2951
Accounting Principles and Reporting Practices for Certain Nonprofit Organizations: A Discussion of the More Important Provisions of the AICPA Statement of Position, 2422
"Accounting: The University View", 1101
"Accurate, Thorough Research Nets Bigger Prospect Dollars: Effective Research Is a Key to More Effective Fund Raising", 3050
"Achieving Quality in Nonprofits", **2603**
"Acquiring Foundation Funds for Health-Related Projects", 3223
Across the Busy Years: Recollections and Reflections, 71
Activists Guide to Religious Funders: Leveraging God's Resources from Her Representatives on Earth. A Working Model, **3200**
Activities of Japanese Nonprofit Organizations in Southeast Asia, 1854
"Ad Agency Helps Non-Profit Become Self-Sufficient", 3987

"Adding Creativity to Public Relations: You Can Do It!", 3555
"Adding It Up", **3067**
"Adding the Human Dimension", **818**
Additional Views of Angier L. Goodwin, 4378
"Administration Rejects Overhaul of 1969 Tax Act", 4068
Admissibility in Evidence of Microfilm Records, 4264
"Advantages of a Community Foundation", 3198
Adventure in Giving: The Story of the General Education Board, 765
"The Adventurous Angels", 316
"Advice and Consent: Before You Hire a PR Consultant, Learn Whether You Need One, Where to Look for One, and What You Can Expect One to Do", 2774
"Advise and Invest", **563**
"Advisory Boards: No Miracle Solution", 2689
Advocacy Is Sometimes an Agency's Best Service: Opportunities and Limits within Federal Law, 4201
"Aetna's National Urban Revitalization Program Investments Reach $15 Million", 1299
"Afro-American Studies Here to Stay, Ford Foundation Report Says", 4823
After the Emergence: Voluntary Support and the Building of American Research Universities, 4848
After Virtue: A Study in Moral Theory, 318
The Age of Reform: From Bryan to F.D.R., **4535**
Agencies for Project Assistance: Sources of Support for Small Church Sponsored Projects in Africa, Asia, Latin America and the Pacific, **1757**
An Agenda for Research on Fund Raising, 3107
"Agent Requires Voluntary Responsibility from Athletes", **3464**
"Agreeing to Disagree", 971
The AIA Story: Two Decades of International Cooperation, 1786
"The AICPA Discussion Draft for Nonprofit Organizations", 2725
Aid and Self-Help: A General Guide to Overseas Aid, 1915
Aide de Fondations aux Universites Americaines (Foundation aid to American universities), 3110

AIDS: An Update for Grantmakers, **523**
"AIDS and the American Health Polity: The History and Prospects of a Crisis of Authority", 4843
"AIDS and the Limits of Insurability", 4861
The AIDS Crisis: Challenges and Opportunities for Grantmakers, 1044
AIDS Funding: A Guide to Giving by Foundations and Charitable Organizations, **621**
"AIDS: Giving Soars for Medical Care, Public Health: Foundation in Lead", **4768**
AIDS Health Services Program, **888**
"AIDS: How a Problem Became a Priority", 1204
"AIDS, Power, and Reason", 4782
Aids to Corporate Support of Higher Education, 1404
Alabama Foundation Directory, **573**
Alcoholism Funding Service: A Directory of Federal, State and Foundation Grants for Alcohol Education, Prevention and Treatment Services, **3219**
Alfred I. Du Pont: The Family Rebel, 241
Alfred P. Sloan Jr., Philanthropist, 493
All Aboard the Grantsmanship: A Bibliography on Government and Proposal Writing, 3997
The All Givers Charitable Deduction, 4357
All in Order: Information Systems for the Arts, 2511
"All in the Family (Well, Mostly)", **1281**
The Alliance Handbook, 1991
Allocations: One Approach, Many Questions, 2034
Alma Mater, 592
"Alternative Funds Emerge As Force in Charitable Campaigns", 2988
Alternative Futures and Human Development: Challenges for the Southwest, 4963
Alternative Investing in Community Development, **2890**
Alternative Investment Strategies for Institutions. Conference Proceedings, **647**
"Alternative Investments: Helping Communities the Old Fashioned Way", **2205**
Alternative Schools, 4890
Alternative Work Schedules: Selecting, Implementing, and Evaluating, 2866
Altruism, Morality and Economic Theory, **380**

TITLE INDEX

"Altruism's Own Rewards", 252
Am I Covered for? A Guide to Insurance for Nonprofit Organizations, 2504
Ambition: The Secret Passion, 145
"America Responds to AIDS", 4772
"An American Abroad", 507
The American As Reformer, 4576
The American Association of Fund-Raising Counsel, Inc.: Its First Thirty Years, 1994
American Business and the Public School: Case Studies of Corporate Involvement in Public Education, 1561
"American Business Provides $506 Million to Arts Organizations in 1982", 1997
"American Cancer Society's Market Planning Process", 3367
American Charities: A Study in Philanthropy and Economics, 490
"American Corporations Contribute Record Amount to Charities", 1303
"American Express Expands 'Cause' Related Marketing Program", 1304
American Firms in Foreign Countries, 1305
American Foundations: A Study of Their Role in the Child Welfare Movement, 623
American Foundations for Social Welfare, 839, 867, 868
The American Giver: A Review of American Generosity, 254
American Giving in the Field of Higher Education, 2998
American Graduate Schools of Education: A View from Abroad, 4881
The American Graduate Student: A Normative Description, 4819
American Grantmaking in South Africa: A Conference Report, 1944
American Heroine: The Life and Legend of Jane Addams, 118
American Learned Societies, 2200
American Philanthropy, 56
American Philanthropy: A Guide for South Africans, 1945
American Philanthropy Abroad: A History, 1785
"American Philanthropy and the National Character", 111
American Philanthropy for Higher Education, 54
American Philanthropy in the Near East, 1820-1960, 1787
American Philanthropy, 1731-1860, 276
American Private Higher Education in Comparative Perspective, 4849
The American Private Philanthropic Foundation and the Public Sphere, 1890-1930, 903
American Sociology, 4977
American Statistical Meeting. Statistics of Income and Related Administrative Record Research: Selected Papers, 2432
An American Transplant: The Rockefeller Foundation and Peking Union Medical College, 1768
American Universities and Federal Research, 4672
"The American Way of Giving", 2363

"American Way of Giving: Inside the World of Charity. Part 2", 26
American Welfare, 122
Americans and the Arts, 1984, 1998
"Americans Giving More: Even If Not Enough", 1021
Americans Volunteer, 1981, 4538
"America's Best-Run Charities", 2201
"America's Centimillionaires", 308
America's Hidden Philanthropic Wealth: Tomorrow's Potential Foundation Giants, 304
America's Most Successful Fund Raising Letters, 3204
America's Newest Foundations, 963
America's Shame, America's Hope: Twelve Million Youth at Risk, 4960
America's Sixty Families, 312
America's Voluntary Spirit: A Book of Readings, 4560
"America's Wealth and the Future of Foundations", 1058
America's Wealthiest People: Their Philanthropic and Nonprofit Affiliations, 305
America's Wealthy and the Future of Foundations, 1059
Amerikanische Stiftungen; Organisation, Kapitalverhaltnisse und Arbeitsweise (American foundations; their organization, financial relations, and modes of operation), 1040
Amherst H. Wilder and His Enduring Legacy to St. Paul, 244
"Among Volunteers, Change in the Suburbs", 4492
The Amount of Total Personal Giving in the United States, 1948-1982 with Projections to 1985, 351
"Analysis and Testing of Acquisition Mailings", 3481
Analysis and Text of the Tax Reform Act of 1976. 2 Vols, 4076
An Analysis of Charitable Contributions by Upper-Income Households for 1986 and 1987, 2994
An Analysis of North Carolina Foundations, 1189
An Analysis of Southern California Charitable Giving: 1986 Member Survey, 13
Analysis of the Economic Recovery Program's Direct Significance for Philanthropic and Voluntary Organizations and the People They Serve, 230
(Analysis of) the Tax Reform Act of 1969, 4150
An Analysis of Trends of the Financial Support by Philanthropic Foundations to General Programs in U.S. Higher Education, 1955-1970, 117
"Analysts Say Cuts in Aid Hurt Young", 4968
"Analyzing Foundations' Leadership and Decision-Making", 801

"Analyzing the Applicant's Financial Statements: A Grantor's Introduction", 739
"Anatomy of Giving: Millionaires in the Late 19th Century", 112
"And What Would You Do about Mr. Gotrocks?", 2443
Andrew Carnegie, 488
Andrew Carnegie, Apostle of Peace, 251
Andrew Carnegie Centenary, 1835-1935, 83
Andrew Carnegie: Educator, 250
Andrew Carnegie Sesquicentenary Gathering, 84
Andrew Carnegie: The Man and His Work, 9
"Annenberg/CPB Will Give $10 Million to Telecommunications Projects", 544
"Anniversaries: Celebrating a Big Birthday for Love and Money", 3843
Announcement of Research Programs in the Division of Information Science and Technology, 4704
Annual Conference, 648, 2479
"The Annual Fund", 3340
Annual Index of Foundation Reports and Appendix, 1985, 988
Annual Report, 3292, 4689, 4720
"Annual Report: A Necessity for Corporate Grant Programs", 1623
"Annual Report Survey. Part 1", 545
"Annual Reports Are 'Winning' Fund-Raising Technique", 2131
"Annual Reports Key to Foundation World View", 1111
"Annual Reports: Making a Good Idea Better", 1255
"Annual Reports, 1983: Cautious and Colorful", 1108
"Annual Reports Often Reveal Giving Priorities", 546
Annual Salary Survey Results, 2002
Annual Survey of Corporate Contributions., 1416
"Another Way: A Look at Alternative Funds", 3004
"Anybody Need a Good Proposal Writer?", 4048
"Appeals Courts Smash 'Commerciality Doctrine'", 2169
"Apple Computer Awards Equipment to Nonprofit Networks: Expansion of Donation Programs Planned", 1310
"Apple Plants Seeds for Community Networking", 4774
"Apples for Nonprofits", 2745
"Applications for Foundation Grants", 534
Applied Empirical Research on Nonprofit Organization Management: Survey and Recommendations, 2491
"Applying the Theory Z Method to the Development Office", 3682
Appreciations of Frederick Paul Keppel by Some of His Friends, 21
Approaching Business for Support of the Arts, 1340
Archaeologia Cantiana. Social Institutions in Kent, 1480-1660, 1864

TITLE INDEX

"Are Changes Needed in Private Foundation Reporting Practices?", 2450
"Are Nonprofits Wolves in Sheep's Clothing?", **2017**
"Are Unrestricted Funds Truly without Strings?", 550
"Are You Feeling Pressure to Take Your Charity 'into Business'? The Museum Experience", **4080**
"Are You Ready for Fund Raising?", 3621
"Arguments Regarding Tax Reform", 4246
Arizona Foundation Directory, **899**
ARL Annual Salary Survey, 1981, 2003
Arnaud Cartwright Marts, 90
Arrowsmith, 948
"Art and Money in a Ballet Conflict", 3495
"The Art and Science of Direct Mail Copywriting", **3264**
"Art Collections Can Showcase Non-Profits", **1624**
Art in Business: The Philip Morris Story, 1507
The Art of Asking: How to Solicit Philanthropic Gifts, **3803**
"The Art of Friendship Entices Unsolicited Donors", 3265
The Art of Fund Raising, 3941
"The Art of Soliciting a Prospective Donor in Person. Part 1", 3010
The Art of Winning Corporate Grants, **1500**
The Art of Winning Foundation Grants, 4024
The Art of Winning Government Grants, **4666**
The Art of Writing Business Reports and Proposals, 4025
"The Artful Banker", 317
Artists in Education Application Guidelines, 4690
The Artists Resource Guide to New England: Galleries, Grants, Services, **673**
Arts Administration: How to Set Up and Run Successful Nonprofit Arts Organizations, 2657
"Arts Administration: Managing the Resources of Arts Organizations", 2892
Arts Advocacy: A Citizen Action Manual, 4604
The Arts and 504: A 504 Handbook for Accessible Arts Programming, 4691
The Arts and the New England Economy, 2264
Arts and the People. A Survey of Public Attitudes and Participation in the Arts Culture in New York State, 4776
The Arts and the U.S. Department of Education: A List of Funded Projects and Activities, 1979, 4754
The Arts and the World of Business, 2613
The Arts As an Industry: Their Economic Importance to the New York-New Jersey Metropolitan Region, 2071
The Arts Catalogue of New Jersey, 2289
Arts Endowment Starts New Grant Program, 4645

"Arts Focus on Business Surveys and New Programs", 1311
"Arts Groups Can Obtain Non-Arts Dollars Too", 3130
"Arts Groups Try New Approaches to Win Corporate Sponsorship", **3767**
An Arts in Education Source Book: A View from the JDR 3rd Fund, 4784
Arts Management: An Annotated Bibliography, 2467, 2510
The Arts Management Reader, 2862
The Arts of Boston, 4966
"Arts Stabilization Is Mission of New Fund", 2006
Artsmoney: Raising It, Saving It, and Earning It, **3467**
Artswork: A System for Program Planning and Design (of an Arts Employment Program), 2713
"As I See It: 'To Be a Good Citizen'", 1484
As It Happened: A Memoir, 368
"As U.S. Aid to Cities Withers, Private Money Gets Bigger Role", 3391
Asa Griggs Candler, 76
Asian American Charitable Giving, **476**
"Asian Invasion!: Japanese Corporate Philanthropy Zooms", **1755**
Asking and Giving: A Report on Hospital Philanthropy, 3181
Asking Corporations for Money, **1599**
"Asking Current Donors for Extra Gifts: Why, How and How Often", 3496
"Asking for Money", 3809
"Aspects of Corporate Giving in Canada", 1756
Aspirations, Enrollments, and Resources: The Challenge to Higher Education in the Seventies, 3298
"Assessing How Gifts to Charity Are Used", 3844
"Assessing the Future Needs of Nonprofit Management", 2568
"Assessing the Strengths and Challenges of Your Group", **2386**
An Assessment for Grantmaking International, 1892
Association Committees, 2050
"Association-Related Foundation: A Fund-Raising Vehicle", **3410**
Associations and Lobbying. A Guide for Non-Profit Organizations, 4473
"At Your Place or Mine? Special Events Are the Sine Qua Non of Arts Fund Raising", **3768**
The Atlanta Nonprofit Sector in a Time of Government Retrenchment, 4678
The Attitudes, Accessibility, and Participation of Blacks and Whites in Work-Site Charitable Payroll Deduction Plans, 3113
"Attitudes That Shape the Fight against AIDS", 4777
Attitudes toward Giving, **14**
"Attorney General Probes Shubert Salaries", **1265**

Attorney General's Report on the Trustees of the Moody Foundation: An Investigation Report to Crawford C. Martin, Attorney General of Texas from Wilmer B. Hunt, Special Assistant Attorney General, 1017
"Attracting and Retaining Talented People", **2675**
Attributes and Context, 2606
The Auction Book: A Comprehensive Fund-Raising Resource for Nonprofit Organizations, **3047**
"Audiovisuals: They Can Add Punch to Your Pitch", **3514**
The Audit Committee: The Board of Trustees of Nonprofit Organizations and the Independent Accountant, 2455
"Audit Your Development Office for Results", 3236
Audits of Certain Nonprofit Organizations, 2437
Audits of Colleges and Universities, 2513
Audits of Voluntary Health and Welfare Organizations, 2514
Autobiography of Andrew Carnegie, 79
"Automating Your Management Information System", 2943
"The Average Gift Size Factor", 3557
"Avoiding Limits on Private Foundation Business Holdings: Planning Possibilities", **4089**
"Avoiding Private Foundation Status", 749
The A.W. Mellon Educational and Charitable Trust: A Report of Its Work for the Fifty Years, 1930-1980, 1005
"Award Winning Performers", 4769
Awards for Senior U.S. Scientists, 1257
The Awkward Embrace: The Creative Artist and the Institution in America, 2036
Ayer Fund-Raising Dinner Guide, 3020
Back to Basics: Planning, 2826
"Back to the Future: Human Resource Planning for Nonprofits", **2295**
Backs against the Wall: Urban-Oriented Colleges and Universities and the Urban Poor and Disadvantaged, 4788
The Backyard Revolution: Understanding the New Citizen Movement, **4491**
"Balance-Sheet Strategy", **2039**
Balancing Quality and Equity: Toward a Grantmaking Program in Pre-Collegiate Public Education, **1202**
"Baltimore's Responses to Difficult Times", 3034
Banking and Private Philanthropy, 487
Banks, Neighborhoods and the Community Reinvestment Act, 4980
The Bar Foundation: Recognizing a Professional and Public Responsibility, 1996
"Base Salary and Incentive Compensation Practices in Not-for-Profit Organizations", 2160
Bashful Billionaire, 806
Basic Computer Knowledge for Nonprofits, 2947

341

TITLE INDEX

Basic Fund Raising, 3123
"Basic Grantsmanship Library", 3041
A Basic Guide to Proposal Development, 4046
"Basic Standards in Philanthropy", 2011
The Battelle Memorial Institute Foundation, 1975-1982: A History and Evaluation, 933
"The Battle for the NEH", 4648
Bay Area Foundation History, 611, 923, 991, 1150, 1180
A Beacon for Philanthropy: The American Association of Fund-Raising Counsel through Fifty Years, 1935-1985, 2354
"Bears and Beggars", **4670**
Before You Give Another Dime, 440
Beginnings. Andrew Carnegie's Peace Endowment: The Tycoon, the President, and Their Bargain of 1910, 737
Beginnings of Sisterhood: The American Woman's Rights Movement, 1800-1850, **4555**
Beloved Lady: A History of Jane Addams' Ideas on Reform and Peace, **149**
"The Benefactory", 1552
"Benefit by Bids: The Gavel Rises", 3053
"The Benevolence of Businessmen", 1458
Bequests, 3474
Die Bereitstellung von Unternehmenskapital fur Stiftungen (The preparation of business funds for foundations), 1904
"Berkshire Hathaway Pleases Shareholders by Letting Them Earmark Corporate Gifts", 1657
"The Beryl Buck Estate and the Future of Philanthropy", 1196
The Best Gift: A Record of the Carnegie Libraries in Ontario, 564
Best Techniques, 3180
Better Brochures, Catalogs and Mailing Pieces, 2731
"Better Coordination of Science and Math Programs Sought by Foundations", 689
Better Giving: The New Needs of American Philanthropy, 279
Better Management of Business Giving, 1345
"Better Performance from 'Nonprofits'", 2329
"Beyond Coping with Crisis: Cooperation for Survival", 3542
Beyond Money: New Dimensions in International Corporate Giving, 1769
Beyond Preference: Liberal Theories of Independent Association, 4523
Beyond Profit: The Complete Guide to Managing the Nonprofit Organization, **2889**
"Beyond the Ask: Ten Other Ways to Involve Faculty in Fund Raising", 3544
Beyond the Bake Sale: A Fund Raising Handbook for Public Agencies, **3641**
Bibliography, 15
Bibliography: Corporate Responsibility for Social Problems, 1316

Bibliography: Development Research Materials, 3872
Bibliography for Fund Raising and Philanthropy, 3328
Bibliography for Hospital Resource Development: A Useful Tool for Fund Raisers and Resource Development Teams, **3653**
Bibliography for Neighborhood Leaders, 4916
Bibliography of Fund Raising and Philanthropy, 3329, 3655
A Bibliography on Arts Administration, 2718
A Bibliography on Historical Organization Practices, 2857
"Big Business Tightens Its Arts Budget", 1668
The Big Foundations, **1050**
"Bill to Cut Excise Tax on Foundations Could Yield $50-Million to Charities", 4235
"Billion Dollar Brains: How Wealth Puts Knowledge in Its Pocket", 3419
A Biography of Robert Alonzo Welch, 98
A Biography of the Nuffield Foundation, 1776
"Bittersweet Charity: The High Cost of Fund-Raising", 3910
"Black Charities Face Opposition", 423
"Black Colleges and Foundations Try 'Hand-Holding'", 740
"Black Fund Raising", 3059
"Black United Funds Battle over Workplace Solicitation", 3465
"Blacks Give to Blacks: For 'Survival Causes'", 377
Block Grants: A Human Services Bibliography, 4734
Blue Blood, **482**
"The Board and Its Executive Director: A Supervisory Checklist", 2908
"The Board Is Key in Strengthening Nonprofit Corporations", 2579
Board Liability: Guide for Nonprofit Directors, **2700**
Board Management Tapes, 2796
The Board Manual Workbook, **2904**
Board Member Manual, **2500**
The Board Member's Book: Making a Difference in Voluntary Organizations, **2805**
The Board of Directors, **2474**
The Board President and the Board of Directors: A Guide, 2909
"The Board's Job Is to Hire the Executive Director in a Responsible Manner", 2794
Bollingen: An Adventure in Collecting the Past, 997
The Bonds of Womanhood: "Woman's Sphere" in New England, 1780-1835, **4505**
Bonnet Brigades, **4550**
A Book of Carnegie Libraries, 286
"Book Reviews: Managing Not-for-Profit Organizations", 2703
Bookkeeping for Nonprofits, 2843

Bookkeeping Handbook for Low-Income Citizens Groups, 2787
Born to Raise. What Makes a Great Fundraiser; What Makes a Fundraiser Great, **3701**
The Bottom Line: Improved Management of Nonprofit Organizations. Proceedings, 2478
"The Bottom Line in Fundraising", **3693**
"Bounty from Beyond, How to Give the Most Good with Your Bequests", 3003
The Brakeley Compensation Report: A Report on the Compensation of Chief Development Officers in Higher Education, **2481**
"Brakeley President Spots Trends in Major-Gift Fund Raising", 3538
The Bread Game, **3994**
"Break a Leg, Cleveland", 4831
"Breaking Down the Barriers: Ten Ways to Promote Partnerships between Alumni Officers and Fund Raisers", 3712
Breaking Even: Financial Management in Human Service Organizations, 2726
"Breaking Ground: Private Interest in Public Job Training", 3076
"Breaking into Foundation Big Time: A Strategy for Seeking Grants from Major Foundations", 3363
Bricks, Mortar and the Performing Arts: Report of the Twentieth Century Fund Task Force on Performing Arts Centers, 2232
Bridge over Troubled Waters: Loan Fund for the Arts, 2045
"Bridging the Cash Flow Gap", 3079
"Bringing High-Tech to Neighborhoods: Here's How High Technology Created a Network That Really Works for Grassroots Organizations", 2331
The Buck Bequest: A Case Study in Philanthropy, 583
"The Buck Trust Petition: A Bid for Philanthropic Self-Regulation", 588
Buck Trust Trial: Copies of the Expert Witnesses Statements, **1054**
Buck Trust Trial: Copies of the Trial Briefs Submitted by Various Parties to the Suit, **1055**
Buck Trust Trial: Judgement and Statement of Decision in Buck Trust Case, 1056
Buck Trust Trial: Text of Agreement, **1057**
The Bucks Start Here: How to Fund Social Service Projects, 3288
"Budget Cuts, Tax Plan May Change Way Firms Contribute to Charities", 1385
"Budget Cuts Threaten Historic Houses", 4873
"Budget-KO'd Scholars Come Back Fighting", 4855
A Budget Primer and Worksheets for Proposal Writers, 4010
Budgeting and Financial Accountability, **2806**
"Budgeting for Development", 3054

TITLE INDEX

Budgeting for Nonprofits, 2844
Budgeting for Not-for-Profit Organizations, **2941**
"Build the Organization You Would like to Have", 2044
Builders of Goodwill: The Story of the State Agents of Negro Education in the South, 1910-1950, 444
Building a Board of Directors, 2485
Building a Corporate Volunteer Program, 1398
"Building a Mailing List: An Introduction", 3266
"The Building Better Boards Project", 2954
"The Building Bloc: Kresge Survey Reveals Who's Doing What in Capital Grantmaking", 3408
"Building Community Partnerships: The Foundation Role", 1276
"Building Momentum in Japan", **1767**
Building Neighborhood Organizations, 2072
Building Networks: Cooperation As a Strategy for Success in a Changing World, **2495**
"Building on Experience: Improving Organizational Capacity to Handle Development Projects", 3093
Building Partnerships, 1641
Building Partnerships with Business: A Guide for Nonprofits, 2388
"Building Strength from Weakness", 3869
"Building the Case for Solid Gift Support", 2836
"Building the Tiers of Your Resource Development Program", 3801
Building Your Own Philanthropic Foundation, **554**
Bulletin of the Russell Sage Foundation Library, 247
Bulletin on Public Relations and Development for Colleges and Universities, 4107
"The Bureaucratization of Begging: A Donor with Shell(out) Shock Looks Back to a Time When the Giving Was Easy", 42
The Burke Foundation, 994
"A Busch Family Heritage", **70**
Business and Social Change, 1611
Business and Society: Concepts and Policy Issues, **1321**
Business and Society: Strategies for the 1980's, 1711
Business and the Arts, 1477
Business and the Arts: From a Mutual Need, a Working Partnership, 1661
Business and the Cities: Programs and Practices, 1741
"The Business Executive As Nonprofit Trustee: A Fish Out of Water?", 2957
The Business for Seminars, 2780
"Business Groups Join in Fight on Lobbying Rules", 4109
Business in the Arts '70, 1354
Business Information: How to Find It, How to Use It, **1555**

"Business Meets Its Social Responsibility", 1594
"The Business of Boards Is Serious Business", 2677
"The Business of Giving Away Money", 731
"The Business of Managing the Arts", 2859
A Business Planning Guide for Not-for-Profit Organizations, **2483**
"Business Sense", **1676**
Business Spinoffs: Planning the Organizational Structure of Business Activities, **2503**
"Business Ventures of Citizen Groups", **2037**
"Business Voluntarism Means Giving People As Well As Money", 4486
"Businesses Urged Not to Forget Charity", 1715
"Businessman Donates $100,000 to Vo-Tech School", 142
A Businessman's Concept of Citizenship, **1665**
The Businessman's Guide to Washington, 4736
"Buy Buildings through Partnerships", 2170
A Buyer's Guide to Microcomputers for Non-Profit Arts Organizations, 2497
"By Any Other Name: Altruism, Self-Help, Charity, Philanthropy, Voluntarism, Nonprofit", 354
"By Itself, Media Isn't Enough", 2459
By-Laws a Guide for New York Not-for-Profit Organizations and Their Lawyers, **4311**
By the People. A History of Americans As Volunteers, **4515**
"Cable Watch Out!", 3732
The California Non-Profit Corporation Handbook, **2743**
Call for Help: How to Raise Philanthropic Funds with Phonothons, 3033
"Calling All Directors: Have You Checked Your Insurance Policy Lately?", 2574
The Campaign Manuals. 2 Vols, **3094**
Campanas para Obtencion de Fondos, 3815
The Campus and the City: Maximizing Assets and Reducing Liabilities, 4791
"Can a Black Be Quarterback?", **2192**
Can Culture Survive the Marketplace?, 3222
"Can Do, Can Do: What a Computer Can Do for Independent Schools", 2819
Can Do 2, 2567
"Can Foundations Support Voter Registration?", 1245
"Can the Best Corporations Be Made Moral?", 1308
"Can the Non-Profit Sector Work Better?", 2066
"Can Two Heads Be Better Than One? Collaborations among Not-for-Profit Corporations", 4302

Canada Gives: Trends and Attitudes Towards Charitable Giving and Voluntarism, **1750**
The Canadian Book of Charities: The Guide to Intelligent Giving, 1771
"The Canadian Centre for Philanthropy: Building Resources North of the Border", 1764
Canadian Directory to Foundations, **1751**
Canadian Index to Foundation Grants, **1752**
"Canadian Society of Fund Raising Executives Created", 1927
"The Capital Campaign", 3908
The Capital Campaign Handbook: How to Maximize Your Fund Raising Campaign, **3381**
Capital Campaign Resource Guide, 3746
Capital Campaigns for Community Organizations, 3132
"Capital Campaigns: Knowing When You're Ready", 3106
"Capital Drives Prosper", 3759
Capital Grant Survey Results, 924
"Capital Ideas: How an Independent College Got State Government Aid", 4748
Capital Ideas. Step by Step: How to Solicit Major Gifts from Private Sources, 3965
Capital Ideas: The Elements and Techniques of a Systematic Approach to Capital Fund Raising. 3 Vols, 3966
The Care of Destitute, Neglected, and Delinquent Children, **157**
Careers in the Nonprofit Sector: Doing Well by Doing Good, 2235
The Carlsberg Foundation, 1918
Carlsbergfondet, 1827
The Carnegie Commission on Higher Education, 993
The Carnegie Corporation and the Development of American College Libraries, 1928-1941, 1095
"The Carnegie Endowment for International Peace", **1770**
Carnegie Hall, the House That Music Built, 378
The Carnegie Millions and the Men Who Made Them: Being the Inside History of the Carnegie Steel Co., 62
"Carnival Time in Hawaii: The Punahou School in Hawaii Has One of the Most Successful of All Special Events", 3193
"Carry on: Making Careful Promises to Donors, Prospects", 3027
"The Case for Cause-Related Marketing", **1731**
"A Case for Constituency Building As a Direct Program Expense", 3061
"The Case for Corporate Giving", **1528**
"A Case for Giving 2% of Pretax Income", 1542
Case Histories of Ten New Medical Schools, 951
Case Readings for Marketing for Nonprofit Organizations, 2694

343

TITLE INDEX

"Case Statements, Feasibility Studies, and Action Plans", 3203
"A Case Study in Federated Fundraising: Aid to Wisconsin Organizations", 3333
A Casebook of Grant Proposals in the Humanities, **4005**
Cash In! Funding and Promoting the Arts, **3769**
"Cash Management for Smaller Non-Profit Organizations", 2559
"Cashing in on Noncash Corporate Support", 1346
Catalog of California State Grants Assistance, **4727**
Catalog of Federal Domestic Assistance, **4761**
"Cataloging Urban Needs: Gifts Catalogs Encourage Private Giving to Cities", 3065
A Catalyst for Action: A National Survey to Mobilize Leadership and Resources for the Prevention of Alcohol and Other Drug Problems among American Youth, 4865
"Catalyst for Dollars and Issues Is Role of Mail", 3959
Catalyst's Guide to Social Change Revolving Loan Funds, **3625**
Catholic Charities in the United States: History and Problems, 365
The Catholic Guide to Foundations, 682
"Catholic Relief Services Involved in Dispute over Spending of Ethiopia Aid", 3064
"Caught between Two Poles: Corporate Grantmakers Must Strike a Balance between Idealism and Institutional Self-Interest", 1563
"Cause-Related Marketing: Blessing or Curse for Philanthropy?", **1347**
"Cause-Related Marketing: Case to Not Leave Home without It", **1328**
"Cause-Related Marketing Does Not Fit All Corporations' Needs", 1348
"Cause-Related Marketing: Savior or Devil for Hospital Fund Raising?", 3026
"Cause-Related Marketing: The New Face of Corporate Philanthropy", **1342, 1349**
"Cedar Rapids Hall Foundation: Pot of Gold for Charities", 560
"Celebrating the Legacy of Andrew Carnegie's Philanthropy", 123
"The Celebrity Auction", 3153
"Centering on the Underdog", **2400**
Centers for Community Education Development and Other Resources, 4812
"A CEO Views Philanthropy and the Fund Raiser", 3334
"Certain Nonprofit Organizations: Proposed Audit Guide", 2706
The CFAE Casebook. A Cross-Section of Corporate Aid-to-Education Programs, 1405
"The Challenge and Rewards of Promoting the Bible", **4939**
The Challenge Grant and Higher Education, 3421

The Challenge Grant Experience: Planning, Development, and Fundraising, 4650
The Challenge of Change, **2680**
"Challenges for the Manager of the One-Person Shop", **3597**
"The Changing Aspirations of Men and Women Volunteers", 4520
Changing Conditions in Public Giving, 18
"The Changing Health Care System: A Challenge for Foundations", 3627
Changing Needs and Social Services in Three Chicago Communities, **2162**
"Changing Patterns in Donations Challenges United Way Methods", 3899
The Changing Position of Philanthropy in the American Economy, **131**
"The Changing Profession of Volunteer Administration", 4524
The Changing Role of Private Foundations: Business As Usual or Creative Innovation?, 977
"The Changing World of Private Foundations: An Interview with Dr. David E. Rogers", **872**
Chapters in My Life, **171**
The Charitable Behavior of Americans: A National Survey, **520**
The Charitable Behavior of Americans: Management Summary, **501**
The Charitable Behavior of San Francisco Bay Area Physicians, 68
Charitable Contributions by Arkansas Businesses, **1512**
Charitable Contributions: The Discretionary Income Hypothesis, 3202
Charitable Deductions and Tax Reform: New Evidence on Giving Behavior, **4085**
Charitable Distribution Requirements for Private Foundations, 4395
Charitable Foundations Conference, 612, 1046, 1047, 1048, 1049
Charitable Foundations Directory of Ohio, **1064**
Charitable Foundations for Business Corporations, 1621
Charitable Giving: A Tax Guide for Individual Donors, **4082**
Charitable Giving and "Excessive" Fundraising, 3781
"Charitable Giving and Financial Planning", 2229
Charitable Giving and Solicitation, **4334**
Charitable Giving and Tax-Exempt Organizations: The Impact of the 1981 Tax Act, 4182
"Charitable Giving and the Tax Bill", 4307
"Charitable Giving at Crossroads: An Interview with Independent Sector's Brian O'Connell", 2275
Charitable Giving in Light of the Economic Recovery Tax Act of 1981, 4339
"Charitable Giving Techniques for Business Owners", 3638
Charitable Giving: What Contributors Want to Know, 347
The Charitable Impulse in Eighteenth Century America: Collected Papers, **415**

The Charitable Lead Trust: A Wise Way to Be a Philanthropist and Pass Wealth to Family Members Free of Gift and Estate Taxes, 4358
"The Charitable Lead Trust: An Update on the Tax Savings Available to Donors", 4126
"The Charitable Lead Trust in the Ten Percent World", 4222
"The Charitable Nonprofit Institution and the Highly Compensated Employee", **4110**
Charitable Real Property Tax Exemptions in New York State: Menace or Measure of Social Progress?, **4349**
Charitable Trust Directory, **1261**
Charitable Trusts, 616
"Charitable Trusts and the Taxman", 4294
Charities, 1910
Charities and Charitable Foundations, **4151**
Charities and Charitable Foundations. Cumulative Supplement, 4152
Charities and Social Aid in Greece and Rome, **196**
Charities and the Fiscal Crisis: Creative Approaches to Income Production, 2375
"Charities, Charitable Trusts and Foundations", 849
"The Charities Come Up Short", 396
"Charities Gear Up for a Fight over the Treasury's Tax Plan", 4368
"Charities in the Marketplace: A Look at Joint-Venture Marketing. Part 1", **1666**
"Charities in the Marketplace: A Look at Joint-Venture Marketing. Part 2", **1667**
The Charities of London, 1480-1660, **1865**
The Charities of Rural England, 1480-1660, 1866
Charity and Dynasty under the Federal Tax System, 4320
"Charity and Social Classes in the United States, 1874-1900", **174**
"Charity Appeals Sharply on Rise", 3900
"A Charity Ball: A Nuts and Bolts Approach", 3468
"Charity Begins at the Pump: The Oil Companies As a Funding Source", 1527
"Charity Begins at Work", 3121
Charity Begins at Work: Alternatives to United Way Dramatically Change the Billion Dollar World of Workplace Fundraising, 3658
Charity Deductions Aren't Subsidies, 4122
"Charity Falls on Hard Times", 406
"Charity in Texas. Part 1: Charity, Inc.", 200
"Charity in Texas. Part 2: Hearts of Gold", 496
Charity in the USA, **514**
"Charity Life Insurance Gifts: Installments and No Probate", 3398
"Charity Links with Commercial Enterprises in the U.K.: A Success Story", **1834**
The Charity Market: Paying Customers and Quality Control, 412

TITLE INDEX

"Charity May Be Stretched Thin over Gulf in Services Dug Out by Reagan", 4545

The Charity of Nations: The Political Economy of Foreign Aid, 1977

"Charity on Their Lips and Larceny in Their Hearts: A Study of New York State's Professional Fund Raisers", 3122

The Charity Organization Movement in the United States: A Study in American Philanthropy, **491**

Charity Statistics, **1896**

Charity Trends, 1986-87, **1897**

Charity Trends, 1987-88, 1898

Charity under Siege: Government Regulation of Fund-Raising, 4183

Charity U.S.A.: An Investigation into the Hidden World of the Multi-Billion Dollar Charity Industry, **27**

"Charles Stewart Mott, 1875-1973", 94

Charters of Philanthropies: A Study of Selected Trust Instruments, Charters, By-Laws and Court Decisions, 610

Charters of Philanthropies: A Study of the Charters of Twenty-Nine American Philanthropic Foundations, 728

"Cheaper by the Dozen", 2956

"Check If Non-Cash Gifts Deductible for Business", 1625

The Checkbook: The Politics and Ethics of Foundation Philanthropy, **334**

The Cheswick Process: Seven Steps to a More Effective Board, **2875**

The Chicago Nonprofit Sector in a Time of Government Retrenchment, 4657

"The Chicago Opera Youth Program: Proposal Writing Exercises", 3998

Chicago's Corporate Foundations: A Directory of Chicago Area and Illinois Corporate Foundations, **1431**

Chief Executive Officer Conference on Corporate Social Responsibility. Report on Proceedings, 1352

Children's Charities. Part 4: Voluntary Foreign Aid Agencies Serving Children and Youth, 93rd Congress, 2nd Session, October 10, 1974, 3921

China Medical Board and Peking Union Medical College: A Chronicle of Fruitful Collaboration, 1914-1951, 742

"The Chocolate Soldiers", **1983**

"Choosing the Right Capital Campaign Consulting Firm", 3129

"Christian Charity: Its Roots, Its Forms, Its Critics", 4901

The Chronically Mentally Ill: Improving the Knowledge Base through Research, 4956

Chronicle of a Generation: An Autobiography, 160

Church Funders List, **3119**

Church Funding Sources for International Projects, **1985**

Church Funding Sources. Resource Guide, **3981**

Church Funds for Social Justice: A Directory, **3342**

Church-Sponsored Higher Education in the United States, 4923

The Church, the State, and the Poor, 1774

Churches As Development Institutions: The Case of Chile, 1973-1980, 1948

"Churches Await Impact of Tax Reform", 4217

"Churches That Face Peril Need Marketing Skills", 2548

The Churches: Their Riches, Revenues, and Immunities, 2212

Cities, Counties and the Arts, 4681

"Citizen Scaife", 1143

Citizen Support for Non-Profit Public Interest Groups, 2113

The Citizen Volunteer: His Responsibility, Role, and Opportunity in Modern Society, **4502**

Citizen Volunteer Program, 4568

"Citizens Rich", **30**

The City and the Grassroots: A Cross-Cultural Theory of Urban Social Movements, **2043**

Civil Rights, Social Justice, and Black America, 4836

"Class Act: More and More Institutions Offer Development Training", 3108

"Clean Your Carpet and Help a Child: The Pros and Cons of Cause Marketing", **1685**

The Clearinghouse for Technical Assistance, 2453

The Cleveland Foundation, 987

Clientele Involvement in Non-Proft Organizations, 2060

The Climate for Giving: The Outlook of Current and Future CEO's, **1742**

"A Close Look at a RAG", 1178

"The Co-Corp: Big Business Can Re-Form Itself", 1367

"Coalition Says Nonprofits Have Unfair Business Edge", 2057

A Collaborative Technical Assistance Strategy for Child Welfare Reform: Implementation Plan, 2048

Collected Newspaper Clippings and Newsreleases, 628

"Collecting Marketing Research Data", 3218

"College and Foundations: Partners or Antagonists?", 1096

College and University Business Administration, 2436

College and University Endowment, 4858

College and University Finance, 2451

The College and University Trustee: A View from the Board Room, 2642

"College Endowments Return a Record 42% in One Year", 3595

College Graduates and Jobs: Adjusting to a New Labor Market Situation, 4792

College: The Undergraduate Experience in America, **4785**

Colorado Corporate Contributions Survey, 1436

Colorado Foundation Directory, **626**

Colorado Non-Profit Wage and Benefits Survey, 1984, 2367

"Combined Federal Campaign, Broad Changes: Will Radical Surgery Cure the CFC or Kill It?", 3860

"The Combined Federal Campaign: Let's Make It Work Better", 3145

"Combined Federal Campaign: New, Final Rules Will Govern 1984 Campaign", 3861

"Combined Federal Campaign: Philanthropy and Politics on the Potomac", 3807

"Coming of Age", **1256, 4877**

Commitment and Community: Communes and Utopias in Sociological Perspective, **4882**

Committee Amendment (in the Nature of a Substitute) Reported by Mr. Long, from the Committee on Finance, to H.R. 13270, an Act to Reform the Income Tax Laws, Calender No. 547, 91st Congress, 1st Session, 4437

"Common Ground: The Marriage of America's Rural and Corporate Workplace", 4902

Common Sense about Fund Raising, 3541

The Commonwealth Activities in Austria, 1923-1929, 796

Commonwealth African Directory of Aid Agencies, 1777

Commonwealth Caribbean Directory of Aid Agencies, 1967

The Commonwealth Fund Fellows and Their Impressions of America, 1102

A Commonwealth Fund Paper: The Financial Condition of New York City Voluntary Hospitals, 4787

Communicating and Moneymaking. A Guide for Using Public Relations to Improve Fund-Raising Success, 2461

Communicating in the '80s: New Options for the Nonprofit Community, 2138

"Communication Is a Board's Job Too. Part 1: Internal Communication", 2886

Communications and Public Affairs Guide, 2528

A Communications Manual for Nonprofit Organizations, **2735**

The Community Arts Council Movement: History, Opinions, Issues, 4649

Community-Based Development: Investing in Renewal, 4967

Community Cash Flow Fund Program: Guidelines, Application, and Sample Cash Flow Application Forms, 3897

Community Changes/Corporate Responses, **106**

Community Chest: A Case Study in Philanthropy, 438

"Community Colleges and Industry Ally to Provide 'Customized' Job Training", 1727

Community Development Block Grant: A Basic Guidebook for Community Groups, 4620

345

TITLE INDEX

Community Development in South Africa: A Guide for American Donors, **1946**
Community Education Funding Guide, 4621
Community Energy Cooperatives: How to Organize, Manage and Finance Them, 3150
The Community Foundation and the Foundations of Community: The H.C. Trexler Estate of Allentown, Pennsylvania—a Preliminary Report, 834
The Community Foundation: Its Historical Background, the Creation of the North Dakota Community Foundation, and a Developmental Framework for Beginning New Community Foundations, 874
"The Community Foundation Movement: An Idea Whose Time Has Come", 893
Community Foundation Resource Manual, 649
Community Foundations, 609, 1169
"Community Foundations Can Be Designed for Local Needs", **1199**
"Community Foundations Take off", **1272**
"Community Foundations Vary from Private in Many Ways", 1112
Community Organization for Social Welfare, 2240
"Community Partnerships at Home and Abroad", 505
The Community Reinvestment Act: A Citizen's Action Guide, 2501
Community Relations: Being a Good Neighbor, 1583
Community Resources Directory, 2516
Community Service Partnerships, 3519
"Community Spirit Lives in Local Arts", 3623
Community Support of the Performing Arts: Selected Problems of Local and National Interest, 2097
"Community Trust Opens a Center to Study Aging", **1224**
Community Trusts in the United States and Canada: A Survey of Existing Trusts with Suggestions for Organizing and Developing New Foundations, 530
Community Trusts or Foundations: United States and Canada. Status of 1949, 1030
"A Community United", **4936**
"Companies' Gifts to Colleges Up over 20% in 1982, Despite Sag in Profits, Survey Finds", 1372
Company Charitable Giving Statistics, **1912**
Company Contributions, 1377
Company Contributions in Canada, 1978
Company Contributions. Part 3: Policies and Procedures, 1378
Company Foundations and the Self-Dealing Rules, **1502**
"Company Gifts Up 8.5%", 1373
Company Giving, 1672
"Company Giving through Foundations", 1671
Company Information: A Model Investigation, 1556
Company Policies on Donations, 1379

Company Policies on Donations. Part 2: Written Statements of Policy, 1380
"Company Programs Illustrate Strong Commitment to the Arts", 1374
Company-Sponsored Foundations, 1381
Company-Sponsored Foundations in Education, 1325
"A Comparative Study of the Tax Treatment of Donors to Charity in Various Countries", **1748**, 1749
Comparing Public and Private Schools: The Puzzling Role of Selectivity Bias, 4908
A Comparison of Joint Efforts by Philanthropic Foundations in Three States, 838
A Comparison of Non-Profit, For-Profit and Public Hospitals in the United States, 1935 to the Present, **2168**
Comparisons of Public and Private Schools: Lessons from the Uproar, 4909
"The Compelling Case for Fund Raising by Objective", 3354
"Compensation and Benefits", 2896
Compensation Differentials in the Nonprofit Sector: An Application to the Day Care Industry, 2299
"Compensation in the Nonprofit Sector", **2411**
Competition between the Nonprofit and For-Profit Sectors, 2290
"The Competitive Market Model: Emerging Strategy for Nonprofits", 2315
Competitive Marketing: A Guide for United Ways and Other Nonprofits, **2936**
"A Compilation of State Laws Regulating Charitable Solicitations", 4131
The Complete Fund Raising Guide, **3634**
The Complete Grants Sourcebook for Higher Education, **3043**
The Complete Guide to Corporate Fund Raising, **1428**
The Complete Guide to Florida Foundations, **635**
The Complete Guide to Money-Making Ventures for Nonprofit Organizations, **2492**
The Complete Guide to Planned Giving, **3014**
The Complete Writing Guide to Preparing Reports, Proposals, Memos, Etc., 4047
"Composing Effective Letters with Word Processing Features", 3568
Composition of Governing Boards, 1985: A Survey of College and University Boards, 2454
"Computer Basics for Nonprofit Organizations", 2762
"Computer Grants May Depend on Whom You Know", 2376
"Computer Industry Shakeout Won't Affect Equipment Donations, Insiders Predict", 1375
"Computer, Other Services Can Be Business-Donated", 1626
Computer Resource Guide for Nonprofits, **3747**

"Computer Subsidy Divides Education", 1376
"Computer Technology and the Connecticut Junior Republic", 3418
"Computerized Information Management Systems for Research Administration: General Issues Affecting Their Implementation", 2882
"Computerized Spreadsheets Offer Objective Mail Analysis", 3080
"Computers and Accounting 2: Accounting Software for Nonprofits", **2748**
"Computers Calculate Volunteer's Future", 4501
Computers for Everybody, 2963
"Computers for Non-Profits? Part 1", 2959
"Computers for Non-Profits? Part 2", 2867
Computers for Nonprofits, **2616**
"Computers for Nonprofits. Computer Equipment: How to Know What You Want", 2538
"Computers in Alumni and Development", 3147
"Computing the Odds in Software", **2195**
"Concepts in Planned Giving: Or, How Property Is like Celery", **3295**
Concepts of Funding for Community Foundations, 650
Conceptual Framework for Financial Accounting and Reporting: Objectives of Financial Reporting by Nonbusiness Organizations, 2582
Conditions and Needs of the Professional American Theatre, 4697
"Conduct of the 'Business' of a Private Foundation under the Tax Reform Act of 1969", 4340
"Conducting a Major Gifts Campaign", 3148
Conducting a Successful Capital Campaign: A Comprehensive Fundraising Guide for Nonprofit Organizations, 3237
Conducting Evaluations: Three Perspectives, 2428
Conducting Good Meetings, **2807**
Conference of Foundations, 636, 637
Conference on Charitable Organizations, 2269
Conference on Philanthropy in Action, 3662
Conference on Voluntary Giving for American Christian Institutions, 3663
Conferences on Wills, Annuities, and Special Gifts, 3664
Confessions of a Fund Raiser: Lessons of an Instructive Career, **3355**
"Confessions of a Grant Writer: The Development of the PREP Project", **4021**
"Confessions of a Grantsperson", **2024**
Conflicts of Interest: Nonprofit Organizations, 2395
Congress and Health: An Introduction to the Legislative Process and Its Key Participants, 4702

346

TITLE INDEX

Congress and Private Foundations: An Historical Analysis, **721**
Congress and the Foundations in the Twentieth Century, **934**
"Congress Debates More Liberal Equipment Donation Rules", 1382
"A Congressional Call for More Accountability", 819
Congressional Yellow Book: A Directory of Members of Congress, Including Their Committees and Key Staff Aides, **4741**
Connecticut Foundation Directory, **593**
Conscience and Convenience: The Asylum and Its Alternatives in Progressive America, **416**
The Conscience of the Corporations, 1366
"Consequences of Corporate Giving", **1735**
Conservation Directory, **3670**
"Conservative Unit Gains from Legacy: Olin Foundation Tells of Plans for Education Activity with Founder's $50 Million", 1225
"Conservatives: A Well-Financed Network", 1019
"Considering the Many Facets of Volunteer/Union Relations", 4527
"Consortium Provides Grants to Help Small Colleges Help Themselves", 3211
The Constant Quest: Raising Billions through Capital Campaigns, 3142
Constituent Involvement in Non-Profit Organizations: A Study of Twelve Participation Experiments, 2061
The Constitution and the Independent Sector, **2178**
"Constitutionality of the Tax on Lobbying by Private Foundations under Section 4945(d)(1) of the Internal Revenue Code", 4324
"Construction Projects: A Source of Income for Nonprofits", 2105
The Consultant's Guide to Proposal Writing, 4026
"A Consumer Guide to Charity: Where to Get More Balm for Your Buck", **2124**
Contemporary European Arts Support Systems: Precedents for Intergovernmental Development in the United States, 4671
"The Continuing Struggle toward a Conceptual Accounting Framework", **2863**
Continuity and Discontinuity: Higher Education and the Schools, 4793
"Continuity Yields Turnaround for Rio Grande College", 3587
"Contractual Protection of Agency's Confidential Data", 2835
"Contributing to the Vitality of Our Community (St. Paul, MN)", 1435
Contributions of Selected Private Philanthropic Foundations for Higher Education Administration, 1966-1975, 574
"Converting an Estate Donor into a Substantial Annual Giver", 3791

Cooperation among Grantmakers: A Guide to Cooperative Associations of Foundations and Corporate Contributors, 651
"Cooperation in Cleveland", **703**
Cooperation in Fiduciary Service, 547
Cooperation: Key to the Future, **1454**
"Cooperation or Collusion?", 3548
Coping with Cutbacks: A Study of the Differential Impact and Response by Voluntary Social Agencies in New York City to Government Funding Reductions, 4746
"Copy Makes Difference in This Salvation Army Appeal", 3244
"Cornell Medical Unit Given $50 Million: Donor Anonymous", 3901
"Corporate Ads on PBS Spark Debate", 1678
Corporate Aid Programs in Twelve Less-Developed Countries, 1891
Corporate and Foundation Research Sources, 964
"Corporate Caring: U.S. Business's Long (and Legal) Tradition", 1689
"Corporate Charity Is Still Spreading", 1580
"Corporate Clubs Can Stimulate Private Giving", 1386
"Corporate Commitment to Philanthropy and Volunteerism", 1387
"Corporate-Community Foundations: The Tie That's Binding", **850**
Corporate Community Involvement, **1642**
Corporate Community Involvement: An Annotated Bibliography, 1980-1986, **1713**
Corporate Contribution Programs: A Sampler of Policies and Statements, **1714**
The Corporate Contributions Function, 1704
"Corporate Contributions of Goods and Services", 1388
"Corporate Contributions of $100,000 or More in 1987 (Including Corporate Foundations)", 1389
Corporate Contributions Outlook, **1537**
The Corporate Contributions Professional, **1538**
Corporate Contributions Report, 1306
Corporate Contributions to the Nonprofit Sector: The Organizations of Giving, and the Influence of the Chief Executive Officer and Other..., 1716
"Corporate Donation Clearinghouse Distributes $20 Million", 1390
"Corporate Donors Can Help Make Contracts", 1627
The Corporate Donor's Handbook, **1609**
Corporate 500: The Directory of Corporate Philanthropy, **1322**
Corporate Foundation Profiles, **1467**
"Corporate Foundations: A Charitable Alternative", 1391
The Corporate Fund Raising Directory, **1652**
"Corporate Funding: An Emerging Revenue Source for Nonprofit Organizations", 1720

The Corporate Funding Guide of Greater Philadelphia, 1541
"Corporate Funding: Who Gets It and Why", **1717**
"Corporate Funding: Why You Did (or Didn't) Get That Grant", **1718**
Corporate Fundraising: Advice from an Expert, 1656
Corporate Fundraising for the Arts, 1350
"Corporate Gift-Giving in Cleveland", 1585
"Corporate Gifts Leveling off", 1581
"Corporate Giving", 1392
"Corporate Giving by Retail Department Stores", 1317
"Corporate Giving Clubs", 1543
"Corporate Giving Clubs on the Rise", 1393
"Corporate Giving Fails to Offset Cuts by U.S.", 1564
"Corporate Giving in Canada", 1779, 1941
Corporate Giving in Chicago, 1980. A Study of the Giving Programs of 51 Major Chicago Corporations, 1365
Corporate Giving in the Reagan Years, **1318**
"Corporate Giving in the United States, 1982", 1394
"Corporate Giving Is on Center Stage in the 1980's", 1548
"Corporate Giving Programs: Some Industries Stand Out", 1395
Corporate Giving: The Views of Chief Executive Officers of Major American Corporations, **1417**
"Corporate Giving: Theory and Policy", 1445
"Corporate Giving to Two-Year Colleges", **1635**
Corporate Giving Yellow Pages. Taft Guide to Corporate Giving Contacts, **1523**
Corporate Handbook of Aid-to-Education Programs, **1403**
The Corporate Investment in Higher Education: State and National Trends in Gift and Tax Support, 1314
"Corporate Leaders Say They Have Obligation to Meet Needs of Their Communities", 1396
"Corporate Matching Gift Program for Schools Underway", 3239
Corporate-Nonprofit Linkages in Minneapolis-St. Paul. Preliminary Findings from Three Surveys, 1471
"Corporate Nonprofit Teamwork", 1639
The Corporate 1000: A Directory of Those Who Manage the Leading 1000 Listed U.S. Companies, **1577**
"Corporate Philanthropists Give Up on the 'Free Lunch'", **1662**
Corporate Philanthropy, **1319**, 1513
Corporate Philanthropy: A Human Services Bibliography, 1645
"Corporate Philanthropy Abroad: How's It Doing?", 1360
"Corporate Philanthropy: Alternate Funding Sources", **1440**

347

TITLE INDEX

Corporate Philanthropy: An Annotated Bibliography, 1452
"Corporate Philanthropy Comes to Europe", 1984
"Corporate Philanthropy: How Much, If at All? Charity and Business Shouldn't Mix", 1550
Corporate Philanthropy in America: New Perspectives for the Eighties, **1570**
Corporate Philanthropy in New England: Maine, **1333**
Corporate Philanthropy in New England: New Hampshire, **1334**
Corporate Philanthropy in New England: Vermont, **1335**
Corporate Philanthropy in the Eighties: Expert Advice for Those Who Give or Seek Funds, **1602**
Corporate Philanthropy: Issues in the Current Literature, 1553
Corporate Philanthropy: Philosophy, Management, Trends, Future, Background, **1418**
"Corporate Planes Transport Cancer Victims", 1536
Corporate Planning in Girl Scouting, 2617
Corporate Power and Social Responsibility: A Blueprint for the Future, 1520
"Corporate Public Involvement: An Interview with John Filer", 1554
Corporate Public/Private Partnerships: Is It a New Time?, **1419**
"Corporate Responsibility and the American Dream", 1510
"Corporate Responsibility and the Competent Board", 1615
Corporate Responsibility in a Changing Society. Essays on Corporate Social Responsibility, 1323
"Corporate Restructuring with a Development Emphasis", **1582**
Corporate Social Investment: Portfolios for Social Wealth, 1682
Corporate Social Programs: Nontraditional Assistance, **1539**
Corporate Social Reporting in the United States and Western Europe, 1712
Corporate Social Responsibility and the Institutional Investor, 1569
Corporate Social Responsibility: Minnesota Strategies, 1482
Corporate Social Responsibility: Policies, Programs and Publications, 1406
Corporate Support for Community Development, 1370
"Corporate Support Key to United College Fund Growth", 1521
"Corporate Support: More Money and Involvement", 1590
Corporate Support of Higher Education, 1407
Corporate Support of Higher Education. 1972-1976, 1408
Corporate Support Program Research Project, 1600
Corporate Tuition Aid Programs, **1614**

Corporate Voluntary Contributions in Europe, 1883
"Corporate Volunteer Programs", 4602
"The Corporation and Its Obligations: An Interview with C. Peter McColough of Xerox Corporation", 1320
The Corporation and the Arts, 1446
The Corporation and the Campus, 1383
Corporation Contributions to Organized Community Welfare Services, 1738
Corporation Giving, **1307**
Corporation Giving in a Free Society, 1447
Corporations and Their Critics, **1327**
"Corporations for Art", 1356
"Corporations Have Something to Offer Those Foundations", **901**
"Corporations Increase Giving to Education in 1982 by Twenty Percent, to $1.3 Billion", 1400
"Corporations May Benefit from Promoting Nonprofits", 1618
"Corporations with a Conscience", **1401**
"Corporatist Culture Ministries", 1607
Corrective Capitalism: The Rise of America's Community Development Corporations, 2285
Cost Principles for Nonprofit Organizations, 4762
"Cost Squeeze, Budget Ax Prods Market Piggybacking Trend", 3685
The Costs and Benefits of Deferred Giving, 3278
"Cotton Mather and the Doing of Good: A Puritan Gospel of Wealth", 39
Cottrell, Samaritan of Science, 75
"Council Bill Seeks to Remove Impediments to Foundation Gifts", 722
The Council on Foundations, **366**
"Council to Develop Community Foundations Technical Assistance Program with Support of Charles Stewart Mott Foundation", 652
Counsellor's Tax Guide to Charitable Contributions, 4359
"Counting the Cost of Giving", 668
"Courses in Philanthropy: A First in U.S. Colleges", **191**
"A Court Approves City's Right to Tax Nonprofit Group", 4166
Court Decision: Erica P. John (DeRance, Inc.) vs. Harry G. John (DeRance, Inc.), 1290
Courtroom Crucible: The Smith Charities, 719
Cousins and Strangers. Comments on America by Commonwealth Fund Fellows from Britain, 1946-1952, 1094
Cracking the Corporations: Finding Corporate Funding for Family Violence Programs, **1439**
Cradle of the Middle Class: The Family in Oneida County, New York. 1790-1865, **4571**
"The Craft of Research Foundations and Corporations", 3962
"Crazy about Families", 3649
Created Equal, 4837

Creating a Media Resource Guide: Communication Resource Handbook Five, 2937
Creating Neighborhood Enterprise: A Primer for Nonprofits, **2917**
Creating Private Alternatives in Higher Education, 4850
"Creating the Nonprofit Entrepreneur", 2193
"Creating the Right Match", **1075**
"Creative Financing for Nonprofits", 3770
Creative Philanthropy: Carnegie Corporation and Africa, 1953-1973, 1901
"Creativity As the Cornerstones of Philanthropy", 736
"Credibility Critical in Celebrity Mail Packages", 3535
"Credit Card Companies Embrace Cause Marketing", **1424**
The Crisis in Higher Education: A Shared Responsibility and a Major Opportunity, 3128
"Criteria for the Appraisal of Directors", 1597
Cross Subsidization by Non-Profit Organizations: Theory, Evidence and Evaluation, 2188
"Cultivating Major Donors As Greatest Untapped Source", 3629
"'Cultivating Relationships' Attracts Foundation Support", 674
"Cultivating the Big Gift", 3490
"Cultivating Your Computer: A Botanical Garden Case Study", 3828
Cultural Directory 2: Federal Funds and Services for the Arts and Humanities, **4630**
Cultural Facilities in Mixed-Use Development, 3839
Culture and Company: A Critical Study of an Improbable Alliance, 1655
"Culture's Hidden Persuaders", 180
The Current Climate and Major Trends in American Philanthropy, **433**
Current Thought on Corporate Giving: A Survey and Analysis of the Literature, 1474
Currents Index, 1975-1984, 4961
"The Curse of Assumptions", **3240**
The Cy Pres Doctrine in the United States, 746
Dance: Application Guidelines, 4692
Dancing, 4886
Danger on the Right, 764
The Dangerous Classes of New York and Twenty Year's Work among Them, **52**
Dare to Chair, **2641**
Daring Goals for a Caring Society: A Blueprint for Substantial Growth in Giving and Volunteering in America, **231**
Daring Venture: The Story of William H. Danforth, 383
Data on Philanthropy in New Jersey: Alternatives for Data Collection and Analysis. Preliminary Report, 159
"Database Creation Helps This School Build Income, Friends", 3267

TITLE INDEX

"Database Marketing Propels Non-Profits into New Age", 3282
David: Report on a Rockefeller, 223
"Day Care: A New Alliance", **3195**
"The Day Trust: The High Cost of a $2,801 Foundation Excise Tax Refund", 4137
DC Directory of Native American Federal and Private Programs, 3715
The de Facto Non-Profit Sector in Yugoslavia, 1903
The Dead Hand: Addresses on the Subject of Endowments and Settlements of Property, 851
"Dealing with the IRS", **4178**
Dear Chris: Advice to a Volunteer Fund Raiser, 3932
Dear Friend. Mastering the Art of Direct Mail Fund Raising, 3536
"Debate Grows over Fundraising Bonuses", **3859**
"Debate over For-Profit vs. Nonprofit Health Providers Heats Up", 2081
Decentralization: A Program for the Arts in New York State, 4726
The Decline of Radicalism: Reflections on America Today, 44
"Deferred Gift Derring-Do", 3068
"Deferred Giving: Accent on Planning", 3397
"Deferred Giving: It's Never Too Late", 3185
"Deferred Giving: Letting the Donor Have His Cake While You Eat It Too", 3835
"Define Your Roles: Nonprofits Must Have Clearly Understood Responsibilities for Their CEO's and Trustees", 2545
"Defining Purpose. Part 2: Writing the Statement of Purpose", 2522
A Degree and What Else? Correlates and Consequences of a College Education, 4985
Delaware Foundations, **1252**
"Delaware Museum Seeks Funds to Support a Du Pont Legacy", 3775
"A Delicate Balance: Foundation Board-Staff Relations", 1060
The Demise of Diversity? A Comparative Profile of Eight Types of Institutions, 4922
Democracy and Social Ethics, **5**
Democracy and the Gospel of Wealth, 271
Democracy in America: Towards Greater Participation, **1043**
"Democrats' Direct Mail Efforts Segment the Issues", 3466
The Dependent Child: A Story of Changing Aims and Methods in the Care of Dependent Children, **4973**
"Depreciation Will Be Required for All Nonprofits: The Discussion in the FASB (Financial Accounting Standards Board)", **2355**
Description of Income Tax Provisions Relating to Private Foundations. Scheduled for Hearings before the Subcommittee on Oversight of the Committee on Ways and Means on June 27, 28, and 30, 1983, 4434
"Designing Volunteer Jobs for Results", 4548
Designs for Fund-Raising: Principles, Patterns and Techniques, 3816
"Despite Long History, Black Philanthropy Gets Little Credit As 'Self-Help' Tool", **87**
Destroying Democracy: How Government Funds Partisan Politics, 4614
"Determining Cost of Services, Break-Even Analysis and Pricing", 2831
Deutsche Stiftungen fur Wissenschaft, Bildung und Kultur (German foundations for science, education and culture), 1905
"Developing a Fundraising Strategy", **3040**
"Developing a Grant Proposal: Some Basic Principles", 4029
Developing a Mass Promotion for Books: How to Use Ads and Direct Mail to Increase Your Sales, 2661
"Developing a Membership Base", 2651
"Developing a Sensible Fund Raising Strategy", 3924
Developing Good Will, 644
The Developing Law of Endowment Funds, 4118
"Developing Leadership in Minority Communities", **2230**
Developing Successful Volunteer Programs: A Guide for Local Government, 4499
Developing Your Community-Based Organization: With Special Emphasis on Economic Development Organizations and Community Action Agencies, 2767
The Development Consultant Program: Kit of Guidelines and Samples, 2918
Development in Science Education: Guide for the Preparation of Proposals, 4705
The Development of American Political Sociology: A Case Study of the Ford Foundation's Role in the Production of Knowledge, 1168
The Development of an Evaluation Procedure for Larger Grants, 1702
Development of the Activity of Foundations. International Field Conference, 1791
Development of the Law and Continuing Legal Issues in the Tax Treatment of Private Foundations, 98th Congress, 1st Session, June 17, 1983, 4407
Development Today: A Fund Raising Guide for Nonprofit Organizations, 3529
"Development Trends at Selected Hospitals", **3527**
"Dialing for Dollars: Using Phone-a-Thons for Renewals", 3217
"Diary of a Homeless Man", 4814
"A Different Way to Start a Nonprofit", **856**
The Difficult Art of Giving: The Epic of Alan Gregg, 373
A Digest of Reports of the Carnegie Commission on Higher Education with an Index of Recommendations and Suggested Assignments of Responsibility for Action, 4794
Digest of Statistics on Higher Education in the United States, 1969-1970, 1973-74, 4825
Dimensions of the Independent Sector: A Statistical Profile, **221, 222**
The Diplomacy of Ideas: U.S. Foreign Policy and Cultural Relations, 1938-1950, **1911**
Direct Mail: A Preliminary View, 3225
Direct Mail and Mail Order Handbook, 2648
"Direct Mail Expectations, Great and Small", 3226
Direct Mail Fund Raising, 3748
"Direct Mail Fund Raising: Sweepstakes and Other Trends", 3697
"Direct Mail Fund Raising: Where Do I Begin?", 3173
"Direct Marketers' Battle Tactic Good Strategy for Fund Raisers", 3733
Direct Marketing: Strategy, Planning, Execution, 2782
"Director Who Remembered to Bring Her Credentials", 38
Directorio de las Fundaciones Espanolas (Directory of Spanish foundations), **1772**
Directorio Nacional de Instituciones Privadas Filantropicas y de Desarrollo Social (National directory of private philanthropic institutions and social development), 1745
Directors' and Officers' Liability: A Crisis in the Making, **2284**
Directors and Officers Liability Insurance, 2529
Directory of Biomedical and Health Care Grants, 3228
Directory of Building and Equipment Grants, 3254
Directory of Campus-Business Linkages: Education and Business Prospering Together, 1453
Directory of Charitable Funds in New Hampshire, **1042**
Directory of Community Services: The Bronx, Manhattan and Staten Island, **2268**
Directory of Corporate Affiliations, 1989, **1433**
Directory of Dallas County Foundations, **848**
Directory of Dayton Area Grantmakers, **1110**
Directory of Directors in the City of New York and Tri-State Area, **1434**
Directory of Evaluation Consultants, **2674**
Directory of Federal Aid for Education, 4633
Directory of Fellowship Awards for the Years 1917-1950, 1132
Directory of Fellowship Awards for the Years 1917-1970, 1133
Directory of Fellowship Awards for the Years 1922-1950, 805

349

TITLE INDEX

Directory of Foundations in Massachusetts, 989

A Directory of Foundations in Utah, **882**

Directory of Foundations of the Greater Washington Area, **634**

Directory of Grant-Making Foundations: Guide to Private Grant Sources, 1816

Directory of Grant-Making Foundations in Rhode Island, **643**

Directory of Grant-Making Trusts, **1775**

Directory of Grantmakers Interested in Precollegiate Education, **653**

Directory of Grants in the Physical Sciences, **3229**

The Directory of Greater Kansas City Foundations, **618**

"Directory of Hispanic Arts Organizations", **2086**

Directory of Historical Societies and Agencies in the United States and Canada, 2236

Directory of Humanities Resource People in New York State, 2714

Directory of Idaho Foundations, **700**

The Directory of Illinois Foundations, **706**

Directory of International Corporate Giving in America, **1524**

Directory of International Fellows, 1925-1965, 633

The Directory of Kansas Foundations, **840**

Directory of Maine Foundations, **608**

Directory of Management Resources for Community Organizations, 2830

Directory of Matching Gift Programs for the Arts, **3099**

Directory of Members, 2797

The Directory of Missouri Foundations, **701**

Directory of Montana and Wyoming Foundations, **1001**

Directory of New and Emerging Foundations, **1066**

The Directory of Oklahoma Foundations, **1206**

Directory of Pennsylvania Foundations, **917**

A Directory of Philanthropic Trusts, 1783

Directory of Philanthropic Trusts in Australia, 1837

Directory of Private Bar Involvement Programs, **2435**

Directory of Private, Nonprofit Preservation Organizations: State and Local Levels, 2259

Directory of Religious Organizations in the United States of America, 2087

A Directory of Rural Organizations, 2258

Directory of Services, **2106**

Directory of Social and Health Agencies of New York City, 2215

Directory of Socially Responsible Investments, **2512**

Directory of Tarrant County Foundations, **1109**

Directory of Texas Foundations, **1264**

The Directory of the Major California Foundations, **956**

Directory of the Major Connecticut Foundations, **957**

The Directory of the Major Florida Foundations, **958**

Directory of the Major Greater Boston Foundations, **959**

The Directory of the Major New Jersey Foundations, **960**

The Directory of the Major Texas Foundations, **961**

Directory of Women's Organizations, 2088

Directory. Three Hundred-Thirty Funded Community Health Centers, 2255

Dirty Business: The Corporate-Political Money-Power Game, 1427

"Disappointed, Large Foundation Dumps Higher Education", **1113**

"Disasters and Charity: Some Aspects of Cooperative Economic Behavior", 3235

"Discouraging Charity", **4267**

Discover Total Resources: A Guide for Nonprofits, **2764**

The Discovery of the Asylum: Social Order and Disorder in the New Republic, **4944**

Discussion Draft of Report and Recommended Program Plan for Measurable Growth in Giving and Volunteering, 232

"Discussions of the Form 990 Advisory Committee: Problems of a Multi-Purpose Form", **4344**

"Disease and Social Order in America: Perceptions and Expectations", 4943

"Disrupted Dimensions of Risk: A Public School Controversy over AIDS", 4917

Dissertations and Discussions, 337

"The Distinctive Nature of the Voluntary Organization Management", 2749

"A Disturbing New Wrinkle from IRS: Exchange of Mailing Lists Is Now Considered Taxable Income", 4184

"The Divestment Dilemma: The South African Divestment Issue's Impact on Fund Raising, PR, and Alumni Relations", 2761

Divestment of South Africa Investments: A Legal Analysis for Foundations, Other Charitable Institutions and Pension Funds, **2929**

"Do Corporations Give Enough?", 1565

Do Government Grants to Charity Reduce Private Donations?, 2310

Do-It-Yourself Marketing Research, 2482

"Do Nonprofit Organizations Compete Unfairly with Business?", 2389

Do or Die: Survival for Nonprofits, 2715

"Do You Need a Computer?", 3972

Doctor Dillard of the Jeanes Fund, 55

"Documenting Needs for the Program Plan", 2633

Documenting Your Organization's Information System: A Manual, 2944

Does the Nonprofit Form Fit the Hospital Industry?, 2054

"Does Your Report Measure Up to the Objectives", 2175

"Does Your System Get in the Way of Your Mission?", 2560

Doing Good: The Limits of Benevolence, **4846**

"Doing Well by Doing Good: Should Business Link Philanthropy to Promotional Schemes?", **1669**

Dollars and Sense: A Community Fundraising Manual for Women's Shelters and Other Non-Profit Organizations, 3955

Dollars for Research: Science and Its Patrons in Nineteenth-Century America, **338**

"Dollars to Donors: Revenue Canada Helps Those Who Help the Charities", 1980

"Donald Young: Unique Loan Finances Modernization Projects", 2561

"Donations Increase to Groups Studying Prevention of War", 1226

Donations, Local Government Spending, and the "New Federalism", **2350**

"The Donor Connection: How to Make It Click", 3792

"Donor/Donee Relationship: Reciprocal Positive Influence", 2291

"Donor Motivation", **3773**

"The Donor Process: Solicitation and Recognition", 3485

"The Donor Profile Survey: A Way to Determine Priorities", 3798

"Donor Pyramid Explained", 3395

Donors and Dollars: Investing in Direct Mail Fund Raising, 3230

Donors and Donees: Sharing Philanthropic Responsibilities, 2788

Donors Forum Members Grant List, **707**

"Donors Must Be Cultivated to Become Major Donors", 3233

"Don't Call It Fund Raising", 3183

"Don't Make the Creative Mistakes That Cut Response", 3565

"Dos and Don'ts in Proposal Writing: How to Increase Your Probability of Obtaining Federal Funding", 4053

"Double Identity: Several Churches and Synagogues Operate Grantmaking Programs Exactly like Private Foundations", 384

"Douglas Fairbanks Jr. to Be Honored at Int'l Ball", 137

Draft European Convention on the Tax Treatment in Respect of Certain Non-Profit Organizations, 1975

"Dramatic Changes in New Planned Giving Tables: New IRS Tables for Charitable Gift Annuities", 4087

Driven from the Tribunal: Judicial Resolution of Internal Church Disputes, 4828

Drug Abuse Funding Service: A Directory of Federal, State and Foundation Grants for Drug Abuse Education, Prevention and Treatment Services, **3220**

Du Pont: Behind the Nylon Curtain, 522

The Du Ponts: From Gunpowder to Nylon, 135

The Du Ponts of Delaware, 86

TITLE INDEX

The Du Ponts: Portrait of a Dynasty, 138
"Due to Circumstances Beyond Our Control", 986
The Dynamics of Educational Change: Toward Responsive Schools, 4851
The Dynamics of Funding, 3942
Early History and Influence of Harvard College's Hollis Professorship of Divinity (the First Endowed Professorial Chair in America), **287**
The Early History of English Poor Relief, 1875
Early Schooling in England and Israel, 4833
Early Schooling in the United States, 4852
"Earth to Board Members: Are We All Clear?", 2690
"Earth, Wind and Loss of Momentum", 2332
"Easing the Bite from Unrelated Business Income Tax", 4093
East-West Philanthropy Conference, 2991
East-West Philanthropy Conference. Philanthropy in the Seventies, 2992
Economic and Empiric Analysis of Fund-Raising Behavior by Nonprofit Firms, 3857
Economic Factors in the Growth of Corporation Giving, 1604
"The Economic Recovery Program and the Non-Profit Sector", 4467
"Economic Research Sponsored by Private Foundations", 1037
The Economics and Financing of Higher Education in the United States, 4760
The Economics of Charity, 239
The Economics of Nonprofit Institutions: Studies in Structure and Policy, **2311**
"Economics of Planned Gifts: Myths Destroy Programs", 3138
The Economics of Public Finance, 65
"EDI: Capital with a Conscience", **1361**
"Educating Communities", **990**
Educating Managers of Nonprofit Organizations, **2822**
"Education, a Capital Investment: Why Corporations Give Billions to Colleges and Universities", **1443**
Education and Development Reconsidered, 4978
Education and the Business Dollar: A Study of Corporate Contributions Policy and American Education, 1616
Education and Training Program Plans and Guidelines, 4756
Education for All People: A Grassroots Primer, 3196
Education for Citizenship: A Foundation's Experience, 1239
"Education Gifts Forecast to Rise Nine Percent a Year", 3255
"The Education of a Philanthropist", **417**
Education Resource Directory, 4667
Educational Fund Raising and the Law, 3035
Educational Fund Raising Manual, 3021, 2990

Edward Stephen Harkness, 1874-1940, 516
Edward Warriner Hazen, 1860-1929: A Biographical Sketch, 425
Edwin Gould: The Man and His Legacy, 642
The Effect of Tax Exemption and Other Factors on Competition between Nonprofit and For-Profit Enterprise, 2152
"The Effect of the Private Foundations Provisions of the Tax Reform Act of 1969 on Community Development Corporations", 4232
Effecting Organizational Renewal in Schools: A Social Systems Perspective, 4983
The Effective Board. 1960, 2658
"Effective Boards in a Time of Transition", 2880
"Effective Budgeting", 2707
Effective Corporate Fundraising, **1331**
Effective Internal Accounting Control for Nonprofit Organizations: A Guide for Directors and Management, 2839, 2840
"Effective Leadership", **2118**
Effective Leadership in Voluntary Organizations, **2808**
The Effective Management of Volunteer Programs, 2966
The Effective Nonprofit Executive Handbook, 2845
"Effective Strategic Planning in Nonprofit Organizations", 2449
Effective Trusteeship: Guidelines for Board Members, 2980
"Effective Use of Volunteers: Who, Why, When and How", 4547
The Effective Voluntary Board of Directors: What Is It and How It Works, **2520**
"The Effects of the Proposed Regulations on Charitable Remainder Trusts", 4228
"Eight Months of Good Intentions, But No Grants to Schools", 3257
"'82 Gifts to Charity a Record, But Rate of Increase Slowed", 464
"Einstein Revealed As Brillant in Youth", 458
Elderly Private/Public Partnerships, 3258
"Electronic Funds Transfer Ideal for Monthly Giving", 3024
"The Electronic Tonic", 3042
"Elements to Test in Direct Mail Packages", 3537
"Eleven Criteria for Evaluating the Executive Director", 2685
Eleven Ways Associations Can Increase Income, 3259
The Elusive Promise of Management Cooperation in the Performing Arts, **2601**
Embarrassing Dollars and Hints to Their Holders, 859
The Emergence of the Philanthropic Foundation As an American Social Institution, 1900-1920, 863
"Emergency Loan Funds: Help for Cash Flow Crisis", 3261
The Emerging Arts: Management Survival and Growth, 2670

"Emerging Pattern in Corporate Giving", 1637
Emma Willard: Daughter of Democracy, 314
"Emotion, Right Price, Prizes Spark Employee Contributions", 3472
"Employee Annual Giving", 3989
"Encourage Donors to Consider Living Trusts", 3756
The Encyclopedia of U.S. Government Benefits, **4656**
"The End of Another Myth", 1544
The Endangered Sector, 357
"Endowment and Foundation Funds Did Better Than Market As Whole in First Half, Data Show", 727
"Endowment. Key Ingredient for Non-Profit Hospitals", 3993
"Endowments", 679
The Energy Conservation Idea Handbook, 4766
Energy Resource Guide, 3661
English Charities. Part 1: Legal Definition, Taxation, and Regulation, 1792
English Philanthropy, 1660-1960, **1916**
The English Poor Law System, 1754
Enterprise in the Nonprofit Sector, 2070
Entrepreneurial Approaches to Revenue Generation in the Voluntary Sector, 2316
Entrepreneurship in the Non-Profit Sector: Preliminary Report, 2263
The Environmental Grantmakers Association Directory, **733**
"The Epidemic of AIDS: A Failure of Public Health Policy", 4891
Equity Syndication: How Does It Work? How Can Cities, Nonprofits Use It?, 3048
"The Esquire Register", 146
An Essential Bibliography for Grassroots Consumer Organizations, 2103
An Essential Grace: Funding Canada's Health Care, Education, Welfare, Religion and Culture, 1880
"Essential Ingredients for Fundraising Planning. Part 2", **3787**
Establishing a Charitable Foundation in Michigan, 1217
"Establishing a Nonprofit Corporation: A Case Study", **2555**
"Establishing a Nursing Education Fund", 3619
"Establishing a Private Foundation", 735, **817**
"Establishing Endowment: A Small College's Survival Kit", 3513
"Estate of Buck: Frustration of a Charitable Purpose", 604
The Estate of George Washington, Deceased, 394
Estate Planning: Quick Reference Outline, 3850
The Ethical Investor: Universities and Corporate Responsibility, 1674
"Ethics and Enterprise: The Values of the Boston Elite, 1800-1860", **183**
"Ethics and Fund Raising Letters: Ten Suggestions", 3445

351

TITLE INDEX

"Ethics and the NMA", 2533
The Ethics of Corporate Grantmaking, **1617**
"Evaluating Development Costs for a Proposal to a Federal Agency", 4665
"Evaluating Fund-Raising Software", **3584**
Evaluating Private Philanthropy: A Practical Guide, 348
"Evaluating Public Relations Effectiveness: A Necessary Function", 2699
Evaluating Results, **2809**
Evaluation Handbook, **2846**
The Evaluation Interview, 2581
"Evaluation, Media Style", **2825**
Evaluator's Handbook, 2775
"An Evening at the Theater to Help AIDS Research", 3420
Everybody's Business, an Almanac: The Irreverent Guide to Corporate America, 1595
"Everyone Benefits When Families Volunteer: A Preview of Volunteer's New Workbook for Involving Families", 4518
"The Evolution of Telephone Fund Raising: 5 Case Studies", 3782
"Evolution of the Philanthropic Foundation", 853
An Examination of Bay Area Corporate Non-Cash Contributions, 1461
"Examining the Role of a Hospital Trustee", 2535
Excellence: Can We Be Equal and Excellent Too?, 4844
"Excerpts from Newman's Report on Higher Education Policy", 4830
Executive Development for Foundation Management: The Results of a National Survey, **2742**
Executive Session: The Best of the Nonprofit Executive, 2580
Exempt Organizations and the Arts, 2721
Exempt Organizations Reporter, 4127
"Expanding Your Board of Directors", 2652
Expansion Arts: Application Guidelines, 4693
Expansion, Entry and Exit in the Nonprofit Sector: The Long and Short of It, **2326**
The Experiment: A Novel, 685
"An Expert Strategy for Saving the Non-Profit Postal Rate", 2104
Explanation of Tax Reform Act of 1969, 4144
An Explanation Selected from CCH Tax Reform Action of 1976 Law and Explanation, 4128
Exploitation from 9 to 5, 4955
An Exploration of Entrepreneurship in the Field of Nursing Home Care for the Elderly: Case Studies, 2140
"Exploratorium Shares Research: Corporations Match Employee Gifts", 3271
"Exploring New Developments in Computerized Fund Raising", 3822

Exploring Volunteer Space: The Recruiting of a Nation, 4573
Exposure Draft: Proposed Guide: The Audits of Certain Nonprofit Organizations, 2438
Externalities, Exclusivity, Stratification, and Cooperation: A Theory of Associative Organizations, 2153
"Exxon Increases Support for Nonprofit Management", 1449
Facilities Funding Finesse. Proceedings. ALA Conference, 2999
"Facing Emergency Needs: Foundations in Other Cities Have Created Emergency Structures", 3231
Factbook: Guide to National Science Foundation Programs and Activities, 4640
"Factors in the Success and Failure of Non-Profit Organizations", **2126**
Facts and Trends 1987: A Resource Guide to Conditions in the USA, **743**
The Facts On File Dictionary of Nonprofit Organization Management, **2823**
"'Fairness' and the Charitable Deduction for Nonitemizers", 233
"Faith, Hope, and Chicanery", **2391**
Faith, Hope and $5,000. The Story of Monsanto: The Trials and Triumphs of the First 75 Years, 1462
The Fall of Public Man, 4950
"Family Secrets", **3114**
Family Security through Estate Planning, 263
"Famous Amos Promotes Literacy Organization on Ice Cream Box", 1450
Famous Givers and Their Gifts, **43**
"A Farewell to Alms", 830
"Farsighted Corporations Focus on Long-Term Gains", **1571**
"FASB's Proposals for 'Nonbusiness' Accounting: Comments from Four Directions", 2686
"Fast and Luce", **60**
Federal Alcohol and Drug Abuse Initiatives: A Special Report, 3745
Federal and Private Foundation Programs Conference, 602
The Federal Budget and the Nonprofit Sector, 4737
Federal Funding Guide. 2 Vols, **4653**
Federal Funding Programs for Social Scientists, 4615
Federal Funds for Research and Development, Fiscal Years 1977, 1978 and 1979. Surveys of Science Resources Studies, 4706
The Federal Government and the Nonprofit Sector: Implications of the Reagan Budget Proposals, 4738
The Federal Government and the Nonprofit Sector: Philanthropy Monthly Reviews, 4745
The Federal Government and the Nonprofit Sector: The Impact of the 1981 Tax Act on Individual Charitable Giving, 4123
Federal Grants for Library and Information Services, 4651

Federal Grants. The National Interest and State Response: A Review of Theory and Research, 4611
"Federal Office of Management and Budget Proposes More Stringent Rules on Advocacy by Nonprofit Groups Receiving Federal Funds", 4145
Federal Patronage of Universities: A Rose by Many Other Names?, 4646
Federal Policy and the Voluntary Sector: A Bibliography, 4510
"Federal Reserve Board Survey Suggests Bright Future for Planned Giving", 3154
"Federal Restrictions on Foundations", 4146
The Federal Role in Postsecondary Education: Unfinished Business, 1975-1980, 4808
"Federal Study Cites Slow Arts Growth", 2247
"Federal Tax on Unrelated Debt-Financed Income", 4111
"Federal Tax Plan Called Devastating to Charitable World", 4147
Federal Tax Policy and Charitable Giving, **4124**
Federal Tax Treatment of Unrelated Business Income, 4224
"Federal Tax Update", 4112, 4113
Federal Yellow Book: A Directory of the Federal Departments and Agencies, **4628**
"Federated Fundraising", 3497
"Feds Crack Down on Nonprofit Income", 2107
"Feeling Charitable? Find Out Where the Money Goes", **2108**
Fidalgos and Philanthropists. The Santa Casa Da Misericordia, 1550-1755, **1935**
"Fierce Competition among Colleges Predicted As Many Gear Up to Seek More Private Money", 3212
The Fifteen Largest United States Foundations: Financial Structure and the Impact of the Tax Reform Act of 1969, 4390
Fifty Years in Review, 606
Fifty Years with the Golden Rule, 374
"Fighting the 'Chill Effect'", **2075**
"Filer Commission Paved Philanthropic Road", 1163
"The Filer Commission Revisited", 918
"Filling Big Hopes with Small Grants", **1227**
"Filling the School Funding Gap", 3066
"Final Regs on Section 4945: Working with the New Rules Restricting Foundations' Activities", 4308
Final Report and Testimony Submitted to Congress by the Commission on Industrial Relations, 64th Congress, 1st Session, 4750
Final Report on Foreign Aid Submitted to Congress by the Select Committee on Foreign Aid, 80th Congress, 2nd Session, 4749
Final Report. 64th Congress, 1st Session, 4751

352

TITLE INDEX

Final Thoughts, 385
"Finally, a Beginning? Philanthropy and the American Indian", **460**
"Finally: A Study on Costs, Benefits of Deferred Gifts", 3279
The Finances of the Performing Arts. Part 1: A Survey of 166 Professional Nonprofit Resident Theaters, Operas, Symphonies, Ballets, and Modern Dance Companies, 2109
Financial Accounting in Nonbusiness Organizations: An Exploratory Study of Conceptual Issues, 2447
Financial Accounting in Nonbusiness Organizations: An Overview of the Research Report by Robert N. Anthony, 2583
"Financial Analysis and Planning: Tools for Non-Profit Organizations", 2832
Financial and Accounting Guide for Nonprofit Organizations, **2624**
Financial and Strategic Management for Nonprofit Organizations, 2493
Financial Management for Nonprofit Organizations, 2518
Financial Management in Nonprofit Organizations, 2948
Financial Management of Nonprofit Organizations: Reference Material, 2798
"Financial Management of Nonprofit Organizations: Selected Topics", 2708
Financial Management Strategies for Arts Organizations, 2930
Financial Planning and Evaluation for the Nonprofit Organization, 2605
"Financial Reporting by Community Foundations", **1210**
Financial Resource Management for Nonprofit Organizations, 2635
Financial Survey of Peace and International Security Organizations: A Preliminary Report, **2406**
Financial Trends in Organized Social Work in New York City, 2174
"Financing Arts Organizations: The Charity As the General Partner in a Limited Partnership", 3276
Financing Higher Education in the United States, 3631
Financing Higher Education, 1969-70, 3482
Financing Humanistic Service, 1881
The Financing of Social Work, 3742
Financing Online Search Services in Publicly Supported Libraries, 3590
"Financing Private Colleges: The Picture Has Changed", 3056
Finding, Developing and Rewarding Good Board Members, **2810**
"Finding Funds for Youth Shelters", **3111**
"Finding Out about Foundations", 1965
"Finding the Real Bottom Line", 1739
"The Fine Art of Funding", **3401**
Fire and Ice. The Story of Charles Revson: The Man Who Built the Revlon Empire, 475
Fireworks, Brass Bands and Elephants: Promotional Events with Flair for Libraries and Other Nonprofit Organizations, 3571
"Firing Up for Funding: A Model Faculty Proseminar in Grants and Contracts", 4013
The First Charity: How Philanthropy Can Contribute to Democracy in America, **253**
"A First for the Cathedral: St. John the Divine Hopes to Emulate the Fund-Raising Successes of the Public Library and the Zoo", 3182
The First Half-Century, 1930-1980: Private Approaches to Public Needs, 908
"First Lady of Theater Always a Pushover for a Good Cause", **4532**
"First Meeting: The Form 990 Advisory Committee", 4332
First Steps in Starting a Foundation, **723**
The First Ten Years: The Story of the Beginning and Achievements of the Physicians' Services Incorporated Foundation during the First Decade from 1970 to 1980, 680
The First Thirty Years: A Report on the Activities of the Kresge Foundation, 1924-1953, 925
The First Twenty Years of Carnegie Corporation, 1087
"Fiscal Agents Can Be Illegal", **2099**
Fiscal Aspects of Foundations and Charitable Donations in European Countries, 1902
The Fiscal Capacity of the Voluntary Sector, 2317
A Fiscal Management Handbook for Small Nonprofit Organizations, 2566
"Fitting the Business to the Non-Profit: Keeping in Control", 2196
"Fitting the Pieces Together", 2717
"$5-Billion Sale Makes Institute Richest Charity", 124
Five Blue-Ribbon Ways to Give Away Your Money, **105**
"Five Challenges Outlined at Battle Creek Gathering", 258
Five Evolving Strategies for Youth Services: A Resource Guide, 2157
"Five Great Gifts", 808
Five Hundred Thirty-Four Ways to Raise Money, 3382
"Five-Page Letter Raises $546,116 from 2,400 Prospects", 3284
Five Percent and Two Percent Clubs in the United States, 1343
"Five Percent Clubs Channel Arts Donations", 1687
"Five Self-Serving Reasons for Foundations to Communicate and a New Service to Help Them Do It", **954**
"Five Steps to Progressive Fundraising", 3789
"Flexibility: Essential Trait for Successful Fund Raising", 3528
"Focus on: Grant Funding", 3710
Folklife and the Federal Government: A Guide to Activities, Resources, Funds and Services, 4624
Fondation Europeenne de la Culture (European Cultural Foundation), 1796
Fondations, 1824
Les Fondations En Europe: Une Etude Comparative, 1906
Fondations: Reconnues D'utilite Publique En France, 1952
Le Fondazioni Italine. Con Un Saggio Sulle Fondazioni Private Nell 'Ordinamento Giurdico Di Dante Cosi, 1797
Food, Money and People. Seminar, 2053
Footprints, 22
"For a Mere Song", 3762
"For a Price, Free Advice: Some Thoughts on the Role of Consultants", 2593
"For All It's Worth: Analyzing Revenue, Assets, and Fundraising Costs", **3558**
"For Fee or Charity?", 2401
For Fun and Funds: Creative Fund-Raising Ideas for Your Organization, 3209
For More Information: A Guide to Arts Management Information Centers, **2149**
"For Nonprofits: What Is Permissible Activity during a Political Campaign", 4154
"For-Profit Activities in the Nonprofit World: Where Do We Draw the Line?", **2347**
"For-Profit Corporation Best Way to Make Money for Association, Provides 'Bottom-Line' Vehicle Needed", 2111
"For RAGs' It's Riches", **752**
For the People of North Carolina: The Z. Smith Reynolds Foundation at Half-Century, 1936-1986, **1289**
For the Soul and the Pocketbook: A Resource Guide for the Arts in Rural and Small Communities, 3936
For the Welfare of Mankind: The Commonwealth Fund and American Medicine, **841**
For the Working Artist: A Survival Guide for Performing, Visual and Media Artists Who Choose to Manage Their Own Careers, 3588
"The Forbes Four Hundred", 158, 1460
"Forbes's List of the Richest", 1535
"The Ford Foundation As a Transnational Actor", **1761**
The Ford Foundation at Work: Philanthropic Choices, Methods, and Styles, 972
"Ford (Foundation) Has a Better Way", 551
"Ford Foundation Leads Delayed Philanthropic Response to AIDS", 1228
"Ford Foundation Plans Sixty Percent Increase in Support for Hispanic Programs", 690
Ford Foundation Support for the Arts in the United States: A Discussion of New Emphasis in the Foundation's Arts Programs, 757
The Ford Foundation: The Men and the Millions, **967**

TITLE INDEX

"Ford Foundation Weighs New Venture in Puerto Rico", 763
The Fords: An American Epic, 100
Foreign Assistance: A View from the Private Sector, 1968
"Foreign Funding of Research", **1872**
"Foreign Policy", **1942**
The Forgotten Half: Pathways to Success for America's Youth and Young Families, **4857**
"The Forgotten Milestone", **1489**
"Form 990 for 1984", 4155
Formal Education of Nonprofit Organization Leaders/Managers, **2663**
Formal Systems of Appraisal of Individual Performance: Some Considerations, Critical Issues, and Application to Non-Profit Organizations, 2031
"Formation and Qualification of a Charitable Organization", 4375
Forming and Operating a Nonprofit Organization, 4103
The Forming of the Charitable Institutions of the West of England: A Study of the Changing Pattern of Social Aspirations on Bristol and Somerset, 1480-1660, 1867
"Fortune 500 Directory: Geographic Breakdown, City", 1463
"Fortune 500 Directory: Geographic Breakdown, State", 1464
"The Fortune Service 500 Directory: Geographic Breakdown, City", 1465
"The Fortune Service 500 Directory: Geographic Breakdown, State", 1466
Forty Years of Carnegie Giving, 298
"Fostering the Voluntary Spirit: Motivating People to Serve", 4508
The Foundation, 910
The Foundation Administrator: A Study of Those Who Manage America's Foundations, **2978**
"Foundation and Corporate Funding: Effecting the Possible", 3290
The Foundation and the Junior College: A Workshop for Junior College Institutional Teams, 529
"The Foundation behind the 'Genius Grants'", 1127
"The Foundation Center: A Valuable Information Resource", 715
"Foundation Center of Gravity Shifting to West?", 775
Foundation Community Representation: An Analysis of the Representation of Community in Pennsylvania Foundation Grant Decisions, 1240
Foundation Compensation Report, **654**
"Foundation Denounces U.S. Education Policy", 776
The Foundation Directory, **769**
Foundation 500: An Index to Foundation Giving Patterns, 777
Foundation for Living: The Story of Charles Stewart Mott and Flint, 521
Foundation Fundamentals: A Guide for Grantseekers, **1099**

"Foundation Funding and Psychiatric Research", **3494**
"Foundation Funding for AIDS Education", **1269**
"Foundation Funding for AIDS Programs", **3954**
"Foundation Funding for Environmental Programs", 578
"Foundation Funding: Information and Resource Guide", 570
Foundation Funding Resource Guide for Programs Serving North Carolina's Handicapped Population, 980
"The Foundation Game: Unwritten Rules", **4020**
"Foundation Grants for Social Science Research", 569
Foundation Grants Guide for Schools, Museums and Libraries: Grants with a Slice for Communications Technology Products, **3291**
Foundation Grants in Hawaii, 1970-1980, 778
The Foundation Grants Index, **1052**
Foundation Grants to Individuals, **928**
"A Foundation Grapples with the Problems of a 'Magnificent Gift'", 691
Foundation Guide for Religious Grant Seekers, **595**
The Foundation Handbook: A Private Foundation Approach to Fundraising at State Colleges and Universities, 3545
The Foundation in the Year 2000, 1076
Foundation Investment Strategies: New Possibilities in the 1981 Tax Law, 4477
"Foundation Management in Transition", **894**
Foundation Management Report, **655**
"Foundation Management Rewards", 1242
"Foundation Operations under the Tax Reform Act", 4341
Foundation Philanthropy in the Southeast, 1139
"Foundation Plans Grants for Preventing War", 1229
Foundation Primer, **3967**
Foundation Profiles, **1835**
Foundation Profiles: A Guide to Foundation Giving in the Health Field, 1097
Foundation Profiles of the Southeast: Alabama, Arkansas, Louisiana, Mississippi, **1219**
Foundation Profiles of the Southeast: Georgia, **1220**
Foundation Profiles of the Southeast: Kentucky, Tennessee, Virginia, **1221**
Foundation Profiles of the Southeast: North Carolina, South Carolina, **1222**
Foundation Radio Funding Guide, **3019**
Foundation Reports to Internal Revenue Service: An Analysis and Evaluation, 535, 4079
"Foundation Role Seen Threatened by U.S. Aid Cuts", 692
"The Foundation Stakes: It's No Horse Race", 885

"Foundation Support of Evaluation", 1184
Foundation Tax Law: History, Problems and Prospects, 4100
Foundation Watcher, **536**
"Foundation Wealth in St. Louis Not Creatively Utilized", 684
Foundation Work May Be Hazardous to Your Mental Health, 1007
"Foundation Work: The Who's and Hows", **779**
"Foundations", **532, 905**
"Foundations: A Time for Review", 1238
The Foundations: An Anatomy of Philanthropic Societies, **1275**
Foundations and Accountability: A Preliminary Exploration of American Philanthropic Foundations and Their Attitudes with Respect to Accountability, 1195
"Foundations and Community Trusts", 537
Foundations and Computer Technology, 656
Foundations and Fund Raising: A Bibliography of Books to 1980, 1008
Foundations and Government: State and Federal Law and Supervision, 4160
Foundations and Health: Opportunities in a Time of Rapid Change, 566
"Foundations and Higher Education", 780
Foundations and Higher Education at Home and Abroad: A Tale of Heroic Efforts Abandoned, **1214**
Foundations and Public Information: A Selection of Articles Reflecting Improved Public Information Performance by Foundations, 781
Foundations and Public Information: Sunshine or Shadow?, 1027
Foundations and Public Policy, **657**
"Foundations and Public Policy: Coming of Age in the 1980's", 902
Foundations and Scholarly Publishing: A Working Paper for the National Enquiry into Scholarly Communication, 1183
"Foundations and the Nation's Health Agenda", **809**
"Foundations and the Private College", 1070
"Foundations and the Supreme Court", **1134**
Foundations and the Tax Bill: Testimony on Title I of the Tax Reform Act of 1969 Submitted by Witnesses Appearing before the United States Senate Finance Committee, October 1969, 4156
Foundations and the Tax Reform Act of 1969, 4157
Foundations and Their Trends, 920
"Foundations and Universities", 1020
"Foundations and Voter Registration", **782**
"Foundations Answer the Economic Distress Call", 1114
"Foundations Asked to Reaffirm Commitment to the Arts", 693
Foundations, Charities and the Law: The Interaction of External Controls and Internal Policies, 4159

TITLE INDEX

"Foundations: Excess Business Holdings", 927
"Foundations Face Growing Worry: Giving Away Money Fast Enough", **783**
"Foundations Face Uncertainty", 4470
"Foundations Hear Invitation to Rejoin U.S. Policy Arena", 784
"Foundations: How Charity Molds Cleveland", 1160
"Foundations: How to Approach and Successfully Solicit Them", **785**
Foundations in Europe: A Comparative Survey, 1955
Foundation(s) in Japan: Their Legal Provisions and Tax Regulations, **1959**
"Foundations in the Twentieth Century", 812
"Foundations in the United Kingdom", **1951**
Foundations in Turkey, 1974
Foundations in Wisconsin: A Directory, **858**
"Foundations Increase Giving for Voter Issues", 791
Foundations Indicating Program-Related Investments As One of Their Types of Support, 770
"Foundations: Learning to Give", 798
"Foundations May Gain from Sun Belt Religious Wealth", 1115
"Foundations Now Provide Grantees with Seminar Help", 1116
"A Foundation's Observations about Its Selection Process", 4062
"Foundations of a Better Society?", 1468
"Foundations on Display: Money, Bias, and Brains", 1211
Foundations: Potential Funding Sources for Speech Pathology and Audiology, 892
Foundations, Private Giving and Public Policy. Report and Recommendations of the Commission on Foundations and Private Philanthropy, **629**
"Foundations: Private Giving for Public Schools", 567
"Foundations Re-Examine Program-Related Investments", 786
"Foundations' Role in Health Policy", **810**
"Foundations Saying 'We All Have a Stake' in Schools", **1065**
"Foundations Seek Links to Congress", 1230
"Foundations Seek Tax Changes", 1231
Foundations Serving the Hudson Valley, 787
"The Foundations: Sources of Educational Variety or Constraint?", 675
"Foundations Spread $10.5 Million through Iowa in '79", 561
Foundations Support for Puerto Ricans, 788
Foundations That Provide Support for Health and Human Services, 877
Foundations That Send Their Annual Report. Book 2, 1092
Foundations That Support Roman Catholic Activities, **1130**
"Foundations: The Quiet $20 Billion", 1268

Foundations: Their Power and Influence, 1293
The Foundations: Their Use and Abuse, 1144
Foundations Today: Current Facts and Figures on Private Foundations, **1100**
Foundations: Twenty Viewpoints, 538
Foundations under Fire, **1104**
"Foundations under IRS Scrutiny", 4105
"Foundations, United States Foreign Policy and African Education, 1945-1975", **1762**
"Foundations, Universities, and Research", **936**
Foundations, Universities, and Social Change, 926
"Foundations Urged to Be More Active on Public Policy Issues", 694
"Foundations Urged to Help Colleges Cope with Financial Hard Times", 1165
"Foundations Warned against Complacency", 1232
"Foundations: What Are They? What Do They Do and Why?", **789**
The Founding Fortunes: A New Anatomy of the Super-Rich Families in America, **10**
"The Four Basic Principles of Fundraising", **3498**
"Four Foundations Aid New Study of Retirement in Academe", 884
"The 400 Richest People in America", 35
"Four Months on the Road to Peace: A Fundraiser's Journey", 1288
"Four More Years: What It Means to Non-Profits", **2227**
"Fourteen Rather Rocky Reasons for a Capital Campaign", 3800
"The Fourteen-Year Itch", 790
FPK: An Intimate Biography of Frederick Paul Keppel, 272
"FRAC: A Lean, Mean Hunger Machine", 4822
"Free Advice: IRS Publications Fill You in on the Rules for Charitable Giving and Getting", 4317
The Free List: Property without Taxes, 4088
Free Spaces: The Sources of Democratic Change in America, **4517**
Freedom and the Foundation: The Fund for the Republic in the Era of McCarthyism, **1105**
Freedom, Education and the Fund: Essays and Addresses, 1946-1956, **870**
"'Freedom' in France Means State Control", 1917
Freedom's Ferment, 481
The FRI Annual Giving Book, 3968
The FRI Idea Pack, 3302
Friendly Visiting among the Poor: A Handbook for Charity Workers, 403
Friends of the Library Handbook: Organization, Administration, Public Relations, Fund Raising, 2452
"Fringes Are Not Frills: Employee Benefits for Nonprofits", **2010**

From Belief to Commitment: The Activities and Finances of Religious Congregations in the United States, 3399
From Charity to Social Work in England and the United States, **515**
"From Family Fortune to Social Change", 1260
"From Perestroika to Philanthropy", **1966**
From Poor Law to Welfare State: A History of Social Welfare in America, **4974**
From the Depths: The Discovery of Poverty in the United States, 57
From the Top Down: The Executive Role in Volunteer Program Success, 4516
From These Beginnings: The Early Philanthropies of Henry and Edsel Ford, 1911-1936, **187**
From Voluntarism to Vendorism: An Organizational Perspective on Contracting, 2207
"From Voluntary to para-Corporate: Today's Nonprofit Spectrum", **2325**
Fruit of an Impulse: Forty-Five Years of the Carnegie Foundation, 1905-1950, **1154**
"The Fruits of a Fortune", 72
"The Function of Lists: A Fund Raising Primer", 3573
"The Functions of Organized Charity in the Progressive Era: Chicago As a Case Study", **2210**
"Fund Raisers' Aim", 969
"Fund-Raisers Are Invited to 'Lend a Hand' with Ad Council Campaign", 3300
Fund Raiser's Guide to Capital Grants, **3389**
Fund Raiser's Guide to Human Service Funding, **3260**
Fund Raiser's Guide to Private Fortunes, **306**
Fund Raiser's Guide to Religious Philanthropy: A Source for Nonprofits Seeking Aid from Religiously Oriented Donors and Organizations, **3390**
The Fund Raiser's Guide to Successful Campaigns, **3045**
Fund Raisers of Academe, **3109**
Fund Raising, **2811**, 3963
Fund-Raising, 3454
Fund Raising: A Basic Reader, **3684**
Fund Raising: A Guide for Non-Profit Organizations, 3706
Fund Raising: A Professional Guide, 3179
"Fund Raising after Tax Reform", **3624**
Fund Raising and Public Relations: A Critical Guide to Literature and Resources, 3188
"Fund Raising and Taxes: When Is a 'Gift' Not a Gift?", 4185
"Fund Raising and the Law: What's Ahead in 1988", **4186**
Fund-Raising by Computer: Basic Techniques, 3969
Fund Raising by Formula: Steps to Make People Give, 3378

TITLE INDEX

"Fund Raising by Phone Comes under Court Attack", 3411
"Fund Raising by Strategic Design", **3135**
"Fund Raising Direct Mail Peaks in December, February", 3799
"Fund Raising Efforts Really Produce Management Strategies", 3359
"Fund Raising Events. Part 4: Starting at Home", 3403
Fund-Raising Events: Strategies and Programs for Success, **3083**
Fund-Raising for Higher Education, 3726
Fund Raising for Museums: The Essential Book for Staff and Trustees, **3379**
Fund Raising for Philanthropy, 3845
Fund-Raising for the Private School: The Alumni Fund, 3157
Fund-Raising for the Private School: The Capital Gifts Campaign, 3158
Fund-Raising for the Private School: The Foundation Approach. 3 Vols, 3159
Fund Raising for the Small Organization, 3825
Fund-Raising, Grants, and Foundations: A Comprehensive Bibliography, **3314**
Fund Raising Handbook, 3301
Fund Raising in California School Districts: A Discussion Paper, 2987
"Fund-Raising in Difficult Times", 3909
Fund Raising in New York State. Second Report: An Analysis of Charitable Organizations Registered in New York State, 1956-57, 3677
Fund Raising in the Black Community: History, Feasibility, and Conflict, 3191
Fund Raising in the Public Interest: A Citizen's Guide to Direct Mail Fund Raising, 3353
Fund Raising in the United States: Its Role in America's Philanthropy, 3184
"Fund Raising Information Is Analyzed by Costs, Benefits", 3823
Fund Raising Letter Collection, 3824
Fund Raising Letters: A Comprehensive Study Guide to Raising Money by Direct Response Marketing, 3446
"Fund Raising Management of the Feasibility Deficient", 3139
"Fund Raising or Business?", 2171
"The Fund Raising Profession", 3576
"Fund Raising Questions from the Supreme Court", 3303
The Fund Raising Resource Manual, **3906**
Fund Raising Review, 3058
"Fund-Raising Software Package Review", 3304
"Fund-Raising Strategies for the Allied Health Professions", **3162**
Fund Raising. The Guide to Raising Money from Private Sources, 3082
"Fund Raising: The Search for Discretionary Income", 3974
"Fund Raising's Future Lies with Creative Visionaries", 3475
"Fund Raising's Revolving Door: How It Can Be Stopped", 3136

"Fund Uncovers Way for Companies to Use Frozen Overseas Assets: Give Them Away", **1429**
Fundaciones Privadas de Venezuela, 1826
Fundamental Practices for Success with Volunteer Board of Non-Profit Organizations: A Self-Assessment and Planning Guide, 2802
Funders' Guide Manual. A Guide to Prevention Programs in Human Services: Focus on Children and Adolescents, **4907**
A Funder's Guide to AIDS Grantmaking: Action Strategies, **741**
Funders' Guide to Voter Registration and Education: How Funders Can Support Non-Partisan Efforts to Increase Citizen Participation in America, **4065**
"Funders Who Are Serious about Self-Sufficiency for Nonprofits Have to Start Thinking Endowment", 3608
"Funding Agency Contacts: Letting Them Help", 3833
Funding Alternatives for Libraries, 3078
"The Funding Crisis: Implications for the Survival of Human Service Institutions", 2101
"Funding Cutbacks Have Nonprofit Groups Scrambling for $$$", 3392
Funding Family Violence Programs: Sources and Potential Sources for Federal Monies, 4688
Funding for Anthropological Research, **605**
Funding for Culture: The Cultural Policy of the City of New York, 4719
Funding for Museums, Archives and Special Collections, **1259**
Funding for Renewable Energy and Conservation Projects, 3102
Funding for Social Change: How to Become an Employer and Gain Tax Exempt Status, 2433
Funding for Women's Programs, 3348
Funding Guide for Native Americans, **3124**
Funding: How to Get Your Fair Share of the $47.74 Billion Given in the U.S. Today, 3639
Funding in Aging: Public, Private and Voluntary, 3141
Funding Information Center Handbook, **3101**
Funding of the Arts in Canada to the Year 2000, **1961**
"Funding Opportunities for Fighting Illiteracy", 3620
"The Funding Partnership: Public and Private Giving in the 80's", 2030
The Funding Process: Grantsmanship and Proposal Development, 4011
Funding Report, **4723**
Funding Report for Microcomputers, 2466
Funding Sources and Financial Aid Techniques for Historic Preservation, 3586
Funding Sources and Technical Assistance for Museums and Historical Agencies: A Guide to Public Programs, 3380

Funding Sources for Cultural Facilities: Private and Federal Support for Capital Projects, 3140
Funding Sources for Neighborhood Groups, 3923
"Funding South of the Border", **1817**
"Funding the AIDS Fight", **4949**
Funding Urban Design, 3461
Funding Volunteer Services: Potential Sources of Dollars to Expand Agency Programs, 4519
"Fundraising: A Marketing Perspective", 3275
"Fundraising and the Meaning of Public Support", 3296
"Fundraising: As Dollars Shrink, Campaigns Grow", 3533
"Fundraising Events. Part 3: Budgeting", 3305
Fundraising for Early Childhood Programs: Getting Started and Getting Results, 3280
Fundraising for Independent Living Centers, **3366**
Fundraising for Non-Profit Groups: How to Get Money from Corporations, Foundations and Government, 3990
Fundraising for Social Change, **3499**
"Fundraising in Rural Communities", 3287
"Fundraising in the Late 80s: Survival May Be the Best Goal", **3500**
"Fundraising Is a Song and Dance", **3365**
"Fundraising Network", **3248**
Fundraising Resource Guide: Annotated Bibliography and Resource List, 3758
Fundraising Strategies for Grassroots Organizations, 3888
Fundraising Terminology: A Glossary, **3306**
Fundraising through Proposal Writing, 4002
Funds and Foundations: Their Policies, Past and Present, **751**
Funds for Hispanics, 3277
"Funds for Peace Are on the Rise", 799
Funds for the Future, 3919
"A Future for the National Charities Information Bureau?", **2356**
"The Future of Communicable Disease Control: Toward a New Concept in Public Health Law", 4854
The Future of Foundations, **847**
The Future of Foundations: Some Reconsiderations, **579**
"The Future of Foundations: The Jeffersonian Potential", 814
"The Future of Fund Raising: An Endangered Species", 3577
The Future of Philanthropic Foundations, 615
The Future of Philanthropy: Part 2, 69
The Future of Private Philanthropy, 300
"The Future of Telethons: Cutting through the Clutter", 3778
"The Future of the Nonprofit Sector", 2320
"The Future of the Voluntary Agency in a Mixed Economy", **289**
"Gaining Clarity in a Time of Change", **1509**

TITLE INDEX

Gaining Momentum for Board Action, **2928**
"Gathering Grants: Financial Boon or Bust?", **3315**
Gaylord Freeman of First Chicago. 2 Vols, 229
General Explanation of the Tax Reform Act of 1969, H.R. 13270, 91st Congress, Public Law 91-172, 4433
"General Support vs. Project Support: A 75-Year-Old Philanthropic Debate", **2073**
"Generating Income for Nonprofit Programs", 2123
"The Generosity Factor: A New Index of Philanthropy", 479
The Generosity of Americans, Its Source, Its Achievements, 324
The Gentle Legions, **2042**
Gentleman in the Outdoors: A Portrait of Max C. Fleischmann, 499
George Eastman, 3
George F. Baker and His Bank, 1840-1955, 955
George Lundy of Iowa, 325
George Peabody, Esq., 509
George Peabody, 1795-1869, **369**
George Washington: Patron of Learning, 208
Gertrude Vanderbilt Whitney, 164
Get the Money and Shoot, **3463**
Getting a Grant: How to Write Successful Grant Proposals, 4035
Getting a Grant in the 1980s: How to Write Successful Grant Proposals, **4036**
"Getting a Star to Help Your Cause", **3197**
Getting Funded: A Complete Guide to Proposal Writing, 4019
"Getting 'Good Visibility'", **1475**
"Getting Grants Independently: A Resource Guide", **912**
"Getting H.R. 911 Passed: How the Process Works and What You Can Do", 4173
"Getting in Gear", 3838
"Getting Management Help to the Nonprofit Sector", 2771
"Getting Management Support to Nonprofits", 2614
Getting Organized: Incorporation and Tax-Exemption for Non-Profit Organizations in New York, **4133**
"Getting over the Fear of Asking. Part 1", 3501
"Getting over the Fear of Asking. Part 2", 3502
Getting Publicity, 2860
"Getting Started in Direct Mail", 3523
"Getting Started: What to Do before You Ask for Money", 3925
"Getting the Employee into the Corporate Giving Act: The Growth of Matching Gifts", 3724
"Getting the Most from a Consultant", **2704**
"Getting to Know You: Post-Grant Evaluation", 596
"Getting to the Source of Problems", 2142

"Getting Your Board Unstuck", 2783
"Getting Your Message on Television News", 3323
Getting Your Share of the R and D Funds, 4605
Getting Yours: A Publicity and Funding Primer for Nonprofit and Voluntary Organizations, 4008
Getting Yours: The Complete Guide to Government Money, **4676**
"Getty Trust Goes National with Push for Art Education", 576
"Gift Computers: Now's the Time", **1675**
The Gift: Forms and Functions of Exchange in Archaic Societies, **329**
Gift Giving Guide: Methods and Tax Implications of Giving Money Away, 4161
"Gift Rating Donors: An Important First Step", 3813
The Gift Relationship: From Human Blood to Social Policy, **474**
Gifts and Bequests to Colleges and Universities in Good Times and Bad Times, 3316
"Gifts-in-Kind Organization Gives Something for Nothing", **1522**
"Gifts to Colleges Down $80 Million", 3934
"Gifts to Education Down 3.5% in 1975", 3165
"Gifts to Education Rose 7.1% in 1983, Study Finds", 3317
"Gifts to Higher Education Reach Record $5.6-Billion: Businesses, Foundations, Individuals All Increase Aid", 3213
"Gifts to Universities Rise 6.2%, Survey Finds", 3902
"Give and Take", 4239
Give-and-Take: The Complete Tax Incentive Guide and the Approved Methods for Donating or Accepting Corporate Gifts of Inventory, **1558**
"Give Me Your Money and We'll Be Partners", 3460
Give! Who Gets Your Charity Dollar?, 269
Giving: A Comparison of the Philanthropic Resources of Seven Metropolitan Areas, **330**
Giving: A Comparison of the Philanthropic Resources of Seven Metropolitan Areas. Supplementary Tables, 331
"Giving a Wealth of Goodwill", **144**
Giving: America's Greatest National Resource, **407**
Giving and Getting: A Chemical Bank Study of Charitable Contributions 1983 through 1988, 95
Giving and Getting: A Chemical Bank Study of Charitable Contributions through 1984, 96
"Giving and Getting. The Non-Profit Outlook, 1983-88", 332
Giving and Taking: Across the Foundation Desk, 1146
"Giving and Volunteering in America: Findings of a Major National Survey", 3884

Giving and Volunteering in New York City, **12**
"Giving Away Money", 3177
"Giving in America", 811
Giving in America: Toward a Stronger Voluntary Sector. Report of the Commission on Private Philanthropy and Public Needs, **102**
Giving in Minnesota, 1977-1978, 343
"Giving in 1982: Colleges Got $8.59 Billion", 3319
"Giving It Away", 800
"Giving More and like It More", 3985
"Giving Rises in 1986, But Future Is in Doubt", 3320
Giving to Higher Education Maintains Its Upward Curve. Report for 1954-55, 3469
Giving to Jewish Philanthropic Causes: A Preliminary Reconnaissance, 441
"Giving to the College of Your Choice", 1576
Giving USA, **176**
Giving with Interest: A Guide to Enlightened Charitable Giving, **3321**
"Global Reach", 1818
A Global View on Philanthropy, 1879
Glossary of Fund-Raising Terms, **3666**
Glossary of Tools and Concepts for Nonprofit Managers, 2879
"Go, Team, Go!", 2874
"Go Ye into All the World: Doane College Used Church Connections to Bring Its Message to Corporations", 3691
God's Gold: The Story of Rockefeller and His Times, 156
"Going Back to Major Donors", **3503**
"Going for the Gold: A Training Manual for Volunteer Fund Raisers", 3581
"Going into Business Can Be 'Taxing' Experience for Nonprofits", 4248
The Golden Donors: A New Anatomy of the Great Foundations, **1051**
"Golden Donor's Hidden Insight", **1647**
Good Deeds in Old Age. Volunteering by the New Leisure Class, **4500**
"Good for the Company: Good for the Community", 4599
"Good Management Requires a Director of Planning and Development", 3178
"Good Professional Contacts: Tapping Your Hidden Resource", 3072
"Good Telemarketers Have Good Databases", 3349
"Good Works and Self-Help", 575
"Goodbye BBC, Hello NHK!", **1830**
The Gospel of Wealth and Other Timely Essays, 80, **81**
Governance Is Governance, **2546**
Governance of Higher Education: Six Priority Problems, 4795
"Governing Boards: A Governing Board Membership Audit for Nonprofits", **2598**
"Government Adopts Foundation Mode", 4659
"Government and Private Roles in Activities for the Public Good", 1907

357

TITLE INDEX

Government Assistance Almanac, 4636
Government Assistance in Eighteenth-Century France, 1889
Government Contracts: Proposalmanship and Winning Strategies, **4668**
"Government Foundations: Worthy But Threatened", 4647
Government Spending and the Nonprofit Sector in Atlanta/Fulton County, 4685
Government Spending and the Nonprofit Sector in Cook County/Chicago, 4658
Government Spending and the Nonprofit Sector in Pittsburgh/Allegheny County, 4686
Government Spending and the Nonprofit Sector in San Francisco, 4663
Government Spending and the Nonprofit Sector in Two Michigan Communities: Flint/Genesee County and Tuscola County, 4687
Government Tax and Expenditure Limitations: Analyses and Impacts, 4134
"Grammar for Grantseekers", 4027
Grant Budgeting and Finance: Getting the Most Out of Your Grant Dollar, 2898
"The Grant Development Process: A Nursing Solution for a Community Health Need", 3309
"A Grant for Every Purpose", 3393
Grant Making Corporations That Publish Guidelines, 1653
Grant Money and How to Get It: A Handbook for Librarians, 3070
The Grant-Seeker's Guide, 3526
The Grant Seekers: The Foundation Fund Raising Manual, 3327
The Grant System, **267**
The Grant Writer's Handbook. 2 Vols, 4006
Grant Writing Made Easy, 4023
"Grantees' Overhead Costs: Should Foundations Pay?", 2592
A Grantmaker's Guide, 619
A Grantmaker's Guide to a New Tool for Philanthropy: Form 990, 4256
Grantmaking for the Elderly: An Analysis of Foundation Expenditures, 1978-1982, **1036**
"Grantmaking in Hard Times", 869
The Grantmaking Process, **658**, 3692
The Grantmaking Process: Setting Priorities, Assessing, Evaluating, **645**
The Grantmaking Process: The Basics. Workshop Handbook, **1192**
"Grantmanship: Winning Foundation Funding", 3982
Grants and Fellowships, **533**
"Grants As a Matter of Law", **4617**
"The Grants Clinic", 4058, **4059**
Grants for Libraries, 3164
Grants for the Arts, 3957
The Grants Game: How to Get Free Money, **3543**
Grants: How to Find Out about Them and What to Do Next, 3958
Grants in the Humanities: A Scholar's Guide to Funding Sources, **624**
The Grants Planner, 3151

Grants Resource Manual, 3559
Grants Resources Directory, 3251
Grants to Higher Education Related to Minorities, 1986-87, 828
Grants: Views from the Campus, 3273
Grantseekers Guide, **1174**
Grantseeking in North Carolina: A Guide to Foundation and Corporate Giving, **1176**
A Grantsman's Bibliography, 3604
Grantsmanship, 3186, **3534**
Grantsmanship and Fundraising, 3031
Grantsmanship Bibliography, 3338
The Grantsmanship Book, **3339**
"Grantsmanship Provides Gains", 3051
Grantsmanship Resources for Problems in Aging, 3084
Grantsmanship Resources for Rehabilitation Programs, 3085
Grantsmanship Resources for the Arts and Humanities, 586
Grantsmanship Training Program, 4018
Graphic Design for Non-Profit Organizations, 2712
The Grass Is Greener: Fund Raising Opportunities under the 1981 Tax Act, 4202
Grass-Roots Fundraising, 3087
The Grass Roots Fundraising Book, **3285**
"Graying Population Means Rosier Fund Raising Ahead", 3983
"Great Family Fortunes", **185**
The Great Getty, 297
"The Great Numbers Debate: And Why It's Important", 835
Great Philanthropic Foundations. 5 Vols, 639
The Great Soul Trial: The Gripping Story of the Prospector Who Left a Fortune to a Study of the Soul, 167
The Greatest Good: A History of the John A. Hartford Foundation, 883
The Greatest Good Fortune, 816
The Green Book. The Official Directory of the City of New York, 4654
Green Sheets, 4542
The Groves of Academe, 996
"Growing by Leaps and Towns", 1136
Growing Up with a City, **51**
Growth Factors in the Development of Community Foundations: A Study Guide for Technical Assistance, **992**
"Growth Is Explosive in Corporations' Gifts of Equipment", 1430
"The Growth of Heartlessness: The Need for Studies in Philanthropy", **152**
"The Growth of Schuller's Television Ministry in Australia", **3241**
The Guggenheims: An American Epic, 120
Guide for Charities, **2206**
A Guide for Charity Trustees, 1838
A Guide for Colleges and Universities Cost Principles and Procedures for Establishing Indirect Cost Rates for Grants and Contracts with the Department of Health, Education, and Welfare, 4661

A Guide for Preparing a Statement of Accountability, 2786
A Guide for Youth Participation and Youth Programs, 4528
Guide to Arkansas Funding Sources, **671**
Guide to Black Organizations, 2143
Guide to California Foundations, **738**
A Guide to Charitable Trusts and Foundations in the State of Hawaii, 528
A Guide to Community Fundraising for Runaway Centers and Other Community-Based Youth Programs, 3609
A Guide to Company Giving, **1913**
Guide to Corporate Giving in Connecticut, **1336**
Guide to Corporate Giving in Massachusetts, **1337**
Guide to Corporate Giving in New Hampshire, **594**
Guide to Corporate Giving in Rhode Island, **1338**
Guide to Corporate Giving in the Arts 4, 1638
Guide to Corporations: A Social Perspective, 1415
Guide to Creative Giving, 462
"A Guide to Dealing with the IRS", 4338
"Guide to Eliminate Confusion of Software Technology Options", 3318
Guide to European Foundations, 1747
Guide to Federal Energy Development and Assistance Programs, 4729
Guide to Federal Funding for Education. 2 Vols, 4735
A Guide to Federal Programs for Rural Development, 4612
Guide to Forming a Non-Profit, Tax-Exempt Organization, 4286
A Guide to Foundation Fund Raising under the Reagan Administration, 3205
A Guide to Funders in Central Appalachia and the Tennessee Valley, **1063**
Guide to Funding Sources for American Indian Library and Information Services, 3116
The Guide to Gifts and Bequests: New York/Florida, **2144**
Guide to Government Resources for Economic Development: A Handbook for Nonprofit Agencies and Municipalities, 4682
"A Guide to Grants", 4629
A Guide to Grants: Governmental and Nongovernmental, **3560**
A Guide to Hispanic Organizations, 2145
A Guide to Information Sources and Services for Voluntary Human Services Agencies, 2328
A Guide to Kentucky Grantmakers, **713**
Guide to Minnesota Foundations and Corporate Giving Programs, **1011**
Guide to New Approaches to Financing Parks and Recreation, 3013
The Guide to Oregon Foundations, **1000**
A Guide to Organizations, Agencies, and Federal Programs for Children, 3591
Guide to Programs, 4707

TITLE INDEX

Guide to Programs: Administered by Office of Higher Education Programs and Fund for Improvement of Post-Secondary Education, **4755**
Guide to Public Relations for Voluntary Organizations, 2521
The Guide to Software for Nonprofits, 2632
Guide to Sponsored Research of the Commission on Private Philanthropy and Public Needs, 630
Guide to Student Fundraising, **3645**
Guide to Successful Fund Raising, **3894**
A Guide to Successful Phonathons, **3171**
The Guide to Texas Foundations, 1193
A Guide to the California Nonprofit Public Benefit Corporation Law, **4373**
The Guide to the Federal Budget, 4626
A Guide to the Making of Grants to Individuals by Private Foundations, **857**
Guide to the National Endowment for the Arts, **4694**
Guide to Using the Form 990, 4244
Guide to Women's Art Organizations and Directory for the Arts, **2260**
Guidelines, 4721
Guidelines and Application, 4715
Guidelines and Application Instructions for the United States Newspaper Projects, 4698
Guidelines for Business Giving, **1414**
Guidelines for Preparing Proposals, **4042**
Guidelines for Publishing a Minimum Annual Report, 659
Guidelines for the Administration of Matching Gift Programs, 2525
"Guidelines for the Selection of Training Programs", 4030
Guidelines: How to Develop an Effective Program of Corporate Support for Higher Education, **1409**
"Guidelines to Deal with Corporate Matching Gift Problems", 3776
Guidelines to Fund Raising: Annual Support, **3270**
Guides to Successful Fund Raising, **3372**
"Guiding Charitable Funds", **2549**
"Gulling the Grantseeker", **1282**
Habits of the Heart: Individualism and Commitment in American Life, **37**
Hammer, **194**
The Handbook for Community Foundations: Their Formation, Development and Operation. 2 Vols, **1207**
Handbook for Development Officers at Independent Schools, 3956
Handbook for Educational Fundraising, **3737**
Handbook of Aid to Higher Education by Corporations, Major Foundations and the Federal Government, 3168
The Handbook of Corporate Social Responsibility: Profiles of Involvement, 1504
Handbook of Institutional Advancement, 3786

A Handbook of Latin-American Foundations: Purposes and Activities, 1954
Handbook of Legal Liabilities for Nonprofit Executives, 4138
Handbook of Publicity and Public Relations for the Nonprofit Organization, **2868**
The Handbook on Private Foundations, **795**
Handbook on Tax-Exempt Organizations, 2127
Handbuch des Stiftungsrecht. Geschichte des Stiftungsrecht. Band 1. (Handbook of foundation laws. History of foundation laws. Vol. 1), 1876
Handicapped Funding Directory, 3253
"Handle with Care: Thirteen Steps to Better Stewardship Reports", 3480
Happy to Be Here, **907**
"Harder Than It Looked", **1283**
"Hardware and Software Needs to Improve Staff Efficiency", 2861
"Hardware and Software: Panic or Panacea", 3784
The Harpur Trust, 1552-1973, 1829
Hartford Foundation for Public Giving: The First Fifty Years, 1262
"Hauck Gives City Money for Pavilion", 202
Healing America, 103
"Health Care for the Elderly: Turning from Coordinated Community-Based Services", 2026
The Health Funds Grants Resource Yearbook, **3796**
Health Giving of Private Foundations, 1975 and 1980, 709
"Health Giving Patterns of Philanthropic Foundations", **710**
Health Giving Patterns of Philanthropic Foundations, 1975, 1980 and 1983, 711
"A Healthy Sign", 4827
Hearing before the Committee on Finance, U.S. Senate, 91st Congress. 1st Session. Improper Payments by Private Foundations to Government Officials, 4393
Hearing before the Select Committee to Investigate Foundations and Other Organizations, 82nd Congress, 2nd Session, 4379
Hearings before a Subcommittee of the Committee on Government Operations. (Federal Agencies and Philanthropies.) 85th Congress, 2nd Session, 4380
Hearings before Subcommittee on the Committee on Interstate and Foreign Commerce, Senate, 80th Congress, 2nd Session. 2 Vols, 4453
Hearings before the Committee on Finance, United States Senate, 91st Congress, 1st Session, on H.R. 13270 to Reform the Income Tax Laws. 3 Vols, 4438
Hearings before the Committee on Ways and Means, House of Representatives, on the Subject of Tax Reform, 91st Congress, 1st Session. 6 Vols, 4396

Hearings before the Committee on Ways and Means, House of Representatives. Part 2: On the Subject of Tax Reform, 91st Congress, 1st Session, 4397
Hearings before the Select Committee to Investigate Tax-Exempt Foundations and Comparable Organizations, 82nd Congress, 2nd Session, 4381
Hearings before the Special Committee to Investigate Tax-Exempt Foundations and Comparable Organizations, 83rd Congress, 2nd Session. 2 Vols, 4382
Hearings before the Subcommittee on Domestic Finance of the Committee on Banking and Currency. Tax-Exempt Foundations and Charitable Trusts: Their Compliance with the Provisions of the Tax Reform Act of 1969, 4391
Hearings before the Subcommittee on Federal Charters, Holidays and Celebrations, 2933
Hearings before the Subcommittee on Foundations of the Committee on Finance. The Role of Private Foundations in Today's Society and a Review of the Impact of Charitable Provisions of the Tax Reform Act of 1969..., 93rd Congress, 1st Session, 4439
"Hearings on Nonprofit 'Competition'", **4187**
Hearings on the Subject of General Tax Reform, 93rd Congress, 1st Session. 3 Vols, 4398
"The Hearings Were Intended to Educate Ways and Means. What Happened?", 1212
The Hearsts. Family and Empire: The Later Years, 93
The Heart of the Matter: Leader-Constituent Interaction, **2607**
"Helen O'Rourke-McClary: She Helped Make Charities Accountable", 449
Help! A Guide to Seeking, Selecting and Surviving an Arts Consultant, 2619
Help: A Working Guide to Self-Help Groups, 2121
The Help Book, 3036
Help-Seeking and the Use of Social Service Providers by Welfare Families in Chicago, **2348**
"Help with Your Problems", **2161**
"Helpful Hints and Observations for Fund Raising Neophytes", 3125
"A Helpful Look Inward", **598**
"Helping Hands: Companies Change the Ways They Make Charitable Donations", 1723
Helping Minority Students Succeed, 4866
Helping Networks: How People Cope with Problems in the Urban Community, **4979**
Helping Others: A Guide to Selected Social Service Agencies and Occupations, 2147
Helping Ourselves: Local Solutions to Global Problems, **4586**
Henry C. Frick Educational Commission, 1909-1974, 1200
Henry Clay Frick: The Man, 201

359

TITLE INDEX

The Henry Luce Foundation: A History, 1936-1986, **832**
Henry P. Davison: The Record of a Useful Life, 291
Henry S. Pritchett: A Biography, 153
"Here Comes the Earthquake: Preliminary Analysis of the Conference Agreement for the 1986 Tax Reform Bill", **4066**
"Here's How Simple Research Tool Audits Communication", 3488
"Heretic, Gadfly, or Prophet?", 2035
Heroes of Peace: A History of the Carnegie Hero Fund Commission, 548
"He's First a Music Lover, Then a Philanthropist", 411
Hidden History, 45
Higher Education: Cooperation with Developing Countries, 1919
Higher Education Finance: A Comparative Study of Matched Samples of Black and White Private Institutions, 4874
Higher Education Prices and Price Indexes, 4859
"Higher Education Receives Lion's Share of Corporate Matching Gifts...", 3396
Higher Education: Who Pays? Who Benefits? Who Should Pay?, 4796
Higher Education: Who Pays? Who Gains? Financing Education Beyond the High School, 3120
"Higher Rates for Charitable Annuities: How Charitable Annuities 'Work'", 3644
Highlights from the Conference Board's Survey of Corporate Contributions, **1622**
Highlights of 1969 Changes in the Tax Law, 4456
Highlights 3: Arts and Business Council Seminar Series for Small Community Arts Organizations, 3012
"Hired Guns: Tips on Finding and Using Consultants", **2473**
"Hiring a Development Director", 3504
"Hispanic Corporate Partnerships: Some Observations and Examples", 1743
Hispanic Theater in the United States and Puerto Rico, **4928**
Hispanics and Grantmakers, 660
Hispanics: Challenges and Opportunities, 4838
Historic House Museums, 4815
An Historical Survey of Jewish Philanthropy, 165
Historiographic Review of Foundation Literature: Motivations and Perceptions, **911**
"The History of American Philanthropy As a Field of Research", **113**
A History of English Philanthropy, 1832
History of the Baron de Hirsch Fund: The Americanization of the Jewish Immigrant, 897
History of the Sage and Slocum Families of England and America, Including the Allied Families of Montague, Wanton, Brown, Josselyn, Standish, Doty, Carver, Jermain or Germain, Pierson, and Howell, 502

A History of the Z. Smith Reynolds Foundation, 833
A History of Western Philosophy, and Its Connection with Political and Social Circumstances from the Earliest Times to the Present Day, 424
"Hit the Ground Running: How the Chief Advancement Officer Can Start a Job and a Capital Campaign in 60 Working Days", 3256
Homelessness: Critical Issues for Policy and Practice, **282**
Homelessness in Chicago: Poverty and Pathology, Social Institutions and Social Change, **4962**
Homer Folks: Pioneer in Social Welfare, **478**
"Honor Thy Donors", 3612
Honorable Richard Shelby before the Subcommittee on Oversight, June 28, 1983, 98th Congress, 1st Session, 4408
The Hooper Directory of Texas Foundations: Supplement, 614
"Hospice Letter", 4871
Hospital Audit Guide, 2439
"Hospital Development Is Growing Up", 3635
"Hospital Marketing Moves into Convenience Shopping Centers", 2333
"Hospital Philanthropy in the Future", 3640
"Hospital Philanthropy: Strengthening the Financial Base of Nonprofit Hospitals", 3961
"Hospitals 'Buy' the Future through Fundraising Efforts", 3593
"Hot for Safe Energy", 983
The House of Getty, 340
The House of Intellect, 33
The Housing Handbook: A Guide to Financing for Non-Profit Organizations, 3343
"How a Computer Thinks (and How It Doesn't)", 2539
"How about Franklin Thomas for Mayor?", 497
"How American Can Came to Martin Luther King Junior High School: A Look at Corporate Responsibility in the USA", 1533
How and What Canadians Contribute to Charity, 1790
"How and Why to Hire a Consultant", **2542**
"How Artists Don't Just Sing for Their Supper", **4258**
"How at One Foundation a Grant Went from Idea to Reality", 568
"How Big Foundations Spend Their Millions", 860
How Can I Help? Stories and Reflections on Service, **4525**
"How Close Is Too Close?", 861
"How Colleges Can Attract Corporate Funding", 1486
"How Colleges Cope with the Red Ink", 3422

"How Companies Respond to Social Demands", 1298
"How Do Private Foundations Spend Their Money? A Description of Health Giving", **712**
How Do We Look? A Guide to Corporate Self Assessment and Ethical Reflection in Nonprofit Homes for the Aging, 2223
"How Ethical Is Creative Accounting?", **2676**
How Firm a Foundation, 686
"How Foundations Undergo the Grantmaking Process", 716
"How I Learned to Love Fund Raising", 3374
"How Impact Statements Can Help Foundations Assess Programs for Their Impact on Women and Girls: Or, How to Tell If You Are Really Being Fair to Women and Girls", 1153
"How Infirm a Foundation", 4180
"How Lockboxes Can Unlock the Fund Raising Gridlock", 3795
"How Many Legitimate Prospects Do You Have?", **3423**
"How Market Piggybacking Affects Your Exempt Status", 4262
"How Much Are Volunteers Worth?", 4552
"How Nonprofits Can Beat the Depreciation Game", **1999**
"How Nonprofits Can Use Television Talk Shows", 3324
"How Paul Newman's Hobby Grew Up into a Major Grantor", 240
"How Sale Helps the Institute", 4969
"How Small Businesses Can Be Big Contributors", **1485**
How Small Grants Make a Difference, 3032
"How Software Helped Humanize the Chore of Statistic Gathering", 3424
How Tax Laws Make Giving to Charity Easy, 4223
"How the Ford Foundation Deals with Social Issues", 1532
"How the J. Paul Getty Trust Will Spend $90 Million a Year", 148
"How to Achieve Real Donor Base Growth", 3522
How to Analyze and Report Annual Giving Campaign Progress, 2872
"How to Approach Foundations", 3425
How to Approach the Corporate Donor: A Guide for Fund Raisers, 3426
"How to Ask for Federal Funding", 4613
How to Assess Board Liability, **4104**
"How to Avoid Pitfalls in Fund Raising Direct (Mail) Response", 3096
"How to Be a Better Board Member: Guidelines for Trustees", 2462
How to Be an Effective Board Member, 2847
How to Become a 501 (c)(3) Organization, 2184
How to Build a Big Endowment, 3749
"How to Capitalize on a Strong Endowment Fund", 3215

TITLE INDEX

How to Collect Triple Profits from Your Hobbies, Skills or Interests!, 3281
"How to Conduct a Marketing Research Project", 2552
How to Conduct a Meeting, **2486**
How to Conduct a Membership Drive, **2487**
"How to Convince Your Prospects to Become Donors", 3427
"How to Create a Film to Increase Fund Raising", 3779
How to Create a Winning Proposal, 3995
How to Create and Use Solid Gold Fund-Raising Letters, **3149**
How to Deal with Goals and Objectives, 2776
"How to Design a Great Major-Gifts Club: Benefits Are the Key, As Mt. Sinai Courts the Big Donors", 3428
How to Develop a Board of Directors, **2488**
How to Develop and Administer a Corporate Scholarship Program, 1410
"How to Develop Your Own Donor Profile", **3429**
How to Establish and Fund an Association Foundation, **999**
"How to Evaluate a Neighborhood Organization", 2194
How to Evaluate Your Fund-Raising Program: A Performance Audit System, **2778**
How to Find Funds to Attend Conferences, 2848
How to Find Information about Companies: The Corporate Intelligence Source Book, 1725
How to Form and Operate a Nonprofit Corporation, **2489**
How to Form Your Own Non-Profit Corporation in One Day, 2958
How to Form Your Own Profit/Non-profit Corporation without a Lawyer, **2444**
How to Fund Media, 4953
How to: Fund Raising Manual, 3834
"How to Get a Celebrity to Attend Your Special Event", 3718
"How to Get Cash without Compromising Ethics", **4919**
How to Get Corporate Grants, **1648**
How to Get Government Grants, 4631
How to Get Money for: Arts and Humanities, Drug and Alcohol Abuse, and Health, 3441
How to Get Money for: Conservation and Community Development, 3442
How to Get Money for Research, **3788**
How to Get Money for: Youth, the Elderly, the Handicapped, Women and Civil Liberties, 3443
"How to Get On-Line with Database Software Programs", 3479
How to Get the Best Results from Management Consultants, 2891
How to Get the Most Out of Being a Volunteer: Skills for Leadership, 4541
The How to Grants Manual, **3044**
"How to Guarantee Success of a Large Gift Club", 3430

"How to Handle Personal Gifts", 3028
How to Have a Successful Career in Fund Raising, 2639
How to Help, 4504
How to Hire the Right Fund Raising Consultant, 3761
How to Increase Corporate Giving to Your Organization, 3836
"How to Interpret and Use Financial Information", 669
"How to Keep the Grant Money Flowing: Some Answers to the Most Commonly Asked Questions about Filling Out the Endowment's Application Forms", 4622
How to Make Big Improvements in the Small PR Shop, 2659
How to Manage a Nonprofit Organization, 2589
How to Manage Cutbacks and Develop Local Funding Sources, 2502
"How to Market Planned Giving", 3115
"How to Match Volunteer Motivation with Job Demands", 4589
"How to Maximize the Return from Your Operational Budget", 2709
How to Organize a Chamber of Commerce Two Percent Club, to Encourage Increased Private Sector Initiative in Your Community, 1493
"How to Organize a Memorial Giving Program", 3431
How to Organize and Manage a Seminar: What to Do and When to Do It, **2779**
"How to Package and Market Major Donor Club Benefits", 3383
"How to Plan a Marketing Research Project", 2553
How to Prepare a Budget, **2490**
How to Prepare a Research Proposal: Guidelines for Funding and Dissertations in the Social and Behavioral Sciences, 4034
How to Present an Evaluation Report, 2777
"How to Raise Funds for a Cause", 3601
How to Raise Money, 3720
How to Raise Money for Anything, 3991
How to Raise Money for Community Action, 3432
"How to Raise Money for Your Hispanic Students? Involve Your Alumni and Their Corporate Contacts", 1693
How to Raise Money for Your Organization, 2531
"How to Raise Money from Churches", **3433**
How to Raise Money: Special Events for Arts Organizations, 3187
How to Rate Your Development Office: A Fund-Raising Primer for the Chief Executive, 3055
"How to Recruit Good Corporate Volunteers", 4536
"How to Reinstate Your Lapsed Donors", **3434**
"How to Select a Fund Raising Software Package", 3892

How to Set Up and Operate a Non-Profit Organization, **2382**
How to Shake the New Money Tree, **3250**
How to Solicit Big Gifts, **3152**
"How to Start a Low-Budget Publicity Program", 2769
How to Start and Manage Your Direct Mail Annual Appeal, 3435
How to Succeed As an Independent Consultant, **2650**
"How to Survive a Capital Campaign: Ways and Means of Using Consultants to Maximize Your Organization's Major Efforts", 3172
"How to Survive Success or Coping with Rapid Growth", 3386
"How to Turn Humble Public Service Ad into a Moneymaker", 3008
How to Use Consultants Once You Have Retained Them, 2666
"How to Use Flowers for Fund Raising", 3029
"How to Use the Media: Getting on the Air", 3436
How to Win Friends and Influence Audiences: Expert Tips in Financing and Promoting Your Session, 3771
How to Win Government Contracts, **4655**
How to Work Smarter, Not Harder: A Manual for Development Officers, 2977
How to Work with Groups: Guidelines for Volunteers, 4587
How to Write a Proposal, **4003**
How to Write Successful Corporate Appeals, **4055**
How to Write Successful Foundation Presentations, 4012
How We Helped, **661**
"How Will Philanthropy Fare in the New Congress?", 228
"How Your Agency Can Organize a Conference", 2543
"How's the Weather in Your Organization?", 2369
H.R. 13270. An Act to Reform the Income Tax Laws, 91st Congress, 1st Session, 4440
Hugh Roy Cullen: A Story of American Opportunity, 275
The Humanities in American Life, 4816
"The Humanities' Message to Grantmakers", 4965
Humanizing American Foreign Policy: Non-Profit Lobbying and Human Rights, 2114
Hunger in America: The Federal Response, 4889
"I Have a Million Dollars to Leave", 3155
I Remember: The Autobiography of Abraham Flexner, **154**
"IBM-Digital Pact at MIT", 1511
"IBM, Digital to Give MIT $50-Million to Develop Computerized Curriculum", 1708
"IBM Increased Its Support of Education More Than Fifty Percent in 1983", 1709
The Idea Book for Colleges and Universities, 4767

361

TITLE INDEX

"Ideas for Expanding Your Mailing List", 3452

"Ideas in Print: Annual Report Review", 2176

"Identifying and Nurturing Core Donors", 3790

"The IEA: Teaching the 'Right' Stuff", 1205

"If Kids Can't Get Summer Jobs, What Can They Do?", 617

If Not for Profit, for What?, **2412**

"If Only We Had an Endowment Fund", 3783

"If Starting a Private Foundation Incurs Legal Headaches, Here Are Alternatives", **4321**

"If You Do Not Have a Planned Giving Program: Use These Guidelines to Gain the Planned Giving Support You Need", **3015**

If You Want Air Time, 3654

I'll Invest My Money in People, 270

"Immortality on the Installment Plan", 3911

Impact Evaluation: A Field Manual, 2425

Impact of Current Economic Crisis on Foundations and Recipients of Foundation Money. Hearings, 93rd Congress, 2nd Session, November 25-26, 1974, 4441

The Impact of Foundations on Higher Education, 603

Impact of Government Funding on the Management of Voluntary Agencies, 2640

The Impact of Public Funding on Organizations in the Arts, 4632

"The Impact of Taxation on Charitable Giving: Some Very Personal Views", 1831

"The Impact of the Civil War on Philanthropy and Social Welfare", **58**

The Impact of the Foundation Provisions of the Tax Reform Act of 1969: Early Empirical Measurements, **4219**

Impact of the Omnibus Budget Reconciliation Act of 1987 on Tax-Exempt Organizations, **4116**

"Impact of TRA '84 on Nonprofits", 4371

"Implementing a Long-Range Plan", 2723

Implementing Joint Urban Ventures: Community Organizations and Organized Philanthropy, 2177

"Implications for Accounting in the Munson Decision", 4200

"The Importance of Marketing Research to the Nonprofit Organization", 2554

"The Importance of Staff Involvement in Volunteer Program Planning", 4581

"Important Information for Persons with 'Private' or 'Family' Foundations", 4231

Important 20th Century Paintings, Watercolors, and Drawings from the Soloman R. Guggenheim Foundation, 875

Imposing Aid: Emergency Assistance to Refugees, **1836**

Improper Payments by Private Foundations to Government Officials. Hearings before the Committee on Finance, United States Senate, 91st Congress, 1st Session on S. 2075, June 4, 1969, 4442

"Improve Communications with Local TV News People", 3325

"Improve Your Mail Solicitation Using Tested Testing Techniques", 3489

"Improving New York's Fund Raising Law", 4069

"Improving Our Prospects", **3599**

"Improving the Direct Mail Program in a Small Development Office", 3297

"Improving Your Program through Evaluation: Besides Program Justification, Evaluation Research Can Provide Information to Help Improve Volunteer Programs", 2014

"In a Secular Society, How Can We Teach People about Philanthropy? A Conversation with Robert L. Payton", **226**

In Art We Trust: The Board of Trustees in the Performing Arts, 2530

In Cold Type: Overcoming the Book Crisis, 4952

In Common Cause: Relations between Higher Education and Foundations, 843

"In Defense of the Federal Grant", 4618

"In Non-Cash World, Barter Emerges As New Development", 1628

"In Peapack, Moroccan Fantasy Benefits Channel 13", 3453

In Pursuit of Happiness and Good Government, **346**

In Return: The Autobiography of Sigmund Samuel, 429

In Search of Cash Cows: Exploring Money-Making Options for Nonprofit Agencies, **2377**

"In Search of More Responsible Philanthropy", **141**

In Search of Partnerships: Black Colleges and Universities/Private Philanthropy, **301**

"In the Company of Choreographers", 2306

"In the Money: A Foundation President's Advice on Foundation Solicitation", 3160

"In the Public Interest", 2015

"In Their Own Style", **116**

Incentives and the Nonprofit Sector, 2413

"The Increased Competition for Private Contributions and Grants", 3156

"Increased Corporate Support for Urban Public Schools", 1701

"Increasing Contributions through Effective Writing", 3052

"Increasing Dollar Levels by Building Relationships", **3780**

Increasing Giving Options in Corporate Charitable Payroll Deduction Programs: Who Benefits?, **1636**

Increasing the Impact, 1980's, **909**

Increasing the Impact of Social Innovations Funded by Grantmaking Organizations, 950

"Increasing What We Know", 46

The Incredible Bread Machine, 67

Indenture of James B. Duke Establishing the Duke Endowment, 717

"The Independent Sector Can Be Strengthened If Boards Assume Their Proper Responsibilities", 2570

"Independent Sector Outlines Plan to Double Giving", 3456

An Independent Sector Resource Directory of Education and Training Opportunities and Other Services, **2622**

Index of Progressive Funders, **1091**

"Indian Bingo: High Stakes Fundraising", 3299

Indiana Foundations: A Directory, **1194**

Indirect Costs, 2494

Indirect Costs: A Guide for Foundations and Nonprofit Organizations, 2856

"Indirect Costs: The Wonder of Never Having to Say Anything", **4037**

"Individual Contributions Expected to Rise by 10% for 1982", 3457

"Individual, Corporate Giving Depends on a Healthy Economy", 388

Individual Giving and Volunteering, 4539

The Industrial Museum, 4935

Industry-College Relations, 1501

"Industry Giving Spotlight: Oil Industry", 1515

Industry Support of Federated Appeals, 1728

"Industry's Role in Academia", 1425

Inequality of Sacrifice: The Impact of the Reagan Budget on Women, 4986

The Influence of Foundations on Education, 1297

The Influence of the Carnegie, Ford and Rockefeller Foundations on American Foreign Policy: The Ideology of Philanthropy, 572

"Influencing Public Policy: The Legal Limits", 724

An Informal Inquiry into Philanthropy in Europe, 1961-1962, 1969

Information Brochure, 641, 3656

Information for Seeking Foundation and Corporate Grants: How to Research, How to Prepare a Proposal, Where to Get More Information, 4009

Information Quarterly. 1972-1974, 947

Information Resources for the Non-Profit Sector. Interphil Conference, 1845

"Information Systems for Fund Raising Development Phase", 3368

"Information: The Key to Making Your Mid-Sized Donors Act Big", 3648

Infrastructure Problems of the Cities of Developing Countries, 1798

"Ingenuity and the Grant Application", 4016

Inherited Wealth: Your Money and Your Life, 203

The Inheritors: A Study of America's Great Fortunes and What Happened to Them, 463

Innovation and Entrepreneurship, 2569

TITLE INDEX

Innovation in Education, 4905

An Inside Look at Foundations and United Ways, **1028**

"The Inside Story on Hopkin's Billet-Doux", 3459

"The Inside Track: What the Experts Say about Seeking Alternative Funding", **3614**

"Inspecting the Damage", 549

"The Institute for Community Economics Where You Can Find Financial Aid, Technical Assistance, and a Firm Philosophical Footing", 2231

Institutional Aid, Federal Support to Colleges and Universities, 4797

Instructions for Form 990-PF. Return of Private Foundation or Section 4947(a)(1) Trust Treated As a Private Foundation, 4457

"Insurance Industry Giving Reaches New High", 1516

"Insurance Industry Issues 11th Annual Social Report, Identifies Trends in Giving", **1517**

Intellectual Life in America, 375

Intelligence Activities and the Rights of Americans. Book 2: Final Report of the Select Committee to Study Governmental Activities, 94th Congress, 4436

"Interaction of the Voluntary and Government Sectors: Toward an Understanding of the Coproduction of Municipal Services", 4569

"Interest in Endowment Campaigns for Arts Growing", 3462

"Interested and Knowledgeable Individuals Say No on Cost Allocation Proposal", 3876

Interface: Growing Initiatives between the Corporation and the Campus toward Greater Mutual Understanding, 1411

Interim Appraisal of the Economic Recovery Program's Impact on Philanthropic and Voluntary Organizations and the People They Serve, 4203

Internal Revenue Code, 4208

International Business Philanthropy, 1448

"International Conference on Fund Raising Keynote Address", 3234, 3589

International Corporate Contributions, **1934**

The International Corporate 1000: A Directory of Those Who Manage the World's Leading 1000 Corporations, **1938**

International Directory of Corporate Affiliations, **1518**

International Directory of Corporate Art Collections, 1503

"International Disaster: Fund Raiser's Dream or Nightmare?", 3852

The International Foundation Directory, **1839**

International Philanthropy: A Compilation of Grants by U.S. Foundations, 906

"International Philanthropy at Ditchley Park", 1819

"International Programs at the Department of Education", 4625

Internationalizing the Curriculum and the Campus: Guidelines for AASCU Institutions, 4862

"Interphil Hosts First U.S. Philanthropy Confab", 1847

"The Interrelationships of Organized Philanthropy", 259

"Interview: Budgeting and Financial Reporting in the Not-for-Profit Sector", **2668**

"Interview Guide for Review of Board Effectiveness", 1309

"An Interview with Susan K. Kinoy, Chief Grants Officer of the Villers Foundation", 878

"An Interview with William E. Simon", 1284

"Interviewing Volunteer Applicants for Skills", **2827**

"An Introduction to Capital Campaigns", 3530

Introduction to Foundation and Public Information: Sunshine or Shadow? A Study of the Public Information Accountability of the Country's Largest Foundations, 1029

Introduction to Fund Accounting, 2729

An Introduction to Fund Raising: The Newcomers' Guide to Development, 3272

Introduction to Nonprofit Organization Accounting, **2645**

An Introduction to Planned Giving Fund Raising through Bequests, Charitable Remainder Trusts, Gift Annuities and Life Insurance, 3930

"An Introduction to Program-Related Investments", **2294**

An Introduction to the American Association of Fund-Raising Counsel, Inc. and AAFRC Trust for Philanthropy, **2993**

An Introduction to the Art of Leadership of Commuity Service Organizations, 2885

An Inventory of Data Sources for Governmental and Other Nonprofit Organizations, 2434

An Inventory of Federal Income Transfer Programs, Fiscal Year 1977, 4674

Investigation Guidelines for Setting Up a Not-for-Profit Tax-Exempt Regional Theatre, 2595

Investing in America: Initiatives for Community and Economic Development, 1643

"Investing in Children", 4860

Investing in Our Children: Business and the Public Schools, 1369

"Investing in Volunteers: A Guide to Effective Volunteer Management", 4482

"Investing Your Foundation's Assets", 792

The Investment History of the Carnegie Corporation of New York, 942

Investment in People: The Story of the Julius Rosenwald Fund, 732

Investment of Charity Funds, **1914**

"Investment Partnerships Can Finance Charitable Activity", 3988

The Investment Policies of Foundations, 1038, 1039

"Investments of Philanthropic Organizations and Social Responsibility", 879

"Investor Involvement: Then and Now", 1444

The Invisible Hand of Planning: Capitalism, Social Science, and the State in the 1920s., **524**

Iowa Directory of Foundations, **854**

"IRIS and SPIN: Using Computers to Identify Funding Sources", **3871**

The Iron Cage Revisited: Conformity and Diversity in Organizational Fields, 2084

"IRS Commentary on Small Business Administration's 'Statistical Profile of the Nonprofit Sector'", 2362

"IRS Eases Foundation Rules for Pass through Foundations", 1164

"IRS Form 990: An Analytical Tool for Donors", 4236

IRS Oversight of Tax-Exempt Foundations, 98th Congress, 1st Session, May 11, 1983, 4394

"IRS Plans Major Research on Tax-Exempt Organizations", 4209

IRS Revenue Procedures on Tipping, 4210

IRS Rulings Re: Tax Reform Act of 1969, 4458, 4459

IRS Rulings Re: Tax Reform Act of 1969. April 1971-October 1971, 4460

"IRS' Special Emphases for Nonprofits in 1988", **4211**

"IRS Strikes Out at Two Property Acquisition Tacts", 4188

"IRS's Crackdown on Art Gifts Gains", 4214

The Irvine Ranch, 620

Is a Good Jew a Contributing Jew? The Relationship between Jewish Identity and Philanthropy, **405**

"Is It Feasible? The Prime Question in Venture Planning: A Case Study Shows How One Nonprofit Found Its Own Answer", **2965**

"Is It Time to Start Acting like a Corporation?", 3976

"Is Marketing Dangerous for Fund Raising?", **3356**

"Is New Regulation Really Needed?", **4189**

"Is Planned Giving Dead?", 3335

"Is Starting a Nonprofit Business for You?", 2214

"Is Technical Assistance Worth Funding?", 2427

Is That It?, **173**

"The Issue That Won't Go Away", 973

Issues and Opportunities Facing the Public-Sector Arts Support Network, 2304

Issues and Trends in Corporate Philanthropy: The American Experience, 1529

"It's about Time: How to Make It and Manage It", 2946

363

TITLE INDEX

It's Fun to Raise Money for World Service, 3546

J. Pierpont Morgan: An Intimate Portrait, 431

James B. Duke, Master Builder: The Story of Tobacco, Development of Southern and Canadian Water Power and the Creation of a University, 248

James Bertram: An Appreciation by Frank Pierce Hill, 219

James Buchanan Duke, 397

"James D. Robinson III on Tax Incentives for Charitable Giving", 4303

James Smithson and His Bequest, 401

James Smithson and the Smithsonian Story, 78

Japan-America Dialogue: A Survey of Organizational Activities, 1973

"Japan Digs Deep to Win the Hearts and Minds of America: A Growing Philanthropic Role Protects Its U.S. Investments and Improves Its Corporate Image", 1882

Japanese-American Yellow Pages, 1859

"Japanese Auto Manufacturers: The Quiet Philanthropists", 1861

"Japanese Corporations Emerging As Key Players in Grantmaking", **1863**

"Japanese Firms Learning Art of Image Polishing: Corporate Charity Is Alien Concept, But Companies Are Adapting to U.S. Rules", **1744**

"Japanese Foundations That Support U.S. Nonprofits", **1923**

Japanese Philanthropy and International Cooperation, **1855**

"Japanese Philanthropy in the United States. Part 1", 242

"Japanese Philanthropy in the United States. Part 2", 243

The Japanese Present Condition of the Philanthropic Activities under Private Initiative, 1860

"Japan's Rockefeller", **1862**

The JDR 3rd Fund and Asia, 1963-1975, 886

"JFS Aids Social Change for $2 Million Annually", **887**

J.K. Lasser's 53 New Plans for Saving Estate and Gift Taxes, 4171

J.M. Foundation. Final Report Evaluation, 1147

Jobs in the Arts and Arts Administration: A Guide to Placement/Referral Services, Career Counseling and Employment Listings, 2046

Jock: The Life and Times of John Hay Whitney, 264

John D.: A Portrait in Oils, 512

John D. Rockefeller Jr.: A Portrait, 161

John Davison Rockefeller, 1839-1937. A Memorial, 409

John Hay Whitney Foundation: Opportunity Fellows, Fulbright and Visiting Professors, 1098

John Hay Whitney Foundation: The John Hay Fellows, 1083

The John Jay and Eliza Jane Watson Foundation, 1949-1964, 1022

John Price Jones: A Memoir by Robert F. Duncan, 139

Johns Hopkins: A Silhouette, 468

"Join the Club: More and More Institutions Use Mega-Gift Clubs to Get Bigger Slice of the Pie", 3628

The Joiners: A Sociological Description of Voluntary Association Membership in the United States, **4531**

"Joint Costs Accounting a Key Issue in the Supreme Court's Munson Decision", 3877

Julius Rosenwald, Benefactor of Mankind, 245

"Just like Jonah Said", 984

"Keep Board Members Motivated and Working", 2534

"Keep It Simple: Overcoming Call Reluctance", **3793**

"Keeping in Touch with Major Donors", **3505**

Keeping Nonprofit Organizations Out of Trouble, 2953

Keeping Pace with the New Television: Public Television and Changing Technology, 4807

"Keeping the Board on a Roll: Interview with Amy Harwell", 2571

"Keeping Track of Volunteers with Micro-Computer", 4578

Keeping Track of What You Spend: The Librarian's Guide to Simple Bookkeeping, 2430

"Keeping Up with the States", 2903

"Key Fund-Raising Statistics", 3492, **3493**

Keys to Making a Volunteer Program Work, 4493

"Kicking the Federal Habit", 4606

King of the Castle, 355

The Kingdom and the Power, 461

"The Klan Basher", **2100**

"Knock, Knock, Who's There: Evaluating Your Board of Directors", 2692

"Know Who Will Be Reading Your Proposal", 4050

"Know Your Goals and How to Achieve Them", 2758

"Knowledge Is Power: Learn about Prospective Donors before You Write Your Proposals", **3337**

The KRC Aide and Advisor to Fund Raising Copywriters, 3483

KRC Computer Book for Fund Raisers, 3893

The KRC Desk Book for Fund Raisers, 3752

KRC Fund Raiser's Manual: A Guide to Personalized Fund Raising, 3060

The KRC Guide to Direct Mail Fund Raising, 3484

The KRC Handbook of Fund Raising Principles and Practices: With Sample Forms and Records, 3520

The KRC Handbook of Fund Raising Strategy and Tactics, 3252

KRC Portfolio of Fund Raising Letters, 3174

"The Kresge Foundation and Capital Grants", 807

Kulturfonder I Sverige: Ett Urval Till Tjanst for Stipendiesokande, 1874

Lady Unknown: The Life of Angela Burdett-Coutts, 206

"The Last Caprice: A Collection of Unusual Wills, Proving That People's Bequests Are Almost As Fascinating As People", 3626

Latin American Foundations, 1789

Latin American Libraries and U.S. Foundation Philanthropy: An Historical Survey, 1884

Law and Taxation: A Guide for Conservation and Other Nonprofit Organizations, 4132

The Law and the Lore of Endowment Funds, 4119

"The Law Limiting Foundation Grant Expenses", 939

The Law of Tax-Exempt Organizations, **4190**

The Law of Tax-Exempt Organizations. Cumulative Supplement, **4191**

The Law of Trusts, 4314

Law Relating to Charities, 1784

A Lawyer's Guide to Private Foundations. Supplement, **4163**

"Laying It on the Line", 1530

A Layman's Guide to Lobbying without Losing Your Tax-Exempt Status, 4243

"Leaders Examine Philanthropy: Stress Need for Greater Education about Its Role in Society", 296

Leadership and Power, **2608**

"Leadership and Voluntary Action", 2237

"Leading Business Spokesmen Argue Strong Case for Corporate Public Involvement", 1557

"Leaping the Cultural Barrier: A Roadmap to Japanese Corporate Philanthropy", 1924

"Learning from Foundation Annual Reports", 940

"Learning from Foundation Reports", **720**, 941, 1223

"Learning from Foundation Reports: The Rosenberg Foundation", 1185

"Learning from Foundation Reports: The San Francisco Foundation", 1069

"Learning the Magic of Asking Via Walt Disney and Joyce Hall", 3596

"Learning to Listen", 581

"Learning to Save Lebanon", **63**

"Learning to Think like Proposal Readers", 4004

"Leave the Left Alone", 4675

Leaving Money to Charity, **359**

Left-Handed Fastballers: Scouting and Training America's Grass-Roots Leaders, 1966-1977, 4918

Legacies: A Practical Guide for Charities, **2804**

TITLE INDEX

The Legacy Today, Andrew Carnegie's Peace Endowment: The Nineteen-Eighties, 607
"Legal Advice", 4234
Legal Aspects of Charitable Trusts and Foundations: A Guide for Philanthropoids, 4218
The Legal Foundations of American Philanthropy, 1776-1844, **4247**
Legal Handbook for Nonprofit Organizations, 4220
Legal Instruments of Foundations, 539
Legal Issues in Nonprofit Organizations, 4237
Legal Issues Involving Competition by Nonprofits with Small Business, 4192
Legislative Activity by Certain Types of Exempt Organizations. Hearings on H.R. 13720, May 3, 4 and 5, to Amend the Internal Revenue Code of 1954 with Respect to Lobbying by Certain Types of Exempt Organizations, 92nd Congress, 2nd Session, 4399
"Lehrfeld on Foundations", 943
"Lending Sources for Nonprofits", 2394
"Length of Stock Market Meltdown Holds Key to How Foundations Will Fair, But Crash Not Seen Curbing Grants, Assets, Soon", **944**
"Lesson from a Community Organizer", 4951
"Lessons Learned from the New Century Campaign", **3388**
Let the People Decide: Neighborhood Organizing in America, **4834**
"Let's Clear the Air about Public Service Announcements", 3617
Letters to a Foundation Trustee: What We Need to Know about Foundations and Their Management, 676
"Letters to the Editor: The Dangers of Research Partnerships with Industry", 1560
A Lexicon for Community Foundations, **1155**
"The Liberal-Conservative Spectrum in Philanthropy", **454**
Libraries: Getting into the Philanthropic Thick of Things, 3570
Library Jobs: How to Fill Them, How to Find Them, 2551
"Life after a Grant: Now the Hard Work Begins for Grantee", 2939
"Life after Tax Reform", **4125**
Life for Dead Spaces: The Development of the Lavanburg Commons, 4853
The Life of Andrew Carnegie. 2 Vols, 209
The Life of Dr. D.K. Pearsons, Friend of the Small College and of Missions, 506
"The Limits of a Model Community Bank", 4856
The Limits of Altruism: An Ecologist's View of Survival, **197**
The Limits of Corporate Responsibility, 1357
Linking Corporate Philanthropy to Corporate Growth, 1584

"Linking Philanthropy to Corporate Marketing", 1567
"The LISC Public-Private Partnership", 3572
List Brokers, 3227
List of Organizations Filing As Private Foundations, 771
"Listening and Learning: Developing Foundation Programs", 844
A Listing of U.S. Non-Profit Organizations in Small Industry Development Assistance Abroad, 1962
The Literature of Philanthropy, **182**
A Literature Review of Altruism and Helping Behavior, 181
Litigation on Behalf of Women, 4783
"Little-Known Funders Give Substantial Amounts", **1568**
"Little Things Mean a Lot: The Care and Feeding of Speakers", 2468
Living with A-122: A Handbook for Nonprofit Organizations. 3 Vols, **4091**
"Lobbying and Political Activities: What Every Nonprofit Should Know", 4245
"Lobbying and Political Activity for Nonprofits: What You Can and Can't Do under Federal Law", 4108
The Local Arts Council Movement, 2233
"Local Foundations: Their Dollar Power and Impact", 1161
"Local Fund Raising: Demonstrating the Value of Libraries", 3615
"Local Funding of Public Libraries", 3046
Local Heroes, **4490**
"Local TV News: De-Mystifying the Medium and Getting Your Stories on the Air", 3326
Locating, Recruiting and Hiring the Disabled, 2853
"Long-Range Process Planning: The First Cut", 2392
"A Look at Some Conservative-Oriented Foundations", 962
"Look Carefully at That Contract before You Sign Up with a Fund-Raising Consultant", 2728
"Look into My Crystal Cathode Ray Tube: Computer Models Make Annual Giving Predictions Easy", 2753
"Looking Ahead: Mobilizing Sources and Resources for the Future", 4574
"Looking Ahead: The Future for Nonprofits", 2357
Looking at Income-Generating Businesses for Small Nonprofit Organizations, 2095
Looking Forward to the Year 2000: Public Policy and Philanthropy, **234**
"Looking Good. Part 2: Speaking the Language", **1990**
"The Looming Battle: Partisan Activities of Tax-Exempt Organizations", 4164
"Lose Art, Jobs, Treasure Revived with Cathedral Plan", 3525
"Loudoun Man at Ninety-Two Leads Rugged Life: Spry Retired Doctor Made Fortune in Land", 220
Louis C. Tiffany: Rebel in Glass, 285

Louise Whitfield Carnegie, 210
"Low Pay, Long Hours", **2020**
"Lower Profits and Economic Uncertainty Threaten Corporate Philanthropy", 1694
The MacArthur Foundation, **921**
"MacArthur Foundation. Part 1: The Chicago School of Philanthropy", 914
"MacArthur Foundation. Part 2: Selling off the Family Business", 915
"MacArthur Foundation. Part 3: The Gold-Plated Charity Machine", 916
"Mail Appeals: But Will They Open the Envelope?", 3506
"Mail Order Influence on Giving Grows According to New Study", 3283
Maine Corporate Foundation Directory, **1332**
Major Challenges to Philanthropy, **370**
"Major Donor Prospecting: 'I Don't Know Anyone with Money'", 3507
"Major Gift Volunteers: A Balanced View", 3944
"Major Gifts: Building an Effective Program", **3939**
"Major Gifts: Three Perspectives", **3611**
"Major Tax Changes Affect Property Gifts", **4337**
Major U.S. Foundations' and Corporations' Responsiveness to Puerto Rican Needs and Concerns, 350
"Make an Average Investment, Get an Average Return", 3736
"Make Crisis Work for You: Wilson College Case History", 3916
Make Your Events Special: How to Produce Successful Events for Nonprofit Organizations, 3311
"Making a Stronger Case for Health Care Philanthropy", 437
"Making Beautiful Music", 3896
"Making Choices: Issues Facing Charities and Donors. Part 1", **2028**
"Making Endowments Greener", 3598
Making Grants Overseas, 1780
"Making It by Doing Good: Nouvelle Society Ladies Win Peer Approval Working for 'the Arts and Diseases'", 97
Making PSAs Work. TV, Radio: A Handbook for Health Communication Professionals, 2934
"Making the Most of Charitable Impulses: An Outright Gift to Your Alma Mater Cuts Your Taxes", 4167
Making the Most of Special Events, 3948
Making the Non-Profit Organization Work: A Financial, Legal and Tax Guide for Administrators, 2816
"Making Your Voice Heard", 2746
"A Man of Arts and Letters", 426
The Man Who Gave Away Millions: The Story of Andrew Carnegie, 151
"Management: A Missing Function?", 2770
"Management Accounting Techniques for Not-for-Profit Enterprises", 2547
The Management and Financing of Colleges, 2738
"Management and the Foundations", 979

365

TITLE INDEX

Management Assistance for the Arts: A Survey of Programs, 2499
"Management Audit: A Key to Cost Control", 2484
Management by Design: Library Management, 2727
Management by Objectives in Mental Health Services, 2960
Management Control in Nonprofit Organizations, 2448
"Management Corporations: The New Trend in Human Services", 2741
Management Indicators in Nonprofit Organizations: Guidelines to Selection and Implementation, 2576
Management of American Foundations: Administration, Policies, and Social Role, 2979
The Management of Carnegie Corporation, **1077**
The Management of Corporate Giving Programs, **1545**
"The Management of Volunteers in Nonprofit Organizations: Theory and Practice", 4522
Management Pamphlets. Series 1, 2431
Management Principles for Nonprofit Agencies and Organizations, 2976
"Management: The Corporate Cezanne", 321
Managers of the Arts, **2556**
"Managers Should Protect the Unique Strengths of the Nonprofit Workplace", 2634
Managing a Business Contributions Program, 1736
"Managing Change: The Challenge for Giving", 871
Managing Corporate Contributions, **1705**
Managing Crisis, 2426
Managing Educational Endowments, 2460
Managing Endowment Capital. The Endowment Conference, 2562, 2563, 2564, 2565
Managing Expectations: What Effective Board Members Ought to Expect from Nonprofit Organizations, 2751
Managing for Impact in Nonprofit Organizations: Corporate Planning Techniques and Applications, **2638**
Managing for Profit in the Nonprofit World, **2588**
Managing Foundation Assets: An Analysis of Foundation Investment and Spending Policies and Performance, **1149**
Managing Nonprofit Agencies for Results: A Systems Approach to Long-Range Planning, **2646**
Managing Nonprofit Organizations, 2475
Managing Online Reference Services, 2457
"Managing Public Library Investments", 2871
Managing Smaller Corporate Giving Programs, **1420**
"Managing the Arts", 2612
Managing the Library Automation Project, 2523

Managing Voluntary Organizations: A Manual for Community Development and Management of Voluntary Organizations, 2604
Managing Volunteers for Results, 2849
Man's Concern for His Fellow Man. A Swift Review of Civilized Man's Philanthropic Nature and Efforts, 326
Manual for Board Members of Not-for-Profit Organizations, 2739
The Manual of Corporate Giving, 1663
Manual of Practical Fund Raising, 4063
A Manual of the Public Benefactions of Andrew Carnegie, 85
A Manual on State Mental Health Planning, 4757
Mapping the Third Sector: Voluntarism in a Changing Social Economy, **4592**
The Marcus L. Ward Home at Maplewood, N.J., 198
The Market for Loving Kindness: Day Care Centers and the Demand for Child Care, 2312
The Market for the Development of Appalachian Kentucky: Government Demand and Nonprofit Supply, 2416
Market the Arts!, 2763
"'Market Yourself' Becoming a Common Cry at Nonprofit Conferences", 2351
"Marketing: A Development Opportunity", 3694
"Marketing Communications in Nonbusiness Situations or Why It's So Hard to Sell Brotherhood like Soap", 3785
"Marketing Demystified: Even Small Nonprofit Organizations Can Use Marketing Tools in Fund Raising", 3090
Marketing for Non-Profit Organizations, **2855**
Marketing for Nonprofit Organizations, 2695
"Marketing for Public and Nonprofit Managers", 3585
"Marketing for Volunteer Service Organizations: A Case Study", 3848
"Marketing Imagination", **3646**
Marketing in the Service Sector, 2858
"Marketing Linked to Charity", 1686
Marketing the Arts, 2772
Marketing the Library, 2716
"Marketplace Only Real Way to Get True Response Results", 3104
"A Marriage of Convenience", 1285
Marshall Field III, 34
"Maryland Approves Private Fund Raising for Schools", 3698
"MAS Program Places Retired Corporate Execs with Nonprofits", 2747
Massachusetts Foundation Directory, 556
Massachusetts Foundation Directory Supplement: Sources of Private Support for Individuals, 557
Massachusetts Grantmakers, **558**
"Matching Business Resources with Neighborhood Needs", 4900

"Matching Executives and Nonprofits: Interview with Aetna Life and Casualty", 4514
Matching Gift Details: Guidebook to Corporate Matching Gift Programs, **1487**
Matching Gifts: Patterns and Practices in Corporate Matching-Gift Programs, 3602
Matching Greater Cleveland's Corporate Philanthropy with Emerging Community Needs, 1480
"Matching Your Needs with Computer Capability", 2899
A Matter of Vision: Community and Economic Development in the Philadelphia Area, **2390**
"Mattox Offers Guidelines for Foundation Trustees", 2913
The Maurice and Laura Falk Foundation: A Private Fortune—a Public Trust, 1201
MBO for Nonprofit Organizations, 2754
McKinney's Consolidated Laws on New York Annotated, 4242
"The Meaning of 1983 for the Mission of 1984", 260
Meaning Well Is Not Enough, 4563
Measurable Growth in Giving and Volunteering, **235**
The Measurement of Organizational Effectiveness, Productivity, Performance, and Success: Issues and Dilemmas in Service and Non-Profit Organizations, 2197
"Measuring Financial Health: Hands-on", **2902**
Measuring Potential and Evaluating Results, 2803
"The Media and Philanthropy", **442**
The Media Book: Making the Media Work for Your Grassroots Group, 2515
"The Media Don't Give Corporations Enough Credit", **1469**
Media Resource Guide, 2594
Mediability: A Guide for Nonprofits, 2471
Medical Research: A Mid-Century Survey. 2 Vols, 4893
The Medicare Hospital Insurance System: An Illustration of Non-Profit Participation in a Federal Government Program, 4644
Medicare's Poor: Filling the Gaps in Medical Coverage for Low-Income Elderly Americans, 4817
Medicine and Public Health: Development Assistance Abroad, 1963
"A Medley of Radio Winners", 4932
Meeting Human Needs: Corporate Programs and Partnerships, **1706**
Meeting Human Needs toward a New Public Philosophy, 335
Meeting the Challenge: Foundation Responses to Acquired Immune Deficiency Syndrome, **1167**
Meeting Today's Fund Raising Challenges, 3038
Mega Gifts: Who Gives Them, Who Gets Them?, **3702**

TITLE INDEX

Megatrends: Ten New Directions Transforming Our Lives, 4912

The Mellon Family: A Fortune in History, 214

Mellon's Millions: The Biography of a Fortune. The Life and Times of Andrew W. Mellon, 363

The Mellons: The Chronicle of America's Richest Family, 288

Members and Library Partners Directory, 525

"Members, Committees, and the Board of Directors", 2591

"Membership Development: Part 2, Attracting New Members", 2653

"Membership Development: Part 3, the Brochure", 3404

Membership Directory, **559**

The Membership Mystique: How to Create Income and Influence with Membership Programs, 2926

Membership Roster, **1045**, 2558

"Memo to Nonprofit Board Members. Re:: What You Should Know about Legal Liability", 2756

"The Memoirs of Frederick T. Gates", 172

Memorandum on Corporate Giving: Including Compendium of Applicable Federal Tax Laws, 1421

A Memorial of the Life and Benefactions of Mary Hemenway, 1820-1894, 473

Mental and Developmental Disabilities Directory of Legal Advocates, 4073

Mental Health: An Interdisciplinary and International Perspective, 4887

Mental Health Funding: A Directory of Federal, State and Foundation Grants for Mental Health Education, Prevention and Treatment Services, 3221

The Mental Hygiene Movement, 4813

Mental Retardation and Society: The Ethics and Politics of Normalization, 4941

Merger: Another Path Ahead: A Guide to the Merger Process for Voluntary Human Service Agencies, 2136

"Mergers Won't Slow Corporate Philanthropy", 1640

"Met Given $1 Million for Armor", **3613**

"Met Museum Seeks Endowed Chairs", 3322

"The Met Sings the Praise of Corporate Sponsorship", 1660

"Metaphor Carried Too Far", 4984

"A Method for Hospice Economic Survival", 3098

"Methods of Evaluating Computer Software Systems", 3743

The Metropolitan Philadelphia Philanthropy Study, 485

The Metropolitan Philadelphia Philanthropy Study. Final Report, 486

The Michigan Foundation Directory, **747**

Michigan Foundations Conference, 768

Mid-Continent Conference on Philanthropy, 336

The Milbank Memorial Fund: Its Leaders and Its Work, 1905-1974, 913

"A Mile High and Still Growing", 935

"Million Dollar and Up Donors", 3632

"Million-Dollar Gifts, Grants, Pledges and Requests of 1986", 341

Minding the Corporate Conscience: Public Interest Groups and Corporate Social Accountability, 1572

Mindpower Match/Double Your Dollar, 3166

"Minds, Money, and Markets", 1592

Minnesota Foundations List, 1010

Minnesota Philanthropic Support for the Disadvantaged: A Report on Who Benefits from Grantmaking, 390

Minnesota Philanthropy and Disadvantaged People: A Report on Who Benefits from Grantmaking, **391**

Minnesota Philanthropy and Disadvantaged People. Supplementary Tables, **342**

A Minor Miracle: An Informal History of the National Science Foundation, 4679

Minority Access to College, 4820

Minority Organizations: A National Directory, 2059

"The Minus and Plus of Partial Funding", **3540**

"Misdirecting Corporate Philanthropy", 1315

Misgivings, **1899**

Mission Accomplished: Automating Your Tax-Exempt Organizations, 2971

Mission Handbook: North American Protestant Missionaries Overseas, 1788

The Mitchell Guide to Foundations, Corporations and Their Managers: Central New York, Including Binghamton, Corning, Elmira, Geneva, Ithaca, Oswego, Syracuse, Utica, **1012**

The Mitchell Guide to Foundations, Corporations and Their Managers: Long Island, Including Nassau and Suffolk Counties, **1013**

The Mitchell Guide to Foundations, Corporations, and Their Managers. New Jersey, **953**

The Mitchell Guide to Foundations, Corporations and Their Managers: Upper Hudson Valley Including Capital Area, Glens Falls, Newburgh, Plattsburgh, Poughkeepsie, Schenectady, **1014**

The Mitchell Guide to Foundations, Corporations and Their Managers: Westchester, Including Putnam, Rockland and Orange Counties, **1015**

The Mitchell Guide to Foundations, Corporations and Their Managers: Western New York, Including Buffalo, Jamestown, Niagara Falls, Rochester, **1016**

"The Mixmasters", 2283

"A Model for Pre-Award Grant Information Management Using a Word Processor: In the Move to Bring Technology to Pre-Award Grant Management, a Word Processor May Be More Cost and Time Effective Than a Computer", 2618

The Modern Corporation and Social Responsibility, 1575

"A Modern Day Noah's Ark", **1181**

The Modern Foundation: Its Dual Character, Public and Private, 904

The Modern Law of Charities, 1870, 1871

"The Modern Philanthropic Foundation: A Critique and a Proposal", 829

Modern Philanthropy: A Study of Efficient Appealing and Giving, 11

"Money and the Board", **2058**

Money and the Church, 2296

Money and Your Church: How to Raise More, How to Manage It Better, 3402

Money Business: Grants and Awards for Creative Artists, 553

The Money Givers: An Examination of the Myths and Realities of Foundation Philanthropy in America, 822

"Money Isn't Everything", 704

Money Isn't Everything: A Survival Manual for Nonprofit Organizations, 2590

Money-Makers: A Systematic Approach to Special Events Fund Raising, 2984

Money Making Marketing, **2705**

"Money Out of the Blue Aiding Individual Thinkers", 705

Money: Raising and Managing Funds for Human Services, 2773

Money Raising Ideas for Exchange Clubs, 3665

"Money-Starved Schools Get Help from Foundations", 978

"Money to Battle AIDS Scarce Despite Recent Surge in Grants", **889**

Money to Burn. What the Great American Philanthropic Foundations Do with Their Money, 640

Money to Work: Grants for Visual Artists, **4608**

"Monitoring Financial Health", 2833

The Montana and Wyoming Foundation Directory, **1002**

The Moral Aspect of Leadership, 2609

"Moral Issues in Investment Policy", 1574

Moral Obligation or Marketing Tool? Examining the Roles of Corporate Philanthropy, 1422

The Morality of Spending: Attitudes toward the Consumer Society in America, 1875-1940, **227**

More and Better Wills: Testamentary Benefactions, 3005

"More Effective and Less Costly AIDS Health Services", 2989

The More Effective Use of Resources, an Imperative for Higher Education, 4798

"More Helpful Cues for a New Position", **3137**

More Money for More Opportunity. Financial Support of Community College Systems, 3945

"More Nonprofit Groups Make Imaginative Aggressive Sales", 1992

367

TITLE INDEX

"More on Munson: State Laws Unconstitutional", **4335**
"More Paperwork on Gifts of Property Worth $5,000", **4225**
"More Than a Salary Survey", **585**
More Than Survival: Prospects for Higher Education in a Period of Uncertainty, 4811
More They Told Barron: Conversations and Revelations of an American Pepys in Wall Street, 31
"A More Thoughtful Path to Preventing Nuclear War: Foundations Are Supporting Research That Goes Beyond Counting Missiles", 929
"More Unrelated Business Tax Issues", 4226
Morgan the Magnificent: The Life of J. Pierpont Morgan, 1837-1913, 513
"Most Big United Ways Shield Executive Salaries from Public", **3062**
"Most Boards Are Still Operating in the 19th Century. Interview with Harvey Newman", 2572
"The Most Generous Living Americans", 418, **419**
"A Mother's Trust", **432**
Motivations for Charitable Giving: A Reference Guide, 3642
Motives in Educational Philanthropy, 517
Motives, Models, and Men: An Exploration of Entrepreneurship in the Nonprofit Sector, 2414
"Mott Advisor Recommends Fund-Raising Strategies", 3643
"Movers and Shakers of Corporate Social Responsibility", **1589**
"Moving Target", **599**
Mr. Anonymous: Robert W. Woodruff of Coca Cola, 143
Mr. Five Percent: The Story of Calouste Gulbenkian, 216
"Much More Than Bricks and Mortar", **527**
"A Multi-Tiered Economy: Industry Outlooks 1981", 1598
"Munson and the Watchdogs", **4336**
"The Munson Case", 3862
"Munson: The Supreme Court Disposes of the Rebuttable Presumption", **4251**
Museum Accounting Handbook, 2541
"The Museum As Employer", 2134
Museum Guide to Federal Programs, 4684
Museum Program, 4695
"Musical Superstars Continue African Charity Relief Effort", 1849
A Must for Effective Corporate Philanthropy: Good Communications, 1402
"Must Non-Profits Be Market Driven?", **2151**
The Mutual Benefit Life Report. Corporate Commitment to Volunteerism, 4557
The Mutual Benefit Life Report 2. Small Business Commitment to Volunteerism and Community Development, 4558

Mutual Insurance Companies and the Theory of Nonprofit and Cooperative Enterprise, 2154
"The Mystique of University Endowments", 3486
The Myth of Unfair Competition by Nonprofit Organizations: A Review of Government Assistance to Small Business, **4475**
"Myths and Maxims about Boards of Directors", 2781
"NAAG Seeks Model Law for Charities", 4253
"NAEIR: A Storehouse of Corporate Gifts", 1359
"NAEIR Members, Donors Both Benefit from Surplus Goods Supply", **1498**
"NAHD Sees Threat to Charitable Contributions Law in Analysis of Philanthropic Issues", 4252
"A Name for the Sector: Suggestions from the Accounting World", 2249
"Names and Numbers: A Survey Shows How Major Universities Go about Prospect Research", **3069**
"A Nation of Groups", 2158
A Nation Prepared: Teachers for the 21st Century, **4810**
National Arts and Humanities Foundations, 4752
"National Arts Stabilization Fund Gets Underway", 2251
National Association of Attorneys General Conference, 4255
The National Climate for Philanthropy and the Private Sector, 218
National Community Foundations Mental Health Project: Final Report, 1031
National Conference on Nonprofit Management and Technical Assistance, 2799
National Conference on Solicitations, 349
"National Conference Sharpens Focus of Volunteer Community", **4483**
National Council on Community Foundations Meeting, 1032, 1033
National Data Book of Foundations, **772**
The National Directory for the Performing Arts and Civic Centers, 2150
The National Directory of Arts and Education Support by Business Corporations, **1451**
National Directory of Arts Support by Business Corporations, 1586
National Directory of Arts Support by Private Foundations, 3633
National Directory of Corporate Charity, **1684**
National Directory of Corporate Public Affairs, 1364
National Directory of Service and Product Providers to Nonprofit Organizations and Resource Center Catalog, 2341
The National Directory of State Agencies, **4635**
"The National Grantmaker Networks. Part 1", 1034

"The National Grantmaker Networks. Part 2", **1035**
National Guide to Foundation Funding in Health, **622**
National Guide to Funding in Aging, **3950**
National Institute of Mental Health Research Support Programs and Activities, 4758
National Survey on Women in the Arts and Humanities, 2384
National Taxonomy of Exempt Entities (NTEE), **2179**
National VLA Directory, **2878**
National Working Conference of Nonprofit Professional Theatres, 4970
"Native Profit", **2226**
The Nature of Leadership, 2119
The Nature of Trusteeship: The Role and Responsibilities of College and University Boards, **2784**
"NCIB Standards Shift to Governance and Program: Less Emphasis on Fund Raising", **2358**
"NCIB's New Standards", **2262**
Nebraska Foundation Directory, **898**
Needs Assessment: A Guide for Planners, Managers, and Funders of Health and Human Care Services, 2938
Needs Assessment: A Model for Community Planning, 2793
"Needy Arts: Where Have All the Patrons Gone?", 358
"Negotiating the Terms of a Grant", 2505
"Neighborhood: Enterprising Organizations", 2132
Neighborhood Grantsmanship: An Approach for Grassroots Self-Reliance in the 1980's, 3161
A Neighborhood Reinvestment Partnership, 2982
"Neighborhood Revitalization Partnerships", 3672
"'Network Call' Helps Nonprofits Save Money Talking to Each Other", 2792
Network Matching: Nonprofit Structure and Public Policy. Chapter 1: Cultural Conflicts and the Roots of Nonprofit Social Structure, 2025
Network of Change-Oriented Foundations, 1081
"Networking in Ohio: The Ohio Association of Grantmakers", 683
Networking: The First Report and Directory, 2724
Nevada Foundation Directory, **855**
"Never Mind the Project Just Give Us a Grant", 3674
The New Accounting Standards for Charitable Organizations and Their Importance to Regulatory Bodies, 2625
"New Aging Foundation Emphasizes Senior-Led Groups", 1041
New Approaches to Increase Private Funds for Neighborhood Organization Development, **3659**
"New Arts Database Will Provide Information Leap", 2007

TITLE INDEX

"New Ball Game for the Foundations", 4259

"New Breed, Meet the Old Creed. The Trend to Be like For-Profit Executives May Have Violated a Basic Rule about Who's in Charge", 2736

New Challenges for Employee Volunteering, 4595

A New Competitive Edge: Volunteers from the Workplace, **4594**

The New Corporate Philanthropy: How Society and Business Can Profit, 1549

New Direction in Funding and Program Priorities for the Aging: The Interrelationship of Government, Private Foundations, Corporate Grantmakers and Unions, 4982

New Directions for Institutional Advancement. Understanding and Increasing Foundation Support, 3524

"The New Face of Volunteerism", 4537

The New Federalism, the Federal Budget, and the Nonprofit Sector, 2321

"New Formulas for Philanthropy", **1459**

"New Fund for the Arts", 758

"New Fund to Make Grants Only to Individual Artists", 695

New Futures Initiative: Strategic Planning Guide, **2049**

"New GAO Study Sees Decline in Foundation Birthrate", 725

New Goals for Corporate Giving to Higher Education, 1412

The New Grants Planner: A Systems Approach to Grantsmanship, 3750

New Haven: A Case Study of Corporate Philanthropy and the Federal Budget Cuts, 1980-1982, 1492

"New Health Care Strategy Outgrowth of Marketing Focus", 2225

"New Horizons for Kids in the Middle", **1476**

The New How to Raise Funds from Foundations, 3206

New Ideas for Foundation Investments: Program-Related Loans, 1129

New Information Technologies for the Nonprofit Sector, **2404**

New Jersey State Aid Catalog for Local Governments, 4718

"New Jewish Philanthropy Aiming at Non-Sectarian Aid for All Poor", **465**

"New Job Training Act: What Does It Mean for Nonprofits?", 4641

"New Law Called 'a Victory'", **4301**

"New Life Insurance Plan Boon to Endowment Fund", 3943

"The New Mexican Umbrella", 2744

New Mexico Private Foundations Directory, **1024**

New Models for Creative Giving, 284

New Models for Financing the Local Church, 3515

New Money for Nonprofits, 2378

The New Morality: A Profile of American Youth in the 70's, 4990

"The New Need for Charity: Can Corporations Cover It?", 1384

"The New 990", 4333

New 1986 Tax Law: Explanation, Year-End Strategies and Charitable Gifts, 4360

"New Nonprofits Are Being Undermined", 48

"New Partnerships in International Corporate Philanthropy", 1820

"A New Philanthropy: Patrons Single Out the Design Field for Support", 1531

The New Political Economy: The Public Use of the Private Sector, **4743**

"New Relief for Tired Fund-Raising Messages", 3091

New Rules: Searching for Self-Fulfillment in a World Turned Upside Down, 4991

"New Service to Make Matches between Corporate Donors and Nonprofits", 1605

New Sources of Revenue: An Ideabook, **3444**

"New Strategy: 'Databased' Donor Personalization", 3350

"New Study Shows Nearly All Major Corporations Give to Charity", 1606

"New Style Philanthropy", 466

"New Tax Bill Creates Crucial Changes in Tax Return: Revisions in 990-PF Call for Greater Detail on Administrative Costs", 4142

The New Tax Law: A Guide for Child Welfare Organizations, 4376

"New Techniques for Upgrading Donors", 3351

"New Technologies Media for Fund Raising Are on the Way", 3651

New Telecommunications Technologies and Programming, 2888

New Tools for Neighborhood Development: A Look at Some Information Providers and Users, **4964**

"New United Fund Cut Charity Drives", 3676

"New Ventures for Antipoverty Agencies", **2018**

"New Ways to Lead", 600, **1292**

"New York: A New Charitable Solicitation Statute", 3842

"New York Adopts Revised Fund-Raising Regulation Law", 3412

New York City Arts Funding Guide, 3117

New York City Arts-in-Education Directory, 2266

The New York Nonprofit Sector in a Time of Government Retrenchment, 4660

New York Not-for-Profit Organization Manual, **4469**

New York State Foundations: A Comprehensive Directory, **1067**

"New York's Own Private Trust Fund", **1278**

"Newman Donates $25G to Connecticut Library", 356

NIB Standards in Philanthropy, 2256

The 1981 Tax Act and Charitable Organizations, 4465

"The 1982 Annual Reports: A Potpourri for the Corporate Watchdog", 1596

"The 1982 Form 990", 4263

"The 1982 Tax Act and the 'New' Minimum Tax: Its Impact on Charitable Contribution Deductions", 4114

"1984 in Philanthropy", 4728

"A 1984 Tax Bill after All: Extensive Provisions Affecting Charitable Nonprofit Organizations", 4345

"1985 Tax Reform Options and Charitable Contributions", 4480

"The 1986 Finance Bill: Increasing Charitable Giving the U.K. Way—a Historical Perspective", **1828**

The 1986 Tax Reform Act: Bad News for Nonprofits, 4106

"1987, the Year of Charity-Bashing", **2172**

"The No-Apologies Budget: How to Justify the Financial Support a Volunteer Program Deserves", 2678

"No Bow and Arrow", 3831

"No Longer a Free Ride: New Regulations on below-Market Loans Are Restrictive", **4168**

No Quick Fix (Planning), **2942**

"No Strings on Gifts to Universities", 3347

Noblesse Oblige: Charity and Cultural Philanthropy in Chicago, 1849-1929, 333

Non-Cash Corporate Philanthropy: A Report on Current Practices with Annotated Bibliography, 1587

Non-Grant Fund Raising: Overall Fund Raising Campaign (Including Case Statement, Feasibility Study, Fund Raising Plan), 1324

"Non-Profit Accounting Concepts Take a Step Forward", 2864

Non-Profit Cultural Organizations, 4287

Non-Profit Enterprise in the Performing Arts, 2637

"Non-Profit Homes for the Aged: How to Avoid Private Foundation Status", 4101

Non-Profit Organizations: Current Issues and Developments, **2298**

"Non-Profit Sector Facing 'Tricky and Delicate' Times", 2199

The Non-Profit Sector in International Perspective: The Case of Sri Lanka, 1850

"The Non-Profit Sector in the Metropolitan (Philadelphia) Economy", **2305**

Non-Profit Service Organizations, 2252

"Non-Profit Software Package Directory", 2795, 3686

"Non-Profit Software Package Directory: Fall '88 Update", **3687**

"Non-Profit Software Package Review: Part 4", 3671

Non-Profit Tax Exempt Corporations: The Alternative Tax Shelter, 2270

"Non-Profits and the U.N.", 1958

"Non Profits in Business", 2343

"Non-Profits Must Consider Ethics in Soliciting Gifts", 3224

"Non-Traditional Corporate Assistance Under Study", 1629

369

TITLE INDEX

"Noncash Giving on Rise to Needy Organizations", 1695
Nonprivate Foundations: A Tax Guide for Charitable Organizations, 4169
"Nonprofit Accounting: A Revolution in Process", 2626
"Nonprofit Accounting: The Continuing Revolution", 2627
"Nonprofit Accounting: The Search for a Solution", 2895
"Nonprofit Agencies Are Turning to Fees to Balance Books", 2271
Nonprofit Arts Organizations: Formation and Maintenance, 2287
Nonprofit Arts Organizations: Formation and Maintenance. Supplement, 2288
The Nonprofit Board Book: Strategies for Organizational Success, 2445
Nonprofit Boards: A Practical Guide to Roles, Responsibilities, and Performance, **2573**
"Nonprofit Boards: They're Going Corporate", **2597**
"Nonprofit Charitable Organizations, 1983", **2164**
Nonprofit Corporations, Organizations, and Associations, 4269
Nonprofit Decline and Dissolution Project Report, 2399
"The Nonprofit Economic Miracle", 2272
The Nonprofit Enterprise in Market Economies, **2189**
Nonprofit Enterprise in the Arts: Studies in Mission and Constraint, **2557**
"Nonprofit Enterprise: Through the Eyes of For-Profit", 2408
The Nonprofit Entrepreneur: Creating Ventures to Earn Income, 2897
Nonprofit Financial Management, 2850
Nonprofit Firms in a Three Sector Economy, 2397
"Nonprofit Group Goes into Business", 2368
"Nonprofit Groups' Answer to High Manhattan Rents", 2198
"Nonprofit Groups Required to Join Social Security", 2281
"Nonprofit Groups Said to Face Big Cuts in U.S. Aid", 4369
"Nonprofit Groups Want Academe to Help Train Their Administrators", 2083
"Nonprofit Hospitals Join to Offer Insurance", 2372
"Nonprofit Loan Funds Diversify Lending to Nonprofits", **2273**
"Nonprofit Loan Funds Emerge with Cash for Crises", 3688
Nonprofit Management: A Report on Current Research and Areas for Development, **2768**
"Nonprofit Memberships of Corporate Board Influence Grants", 2801
The Nonprofit Organization: An Operating Manual, **2967**
Nonprofit Organization Governance: A Challenge in Turbulent Times, **2687**

The Nonprofit Organization Handbook, **2519**
Nonprofit Organization Handbook: A Guide to Fundraising, Grants, Lobbying, Membership Building, Publicity and Public Relations, 2602
Nonprofit Organizational Effectiveness Study, 2180
Nonprofit Organizations and Liability Insurance: Problems, Options and Prospects, **2076**
Nonprofit Organizations and Socioeconomic Development in Columbia, **2339**
Nonprofit Organizations As Opposition to Authoritarian Rule: The Case of Human Rights Organizations and Private Research Centers in Chile, **2117**
"Nonprofit Organizations, Business Ventures, and the IRS: Your Guide to the Unrelated Business Income Tax Law", **4139**
Nonprofit Organizations: Laws and Regulations Affecting Establishment and Operation, 4153
"Nonprofit Organizations: Management, Not Charity", 2636
Nonprofit Organizations: Why Do They Exist in Market Economies?, 2016
Nonprofit Piggy Goes to Market: How the Denver Children's Museum Earns $600,000 Annually, 3830
The Nonprofit Research Institute: Its Origins, Operations, Problems and Prospects, 2280
The Nonprofit Sector: A Research Handbook, **2297**
The Nonprofit Sector and the New Federal Budget, 4603
The Nonprofit Sector and the Rise of Third-Party Government: The Scope, Character, and Consequences of Government Support of Nonprofit Organizations, **4739**
"The Nonprofit Sector in the New York Area", **2274**
"Nonprofit Umbrella Group Offers New Services to Members", 2248
"Nonprofits and Free Speech: Where Are the Boundaries?", 4193
"Nonprofits and the Federal Budget: Deeper Cuts Ahead", 4740
"Nonprofits Find Going into Business Can Be Taxing Experience", 4249
Nonprofits' Handbook on Lobbying: The History and Impact of the New 1976 Lobbying Regulations of the Activities of Nonprofit Organizations, 4172
"Nonprofits in the Business of Business: A Cautionary Look at Raising Money through For-Profit Ventures", 2038
"Nonprofits, Meet the Computer, Computer, Meet the Nonprofits", 2681
"'Nonprofits' Need Surplus Too", 2973
"NOPEC Works to Conserve Energy Costs", 4920
North Carolina and South Carolina Foundation Directory, 718

The Not-for-Profit Organization Reporting Entity: An Exploratory Study of Current Practice, **2649**
Not-for-Profit Organizations and Community: A Review of the Sociological Literature, 2242
"Not Passing the Bucks: Study Finds Arts Are Relatively Unscathed by Funding Cuts", 3232
"Not Yet a Profession", **845**
Notes on the Literature of Charities, 4
Notes on the Policies and Practices of Foundations, 823
"Notes: The Philharmonic Reaches Out", 3569
Notre Dame Institute on Charitable Giving, Foundations, and Trusts, 360
"Now Foundations Are Broadening Their Social Aims", 1172
"Now That We're in an Age of Partnership, Let's Take a New Look at Those Five Phases of Grantsmanship", **1610**
"The 'Now' Value of Deferred Gifts", 3310
"Nuclear Anonymity", 1103
"Nuclear-War Studies Get $1.4 Million from Carnegie", 696
The Oberlaender Trust, 1931-1953, 825
Objectives of Financial Reporting by Nonbusiness Organizations, 2584
Observations in the Financial Conditions of Colleges and Universities, 4775
"Obtaining a Grant: A Collaborative Effort", **3705**
Obtaining Funds for Therapeutic Recreation and the Creative Art Therapies, 3933
"Obtaining Grants in the Electronic Age: The Impact of the Federal Program Information Act", 4642
"Obtaining Pledges through Electronic Funds Transfer", **3487**
"Obtaining Results for the Nonprofit Group", 2238
"Obtaining U.S. Financing to Support Foreign Charities", 1853
"Of $41.4-Billion Donated to Churches, Almost Half Goes to Charitable Work", **448**
"Of Lasting Duration", **793**
Of Men and Dreams, 446
"Of Partnerships, Profits and Philanthropy", **364**
Off Your Duffs and Up the Assets: Common Sense for Non-Profit Managers, **2465**
Oh No, Not Another Proposal!, 4049
"Okay, We Need One. Now What?", 2893
Oklahoma Foundations Directory, **1106**
Older Volunteers in Church and Community, 4551
"The Olympics Are Coming! The Olympics Are Coming!", 3245
Olympus on Main Street: A Process for Planning a Community Arts Facility, 2620
"On Being a Trustee", 2577

TITLE INDEX

"On Building a Foundation", **1135**
"On Complying with the 1987 Tax Act: Even the IRS Has As Many Questions As Answers", **4271**
"On Giving: To Whom and Why", 443
"On-Line Databanks Provide Valuable Information Link", 2458
"On-Line Database System Raises ALA's Fund Raising Capabilities", 3547
"On Nonprofits, Marketing, Competition and Sales", 1993
"On-Target Marketing Programs Key to Successful Arts Funding", 3772
"On Target: The Anatomy of an Effective Direct-Mail Appeal", **3695**
On Technical Assistance Programs. A Directory of Resources for New York City Nonprofit Organizations, 2821
"On Using Professional Fund-Raising Counsel", 2496
One Hundred and One Ways to Raise Resources, **3935**
One Man's Vision: The Story of the Joseph Rowntree Village Trust, 1933
"One More Try", 1286
"One Worthwhile Coffee Klatch", 4897
Only by Public Consent. American Corporations Search for Favorable Opinion, 1479
"Only Crazy People Write Fund-Raising Copy", 4064
"An Open and Shut Case", **211**
Open Studio Event: An Artist's Planning Guide, 3011
Open the Books. How to Research a Corporation, **1371**
Operating Effective Committees, 2812
Operating Principles of Larger Foundations, 2683
"Operation of a Business by Non-Profit, Tax Exempt Organizations", 2550
Opportunities for Women in Higher Education: Their Current Participation Prospects for the Future, and Recommendations for Action, 4799
Opportunities in Non-Profit Organizations, 1988
"Opportunity or Imposition?", 3331
Options for Institutions: Charitable Organizations, 2442
The Organization of American Culture, 1700-1900: Private Institutions, Elites, and the Origins of American Nationality, **1490**
Organizational Change: The Political Economy of the YMCA, **2417**
"Organizational Ethics, What Is It and What Does It Mean for Nonprofits?", 2250
"Organizational Momentum", 2759
"Organizational Tools for a Small Development Office", 3268
Organizations, Clubs, Action Groups: How to Start Them, How to Run Them, 2969
"Organizations That Make Loans to Nonprofits", 2279

Organized for Action: Commitment in Voluntary Associations, **4543**
Organizing for Local Fundraising: Self-Sufficiency for the 80s, 3470
Organizing for Neighborhood Development: A Handbook for Citizen Groups, 2047
Organizing the Library's Support: Donors, Volunteers, Friends, 3521
"Organizing Your Operation", 3797
Organizing Your Way to Dollars, 2665
Orientation Packet for the Newcomer to Philanthropy, 708
The Original Has This Signature, W.K. Kellogg, 389
Origins, Dimensions and Impact of America's Voluntary Spirit, 4561
Orpheus in the New World: The Symphony Orchestra As an American Cultural Institution, 2159
The Other America: Poverty in the United States, **4864**
"The Other Bottom Line: One Central Question Determines Whether a Project Is Right for Your Foundation: Does It Build Community?", 1137
Other Than Grants: A Sampling of Southern California's Corporate Gift Matching, Volunteer, and in-Kind Giving Programs, **1344**
Our Crowd: The Great Jewish Families of New York, 40
"Our Ladies of Charity", 3416
Our Organization, 2276
"Out of the Shadows", 974
Outcast London: A Study in the Relationship between Classes in Victorian Society, **4878**
Outline of Testimony of Malcolm L. Stein before the Subcommittee on Oversight, June 28, 1983, 98th Congress, 1st Session, 4409
The Outlook for Gifts to Colleges and Philanthropy, 327
"An Overall Look at Planned Giving", 3385
"Overcompensating", 2824
The Overseas List: Opportunities for Living and Working in Developing Countries, **1760**
Overview of Endowment Programs, **4699**
"Oxfam Leads the Way", 2278
"Packaged Goods Techniques Work in Fund Raising As Well", 3858
"The Pact Is Broken! Corporations Now Prefer Governmental Higher Ed", **1649**
Papers in Educational Fund Raising, 3214
Papers on Corporate Philanthropy, **1423**
"Parents Chip in to Keep School Programs Afloat", 3458
Parliamentary Law for Nonprofit Organizations, 4270
Participation, Associations, Development, and Change, **4554**
Partners, 3373
Partners: A Practical Guide to Corporate Support of the Arts, **1426**

Partners for the 80's: Business and Education, 1603
"Partners in Neighborhood Growth", 1664
Partners in Public Service: Government and the Nonprofit Sector in Rhode Island, 4634
"Partnership: Lincoln Center's Consolidated Corporate Fund Drive Provides Business Support for the Arts", 1441
"Partnerships: Corporate Nonprofit Teamwork", 1438
"Partnerships in Education: Executive Department/Agency Partnership Programs", 2282
"Partnerships with Industry and Government Propel an Engineering School toward Its Goal", 3095
"The Party Line Returns", 2190
"Passing the Torch: John Gardner Steps Down As Chairman of Independent Sector", 2148
"Patent Fight: Inventor's Battle for Cable Cements His Fame, Fortune", 4845
"The Path to Iona House", **2078**
Patman and Foundations: Review and Assessment, 540
Patman Report, 4383
Patrons Despite Themselves: Taxpayers and Arts Policy, 4832
Patterns for Lifelong Learning: A Report of Explorations Supported by the W.K. Kellogg Foundation, 4867
"Patterns of Benevolence: Associated Philanthropy in the Cities of New York, 1830-1860", 204
"Patterns of Benevolence: Charity and Morality in Rural and Urban New York, 1783-1830", 205
Patterns of Concentration in Large Foundations' Grants to U.S. Colleges and Universities, 3143
Patterns of Corporate Philanthropy, **1612**
Patterns of Foundation Giving in the Criminal Justice Field, 831
Patterns of Giving to Higher Education: An Analysis of Contributions and Their Relation to Tax Policy, 3552
Patterns of Giving to Higher Education. Part 2: Analysis of Voluntary Support of American Colleges and Universities, 1970-71, 3553
Patterns of Giving to Higher Education. Part 3: An Analysis of Voluntary Support of American Colleges and Universities, 1973-74, 3554
"Paul Mellon", 215
"Paying for Keeps", 4095
"Paying for the Arts", 249
"The Payoff in Nonprofits", 2217
Pensions for Professors, 4948
"People First: A Requirement for the Success of Any Planned Giving Program", 3931
People in Philanthropy: A Guide to Funding Connections, **212**

371

TITLE INDEX

People/Profits: The Ethics of Investment, 2837

"Percentage Fundraising: Is an Ethical Code Giving Way to Expediency?", **3707**

The Perfect Development Officer: From Harvard Business Review, 3708

The Perfect Development Officer: Skills and Characteristics for Success, 3709

"The Perfect Fit: When Albert Kunstadter Sold His Famous Corset and Brassiere Firm and Started a Foundation, He Couldn't Have Known What a Model It Would Become", **323**

"The Perfect Gift: Examples of Noncash Corporate Philanthropy", **1588**

"Perfecting Your 'Case' Statement", 3889

Performance and Reward in Nonprofit Organizations: Evaluation, Compensation, and Personnel Incentives, **2415**

"Performance-Based Certification: An Avenue for Professional Development and Recognition", 4509

Performance Evaluation: A Management Basic for Librarians, 2722

Performance Norms in Non-Market Organizations: An Exploratory Survey, 2098

The Performing Arts: Problems and Prospects, 2309

Performing Arts, the Economic Dilemma: A Study of Problems Common to Theater, Opera, Music, and Dance, **2012**

"The Perils and Promise of Life Insurance Policies", 3817

The Permanent Charitable Contributions Legislation, 4204

"Permissible Activities of 501(c)(3) Organizations during a Political Campaign", 4284

Personal and Organizational Renewal, 2120

Personal Deductions in the Federal Income Tax, 4215

"The Personal Experience of a Canvasser: Through Rain, Sleet and Snow", 3938

Personal Recollections of Andrew Carnegie, 315

"Personal Values: The Reason for Philanthropic Exchange", **61**

"Personality Type Theory Weds Programs, Motivation", **3683**

"Personalizing Fundraising Appeals", 3405

Personnel Matters in the Nonprofit Organization, **2446**

"Perspective on the Arts in GNP", 2286

Perspectives on Collaborative Funding: A Resource for Grantmakers, **3711**

Peter Cooper: Citizen of New York, 319

"A Phenomenal Phonathon", 3175

Philadelphia Gentlemen: The Making of a National Upper Class, **28**

Philanthropic Activity in the Greater Cleveland Area, 1979-1991, 1481

"Philanthropic Employment Growth from 1972 to 1982", 422

"Philanthropic Entrepreneurs", 1138

"A Philanthropic Foundation at Work: Gunnar Myrdal's *American Dilemma* and the Carnegie Corporation", **930**

Philanthropic Foundations, **541**

Philanthropic Foundations and Higher Education, 224

Philanthropic Foundations and Public Policy: The Political Role of Foundations, 627

"Philanthropic Foundations and the Development of the Social Sciences in the Early Twentieth Century: A Reply to Donald Fisher", **590**

Philanthropic Foundations in Latin America, 1957

Philanthropic Fund Raising As a Profession, 3131

Philanthropic Giving, **16**

The Philanthropic Impulse and the Democratization of Tradition in America, 268

"Philanthropic Index Projects Charitable Giving Will Double by 1990", 381

"Philanthropic Outlook Somber", 1696

Philanthropic Trusts in Australia, 1758

"Philanthropies Focus Concern on Arms Race", 1233

"Philanthropist Joan Pavlevsky's Heart Is in Giving and Research", 361

The Philanthropoids: Foundations and Society, **500**

"Philanthropy: A Much Underused Hospital Resource", 3913

Philanthropy and American Society: Selected Papers, **428**

Philanthropy and Cultural Imperialism: The Foundations at Home and Abroad, **552**

Philanthropy and Culture: The International Foundation Perspective, **1886**

"Philanthropy and Estate Planning", **4361**

Philanthropy and International Affairs: A Typology and Study of Grantmaking by San Francisco Bay Area Foundations, **66**

Philanthropy and Jim Crow in American Social Science, **445**

Philanthropy and Learning: With Other Papers, 273

Philanthropy and Marketing: New Strategies for Fund Raising, 3582

Philanthropy and Public Policy, **132**

Philanthropy and Public Schools: One Foundation's Evolving Perspective, 1003

Philanthropy and Social Progress: Seven Essays, 6

"Philanthropy and Social Science in the 1920s: Beardsley Ruml and the Laura Spelman Rockefeller Memorial, 1922-29", **591**

Philanthropy and the Business Corporation, **1470**

Philanthropy and the Civil Rights Movement, **170**

Philanthropy and the Environment: A Report on Nature and Extent of Philanthropic Activity in the Environmental Field, 511

Philanthropy and the Individual, **677**

Philanthropy and the Spirit of Voluntarism, 41

Philanthropy and the State, or Social Politics, 1833

Philanthropy and Voluntarism: An Annotated Bibliography, **294**

"Philanthropy As News: Let the Media Be the Judge", 452

"The Philanthropy Business", 3837

"Philanthropy Considered", 508

"Philanthropy Courses and Tax Incentive Backed by Fund-Raisers' Trust", 125

Philanthropy for the Future, 19

Philanthropy: Four Views, 371

"Philanthropy Goes to Congress", 1074

"Philanthropy 'Has to Be Talked about on Campus,' Foundation Head Says", 126

"Philanthropy: How Much Should Business Do?", 1473

Philanthropy in Action, **362**

Philanthropy in America, 246

Philanthropy in America: The Need for Action. Fiscal Issues 2, 73

Philanthropy in an Age of Transition: The Essays of Alan Pifer, **386**

Philanthropy in England, 1480-1660, **1868**

"Philanthropy in Germany", **1908**

Philanthropy in Japan, 1856

Philanthropy in Japan '83: Private Nonprofit Activities in Japan, **1960**

"Philanthropy in Support of Democracy and Its Institutions", 1117

Philanthropy in the History of American Higher Education, 436

Philanthropy in the 70's: An Anglo-American Discussion, 107

Philanthropy in the Seventies. The Tax Reform Act of 1969 As It Affects Foundations and Charitable Contributions, 4121

Philanthropy in the Shaping of American Higher Education, **114**

Philanthropy in the United States: History and Structure, **17,** 542

Philanthropy Is... , 344

"Philanthropy Is Both Giving and Receiving", 162

"The Philanthropy Marketplace", **2407**

"Philanthropy May Benefit Corporations", 1329

The Philanthropy of Organized Religion, **108**

"The Philanthropy of Organized Religion: What It Is, What It Does, and How It Relates to the Work Being Done by Private Foundations and Corporate Grantmakers", 398

"Philanthropy 1, 2, 3: The Past, Present, and Future of Philanthropy", **382**

Philanthropy: Private Means, Public Ends, **470**

"Philanthropy Provides Fiscal Edge, Leverage", 3914

TITLE INDEX

"Philanthropy: Shareholders and Capital Formation for Hospitals", 3105

Philanthropy Today: An Interim Report, 255

Philanthropy: Tradition and Change, 439

"Philanthropy under Attack, Foundation Head Charges", 4140

Philanthropy, Voluntary Action and the Public Good, 236

Philanthropy. Voluntary Action for the Public Good, **372**

Philanthropy's Role in Civilization: Its Contribution to Human Freedom, **328**

Philippine Directory of Foundations, 1877

A Philosophy for a Foundation, 766

"Phonathon Spurs Parents' Fund, Increasing Donors from 19 to 140", 3439

Pitfalls and Ideals in Communicating for Foundations, 975

The Pittsburgh Nonprofit Sector in a Time of Government Retrenchment, 4662

Pity the Poor Rich, 186

"The Place and Functions of Voluntary Associations", **4533**

The Place and Power of Non-Profit Boards of Directors, **2241**

"Placements and Salaries, 1982", 4894

"Placements and Salaries, 1986: An Upswing", **2213**

"The Plain Fact Is Our Colleges and Universities Are Facing What Might Easily Become a Crisis", 3722

Plain Talk about Grants. A Basic Handbook, **3313**

Planned Gift Fund Raising: A Programmed Instructional Text, 3723

"Planned Giving", 3022

"Planned Giving: A Look at the Eighties", 3163

"Planned Giving: A Training Aid to Help Volunteers Qualify Gift Leads", 3865

"Planned Giving: An Introduction", **3917**

"Planned Giving: How to Qualify Planned Gift Leads Promptly", 3866

The Planned Giving Idea Book, 3818

"Planned Giving in a One Person Shop", **3016**

"Planned Giving Instruments: The Great Circle Route", 3086

"Planned Giving: It's for Everyone", **3413**

"Planned Giving: Key to Prosperity, Professionalism", 3819

"A Planned Giving Program for the Small Development Office", 3637

"Planned Giving Success Starts with Your Board", **3017**

"Planned Giving: Untapped Sources", **3023**

"Planning a Funding Search: How to Identify a Foundation That Could Fund Your Project", 3308

Planning an Income-Generating Food Service Enterprise, 2220

"Planning and Marketing Development Programs in the Future", 3089

Planning and Setting Objectives, 2693

Planning, Conducting, and Evaluating Workshops: A Practitioner's Guide to Adult Education, 2544

Planning Consultant Roster, 2441

"Planning: Essential Ingredient of Time Management Formula", 2734

Planning for the Planned Gift, **3037**

"Planning Is Key to Public Relations Efforts in 1984", 2834

"Planning: The Key to Nonprofit Success", 2596

Playing Their Game Our Way. Using the Political Process to Meet Community Needs, 4329

Please Buy My Violets: Or How to Raise Money for Your Causes, 3947

"Plight of the EDP Manager", 1608

"Policies Clear Up Confusion for Board, Staff, Committees", 3727

Policies Underlying Corporate Giving, 1699

"A Policy for the Advancement of Science: The Rockefeller Foundation, 1924-29", **919**

Policy Grants Directory: A Directory Describing Governmental and Private Funding Sources for Policy Studies Research, 3652

"Political Advocacy Again: Revamping the Combined Federal Campaign", 3863

"'Political' Advocacy by Non-Profits", 4346

The Politics of Altruism: A Study of the Political Behaviour of Voluntary Development Agencies, 1878

The Politics of Human Services: Radical Alternatives to the Welfare State, 2405

"The Politics of Knowledge: The Carnegie Corporation and the Formulation of Public Policy", 931

"The Politics of Planned Giving: Alligators in the Swimming Pool", 3603

"Pooled Income Funds", 3100

"Pooling Lending Resources", **601**

Poor Devils, 730

Population Programmes and Projects. 2 Vols, 1971

Portrait of the Artist, 1987. Who Supports Him/Her?, 4609

"A Portrait of the Donor: For a Connoisseur, Living Well Can Also Be a Work of Art", 99

"Portrait of the Producer As Artist", **4847**

"Position-by-Position Salary Data. Part 3", 2383

Post-Mortem Use of Wealth, 400

"The Postal Rate Wars", 3734

Poverty and Dependency, 175

Poverty in America: The Impact of Changing Attitudes and Public Policies on the Poor. Proceedings of the Conference of the National Assembly and the National Conference on Social Welfare, 4929

Power: A Repossession Manual. Organizing Strategies for Citizens, 2346

Power in the States: The Changing Face of Politics across America, 4732

"The Power of Giving: What's What in Canada's World of Foundations", **1753**

The Power of "Perceptual Marketing": An Analysis of Sponsorships As Components of Marketing-Support and Corporate Relations Programs, **1673**

"The Power of Purpose", 2629

Praise the Lord for Tax Exemption, 4221

Pre-Conditions, Benefits and Costs of Privatized Public Services: Lessons from the Dutch Educational System, 1851

"Prediction for 1987: A Year of Intense Change", **3447**

"Predictions for 1988: The Worst Is Yet to Come!", **3448**

Predictions on the Effect of a Value-Added Tax on Charitable Contributions, 4090

A Preface to Grants Economics: The Economy of Love and Fear, **49**

"Premiums: An Innovative Way to Increased Gift Giving", 3579

"The Preoccupations of Boards", 2884

"Preparation of the Research-Grant Application: Opportunities and Pitfalls", 4015

"Preparing an Annual Report: Your Creative Calling Card", 2760

Preparing Instructional Objectives, 4039

Prescription for Change, 4821

Presence of the Past: A History of the Preservation Movement in the United States before Williamsburg, 4870

Presenting Performances: A Handbook for Sponsors, 2968

"Preservation and the Neighborhoods", 3738

"President Asks $125 Million for Arts in '84", 3127

"The President's Role in the Capital Campaign", 3622

Press Clippings, 109

Press Comment on Foundation Proposals in the Tax Reform Bill, 4158

Press Release Announcing Tentative Decisions to Date on Tax Reform Subjects As Announced by Chairman Wilbur D. Mills on May 27, 1969, 91st Congress, 1st Session, 4400

Prevalence of Nonprofit Organizations in the Broadcast Media, 2327

"Preventing the No. How to Spot, and Work with, a Donor's Mental Anchors", 3973

Prevention of Nuclear War: Funders' Guide to Non-Partisan Voter Education Activities, **2301**

"Preventive Measures", 2221

"A Primer on Mailing Lists", 3001

"Primer on Tried and True List Testing Techniques", 3269

"A Prince Whose Mission Is UNICEF", 169

"The Princess of Playboy", 498

"Principles and Practices Prescribed for Foundations", **1086**

"Principles of Public Giving", **1140**

The Principles of Relief, 130

373

TITLE INDEX

Priorities for Action, 4800
Priorities in Social Services: A Guide for Philanthropic Funding, 3675
"PRI's: An Anniversary", 759
"Private Aid Keeps UK OK Abroad", 1922
Private and Community Foundation Grants for Local Community Economic Development, **565**
The Private Charitable Foundation: Its Role in Federal Income Tax Planning, 846
Private Charitable Foundations, 1266, 1267
"Private Contributions to the Arts Increase", 3636
Private Education: Studies in Choice and Public Policy, **4895**
Private Financing in Public Parks: A Handbook, 2986
Private Foreign Aid: U.S. Philanthropy for Relief and Development, **1765**
The Private Foundation and the Tax Reform Act, 4290
"Private Foundation Information Returns, 1982", **1125**
"A Private Foundation Profile for 1983", **1126**
"The Private Foundation Question: Problems and Solutions for CBOS", 4096
"Private Foundations: A Tour through the Labyrinth Created by the '69 Act", 4181
"Private Foundations and Social Science Research", 1131
Private Foundations and the Problem of "Tipping": A Description of the Problem and Some Practical Suggestions for Use in Grantmaking, **4179**
Private Foundations and the Requirement to Exercise Expenditure Responsibility, 922
"Private Foundations and the Tax Reform Act", 4291
"Private Foundations and the Tax Reform Act of 1969", 4297
Private Foundations: Before and after the Tax Reform Act of 1969, 4327
"Private Foundations, Government, and Social Change: Home and Community-Based Care for the Elderly", **4829**
"Private Foundations in the Post-69 Era: Have Controls Spawned a Trend to Orthodoxy?", 4227
"Private Foundations Keep Secrecy Lid on Despite Law", 1148
Private Foundations. Supporting Health Manpower Education and Training: An Inventory, 1971, 1246
Private Foundations: The Payout Requirement..., 1107
"Private Funding and Public Libraries", 3092
Private Funding for Rural Programs: Foundations and Other Private Sector Resources, 1203
"Private Grantmaking in Japan", **1821**
"Private Groups Aid Budgets for Schools", 2110

"Private Help for Public Schools", 1182
"Private Higher Education Focus of New Corporate/Private Foundation Effort", 1644
Private Initiatives and the Cohesion of the Western Democracies: Directory of Organizations, 1841
Private Initiatives and the Cohesion of the Western Democracies: Findings, Conclusions, Recommendations, 1842
Private Initiatives and the Cohesion of the Western Democracies: Notes and Documentation, 1843
Private Keepers of the Public Interest, 1497
Private Money and Public Service: The Role of Foundations in American Society, **678**
"Private Philanthropy and Public Needs", 1277
Private Philanthropy and Public Welfare: The Joseph Rowntree Memorial Trust, 1954-1979, 1976
Private Philanthropy and the Making of Public Policy, 895
"Private Philanthropy in Support of Health Service Demonstrations and Research", 3216
Private Philanthropy: Vital and Innovative or Passive and Irrelevant?, 631
Private Power for the Public Good: A History of the Carnegie Foundation for the Advancement of Teaching, **932**
The Private Provision of Public Services: A Comparison of Sweden and Holland, 1852
"Private-Religious Collaboration: Asking the Right Questions Together", 4880
Private Resources and Public Needs: Los Angeles in the Twenty-First Century, **2345**
Private Responsibility for Public Management, 1591
Private Sector Giving, Greater Worcester Area: A Directory and Index, **1187**
Private Sector Giving Report: Greater Worcester Area, 1188
Private Sector, Public Control and the Independent University, 2125
Private Sectors in Higher Education, **2122**
Private Universities in the Seventies: The Financial Crisis, 1368
Private Versus Public Financing of Higher Education: U.S. Policy in Comparative Perspective, 4677
"Private Welfare in the Welfare State: Recent U.S. Patterns", **188**
"Private Welfare: Its Future in the Welfare State", **189**
"Proactive Prospecting", 3387
"The Problem of Being the Ford Foundation", 1088
"The Problem Proposal", **3741**
"The Problem That Knows No Boundaries", 1158
"The Problem That Won't Go Away", 4770

Problems of the Charitable Foundation. New York Institute on Federal Taxation Conference, 4261
"Problems with Matching-Grant Charity", 4313
Proceedings, 3660
Proceedings: A Symposium on Financing Higher Education, 3847
A Process for Development of Ideas, **4000**
"The Process of Developing Innovation and Leadership", 3875
"Procuring Incentives for Community Health Promotion Programs", **3263**
The Professional Altruist: The Emergence of Social Work As a Career, 1880-1930, **310**
Professional Forum Conference. Proceedings, **2664**
"The Professional Fund Raiser's Contract", 3414
Professionalism and Non-Profit Organizations, 2224
"Professionalizing Technical Assistance: The Nonprofit Management Association", 2842
The Professionals' Guide to Fund-Raising, Corporate Giving, and Philanthropy: People Give to People, **2981**
"Professors Can Land Corporate Sponsors for Research, If They Follow the Rules", 1620
"Profile of a Major Donor", **1534**, 3508, 3744
"Profile of a Major Donor. No. 2", 3509
"Profile of a Small Donor", 3510
A Profile of Corporate Contributions, **1677**
"Profiles: Blue Chip off the Old Block (Stewart Rawlings Mott)", 265
"Profiles in Philanthropy: Opportunities for Gifts", **4229**
Profiles of Effective Corporate Giving Programs, **1546**
Profiles of Financial Assistance Programs, **4759**
Profiles of Involvement. 3 Vols, 3440
"Profiles: Resources and Responsibilities", 266
"Profit-Making and Risk-Taking in the Nonprofit Sector", 2228
Profit Making by Non-Profits, **2135**
"Profit Making Subsidiaries, Are They for You?", **2429**
"Profit: Spur for Solving Social Ills", 1578
Profitable Careers in Nonprofit, **2219**
"Profits", 2338
Program Evaluation. A Conceptual Tool Kit for Human Service Delivery Managers, 2755
Program for Certification of Fund Raising Executives: Study Guide Outline, 3667
A Program for Renewed Partnership. The Report of the Sloan Commission on Government and Higher Education, 4957
A Program for Renewed Partnerships. The Report of the Sloan Commission on Government and Higher Education: An Overview, 4958

TITLE INDEX

Program Guidelines. Supplement, 4724
Program Information, 4716
Program on Non-Profit Organizations Working Papers Series: Index, #1-25, 2185
Program Plan, 2181
Program Planning and Proposal Writing, 4031
"Program Planning and Proposal Writing: Introductory Version", **4032**
Program-Related Investments, 760, 2096
Program Related Investments, 2302
Program-Related Investments: A Primer, **1080**
Progress and Problems in Medical and Dental Education: Federal Support Versus Federal Control, 4809
"A Progress Report on the Filer Commission", 1089
"Progress toward Change in Financial Reporting by Nonbusiness Organizations", **2865**
The Progressives and the Slums: Tenement House Reforms in New York City, 1890-1917, **311**
Project Bank Information Form, 4566
Project Excellence. Perceptions of Corporate Social Involvement: A Survey of 64 Cities, **1326**
Project Excellence. Supplement, 1351
"A Project to Assess the Effectiveness and Efficiency of Philanthropic Programs", 2393
"Projected 1985 Levels of Charitable Giving", 4292
Projections. Calendar Years 1985-1992: Number of Returns to Be Filed, 4461
Promoting Issues and Ideas, 2303
"A Proper Upbringing", 837
Prophet of Progress: Selections from the Speeches of Charles F. Kettering, 274
Proposal for a Study of the Role of Foundations in the Third Sector, 1175
Proposal Preparation, 4061
"Proposal Preparation in a Dry Season", 4043
The Proposal Writer's Swipe File, **4028**
"Proposalese Spoken Here: How to Survive in the Wonderful World of Grants", 4041
"Proposed Model Act: Brave New World for Nonprofits?", **2064**
"Proposed Tax Change Would Send High Tech Product Donations Soaring", **1646**
"Proposed Tax Changes Prompt Giving in 1985", 4094
Prospect Research: A How-to Guide, **3873**
Prospecting: Searching Out the Philanthropic Dollar, **3394**, 3517
"Prospects for Private Arts Support", 3400
"Protecting Personal Information: What Every Nonprofit Should Know", 2456
"Protecting Volunteers from Suit: A Look at State Legislation", **4553**
"Psst, Wanna Make a Donation?", 3002
"The Psychology of Money", 53

Public Accountability of Foundations and Charitable Trusts, 1218
The Public and Its Problems, **4824**
"Public and Private Philanthropy in the Eighties", 1979
Public and Private Sources of Funding for Sexual Assault Treatment Programs, 3657
Public College and University Development, **3986**
The Public Good: Philanthropy and Welfare in the Civil War Era, **59**
Public Information Handbook for Foundations, 1118
Public Information Reporting by Tax-Exempt Private Foundations Needs More Attention by IRS, 1090
Public Inspection of IRS Private Letter Rulings. Hearing before the Subcommittee on Administration of the Internal Revenue Code, 94th Congress, 4443
Public Interest Law in the Bay Area, 804
Public Law 91-172, 91st Congress, H.R. 13270, December 30, 1969: An Act to Reform the Income Tax Laws, 4384
"Public Libraries: Getting into the Philanthropic Thick of Things", 3890
"Public Library under Gregorian Celebrating a Good Year", 4790
Public Policy and Its Impact on Giving and Volunteering, 876
Public Policy and the Dead Hand: The Thomas Cooley Lectures, 4319
Public/Private Cooperation: Funding for Small and Emerging Arts Programs, 803
Public-Private Partnership in American Cities, 2115
Public-Private Partnership: New Opportunities for Meeting Social Needs, **1330**
"Public/Private Partnerships Bring a Building to Harlem", 3618
"Public-Private Partnerships: Helping to Achieve Common Goals", 3134
"Public/Private Partnerships: Useful But Sterile", 3473
Public Relief and Private Charity, 309
"Public Schools Emerge As Fund Raisers", **3751**
The Public Service Budget of Arts and Cultural Organizations: A Better Measure of Full Financial Need, 4610
"Public Speaking As a Fund Raising Tool", 3832
Public Statement on OMB Circular A-122, 4268
Public Support for the Performing Arts in Western Europe and the United States: History and Analysis, 1900
"The Public Thoughts of a Private Foundation Leader: A Conversation with Alvin Tarlov", **873**
A Public Trust, 4806
"Public TV's CIA Show", 797
Public vs. Private Arts Subsidies: Are They Equivalent?, 3699

Public Welfare Directory, **4764**
Publicity for Volunteers, 2476
Publicity Guidelines for Fundraisers, 2961
"Publisher Tries New Twist in Fund Raising", **3345**
Pulling Yourself Up by Your Bootstrap: The Evolution of Black Philanthropic Activity, 88
The Purposes and the Performances of Higher Education in the United States: Approaching the Year 2000, 4801
"The Push-Pull of Foundation Dollars", 672
"Putting the Fun in Fund-Raising", 3714
Putting the Fun in Fund Raising: 500 Ways to Raise Money for Charity, 3242
"Putting Your Campus Assets to Work Full Time", 4868
"Putting Your Case to the Family Foundation", 881
A Quantitative Profile of the Nonprofit Sector, 2318
"Quarantine and the Problem of AIDS", 4911
Queens Arts Manager's Survival Guide: A Directory of Services, Arts Resources, and Publicity Outlets, **2785**
"The Quest for Funds: Dialing for Data and Dollars", **2927**
Quest for Funds: Insider's Guide to Corporate and Foundation Funding, **3077**
"The Question of Revising the Tax Status of Foundations: Pro and Con", 4293
"The Questionable Testamentary Gift to Charity: A Suggested Approach to Judicial Decision", 3592
"Questioning the Conventional Wisdom", **3580**
"Questions and Answers Regarding the Impact of the U.S. Treasury's Tax Plan on Charitable Giving", 4205
"Questions Donors Ask and How They Can Be Answered by the Financial Statements of Not-for-Profit Organizations", 2720
"The Questions Nonprofits Ask", **1925**
A Quick Guide to Loans and Emergency Funds, 3754
The Quick Proposal Workbook, **4007**
Race and the Third World City, 1799
Racial Segregation: Two Policy Views, **4730**
"Raffle of a Co-Op Is Planned", 3952
"Raffles: A Chancy Thing for Homeowners", 3953
"Raise More Money, Easier with EFT", 3802
"Raising Funds for Women's Causes: The New Frontier", 3960
Raising Funds from America's 2,000,000 Overlooked Corporations, 1634
Raising Funds with Souvenir Journals, 3757
Raising Money for the Arts. Conference Report, 2996
"Raising Money from Churches", 3201
"Raising Money from Members: Who Needs What You Do?", 3286

375

TITLE INDEX

Raising Money through an Institutionally Related Foundation, **3766**
The Raising of Money: Thirty-Five Essentials Every Trustee Should Know, **3583**
Random Reminiscences of Men and Events, 408
The Rape of the Taxpayer, 1683
"Rapidly Growing Women's Funds", 3760
Rating America's Corporate Conscience: A Provocative Guide to the Companies behind the Products You Buy Every Day, **1573**
Rating Board Performance, 2876
"Rating Gift Capacity through Screening Sessions", 3600
Ratio Analysis in Libraries, 2828
Ratio Analysis in Voluntary Health and Welfare Organizations, 2829
The Rationale for Exempting Nonprofit Organizations from Corporate Income Taxation, 4174
Rationalizing Non-Profit Corporation Law, 4175
Raymond Blaine Fosdick, 199
"Reach Out and Touch Someone", 3650
"The Readiest Reference: When It Comes to Providing the Facts about Foundations, No One Can Match the Foundation Center", 3970
"Reagan Administration Does It Again", 3071
The Reagan Economic Program: A Working Paper for Grantmakers, 4683
The Reagan Experiment: An Examination of Economic and Social Policies under the Reagan Administration, 4731
"Reagan Hatches Plan to Gag Nonprofit Groups", 4295
"Reagan Restricts Lobbying by Charities with Federal Grants", 4296
"Reagan's Second Thoughts on Corporate Giving", 1613
"Real Estate Essentials for Nonprofits", **2128**
"Reassessing the Earthquake", 4067
Rebuilding America: A Blueprint for the New Economy, **4771**
"The Rebuttable Presumption Is a Key Issue: The Munson Case Attracts Friends of the Court", 3763
"Recent Challenges to Nonprofits: Some Questions", **2063**
Recent Trends in Higher Education in the United States: With Special Reference to Financial Support for Private Colleges and Universities, 3009
Recommendation to Foundations Regarding Technical Assistance, 2915
Recommendations for Improving Trustee Selection in Private Colleges and Universities, 2420
Recommended Principles and Practices for Effective Grantmaking, 662
"Record Keeping for Fundraisers: How to Get Lost in the Shuffle", 3511

"Record-Keeping for Membership Campaigns", 2654
"Record Keeping Is Important", 2623
Recruiting, Encouraging and Evaluating the Chief Staff Officer, 2813
"Redefinition of Nonprofit Accounting", **2340**
Redistribution through the Financial System: The Grants Economics of Money and Credit, 50
Reference Book: Corporation Aid to American Higher Education, 1413
Reference Book of Corporate Managements, 1437
"Reference Guide 1989: Tax and Reporting Compliance for Nonprofit Organizations", **4216**
"Refine Your Approach to Fundraising", **2643**
The Reform of Secondary Education, 4914
Reform on Campus, Changing Students, Changing Academic Programs, 4802
Reforming Nonprofit Corporation Law, 4176
"Region Foundation Councils Still Growing, Learning", 1119
The Regional Arts Organization Movement, 2004
Regional Associations of Grantmakers: Program Primer, 663
"Regional Film Grants", 3765
"Regulating Religion", 4298
"Regulating the Political Activity of Foundations", 4299
Regulating the Poor: The Functions of Public Welfare, **4926**
Regulation of Charitable Trusts and Solicitations: Summary of the Special Meeting of the Subcommittee on Charitable Trusts and Solicitations, 4254
Rehabilitating Older and Historic Buildings: Law, Taxation, Strategies, **4883**
Rehabilitating Older and Historic Buildings. Supplement, **4884**
"The Relationship between Marketing and Development", 3364
Religion and Philanthropy, 237
Religion and Philanthropy Project: Progress Report, May 15, 1987, 238
"Religion Gives As Well As It Gets", **4888**
Religious and Ethical Issues on Tax Policy, 4281
"Religious Congregations As Social Service Agencies: How Extensive Are They?", 4945
"Religious Groups Lead in Philanthropy", **399**
Religious Philanthropy in New England: A Sourcebook, **3097**
"Religious Philanthropy's Distinctive Mission", **495**
"The Reluctant Fund-Raisers: Getting Physicians into the Act", **3088**
The Reluctant Patron: The United States Government and the Arts, 1943-1965, 4673

"A Remarkable Rally", 3870
Remarks, 4250
Remarks of David E. Rogers, M.D., President, the Robert Wood Johnson Foundation before the Subcommittee on Oversight, June 28, 1983, 98th Congress, 1st Session, 4410
The Remembered Gate. Origins of American Feminism: The Woman and the City, 1800-1860, **4488**
Renewing: The Leader's Creative Task, **2610**
"Rents Bedevil Arts Groups: Compromise Gained with City Eases Plight", 2335
Report, **4700**
Report and Recommendations Concerning Federal and Tax Rules Governing Private Foundations, 98th Congress, 1st Session, September 28, 1983, 4411
Report and Recommendations to the Commission on Private Philanthropy and Public Needs on Private Philanthropic Foundations, 110
"Report by Philanthropic Group Proposes Ways to Spur Giving", 1170
Report from His Majesty's Commissioners for Inquiry Into the Administration and Practical Operation of the Poor Laws, 1929
"Report from the People", 976
Report of Corporate Non-Cash Contributions, 1722
Report of New York City Task Force on the Exemption of Non-Profit Organizations from Real Property Tax, 4260
Report of Special Committee to Study the Laws of This State (Rhode Island) with Respect to and Governing Charitable-Trusts, 4130
Report of the Charity Commissioners for England and Wales, 1930
Report of the Committee on the Foundation Field, 802
Report of the Committee on the Law and Practice Relating to Charitable Trusts. (Nathan Report), 1931
Report of the Committee on Ways and Means, U.S. House of Representatives on H.R. 4170, Title III, 98th Congress, 1st Session, 4412
"Report of the Marshalling Human Resources Committee", 4567
The Report of the New Jersey Committee for the Humanities, 1980-1983, 4717
Report of the President, 1844
Report of the Princeton Conference on the History of Philanthropy in the United States, 427
Report of the Study of the Ford Foundation on Policy and Program, 761
Report on Activities, 1977-78, 1397
"A Report on American Philanthropy", 4285
"Report on Company Contributions", 1729
Report on Corporate Giving, 1339
"Report on Nonprofit Accounting", 2628

376

TITLE INDEX

Report to the Commission on Private Philanthropy and Public Needs, 2421
Report to the President, 4733
Reporting Characteristics. Forms 990 and 990-PF: Returns of Organizations and Private Foundations Exempt from Income Tax for 1973, 1248
Reporting of Service Efforts and Accomplishments, 2480
"Repositioning a Non-Profit Requires Prospect Strategy", 3176
"Repositioning Development in a Corporate Reorganization", 3417
Representing Artists, Collectors, and Dealers, 2838
"Research about Development: Reasons for It, Obstacles to It", 3704
Research and Development and Its Impact on the Economy, 4915
Research and Project Funding for the Uninitiated, **4040**
Research Centers Directory. 2 Vols, **2094**
Research for Action: A Guidebook to Public Records Investigation for Community Activists, 2940
Research in Progress, 1985-1986. A National Compilation of Research Projects on Philanthropy, Voluntary Action, and Non-Profit Activity, **2182**
Research in the Humanistic and Social Sciences, 4921
Research in Undergraduate Institutions, 4708
Research Institutions in Japan, 1857
"Research Is the Bane of My Existence", 3512
"Research on the Impact on Charitable Giving of the U.S. Treasury's November 1984 Tax Reform Proposal", 4300
Research Opportunities for Minority Scientists and Engineers, 4709
Research Opportunities for Women, 4710
Research Papers. 5 Vols, 632
Research Universities and the National Interest. A Report from Fifteen University Presidents, 4839
Researching Foundations: A to $, **4051**
Resource Directory, **2074**
The Resource Directory for Funding and Managing Nonprofit Organizations, 2647
Resource Guide for Rural Development: Handbook for Accessing Government and Private Funding Sources, 3678
"Resource Raising Calls for New Fund Raising Mind-Set", 1630
Resource Raising: The Role of Non-Cash Assistance in Corporate Philanthropy, **1631, 1632**
Resources for Adult Learning Services, 4725
Responding to Community Needs: The Missions and Programs of Chicago Nonprofit Organizations, **2141**
"Responsibility for Social Change", 1313
Responsible Choices in Taxation, 1659
Responsiveness of the U.S. Foundations to Hispanic Needs and Concerns, 937

Restatement of the Law of Trusts As Adopted and Promulgated by the American Law Institute, 4075
"A Restless Philanthropist", 115
"Restoring the Faith", **891**
"The Results Are Coming in", 2322
"Resurrecting Denver's Lost Neighborhood", **4892**
"Rethinking Development: Women As Catalysts for Change", 4972
Return of Organizations Exempt from Income Tax, 4462
"Return of the Givers: Happy Surprise for Colleges", 3774
Returns for Private Foundations Exempt from Income Tax, 1973, 4463
"Revenue Enhancement Part of Wider Look at Fund Raising", 3415
"Reversing the Old Order", **3073**
Review and Evaluation of Maurice Falk Medical Fund, 1209
Review of Approaches to Productivity, Performance, and Organizational Effectiveness in the Public Sector: Applicability to Non-Profit Organizations, 2032
A Review of Federal Programs Supporting the Arts in Education, 4638
Review of Federal Programs to Alleviate Rural Deprivation, 4623
A Review of Projects in the Arts, 4639
A Review of the Literature on Non-Profit Organizations in Nursing Home Care for the Elderly, 2009
"The Review Process: From the Viewpoint of the Unsuccessful Grant Applicant", 4022
Revised Model Nonprofit Corporation Act. Exposure Draft, **4072**
Revised Model Nonprofit Corporation Act: Official Text with Official Comments and Statutory Cross-References, **4074**
Revised OMB Proposal to Amend Circular A-122 Treatment of Lobbying Expenditures, 4117
"Rewarding Innovation: The Beginnings of a Foundation's Awards Program", **1270**
The Rich: A Study of the Species, 121
The Rich: Are They Different?, 280
The Rich Get Richer and the Poor Write Proposals, **4044**
"The Rich List of 1845", 402
Riches, Class, and Power before the Civil War, **376**
Rights and Remedies under Federal Grants, 4619
The Rise of the Arts on the American Campus, 4906
"A Rising Tide? International Grants Appear to Be Growing Steadily", 1822
Risk Management Guide for Nonprofits, **2673**
"Risk-Taking Grantmakers Make Commendable Efforts", 1120

The Road Map to Success: A Unique Development Guide for Small Arts Groups, 2508
The Robber Barons: The Great American Capitalists, 1861-1901, 262
"Robert Wood Johnson Identifies Emerging Health Issues", 1128
Robin Hood Was Right: A Guide to Giving Your Money for Social Change, 1254
The Rockefeller Billions: The Story of the World's Most Stupendous Fortune, 2
"The Rockefeller Foundation and the Development of Scientific Medicine in Great Britain", **1795**
The Rockefeller Inheritance, 345
Rockefeller Medicine Men: Medicine and Capitalism in America, **587**
Rockefeller Power: America's Chosen Family, 290
The Rockefeller Syndrome, 313
The Rockefellers: An American Dynasty, **101**
"Rockefeller's Magnificent Amateur: Peter Goldmark Mastered Budgets and Bridges on the Job. Now He's Going to Run the Rockefeller Foundation", **1162**
"Rockefellers Restyle Fund for the 1980's", 1234
"The Role of Business in Community Service", 1721
The Role of Business in Society, 1432
"The Role of Foundations in the Future Financing of Higher Education", 1071
The Role of Foundations Today and the Effect of the Tax Reform Act of 1969 upon Foundations. Testimony Presented October 1-2, 1973, 93rd Congress, 1st Session, 4451
The Role of Non-Profit Enterprise, **2155**
The Role of Non-Profit Organizations in Foreign Aid: A Literature Survey, 1825
"The Role of Philanthropic Foundations in the Reproduction and Production of Hegemony: Rockefeller Foundation and the Social Sciences", **748**
The Role of Philanthropy in International Cooperation, **1858**
The Role of Politicians in Public Charities, 794
The Role of Private Foundations in Our Society in the 1970's, 1068
Role of Private Foundations in Public Broadcasting. Hearings before the Subcommittee on Foundations, 93rd Congress, 2nd Session, 4452
Role of Private Foundations in Today's Society and a Review of the Impact of the Tax Reform Act of 1969. Hearings, 4444
The Role of Privatization in Florida's Growth, **2055**
The Role of the Board and Board Members, **2814**
"The Role of the Charitable Foundation in a Changing Society", **1920**
The Role of the Foundation in American Life, 1145

377

TITLE INDEX

"The Role of the Volunteer", 4591
"The Role of Viewpoint Neutrality in Nonpublic Fora Access Restrictions: Cornelius v. NAACP Legal Defense and Educational Fund", 3476
The Role of Voluntary Agencies in International Assistance, 1972
"The Role of Volunteers in Canadian Society", 1782
The Roles and Relationships of the Chief Volunteer and Chief Staff Officers, Board, and Staff: Who Does What?, **2815**
"A Roof and a Future", **2349**
The Rotch Travelling Scholarship, 1142
"Round Two: Waldemar Nielsen and the Large Foundations", 1213
Royal Dunfermline. A Historical Guide to the City and Its Antiquities: With an Account of the Carnegie Benefactions, 1928
"The Rules and Reasons for Creating Private Foundations", **864**
Rural Development and Higher Education: The Linking of Community and Method, 4885
Rural Development Programs: A Citizen's Action Guide, 3118
Rural Resources Guide: A Directory of Public and Private Assistance for Small Communities, **3922**
Russell Sage Foundation, 1907-1946, 813
The Russell Sage Foundation: Social Research and Social Action in America, 1907-1947. Guide to the Microfiche Collection, **968**
Russell Sage: The Money King, 430
"Rx for Getting a Grant", **3630**
Saatiohakemisto (Finnish foundations), 1794
"Salaries of the Top Officials at the Largest Foundations", 1294
The Salary and Benefits Survey of National Voluntary Human Service Organizations, 1981, 2324
Salary Survey Report, 1982, 2137
"Salary Wars", **2021**
"Salary Wars Boost Pay across Nonprofit Sector", **2022**
Samuel Fels of Philadelphia, 379
San Diego County Foundation Directory, **1151**
The San Francisco Bay Area Nonprofit Sector in a Time of Government Retrenchment, 4664
"Saving the Postal Subsidy", 2307
"Saving the Schools: How Business Can Help", **1619**
Scarcity and Community: A Resource Allocation Theory of Community and Mass Society Organizations, 2243
Scene of Change: A Lifetime in American Science, 494
Scenes from the Life of Benjamin Franklin, 225
Scholarly Communication: The Report of the National Enquiry, 4773
"Scholars Debate Need to Aid Arts", 2130

Scholars, Dollars, and Public Policy: New Frontiers in Corporate Giving, 1559
"School Advertises for New Trustees", 2883
The School-Based Adolescent Health Care Program, 4876
"School Initiative", 3805
"Schooled in Cooperation", **1562**
Schools in Transition: The Practitioner As Change Agent, **4975**
"Schools Using Tax Bill to Prod Donors to Give", 4233
"Science and Engineering Academies Get Two Large Gifts for California Center", 697
Science in the Federal Government: A History of Policies and Activities to 1940, 4637
Science: The Endless Frontier, 4616
Scientific Research Expenditures by the Larger Private Foundations, 543
"Scientist Donates $40-Million to U. of Illinois for Research on Intelligence", 147
"Screen Your Prospects for Major Giving", **3018**
Screening Requests for Corporate Contributions, **1540**
"Scripting for Successful Telemarketing Campaigns", 3605
The Search for an American Law of Charity, **518**
"The Search for New Tax Revenues", 4315
The Search for Order, 1877-1920, **504**
"A Search for Scandal Boomerangs in House Foundation Hearings", 4316
Search for Security: A Guide to Grantmaking in International Security and the Prevention of Nuclear War, **434**
Search for Security: A Study of Philanthropy in International Security and the Prevention of Nuclear War, 435
The Search for the Public Interest, 714
"Searching for Excellence", **1197**
"Seasonality Study Category: Fund Raising", 3811
The Second American Revolution: Some Personal Observations, 2308
"Second Thoughts on the Felstein Findings", 4305
"Secondary Market Research: A First Step in the Process", **3369**
Secretary of State of Maryland v. Joseph H. Munson Co., Inc., 3455
"Secrets of Computer-Based Direct Mail Fund Raising", 3851
Secrets of Foundation Fund Raising, 3891
"Secrets of Success in Special Events", **3189**
"Secrets to a Successful Major Gift Program", **3238**
"Secrets to a Successful Special Event", **3531**
Sectarian Welfare Federation among Protestants, 451

Securing Your Organization's Future: A Complete Guide to Fundraising Strategies, **3812**
Seed Money: The Guggenheim Story, 302
"Seed Planting, Community Foundation Style", **1208**
Seeds of Southern Change: The Life of Will Alexander, 140
Seedtime of Reform: American Social Service and Social Action, 1918-1933, **92**
Seeking Foundation Funds: A Brief Guide for Nonprofit Groups in Indiana, 3194
Seeking the Competitive Dollar: College Management in the Seventies, 3549
Selected Bibliographies, 664
Selected Bibliography on Grantsmanship, 3561, 3562
A Selected Chronology of the Ford Foundation, 762
Selected Press Coverage: Philanthropy, 1166
"Selecting a Computer System for Fund Raising", 3764
"Selecting a Special Event", **3575**
"Selecting the Right Management Training Program", **2719**
Selective Giving: An Account of the Ittleson Family Foundation, 880
"Selective Selectivity", 2599
Self Help: Earned Income Opportunities for Cultural Organizations, 2330
The Self-Made Man in America: The Myth of Rags to Riches, 519
Semillas de Prosperidad or How to Cultivate Resources from the Private Sector, 3360
"The Serious Problem of State and Local Barriers to Fund Raising: Are We Creating Walled States?", **3814**
"Service Companies Posting Record Profits May Give More", **1670**
"Service Corporations: The Profit Side of Nonprofits", 2019
Service for Givers: The Story of the National Information Bureau, Inc, 2257
"Service Unlimited", 753
Services for Sexually Active, Pregnant and Parenting Adolescents in New York City: Planning for the Future, 2033
"Serving Better by Cooperating More", 734
Serving Community Needs: The Nonprofit Sector in an Era of Governmental Retrenchment, 4763
"Serving God and Mammon: Financing Alternatives for Nonprofit Cultural Enterprises", 2218
"Serving People Needs", **3208**
"Serving 'the Least of These'", **4879**
"Setting Priorities for the 1980's", 562
"Setting Up a Canvass", 3126
"Seven Hundred Forty-Three Acres Given by Rockefellers for a State Park", 150
The Seven Laws of Money, 3717
"The Seven Sins of Direct Mail Fund Raising", 3721
Seven Ways to Contact Corporate Funding Executives, 1650
Shaping the Future, 4559

TITLE INDEX

The Share of the Top Wealth Holders in National Wealth, 1922-1956, 292
"Shifting Contributions from Corporation to Shareholder", **2040**
Short-Staffed! The Personnel Crisis in New York City's Voluntary Human Service Agencies, **2667**
"Should Business Give Money to Charity?", 1547
"Should Business Tackle Society's Problems", 1495
"Should For-Profit Go Non-Profit?", 2359
"Should I Buy a Personal Computer?", 2962
"Should Not-for-Profits Go into Business?", 2336
Should You Incorporate?, 2069
"Should You Leave All to the Children?", **278**
"Should Your Foundation (or Nonprofit) Go Hi-Tech?", 3409
"Show Prospective Donors the Way and They Can Provide the Will for Deferred Gifts and Bequests", 3190
"Shubert Foundation in Routine State Review", 1177
Significance of Employment and Earnings in the Philanthropic Sector, 1972-1982, 2319
Significant Private Foundations and the Need for Public Selection of Their Trustees, 952
"Simple Financial Ratios Can Show You Not Only How Your Organization Is Doing: But Also Where You're Heading", 2817
"Situation Analysis for Nonprofit Marketing Planning", **2672**
"Six Heresies and a New Reality", 2211
"Six Questions to Ask before Becoming a Trustee", **2600**
"The Six R's of Fund Raising: The Toil of Getting Grants", 3564
"Six Trends Shaping Philanthropy's Future", 896
"Sixteen Questions Every Nonprofit Director Should Ask", 2869
The Sixth Commandment, 1152
"Sixty-Six Nonprofit Groups Assail Lobbying Curbs", 4322
Skibo, 489
"Skill in Communication: A Vital Element in Effective Management", **2423**
"Skills Called for in Managing Prospect Research", 3384
The Slippery Slope, and Other Papers on Social Subjects, 25
"Small Can Be Beautiful: Tips on How to Win Grants from Regional, Community and Family Foundations", 3929
Small Change from Big Bucks: A Report and Recommendations on Bay Area Foundations and Social Change, **526**
The Small College Advancement Program: Managing for Results, 2964
"Small Companies: Patterns and Attitudes of Charitable Giving", **1947**
"Small Foundation Tactic: Pooling for Grassroots Causes", 1253
"Small Wonders: Personifying the Playboy Philosophy", 985
So Now You're a Fund Raiser, 3668
"So Why Not Start a Foundation?", 754
"So You Want to Get a Grant: Some Advice from the Experts", 3025
"So You Want to Run a Foundation?", 966
"So, You Want Your Board to Raise Money", **2655**, 2656
Social Aspects of Marketing, 2955
"Social Change in a 'Conservative' Setting", 4765
Social Diagnosis, **404**
The Social Institutions of Lancashire: A Study of the Changing Patterns of Aspirations in Lancashire, 1480-1660, 1869
Social Investing through Program-Related Investments: A Report to the Ford Foundation, **2112**
Social Organization of an Urban Grants Economy: A Study of Business Philanthropy and Nonprofit Organizations, **1472**
Social Planning and Human Service Delivery in the Voluntary Sector, **4590**
Social Report of the Life and Health Insurance Business, 1362
Social Report of the Life and Health Insurance Business, 1981, 1363
Social Report of the Life and Health Insurance Business, 1986, **1353**
The Social Responsibilities of Business: Company and Community, 1900-1960, **1494**
Social Responsibility and the Business Predicament, 1579
"Social Science Research: Shifting Infatuation with a Critical Resource", 4937
Social Strategy and Corporate Structure, 1358
The Social Thought of Jane Addams, **293**
"Social Welfare Agencies Survive Cuts in U.S. Aid", 3903
"Socialist Sweden Tries to Reinvent Philanthropy", 1793
Socially Responsible Investment, **2952**
Society's Stake in the Communications Future: What Can Grant-Makers Do?, 1241
"Soft Sheen Goes to the Top of Black Hair-Care Industry", 1483
"A Software Primer: What the Chief Development Officer Needs to Know", 3713
Sold Out: A Publicity and Marketing Guide, 2733
The Solicitation and Collection of Funds for Charitable Purposes: Article 7-A of the Executive Law, 2342
"Solicitation by Telephone: A Constitutional Perspective", 3103
"Soliciting Mega Gifts from the Wealthy", 3840
"Soliciting Patients: The Best New Source of Prospects", 3332
"Solicitor's Guide: Prepared for the Volunteer Fund Raiser", 3841
"Solving the Funding Puzzle", 3249
"Some ABC's of Indirect Cost for the Uninitiated: Philosophies and Development of University Indirect Cost", 2900
"Some Advice for Corporate Givers", 1724
Some American Pioneers in Social Welfare: Select Documents with Editorial Notes, **1**
Some Aspects of Educational Fund Raising, 3574
Some Aspects of Philanthropy in the United States, Scope and Trends, 483
"Some Athletes Build on Solid Foundations", **3827**
"Some Considerations on Funding Policy Research", 4946
"Some Limitations of Standard Setting", **2360**
"Some Thoughts on Voluntarism in the 80's", 4598
Something Ventured, Something Gained: A Business Development Guide for Non-Profit Organizations, 2702
The Source: A Directory of Cincinnati Foundations, **1190**
Source Book Profiles, **773**
Sourcebook of Aid for the Mentally and Physically Handicapped, **3689**
Sources of Funds to Colleges and Universities: A Technical Report, 3696
Sources of State Information on Corporations, 1726
"South African Giving Gets a Voice", 1953
South Carolina Foundation Directory, **1279**
The South Dakota Grant Directory, **1191**
Spacesearch: A Guide to Cultural Facilities in New York City, 2536
Speakers in the Humanities: A Free Resource, 4722
Speaking Out: Reflections on Thirty Years of Foundation Work, **1078**
Spearheads for Reform: The Social Settlements and the Progressive Movement, 1890-1914, **119**
"Special Conference Report: Independent Sector Explores Giving Trends and Structures", 3849
"Special Events Face New Challenge in 1987", **3820**
Special Events: Planning for Success, **3376**
Special Events Survival Kit, 3167
Special Report, 395
A Special Report Summarizing Self-Study Methods for the Philanthropic Programs of Twelve Corporations, 1601
Special Treatment of Churches under the Internal Revenue Code, 4212
"Spelling for Dollars: An Educational Way to Raise Funds for School Programs", 3927

TITLE INDEX

"Spinning the Web of Partnership: Binding Public and Private Sectors", 3753
The Spirit of Chinese Philanthropy, 1970
"The Spirit of Corporate Giving", 1566
"Splitting the Profits of a Business: Nonprofit Joint Venture", 2352
Sponsored Research of the Carnegie Commission on Higher Education, 4803
Sponsored Research Policy of Colleges and Universities, 2997
"Sponsoring PBS: Selling an Image, Tastefully", 1679
Spread the Word! A Publicity Handbook for Rhode Island Nonprofit Agencies, 2191
Stability and Change in Economic Hardship: Chicago, 1983-1985, **2065**
"Staff and Volunteer Motivation: Helping People Overcome Discouragement", 2682
Staff Directory: State Chambers of Commerce and Associations of Commerce and Industry, **1710**
Staff Reference Manual, 2506, 2507
Staffing American Colleges and Universities, 4940
Stalking the Large Green Grant, 4713
Standard and Poor's Register of Corporations, Directors and Executives, **1680**
Standard and Poor's Register of Corporations, Directors and Executives. Cumulative October Supplement, 1681
"A Standard for Citizenship", **4513**
Standards for Charitable Solicitations, 2067
Standards in Philanthropy, 2254
Standards of Accounting and Financial Reporting for Voluntary Health and Welfare Organizations, **2789**
"Stanford and Industry Forge New Research Link", 1654
"Stars Strew Megabucks", **890**
"Start Your Own Medical Foundation", 1179
The Starter Kit: A Resource Program for New Community Cultural Organizations, 2537
Starting a Foundation, 531
Starting a Local Conservation and Passive Solar Retrofit Program: An Energy Planning Sourcebook, 4780
Starting and Running a Nonprofit Organization, **2662**
"Starved Cities Hunger for Corporate Aid", 1496
The State and the Voluntary Sector: A Report of New York State Project 2000, **2077**
State Arts Agencies in Transition: Purpose, Program, and Personnel, 4607
The State Arts Council Movement, 2005
"State Campaigns Open Up to Broader Range of Charities", 3853
"State Eyes Fund Drive for Cancer", 447
"State Government and Community Partnerships", 3243

"State-Imposed Fund Raising Limitations Struck Down by Supreme Court", 3854
"State Income Tax Reform and Charitable Giving: The Case of Wisconsin", 4312
"State Laws Regulating Charitable Solicitations (As of December 1, 1986)", **4070**
"State Laws Regulating Charitable Solicitations: As of December 31, 1987", **4330**
"The State of Fundraising in 1985", 3855
"The State of the Arts", 2080
The State of the Arts and Corporate Support, 1355
"The State Solution", 815
Statement by Congressman Mickey Leland, Hearings of the Subcommittee on Oversight, June 28, 1983, 98th Congress, 1st Session, 4413
A Statement from the Field Foundation, 744
Statement of Financial Accounting Concepts. No. 2: Qualitative Characteristics of Accounting Information, 2585
Statement of Financial Accounting Concepts. No. 3: Elements of Financial Statements of Business Enterprises, 2586
Statement of Financial Accounting Concepts. No. 4: Objectives of Financial Reporting by Nonbusiness Organizations, 2587
Statement of Johnny C. Finch, Associate Director, U.S. General Accounting Office before the Subcommittee on Oversight, June 28, 1983, 98th Congress, 1st Session, 4414
Statement of Joseph J. DioGuirdi, C.P.A., Tax Partner Arthur Andersen and Co. before the Subcommittee on Oversight, Committee on Ways and Means. Hearings, June 28, 1983, 98th Congress, 1st Session, 4415
Statement of Millie Torres before the Subcommittee on Oversight, June 15, 1983, 98th Congress, 1st Session, 4416
Statement of Peter G. Peterson, Chairman, Commission on Foundations and Private Philanthropy before the Senate Finance Committee, 1073
Statement of Position (on) Accounting Principles and Reporting Practices for Certain Nonprofit Organizations: A Proposed Recommendation to the Financial Accounting Standards Board, 2440
Statement of the Honorable James P. Shannon before the Subcommittee on Oversight, June 28, 1983, 98th Congress, 1st Session, 4417
Statistical Analysis of the Operations and Activities of Private Foundations, 1250
Statistical Handbook on Aging Americans, **4947**
Statistics of Higher Education: Faculty, Students and Degrees, 1951-52, 4778

Statistics of Higher Education: Receipts, Expenditures, and Property, 1951-52, 4779
Statistics of Income: Exempt Organization Studies, **4464**
Statistics of Income: Private Foundations, 1974-1978, 1249
Status of Community Foundations in 1984, **1156**
The Status of Philanthropy in Latin America and the Caribbean, **1781**
Steering Nonprofits, 2740
"Steering through Hard Times", **1740**
Step by Step. Management of the Volunteer Program in Agencies, 2732
Stephen Girard: Founder, 213
Steps and Strategies of Good Grantsmanship, 3477
"Stewardship: A Future Direction for Catholic Fund Raising?", **3883**
Stewardship and Philanthropy: The Unique Ministry of the Endowed Parish, **283**
"Stewardship/Fund Raising Topic in Christian Conference", 3868
Stiftung und Unternehmen im Spannungs-Verhaltnis (The relationship of the foundation and business), 1982
Stiftungen im Gesellschaftlichen Prozess (Foundations in the social process), 1937
Stiftungen in Europa: Eine Vergleichende Ubersicht (Foundations in Europe: A comparative survey), 1956
Stiftungen und Bildungswesen in den USA (Foundations and matters of education in the U.S.A.), 900
Stimulating Joint Urban Ventures: Community Organizations and Organized Philanthropy, 2353
"Stirrings in the Shadows", **64**
"Stock Market Helps Mott Foundation Set Assets Record", 824
Stock Market Trends: Their Effects upon Fund Raising for Education, 3610
The Story of a Good Woman: Jane Lathrop Stanford, 257
"The Story of the Charles E. Merrill Trust: A Marxist Account of the Disposition of a Capitalist Fortune", **455**
The Story of the Charles Hayden Foundation, 842
The Story of the Davella Mills Foundation, 1935-1955, 1009
The Story of the Rockefeller Foundation, 767
The Story of Woodrow Wilson, 307
"Straight Talk about a Nagging Problem: How to Improve Nonprofit Management", **2818**
"Straight Talk about Our Future", **2820**
Strangers in the Philanthropic World: The Limited Latino Share of Chicago Grants, **938**
"Strategic Foundation Plan Requires Thoughtful Process", 1082
"Strategic Income Unit Indicators Identify Most Profitable Paths", 3049

380

TITLE INDEX

Strategic Marketing for Nonprofit Organizations, 2696
Strategic Marketing for Not-for-Profit Organizations, **2711**
"Strategic Philanthropy: New and More Imaginative Ways of Giving Away Money Are Paying off for Both Recipients and Corporate Donors", **1505**
"Strategic Planning for Nonprofit Health Care Organization Funding", 3274
Strategic Planning Workbook for Nonprofit Organizations, **2008**
"Strategies for Giving: Developed by the Contributions Strategies Committee", 3874
"Strategies for Individuals Contributing to Charitable Organizations under the Old Tax Law As Compared to New Law in 1987", **453**
Strategies for Individuals under the Old Tax Law As Compared to New Law in 1987, 4071
"Strategies for Leaner Times", **1658**
Strategy for the Conquest of Hunger, 4863
"Streamlining Foundation Tax Forms: Recent Changes Make Form 990-PF Easier to Complete, More Information for Grantseekers", 4143
"Strengthening Chair, CEO Relationships", 2679
Strengthening Philanthropy and Voluntary Initiative. An Independent Sector Program for Candidates for National Office and for the New Administration and Congress, 2183
Strengthening the Voluntary Sector, 745
"Stress: A Fact of Life", 2791
Stretch: A Resource Directory of Technical Assistance Providers, 2949
"Stretching the Career Ladder", **755**
"Striving for Peace: Symbolic Doves at Hiroshima Strengthen Kroc's Resolve", **1186**
"Structure and Change: A Funder's Perspective on Multicultural Support", **2234**
Structure and Process in Self-Help Organizations, 2244
The Structure of Funding Arenas for Community Self-Help Organizations, 2245
"Structuring a Nonprofit's Role in Real Estate Syndications", **2027**
Struggling through Tight Times: A Handbook for Women's and Other Nonprofits, 2133
"Study Details Rise in New Foundations", 577
Study in Power: John D. Rockefeller, Industrialist and Philanthropist. 2 Vols, **353**
A Study of Financial Management Issues and Reporting Requirements of South Bronx Community Organizations, 2688
A Study of Foundation Awards to Hispanic-Oriented Organizations in the U.S., 1981-1982. Preliminary Report, **1198**
"Study of Foundations Reveals Many Omit Critical Tax Data", 1235
A Study of Oklahoma-Based Private Philanthropic Foundations and Their Impact on Higher Education, 584
A Study of the Admissions Policies and Practices of Eight Local United Way Organizations, 2293
A Study of the Demand for a Greater New York Association of Foundations, 1296
Studying and Addressing Community Needs: A Corporate Case Book, **1707**
"Studying Philanthropy: Bibliographies and Beginnings", 295
Subscribe Now: Building Arts Audiences through Dynamic Subscription Promotion, 3679
The Subsidized Muse: Public Support for the Arts in the United States, 4714
The Successful Capital Campaign: From Planning to Victory Celebration, **3755**
"The Successful Fund Raiser: Born or Made?", 3057
"Successful Fund Raising Using Simple Engineering", **3846**
Successful Fundraising: A Handbook of Proven Strategies and Techniques, 3341
"Successful Grant-Seeking Techniques for Obtaining Private Grants: How to Contact a Private Funding Source", **3999**
"Successful Involvement of Volunteers Uses Phone", 3700
Successful Public Relations Techniques, **2851**
Successful Resources Fairs: Guidelines for Planning, 2945
Successful Seminars, Conferences and Workshops, **2852**
"Successful Small Shop Approaches to Foundations", 3977
"Successful Strategies for Institutionalizing Grants", **4038**
The Successful Volunteer Organization: Getting Started and Getting Results in Nonprofit, Charitable, Grass Roots and Community Groups, **4521**
Suggested Clauses for Wills and Trust Agreements, 4342
"Suggestions for Future Accounting Treatment of Non-Profit...", 2905
"Suggestions to Change Form 990", 4343
"Suite Charity: The Big Business of Corporate Philanthropy in Chicago", **1457**
Summary Guide to Educational Foundations: Europe (Excluding U.K.), 1986
Summary Guide to Educational Foundations: United Kingdom, 1987
Summary of H.R. 13270 Tax Reform Act of 1969. As Reported by the Committee on Finance, Russell B. Long, Chairman, 91st Congress, 1st Session, 4445
Summary of H.R. 13270, the Tax Reform Act of 1969 (As Passed by the House of Representatives), 91st Congress, 1st Session, 4446
Summary of Provisions of the Tax Reform Act of 1969 and 1976 Relating to Private Foundations, 4135
Summary. Senate Finance Committee's Subcommittee on Foundations, 1079
"Summer in the Non-Profit World", 3406
"Super Santas of '84", **459**
Supervision, 2921
"Supplement Your Fund Raising with a Direct Mail Campaign", 2985
Support for Museums and Historical Organizations, 4701
Support for the Arts from Independent Foundations, **699**
"Supporters Finding New Ways to Assist the Arts", 3885
Supporting the Arts: An International Comparative Study, **1939**
"Survey Dispels Myth That Blacks Receive But Do Not Give to Charity", **89**
"Survey Finds Religious Groups Strongly Favor More Collaboration", **4904**
"Survey Finds Significant Shift in Corporate Giving in 1982", 1691
"Survey Indicates Fund Raising Continues on Upward Swing", 3886
Survey, 1979, 2370
Survey of Arts Administration Training, **2498**
A Survey of Arts and Cultural Activities in Chicago, 1977, 4818
A Survey of Arts-in-Education in New York City, 2267
A Survey of European Programs: Education for Urbanization in the Developing Countries, 1800
A Survey of Financial Reporting and Accounting Practices of Private Foundations, 1085
Survey of Financial Reporting and Accounting Practices of Private Foundations, 2841
Survey of Foundation and Government Grants for Women's Rights and Opportunities, 1971-75, 3289
A Survey of Foundations Involved in U.S. Health R and D, 1247
Survey of Giving Report, Fiscal Year 1985, **3703**
Survey of Grant Making Foundations with Assets of over $1,000,000 or Grants of over $100,000, 1983-84, 1093
"Survey of Grants Activities at Selected Children's Hospitals", 4989
Survey of Human Resource Policies and Practices among Non-Profit Organizations in New York City, **2041**
Survey of Michigan Foundation Philanthropy, 1988, **646**
Survey of Philanthropy, **1025**
Survey of Record Keeping Practices in Foundations, 1291
Survey of State Laws Regulating Charitable Solicitation, 4348
Survey of the Public's Recollection of 1978 Charitable Donations, 168

381

TITLE INDEX

Survey of the Public's Recollection of 1981 Charitable Donations, **104**
Survey of United States and Foreign Government Support for Cultural Activities, 4753
"Survey: Rapidly Growing Alternative Funds Raise $13.7 Million. Supplement", 3887
"Survey Says Companies Gave Record Amount to Charities", 1697
A Survival Kit for Invisible Colleges, or What to Do until Federal Aid Arrives, 3438
"Survival Time for Nonprofits", 2337
"Sweet Charities", **387**
"Sweet Charity: Building an Approach to Foundation Money", 3361
Symposium, 1995
Symposium on Strategy for the Conquest of Hunger. Proceedings, 4938
A System of Scientific Medicine: Philanthropic Foundations in the Flexner Era, **571**
"System Selection: Staff Input Assures Best Computer Output", 2920
Taft Corporate Giving Directory, **1525**
Taft Directory of Nonprofit Organizations: Profiles of America's Major Charitable Institutions, 2102
Taft Foundation Reporter, **729**
"Taft Survey Finds: Corporate Giving Could Go Up in 1983", 1692
"Tainted Money", **177**
"'Take Care': The Legal Duties of Board Members", 2972
"Take Custody of Your Assets", **2710**
Taken at the Flood: The Story of Albert D. Lasker, 190
"Taken under Advisement", **965**
Taking Charge: Management and Marketing for the Media Arts, 2912
Taking Stock: Rural People and Poverty from 1970 to 1983, 4872
"Taking the Initiative for Corporate Public Involvement", 1442
"Taking the Lead with a Potential Grantee: How Much Is Too Much?", 1216
"A Tale of Two Donors: Claiming Charitable Deductions", 4362
"Tales of Sonnenberg", 413
Tales of the Phelps-Dodge Family: A Chronicle of Five Generations, **133**
"Tales Out of School: A Wry Look at How Not to Succeed in Fund Raising", 3346
"Talking to a Corporate Donor", **1312**
"Taming the Cost of Health Care", 4976
"Tao House Calendar", **3992**
"Tapping into the Power Base of Corporate Philanthropy", **1719**
The Tasks of Leadership, **2611**
"Tax Act May Hurt Charitable Giving", 4372
Tax Administration: Information on Lobbying and Political Activities of Tax-Exempt Organizations, **4418**

Tax Aspects of Charitable Giving and Receiving, 4257
Tax Aspects of Individual Charitable Giving, 4288, 4289
"Tax Breaks for Not-for-Profits", 4099
"Tax Changes Swell the 'Products' Package", 1690
The Tax Climate for Philanthropy, 4199
Tax Considerations in Charitable Giving, 4083
"The Tax-Deduction Issue", **4328**
"Tax Deductions for Volunteers", 4350, 4588
Tax Economics of Charitable Giving, **4084**
Tax Equity and Fiscal Responsibility Act of 1982, 4282
Tax-Exempt Charitable Organizations, **4374**
The Tax-Exempt Foundations, 998
Tax-Exempt Foundations and Charitable Trusts: Their Impact on Our Economy, 4385, 4386, 4387, 4392, 4431
Tax-Exempt Foundations: Their Impact on Small Business, 4432
Tax-Exempt Organizations' Lobbying and Political Activities Accountability Act of 1987: A Guide for Volunteers and Staff of Nonprofit Organizations, 4098
Tax-Exempt Organizations. 2 Vols, **4240**
"Tax-Exempt Status Threatened by Fund Raising?", 4194
Tax Exemptions for Charitable Organizations Affecting Poverty Programs: Examination of Internal Revenue Service Decision to Deny Tax-Exempt Status to Charitable Organizations Which Engage in Litigation Affecting Poverty Programs. Hearings, 91st Congress, 2nd Session, November 16-17, 1970, 4454
Tax Free, 4323
A Tax Guide for Artists and Arts Organizations, 4230
"A Tax Guide to Contributions", **4363**
Tax Impacts on Philanthropy. Tax Institute of America Conference, 4351
Tax Incentives for Charitable Donations: Deeds of Covenant and Charitable Contribution Deductions, 1940
"Tax-Induced Fund Raising: New Techniques to Prosperity", 3081
"Tax Law Spurs Giving in '81", 4081
"Tax Laws Aiding Arts Faulted by Foundation", 4241
"The Tax Man Cometh", **4304**
"Tax Plan Draws Jeers from Art World", 2013
Tax Planning for Foundations and Charitable Giving, 4120
Tax Policies and United Ways, 4466
Tax Policy and Private Support for the Arts in the U.S., Canada and Great Britain, 4310
Tax Policy: Competition between Taxable Businesses and Tax-Exempt Organizations, **4435**
Tax Reform Act of 1969, 4129

Tax Reform Act of 1969. Conference Report (to Accompany H.R. 13270) 91st Congress, 1st Session, December 21, 1969, 4389
"Tax Reform Act of 1969: An Overview", 4309
"Tax Reform Act of 1969 and the Treatment of Accumulation Trusts", 4331
Tax Reform Act of 1969. Compilation of Decisions Reached in Executive Session, 4447
Tax Reform Act of 1969. H.R. 13270. Part A: Testimony to Be Received Tuesday, September 9, 1969. Part B: Additional Statements (Topic: Foundations), 91st Congress, 1st Session, 4448
Tax Reform Act of 1969. H.R. 13270: Testimony to Be Received Wednesday, October 22, 1969 (Topic: Foundations), 91st Congress, 1st Session, 4449
Tax Reform Act of 1969. News Clippings and Press Comment, 4352
Tax Reform Act of 1969: Report of the Committee on Ways and Means to Accompany H.R. 13270, a Bill to Reform the Income Tax Laws with Separate and Supplemental Views, 91st Congress, 1st Session. 2 Vols, 4401
"Tax Reform Act of 1976: Effects on Charitable Giving", 4364
Tax Reform Act of 1976. Supplemental Report, 4450
Tax Reform Act of 1976: Tax Considerations for Individuals, 4283
Tax Reform Act of 1983. H.R. 4170, Title III, 98th Congress, 1st Session, 4388
"Tax Reform Act of 1984 Begets Many Changes for Non-Profits: Part 1", 4195
"Tax Reform Act of 1984 Begets Many Changes for Non-Profits: Part 2", 4196
The Tax Reform Act of 1986, **4265**
Tax Reform Act of 1986. Conference Committee Bill and Report. 2 Vols, 4353
"Tax Reform Act: Public Charities, Lobbying", 4141
Tax Reform and Individual Giving to Higher Education, **4086**
Tax Reform and the Crisis of Financing Higher Education: A Report of the Association of American Universities, 4266
"Tax Reform and the Foundations", 4077
Tax Reform in Review. Selected Articles, 4354
Tax Reform Proposals Contained in the Message from the President on April 21, 1969 and Presented by Representatives of the Treasury Department to the Committee on Ways and Means, April 22, 1969, 91st Congress, 1st Session, 4402
Tax Reform Studies and Proposals U.S. Treasury Department: Joint Publication Committee on Ways and Means of the House and Committee on Finance of the Senate, February 5, 1969, 91st Congress, 1st Session. 3 Vols, 4455

TITLE INDEX

Tax Rules Governing Foundations. 98th Congress, 1st Session. 2 Vols, **4403**
Tax Techniques for Foundations and Other Exempt Organizations. 5 Vols, 4474
Tax Techniques in Fund-Raising, 4365
Taxation and Education, 4149
"Taxation and Private Foundations: Special Issues", 4355
Taxation of Charitable Giving, 4165
The Taxation of Nonprofits: A State-by-State Summary, **4206**
"Taxation 101", 4078
"Taxing Charitable Giving Undermine Our Worthiest Institutions", 4356
"Taxing Educational Gifts", 4213
"A Taxonomy of the Tax-Exempt", **2364**
The Taxpayers' Revolt and the Arts: A U.S. Conference of Mayors' Position Paper, 4377
Teachers on Individualism: The Way We Do It, 4954
"Teaching Doctors to Fund Raise", 3312
"Teaching Volunteers the Art of Asking", **3330**
"The Team Approach", 1053
"The Team Approach Leads to Better Fund Raising", 3907
"Team Building May Enhance Development Effectiveness", 2621
"Team Building within Your Organization", 2919
Technical Assistance Guide (TAG). A Directory of Resources for New York Non-Profit Organizations, **2517**
Technical Assistance Pamphlet (TAP), 2975
"Technical Assistance: Tea and Sympathy?", 2916
"Technical Assistance: What Role for Foundations and Corporations", 2470
Technical Memorandum on Corporate Giving. Corporate Foundations vs. Corporate Giving Programs: Compendium of Applicable Federal Tax Laws, **4136**
The Technique for Proper Giving, 207
"The Technique of Soliciting", 3777
The Teen Parent Collaboration: A Cooperative Venture between National and Community Foundations, **4930, 4931**
The Teen Parent Collaboration: Reaching and Serving the Teenage Father, **2203, 2204**
The Teen Parent Collaboration: Strengthening Services for Teen Mothers, 4933, 4934
Telecommunications for Library Management, **2477**
Telecommunications Networks: Issues and Trends, **2669**
"Telemarketing Fund Raising Can Have Giving Drawbacks", 3594
"Telemarketing: The Key to Successful Fund Raising", 3821
"Telemarketing Variables Work Together for Campaign Success", 3949
"Telephone Fundraising Strategies", 3563

Telepledge: The Complete Guide to Mailphone Fund Raising, 3808
"Telethons and Radiothons: Tales from the Toteboard", 3246
"A Tempting Target", **36**
"The Ten Cardinal Rules of Writing Fund Raising Copy", 3905
Ten for the Eighties: What Every Nonprofit Executive Should Know, 2911
Ten Largest Foundations Ranked by Grants and Assets: New York City, Boston, Chicago, Cleveland, and San Francisco, 774
The Ten Lost Commandments of Fund Raising, 2644
"The Ten Most Common Organizational Problems: Getting to Their Source", 2630
Ten Prerequisites for Successful Fund Raising, 3690
"Ten Questions for the Thinking Board Member", 2752
"Ten Significant Questions You Might Have to Answer", **2701**
"Ten Ways That Institutions Are Raising New Resources", 2365
"The Ten Wealthiest People in the USA", 467
The Tennessee Directory of Foundations and Corporate Philanthropy, 1006
Tennessee Directory of Foundations and Corporate Philanthropy, **1236**
"Termination of Private Foundations", 4102
"Test Yourself!", 3946
Tested Ways to Successful Fund Raising, 3074
Testimony of Brian O'Connell, President, Independent Sector, before the Subcommittee on Oversight, June 27, 1983, 98th Congress, 1st Session, 4419
"Testimony of Brian O'Connell, President, Independent Sector, on the Impact of the President's Tax Proposals on Charities", 4207
Testimony of Dorothy A. Johnson, Executive Director, Council of Michigan Foundations, Hearings before Subcommittee on Oversight, 98th Congress, 1st Session, June 28, 1983, 4420
Testimony of J. Stoddard Hayes, Jr. on Behalf of the American Bankers Association before the Subcommittee on Oversight, June 28, 1983, 98th Congress, 1st Session, 4421
Testimony of James P. Shannon, Executive Director of General Mills Foundation before Subcommittee on Oversight, 98th Congress, 1st Session, June 28, 1983, 4422
Testimony of Janet C. Taylor, Executive Director, Associated Grantmakers of Massachusetts before the Subcommittee on Oversight, 98th Congress, 1st Session, June 28, 1983, 4423

Testimony of John L. Currin, Counselor and Secretary on Behalf of Richard F. Schubert, President, the American Red Cross, before the House Subcommittee on Oversight of the Committee on Ways and Means, 98th Congress, 1st Session, 4424
Testimony of Marjorie P. Allen, President of the Powell Family Foundation. Hearings before the House Subcommittee on Oversight, Committee on Ways and Means, 98th Congress, 1st Session, 4425
Testimony of Norman B. Ture, Chairman, Institute for Research on the Economics of Taxation before the Subcommittee on Oversight, June 28, 1983, 98th Congress, 1st Session, 4426
Testimony of Pablo Eisenberg, President, Center for Community Change, before the Subcommittee on Oversight, June 28, 1983, 98th Congress, 1st Session, 4427
Testimony of Robert O. Bothwell. Miscellaneous Revisions to Improve Federal Tax Laws Especially Regarding Elimination of Certain Overlapping Reporting Requirements in the Case of Private Foundations and Generally Increasing Public Access, 4097
Testimony of Thomas R. Buckman, President, the Foundation Center before the Commerce, Consumer, and Monetary Affairs Subcommittee of the Committee on Government Operations, 589
Testimony of Wilbur D. Mills, Counsel, Shea and Gould before the Oversight Subcommittee, 98th Congress, 1st Session, 4428
Testimony of William L. Bondurant before the Oversight Subcommittee, June 28, 1983, 98th Congress, 1st Session, 4429
Testimony Presented before the Oversight Subcommittee of the House Ways and Means Committee by Christopher F. Edley, Presented on Behalf of the United Negro College Fund, 98th Congress, 1st Session, 4430
"Testing: A Conduit to Solid Development Growth", 3437
"Testing Increases Contributions in Telemarketing Campaigns", 3606
"Testing Telemarketing Reveals Donor Efficiencies", 3607
"Thank You, Japan", **74**
"Thanks a Million", 414
Theater Profiles 8, 2186
Theater Program: Application Guidelines, 4696
Theatre Directory, **4971**
"Theatre Facts 86", 2166
"Theatre Facts 87", **2419**
Their Sister's Keepers: Women's Prison Reform in America, 1830-1930, **163**
A Theology for Christian Stewardship, 3478
"The Theory of a Positive Crisis", 3352
"There's More Asking and More Giving: Individual Donations Top $61-Billion", 127

TITLE INDEX

"There's More to Special Events Than Raising Money", **3647**

"There's More Work in Making Grants to Individuals", 1121

There's Plenty of Money for Nonprofit Groups Willing to Earn Their Shares: How to Do It Successfully, **3739**

"There's $10 Million in Religious Foundations in Texas", 1018

"These Phenomenally Orthodox Donors", 1981

They Told Barron: Conversations and Revelations of an American Pepys in Wall Street, 32

"A Thing of Beauty Is a Profit Forever", 1698

"Think before You Plunge: Advance Planning for Fundraisers", 3407

"Think Youth: The Challenge of Youth Volunteerism", 4496

"Thinking the Unthinkable: Should We Go on?", 2029

"The Third Sector", **410**

"A Third Sector Headquarters", 1237

The Third Sector: New Tactics for a Responsive Society, **299**

The Thirteen Most Common Fund-Raising Mistakes and How to Avoid Them, 3804

A Thirty Year Catalog of Grants, during the Period November 10, 1911 to September 30, 1941, 945

This Old Neighborhood: A Business and Community Guide to Neighborhood Revitalization, 3146

Those Were the Days: Tales of a Long Life, 217

"The Thoughtful Marketing of Foster Parents Plan", 3716

"Thoughts of a Corporate Gadfly: On Community Groups and Corporate Giving", 1700

"Thoughts on the Supervision of Volunteers", 4494

"Three Checklists: Marketing Your Volunteer Program to Recruit Volunteers", **2757**

"Three Common Problems Faced in Capital Campaigns", 3806

"The Thrift Shop Dilemma: Fund Raising or Business Venture?", 3864

"Throw Away Berlitz! Just Memorize These Terms", **472**

"Tightwads, Ltd.", **1885**

"Time for a Hard Look, at Ourselves", **2292**

"Time for the Annual Headache: The Annual Report", 2371

"Time to Listen", 339

"Times Cause Exxon to Give More, Smaller Grants", 1633

Tips for Proposal Writers, 4001

Tips on Charitable Giving: How to Give But Give Wisely, **2068**

"Tisch, Tisch: The Billionaire Brothers Built Loews with One Strategy: Wait and Seize", 367

"To Africa, with Love", **1950**

"To Be a Better Trustee", 2877

To Be or Not to Be: An Artist's Guide to Not-for-Profit Incorporation, 2387

To Cast Our Mite on the Altar of Benevolence: Women Begin to Organize, **4577**

To Empower People: The Role of Mediating Structures in Public Policy, **4489**

"To Get Grants, Universities Use Applied Political Science", 4318

To Have or to Be?, **166**

To Light One Candle: A Handbook for Organizing, Funding and Maintaining Public Service Activities, 3556

"To Live on This Earth", 4898

To Preserve an Independent Sector. Organizing Committee Report, 2056

"To Some Celebrities, Stints for Charities Are Strictly Business", 3471

Today's Planning, Creating, Operating and Reporting for Foundations, 613

Too Many Clients, Too Little Time: A Guide to Planning and Managing a Legal Services Program, 2766

"Top Consultants Tell All", **1703**

The Top Fifty Grant Awarding Foundations in 1982, 946

Total Corporate Responsibility in the 80's, **1341**

"Total for United Way in 1983 Was $15.5 Million, a 12% Rise", 3912

"Total Giving Continues to Climb, But Corporate Donations Are Flat: Giving USA Report", **450**

"Total Giving, 1955-84. The Growth of Philanthropy, 1968-84", 477

Total Proposal Building, **4060**

The Touche Ross Survey of Business Executives on Non-Profit Boards, **2924**

"Touring Rosters and Funding Support", **2373**

Toward a Contingency Model of Board-Executive Relations in Nonprofit Organizations, 2697

Toward a Learning Society: Alternative Channels to Life, Work, and Service, 4804

Toward Ending Poverty among the Elderly and Disabled: Policy and Financing Options, 2418

"Toward Fairer Competition between For-Profit and Non-Profits", 2374

Toward Greatness in Higher Education, 4840

Toward Reform of Program Evaluation: Aims, Methods, and Institutional Arrangements, 2532

Toward the Future. National Conference Report, **2800**

Toward the Well-Being of Mankind: Fifty Years of the Rockefeller Foundation, 1173

Towards a Rationale for Private Non-Profit Organizations: A Review of Current Theory, 2092

"TRA '69: Coming Up on 10 Years", 4468

"TRA '84 Provisions Affecting Charities and Donors", 4366

"Training Volunteers: The Trainer As Teacher, a Personal Perspective", 4495

Traite des Fondations D'utilite Publique, 1921

Transactions Costs and a Theory of the Non-Profit Organization, **2698**

Transfers to Charities under the Tax Reform Act of 1969, 4092

Transforming Work: A Collection of Organizational Transformation Readings, 2424

"Traversing the Spectrum", 820

Treasury Department Report on Private Foundations. 89th Congress, 1st Session, 4404

A Treasury of Successful Appeal Letters, **3207**

"Treasury Tax-Reform Proposal", **4197**

"The Trend Away from Perpetuities", 1141

"Trendlines: Foundation Support of Higher Education", 1243

Trends and Developments in Federal and Foundation Grants for Health, 1244

Trends Document, 665

"Trends in Corporate Giving", 1526

Trends in Health Philanthropy: A Survey of Private or Independent Foundations, Corporations, and Community Foundations Engaged in Health Grantmaking, 826

"Trends in Hospital Philanthropy: Reacting to Current Changes", 510

Trends in Nonprofit Public Relations, 2463

Trends in Philanthropy: A Study in a Typical American City, 277

Tribal Economic Development Directory, **2051**

Triennial Salary Survey, 2901

"The Triumph of a Prodigal Son", 420

Triumphant Democracy, 82

Troubled Youth and the Arts: A Resource Guide, 3719

Trust for All Time: The Story of the Cleveland Foundation and the Community Trust Movement, 862

"Trust vs. Corporate Form", **4326**

"Trustee Leadership Succession: The Key to Long-Term Stability", 2684

Trustee Orientation Packet, 666

"Trustees and the Fund-Raising Role: Facing the Hard Truth", 2660

Trustees and the Future of Foundations, **1026**

"Trustees' Role in a Major Campaign", 2524

Trustees, Trusteeship, and the Public Good: Issues of Accountability for Hospitals, Museums, Universities and Libraries, **2464**

Trusteeship and the Management of Foundations, 2974

Trusteeship of American Endowments, 2970

Trusts and Foundations: A Select Guide to Organizations and Grant-Making Bodies

TITLE INDEX

Operating in Great Britain and the Commonwealth, 1873
Trusts and Foundations in Europe: A Comparative Survey, 1909
Trusts and Trusteeships, 20
"The Truth about Nonprofit Managers", **2631**
"Truth Telling Pays off in Development Game Plan", 3030
"Try Innovative Giving, Despite Government Cuts", 1122
Tudor on Charities, 1895
Tuition, 4805
"Turn on the Light", 3895
"The Turnaround", 2334
"The Twelve Best Things You Can Do to Strengthen Your Development Program: In a World of Priorities", 3000
"Twelve Suggestions about Fund-Raising Packages", **3449**
Twelve Tips on Use of Consultants, 2931
"Twelve Tips Will Help When Compiling Proposals", 4014
Twenty Company-Sponsored Foundations. Programs and Policies, 1730
Twenty-Eight Years: A Narrative Report of the Foundation's Activities, 1952-1980, 750
"The $25 Billion Giveaway: America Perfects the Fine Art of Fund Raising", 3112
"Twenty-Five Years and Change", **995**
Twenty-Five Years of Giving in New York City: The Vincent Astor Foundation, 23
"Twenty-Five Years' Worth", 836
Twenty-Four Ways to Improve Your Direct Mail Results: A Dartnell Report for Direct Mail and Mail Order Advertising Executives, 3516
Twenty Master Keys to Increase Giving, 3920
"$20 Million Private Project to Aid Homeless", 4924
"Twenty-Nine Ways That Board Members (and Other Volunteers) Can Raise about $500 without Very Much Effort", 2691
"Twenty Recipients of President's Volunteer Action Awards Honored", 4556
"Twenty-Two Predictions on the Future of Direct Mail Fund Raising", 3450
Twenty Years at Hull House, with Autobiographical Notes, **7**
Twigs for an Eagle's Nest. Government and the Arts, 1965-1978, 4744
The Twin Cities Nonprofit Sector in a Time of Government Retrenchment, 4680
Two Cheers for Capitalism, 1551
"Two Executives Talk about the Reagan Cuts and One Company's Response", 1499
Two Perspectives on Our Future, 480
"Two Shots in the Arm", **821**
"Two Standards for Charities' Lobbying OKd", 4238
"Two Surefire Ways to Increase Annual Giving", 3915

"The Typewritten Request for the Grail: Grants in Fiction", 1295
"The Ultimate Gift: The Biggest Gifts of All Take a Special Kind of Fund Raising", **3247**
The Uncertain Consequences of Tuition Tax Credits: An Analysis of Student Achievement and Economic Incentives, 4910
Understanding and Obtaining Federal Grants, 4643
"Understanding Evaluation of Research Proposals: The First Step toward More Effective Writing", 4054
Understanding Foundation Support for Higher Education, 1023
Understanding Foundations: Dimensions in Fund Raising, 1215
"Understanding Fund Raising: The Media Obstacle", 3878
"Understanding International Philanthropy", 1823
"Understanding Nonprofit Financial Statements. Part 1", **2526**
"Understanding Nonprofit Financial Statements. Part 2", 2527
"Understanding Software", 2578
"Understanding the Philanthropic Partnership", **1300**
The Uneasy Partnership: Social Science and the Federal Government in the Twentieth Century, 4896
Unfair Competition and Corporate Income Taxation, 2313
"'Unfair Competition': Business vs. Nonprofits", 2167
Unfair Competition by Nonprofit Organizations with Small Business: An Issue for the 1980's, 2380
The Unfinished Agenda: The Citizen's Guide to the Environmental Issues, 4781
"Unforgettable Characters in Fund Raising: Charles R. Hook, William Allen White", 3491
Unintended Consequences: Regulating the Quality of Subsidized Day Care, 4942
"A Unique Calling", 1159
United Arts Fundraising, 3728
United Arts Fundraising. Campaign Analysis, 1980, 3729
United Arts Fundraising Manual, 3730
United Arts Fundraising Policybook, 3731
United Charities: An Economic Analysis, **2314**
"The United Way", **3951**
"The United Way and the Issue of Admissions", 3725
"United Way Results for 1982", 3879
"United Way Results for 1983", 3880
"United Way Results, 1984", 3881
The United Way: The Next Hundred Years, **2000**
"United Way: Who Are Its Critics?", 3794
"United Way's President Talks about Restructuring, Alternative Funds", **2023**
"Universities and High Technology Industry", 3829

"Universities Come to the Aid of Neighboring Communities", 2381
Universities, Foundations, and Government, 1084
"Universities Take Lead in New Volunteer Efforts", 4497
University-Connected Research Foundations, 2540
University/Industry Research Relationships: Myths, Realities and Potentials, 4711
The University of Chicago Biographical Sketches, 184
"Unlocking the Power of Computers: Statistics for Nonprofits", **2730**
The Unofficial Commonwealth: The Story of the Commonwealth Foundation, 1965-1980, 1773
"The Unrelated Business: Concerns for Profits and Losses", 2409
The Unrelated Business Income Tax, 4162
"The Unrelated Business: The Myth of 'Stare Decises'", 2410
"The 'Unseen' Sector", 2090
"The Untapped Resource: Corporate Matching Gifts", 3192
Up Your Account-Ability: How to Up Your Serviceability and Funding Credibility by Upping Your Accounting Ability, 2469
Uplift. What People Themselves Can Do, 2379
The Urban Funding Guide: Sources of Funds for Urban Programs at Colleges and Universities, 2995
"Urban Hospital's Rehab Efforts Lead Health Trend", 2239
Urbanization in Brazil, 1801
Urbanization in Chile, 1802
Urbanization in Colombia, 1803
Urbanization in India, 1804
Urbanization in Jamaica, 1805
Urbanization in Kenya, 1806
Urbanization in Morocco, 1807
Urbanization in Nigeria: A Planning Commentary, 1808
Urbanization in Peru, 1809
Urbanization in Thailand, 1810
Urbanization in the Developing Countries: The Response of International Assistance, 1811
Urbanization in Tropical Africa: A Demographic Introduction, 1812
Urbanization in Turkey, 1813
Urbanization in Venezuela, 1814
Urbanization in Zambia, 1815
U.S. and Canadian Nonprofit Organizations (PVOs) As Transitional Development Institutions, 1949
U.S. Facilities and Programs for Children with Severe Mental Illness: A Directory, 4703
"U.S. Finds Foundations Failing to Comply with Disclosure Law", 970
U.S. Foundation Giving to Enhance Educational Opportunities for Black South Africans: An Analysis of the

385

TITLE INDEX

Present State of Foundation Funding and a Foundation Inventory, **1893**
"U.S. Foundations and International Concerns", 1887
U.S. Foundations and Minority Group Interests, 1251
U.S. Funding for Biomedical Research, 580
"U.S. Is Upheld in Charity Drive Curb", 3344
U.S. Non-Profit Organizations, Voluntary Agencies, Missions, and Foundations Participating in Technical Assistance Abroad: A Directory, 1964
U.S. Nonprofit Organizations in Development Assistance Abroad: Directory, **1766**
U.S. Philanthropic Foundations: Their History, Structure, Management and Record, **1263**
U.S. Philanthropy: Grantmaking for International Purposes, 1894
"U.S. Seeks Curbs on Foundations", 1171
"USA for Africa Decides to Disburse $17 Million", 1890
"The Use and Abuse of Endowments", 3740
"The Use and Misuse of Consultants", 2737
"Use Good Marketing for Fund Raising Success", 3370
"The Use of Charts: A Tool for Management", 3144
"The Use of Sweepstakes and Other Donor Promotions", 3362
The Use of the Mail in Philanthropic Finance: A Compilation of the Theory and Practice of the Use of the Mail in Fund Raising for the Use of Philanthropic and Social Service Organizations Accompanied by a Collection of Successful Fund Raising Letters. 2 Vols, 3680
"Use Persuasion Theory to Raise More Money", 3904
"USF and G: A Heritage of Giving", **1593**
"Using a Consumer-Oriented Approach: A Personal and Professional Perspective", **2923**
Using Microcomputers in Social Agencies, 2914
Using Publicity to Best Advantage, 2881
"Using the Buddy System to Survive Computerization", 2870
"Using the Charitable Remainder Unitrust", 4170
"Using Your Donor Surveys to Find New Donors", 3926
Valuation Guide for Donated Goods, 1514
"Value of 202 Endowments on June 30, 1983", 3928
The Variability of the Charitable Giving of the Wealthy, 24
"Varied Scherman Foundation: A Broad Philanthropic Model", 1123
"Vehicles for Urban Survival", 1258
"Venture Capital Ideas for Schools and Other Nonprofits", 2277

Venture Capital, Where to Find It. Membership Directory, 4913
"Venture Censure", 2385
A Venture in Industry Aid to Public Secondary Education, 1519
"Verisimilitude, Benefit and Clarity: Your Copy Umbrella", 3566
"The Very Expensive Education of McGeorge Bundy: A Study in the Uses of Power and How It Is Manipulated in the Upper Reaches Where the Nation's Elite Operates", 193
The Very Rich: A History of Wealth, 471
The Very Rich Book. America's Super-Millionaires and Their Money: Where They Got It, How They Spend It, 469
Video Service Profiles: A Guide to Services for the New York State Video Community, 2671
"A View from Both Sides of the Fence", 3856
"Vintage Victorian: Swiss Avenue's Wilson Block Is Restored to New Life", 4835
Virginia Foundations, **827**
Visiting Professorships for Women, 4712
The Vital Margin of Voluntary Support, 3294
"Voluntarism and Reagan", 4652
Voluntarism and the Business Community, 4600
Voluntarism at the Crossroads, **4549**
"Voluntarism Challenges", 4575
Voluntarism, Tax Reform, and Higher Education, 4506
Voluntary Action: A Report on Methods of Social Advance, 1763
Voluntary Action Research, **4583**
"Voluntary Agencies and Community Partnerships", 3006
Voluntary Agencies in the Welfare State, 2208
The Voluntary Agency in a Mixed Economy: Dilemmas of Entrepreneurialism and Vendorism, 2209
Voluntary and Public Hospitals in England and Wales, 1840
Voluntary Associations: A Study of Groups in Free Societies, **4570**
Voluntary Associations, Nomos XI, **4564**
Voluntary Associations: Perspectives on the Literature, **4582**
Voluntary Associations: Socio-Cultural Analyses and Theological Interpretation, **4481**
Voluntary Foreign Aid Programs, 1746
Voluntary Health Agencies, 2146
Voluntary Health and Welfare Agencies in the United States: An Exploratory Study, **1989**
Voluntary Nonprofit Enterprise Management, 2750
The Voluntary Nonprofit Sector: An Economic Analysis, **1732**
Voluntary Organizations and the Crisis of the Welfare State, **2323**

The Voluntary Sector Overseas: Notes from the Field, **1888**
Voluntary Sector Policy Research Needs, **4584**
Voluntary Support for Public Higher Education, 3075
Voluntary Support of America's Colleges and Universities, **3169**
"Voluntary Support of Colleges Drops $80 Million in Year", 3810
The Volunteer Board Member in Philanthropy: Responsibilities, Achievements, Special Problems, **2790**
"Volunteer Executives Find Jobs Make Tough Demands", 4580
"The Volunteer Key to Successful Fund Raising", 3199
The Volunteer Leader: Essays on the Role of Trustees of Nonprofit Facilities and Services for the Aging, **2509**
The Volunteer Skillsbank: An Innovative Way to Connect Individual Talents to Community Needs, 4572
Volunteer to Career: A Study of Student Volunteerism and Employability and a Directory of Employers Recognizing the Volunteer Experience of Recent College Graduates, 4487
Volunteer Values, 4512
"Volunteering and Unemployment: The Flint Conference", 4596
"Volunteering in America", 4484
"Volunteering in America, 1982-83", 4485
"Volunteering: The Policy-Maker's Role", 4593
"Volunteerism", 4529
Volunteerism: A Directory of Special Collections, 4562
Volunteerism Corporate Style, **1399**
Volunteerism in the Eighties: Fundamental Issues in Voluntary Action, **4530**
"Volunteerism in the '80's: Takes Steps to Erase 'Miss Goody Two Shoes' Image", 4507
"Volunteerism, Third Sector Are Indeed Alive and Growing", 4565
Volunteers, 4544
Volunteers: A Valuable Resource, 4579
Volunteers As Managers: A Philosophy and Plan for Involvement and Leadership, **4585**
"Volunteers Bank Their Skills", 4511
Volunteers from the Workplace, 1301
Volunteers in Libraries: 2, 4597
Volunteers: The Untapped Potential, 4498
"Volunteers Try to Raise Sports Funds", 3937
"Want a Japanese Grant? Cultivate These Third Parties First", **1926**
"Want a Photographic Grant?", 688
"Wanted: More Minorities for Top Fundraising Jobs", **3063**
"Wanted: More Trustees with Certain Wallop", 2854
The Waqfiyah of 'Ahmed Pasa, 1943
Washington Embassies: A Guide for the Private Sector, 1759

TITLE INDEX

Washington Information Directory, **4627**
The Washington Lobby, 4471
Washington Non-Profit Tax Conference, 4272, 4273, 4274, 4275, 4276, 4277, 4278, 4279, 4280
"The Wave of Self-Help", 2402
"Ways and Means Committee Votes to Eliminate Impediments to Foundation Gifts, Operations", 726
"Ways and Means Subcommittee Releases UBIT Options", **4472**
Ways to Find Private Sector Funding for Schools, 3518
"We Have Much to Learn from Our International Friends", **1936**
Wealth and Culture: A Study of One Hundred Foundations and Community Trusts and Their Operations during the Decade, 1921-1930, 949
Wealth Holders of America, 492
The Wealth of the American People: A History of American Affluence, 195
"The Wealthiest Americans", 421
"Wealthy, Rightest Foundation Plans 24-Hour-a-Day Cable TV Network", 670
The Welcome Mat Is Out, 1491
Welcome to the Club! (No Women Need Apply). Removing Financial Support from Private Clubs That Discriminate against Women, 1157
Welfare in America, 47
Welfare in Trust: A History of the Carnegie United Kingdom Trust, 1913-1963, 1932
West Virginia Foundation Directory, **1271**
What American Corporations Are Doing to Improve the Quality of Precollege Education: A CFAE Sampler, **1733**
What Americans Think: Views on Development and U.S.-Third World Relations, 1778
"What Appeals to Whom?", **3550**
"What Are Your Responsibilities As a Professional Fund Raiser?", 3039
"What Corporations Want to Know about You", 1734
"What Do They Think of Us?", **1488**
"What Do You Do after All Your Donors Are Dead?", **3451**
"What Do You Do with a Do-Nothing Board Member?", **2472**
"What Does (or Should) Society Want from Non-Profits?", **2361**
"What Fund Raisers Should Know about Planned Giving", 3336
"What Fund Raisers Should Know about TV Talk Shows", 3357
"What Hath Geldof Wrought?", **3971**
"What Is a Church?", **4981**
"What Is a National Taxonomy for?", **2165**
"What Is Fair Market Value?", **4789**
"What Is My Database?", 2894
"What Is the Ad Council and How Does It Work?", 4927
What Is the Appropriate Structure for Nonprofit Corporation Law? A Response to Ellman, 2156

"What Is the Economic Outlook for Philanthropy?", 456
What Kind of Society Shall We Have?, 2222
What Kinds of Groups Receive Colorado's Foundation Grants? A Study of the Grants of the Twenty-Five Largest Private Foundations from 1974-1976, 625
"What Leads to Yes: Applying the Psychology of Influence to Fund Raising, Alumni Relations, and PR", **3133**
What Lies Ahead for Philanthropy, 261
What Lies Ahead: Looking toward the 90's, **484**
"What Lies Ahead: Looking toward the '90s", **2079**
"What Makes a Good Nonprofit Manager?", 2887
"What Makes a Rich Man Happy?", 392
"What Makes a Successful Chief Development Officer?", 3964
"What Makes Projects Different?", 2216
"What Motivates Giving to Christian Organizations?", **3262**
"What TV Stations Want in Public Service Announcements", 3616
What Volunteers Should Know for Successful Fund Raising, 3358
"What, When, How Much Primer on the Reagan Tax-Reform Plan", **4198**
"What Worked in 1970 Won't Work Anymore in 1990", 3567
"What Would Andrew Carnegie Think about How His Money Is Used Today?", 128
"What's at Stake in Government Regulation of Fund Raising: A Story in Five Parts", 3882
"What's Happening to the Neighborhood Movement?", 4875
"What's on Your Prospective Planned Gift Donor's Mind?", 3867
"What's Your Organizational Posture?", **2615**
"When a Donor Asks 'Will the Charity's Re-Sale Price Undermine My Appraisal?' What Do You Tell Him?", 4115
"When a Foundation Goes to School", 1004
"When a Grantee Seeks Money for Project A, and You Know It's Really for Project B", 1273
"When Associations Become Entrepreneurs", 2089
When Development Directors Fail, 2910
"When Donors Give: How Giving Changes in Good and Bad Economic Times", 3551
"When It's Cutback Time at NIH", 4742
"When May Conditional Pledges of Support Become 'Receivables' on Your Books?", **2906**
"When Money Isn't the Problem", **2202**
"When Non-Profits Should Use Subsidiaries", 2173

"When Nonprofits Fit into Marketing Strategy", **1651**
"When Should the Profits of Nonprofits Be Taxed?", 2396
"When the Buck Stopped", **1287**
Where America's Large Foundations Make Their Grants, 687
"Where Is IRS Likely to Look in 'Unrelated Business Income' Audits?", 4148
"Where Is the Private Money President Reagan Promised?", 178
"Where Non-Profits Stand: Barber Conable Looks Back", 2062
"Where Proposals Fail: A Foundation Executive's Basic List of What to Do and Not Do When Requesting Funding", 4056
Where the Money Is: A Grantsmanship Handbook for Non-Profit Agencies and Organizations in Dutchess County, 1274
Where the Money Is and How to Get It, 3681
"Where to Find Money in New York", **4826**
Wherewithal: A Guide to Resources for Museums and Historical Societies in New York State, 3375
White Paper on Self-Care, 4903
"Who Funds the Arts?", 2116
Who Knows Who, **1478**
"Who Needs D and O Insurance?", **2398**
Who Owns Information, 4786
"Who Profits from Nonprofits?", **2163**
"Who Speaks for Philanthropy?", 457
"Who Took the Fun Out of Fundraising?", 3735
Whole Arts Directory, **2261**
"Who's Watching the Watchdogs?", **2139**
Who's Who in American Public-Private Partnerships, 503
Who's Who in Fund-Raising, 3669
"Whose Move Is It? A Computer Program Helps SMU Win at the Game of Donor Cultivation", 3918
Why a New Goal for Corporate Giving to Higher Education?, 1456
Why Are Non-Profit Organizations Exempted from Corporate Income Taxation?, 4177
"Why Britain Is Slow to Grasp Ethnic Needs", **1848**
Why Charity? The Case for the Third Sector, **136**
Why Charity: Towards a Rationale for the Third Sector, 2093
"Why College Donors Are Uptight: House-Passed Tax Bill Would Change Rules on Donations and Could Reduce Gifts", 4476
Why Corporations Need to Do More, 1455
"Why Corporations Support Employee Volunteering", **4601**
"Why Do People Make Gifts? Here Are the Main Reasons", 3539
Why Do Universities Have Endowments?, **3371**

TITLE INDEX

"Why Don't We Set Up a Profit-Making Subsidiary?", 2403
Why Establish a Private Foundation?, 865, **866**
"Why Foundations Should Support Advocacy Groups", 555
"Why Foundations Should Support the Projects of Religious Organizations", 702
"Why Give to the Arts", **3578**
"Why Has the Cost of Directors and Officers Liability Insurance Gone through the Ceiling?", 2907
"Why Is Munson a Liberal-Conservative Issue?", **4347**
"Why Not a Program-Related Investment?", 1072
Why People Give, 77
"Why Philanthropy Will Overcome Tax Reform", **4370**
"Why Should the Private Sector Support Public Education?", 582
Why They Give: American Jews and Their Philanthropies, 179
"Why We Need Better Marketing", 2366
The Wichita Experience. Mobilizing Corporate Resources to Meet Community Needs, 1302
Wildlife and the Public Interest: Nonprofit Organizations and Federal Wildlife Policy, 4747
Will Hogg: Texan, 303
Will It Make a Theatre, 2575
"Will the Patient Live?", 4899
"Will the Tax Act Hurt Giving?", 4306
William Henry Welch and the Heroic Age of American Medicine, 155
The William T. Grant Foundation: The First Fifty Years, 1936-1986, 597
Williams-Waterman Fund for the Combat of Dietary Diseases: A History of the Period 1935 through 1955, 1280
A Willingness of Hearts: Volunteerism and the Non-Profit Organization in the American Society, 4526
Wills and Willmakers, 3377
"Wilmer Shields Rich: The First Lady of Organized Foundations", 320
A Window on the World of Philanthropy: A Compilation of Insights, 1973-1983, **134**
"Winds of Change from the West", 4959
Winning Techniques for Athletic Fund Raising, 2983
Winning the Money Game: A Guide to Community-Based Library Fundraising, 3975
"Winning Tickets: Capital Campaign Strategies That Helped Rally Support for Seven Community Colleges", 3293
Winterfare, **2001**
"With Cutbacks in the Air, Grantee Health Monitored", 1124
"With Most of Its Assets Missing, Swanson Fund Faces Uncertain Future", 698
"With $2.2-Billion in Its Till, Getty Aims to Make World a Better Place for Art", 129

Woman's Day Book of Fund Raising, 3007
Women and Economic Independence Conference, 4987
Women and Philanthropy in Nineteenth Century England, **393**
Women and Philanthropy: Past, Present and Future, **91**
Women, Children, and Poverty in America, 4841
Women in Organizations: An Analysis of the Role and Status of Women in American Voluntary Organizations, 2344
"Women in the Eighties: The Future", 4988
Women in the White Collar Non-Profit Sector: The Best Option or the Only Option, 2300
Women in the World, 4842
Women of Color: Building Bridges between Resources and Needs, **852**
Women Volunteering: The Pleasure, Pain, and Politics of Unpaid Work from 1830 to the Present, 4540
Women, Work, and Volunteering, 4546
Women Working: Toward a New Society, 4925
"Women's Funds: A Growing Response to Poverty, Abuse, and Discrimination", 3978
"Women's Funds: A New Movement", **3979**
"Women's Funds in the U.S.", **3980**
Women's Organizations: A National Directory, **2091**
Women's Organizations: A New York City Directory, **2265**
"Word Processing May Promote Better Donor Record Use", 3307
"Work and Work Force Characteristics in the Nonprofit Sector", 2246
Working Conference on Financial Aid to Education, 3170
A Working Guide for Directors of Not-for-Profit Organizations, 2950
Working in Foundations: Career Patterns of Women and Men, **1061**, **1062**
Working Papers of the Subcommittee on the Case Statement for Community Foundations, **667**
A World in Need, Opportunities and Changing Roles for Philanthropy, 1846
The World of Andrew Carnegie, 1865-1901, 192
"The World of Philanthropy in the Eighties", 281
Worldly Goods: The Wealth and Power of the American Catholic Church, the Vatican, and the Men Who Control the Money, 2129
"World's Fastest Fund Raisers", 3984
Worth and Wealth: A Collection of Maxims, Morals and Miscellanies for Merchants and Men of Business, **1506**
"Write on the Money: The Basics of Effective Proposal Writing, from Content to Structure to Length", 4033

"Writing a Proposal: A Conceptual Framework", 4057
"Writing a Winning Grant Proposal", **4045**
Writing on the Job: A Handbook for Business and Government, 4052
"Writing Proposals Grows More Exacting As the Competition for Grants Heats Up", 3996
Writing Winning Proposals, 4017
Written Statements by Interested Individuals and Organizations on Treasury Department Report on Private Foundations Issued on February 2, 1964, Submitted to Committee on Ways and Means, 89th Congress, 1st Session, 4405
Written Statements Submitted by Witnesses Scheduled to Appear before the Committee on Ways and Means at Hearings on the Subject of Tax Reform on February 18-24, 1969, 91st Congress, 1st Session. 5 Vols, 4406
Wyoming Foundations Directory, **681**
Yankee Reformers in the Urban Age: Social Reform in Boston, 1880-1900, **322**
Yardsticks for Corporation Gifts to Community Chests, 1688
Yearbook of American and Canadian Churches, **2187**
Yearbook of New York State Charitable Organizations: Fund-Raising and Expense Information As Reported by Charitable, Civic, Health, Fraternal, and Other Organizations, **2253**
The Yearbook of Philanthropy, 1940-1948. 9 Vols, 256
YMCA Capital Development. Key Planning Steps Leading to a Capital Campaign, 3673
You Can Be a Philanthropist: Ten Painless Ways, 4367
"You Have to Be Rude", **29**
"You Name It, They Do It", 756
"Young Unwed Mothers Learn a Trade", **4992**
"Your Board Members Will Raise Funds Effectively, But They Do Need Your Help", 2932
"Your Family's Financial Future. Impact of New Tax Law: An Interview with Conrad Teitell", 4479
"Your Financial Report: Fact and Fiction", 2085
"Your Introduction to Endowments", 3826
"Your Money: Rules of I.R.S. on Donations", 4325
Your Personal Guide to Marketing a Nonprofit Organization, **2922**
"Your Program Is Worth More Than You Think: An Introduction to Volunteer Program Cost Accountability", 4534
Your Will and What Not to Do about It, 4478
"Your Worst Fears Realized, or What to Do When the Corporation or Foundation Declines Your Proposal", **3532**

TITLE INDEX

Youth Service: A Guidebook for Developing and Operating Effective Programs, **4503**
Youthbook: Models and Resources for Neighborhood Use, 2052
"Zero Based Budgeting Gives You the Big Picture", **2873**
"Zero-Based Goal-Setting for Your Community Campaign", 3940

PART FIVE

FOUNDATION CENTER SERVICES

THE FOUNDATION CENTER COOPERATING COLLECTIONS NETWORK

The Foundation Center is an independent national service organization established by foundations to provide an authoritative source of information on private philanthropic giving. The Center disseminates information on private giving through public service programs, publications and through a national network of library reference collections for free public use. The New York, Washington, DC, Cleveland and San Francisco reference collections operated by The Foundation Center offer a wide variety of services and comprehensive collections of information on foundations and grants. Cooperating Collections are libraries, community foundations and other nonprofit agencies that provide a core collection of Foundation Center publications and a variety of supplementary materials and services in areas useful to grantseekers.

Over 100 of the network members have sets of private foundation information returns (IRS Form 990-PF) for their states or regions which are available for public use. A complete set of U.S. foundation returns can be found at the New York and Washington, DC offices of The Foundation Center. The Cleveland and San Francisco offices contain IRS returns for those foundations in the midwestern and western states, respectively.

Because the collections vary in their hours, materials and services, IT IS RECOMMENDED THAT YOU CALL EACH COLLECTION IN ADVANCE. To check on new locations or current information, call toll-free 1-800-424-9836.

Those collections marked with a bullet (●) have sets of private foundation information returns (IRS Form 990-PF) for their states or regions, available for public reference. Reference collections operated by The Foundation Center are in **boldface.**

ALABAMA

● Birmingham Public Library
2100 Park Place
Birmingham 35203
205-226-3600

Huntsville Public Library
915 Monroe St.
Huntsville 35801
205-532-5940

University of South Alabama
Library Reference Dept.
Mobile 36688
205-460-7025

● Auburn University at
  Montgomery Library
I-85 @ Taylor Rd.
Montgomery 36193-0401
205-271-9649

ALASKA

Juneau Public Library
242 Marine Way
Juneau 99801
907-586-5249

● University of Alaska
Anchorage Library
3211 Providence Drive
Anchorage 99508
907-786-1848

ARIZONA

● Phoenix Public Library
Business & Sciences Dept.
12 East McDowell Road
Phoenix 85257
602-262-4636

● Tucson Public Library
200 South Sixth Avenue
Tucson 85726-7470
602-791-4393

ARKANSAS

● Westark Community College
  Library
5210 Grand Avenue
Fort Smith 72913
501-785-7000

● Central Arkansas Library System
Reference Services
700 Louisiana Street
Little Rock 72201
501-370-5950

CALIFORNIA

● California Community
  Foundation
Funding Information Center
3580 Wilshire Blvd., Suite 1660
Los Angeles 90010
213-413-4042

● Community Foundation for
  Monterey County
420 Pacific Street
Monterey 93940
408-375-9712

California Community
  Foundation
13252 Garden Grove Blvd.
Garden Grove 92643
714-750-7794

Riverside Public Library
3581 7th Street
Riverside 92501
714-782-5201

California State Library
Reference Services, Rm. 309
914 Capital Mall
Sacramento 95667
916-322-4570

● San Diego Community
  Foundation
525 "B" Street, Suite 410
San Diego 92101
619-239-8815

● **The Foundation Center**
312 Sutter Street, Room 312
San Francisco 94108
415-397-0902

● Grantsmanship Resource Center
1762 Technology Dr., Suite 225
San Jose 95110
408-452-8181

● Orange County Community
  Developmental Council
1695 W. MacArthur Blvd.
Costa Mesa 92626
714-540-9293

● Peninsula Community
  Foundation
1204 Burlingame Avenue
Burlingame 94011-0627
415-342-2505

● Santa Barbara Public Library
40 East Anaparnu
Santa Barbara 93102
805-962-7653

Santa Monica Public Library
1343 Sixth Street
Santa Monica 90401-1603
213-451-8859

Tuolumne County Free Library
480 Greenley Rd.
Sonora 95370
209-533-5507

COLORADO

Pikes Peak Library District
20 North Cascade Avenue
Colorado Springs 80901
719-473-2080

● Denver Public Library
Sociology Division
1357 Broadway
Denver 80203
303-571-2190

CONNECTICUT

Danbury Public Library
170 Main Street
Danbury 06810
203-797-4527

● Hartford Public Library
Reference Department
500 Main Street
Hartford 06103
203-293-6000

D.A.T.A.
25 Science Park
Suite 502
New Haven 06511
203-786-5225

DELAWARE

● University of Delaware
Hugh Morris Library
Newark 19717-5267
302-451-2965

DISTRICT OF COLUMBIA

● **The Foundation Center**
1001 Connecticut Avenue, NW
Washington 20036
202-331-1400

FLORIDA

Volusia County Library Center
City Island
Daytona Beach 32014-4484
904-255-3765

● Jacksonville Public Libraries
Business, Science & Documents
122 North Ocean Street
Jacksonville 32206
904-630-2665

● Miami–Dade Public Library
Humanities Department
101 W. Flagler St.
Miami 33130
305-375-2665

● Orange County Library System
101 E. Central Blvd.
Orlando 32801
407-425-4694

Selby Public Library
1001 Boulevard of the Arts
Sarasota 33577
813-951-5501

● Leon County Public Library
Funding Resource Center
1940 North Monroe Street
Tallahassee 32303
904-487-2665

Palm Beach County Community
  Foundation
324 Datura Street, Suite 340
West Palm Beach 33401
407-659-6800

GEORGIA

● Atlanta–Fulton Public Library
Ivan Allen Department
1 Margaret Mitchell Square
Atlanta 30303-1089
404-688-4636

HAWAII

● University of Hawaii
Thomas Hale Hamilton Library
2550 The Mall
Honolulu 96822
808-948-7214

Hawaiian Community
  Foundation
Hawaii Resource Room
212 Merchant Street
Suite 330
Honolulu 96813
808-599-5767

IDAHO

● Boise Public Library
715 S. Capitol Blvd.
Boise 83702
208-384-4466

- Caldwell Public Library
  1010 Dearborn Street
  Caldwell 83605
  208-459-3242

ILLINOIS

Belleville Public Library
121 East Washington Street
Belleville 62220
618-234-0441

DuPage Township
241 Canterbury Lane
Bolingbrook 60439
312-759-1317

- Donors Forum of Chicago
  53 W. Jackson Blvd., Rm. 430
  Chicago 60604
  312-431-0265

- Evanston Public Library
  1703 Orrington Avenue
  Evanston 60201
  312-866-0305

- Sangamon State University
  Library
  Shepherd Road
  Springfield 62794-9243
  217-786-6633

INDIANA

Allen County Public Library
900 Webster Street
Fort Wayne 46802
219-424-7241

Indiana University Northwest
Library
3400 Broadway
Gary 46408
219-980-6580

- Indianapolis–Marion County
  Public Library
  40 East St. Clair Street
  Indianapolis 46206
  317-269-1733

IOWA

- Public Library of Des Moines
  100 Locust Street
  Des Moines 50308
  515-283-4259

KANSAS

- Topeka Public Library
  1515 West Tenth Street
  Topeka 66604
  913-233-2040

- Wichita Public Library
  223 South Main
  Wichita 67202
  316-262-0611

KENTUCKY

Western Kentucky University
Helm-Cravens Library
Bowling Green 42101
502-745-6125

- Louisville Free Public Library
  Fourth and York Streets
  Louisville 40203
  502-561-8600

LOUISIANA

- East Baton Rouge Parish Library
  Centroplex Branch
  120 St. Louis Street
  Baton Rouge 70802
  504-389-4960

- New Orleans Public Library
  Business and Science Division
  219 Loyola Avenue
  New Orleans 70140
  504-596-2583

- Shreve Memorial Library
  424 Texas Street
  Shreveport 71120-1523
  318-226-5894

MAINE

- University of Southern Maine
  Office of Sponsored Research
  246 Deering Ave., Rm. 628
  Portland 04103
  207-780-4871

MARYLAND

- Enoch Pratt Free Library
  Social Science and History
  Department
  400 Cathedral Street
  Baltimore 21201
  301-396-5320

MASSACHUSETTS

- Associated Grantmakers of
  Massachusetts
  294 Washington Street
  Suite 840
  Boston 02108
  617-426-2608

- Boston Public Library
  666 Boylston St.
  Boston 02117
  617-536-5400

- Western Massachusetts Funding
  Resource Center
  Campaign for Human
  Development
  73 Chestnut Street
  Springfield 01103
  413-732-3175

- Grants Resource Center
  Worcester Public Library
  Salem Square
  Worcester 01608
  508-799-1655

MICHIGAN

- Alpena County Library
  211 North First Avenue
  Alpena 49707
  517-356-6188

University of Michigan–Ann
Arbor
209 Hatcher Graduate Library
Ann Arbor 48109-1205
313-764-1149

- Henry Ford Centennial Library
  16301 Michigan Avenue
  Dearborn 48126
  313-943-2337

- Wayne State University
  Purdy-Kresge Library
  Detroit 48202
  313-577-4040

- Michigan State University
  Libraries
  Reference Library
  East Lansing 48824-1048
  517-353-8818

- Farmington Community Library
  32737 West 12 Mile Road
  Farmington Hills 48018
  313-553-0300

- University of Michigan–Flint
  Library
  Reference Department
  Flint 48502-2186
  313-762-3408

- Grand Rapids Public Library
  Business Dept.
  60 Library Plaza
  Grand Rapids 49503
  616-456-3600

- Michigan Technological
  University Library
  Highway U.S. 41
  Houghton 49931
  906-487-2507

- Sault Ste. Marie Area
  Public Schools
  Office of Compensatory
  Education
  460 W. Spruce St.
  Sault Ste. Marie 49783-1874
  906-635-6619

MINNESOTA

- Duluth Public Library
  520 W. Superior Street
  Duluth 55802
  218-723-3802

- Southwest State University
  Library
  Marshall 56258
  507-537-7278

- Minneapolis Public Library
  Sociology Department
  300 Nicollet Mall
  Minneapolis 55401
  612-372-6555

Rochester Public Library
11 First Street, SE
Rochester 55902-3743
507-285-8002

St. Paul Public Library
90 West Fourth Street
Saint Paul 55102
612-292-6307

MISSISSIPPI

Jackson Metropolitan Library
301 North State Street
Jackson 39212
601-968-5803

MISSOURI

- Clearinghouse for Midcontinent
  Foundations
  Univ. of Missouri
  Law School, Suite 1-300
  52nd Street and Oak
  Kansas City 64113-0680
  816-276-1176

- Kansas City Public Library
  311 East 12th Street
  Kansas City 64106
  816-221-9650

- Metropolitan Association for
  Philanthropy, Inc.
  5585 Pershing Avenue
  Suite 150
  St. Louis 63112
  314-361-3900

- Springfield–Greene County
  Library
  397 East Central Street
  Springfield 65801
  417-866-4636

MONTANA

- Eastern Montana College Library
  1500 N. 30th Street
  Billings 59101-0298
  406-657-1662

- Montana State Library
  Reference Department
  1515 E. 6th Avenue
  Helena 59620
  406-444-3004

NEBRASKA

- University of Nebraska
  106 Love Library
  14th & R Streets
  Lincoln 68588-0410
  402-472-2848

- W. Dale Clark Library
  Social Sciences Department
  215 South 15th Street
  Omaha 68102
  402-444-4826

NEVADA

- Las Vegas–Clark County Library
  District
  1401 East Flamingo Road
  Las Vegas 89119-6160
  702-733-7810

- Washoe County Library
  301 South Center Street
  Reno 89501
  702-785-4012

NEW HAMPSHIRE

- New Hampshire Charitable Fund
  One South Street
  Concord 03301
  603-225-6641

Littleton Public Library
109 Main Street
Littleton 03561
603-444-5741

NEW JERSEY

Cumberland County Library
800 E. Commerce Street
Bridgeton 08302-2295
609-453-2210

The Support Center
17 Academy Street, Suite 1101
Newark 07102
201-643-5774

County College of Morris
Masten Learning Resource
 Center
Route 10 and Center Grove Rd.
Randolph 07869
201-361-5000 ext. 470

• New Jersey State Library
Governmental Reference
185 West State Street
Trenton 08625
609-292-6220

NEW MEXICO

Albuquerque Community
 Foundation
6400 Uptown Boulevard N.E.
Suite 500-W
Albuquerque 87105
505-883-6240

• New Mexico State Library
325 Don Gaspar Street
Santa Fe 87505
505-827-3824

NEW YORK

• New York State Library
Cultural Education Center
Humanities Section
Empire State Plaza
Albany 12230
518-474-5161

New York Public Library
Bronx Reference Center
2556 Bainbridge Avenue
Bronx 10458
212-220-6575

Brooklyn in Touch
One Hanson Place
Room 2504
Brooklyn 11243
718-230-3200

• Buffalo and Erie County Public
 Library
Lafayette Square
Buffalo 14202
716-846-7103

Huntington Public Library
338 Main Street
Huntington 11743
516-427-5165

• Levittown Public Library
One Bluegrass Lane
Levittown 11756
516-731-5720

• **The Foundation Center**
79 Fifth Avenue
New York 10003
212-620-4230

SUNY/College at Old Westbury
 Library
223 Store Hill Road
Old Westbury 11568
516-876-3156

• Plattsburgh Public Library
15 Oak Street
Plattsburgh 12901
518-563-0921

Adriance Memorial Library
93 Market Street
Poughkeepsie 12601
914-485-3445

Queens Borough Public Library
89-11 Merrick Boulevard
Jamaica 11432
718-990-0700

• Rochester Public Library
Business Division
115 South Avenue
Rochester 14604
716-428-7328

Staten Island Council on the Arts
One Edgewater Plaza, Rm. 311
Staten Island 10305
718-447-4485

• Onondaga County Public Library
 at the Galleries
447 S. Salina Street
Syracuse 13202-2494
315-448-4636

• White Plains Public Library
100 Martine Avenue
White Plains 10601
914-682-4480

• Suffolk Cooperative Library
 System
627 North Sunrise Service Road
Bellport 11713
516-286-1600

NORTH CAROLINA

Asheville-Buncomb Technical
 College
Learning Resource Center
340 Victoria Rd.
Asheville 28801
704-254-1921 x300

• The Duke Endowment
200 S. Tryon Street, Ste. 1100
Charlotte 28202
704-376-0291

Durham County Library
300 N. Roxboro Street
Durham 27701
919-683-2626

• North Carolina State Library
109 East Jones Street
Raleigh 27611
919-733-3270

• The Winston-Salem Foundation
229 First Union Bank Building
Winston-Salem 27101
919-725-2382

NORTH DAKOTA

Western Dakota Grants Resource
 Center
Bismarck State Community
 College
Bismarck 58501
701-224-5400

• The Library
North Dakota State University
Fargo 58105
701-237-8886

OHIO

• Public Library of Cincinnati and
 Hamilton County
Education Department
800 Vine Street
Cincinnati 45202-2071
513-369-6940

• **The Foundation Center**
Kent H. Smith Library
1442 Hanna Building
Cleveland 44115
216-861-1933

The Public Library of Columbus
 and Franklin County
96 S. Grant Avenue
Columbus 43215
614-645-2275

• Dayton and Montgomery County
 Public Library
Grants Information Center
215 E. Third Street
Dayton 45402-2103
513-227-9500 ext. 211

• Toledo–Lucas County Public
 Library
Social Science Department
325 Michigan Street
Toledo 43623-1614
419-259-5245

Ohio University–Zanesville
Community Education and
 Development
1425 Newark Road
Zanesville 43701
614-453-0762

Stark County District Library
715 Market Avenue North
Canton 44702-1080
216-452-0665

OKLAHOMA

• Oklahoma City University
 Library
2501 North Blackwelder
Oklahoma City 73106
405-521-5072

• Tulsa City–County Library
 System
400 Civic Center
Tulsa 74103
918-596-7944

OREGON

• Multnomah County Library
Government Documents Room
801 S.W. Tenth Avenue
Portland 97205
503-223-7201

Oregon State Library
State Library Building
Salem 97310
503-378-4274

Pacific Non-Profit Network
Grantsmanship Resource Library
33 N. Central, Ste. 211
Medford 97501
503-779-6044

PENNSYLVANIA

Northampton Community College
Learning Resources Center
3835 Green Pond Road
Bethlehem 18017
215-861-5360

• Erie County Public Library
3 South Perry Square
Erie 16501
814-451-6927

• Dauphin County Library System
101 Walnut Street
Harrisburg 17101
717-234-4961

Lancaster County Public Library
125 North Duke Street
Lancaster 17602
717-394-2651

• The Free Library of Philadelphia
Logan Square
Philadelphia 19103
215-686-5423

• University of Pittsburgh
Hillman Library
Pittsburgh 15260
412-648-7722

Economic Development Council
 of Northeastern Pennsylvania
1151 Oak Street
Pittston 18640
717-655-5581

RHODE ISLAND

• Providence Public Library
Reference Department
150 Empire Street
Providence 02903
401-521-7722

SOUTH CAROLINA

• Charleston County Library
404 King Street
Charleston 29403
803-723-1645

• South Carolina State Library
Reference Department
1500 Senate Street
Columbia 29211
803-734-8666

SOUTH DAKOTA

• South Dakota State Library
800 Governors Drive
Pierre 57501-2294
605-773-3131
800-592-1841 (SD residents)

Sioux Falls Area Foundation
321 S. Phillips Avenue, Rm. 404
Sioux Falls 57102-0781
605-336-7055

TENNESSEE

• Knoxville–Knox County Public
 Library
500 West Church Avenue
Knoxville 37902
615-544-5750

• Memphis & Shelby County
 Public Library
1850 Peabody Avenue
Memphis 38104
901-725-8876

• Public Library of Nashville and
 Davidson County
8th Ave. N. and Union St.
Nashville 37211
615-259-6256

TEXAS

Amarillo Area Foundation
70 1st National Place I
800 S. Fillmore
Amarillo 79101
806-376-4521

• Hogg Foundation for Mental
Health
University of Texas
Austin 78713
512-471-5041

Community Foundation of Abilene
Funding Information Library
708 NCNB Bldg.
402 Cypress
Abilene 79601
915-676-3883

• Corpus Christi State University
Library
6300 Ocean Drive
Corpus Christi 78412
512-994-2608

• El Paso Community Foundation
201 E. Main
El Paso 79901
915-533-4020

• Texas Christian University
Library
Funding Information Center
Ft. Worth 76129
817-921-7664

• Houston Public Library
Bibliographic Information Center
500 McKinney Avenue
Houston 77002
713-236-1313

• Lubbock Area Foundation
502 Commerce Bank Building
Lubbock 79401
806-762-8061

• Funding Information Library
507 Brooklyn
San Antonio 78215
512-227-4333

• Dallas Public Library
Grants Information Service
1515 Young Street
Dallas 75201
214-670-1487

• Pan American University
Learning Resource Center
1201 W. University Drive
Edinburg 78539
512-381-3304

UTAH

• Salt Lake City Public Library
Business and Science Dept.
209 East Fifth South
Salt Lake City 84111
801-363-5733

VERMONT

• Vermont Dept. of Libraries
Reference Services
109 State Street
Montpelier 05602
802-828-3268

VIRGINIA

• Hampton Public Library
Grants Resources Collection
4207 Victoria Blvd.
Hampton 23669
804-727-1154

• Richmond Public Library
Business, Science, & Technology
101 East Franklin Street
Richmond 23219
804-780-8223

Roanoke City Public Library
System
Central Library
706 S. Jefferson Street
Roanoke 24014
703-981-2477

WASHINGTON

• Seattle Public Library
1000 Fourth Avenue
Seattle 98104
206-386-4620

• Spokane Public Library
Funding Information Center
West 906 Main Avenue
Spokane 99201
509-838-3364

WEST VIRGINIA

• Kanawha County Public Library
123 Capital Street
Charleston 25304
304-343-4646

WISCONSIN

• Marquette University
Memorial Library
1415 West Wisconsin Avenue
Milwaukee 53233
414-224-1515

• University of Wisconsin–Madison
Memorial Library
728 State Street
Madison 53706
608-262-3242

WYOMING

• Laramie County Community
College Library
1400 East College Drive
Cheyenne 82007-3299
307-778-1205

AUSTRALIA

ANZ Executors & Trustees Co.
Ltd.
91 William St., 7th floor
Melbourne VIC 3000
648-5768

CANADA

Canadian Centre for
Philanthropy
74 Victoria Street, Suite 920
Toronto, Ontario M5C 2A5
416-368-1138

ENGLAND

Charities Aid Foundation
18 Doughty Street
London WC1N 2PL
01-831-7798

JAPAN

Foundation Center Library
of Japan
Elements Shinjuku Bldg. 3F
2-1-14 Shinjuku, Shinjuku-ku
Tokyo 160
03-350-1857

MEXICO

Biblioteca Benjamin Franklin
American Embassy, USICA
Londres 16
Mexico City 6, D.F. 06600
905-211-0042

PUERTO RICO

University of Puerto Rico
Ponce Technological College
Library
Box 7186
Ponce 00732
809-844-4150

Universidad Del Sagrado
Corazon
M.M.T. Guevarra Library
Correo Calle Loiza
Santurce 00914
809-728-1515 ext. 357

U.S. VIRGIN ISLANDS

University of the Virgin Islands
Paiewonsky Library
Charlotte Amalie
St. Thomas 00802
809-776-9200 ext. 1487

THE FOUNDATION CENTER AFFILIATES PROGRAM

As participants in the cooperating collection network, affiliates are libraries or nonprofit agencies that provide fundraising information or other funding-related technical assistance in their communities. Affiliates agree to provide free public access to a basic collection of Foundation Center publications during a regular schedule of hours, offering free funding research guidance to all visitors. Many also provide a variety of special services for local nonprofit organizations using staff or volunteers to prepare special materials, organize workshops, or conduct library orientations.

The affiliates program began in 1981 to continue the expansion of The Foundation Center's funding information network of 90 funding information collections. Since its inception, over 80 organizations have been designated Foundation Center affiliates. Affiliate collections have been established in a wide variety of host organizations, including public and university libraries, technical assistance agencies, and community foundations. The Center maintains strong ties with its affiliates through regular news bulletins, the provision of supporting materials, the sponsorship of regional meetings, and by referring the many nonprofits that call or write to The Foundation Center to the affiliate nearest them.

The Foundation Center welcomes inquiries from agencies interested in providing this type of public information service. If you are interested in establishing a funding information library for the use of nonprofit agencies in your area or in learning more about the program, we would like to hear from you.

The first step is for the director of your organization to write, explaining why the collection is needed and how the responsibilities of network participation would be met. The Center will contact you to review the details of the relationship. If your agency is designated an affiliate, you will then be entitled to purchase a core collection of Foundation Center materials at a 20% discount rate (annual cost of approx. $500). Center staff will be happy to assist in identifying supplementary titles for funding information libraries. A core collection, which must be maintained from year to year, consists of current editions to the following publications (subject to change):

Corporate Giving Directory
The Foundation Directory
The Foundation Directory Supplement
The Foundation Grants Index
The Foundation Grants Index Bimonthly

Source Book Profiles
The National Data Book
Foundation Fundamentals
Foundation Grants to Individuals

For more information, please write to: Anne J. Borland, The Foundation Center, 79 Fifth Avenue, New York, NY 10003.

Publications and Services of the Foundation Center

The Foundation Center is a national service organization founded and supported by foundations to provide a single authoritative source of information on foundation giving. The Center's programs are designed to help grantseekers as they begin to select those foundations which may be most interested in their projects from the over 27,000 active U.S. foundations. Among its primary activities toward this end are publishing reference books on foundations and foundation grants, and disseminating information on foundations through a nationwide public service program.

Publications of the Foundation Center are the primary working tools of every serious grantseeker. They are also used by grantmakers, scholars, journalists, regulators, and legislators—in short, everyone seeking any type of factual information on foundation philanthropy. All private foundations actively engaged in grantmaking, regardless of size or geographic location, are included in one or more of the Center's publications. The publications are of three kinds: directories which describe specific foundations, characterizing their program interests and providing fiscal and personnel data; grants indexes which list and classify by subject recent foundation awards; and guides, brochures, monographs, and bibliographies which introduce the reader to funding research, elements of proposal writing, and nonprofit management issues.

Foundation Center publications may be ordered from the Foundation Center, 79 Fifth Avenue, New York, NY 10003. For more information about any aspect of the Center's program or for the name of the Center's library collection nearest you, call toll-free (800) 424-9836.

THE FOUNDATION DIRECTORY, 11th EDITION

The Foundation Directory has been widely known and respected in the field for 25 years. It includes the latest information on all foundations whose assets exceed $1 million or whose annual grant total is $100,000 or more. The new 11th Edition is the biggest ever: 5,148 foundations are included, 983 of which are new to this edition, and 781 of which are corporate foundations. *Directory* foundations hold over $89 billion in assets and award $5.3 billion in grants annually, accounting for 92% of all U.S. foundation dollars awarded in 1985 and 1986.

Each *Directory* entry now contains more precise information on application procedures, giving limitations, types of support awarded, the publications of each foundation, and foundation staff—all this in addition to such vital data as the grantmakers' giving interests, financial data, grant amounts, addresses and telephone numbers. The Foundation Center works closely with foundations to ensure the accuracy and timeliness of the information provided.

The *Directory* includes indexes by foundation name; subject areas of interest; names of donors, trustees, and officers; geographic location; and the types of support awarded. Also included are analyses of the foundation community by geography, asset and grant size, different types of foundations, trends in foundation establishment, and information on the effects of inflation on the field since 1975.

11th Edition, Oct. 1987
ISBN 0-87954-199-7 / $85 / 1001 pages

THE FOUNDATION DIRECTORY SUPPLEMENT

Updates detailing significant changes in the entries for over 2,000 of the *Directory* foundations are listed in **The Foundation Directory Supplement**, Edition 11. The *Supplement* is published in the interim year of *The Foundation Directory*'s two year cycle, and highlights foundation changes in bold type for quick reference.

Foundation Directory Supplement, 11th Edition / Oct. 1988
ISBN 0-87954-242-X / $50 / 477 pages

COMSEARCH PRINTOUTS

This popular series of computer-produced guides to foundation giving derived from the Foundation Center Database is now issued in four separate categories:

COMSEARCH: Broad Topics

This series indexes and analyzes recent foundation grants in 27 broad subject categories. Each listing includes all grants in the particular subject area reported to the Foundation Center during the preceding year, along with an index listing name and geographic location of organizations which have received grants, a geographic index arranged by state of the recipient organization, and a key word index listing descriptive words and phrases which link foundation giving interests with your organization's field. Write for the complete listing of 27 Broad Topics.

Series published annually in July. $40 each

COMSEARCH: Subjects

This series includes 31 specially focused subject listings of grants reported to the Foundation Center during the preceding year. Listings are arranged by the state where the foundation is located and then by foundation name, and include complete information on the name and location of the grant recipient, the amount awarded, and the purpose of the grant. *COMSEARCH: Subjects* may be purchased as a complete set on microfiche or individually by particular subject area of interest in paper or microfiche form. Write for the complete listing of 31 subject categories.

Series published annually in July. $125 microfiche set; $20 per subject on paper; $8 per subject on microfiche

COMSEARCH: Geographics

This series provides customized listings of grants received by organizations in two cities, eleven states, and seven regions. These listings make it easy to see which major foundations have awarded grants in your area, to which nonprofit organizations, and what each grant was intended to accomplish. Write for the complete listing of geographic locations.

Series published annually in July. $35 each

COMSEARCH: Special Topics

These are three of the most frequently requested special listings from the Center's computer databases. The three special listings are:
- The 1,000 Largest U.S. Foundations by Asset Size
- The 1,000 Largest U.S. Foundations by Annual Grants Total
- The over 2,000 Operating Foundations which Administer Their Own Projects or Programs

Series published annually in July. $20 each

THE FOUNDATION GRANTS INDEX ANNUAL, 17TH EDITION

The Foundation Grants Index Annual lists the grants of $5,000 or more awarded to nonprofit organizations by 465 foundations. It is the most thorough subject index of actual grants of major U.S. foundations available, and includes the top 100 grantmakers.

The 17th Edition is the largest annual *Index* ever, with an expanded analytical introduction, an improved and enlarged subject index, and more grant descriptions than ever before—more than 43,000 grants of $5,000 or more made to nonprofit organizations reported to the Center in 1986/1987. The volume is arranged alphabetically by state, then by foundation name. Each entry includes the amount and date of the grant, name and location of the recipient, a description of the grant, and any known limitations of the foundation's giving pattern. The grants are indexed by subject and geographic location, by the names of the recipient organizations, and by a multitude of key words describing all aspects of each grant. The grants total over $2 billion and represent about 45% of all foundation giving, making this the most comprehensive grants compilation available.

The Foundation Grants Index Annual is the reference used by educators, librarians, fundraisers, medical personnel, and other professionals interested in learning about foundation grants. It shows you what kind of organizations and programs the major foundations have been funding.

17th Edition, July 1988 / ISBN 0-87954-241-1 / $55 / 1032 pages

THE FOUNDATION GRANTS INDEX BIMONTHLY

This unique subscription service keeps your fundraising program up-to-date, bringing you important new information on foundation funding every other month. Each issue of *The Foundation Grants Index Bimonthly* brings you descriptions of over 2,000 recent foundation grants, arranged by state and indexed by subjects and recipients. This enables you to zero in on grants made in your subject area within your geographic region. You can use the *Bimonthly* to target potential sources of funding for medical schools in Washington, D.C., for example, modern dance troupes in New York, or any other combination of factors.

The *Bimonthly* also contains updates on grantmakers, noting changes in foundation address, personnel, program interests, and application procedures. Also included is a list of grantmakers' publications—annual reports, information brochures, grants lists, and newsletters. *The Foundation Grants Index Bimonthly* is a trusted current-awareness tool used by professional fundraisers.

Annual subscription $36 / 6 issues ISSN 0735-2522

SOURCE BOOK PROFILES

Source Book Profiles is an annual subscription service offering detailed descriptions of the 1,000 largest foundations, analyzing giving patterns by subject area, type of support, and type of recipient. The service operates on a two-year publishing cycle, with each one-year series covering 500 foundations. Each quarterly installment includes 125 new profiles as well as information on changes occurring in foundations profiled earlier in the year, including revised information on address, telephone, personnel, and program interests. Also included is a revised cumulative set of indexes to all 1,000 foundations covered in the two-year cycle by name, subject interest, type of grants awarded, and city and state location or concentration of giving.

1989 Subscription (500 Profiles) / $295 / ISBN 0-87954-238-1
1988 Cumulative Volume (500 Profiles) / $295 / ISBN 0-87954-235-7
1988–1989 Set (1000 Profiles) / $530

CORPORATE FOUNDATION PROFILES, 5TH EDITION

This newly updated volume includes comprehensive information on corporate direct giving programs and company-sponsored foundations. A total of 771 grantmakers with assets of $1 million or annual giving of $100,000 or more are listed with full subject, types of support, and geographic indexes. Detailed profiles of the largest corporate foundations and timely information on foundation policies, guidelines, representative grants, and application procedures are included in the listing. Financial data provides a summary of the size and grant-making capacity of each foundation and contains a list of assets, gifts or contributions, grants paid, operating programs, expenditures, scholarships, and loans.

5th Edition / Feb. 1988 / ISBN 0-87954-237-3 / $75 / 688 pages

DIRECTORY OF NEW AND EMERGING FOUNDATIONS

The *Directory of New and Emerging Foundations* provides complete data on America's top new funding resources. The product of a year's research by the editors of *The Foundation Directory,* this essential volume describes 768 major new funders in one convenient source. Included are vital facts on close to 300 newly-formed foundations—all foundations meeting the *Foundation Directory* criteria of holding assets of $1 million or more or awarding $100,000 or more annually. Also included are over 450 new-growth foundations whose recent increases in funding capabilities meet the criteria for inclusion in this volume. Five time-saving indexes help fundraisers to identify new foundations quickly according to their subject interests, foundation name, geographic area, types of support provided, and names of donors, officers and trustees.

November 1988 / ISBN 0-87954-282-9 / $75 / 126 pages

NEW YORK STATE FOUNDATIONS: A Comprehensive Directory

New York State Foundations offers fundraisers, for the first time, complete coverage of independent, corporate and community foundations throughout New York State—all in one comprehensive source. This information-packed volume will help fundraisers to identify the giving interests and funding policies of this very important segment of the foundation world—the over 4,500 foundations which, combined, hold assets of $26 billion and award $1.4 billion annually to thousands of nonprofit organizations throughout New York State. Fundraisers will find carefully researched data on every known New York foundation, small and large, with funding policies that cover a broad range of program areas. Every foundation entry in this directory has been drawn from the most current sources of information available on New York-based foundations, including IRS 990-PF foundation tax returns and, in many cases, foundations themselves. Along with over 4,500 entries, are complete or sample grants lists for over 3,000 foundations; convenient arrangement of foundations by county of origin; close to 100 grantmakers outside of New York State which fund nonprofits in New York State; and critical foundation facts to help fundraisers pinpoint potential funders. Five time-saving indexes offer quick access to foundations according to their fields of interest; types of support awarded; city and county; names of donors, officers, and trustees; and foundation names.

December 1988 / ISBN 0-87954-245-4 / $150 / 855 pages

THE NATIONAL GUIDE TO FUNDING IN AGING

This comprehensive reference is the result of a unique collaborative effort between the Foundation Center, Long Island University, and the Nassau County, New York, Department of Senior Citizen Affairs. Carefully researched, up-to-date, and truly comprehensive, *The National Guide to Funding in Aging* is the only funding tool to cover all public and private sources of funding support and technical assistance for programs for the aging. Areas of support categorized are: federal funding programs, with detailed profiles of 99 funding programs in 15 areas of service; state government funding programs, including programs and up-to-date listings for all 50 states and U.S. territories; foundations, covering 369 private and community grantmakers with an expressed interest in the field of the aging, *plus* a complete list of all grants reported to the Foundation Center for aging in 1985; and *Private* Organizations, with 78 profiles of academic, religious, and service agencies offering funding and technical aid.

January 1987 / ISBN 0-87954-191-1 / $35 / 280 pages

THE NATIONAL GUIDE TO FOUNDATION FUNDING IN HEALTH

For the first time, those seeking foundation support or tracking health giving patterns can have immediate access to information on the top health funders in the nation in one convenient source. The *National Guide to Foundation Funding in Health* contains essential facts on more than 2,000 foundations which have a history of awarding grant dollars to hospitals, universities, research institutes, community-based agencies, and national health associations for a broad range of health-related programs and services. With competition on the rise for the funding of crucial health programs, fundraisers need the best information available about foundations in order to direct their proposals to appropriate funders. Included in this volume is a wealth of information on the programs and policies of more than 2,000 health funders, plus additional information on leading grantmakers who award in health—including actual grants lists. This all-in-one source of essential foundation data includes facts on foundation program interests, contact persons, application guidelines, listings of board members, and much more. And, three indexes help fundraisers find foundation entries easily according to their state, subject interest, or foundation name. A useful bibliography of publications on health issues and philanthropic initiatives in the field is included as a guide to further study.

December 1988 / ISBN 0-87954-247-0 / $95 / 603 pages

ALCOHOL AND DRUG ABUSE FUNDING: An Analysis of Foundation Grants 1983–1987

This new report provides an authoritative study of independent, corporate, and community foundation grants awarded between 1983–1987 for drug and alcohol abuse programs. The study presents the complete picture of private funding, as it examines the historical background, present status, and future directions of grantmaking in this critical field. Designed for foundation policymakers, grantseekers, and researchers in the fields of health care and prevention, education, and social service.

March 1988 / $40

AIDS FUNDING: A Guide to Giving by Foundations and Charitable Organizations

In the summer of 1987, the Foundation Center surveyed over 500 foundations and discovered 85 funders which had awarded more than 250 grants totaling over $18 million in AIDS-related grants. In this newly updated report on AIDS funding, our researchers have uncovered data on 72 additional foundations with AIDS-related programs and services for a total of nearly 600 grants—a figure up 50% from our 1987 report. In addition to these foundations, public foundations, and an analysis of AIDS grantmaking by charitable organizations outside of the U.S. have been included for the first time. Fundraisers seeking information on foundations awarding grants in this area will find a wealth of information on grantmakers' interests, purposes, and limitations, plus detailed information on the hundreds of AIDS grants awarded.

November 1988 / ISBN 0-87954-243-8 / $35 / 133 pages

FOUNDATION GRANTS TO INDIVIDUALS, 6TH EDITION

The only publication devoted entirely to specialized foundation grant opportunities for qualified individual applicants. The 6th Edition provides full descriptions of the programs specifically designated for individuals of over 1,200 foundations. Entries also include foundation addresses and telephone numbers, financial data, giving limitations, and application guidelines. This volume can save individuals seeking grants countless hours of research.

July 1988 / ISBN 0-87954-244-6 / $24 / 360 pages

AMERICA'S VOLUNTARY SPIRIT: A Book of Readings

In this thoughtful collection, Brian O'Connell, President of INDEPENDENT SECTOR, brings together 45 selections which celebrate and examine the richness and variety of America's unique voluntary sector. O'Connell researched nearly 1,000 selections spanning over 300 years of writing to identify those speeches, articles, chapters, and papers which best define and characterize the roles that philanthropy and voluntary action play in our society. Contributors as diverse as de Tocqueville, and John D. Rockefeller, Thoreau, and Max Lerner, Erma Bombeck, and Vernon Jordan are unified in a common examination of this unique dimension of American life. The anthology includes a bibliography of over 500 important writings and a detailed subject index.

October 1983 / ISBN 0-87954-079-6 (hardcover) / $19.95
SBN 0-87954-081-8 (softcover) / $14.95

PHILANTHROPY IN AN AGE OF TRANSITION

The Essays of Alan Pifer

This is a collection of essays by one of the most respected and well-known individuals in philanthropy. In these essays, Alan Pifer analyzes issues of great concern to all Americans; the responsibilities of higher education, charitable tax deductions, women in the work force, the financial straits of the nonprofit sector, the changing age composition of the American population, bilingual education, the progress of blacks, and more. The essays have been collected from the annual reports of Carnegie Corporation, from 1966-82, one of the most turbulent periods of social change in American history.

Alan Pifer is President Emeritus of Carnegie Corporation of New York where he was President for over seventeen years.

April 1984 / ISBN 0-87954-104-0 / $12.50 / 270 pages

THE BOARD MEMBER'S BOOK

by Brian O'Connell, President, INDEPENDENT SECTOR

Based on his extensive experience working with and on the boards of voluntary organizations, Brian O'Connell has developed this practical guide to the essential functions of voluntary boards. O'Connell offers practical advice on how to be a more effective board member and how board members can help their organizations make a difference. This is an invaluable instructional and inspirational tool for anyone who works on or with a voluntary board. Includes an extensive reading list.

May 1985 / ISBN 0-87954-133-4 / $16.95 / 208 pages

MANAGING FOR PROFIT IN THE NONPROFIT WORLD

by Paul B. Firstenberg

How can service-oriented nonprofits expand their revenue bases? In this title in our series on nonprofit management, author Paul B. Firstenberg shares his view that a vital nonprofit is an entrepreneurial nonprofit. Drawing upon his 14 years of experience as a professional in the nonprofit sector—at the Ford Foundation, Princeton, Tulane, and Yale Universities, and Children's Television Workshop—as well as his extensive for-profit experience, Firstenberg outlines innovative ways in which nonprofit managers can utilize the same state-of-the-art mangement techniques as the most successful for-profit enterprises.

September 1986 / ISBN 0-87954-159-8 / $19.95 / 253 pages

SECURING YOUR ORGANIZATION'S FUTURE: A Complete Guide to Fundraising Strategies

by Michael Seltzer

Michael Seltzer, a well-known pioneer in the field of nonprofit management, uses compelling case studies and bottom-line facts to demonstrate how fundraisers—whether beginners or seasoned pros—can help their nonprofit organizations achieve long-term financial well-being. Seltzer uses a step-by-step approach to guide fundraisers through the world of money and shows how to build a network of support from among the wide variety of funding sources available today. Seltzer's work is supplemented with easy-to-follow worksheets and an extensive bibliography of selected readings and resource organizations. Highly recommended for use as a text in nonprofit management programs at colleges and universities.

February 1987 / ISBN 0-87954-190-3 / $19.95 / 52 pages

THE NONPROFIT ENTREPRENEUR: Creating Ventures to Earn Income

Edited by Edward Skloot

Nonprofit consultant and entrepreneur Edward Skloot, in a well-organized topic-by-topic analytical approach to nonprofit venturing, demonstrates how nonprofits can launch successful earned income enterprises without compromising their missions. Skloot has compiled a collection of writings by the nation's top practitioners and advisors in nonprofit enterprise. Topics covered include legal issues, marketing techniques, business planning, avoiding the pitfalls of venturing for smaller nonprofits, and a special section on museums and their retail operations.

March 1988 / ISBN 0-87954-239-X / $19.95 / 170 pages

WORKING IN FOUNDATIONS: Career Patterns of Women and Men

By Teresa Jean Odendahl, Elizabeth Trocolli Boris, and Arlene Kaplan Daniels

This publication is the result of a groundbreaking study of foundation career paths of women and men undertaken by Women and Foundations/Corporate Philanthropy with major funding from the Russell Sage Foundation. This book offers a detailed picture of the roles and responsibilities of foundation staff members, employment opportunities in philanthropy, and the management styles and grantmaking processes within foundations.

April 1985 / ISBN 0-87954-134-2 / $12.95 / 115 pages

FOUNDATION FUNDAMENTALS: A Guide for Grantseekers

By Patricia Read

This comprehensive, easy-to-read guidebook presents the facts you need to understand the world of foundations, and to identify foundation funding sources for your organization. Over 45 illustrations take you step-by-step through the funding research process, and worksheets and checklists are provided to help you get started in your search for funding. Comprehensive bibliographies and detailed research examples are also supplied.

Revised edition, September 1986/ISBN 0-87954-100-8/ $9.95 / 239 pages

PROMOTING ISSUES AND IDEAS: A Guide to Public Relations for Nonprofit Organizations

by Public Interest, Public Relations, Inc. (PIPR)

PIPR, specialists in promoting the issues and ideas of nonprofit groups, present proven strategies which will put your organization on the map and attract the interest of the people you wish to influence and inform. Included are the "nuts-and-bolts" of advertising, publicity, speechmaking, lobbying, and special events; how to write and produce informational literature that leaps off the page; public relations on a shoestring budget; how to plan and evaluate "pr" efforts, and the use of new communication technologies.

March 1987 / ISBN 0-87954-192-X / $19.95 / 183 pages

AMERICA'S WEALTHY AND THE FUTURE OF FOUNDATIONS

Edited by Teresa J. Odendahl
Co-sponsored by the Council on Foundations and the Yale University Program on Non-Profit Organizations

Recent studies indicate that the "big foundations" with

giant assets and high public profiles are declining in popularity as charitable vehicles of the rich. *America's Wealthy* poses the compelling question: What impact will the declining birthrate of "big foundations" have on the future of philanthropy and the social programs it supports? It also takes us behind the scenes for a firsthand look at the culture of the wealthy and reveals a complex set of attitudes, motivations, economic forces, and policy regulations that offer insight into how and why America's wealthy commit their private resources for the public good. A must-read for all concerned with philanthropy in America.

March 1987 / ISBN 0-87954-194-6 / $24.95 / 325 pages—paperbound
ISBN 0-87954-197-0 / $34.95—hardbound

PHILANTHROPY IN ACTION

by Brian O'Connell, President, INDEPENDENT SECTOR

Goddard's rocketry research. The suffrage and civil rights movements. Salk's polio vaccine. Historic Williamsburg. *Philanthropy in Action* tells the fascinating stories of hundreds of grants which have made a difference, revealing the history, role, and impact of philanthropy in our society. O'Connell captures the remarkable relationships between donors and grantees as he presents philanthropy according to nine roles, including discovering new frontiers of knowledge, supporting and encouraging excellence, relieving human misery, and making communities a better place to live. The stories of the invaluable contributions made by community foundations, cooperative benevolence associations, and corporate giving programs are also narrated. Lively, entertaining, and informative, *Philanthropy in Action* is both an essential resource tool for students, teachers, writers, and scholars of philanthropy, and a collection of great stories, masterfully told.

September 1987 / ISBN 0-87954-231-4 / $19.95 / 337 pages—paperbound
ISBN 0-87954-230-6 / $24.95—hardbound

PHILANTHROPY AND VOLUNTARISM: An Annotated Bibliography

by Daphne N. Layton
for the Association of American Colleges

Finally, a comprehensive bibliography on philanthropy and voluntarism to aid students, scholars, and the general public in understanding the field. All of the best and most important works can be found here, including over 1,600 books and articles which analyze aspects of the philanthrophic tradition in the U.S. and abroad.

Among these are 250 extensively annotated scholarly works particularly useful as texts or background reading for undergraduate study and research in philanthropy.

June 1987 / ISBN 0-87954-198-9 / $18.95 / 308 pages

MAPPING THE THIRD SECTOR: Voluntarism in a Changing Social Economy

by Jon Van Til

Over 700,000 nonprofit organizations. Over 15 million volunteers. What impact do they have on society today? Professor Jon Van Til, Editor of the *Nonprofit Voluntary Sector Quarterly*, raises this compelling question in his scholarly new work as he sets the stage for a coherent view of the voluntary sector. His review of historical and contemporary models of voluntary action paves the way for one that stresses the need for a new conception of how to preserve, extend, and experience community within the interactive web of modern society.

March 1988 / ISBN 0-87954-240-3 / $24.95 / 270 pages

MANAGING FOUNDATION ASSETS: An Analysis of Foundation Investment and Payout Procedures and Performance

by Lester M. Salamon and Kenneth P. Voytek

In their new study, Salamon and Voytek address some of the most critical questions from the foundation community on foundation investing and payout procedures, including: how do foundations manage the immense wealth in their control?, how does the payout requirement affect foundation investment operations?, what impact has the change in the payout requirement of 1981 had on both the investment and payout performance of foundations? After addressing these questions, Salamon offers insight into key topics: the process foundations use to make their payout decisions and manage their investments, the rate of return they have achieved and the payout rates foundations have adopted.

March 1989 / ISBN 0-87954-283-7 / $19.95

FOUNDATION TRUSTEESHIP: Service in the Public Interest

by John W. Nason

Changing public expectations of foundations and new challenges for foundation board members necessitate a fresh approach and an expert guide through the complexities of foundation trusteeship. John Nason, calling upon his years of experience as a trustee, has identified the problem areas and provides insight into many topics of interest to foundations and their board members. Dr.

Nason includes chapters covering the roles of foundations and their trustees as well as the changing programs in today's changing society.

Spring 1989 / ISBN 0-87954-285-3 / $19.95

A HISTORIOGRAPHIC REVIEW OF FOUNDATION LITERATURE

by Joseph C. Kiger

An historical overview of literature on the foundation field from 1894 to the present, this book is an excellent resource for anyone interested in foundation history, both in itself and as a guide to further reading.

October 1987 / ISBN 0-87954-233-0 / $7.50

ASSOCIATES PROGRAM

"Direct Line to Fundraising Information"

The Associates Program puts important facts and figures on your desk through a toll-free telephone reference service helping you to:

- identify potential sources of foundation funding for your organization,
- gather important information to target and present your proposals most effectively.

Your annual membership in the Associates Program gives you vital information on a timely basis, saving you hundreds of hours of research time.

- Membership in the Associates Program puts important funding information on your desk, including information from:
  - foundation annual reports, information brochures, press releases, grants lists, and other documents
  - IRS 990-PF information returns for all 27,000 U.S. foundations—often the only source of information on small foundations
  - books and periodicals chronicling foundation and philanthropic history and regulations
  - files filled with news clippings about foundations
  - The Foundation Center's own publications: *Foundation Directory* and *Supplement, Foundation Grants Index*—annual and bimonthly, *Source Book Profiles, Corporate Foundation Profiles, National Data Book, COMSEARCH Printouts, Foundation Fundamentals, Grants to Individuals,* and *Special Topics.*

- The Associates Program puts this vital information on your desk through a *toll-free telephone call*. The annual fee of $375 for the Associates Program grants you *10 free calls, or 2½ hours* worth of answers per month.

- Membership in the Associates Program allows you to request *custom searches of The Foundation Center's computerized databases* which contain information on *all 27,000* active U.S. foundations.

Thousands of professional fundraisers find it extremely cost effective to rely on the Center's Associates Program. Put our staff of experts to work for your fundraising program. For more information call TOLL-FREE 800-424-9836.

FOUNDATION CENTER COMPUTER DATABASES

Foundation and Grants Information Online

As the only nonprofit oranization whose sole purpose is to provide information on philanthropic activity, the Foundation Center offers three important databases online—Foundation Directory, Foundation Grants Index, and National Foundations. The databases correspond in form and content to the printed volumes: *The Foundation Directory, The foundation Grants Index,* and the *National Data Book.* Online retrieval provides vital information on funding sources, philanthropic giving, grant application guidelines, and the financial status of foundations to:

>Nonprofit organizations seeking funds
>Grantmaking institutions
>Corporate contributors
>Researchers
>Journalists
>Legislators

Searches of the Center's databases can provide comprehensive and timely answers to your questions, such as . . .

- Which New York foundations support urban projects? Who are their officers and trustees?
- What are the program interests of the ten largest corporate foundations? Which ones publish annual reports?
- Which foundations have given grants in excess of $100,000 in the past two years for continuing education for women?
- Which foundation would be likely to fund a cancer research project at a California hospital?
- Which are the ten largest foundations in Philadelphia by annual grants amount?
- What are the names and addresses of smaller foundations in the 441 zip code range?

The Center's up-to-date and authoritative data is available online through DIALOG Information Services, and on the Telecommunications Cooperative Network's (TCN) DIALCOM System. For additional information about the contents of the Foundation Center's databases, call the Foundation Center at (212) 620-4230. For information on how to access our databases, contact DIALOG at (415) 858-2700 or the Telecommunications Cooperative Network at (212) 714-9780.